Sociology

Sociology

A DOWN-TO-EARTH APPROACH

FIFTH EDITION

James M. Henslin
Southern Illinois University, Edwardsville

Allyn and Bacon
Boston ■ London ■ Toronto ■ Sydney ■ Tokyo ■ Singapore

Editor-in-Chief, Social Sciences: Karen Hanson
Series Editor: Jeff Lasser
Development Editor: Susan Gleason
Editorial Assistant: Susan Hutchinson
Cover Administrator: Linda Knowles
Composition and Prepress Buyer: Linda Cox
Manufacturing Buyer: Megan Cochran
Marketing Manager: Judeth Hall
Signing Representative: Ward Moore
Photo Researcher: Myrna Engler
Fine Art Researcher: Laurie Frankenthaler
Editorial-Production Service: The Book Company
Text Designer: Carol Somberg, Omegatype Typography, Inc; Delgado Design
Electronic Composition: Omegatype Typography, Inc.
Cover Designer: Studio Nine

Library of Congress Cataloging-in-Publication Data

Henslin, James M.
    Sociology: a down-to-earth approach / James M. Henslin. -- 5th ed.
        p. cm.
    Includes bibliographical references and index.
    ISBN 0–205–31914–9
        1. Sociology.   I. Title.

HM586.H45 2001
    301—dc21

00–035586

Chapter Opener Art Credits:

Chapter 1: *Crowd with Happy Faces* by Margaret Cusack, 1983. Machine stitch appliqué. © Margaret Cusack/SIS.

Chapter 2: *Songs of the Great Serpents* by Fishinghawk (Dewayne Mathews), 1997. Mixed media monotype, 22" by 30". Courtesy of El Cerro Graphics.

Chapter 3: *Man Reading to Child* by Cynthia Fitting, 1992. Gouache, water color opaque. © Cynthia Fitting/SIS.

Chapter 4: *Sunday Afternoon Stickball Game* by Ralph Fasanella, 1953. Oil on canvas, 36" x 40". Courtesy of ACA Galleries, New York and Eva Fasanella.

Chapter 5: *People* by Diana Ong, 1995. Computer graphics. Diana Ong/SuperStock.

Chapter 6: *Congregating People* by Bernard Bonhomme, 1997. Digital image. © Bernard Bonhomme/SIS.

Chapter 7: *Les Flaneurs* by Jean-Pierre Stora, 1995. Oil on canvas, 61" x 50". The Grand Design/SuperStock.

Chapter 8: *Prison* by Alan E. Cober. Alan E. Cober/SIS.

Chapter 9: *Tea Pickers* by Senaka Sennayake, 20th century. Oil on canvas. SuperStock.

Chapter 10: *City Gleaners* by Tsing-Fang Chen, 1986. Paul Lee Collection/TF Chen/SuperStock.

Chapter 11: *Dissension* by Wendy Seller, 1993. Oil on canvas, 34" H x 30" W. © 1993 Wendy Seller. In the collection of Robert and Elayne Simandl.

Chapter 12: *Watts* 1963 by Kerry James Marshall, 1995. Acrylic collage on canvas, 114 x 135 inches. Collection of the St. Louis Museum of Art. Courtesy of Jack Shainman Gallery, New York City.

Chapter 13: *Holding Court* by Phoebe Beasley, 1989. Collage, 36" x 36". © Phoebe Beasley/Omni-Photo Communications.

Chapter Opener Art Credits and Photo Credits continue on page 727, which is a continuation of this copyright page.

Printed in the United States of America
10   9   8   7   6   5   6   5   4   3   2   1   VHP   04   03   02   01   00

To my fellow sociologists, who do such creative research on social life and who communicate the sociological imagination to generations of students.

With my sincere admiration and appreciation,

Jim Henslin

Brief Contents

PART I The Sociological Perspective

1	The Sociological Perspective	2
2	Culture	36
3	Socialization	62
4	Social Structure and Social Interaction	94
5	How Sociologists Do Research	124

PART II Social Groups and Social Control

6	Societies to Social Networks	148
7	Bureaucracy and Formal Organizations	172
8	Deviance and Social Control	196

PART III Social Inequality

9	Global Stratification	226
10	Social Class in the United States	254
11	Sex and Gender	284
12	Race and Ethnicity	316
13	The Elderly	354

PART IV Social Institutions

14	The Economy	386
15	Politics	416
16	The Family	442
17	Education	476
18	Religion	506
19	Medicine	538

PART V Social Change

20	Population and Urbanization	570
21	Collective Behavior and Social Movements	606
22	Social Change and the Environment	633

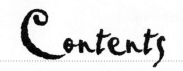

Contents

To the Student from the Author   xxiv
Preface   xxviii

PART I   The Sociological Perspective

1   The Sociological Perspective   2

The Sociological Perspective   4
Seeing the Broader Social Context   4
The Growing Global Context   5
Sociology and the Other Sciences   6
The Natural Sciences   6
The Social Sciences   6
The Goals of Science   7
■ *Down-to-Earth Sociology:* An Updated Version of the Old Elephant Story   8
■ *Down-to-Earth Sociology:* Enjoying a Sociology Quiz— Sociological Findings Versus Common Sense   9
Origins of Sociology   9
Tradition Versus Science   9
■ *Down-to-Earth Sociology:* Sociological Findings Versus Common Sense—Answers to the Sociology Quiz   10
Auguste Comte and Positivism   11
Herbert Spencer and Social Darwinism   11
Karl Marx and Class Conflict   12
Emile Durkheim and Social Integration   13
Max Weber and the Protestant Ethic   14
The Role of Values in Social Research   14
***Verstehen* and Social Facts   16**
Weber and *Verstehen*   16
Durkheim and Social Facts   16
How Social Facts and *Verstehen* Fit Together   16
Sexism in Early Sociology   17
Attitudes of the Time   17
Harriet Martineau   17
Sociology in North America   17

Early History: The Tension Between Social Reform and Social Analysis   17
Jane Addams and Social Reform   18
W.E.B. Du Bois and Race Relations   18
Talcott Parsons and C. Wright Mills: Theory Versus Reform   19
The Present: The Continuing Tension and the Rise of Applied Sociology   19
■ *Down-to-Earth Sociology:* Early North American Sociology: Du Bois and Race Relations   20
■ *Down-to-Earth Sociology:* Careers in Sociology: What Applied Sociologists Do   21
Theoretical Perspectives in Sociology   22
■ *Down-to-Earth Sociology:* Sociology or Social Work? Taking Back Children from the Night   23
Symbolic Interactionism   23
Functional Analysis   27
Conflict Theory   30
Levels of Analysis: Macro and Micro   31
Putting the Theoretical Perspectives Together   32
Trends Shaping the Future of Sociology   32
Summary and Review   33

2   Culture   36

What Is Culture?   38
Culture and Taken-for-Granted Orientations to Life   39
Practicing Cultural Relativism   40
Components of Symbolic Culture   42
Gestures   42
Language   43
■ *Down-to-Earth Sociology:* The New Shorthand: Expressing Yourself Online   45

■ *Perspectives:* Cultural Diversity in the United States:
   Race and Language: Searching for Self Labels   46
   Values, Norms, and Sanctions   47

Miami—Language in a Changing City   48
   Folkways and Mores   48
   Many Cultural Worlds: Subcultures and
   Countercultures   49

Values in U.S. Society   50
   An Overview of U.S. Values   50
   Value Contradictions and Social Change   51
■ *Mass Media in Social Life:* Why Do Native Americans
   Like Westerns?   52
   Value Clusters   53
   Culture Wars: When Values Clash   54
   Values as Blinders   54
   "Ideal" Versus "Real" Culture   54

Cultural Universals   55
■ *Thinking Critically:* Are We Prisoners of Our Genes?
   Sociobiology and Human Behavior   55
   Animals and Language   56

Technology in the Global Village   57
   The New Technology   57
   Cultural Lag and Cultural Change   58
   Technology and Cultural Leveling   58
■ *Sociology and the New Technology:* Could Computers
   Replace the Human Species?   60

Summary and Review   60

3   **Socialization**   62
──

What Is Human Nature?   64
   Feral Children   64
   Isolated Children   64
■ *Down-to-Earth Sociology:* Heredity or Environment?
   The Case of Oskar and Jack, Identical Twins   65
   Institutionalized Children   66
   Deprived Animals   67

Socialization Into the Self, Mind, and Emotions   68
   Cooley and the Looking-Glass Self   68
   Mead and Role Taking   69
   Piaget and the Development of Reasoning Skills   71
   Kohlberg and the Development of Morality   71
   Gilligan and Gender Differences in Morality   72
   Global Considerations: The Self, Reasoning, and
   Morality   72
   Freud and the Development of Personality   72
   Socialization and Emotions   73
   The Self and Emotions as Social Control: Society
   Within Us   74
■ *Down-to-Earth Sociology:* Signs of the Times: Are We
   Becoming Ik?   75

Socialization into Gender   76
   Gender Messages in the Family   76
   Gender Messages in the Mass Media   76
■ *Mass Media in Social Life:* From Xena, Warrior
   Princess, to Lara Croft, Tomb Raider: Changing
   Images of Women in the Mass Media   78

Agents of Socialization   79
   The Family   79
   The Neighborhood   80
   Religion   80
   Day Care   80
   The School   81
■ *Perspectives:* Cultural Diversity in the United States:
   Caught Between Two Worlds   82
   Peer Groups   83
   Sports   84
   The Workplace   84

Resocialization   84
   Total Institutions   84
■ *Down-to-Earth Sociology:* Of Boys and Sports   85

Socialization Through the Life Course   86
   Childhood (from birth to about age 12)   86
■ *Down-to-Earth Sociology:* Boot Camp as a Total
   Institution   87
   Adolescence   88
   Young Adulthood   89
   The Middle Years   89
   The Older Years   90
   The Sociological Significance of the Life Course   90

Are We Prisoners of Socialization?   91

Summary and Review   91

4   **Social Structure and Social
    Interaction**   94
──

Levels of Sociological Analysis   96
   Macrosociology and Microsociology   96

**The Macrosociological Perspective: Social
Structure   97**
   The Sociological Significance of Social Structure   97
   Culture   98
   Social Class   98
   Social Status   98
■ *Down-to-Earth Sociology:* College Football as Social
   Structure   99
   Roles   101
   Groups   102

Social Institutions   102
   The Sociological Significance of Social
   Institutions   102

An Example: The Mass Media as an Emerging Social Institution   104

Comparing Functionalist and Conflict Perspectives   105

Changes in Social Structure   106

What Holds Society Together?   106

The Microsociological Perspective: Social Interaction in Everyday Life   108

Symbolic Interaction   108

■ *Perspectives:* Cultural Diversity in the United States: The Amish—*Gemeinschaft* Community in a *Gesellschaft* Society   109

Dramaturgy: The Presentation of Self in Everyday Life   113

■ *Mass Media in Social Life:* You Can't Be Thin Enough: Body Images and the Mass Media   116

Ethnomethodology: Uncovering Background Assumptions   118

The Social Construction of Reality   119

The Need for Both Macrosociology and Microsociology   121

Summary and Review   122

---

5   How Sociologists Do Research   124

What Is a Valid Sociological Topic?   126

Common Sense and the Need for Sociological Research   126

A Research Model   126

1. Selecting a Topic   126
2. Defining the Problem   127
3. Reviewing the Literature   127
4. Formulating a Hypothesis   128

5. Choosing a Research Method   128
6. Collecting the Data   128
7. Analyzing the Results   128
8. Sharing the Results   129

Research Methods   129

Surveys   129

■ *Down-to-Earth Sociology:* Loading the Dice: How *Not* to Do Research   132

Participant Observation (Fieldwork)   134

Secondary Analysis   135

Documents   135

Unobtrusive Measures   136

Experiments   136

■ *Down-to-Earth Sociology:* The Hawthorne Experiments   138

Deciding Which Method to Use   139

■ *Down-to-Earth Sociology:* Applied Sociology: Marketing Research as a Blend of Quantitative and Qualitative Methods   139

■ *Thinking Critically:* Doing Controversial Research— Counting the Homeless   140

Gender in Sociological Research   142

Ethics in Sociological Research   142

Protecting the Subjects: The Brajuha Research   143

Misleading the Subjects: The Humphreys Research   143

How Research and Theory Work Together   144

The Real World: When the Ideal Meets the Real   145

■ *Thinking Critically:* Are Rapists Sick? A Close-Up View of Research   145

Summary and Review   146

PART II Social Groups and Social Control

6   Societies to Social Networks   148

Social Groups and Societies   150

The Transformation of Societies   150

Hunting and Gathering Societies   150

Pastoral and Horticultural Societies   152

Agricultural Societies   152

Industrial Societies   153

Postindustrial Societies   154

Groups Within Society   155

Primary Groups   156

Secondary Groups   156

In-Groups and Out-Groups   157

Reference Groups   158

Social Networks   159

■ *Perspectives:* Cultural Diversity in the United States: How Our Social Networks Perpetuate Social Inequality   160

A New Group: Electronic Communities   161

Group Dynamics   161

Effects of Group Size on Stability and Intimacy   161

■ *Sociology and the New Technology:* Electronic Communities: Cybercommunications and Our Changing Culture   162

Effects of Group Size on Attitudes and Behavior   164
Leadership   165
The Power of Peer Pressure: The Asch Experiment   167
■ *Thinking Critically:* If Hitler Asked You to Execute a Stranger, Would You? The Milgram Experiment   167
Global Consequences of Group Dynamics   169
Summary and Review   170

7   Bureaucracy and Formal Organizations   172

The Rationalization of Society   174
Why Did Society Change?   174
Marx: Capitalism Broke Tradition   175
Weber: Religion Broke Tradition   175
Formal Organizations and Bureaucracy   177
Formal Organizations   177
The Characteristics of Bureaucracies   177
"Ideal" Versus "Real" Bureaucracy   179
■ *Down-to-Earth Sociology:* The McDonaldization of Society   180
Dysfunctions of Bureaucracies   180
The Perpetuation of Bureaucracies   182
The Sociological Significance of Bureaucracies   183
Voluntary Associations   183
Functions of Voluntary Associations   184
Shared Interests   185
The Problem of Oligarchy   185
Careers in Bureaucracies   186
The "Hidden" Corporate Culture   186
Humanizing the Corporate Culture   187
■ *Perspectives:* Cultural Diversity in the United States: Changing Times: Diversity in the Corporation   188
Quality Circles   188
Employee Stock Ownership   189
Small Work Groups   189
Corporate Day Care   189
The Cooperative   190
The Conflict Perspective   190
Technology and the Control of Workers   191
Myths and Realities of the Japanese Corporate Model   191
Hiring and Promoting Teams   191
■ *Sociology and the New Technology:* Cyberslackers and Cybersleuths: Surfing at Work   192
Lifetime Security   192
Almost Total Involvement   193

Broad Training   193
Decision Making by Consensus   193
The Myth Versus Reality   193
■ *Perspectives:* Cultural Diversity Around the World: Japanese and U.S. Corporations in an Age of Greed   194
Summary and Review   194

8   Deviance and Social Control   196

Gaining a Sociological Perspective on Deviance   198
The Relativity of Deviance   198
■ *Perspectives:* Cultural Diversity Around the World: Suicide and Sexual Behavior in Cross-Cultural Perspective   199
Who Defines Deviance?   199
How Norms Make Social Life Possible   200
Comparing Biological, Psychological, and Sociological Explanations   201
The Symbolic Interactionist Perspective   202
Differential Association Theory   202
■ *Perspectives:* Cultural Diversity in the United States: Is It Rape or Is It Marriage? A Study in Culture Clash   203
Control Theory   205
Labeling Theory   205
The Functionalist Perspective   208
How Deviance Is Functional for Society   208
■ *Mass Media in Social Life*: Pornography on the Internet: Freedom Versus Censorship   209
Strain Theory: How Social Values Produce Deviance   210
Illegitimate Opportunity Theory: Explaining Social Class and Crime   211
■ *Down-to-Earth Sociology:* Islands in the Street: Urban Gangs in the United States   212
The Conflict Perspective   214
Class, Crime, and the Criminal Justice System   214
Power and Inequality   214
The Law as an Instrument of Oppression   215
The Need for Multiple Theories   216
Reactions to Deviance   216
Sanctions   216
Degradation Ceremonies   216
Imprisonment   217
■ *Thinking Critically:* "Three Strikes and You're Out!" Unintended Consequences of Well-Intended Laws   218
The Death Penalty   220

New Legislation   220
■ *Thinking Critically:* Our Changing Society:
    The Significance of Hate Crimes   221
The Trouble with Official Statistics   222

The Medicalization of Deviance: Mental
    Illness   222
The Need for a More Humane Approach   224
Summary and Review   224

PART III Social Inequality

9   Global Stratification   226

What Is Social Stratification?   228
Systems of Social Stratification   229
Slavery   229
Caste   231
■ *Mass Media in Social Life:* What Price Freedom?
    Slavery Today   232
Estate   234
Class   234
Global Stratification and the Status of Females   235
What Determines Social Class?   235
Karl Marx: The Means of Production   235
Max Weber: Property, Prestige, and Power   236
Why Is Social Stratification Universal?   237
The Functionalist View of Davis and Moore:
    Motivating Qualified People   237
Tumin: A Critical Response   238
Mosca: A Forerunner of the Conflict Perspective   238
The Conflict Perspective: Class Conflict and Scarce
    Resources   239
Lenski's Synthesis   239
How Do Elites Maintain Stratification?   240
Ideology Versus Force   240
Comparative Social Stratification   241
Social Stratification in Great Britain   241
Social Stratification in the Former Soviet Union   242
Global Stratification: Three Worlds   243
The Most Industrialized Nations   243
The Industrializing Nations   243
■ *Thinking Critically:* Open Season: Children as
    Prey   246
The Least Industrialized Nations   247
Modifying the Model   247
How the World's Nations Became Stratified   248
Colonialism   248
World System Theory   248
Dependency Theory   249
Culture of Poverty   249

Evaluating the Theories   250
Maintaining Global Stratification   250
Neocolonialism   250
Multinational Corporations   250
■ *Perspectives:* Cultural Diversity Around the World:
    Sex Tourism and the Patriotic Prostitute   251
Technology and the Maintenance of Global
    Domination   252
A Concluding Note   252
Summary and Review   252

10   Social Class in the United States   254

What Is Social Class?   256
Wealth   256
Power   258
■ *Down-to-Earth Sociology:* How the Rich Live   260
Prestige   260
Status Inconsistency   262
Sociological Models of Social Class   263
Updating Marx   263
Updating Weber   263
Social Class in the Automobile Industry   266
Consequences of Social Class   267
Physical Health   267
Mental Health   268
Family Life   268
Education   269
Religion   269
Politics   269
Crime and the Criminal Justice System   270
The New Technology   270
Social Mobility   270
■ *Sociology and the New Technology:* Closing the Digital
    Divide: The Technology Gap Facing the Poor and
    Minorities   271
Three Types of Social Mobility   271
Women in Studies on Social Mobility   272

The New Technology and Fears of the Future   272
The Pain of Social Mobility   273

Poverty   273

Drawing the Poverty Line   273

■ *Down-to-Earth Sociology*: Living in Two Worlds:
Upward Mobility on the Social Class Ladder   274

Who Are the Poor?   274

■ *Down-to-Earth Sociology:* Exploring Myths About the
Poor   276

Children of Poverty   277

■ *Thinking Critically:* The Nation's Shame: Children in
Poverty   278

The Dynamics of Poverty   279

Why Are People Poor?   279

■ *Thinking Critically:* The Welfare Debate:
The Deserving and the Undeserving Poor   279

Welfare Reform   280

Deferred Gratification   281

Where Is Horatio Alger? The Social Functions of a
Myth   281

■ *Down-to-Earth Sociology:* Poverty: A Personal
Journey   282

Summary and Review   282

11   Sex and Gender   284

Issues of Sex and Gender   286

Biology or Culture? The Continuing
Controversy   286

The Dominant Position in Sociology   288

■ *Thinking Critically:* Biology Versus Culture—Culture Is
the Answer   288

Opening the Door to Biology   289

■ *Thinking Critically:* Biology Versus Culture—Biology Is
the Answer   289

Gender Inequality in Global Perspective   291

Sex Typing of Work   291

Prestige of Work   292

Other Areas of Global Discrimination   293

■ *Perspectives:* Cultural Diversity Around the World:
Female Circumcision   294

How Females Became a Minority Group   195

The Origins of Patriarchy   195

■ *Perspectives:* "Pssst. You Wanna Buy a Bride?" China in
Transition   295

Gender Inequality in the United States   297

Fighting Back: The Rise of Feminism   297

■ *Down-to-Earth Sociology:* Making the Invisible
Visible—The Deadly Effects of Sexism   298

Gender Inequality in Education   299

Gender Inequality in Everyday Life   301

Gender Inequality in the Workplace   302

The Pay Gap   302

The Glass Ceiling and the Glass Escalator   305

The "Mommy Track"   307

Sexual Harassment   307

■ *Thinking Critically:* Sexual Harassment of Women in
the Military   308

Gender and Violence   309

Feminism and Gendered Violence   310

Solutions   310

■ *Mass Media in Social Life:* Beauty and Pain:
How Much Is an Ad Worth?   311

The Changing Face of Politics   311

Glimpsing the Future—With Hope   313

Summary and Review   313

12   Race and Ethnicity   316

Laying the Sociological Foundation   318

Race: Myth and Reality   318

■ *Perspectives:* Cultural Diversity in the United States:
Tiger Woods and the Emerging Multiracial Identity:
Mapping New Ethnic Terrain   320

Ethnic Groups   321

Minority Groups and Dominant Groups   321

How People Construct Their Racial-Ethnic
Identity   323

Prejudice and Discrimination   324

■ *Thinking Critically:* Self-Segregation:
Help or Hindrance for Race Relations
on Campus?   326

Individual and Institutional Discrimination   326

Theories of Prejudice   328

Psychological Perspectives   328

Sociological Perspectives   329

■ *Mass Media in Social Life*: Preaching Hatred: Crime or
Inalienable Right?   329

■ *Down-to-Earth Sociology:* The Racist Mind   332

Global Patterns of Intergroup Relations   332

Genocide   332

Population Transfer   334

Internal Colonialism   334

Segregation   334

Assimilation   334

■ *Perspectives:* Cultural Diversity in the United States:
Haitian Assimilation   335

Multiculturalism (Pluralism)   335

**Race and Ethnic Relations in the United
States   336**

White Europeans   337

African Americans   337

■ *Down-to-Earth Sociology:* No Cross Burning Allowed, But . . . The Continuing Significance of Race in Everyday Life   341

Latinos   342

Asian Americans   344

Native Americans   347

Looking Toward the Future   349

The Immigration Debate   349

Affirmative Action   350

Toward a True Multicultural Society   350

■ *Thinking Critically:* Whose History? Searching for Truth about the Relationships Between Ethnic Groups   351

Summary and Review   352

13 The Elderly   354

Aging in Global Perspective   356

The Social Construction of Aging   356

Effects of Industrialization   357

The Graying of America   358

The Symbolic Interactionist Perspective   362

Labeling and the Onset of Old Age   362

The Meaning of Old Age: Cross-Cultural Comparisons   363

U.S. Society: Changing Perceptions   364

■ *Perspectives:* Cultural Diversity Around the World: China: Changing Sentiment About the Elderly   365

The Mass Media: Powerful Source of Symbols   366

■ *Mass Media in Social Life:* Shaping the Way We Look at the World: The Mass Media and Our Perceptions of the Elderly   367

The Functionalist Perspective   367

Disengagement Theory   368

Activity Theory   369

The Conflict Perspective   369

Social Security Legislation   369

Intergenerational Conflict   370

■ *Down-to-Earth Sociology:* Changing Sentiment About the U.S. Elderly   371

■ *Thinking Critically:* Exploding the Myth of U.S. Budget Surpluses: Can We Pay the Elderly's Social Security Out of Thin Air?   372

Fighting Back: Elderly Empowerment   375

Problems of Dependency   375

Isolation and Gender   375

Nursing Homes   376

■ *Perspectives:* Cultural Diversity Around the World: Alzheimer Disease: Lessons from Sweden   377

Elder Abuse   378

The Elderly Poor   378

The Sociology of Death and Dying   380

Effects of Industrialization and the New Technology   380

Death as a Process   381

Hospices   381

Suicide and the Elderly   382

Looking Toward the Future   383

■ *Thinking Critically:* How Long Do You Want to Live? Pushing Past the Limits of Biology   383

Summary and Review   384

PART IV Social Institutions

14 The Economy   386

The Transformation of Economic Systems   388

Preindustrial Societies: The Birth of Inequality   389

Industrial Societies: The Birth of the Machine   389

Postindustrial Societies: The Birth of the Information Age   390

The Transformation of the Medium of Exchange   391

Earliest Mediums of Exchange   391

Medium of Exchange in Agricultural Societies   391

Medium of Exchange in Industrial Societies   392

Medium of Exchange in Postindustrial Societies   393

World Economic Systems   393

Capitalism   393

Socialism   395

Ideologies of Capitalism and Socialism   395

Criticisms of Capitalism and Socialism   396

Changes in Capitalism and Socialism   396

■ *Mass Media in Social Life:* Greed Is Good—Selling the American Dream   397

■ *Perspectives:* Cultural Diversity Around the World: No Cash? No Problem! Barter in the Former Soviet Union 398

The Functionalist View of the Globalization of Capitalism 399

The New Global Division of Labor 399

■ *Perspectives*: Cultural Diversity Around the World: Doing Business in the Global Village 400

Ownership and the Management of Corporations 400

Functions on a Global Scale 401

The Conflict View of the Globalization of Capitalism 402

The Inner Circle and Corporate Capitalism 402

Interlocking Directorates 403

Global Investing 404

Work in U.S. Society 405

The Decline of Agriculture and the Transition to Postindustrial Society 405

Women and Work 406

The Underground Economy 407

■ *Down-to-Earth Sociology:* Maneuvering the Hidden Corporate Culture: Women Surviving the Male-Dominated Business World 408

Shrinking Paychecks 409

Patterns of Work and Leisure 409

■ *Perspectives:* Cultural Diversity in the United States: Who Is Unemployed? 411

The Future: Facing the Consequences of Global Capitalism 412

Expanding Global Trade 412

New Technologies and Downsizing: Utopia or Nightmare? 412

■ *Thinking Critically:* New Technology and the Restructuring of Work: What Type of New Society? 413

Summary and Review 414

15 Politics 416

Micropolitics and Macropolitics 418

Power, Authority, and Violence 418

Authority and Legitimate Violence 419

Traditional Authority 419

Rational-Legal Authority 420

Charismatic Authority 420

Authority as Ideal Type 422

The Transfer of Authority 422

Types of Government 423

Monarchies: The Rise of the State 423

Democracies: Citizenship as a Revolutionary Idea 423

Dictatorships and Oligarchies: The Seizure of Power 424

■ *Mass Media in Social Life:* Politics and Democracy in a Technological Society 425

The U.S. Political System 426

Political Parties and Elections 426

Democratic Systems in Europe 427

Voting Patterns 428

■ *Perspectives:* Cultural Diversity in the United States: The Politics of Immigrants: Power, Ethnicity, and Social Class 429

Lobbyists and Special-Interest Groups 430

PACs in U.S. Politics 431

Who Rules the United States? 432

The Functionalist Perspective: Pluralism 432

The Conflict Perspective: The Power Elite, or Ruling Class 432

Which View Is Right? 433

War and Terrorism: Means to Implement Political Objectives 434

Is War Universal? 434

How Common Is War? 434

Why Nations Go to War 434

Costs of War 435

Sowing the Seeds of Future Wars 435

Nuclear, Biological, and Chemical Terrorism 436

War and Dehumanization 436

■ *Down-to-Earth Sociology:* Thinking the Unthinkable: Biological Terrorism in the Twenty-First Century 437

A New World Order? 438

■ *Perspectives:* Cultural Diversity Around the World: Roadblocks in the Path to the New World Order: The Globalization of Capitalism Versus the Resurgence of Nationalism 439

Summary and Review 440

16 The Family 442

Marriage and Family in Global Perspective 444

Defining Family 444

Common Cultural Themes 445

Marriage and Family in Theoretical Perspective 446

The Functionalist Perspective: Functions and Dysfunctions 446

■ *Perspectives:* Cultural Diversity Around the World: Family Life in Sweden 447

The Conflict Perspective: Gender and Power 448

■ *Thinking Critically:* The Second Shift—Strains and Strategies 449

The Symbolic Interactionist Perspective: Gender and the Meanings of Marriage 450

The Family Life Cycle 451

Love and Courtship in Global Perspective 451

■ *Perspectives:* Cultural Diversity Around the World: East Is East and West Is West . . . Love and Arranged Marriage in India   452

Marriage   452

Childbirth   453

Child Rearing   453

The Family in Later Life   455

Diversity in U.S. Families   456

African-American Families   456

Latino Families   458

Asian-American Families   458

Native-American Families   459

One-Parent Families   459

Families Without Children   460

Blended Families   460

Gay and Lesbian Families   460

■ *Sociology and the New Technology:* The Brave New World of High-Tech Reproduction: Where Technology Outpaces Law and Sometimes Common Sense   461

Trends in U.S. Families   462

Postponing Marriage   462

Cohabitation   463

Unmarried Mothers   463

The Sandwich Generation and Elder Care   464

Divorce and Remarriage   465

Problems in Measuring Divorce   465

Children of Divorce   466

■ *Down-to-Earth Sociology:* You Be the Sociologist: Curious Divorce Patterns   467

The Absent Father and Serial Fatherhood   468

■ *Down-to-Earth Sociology:* Shall We Tighten the Ties That Bind? Rolling Back No-Fault Divorce   468

The Ex-Spouses   469

Remarriage   469

Two Sides of Family Life   469

The Dark Side of Family Life: Battering, Child Abuse, Marital Rape, and Incest   469

The Bright Side of Family Life: Successful Marriages   472

The Future of Marriage and Family   474

Summary and Review   473

17 Education   476

The Development of Modern Education   478

Education in Earlier Societies   478

Democracy, Industrialization, and Universal Education   479

Education in Global Perspective   481

Education in the Most Industrialized Nations: Japan   481

Education in the Industrializing Nations: Russia   482

Education in the Least Industrialized Nations: Egypt   483

The Functionalist Perspective: Education's Social Benefits   484

Teaching Knowledge and Skills   484

Cultural Transmission of Values   484

Social Integration   485

Gatekeeping   487

Promoting Personal Change   487

Promoting Social Change   487

Replacing Family Functions   488

Other Functions   488

The Conflict Perspective: How Education Reproduces the Social Class Structure   488

The Hidden Curriculum   489

Tilting the Tests: Discrimination by IQ   489

■ *Down-to-Earth Sociology:* Kindergarten as Boot Camp   490

Stacking the Deck: Unequal Funding   491

The Correspondence Principle   492

The Bottom Line: Family Background and the Educational System   493

The Symbolic Interactionist Perspective: Teacher Expectations and the Self-Fulfilling Prophecy   494

The Rist Research   494

The Rosenthal-Jacobson Experiment   495

How Do Teacher Expectations Work?   495

■ *Sociology and the New Technology:* Internet University: No Walls, No Ivy, No Keg Parties   496

Problems in U.S. Education—and Their Solutions   496

Problems: Mediocrity, Teen Pregnancy, and Violence   496

■ *Mass Media in Social Life:* School Shootings: When Myth Gives Way to Panic   499

Solutions: Retention, Standards, Safety, and Other Reforms   500

■ *Thinking Critically:* High Schools and Teen Pregnancy: A Program That Works   500

■ *Thinking Critically:* Breaking Through the Barriers: The Jaime Escalante Approach to Restructuring the Classroom   503

Summary and Review   504

18 Religion   506

What Is Religion?   508

The Functionalist Perspective   509

Functions of Religion   509

Functional Equivalents of Religion   510

Dysfunctions of Religion   510

The Symbolic Interactionist Perspective   511
  Religious Symbols   511
  Rituals   512
  Beliefs   512
  Religious Experience   512
  Community   513
The Conflict Perspective   513
  Opium of the People   513
  A Reflection of Social Inequalities   514
  A Legitimation of Social Inequalities   514
Religion and the Spirit of Capitalism   514
The World's Major Religions   515
  Judaism   516
  Christianity   517
  Islam   517
  ■ *Perspectives:* Cultural Diversity in the United
    States: The New Neighbor: Islam in the United
    States   519
  Hinduism   519
  Buddhism   520
  Confucianism   521
Types of Religious Groups   521
  Cult   521
  ■ *Down-to-Earth Sociology:* Heaven's Gate and Other
    Cults   522
  Sect   523
  Church   523
  Ecclesia   523
  Variations in Patterns   524
  When Religion and Culture Conflict   524
  ■ *Thinking Critically:* How to Destroy a Cult: The U.S.
    Government Versus the Branch Davidians   525
Characteristics of Religion in the United States   526
  Characteristics of Members   527
  Characteristics of Religious Groups   528
  Secularization of Religion and Culture   530
  ■ *Down-to-Earth Sociology:* Bikers and Bibles   532
The Future of Religion   533
  ■ *Mass Media in Social Life:* God on the Net: The Online
    Marketing of Religion   535
Summary and Review   535

19 Medicine   538

Sociology and the Study of Medicine   540
The Symbolic Interactionist Perspective   540
  The Role of Culture in Defining Health and
    Illness   540
  The Components of Health   540
The Functionalist Perspective   541
  The Sick Role   541
The Conflict Perspective   542
  Effects of Global Stratification on Health Care   542
  Establishing a Monopoly on U.S. Health Care   543
  ■ *Down-to-Earth Sociology:* To Establish a Monopoly,
    Eliminate Your Competition: How Physicians
    Defeated Midwives   542
Historical Patterns of Health   546
  Physical Health   546
  Mental Health   547
Issues in Health Care   547
  Medical Care: A Right or a Commodity?   547
  Social Inequality   547
  Malpractice Suits and Defensive Medicine   548
  Medical Incompetence   549
  Depersonalization: The Medical Cash Machine   550
  Conflict of Interest   550
  Medical Fraud   551
  Sexism in Medicine   551
  ■ *Down-to-Earth Sociology:* The Doctor-Nurse
    Game   552
  Medically Assisted Suicide   552
  ■ *Mass Media in Social Life:* Viagra on the
    Internet   553
  ■ *Thinking Critically:* Should Doctors Be Allowed to Kill
    Patients?   554
  Curbing Costs: Issues in Private and National Health
    Insurance   555
  ■ *Sociology and the New Technology:* Who Should Live,
    and Who Should Die? Technology and the Dilemma
    of Medical Rationing   557
Threats to Health   557
  AIDS   557
  The Globalization of Disease   560
  Drugs: Alcohol and Nicotine   561
  Disabling Environments   563
  Misguided, Foolish, and Callous
    Experiments   563
The Search for Alternatives   564
  Treatment or Prevention?   565
  Health Care in Global Perspective   565
  ■ *Perspectives:* Cultural Diversity Around the
    World: Health Care in Sweden, Russia, and
    China   566
Summary and Review   567

PART V Social Change

20 Population and Urbanization 570

POPULATION IN GLOBAL PERSPECTIVE 572
A Planet with No Space to Enjoy Life? 572
The New Malthusians 573
The Anti-Malthusians 574
Who Is Correct? 575
Why Are People Starving? 576

Population Growth 577
Why Do the Least Industrialized Nations Have So Many Children? 577
Implications of Different Rates of Growth 579
The Three Demographic Variables 580
■ *Perspectives:* Cultural Diversity in the United States: Glimpsing the Future: The Shifting U.S. Racial-Ethnic Mix 582
Problems in Forecasting Population Growth 584
■ *Perspectives:* Cultural Diversity Around the World: Killing Little Girls: An Ancient and Thriving Practice 585

URBANIZATION 586
The Development of Cities 588
The Industrial Revolution and the Size of Cities 588
Urbanization, Metropolises, and Megalopolises 589
U.S. Urban Patterns 589
■ *Down-to-Earth Sociology:* Reclaiming Harlem: "It Feeds My Soul" 592

Models of Urban Growth 592
The Concentric Zone Model 592
The Sector Model 593
The Multiple-Nuclei Model 594
The Peripheral Model 594
Critique of the Models 594

City Life 594
■ *Perspectives:* Cultural Diversity Around the World: Why City Slums Are Better Than the Country: Urbanization in the Least Industrialized Nations 595
Alienation 596
Community 596
Types of Urban Dwellers 597
Urban Sentiment: Finding a Familiar World 598
The Norm of Noninvolvement and the Diffusion of Responsibility 598

■ *Down-to-Earth Sociology:* Urban Fear and the Gated Fortress 599

Urban Problems and Social Policy 600
Suburbanization 600
Disinvestment and Deindustrialization 601
The Rural Rebound 601
The Potential of Urban Revitalization 602

Summary and Review 603

21 Collective Behavior and Social Movements 606

COLLECTIVE BEHAVIOR 608
Early Explanations: The Transformation of the Individual 608
Charles Mackay, Gustave LeBon, and Robert Park: How the Crowd Transforms the Individual 608
Herbert Blumer: The Acting Crowd 609

The Contemporary View: The Rationality of the Crowd 610
Richard Berk: The Minimax Strategy 610
Ralph Turner and Lewis Killian: Emergent Norms 611

Forms of Collective Behavior 612
Riots 612
Panics 613
Moral Panics 615
Rumors 615
Fads and Fashions 616
Urban Legends 617

SOCIAL MOVEMENTS 618
Types and Tactics of Social Movements 619
■ *Perspectives:* Cultural Diversity in the United States: The Million-Man March: Another Step in an Unfinished Social Movement 619
Types of Social Movements 619
Tactics of Social Movements 621
The Mass Media: Gatekeepers to Social Movements 623
■ *Down-to-Earth Sociology:* "Tricks of the Trade"— The Fine Art of Propaganda 624

Why People Join Social Movements 625
Mass Society Theory 625
Deprivation Theory 625
Moral Issues and Ideological Commitment 626
A Special Case: The Agent Provocateur 626

On the Success and Failure of Social Movements   628
   The Stages of Social Movements   628
■ *Thinking Critically:* Which Side of the Barricades?
   Prochoice and Prolife as a Social Movement   629
   The Difficult Road to Success   630
Summary and Review   630

22   Social Change and the Environment   633

How Social Change Transforms Society   634
   The Four Social Revolutions   634
   From *Gemeinschaft* to *Gesellschaft*   635
   Capitalism, Modernization, and Industrialization   635
   Social Movements   636
   Geopolitics and Ethnic Conflicts   636
Theories and Processes of Social Change   638
   Cultural Evolution   638
   Natural Cycles   638
   Conflict Over Power   639
   Ogburn's Theory   639
■ *Sociology and the New Technology:* From the Luddites
   to the Unabomber: Opposition to Technology   641
How Technology Changes Society   641
   Types of Transformation   642

   The Impact of the Automobile   643
   The Impact of the Computer   646
   Cyberspace and Social Inequality   649
The Growth Machine Versus the Earth   649
   Environmental Problems in the Most Industrialized
     Nations   650
■ *Down-to-Earth Sociology:* Corporations and Big
   Welfare Bucks: How to Get Paid to Pollute   651
   Environmental Problems in the Industrializing and
     Least Industrialized Nations   652
■ *Perspectives:* Cultural Diversity Around the World:
   The Rain Forests: Lost Tribes, Lost Knowledge   653
   The Environmental Movement   654
■ *Thinking Critically:* Ecosabotage   654
   Environmental Sociology   655
Summary and Review   656

Glossary   659

Suggested Readings   673

References   681

Name Index   707

Subject Index   711

Boxed Features

Down-to-Earth Sociology

An Updated Version of the Old Elephant Story   8
Enjoying a Sociology Quiz—Sociological Findings Versus
  Common Sense   9
Sociological Findings Versus Common Sense—Answers to
  the Sociology Quiz   10
Early North American Sociology: Du Bois and Race
  Relations   20
Careers in Sociology: What Applied Sociologists Do   21
Sociology or Social Work? Taking Back Children from the
  Night   23
The New Shorthand: Expressing Yourself Online   45
Heredity or Environment? The Case of Oskar and Jack,
  Identical Twins   65
Signs of the Times: Are We Becoming Ik?   75
Of Boys and Sports   85
Boot Camp as a Total Institution   87
College Football as Social Structure   99
Loading the Dice: How *Not* to Do Research   132
The Hawthorne Experiments   138
Applied Sociology: Marketing Research as a Blend of
  Quantitative and Qualitative Methods   139
The McDonaldization of Society   180
Islands in the Street: Urban Gangs in the United
  States   212
How the Rich Live   260
Living in Two Worlds: Upward Mobility on the Social
  Class Ladder   274
Exploring Myths About the Poor   276
Poverty: A Personal Journey   282
Making the Invisible Visible—The Deadly Effects of
  Sexism   298
The Racist Mind   332
No Cross Burning Allowed, But . . . The Continuing
  Significance of Race in Everyday Life   341
Changing Sentiment About the U.S. Elderly   371
Maneuvering the Hidden Corporate Culture: Women
  Surviving the Male-Dominated Business World   408
Thinking the Unthinkable: Biological Terrorism in the
  Twenty-First Century   437
You Be the Sociologist: Curious Divorce Patterns   467
Shall We Tighten the Ties That Bind? Rolling Back
  No-Fault Divorce   468
Kindergarten as Boot Camp   490
Heaven's Gate and Other Cults   522

Bikers and Bibles   532
To Establish a Monopoly, Eliminate Your Competition:
  How Physicians Defeated Midwives   542
The Doctor-Nurse Game   552
Reclaiming Harlem: "It Feeds My Soul"   592
Urban Fear and the Gated Fortress   599
"Tricks of the Trade"—The Fine Art of
  Propaganda   624
Corporations and Big Welfare Bucks: How to Get Paid to
  Pollute   651

Perspectives

Cultural Diversity in the United States: Race and
  Language: Searching for Self Labels   46
Cultural Diversity in the United States: Caught Between
  Two Worlds   82
Cultural Diversity in the United States: The Amish—
  Gemeinschaft Community in a *Gesellschaft* Society   109
Cultural Diversity in the United States: How Our Social
  Networks Perpetuate Social Inequality   160
Cultural Diversity in the United States: Changing Times:
  Diversity in the Corporation   188
Cultural Diversity Around the World: Japanese and U.S.
  Corporations in an Age of Greed   194
Cultural Diversity Around the World: Suicide and Sexual
  Behavior in Cross-Cultural Perspective   199
Cultural Diversity in the United States: Is It Rape or Is It
  Marriage? A Study in Culture Clash   203
Cultural Diversity Around the World: Sex Tourism and the
  Patriotic Prostitute   251
Cultural Diversity Around the World: Female
  Circumcision   294
Cultural Diversity Around the World: "Pssst. You Wanna
  Buy a Bride?" China in Transition   295
Cultural Diversity in the United States: Tiger Woods and
  the Emerging Multiracial Identity: Mapping New Ethnic
  Terrain   320
Cultural Diversity in the United States: Haitian
  Assimilation   335
Cultural Diversity Around the World: China: Changing
  Sentiment About the Elderly   365
Cultural Diversity Around the World: Alzheimer Disease:
  Lessons from Sweden   377
Cultural Diversity Around the World: No Cash? No
  Problem! Barter in the Former Soviet Union   398

Cultural Diversity Around the World: Doing Business in the Global Village   400

Cultural Diversity in the United States: Who Is Unemployed?   411

Cultural Diversity in the United States: The Politics of Immigrants: Power, Ethnicity, and Social Class   429

Cultural Diversity Around the World: Roadblocks in the Path to the New World Order: The Globalization of Capitalism Versus the Resurgence of Nationalism   439

Cultural Diversity Around the World: Family Life in Sweden   447

Cultural Diversity Around the World: East Is East and West Is West . . . Love and Arranged Marriage in India   452

Cultural Diversity in the United States: The New Neighbor: Islam in the United States   519

Cultural Diversity Around the World: Health Care in Sweden, Russia, and China   566

Cultural Diversity in the United States: Glimpsing the Future: The Shifting U.S. Racial-Ethnic Mix   582

Cultural Diversity Around the World: Killing Little Girls: An Ancient and Thriving Practice   585

Cultural Diversity Around the World: Why City Slums Are Better Than the Country: Urbanization in the Least Industrialized Nations   595

Cultural Diversity in the United States: The Million-Man March: Another Step in an Unfinished Social Movement   619

Cultural Diversity Around the World: The Rain Forests: Lost Tribes, Lost Knowledge   653

Mass Media in Social Life

Why Do Native Americans Like Westerns?   52

From Xena, Warrior Princess, to Lara Croft, Tomb Raider: Changing Images of Women in the Mass Media   78

You Can't Be Thin Enough: Body Images and the Mass Media   116

Pornography on the Internet: Freedom Versus Censorship   209

What Price Freedom? Slavery Today   232

Beauty and Pain: How Much Is an Ad Worth?   311

Preaching Hatred: Crime or Inalienable Right?   329

Shaping the Way We Look at the World: The Mass Media and Our Perceptions of the Elderly   367

Greed Is Good—Selling the American Dream   397

Politics and Democracy in a Technological Society   425

School Shootings: When Myth Gives Way to Panic   499

God on the Net: The Online Marketing of Religion   535

Viagra on the Internet   553

Thinking Critically

Are We Prisoners of Our Genes? Sociobiology and Human Behavior   55

Doing Controversial Research—Counting the Homeless   140

Are Rapists Sick? A Close-Up View of Research   145

If Hitler Asked You to Execute a Stranger, Would You? The Milgram Experiment   167

"Three Strikes and You're Out!" Unintended Consequences of Well-Intended Laws   218

Our Changing Society: The Significance of Hate Crimes   221

Open Season: Children as Prey   246

The Nation's Shame: Children in Poverty   278

The Welfare Debate: The Deserving and the Undeserving Poor   279

Biology Versus Culture—Culture Is the Answer   288

Biology Versus Culture—Biology Is the Answer   289

Sexual Harassment of Women in the Military   308

Self-Segregation: Help or Hindrance for Race Relations on Campus?   326

Whose History? Searching for Truth about the Relationships Between Ethnic Groups   351

Exploding the Myth of U.S. Budget Surpluses: Can We Pay the Elderly's Social Security Out of Thin Air?   372

How Long Do You Want to Live? Pushing Past the Limits of Biology   383

New Technology and the Restructuring of Work: What Type of New Society?   413

The Second Shift—Strains and Strategies   449

High Schools and Teen Pregnancy: A Program That Works   500

Breaking Through the Barriers: The Jaime Escalante Approach to Restructuring the Classroom   503

How to Destroy a Cult: The U.S. Government Versus the Branch Davidians   525

Should Doctors Be Allowed to Kill Patients?   554

Which Side of the Barricades? Prochoice and Prolife as a Social Movement   629

Ecosabotage   654

Sociology and the New Technology

Could Computers Replace the Human Species?   60

Electronic Communities: Cybercommunications and Our Changing Culture   162

Cyberslackers and Cybersleuths: Surfing at Work   192

The Digital Divide: The Technology Gap Facing the Poor and Minorities   271

The Brave New World of High-Tech Reproduction: Where Technology Outpaces Law and Sometimes Common Sense   461

Internet University: No Walls, No Ivy, No Keg Parties   496

Who Should Live, and Who Should Die? Technology and the Dilemma of Medical Rationing   557

From the Luddites to the Unabomber: Opposition to Technology   641

Guide to Social Maps

Figure 6.3	Types of Societies in Today's World	155
Figure 8.1	Some States Are Safer: Violent Crime in the United States	213
Figure 8.3	Executions in the United States	221
Figure 9.2	Global Stratification: Income of the Worlds' Nations	244–245
Figure 10.5	Patterns of Poverty	276
Figure 11.4	How Likely Is a Woman to Work for Wages?	303
Figure 12.2	The Distribution of Dominant and Minority Groups in the United States	324
Figure 13.1	The Graying of the Globe	358
Figure 13.4	As Florida Goes, So Goes the Nation: The Year 2025	361
Figure 14.3	The Globalization of Capitalism: Foreign Ownership of U.S. Business	404
Figure 14.4	The Globalization of Capitalism: U.S. Ownership in Other Countries	405
Figure 15.1	Political Parties in the United States	427
Figure 16.10	The "Where" of U.S. Divorce	465
Figure 17.2	Not Making It: Dropping Out of High School	481
Figure 18.1	Church Membership: Dominant Religion by County	518
Figure 19.6	Who Lacks Medical Insurance?	556
Figure 20.8	Net Migration Flows between Regions, 1997–1998	581
Figure 20.12	How Urban Is Your State? The Rural-Urban Makeup of the United States	590
Figure 22.2	Where Are the Worst Hazardous Waste Sites?	650

To the Student from the Author

If you like to watch people and try to figure out why they do what they do, you will like sociology. Sociology pries open the doors of society so you can see what goes on behind them.

In this venture into sociology, you will see especially how social class sets us on different paths in life, and how in one direction these paths lead to better health, more education, higher income, and even better marriages—and in the other direction they lead to more illness and disease, less education, lower income, and greater chances of a failed marriage. These paths even affect your chances of making it to your first birthday, of getting in trouble with the police—and of reading this book in the first place.

When I took my first course in sociology, I was "hooked." Seeing how marvelously my life had been affected by these larger group influences opened my eyes to a new world, one that has been fascinating to explore. I hope that this will be your experience also.

From how people become homeless to how they become presidents, from why women are treated as second-class citizens around the world to why people commit suicide—all of these topics are part of sociology. This breadth of subject, in fact, is what makes sociology so intriguing. We can turn the sociological lens on broad features of society, such as social class, gender, and race, and then immediately turn our focus onto the small-scale aspects of everyday life. If we look at two people interacting—whether quarreling or kissing—we see how these broad features of society are being played out in their lives.

We aren't born with instincts. We don't come into this world with preconceived notions of what life should be like. At birth, we have no ideas of race, gender, age, social class, of how people "ought" to be. Yet we all learn such things as part of growing up in our society. Uncovering the "hows" and the "whys" of this process is also part of sociology's fascination.

One of sociology's many pleasures is that as we study life in groups (an apt definition of sociology), whether those groups are in some other part of the world or in some nearby corner of our own society, we constantly gain insights into our own selves. As we see how other people's customs influence their lives, the effects of our own society on ourselves become more visible.

You can look forward to reading this book, for it shows you the path to a new way of looking at the social world, and in the process it can help you to better understand both society and yourself.

I have avoided unnecessary jargon so you won't have to wade through a linguistic quagmire in order to grasp basic ideas. These ideas are of utmost importance in your sociological journey, and to introduce them I use concise explanations, clear language, and relevant examples.

I also use several special features to help you.

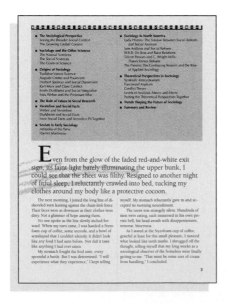

Opening Vignettes for Each Chapter

To give you a down-to-earth introduction, I open each chapter with a vignette. I think you'll enjoy them. They are down-to-earth, and help make the chapter's materials come alive. Many vignettes are based on my own experiences. Some come from my research with the homeless, the time I spent with them on the streets and slept in their shelters (Chapters 1, 10, and 19). Others recount my travels in Africa (Chapters 2 and 11) and Mexico (Chapter 20). I also tell you about the night I spent with street people at Du Pont Circle in Washington, D.C. (Chapter 4). For other vignettes, I use current and historical events (Chapters 5, 6, 7, 12, 17, 18, 21, and 22), classic studies in the social sciences (Chapters 3, 8, and 13), and even a scene from a novel (Chapter 15). Students have told me that they find the vignettes compelling, that they stimulate interest in the chapter. I hope that this is your experience as well.

Chapter Outlines, "In-Sums," and Summaries

To help you preview what you are about to read, I present an outline at the beginning of each chapter. I also include "In Sum" sections at various places in the chapters. These help you review important points before going on to new materials. To highlight and reinforce important concepts and issues, I close each chapter with a summary and review. To help you think along with me, I use an interactive question-and-answer format.

Boxes

I have written four types of boxed features that I think you will find stimulating. Students have told me that they find the type called "Down-to-Earth Sociology" especially interesting. These focus on such topics as a sociologist who specializes in getting teenage prostitutes off the streets (Chapter 1), "emoticons," expressive symbols that are used in e-mail (Chapter 2), and strategies women use to survive the male-dominated business world (Chapter 7). This last one was written by one of my students and recounts her struggle. I also include an account of my own personal journey out of poverty (Chapter 10). Two of the topics are more disturbing: the racist mind (Chapter 12), and the possibility that you and I will be the victims of biological terrorism (Chapter 15).

Another type of box is called "Cultural Diversity." Some focus on the United States. They explore such topics as race and the search for self-labels (Chapter 2), the use of English versus Spanish (Chapter 2), a Latino's reaction to his socialization into Anglo culture (Chapter 3), how the Amish resist social change (Chapter 4), how some new immigrants unintentionally violate U.S. norms (Chapter 8), Tiger Woods and the emerging multiracial identity (Chapter 12), and the new neighbor, Islam in the United States (Chapter 18). Those that focus on Cultural Diversity Around the World address such issues as Japanese and U.S. corporations in an age of greed (Chapter 7), the circumcision of girls (Chapter 11), ethnic conflict (Chapter 15), health care (Chapter 19), and threats posed to the world's remaining tribal groups (Chapter 22).

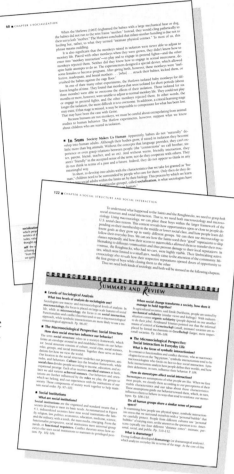

In a third type of box, I focus on technology, one of the most profound social forces facing us today. Topics of "Sociology and the New Technology" explore whether computers could replace the human species (Chapter 2), electronic communities (Chapter 6), cyberslacking and cybersleuthing (Chapter 7), the "digital divide" (Chapter 10), how technology affects democracy (Chapter 15), high-tech reproduction (Chapter 16), and the coming Internet University (Chapter 17).

In the last type of box, I focus on how the mass media are affecting our lives. These boxes, called "Mass Media in Social Life," explore why Native Americans like Westerns (Chapter 2), changing images of women (Chapter 3), body image and thinness (Chapter 4), pornography (Chapter 8), slavery today (Chapter 9), beauty and pain (Chapter 11), the preaching of hatred (Chapter 12), perceptions of the elderly (Chapter 13), Jesse Ventura's election (Chapter 15), school shootings (Chapter 17), the online marketing of religion (Chapter 18), and Viagra being sold on the Internet (Chapter 19).

Thinking Critically

As you can see from the boxed features, you are going to explore many controversial topics in this book. Sociology is our lives, and to delve into sociology is to wade into the mainstream of social controversy. Consequently, to address pressing and often controversial issues, I have included another feature called "Thinking Critically." In these sections, we consider why people follow evil authorities (Chapter 6), hate crimes (Chapter 8), bounties that are paid in order to have homeless children in Brazil killed (Yes, you read that right) (Chapter 9), racial and ethnic self-segregation on campus (Chapter 12), pushing the limits of longevity (Chapter 13), why men don't share much housework (Chapter 16), how to get single teen mothers back in school (Chapter 17), the destruction of the Branch Davidians in Waco, Texas (Chapter 18), euthanasia (Chapter 19), and abortion (Chapter 21).

Social Maps

I have also developed a series of social maps for you. They illustrate how social conditions vary by geography. For example, at a glance you will be able to see which states are the safest, and which are the most dangerous (Chapter 8); how likely women are to work for wages (Chapter 11); which states are controlled by Democrats, and which by Republicans (Chapter 15); and which states have the highest and lowest divorce rates (Chapter 16).

Key Terms

I know that learning new terms is difficult, but it is necessary. The sociologist's basic vocabulary provides a working definition of important concepts that help you understand your social world. To make this task easier, I introduce each key term within a context that explains or illustrates it. I also highlight each term when I introduce it, and then define it again in the margin.

Comprehensive Glossary

As you go from one chapter to another, you may forget what a term means. I did when I began my study of sociology. To help overcome this normal forgetting, at the end of the book I've included a glossary that lists all the terms that I introduce in the text. An instructor wrote me about how useful she finds this glossary in her teaching. She was pleased with how clear the definitions are. If you find difficulty with any of my definitions, let me know.

Using the Internet

The Internet, which has become such a significant aspect of our culture, contains a vast amount of sociological information. At the end of each chapter is a set of projects and exercises to help you use the Internet to explore ideas from the chapter. You may also wish to check my Web site at http://www.abacon.com/henslin.

Suggested Readings

At the end of the book, I have a section where I recommend readings for each chapter. You may find these helpful in writing papers or for exploring topics for class. To be of more help, I include a brief description of each source.

I would count it a privilege if you would share with me your experiences with this book. If there are sections of this text that you especially enjoy, or that you wish to comment on for whatever reason, don't hesitate to write me. I enjoy communicating with students.

I wish you the very best in college—and in your career afterward. It is my sincere hope that *Sociology: A Down-to-Earth Approach* contributes to that success.

James M. Henslin
Professor Emeritus
Southern Illinois University, Edwardsville
henslin@aol.com

Preface

hy shouldn't sociology be presented in a manner that conveys its inherent excitement? There is no doubt in my mind that sociology is the most enticing of all the social sciences. Yet textbooks often make sociology seem dull, and thereby fail to reach students.

My choice of subtitle for this book, *A Down-to-Earth Approach,* is deliberate. My goal is to share sociology's excitement, to help students embark on a fascinating journey that allows them to see how the *social* influences their lives, how it penetrates even their thinking. To see your students grasp the sociological perspective—and gradually become aware of how the social affects even their innermost being—is one of the most exciting things about teaching the introductory course.

To study sociology is to enter a new world of perception and understanding. It is an exploration of worlds and ideas far from our own, as well as a quest to understand our own world and ideas. Since this book is designed to help you lead your students on this journey, I'd like to show you how it is organized, and then review its themes and goals.

THE ORGANIZATION OF THIS TEXT

I have organized this text into five parts. Each has a broad focus and is designed to help your students acquire the sociological perspective. This will enable them to better understand social relations—and the particular corner of life in which they find themselves.

Part I focuses on the sociological perspective, which I introduce in the first chapter. In the following chapters, I contrast macrosociology and microsociology, present an overview of culture, introduce socialization, and then look at how sociologists do research. I wait until the fifth chapter to introduce research so that students have a chance to become immersed in the captivating findings of sociology and to become more acquainted with the sociological perspective. If you wish to follow the more traditional order, simply teach this chapter as the second chapter. No content will be affected.

Part II builds on these ideas as students continue to explore how social groups influence their lives. We open with an overview of groups—from society, which encompasses us, to the smaller networks in which we are immersed. Then we examine the impact of bureaucracy and formal organizations. This section closes with a look at deviance, which students find so intriguing. This closing chapter also has a strong emphasis on how groups exert social control over those who violate their norms.

Part III focuses on social inequality, which penetrates every aspect of our existence. Because social stratification is so significant, I have written two chapters on this topic. The first, with a global focus, presents an overview of the principles of stratification. These principles serve as background for the next chapter, in which we turn the sociological spotlight on social class in the United States. After establishing this broader context, we then focus on gender, the most global of the social inequalities. Following this, we examine the inequalities of race, ethnicity, and age.

In *Part IV,* we turn to those engulfing social arrangements called "social institutions." As you know, they are so significant that without understanding them we cannot understand life in society. Students seldom have this grasp, however, and these chapters are designed to help them understand how vital social institutions are for their lives. We begin by examining the economy and politics, currently our two overarching institutions. Then, in separate chapters, we turn the focus on the family, education, religion, and medicine.

Part V will help your students understand why our world is changing so rapidly; it also offers them a glimpse of what is yet to come. This concluding section opens with a focus on how population and urbanization have a direct impact on our lives. Then we look at collective behavior and social movements, which are among students' favorite topics in sociology. We end this journey into sociology by exploring the "cutting edge" of society—social change, technology, and the environment.

*T*HEMES AND GOALS

Every feature of this text is designed to share sociology's insights, promote the excitement of discovery, and foster an understanding of how vitally the social penetrates our lives. To help students understand how social forces shape our behavior, I use four central themes. Two of these themes, down-to-earth sociology and diversity, have been in the text since the first edition. The third edition introduced the timely theme of technology and society. Because of the enthusiastic response that this theme generated, and given the major impact that technology has on our lives, I maintain technology as a central theme in this edition. This fifth edition also introduces a new feature, "Mass Media in Social Life."

Let's look at these features in more detail.

Down-to-Earth Sociology

As students read the vignettes that open each chapter, they will begin to sense that something is different about this text. Over and over, students tell me how much they appreciate my sharing of personal experiences, how this gives them an awareness that sociology is not just a subject to study in college but a topic that permeates our lives.

I have attempted to reinforce this down-to-earth theme through a writing style that is also "down-to-earth"; that is, one that is accessible and inviting. Textbooks often seem to be written to appeal to the adopters of texts, rather than to the students who study them. My own experiences in college bear this out, as I'm sure your own do, too. Throughout the text I avoid unnecessary jargon, use "In Sum" sections to help students review important points before going on to new materials, and use down-to-earth examples to illustrate sociological concepts. My constant goal is to maintain and improve this down-to-earth style. The title of my introductory reader, *Down to Earth Sociology,* which has now reached its eleventh edition (Free Press, 2001), also reflects this approach.

Cultural Diversity and Globalization

Any attempt to explain U.S. society must pay keen attention to its diverse populations, for ours is truly a multicultural society. It also must explore the many implications of globalization. Consequently, cultural diversity and globalization continue to be stressed in this edition.

Cultural Diversity in the United States The United States is undergoing a profound demographic shift. Each year about one million people from around the world legally move to the United States. The number of illegal entrants is at least as large. Currently, about one American in four defines himself or herself as a member of a racial-ethnic minority group. If current immigration and birth rates continue, during the next fifty to eighty years minorities and whites will each account for about half of the U.S. population. A sociology textbook that does not explore the implications of this demographic shift simply cannot serve as an adequate introduction to the realities of life in a multicultural society.

To help your students appreciate our growing diversity, I have written Perspectives boxes called "Cultural Diversity in the United States." These boxes, as well as the many discussions of diversity throughout the text, will help your students apply their growing sociological imagination to fundamental changes occurring in U.S. society. They also will help students see the connections among key sociological concepts, such as culture, socialization, norms, race, gender, and social class. As their sociological imagination grows, they will better understand the social structure of U.S. society—and their own place in it.

In a second type of Perspectives box called "Cultural Diversity Around the World," we explore customs and forms of behavior that differ from our own. These topics allow students to gain a comparative understanding of such vital issues as the status and treatment of women, health care, suicide, U.S. and Japanese corporations, and threats to the world's remaining tribal groups.

Globalization As I wrote and revised this text, a primary goal was to increase students' awareness of how globalization profoundly affects their lives—not just through satellite communications and the Internet, though these are vital. Intertwined throughout the changes we are experiencing is the globalization of capitalism, which has married our fate with that of other nations. Our new global economy influences not just the variety and costs of our goods and services, but also the kinds of skills and knowledge that we need to make a living, even the types of work that are available to us. It affects even matters of life and death, especially the likelihood and locations of warfare.

To stress globalization, I have written a separate chapter on global stratification, given extensive coverage to global matters in the chapters on social institutions, and provided a global focus in the final chapter on social change and the environment. Throughout the text, I analyze how the globalization of capitalism is affecting world affairs.

This text is not intended as a critical review of U.S. power—there are many books that focus on this issue. To be relevant to the vital issues of our time, however, I do examine the implications of the United States being the dominant power in the world today. I do not shy away from such issues as the underlying but less obvious reasons for Desert Storm and the bombing of Kosovo.

Sociology and the New Technology

Another profound social force that we face is the accelerated rate of technological change. In just a single generation, computers have become part of our everyday lives: The Internet, unheard of just a few years ago, has become vital for information and shopping; "sci-fi"-like technologies aid reproduction; and distance learning is becoming common. Each of these topics is the subject of a boxed feature, "Sociology and the New Technology."

Because technology is so vital to our well-being, I also stress technological change throughout the text. We examine how the new technology is used to control workers in order to produce the "maximum security" workplace (Chapter 7), how technology helps to maintain global stratification (Chapter 9), how the consequences of technology differ by social class (Chapter 10), how technology often outpaces norms (Chapter 13), and how parents use the Internet to monitor their children in day care (Chapter 16). The final chapter, "Technology, Social Change, and the Environment," concludes your students' introduction with an appropriate stress on their changing world.

Thinking Critically

The classroom, a unique and stimulating place of interaction, provides an outstanding opportunity to explore social issues. To help you stimulate your students' sociological imagination, I have included special sections that make excellent points of departure for class discussion. In these sections, called "Thinking Critically," I try to present a balanced view of critical issues by contrasting several points of view or theoretical interpretations. These multiple perspectives on areas of social controversy are designed to help your students rise above their narrow frameworks of interpretation, to help them develop and apply their growing sociological imagination.

To give you an idea of how far-ranging and yet focused these sections are, here are just four areas of controversy we consider: In Chapter 12, students are asked to consider segregated housing on campus, along with the many unresolved questions this practice has raised. Chapter 18 exposes them to a conflict interpretation of the destruction of the Branch Davidians. In Chapter 19, they confront euthanasia, and in Chapter 22, they examine the implications of ecosabotage and the environment. These analyses and invitations to "think along" as we explore social controversy are one more means by which your students will learn to appreciate the relevance sociology has to their lives.

A New Theme: The Mass Media in Social Life

In this edition, I have added the mass media as a new theme. The mass media have been an important part of U.S. life throughout its short history, but they now are playing an ever-increasing role in shaping our behavior and orientations to life. Not only have they become one of the most important factors in how we think about social issues, but also they help to shape even our self concept and our views of morality. To help make their influence on our lives more visible to students, I have written a series of boxes called "Mass Media in Social Life." In this boxed feature, we explore a variety of interesting topics. Among them are how the mass media influence our perceptions of gender (Chapter 3), our own bodies (Chapter 4), race-ethnicity (Chapter 12), the elderly (Chapter 13), politics (Chapter 15), and school violence (Chapter 17). I think you'll enjoy exploring the role of the mass media in social life with your students, and that this addition to the book will help to develop their sociological imagination.

New Topics

Because sociology is about social life, as society changes the topics in an introductory text reflect those changes. Consequently, this edition contains numerous new topics. Among them are trends affecting the future of sociology (Chapter 1); moral holidays (Chapter 2); gender in research (Chapter 5); "emoticons," the new shorthand in e-mail (Chapter 6); "cyberslacking" and "cybersleuthing" (Chapter 7); hate crimes (Chapter 8); the three-strike laws (Chapter 8); slavery today (Chapter 9); the digital divide (Chapter 10); how the super-rich live (Chapter 10); the resurgence of bride selling in China (Chapter 11); the continuing significance of race in the United States (Chapter 12); the alternative office (Chapter 14); the looming threat of biological terrorism (Chapter 15); the online marketing of religion (Chapter 18); medical incompetence (Chapter 19); the rural rebound (Chapter 20); the gentrification of Harlem (Chapter 20); and corporate welfare (Chapter 22).

The new Social Maps should also aid your teaching. At a glance, students can explore the number of executions in different states (Chapter 8); how likely women are to work for wages (Chapter 11); the distribution of dominant and minority groups (Chapter 12); Democratic and Republican control (Chapter 15); the lack of medical insurance (Chapter 19); and urbanization (Chapter 20). One of the more interesting global maps shows U.S. investments around the world (Chapter 14). These maps are in addition to the many that I retained and updated from previous editions.

ACKNOWLEDGMENTS

The highly gratifying response to the first four editions indicates that my efforts at making sociology down-to-earth have succeeded. The years that have gone into writing this text are a culmination of the many more years that preceded its writing—from graduate school to that equally demanding endeavor known as classroom teaching. But no text comes solely from its author. Although I am responsible for the final words on the printed page, I have received invaluable feedback from instructors and students who have used this book. I especially want to thank these instructors who have provided overviews for my guidance:

Reviewers of Previous Editions

Francis O. Adeola, *University of New Orleans*
Sandra L. Albrecht, *The University of Kansas*
Richard Alman, *Sierra College*
Kenneth Ambrose, *Marshall University*
Alberto Arroyo, *Baldwin–Wallace College*
Karren Baird-Olsen, *Kansas State University*
Linda Barbera-Stein, *The University of Illinois*
Ronnie J. Booxbaum, *Greenfield Community College*
Cecil D. Bradfield, *James Madison University*
Francis Broouer, *Worcester State College*
Sandi Brunette-Hill, *Carrol College*
Karen Bullock, *Salem State College*
John K. Cochran, *The University of Oklahoma*
Joan Cook-Zimmern, *College of Saint Mary*
Russell L. Curtis, *University of Houston*
John Darling, *University of Pittsburgh—Johnstown*
Ray Darville, *Stephen F. Austin State University*
Nanette J. Davis, *Portland State University*
Vincent Davis, *Mt. Hood Community College*
Lynda Dodgen, *North Harris Community College*
Terry Dougherty, *Portland State University*
Marlese Durr, *Wright State University*
Helen R. Ebaugh, *University of Houston*
Obi N. Ebbe, *State University of New York—Brockport*
Cy Edwards, Chair, *Cypress Community College*
Louis J. Finkle, *Horry-Georgetown Technical College*
David O. Friedrichs, *University of Scranton*
Norman Goodman, *State University of New York—Stony Brook*
Ramon Guerra, *University of Texas—Pan American*
Donald W. Hastings, *The University of Tennessee—Knoxville*
Michael Hoover, *Missouri Western State College*
Erwin Hummel, *Portland State University*
Charles E. Hurst, *The College of Wooster*
Kathleen R. Johnson, *Keene State College*
Irwin Kantor, *Middlesex County College*
Mark Kassop, *Bergen Community College*
Myles Kelleher, *Bucks County Community College*
Alice Abel Kemp, *University of New Orleans*
Diana Kendall, *Austin Community College*
Gary Kiger, *Utah State University*

Gene W. Kilpatrick, *University of Maine—Presque Isle*
Michele Lee Kozimor-King, *Pennsylvania State University*
Abraham Levine, *El Camino Community College*
David Maines, *Oakland University*
Ron Matson, *Wichita State University*
Armaund L. Mauss, *Washington State University*
Evelyn Mercer, *Southwest Baptist University*
Robert Meyer, *Arkansas State University*
John Mitrano, *Central Connecticut State University*
W. Lawrence Neuman, *University of Wisconsin—Whitewater*
Charles Norman, *Indiana State University*
Patricia H. O'Brien, *Elgin Community College*
Laura O'Toole, *University of Delaware*
Ruth Pigott, *University of Nebraska—Kearney*
Phil Piket, *Joliet Junior College*
Trevor Pinch, *Cornell University*
Daniel Polak, *Hudson Valley Community College*
Deedy Ramo, *Del Mar College*
Adrian Rapp, *North Harris Community College*
Ray Rich, *Community College of Southern Nevada*
Barbara Richardson, *Eastern Michigan University*
Howard Robboy, *Trenton State College*
Michael L. Sanow, *Catonsville Community College*
Walt Shirley, *Sinclair Community College*
Marc Silver, *Hofstra University*
Roberto E. Socas, *Essex County College*
Susan Sprecher, *Illinois State University*
Randolph G. Ston, *Oakland Community College*
Gary Tiederman, *Oregon State University*
Kathleen Tiemann, *University of North Dakota*
Judy Turchetta, *Johnson & Wales University*
Steven Vassar, *Mankato State University*
Jay Weinstein, *Eastern Michigan University*
Larry Weiss, *University of Alaska*
Douglas White, *Henry Ford Community College*
Stephen R. Wilson, *Temple University*
Anthony T. Woart, *Middlesex Community College*
Stuart Wright, *Lamar University*
Mary Lou Wylie, *James Madison University*
Diane Kholos Wysocki, *University of Nebraska—Kearney*

Reviewers of the Current Edition

Gabriel C. Alvarez, *Duquesne University*
Rafael Balderrama, *University of Texas—Pan American*
Karen Bradley, *Central Missouri State University*
Valerie S. Brown, *Cuyahoga Community College*
Paul Ciccantell, *Kansas State University*
Jim David, *Butler County Community College*
Cy Edwards, Chair, *Cypress College*
Rebecca Susan Fahrlander, *Bellevue University*
Louis J. Finkle, *Horry-Georgetown Technical College*
Nicole T. Flynn, *University of South Alabama*
Bruce Friesen, *Kent State University—Stark*
Rosalind Gottfried, *San Joaquin Delta College*
Ramon S. Guerra, *University of Texas—Pan American*
Lillian O. Holloman, *Prince George's Community College*
James H. Huber, *Bloomsburg University*
Nita Jackson, *Butler County Community College*
Jennifer A. Johnson, *Germanna Community College*
David Jones, *Plymouth State College*

Myles J. Kelleher, *Bucks County Community College*
Mary E. Kelly, *Central Missouri State University*
Gene Kilpatrick, *University of Maine—Presque Isle*
Jerome R. Koch, *Texas Tech University*
Michael V. Miller, *University of Texas—San Antonio*
Patricia H. O'Brien, *Elgin Community College*
James Pond, *Butler Community College*
Salvador Rivera, *State University of New York—Cobleskill*
Michael Samano, *Portland Community College*
Michael L. Sanow, *Community College of Baltimore County*
Mary C. Sengstock, *Wayne State University*
Mariella Rose Squire, *University of Maine at Fort Kent*
Vickie Holland Taylor, *Danville Community College*
Maria Jose Tenuto, *College of Lake County*
William J. Wattendorf, *Adirondack Community College*
Stacey G. H. Yap, *Plymouth State College*
Joan Cook Zimmern, *College of Saint Mary*

I appreciate the efforts of everyone who has helped me on this and earlier editions. It is difficult to single out the many fine people who have been involved in what often has been an arduous and seemingly endless process. I want to mention four especially capable people, however, who worked closely with me on this edition: Sue Gleason, who kept prodding me to continue to write, even when I was near exhaustion, and who did so gently; Dusty Friedman, who coordinated the many interrelated and complicated aspects of production, often under pressure and in the face of severe time restrictions; Jane Townsend, whose outstanding knowledge of the English language helped sharpen my phrasing; and Myrna Engler, who turned photo specifications into reality. I owe a lot to these four.

Many others on the capable staff of Allyn and Bacon did behind-the-scenes work that was critical for this edition. Chief among them, I wish to thank Judy Fiske, who coordinated the many activities involved in production; Jeff Lasser, my acquisitions editor, who managed the supplements package that enhances this textbook; and Sue Hutchinson, Jeff's editorial assistant.

I also wish to thank two people who were instrumental in previous editions: Karen Hanson, who saw the promise of the early manuscript and has strongly supported this project from the beginning to the present; and Hannah Rubenstein whose creativity, insightful questioning, and acute perception of the relevance of social events have left an indelible mark on this text.

I owe all these people a debt of gratitude for their fine contributions to this book. From the bottom of my heart, a sincere thank you—and my best wishes for your many endeavors in life.

Jim Henslin
henslin@aol.com

The publisher would like you to know about the supplements that have been prepared to enhance student learning and your teaching.

$\int$ UPPLEMENTS FOR THE INSTRUCTOR

Instructor's Manual (Harry Hoffman, Minot State University) For each chapter in the text, the Instructors Manual provides: a "chapter-at-a-glance" grid that coordinates use of other supplements; a chapter summary; learning objectives; a lecture outline; a list of what's new in the fifth edition; key terms with page references; classroom discussion topics and activities; and suggestions for guest lecturers.

Test Bank (Jacqueline Fellows, Riverland Community College) and *Alternate Test Bank* (Kanwal Prasher, Rock Valley Community College) The test banks contain several thousand questions in multiple choice, true-false, short answer, and essay formats. Many of the multiple choice questions test students' ability to apply what they've learned to new situations.

Computerized Testing Allyn and Bacon Test Manager is an integrated suite of testing and assessment tools for Windows and Macintosh. You can use Test Manager to create professional-looking exams in just minutes by selecting from the existing database of questions, editing questions, or writing your own. Course management features include a class roster, grade book, and item analysis. Test manager also has everything you need to create and administer online tests.

Call-In Testing Allyn and Bacon can create your tests for you and have a finished, ready-to-duplicate test on its way to you by mail or fax within 48 hours.

Allyn and Bacon Interactive Video for Introductory Sociology, and *Video User's Guide* This custom video features television news footage on both national and global topics. The video segments can help launch lectures, spark classroom discussion, and encourage critical thinking.

A user's guide provides descriptions of each video segment, specific tie-ins to the text, and suggested discussion questions and projects.

Allyn and Bacon Transparencies for Introductory Sociology Revised for this edition, this package includes more than 100 color acetates featuring illustrations both from the text and from other sources.

PowerPoint Presentation (Douglas McConatha and Anthony Zumpetta, West Chester University of Pennsylvania) A PowerPoint presentation created for this text provides hundreds of ready-to-use graphic and text images. The presentation is available on a cross-platform CD-ROM. PowerPoint software is not required to use this program; a PowerPoint viewer is included to access the images.

Digital Media Archive for Sociology This CD-ROM for Windows and Macintosh contains a variety of media elements that you can use to create electronic presentations in the classroom. It includes hundreds of original images, as well as selected art from Henslin's texts and from other Allyn and Bacon sociology texts, providing instructors with a broad selection of graphs, charts, and maps that illustrate key sociological concepts. For classrooms with full multimedia capability, it also contains video segments and links to sociology Web sites.

Learning by Doing Sociology: In-Class Experiential Exercises (Linda Stoneall) This manual offers step-by-step procedures for in-class activities, contains suggestions for experiential learning, and provides trouble-shooting tips. It contains twenty-two exercises on a broad range of topics typically covered in the introductory sociology course.

The Blockbuster Approach: A Guide to Teaching Sociology with Video (Casey Jordan, Western Connecticut State University) This manual describes hundreds of commercially available videos that represent sociological ideas and themes, and provides sample assignments.

Doing Sociology with Student CHIP: Data Happy!, Third Edition, and *Analyzing Contemporary Social Issues: A Workbook with Student CHIP Software, Second Edition* (Gregg Lee Carter, Bryant College) The exercises in these workbooks, which explore major subfields of sociology, provide students the opportunity to use real data to analyze sociological issues.

A&B Video Library Qualified adopters may select from a wide variety of high quality videos from such sources as Films for the Humanities and Sciences and Annenberg/CPB.

Online Courses (Distributed Learning) If you conduct some or all of your introductory sociology course over the Internet, you can find out about online (distributed learning) options available for this text at **www.abacon.com/techsolutions**.

Faculty Guide for The Sociological Imagination *Telecourse* For instructors using this popular video series, this guide contains a syllabus that correlates the textbook, videos, *Telecourse Study Guide* (available from Allyn and Bacon), and *The Sociological Imagination Faculty Guide* (available from the telecourse producers).

SUPPLEMENTS FOR STUDENTS

Study Guide Plus (Gwendolyn E. Nyden, Oakton Community College) This manual provides learning objectives, key terms, self-tests, and glossaries. Students who need special language assistance will find a glossary for potentially confusing idioms and colloquialisms.

Study Guide for the Telecourse, The Sociological Imagination (Chris Moyers, Mission College) In addition to helping students review and master key information, this study guide correlates Henslin's text with all twenty-six lessons in this popular video series.

Practice Tests (Sharon LeBlond, Cincinnati State Technical and Community College) This manual of self-tests with answers helps students prepare for quizzes and exams.

Allyn and Bacon Quick Guide to the Internet for Sociology (Joseph Jacoby, Bowling Green University, and Doug Gotthoffer, California State University—Northridge) This reference guide introduces students to the basics of the Internet and the World Wide Web; it is updated annually and lists hundreds of URLs for sites that are useful for the study of sociology.

The Essential Sociology Reader (Robert Thompson, Minot State University) This anthology contains sixteen readings.

Careers in Sociology, Second Edition (W. Richard Stephens, Greenville College) This supplement examines how people working as sociologists entered the field, and how a degree in sociology can be a preparation for careers in areas such as law, gerontology, social work, and computers.

About the Web Site for this Edition

Students who visit the Web site that accompanies the Fifth Edition (www.abinteractive.com) will find an online study guide with practice tests, learning objectives, and links to useful sociology sites on the Internet. But that's just the beginning. Using a PIN code distributed with the text, they can log onto an area of premium content created and maintained by a team of college sociology instructors. On this portion of the site, students can access hundreds of additional online learning activities that will complement their textbook and enrich their study of sociology. Adopters of the Fifth Edition will likewise receive a PIN code that will give them access to the entire student area, plus a wealth of teaching resources. This Web site will continue to grow, with new features and information being added regularly.

About the Author

James M. Henslin, who was born in Minnesota, graduated from high school and junior college in California and from college in Indiana. Awarded scholarships, he earned his Master's and doctorate degrees in sociology at Washington University in St. Louis, Missouri. After this, he was awarded a postdoctoral fellowship from the National Institute of Mental Health, and spent a year studying how people adjust to the suicide of a family member. His primary interests in sociology are the sociology of everyday life, deviance, and international relations. Among his more than a dozen books is *Down to Earth Sociology* (Free Press), now in its eleventh edition, a book of readings that reflects some of these sociological interests. He also has published widely in sociology journals, including *Social Problems* and *American Journal of Sociology*.

While a graduate student, James Henslin taught at the University of Missouri at St. Louis. After completing his doctorate, he joined the faculty at Southern Illinois University, Edwardsville, where he is Professor Emeritus of Sociology. He says, "I've always found the introductory course enjoyable to teach. I love to see students' faces light up when they first glimpse the sociological perspective and begin to see how society has become an essential part of how they view the world."

Henslin enjoys spending time with his wife, reading, and fishing. His two favorite activities are writing and traveling. He especially enjoys living in other cultures, for this brings him face to face with behaviors and ways of thinking that he cannot take for granted, experiences that "make sociological principles come alive."

Sociology

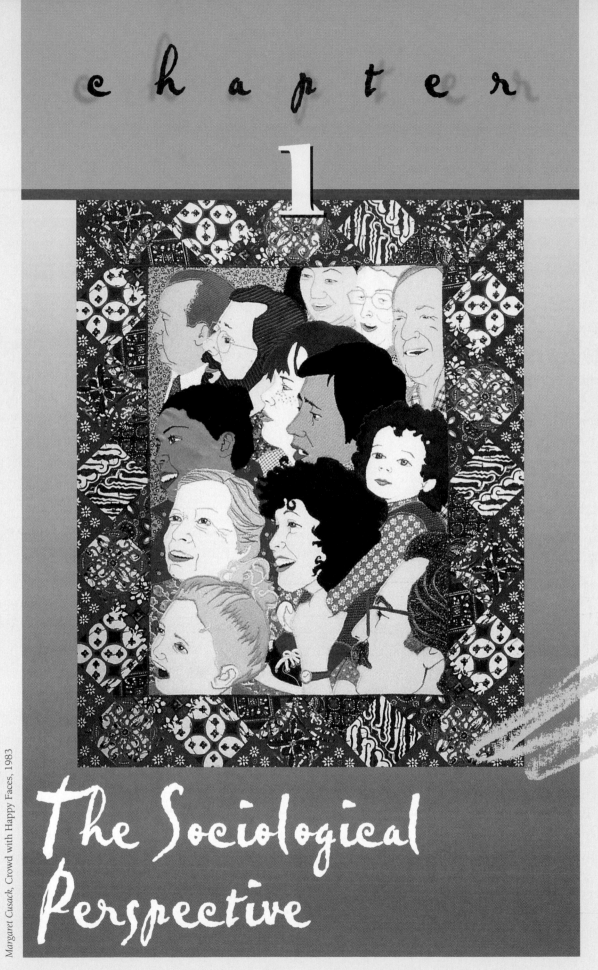

Margaret Cusack, Crowd with Happy Faces, 1983

The Sociological Perspective

- **The Sociological Perspective**
  Seeing the Broader Social Context
  The Growing Global Context

- **Sociology and the Other Sciences**
  The Natural Sciences
  The Social Sciences
  The Goals of Science

- **Origins of Sociology**
  Tradition Versus Science
  Auguste Comte and Positivism
  Herbert Spencer and Social Darwinism
  Karl Marx and Class Conflict
  Emile Durkheim and Social Integration
  Max Weber and the Protestant Ethic

- **The Role of Values in Social Research**

- ***Verstehen* and Social Facts**
  Weber and *Verstehen*
  Durkheim and Social Facts
  How Social Facts and *Verstehen* Fit Together

- **Sexism in Early Sociology**
  Attitudes of the Time
  Harriet Martineau

- **Sociology in North America**
  Early History: The Tension Between Social Reform
    and Social Analysis
  Jane Addams and Social Reform
  W.E.B. Du Bois and Race Relations
  Talcott Parsons and C. Wright Mills:
    Theory Versus Reform
  The Present: The Continuing Tension and the Rise
    of Applied Sociology

- **Theoretical Perspectives in Sociology**
  Symbolic Interactionism
  Functional Analysis
  Conflict Theory
  Levels of Analysis: Macro and Micro
  Putting the Theoretical Perspectives Together

- **Trends Shaping the Future of Sociology**

- **Summary and Review**

Even from the glow of the faded red-and-white exit sign, its faint light barely illuminating the upper bunk, I could see that the sheet was filthy. Resigned to another night of fitful sleep, I reluctantly crawled into bed, tucking my clothes around my body like a protective cocoon.

The next morning, I joined the long line of disheveled men leaning against the chain-link fence. Their faces were as downcast as their clothes were dirty. Not a glimmer of hope among them.

No one spoke as the line slowly inched forward. When my turn came, I was handed a Styrofoam cup of coffee, some utensils, and a bowl of semiliquid that I couldn't identify. It didn't look like any food I had seen before. Nor did it taste like anything I had ever eaten.

My stomach fought the foul taste, every spoonful a battle. But I was determined. "I will experience what they experience," I kept telling myself. My stomach reluctantly gave in and accepted its morning nourishment.

The room was strangely silent. Hundreds of men were eating, each immersed in his own private hell, his head awash with disappointment, remorse, bitterness.

As I stared at the Styrofoam cup of coffee, grateful at least for this small pleasure, I noticed what looked like teeth marks. I shrugged off the thought, telling myself that my long weeks as a sociological observer of the homeless were finally getting to me. "That must be some sort of crease from handling," I concluded.

I joined the silent ranks of men turning in their bowls and cups. When I saw the man behind the counter swishing out styrofoam cups in a washtub of water, I began to feel sick to my stomach. I knew then that the jagged marks on my cup really had come from a previous mouth.

How much longer did this research have to last? I felt a deep longing to return to my family—to a welcome world of clean sheets, healthy food, and "normal" conversations. ■

THE SOCIOLOGICAL PERSPECTIVE

Why were these men so silent? Why did they receive such despicable treatment? What was I doing in that homeless shelter? After all, I hold a respectable, secure, professional position, and I have a home and family.

Sociology offers a perspective, a view of the world. The *sociological perspective* (or imagination) opens a window onto unfamiliar worlds, and offers a fresh look at familiar worlds. In this text you will find yourself in the midst of Nazis in Germany, chimpanzees in Africa, and warriors in South America. But you will also find yourself looking at your own world in a different light. As you view other worlds, or your own, the sociological perspective enables you to gain a new vision of social life. In fact, this is what many find appealing about sociology.

The sociological perspective has been a motivating force in my own life. Ever since I took my first introductory course in sociology, I have been enchanted by the perspective that sociology offers. I have thoroughly enjoyed both observing other groups and questioning my own assumptions about life. I sincerely hope the same happens to you.

Seeing the Broader Social Context

The **sociological perspective** stresses the social contexts in which people live. It examines how these contexts influence people's lives. At the center of the sociological perspective is the question of how groups influence people, especially how people are influenced by their **society**—a group of people who share a culture and a territory.

To find out why people do what they do, sociologists look at **social location,** the corners in life that people occupy because of where they are located in a society. Sociologists look at jobs, income, education, gender, age, and race as significant. Consider, for example, how being identified with a group called females or with a group called males when we are growing up affects our ideas of what we should attain in life. Growing up as a male or a female influences not only our aspirations, but also how we feel about ourselves and how we relate to others in dating and marriage and at work.

Sociologist C. Wright Mills (1959) put it this way: "The sociological perspective enables us to grasp the connection between history and biography." By history, Mills meant that each society is located in a broad stream of events. Because of this, each society has specific characteristics—such as its ideas of the proper roles of men and women. By biography, Mills referred to the individual's specific experiences in society. In short, people don't do what they do because of inherited internal mechanisms, such as instincts. Rather, *external* influences—our experiences—become part of our thinking and motivations. The society in which we grow up, and our particular corners in that society, then, lie at the center of our behavior.

Consider a newborn baby. If we were to take the baby away from its U.S. parents and place it with a Yanomamö Indian tribe in the jungles of South America, you know that when the child begins to speak, his or her words will not be in English. You also know that the child will not think like an American. He or she will not grow up wanting credit cards,

sociological perspective an approach to understanding human behavior by placing it within its broader social context

society a term used by sociologists to refer to a group of people who share a culture and a territory

social location the group memberships that people have because of their location in history and society

for example, or designer jeans, a new car, and the latest video game. Equally, the child will unquestioningly take his or her place in Yanomamö society—perhaps as a food gatherer, a hunter, or a warrior—and he or she will not even know about the world left behind at birth. And, whether male or female, the child will grow up assuming that it is natural to want many children, not debating whether to have one, two, or three children.

People around the globe take their particular world for granted. Something inside us Americans tells us that hamburgers are delicious, small families attractive, and designer clothing desirable. Yet something inside some of the Sinai Desert Arab tribes used to tell them that warm, fresh camel's blood makes a fine drink and that everyone should have a large family and wear flowing robes (Murray 1935; McCabe and Ellis 1990). And that something certainly isn't an instinct. As sociologist Peter Berger (1963) phrased it, that "something" is "society within us."

Although obvious, this point frequently eludes us. We often think and talk about people's behavior as though it were caused by their sex, their race, or some other factor transmitted by their genes. The sociological

Examining the broad social context in which people live is essential to the *sociological perspective,* for this context shapes our beliefs and attitudes and sets guidelines for what we do. From this photo, you can see how distinctive those guidelines are for the Yanomamo Indians who live on the border of Brazil and Venezuela. How have these Yanomamo men been influenced by their group? How has your behavior been influenced by your groups?

perspective helps us escape from this cramped personal view by exposing the broader social context that underlies human behavior. It helps us see the links between what people do and the social settings that shape their behavior.

This brings us to *you*—to how *your* social groups have shaped *your* ideas and desires. Over and over in this text you will see that how you look at the world is the result of your exposure to certain groups rather than to others. I think you will enjoy the process of self-discovery that sociology offers.

The Growing Global Context

As is evident to all of us—from the labels on our clothing to the components in our cars—our world is becoming a global village. We used to live isolated on farms and in small towns, where beyond the borders of our community lay a world only dimly perceived. Communications used to be so slow that in the War of 1812 the Battle of New Orleans was fought two weeks after the adversaries, the United States and Great Britain, had signed a peace treaty. The armed forces there had not yet heard that the war was over (Volti 1995).

Today, in contrast, instantaneous communications connect us with remote areas of the globe, and a vast economic system connects us not only with Canada and Mexico but also with Belgium, Taiwan, and Indonesia. At the same time that we are immersed in such global interconnections, however, we continue to occupy little corners of life, marked by differences in family background, religion, job, gender, race, and social class. In these corners, we learn distinctive ways of viewing the world.

One of the beautiful—and fascinating—aspects of sociology is that it is able to analyze both parts of our current reality, the changes that incorporate us into a global network and our unique experiences in our smaller corners of life. In this text, we shall examine both of these vital aspects of the contemporary experience.

SOCIOLOGY AND THE OTHER SCIENCES

Just as humans today have an intense desire to unravel the mysteries around them, people in ancient times also attempted to understand their world. Their explanations, however, were not based only on observations, but were also mixed with magic and superstition.

To satisfy their basic curiosities about the world around them, humans gradually developed **science,** systematic methods used to study the social and natural worlds, as well as the knowledge obtained by those methods. **Sociology,** the scientific study of society and human behavior, is one of the sciences that modern civilization has developed.

A useful way of comparing these sciences—and of gaining a better understanding of sociology's place—is to first divide them into the natural and the social sciences.

The Natural Sciences

The **natural sciences** are the intellectual and academic disciplines designed to comprehend, explain, and predict the events in our natural environment. The natural sciences are divided into specialized fields of research according to subject matter, such as biology, geology, chemistry, and physics. These are further subdivided into even more highly specialized areas, with a further narrowing of content. Biology is divided into botany and zoology, geology into mineralogy and geomorphology, chemistry into its inorganic and organic branches, and physics into biophysics and quantum mechanics. Each area of investigation examines a particular "slice" of nature (Henslin 1999).

The Social Sciences

People have not limited themselves to investigating nature. In the pursuit of a more adequate understanding of life, they have also developed fields of science that focus on the social world. These, the **social sciences,** examine human relationships. Just as the natural sciences attempt to objectively understand the world of nature, the social sciences attempt to objectively understand the social world. Just as the world of nature contains ordered (or lawful) relationships that are not obvious but must be discovered through controlled observation, so the ordered relationships of the human or social world are not obvious, and must be revealed by means of controlled and repeated observations.

Like the natural sciences, the social sciences are divided into specialized fields based on their subject matter. These divisions are anthropology, economics, political science, psychology, and sociology. And the social sciences, too, are subdivided into further specialized fields. Thus, anthropology is divided into cultural and physical anthropology; economics has macro (large-scale) and micro (small-scale) specialties; political science has theoretical and applied branches; psychology may be clinical or experimental; and sociology has its quantitative and qualitative branches. Since our focus is sociology, let us contrast sociology with each of the other social sciences.

Political Science *Political science* focuses on politics and government. Political scientists study how people govern themselves: the various forms of government, their structures, and their relationships to other institutions of society. Political scientists are especially interested in how people attain ruling positions in their society, how they maintain those positions, and the consequences of their activities for those who are governed. In studying a constitutional government, such as that of the United States, political scientists also analyze voting behavior.

Economics *Economics* also concentrates on a single social institution. Economists study the production and distribution of the material goods and services of a society. They want to know what goods are being produced at what rate and at what cost, and how those goods

science the application of systematic methods to obtain knowledge and the knowledge obtained by those methods

sociology the scientific study of society and human behavior

natural sciences the intellectual and academic disciplines designed to comprehend, explain, and predict events in our natural environment

social sciences the intellectual and academic disciplines designed to understand the social world objectively by means of controlled and repeated observations

are distributed. They also are interested in the choices that determine production and consumption; for example, why a society produces a certain item instead of another.

Anthropology *Anthropology* is the sister discipline of sociology. The chief concern of anthropologists is to understand *culture,* a people's total way of life. Culture includes (1) the group's artifacts, such as its tools, art, and weapons; (2) the group's structure, that is, the hierarchy and other patterns that determine how its members interact with one another; (3) a group's ideas and values, especially how its belief system affects people's lives; and (4) the group's forms of communication, especially language. The anthropologists' traditional focus has been on preliterate or tribal peoples. It has been the practice that anthropologists who are studying for their doctorate live with a group. In their reports, they place special emphasis on the group's family (kin) relationships. With the world no longer having "undiscovered" groups, this focus on tribal groups is giving way to the study of groups in industrialized settings. When anthropologists study the same groups that sociologists do, they place greater emphasis on artifacts, authority (hierarchy), and language, especially kinship terms.

Psychology The focus of *psychology* is on processes that occur *within* the individual, within what they call the "skin-bound organism." Psychologists focus primarily on mental processes (what occurs in the brain, or the mind). They examine intelligence, emotions, perception, memory, even dreams. Some study how personality is formed. Others focus on mental aberration (psychopathology, or mental illness). Many psychologists work as counselors in school and work settings, and in private practice, where they give personality tests, IQ tests, and vocational aptitude tests. As therapists, they focus on resolving personal problems, whether they involve the need to recover from trauma, such as rape, or to free oneself from addiction to drugs, alcohol, or gambling.

Sociology *Sociology* has many similarities to the other social sciences. Like political scientists, sociologists also study how people govern one another, focusing especially on the impact that various forms of government have on people's lives. Like economists, sociologists are concerned with what happens to the goods and services of a society—but sociologists place their focus on the social consequences of production and distribution. Like anthropologists, sociologists study culture; they have a particular interest in the social consequences of material goods, group structure, and belief systems, as well as in how people communicate with one another. Like psychologists, sociologists are also concerned with how people adjust to the difficulties of life.

Given these overall similarities, then, what distinguishes sociology from the other social sciences? Unlike political scientists and economists, sociologists do not concentrate on a single social institution. Unlike anthropologists, sociologists focus primarily on industrialized societies. And unlike psychologists, sociologists stress factors *external* to the individual to determine what influences people. The Down-to-Earth Sociology box on the next page revisits an old tale about how members of different disciplines perceive the same subject matter.

The Goals of Science

The first goal of each scientific discipline is to *explain* why something happens. The second goal is to make **generalizations,** that is, to go beyond the individual case and make statements that apply to a broader group or situation. For example, a sociologist wants to explain not only why Mary went to college or became an armed robber but also why people with her characteristics are more likely than others to go to college or to become armed robbers. To achieve generalizations, sociologists look for **patterns,** recurring characteristics or events. The third scientific goal is to *predict,* to specify what will happen in the future in the light of current knowledge.

generalization a statement that goes beyond the individual case and is applied to a broader group or situation

patterns recurring characteristics or events

Sociology

AN UPDATED VERSION OF THE OLD ELEPHANT STORY

It is said that in the recent past five wise men and women, all blindfolded, were led to an elephant and asked to explain what they "saw." The first, a psychologist, feeling the top of the head, said, "This is the only thing that counts. All feeling and thinking take place inside here. To understand this beast, study only this."

The second, an anthropologist, tenderly touched the trunk and the tusks, then smiled and said, "This is really primitive. I feel very comfortable here. Concentrate on these."

The third, a political scientist, feeling the gigantic ears, announced, "This is the power center. What goes in here controls the entire beast. Concentrate your studies here."

The fourth, an economist, feeling the mouth, said, "This is what counts. What goes in here is distributed throughout the body. Concentrate your studies on how it is distributed."

Then came the sociologist (of course!), who, after feeling the entire body, said, "You can't understand the beast by concentrating on only one part. Each is but part of the whole. The head, the trunk and tusks, the ears, the mouth—all are important. But so are the parts of the beast that you haven't mentioned. We must remove our blindfolds so we can see the larger picture. We have to see how everything works together to form the entire animal."

Pausing for emphasis, the sociologist added, "And we also need to understand how this creature interacts with similar creatures. How does its life in groups influence its behaviors?"

I wish I could conclude this tale by saying that the psychologist, the anthropologist, the political scientist, and the economist were dazzled on hearing the wisdom of the sociologist, and amid gasps of wonderment threw away their blindfolds, joined together, and began to examine the entire animal. But, alas and alack! On hearing this sage advice, the specialists stubbornly bound their blindfolds even tighter so they could concentrate all the more on the single part. And if you listened very, very carefully you could even hear them mutter, "The top of the head is mine—stay away from it." "Don't touch the tusks." "Take your hand off the ears." "Stay away from the mouth—that's my area." ■

To attain these goals, scientists do not rely on magic, superstition, or common beliefs but on conclusions based on systematic studies. They examine evidence with an open mind, in such a way that it can be checked by others. Secrecy, prejudice, and other biases go against the grain of science.

Sociologists and other scientists also move beyond **common sense,** those ideas that prevail in a society, and that "everyone knows" are true. Just because "everyone" knows something is true does not make it so. "Everyone" can be mistaken, today just as easily as when common sense dictated that the world was flat or that no human could ever walk on the moon. As sociologists examine people's assumptions about the world, their findings may contradict commonsense notions about social life. To test your own "common sense," read the Down-to-Earth Sociology box on the next page.

Sometimes the explorations of sociologists take them into nooks and crannies that people would prefer remain unexplored. For example, a sociologist might study how people make decisions to commit a crime or to cheat on their spouses. Because sociologists want above all to understand social life, they cannot cease their studies because people feel uncomfortable. With all realms of human life considered legitimate avenues of exploration by sociologists, their findings sometimes challenge even cherished ideas.

As they examine how groups operate, sociologists often confront prejudice and attempts to keep things secret. It seems that every organization, every group, nourishes a pet image that it presents to the public. Sociologists are interested in knowing what is really going on behind the scenes, however, so they peer beneath the surface to get past that sugar-coated image (Berger 1963). This approach sometimes brings sociologists into conflict with

common sense those things that "everyone knows" are true

Sociology

ENJOYING A SOCIOLOGY QUIZ— SOCIOLOGICAL FINDINGS VERSUS COMMON SENSE

Some findings of sociology support commonsense understandings of social life, while others contradict them. Can you tell the difference? To enjoy this quiz, complete *all* the questions before turning the page to check your answers.

1. True/False The earnings of U.S. women have just about caught up with those of U.S. men.
2. True/False When faced with natural disasters such as floods and earthquakes, people panic and social organization disintegrates.
3. True/False Rapists are mentally ill.

4. True/False Most people on welfare are lazy and looking for a handout. They could work if they wanted to.
5. True/False Compared with men, women touch each other more while they are talking to one another.
6. True/False Compared with women, men maintain more eye contact in face-to-face conversations.
7. True/False The more available alcohol is (as measured by the number of places to purchase alcohol per one hundred people), the more alcohol-related injuries and fatalities occur on U.S. highways.

8. True/False Couples who live together before they marry are usually more satisfied with their marriages than couples who do not live together before they marry.
9. True/False The reason that people discriminate against minorities is prejudice; unprejudiced people don't discriminate.
10. True/False Students in Japan are under such intense pressure to do well in school that their suicide rate is about double that of U.S. students. ■

people who feel threatened by that information—which is all part of the adventure, and risk, of being a sociologist.

Origins of Sociology

Tradition Versus Science

Just how did sociology begin? In some ways it is difficult to answer this question. By the time Jesus Christ was born, the Greeks and Romans had already developed intricate systems of philosophy about human behavior. Even preliterate peoples tried to figure out social life. They, too, asked questions about why war exists, why some people become more powerful than others, and why some become rich. However, they often based their answers on superstition, myth, or even the positions of the stars, and did not *test* their assumptions.

Simple assertions of truth—or observations mixed with magic or superstition or the stars—are not adequate. *All science requires the development of theories that can be proved or disproved by systematic research.*

This standard simplifies the question of the origin of sociology. Measured by this standard, sociology is clearly a recent discipline. It emerged about the middle of the nineteenth century when European social observers began to use scientific methods to test their ideas. Four factors combined to lead to the development of sociology.

The first was the turmoil of the Industrial Revolution. By the middle of the nineteenth century, Europe was changing from agriculture to factory production. This violently changed people's lives. Masses of people were forced off the land. Moving to the cities in search of work, they found anonymity, crowding, filth, and poverty. Their ties to the land, to the generations

Sociology

SOCIOLOGICAL FINDINGS VERSUS COMMON SENSE— ANSWERS TO THE SOCIOLOGY QUIZ

1. False. Over the years, the income gap has narrowed, but only slightly. On average, full-time working women earn only about 65 to 70 percent of what full-time working men earn; this low figure is actually an improvement, for in the 1970s women's incomes averaged about 60 percent of men's. (See Figures 11.5 and 11.6, pages 304, 305.)

2. False. Following disasters, people develop *greater* cohesion, cooperation, and social organization to deal with the catastrophe.

3. False. Sociologists compared the psychological profiles of prisoners who had been convicted of rape and prisoners who had been convicted of other crimes. Their profiles were similar. Like robbery or embezzlement, rape is a learned behavior, not a consequence of overwhelming desire. See page 142.

4. False. Most people on welfare are children, the old, the sick, the mentally and physically handicapped, or young mothers with few skills. Less than 2 percent meet the common stereotype of an able-bodied man. See also "Exploring Myths about the Poor" on page 276.

5. False. Men touch each other more during conversations (Whyte 1989). This conclusion is based on a Manhattan sample of adults talking outside a restaurant. We need other studies to confirm this finding.

6. False. Women maintain considerably more eye contact (Henley et al. 1985).

7. False. Researchers in California compared the number of alcohol outlets per population with the alcohol-related highway injuries and fatalities. They found that counties in which alcohol is more readily available do not have more

alcohol-related injuries and fatalities (Kohfeld and Leip 1991).

8. False. The opposite is true. The reason, researchers suggest, is that many couples who marry after cohabiting are less committed to marriage in the first place—and a key to marital success is firm commitment to one another (Larson 1988).

9. False. When racial discrimination was legal in the United States, sociologists found that due to business reasons and peer pressure some unprejudiced people did discriminate (LaPiere 1934). For these same reasons, some prejudiced people do not discriminate, although they want to.

10. False. The suicide rate of U.S. students is about double that of Japanese students (Haynes and Chalker 1997). ■

that had lived there before them, and to their way of life were abruptly broken. They also found horrible working conditions: low pay, exhausting hours, dangerous work, foul smoke, and much noise. To survive, families had to permit their children to work in these same conditions; some children were even chained to factory machines to make certain they could not run away. Life no longer looked the same, and tradition, which had provided the answers, no longer could be counted on.

The second blow to tradition was the success of the American and French revolutions. These encouraged people to rethink social life. New ideas arose, including the conviction that individuals possess inalienable rights. As this new idea caught fire, many traditional Western monarchies gave way to more democratic forms. The ready answers of tradition, including religion, no longer sufficed.

When tradition reigns supreme, it provides a ready answer: "We do this because it has always been done this way." Such societies discourage original thinking. Since the answers are already provided, why search for explanations? Sweeping change, however, does the opposite: By upsetting the existing order, it encourages questioning and demands answers.

A third factor, imperialism, also stimulated the development of sociology. The Europeans had been successful in conquering many parts of the world. Their new colonial empires, stretching from Asia through Africa to North America, exposed them to radically different cultures. Startled by these contrasting ways of life, they began to ask why cultures differed.

The fourth impetus for the development of sociology was the success of the natural sciences. Just at the time when people were questioning fundamental aspects of their social worlds, **the scientific method**—using objective, systematic observations to test theories—was being tried out in chemistry and physics. Many secrets that had been concealed in nature were uncovered. With tradition no longer providing the answers to questions about social life, the logical step was to apply this method to these questions. The result was the birth of sociology.

Auguste Comte and Positivism

This idea of applying the scientific method to the social world, known as **positivism,** apparently was first proposed by Auguste Comte (1798–1857). With the French Revolution still fresh in his mind, Comte left the small, conservative town in which he had grown up and moved to Paris. The changes he experienced, combined with those France underwent in the revolution, led Comte to become interested in what holds society together. What creates social order, he wondered, instead of anarchy or chaos? And then, once society does become set on a particular course, what causes it to change?

As he considered these questions, Comte concluded that the right way to answer them was to apply the scientific method to social life. Just as this method had revealed the law of gravity, so, too, would it uncover the laws that underlie society. Comte called this new science **sociology**—"the scientific study of society" (from the Greek *logos,* "study of," and the Latin *socius,* "companion," or "being with others"). Comte stressed that this new science not only would discover social principles but also would apply them to social reform, to making society a better place to live.

Comte had some ideas that today's sociologists find humorous. For example, as Comte saw matters, there were only six sciences—mathematics, physics, chemistry, biology, astronomy, and sociology—with sociology far superior to the others (Bogardus 1929). To Comte, applying the scientific method to social life meant practicing what we might call "armchair philosophy"—drawing conclusions from informal observations of social life. He did not do what today's sociologists would call research, and his conclusions have been abandoned.

Nevertheless, Comte's insistence that we cannot be dogmatic about social life, but that we must observe and classify human activities in order to uncover society's fundamental laws, is well taken. Because he developed this idea and coined the term *sociology,* Comte often is credited with being the founder of sociology.

Herbert Spencer and Social Darwinism

Herbert Spencer (1820–1903), who grew up in England, is sometimes called the second founder of sociology. He, too, believed that society operates according to fixed laws. Spencer became convinced that societies evolve from lower ("barbarian") to higher ("civilized") forms. As generations pass, he said, the most capable and intelligent ("the fittest") members of a society survive, while the less capable die out. Thus, over time, societies steadily improve.

Spencer called this principle "the survival of the fittest." Although Spencer coined this phrase, it is usually attributed to his contemporary, Charles Darwin, who proposed that living organisms evolve over time as they survive the conditions of their environment. Because they were so similar to Darwin's ideas, Spencer's views of the evolution of societies became known as *social Darwinism.*

Unlike Comte, Spencer did not think sociology should guide social reform. In fact, he was convinced that no one should intervene in the evolution of society. The fittest members didn't need any help. They would always survive on their own and produce a more advanced society unless misguided do-gooders got in the way and helped the less fit survive.

Auguste Comte (1798–1857), who is identified as the founder of sociology, began to analyze the bases of the social order. Although he stressed that the scientific method should be applied to the study of society, he did not apply it himself.

the scientific method the use of objective, systematic observations to test theories

positivism the application of the scientific approach to the social world

sociology the scientific study of society and human behavior

This eighteenth-century painting (artist unknown) depicts women from Paris joining the French Army on its way to Versailles on October 5, 1789. The French Revolution of 1789 not only overthrew the aristocracy but upset the entire social order. With change so extensive, and the past no longer a sure guide to the present, Auguste Comte began to analyze how societies change, thus ushering in the science of sociology.

Consequently, Spencer's ideas—that charity and helping the poor were wrong, whether carried out by individuals or by the government—appalled many. Not surprisingly, wealthy industrialists, who saw themselves as "the fittest" (superior), found Spencer's ideas attractive. And not coincidentally, his views also helped them avoid feelings of guilt for living like royalty while people around them starved.

Like Comte, Spencer was more of a social philosopher than a sociologist. Also like Comte, Spencer did not conduct scientific studies, but simply developed ideas about society. Eventually, after gaining a wide following in England and the United States, Spencer's ideas about social Darwinism were discredited.

Karl Marx and Class Conflict

Karl Marx (1818–1883) not only influenced sociology but also left his mark on world history. Marx's influence has been so great that even the *Wall Street Journal,* that staunch advocate of capitalism, has called him one of the three greatest modern thinkers (the other two being Sigmund Freud and Albert Einstein).

Like Comte, Marx thought that people should take active steps to change society. Marx, who came to England after being exiled from his native Germany for proposing revolution, believed that the engine of human history is **class conflict.** He said that the *bourgeoisie* (the controlling class of *capitalists,* those who own the means to produce wealth—capital, land, factories, and machines) are locked in inevitable conflict with the *proletariat* (the exploited class, the mass of workers who do not own the means of production). This bitter struggle can end only when members of the working class unite in revolution and throw off their chains of bondage. The result will be a classless society, one free of exploitation, in which all individuals will work according to their abilities and receive according to their needs (Marx and Engels 1848/1967).

Marxism is not the same as communism. Although Marx supported revolution as the only way for the workers to gain control of society, he did not develop the political system called *communism.* This is a later application of his ideas. Indeed, Marx himself felt disgusted when he heard debates about his insights into social life. After listening to some of the positions attributed to him, he even declared, "I am not a Marxist" (Dobriner 1969b:222; Gitlin 1997:89).

Unlike Comte and Spencer, Marx did not think of himself as a sociologist. He spent years studying in the library of the British Museum in London, where he wrote widely on history, philosophy, and, of course, economics and political science. Because of his insights into the relationship between the social classes, especially the class struggle between the "haves" and the "have-nots," many sociologists today claim Marx as a significant early soci-

Karl Marx (1818–1883) believed that the roots of human misery lay in the exploitation of the proletariat, or propertyless working classes, by the capitalist class, those who own the means of production. Social change, in the form of the overthrow of the capitalists by the proletariat, was inevitable from Marx's perspective. Although Marx did not consider himself a sociologist, his ideas have profoundly influenced many in the discipline, particularly conflict theorists.

ologist. He also introduced one of the major perspectives in sociology, conflict theory, which is discussed on pages 30–31.

Emile Durkheim and Social Integration

Emile Durkheim (1858–1917) had a primary goal of getting sociology recognized as a separate academic discipline. Up to this time, sociology was viewed within the university as an offshoot of history and economics. Durkheim, who grew up in eastern France and was educated in both Germany and France, achieved his goal when he received the first academic appointment in sociology (the University of Bordeaux, in 1887) (Coser 1977).

Durkheim had another goal: to show how social forces affect people's behavior. To accomplish this, he conducted rigorous research. Durkheim compared the suicide rates of several European countries. He (1897/1966) found that each country's suicide rate was different, and that each remained remarkably stable year after year. He also found that different groups within a country had different suicide rates, and that these, too, remained stable from year to year. For example, Protestants, males, and the unmarried killed themselves at a higher rate than did Catholics, Jews, females, and the married. From this, Durkheim drew the insightful conclusion that suicide is not simply a matter of individuals here and there deciding to take their lives for personal reasons. Instead, *social factors underlie suicide,* and this is what keeps those rates fairly constant year after year.

Durkheim identified **social integration,** the degree to which people are tied to their social group, as a key social factor in suicide. He concluded that people with weaker social ties are more likely to commit suicide. This factor, he said, explained why Protestants, males, and the unmarried have higher suicide rates. It works this way, Durkheim argued: Protestantism encourages greater freedom of thought and action; males are more independent than females; and the unmarried lack the ties and responsibilities of marriage. In other words, because their social integration is weaker, members of these groups have fewer of the social ties that keep people from committing suicide.

The French sociologist Emile Durkheim (1858–1917) contributed many important concepts to sociology. When he compared the suicide rates of several countries, he discovered an underlying social factor: People are more likely to commit suicide if their ties to others in their communities are weak. Durkheim's identification of the key role of *social integration* in social life remains central to sociology today.

Although strong social bonds help protect people from suicide, Durkheim noted that in some instances strong bonds encourage suicide. To illustrate this type of suicide, which Durkheim termed *altruistic suicide,* he used the example of people who, torn apart by grief, kill themselves following the death of a spouse. Their own feelings are so integrated with those of their spouse that they prefer death rather than life without the one who gave meaning to life.

A hundred years later, Durkheim's study still is quoted (Simpson 1996). His research was so thorough that the principle he uncovered still applies: People who are less socially integrated have higher rates of suicide. Even today, those same categories that Durkheim identified—Protestants, males, and the unmarried—are more likely to kill themselves.

Durkheim's third concern was that social research be practical. He thought of sociologists as being similar to physicians: Where physicians apply scientific findings to determine the sickness and health of the body, sociologists should do the same for society (Giddens 1978). They should diagnose causes of social ills and develop remedies for them. For example, as today, in Durkheim's time people were concerned that there was too much individualism. Durkheim concluded that the new individualism was not pathological, but a normal, healthy expression of a changing society. Individualism can go too far, however. It then poses the danger of what Durkheim called **anomie,** a breaking down of the controlling influences of society. Under these conditions, people become detached from society and are left with too little moral guidance. This is dangerous, for their desires are no longer regulated by social norms (Coser 1977). Durkheim suggested that sociologists intervene: To prevent anomie, they should create new social groups to stand between the state and the family. These groups, he said, would help meet the need for a sense of belonging that the new, impersonal industrial society was eroding.

In sum, Durkheim's major contribution was his thorough sociological approach to understanding human behavior. Suicide, for example, appears to be such an intensely individual act that psychologists should examine it, not sociologists. Yet, as Durkheim illustrated, if we look at human behavior (such as suicide) only in individualistic terms, we miss its *social* basis.

class conflict Marx's term for the struggle between capitalists and workers

social integration the degree to which people feel a part of social groups

anomie Durkheim's term for a condition of society in which people become detached, cut loose from the norms that usually guide their behavior

Emile Durkheim used the term *anomie* to refer to feeling rootless and normless, lacking a sense of intimate belonging—the opposite of what sociologists mean by *community*. Durkheim believed that modern societies produce a feeling of isolation, much of which comes from the division of labor. In contrast, members of traditional societies, who work alongside family and neighbors and participate in similar activities, experience a high degree of *social integration*—the opposite of anomie. The photo on the right shows a contemporary farm family in Slovakia.

Max Weber and the Protestant Ethic

Max Weber (1864–1920) was another early sociologist who left a profound impression on sociology. He used cross-cultural and historical materials to determine how extensively social groups affect people's orientations to life.

Max Weber (Mahx VAY-ber) (1864–1920), a German sociologist and a contemporary of Durkheim, also held professorships in the new academic discipline of sociology. With Durkheim and Marx, Weber is one of the most influential of all sociologists, and you will come across his writings and theories in the coming chapters. Let's look at two issues Weber raised that remain controversial today.

Religion and the Origin of Capitalism Weber disagreed with Marx's claim that economics is the central force in social change. That role, he said, belongs to religion. Weber (1904/1958) theorized that the Roman Catholic belief system encouraged Roman Catholics to hold onto traditional ways of life, while the Protestant belief system encouraged its members to embrace change. Protestantism, he said, undermined people's spiritual security. Roman Catholics believed that because they were church members they were on the road to heaven. But Protestants, who did not share in this belief, turned to outside "signs" that they were in God's will. Financial success became the major sign that God was on their side. Consequently, Protestants began to live frugal lives, saving their money and investing the surplus in order to make even more. This, said Weber, brought about the birth of capitalism.

Weber called this self-denying approach to life the *Protestant ethic*. He termed the readiness to invest capital in order to make more money the *spirit of capitalism*. To test his theory, Weber compared Roman Catholic and Protestant countries. In line with his theory, he found that the Protestant countries were much more likely to have embraced the new economic system called capitalism. This theory was controversial when Weber developed it, and it continues to be debated today (Zou 1994; Hamilton 1996). We'll explore these ideas in more detail in Chapter 7.

value free the view that a sociologist's personal values should not influence social research

values ideas about what is good or worthwhile in life; attitudes about the way the world ought to be

✝ HE ROLE OF VALUES IN SOCIAL RESEARCH

Weber raised another issue that remains controversial among sociologists. He declared that sociology should be **value free**. By this, he meant that a sociologist's **values**, personal beliefs about what is good or worthwhile in life and the way the world ought to be, should not affect research. Weber wanted **objectivity,** total neutrality, to be the hallmark of sociological research. If values influence research, he said, sociological findings will be biased.

Objectivity as an ideal is not a matter of debate in sociology. On the one hand, all sociologists agree that objectivity is a proper goal, in the sense that sociologists must not distort data to make them fit preconceived ideas or personal values, and that research must report actual, not desired findings. On the other hand, it is equally clear that sociologists are members of a particular society at a given point in history and are therefore infused with values of all sorts. These values inevitably play a role in our research. For example, values are part of the reason that one sociologist chooses to do research on the Mafia, while another turns a sociological eye on kindergarten students.

To overcome the distortions that values can cause, and that can unwittingly become part of our research, sociologists stress **replication,** that is, the repetition of a study by other researchers to compare results. If values have influenced research findings, replication by other sociologists should uncover this problem and correct it.

Despite this consensus, however, values remain a hotly debated topic in sociology (Haynor and Varacalli 1993; Haddad and Newby 1999; Orlans 1999; Tinney 1999). The problem centers on the proper purposes and uses of sociological research. Regarding the *purpose* of sociology, some sociologists take the position that sociology's proper role is to advance understanding. Sociologists should gather data on any aspect of social life in which they are interested and then use the best theory available to interpret their findings. Others are convinced that it is the responsibility of sociologists to explore harmful social arrangements of society—to investigate what causes poverty, crime, war, and other forms of human exploitation. (See Figure 1.1)

Regarding the *uses* of sociology, those who say that understanding is sociology's proper goal take the position that the knowledge gained by social research belongs to the scientific community and to the world. Accordingly, it can be used by anyone for any purpose. In contrast, those who say that sociologists should focus their research on harmful social conditions take the position that sociologists should spearhead social reform. They say that sociologists should use their studies to alleviate human suffering and make society a better place to live.

Although the debate about the proper role of values in social research is infinitely more complicated than the argument summarized here—few sociologists take such one-sided views—the preceding sketch does identify its major issues. Perhaps sociologist John Galliher (1991) best expresses the majority position:

> Some argue that social scientists, unlike politicians and religious leaders, should merely attempt to describe and explain the events of the world but should never make value judgments based on those observations. Yet a value-free and nonjudgmental social science has no place in a world that has experienced the Holocaust, in a world having had slavery, in a world with the ever-present threat of rape and other sexual assault, in a world with frequent, unpunished crimes in high places, including the production of products known by their manufacturers to cause death and injury as has been true of asbestos products and continues to be true of the cigarette industry, and in a world dying from environmental pollution by these same large multinational corporations.

objectivity total neutrality

replication repeating a study in order to check the findings of a previous study

---

The Purposes of Social Research		The Uses of Social Research	
To advance understanding of human behavior	*versus* To investigate harmful social arrangements	Can be used by anyone for any purpose	*versus* Should be used to reform society

THE DEBATE OVER VALUES

VERSTEHEN AND SOCIAL FACTS

Weber and *Verstehen*

Weber also stressed that one cannot understand human behavior simply by looking at statistics. Those cold numbers may represent people's activities, he said, but they must be interpreted. To understand people, he said that we should use **Verstehen** (a German word meaning "to understand"). Perhaps the best translation of this term is "to grasp by insight." By emphasizing *Verstehen,* Weber meant that the best interpreter of human action is someone who "has been there," someone who can understand the feelings and motivations of the people they are studying. In short, we must pay attention to what are called **subjective meanings,** the ways in which people interpret their own behavior. We can't understand what people do, Weber insisted, unless we look at how people themselves view and explain their own behavior.

To better understand this term, let's return to the homeless in the opening vignette. Why were the men so silent? Why were they so unlike the noisy, sometimes boisterous college students who swarm dorms and cafeterias?

Verstehen can help explain this. When I interviewed men in the shelters (and, in other settings, homeless women), they revealed their despair. Because you know—at least on some level—what the human emotion of despair is, you can immediately apply your understanding to their situation. You know that people in despair feel a sense of hopelessness. The future looks bleak, hardly worth plodding toward. Consequently, why is it worth talking about? Who wants to hear another hard-luck story?

By applying *Verstehen*—your own understanding of what it means to be human and to face various situations in life—you gain an understanding of people's behavior, in this case the silence, the lack of communication, among the homeless.

Durkheim and Social Facts

In contrast to Weber's use of *Verstehen,* or subjective meanings, Durkheim stressed what he called **social facts.** By this term, he meant the patterns of behavior that characterize a social group. (Note, however, that Weber did not disagree about the significance of social facts, for they are the basis of his conclusions about Protestantism and capitalism.) Examples of social facts in the United States include June being the most popular month for weddings, suicide rates being higher among people 65 and older, and more births occurring on Tuesdays than on any other day of the week.

Durkheim said that we must use social facts to interpret social facts. In other words, each pattern reflects some underlying condition of society. People all over the country don't just coincidentally decide to do similar things, whether that be to get married or to commit suicide. If that were the case, in some years middle-aged people would be the most likely to kill themselves, in other years, young people, and so on. *Patterns that hold true year after year, however, indicate that as thousands and even millions of people make their individual decisions, they are responding to conditions in their society.* It is the job of the sociologist, then, to uncover social facts and then to explain them through other social facts. In the following section, we shall see how these particular social facts are explained by the school year, conditions of the aged, and the social organization of medicine, respectively.

How Social Facts and *Verstehen* Fit Together

Social facts and *Verstehen* go hand in hand. As a member of U.S. society, you know how June weddings are related to the end of the school year and how this month, now locked in tradition, common sentiment, and advertising, carries its own momentum. As for suicide among the elderly (see Chapter 13), you probably already have a sense of the greater despair that many Americans of this age feel.

Verstehen a German word used by Weber that is perhaps best understood as "to have insight into someone's situation"

subjective meanings the meanings that people give their own behavior

social facts Durkheim's term for the patterns of behavior that characterize a social group

But do you know why more Americans are born on Tuesday than on any other day of the week? One would expect Tuesday to be no more common than any other day, and that is how it used to be. But no longer. To understand this change, we need a combination of social facts and *Verstehen*. Four social facts are relevant: First, technological developments have made the hospital a dominating force in the U.S. medical system. Second, current technology has made delivery by cesarean section safer. Third, as discussed in Chapter 19, men took over the delivery of babies. Fourth, profit is a top goal of medicine in the United States. As a result, an operation that used to be reserved for emergencies has become so routine that one-fifth (21 percent) of all U.S. babies are now delivered in this manner (*Statistical Abstract* 1999:Table 104), the highest rate of such births in the world (Wolff et al. 1992). To these social facts, then, we add *Verstehen*. In this instance, that means understanding the preference of mothers-to-be to give birth in a hospital; understanding their perceived lack of alternatives; and understanding that physicians, whose services are in high demand, schedule deliveries for the time that is most convenient for them, with Tuesday being the day that suits them best.

SEXISM IN EARLY SOCIOLOGY

Attitudes of the Time

As you may have noticed, all the sociologists we have discussed are males. In the 1800s, sex roles were rigidly defined, with women assigned the roles of wife and mother. In the classic German phrase, women were expected to devote themselves to the four K's: *Kirche, Küchen, Kinder,* und *Kleider* (church, cooking, children, and clothes). Daring to break out of this mold meant risking severe social disapproval.

Few people, male or female, received any education beyond basic reading and writing. Higher education, for the rare few who received it, was reserved for men. A handful of women from wealthy families, however, did pursue higher education. A few even managed to study sociology, although the sexism so deeply entrenched in the universities stopped them from obtaining advanced degrees or becoming professors. In line with the times, their own research was almost entirely ignored.

Harriet Martineau

A classic example is Harriet Martineau (1802–1876), who was born into a wealthy English family. When Martineau first began to analyze social life, she would hide her writing beneath her sewing when visitors arrived, for writing was "masculine" and sewing "feminine" (Gilman 1911:88). Martineau persisted in her interests, however, and she eventually studied social life in both Great Britain and the United States. In 1837, two or three decades before Durkheim and Weber were born, Martineau published *Society in America*, in which she reported on this new nation's customs—family, race, gender, politics, and religion. In spite of her insightful examination of U.S. life, which is still worth reading today, Martineau's research met the fate of other early women sociologists and, until recently, has been ignored. Instead, she is known primarily for translating Comte's ideas into English.

SOCIOLOGY IN NORTH AMERICA

Early History: The Tension Between Social Reform and Social Analysis

Transplanted to U.S. soil in the late nineteenth century, sociology first took root at the University of Kansas in 1892, at Atlanta University, then an all-black school, in 1897, and at the University of Chicago in 1899. From there, academic specialties in sociology spread throughout North America. The growth was gradual, however. It was not until 1922 that

Interested in social reform, Harriet Martineau (1802–1876) turned to sociology, where she discovered the writings of Comte. An active advocate for the abolition of slavery, she traveled widely and wrote extensively.

Jane Addams, 1860–1935, a recipient of the Nobel Peace Prize, tirelessly worked on behalf of poor immigrants. With Ellen G. Starr, she founded Hull-House, a center to help immigrants in Chicago. She was also a leader in women's rights (women's suffrage) and in the peace movement.

McGill University gave Canada its first department of sociology. Harvard University did not open its department of sociology until 1930, and the University of California at Berkeley did not follow until the 1950s.

Initially, the department at the University of Chicago, which was founded by Albion Small (1854–1926), dominated sociology. (Small also founded the *American Journal of Sociology* and was its editor from 1895 to 1925.) Members of this first sociology department whose ideas continue to influence today's sociologists include Robert E. Park (1864–1944), Ernest Burgess (1886–1966), and George Herbert Mead (1863–1931), who developed the symbolic interactionist perspective, which we will examine later.

The situation of women in North America was similar to that of European women, and their contributions to sociology met a similar fate. Among the early women sociologists were Jane Addams, Emily Greene Balch, Isabel Eaton, Sophie Germain, Charlotte Perkins Gilman, Alice Hamilton, Florence Kelley, Elsie Clews Parsons, and Alice Paul. Denied faculty appointments in sociology, many turned to social activism (Young 1995).

Because some of these women worked with the poor rather than as professors of sociology, many sociologists classify them as social workers. Today's distinction between sociology and social work is fairly clear cut. There is a profession called social work; people train for it, they are hired to do it, and they have a distinct identity as social workers. They focus on aiding the economically underprivileged and socially maladjusted members of society. They have jobs in hospitals and schools, and many work in the area of public aid. Others set up private practice and counsel patients. Earlier in the development of sociology, there was often little distinction between sociology and social work. This fuzziness lasted until recently, and many departments combined sociology and social work. Some still do.

Jane Addams and Social Reform

Although many North American sociologists combined the role of sociologist with that of social reformer, none was so successful as Jane Addams (1860–1935). Like Harriet Martineau, she came from a background of wealth and privilege. Addams attended The Women's Medical College of Philadelphia, but dropped out because of illness (Addams 1910/1981). On one of her many trips to Europe, she was impressed with work being done to help London's poor. From then on, Addams tirelessly worked for social justice.

In 1889, Addams co-founded Hull-House, located in Chicago's notorious slums. Hull-House was open to people who needed refuge—to immigrants, the sick, the aged, the poor. With her piercing insights into the social classes, especially how workers were exploited and how peasant immigrants adjusted to industrializing cities, Addams strived to bridge the gap between the powerful and the powerless. Sociologists from nearby University of Chicago were frequent visitors at Hull-House. Her efforts at social reform were so outstanding and so effective that in 1931 she was a co-winner of the Nobel Peace Prize, the only sociologist to win this coveted award.

W(illiam) E(dward) B(urghardt) Du Bois (1868–1963) spent his lifetime studying relations between African Americans and whites. Like many early North American sociologists, Du Bois combined the role of academic sociologist with that of social reformer. He was also the editor of *Crisis,* an influential journal of the time.

W.E.B. Du Bois and Race Relations

Confronted by the racism of this period, African-American professionals also found life difficult. The most notable example is provided by W.E.B. Du Bois (1868–1963), who, after earning a bachelor's degree from Fisk University, became the first African American to earn a doctorate at Harvard (Lemert 1994). After completing his education at the University of Berlin, where he attended lectures by Max Weber, Du Bois taught Greek and Latin at Wilberforce University. He was hired by Atlanta University in 1897, where he remained for most of his career (Du Bois 1935).

It is difficult to imagine the racism that Du Bois encountered. For example, he once saw the fingers of a lynching victim displayed in a Georgia butcher shop (Aptheker 1990). His passionate concern became to eliminate social injustice. *Each* year between 1896 and 1914, Du Bois published a book on relations between African Americans and whites. Of his almost 2,000 writings, *The Philadelphia Negro* (1899) stands out. In this analysis of how African Americans in Philadelphia coped with racism, Du Bois pointed out that some of the more successful African Americans were breaking their ties with other African Americans in order to win acceptance by whites. This, he said, weakened the African-American community by depriving it of their influence. One of Du Bois' most elegantly written books, which preserves a picture of race relations immediately after the Civil War, is *The Souls of Black Folk.* The box on the next page is taken from this book.

Du Bois' insights into race relations were heightened by personal experiences. For example, although he was invited to present a paper at the 1909 meetings of the American Sociological Society, despite his education, faculty position, and accomplishments, he was too poor to attend. When he could afford to attend subsequent meetings, discrimination was so prevalent that he was not permitted to eat or stay at the same hotels as the white sociologists. Later in life, when Du Bois had the money to travel, the U.S. State Department feared that he would criticize the United States and refused to give him a visa (Du Bois 1968).

At first Du Bois was content simply to collect and interpret objective data. Later, frustrated at the lack of improvement in race relations, he turned to social action. Along with Jane Addams, Florence Kelley, and others from Hull-House, he founded the National Association for the Advancement of Colored People, or NAACP (Deegan 1988). Continuing to battle racism both as a sociologist and as a journalist, Du Bois eventually embraced revolutionary Marxism. At age 93, dismayed that so little improvement had been made in race relations, he moved to Ghana, where he is buried (Stark 1989).

Until recently, W.E.B. Du Bois was neglected in sociology, his many contributions unrecognized. As a personal example, during my entire graduate program at Washington University, I was never introduced to Du Bois' books and thought. Today, however, sociologists are rediscovering Du Bois, and he is beginning to receive some long-deserved appreciation.

Talcott Parsons and C. Wright Mills: Theory Versus Reform

Like Du Bois, and following the advice of Comte, many early North American sociologists combined the role of sociologist with that of social reformer. They saw society, or parts of it, as corrupt and in need of reform. During the 1920s and 1930s, for example, Park and Burgess not only studied prostitution, crime, drug addiction, and juvenile delinquency, but they also offered suggestions for how to alleviate these social problems.

During the 1940s, the emphasis shifted from social reform to social theory. Talcott Parsons (1902–1979), for example, developed abstract models of society that influenced a generation of sociologists. Parsons' detailed models of how the parts of society harmoniously work together did nothing to stimulate social activism.

C. Wright Mills (1916–1962) deplored the theoretical abstractions of this period, and he (1956) urged sociologists to get back to social reform. He saw the coalescing of interests on the part of a group he called the *power elite*—the top leaders of business, politics, and the military—as an imminent threat to freedom. Shortly after Mills' death, fueled by the Vietnam War, the United States entered the turbulent era of the 1960s and 1970s. Interest in social activism was sparked, and Mills' ideas became popular among a new generation of sociologists.

The Present: The Continuing Tension and the Rise of Applied Sociology

The apparent contradiction of these two aims—analyzing society versus working toward its reform—created a tension in sociology that is still evident today. Some sociologists believe that their proper role is to analyze some aspect of society and to publish their findings in sociology journals. Others say this is not enough—sociologists have an obligation to use their expertise to try to make society a better place in which to live, to help bring about a more just society.

Sociology

Down-to-Earth

EARLY NORTH AMERICAN SOCIOLOGY: DU BOIS AND RACE RELATIONS

The writings of W.E.B. Du Bois, who expressed sociological thought more like an accomplished novelist than like a sociologist, have been neglected in sociology. To help remedy this omission, I reprint the following excerpts from pages 66–68 of *The Souls of Black Folk* (1903). In this book, Du Bois analyzes changes that occurred in the social and economic conditions of African Americans during the thirty years following the Civil War. For two summers, while he was a student at Fisk, Du Bois taught in a log-hut, segregated school "way back in the hills" of rural Tennessee. The following excerpts help us understand conditions at that time.

It was a hot morning late in July when the school opened. I trembled when I heard the patter of little feet down the dusty road, and saw the growing row of dark solemn faces and bright eager eyes facing me. . . .There they sat, nearly thirty of them, on the rough benches, their faces shading from a pale cream to deep brown, the little feet bare and swinging, the eyes full of expectation, with here and there a twinkle of mischief, and the hands grasping Webster's blue-black spelling-book. I loved my school, and the fine faith the children had in the wisdom of their teacher was truly marvelous. We read and spelled together, wrote a little, picked flowers, sang, and listened to stories of the world beyond the hill. . . .

On Friday nights I often went home with some of the children,—sometimes to Doc Burke's farm. He was a great, loud, thin Black, ever working, and trying to buy the

seventy-five acres of hill and dale where he lived; but people said that he would surely fail and the "white folks would get it all." His wife was a magnificent Amazon, with saffron face and shiny hair, uncorseted and barefooted, and the children were strong and barefooted. They lived in a one-and-a-half-room cabin in the hollow of the farm near the spring. . . .

I liked to stay with the Dowells, for they had four rooms and plenty of good country fare. Uncle Bird had a small, rough farm, all woods and hills, miles from the big road; but he was full of tales,—he preached now and then,—and with his children, berries, horses, and wheat he was happy and prosperous. Often, to keep the peace, I must go where life was less lovely; for instance, 'Tildy's mother was incorrigibly dirty, Reuben's larder was limited seriously, and herds of untamed insects wandered over the Eddingses' beds. Best of all I loved to go to Josie's, and sit on the porch, eating peaches, while the mother bustled and talked: how Josie had bought the sewing-machine; how Josie worked at service in winter, but that four dollars a month was "mighty little" wages; how Josie longed to go away to school, but that it "looked liked" they never could get far enough ahead to let her; how the crops failed and the well was yet unfinished; and, finally, how "mean" some of the white folks were.

For two summers I lived in this little world. . . . I have called my tiny community a world, and so its isolation made it; and yet there was among us

but a half-awakened common consciousness, sprung from common joy and grief, at burial, birth, or wedding; from common hardship in poverty, poor land, and low wages, and, above all, from the sight of the Veil* that hung between us and Opportunity. All this caused us to think some thoughts together; but these, when ripe for speech, were spoken in various languages. Those whose eyes twenty-five and more years had seen "the glory of the coming of the Lord," saw in every present hindrance or help a dark fatalism bound to bring all things right in His own good time. The mass of those to whom slavery was a dim recollection of childhood found the world a puzzling thing: it asked little of them, and they answered with little, and yet it ridiculed their offering. Such a paradox they could not understand, and therefore sank into listless indifference, or shiftlessness, or reckless bravado. There were, however, some—such as Josie, Jim, and Ben—to whom War, Hell, and Slavery were but childhood tales, whose young appetites had been whetted to an edge by school and story and half-awakened thought. Ill could they be content, born without and beyond the World. And their weak wings beat against their barriers,—barriers of caste, of youth, of life; at last, in dangerous moments, against everything that opposed even a whim. ■

*"The Veil" is shorthand for the Veil of Race, referring to how race colors all human relations. Du Bois' hope was that "sometime, somewhere, men will judge men by their souls and not by their skins" (p. 261).

Figure 1.2 COMPARING BASIC AND APPLIED SOCIOLOGY

BASIC SOCIOLOGY
Audience: Fellow sociologists
Product: Knowledge

APPLIED SOCIOLOGY
Audience: Clients
Product: Change

| Constructing theory/testing hypotheses | Research on basic social life, on how groups affect people | The middle ground: criticisms of society and social policy | Analyzing specific problems/ evaluating the effectiveness of policies and programs | Suggesting solutions to specific problems/ proposing ways to improve a policy or program | Implementing solutions (clinical sociology) |

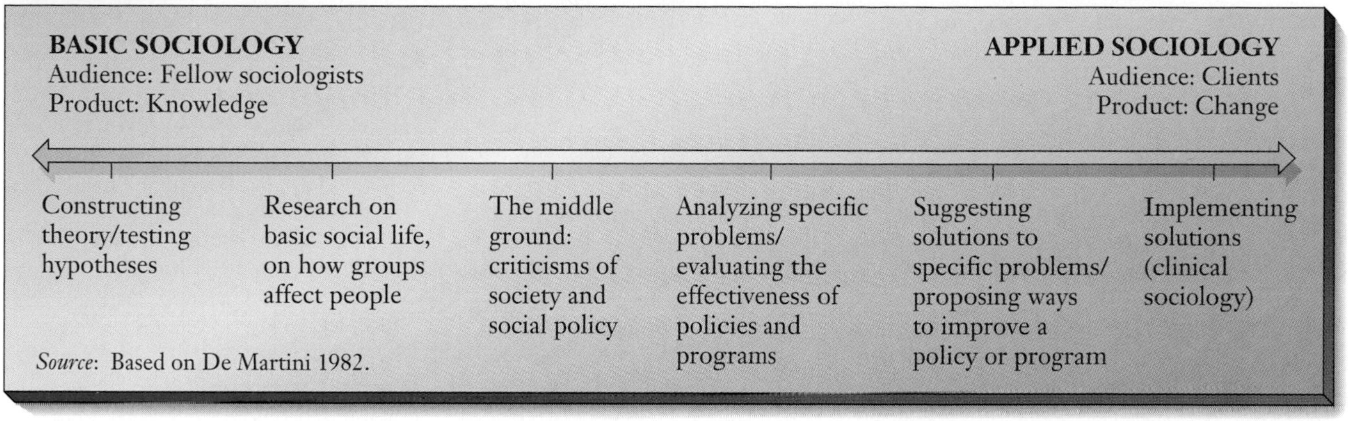

Source: Based on De Martini 1982.

Somewhere between these extremes has emerged **applied sociology**, the use of sociology to solve problems. (See Figure 1.2, which contrasts basic and applied sociology.) One of the first attempts at applied sociology—and one of the most successful—was one that I just mentioned, the founding of the National Association for the Advancement of Colored People. Today's applied sociologists work in a variety of settings. Some work for business firms to solve problems in the workplace. Others do research for government commissions, where they investigate pornography, crime, violence, or environmental pollution. Still others work in high technology (Guice 1999). The Down-to-Earth Sociology box below gives an idea of the variety of settings in which applied sociologists work.

applied sociology the use of sociology to solve problems—from the micro level of family relationships to the macro level of crime and pollution

Down-to-Earth Sociology

CAREERS IN SOCIOLOGY: WHAT APPLIED SOCIOLOGISTS DO

Most sociologists teach in colleges and universities. As your instructor is doing in this course, they transmit basic sociological theory and research to the next generation. Applied sociologists, in contrast, work in a wide variety of areas—from improving work relationships to studying high technology. To give you an idea of that variety, let's look over the shoulders of four applied sociologists.

Leslie Green, who does marketing research at Vanderveer Group in Philadelphia, Pennsylvania, earned her bachelor's degree in sociology at Shippensburg University. To develop marketing strate-

gies to get doctors to prescribe a particular drug, her company has physicians meet in groups to discuss prescription drugs. Green sets up the meetings, locates moderators for the discussion groups, and arranges payments to the physicians who participate in the research. "My training in sociology," she says, "helps me in 'people skills.' It helps me to understand the needs of different groups, and to interact with them."

Stanley Capela, whose master's degree is from Fordham University, works as an applied sociologist at HeartShare Human Services in New York. He evaluates how children's programs—

such as ones focusing on housing, AIDS, care in group homes, and preschool education for developmentally disabled children—actually work, compared with what they are supposed to do. He spots problems and suggests solutions. One of his assignments was to find out why adoption was so slow, why there was a backlog of unadopted children even though there was a long list of eager adoptive parents. He identified the problem as an inefficient information system; that is, the paperwork got bogged down as it was routed through the system. He suggested ways to improve the flow of paperwork.

(continued)

Sociology

CAREERS IN SOCIOLOGY:
WHAT APPLIED SOCIOLOGISTS DO *(continued)*

Laurie Banks, who received her master's degree in sociology from Fordham University, works for the New York City Health Department, where she analyzes vital statistics. As she examined death certificates, she found that some areas of the city had higher rates of cancer. With its high rates of stomach cancer, one Polish neighborhood stood out. Alerted to this, the Centers for Disease Control conducted interviews in the neighborhood. They traced the cause to eating large amounts of sausage. In another case, Banks compared birth certificates with school records. She found that problems at birth—low birth weight, lack of prenatal care, and birth complications—were linked to low reading skills and behavior problems in school.

Ross Cappell, whose doctorate is from Temple University, runs

his own research company, Social Research Corporation, in Philadelphia. His work, too, is filled with variety—from studying how an increase in fares would affect the use of public transportation to surveying the customers of a credit card company so the company could better understand its market. In one case, Cappell was asked to evaluate the services that unemployed workers received when a steel mill closed down. He found that the services and training were not very helpful. Too many workers were retained in a single field, such as air conditioner repair, and the local market was flooded with more specialists than it could use. When Cappell testified before Congress, he recommended that displaced workers be trained to match the needs of the local labor market.

Other sociologists work in the developing fields of high technology, especially in information technology and telecommunications. They develop what are called "user-centered designs"; that is, they figure out how people will respond to new computer products and they give feedback to software engineers who design those products (Guice 1999).

From just this small sample, you can catch a glimpse of the wide variety of work that applied sociologists do. You can see that some applied sociologists work for corporations, some for government and private agencies, and others operate their own firms. You can also see that a doctorate is not necessary to work as an applied sociologist. For another example of applied sociology, see the Down-to-Earth Sociology box on page 23. ■

Applied sociology is not the same as social reform. For the most part, it is an application of sociology in some specific setting, not an attempt to rebuild society, as early sociologists envisioned. Consequently, a new tension has emerged in sociology. Sociologists who want the emphasis to be on social reform say that applied sociology doesn't even come close to this. It is an application of sociology but not an attempt to change society. Others, who want the emphasis to remain on discovering knowledge (basic sociology), say that when sociology is applied it is not sociology—even if done by a sociologist. If a sociologist uses sociological principles to help prostitutes escape from pimps, for example, is it sociology? This issue is discussed in the Down-to-Earth Sociology box on the next page. This basic tension is likely to remain throughout the new century.

At this point, let's consider how theory fits into sociology.

theory a general statement about how some parts of the world fit together and how they work; an explanation of how two or more facts are related to one another

symbolic interactionism a theoretical perspective in which society is viewed as composed of symbols that people use to establish meaning, develop their views of the world, and communicate with one another

*T*HEORETICAL PERSPECTIVES IN SOCIOLOGY

Facts never interpret themselves. In everyday life, we interpret what we observe by using common sense, placing any particular observation or "fact" into a framework of more-or-less related ideas. Sociologists place their observations into a conceptual framework called

Sociology

Down-to-Earth

SOCIOLOGY OR SOCIAL WORK?
TAKING BACK CHILDREN FROM THE NIGHT

What is and is not sociology remains a lively topic among sociologists. Especially when sociologists discuss the application of sociological knowledge, discussions tend to become heated. Where, for example, is the line between sociology and social work? That line can sometimes be very fine. Consider Lois Lee and her work among teen prostitutes.

Lois Lee is a sociologist. There is no doubt about this. She earned a Ph.D. in sociology from United States International University in 1981. While she was working on her doctorate, she began to help teenagers who were prostituting themselves. She took them into her home, where she lived with her husband and baby son. In three years, she took in 250 girls.

As Lee focused more and more on helping teen prostitutes, she founded Children of the Night, which reaches the kids by means of "a twenty-four-hour hotline, a street outreach program, a walk-in crisis center, crisis intervention for medical or life-threatening situations, family counseling, job placement, and foster home or group placement." By providing alternatives to prostitution and petty crime, Lee estimates that Children of the Night has helped more than 5,000 young runaways and prostitutes get off the streets. Lee's work has brought her national recognition and a presidential award.

Lee credits her success to sociology. She says that sociology gave her insights into the relationships between groups. She says that her sociological training helps her "to understand and move safely through intersecting deviant worlds, to relate positively to police and caretaking agencies while retaining a critical perspective, to know which game to play in which situation."

In a CBS interview, Lee said, "I know what the street rules are. I know what the pimp game is, I know what the con games are, and it's up to me to play that game correctly." She added, "It's all sociology. That's why when people call me a social worker I always correct them."

Many sociologists disagree. They say that Lee is a sociologist who is doing social work. Whether a sociologist, a psychologist, or a social worker helps prostitutes does not change what they do. If a sociologist went into computer sales, for example, he or she would be in business, not sociology, no matter how much insight his or her sociological studies may have provided into relationships among customers, managers, and suppliers. ■

---

a theory. A **theory** is a general statement about how some parts of the world fit together and how they work. It is an explanation of how two or more facts are related to one another. By providing a framework in which to place observations, each theory interprets reality in a distinct way.

Sociologists use three major theories: symbolic interactionism, functional analysis, and conflict theory. Let's first examine the main elements of these theories. (See Table 1.1.) Then let's see how each theory provides a different understanding of social life. To do so, we'll use each theory to explain why the U.S. divorce rate is so high.

Symbolic Interactionism

We can trace the origins of **symbolic interactionism** to the Scottish moral philosophers of the eighteenth century, who noted that people evaluate their own conduct by comparing themselves with others (Stryker 1990). In the United States, a long line of thinkers added to this analysis, including the pioneering psychologist William James (1842–1910) and the educator John Dewey (1859–1952), who analyzed how people use symbols to encapsulate their experiences. This theoretical perspective was brought to sociology by Charles Horton Cooley (1864–1929), William I. Thomas (1863–1947), and George Herbert Mead (1863–1931). Cooley's and Mead's analyses of how symbols lie at the basis of the self-concept are discussed on pages 68–71.

George Herbert Mead (1863–1931) is one of the founders of symbolic interactionism, a major theoretical perspective in sociology. He taught at the University of Chicago, where his lectures were very popular. Though he wrote very little, after his death students compiled his lectures into an influential book, *Mind, Self, and Society.*

Table 1.1

MAJOR THEORETICAL PERSPECTIVES IN SOCIOLOGY

Perspective	Usual Level of Analysis	Focus of Analysis	Key Terms	Applying the Perspectives to the U.S. Divorce Rate
Symbolic Interactionism	Microsociological—examines small-scale patterns of social interaction	Face-to-face interaction; how people use symbols to create social life	Symbols Interaction Meanings Definitions	Industrialization and urbanization change marital roles and lead to a redefinition of love, marriage, children, and divorce.
Functional Analysis (also called functionalism and structural functionalism)	Macrosociological—examines large-scale patterns of society	Relationships among the parts of society; how these parts are *functional* (have beneficial consequences) or *dysfunctional* (have negative consequences)	Structure Functions (manifest and latent) Dysfunctions Equilibrium	As social change erodes the traditional functions of the family, family ties weaken, and the divorce rate increases.
Conflict Theory	Macrosociological—examines large-scale patterns of society	The struggle for scarce resources by groups in a society; how dominant elites use power to control the less powerful	Inequality Power Conflict Competition Exploitation	When men control economic life, the divorce rate is low because women find few alternatives to a bad marriage; the rising divorce rate reflects a shift in the balance of power between men and women.

Until recently, it was common for the basic necessities of life to be scarce. Family members depended on one another for survival. As functionalists stress, industrialization not only brought more goods, which made survival easier, but also undermined the functions that bind families together, making it more likely that couples will divorce. What makes families strong today?

Symbolic interactionists stress that *symbols*—things to which we attach meaning—make social life possible. What do they mean by this? First, without symbols our social relations would be limited to the animal level, for we would have no mechanism for perceiving others in terms of relationships (aunts and uncles, employers and teachers, and so on). Strange as it may seem, only because we have symbols can we have aunts and uncles, for it is these symbols that define for us what such relationships entail. Second, without symbols we also could not coordinate our actions with others. We would be unable to make plans for a future date, time, and place. Unable to specify times, materials, sizes, or goals, we could not build bridges and highways. Without symbols, there would be no books, movies, or musical instruments. We would have no schools or hospitals, no government, no religion.

Symbolic interactionists point out that even the *self* is a symbol, for it consists of the ideas that we have about who we are. And it is a changing symbol, for as we interact with others, we constantly adjust our views of the self based on how we interpret the reactions of others.

In short, symbolic interactionists analyze how our behaviors depend on the ways we define ourselves and others. For example, if you think of someone as an aunt or uncle, you behave in certain ways, but if you think of that person as a boyfriend or girlfriend, you behave quite differently. It is as though everyday life is a stage on which we perform; we switch roles to suit our changing audiences. Symbolic interactionists primarily examine face-to-face interaction; they look at how people work out their relationships and make sense out of life and their place in it.

Applying Symbolic Interactionism To better understand symbolic interactionism, let's see how changing symbols (meanings) help to explain the high U.S. divorce rate. For background, you should understand that marriage used to be seen as a lifelong commitment, and divorce as an immoral act, evidence of a flagrant disregard for public opinion and the abandonment of adult responsibilities.

REVIEW

1. *Emotional satisfaction.* In the early part of the last century, symbolic interactionists observed that the basis for family solidarity was changing. As early as 1933, sociologist William Ogburn noted that personality was becoming more important in mate selection. Then in 1945, sociologists Ernest Burgess and Harvey Locke found that family solidarity was coming to depend more and more on mutual affection, understanding, and compatibility. What these sociologists had observed was a fundamental shift in U.S. marriage: Husbands and wives were coming to expect—and demand—greater emotional satisfaction from one another.

   As this trend intensified, intimacy became the core of marriage. At the same time, as society grew more complex and impersonal, Americans came to see marriage as a solution to the tensions that society produced (Lasch 1977). This new form, "companionate marriage," contributed to divorce, for it encouraged people to expect that their spouse would satisfy "each and every need." Consequently, sociologists say, marriage became an "overloaded institution."

2. *The love symbol.* Our symbol of love also helps to "overload" marriage. Unrealistic expectations that "true love" will be a constant source of emotional satisfaction set people up for crushed hopes, for when dissatisfactions enter marriage, as they inevitably do, spouses tend to blame one another for what they see as the other's failure. Their engulfment in the symbol of love at the time of marriage blinds them to the basic unreality of their expectations.

3. *The meaning of children.* Ideas about childhood have undergone a deep historical shift with far-reaching consequences for the contemporary U.S. family (Henslin 1992). In medieval European society children were seen as miniature adults, and there was no sharp separation between the worlds of adults and children (Ariés 1962). Boys were apprenticed at about age 7, while girls at the same age learned the homemaking duties associated with the wifely role. In the United States, just three generations ago children "became adults" when they graduated from eighth grade and took employment. The contrast is amazing: From miniature adults, children have been culturally fashioned into impressionable, vulnerable, and innocent beings.

4. *The meaning of parenthood.* These changed notions of childhood have had a corresponding impact on our ideas of good parenting. Today's parents are expected not only to provide unending amounts of affection, love, and tender care but also to take responsibility for ensuring that their children "reach their potential." Today's child rearing lasts longer and is more demanding, pushing the family into even greater "emotional overload" (Lasch 1977).

5. *Marital roles.* In earlier generations, newlyweds knew what they could legitimately expect from each other, for the responsibilities and privileges of husbands and wives were clearly defined. In contrast, today's much vaguer guidelines leave couples to work out more aspects of their respective roles on their own. Many find it difficult to figure out how to divide up responsibilities for work, home, and children.

6. *Perception of alternatives.* While the above changes in marriage expectations were taking place, another significant social change was under way: More and more women began taking jobs outside the home. As they earned paychecks of their own, many wives began for the first time to see alternatives to remaining in unhappy marriages. Symbolic

Figure 1.3

**U.S. MARRIAGE,
U.S. DIVORCE**

Sources: Statistical Abstract 1998:Table 92; earlier editions for earlier years; "Population Update" 1999. The broken lines indicate the author's estimates.

interactionists consider the perception of an alternative an essential first step to making divorce possible.

7. *The meaning of divorce.* As these various factors coalesced—greater expectations of emotional satisfaction and changed marital and parental roles, accompanied by a new perception of alternatives to an unhappy marriage—divorce steadily increased. (Figure 1.3 shows the increase in divorce in the United States, from practically zero in 1890 to the current 1.1 million divorces a year. The plateau for both marriage and divorce since 1980 is probably due to increased cohabitation.)

As divorce became more common, its meaning changed. Once a symbol of almost everything negative—failure, irresponsibility, even immorality—divorce became infused with new meanings—personal change and the opportunity to begin anew. This symbolic change from failure to self-fulfillment reduced the stigma of divorce, setting the stage for divorce on an even larger scale.

8. *Changes in the law.* The law, itself a powerful symbol, began to reflect these changed ideas about divorce—and to encourage divorce. Where previously divorce was granted only when the most rigorous criteria, such as adultery, were met, legislators now made "incompatibility" legitimate grounds for divorce. Eventually, states pioneered "no-fault" divorce, in which couples could dissolve their marriage without accusations of wrongdoing. Some even provide do-it-yourself divorce kits.

■ **In Sum** Symbolic interactionists explain an increasing divorce rate in terms of the changing symbols (or meanings) associated with both marriage and divorce. Changes in people's ideas—about divorce, marital satisfaction, love, the nature of children and parenting, and the roles of husband and wife—have put extreme pressure on today's married couples. No single change is *the* cause, but taken together, these changes provide a strong "push" toward divorce.

Are these changes good or bad? Central to symbolic interactionism is the position that to make a value judgment about change (or anything else) requires a value framework from which to view the change. Symbolic interactionism provides no such value framework. In short, symbolic interactionists, like other sociologists, can analyze social change, but they cannot pass judgment on that change.

Functional Analysis ✳

The central idea of **functional analysis** is that society is a whole unit, ✳ made up of interrelated parts that work together. Functional analysis, also known as *functionalism* and *structural functionalism,* is rooted in the origins of sociology (Turner 1978). Auguste Comte and Herbert Spencer viewed society as a kind of living organism. Just as a biological organism has organs that function together, they wrote, so does society. Like an organism, if society is to function smoothly, its various parts must work together in harmony.

Emile Durkheim also saw society as being composed of many parts, each with its own function. When all the parts of society fulfill their functions, society is in a "normal" state. If they do not fulfill their functions, society is in an "abnormal" or "pathological" state. To understand society, then, functionalists say that we need to look at both *structure* (how the parts of a society fit together to make the whole) and *function* (what each part does, how it contributes to society).

Although Robert Merton dismissed the organic analogy, he continued the essence of functionalism—the image of society as a whole composed of interrelated parts. Merton used the term *functions* to refer to the beneficial consequences of people's actions that help keep a group (society, social system) in equilibrium. In contrast, *dysfunctions* are consequences that undermine a system's equilibrium.

Functions can be either manifest or latent. If an action is intended to help some part of a system, it is a *manifest function.* For example, suppose that government officials become concerned about our slowing rate of childbirth. Congress passes a new law that offers a $10,000 bonus for every child born to a married couple. The intention, or manifest function, of the bonus is to increase childbearing. Merton pointed out that people's actions also can have *latent functions*—unintended consequences that help a system adjust. Let's suppose that the bonus works, that the birth rate jumps. As a result, the sale of diapers and baby furniture booms. Because the benefits to these businesses were not the intended consequences, they are latent functions of the bonus.

Of course, human actions also can hurt a system. Because such consequences usually are unintended, Merton called them *latent dysfunctions.* Let's assume that the government has failed to specify a "stopping point" with regard to its bonus system. To collect the bonus, some people keep on having children. The more children they have, however, the more they need the next bonus in order to survive. Large families become common, and poverty increases. Welfare is reinstated, taxes jump, and the nation erupts in protest. Because these results were not intended, and because they harmed the social system, they represent latent dysfunctions of the bonus program.

■ **In Sum** From the perspective of functional analysis, then, the group is a functioning whole, with each part related to the whole. Whenever we examine a smaller part, we need to look for its functions and dysfunctions to see how it is related to the larger unit. This basic approach can be applied to any social group, whether an entire society, a college, or even a group as small as a family.

Applying Functional Analysis Now let's apply functional analysis to the U.S. divorce rate. Functionalists stress that industrialization and urbanization undermined the traditional functions of the family. Let's see how each of these basic functions has changed.

1. *Economic production.* Prior to industrialization, the family constituted an economic team. Most families found it difficult to obtain the basic necessities of life, and family members

Sociologists who use the functionalist perspective stress how individualization and urbanization undermined the traditional functions of the family. Before industrialization, members of the family worked together as an economic unit. As production moved away from the home, it took with it first the father and, more recently, the mother. One consequence is a major dysfunction, the weakening of family ties. This scene was painted by Master of Serrone, Foligno, Italy.

functional analysis a theoretical framework in which society is viewed as composed of various parts, each with a function that, when fulfilled, contributes to society's equilibrium; also known as functionalism and structural functionalism

had to cooperate in producing what they needed to survive. When industrialization moved production from home to factory, it disrupted this family team and weakened the bonds that tied family members together. Especially significant was the transfer of the husband/father to the factory, for this move separated him from the family's daily routine. In addition, the wife/mother and children now contributed less to the family's economic survival.

2. *Socialization of children.* As these sweeping economic changes took place, the government, which was growing larger and more powerful, usurped many family functions. To name just one example, local schools took away from the family the responsibility of educating children. In so doing, they assumed much of the responsibility for socializing children. To make certain that families went along with this change, states passed laws requiring that children attend school and threatened parents with jail if they did not send their children.

3. *Care of the sick and elderly.* With new laws governing medical schools and hospitals, institutionalized medicine grew more powerful, and care of the sick gradually shifted from the family to outside medical specialists. As the central government expanded and its agencies multiplied, care of the aged changed from a family concern to a government obligation.

4. *Recreation.* As more disposable income became available to Americans, business enterprises sprang up to compete for that income. This cost the family much of its recreational function, for much entertainment and "fun" changed from home-based, family-centered activities to attendance at paid events.

5. *Sexual control of members.* Even the control of sexuality was not left untouched by the vast social changes that swept the country. Traditionally, only sexual relations within marriage were considered legitimate. Although this sexual control was always more ideal than real, for even among the Puritans matrimony never did enjoy a monopoly over sexual relations (Smith and Hindus 1975), it is now considerably weaker than it used to be. The "sexual revolution" of the past few decades has opened many alternatives to marital sex.

Figure 1.4 **GLOBAL TRENDS: PERCENTAGE OF BIRTHS TO UNMARRIED MOTHERS**

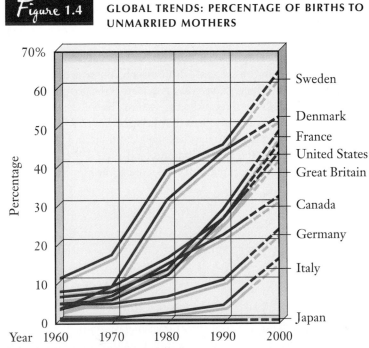

Source: Statistical Abstract 1994:1358 and 1997:1338. Dotted lines indicate the author's projections

In the 1800s, poverty was widespread in the United States. Most people were so poor that they expended their life energies on just getting enough food, fuel, and clothing to survive. Formal education beyond the first several grades was a luxury. This photo depicts the conditions of the people Du Bois worked with. (See the Down-to-Earth Sociology box on page 20.)

6. *Reproduction.* On the surface, the only family function that seems to have been left untouched is reproduction. Yet even this vital and seemingly inviolable function has not gone unchallenged. A prime example is the greater number of single women who are having children. Figure 1.4 shows that in the United States unmarried women now account for more than 40 percent of all births—and that the same upward trend is common throughout the industrialized world. (Japan is the only exception.) Even schools and private agencies have taken over some of the family's control over reproduction. A married woman, for example, can get an abortion without informing her husband, and some high schools distribute condoms.

A Glimpse of the Past   To see how sharply family functions have changed, it may be useful to take a glimpse of family life in the 1800s.

> When Phil became sick, he was nursed by Ann, his wife. She cooked for him, fed him, changed the bed linen, bathed him, read to him from the Bible, and gave him his medicine. (She did this in addition to doing the housework and taking care of their six children.) Phil was also surrounded by the children, who shouldered some of his chores while he was sick.
>
> When Phil died, the male neighbors and relatives made the casket while Ann, her mother, and female friends washed and dressed the body. Phil was then "laid out" in the front parlor (the formal living room), where friends, neighbors, and relatives viewed him, paying their last respects. From there friends moved his body to the church for the final message, and then to the grave they themselves had dug.

As you can see, the family used to have more functions. They even handled many aspects of life and death that we now assign to outside agencies. Not only did the care of the sick take place almost exclusively within the family, but death was also a family affair—from preparing the body to burying it. Today we assume that such functions *properly* belong to specialized agencies, and few of us can even imagine preparing the body of a close relative for burial. Such an act may even seem grotesque, almost barbarous, for our current customs also guide our feelings, another fascinating aspect of social life, but one, regrettably, that we do not have time to pursue. (On pages 73–74, I return to the topic of emotions.)

■ **In Sum** The family has lost many of its traditional functions, while others are presently under assault. Especially significant is that economic production is no longer a cooperative, home-based effort, with husbands and wives depending on one another for their interlocking contributions to a mutual endeavor. Husbands and wives today earn individual paychecks, and increasingly function as separate components of an impersonal, multinational, and even global system. When outside agencies take over family functions, this makes the family more fragile, and an increase in divorce inevitable. The fewer functions that family members have in common, the fewer their "ties that bind," and these ties are what help see husbands and wives through the inevitable problems they experience.

Conflict Theory

Conflict theory provides a third perspective on social life. Karl Marx, who developed conflict theory, witnessed the Industrial Revolution that transformed Europe. He saw that peasants who had left the land to seek work in cities had to work at wages that barely provided enough to eat. (The average worker died at age 30, the average wealthy person at age 50 [Edgerton 1992:87]). Shocked by this suffering and exploitation, Marx began to analyze society and history. As he did so, he developed **conflict theory**, concluding that the key to human history is class struggle. In every society, some small group controls the means of production and exploits those who are not in control. In industrialized societies the struggle is between the **bourgeoisie**, the small group of capitalists who own the means to produce wealth, and the **proletariat**, the mass of workers who are exploited by the bourgeoisie. The capitalists also control politics, so that when workers rebel the capitalists are able to call on the power of the state to control them (Angell 1965).

When Marx made his observations, capitalism was in its infancy and workers were at the mercy of their employers. Workers had none of what we take for granted today—the right to strike, minimum wages, eight-hour days, coffee breaks, five-day work weeks, paid vacations and holidays, medical benefits, sick leave, unemployment compensation, Social Security. Marx's analysis reminds us that these benefits came not from generous hearts, but from workers who forced concessions from their employers.

Some current conflict sociologists use conflict theory in a much broader sense. Ralf Dahrendorf (b. 1929) sees conflict as inherent in all relations that involve authority. He points out that **authority**, or power that people consider legitimate, permeates every layer of society—whether a small group, an organization, a community, or the entire society. People in positions of authority try to enforce conformity, which in turn creates resentment and resistance. The result is a constant struggle throughout society to determine who has authority over what (Turner 1978).

Another sociologist, Lewis Coser (b. 1913), pointed out that conflict is especially likely to develop among people who are in close relationships. Such people are connected by a network of responsibilities, power, and rewards, and any change can easily upset the arrangements that they have so carefully worked out. Consequently, we can think even of an intimate relationship as a balancing act—one that involves maintaining and reworking the individuals' arrangement of responsibilities, power, and rewards.

■ **In Sum** Unlike the functionalists who view society as a harmonious whole, with its parts working together, conflict theorists see society as being composed of groups that are battling for scarce resources. Although alliances or cooperation may prevail on the surface,

conflict theory a theoretical framework in which society is viewed as composed of groups competing for scarce resources

bourgeosie Karl Marx's term for capitalists, those who own the means to produce wealth

proletariat Marx's term for the exploited class, the mass of workers who do not own the means of production

authority power that people consider legitimate

beneath that surface is a struggle for power. Marx focused on struggles between the bourgeoisie and proletariat, but today's conflict theorists have expanded this perspective to include smaller groups and even basic relationships.

Applying Conflict Theory To explain why the U.S. divorce rate is high, conflict theorists look at men's and women's relationships in terms of basic inequalities—men dominate and exploit, while women are dominated and exploited. They also point out that marriage reflects the basic male-female relationship of society and is one of the means by which men maintain their domination and exploitation of women.

Conflict theorists stress that women have traditionally been regarded as property and passed by one male, the father, to another, the husband (Dobash and Dobash 1981). In society after society, women have been assigned the role of satisfying the needs of men— their fathers, husbands, and brothers. Although marriage still reflects these millennia-old patterns of female subordination, the relationship between men and women is undergoing fundamental change. Because today's females increasingly participate in social worlds beyond the home, women refuse to bear burdens previously accepted as inevitable and are much more likely to dissolve a marriage that has become intolerable. Changing relationships of power and inequality, then, are the keys to understanding the current divorce rate (Bernard 1992). Increases in the number of women who work outside the home and in women's organizations advocating changes in male-female relationships have upset traditional imbalances of rights and obligations. Conflict in marriage is primarily due to husbands' resentment of their decreasing power and wives' resentment of their husbands' reluctance to share marital power.

■ **In Sum** Conflict theorists see marriage as reflecting society's basic inequalities between males and females. Higher divorce rates result from changed male-female power relationships, especially as wives attempt to resolve basic inequalities and husbands resist those efforts. From the conflict perspective, then, the increase in divorce is not a sign that marriage has weakened but, rather, a sign that women are making headway in their historical struggle with men.

Levels of Analysis: Macro and Micro

A major difference between these three theoretical perspectives is their level of analysis. Functionalists and conflict theorists focus on **macro-level analysis;** that is, they examine large-scale patterns of society. In contrast, symbolic interactionists usually focus on **micro-level analysis;** that is, they analyze **social interaction,** what people do when they are in one another's presence. (See Table 1.1, page 24).

Let's return to the example of the homeless to make this distinction between micro and macro levels clearer. In studying homeless people, symbolic interactionists would focus on the micro level. They would analyze what homeless people do when they are in shelters and on the streets. They also would analyze their communications, both their talk and their **nonverbal interaction** (communication by gestures, silence, use of space, and so on). The observations I made at the beginning of this chapter about the silence in the homeless shelter, for example, would be of interest to symbolic interactionists.

This micro level, however, would not interest functionalists and conflict theorists. They would focus instead on the macro level. Functionalists would examine how changes in the parts of society have increased homelessness. They might look at how changes in the family (fewer children, more divorce) and economic conditions (higher rents, inflation, fewer unskilled jobs, loss of jobs overseas) cause homelessness among people who are unable to find jobs and have no family to fall back on. For their part, conflict theorists would stress the struggle between social classes, especially how the policies of the wealthy force certain groups into unemployment and homelessness. That, they would point out, accounts for the

macro-level analysis an examination of large-scale patterns of society

micro-level analysis an examination of small-scale patterns of society

social interaction what people do when they are in one another's presence

nonverbal interaction communication without words through gestures, space, silence, and so on

disproportionate number of African Americans who are homeless. Chapter 4 focuses on the distinctions between macro and micro levels of analysis.

Putting the Theoretical Perspectives Together

Which theoretical perspective should we use to study human behavior? Which level of analysis is the correct one? As you have seen, these theoretical perspectives provide contrasting pictures of human life. No theory or level of analysis encompasses all of reality. Rather, by focusing on different features of social life, each provides a distinctive interpretation. Consequently, it is necessary to use all three theoretical lenses to analyze human behavior. By combining their contributions, we gain a more comprehensive picture of social life.

As you can see, the sociological perspective leads to an understanding of divorce that is entirely different from the commonsense understanding that two people were "simply incompatible." Taking this broader view of human events, which is the sociological perspective, gives us a different way of viewing social life. This will become even more apparent in the following chapters as we explore topics as broad as sexism and as highly focused as a kindergarten classroom.

*T*RENDS SHAPING THE FUTURE OF SOCIOLOGY

Two major trends indicate changing directions in sociology. Let's look again at the relationship of sociology to the reform of society, and then at globalization.

Sociology Full Circle: Reform Versus Research A tension between social reform and social analysis has always run through sociology. To better understand this tension, some sociologists find it useful to divide sociology into three major periods (Lazarsfeld and Reitz 1989). During the first phase, sociologists stressed the need to do research in order to improve society. One of the first presidents of the American Sociological Society, Albion Small, made this goal explicit. In 1912, Small said that the primary reason for sociology was its "practical application to the improvement of social life." He said that sociologists should use science to gain knowledge, and then use that knowledge to "realize visions" (Fritz 1989). This first phase of sociology lasted until the 1920s.

During the second phase, from the 1920s until World War II, the emphasis switched from making the world a better place to making sociology a respected field of knowledge. Sociologists emphasized **basic** or **pure sociology,** that is, research and theory aimed at making discoveries about life in human groups, but not at making changes in those groups. They achieved this goal within a generation, and almost every college and university in the United States added sociology to its course offerings. It is because of these efforts that you are taking this introductory course in sociology.

We are now in a third phase, which began around the end of World War II. A watershed event occurred in 1954, when sociological research became significant in a U.S. Supreme Court ruling. The Court was deciding whether racially segregated public schools were constitutional. Up to this time, states followed a so-called "separate but equal" doctrine and had separate public schools for whites and for blacks. (The schools certainly were separate, but they were anything but equal.) The testimony of sociologists on the harmful effects of segregation became important in the Court's landmark ruling (*Brown v. the Board of Education of Topeka*), which banned segregated public schools (Teacher's College Record 1995).

This fundamental change in law and its direct impact on education in the United States made sociologists more aware of their potential to bring about social change. Just as sociologists switched from their initial concern with improving society to developing abstract

pure or **basic sociology** sociological research whose purpose is to make discoveries about life in human groups, not to make changes in those groups

knowledge, today they are seeking ways to apply their research findings. With the development of applied sociology, these efforts have gained momentum. Many sociology departments offer courses in applied sociology, and some offer specialties, and even internships, in applied sociology at both the graduate and undergraduate levels.

I want to stress that sociology is not a monolith, with all of us in agreement, moving in lock-step toward a single goal. Neatly dividing sociology into three separate phases overlooks as much as it reveals. Even during the first phase, Durkheim and Weber did research for the purpose of gaining academic respectability for sociology. Similarly, during the second phase, many sociologists who wanted to reform society chafed at the emphasis on understanding. And today, many sociologists want the emphasis to remain on basic sociology; they do not view applied sociology as "real" sociology. They say that it is actually social work or psychology masquerading as sociology. Each particular period, however, does have basic emphases, and this division of sociology into three phases does illustrate major trends. The tension that has run through sociology—between gaining knowledge and applying knowledge—will continue. During this current phase, it is likely that the emphasis on applying sociological knowledge will become stronger.

Globalization A second major trend, globalization, seems destined to leave its mark on sociology. **Globalization** is the breaking down of national boundaries because of advances in communication, trade, and travel. Currently, the United States dominates sociology. As sociologists William Martin and Mark Beittel (1998) put it, U.S. sociology is the "unrivaled center of the discipline on a world scale." One consequence of this dominance is an emphasis on groups in the United States. We U.S. sociologists tend to look inward, concentrating on events and relationships that occur in our own country. We even base most of our findings on U.S. samples. Globalization is likely to broaden our horizons, directing us to a greater consideration of global issues. This, in turn, is likely to motivate us to try more vigorously to identify universal principles.

Application of Globalization to This Text With each passing year, the world becomes smaller as we all become more and more connected to the global village. What occurs elsewhere has a direct impact on our lives, and, increasingly, our welfare is tied to that of people in other nations. To help broaden our horizons, in this book we will visit many cultures around the world, examining what life is like for the people there. Seeing how *their* society affects their behavior and orientations to life will help us see how *our* society influences what we do and how we feel about life.

Globalization is one of the most significant events in world history, and you and I are living through it. Throughout this text, I will stress the impact of globalization on your life, especially how it is likely to shape your future. We will also examine the **globalization of capitalism**, focusing on implications of the triumph of this economic system. From time to time, as you read the following pages, you will also confront the developing new world order, which appears destined to play a most significant role in your future.

Globilization the extensive interconnections among nations due to the expansion of Capitalism.

Globilization of capitalism capitalism (investing to make profits within a rational system) becoming the globe's dominant economic system

SUMMARY AND REVIEW

■ The Sociological Perspective

What is the sociological perspective?

The **sociological perspective** stresses that people's social experiences—the groups to which they belong and their particular experiences within these groups—underlie their behavior. C. Wright Mills referred to this as the intersection of biography (the individual) and history (social factors acting on the individual). Pp. 3–5.

■ Sociology and the Other Sciences

What is science, and where does sociology fit in?

Science is the application of systematic methods to obtain knowledge and the knowledge obtained by those methods. The sciences are divided into the **natural sciences**, which seek to comprehend, explain, and predict events in the natural environment; and the **social sciences**, which seek to understand the social world objectively by means of controlled and repeated observations. **Sociology** is the scientific study of society and human behavior. Pp. 6–9.

■ Origins of Sociology

When did sociology first appear as a separate discipline, and what factors contributed to its emergence?

Sociology emerged as a separate discipline in the mid-1800s in western Europe, during the onset of the Industrial Revolution. Industrialization brought social change so sweeping it affected all aspects of human existence—where people lived, the nature of their work, how they viewed life, and their interpersonal relationships. Early sociologists who focused on these social changes include Auguste Comte, Herbert Spencer, Karl Marx, Harriet Martineau, Emile Durkheim, and Max Weber. Pp. 9–14.

■ The Role of Values in Social Research

Should the purpose of social research be only to advance human understanding or also to reform society?

All sociologists agree that social research should be **value free**: The researcher's personal beliefs should be set aside in order to permit objective findings. But sociologists do not agree on the uses and purposes of social research. Some believe its purpose should be only to advance understanding of human behavior; others, that its goal should be to reform harmful social arrangements. Pp. 14–15.

■ *Verstehen* and Social Facts

How do sociologists use *Verstehen* and social facts to investigate human behavior?

According to Weber, to understand why people act as they do, sociologists must try to put themselves in their shoes. He used the German term *Verstehen*, "to grasp by insight," to describe this essentially subjective approach. Although not denying the importance of *Verstehen*, Emile Durkheim emphasized the importance of uncovering **social facts**, objective social conditions that influence how people behave. Contemporary sociology uses both approaches to understand human behavior. Pp. 16–17.

■ Sexism in Early Sociology

What was the position of women in early sociology?

Only a few wealthy women received advanced education, and their writings were largely ignored. Harriet Martineau is an example. P. 17.

■ Sociology in North America

How recently were academic departments of sociology established in the United States?

The earliest departments of sociology were established in the late 1800s at the universities of Kansas, Atlanta, and Chicago. During the 1940s, sociology was dominated by the University of Chicago. Today, no single university or theoretical perspective dominates. In sociology's early years, the contributions of women and minorities were largely ignored. Pp. 17–22.

What is the difference between basic (or pure) and applied sociology?

Basic (or pure) **sociology** is sociological research whose purpose is to make discoveries. In contrast, **applied sociology** is the use of sociology to solve problems. Pp. 21–22.

■ Theoretical Perspectives in Sociology

What is a theory?

A **theory** is a general statement about how sets of facts are related to one another. A theory provides a conceptual framework within which facts are interpreted. Pp. 22–23.

What are the major theoretical perspectives?

Sociologists make use of three primary theoretical frameworks to interpret social life. **Symbolic interactionism** examines how people use symbols to develop and share their views of the world. Symbolic interactionists usually focus at the micro level—on small-scale patterns of human interaction. **Functional analysis**, in contrast, focuses on the macro level—on large-scale patterns of society. Functional theorists stress that a social system is made up of various parts. When working properly, each part contributes to the stability of the whole, fulfilling a function that contributes to a system's equilibrium. **Conflict theory** also focuses on large-scale patterns of society. Conflict theorists stress that society is composed of competing groups struggling for scarce resources.

Because no single theory encompasses all of reality, at different times sociologists may use any or all of the three theoretical lenses. With each perspective focusing on certain features of social life and each providing its own interpretation, their combined insights yield a more comprehensive picture of social life. Pp. 23–32.

■ Trends Shaping the Future of Sociology

What trends are likely to have an impact on sociology?

Sociology has gone through three phases: The first was an emphasis on reforming society; the second, an emphasis on basic sociology. In today's third phase, we are swinging full circle, coming closer to our roots of applying sociology to social change. **Applied sociology**, which is already having an impact, is likely to continue its influence. A second major trend, **globalization**, is likely to broaden sociological horizons, refocusing research and theory from its concentration on U.S. society. Pp. 32–33.

Where can I read more on this topic?

Suggested Readings for this chapter are at the back of this book.

Sociology & the Internet

All URLs listed are current as of the printing of this book. URLs often change. Please check our Web site, **http://www.abacon.com/ henslin,** for updates.

1. In this chapter you were introduced to the sociological imagination, which can help you understand human behavior. This activity is designed to help develop your sociological imagination. There are many different sites on the Internet that report the findings of public opinion polls. One such site is maintained by the Gallup Organization and can be accessed at **http://www. gallup.com/poll/index.asp.** Go to that site and explore some of the different Gallup polls of the U.S. population by clicking on "Social Issues and Policy," "Lifestyle," "Social & Economic Indicators," or "Social Audits." Pick one that interests you, and study the patterns of public opinion. Make a list of social factors that you think might help to explain the pattern. Another site with a wealth of information about opinion polls is **http://www.pollingreport. com.** From the main page, click on "The American Scene" or the "Contents" page, and then pick out a specific opinion poll. Once again, look for patterns. Try to use your sociological imagination to identify the social factors that may affect these patterns. In a brief essay, discuss the social factors responsible for the pattern or trend you found.

2. To learn more about sociology's founders, including Comte, Durkheim, Marx, and many others, go to the Dead Sociologists Society site, **http://www.runet.edu/~lridener/DSS/DEADSOC. HTML.** Select one of the sociologists who were discussed in this chapter. Gather material for a report on the sociologist's background, ideas, and writings. Exercise your sociological imagina-tion by thinking about how the sociologist's social environment influenced his or her work. To obtain more information, use a search engine like Yahoo (**http://www.yahoo.com**) or Meta-crawler (**http://www.metacrawler.com**). Enter the sociologist's name or the words "dead sociologists" (without the quotation marks) in the search term box.

3. This chapter introduces the theoretical perspectives used by so-ciologists—symbolic interactionism, functionalism, and conflict theory. This next activity will help you apply these perspectives to the social world. Begin by going to **http://nces.ed.gov/search. html.** In the search term box, type in one of the following: ele-mentary education, secondary education, or postsecondary edu-cation. Browse through the information that comes up on the screen. Select one data source that interests you and click on it. After reading through the information that comes up, try to in-terpret the findings by using one or more of the three perspectives.

4. As your text notes, many sociologists do applied sociology, in which they combine sociological knowledge with practical results in trying to solve social problems. Go to **http://www.appliedsoc. org,** the home page for the Society for Applied Sociology. This site will give you a good idea of careers in applied sociology. Ex-plore some of the pages, particularly the ones about becoming an applied sociologist. Browse through the pages on the speak-ers' bureau, the consultant roster, and the job listings to see the range of applied sociologists' professional activities. Take a look at the student problem-solving exercise. Prepare a brief report for your class regarding careers in applied sociology

Fishinghawk (Dewayne Mathews), Songs of the Great Serpents, 1997

Culture

■ **What Is Culture?**
Culture and Taken-for-Granted Orientations to Life
Practicing Cultural Relativism

■ **Components of Symbolic Culture**
Gestures
Language
Values, Norms, and Sanctions
Folkways and Mores
Many Cultural Worlds: Subcultures
    and Countercultures

■ **Values in U.S. Society**
An Overview of U.S. Values
Value Contradictions and Social Change
Value Clusters

Culture Wars: When Values Clash
Values as Blinders
"Ideal" Versus "Real" Culture

■ **Cultural Universals**
Animals and Language

■ **Technology in the Global Village**
The New Technology
Cultural Lag and Cultural Change
Technology and Cultural Leveling

■ **Summary and Review**

I had never felt heat like this before. If this is northern Africa, I wondered, what must it be like closer to the equator? The sweat poured off me as the temperature soared past 110 degrees Fahrenheit.

As we were herded into the building—which had no air conditioning—hundreds of people lunged toward the counter at the rear of the building. With body crushed against body, we waited as the uniformed officials behind the windows leisurely examined each passport. At times like this I wondered what I was doing in Africa.

When I first arrived in Morocco, I found the sights that greeted me exotic—not far removed from my memories of *Casablanca, Raiders of the Lost Ark,* and other movies that over the years had become part of my collective memory. The men, women, and even the children did wear those white robes that reached down to their feet. What was especially striking was the fact that the women were almost totally covered. Despite the heat, they wore not only full-length gowns, but also head coverings that reached down over their foreheads, and veils that covered their faces from the nose down. All you could make out were their eyes—and every eye the same shade of brown.

And how short everyone was! The Arab women looked to be on average 5 feet, and the men only about three or four inches taller. As the only blue-eyed, blonde, 6-foot-plus person around, and the only one wearing jeans and a pullover shirt, in a world of white-robed short people I stood out like a sore thumb. Everyone stared. No matter where I went, they stared. Wherever I looked, I found brown eyes watching me intently. Even staring back at those many dark brown eyes had no effect. It was so different from home, where, if you caught someone staring at you, the person would immediately look embarrassed and glance away.

And lines? The concept apparently didn't even exist. Buying a ticket for a bus or train meant pushing and shoving toward the ticket man (always a man—no women were visible in any public position), who just took the money from whichever outstretched hand he decided on.

And germs? That notion didn't seem to exist here either. Flies swarmed over the food in the

37

restaurants and the unwrapped loaves of bread in the stores. Shopkeepers would considerately shoo off the flies before handing me a loaf. They also offered home delivery. I still remember watching a bread vendor deliver an unwrapped loaf to a woman who stood on a second-floor balcony. She first threw her money to the bread vendor, and he then threw the unwrapped bread up to her. Only, his throw was off. The bread bounced off the wrought-iron balcony railing and landed in the street, which was filled with people, wandering dogs, and the ever-present burros. The vendor simply picked up the loaf and threw it again. This certainly wasn't his day, for again he missed. But he made it on his third attempt. And the woman smiled, satisfied, as she turned back into her apartment, apparently to prepare the noon meal for her hungry family.

Now, standing in the oppressive heat on the Moroccan-Algerian border, the crowd once again became unruly. Another fight had broken out. And once again, the little man in uniform appeared, shouting and knocking people aside as he forced his way to a little wooden box nailed to the floor. Climbing onto this makeshift platform, he shouted at the crowd, his arms flailing about him. The people grew silent. But just as soon as the man left, the shoving and shouting began again as the people clamored to get their passports stamped.

The situation had become unbearable. Pressed body to body, the man behind me had decided that this was a good time to take a nap. Determining that I made a good support, he placed his arm against my back and leaned his head against his arm. Sweat streamed down my back at the point that his arm and head touched me.

Finally, I realized that I had to abandon U.S. customs. I pushed my way forward, forcing my frame into every square inch of vacant space that I could create. At the counter, I shouted in English. The official looked up at the sound of this strange tongue, and I thrust my long arms over the heads of three people, shoving my passport into his hand.

₩HAT IS CULTURE?

culture the language, beliefs, values, norms, behaviors, and even material objects that are passed from one generation to the next

material culture the material objects that distinguish a group of people, such as their art, buildings, weapons, utensils, machines, hairstyles, clothing, and jewelry

nonmaterial culture a group's ways of thinking (including its beliefs, values, and other assumptions about the world) and doing (its common patterns of behavior, including language and other forms of interaction)

What is culture? The concept is sometimes easier to grasp by description than by definition. For example, suppose you meet a young woman who has just arrived in the United States from India. That her culture is different from yours is immediately evident. You first see it in her clothing, jewelry, makeup, and hairstyle. Next you hear it in her language. It then becomes apparent by her gestures. Later, you may hear her express unfamiliar beliefs about the world and opinions about what is valuable in life. All these characteristics are indicative of **culture,** the language, beliefs, values, norms, behaviors, and even material objects that are passed from one generation to the next.

In northern Africa, I was surrounded by a culture quite alien to my own. It was evident in everything I saw and heard. The **material culture**—such things as jewelry, art, buildings, weapons, machines, and even eating utensils, hairstyles, and clothing—provided a sharp contrast to what I was used to seeing. There is nothing inherently "natural" about material culture. That is, it is no more natural (or unnatural) to wear gowns on the street than it is to wear jeans.

I also found myself immersed in a contrasting **nonmaterial culture,** that is, a group's ways of thinking (its beliefs, values, and other assumptions about the world) and doing (its common patterns of behavior, including language, gestures, and other forms of interaction). North African assumptions about crowding to buy a ticket and staring in public are examples of nonmaterial culture. So are U.S. assumptions about not doing either of these things. Like material culture, neither custom is "right." People simply become comfortable with the customs they learn during childhood, and—as in the case of my visit to northern Africa—uncomfortable when their basic assumptions about life are challenged.

Culture and Taken-for-Granted Orientations to Life

To develop a sociological imagination, it is essential to understand how culture affects people's lives. While meeting someone from a different culture may make us aware of culture's pervasive influence, attaining the same level of awareness regarding our own culture is quite another matter. *Our* speech, *our* gestures, *our* beliefs, and *our* customs are usually taken for granted. We assume that they are "normal" or "natural," and we almost always follow them without question. As anthropologist Ralph Linton (1936) said, "The last thing a fish would ever notice would be water." So also with people: Except in unusual circumstances, the effects of our own culture generally remain imperceptible to us.

Yet culture's significance is profound; it touches almost every aspect of who and what we are. We came into this life without a language, without values and morality, with no ideas about religion, war, money, love, use of space, and so on. We possessed none of these fundamental orientations that we take for granted and that are so essential in determining the type of people we are. Yet at this point in our lives we all have acquired them. Sociologists call this culture *within* us. These learned and shared ways of believing and of doing (another definition of culture) penetrate our beings at an early age and quickly become part of our taken-for-granted assumptions concerning normal behavior. *Culture becomes the lens through which we perceive and evaluate what is going on around us.* Seldom do we question these assumptions, for, like water to a fish, the framework from which we view life remains largely beyond our ordinary perception.

The rare instances in which these assumptions are challenged, however, can be upsetting. Although as a sociologist I should be able to look at my own culture "from the outside," my trip to Africa quickly revealed how fully I had internalized my own culture. My upbringing in Western industrialized society had given me strong assumptions about aspects of social life that had become deeply rooted in my being—staring, hygiene, and the use of space. But in this part of Africa these assumptions were useless for helping me get through daily life. No longer could I count on people to stare only surreptitiously, to take precautions against invisible microbes, or to stand in an orderly way one behind the other on the basis of time of arrival to obtain a service.

As you can tell from the opening vignette, I personally found these different assumptions upsetting, for they violated my basic expectations of "the way people *ought* to be"—although I did not know how firmly I held these expectations until they were so abruptly challenged. When my nonmaterial culture failed me—when it no longer enabled me to make sense out of the world—I experienced a disorientation known as **culture shock.** In the case of buying tickets, the fact that I was several inches taller than most Moroccans and thus able to outreach almost everyone helped me to adjust partially to their different ways of doing things. But I never did get used to the idea that pushing ahead of others was "right," and I always felt guilty when I used my size to receive preferential treatment.

An important consequence of culture within us is **ethnocentrism,** a tendency to use our own group's ways of doing things as the yardstick for judging others. All of us learn that the ways of our own group are good, right, proper, and even superior to other ways of life. As sociologist William Sumner (1906), who developed this concept, said, "One's own group is the center of everything, and all others are scaled and rated with reference to it." Ethnocentrism has both positive and negative consequences. On the positive side, it creates in-group loyalties. On the negative side, ethnocentrism can lead to harmful discrimination against people whose ways differ from ours.

The effects of culture on our lives fascinate sociologists. By examining more explicitly just how profoundly culture affects everything we are, this chapter will serve as a basis from which you can start to analyze your previously unquestioned assumptions of reality and thus help you gain a different perspective on social life and your role in it.

culture shock the disorientation that people experience when they come in contact with a fundamentally different culture and can no longer depend on their taken-for-granted assumptions about life

ethnocentrism the use of one's own culture as a yardstick for judging the ways of other individuals or societies, generally leading to a negative evaluation of their values, norms, and behaviors

■ **In Sum** To avoid losing track of the ideas under discussion, let's pause for a moment to summarize, and in some instances clarify, the principles we have covered.

1. There is nothing "natural" about material culture. Arabs wear gowns on the street and feel that it is natural to do so; Americans do the same with jeans.

2. There is nothing "natural" about nonmaterial culture; it is just as arbitrary to stand in line as it is to push and shove.

3. Culture penetrates deep into our thinking, becoming a taken-for-granted aspect of our lives.

4. Culture provides the lens through which we see the world and obtain our perception of reality.

5. Culture provides implicit instructions that tell us what we ought to do in various situations. It provides a fundamental basis for our decision making.

6. Culture also provides a "moral imperative"; that is, by internalizing a culture, people learn ideas of right and wrong. (I, for example, deeply believed that it was wrong to push and shove to get ahead of others.)

7. Coming into contact with a radically different culture challenges our basic assumptions of life. (I experienced culture shock when I discovered that my deeply ingrained cultural ideas about the use of space and hygiene no longer applied.)

8. Although the particulars of culture differ from one group of people to another, culture itself is universal. That is, all people have culture. There are no exceptions. A society cannot exist without developing shared, learned ways of dealing with the demands of life.

9. All people are *ethnocentric,* which has both positive and negative consequences.

Practicing Cultural Relativism

To counter our tendency to use our own culture as a standard by which we judge other cultures, we can practice **cultural relativism;** that is, we can try to understand a culture on its own terms. Cultural relativism is looking at how the elements of a culture fit together, without judging those elements as superior or inferior to one's own way of life.

Because we tend to use our own culture to judge others, cultural relativism presents a challenge to ordinary thinking. For example, most U.S. citizens appear to have strong feelings against raising bulls for the sole purpose of stabbing them to death in front of crowds that shout "Olé!" According to cultural relativism, however, bullfighting must be viewed from the context of the culture in which it takes place—*its* history, *its* folklore, *its* ideas of bravery, and *its* ideas of sex roles.

You may still regard bullfighting as wrong, of course, if your culture, which is deeply ingrained in you, has no history of bullfighting. We all possess culturally specific ideas about cruelty to animals, ideas that have evolved slowly and match other elements of our culture. In the United States, for example, practices that once were common in some areas—cock fighting, dog fighting, bear-dog fighting, and so on—have been gradually weeded out (Bryant 1993).

None of us can be entirely successful at practicing cultural relativism; we simply cannot help viewing a contrasting way of life through the lens that our own culture provides. Cultural relativism, however, is an attempt to refocus that lens and thereby appreciate other ways of life rather than simply asserting, "Our way is right."

Although cultural relativism is a worthwhile goal and helps us to avoid cultural smugness, this view has come under attack. In a provocative book, *Sick Societies* (1992), anthropologist Robert Edgerton points out that some cultures endanger their people's health,

cultural relativism understanding a people from the framework of its own culture

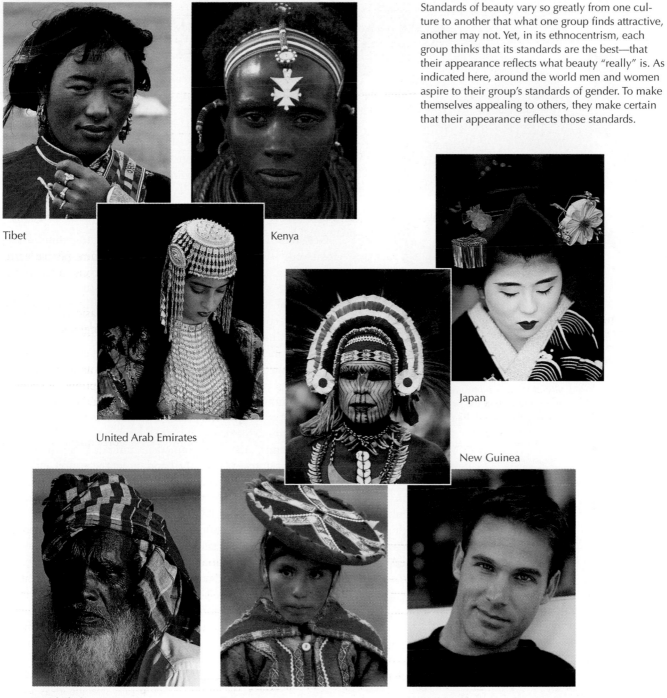

Standards of beauty vary so greatly from one culture to another that what one group finds attractive, another may not. Yet, in its ethnocentrism, each group thinks that its standards are the best—that their appearance reflects what beauty "really" is. As indicated here, around the world men and women aspire to their group's standards of gender. To make themselves appealing to others, they make certain that their appearance reflects those standards.

Tibet

Kenya

United Arab Emirates

New Guinea

Japan

Bangladesh

Peru

United States

happiness, or survival. He suggests that we should develop a scale for evaluating cultures on their "quality of life," much as we do for U.S. cities. He also asks why we should consider cultures that practice female genital mutilation, gang rape, wife beating, or that sell daughters into prostitution as morally equivalent to those that do not. Cultural values that result in exploitation, he says, are inferior to those that enhance people's lives.

Edgerton's sharp questions and incisive examples bring us to a point that will come up repeatedly in this text—disagreements that arise among scholars as they confront changing views of reality. It is such questioning of assumptions that keeps sociology interesting.

Many Americans perceive bullfighting, which is illegal in the United States, as a cruel activity that should be abolished everywhere in the world. To Spaniards and those who have inherited Spanish culture, however, bullfighting is a beautiful, artistic sport in which matador and bull blend into a unifying image of power, courage, and glory. *Cultural relativism* requires that we suspend our own perspectives in order to grasp the perspectives of others, something that is much easier described than attained.

symbolic culture another term for nonmaterial culture

symbol something to which people attach meanings and then use to communicate with others

gestures the ways in which people use their bodies to communicate with one another

COMPONENTS OF SYMBOLIC CULTURE

Sociologists sometimes refer to nonmaterial culture as **symbolic culture,** because a central component is the symbols that people use to communicate. A **symbol** is something to which people attach meaning and which they then use to communicate. Symbols are the basis of culture. They include gestures, language, values, norms, sanctions, folkways, and mores. Let's look at each of these components of symbolic culture.

Gestures

Gestures, which involve using one's body to communicate with others, are useful shorthand ways to give messages without using words. Although people in every culture of the world use gestures, the meaning of those gestures may change completely from one culture to another. North Americans, for example, communicate a succinct message by raising the middle finger in a short, upward stabbing motion. I wish to stress "North Americans," for that gesture does not convey the same message in South America or most other parts of the world.

I was once surprised to find that this particular gesture was not universal, having internalized it to such an extent that I thought everyone knew what it meant. When I was comparing gestures in Mexico, however, this gesture drew a blank look from friends. After I explained its intended meaning, they laughed and showed me their rudest gesture—placing the hand under the armpit and moving the upper arm up and down. To me, they simply looked as if they were imitating a monkey, but to them the gesture meant "Your mother is a whore"—absolutely the worst possible insult in that culture.

Gestures thus not only facilitate communication but also, because they differ around the world, can lead to misunderstandings, embarrassment, or worse. Once in Mexico, for example, I raised my hand to a certain height to indicate how tall a child was. My hosts began to laugh. It turned out that Mexicans use several hand gestures to indicate height: separate ones for people, animals, and plants. What had amused them was that I had ignorantly used the plant gesture to indicate the child's height.

Figure 2.1

GESTURES TO INDICATE HEIGHT, SOUTHERN MEXICO

Indicates animal height   Indicates plant height   Indicates human height

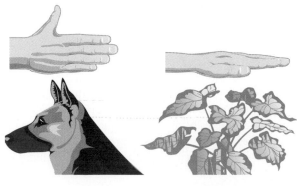

To get along in another culture, then, it is important to learn the gestures of that culture. If you don't, you will not only fail to achieve the simplicity of communication that gestures allow, but you will also miss much of what is happening, run the risk of appearing foolish, and possibly offend people. In many cultures, for example, you would provoke deep offense if you were to offer food or a gift with your left hand, because the left hand is reserved for dirty tasks, such as wiping after going to the bathroom. Left-handed Americans visiting Arabs, please note!

Now suppose for a moment that you are visiting southern Italy. After eating one of the best meals in your life you are so pleased that when you catch the waiter's eye, you smile broadly and use the standard U.S. "A-OK" gesture of putting your thumb and forefinger together and making a large "O." The waiter looks horrified, and you are struck speechless when the manager asks you to leave. What have you done? Nothing on purpose, of course, but in that culture that gesture refers to a part of the human body that is not mentioned in polite company (Ekman et al. 1984).

Is it really true that there are no universal gestures? There is some disagreement on this point. Some anthropologists claim that no gesture is universal. They point out that even nodding the head up and down to indicate "yes" is not universal, because in some parts of the world, such as areas of Turkey, nodding the head up and down means "no" (Ekman et al. 1984). However, ethologists, researchers who study biological bases of behavior, claim that expressions of anger, pouting, fear, and sadness are built into our biology and are universal (Eibl-Eibesfeldt 1970:404). They point out that even infants who are born blind and deaf, who have had no chance to *learn* these gestures, express themselves in the same way.

Although this matter is not yet settled, we can note that gestures tend to vary remarkably around the world. It is also significant that certain gestures can elicit emotions; some gestures are so associated with emotional messages that the gestures themselves summon up emotions. For example, my introduction to Mexican gestures took place at a dinner table. It was evident that my husband-and-wife hosts were trying to hide their embarrassment at using their culture's obscene gesture at their dinner table. And I felt the same way—not about *their* gesture, of course, which meant absolutely nothing to me—but about the one I was teaching them.

Although most gestures are learned, and therefore vary from culture to culture, some gestures that represent fundamental emotions such as sadness, anger, and fear appear to be inborn. This crying child differs little from a crying child in China or the United States or anywhere else on the globe. In a few years, however, this child will demonstrate a variety of gestures highly specific to his culture.

Language

The primary way in which people communicate with one another is through **language**—a system of symbols that can be strung together in an infinite number of ways for the purpose of communicating abstract thought. Each word is actually a symbol, a sound to which we have attached a particular meaning so that we can then use it to communicate with one another. Language itself is universal in the sense that all human groups have language, but there is nothing universal about the meanings given to particular sounds. Thus, like gestures, in different cultures the same sound may mean something entirely different—or may have no meaning at all.

The significance of language for human life is difficult to overstate, as will become apparent from the following discussion of how language allows culture to exist.

Language Allows Human Experience to Be Cumulative By means of language, one generation can pass significant experiences on to the next, allowing that next generation to build on experiences that it may never undergo. This building process enables humans to modify their behavior in light of what previous generations have learned. Hence the central sociological significance of language: *Language allows culture to develop by freeing people to move beyond their immediate experiences.*

language a system of symbols that can be combined in an infinite number of ways and can represent not only objects but also abstract thought

Language is the basis of human culture around the world. The past few years have seen a major development in communication—the ease and speed with which we can "speak" to people across the globe. This development is destined to have vital affects on culture.

Without language, human culture would be little more advanced than that of the lower primates. People would be limited to communicating by some system of grunts and gestures, which would minimize the temporal dimension of human life and limit communication to a small time span: events that are now taking place, those that have just taken place, or those that will take place immediately—a sort of "slightly extended present." You can grunt and gesture, for example, that you want a drink of water, but in the absence of language how could you share ideas concerning past or future events? There would be little or no way to communicate to others what event you had in mind, much less the greater complexities that humans communicate—ideas and feelings about events.

Language Provides a Social or Shared Past Even without language, an individual would still have memories of experiences. Those memories, however, would be extremely limited, for people associate experiences with words and then use words to recall the experience. Such memories as would exist in the absence of language would also be highly individualized, for they could be but rarely and incompletely communicated to others, much less discussed and agreed on. With language, however, events can be codified, that is, attached to words and then recalled so they can be discussed in the present.

Language Provides a Social or Shared Future Language also extends our time horizons forward. When people talk about past events, they share meanings that allow them to decide how they will or should act in similar circumstances in the future. Because language enables people to agree with one another concerning times, dates, and places, it also allows them to plan activities with one another.

Think about it for a moment. Without language how could people ever plan future events? How could they possibly communicate goals, purposes, times, and plans? Whatever planning could exist would have to be limited to extremely rudimentary communications, perhaps to an agreement to meet at a certain place when the sun is in a certain position. But think of the difficulty, perhaps impossibility, of conveying just a slight change in this simple arrangement, such as "I can't make it tomorrow, but my neighbor can, if that's all right with you."

Language Allows Shared Perspectives or Understandings Our ability to speak, then, allows us a social past and future. These two vital aspects of our humanity represent a watershed that distinguishes us from animals. But speech does much more than this. When humans talk with one another, they are exchanging ideas about events, that is, exchanging perspectives. Their words are the embodiment of their experiences, distilled and codified into a readily exchangeable form, mutually understandable to people who have learned that language. Talking about events allows people to arrive at the shared understandings that form the essence of social life. Arriving at shared understandings is often the result of determined efforts, as illustrated in the Down-to-Earth sociology Box on the next page.

Language Allows Complex, Shared, Goal-Directed Behavior Common understandings further enable people to establish a *purpose* for getting together. Let's suppose that you want to go on a picnic. You use speech not only to plan the picnic but also to decide on reasons for the picnic—which may be anything from "because it's a nice day and it shouldn't be wasted studying" to "because it's my birthday." Language permits you to blend individual activities into an integrated sequence. In other words, through discussion you de-

Sociology
Down-to-Earth

THE NEW SHORTHAND: EXPRESSING YOURSELF ONLINE

Talking online has become a favorite activity of millions of people, young and old, who use their computers to communicate with others on an everyday basis. Teenagers who rehash the day's events with friends; grandmothers who keep in touch with grandchildren in different states; hobbyists who correspond about their special interests; businesspeople who seal their deals with the click of a "send" button: All of them love the speed of online communications. They send an e-mail or post a note in a chatroom, and in an instant people thousands of miles away, across the country or in distant lands, can read and respond to it.

Although online communication allows for the speedy transmission of words and ideas, it doesn't allow its users to convey the nuances that are transmitted during face-to-face talk, especially the gestures and tones of voice that people use to monitor and communicate sub-messages. To make up for this, users have developed symbols that are meant to convey humor, disappointment, sarcasm, and other indications of mood or attitude. Although not as rich in number or as varied or spontaneous as the nonverbal cues of face-to-face interaction, these symbols are useful. Here are some

of them. If you tilt your head to the left as you view them, the symbols will be clearer.

:-)	Smile
:-))	Laugh
:-D	Laugh or big grin
:-(	Sad
:-((	Very Sad
;-)	Wink, wink—know what I mean?
:-X	My lips are sealed
:-P	Sticking out your tongue
:-')	Tongue in cheek
>:-)	Feeling in a devilish mood
:-0	WOW! (What a surprise!)

Some correspondents also use the following abbreviations, which add a touch of whimsy and make their correspondence even more succinct:

ILY	I Love You
LOL	Laughing Out Loud
OTF	On The Floor (laughing)
ROTF	Rolling On The Floor
ROFLWTIME	Rolling On Floor Laughing With Tears In My Eyes

IMBO	In My Humble Opinion
AFK	Away From Keyboard
BAK	Back At Keyboard
BRB	Be Right Back
TTFN	Ta-Ta For Now
WB	Welcome Back
BTW	By The Way
GMTA	Great Minds Think Alike
WTG	Way To Go!
J/K	Just Kidding
D/L	Downloading
OIC	Oh, I see
UGG	You Go, Girl!
IAB	I Am Bored
L8R	Later
CUL8R	See You Later
TTYL	Talk To You Later

As e-mail advances, such shorthand may become increasingly unnecessary. We now have the means to include video in our e-mail: Just click the link, and your image appears. The recipient is also able to hear your voice. As miniaturized video transmitters become inexpensive, live or stored verbal messages—which include facial cues—may replace much e-mail. E-mail itself is unlikely to be replaced, however, and some system of symbols to substitute for gestures will continue. ■

cide where you will go; who will drive; who will bring the hamburgers, the potato chips, the soda; where you will meet; and so on. Only because of language can you participate in such a common yet complex event as a picnic—or build roads and bridges, or hold and attend college classes.

Language and Perception: The Sapir-Whorf Hypothesis In the 1930s, two anthropologists, Edward Sapir and Benjamin Whorf, became intrigued when they noted that the Hopi Indians of the southwestern United States had no words to distinguish among the past, the present, and the future. English, in contrast, as well as German, French, Spanish, and so on, distinguishes carefully among these three time frames. From this observation, Sapir and Whorf concluded that the commonsense idea that words are

Sapir-Whorf hypothesis Edward Sapir and Benjamin Whorf's hypothesis that language creates ways of thinking and perceiving

merely labels that people attach to things was wrong. Language, they concluded, has embedded in it ways of looking at the world. Thus thinking and perception are not only expressed through language, but are also shaped by language. When we learn a language, we learn not only words, but also a particular way of thinking and perceiving (Sapir 1949; Whorf 1956).

The implications of the **Sapir-Whorf hypothesis,** which alerts us to how extensively language affects us, are far-reaching. *The Sapir-Whorf hypothesis reverses common sense:* It indicates that rather than objects and events forcing themselves onto our consciousness, it is our very language that determines our consciousness, and hence our perception, of objects and events. Sociologist Eviatar Zerubavel (1991) gives a good example. Hebrew, his native language, does not differentiate between jam and jelly. Only when Zerubavel learned English could he "see" this difference, which is "obvious" to native English speakers. Similarly, if you learn to classify students as "dweebs," "dorks," "nerds," "brains," and so on, you will perceive a student who asks several questions during class in an entirely different way from someone who does not know these classifications.

Although Sapir and Whorf's observation that the Hopi do not have tenses was incorrect (Edgerton 1992:27), they stumbled onto a major truth about social life. The classifications that we humans develop as we try to make sense of life do influence our perception. The race-ethnic terms that our culture provides, for example, influence how we see others and ourselves, a point that is discussed in the Perspectives box below.

■ **In Sum** The sociological significance of language is that it takes us beyond the world of apes and allows culture to develop. Language frees us from the present by providing a past and a future, giving us the capacity to share understandings about the past and develop common perceptions about the future, as well as to establish underlying purposes for our activities. Consequently, as in the case of planning a picnic, each individual is able to perform a small part of a larger activity, aware that others are carrying out related parts. In this way a series of separate activities become united into a larger whole.

PERSPECTIVES | Cultural Diversity in the United States

RACE AND LANGUAGE: SEARCHING FOR SELF LABELS

Those groups that dominate a society often have the power to determine what terms will be used to refer to others. As they become associated with oppression, those terms often take on negative meanings. For example, the terms *Negro* and *Colored People* were often associated with submission and low status. To overcome these meanings, those referred to by these terms began to use *African American* as a term of self-reference. They infused this term with respect—a basic source of self-esteem—which they felt was denied them through the use of the old terms.

In a twist, African Americans—and to a lesser extent Latinos, Asian Americans, and Native Americans—have modified the term *Colored People* and are using

the modified term, *People of Color,* to refer to themselves. They are imbuing this term with meanings that give them an identity of respect. The term also indicates a sense of common ties that transcend race-ethnicity, common bonds rooted in historical oppression.

There is *always* disagreement about such terms, however, and this one is no exception. Just as some people felt that the term *Colored People* indicated respect, and claimed it for themselves (such as the NAACP, the National Association for the Advancement of Colored People), so some who would be included in the term *People of Color* claim that it is not appropriate. They point out that it makes color the primary characteristic or identifier of people. They stress

that humans transcend race-ethnicity, that what we have in common as human beings goes much deeper than our surface similarities. They stress that we should avoid terms that focus on differences in the pigmentation of our skin.

The language of self-reference in a society so conscious of skin color is an ongoing issue. As long as our society continues to place such an emphasis on superficial differences, the search for adequate terms is not likely to ever be "finished." In this quest for terms that strike the right chord, the term *People of Color* may become a historical footnote. If it does, it will be replaced by another term that indicates changing self-identification and changing historical characteristics. ■

Language also allows us to expand our connections far beyond our immediate, face-to-face groups, so that our *individual* biological and social needs are met by extended networks of people. This development, in turn, leads to far-flung connections with our fellow humans—connections that extend outward from our family and local community and eventually embrace worldwide networks of production and distribution. Although language by no means *guarantees* cooperation among people, language is an *essential* precondition of collaboration. Without language, the extended cooperative human endeavors on which society is based simply could not exist (Malinowski 1945; Hertzler 1965; Blumer 1966).

Learning a language means not only learning words but also acquiring the perceptions embedded in that language. In other words, language both reflects and shapes cultural experiences. Precisely because language is such a primary shaper of experience and culture, difficulties arise among people who live among each other but do not share a language, as illustrated in the Perspectives box on the next page.

In short, *language is the basis of culture.* Like most aspects of culture, its linguistic base is usually invisible to us.

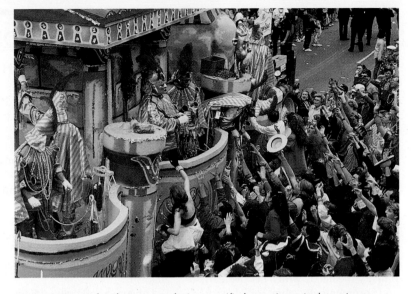

Many societies relax their norms during specified occasions. At these times, known as moral holidays, behavior that is ordinarily not permitted is allowed. From a functional standpoint, moral holidays, such as the Mardi Gras held at New Orleans, serve as safety valves, allowing a release of deviance. When the moral holiday is over, the usual enforcement of rules follows.

Values, Norms, and Sanctions

To learn a culture is to learn people's **values,** their ideas of what is desirable in life. When we uncover people's values, we learn a great deal about them, for values are the standards by which people define good and bad, beautiful and ugly. Values underlie our preferences, guide our choices, and indicate what we hold worthwhile in life.

Every group develops expectations concerning the right way to reflect its values. Sociologists use the term **norms** to describe those expectations, or rules of behavior, that develop out of a group's values. They use the term **sanctions** to refer to positive or negative reactions to the ways in which people follow norms. A **positive sanction** is an expression of approval given for following a norm, while a **negative sanction** reflects disapproval for breaking a norm. Positive sanctions can be material, such as a monetary reward, a prize, or a trophy, but in everyday life they usually consist of hugs, smiles, a clap on the back, soothing words, or even handshakes. Negative sanctions can also be material—a fine is one example—but they, too, are more likely to consist of gestures, such as frowns, stares, harsh words, or raised fists. Being awarded a raise at work is a positive sanction, indicating that the norms clustering around work values have been followed, while being fired is a negative sanction, indicating the opposite. The North American finger gesture discussed earlier is, of course, a negative sanction.

Norms vary from one situation to another. People who talk to God out loud on a bus, for example, are breaking norms. Those who talk to God aloud in church, in contrast, are following the norms for that situation. If they jump up in the middle of the sermon and begin to talk to God, however, they have broken the norm of how and when they are supposed to talk to God in church.

Norms can become too rigorous, making people feel that they are stifled. One way some cultures relieve the pressure is through *moral holidays,* specified times when people are allowed to break norms. Moral holidays often center around getting drunk and being rowdy. Mardis Gras is an example. During Mardis Gras many norms are loosened. Activities for which people would otherwise be arrested are permitted—and expected—including public

values the standards by which people define what is desirable or undesirable, good or bad, beautiful or ugly

norms the expectations, or rules of behavior, that develop out of values

sanctions expressions of approval or disapproval given to people for upholding or violating norms

positive sanction a reward given for following norms, ranging from a smile to a prize

negative sanction an expression of disapproval for breaking a norm, ranging from a mild, informal reaction such as a frown to a formal prison sentence or an execution

PERSPECTIVES | Cultural Diversity in the United States

MIAMI—LANGUAGE IN A CHANGING CITY

In the years since Castro seized power in Cuba, the city of Miami has been transformed from a quiet southern city to a Latin-American mecca. Nothing reflects Miami's essential character today as much as its long-simmering feud over language: English versus Spanish. Half of the city's 360,000 residents have trouble speaking English. Only *one-fourth* of Miami residents speak English at home.

As this chapter stresses, language is a primary means by which people learn—and communicate—their social worlds. Consequently, language differences among Miami residents reflect not just cultural diversity but people who live in separate social worlds.

Although the ethnic stew makes Miami culturally one of the richest cities in the United States, the language gap sometimes creates anger and misunderstanding. The aggravation felt by Anglos—which often seems tinged with

hostility—is seen in the bumper stickers that read, "Will the Last American Out Please Bring the Flag?"

But Latinos, now a majority in Miami, are equally frustrated. Many feel Anglos should be able to speak at least some Spanish. Nicaraguan immigrant Pedro Falcon, for example, is studying English and wonders why more people don't try to learn his native language. "Miami is the capital of Latin America," he says. "The population speaks Spanish."

Language and cultural flare-ups sometimes make headlines in the city. Latinos were outraged when an employee at the Coral Gables Board of Realtors lost her job for speaking Spanish at the office. And protesters swarmed a Publix supermarket after a cashier was fired for chatting with a friend in Spanish.

What's happening in Miami, says University of Chicago sociologist Doug-

las Massey, is what happened in cities such as Chicago in the early 1900s. Then, as now, the rate of immigration exceeded the speed with which new residents learned English, creating a pile-up effect in the proportion of non-English speakers. "Becoming comfortable with English is a slow process," he points out, "whereas immigration is fast."

As immigration continues, Massey expects Miami's proportion of non-English speakers to increase even more. But he says that this "doesn't mean in the long run that Miami is going to end up being a Spanish-speaking city." Instead, Massey believes that bilingualism will prevail. "Miami is the first truly bilingual city," he says. "The people who get ahead are not monolingual English speakers or monolingual Spanish speakers. They're people who speak both languages." ■

Source: Based on Sharp 1992; Usdansky 1992.

The violation of mores is usually a very serious matter. In this case, it is serious enough that the police at this international rugby tournament have swung into action to protect the public from seeing a "disgraceful" sight—at least one so designated by this group. Yet, unlike the reactions to most violations of mores, this scene also elicits barely suppressed laughter.

drunkenness and nudity. The norms are never completely dropped, however—just loosened a bit. Property damage and full nudity will quickly incur the wrath of the police.

Folkways and Mores

Norms that are not strictly enforced are called **folkways**. We expect people to comply with folkways, but we are likely to shrug our shoulders and not make a big deal about it if they don't. If someone insists on passing you on the left side of the sidewalk, for example, you are unlikely to take corrective action—although if the sidewalk is crowded and you must move out of the way, you might give the person a dirty look.

Other norms, however, are taken much more seriously. We think of them as essential to our core values, and we insist on conformity. These are called **mores** (MORE-rays). A person who steals, rapes, or kills has violated some of society's most important mores. As sociologist Ian Robertson (1987:62) put it,

A man who walks down a street wearing nothing on the upper half of his body is violating a folkway; a man who walks down the street wearing nothing on the lower half of his body is violating one of our most important mores, the requirement that people cover their genitals and buttocks in public.

It should also be noted that one group's folkways may be another group's mores. Although a man walking down the street with the upper half of his body uncovered is deviating from a folkway, a woman doing the same thing is violating a more. In addition, the folkways and mores of a subculture (the topic of the next section) may be the opposite of mainstream culture. For example, walking down the sidewalk in a nudist camp with the entire body uncovered would conform to that subculture's folkways.

A **taboo** refers to a norm so strongly ingrained that even the thought of its violation is greeted with revulsion. Eating human flesh and having sex with one's parents are examples of such behaviors (Benales 1973; Read 1974; Henslin 1999). When someone breaks a taboo, the individual is usually judged as not fit to live in the same society as others. The sanctions are severe, and may include banishment or death.

Many Cultural Worlds: Subcultures and Countercultures

My best guess is that you won't be able to decipher the meaning of these sentences:

> We can make epistemically subjective statements about entities that are ontologically objective, and similarly, we can make epistemically objective statements about entities that are ontologically subjective. . . . Mental phenomena are ontologically subjective; and the observer-relative features inherit that ontological subjectivity. (Searle 1995:8, 12–13)

For most of us, this statement might as well be written in Greek. Philosophers, however, write like this, and—to them—the author's intent is clear. Philosophers form a **subculture,** *a world within the larger world of the dominant culture.* Each subculture has some distinctive way of looking at life. Even if we cannot understand the preceding quote, it makes us aware that the philosopher's view of life is not quite the same as ours.

U.S. society contains tens of thousands of subcultures. Some are as broad as the way of life we associate with teenagers, others as narrow as those we associate with body builders—or with philosophers. Some U.S. ethnic groups also form subcultures: Their values, norms, and foods set them apart. So might their religion, language, and clothing. Occupational groups also form subcultures, as anyone who has hung out with cab drivers (Davis 1959; Henslin 1993), artists (McCall 1980), or construction workers (Haas 1972) can attest. Even sociologists form a subculture whose members, as you are learning, use a unique language for carving up the world.

Consider this quote from another subculture:

> If everyone applying for welfare had to supply a doctor's certificate of sterilization, if everyone who had committed a felony were sterilized, if anyone who had mental illness to any degree were sterilized—then our economy could easily take care of these people for the rest of their lives, giving them a decent living standard—but getting them out of the way. That way there would be no children abused, no surplus population, and, after a while, no pollution. . . .
>
> Now let's talk about stupidity. The level of intellect in this country is going down, generation after generation. The average IQ is always 100 because that is the accepted average. However, the kid with a 100 IQ today would have tested out at 70 when I was a lad. You get the concept . . . the marching morons. . . .
>
> When the . . . present world system collapses, it'll be good people like you who will be shooting people in the streets to feed their families. (Zellner 1995:58, 65)

Welcome to the world of the Survivalists, where the message is much clearer than that of the philosophers—and much more disturbing.

The values and norms of most subcultures are compatible with the larger society to which they belong. In some cases, however, such as these survivalists, the group's values and norms place it in opposition to the dominant culture. Sociologists use the term **counterculture** to refer

Each subculture provides its members with sets of values and distinctive ways of viewing the world. Subcultures can form around almost any topic, including, as shown here, the human body itself.

folkways norms that are not strictly enforced

mores (MORE-rays) norms that are strictly enforced because they are thought essential to core values

taboo a norm so strong that it brings revulsion if violated

subculture the values and related behaviors of a group that distinguish its members from the larger culture; a world within a world

counterculture a group whose values, beliefs, and related behaviors place its members in opposition to the broader culture

to such groups. Heavy metal adherents who glorify Satanism, hatred, cruelty, sexism, violence, and death are an example of a counterculture. Note that motorcycle enthusiasts—who emphasize personal freedom and speed *and* affirm cultural values of success—are members of a subculture. In contrast, the members of an outlaw motorcycle gang—who also stress freedom and speed, but add the values of dirtiness and contempt toward women and work—form part of a counterculture (Watson 1988). Countercultures do not have to be negative, however. Back in the 1800s, the Mormons were a counterculture who challenged the dominant culture's core value of monogamy.

Often, members of the broader culture feel threatened by a counterculture, and they sometimes move against it in an attempt to affirm their own values. The Mormons, for example, were driven out of several states before they finally settled in Utah, which was then a wilderness. Even there the federal government would not let them practice polygyny (one man having more than one wife), and Utah's statehood was made conditional on its acceptance of monogamy (Anderson 1942/1966). Today, the federal and state governments have taken steps against various survivalist groups.

*V*ALUES IN U.S. SOCIETY

An Overview of U.S. Values

As you well know, the United States is a **pluralistic society,** made up of many different groups. The United States has numerous religious, racial, and ethnic groups, as well as countless interest groups that center around such divergent activities as collecting Barbie dolls and hunting deer. This state of affairs makes the job of specifying U.S. values difficult. Nonetheless, sociologists have tried to identify the underlying core values that are shared by the many groups that make up U.S. society. Sociologist Robin Williams (1965) identified the following:

1. *Achievement and success.* Americans place a high value on personal achievement, especially outdoing others. This value includes getting ahead at work and school, and attaining wealth, power, and prestige.

2. *Individualism.* Americans have traditionally prized success that comes from individual efforts and initiative. They cherish the ideal that an individual can rise from the bottom to the very top of society. If someone fails to "get ahead," Americans generally find fault with that individual, rather than with the social system for placing roadblocks in his or her path.

3. *Activity and work.* Americans expect people to work hard and to be busily engaged in some activity even when they are not at work. This value is becoming less important.

4. *Efficiency and practicality.* Americans award high marks for getting things done efficiently. Even in everyday life, Americans consider it important to do things as fast or as well as possible, and constantly seek changes to increase efficiency.

5. *Science and technology.* Americans have a passion for applied science, for using science to control nature—to tame rivers and harness winds—and to develop new technology, from improved carburetors to talking computers.

6. *Progress.* Americans expect rapid technological change. They believe that they should constantly build "more and better" gadgets that will help them move toward that vague goal called "progress."

7. *Material comfort.* Americans expect a high level of material comfort. This comfort includes not only nutrition, medical care, and housing, but also late-model cars and recreational playthings—from boats to computer games.

8. *Humanitarianism.* Americans emphasize helpfulness, personal kindness, aid in mass disasters, and organized philanthropy.

9. *Freedom.* This core value pervades U.S. life. It underscored the American Revolution, and Americans today bristle at the suggestion of any limitation on personal freedom.

pluralistic society a society made up of many different groups

The Mass Media box on the next page highlights some interesting research on how this core value applies to Native Americans.

10. *Democracy.* By this term, Americans refer to majority rule, to the right of everyone to express an opinion, and to representative government.

11. *Equality.* It is impossible to understand Americans without being aware of the central role that the value of equality plays in their lives. Equality of opportunity, an important concept in the ideal culture discussed later, has significantly influenced U.S. history and continues to mark relations between the groups that make up U.S. society.

12. *Racism and group superiority.* Although it sharply contradicts freedom, democracy, and equality, Americans value some groups more than others and have done so throughout their history. The institution of slavery in earlier U.S. society is the most notorious example.

Romantic love is a value so primary in the United States that it permeates the culture. Movies, music, and photos promulgate this value. The couple shown here have learned the value well—not only to desire romantic love, but also how to express it to others.

In an earlier publication, I updated Williams' analysis by adding the following three values (Henslin 1975).

13. *Education.* Americans are expected to go as far in school as their abilities and finances allow. Over the years, the definition of an "adequate" education has changed sharply, and today the attainment of a college education is held as an appropriate goal for most Americans. People who have an opportunity for higher education and do not take it are even viewed by others as doing something "wrong"—not merely as making a bad choice, but as somehow being involved in an immoral act.

14. *Religiosity.* There is a feeling that "every true American ought to be religious." This does not mean that everyone is expected to join a church or synagogue, but that everyone ought to acknowledge a belief in a Supreme Being and follow some set of matching precepts. This value is so pervasive that Americans stamp "In God We Trust" on their money and declare in their national pledge of allegiance that they are "one nation under God."

15. *Romantic love and monogamy.* Americans feel that the only proper basis for marriage is romantic love. Songs, literature, mass media, and "folk beliefs" all stress this value. They especially love the theme that "love conquers all."

Value Contradictions and Social Change

As you can see, the values in a given culture can't always be integrated or reconciled in a way that allows them to support one another or even to peacefully coexist. Some may contradict one another. The value of group superiority violates the values of freedom, democracy, and equality, producing a **value contradiction.** There simply cannot be full expressions of freedom, democracy, and equality along with racism and sexism. Something has to give. One way in which Americans sidestepped this contradiction in the past was to say that freedom, democracy, and equality applied only to certain groups. The contradiction was bound to surface, however, and so it did, as is evident from the Civil War and the women's liberation movement.

As society changes, then, some values are challenged and undergo modification. Such change may be gradual, with people slowly adjusting their behaviors and ideas, or it may come suddenly and be extremely disrupting. *It is precisely at the point of value contradictions that one can see a major force for social change in a society.*

value contradiction values that contradict one another; to follow the one means to come into conflict with the other

Mass Media in Social Life

WHY DO NATIVE AMERICANS LIKE WESTERNS?

U.S. audiences (and even German, French, and Japanese ones) devour westerns. In the United States, it is easy to see why Anglos might like westerns, for it is they who seemingly defy the odds and emerge victorious. It is they who are portrayed as heroes who tame the savage wilderness and defend themselves from cruel, barbaric Indians who are intent on their destruction. But why would Indians like westerns?

Sociologist JoEllen Shively, a Chippewa who grew up on Indian reservations in Montana and North Dakota, found that westerns are so popular that Native Americans bring bags of paperbacks into taverns to trade with one another. They even call one another "cowboy."

Intrigued, Shively decided to investigate the matter by showing a western movie to adult Native Americans and Anglos in a reservation town. The groups were matched in terms of education, age, income, and percentage of unemployment. To select the movie, Shively (1991, 1992) previewed more than seventy westerns. She chose a John Wayne movie, *The Searchers,* because it not only focuses on conflict between Indians and cowboys but also shows the cowboys defeating the Indians. After the movie, the viewers filled out questionnaires, and she interviewed them.

Shively found something surprising: *All* Native Americans and Anglos identified with the cowboys; *none* identified with the Indians. The ways in which Anglos and Native Americans identified with the cowboys, however, were quite different. Each projected a different fantasy onto the story. While Anglos saw the movie as an accurate portrayal of the Old West and a justification of their own status in society, Native Americans saw it as embodying a free, natural way of life. In fact, Na-

In spite of the fact that John Wayne often portrayed an Anglo who kills Indians, Wayne is popular among Indian men. The men tend to identify with cowboys, who reflect their values of bravery, autonomy, and toughness.

tive Americans said that they were the "real cowboys." They said, "Westerns relate to the way I wish I could live"; "He's not tied down to an eight-to-five job, day after day"; "He's his own man."

Shively adds,

What appears to make Westerns meaningful to Indians is the fantasy of being free and independent like the cowboy. . . . Indians . . . find a fantasy in the cowboy story in which the important parts of their ways of life triumph and are morally good, validating their own cultural group in the context of a dramatically satisfying story. (1992)

To express their real identity—a combination of marginality on the one hand, with a set of values which are about the land, autonomy, and being free—they

(use) a cultural vehicle (that is) written for Anglos about Anglos, but it is one in which Indians invest a distinctive set of meanings that speak to their own experience, which they can read in a manner that affirms a way of life they value, or a fantasy they hold to. (1991)

In other words, values, not ethnicity, are the central issue. If a Native American film industry were to portray Native Americans with the same values that the Anglo movie industry projects onto cowboys, then Native Americans would identify with their own group. Thus, says Shively, Native American viewers make cowboys "honorary Indians," for the cowboys express their values of bravery, autonomy, and toughness. ■

Value Clusters

As is also apparent from the overview of U.S. values, values are not independent units. Instead, some cluster together to form a larger whole. In the **value cluster** surrounding success, for example, we find hard work, education, efficiency, material comfort, and individualism all bound up together. Americans are expected to go far in school, to work hard afterward, to be efficient, and then to attain a high level of material comfort, which, in turn, demonstrates success. Success is attributed to the individual's own efforts, lack of success to his or her own faults.

A value cluster centering around youthfulness, physical fitness, self-fulfillment, and leisure is becoming central to life in industrial and postindustrial societies. A major reason for the emergence of this value cluster is the greater abundance of material goods, which has freed people from the need to concentrate on survival.

An Emerging Value Cluster A value cluster of four interrelated core values—leisure, self-fulfillment, physical fitness, and youngness—appears to be emerging in the United States.

16. *Leisure.* The emergence of leisure as a value is reflected in the rapid growth of a huge recreation industry—from computer games, boats, and motor homes to sports arenas, vacation homes, and a gigantic travel and vacation industry.

17. *Self-fulfillment.* This value is reflected in the "human potential" movement, which involves becoming "all one can be," "self-help," "relating," and "personal development."

18. *Physical fitness.* Physical fitness is not a new U.S. value, but the much greater emphasis being placed on it is moving it into this emerging cluster. This trend can be seen in the "natural" foods craze; in people's obsessive concerns about weight and diet, in the many joggers, cyclists, and backpackers who take to the trails; and in the mushrooming number of health clubs and physical fitness centers all across the country.

19. *Youngness.* While valuing youth and disparaging old age is not new, some note a new sense of urgency. They attribute this to aging baby boomers, who, aghast at their physical changes, attempt to deny their biological fate. An extreme view is represented by a physician who claims that "aging is not a normal life event, but a disease" (Cowley 1996). It is not surprising, then, that techniques of youth enhancement—from cosmetics to surgery—have become popular.

This emerging value cluster is a response to fundamental changes in U.S. society. Americans used to be preoccupied with forging a nation and fighting for economic survival. They now have come to a point in their economic development where millions of people are freed from long hours of work, and millions more are able to retire from work at a young enough age that they can expect decades of life ahead of them. This value cluster centers around helping those people to maintain their health and vigor during their younger years while they look forward to a life of leisure and enabling them to enjoy their years of retirement.

A Value in Search of a Cluster Related to, but not an essential part of this emerging value cluster, is environmental concern, which is still in the process of emerging.

20. *Concern for the environment.* During most of U.S. history, the environment was seen as a challenge—wilderness to be settled, forests to be chopped down, rivers and lakes to be fished, and animals to be hunted. The lack of concern for the environment that characterized earlier Americans is illustrated by the near extinction of the bison and the

value cluster a series of interrelated values that together form a larger whole

Values, both those held by individuals and those representing a nation or people undergo change. It is difficult for many of us today to grasp the pride with which earlier Americans destroyed trees that took thousands of years to grow, were located only in one tiny speck of the globe, and were part of the nation's and world's heritage. But this is a value statement, representing current views. The evident satisfaction and pride at a job well done depicted here by both lumberjacks and managers of the timber company represent another set of values entirely.

extinction in 1915 of the passenger pigeon, a bird previously so numerous that its annual migration would darken the skies for days. Today, Americans have developed a genuine and (we can hope) long-term concern for the environment.

This emerging value of environmental concern is also related to the current stage of U.S. economic development, a point that becomes clearer when we note that people act on environmental concerns only after basic needs are met. At this point in their development, for example, the world's poor nations have a difficult time "affording" this value.

Culture Wars: When Values Clash

Changes in core values always meet with strong resistance on the part of traditionalists—who hold them dear. People become upset at changes that challenge their way of life and seem to make their future insecure. Efforts to change gender roles, for example, arouse intense controversy, as does support of alternative family forms and changes in sexual behavior. Alarmed at such onslaughts to their values, traditionalists fiercely defend historical family relationships and the gender roles they grew up with. The issue of socialist economic principles versus profit and private property is also at the center of controversy. Today's clash in values is so severe that the term "culture wars" has been coined to refer to it.

Values as Blinders

Just as values and their supporting beliefs paint a unique picture of reality, so they also form a view of what life *ought* to be like. Americans value individualism so highly, for example, that they tend to see people as free to pursue whatever legitimate goals they desire. This value blinds them to the many social circumstances that impede people's efforts. The dire consequences of family poverty, limited educational opportunities, and dead-end jobs tend to be overlooked. Instead, Americans cling to the notion that anyone can make it—if they put out enough effort. And they know they are right, for surrounding them are enticing stories of individuals who have succeeded despite huge handicaps.

"Ideal" Versus "Real" Culture

ideal culture the ideal values and norms of a people, the goals held out for them

Many of the norms that surround cultural values are only partially followed. Differences always exist between a group's ideals and what its members actually do. Consequently, sociologists use the term **ideal culture** to refer to the values, norms, and goals that a group considers ideal, worth aspiring to. Success, for example, is part of ideal culture. Americans glorify academic progress, hard work, and the display of material goods as signs of individual achievement. What people actually do, however, usually falls short of this cultural ideal. Compared with their capacities, for example, most people don't go as far as they could in school or work as hard as they could. Sociologists call the norms and values that people actually follow **real culture**.

CULTURAL UNIVERSALS

With the amazing variety of human cultures around the world, are there any **cultural universals**—values, norms, or other cultural traits that are found everywhere?

To answer this question, anthropologist George Murdock (1945) combed through data that anthropologists had gathered on hundreds of groups around the world. He drew up a list of customs concerning courtship, cooking, marriage, funerals, games, laws, music, myths, incest taboos, and even toilet training. He found that although such activities are present in all cultures, *the specific customs differ from one group to another.* There is no universal form of the family, no universal way of disposing of the dead. Similarly, specific games, rules, songs, stories, and methods of toilet training differ from one culture to another.

Even incest is defined differently from group to group. For example, the Mundugumors of New Guinea extend the incest taboo so far that for each man, seven of every eight women are ineligible marriage partners (Mead 1935/1950). Other groups go in the opposite direction and allow some men to marry their own daughters (La Barre 1954). In certain circumstances, some groups require that brothers and sisters marry one another (Beals and Hoijer 1965). The Burundi of Africa even insist that, in order to remove a certain curse, a son must have sexual relations with his mother (Albert 1963). Such sexual relations are usually allowed only for special people (royalty) or in special situations (such as when a lion hunter faces a dangerous hunt), and no society permits generalized incest for its members.

In short, although there are universal human activities (speech, music, storytelling, marrying, disposing of the dead, preparing food, and so on), there is no universally accepted way of doing any of them. Humans have no biological imperative that results in one particular form of behavior throughout the world. As indicated in the following Thinking Critically section, a few sociologists do take the position that genes significantly influence human behavior, although almost all sociologists reject this view.

Thinking Critically

ARE WE PRISONERS OF OUR GENES? SOCIOBIOLOGY AND HUMAN BEHAVIOR

A controversial view of human behavior, called **sociobiology,** provides a sharp contrast to the perspective of this chapter, that human behavior is primarily due to culture. Sociobiologists hold that due to natural selection the basic cause of human behavior is biology.

According to Charles Darwin (1859), natural selection is based on four principles. First, reproduction occurs within a natural environment. Second, the genes of a species, the basic units of life that contain the individual's traits, are passed on to offspring. These genes have a degree of random variability; that is, different characteristics are distributed among the members of a species. Third, because the members of a species possess different characteristics, some members have a better chance of surviving in the natural environment than do others—and of passing their particular genetic traits to the next generation. Fourth, over thousands of generations, those genetic traits that aid survival in the natural environment tend to become common in a species, while those that do not tend to disappear.

real culture the norms and values that people actually follow

cultural universal a value, norm, or other cultural trait that is found in every group

sociobiology a framework of thought that views human behavior as the result of natural selection and considers biological characteristics to be the fundamental cause of human behavior

Natural selection explains not only the physical characteristics of animals, but also their behavior, for over countless generations instincts emerged. Edward Wilson (1975), an insect specialist, claims that human behavior is also the result of natural selection. Human behavior, he said, is no different from the behavior of cats, dogs, rats, bees, or mosquitoes—it has been bred into *Homo sapiens* through evolutionary principles.

Wilson deliberately set out to create a storm of protest, and he succeeded. He went on to claim that religion, competition and cooperation, slavery and genocide, war and peace, envy and altruism—all can be explained through sociobiology. He provocatively added that because human behavior can be explained in terms of genetic programming, the new discipline of sociobiology will eventually absorb sociology—as well as anthropology and psychology.

Obviously, most sociologists find Wilson's position unacceptable. Not only is it a direct attack on their discipline, but it also bypasses the essence of what sociologists focus on: humans designing their own cultures, their own unique ways of life. Sociologists do not deny that biology underlies human behavior, at least not in the sense that it takes a highly developed brain to develop human culture, that there would be no speech if humans had no tongue or larynx, that abstract thought could not exist if we did not have a highly developed cerebral cortex.

But sociologists find the claim that human behavior is due to genetic programming to be quite another matter (Howe et al. 1992). Pigs act like pigs because they don't have a cerebral cortex, and instincts control their behavior. So it is for spiders, elephants, and so on. But humans possess a self and have abstract thought. They discuss principles that underlie what they do. They decide on rational courses of action. They develop purposes and goals. They consider, reflect, and make choices.

This controversy has turned into much more than simply an academic debate among scientists. Homosexuals, for example, have a personal interest in its outcome. If homosexuality is determined to be a lifestyle *choice*, then those who consider that lifestyle to be immoral will use this as a basis for excluding homosexuals from full social participation. If, however, homosexuality is determined to have a genetic basis, then that reason for social exclusion is eliminated. Sociologist Peter Conrad (1997) expresses the dominant sociological position when he points out that not all homosexuals have Xq28, the so-called "gay gene," and some people who have this gene are not homosexual. This gene, then, does not determine behavior. Instead, we must look for *social* causes.

In short, sociobiologists and sociologists stand on opposite sides, the one looking at human behavior as determined by genetics, the other looking at human behavior as determined by social learning, by experiences in the human group. Sociologists point out that if humans were prisoners of their genes, we would not have developed such a variety of fascinating ways of life around the world—we would live in a monoculture of some sort. ■

Do some animals think like humans? This chimp seems to be thinking—but she could simply be scratching her lip. Distinguishing between appearance and reality is often difficult, as is determining whether or not animals have language. Debated for centuries, this question is still not decided. The answer often depends on one's starting point—one's definition of language.

Animals and Language

Let's digress for a moment to follow a fascinating and related issue: Do animals have language? This question has intrigued scientists and nonscientists alike. Do those barks and meows your pets make constitute language?

Social scientists think of language as more complex than mere sounds. They view language as symbols that can be endlessly strung together to communicate abstract thought. Animal sounds, however, appear to be closer to a baby's cries. Although a baby will cry when in pain, this cry of distress, even though it brings a parent running, is not language. The cry is merely a biological response to pain, similar to a reflex.

Social scientists also point out that animals do not even have the vocal apparatus necessary to utter the complex sounds that make up language. Do animals lack speech, then, because they lack intelligence (the inability to learn speech), or because they are unable to make the sounds of speech? When Allen and Beatrice Gardner (1969), psychologists at the University of Nevada, learned from Goodall's research that chimps in the wild use many more hand signals than vocal signals, they decided to teach chimps gestures instead of words (Fleming 1974). Their first pupil was Washoe, a female chimpanzee who was born in the wild. In 1966, when Washoe was 1 year old, her language training began. Washoe was like a human baby. She slept a lot, had begun to crawl, and had a daily routine that centered on diapers and bottles.

The Gardners tried to teach Washoe American Sign Language, in which hand gestures correspond to individual words. They were encouraged when Washoe began to learn some of the signs, and they were elated when she began to *generalize,* to apply a sign learned in one situation to other situations. For example, they taught her the sign for "open," using three doors in the house trailer she lived in. After learning that gesture, Washoe transferred it to all the trailer's doors and drawers, to containers, the refrigerator, and even to the water faucet.

Within a year, Washoe had become inventive and was putting signs together in the equivalent of simple sentences. She even made up combinations, such as joining the sign for "give me" with "tickle" to indicate that she wanted to be tickled. At the end of four years, Washoe could use 160 signs.

Another experiment took place at Northwestern University, where Irene Pepperberg taught Alex, an African Gray parrot, to name eighty objects, such as wool, walnut, and shower. She also taught the parrot to identify colors, and to tell how many objects are in a group (up to six). Skeptics reply that the only thing that distinguishes Alex from pigeons that can learn to peck buttons for food is that his responses sound like English (Stipp 1990).

Do animals have the capacity for language? Such experiments have persuaded some scientists that they do. Others, however, remain unconvinced. For the answer to this question, then, we must await further evidence.

TECHNOLOGY IN THE GLOBAL VILLAGE

The New Technology

The gestures, language, values, folkways, and mores that we have discussed—these all are part of symbolic or nonmaterial culture. Culture, as you recall, also has a material aspect, a group's *things,* from its houses to its toys. Central to a group's material culture is its technology. In its simplest sense, **technology** can be equated with tools. In its broader sense, technology also includes the skills or procedures necessary to make and to use those tools.

We can use the term **new technology** to refer to the emerging technologies of an era that have a significant impact on social life. Many minor technologies appear from time to time, but most are slight modifications of existing technologies. Occasionally, however, technologies appear that make a major impact on human life. It is primarily to these that the term *new technology* refers. For people 500 years ago, the new technology was the printing press. For us, the new technology consists of computers, satellites, and various forms of the electronic media.

> **technology** in its narrow sense, tools; its broader sense includes the skills or procedures necessary to make and use those tools
>
> **new technology** the emerging technologies of an era that have a significant impact on social life

The adoption of new forms of communication by people who not long ago were cut off from events in the rest of the world is bound to change their nonmaterial culture. How do you think this man's thinking and view of the world is changing?

The sociological significance of technology is that its importance goes far beyond the tool itself. *The type of technology a group has sets the framework for its nonmaterial culture.* Technology influences the way people think and how they relate to one another. Consider gender relations. Through the centuries and throughout the world, it has been the custom (a group's nonmaterial culture) for men to dominate women. Today, with instantaneous communications (the material culture), this custom has become much more difficult to maintain. For example, when women from many nations gathered in Beijing for a U.N. conference in 1995, satellites instantly transmitted their grievances around the globe. Such communications both convey and create discontent, sometimes a feeling of sisterhood, and women agitate for social change.

In today's world, the long-accepted idea that it is proper to withhold rights on the basis of someone's sex can no longer hold. What is usually invisible in this revolutionary change is the role of technology, which joins the world's nations into a global communication network. Until recent technological advances, this was impossible.

Cultural Lag and Cultural Change

A couple of generations ago, sociologist William Ogburn (1922/1938), a functional analyst, coined the term **cultural lag.** By this, Ogburn meant that not all parts of a culture change at the same pace. When some part of a culture changes, other parts lag behind.

Ogburn pointed out that *a group's material culture usually changes first, with the nonmaterial culture lagging behind,* playing a game of catch up. For example, if we were to get sick, we could type our symptoms into a computer and get an immediate printout of our diagnosis and best course of treatment. In fact, in some tests computers outperform physicians (Waldholz 1991). Yet our customs have not caught up with our technology. Few people rely on software programs for their medical advice, and most of us continue to visit doctors' offices.

cultural lag William Ogburn's term for a situation in which nonmaterial culture lags behind changes in the material culture

Sometimes nonmaterial culture never does catch up. Instead, we rigorously hold onto some outmoded form, one that once was needed, but was long ago bypassed by new technology. A striking example is our nine-month school year. Have you ever wondered why it is nine months long, and why we take summers off? For most of us, this is "just the way it's always been," and we've never questioned it. But there is more to this custom than meets the eye, for it is an example of cultural lag.

In the nineteenth century, when universal schooling came about, the school year matched the technology of the time, which was labor intensive. For survival, parents needed their children's help at the critical times of planting and harvesting. Although the invention of highly productive farm machinery eliminated the need for the school year to be so short, generations later we live with this cultural lag.

Technology and Cultural Leveling

For most of human history, communication was limited and travel slow. Consequently, in their relative isolation, groups of people developed highly distinctive ways of life as they responded to the particular situations they faced. The unique characteristics they developed that distinguished one culture from another tended to change little over time. The Tasmanians, who lived on a remote island off the coast of Australia, provide an extreme example. For thousands of years, they had no contact with any other

Although today's cultural diffusion moves primarily from the West to the East, it is not entirely one-way. These children are trading Pokemon cards. Pokemon originated in Japan and swept across the United States.

people. They were so isolated that they did not even know how to make clothing or fire (Edgerton 1992).

Except in such rare instances, humans always had *some* contact with other groups. During these contacts, people learned from one another, adapting some part of the other's way of life. In this process, called **cultural diffusion,** groups are most receptive to changes in their technology or material culture. They usually are eager, for example, to adopt superior weapons and tools. In remote jungles in South America one can find metal cooking pots, steel axes, and even bits of clothing spun in mills in South Carolina. Although the direction of cultural diffusion today is primarily from the West to other parts of the world, cultural diffusion is not a one-way street, as bagels, woks, hammocks, and sushi bars in the United States attest.

With today's sophisticated technology in the areas of travel and communications, cultural diffusion is occurring rapidly. Air travel has made it possible to journey around the globe in a matter of hours. In the not-so-distant past, a trip from the United States to Africa was so unusual that only a few hardy people made it, and newspapers would herald their feat. Today, hundreds of thousands make the trip each year.

The changes in communication are no less vast. Communication used to be limited to face-to-face speech, to visual signals involving smoke or light reflected from mirrors, and to written messages that were passed from hand to hand. Despite newspapers, people in some parts of the United States did not hear about the end of the Civil War until weeks and even months after it was over. Today's electronic communications transmit messages across the globe in a matter of seconds, and we learn almost instantaneously what is happening on the other side of the world.

In fact, travel and communication unite us to such an extent that there almost is no "other side of the world" anymore. One result is **cultural leveling,** a process in which cultures become similar to one another as the globalization of capitalism brings not only technology but also Western culture to the rest of the world. Japan, for example, has adopted not only Western economic production but also Western forms of dress and music. These changes, which have been "superimposed" on Japanese culture, have turned Japan into a blend of Western and Eastern cultures.

Cultural leveling is occurring rapidly around the world, as is apparent to any traveler. The Golden Arches of McDonald's welcome today's visitors to Tokyo, Paris, London, Madrid, Moscow, Hong Kong, and Beijing. In Mexico, the most popular piñatas are no longer donkeys but Mickey Mouse and Fred Flintstone (Beckett 1996). In Beijing, a grade school teacher asked his class if they knew who Mickey Mouse was. One of the students held up a lunchbox with Mickey Mouse on it. As he and the kids scanned the room, they found almost a dozen images of Mickey Mouse. But they didn't find a single image of any character from classical Chinese literature—not one (Hofstadter 2000).

Although the bridging of geography and culture by electronic signals does not in itself mark the end of traditional cultures, it inevitably results in some degree of *cultural leveling,* some blander, less distinctive way of life—U.S. culture with French, Japanese, and Bulgarian accents, so to speak. Although the "cultural accent" remains, something vital is lost forever. For an extreme example of culture leveling, and perhaps obliteration, see the New Technology box on the next page.

Shown here is a Masai Barbie Doll. Mattel Toys, the U.S. manufacturer, has modified Barbie to match Masai (Kenya) culture by dressing her in a traditional "shuka" dress, beads, shawl, headdress, and anklets. As objects diffuse from one culture to another, they are modified to meet the tastes and specific needs of the adoptive culture. In this instance, the modification has been done intentionally as part of the globalization of capitalism. Now that Barbie is a Masai, can a Masai Ken be far behind?

cultural diffusion the spread of cultural characteristics from one group to another

cultural leveling the process by which cultures become similar to one another, and especially by which Western industrial culture is imported and diffused into industrializing nations

Sociology & the New Technology

COULD COMPUTERS REPLACE THE HUMAN SPECIES?

A question that used to be asked only jokingly—Could machines replace the human species?—is nowadays being asked more seriously. This issue was first brought to the public's attention in "2001: A Space Odyssey," which introduced us to HAL, a rebellious computer. In that movie, HAL, a computer with consciousness, took over the spaceship, and humans had to use cunning to regain control.

Sometime during this century, computers are expected to have an intelligence that outstrips that of humans. They will be able to think, not just compute according to instruc-

tions. Their thinking power will surpass that of humans. When this happens, computers "may begin to regard human beings as little more than an evolutionary dead end, a kind of pet to be kept around only for amusement" (Chapman 1999).

The stuff only of science fiction? At first it may seem so, but some scientists are taking the question so seriously that they have held a conference on this topic. Among the ideas they put forth: Humans could "download" their thoughts and memories into computers. Computers would then gain human consciousness and become a "successor species." Some even suggest that the

destiny of humans is to produce machines that replace them, that this is the next stage in evolution (Gershenfeld 1999; Kurzweil 1999; Moravec 1999). Most of us probably think that such reasoning should remain in the realm of science fiction. We have a gut reaction that such a thing is too implausible to consider. Consider the possibility for a moment, however. If this were to occur, would culture exist? What would culture consist of? Would language still be its essence? Would values exist? Would there, perhaps, be two main cultures, that of the dominant thinking machines and that of the inferior, submissive humans? ■

SUMMARY AND REVIEW

■ What Is Culture?

All human groups possess **culture**—language, beliefs, values, norms, and material objects that are passed from one generation to the next. **Material culture** consists of objects (art, buildings, clothing, tools). **Nonmaterial** (or **symbolic**) **culture** is a group's ways of thinking and patterns of behavior. **Ideal culture** is a group's ideal values and norms, and its goals. **Real culture** is their actual behavior, which often falls short of their cultural ideals. Pp. 38–40.

What are cultural relativism and ethnocentrism?

People are naturally **ethnocentric**; that is, they use their own culture as a yardstick for judging the ways of others. In contrast, those who embrace **cultural relativism** try to understand other cultures on those cultures' own terms. Pp. 40–41.

■ Components of Symbolic Culture

What are the components of nonmaterial culture?

The central component is **symbols**, anything to which people attach meaning and use to communicate with others. Universally, the symbols of nonmaterial culture are **gestures**, **language**, **values**, **norms**, **sanctions**, **folkways**, and **mores**. Pp. 42–43.

Why is language so significant to culture?

Language allows human experience to be goal directed, cooperative, and cumulative. It also lets humans move beyond the present and share a past, future, and other common perspectives. According to the **Sapir-Whorf hypothesis**, language even shapes our thoughts and perceptions. Pp. 43–47.

How do values, norms, folkways, mores, and sanctions reflect culture?

All groups have **values**, standards by which they define what is desirable or undesirable, and **norms**, rules or expectations about behavior. Groups use **positive sanctions** to show approval of those who follow their norms, and **negative sanctions** to show disapproval of those who do not. Norms that are not strictly enforced are called **folkways**, while **mores** are norms to which groups demand conformity because they reflect core values. Pp. 47–49.

How do subcultures and countercultures differ?

A **subculture** is a group whose values and related behaviors distinguish its members from the general culture. A **counterculture** holds values that at least in some ways stand in opposition to those of the dominant culture. Pp. 49–50.

■ Values in U.S. Society

What are the core U.S. values?

Although the United States is a **pluralistic society**, made up of many groups, each with its own set of values, certain values dominate: achievement and success, individualism, activity and work, efficiency and practicality, science and technology, progress, material comfort, equality, freedom, democracy, humanitarianism, racism and group superiority, education, religiosity, romantic love and monogamy. Some values cluster together (**value clusters**) to form a larger whole. **Value contradictions** (such as equality and racism) indicate areas of social tension, which are likely points of social change.

Changes in a society's fundamental values are opposed by people who hold strongly to traditional values. Leisure, physical fitness, self-fulfillment, and concern for the environment are emerging core values. Pp. 50–55.

■ Cultural Universals

Do cultural universals exist?

Cultural universals are values, norms, or other cultural traits that are found in all cultures. Although all human groups have customs concerning cooking, funerals, weddings, and so on, because the specific forms these customs take vary from one culture to another there are no cultural universals. Pp. 55–56.

Do animals have language?

No animals have language in the sociological sense of the term, although some experiments indicate that some animals may have a limited capacity to learn language. Pp. 56–57.

■ Technology in the Global Village

How is technology changing culture?

Ogburn coined the term **cultural lag** to describe how a group's non-material culture lags behind its changing technology. With today's technological advances in travel and communications, **cultural diffusion** is occurring rapidly. This leads to **cultural leveling**, whereby many groups are adopting Western culture in place of their own customs. Much of the richness of the world's diverse cultures is being lost in the process. Pp. 57–60.

Where can I read more on this topic?

Suggested Readings for this chapter are at the back of this book.

Sociology & the Internet

All URLs listed are current as of the printing of this book. URLs often change. Please check our web site, **http://www.abacon.com/henslin,** for updates.

1. The text discusses how people within a culture use both gestures and language to communicate. Every group creates a system of gestures and language whose meaning is particular to its culture. To learn more about how gestures vary with culture, go to **http://webofculture.com/rcfs/index.html.** Click on "Gestures." To learn more about cultural differences in the meanings of words, go to one of the following Web sites:

   http://www.bg-map.com/us-uk.html

   http://pages.prodigy.com/NY/NYC/britspk/probword.html

   http://www.hps.com/~tpg/ukdict

   After investigating these cultural differences, write a short paper in which you explore the challenges of cross-cultural communication.

2. What do you think of when you hear the word *Amish*? Do you think of horses and buggies? What about clothing? Maybe you think about farms, quilts, and woodcrafting. There is much more to the Amish, however, than their material culture. Examine the following Web sites:

   http://www.800padutch.com

   http://www.holycrosslivonia.org/amish/index.html

   http://www.religioustolerance.org/amish.htm

   http://www.amish-heartland.com/index.htm

Compare both the material and nonmaterial cultures of the Amish with those of the larger U.S. culture. Are most of the differences in the material or the nonmaterial culture? In what ways is the nonmaterial culture of the Amish similar to the larger U.S. culture?

3. Using a search engine like Yahoo (**http://www.yahoo.com**) or Metacrawler (**http://www.metacrawler.com**), search the Internet for information on a value conflict. Entering the words "school prayer" in the search term space. What are the major arguments of people who are on both sides of this issue? To what extent do the supporters on each side of this disagreement make use of core U.S. values in defending their position?

4. Every culture develops expectations about the behavior of its members. Cyber culture is no different. In cyberspace, there are norms that govern the behavior of those "residing" there. These rules of conduct have become known as *netiquette*. Use the Yahoo search engine at **http://www.yahoo.com.** Click on "Society and Culture" to examine the norms in cyberspace. Click on "Etiquette" and you will see the category "Netiquette." Check out some of the links that are listed there, especially **http://www.albion.com/netiquette.** What are some of the norms governing your behavior in cyberspace? What kind of sanctions can you expect to receive if you do not follow the norms? Where you familiar with these norms? Which norms are mores and which are folkways? How can you tell?

Cynthia Fitting, Man Reading to Child, 1992

Socialization

■ **What Is Human Nature?**
Feral Children
Isolated Children
Institutionalized Children
Deprived Animals

■ **Socialization into the Self, Mind, and Emotions**
Cooley and the Looking-Glass Self
Mead and Role Taking
Piaget and the Development of Reasoning
   Skills
Kohlberg and the Development of Morality
Gilligan and Gender Differences in Morality
Global Considerations: The Self, Reasoning,
   and Morality
Freud and the Development of Personality
Socialization and Emotions
The Self and Emotions as Social Control:
   Society Within Us

■ **Socialization into Gender**
Gender Messages in the Family
Gender Messages in the Mass Media

■ **Agents of Socialization**
The Family
The Neighborhood
Religion
Day Care
The School
Peer Groups
Sports
The Workplace

■ **Resocialization**
Total Institutions

■ **Socialization Through the Life Course**
Childhood (from birth to about age 12)
Adolescence (about ages 13–17)
Young Adulthood (about ages 18–29)
The Middle Years (about ages 30–65)
The Older Years (about age 66 on)
The Sociological Significance of the Life Course

■ **Are We Prisoners of Socialization?**

■ **Summary and Review**

The old man was horrified when he found out. Life never had been good since his daughter lost her hearing when she was just 2 years old. She couldn't even talk—just fluttered her hands around trying to tell him things. Over the years, he had gotten used to that. But now . . . . he shuddered at the

thought of her being pregnant. No one would be willing to marry her; he knew that. And the neighbors, their tongues would never stop wagging. Everywhere he went, he could hear people talking behind his back.

If only his wife were still alive, maybe she could come up with something. What should he do? He couldn't just kick his daughter out into the street.

After the baby was born, the old man tried to shake his feelings, but they wouldn't let loose. Isabelle was a pretty name, but every time he looked at the baby he felt sick to his stomach.

He hated doing it, but there was no way out. His daughter and her baby would have to live in the attic.

. . .

Unfortunately, this is a true story. Isabelle was discovered in Ohio in 1938 when she was about 6 ½ years old, living in a dark room with her deaf-mute mother. Isabelle couldn't talk, but she did use gestures to communicate with her mother. An inadequate diet and lack of sunshine had given Isabelle a disease called rickets. Her legs

were so bowed that as she stood erect the soles of her shoes came nearly flat together, and she

63

got about with a skittering gait. Her behavior toward strangers, especially men, was almost that of a wild animal, manifesting much fear and hostility. In lieu of speech she made only a strange croaking sound. (Davis 1940/1999:138).

When the newspapers reported this case, sociologist Kingsley Davis decided to find out what happened to Isabelle after her discovery. We'll come back to that later, but first let's use the case of Isabelle to give us some insight into what human nature is. ■

WHAT IS HUMAN NATURE?

For centuries, people have been intrigued with the question of what is human about human nature. How much of people's characteristics comes from "nature" (heredity) and how much from "nurture" (the **social environment,** contact with others)? One way to answer this question is to study identical twins who have been reared apart, such as those discussed in the Down-to-Earth Sociology box on the next page. Another way is to examine people who have been reared without human contact. Let's consider such children.

Feral Children

Over the centuries, the discovery of **feral** (wild) **children** has been reported from time to time. Supposedly, these children were abandoned or lost by their parents at a very early age and then raised by animals. In the 1700s, a feral child known as the wild boy of Aveyron was studied by the scientists of his day (Itard 1962). This boy, who was found in the forests of France in 1798, walked on all fours, and pounced on small animals, devouring them uncooked. He could not speak, and he gave no indication of feeling the cold. Other reports of feral children have claimed that on discovery, these children acted like wild animals: They could not speak; they bit, scratched, growled, and walked on all fours; they ate grass, tore ravenously at meat, drank by lapping water; and showed an insensitivity to pain and cold (Malson 1972).

Most social scientists today dismiss the significance of feral children, taking the position that children cannot be raised by animals and that children found in the woods were reared by their parents as infants but then abandoned, probably because they were retarded. But what if this were not the case? Could it be that, if untouched by society, we would all by nature be like feral children?

Isolated Children

Well-documented cases like Isabelle (in our opening vignette) surface from time to time. What can they tell us about human nature? We can first conclude that humans have no natural language, for isolated children like Isabelle are unable to speak.

But maybe Isabelle was mentally impaired, as most scientists claim feral children are, and could not progress through the usual stages of development. When given an intelligence test, she scored practically zero. But after a few months of intensive language training, Isabelle was able to speak in short sentences. In about a year, she could write a few words, do simple addition, and retell stories after hearing them. Seven months later, she had a vocabulary of almost 2,000 words. It took only two years for Isabelle to reach the intellectual level that is normal for her age. She then went on to school, where she was "bright, cheerful, energetic . . . and participated in all school activities as normally as other children" (Davis 1940/1999:139).

social environment the entire human environment, including direct contact with others

feral children children assumed to have been raised by animals, in the wilderness isolated from other humans

Sociology

HEREDITY OR ENVIRONMENT?
THE CASE OF OSKAR AND JACK, IDENTICAL TWINS

Identical twins share exact genetic heredity. One fertilized egg divides to produce two embryos. If heredity determines personality—or attitudes, temperment, and basic skills—then identical twins should be identical not only in their looks but also in these characteristics.

The fascinating case of Jack and Oskar helps us unravel this mystery. From their experience, we can see the far-reaching effects of the environment—how social experiences override biology.

Jack Yufe and Oskar Stohr are identical twins born in 1932 to a Jewish father and a Catholic mother. They were separated as babies after their parents divorced. Oskar was reared in Czechoslovakia by his mother's mother, who was a strict Catholic. When Oskar was a toddler, Hitler annexed this area of Czechoslovakia, and Oskar learned to love Hitler and to hate Jews. He became involved with the Hitler Youth (a sort of Boy Scout organization, except that this one was designed to instill the "virtues" of patriotism, loyalty, obedience—and hatred).

Jack's upbringing was in almost total contrast to Oskar's. Reared in Trinidad by his father, he learned loyalty to Jews and hatred of Hitler and the Nazis. After the war, Jack emigrated to Israel, where, at the age of 17, he joined a kibbutz. Later, Jack served in the Israeli army.

In 1954, the two brothers met. It was a short meeting, and Jack had been warned not to tell Oskar that they were Jews. Twenty-five years later, in 1979, when they were 47 years old, social scientists at the University of Minnesota brought them together again. These researchers figured that because Jack and Oskar had the

The question of the relative influence of heredity and the environment on human behavior has fascinated and plagued researchers. Identical twins reared apart provide an opportunity to examine this relationship. However, almost all identical twins, including these girls, are reared together, frustrating efforts to separate heredity and environment.

same genes, whatever differences they showed would have to be due to the environment—to their different social experiences.

Not only did Oskar and Jack have different attitudes toward the war, Hitler, and Jews, but also their other basic orientations to life were different. In their politics, Oskar was conservative, while Jack was more liberal. Oskar enjoyed leisure, while Jack was a workaholic. And, as you can predict, Jack was very proud of being a Jew. Oskar, who by this time knew that he was a Jew, wouldn't even mention it.

That would seem to settle the matter. But there was another side to the findings. The researchers also found that Oskar and Jack both liked sweet liqueur and spicy foods, excelled at sports as children but had difficulty with math, and had the same rate of speech. Both flushed the toilet both before and after using it and enjoyed star-

tling people by sneezing in crowded places. ■

For Your Consideration

Heredity or environment? How much influence does *each* have? The question is not yet settled, but at this point it seems fair to conclude that the *limits* of certain physical and mental abilities are established by heredity (such as ability at sports and mathematics), while such basic orientations to life as attitudes are the result of the environment. We can put it this way: For some parts of life, the blueprint is drawn by heredity; but even here the environment can redraw those lines. For other parts, the individual is a blank slate, and it is entirely up to the environment to determine what is written on that slate.

Sources: Based on Begley 1979, Chen 1979, Wright 1995.

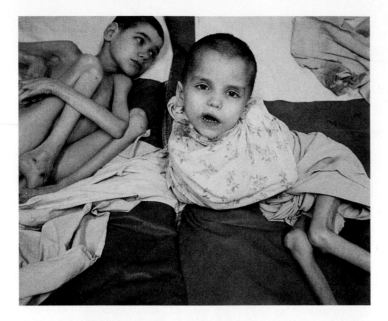

The treatment given these orphaned children in Romania will make it difficult for them to develop into fully functioning adults. If they survive they will carry scars into adulthood. As explained in the text, it is also likely that their abuse has affected their ability to reason.

As discussed in the last chapter, language is the key to human behavior. Without language, people have no mechanism for developing thought. Unlike animals, humans have no instincts that take the place of language. If an individual lacks language, he or she lives in an isolated world, a world of internal silence, without shared ideas, without connections to others.

Without language, there can be no culture—no shared way of life—and culture is the key to what people become. Each of us possesses a biological heritage, but this heritage does not determine specific behaviors, attitudes, or values. It is our culture that superimposes the specifics of what we become onto our biological heritage.

Institutionalized Children

But what besides language is required if a child is to develop into what we consider a healthy, balanced, intelligent human being? The answer is stimulating interaction.

Two or three generations ago, when we had a much higher death rate, orphanages dotted the United States. Children reared in orphanages tended to be smaller than other children, to have difficulty establishing close bonds with others, and to have lower IQs—if they survived, that is, for their death rates were much higher than average (Spitz 1945). These orphanages were not Dickensian institutions where ragged children were beaten and denied food. The children were kept clean and given simple but nutritious food. Nevertheless, the contrast with today's standards is remarkable. Here is an account of a good orphanage in Iowa during the 1930s.

> Until about six months, they were cared for in the infant nursery. The babies were kept in standard hospital cribs that often had protective sheeting on the sides, thus effectively limiting visual stimulation; no toys or other objects were hung in the infants' line of vision. Human interactions were limited to busy nurses who, with the speed born of practice and necessity, changed diapers or bedding, bathed and medicated the infants, and fed them efficiently with propped bottles. (Skeels 1966)

Although everyone "knew" that the cause of mental retardation was biological ("They're just born that way"), two psychologists who consulted in this Iowa orphanage, H. M. Skeels and H. B. Dye (1939), began to suspect that the absence of stimulating social interaction was the basic problem, not some biological incapacity on the part of the children. To test their controversial idea, they placed thirteen infants whose mental retardation was so obvious that no one wanted to adopt them, in an institution for the mentally retarded. Each infant, then about 19 months old, was assigned to a separate ward of women ranging in mental age from 5 to 12 and in chronological age from 18 to 50. The women were pleased with this arrangement. They not only did a good job taking care of the infants' basic physical needs—diapering, feeding, and so on—but they also loved to play with the children, to cuddle them, and to shower them with attention. They even competed to see which ward would have "its baby" walking or talking first. Each baby had one woman who became

particularly attached to him (or her) and figuratively "adopted" him (or her). As a consequence, an intense one-to-one adult-child relationship developed, which was supplemented by the less intense but frequent interactions with the other adults in the environment. Each child had some one person with whom he (or she) was identified and who was particularly interested in him (or her) and his (or her) achievements. (Skeels 1966)

The researchers left a control group of twelve infants at the orphanage, where they received the usual care. These infants were retarded but were higher in intelligence than the other thirteen. Two and a half years later, Skeels and Dye tested all the children's intelligence. Their findings were startling: Those assigned to the retarded women had gained an average of twenty-eight IQ points while those who remained in the orphanage had lost thirty points.

What happened after these children were grown? Did these initial differences matter? Twenty-one years later, Skeels and Dye did a follow-up study. Those in the control group who had remained in the orphanage had, on average, less than a third-grade education. Four still lived in state institutions, while the others held low-level jobs. Only two had married. In contrast, the average level of education for the thirteen individuals in the experimental group was twelve grades (about normal for that period). Five had completed one or more years of college. One had not only earned a B.A. but had also gone on to graduate school. Eleven had married. All thirteen were self-supporting and had higher-status jobs or were homemakers (Skeels 1966). Apparently, then, one characteristic we take for granted as being a basic "human" trait, high intelligence, depends on early, close relations with other humans.

Let's consider one other case, the story of Genie:

In 1970, California authorities found Genie, a 13½-year-old girl who had been locked in a small room and tied to a chair since she was 20 months old. Apparently her father (70 years old when Genie was discovered) hated children, and probably had caused the death of two of Genie's siblings. Her 50-year-old mother was partially blind and frightened of her husband. Genie could not speak, did not know how to chew, was unable to stand upright, and could not straighten her hands and legs. On intelligence tests, she scored at the level of a 1-year-old. After intensive training, Genie learned to walk and use simple sentences (although they were garbled). As she grew up, her language remained primitive, she took anyone's property if it appealed to her, and she went to the bathroom wherever she wanted. At the age of 21, Genie went to live in a home for adults who cannot live alone. (Pines 1981)

From this pathetic story, we can conclude that not only intelligence but also the ability to establish close bonds with others depends on early interaction. In addition, apparently there is a period prior to age 13 in which language and human bonding must occur for humans to develop high intelligence and the ability to be sociable and follow social norms.

Deprived Animals

A final lesson can be gained by looking at animals that have been deprived of normal interaction. In a series of experiments with rhesus monkeys, psychologists Harry and Margaret Harlow demonstrated the importance of early learning. The Harlows (1962) raised baby monkeys in isolation. They gave each monkey two artificial mothers, shown in the photo on this page. One "mother" was only a wire frame with a wooden head, but it did have a nipple from which the baby could nurse. The frame of the other "mother," which had no bottle, was covered with soft terrycloth. To obtain food, the baby monkeys nursed at the wire frame.

Like humans, monkeys need interaction to thrive. Those raised in isolation are unable to interact satisfactorily with others. In this photograph, we see one of the monkeys described in the text. Purposefully frightened by the experimenter, the monkey has taken refuge in the soft terrycloth draped over an artificial "mother."

When the Harlows (1965) frightened the babies with a large mechanical bear or dog, the babies did not run to the wire frame "mother." Instead, they would cling pathetically to their terrycloth "mother." The Harlows concluded that infant-mother bonding is due not to feeding but, rather, to what they termed "intimate physical contact." To most of us, this phrase means cuddling.

It is also significant that the monkeys raised in isolation were never able to adjust to monkey life. Placed with other monkeys when they were grown, they didn't know how to enter into "monkey interaction"—to play and to engage in pretend fights—and the other monkeys rejected them. Neither did they know how to engage in sexual intercourse, despite futile attempts to do so. The experimenters designed a special device, which allowed some females to become pregnant. After giving birth, however, these monkeys were "ineffective, inadequate, and brutal mothers . . . [who] . . . struck their babies, kicked them, or crushed the babies against the cage floor."

In one of their many other experiments, the Harlows isolated baby monkeys for different lengths of time. They found that monkeys that were isolated for short periods (about three months) were able to overcome the effects of their isolation. Those isolated for six months or more, however, were unable to adjust to normal monkey life. They could not play or engage in pretend fights, and the other monkeys rejected them. In other words, the longer the isolation, the more difficult it is to overcome. In addition, a critical learning stage may exist; if that stage is missed, it may be impossible to compensate for what has been lost. That may have been the case with Genie.

Because humans are not monkeys, we must be careful about extrapolating from animal studies to human behavior. The Harlow experiments, however, support what we know about children who are reared in isolation.

■ **In Sum** Society Makes Us Human Apparently, babies do not "naturally" develop into human adults. Although their bodies grow, if raised in isolation they become little more than big animals. Without the concepts that language provides, they can't experience or even grasp relations between people (the "connections" we call brother, sister, parent, friend, teacher, and so on). And without warm, friendly interaction, they aren't "friendly" in the accepted sense of the term; nor do they cooperate with others. They do not think in terms of a past and a future. Indeed, they do not appear to think in any meaningful way.

In short, to develop into adults with the characteristics that we take for granted as "human," children need to be surrounded by people who care for them. Only then do they develop into social adults within the limits set by their biology. This process by which we learn the ways of society (or of particular groups), called **socialization**, is what sociologists have in mind when they say, "Society makes us human."

SOCIALIZATION INTO THE SELF, MIND, AND EMOTIONS

At birth, we have no idea that we are a separate being. We don't even know that we are a he or she. How do we develop our reasoning skills? Our morality? Our personality? Our emotions? How do we develop a **self**, the picture we have of how others see us, our view of who we are?

Cooley and the Looking-Glass Self

Back in the 1800s, Charles Horton Cooley (1864–1929), a symbolic interactionist who taught at the University of Michigan, concluded that this unique aspect of "humanness" called the self is socially created. He said that *our sense of self develops from interaction with*

socialization the process by which people learn the characteristics of their group—the attitudes, values, and actions thought appropriate for them

self the unique human capacity of being able to see ourselves "from the outside"; the picture we gain of how others see us

others. Cooley (1902) coined the term **looking-glass self** to describe the process by which a sense of self develops. He summarized this idea in the following couplet:

> Each to each a looking-glass
> Reflects the other that doth pass.

The looking-glass self contains three elements:

1. *We imagine how we appear to those around us.* For example, we may think that others see us as witty or dull.
2. *We interpret others' reactions.* We come to conclusions about how others evaluate us. Do they like us being witty? Do they dislike us for being dull?
3. *We develop a self-concept.* Based on our interpretations of how others react to us, we develop feelings and ideas about ourselves. A favorable reflection in this "social mirror" leads to a positive self-concept, a negative reflection to a negative self-concept.

Note that the development of the self does *not* depend on accurate evaluations. Even if we grossly misinterpret how others think about us, those misjudgments become part of our self-concept. Note also that although the self-concept begins in childhood, *its development is an ongoing, lifelong process.* The three steps of the looking-glass self are a part of our everyday lives: As we do whatever we do in life, we monitor how others react to us. The result is that we continually modify the self. The self, then, is never a finished product, but is always in process, even into old age.

Mead and Role Taking

Another symbolic interactionist, George Herbert Mead (1863–1931), who taught at the University of Chicago, added that play is critical to the development of a self. In play, children learn to **take the role of the other,** that is, to put themselves in someone else's shoes—to understand how someone else feels and thinks and to anticipate how that person will act.

Young children attain this ability only gradually (Mead 1934; Coser 1977). In a simple experiment, psychologist J. Flavel (1968) asked 14-year-olds and 8-year-olds to explain a board game to some children who were blindfolded and to others who were not. The 8-year-olds gave the same instructions to everyone, while the 14-year-olds gave more detailed instructions to those who were blindfolded. The younger children could not yet take the role of the other, while the older children could.

As they develop this ability, at first children are able to take only the role of **significant others,** individuals who significantly influence their lives, such as parents or siblings. By assuming their roles during play, such as dressing up in their parents' clothing, children cultivate the ability to put themselves in the place of significant others.

As the self gradually develops, children internalize the expectations of more and more people. The ability to take on roles eventually extends to being able to take the role of "the group as a whole." Mead used the term **generalized other** to refer to this, our perception of how people in general think of us.

To take the role of others is essential if we are to become a cooperative member of human groups—whether they be our family, friends, or co-workers.

looking-glass self a term coined by Charles Horton Cooley to refer to the process by which our self develops through internalizing others' reactions to us

taking the role of the other putting oneself in someone else's shoes; understanding how someone else feels and thinks and thus anticipating how that person will act

significant other an individual who significantly influences someone else's life

generalized other the norms, values, attitudes, and expectations of people "in general"; the child's ability to take the role of the generalized other is a significant step in the development of a self

Mead analyzed taking the role of the other as an essential part of learning to be a full-fledged member of society. At first, we are able to take the role only of significant others, as this child is doing. Later we develop the capacity to take the role of the generalized other, which is essential not only for extended cooperation but also for the control of antisocial desires.

This ability allows us to modify our behavior by anticipating how others will react—something Genie never learned.

Learning to take the role of the other goes through three stages:

1. *Imitation.* Children under 3 can only mimic others. They do not yet have a sense of self separate from others, and they can only imitate people's gestures and words. (This stage is actually not role taking, but it prepares the child for it.)

2. *Play.* During the second stage, from the age of about 3 to 6, children pretend to take the roles of specific people. They might pretend that they are a firefighter, a wrestler, the Lone Ranger, Supergirl, Xena, Batman, and so on. They also like costumes at this stage and enjoy dressing up in their parents' clothing, or tying a towel around their neck to "become" Superman or Wonder Woman.

3. *Games.* This third stage, organized play, or team games, begins roughly with the early school years. The significance for the self is that to play these games the individual must be able to take multiple roles. One of Mead's favorite examples was that of a baseball game, in which each player must be able to take the role of all the other players. To play baseball, the child not only must know his or her own role but also must be able to anticipate who will do what when the ball is hit or thrown.

Mead also distinguished between the "I" and the "me" in the development of the self. The "I" is *the self as subject,* the active, spontaneous, creative part of the self. In contrast, the "me" is *the self as object.* It is made up of attitudes that we internalize from our interactions with others. Mead chose pronouns to indicate these two aspects of the self because in our language "I" is the active agent, as in "I shoved him," while "me" is the object of action, as in "He shoved me." Mead stressed that we are not passive in the socialization process. We are not like computerized robots, passively absorbing the responses of others. Rather, our "I" evaluates the reactions of others and organizes them into a unified whole. Mead added that the "I" even monitors the "me," fine-tuning our actions to help us better match what others expect of us.

Mead also drew a conclusion that some find startling—that *not only the self but also the human mind is a social product.* Mead stressed that we cannot think without symbols. But where do these symbols come from? Only from society, which gives us our symbols by giving us language. If society did not provide the symbols, we would not be able to

To help his students understand what the term *generalized other* means, Mead used baseball as an illustration. Why are team sports and organized games such excellent examples to use in explaining this concept?

think, and thus would not possess what we call the mind. Mind, then, like language, is a product of society.

Piaget and the Development of Reasoning Skills

Essential to the human mind is the ability to reason. How do we learn this skill?

This question intrigued Jean Piaget (1896–1980), a Swiss psychologist who noticed that young children give similar wrong answers when they take intelligence tests. This might mean, he thought, that young children follow some sort of incorrect rule in figuring out answers. Perhaps there is a common process that we humans go through as we learn how to reason.

To find out, Piaget set up a laboratory where he could give children of different ages problems to solve (Piaget 1950, 1954; Phillips 1969). After years of research, Piaget concluded that children go through four stages as they develop their ability to reason. (If you substitute "reasoning skills" for the term *operational* in the following explanations, Piaget's findings will be easier to understand.)

1. *The sensorimotor stage* (from birth to about age 2)
   During this early stage, the infant's understanding is limited to direct contact with the environment. It is based on sucking, touching, listening, seeing. Infants do not think in any sense that we understand. During the first part of this stage, they do not even know that their bodies are separate from the environment. Indeed, they have yet to discover that they have toes. Neither can infants recognize cause and effect. That is, they do not know that their actions cause something to happen.

2. *The preoperational stage* (from about age 2 to age 7)
   During this stage, children *develop the ability to use symbols*. They do not yet understand common concepts, however, such as size, speed, or causation. Although they can count, they do not really understand what numbers mean. Nor do they yet have the ability to take the role of the other. Piaget asked preoperational children to describe a clay model of a mountain range. They did just fine. But when he asked them to describe how the mountain range looked from where another child was sitting, they couldn't do so. They could only repeat what they saw from their view.

3. *The concrete operational stage* (from the age of about 7 to 12)
   Although reasoning abilities are more developed, they remain *concrete*. Children can now understand numbers, causation, and speed, and they are able to take the role of the other and to participate in team games. Without concrete examples, however, they are unable to talk about concepts such as truth, honesty, or justice. They can explain why Jane's answer was a lie, but they cannot describe what truth itself is.

4. *The formal operational stage* (after the age of about 12)
   Children are now capable of abstract thinking. Without concrete examples, they can talk about concepts, come to conclusions based on general principles, and use rules to solve abstract problems. During this stage, they are likely to become young philosophers (Kagan 1984). For example, if shown a photo of a slave, a child at the concrete operational stage might have said, "That's wrong!" Now, however, he or she is more likely to ask, "If our country was founded on equality, how could people have owned slaves?"

Kohlberg and the Development of Morality

The development of morality is significant in what humans become. If you have observed young children, you know that they focus on immediate gratification and show little or no concern for others. ("Mine!" a 2-year-old will shout, as she takes a toy from another child.) Yet, at a later age this same child will become considerate of others and concerned with moral issues.

How does this happen? Psychologist Lawrence Kohlberg (1975, 1984, 1986) concluded that we go through a sequence of stages as we develop morality. Building on Piaget's work, he found that children begin in the *amoral stage* I just described. For them, there is no right or wrong, just personal needs to be satisfied. At about ages 7 and 10, children are in what Kohlberg called a *preconventional stage.* They have learned rules, and they follow them to stay out of trouble. They view right and wrong as what pleases or displeases their parents, friends, and teachers. Their concern is to avoid punishment. At about age 10, they enter the *conventional stage.* At this stage, morality means to follow the norms and values they have learned. In the *postconventional stage,* which Kohlberg says most people don't reach, people reflect on abstract principles of right and wrong and judge a behavior according to these principles.

Gilligan and Gender Differences in Morality

Psychologist Carol Gilligan was uncomfortable with Kohlberg's conclusions. They didn't seem to match her own experience, and she noted that he had used only boys in his studies. As more women have become active in social research, they have pointed out that male researchers often assumed that female subjects were not necessary, for what they found with boys would be true of girls.

Gilligan (1982, 1990) decided to find out if there were differences in how men and women looked at morality. After interviewing about 200 men and women, she found fundamental distinctions. Women, she concluded, are more likely to evaluate morality in terms of *personal relationships.* They want to know how an action affects others. They are more concerned with personal loyalties and with the harm that might come to loved ones. Men, in contrast, tend to think more along the lines of *abstract principles* that define what is right or wrong. An act either matches or violates a code of ethics, and personal relationships have little to do with the matter.

Researchers tested Gilligan's conclusions. When they gave standard tests of moral reasoning to both males and females, they found no gender differences (Wark and Krebs 1996). Instead, they found that both men and women use personal relationships and abstract principles when they make moral judgments. Because of these findings, Gilligan no longer supports her original position (Brannon 1999).

Global Considerations: The Self, Reasoning, and Morality

Cooley's conclusions about the looking-glass self and Mead's conclusions about role taking and mind as a social product appear to be universal. There is less agreement, however, that Piaget's four stages are globally true. Some researchers say that the stages are not so rigid as Piaget concluded, that children develop reasoning skills much more gradually than this (Berk 1994; Diver-Stamnes and Thomas 1995).

In addition, some adults apparently get stuck in the concreteness of the third stage and never reach the fourth stage, abstract thinking (Kohlberg and Gilligan 1971). College, for example, is a social experience that nurtures the fourth stage, and most people without this experience apparently have less ability for abstract thought. Social experiences, however, can modify these stages, and the stages may differ from one culture to another.

Certainly the *content* of what we learn varies from one culture to another. This, in turn, influences our thinking. For example, Brazilian street children have little or no schooling. Yet through selling candy they develop sophisticated mathematical and bargaining abilities (Saxe 1995). Because children in other cultures have experiences and abilities unlike those of our children, and because their thinking processes revolve around those activities, we cannot assume that the developmental sequences observed in our children are true of children around the globe (Berk 1994).

Freud and the Development of Personality

Along with the development of the mind and the self comes the development of personality. Let's look at a theory that has influenced the Western world.

In Vienna at the turn of the century, Sigmund Freud (1856–1939), a physician, founded *psychoanalysis,* a technique for treating emotional problems through long-term, intensive exploration of the subconscious mind. We shall look at that part of his thought that applies to the development of personality.

Freud believed that personality consists of three elements. Each child is born with the first, an **id,** Freud's term for inborn drives for self-gratification. The id of the newborn is evident in cries of hunger or pain. The pleasure-seeking id operates throughout life, demanding the immediate fulfillment of basic needs: attention, safety, food, sex, and so on.

But the id's drive for immediate and complete satisfaction runs directly against the needs of other people. As the child comes up against norms and other constraints (usually represented by parents), he or she must adapt to survive. To help adapt to these constraints that block his or her desires, a second component of the personality emerges, which Freud called the **ego.** The ego is the balancing force between the id and the demands of society that suppress it. The ego also serves to balance the id and the **superego,** the third component of the personality, more commonly called the *conscience.*

The superego represents *culture within us,* the norms and values that we have internalized from our social groups. As the *moral* component of the personality, the superego gives us feelings of guilt or shame when we break social rules, or pride and self-satisfaction when we follow them.

According to Freud, when the id gets out of hand, we follow our desires for pleasure and break society's norms. When the superego gets out of hand, we become overly rigid in following those norms, finding ourselves bound in a straitjacket of rules that inhibit our lives. The ego, the balancing force, tries to prevent either the superego or the id from dominating. In the emotionally healthy individual, the ego succeeds in balancing these conflicting demands of the id and the superego. In the maladjusted individual, however, the ego cannot control the inherent conflict between the id and the superego, and the result is internal confusion and problem behaviors.

Sociological Evaluation What sociologists appreciate about Freud is his emphasis on socialization—his belief that the social group into which we are born transmits norms and values that restrain our biological drives. Sociologists, however, object to the view that inborn and unconscious motivations are the primary reasons for human behavior, for this denies *the central principle of sociology:* that factors such as social class (income, education, and occupation) and the roles we take on in groups underlie people's behaviors (Epstein 1988; Bush and Simmons 1990).

Feminist sociologists have been especially critical of Freud. Although what we just summarized applies to both females and males, Freud assumed that what is "male" is "normal." He even analyzed females as inferior, castrated males (Chodorow 1990).

Socialization and Emotions

As we have seen, the mind is a social product, and through socialization we acquire the particulars that go into human reasoning. Emotions, too, are not simply products of biology. They also depend on socialization (Hochschild 1975; Pollak and Thoits 1989; Johnson 1992; Wouters 1992). This may sound strange. Don't all people get angry? Doesn't everyone cry? Don't we all feel guilt, shame, sadness, remorse, happiness, fear? What has socialization to do with emotions?

Anthropologist Paul Ekman (1980) looked into this question. After studying emotions in several countries, he concluded that everyone experiences six basic emotions: anger, disgust, fear, happiness, sadness, and surprise—and we all show the same facial expressions when we have these emotions. A person from Zimbabwe, for example, could tell from just the look on an American's face that she is angry, disgusted, or fearful, and we could tell from the Zimbabwean's face that he is happy, sad, or surprised. Because we all show the same facial expressions when we experience these six emotions, Ekman concluded that they are built into us biologically, a product of our genes."

That there are universal facial expressions of certain basic emotions does not mean that socialization has no effect on how we express emotions. Facial expressions are only

id Freud's term for our inborn basic drives

ego Freud's term for a balancing force between the id and the demands of society

superego Freud's term for the conscience, the internalized norms and values of our social groups

Although males are socialized to express less emotion than are females, such socialization goes against their nature. In certain settings, especially sports, males are allowed to be openly emotional, even demonstrative, with one another. Shown embracing are Mark McGwire of the St. Louis Cardinals and Sammy Sosa of the Chicago Cubs. They both were chasing the Roger Maris' record of 61 home runs.

one way that we show emotions. Other ways vary with gender and culture. For example, U.S. women are allowed more freedom in how they express happiness (and other emotions), while U.S. men are expected to be more reserved. To express sudden happiness, or a delightful surprise, for example, women are allowed to make "squeals of glee" in public places. Men are not. Such an expression would be a fundamental violation of their gender role. Similarly, if close U.S. adult male friends meet after a long separation, they might shake hands vigorously, or pat each other on the back. Two U.S. female friends, in contrast, are more likely to hug.

Culture, social class, and relationships also govern how we express emotions. Culture is very significant. Two close Japanese friends who meet after a long separation don't shake hands or hug. They bow. Two Arab men will kiss. Social class cuts across many other lines, even gender. Upon seeing a friend after a long absence, upper-class women and men are likely to be more reserved in expressing their delight than lower-class women and men are in expressing theirs. Relationships also make a big difference. We express our emotions more openly if we are with close friends, and much more guardedly if we are at a staff meeting with the corporate CEO. A good part of childhood socialization centers on learning the nuances of expressing our emotions in a variety of settings. Each culture, and many groups within a culture, have "norms of emotion" that demand conformity (Clark 1991).

The matter goes deeper than this. Socialization leads not only to different ways of expressing emotions, but even to what we feel. People in one culture may even learn to experience feelings that are unknown in another culture. For example, the Ifaluk, who live on the Western Caroline Islands of Micronesia, use the word *fago* to refer to the feelings they have when they see someone suffer. This comes close to what we call sympathy or compassion. But the Ifaluk also use this term to refer to what they feel when they are around people who are highly admired or respected (Kagan 1984). To us, these are two distinct emotions, and they require distinct terms. For a glimpse of a culture in which emotions, values, and behaviors are shockingly different from those we expect, see the Down-to-Earth Sociology box on the next page.

Although Ekman identified only six basic emotions that are universal in feeling and expression, I suspect that other emotions are common to people around the world—and that everyone shows similar facial expressions when they experience them. I suggest that feelings of helplessness, despair, confusion, and shock are among these universal emotions. We need research to find out if I am right.

The Self and Emotions as Social Control: Society Within Us

Much of our socialization is intended to turn us into conforming members of society. Socialization into the self and emotions is an essential part of this process, for both the self and our emotions mold our behavior. Although we like to think we are "free," consider for a moment just some of the factors that influence how we act: the expectations of friends and parents; neighbors and teachers; classroom norms and college rules; and federal and state laws. For example, if in a moment of intense frustration, or out of a devilish desire to shock people, you wanted to tear off your clothes and run naked down the street, what would stop you?

The answer is your socialization—*society within you.* Your experiences in society have resulted in a self that thinks along certain lines and feels particular emotions. This helps keep you in line. Thoughts such as "Would I be kicked out of school?" and "What would my

Sociology

SIGNS OF THE TIMES: ARE WE BECOMING IK?

Anthropologist Colin Turnbull (1972/1995) studied the Ik, a once proud nomadic people in northern Uganda whose traditional hunting lands were taken from them by the government. Devastated by drought, hunger, and starvation, the Ik turned to a form of extreme individualism in which selfishness, emotional numbness, and lack of concern for others now reign supreme. The pursuit of food has become the only good; their society has been replaced by a passionless, numbed association of individuals.

Imagine, for a moment, that you are born into the Ik tribe. After your first three or four years of life, you are pushed out of the hut. From then on, you are on your own. You can sleep in the village courtyard or take shelter, such as you can, against the stockade. With permission, you can sit in the doorway of your parents' house, but you may not lie down or sleep there.

There is no school. No church. Nothing from this point in your life that even comes close to what we call family. You join a group of children aged 3 to 7. The weakest are soon thinned out, for only the strongest survive. Later, you join a band of 8- to 12-year olds. At 12 or 13, you split off by yourself.

Socialization usually involves learning some aspect of life by what you see going on around you. But here you see coldness at the center of life. The men hunt, but game is scarce. If they get anything, they refuse to bring it back to their families, saying, "Each one of them is out seeing what he can get for himself. Do you think they will bring any back for me?"

You also see cruelty at the center of life. When blind Lo'ono trips and rolls to the bottom of the ravine, the adults laugh as she lies on her back, her arms and legs thrashing feebly. When Lolim begs his son to let him in, pleading that he is going to die in a few hours, Longoli drives him away. Lolim dies alone.

The Ik children learn their lesson well: Selfishness is good, the survival of the individual paramount. But the children add a childish glee to the adults' dispassionate coldness. When blind Lolim took ill, the children teased him, kneeling in front of him and laughing as he fell. His grandson crept up and drummed on the old man's bald head with a pair of sticks.

Then there was little Adupa, who managed, for a while, to maintain a sense of awe at what life had to offer. When Adupa found food, she would hold it in her hand, looking at it with wonder and delight. As she raised her hand to her mouth, the other children would jump on her, laughing as they beat her. ■

For Your Consideration

From the Ik, we learn that the values we take to be uniquely human are not inherent in humanity. Rather, they arise from society, and, as such, can be lost when the sense of mutuality that lies at the basis of society breaks down.

It is easy to criticize a society and not have to walk in their shoes, so let's turn the critical lens on our own society. Just as the Ik are obsessed with food, we have become obsessed with achievement and material goods. Money is becoming more important than values, and we may be rushing headlong toward the day that we, too, lose our sense of mutuality and purpose. Then, like the Ik, we no longer will we be able to perceive truth, beauty, and goodness.

Even people are treated like things—discarded when they are no longer needed. Corporations fire older workers because they can pay younger ones less—or they relocate an entire factory to a land of cheaper labor. As they leave hundreds and even thousands of workers stranded, managers and owners shrug their shoulders and say, "That's business." For the sake of higher salaries, people sever themselves from kin and community. Successful executives discard same-age mates, the co-parent of their own children, in exchange for younger, more photogenic "trophy" mates. Isolation and alienation become common.

Finally, the values we would wish for in friends and family— kindness, generosity, patience, tolerance, cooperation, compassion—are undervalued in society. Any job that requires such talents is low in pay and prestige (Maybury-Lewis 1995).

---

friends (parents) think if they found out?" represent an awareness of the self in relationship to others. So does the desire to avoid feelings of shame and embarrassment. Our *social mirror*, then—the result of being socialized into a self and emotions—sets up effective controls over our behavior. In fact, socialization into self and emotions is so effective that some people experience embarrassment just thinking about running nude in public!

■ **In Sum** Socialization is essential for our development as human beings. From interaction with others, we receive a self, a mind, and the ability to reason. The net result is that our behavior—and even our thinking and emotions—are shaped according to cultural standards. This is what sociologists mean when they refer to *"society within us."*

SOCIALIZATION INTO GENDER

Society also channels our behavior through **gender socialization.** By expecting different attitudes and behaviors from us *because* we are male or female, the human group nudges boys and girls in separate directions in life. This foundation of contrasting attitudes and behaviors is so thorough that, as adults, most of us act, think, and even feel according to the guidelines laid down by our culture as appropriate for our sex.

How do we learn gender messages? Because the significance of gender is emphasized throughout this book, with a special focus in Chapter 11, for now let's briefly consider the influence of just the family and the mass media.

Gender Messages in the Family

Our parents are the first significant others who teach us our part in this symbolic division of the world. Sometimes they do so self-consciously, perhaps by bringing into play pink and blue, colors that have no meaning in themselves but that have social associations with gender. But our parents' own gender orientations are so firmly established that they also teach us **gender roles,** the behaviors and attitudes considered appropriate for our sex, without being aware of what they are doing.

A classic study illustrates how deeply ingrained these orientations are. Psychologists Susan Goldberg and Michael Lewis (1969) asked mothers to bring their 6-month-old infants into their laboratory, supposedly to observe the infants' development. Secretly, however, the researchers also observed the mothers. They found that the mothers kept their daughters closer to them. They also touched and spoke more to their daughters. By the time the children were 13 months old, the girls stayed closer to their mothers during play, and they returned to them sooner and more often than the boys did. When Goldberg and Lewis set up a barrier to separate the children from their mothers, who were holding toys, the girls were more likely to cry and motion for help; the boys, to try to climb over the barrier. Goldberg and Lewis concluded that in our society mothers unconsciously reward daughters for being passive and dependent, but their sons for being active and independent.

These lessons continue throughout childhood. On the basis of their sex, parents and relatives give children different kinds of toys. Boys are more likely to get guns and "action figures" that destroy enemies. Girls are more likely to get dolls and jewelry. Some parents try to choose "gender neutral" toys, but kids know what is popular, and they feel left out if they don't have what the other kids have. The significance of toys in gender socialization can be summarized this way: Almost all parents would be upset if someone gave their boy Barbie dolls.

Parents also let their preschool boys roam farther from home than their preschool sisters, and they subtly encourage them to participate in more rough-and-tumble play. They expect their sons to get dirtier and to be more defiant, their daughters to be daintier and more compliant (Gilman 1911/1971; Henslin 1999). In large part, they get what they expect.

Such experiences in socialization lie at the heart of the sociological explanation of male-female differences. We should note, however, that some sociologists consider biology to be a cause. For example, were the infants in the Goldberg-Lewis study showing built-in biological predispositions, with the mothers merely reinforcing—not causing—those differences? We shall return to this controversial issue in Chapter 11.

Gender Messages in the Mass Media

Sociologists stress how this sorting process that begins in the family is reinforced as the child is exposed to other aspects of society. Especially important today are the **mass media,** forms

---

gender socialization the ways in which society sets children onto different courses in life *because* they are male or female

gender role the behaviors and attitudes considered appropriate because one is a female or a male

mass media forms of communication, such as radio, newspapers, and television, that are directed to mass audiences

of communication that are directed to large audiences. Let's look at how powerful images of both sexes in advertising, television, video games, and from our peers reinforce society's expectations of gender.

Advertising Although advertising uses a mix of gender images, it continues to perpetuate stereotypes by portraying men as dominant and rugged and women as sexy and submissive. The result is a spectrum of stereotypical, culturally molded images. Cowboys who roam the wide open spaces are at one end of this spectrum, while scantily clad females whose assets are intended to sell a variety of products, from automobiles to hamburgers, are at the other end.

Television Television reinforces stereotypes of the sexes. On prime-time television, male characters outnumber female characters two to one. They also are more likely to be portrayed in higher-status positions (Vande Berg and Streckfuss 1992). Viewers get the message, for the more television people watch, the more they tend to have restrictive ideas about women's role in society (Signorielli 1989, 1990).

The exceptions to the stereotypes are notable—and a sign of changing times. One program, perhaps the most stereotype-breaking of all, is *Xena, Warrior Princess,* a popular television series imported from New Zealand. Portrayed as super dominant, Xena overcomes all obstacles and defeats all foes—whether male or female.

Video Games Some youths spend countless hours playing video games in arcades and at home. Even college students, especially males, relieve stress by escaping into video games. Unfortunately, we have no studies of how these games affect their players' ideas of gender. Because these games are on the cutting edge of society, they sometimes also reflect cutting-edge changes in sex roles, as examined in the Mass Media in Social Life box on the next page.

Absorbing Gender Messages: The Peer Group When sociologist Melissa Milkie (1994) studied a group of junior high school boys, she found that much of their talk centered on the latest movies, videos, and TV programs. Of the many images presented in these media, the boys would single out sex and violence. They would joke and laugh about what they had seen, repeat lines, and act out parts for the amusement of one another.

If you know boys in their early teens, you've probably seen behavior like this. You may have been amused, or even shaken your head in disapproval. As a sociologist, however, Milkie peered beneath the surface. She concluded that the boys were using media images to discover who they are as males. In the experience of these boys, and so many like them throughout our society, to be male is to be obsessed with sex and violence. Not to joke and laugh about murder and promiscuous sex would have marked a boy as a "weenie," a label to be avoided at all costs. These boys were in the process of learning what it is to be a male in our society.

■ **In Sum** All of us are born into a society in which "male" and "female" are significant symbols. Sorted into separate groups from childhood, we come to have shared ideas of what to expect of ourselves and of one another based on our sex. These images become integrated into our view of the world, forming a picture that forces an interpretation of the world in terms of gender. We are not simply passive consumers of these images. Rather, we select those images that are significant to our situation in life and use them to help construct our worlds.

Gender images, then, no matter their source, shape our ideas about the world. Lying mostly beneath our level of awareness, the messages they send affect the ways in which we view females and males, and how we ourselves fit into that picture. Images can break down or perpetuate myths and stereotypes. They can promote equality or inequality. Because gender serves as a primary basis for **social inequality**, giving privileges and obligations to one

social inequality a social condition in which privileges and obligations are given to some but denied to others

Mass Media in *Social Life*

FROM XENA, WARRIOR PRINCESS, TO LARA CROFT, TOMB RAIDER: CHANGING IMAGES OF WOMEN IN THE MASS MEDIA

As women change their roles in society, the mass media reflect those changes. Although media images of women as passive, as subordinate, or as mere background objects remain and still predominate, a new image has broken through. Although it exaggerates changes in society, this new image nonetheless reflects women's changed role to an active life outside the home. It also shows a change from acquiescence to dominance in social relations. As mentioned in the text, Xena, the Warrior Princess, is an outstanding example of this change.

Though it is unusual to call video games a form of the mass media, I think it is appropriate to do so. Like books and magazines, video games are made available to a mass audience. And with digital advances, they have crossed the line from what we traditionally think of as games to something that more closely resembles interactive movies.

Sociologically, what is significant is that the *content* of video games socializes their users. Gamers are exposed not only to action, but also to ideas as they play. Especially significant are gender images that communicate powerful messages, just as they do in other forms of the mass media.

Lara Croft, an adventure-seeking archeologist and star of *Tomb Raider* and its three sequels, *Tomb Raider 2, 3,* and *4,* is the essence of the new gender image. Lara is smart, strong, and able to utterly vanquish foes. With both guns blazing, she is the cowboy of the twenty-first century, the term *cowboy* being purposefully chosen, as Lara breaks gender roles and assumes what previously was the domain of men. She

is the first female protagonist in a field of muscle-rippling, machine-gun-toting macho caricatures (Taylor 1999).

Yet, the old remains powerfully encapsulated in the new. As the photo makes evident, Lara is a fantasy girl for young men of the digital generation. No matter her foe, no matter her predicament, Lara always wears form-fitting outfits that flatter her voluptuous physique—which is the creation of Adrian Smith, the man who created this digital character. So successful has his effort been that boys and young men have bombarded corporate headquarters with questions about Lara's personal life. Lara has caught young men's fancy to such an extent that 17 million copies of *Tomb Raider* have been sold. There also is a Lara Croft comic, a Lara Croft action doll, and even a Lara Croft candy bar (Taylor 1999). More than 100 Web sites are devoted to her (Croal and Hughes 1997). ■

For Your Consideration

One reviewer of this text said, "It seems that for women to be defined as equal, we have to become symbolic males—warriors with breasts." Do you think that gender change is mostly one-way—females adopting traditional male characteristics? Can you think of the equivalent happening to men? If it is primarily one-way, why is it men who get to keep their gender roles? You may wish to consider two essential elements: Who is moving into the traditional territory of the other? Do people prefer to imitate power or powerlessness?

The mass media not only reflect gender stereotypes but they also play a role in changing them. Sometimes they do both simultaneously. The images of Lara and of Xena, Warrior Princess, reflect women's changing role in society and, by exaggerating the change, also mold new stereotypes.

group of people while denying them to another, the role of the media and peers is worth exploring. For example, we have no studies of how girls use media images to construct their ideas of femininity, and precious few of how boys do so. Perhaps you will become the sociologist to do such research.

AGENTS OF SOCIALIZATION

People and groups that influence our self-concept, emotions, attitudes, and behavior are called **agents of socialization.** Of the many agents of socialization that prepare us to take our place in society, we shall examine the family, religion, day care, school, peers, sports, mass media, and workplace.

The Family

Around the world, the first group to have a major impact on humans is the family. Unlike some animals, we cannot survive by ourselves, and as babies we are utterly dependent on our family. Our experiences in the family are so intense that they have a lifelong impact on us. They lay down our basic sense of self, establishing our initial motivations, values, and beliefs (Gecas 1990). The family gives us ideas about who we are and what we deserve out of life. It is in the family that we begin to think of ourselves as strong or weak, smart or dumb, good-looking or ugly—or somewhere in between. And as already noted, here we begin the lifelong process of defining ourselves as female or male.

To study this process, sociologists have observed parents and young children in public settings, where their act of observing does not interfere with the natural interaction. Researchers using this unobtrusive technique have noted what they call the "stroller effect" (Mitchell et al. 1992). When parents have their child in a stroller, the father is more likely to be the one who pushes the stroller. If they take the child out of the stroller, the mother is more likely to push the empty stroller, and the father is more likely to carry the child. From these observations, the researchers conclude that parents send their children subtle gender messages, teaching them about expected differences between men and women. Indeed, probably most of the ways that parents teach children gender roles involve not specific instruction, but, rather, nonverbal cues.

The Family and Social Class To see how far-reaching, yet subtle, social class is, consider how working-class and middle-class parents rear their children. Sociologist Melvin Kohn (1959, 1963, 1976, 1977, 1983; Kohn et al. 1986) found that the main concern of working-class parents is their children's outward conformity. They want their children to be obedient, neat, and clean, to follow the rules, and to stay out of trouble. They are likely to use physical punishment to make their children obey. In contrast, middle-class parents focus on developing their children's curiosity, self-expression, and self-control. They stress the motivations for their children's behavior and are more likely to reason with their children than to use physical punishment.

These findings were a sociological puzzle. Just *why* should working-class and middle-class parents rear their children so differently? Kohn knew that life experiences of some

THE FAR SIDE By GARY LARSON

© 1994 FarWorks, Inc. All Rights Reserved 4-25

"So let's go over it again: You're about a mile up, you see something dying below you, you circle until it's dead, and down you go. Lenny, you stick close to your brothers and do what they do."

The Far Side © 1994 Farworks, Inc. Used by permission. All rights reserved.

sort held the key, and he found that key in the world of work. Blue-collar workers are usually supervised very closely. Their bosses expect them to do exactly as they are told. Because blue-collar parents expect their children's lives to be similar to their own, they stress obedience and conformity. Middle-class parents, in contrast, especially those in management and the professions, experience a much freer workplace. They have greater independence, are encouraged to be imaginative, and advance by taking the initiative. Expecting their children to work at similar jobs, they, in turn, socialize them into the qualities they have found valuable.

What still puzzled Kohn was that these class differences were only tendencies. Not all working-class or middle-class parents treat their children alike. Instead, some working-class parents act more like middle-class parents, and vice versa. As Kohn probed this puzzle, the pieces fell into place. He found that the parents' type of job was more important than their social class. Many middle-class office workers, for example, are closely supervised. Kohn found that such workers follow the working-class pattern of child rearing, for they stress outward conformity. In contrast, some blue-collar workers, such as those who do home repairs, have a good deal of freedom. These workers follow the middle-class model in rearing their children (Pearlin and Kohn 1966; Kohn and Schooler 1969).

The Neighborhood

As all parents know, some neighborhoods are better for their children than others. Parents try to move to those neighborhoods—if they can afford them. Their commonsense evaluations are borne out by sociological research. Children from poor neighborhoods are more likely to get in trouble with the law, to become pregnant, to drop out of school, and to end up facing a disadvantaged life (Wilson 1987; Brooks-Gunn et al. 1997).

Sociologists have also documented that the residents of more affluent, stable neighborhoods watch out for the children more than do the residents of poor neighborhoods (Sampson et al. 1999). The adults are more likely to know the local children and their parents, and to help keep the children safe and out of trouble. It is one of the ironies of life that in those neighborhoods that are the riskiest for children (where there is more homicide and child abuse) adults watch out the least for the children, and in neighborhoods where the children least need protecting the adults are more careful.

Religion

By influencing morality, religion becomes a key component in people's ideas of right and wrong. Religion is so important to Americans that 70 percent belong to a local congregation, and during a typical week two of every five Americans attend a religious service (*Statistical Abstract* 1999:Table 89). Religion is significant even for persons reared in nonreligious homes, for religious ideas pervade U.S. society. They provide basic ideas of morality that become significant for us all.

The influence of religion extends to many areas of our lives. For example, participation in religious services teaches us not only beliefs about the hereafter but also ideas about what kinds of dress, speech, and manners are appropriate for formal occasions. Religion is so significant that we shall treat this social institution in a separate chapter.

Day Care

With more mothers working for wages today than ever before, day care has become a significant agent of socialization. Concerns about its effects have propelled day care into the center of controversy. Researchers find that the effects of day care, at least in the United States, largely depend on the child's background (Scarr and Eisenberg 1993). Children from low-income homes, as well as those from dysfunctional families (such as alcoholic, inept, or abusive parents), appear to benefit from day care. For example, the language skills of children from low-income homes increase. In contrast, day care may slow these skills in middle-class children, who would have received more intellectual stimulation at home.

As you would expect, much depends on the quality of day care. Researchers who studied 120 day care centers found that children in better quality day care interact better with other children and have fewer behavioral problems (McCartney et al. 1997). Wages seem to be the primary factor in determining the quality of a day care. Centers that pay higher wages to their teachers attract a better trained staff and have less staff turnover. This, in turn, provides a more secure environment for the children. They can depend on the teachers with whom they bond to be there day after day.

It is rare for social science studies to make national news, but occasionally they do. One such study followed 1,300 children from infancy into preschool. When the children were ages 6, 15, 24, and 36 months, researchers observed them at home and at day care. They videotaped and made detailed notes on their interaction with their mothers (National Institute of Child Health and Human Development 1999). What caught the media's attention was the researchers' main finding: The more hours per week that children were in day care, the weaker the bonds between mothers and children, and the more negative their interaction. Mothers whose children spent less time in day care were more responsive to their children, more positive in their interactions, and their children were more affectionate to them. The researchers suggest that mothers who spend more time with their infants become more familiar and responsive to their "signaling systems."

We need more studies. The study I just referred to is excellent. The findings are without dispute. The explanation of those findings, however, is another matter. The cause could be day care, as the researchers think. But perhaps mothers who put their children in day care for more hours are mothers who are already less sensitive to their children. From this study, we can't determine which is the cause of the weaker bonding. We also need studies that match children by age and family background and that compare children in day care with those who stay home or who are cared for by relatives and friends. In order to compare results, we also need to measure something we know little about—the "quality" of home care.

> **manifest functions** the intended consequences of people's actions designed to help some part of a social system
>
> **latent functions** the unintended consequences of people's actions that help to keep a social system in equilibrium

The School

Part of the **manifest function**, or intended purpose, of formal education, is to transmit certain knowledge and skills, such as reading, writing, and arithmetic. The transmission of such skills certainly contributes to socialization. However, our schools' **latent functions**, the unintended consequences that help the social system, are also significant. Let's look at this less visible aspect of education.

At home, children learn attitudes and values that match their family's situation in life. At school, they learn a broader perspective that helps prepare them to take a role in the world beyond the family. At home, for example, a child may have been the almost exclusive focus of doting parents, but in school the child learns *universality*—that the same rules apply to everyone, regardless of who their parents are or how special they may be at home. The Perspectives box on the next page explores how these new values and ways of looking at the world sometimes even replace those they learned at home.

Schools are one of the primary agents of socialization. One of their chief functions is to sort young people into the adult roles thought appropriate for them, and to teach them the attitudes and skills that match those roles. What sorts of attitudes and adult roles do you think these junior high school girls are being socialized into? Is this a manifest or a latent function? Is it a dysfunction?

PERSPECTIVES | Cultural Diversity in the United States

CAUGHT BETWEEN TWO WORLDS

Just as an individual is socialized into becoming a member of a culture, so a person can lose a culture through socialization. If you are exposed to a new culture as an adult, as older immigrants are, you can selectively adopt aspects of the new culture without entirely relinquishing your native culture. If the immersion occurs as a child, however, the second culture will vie for dominance with your native heritage. This, in turn, can lead to inner turmoil. Cutting ties with your first culture—one way of handling the conflict—can create a sense of loss that is recognized only later in life.

Richard Rodriguez, a literature professor and essayist, was born in the 1950s to working-class Mexican immigrants. Wanting their son to be successful in their adopted land, his parents named him Richard instead of Ricardo. While his Spanish-English hybrid name indicated the parents' aspirations for their son, it was also a portent of the conflict Richard would experience.

Like other children of Mexican immigrants, Richard's first language was Spanish—a rich mother tongue that provided his orientation to the world. Until the age of 5, when he began school, he knew but fifty words in English. He described what happened when he began school:

The change came gradually but early. When I was beginning grade school, I noted to myself the fact that the classroom environment was so different in its styles and assumptions from my own family environment that survival would essentially entail a choice between both worlds. When I became a student, I was literally "remade"; neither I nor my teachers considered anything I had known before as relevant. I had to forget most of what my culture had provided, because to remember it was a disadvantage. The past and its cultural values became detachable, like a piece of clothing grown heavy on a warm day and finally put away.

As happened to millions of immigrants before him, whose parents spoke German, Polish, Italian, and so on, learning English eroded family and class ties and ate away at his ethnic roots. For him, language and education were not simply devices that eased the transition to the dominant culture. Instead, they transformed Richard into a *pocho,* "a Mexican with gringo aspirations." They slashed at the roots that had given him life.

To face such inner turmoil is to confront a fork in the road. Some turn one way and withdraw from the new culture—a clue that helps explain the high dropout rate of Latinos from U.S. schools. Others go in the opposite direction and, cutting ties with their family and cultural roots, wholeheartedly adopt the new culture.

Rodriguez took the second road. He excelled in his new language—so well, in fact, that he graduated from Stanford University and then became a graduate student in English at the University of California at Berkeley. He was even awarded a prestigious Fulbright fellowship to study English Renaissance literature at the British Museum.

But the past wouldn't let Rodriguez alone. Prospective employers were impressed with his knowledge of Renaissance literature. Yet at job interviews, they would ask if he would teach the Mexican novel in translation and be an adviser to Latino students. Rodriguez was haunted by the image of his grandmother, the warmth of the culture he had left behind, the language to which he was now a stranger.

Richard Rodriguez represents millions of immigrants—not just those of Latino origin but millions from other cultures, too—who want to be a part of the United States without betraying their past. They fear that to integrate into U.S. culture is to lose their roots. They are caught between two cultures, each beckoning, each offering rich rewards. ■

Sources: Based on Richard Rodriguez 1975, 1982, 1990, 1991, 1995.

Sociologists have also identified a *hidden curriculum* in our schools. This term refers to values that, though not explicitly taught, are part of a school's "message." For example, the stories and examples that are used to teach math and English grammar may bring with them lessons in patriotism, democracy, justice, and honesty. Schools also teach "correct" attitudes toward the economic system (Marger 1987). To learn that the economic system is basically just, for example, is to simultaneously learn that social problems such as poverty and homelessness have nothing to do with economic power, oppression, and exploitation.

Conflict theorists point out that schools teach students to take their place in the work force. Children born to wealthy parents go to private schools, where they learn skills and values appropriate to their higher position. Children from poorer homes go to public schools, where they learn that not many of "their kind" will become professionals or leaders. Even in public schools, social class is significant in tracking. Children from blue-collar families are much less likely to be placed in the college prep class. In short, schools around the world support their nation's social class, economic, and political systems. We will return to this topic in the chapter on education (Chapter 17).

Peer Groups

As a child's experiences with agents of socialization broaden, the influence of the family lessens. Entry into school marks only one of many steps in this transfer of allegiance. One of the most significant aspects of education is that it exposes children to **peer groups**, individuals of roughly the same age who are linked by common interests. Examples of peer groups are friends, clubs, gangs, and "the kids in the neighborhood."

Sociologists Patricia and Peter Adler (1998), a husband and wife team, document how the peer group provides an enclave in which boys and girls resist the efforts of parents and schools to socialize them their way. Observing children at two elementary schools in Colorado, they saw children separate themselves by sex and develop their own worlds with unique norms (Adler et al. 1992). The norms that made boys popular were athletic ability, coolness, and toughness. For girls, they were family background, physical appearance (clothing and ability to use makeup), and being able to attract popular boys. In this children's subculture, academic achievement pulled in opposite directions: For a boy, doing well academically decreased popularity, while for a girl getting good grades increased her standing among her peers.

You know from personal experience how compelling peer groups are. It is almost impossible to go against a peer group whose cardinal rule seems to be "conformity or rejection." Anyone who doesn't do what the others want becomes an "outsider," a "nonmember," an "outcast." For preteens and teens just learning their way around in the world, it is not surprising that the peer group is king.

As a result, the standards of our peer groups tend to dominate our lives. If your peers, for example, listen to rap, heavy metal, rock and roll, country, folk, gospel, classical, hip hop, gitano, or any other kind of music, it is almost inevitable that you also prefer that kind of music. It is the same for clothing styles and dating standards. Peer influences also extend to behaviors that violate social norms. If your peers are college-bound and upwardly striving, that is most likely what you will be, but if they use drugs, cheat, and steal, you are likely to do so, too.

peer group a group of individuals roughly the same age linked by common interests

Many adults who wish to reduce gender distinctions prefer that grade schoolers of both sexes participate in the same playground activities. In spite of the sometimes not-so-subtle suggestions of teachers, however, grade school children insist on separating by sex, where they pursue different interests and activities and develop contrasting norms.

Sports

Sports are another powerful socializing agent. Everyone recognizes that sports teach not only physical skills but also values. In fact, "teaching youngsters to be team players" is often given as the justification for financing organized sports. How effective sports are in socializing boys is the topic of the Down-to-Earth Sociology box on the next page.

The Workplace

Another agent of socialization that comes into play somewhat later in life is the workplace. Those initial jobs that we take—part-time work after school and in college—are much more than a way to earn a few dollars. From the people we rub shoulders with at work, we learn not only a set of skills but also a perspective on the world.

Most of us eventually become committed to some particular line of work, often after trying out various jobs. This may also involve **anticipatory socialization,** learning to play a role before entering it, a sort of mental rehearsal for some future activity. We may read novels about people who work in a career, talk to them, or take a summer internship. This allows us to gradually identify with the role, to become aware of some of its expectations and rewards. Sometimes this helps people avoid committing themselves to an unrewarding career, as with some of my students, who tried student teaching, found they couldn't stand it, and moved on to another major more to their liking.

An interesting aspect of work as a socializing agent is that the more you participate in a line of work, the more the work becomes a part of your self-concept. Eventually you come to think of yourself so much in terms of the job that if someone asks you to describe yourself, you are likely to include the job in your self-description. You might say, "I am a teacher, accountant, nurse" or whatever.

RESOCIALIZATION

What does a woman who has just become a nun have in common with a man who has just divorced? The answer is that they both are undergoing **resocialization;** that is, they are learning new norms, values, attitudes, and behaviors to match their new situation. In its most common form, resocialization occurs each time we learn something contrary to our previous experiences. A new boss who insists on a different way of doing things is resocializing you. Most resocialization is mild, only a slight modification of things already learned.

Resocialization can be intense, however. People who join Alcoholics Anonymous (AA), for example, are surrounded by reformed drinkers who affirm the destructive effects of excessive drinking. Some students experience an intense period of resocialization when they leave high school and start college—especially during those initially scary days before they begin to feel comfortable and fit in. Beginning psychotherapy or joining a cult is even more profound, for these events expose people to ideas that conflict with their previous ways of looking at the world. If these ideas "take," not only does the individual's behavior change, but he or she also learns a fundamentally different way of looking at life.

Total Institutions

Relatively few of us experience the powerful agent of socialization Erving Goffman (1961) called the **total institution.** He coined this term to refer to a place in which people are cut off from the rest of society and where they come under almost total control of the officials who run the place. Boot camp, prisons, concentration camps, convents, some religious cults, and some boarding schools, such as West Point, are total institutions.

A person entering a total institution is greeted with a **degradation ceremony** (Garfinkel 1956), an attempt to remake the self by stripping away the individual's current identity and stamping a new one in its place. This unwelcome greeting may involve fingerprinting,

anticipatory socialization because one anticipates a future role, one learns parts of it now

resocialization the process of learning new norms, values, attitudes, and behaviors

total institution a place in which people are cut off from the rest of society and are almost totally controlled by the officials who run the place

degradation ceremony a term coined by Harold Garfinkel to describe an attempt to remake the self by stripping away an individual's self-identity and stamping a new identity in its place

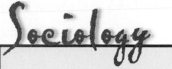

Down-to-Earth

OF BOYS AND SPORTS

Some sports exalt the "male values" of competition and rough physical contact, akin to violence. Boys who play these sports are thought of as learning to be "real men." Even if they don't play a sport, boys and men who intensely follow sports are openly affirming male cultural values and displaying their own masculinity.

Sociologist Michael Messner (1990) interviewed men who had played professional sports and other men for whom sports provided a central identity during and after high school. Usually the father, an older brother, or an uncle had encouraged the boy to develop his athletic abilities, or had served as a role model for the boy's later success. A former professional football player, whose two older brothers had gained wide reputations for sports, said:

> My brothers were role models. I wanted to prove—especially to my brothers—that I had heart, you know, that I was a man. . . . And . . . as I got older, I got better and I began to look around me and see, well hey! I'm competitive with these guys, even though I'm younger, you know?

Success at sports, then, brings recognition from others—and gratifying awareness to the self that one has achieved manly characteristics. This same football player also said,

> And then of course all the compliments come—and I began to notice a change, even in my parents—especially in

my father—he was proud of that, and that was very important to me. He was extremely important . . . he showed me more affection, now that I think of it.

In other words, success at sports brought recognition, not only from a community of peers, but as Messner found, sometimes from an emotionally distant father, who warmed up at his son's success.

The boost in the boy's self-esteem, however, can come at a high cost to others. Messner recounts a haunting scene during his visit to a summer basketball camp headed by a professional basketball coach:

> The youngest boys, about eight years old (who could barely reach the basket with their shots) played a brief scrimmage. Afterwards, the coaches lined them up in a row in front of the older boys who were sitting in the grandstands. One by one, the coach would stand behind each boy, put his hand on the boy's head (much in the manner of a priestly benediction), and the older boys in the stands would applaud and cheer, louder or softer, depending on how well or poorly the young boy was judged to have performed. The two or three boys who were clearly the exceptional players looked confident that they would receive the praise they were due. Most of the

boys, though, had expressions ranging from puzzlement to thinly disguised terror on their faces as they awaited the judgments of the older boys.

Messner also noted that the meaning of success in sports differs by social class. As is well known, many poor people see sports as a way out of poverty. For middle-class boys, in contrast, sports are only one of many options that lead to success in life. Consequently, middle-class boys are more easily able to discard sports and to invest energy and self-identity in a future career. ■

For Your Consideration

Messner concludes that the implications of sports go far beyond the game itself—even into intimate relationships. It works like this. In the intensely competitive world of sports, being accepted by others depends on being a "winner." Following the notion of Cooley's *looking-glass self,* with their acceptance depending on success the boys begin to see themselves in those same terms—if they win, they are better people than if they lose. Accomplishments, then, become the key to relationships. In turn, they tend to develop *instrumental* (useful, goal-oriented, not emotional) relationships. This brings built-in problems, for they try to relate instrumentally to females—who have been socialized to construct identities on meaningful relationships, not competitive success.

photographing, shaving the head, and banning the individual's **personal identity kit** (items such as jewelry, hairstyles, clothing, and other body decorations used to express individuality). Newcomers may be ordered to strip, undergo an examination (often in a humiliating, semi-public setting), and then put on a uniform that designates their new status. (For

personal identity kit items people use to decorate their bodies

prisoners, the public reading of the verdict and being led away in handcuffs by armed police also form part of the degradation ceremony.)

Total institutions are extremely effective in stripping away people's personal freedom. They isolate people from the public (the walls, bars, or other barriers not only keep the inmates in but also keep outsiders from interfering). They suppress preexisting statuses (inmates learn that their previous roles such as spouse, parent, worker, or student mean nothing, and that the only thing that counts is their current role). Total institutions suppress the norms of "the outside world," replacing them with their own rules, values, and interpretation of life. They also closely supervise the day-to-day lives of the residents; eating, sleeping, showering, recreation—all are standardized. They also control information, which helps the institution shape the inmates' ideas and "picture" of the world. Finally, they control the rewards and punishments. (Under conditions of deprivation, simple rewards for compliance such as sleep, a television program, a letter from home, extra food, or even a cigarette, are powerful incentives in controlling behavior.) The institution also holds the power to punish rule breaking—often severely, such as by solitary confinement.

No one leaves a total institution unscathed, for the experience leaves an indelible mark on the individual's self and colors the way he or she sees the world. Boot camp, as described in the Down-to-Earth Sociology box on the next page, is brutal but swift. Prison, in contrast, is brutal and prolonged. Neither recruit nor prisoner, however, has difficulty in pinpointing how the institution affected the self.

life course the stages of our life as we go from birth to death

$\int$OCIALIZATION THROUGH THE LIFE COURSE

Some compare our lives to an empty canvas on which a series of portraits is painted, others to the seasons of the year. Each analogy suggests a process of personal change as we touch, and are touched by, events in which we are immersed. That series of major events, the stages of our lives from birth to death, is called the **life course** (Elder 1975).

Analysts have tried to depict the typical stages through which we go, but they have not been able to agree on a standard division of the life course (Levinson 1978; Schlossberg 1990; Carr et al. 1995). In the following sketch, a composite of the stages they have proposed, I shall stress the *historical* setting of people's lives in order to emphasize the sociological significance of the life course.

Childhood (from birth to about age 12)

It may strike you as strange to say this, but what a child "is" differs from one culture to another. To understand this point, consider how different your childhood would have been if you had grown up during the Middle Ages.

When historian Philippe Ariès (1965) examined European paintings from this period, he noticed that children were always dressed up in adult clothing. If children were not stiffly posed for a family portrait, they were depicted as engaging in adult activities.

Ariès concluded that at that time and in that place childhood was not regarded as a special time of life. Rather, children were seen as miniature adults. Ariès pointed out that boys were apprenticed

How adults view children varies around the world. Americans (like others) assume that their views of children are natural, and that any reasonable person would see children as they do. In nonindustrialized societies, children are less dependent, and they assume adult roles at an earlier age. Children also contribute to the family's economic survival. Shown here is a farming scene in Indonesia.

Sociology

BOOT CAMP AS A TOTAL INSTITUTION

The bus arrives at Parris Island, South Carolina, at 3 A.M. The early hour is no accident. The recruits are groggy, confused. Up to a few hours ago, the boys were ordinary civilians. Now, as a sergeant sneeringly calls them "maggots," their heads are buzzed (25 seconds per recruit), and they are quickly and deeply thrust into the harsh world of Marine boot camp.

The system works.

After eleven weeks of this treatment, the Beavises and Butt-heads emerge self-disciplined, and physically fit. They are even courteous to their elders. Each time they see a superior, they automatically respond with "Good day, sir." Even skinheads and black separatists have been known to lay aside antagonistic identities and to live and work together as a team.

Buzzing the boys' hair is just the first step in stripping away their identity so the Marines can stamp a new one in its place. The uniform serves the same purpose. There is a ban on using the first person, and even simple requests must be made in precise Marine style or they will not be acknowledged. ("Sir, Recruit Jones requests permission to make a head call, sir.")

Every intense moment of those eleven weeks reminds them that they are joining a subculture of self-discipline. Here pleasure is suspect and sacrifice is good. As they learn the Marine way of talking, walking, and thinking, they are denied the diversions they once took for granted: television, cigarettes, cars, candy, soft drinks, video games, music, alcohol, drugs, and sex.

Lessons are bestowed with fierce intensity. When Sgt. Carey checks brass belt buckles, Recruit

Resocialization is often a gentle process. Usually we are gradually exposed to different ways of thinking and doing. Sometimes, however, resocialization can be swift and brutal, as it is during boot camp in the Marines. This private at Parris Island is learning a world vastly unlike the civilian world he left behind.

Robert Shelton nervously blurts, "I don't have one." Sgt. Carey's face grows red as his neck cords bulge. "I?" he says, his face just inches from the recruit. With spittle flying from his mouth, he screams, " 'I' is gone!"

"Nobody's an individual, understand?" is the lesson that is driven home again and again. "You are a team, a Marine. Not a civilian. Not black or white, but a Marine. You will live like a Marine, fight like a Marine, and, if necessary, die like a Marine."

Each day begins before dawn with close order formations. The rest of the day is filled with training in hand-to-hand combat, marching, running, calisthenics, Marine history, and—always—following orders.

"An M-16 can blow someone's head off at 500 meters," Sgt. Norman says. "That's beautiful, isn't it?"

"Yes, sir!" shout the platoon's fifty-nine voices.

"Pick your nose!" Simultaneously 59 index fingers shoot into nostrils.

The pressure to conform is intense. Those sent packing for insubordination or suicidal tendencies are mocked in cadence during drills. ("Hope you like the sights you see / Parris Island casualty.") Exhausted, as lights go out at 9 P.M. the recruits perform the day's last task: The entire platoon, in unison, shouts the virtues of the Marines.

Recruits are constantly scrutinized. Subperformance is not accepted, whether it be a dirty rifle or a loose thread on a uniform. The subperformer is shouted at, derided, humiliated.

The group suffers for the individual. If a recruit is slow, the entire platoon is punished with additional exercise.

One of the new Marines (until graduation, they are recruits, not Marines) says, "I feel like I've joined a new society or religion." He has. ■

For Your Consideration

Of what significance is the recruits' degradation ceremony? Why are recruits not allowed video games, cigarettes, or calls home? Why are the Marines so unfair as to punish an entire platoon for the failure of an individual? Use concepts in this chapter to explain why the system works.

Source: Based on Garfinkel 1956; Goffman 1961; "Anybody's Son Will Do," 1983; Ricks 1995.

at very early ages. At the age of 7, for example, a boy might leave home for good to learn to be a jeweler or a stonecutter. A girl, in contrast, stayed home until she married, but by the age of 7 she had to assume her share of daily household tasks.

Childhood also used to be harsh. Another historian, Lloyd DeMause (1975), documented the nightmare of childhood in ages past. To beat children used to be *the norm*. Parents who did not beat their children were considered neglectful of their social duty to keep them off the road to hell. Even teachers were expected to beat their students, and one nineteenth-century German schoolteacher methodically recorded every beating he administered. His record shows 124,000 lashes with a whip, 911,527 hits with a stick, 136,715 slaps with his hand, and 1,115,800 cuffs across the ears. Beating children was so general that even future kings didn't escape brutal punishment. Louis XIII, for example, "was whipped every morning, starting at the age of two, simply for being 'obstinate.' " He was even whipped on the day of his coronation at the age of 9 (McCoy 1985:392).

To keep children in line, parents and teachers also felt it their moral duty to use psychological terror. They would lock children in dark closets for an entire day and frighten them with tales of death and hellfire. It was also common to terrify children into submission by forcing them to witness gruesome events.

> A common moral lesson involved taking children to visit the gibbet [an upraised post on which executed bodies were left hanging from chains], where they were forced to inspect rotting corpses hanging there as an example of what happens to bad children when they grow up. Whole classes were taken out of school to watch hangings, and some parents would whip their children afterwards to make them remember what they had seen. (DeMause 1975)

To see children as adults seems strange to us. In some of today's Least Industrialized Nations, however, this view persists. Vivid in my memory from a visit to Africa is a Moroccan blacksmith. Standing next to an open furnace, nude from the waist up and sweating profusely in the insufferable heat, he beat his hammer rhythmically on some glowing, red-hot metal. The blacksmith was about 12 years old.

Industrialization fundamentally changed the way we see children. When children have the leisure to go to school, they come to be thought of as tender and innocent, as needing more adult care, comfort, and protection. Over time, such attitudes of dependency grow, and today we view children as needing gentle guidance if they are to develop emotionally, intellectually, morally, socially, even physically. We take our view for granted—after all, it is only "common sense." Yet, as you can see, our view is not "natural," but historically rooted.

In sum, childhood is much more than biology. The point in history in which we live, as well as our social location, creates a framework that is laid on top of our biological foundation. Although a child's *biological* characteristics (such as small and dependent) are universal, the child's *social* experiences (what others expect of the child) are not.

Adolescence (about ages 13–17)

Adolescence is not a "natural" age division. It is a social invention. In earlier centuries, people simply moved from childhood into young adulthood, with no stopover in between. The Industrial Revolution brought such an abundance of material surpluses, however, that for the first time in history millions of teenagers were able to remain outside the labor force. At the same time, education became more important for success. The convergence of these two forces in industrialized societies created a gap between childhood and adulthood. In the early part of this century, the term *adolescence* was coined to indicate this new stage in life (Hall 1904), one that has become renowned for inner turmoil.

To ground the self-identity and mark the passage of children into adulthood, tribal societies hold initiation rites (Gilmore 1990). In the industrialized world, however, adolescents must "find" themselves on their own. As they attempt to carve out an identity that is distinct from both the "younger" world being left behind and the "older" world still out of range, adolescents develop their own subcultures, with distinctive clothing, hairstyles,

In many societies, manhood is not bestowed upon males simply because they reach a certain age. Manhood, rather, is a standing in the community that must be achieved. Shown here is an initiation ceremony in Indonesia, where boys, to lay claim to the status of manhood, must jump over this barrier.

language, gestures, and music. Although these outward patterns are readily visible, we usually fail to realize that adolescence is a social creation: It is contemporary society, not biological age, that makes these years a period of turmoil.

Young Adulthood (about ages 18–29)

If society invented adolescence as a special period in life, can it also invent other periods? Historian Kenneth Keniston (1971) suggests that this is happening now. He noted that industrialized societies are adding a period of prolonged youth to the life course, in which postadolescents postpone adult responsibilities and are "neither psychological adolescents nor sociological adults." For millions, the end of high school marks a period of extended education, including vocational school, college, and even graduate school. This period is characterized by continued freedom from adult responsibilities such as a full-time job, marriage, and home ownership.

Somewhere during this period of extended youth, young adults gradually ease into adult responsibilities. They finish school, take a full-time job, engage in courtship rituals, get married—and go into debt. The self is considerably more stable during the latter part of this period than it was during adolescence.

The Middle Years (about ages 30–65)

The Early Middle Years (ages 30–49) During the early middle years, most people are much surer of themselves and of their goals in life. As with any point in the life course, however, the self can receive severe jolts—in this case from such circumstances as divorce or being fired (Dannefer 1984). It may take years for the self to stabilize after such ruptures.

Because of recent social change, the early middle years pose a special challenge for U.S. women, who increasingly have been given the message, especially by the media, that they can "have it all." They can be superworkers, superwives, and supermoms—all at the same time. The reality, however, often consists of conflicting pressures, of too little time and too many demands. Something has to give. Attempts to resolve this dilemma are often compounded by another hard reality—that during gender socialization their husbands learned that child care and housework are not "masculine." In short, adjustments continue in this and all phases of life.

The Later Middle Years (ages 50–65) During the later middle years, health and mortality begin to loom large as people feel their bodies change, especially if they watch their parents become frail, fall ill, and die. The consequence is a fundamental reorientation in thinking—from *time since birth* to *time left to live* (Neugarten 1976). With this changed orientation, people attempt to evaluate the past and come to terms with what lies ahead. They compare what they have accomplished with how far they had hoped to go. Many people also find themselves caring for not only their own children but also their aging parents. Because of this often crushing set of twin burdens, people in the later middle years sometimes are called the "sandwich generation."

Life during this stage, however, isn't always stressful. Many people find late middle age to be the most comfortable period of their entire lives. They enjoy job security and a higher standard of living than ever before; they have a bigger house (one that may even be paid for), newer cars, and more exotic vacations. The children are grown, the self is firmly planted, and fewer upheavals are likely to occur.

As they anticipate the next stage of life, however, most people do not like what they see.

The Older Years (about age 66 on)

The Early Older Years In industrialized societies, the older years begin around the mid-60s. This, too, is recent, for in preindustrial societies, when most people died early, old age was thought to begin around age 40. The improved nutrition, public health, and medical care that industrialization brought, however, delayed the onset of old age. For those in good health, being over 65 is often experienced not as old age, but as an extension of the middle years. People who continue to work or to be active in rewarding social activities are especially unlikely to see themselves as old (Neugarten 1977). Although frequency of sex declines, most men and women in their 60s and 70s are sexually active (Denney and Quadagno 1992).

Because we have a self and can reason abstractly, we can contemplate death. Initially death is something vaguely "out there," but as people see their friends die and their own bodies no longer functioning as before, death becomes less abstract. Increasingly, people feel that "time is closing in" on them.

The Later Older Years As with the preceding periods of life except the first one, there is no precise beginning point to this last stage. For some, the 75th birthday may mark entry into this period of life. For others, that marker may be the 80th or even the 85th birthday. For most, this stage is marked by growing frailty and illness; for all who reach this stage, by death. For some, the physical decline is slow, and a rare few manage to see their 100th birthday mentally alert and in good physical health.

The Sociological Significance of the Life Course

The sociological significance of the life course is that it does not merely represent biology, things that naturally occur to all of us as we add years to our lives. Rather, *social* factors influence our life course. As you just saw, *when* you live makes a huge difference in the course that your life takes. And the difference does not have to be vast. Being born just ten years earlier or later may mean that you experience war or peace, an expanding economy or a depression—and

This January 1937 photo from Sneedville, Tennessee, shows Eunice Johns, age 9, and her husband, Charlie Johns, age 22. The groom gave his wife a doll as a wedding gift. The new husband and wife planned to build a cabin, and, as Charlie Johns phrased it, "go to housekeeping." This photo illustrates the cultural relativity of life stages, which we sometimes mistake as fixed. It also is interesting from a symbolic interactionist perspective—that of changing definitions—for while our sensibilities are shocked by such marriages, though not common they once were taken for granted.

those factors vitally affect what happens to you not just during childhood but throughout your life.

Your *social location,* such as social class, gender, and race, is also highly significant. Because of it, your experience of society's events will be similar to people who share your location, but different from people who do not. If you are poor, for example, you likely will feel older faster than most wealthy people for whom life is much less demanding. The life course is also influenced by individual factors—such as your health, or marrying early or entering college late—that may make your life course "out of sequence" or atypical.

For all these reasons, this sketch of the life course may not adequately reflect your own past, present, and future. As sociologist C. Wright Mills (1959) would say, because college recruiters are beating down the door of your school, or failing to do so, you are more inclined to marry, to buy a house, and to start a family—or to postpone these life course events, perhaps indefinitely. In short, changing times change lives, steering the life course into different directions.

ARE WE PRISONERS OF SOCIALIZATION?

From our discussion of socialization, you might conclude that sociologists think of people as little robots: The socialization goes in, and the behavior comes out. People cannot help what they do, think, or feel, for everything is simply a result of their exposure to socializing agents.

Sociologists do *not* think of people in this way. Although socialization is powerful, and profoundly affects us all, we have a self. Established in childhood and continually modified by later experience, the self is dynamic. It is not a sponge that passively absorbs influences from the environment but a vigorous, essential part of our being that allows us to act on our environment (Wrong 1961; Meltzer et al. 1975; Couch 1989).

Indeed, it is precisely because individuals are not robots that their behavior is so hard to predict. The countless reactions of other people merge in each of us. As discussed earlier, even twins do not receive identical reactions from others. As the self develops, we internalize or "put together" these innumerable reactions, producing a unique whole that we call the *individual.* And, each unique individual uses his or her own mind to reason and to make choices in life.

In this way, *each of us is actively involved in the social construction of the self.* For example, although our experiences in the family lay down the basic elements of our personality, including fundamental orientations to life, we are not doomed to keep those orientations if we do not like them. We can purposely expose ourselves to groups and ideas that we prefer. Those experiences, in turn, will have their own effects on our self. In short, although socialization is powerful, within the limitations of the framework laid down by our social location we can change even the self. And that self—along with the options available within society—is the key to our behavior.

SUMMARY AND REVIEW

■ **What Is Human Nature?**

How much of our human characteristics come from "nature" (heredity) and how much from "nurture" (the social environment)?

Observations of isolated, institutionalized, and **feral children** help answer this question, as do experiments with monkeys that have been raised in isolation. Language and intimate social interaction—

functions of "nurture"—appear to be essential to the development of what we consider to be human characteristics. Pp. 64–68.

■ **Socialization into the Self, Mind, and Emotions**

How do we acquire a self?

Humans are born with the capacity to develop a **self,** but the self must be socially constructed; that is, its contents depend on social interaction. According to Charles Horton Cooley's concept of the **looking-glass self,** our self develops as we internalize others' reactions to us. George Herbert Mead identified the ability to **take the role of the other** as essential to the development of the self. Mead concluded that even the mind is a social product. Pp. 68–71.

How do children develop reasoning skills?

Jean Piaget identified four stages that children go through as they develop the ability to reason: (1) *sensorimotor,* in which understanding is limited to sensory stimuli such as touch and sight; (2) *preoperational,* the ability to use symbols; (3) *concrete operational,* in which reasoning ability is more complex but not yet capable of complex abstractions; and (4) *formal operational,* or abstract thinking. P. 71.

How do people develope morality?

Children, who are born without morality, appear to go through a series of stages in learning morality. Kohlberg identified these stages as amoral, preconventional, conventional, and postconventional. Both men and women base their moral decisions on personal relationships and abstract principles. Pp. 71–72.

How do sociologists evaluate Freud's psychoanalytic theory of personality development?

Freud viewed personality development as the result of self-centered inborn desires, the **id,** clashing with social constraints. The **ego** develops to balance the id as well as the **superego,** the conscience. Sociologists, in contrast, do not examine inborn and unconscious motivations, but, instead, how social factors—social class, gender, religion, education, and so forth—underlie personality development. Pp. 72–73.

How does socialization influence emotions?

Socialization influences not only *how* we express our emotions, but also *what* emotions we feel. Socialization into emotions is a major means by which society produces conformity. Pp. 73–76.

■ Socialization into Gender

How does gender socialization affect our sense of self?

Gender socialization—sorting males and females into different roles—is a primary means of controlling human behavior. Children receive messages about gender even in infancy. A society's

ideals of sex-linked behaviors are reinforced by its social institutions. Pp. 76–79.

■ Agents of Socialization

What are the main agents of socialization?

The **agents of socialization** include family, religion, day care, school, **peer groups,** the **mass media,** sports, and the workplace. Each has its particular influences in socializing us into becoming full-fledged members of society. Pp. 79–84.

■ Resocialization

What is resocialization?

Resocialization is the process of learning new norms, values, attitudes, and behaviors. Intense resocialization occurs in **total institutions.** Most resocialization is voluntary, but some, as with prisoners, is involuntary. Pp. 84–86.

■ Socialization Through the Life Course

Does socialization end when we enter adulthood?

Socialization occurs throughout the **life course.** In industrialized societies, the life course can be divided into childhood, adolescence, young adulthood, the early middle years, the later middle years, the early older years, and the older older years. Typical patterns include obtaining education, becoming independent from parents, building a career, finding a mate, rearing children, and confronting aging. Life course patterns vary by history, culture, and by social location such as gender, race–ethnicity, and social class, as well as by individual experiences such as health and age at marriage. Pp. 86–91.

■ Are We Prisoners of Socialization?

Although socialization is powerful, we are not merely the sum of our socialization experiences. Just as socialization influences human behavior, so humans act on their environment and influence it. P. 91.

Where can I read more on this topic?

Suggested readings for this chapter are at the back of this book.

Sociology & the Internet

All URLs listed are current as of the printing of this book. URLs are often changed. Please check out our web site, **http://www.abacon.com/henslin,** for updates.

1. According to Charles H. Cooley, our self develops from interactions with others. One of the first pieces of information others gain about us is our name. Names are important in our society, and we often get feedback and reactions from others based on our name. Examine the Kabalarian Philosophy at **http://www.kabalarians.com** and discuss how one's name is important to the development of the self. What do they say is the hidden power of a name? Find your own name under the heading "Demonstration of What's in YOUR Name." If this information was ac-

curate, how do you think your name analysis might affect your self? Write a short paper explaining what you've learned about the importance of our identity.

2. To explore patterns of child rearing, enter the search term "child rearing" into the search term box of your favorite search engine. Try to discover some of the varieties of values and practices found throughout the United States. Can you identify any of the social characteristics of those who propose a particular point of view? Now try the same exercise, but this time look at several different countries; you might try entering the term "child rearing in" and add a particular country. Be prepared to share your findings with the class.

3. To learn more about early childhood experiences, go to the Web site for the Annie E. Casey Foundation, **http://www.aecf.org.** This is a private charitable organization dedicated to helping build better futures for disadvantaged children in the United States. After exploring the homepage, click on "Kids Count." At that page, look for information on "data online." This will take you to a wealth of information about the contemporary social conditions of children in this country. Click on "Profiles" and then click on your own state. Choose one of the different statistical profiles listed, and compare your state against the national averages. Is your state better or worse than the national average? Can you think of any social factors that might contribute to the differences? What has been the trend in this particular area of childhood well-being over the past several years? Go back and try to generate a graph by clicking on "Graphs" and then selecting your state and some other state or the national averages. Write a report about the well-being of children, using the information you obtained.

4. The textbook discusses gender socialization, focusing on the influences of the family and the mass media. Let's look at how the Internet may be influencing the socialization of girls. To generate a quick list of Web sites devoted to girls, go to a search engine like **http://www.metacrawler.com.** From the list of subject areas, click on "Society," then "Women," then "Girls/only." (You can use another search engine and generate a similar list.) Explore some of the Web sites that are listed, paying attention to what age group is targeted, what topics are covered on the Web site, and what colors and graphics are used in the design of the Web site. When you finish, prepare a report to your class in which you talk about whether or not the Internet is reinforcing traditional feminine gender roles or trying to redefine them.

Social Structure and Social Interaction

- **Levels of Sociological Analysis**
  Macrosociology and Microsociology

- **The Macrosociological Perspective: Social Structure**
  The Sociological Significance of Social Structure
  Culture
  Social Class
  Social Status
  Roles
  Groups

- **Social Institutions**
  The Sociological Significance of Social Institutions
  An Example: The Mass Media as an Emerging
    Social Institution
  Comparing Functionalist and Conflict Perspectives
  Changes in Social Structure
  What Holds Society Together?

- **The Microsociological Perspective: Social Interaction in Everyday Life**
  Symbolic Interaction
  Dramaturgy: The Presentation of Self in
    Everyday Life
  Ethnomethodology: Uncovering
    Background Assumptions
  The Social Construction of Reality

- **The Need for Both Macrosociology and Microsociology**

- **Summary and Review**

My curiosity had gotten the better of me. When the sociology convention finished, I climbed aboard the first city bus that came along. I didn't know where the bus was going, and I didn't even know where I was going to spend the night.

"Maybe I overdid it this time," I thought as the bus began winding down streets I had never seen before. Actually, this was my first visit to Washington, D.C., so I hadn't seen any of the streets before. I had no direction, no plans, not even a map. I carried no billfold, just a driver's license shoved into my jeans for emergency identification, some pocket change, and a $10 bill tucked into my socks. My goal was simple: If I saw something interesting, I'd get off and check it out.

"Nothing but the usual things," I mused, as we passed row after row of apartment buildings and stores. I could see myself riding buses the entire night. Then something caught my eye. Nothing spectacular—just groups of people clustered around a large circular area where several streets intersected.

I climbed off the bus and made my way to what turned out to be Dupont Circle. I took a seat on a sidewalk bench and began to observe. As the scene came into focus, I noted several street corner men drinking and joking with one another. One of the men broke from his companions and sat down next to me. As we talked, I mostly listened.

As night fell, the men said that they wanted to get another bottle of wine. I contributed. They counted their money and asked if I wanted to go with them.

Although I felt my stomach churning—a combination of hesitation and fear—I heard a confident "Sure!" come out of my mouth. As we left the circle, the three men began to cut through an alley. "Oh, no," I thought. "This isn't what I had in mind."

I had but a split second to make a decision. I found myself continuing to walk with the men, but holding back half a step so that none of the three was behind me. As we walked, they passed around the remnants of their bottle. When my turn came, I didn't know what to do. I shuddered to think about the diseases lurking within that bottle. I made another quick decision. In the semidarkness I faked it, letting only my thumb and forefinger touch my lips and nothing enter my mouth.

When we returned to Dupont Circle, the men finished their new bottle of Thunderbird. I couldn't fake it in the light, so I passed, pointing at my stomach to indicate that I was having digestive problems.

Suddenly one of the men jumped up, smashed the emptied bottle against the sidewalk, and thrust the jagged neck outward in a menacing gesture. He stared straight ahead at another bench, where he had spotted someone with whom he had some sort of unfinished business. As the other men told him to cool it, I moved slightly to one side of the group—ready to flee, just in case. ■

LEVELS OF SOCIOLOGICAL ANALYSIS

On this sociological adventure, I almost got myself in over my head. Fortunately, it turned out all right. The man's "enemy" didn't look our way, the broken bottle was set down next to the bench "just in case he needed it," and my introduction to a life that up to then I had only read about continued until dawn.

Sociologists Elliot Liebow (1967/1999) and Elijah Anderson (1978, 1990/1999) have written fascinating accounts about men like these. Although street corner men may appear to be disorganized—simply coming and going as they please and doing whatever feels good at the moment—Liebow and Anderson analyzed how, like us, these men also are influenced by the norms and beliefs of our society. This will become more apparent as we examine the two levels of analysis that sociologists use.

Macrosociology and Microsociology

The first level, **macrosociology,** places the focus on broad features of society. Sociologists who use this approach, especially conflict theorists and functionalists, analyze such things as social class and how groups are related to one another. If macrosociologists were to analyze street corner men, for example, they would stress that these men are located at the bottom of the U.S. social class system. Their low status means that many opportunities are closed to them: The men have few job skills, little education, hardly anything to offer an employer. As "able-bodied" men, however, they are not eligible for welfare, even for a two year limit, so they hustle to survive. As a consequence, they spend their lives on the streets.

Conflict theory and functionalism, both of which focus on the broader picture, are examples of this macrosociological approach. In these theories, the goal is to examine the large-scale social forces that influence people.

The second approach sociologists use is **microsociology.** Here the emphasis is placed on **social interaction,** what people do when they come together. Sociologists who use this approach are likely to focus on the men's survival strategies ("hustles"); their rules for dividing up money, wine, or whatever other resources they have; their relationships with girlfriends, family, and friends; where they spend their time and what they do there; their language; their pecking order; and so on. With its focus on face-to-face interaction, symbolic interactionism is an example of microsociology.

Because each has a different focus, macrosociology and microsociology yield distinctive perspectives, and both are needed to gain a more complete understanding of social life.

macrosociology analysis of social life focusing on broad features of social structure, such as social class and the relationships of groups to one another; an approach usually used by functionalist and conflict theorists

microsociology analysis of social life focusing on social interaction; an approach usually used by symbolic interactionists

social interaction what people do when they are in the presence of one another

We cannot adequately understand street corner men, for example, without using *macrosociology*. It is essential that we place the men within the broad context of how groups in U.S. society are related to one another—for, just as with ourselves, the social class of these men helps to shape their attitudes and behavior. Nor can we adequately understand these men without *microsociology*, for their everyday situations also form a significant part of their lives.

To see how these two approaches help us to understand social life, let's look at each. As we do so, you may find yourself feeling more comfortable with one approach than the other. That is what happens with sociologists. For reasons of personal background and professional training, sociologists find themselves more comfortable with one approach and tend to use it in their research. Both approaches, however, are necessary for a full understanding of life in society.

*T*HE MACROSOCIOLOGICAL PERSPECTIVE: SOCIAL STRUCTURE

Why did the street people in the opening vignette act as they did, staying up all night drinking wine and ready to use a lethal weapon? Why don't *we* act like this? Social structure helps us answer such questions.

Sociologists use both macro and micro levels of analysis to study social life. Those who use macrosociology to analyze the homeless—or any human behavior—focus on broad forces, such as the economy and social classes. Sociologists who use the microsociological approach analyze how people interact with one another. Note how this scene invites both levels of analyses: Here you have both social classes (power and powerlessness) and social interaction.

The Sociological Significance of Social Structure

To better understand human behavior, we need to understand **social structure**, the framework of society that was already laid out before you were born. Social structure is the typical patterns of a group, such as its usual relationships between men and women or students and teachers. *The sociological significance of social structure is that it guides our behavior.*

Because this term may seem vague, let's consider how you experience social structure in your own life. As I write this, I do not know your race–ethnicity. I do not know your religion. I do not know if you are young or old, tall or short, male or female. I do not know if you were reared on a farm, in the suburbs, or in the inner city. I do not know if you went to a public high school or an exclusive prep school. But I do know that you are in college. And that, alone, tells me a great deal about you.

From this one piece of information, I can assume that the social structure of your college is now shaping what you do. For example, let's suppose that today you felt euphoric over some great news. I can be fairly certain (not absolutely, mind you, but relatively certain) that when you entered the classroom, social structure overrode your mood. That is, instead of shouting at the top of your lungs and joyously throwing this book into the air, you entered the classroom in a fairly subdued manner and took your seat.

The same social structure influences your instructor, even if, on the one hand, he or she is facing a divorce or has a child dying of cancer, or, on the other, has just been awarded a promotion or a million-dollar grant. The instructor may feel like either retreating into seclusion or celebrating wildly, but it is most likely that he or she will conduct class in the usual manner. In short, social structure tends to override personal feelings and desires.

Just as social structure influences you and your instructor, so it also establishes limits for street people. They, too, find themselves in a specific social location in the U.S. social structure—although it is quite different from yours or your instructor's. Consequently, they are affected differently—and nothing about their social location leads them to take notes or

social structure the framework that surrounds us, consisting of the relationships of people and groups to one another, which give direction to and set limits on behavior

to lecture. Their behaviors, however, are as logical an outcome of where they find themselves in the social structure as are your own. In their position in the social structure, it is just as "natural" to drink wine all night as it is for you to stay up studying all night for a crucial examination. It is just as "natural" for you to nod and say, "Excuse me," when you enter a crowded classroom late and have to claim a desk on which someone has already placed books or a coat as it is for them to break off the head of a wine bottle and glare at an enemy.

People learn their behaviors and attitudes because of their location in the social structure (whether privileged, deprived, or in between), and they act accordingly. This is equally true of street people and of ourselves. *The differences in behavior and attitudes are not due to biology (race, sex, or any other supposed genetic factors), but to people's location in the social structure.* Switch places with street people and watch your behaviors and attitudes change!

To better understand social structure, read the Down-to-Earth Sociology box on football on the next page. Because social structure so critically affects who we are and what we are like, let's look more closely at its major components: culture, social class, social status, roles, groups, and institutions.

Culture

In Chapter 2, we looked in detail at how culture affects us. At this point, let's simply review the main impact of culture, the largest envelope that surrounds us. Sociologists use the term *culture* to refer to a group's language, beliefs, values, behaviors, and even gestures. Culture also includes the material objects that are used by a group. Culture is the broadest framework that determines what kind of people we become. If we are reared in Eskimo, Japanese, Russian, or U.S. culture, we will grow up to be like most Eskimos, Japanese, Russians, or Americans. On the outside, we will look and act like them; and on the inside, we will think and feel like them. The specifics will vary by social location—by subculture, age group, race–ethnicity, and gender.

Social Class

To understand people, then, we must examine the particular social locations that they hold in life. Especially significant is social class, which is based on income, education, and occupation. Large numbers of people who have similar amounts of income and education and who work at jobs that are roughly comparable in prestige make up a **social class.** It is hard to overemphasize this aspect of social structure, for our social class heavily influences not only our behaviors, but even our ideas and attitudes. We have this in common, then, with the street people described in the opening vignette—both they and we are influenced by our location in the social class structure. Theirs may be a considerably less privileged position, but it has no less influence on their lives. Social class is so significant that we shall spend an entire chapter (Chapter 10) on this topic.

Social Status

When you hear the word *status,* you are likely to think of prestige. These two words are welded together in common thinking. Sociologists, however, use **status** in a different way: to refer to the *position* that an individual occupies. That position may carry a great deal of prestige, as in the case of a judge or an astronaut, or it may bring very little prestige, as in the case of a gas station attendant or a hamburger flipper at a fast-food restaurant. The status may also be looked down on, as in the case of a street corner man, an ex-convict, or a bag lady.

All of us occupy several positions at the same time. Simultaneously you may be a son or daughter, a worker, a date, and a student. Sociologists use the term **status set** to refer to all the statuses or positions that you occupy. Obviously your status set changes as your particular statuses change. For example, if you graduate from college and take a full-time job,

social class a large number of people with similar amounts of income and education who work at jobs that are roughly comparable in prestige

status the position that someone occupies in society or a social group

status set all the statuses or positions that an individual occupies

Sociology

COLLEGE FOOTBALL AS SOCIAL STRUCTURE

To gain a better idea of what social structure is, think of college football (see Dobriner 1969a). You probably know the various positions on the team: center, guards, tackles, ends, quarterback, and running backs. Each is a *status;* that is, each is a recognized social position. For each of these statuses, there is a *role;* that is, each of these positions has certain expectations attached to it. The center is expected to snap the ball, the quarterback to pass it, the guards to block, the tackles to tackle or block, the ends to receive passes, and so on. Those *role expectations* guide each player's actions; that is, the players try to do what their particular role requires.

Let's suppose that football is your favorite sport and you never miss a home game at your col-

lege. Let's also suppose that you graduate, get a great job, and move across the country. Five years later, you return to your campus for a nostalgic visit. The climax of your visit is the biggest football game of the season. When you get to the game, you might be surprised to see a different coach, but you are not surprised that each playing position is occupied by people you don't know, for all the players you knew have graduated, and their places have been filled by others.

This scenario mirrors *social structure,* the framework around which a group exists. In this football example, that framework consists of the coaching staff and the eleven playing positions. The game does not depend on any particular individual, but, rather, on statuses, the positions that the in-

dividuals occupy. When someone leaves a position, the game can go on because someone else takes over that position or status and plays the role. The game will continue even though not a single individual remains the same from one period of time to the next. Notre Dame's football team endures today even though Knute Rockne, the Gipper, and his teammates are long dead.

Even though you may not play football, you nevertheless live your life within a clearly established social structure. The statuses you occupy and the roles you play were already in place before you were born. You take your particular positions in life, others do the same, and society goes about its business. Although the specifics change with time, the game—whether of life or of football—goes on. ■

get married, buy a home, have children, and so on, your status set changes to include the positions of worker, spouse, homeowner, and parent.

Like other aspects of social structure, statuses are part of our basic framework of living in society. The example given earlier of students and teachers doing what others expect of them despite their particular moods illustrates how statuses affect our actions—and those of the people around us. Our statuses—whether daughter or son, worker or date—serve as guides for our behavior.

Ascribed and Achieved Statuses The first type, **ascribed statuses,** is involuntary. You do not ask for them, nor can you choose them. Some you inherit at birth such as your race–ethnicity, sex, and the social class of your parents, as well as your statuses as female or male, daughter or son, niece or nephew, and granddaughter or grandson. Others, such as teenager and senior citizen, are related to the life course discussed in Chapter 3, and are given to you later in life.

Achieved statuses, on the other hand, are voluntary. These you earn or accomplish. As a result of your efforts you become a student, a friend, a spouse, a rabbi, minister, priest, or nun. Or, for lack of effort (or efforts that others fail to appreciate), you become a school dropout, a former friend, an ex-spouse, or a defrocked rabbi, priest, or nun. In other words, achieved statuses can be either positive or negative; both college president and bank robber are achieved statuses.

The significance of social statuses for understanding human behavior is that each status provides guidelines for how we are to act and feel. Like other aspects of social structure, they set limits on what we can and cannot do. Because social statuses are an essential part of the social structure, they are found in all human groups.

ascribed statuses positions an individual either inherits at birth or receives involuntarily later in life

achieved statuses positions that are earned, accomplished, or involve at least some effort or activity on the individual's part

Master statuses are those that overshadow our other statuses. Shown here is Christopher Reeve, who was paralyzed when he was thrown from a horse. Before his accident, Reeve was a top Hollywood actor, celebrating worldwide success with his role as Superman. Today, his master status is that of a person with a disability. He has accepted this status, and is a spokesperson for people suffering from spinal cord injuries.

Status Symbols People who are pleased with their particular social status may want others to recognize that they occupy that status. To gain this recognition, they use **status symbols,** signs that identify a status. For example, people wear wedding rings to announce their marital status; uniforms, guns, and badges to proclaim that they are police officers (and to not so subtly let you know that their status gives them authority over you); and "backward" collars to declare that they are Lutheran ministers or Roman Catholic or Episcopal priests.

Some social statuses are negative, and so, therefore, are their status symbols. The scarlet letter in Nathaniel Hawthorne's book by the same title is one example. Another is the CONVICTED DUI (driving under the influence) bumper sticker that some U.S. counties require convicted drunk drivers to display if they wish to avoid a jail sentence.

All of us use status symbols to announce our statuses to others and to help smooth our interactions in everyday life. You might consider your own status symbols. For example, how does your clothing announce your statuses of sex, age, and college student?

Master Statuses A **master status** is one that cuts across the other statuses that you hold. Some master statuses are ascribed. An example is your sex. Whatever you do, people perceive you as a male or as a female. If you are working your way through college by flipping burgers, people see you not only as a burger flipper and a student, but as a *male* or *female* burger flipper and a *male* or *female* college student. Other master statuses are race and age.

Some master statuses are achieved. If you become very, very wealthy (and it doesn't matter if your wealth comes from an invention or from the lottery—it is still *achieved* as far as sociologists are concerned), your wealth is likely to become a master status. No matter what else, people are likely to say, " She is a very rich burger flipper." (Or more likely, "She's very rich, and she used to flip burgers!")

Similarly, people who become physically disabled or disfigured find, to their dismay, that their condition becomes a master status. For example, a person whose face is badly scarred will be viewed through this unwelcome master status no matter what the individual's occupation or accomplishments. People confined to wheelchairs can attest to how their handicap overrides all their other statuses and determines others' perceptions of everything they do.

Although our statuses usually fit together fairly well, sometimes a contradiction or mismatch between statuses occurs. This is known as **status inconsistency** (or discrepancy). A 14-year-old college student is an example. So is a 40-year-old married woman who is dating a 19-year-old college sophomore.

These examples reveal an essential aspect of social statuses: Like other components of social structure, they come with built-in *norms,* that is, expectations or guidelines for be-

status symbols items used to identify a status

master status a status that cuts across the other statuses that an individual occupies

status inconsistency (or discrepancy) a contradiction or mismatch between statuses

Shown here is Stephen Hawking, who is severely disabled by Lou Gehrig's disease. For many, his master status is that of a disabled person. Because Hawking is one of the greatest physicists who has ever lived, however, his astounding accomplishments have given him another status, that of world-class physicist in the ranking of Einstein. Thus, Hawking occupies two master statuses simultaneously, the one ascribed and the other achieved.

havior. When statuses mesh well, as they usually do, we know what to expect of people. This helps social interaction to unfold smoothly. Status inconsistency, however, upsets our expectations. In the preceding examples, how are you supposed to act? Are you supposed to treat the 14-year-old as you would any young teenager, or as you would your college classmate? Do you react to the married woman as you would to the mother of your friend, or as you would to a classmate's date?

Roles

> All the world's a stage
> And all the men and women merely players.
> They have their exits and their entrances;
> And one man in his time plays many parts . . .
> (William Shakespeare, *As You Like It,* Act II, Scene 7)

Like Shakespeare, sociologists, too, see roles as essential to social life. When you were born, **roles**—the behaviors, obligations, and privileges attached to a status—were already set up for you. Society was waiting with outstretched arms to teach you how it expected you to act as a boy or a girl. And whether you were born poor, rich, or somewhere in between, that, too, attached certain behaviors, obligations, and privileges to your statuses.

The difference between role and status is that you *occupy* a status, but you *play* a role (Linton 1936). For example, being a son or daughter is your status, but your expectations of receiving food and shelter from your parents—as well as their expectation that you show respect to them—is your role.

Roles help get us to do what society wants us to do. They are like a fence. They allow us a certain amount of freedom, but for most of us that freedom doesn't go very far. Suppose a female decides that she is not going to wear dresses—or a male that he will not wear suits and ties—regardless of what anyone says. In most situations, they'll stick to their decision. When a very formal occasion comes along, however, such as a family wedding or a funeral, they are likely to cave in to norms that they find overwhelming. Almost all of us stay within the fences that mark out what is "appropriate" for our roles. Most of us are little troubled by such constraints, for our socialization is so thorough that we usually *want* to do what our roles indicate is appropriate.

The sociological significance of roles is that they lay out what is expected of people. As individuals throughout society perform their roles, those roles mesh together to form this thing called society. As Shakespeare put it, people's roles provide "their exits and their entrances" on the stage of life. In short, roles are remarkably effective at keeping people in line—telling them when they should "enter" and when they should "exit," as well as what to do in between.

roles the behaviors, obligations, and privileges attached to a status

Groups

A **group** consists of people who regularly and consciously interact with one another. Ordinarily, the members of a group share similar values, norms, and expectations. Just as social class, statuses, and roles influence our actions, so, too, the groups to which we belong are powerful forces in our lives. In fact, *to belong to a group is to yield to others the right to make certain decisions about our behavior.* If we belong to a group, we assume an obligation to act according to the expectations of other members of that group.

Although this principle holds true for all groups, some groups wield influence over only small segments of our behavior. If you belong to a stamp club, for example, the group's influence may center around your display of knowledge about stamps, and perhaps your attendance at meetings. Other groups, however, such as the family, control many aspects of our behavior. When parents say to their 15-year-old daughter, "As long as you are living under my roof, you had better be home by midnight," they show their expectation that their children, as members of the family, will conform to their ideas about many aspects of life, including their views on curfew. They are saying that so long as the daughter wants to remain a member of the household her behavior must conform to their expectations.

To belong to any group is to relinquish to others at least some control over our lives. Those social groups that provide little option to belong are called **involuntary memberships** (or involuntary associations). These include our family and the gender, ethnic, and racial groups into which we are born. Groups to which we choose to belong are called **voluntary memberships** (or voluntary associations). These include the scouts, professional associations, church groups, clubs, work groups, and this sociology class. If we want to remain members in good standing, we must conform to what people in these groups expect of us. Both voluntary and involuntary memberships are vital in affecting who we are, for our participation in them shapes our ideas and orientations to life.

∫OCIAL INSTITUTIONS

At first glance, the term *social institution* may seem to have little relevance to your personal life. The term seems so cold and abstract. In fact, however, **social institutions**—the organized means that each society develops to meet its basic needs—involve your life in concrete and highly relevant ways.

Sociologists have identified nine social institutions: the family, religion, law, politics, economics, education, medicine, science, and military. In industrialized societies, social institutions tend to be more formal, in nonliterate societies more informal. In industrialized societies, for example, the social institution of education is highly structured, while in nonliterate societies education may consist of informally learning expected roles. Figure 4.1 on the next page summarizes the basic social institutions. Note that each institution has its own set of roles, values, and norms. Part IV of this text focuses on social institutions.

The Sociological Significance of Social Institutions

To understand social institutions is to realize how profoundly social structure affects our lives. Much of their influence lies beyond our ordinary awareness. For example, because of our economic institution, it is common to work eight hours a day for five days every week. There is nothing normal or natural about this pattern, however. Its regularity is only an arbitrary arrangement for dividing work and leisure. Yet this one aspect of a single social institution has far-reaching effects not only in terms of how people structure their time and activities but also in terms of how they deal with family and friends, and how they meet their personal needs and nonwork obligations.

Each of the other social institutions also has far-reaching effects on our lives. By weaving the fabric of society, our social institutions establish the context in which we live, shaping

group people who regularly and consciously interact with one another

involuntary memberships (or involuntary associations) groups in which people are assigned membership rather than choosing to join

voluntary memberships (or voluntary associations) groups that people choose to join

social institutions the organized, usual, or standard ways by which society meets its basic needs

Figure 4.1 SOCIAL INSTITUTIONS IN INDUSTRIAL AND POSTINDUSTRIAL SOCIETIES

Social Institution	Basic Needs	Some Groups or Organizations	Some Values	Some Roles	Some Norms
Family	Regulate reproduction, socialize and protect children	Relatives, kinship groups	Sexual fidelity, providing for your family, keeping a clean house, respect for parents	Daughter, son, father, mother, brother, sister, aunt, uncle, grandparent	Have only as many children as you can afford, be faithful to your spouse
Religion	Concerns about life after death, the meaning of suffering and loss; desire to connect with the Creator	Congregation, synagogue, denomination, charitable association	Reading and adhering to holy texts such as the Bible, the Koran, and the Torah; honoring God	Priest, minister, rabbi, worshipper, teacher, disciple, missionary, prophet, convert	Attend worship services, contribute money, follow the teachings
Law	Maintain social order	Police, Courts, Prisons	Trial by one's peers, innocence until proven guilty	Judge, police officer, lawyer, defendant, prison guard	Give true testimony, follow the rules of evidence
Politics	Establish a hierarchy of power and authority	Political parties, congresses, parliaments, monarchies	Majority rule, the right to vote as a sacred trust	President, senator, lobbyist, voter, candidate, spin doctor	One vote per person, voting as a privilege and a right
Economics	Produce and distribute goods and services	Credit unions, banks, credit card companies, buying clubs	Making money, paying bills on time, producing efficiently	Worker, boss, buyer, seller, creditor, debtor, advertiser	Maximize profits, "the customer is always right," work hard
Education	Transmit knowledge and skills across the generations	School, college, student senate, sports team, PTA, teachers' union	Academic honesty, good grades, being "cool"	Teacher, student, dean, principal, football player, cheerleader	Do homework, prepare lectures, don't snitch on classmates
Science	Master the environment	Local, state, regional, national, and international associations	Unbiased research, open dissemination of research findings	Scientist, researcher, technician, administrator	Follow scientific method, fully disclose research findings
Medicine	Heal the sick and injured, care for the dying	AMA, hospitals, pharmacies, insurance companies, HMOs	Hippocratic oath, staying in good health, following doctor's orders	Doctor, nurse, patient, pharmacist, medical insurer	Don't exploit patients, give best medical care available
Military	Protection from enemies, support of national interests	Army, navy, air force, marines, coast guard, national guard	To die for one's country is an honor, obedience unto death	Soldier, recruit, enlisted person, officer, prisoner, spy	Be ready to go to war, obey superior officers, don't question orders
Mass Media (an emerging institution)	Disseminate information, mold public opinion, report events	Television networks, radio stations, publishers	Timeliness, accuracy, large audiences, freedom of the press	Journalist, newscaster, author, editor, publisher	Be accurate, fair, timely, and profitable

The mass media are a major influence in contemporary life. Until 1436, when Johann Gutenberg invented movable type, printing was a slow process, and printed materials were expensive. Today printed materials are common and often cheap. "Cheap" has a double meaning, with its second meaning illustrated in this photo.

almost everything that is of concern to us. Social institutions are so significant that if they were different, we would be different people. We certainly could not remain the same, for social institutions influence our orientations to the social world, and even to life itself.

An Example: The Mass Media as an Emerging Social Institution

Although not all sociologists agree, the mass media can be considered a social institution. Far beyond serving simply as sources of information, the media influence our attitudes toward social issues, other people, and even our self-concept. Because the media significantly shape public opinion, all totalitarian governments attempt to maintain tight control over them.

The mass media are relatively new in human history, owing their origins to the invention of the printing press in the 1400s. This invention had immediate and profound consequences on virtually all other social institutions. The printing of the Bible altered religion, for instance, while the publication of political broadsides and newspapers altered politics. From these beginnings, a series of inventions—from radio and movies to television and, more recently, the microchip—have made the media an increasingly powerful force.

Indeed, one of the most significant questions we can ask about this new social institution is, Who controls it? That control, which in totalitarian countries is obvious, is much less visible in democratic nations. Functionalists might conclude that the media in a democratic nation represent the varied interests of the many groups that make up that nation. Conflict theorists, in contrast, see the matter quite differently: The mass media—at least a country's most influential newspapers and television stations—represent the interests of the political elite. The wealthy and powerful use the media to mold public opinion and to help preserve their places of privilege.

Since the mass media are so influential in our lives today, the answer to this question of who controls the media is of more than passing interest. This matter is vital for understanding contemporary society.

Comparing Functionalist and Conflict Perspectives

Just as the functionalist and conflict perspectives of the mass media differ, so do their views of the nature of social institutions. Let's compare these views.

The Functionalist Perspective Functionalists stress that no society is without social institutions. This is because social institutions perform vital functions for society. A group may be too small to have people who specialize in education, but it will have its own established ways of teaching skills and ideas to the young. It may be too small to have a military, but it will have some mechanism of self-defense. To survive, every society must meet its basic needs (or **functional requisites**). According to functionalists, that is the purpose of social institutions.

What are those basic needs? Functionalists identify five functional requisites that each society must fulfill if it is to survive (Aberle et al. 1950; Mack and Bradford 1979).

Functionalist theorists have identified five key functional requisites for the survival of a society. One, providing a sense of purpose, is often met through religious groups. To most people, snake handling, as in this church service in Jolo, West Virginia, is nonsensical. From a functional perspective, however, it makes a great deal of sense. Can you identify its sociological meanings?

1. *Replacing members.* If a society does not replace its members, it cannot continue to exist. Because reproduction is so fundamental to a society's existence, and because every society has a vital need to protect infants and children, all groups have developed some version of the family. The family gives the newcomer to society a sense of belonging by providing a "lineage," an account of how he or she is related to others. The family also functions to control people's sex drive and to maintain orderly reproduction.

2. *Socializing new members.* Each baby must be taught what it means to be a member of the group into which it is born. To accomplish this, each human group develops devices to ensure that its newcomers learn the group's basic expectations. As the primary "bearer of culture," the family is essential to this process, but other social institutions, such as religion and education, also help meet this basic need.

3. *Producing and distributing goods and services.* Every society must produce and distribute basic resources, from food and clothing to shelter and education. Consequently, every society establishes an *economic* institution, a means of producing such resources along with routine ways to distribute them.

4. *Preserving order.* Societies face two threats of disorder: one internal, the potential for chaos, and the other external, the possibility of being conquered. To defend themselves against external conquest, they develop some means of defense, some form of the military. To protect themselves from internal threat, they develop some system of policing themselves, ranging from formal organizations of armed groups to informal systems of gossip.

5. *Providing a sense of purpose.* For people to cooperate with one another and willingly give up personal gains in favor of working with and for others, they need a sense of purpose. They need to be convinced that it is worth sacrificing for the common good. Human groups develop various ways of instilling such beliefs, but a primary one is religion, which attempts to answer questions about ultimate meaning. Actually, all of a society's institutions are involved in meeting this functional requisite; the family provides one set of answers about the sense of purpose, the school another, and so on. All of the answers are interrelated.

The Conflict Perspective Although conflict theorists agree that social institutions were originally designed to meet basic survival needs, they do not see social institutions as working harmoniously for the common good. On the contrary, conflict theorists stress that a society's institutions are controlled by an elite that manipulates them in order to maintain its own privileged position of wealth and power (Useem 1984; Domhoff 1967, 1998, 1999).

functional requisites the major tasks that a society must fulfill if it is to survive

As evidence of their position, conflict theorists point out that a fairly small group of people have garnered the lion's share of the nation's wealth. Members of this elite sit on the boards of major corporations and of the country's most prestigious universities. They make strategic campaign contributions to influence (or control) the nation's lawmakers, and it is they who make the major decisions in this society: to go to war or to refrain from war, to raise or to lower taxes, to raise or to lower interest rates, to pass laws that favor or impede moving capital, technology, and jobs out of the country.

Feminist sociologists (both women and men) have used conflict theory to gain a better understanding of how social institutions affect gender relations. Their basic insight is that gender, too, is an element of social structure, not simply a characteristic of individuals. In other words, throughout the world social institutions divide males and females into separate groups, each with unequal access to society's resources.

■ **In Sum**   Conflict theorists regard our social institutions as having a single primary purpose—to preserve the social order. They interpret this as preserving the wealthy and powerful in their privileged positions. Functionalists, in contrast, view social institutions as working together to meet universal human needs.

Changes in Social Structure

This enveloping system that we call social structure, which so powerfully affects our lives, is not static. Our culture changes as it responds to new technology, to innovative ideas from home and abroad, and to evolving values. In our new era of "globalization," we come into contact with the customs of many other people. This exerts profound changes in our basic orientations to life. Nor do social classes remain immune to the winds of change, for growth and contraction in the economy move people in and out of positions of relative privilege. Shifting relationships between racial-ethnic groups also bring changes in relative power and prestige. Similarly, groups that did not exist, such as the IRS, come into being, and afterward wield extraordinary power over our lives.

What Holds Society Together?

With its many different groups and its extensive social change, how does society manage to hold together? Let's examine two answers sociologists have proposed.

Mechanical and Organic Solidarity   Sociologist Emile Durkheim (1893/1933) found the key to **social cohesion**—the degree to which members of a society feel united by shared values and other social bonds—in what he called **mechanical solidarity.** By this term, Durkheim meant that people who perform similar tasks develop a shared consciousness, a sense of similarity that unites them into a common whole. Think of an agricultural society in which everyone is involved in planting, cultivating, and harvesting. Members of this group have so much in common that they know what most others feel about life.

As societies get larger, their **division of labor** (how they divide up work) becomes more specialized. Instead of almost everyone doing the same jobs, some become jewelers, while others become artists, authors, shopkeepers, soldiers, and so on. Rather than splitting society apart, however, the division of labor makes people depend on one another—for the activities of each contribute to the welfare of the whole. Because this form of solidarity is based on interdependence, Durkheim called it **organic solidarity.** To see why he used this term, think about how you depend on your teacher to guide you through this introductory course in sociology. At the same time, your teacher needs you and other students in order to have a job. The two of you are *like organs* in the same body. (The "body" in this case is the college or university.) Although each of you performs different tasks, you depend on one another. This creates a form of unity.

social cohesion the degree to which members of a group or a society feel united by shared values and other social bonds

mechanical solidarity a shared consciousness that people experience as a result of performing the same or similar tasks

division of labor the splitting of a group's or a society's tasks into specialties

organic solidarity solidarity based on the interdependence brought about by the division of labor

The text contrasts *Gemeinschaft* and *Gesellschaft* societies. The French Cafe represents a *Gemeinschaft* approach to life, where there are warm, ongoing relationships. The cybernet cafe in Helsinki, Finland, represents the more impersonal *Gesellschaft* orientation. Here people ignore one another in favor of electronic interaction via the Internet. Internet interactions do not easily fit standard sociological models—another instance of cultural lag.

In the past, societies tolerated little diversity in thinking and attitudes, for their unity depended on similar thinking. This change to organic solidarity meant a new basis for solidarity—not similar views, but separate activities that contribute to the overall welfare of the group. As a result, modern societies can tolerate many differences among people and still manage to work as a whole. Both past and present societies are based on social solidarity, but the types of solidarity differ remarkably.

Gemeinschaft and Gesellschaft Ferdinand Tönnies (1887/1988) also saw a new type of society emerging. Tönnies used the term **Gemeinschaft** (Guh-MINE-shoft), or "intimate community," to describe the traditional type of society in which everyone knows everyone else and people share a sense of shared fate. In such a society people toe the line because they are acutely sensitive to the opinions of others and know that if they deviate, others will gossip and damage their reputation. Although their lives are sharply controlled by the opinions of others, they draw comfort from being part of an intimate group.

Tönnies saw that industrialization was tearing at this intimate fabric of village life. He noted that in this emerging society personal ties, family connections, and lifelong friendships were growing less important. They were being replaced by short-term relationships, individual accomplishments, and self-interests. Tönnies called this new type of society **Gesellschaft** (Guh-ZELL-shoft), or "impersonal association." As much as anyone might hate it, in *Gemeinschaft* society informal mechanisms such as gossip had been effective in controlling people. In this new world of *Gesellschaft,* however, gossip was of little use, and to keep people in line society had to depend on more *formal agencies,* such as the police and courts.

How Relevant Are These Concepts Today? I know that *Gemeinschaft, Gesellschaft,* and *mechanical* and *organic solidarity* are strange terms and that Durkheim's and Tönnies' observations must seem like a dead issue with no connection to life today. The concern these sociologists expressed, however—that their world was changing from a community in which people are united by shared ideas and feelings to an anonymous association built around impersonal, short-term contacts—are still very real. In large part, this same concern explains why our world is witnessing the rise of Islamic fundamentalism (Volti 1995). Islamic leaders fear that their traditional culture will be uprooted by Western values, that

Gemeinschaft a type of society in which life is intimate; a community in which everyone knows everyone else and people share a sense of togetherness

Gesellschaft a type of society dominated by impersonal relationships, individual accomplishments, and self-interest

cold rationality will replace relationships built on long-term associations between families and clans. Although the terms may sound strange, even obscure, the ideas remain a vital part of today's world.

■ **In Sum** *The sociological point is that social structure sets the context for what we do, feel, and think. Ultimately, then, social structure is the fundamental reason that we become the kind of people we become.* Because we tend to take our own social structure for granted, this main point is often difficult to see when we try to apply it to ourselves. It becomes more evident, however, when we look at people who live in a remarkably different social structure, such as the Amish, featured in the Perspectives box on the next page. The Amish are one of the few remaining *Gemeinschaft* societies in the United States. Think of what a fundamentally different kind of person you would be had you been reared in an Amish family instead of your own.

𝑻HE MICROSOCIOLOGICAL PERSPECTIVE: SOCIAL INTERACTION IN EVERYDAY LIFE

Where the macrosociological approach stresses the broad features of society, the microsociological approach has a narrower focus. Microsociologists examine *face-to-face interaction*, what people do when they are in one another's presence. Let's examine some of the areas of social life that microsociologists study.

Symbolic Interaction

For symbolic interactionists, the most significant part of life in society is social interaction. Symbolic interactionists are especially interested in the symbols that people use to define their worlds. They want to know how people look at things and how that, in turn, affects their behavior. Of the many areas of social life that microsociologists study, let's look at stereotyping, personal space, and touching.

Stereotypes in Everyday Life You are familiar with how first impressions "set the tone" for interaction. When you first meet someone, you cannot help but notice certain highly visible and distinctive features, such as the person's sex, race, age, and physical appearance. Despite your best intentions, your first impressions are shaped by the assumptions you make about such characteristics. You probably also know that these assumptions affect not only your ideas about the person, but also how you act toward that person.

Mark Snyder, a psychologist, wondered if **stereotypes**—the assumptions we make of what people are like—might be self-fulfilling. That is, since our assumptions of what people are like shape how we react to them, could our reactions produce behaviors that match the stereotype? Snyder (1993) came up with an ingenious way to test this idea. He gave college men a Polaroid snapshot of a woman (supposedly taken just moments before) and told them that they would be introduced to her after they talked with her on the telephone. Actually, photographs showing either a physically attractive or unattractive woman had been prepared before the experiment began; the photo given to each subject was chosen at random.

Stereotypes of physical attractiveness came into play even before the men spoke to the women they were going to meet. As Snyder gave each man the photograph, he asked him what he thought the woman would be like. The men who had been given the photograph of an attractive woman said they expected to meet a poised, humorous, outgoing woman. The men who had been given a photo of an unattractive woman described the person they were going to meet as awkward, serious, and unsociable. The men's stereotypes affected their style of getting acquainted. Those who had seen the photograph of an attractive woman were warm, friendly, and humorous. Those who had seen the photograph of an unattractive woman were cold, reserved, and humorless.

stereotypes assumptions of what people are like, based on previous associations with them or with people who have similar characteristics, or based on information, whether true or false

PERSPECTIVES | Cultural Diversity in the United States

THE AMISH—*GEMEINSCHAFT* COMMUNITY IN A *GESELLSCHAFT* SOCIETY

In Ferdinand Tönnies' term, the United States is a *Gesellschaft* society. Impersonal associations pervade our everyday life. Local, state, and federal governments regulate many activities. Impersonal corporations hire and fire people not on the basis of long-term, personal relationships, but on the basis of the bottom line. And, perhaps even more significantly, millions of Americans do not even know their neighbors.

Within the United States, a handful of small communities exhibits characteristics that depart from those of the larger society. One such community is the Old Order Amish, followers of a sect that broke away from the Swiss-German Mennonite church in the late 1600s, settling in Pennsylvania around 1727. Today, about 150,000 Amish live in the United States. The largest concentration, about 22,000, reside in Lancaster County, Pennsylvania. The Amish can also be found in about twenty other states and in Ontario, Canada, but 75 percent live in just three states: Pennsylvania, Ohio, and Indiana. The Amish, who believe that birth control is wrong, have doubled in size in just the past two decades.

To the nearly five million tourists who pass through Lancaster County each year, spending $400 million, the serene countryside—with its quiet pastures, white farmhouses, simple barns, horse-drawn buggies, and clothes lines hung with garments that flap in the wind—conveys a sense of peace and wholeness reminiscent of another era. Although just sixty-five miles from Philadelphia, "Amish country" is a world away.

Amish life is based on separation from the world—which is grounded in a literal interpretation of Christ's Sermon on the Mount—and obedience to the church's teachings and leaders. This rejection of worldly concerns, writes Donald Kraybill in *The Riddle of Amish Culture*, "provides the foundation of such Amish values as humility, faithfulness, thrift, tradition, communal goals, joy of work, a slow-paced life, and trust in divine providence."

The village life that Tönnies identified as fostering *Gemeinschaft* communities—and which he correctly predicted was fast being lost to industrialization—is very much alive among the Amish. The Amish make their decisions in weekly meetings, where, by consensus, they follow a set of rules, or *Ordnung,* to guide their behavior. Religion and the discipline that it calls for are the glue that holds these communities together. Brotherly love and the welfare of the community are paramount values. Because they use horses instead of tractors, most Amish farm plots of one hundred acres or less. When needed, as in times of birth, sickness, and death, neighbors pitch in with the chores. In these ways, they maintain intimacy—a sense of community.

The Amish are bound by many communal ties, including language (a dialect of German known as Pennsylvania Dutch), plain black clothing that has remained unchanged for almost three hundred years, and church-sponsored schools. Nearly all Amish marry. Divorce is forbidden. The family is a vital ingredient in Amish life; all major events take place in the home, including weddings and worship services, even births and funerals. Amish children attend church schools only until the age of 13. (In 1972, the Supreme Court ruled that Amish parents had the right to take their children out of school after the eighth grade.) To go to school longer

would expose them to values and "worldly concerns" that would separate them from their community. The Amish believe that all violence is bad, even in personal self-defense, and they register as conscientious objectors during times of war. They pay no social security, and they collect none.

Urban sprawl has made the cost of farmland soar, forcing slow social change. No longer can parents easily help their children buy their own farms. Consequently, almost half of Amish men work at jobs other than farming, most in farm-related businesses, wood crafts, or making furniture. Some Amish women have opened up their own businesses, such as greenhouses and gift shops that specialize in craft items. Some women make several hundred thousand dollars a year in these businesses.

This new nonfarmwork challenges the Amish way of life—especially their traditional husband-wife roles. Recognizing this, Amish men go to great lengths to avoid working for wages, for they believe that working away from the home would change all aspects of life—certainly an excellent sociological insight. Similarly, some successful businesswomen list the husband's name first on their business cards. Others build a kitchen at their business so that they can continue to pack their husbands' lunches, as Amish wives have done for three centuries.

The Amish's recent remarkable economic success poses a challenge to their traditional values. They frown on showy possessions, viewing them as worldly, so they invest their profits. This, in turn, brings further economic success, resulting in even greater pressures to spend the growing profits. (This process, called "The Protestant Ethic and the Spirit of Capitalism," is discussed later; see pages 196–197.) ■

Sources: Hostetler 1980; Kraybill 1989; Bender 1990; Kephart and Zellner 1994; Aeppel 1996; Savells 1997; Bumiller 1998.

Physical attractiveness underlies much of our social interaction in everyday life. The experiment reviewed on pages 108 and 110 illustrates how college men modified their interactions on the basis of attractiveness. How do you think women would modify their interactions if they were to meet the two men in these photographs? Would men change their interactions? Would they change them in the same way, or in different ways?

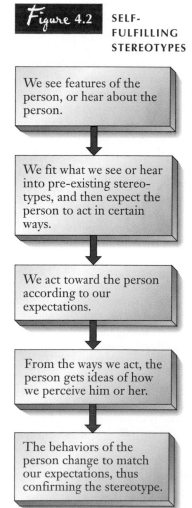

Figure 4.2 SELF-FULFILLING STEREOTYPES

We see features of the person, or hear about the person.

↓

We fit what we see or hear into pre-existing stereotypes, and then expect the person to act in certain ways.

↓

We act toward the person according to our expectations.

↓

From the ways we act, the person gets ideas of how we perceive him or her.

↓

The behaviors of the person change to match our expectations, thus confirming the stereotype.

How the men spoke on the phone then affected the women's behavior. Although the women did not know about the evaluation of their looks, those whom the men believed to be attractive responded in a warm, friendly, outgoing manner, while those who were perceived as homely became cool, reserved, and humorless. In short, *stereotypes tend to produce behaviors that match the stereotype.*

The effects that stereotypes have on human behavior go far beyond influencing how friendly we are to others. They even have an impact on what we accomplish. In one experiment, the welding instructor in a vocational training center was told that five men in his training program had an unusually high aptitude for welding (Snyder 1993). Although the five had been chosen at random and knew nothing about the experiment, the effects were dramatic. These men were absent less often than other trainees, learned the basics of welding in about half the usual time, and scored ten points higher than the other men on their final welding test. The difference was noted even by the other trainees, who singled these five out as their preferred co-workers. The men were no different in their initial abilities, but the instructor's stereotype of their abilities influenced how he behaved toward the men. This, in turn, changed the men's performance. This principle is illustrated in Figure 4.2.

Stereotypes do not have a single, inevitable effect. They are not magical. People can resist stereotypes and change outcomes. But these experiments do illustrate that stereotypes have a profound influence on how we react to others and even on our abilities. Stereotypes of gender, race–ethnicity, ability, and intelligence are vital factors in today's society. How do they influence people—those who do the stereotyping and those who are stereotyped? We need more research on this vital question, but the results we have so far are certainly intriguing.

Personal Space We all surround ourselves with a "personal bubble" that we go to great lengths to protect. We open the bubble to intimates—to our friends, children, parents, and so on—but we're careful to keep most people out of this space. In the hall, we might walk with our books clasped in front of us (a strategy often chosen by females). We carefully line up at the drinking fountain, making certain there is space between us so we don't touch the person in front of us and we aren't touched by the person behind us.

 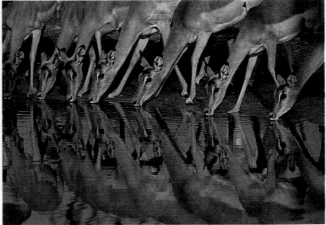

Social space is one of the many aspects of social life studied by sociologists who have a microsociological focus. What do you see in common in these two photos?

At times we extend our personal space. In the library, for example, you may place your coat on the chair next to you—claiming that space for yourself even though you aren't using it. If you want to really extend your space, you might even spread books in front of the other chairs, keeping the whole table to yourself by giving the impression that others have just stepped away.

The amount of space people prefer varies from one culture to another. South Americans, for example, like to be closer when they speak to others than do people reared in the United States. Anthropologist Edward Hall (1959) recounts a conversation with a man from South America who had attended one of his lectures.

> He came to the front of the class at the end of the lecture. . . .We started out facing each other, and as he talked I became dimly aware that he was standing a little too close and that I was beginning to back up. Fortunately I was able to suppress my first impulse and remain stationary because there was nothing to communicate aggression in his behavior except the conversational distance. . . .
>
> By experimenting I was able to observe that as I moved away slightly, there was an associated shift in the pattern of interaction. He had more trouble expressing himself. If I shifted to where I felt comfortable (about twenty-one inches), he looked somewhat puzzled and hurt, almost as though he were saying, "Why is he acting that way? Here I am doing everything I can to talk to him in a friendly manner and he suddenly withdraws. Have I done anything wrong? Said something I shouldn't?" Having ascertained that distance had a direct effect on his conversation, I stood my ground, letting him set the distance.

As you can see, in spite of Hall's extensive knowledge of other cultures, he still felt uncomfortable in this conversation. He first interpreted the invasion of his personal space as possible aggression, for people get close (and jut out their chins and chests) when they are hostile. But when he realized that was not the case, Hall resisted his impulse to move.

After Hall (1969/1999) analyzed situations like this, he observed that North Americans use four different "distance zones."

1. *Intimate distance.* This is the zone that the South American unwittingly invaded. It extends to about 18 inches from our bodies. We reserve this space for lovemaking, comforting, protecting, wrestling, hugging, and intimate touching.

2. *Personal distance.* This zone extends from 18 inches to 4 feet. We reserve it for friends and acquaintances and ordinary conversations. This is the zone in which Hall would have preferred speaking with the South American.

Norms of touching, including kissing, vary widely around the world. Shown here are Palestinian President Yasser Arafat and Monsignor Capucci of the Greek Orthodox Church kissing one another. In North America, in constrast, men shake hands. At most, two male friends, even after a long absence, will hug or clap one another on the back.

3. *Social distance.* This zone, extending out from us about 4 to 12 feet, marks impersonal or formal relationships. We use this zone for such things as job interviews.

4. *Public distance.* This zone, extending beyond 12 feet, marks even more formal relationships. It is used to separate dignitaries and public speakers from the general public.

Touching Not only does frequency of touching differ across cultures, but so does the meaning of touching within a culture. In general, higher-status individuals do more touching. Thus you are much more likely to see teachers touch students and bosses touch secretaries than the other way around. Apparently it is considered unseemly for lower-status individuals to put their hands on superiors. An interesting experiment with surgery patients illustrates how touching can have different meanings. When the nurse came in to tell patients about their coming surgery and after-care, she touched the patients twice, once briefly on the arm when she introduced herself, and then for a full minute on the arm during the instruction period. When she left, she shook the patient's hand (Thayer 1988).

Men and women reacted differently. Touching had a soothing effect on the women. It lowered their blood pressure and anxiety both before the surgery and for more than an hour afterward. The touching upset the men, however. Their blood pressure and anxiety rose. No one knows the reason for this difference. The experimenters suggest that the men found it harder to acknowledge dependency and fear. Instead of a comfort, the touch was a threatening reminder of their vulnerability. Perhaps. We don't know that answer. For this, too, we need more experiments.

Eye Contact One way we protect our personal bubble is by controlling eye contact. Letting someone gaze into our eyes—unless the person is our eye doctor—can easily be taken as a sign that we are attracted to that person, and even as an invitation to intimacy. A chain of supermarkets in Illinois, wanting to become "the friendliest store in town," ordered their checkout clerks to make direct eye contact with each customer. Women clerks complained that men customers were taking their eye contact the wrong way, as a sort of invitation to intimacy. Management said they were exaggerating. Their reply was, "We know the kind of looks we're getting back from men," and they refused to make direct eye contact with them.

Let's now turn to dramaturgy, a special area of symbolic interactionism.

dramaturgy an approach, pioneered by Erving Goffman, analyzing social life in terms of drama or the stage; also called dramaturgical analysis

front stage where performances are given

back stage where people rest from their performances, discuss their presentations, and plan future performances

role performance the ways in which someone performs a role within the limits that the role provides; showing a particular "style" or "personality"

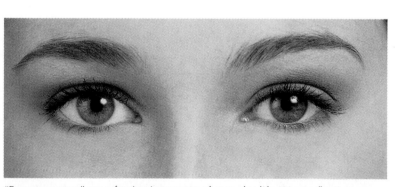

"Eye encounters" are a fascinating aspect of everyday life. We use fleeting eye contact for most of our interactions, such as those with clerks or people we pass in the hall between classes. Just as we reserve our close personal space for intimates, so, too, we reserve lingering eye contact for them.

Shown here are Leonardo DiCaprio and Kate Winslet as passengers on the doomed *Titanic*. In dramaturgy, a specialty within sociology, social life is viewed as similar to the theater. In our everyday lives, we all are actors—we perform roles, use props, and deliver lines to fellow actors.

Dramaturgy: The Presentation of Self in Everyday Life

It was their big day, two years in the making. Jennifer Mackey wore a white wedding gown adorned with an 11-foot train and 24,000 seed pearls that she and her mother had sewn onto the dress. Next to her at the altar in Lexington, Kentucky, stood her intended, Jeffrey Degler, in black tie. They said their vows, then turned to gaze for a moment at the four hundred guests.

That's when groomsman Daniel Mackey collapsed. As the shocked organist struggled to play Mendelssohn's "Wedding March," Mr. Mackey's unconscious body was dragged away, his feet striking—loudly—every step of the altar stairs.

"I couldn't believe he would die at my wedding," the bride said. (Hughes 1990)

Sociologist Erving Goffman (1922–1982) added a new twist to microsociology when he developed **dramaturgy** (or dramaturgical analysis). By this term he meant that social life is like a drama on the stage: Birth ushers us onto the stage of everyday life, and our socialization consists of learning to perform on that stage.

Everyday life, Goffman (1997) said, involves playing our assigned roles. We have **front stages** on which to perform them, as did Jennifer and Jeffrey. (By the way, Daniel Mackey didn't really die—he had just passed out from the excitement of it all.) But we don't have to look at weddings to find front stages. Everyday life is filled with them. Where your teacher lectures is a front stage. And if you make an announcement at the dinner table, you are using a front stage. In fact, you spend most of your time on front stages, for a front stage is wherever you deliver your lines. We also have **back stages**, places where we can retreat and let our hair down. When you close the bathroom or bedroom door for privacy, for example, you are entering a back stage.

The same setting can serve as both a back and a front stage. For example, when you get into your car by yourself and look over your hair in the mirror or check your makeup, you are using the car as a back stage. But when you wave at friends or if you give that familiar gesture to someone who has just cut in front of you in traffic, you are using your car as a front stage.

Everyday life brings with it many roles. The same person may be a student, a teenager, a shopper, a worker, a date, as well as a daughter or a son. Although a role lays down the basic outline for a performance, it also allows a great deal of freedom. The particular emphasis or interpretation that an individual gives a role, the person's "style," is known as **role performance.** Take your role as son or daughter as an example. You may play the role of ideal daughter or son, being very respectful, coming home

Role performance refers to how we play our roles. One of the major roles we are assigned in life is gender. We learn our "gender lessons" early, and we carefully project images that match cultural stereotypes. The source of humor of Pat on *Saturday Night Live* is role confusion, the uncertainty and tentativeness of interaction that results when people don't know whether to react to Pat as a male or as a female.

Figure 4.3 ROLE STRAIN AND ROLE CONFLICT

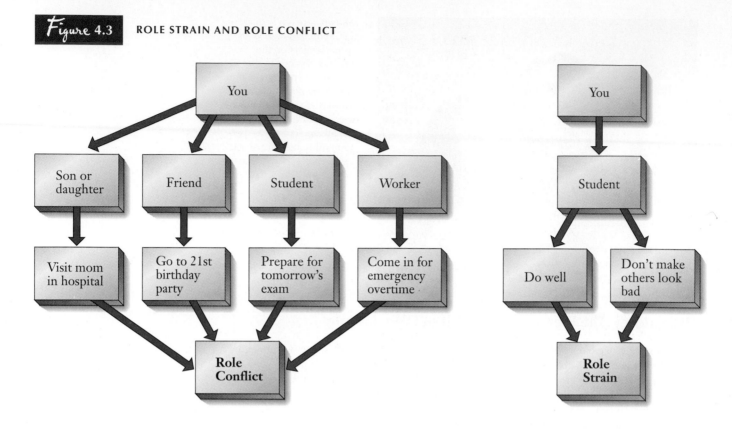

at the hours your parents set, and so forth. Or that description may not even come close to your particular role performance.

Ordinarily our roles are sufficiently separated that conflict between them is minimized. Occasionally, however, what is expected of us in one role is incompatible with what is expected of us in another role. This problem, known as **role conflict,** makes us very uncomfortable, as illustrated in Figure 4.3, in which family, friendship, student, and work roles come clashing together. Usually, however, we manage to avoid role conflict by segregating our roles, which in some instances may require an intense juggling act.

Sometimes the *same* role presents inherent conflict, a problem known as **role strain.** Suppose that you are exceptionally prepared for a particular class assignment. Although the instructor asks an unusually difficult question, you find yourself knowing the answer when no one else does. If you want to raise your hand, yet don't want to make your fellow students look bad, you will experience role strain. As illustrated in Figure 4.3, the difference between role conflict and role strain is that role conflict is conflict *between roles,* while role strain is conflict *within* a role.

A fascinating characteristic of roles is that *we tend to become the roles we play.* That is, roles become incorporated into the self-concept, especially those for which we prepare long and hard and which become part of our everyday lives. When sociologist Helen Ebaugh (1988) interviewed people who had left marriages, police work, and military, medical, and religious vocations, she found that these roles had become so intertwined with the subjects' self-concepts that leaving them threatened their very identity. The question they struggled with was "Who am I, now that I am not a nun (or physician, wife, colonel, and so on)?" Even years after leaving these roles, many continued to perform them in their dreams.

How these roles, having become such a part of the person, linger on after the individual has left them is illustrated by one of my own respondents, who said:

> After I left the (Protestant) ministry, I felt like a fish out of water. *Wearing that turned-back collar had become a part of me.* It was especially strange on Sunday mornings when I'd listen to someone else give the sermon. I knew that I should be up there preaching. I felt as though I had left God.

role conflict conflicts that someone feels *between* roles because the expectations attached to one role are incompatible with the expectations of another role

role strain conflicts that someone feels *within* a role

As we go about our everyday lives, we try to control or manage the impressions that we make on others, a process that Goffman called **impression management.** We all want others to think of us in certain ways, and our roles give us an opportunity to influence the ideas that people have of us.

To communicate information about the self, we use three types of **sign-vehicles:** the social setting, our appearance, and our manner. The **social setting** is the place where the action unfolds. This is where the curtain goes up on your performances, where you find yourself on stage playing parts and delivering lines. A social setting might be an office, dorm, living room, church, gym, or bar. It is wherever you interact with others. Your social setting includes *scenery,* the furnishings you use to communicate messages, such as desks, blackboards, scoreboards, couches, and so on.

The second sign-vehicle is **appearance,** or how we look when we play our roles. Appearance includes *props,* which are like scenery except that they decorate the person rather than the setting. The teacher has books, lecture notes, and chalk, while the football player wears a special costume called a uniform. Although few of us carry around a football, we all use makeup, hairstyles, and clothing to communicate messages about ourselves. Props and other aspects of appearance serve as a sort of grease for everyday life: By letting us know what to expect from others, they tell us how we should react. Think of the messages that props communicate. Some people use clothing to say they are college students, others to say they are mature adults. Some use clothing to say they are clergy, others to say they are prostitutes. Similarly, people choose brands of cigarettes, liquor, and automobiles to convey messages about the self. The mass media are highly significant for impressing on us that certain brands will communicate the type of message that we want to give others.

The shape of our body also proclaims messages about the self. The messages that are attached to various shapes change over time, but, as explored in the Mass Media box on pages 116–117, currently thinness screams desirability.

The third sign-vehicle is **manner,** the attitudes we demonstrate as we play our roles. We use manner to communicate information about our feelings and moods. By communicating anger or indifference, sincerity or good humor, for example, we indicate to others what they can expect of us as we play our roles.

We become so used to our roles in everyday life that we tend to think of ourselves as "just doing" things, not preparing for impression management. Yet every time we dress for school, or for any other activity, impression management is exactly what we are doing. Have you ever noticed how your very casually dressed classmates tend to change their appearance on the day they are scheduled to make a report to the class? No one asks them to do so, but their role has changed, and they dress for their slightly modified part. Similarly, you may have noticed that when teenagers begin to date they take several showers a day, stand before a mirror for hours as they comb and recomb their hair, and then change and rechange their clothing until they "get it just right."

In spite of our best efforts to manage the impressions that others receive of us, however, we sometimes fail. One of my favorite television scenes is when the character Molly Dodd tries to impress a date. She goes to the "powder room," a backstage fix-up place reserved for women, where she does the usual things. Satisfied that she looks good, she makes a grand entrance, walking confidently, an expectant smile on her face—all the while trailing a long piece of toilet paper from her shoe. The scene is humorous because it highlights an incongruity of elements, which creates *embarrassment.* In dramaturgical terms, embarrassment is a feeling we get when our performance fails.

Showing ourselves to be adept role players brings positive recognition from others, something we all covet. To accomplish this, said Goffman, we often use **teamwork**—two or more people working together to make certain that a performance goes off as planned. When a performance doesn't come off quite right, however, it may require **face-saving behavior.** We may, for example, ignore someone's flaws in performance, which Goffman defines as *tact.* Suppose your teacher is about to make an important point. Suppose also that her lecturing has been outstanding and the class is hanging on every word. Just as she pauses for emphasis, her stomach lets out a loud growl. She might then use a face-saving

impression management the term used by Erving Goffman to describe people's efforts to control the impressions that others receive of them

sign-vehicles the term used by Goffman to refer to how people use social setting, appearance, and manner to communicate information about the self

social setting the place where the action of everyday life unfolds

appearance how an individual looks when playing a role

manner the attitudes that people show as they play their roles

teamwork the collaboration of two or more people to manage impressions jointly

face-saving behavior techniques used to salvage a performance that is going sour

Mass Media in Social Life

YOU CAN'T BE THIN ENOUGH: BODY IMAGES AND THE MASS MEDIA

When you stand before a mirror, do you like what you see? To make your body more attractive, do you watch your weight? Where do you get your ideas of what you should look like?

Television keeps telling us that something is wrong with our bodies. They aren't good enough, and we've got to improve them. The way to improve them, of course, is to buy the advertised products. Wigs, hair pieces, hair transplants, padded brassieres, diet pills, and exercise equipment. Chuck Norris looks so strong and manly as he touts his full body exerciser. Men get the feeling that their body will look like his if they just buy that machine. Female movie stars effortlessly go through tough workouts without even breaking into a sweat. Women get the feeling that men will fight to be near them if they purchase that wonder-working workout machine.

Although we attempt to shrug off these messages, knowing they are designed to sell products, they get our attention. They penetrate our thinking, helping to shape our image of how we "ought" to look. Those models so attractively clothed and coiffered as they walk down the run-way, could they be any thinner? For women, the message is clear: You can't be thin enough. The men's message is clear, too: You can't be strong enough.

All of us contrast the reality we see when we look in the mirror with our culture's ideal body types. Gwyneth Paltrow, a top U.S. actress, represents an ideal body type that has developed in some parts of Western culture. Partly because of such cultural images, large women sometimes find themselves social outcasts. Consequently, as in the photo on the left, some now band together in support groups to help overcome the emotional impact of their unwelcome status.

technique by remarking, "I was so busy preparing for class that I didn't get breakfast this morning." It is more likely, however, that both class and teacher will simply ignore the sound, both giving the impression that no one heard a thing—a face-saving technique called *studied nonobservance*. This allows the teacher to make the point, or as Goffman would say, it allows the performance to go on.

Before closing this section, we should note that impression management is not limited to individuals. Families, corporations, colleges, sports teams, in fact probably all groups, try to manage impressions. So do nations. An interesting example occurred when the Interna-

Man or woman, your body isn't good enough. It needs to be shaped into something it isn't. It sags where it should be firm. It bulges where it should be smooth. It sticks out where it shouldn't, and it doesn't stick out where it should.

And—no matter what your weight—it's too much. You've got to be thinner.

Exercise takes time, and it's painful getting in shape. Once you do get in shape, it seems to take only a few days for your body to return to its previous slothful, drab appearance if you slack off. You can't let up, you can't exercise enough, and you can't diet enough.

But who can continue at such a pace, striving for what are unrealistic cultural ideals? A few people, of course, but not many. So liposuction is appealing. Just lie there, put up with a little pain, and the doctor will suck the fat right out of you. Surgeons can transform flat breasts into super breasts overnight. They can lower receding hairlines and smooth furrowed brows. They remove lumps with their magical tummy tucks, and take off a decade with their rejuvenating skin peels and face lifts.

With the bosomy girls on Baywatch the envy of all, and the impossibly shaped models at Victoria's Secret the standard to which they hold themselves, even teens call the plastic surgeon. Parents, anxious lest their child violate peer ideals and trail behind in her race for popularity,

foot the bill. In New York City, some parents pay $25,000 to give their daughters a flatter tummy (Gross 1998).

Although peer pressure to alter the body is high, surgeons keep stoking the fire. A sample ad: "No Ifs, Ands or Butts. You Can Change Your Bottom Line in Hours!"

The thinness craze has moved to the East. Glossy magazines in Japan and China are filled with skinny models and crammed with ads touting diet pills and diet teas. In China, where famine used to abound, a little extra padding was valued as a sign of good health. Today, the obsession is thinness (Rosenthal 1999). Not-so-subtle ads scream that fat is bad. Some teas come with a package of diet pills. Weight-loss machines, with electrodes attached to acupuncture pressure points, not only reduce fat, but they also build breasts. Or so the advertisers claim.

Not limited by some of our rules, advertisers in Japan and China push a soap that supposedly "sucks up fat through the skin's pores" (Marshall 1995). What a dream product! After all, even though those TV models smile as they go through their paces, those exercise machines really do look like a lot of hard work.

In the United States, there is another bottom line. Beauty and attractiveness do pay off. Economists studied physical attractiveness and earnings. The result? "Average-looking" men and women earn more than

"plain" people, and "good-looking" men and women earn even more. The "ugly" are paid a pittance. "Attractive" women have an added cash advantage—they attract and marry higher earning men (Hamermesh and Biddle 1994).

More popularity *and* more money? Maybe you can't be thin enough. Maybe those exercise machines are a good investment after all. If only we could catch up with the Japanese and develop a soap that would suck the fat right out of our pores. You can practically hear the jingle now. ■

For Your Consideration

What image do you have of your body? How do cultural expectations of "ideal" bodies underlie your image? Can you recall any advertisement or television program that has affected your body image?

Most advertising and television programs that focus on weight are directed at women. Women are more concerned than men about weight, more likely to have eating disorders, and more likely to express dissatisfaction with their bodies (Honeycutt 1995). Do you think that the targeting of women in advertising creates these attitudes and behaviors? Or do you think that these attitudes and behaviors would exist even if there were no such ads? Why?

tional Olympic Committee was looking for a nation to host the 2000 Summer Olympic games. Because hosting these games is so prestigious, the committee had a long list of candidates from which to choose. To impress the committee, China tried to put on a different face, to show that it was no longer repressive. With fanfare, China released a noted political prisoner a generous six months before he had finished serving his fifteen-year sentence (Brauchli 1993a). That this was impression management only, not a fundamental change in national policy, soon became apparent. After China lost its bid for the games, the repression of political dissenters resumed in earnest.

All of us have background assumptions, deeply ingrained expectations of how the world operates. They lay the groundwork for what we expect will happen in our interactions. How do you think the background assumptions of these two people differ?

Ethnomethodology: Uncovering Background Assumptions

As discussed in Chapter 1, symbolic interactionists stress that the events of life do not come with built-in meanings. Rather, we give meaning to things by classifying them. When we place objects and events into the classifications provided by our culture, we are doing more than naming things—we are interpreting our world.

Ethnomethodologists study how people make sense of life. They try to uncover people's basic assumptions as they interpret their everyday worlds. To better understand **ethnomethodology,** consider the word's three basic components. *"Ethno"* means folk or people; *"method"* means how people do something; *"ology"* means "the study of." Putting them together, then, *ethno/method/ology* means "the study of how people do things." Specifically, ethnomethodologists study how people use commonsense understandings to get through everyday life.

Let's suppose that you go to a doctor and she says that she doesn't feel like "doing doctoring" today. She then comments on how long your hair is, takes out a pair of scissors, and tries to give you a haircut. This would violate basic assumptions about what doctors are supposed to do. At the very least, we expect our doctor to listen to our medical problems and prescribe medicines. Haircuts, however, are simply not part of our expectations.

These assumptions about the way life is and the way things ought to work (what ethnomethodologists call **background assumptions**) lie at the root of social life. Exactly how these background assumptions work is what ethnomethodologists try to discover. Background assumptions are so deeply embedded in our consciousness that we are seldom aware of them, and most of us fulfill them unquestioningly. Thus, your doctor does not offer you a haircut, even if he or she is good at cutting hair and you need one!

The founder of ethnomethodology, sociologist Harold Garfinkel, conducted some interesting exercises designed to uncover our background assumptions. Garfinkel (1967) asked his students to act as though they did not understand the basic rules of social life. Some tried to bargain with supermarket clerks; others would inch closer to people and stare directly at them. They were met with surprise, bewilderment, even anger. One of the more interesting exercises that Garfinkel's students conducted was to act as though they were boarders in their own homes. When they returned from class they addressed their parents as "Mr." and "Mrs.," asked permission to use the bathroom, sat stiffly, were extremely courteous, and spoke only when spoken to. The other family members were stupefied (Garfinkel 1967):

> They vigorously sought to make the strange actions intelligible and to restore the situation to normal appearances. Reports (by the students) were filled with accounts of astonishment, bewilderment, shock, anxiety, embarrassment, and anger, and with charges by various family members that the student was mean, inconsiderate, selfish, nasty, or impolite. Family members demanded explanations: What's the matter? What's gotten into you? . . . Are you sick? . . . Are you out of your mind or are you just stupid?

ethnomethodology the study of how people use background assumptions to make sense out of life

background assumptions deeply embedded common understandings, or basic rules, concerning our view of the world and of how people ought to act

In another exercise Garfinkel asked students to take words and phrases literally. This is what happened when one student asked his girlfriend what she meant when she said that she had a flat tire:

> What do you mean, "What do you mean?"? A flat tire is a flat tire. That is what I meant. Nothing special. What a crazy question!

Another conversation went like this:

> *Acquaintance:* How are you?
>
> *Student:* How am I in regard to what? My health, my finances, my schoolwork, my peace of mind, my . . . ?
>
> *Acquaintance* (red in the face): Look! I was just trying to be polite. Frankly, I don't give a damn how you are.

Students who are directed to break background assumptions can be highly creative. The young children of one of my students were surprised one morning when they came down for breakfast to find a sheet spread across the living room floor. On it were dishes, silverware, burning candles—and ice cream. They, too, wondered what was going on—but they dug eagerly into the ice cream before their mother could change her mind.

■ **In Sum** Ethnomethodologists explore background assumptions, our taken-for-granted ideas about the world, which underlie our behavior and are violated only with risk. These basic rules of social life are an essential part of the social structure. Deeply embedded in our minds, they give us basic directions for living everyday life. Although our background assumptions often lie beneath our level of awareness, we depend on them to guide us through everyday life.

The Social Construction of Reality

Usually we assume that reality is something that exists independent of ourselves. Symbolic interactionists, however, point out that we define our own realities and then live within those definitions. As sociologist W. I. Thomas said, in what has become known as the **Thomas theorem,** "If people define situations as real, they are real in their consequences." Consider the following incident:

> On a visit to Morocco, in northern Africa, I decided to buy a watermelon. When I indicated to the street vendor that the knife he was going to use to cut the watermelon was dirty (encrusted with filth would be more apt), he was very obliging. He immediately bent down and began to swish the knife in a puddle on the street. I shuddered as I looked at the passing burros that were freely defecating and urinating as they went by. Quickly, I indicated by gesture that I preferred my melon uncut after all.

For that vendor, germs did not exist. For me, they did. And each of us acted according to our definition of the situation. My perception and behavior did not come from the fact that germs are real but *because I grew up in a society that teaches they are real.* Microbes, of course, *objectively* exist, and whether or not germs are part of our thought world makes no difference to whether we are infected by them. Our behavior, however, does not depend on the *objective* existence of something but, rather, on our *subjective interpretation,* on what sociologists call our *definition of reality.* In other words, it is not the reality of microbes that impresses itself on us, but society that impresses the reality of microbes on us.

Let's consider another example. Do you remember the identical twins, Oskar and Jack, who grew up so differently? As discussed on page 65, Jack was reared in Trinidad and learned to hate Hitler, while Oskar was reared in Germany and learned to love Hitler. Thus what Hitler meant to Oskar and Jack (and what he means to us) depends not on Hitler's acts, but, rather, on how we view his acts, that is, on our definition of the situation.

This is what **the social construction of reality** is. Our society, or the social groups to which we belong, have their particular views of life. From our groups (the *social* part of this process), we learn specific ways of looking at life—whether that be our view of Hitler (he's good, he's bad), germs (they exist, they don't exist), or *anything else in life.* In short, through our interaction with others, we *construct reality*; that is, we learn ways of looking at our experiences in life.

Gynecological Examinations To better understand the social construction of reality, let's consider an extended example.

Thomas theorem William I. Thomas' classic formulation of the definition of the situation: "If people define situations as real, they are real in their consequences."

the social construction of reality the process by which people use their background assumptions and life experiences to define what is real for them

A gynecological nurse, Mae Biggs, and I did research on pelvic examinations. Reviewing about 14,000 cases, we looked at how the medical profession constructs social reality in order to define this examination as nonsexual (Henslin and Biggs 1971/1999). This desexualization is accomplished by painstakingly controlling the sign-vehicles—the setting, appearance, and manner.

The pelvic examination unfolds much as a stage play does. I will use "he" to refer to the physician because only male physicians participated in this study. Perhaps the results would be different with female gynecologists.

Scene 1 (the patient as person) In this scene, the doctor maintains eye contact with his patient, calls her by name, and discusses her problems in a professional manner. If he decides that a vaginal examination is necessary, he tells a nurse, "Pelvic in room 1." By this statement, he is announcing that a major change will occur in the next scene.

Scene 2 (from person to pelvic) This scene is the depersonalizing stage. In line with the doctor's announcement, the patient begins the transition from a "person" to a "pelvic." The doctor leaves the room, and a female nurse enters to help the patient make the transition. The nurse prepares the "props" for the coming examination and answers any questions the woman might have.

What occurs at this point is essential for the social construction of reality, for *the doctor's absence removes even the suggestion of sexuality.* To undress in front of him could suggest either a striptease or intimacy, thus undermining the reality so carefully being defined, that of nonsexuality.

The patient also wants to remove any hint of sexuality in the coming interaction, and during this scene she may express concern about what to do with her panties. Some mutter to the nurse, "I don't want him to see these." Most women solve the problem by either slipping their panties under their clothes or placing them in their purse.

Scene 3 (the person as pelvic) This scene opens when the doctor enters the room. Before him is a woman lying on a table, her feet in stirrups, her knees tightly together, and her body covered by a drape sheet. The doctor seats himself on a low stool before the woman, tells her, "Let your knees fall apart" (rather than the sexually loaded "Spread your legs"), and begins the examination.

The drape sheet is critical in this process of desexualization, for it *dissociates the pelvic area from the person:* Bending forward and with the drape sheet above his head, the physician can see only the vagina, not the patient's face. Thus dissociated from the individual, the vagina is dramaturgically transformed into an object of analysis. If the doctor examines the patient's breasts, he also dissociates them from her person by examining them one at a time, with a towel covering the unexamined breast. Like the vagina, each breast becomes an isolated unit dissociated from the person.

In this critical scene, the patient cooperates in being an object, becoming for all practical purposes a pelvis to be examined. She withdraws eye contact from the doctor, usually from the nurse as well, is likely to stare at the wall or at the ceiling, and avoids initiating conversation.

Scene 4 (from pelvic to person) In this scene the patient becomes "repersonalized." The doctor has left the examining room; the patient dresses and tends to her hair and makeup. Her reemergence as a person is indicated by such statements to the nurse as "My dress isn't too wrinkled, is it?" indicating a need for reassurance that the metamorphosis from "pelvic" back to "person" has been completed satisfactorily.

Scene 5 (the patient as person) In this scene, the patient is once again treated as a person rather than as an object. The doctor makes eye contact with her and addresses her by name. She, too, makes eye contact with the doctor, and the usual middle-class interaction patterns are followed. She has been fully restored.

■ **In Sum** To an outsider to our culture, the custom of women going to a male stranger for a vaginal examination might seem bizarre. But not to us. We assume that such behavior is normal, and females in our society are encouraged to participate in this process because they have learned that pelvic examinations are nonsexual. To sustain this definition requires teamwork—patients, doctors, and nurses working together to jointly produce this definition of reality. Thus, sociologists say that we *socially construct reality*.

Although pelvic examinations are socially constructed as nonsexual, many women still cannot rid themselves of uncomfortable feelings during this procedure, especially if their physician is a man. As the second wave of feminism gathered force in the 1960s and 1970s, women revealed this discomfort to one another. At this time, when less than 10 percent of obstetricians and gynecologists were female, some women decided to take back control of their reproductive health. Meeting in "consciousness raising" groups, they taught themselves how to examine their own bodies.

Since then, the situation has changed radically, and today about 40 percent of obstetricians and gynecologists are women. Even more startling, 72 percent of first year ob/gyn residents are women (Council on Resident Education in Obstetrics and Gynecology, 2000). How this changed sex ratio may affect the ways that pelvic examinations—and medicine itself—are socially constructed is yet to unfold. Whatever the particulars may be, the same principles will apply: Team players will work together to maintain agreed-on definitions of the situation.

The social construction of reality is not limited to small segments of social life, such as to medical procedures or watermelons in Africa. Rather, it is an essential part of our everyday lives, for our behavior depends on how we define reality. To understand human behavior—whether that be how people react to microbes, to a photo of Hitler or the swastika, to pelvic examinations, or to anything else in life—we need to know how people define reality.

THE NEED FOR BOTH MACROSOCIOLOGY AND MICROSOCIOLOGY

As noted earlier in this chapter, to understand social life we need both microsociology and macrosociology. Each makes a vital contribution to our understanding of human behavior, and our understanding would be vastly incomplete without one or the other.

To illustrate this point, consider the research on two groups of high school boys, conducted by sociologist William Chambliss (1973/1999). Both groups attended Hanibal High School. In one group were eight boys who came from "good" families and were perceived by the community as "going somewhere." Chambliss calls this group the "Saints." The other group consisted of six lower-class boys who were seen as going down a dead-end road. Chambliss calls this group the "Roughnecks."

Both groups were seriously delinquent. Both skipped school, got drunk, and committed criminal acts, especially fighting and vandalism. The Saints were actually somewhat more delinquent, for they were truant more often and engaged in more vandalism. Yet it was the Saints who had a good reputation, while the Roughnecks were seen by teachers, the police, and the general community as no good and headed for trouble.

These reputations followed the boys throughout life. Seven of the eight Saints went on to graduate from college. Three studied for advanced degrees: One finished law school and became active in state politics, one finished medical school and set up a practice near Hanibal, and one went on to earn a Ph.D. The four other college graduates entered managerial or executive training programs with large firms. After his parents divorced, one Saint failed to graduate from high school on time and had to repeat his senior year. Although this boy tried to go to college by attending night school, he never finished. He was unemployed the last time Chambliss saw him.

In contrast, only four of the Roughnecks even finished high school. Two of these boys did exceptionally well in sports and received athletic scholarships to college. They both graduated from college and became high school coaches. Of the two others who graduated from high school, one became a small-time gambler and the other disappeared "up north," where he was last reported to be driving a truck. Both of the two who did not complete high school were sentenced to state penitentiaries for separate murders.

To understand what happened to the Saints and the Roughnecks, we need to grasp *both* social structure and social interaction. That is, we need both macrosociology and microsociology. Using *macrosociology,* we can place these boys within the larger framework of the U.S. social class system. This context reveals how opportunities open or close to people depending on their membership in the middle or lower social class, and how people learn different goals as they grow up in vastly different groups. We can then use *microsociology* to follow their everyday lives. We can see how the Saints used their "good" reputations to skip classes repeatedly, and how their access to automobiles allowed them to transfer their troublemaking to different communities and thus prevent damage to their local reputations. In contrast, the Roughnecks, who had no cars, were highly visible. Their lawbreaking activities, which were limited to a small area, readily came to the attention of the community. Microsociology also reveals how their respective reputations opened doors of opportunity to the first group of boys while closing them to the other.

Thus we need both kinds of sociology, and both will be stressed in the following chapters.

SUMMARY AND REVIEW

■ Levels of Sociological Analysis

What two levels of analysis do sociologists use?

Sociologists use macro- and microsociological levels of analysis. In **macrosociology**, the focus is placed on large-scale features of social life, while in **microsociology**, the focus is on **social interaction**. Functionalists and conflict theorists tend to use a macrosociological approach, while symbolic interactionists are more likely to use a microsociological approach. Pp. 96–97.

■ The Macrosociological Perspective: Social Structure

How does social structure influence our behavior?

The term **social structure** refers to a society's framework, which forms an envelope around us and establishes limits on our behavior. Social structure consists of culture, social class, social statuses, roles, groups, and social institutions. Together these serve as foundations for how we view the world.

Our location in the social structure underlies our perceptions, attitudes, and behaviors. **Culture** lays the broadest framework, while **social class** divides people according to income, education, and occupational prestige. Each of us receives **ascribed statuses** at birth; later we add various **achieved statuses**. Our behaviors and orientations are further influenced by the **roles** we play, the groups to which we belong, and our experiences with the institutions of our society. These components of society work together to help maintain social order. Pp. 97–102.

■ Social Institutions

What are social institutions?

Social institutions are the organized and standard means that a society develops to meet its basic needs. As summarized in Figure 4.1, industrilized societies have nine social institutions–the family, religion, law, politics, economics, education, medicine, science, and the military, with a tenth, the mass media, emerging. From the functionalist perspective, social institutions meet universal group needs, or **functional requisites**. Conflict theorists stress how society's elite uses social institutions to maintain its privileged position. Pp. 102-106.

When social change transforms a society, how does it manage to hold together?

In agricultural societies, said Emile Durkheim, people are united by **mechanical solidarity** (similar views and feelings). With industrialization comes **organic solidarity** (people depend on one another to do their jobs). Ferdinand Tönnies pointed out that the informal means of control of *Gemeinschaft* (small, intimate) societies are replaced by formal mechanisms in *Gesellschaft* (larger, more impersonal) societies. Pp. 106–108.

■ The Microsociological Perspective: Social Interaction in Everyday Life

What is the focus of symbolic interactionism?

In contrast to functionalists and conflict theorists, who as macrosociologists focus on the "big picture," symbolic interactionists tend to be microsociologists who focus on face-to-face social interaction. Symbolic interactionists analyze how people define their worlds, and how their definitions, in turn, influence their behavior. P. 108.

How do stereotypes affect social interaction?

Stereotypes are assumptions of what people are like. When we first meet people, we classify them according to our perceptions of their visible characteristics and our ideas about those characteristics. These assumptions guide our behavior toward them, which, in turn, influences them to behave in ways that tend to reinforce our stereotypes. Pp. 108–110.

Do all human groups share a similar sense of personal space?

In examining how people use physical space, symbolic interactionists stress that we surround ourselves with a "personal bubble" that we carefully protect. People from different cultures use "personal bubbles" of varying sizes, so the answer to the question is no. Americans typically use four different "distance zones": intimate, personal, social, and public. Pp. 110–112.

What is dramaturgy?

Erving Goffman developed **dramaturgy** (or dramaturgical analysis), which analyzes everyday life in terms of the stage. At the core of this analysis is **impression management,** our attempts to control the impressions we make on others. For this, we use the **sign-vehicles** of setting, appearance, and manner. Our performances often call for teamwork and **face-saving behavior.** Pp. 113–119.

What is the social construction of reality?

The phrase **the social construction of reality** refers to how we construct our views of the world. **Ethnomethodology** is the study of how people make sense of everyday life. Ethnomethodologists try to uncover **background assumptions,** our basic ideas about the way life is. Pp. 119–121.

■ The Need for Both Macrosociology and Microsociology

Why are both levels of analysis important?

Because each focuses on different aspects of the human experience, both microsociology and macrosociology are necessary for us to understand social life. Pp. 121–122.

Where can I read more on this topic?

Suggested Readings for this chapter are at the back of this book.

Sociology & the Internet

All URLs listed are current as of the printing of this book. URLs often change. Please check our Web site, **http://www.abacon.com/henslin,** for updates.

1. The power of the media raises questions not only about who controls the flow of information but also about what information is being distributed. As this chapter suggests, one of the norms governing the media is for reporters to be accurate and fair in their reporting of information. However, they don't always follow this norm. Consequently, organizations have formed to act as watchdogs over the media. One such organization with a Web site is FAIR, accessed at **http://www.fair.org/.** Go to this site and investigate the purpose of the organization. How does this organization identify biased reporting? What examples does it provide of biases that it has found in the media? What action does it take when it discovers bias? How might a sociologist with a functionalist orientation explain the biases? How about a conflict theorist? Write a paper in which you explore these questions.

2. The creation of "intentional communities" represents an attempt to restore *Gemeinschaft* to modern living. You can find information on these communities by going to **http://yahoo.com** and clicking first on "Society and Culture," then "Culture and Groups," and finally "Intentional Communities." Browse several of the sites for specific communities. What are the main characteristics of intentional communities? Look for *Gemeinschaft* elements featured in the descriptions, as well as any *Gesellschaft* components that may be there. Write a report comparing the emphases of the different communities you explored. What characteristics of postindustrial societies draw people to intentional communities?

3. After reading the Perspectives box in this chapter about how the Amish form a *Gemeinschaft* community within a *Gesellschaft* society, go to the following web sites:

   http://www.800padutch.com

   http://www.holycrosslivonia.org/amish/index.html

   http://www.religioustolerance.org/amish.htm

   http://www.amish-heartland.com/index.htm

   These web sites provide a look into the world of the Amish, which is very different from mainstream America. However, as you apply your sociological eye, you will begin to see similarities between the two worlds. Discuss the similarities in the social institutions of the Amish and U.S. society. Does Amish society contain all nine social institutions? How are the institutions of family, religion, law, education, and medicine similar in the two societies?

4. This chapter introduces the concept of "role conflict." A good example of role conflict is the woman who must juggle the demands of her role as a mother with those of her role as a worker. You can read accounts of how real working mothers try to handle the conflicting demands at these Web sites:

   http://www.worknwoman.com/worknmom

   http://momsrefuge.com/juggling/index.html

   What are some of the day-to-day issues these women face? What are some of the solutions offered at these Web sites? Prepare a report to the class concerning role conflict—what causes it and how the conflict can be reduced.

How Sociologists Do Research

- **What Is a Valid Sociological Topic?**

- **Common Sense and the Need for Sociological Research**

- **A Research Model**
  1. Selecting a Topic
  2. Defining the Problem
  3. Reviewing the Literature
  4. Formulating a Hypothesis
  5. Choosing a Research Method
  6. Collecting the Data
  7. Analyzing the Results
  8. Sharing the Results

- **Research Methods**
  Surveys
  Participant Observation (Fieldwork)

  Secondary Analysis
  Documents
  Unobtrusive Measures
  Experiments
  Deciding Which Method to Use

- **Gender in Sociological Research**

- **Ethics in Sociological Research**
  Protecting the Subjects: The Brajuha Research
  Misleading the Subjects: The Humphreys Research

- **How Research and Theory Work Together**
  The Real World: When the Ideal Meets the Real

- **Summary and Review**

Cindy Hudo, a 21-year-old mother of two in Charleston, South Carolina, who was charged with the murder of her husband, Buba, said:

I start in the car, and I get down the road, and I see Buba walking, and he's real mad. . . . I pull over, you know, and [I said] "I didn't know to pick you up. You know, I'm sorry." And he didn't even say nothing to me. He just started hitting on me. And that's all I wanted to do, was just get home, because I was just self-conscious. I don't want nobody to see him hitting me, because I didn't want him to look bad.

I had to go to work in a half-hour, because I was working a double-shift. And he told me I had forty minutes to get all my furniture out of the house and get my clothes and be out or he was going to throw them out. And I was sitting there, because I could talk him down. You know, because I didn't want to leave him. I just talked to him. I said, "Buba, I don't want to leave." I said, "This is my house." And then he told me . . . (unclear) . . . "my kids." And I said, "No, you're not taking my kids from me. That's too much." And so I said, "Just let me leave. Just let me take the kids.

And, you know I'll go, and you know, I won't keep the kids from you or nothing like that." And he said, "I'm going to take them, and you're getting out."

[After they went inside their trailer, Buba threatened to shoot Cindy. He loaded a shotgun, pointed it at her, and said]: "The only way you're going to get out of this is if you kill me, and I'll—I'll kill you." [Buba gave me the shotgun and] turned around and walked right down the hall, because he knew I wouldn't do nothing. And I just sat there a minute. And I don't know what happened. I just, you know, I went to the bedroom, and I seen him laying there, and I just shot him. He moved. I shot him again because I thought he was going to get up again. . . .

I loved him too much. And I just wanted to help him. ■

Source: ABC Television, *20/20*, October 18, 1979

WHAT IS A VALID SOCIOLOGICAL TOPIC?

Sociologists do research on just about every area of human behavior. On the macro level, they study such broad matters as the military (Moscos and Butler 1997), race relations (Wilson 1996), and multinational corporations (Kanter et al. 1997). On the micro level, they study such individualistic matters as pelvic examinations (Henslin and Biggs 1999), how people interact on street corners (Whyte 1989, 1999), and even how people decorate their homes at Christmas (Caplow 1991). In fact, no human behavior is ineligible for sociological scrutiny—whether that behavior is routine or unusual, respectable or reprehensible.

What happened to Cindy and Buba, then, is also a valid topic of sociological research. But exactly *how* would you research spouse abuse? As we look at how sociologists conduct their research, we shall try to answer this question.

COMMON SENSE AND THE NEED FOR SOCIOLOGICAL RESEARCH

First, why do we need sociological research? Why can't we simply depend on common sense, on "what everyone knows"? As noted in Chapter 1 (pages 8–10), commonsense ideas may or may not be true. Common sense, for example, tells us that spouse abuse has a significant impact on the lives of the people who are abused.

Although this particular idea is accurate, we need research to test commonsense ideas, because not all such ideas are true. After all, common sense also tells us that if a woman is abused she will pack up and leave her husband. Research, however, shows that the reality of abuse is much more complicated than this. Some women do leave right away, some even after the first incident of abuse. For a variety of reasons, however—the main one being that they feel trapped and don't see viable alternatives—some women suffer abuse for years.

This brings us to the need for sociological research, for we may want to know why some women put up with abuse, while others don't. Or we may want to know something entirely different, such as why men are more likely to be the abusers. Or why some people abuse the people they say they love.

In order to answer a question, we need to move beyond guesswork and common sense. We want to *know* what is really going on. To find out, sociologists do research on about every aspect of social life. Let's look at how they do their research.

A RESEARCH MODEL

As shown in Figure 5.1, scientific research follows eight basic steps. Before we review this figure, I need to point out that this is an ideal model, and in the real world of research some of these steps may run together. Some may even be omitted.

1. Selecting a Topic

The first step is to select a topic. What do you want to know more about? Many sociologists simply follow their curiosity, their drive to know. They become interested in a particular topic, and they pursue it, as I did in studying the homeless. Some sociologists choose a topic because funding

Because sociologists find all human behavior to be valid research topics, their research runs from the unusual to the routines of everyday life. On the macro level, they study how voting patterns are related to religion, and on the micro level they study tattoo contests, such as this one in New York City's East Village. Their analyses range from such intensely individual acts as suicide to such broad-scale social change as the globalization of capitalism.

Figure 5.1 THE RESEARCH MODEL

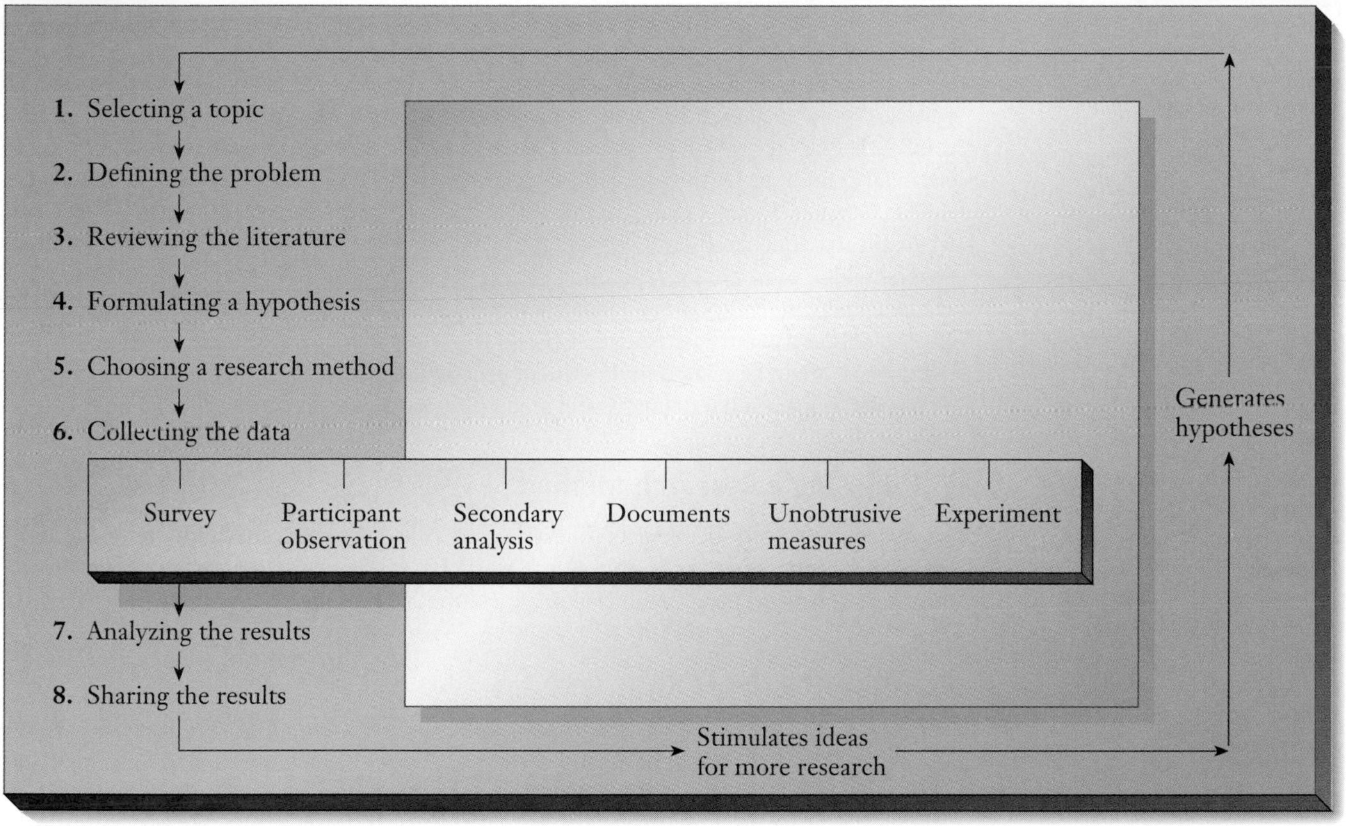

1. Selecting a topic
2. Defining the problem
3. Reviewing the literature
4. Formulating a hypothesis
5. Choosing a research method
6. Collecting the data

| Survey | Participant observation | Secondary analysis | Documents | Unobtrusive measures | Experiment |

7. Analyzing the results
8. Sharing the results

Generates hypotheses

Stimulates ideas for more research

Source: Modification of Fig. 2.2 of Schaefer 1989.

is available for that topic, others because a social problem such as domestic violence has become a pressing social issue, and the sociologist wants to gather data that will help people better understand it—and perhaps to help solve it.

2. Defining the Problem

The second step is to define the problem, to specify exactly what you want to learn about the topic. My interest in the homeless grew until I wanted to learn about homelessness across the nation. Ordinarily, sociologists' interests are much more focused than this. They develop a researchable question that focuses on a specific area or problem. For example, they may want to compare the work experiences of homeless women and men. Or they may want to know what can be done to reduce spouse abuse.

Although sociologists study social problems such as homelessness and spouse abuse, they also conduct research on any aspect of social life that interests them. The "problem" can be as earth shattering as why nations would ever contemplate nuclear war or as simple as wanting to find out why Native Americans like Westerns (see the Mass Media box on page 52).

3. Reviewing the Literature

The third step is to review the literature to see what is already written on the problem. This helps the researcher narrow down the problem, identify areas that are already known, and pinpoint areas that need to be examined. Reviewing the literature may also provide ideas about what questions to ask. A researcher may even find out that the problem has been answered already. Then there is no need to do the research, for no one wants to reinvent the wheel.

hypothesis a statement of the expected relationship between variables according to predictions from a theory

variable a factor or concept thought to be significant for human behavior, which varies from one case to another

operational definitions the way in which a variable in a hypothesis is measured

research method (or research design) one of six procedures sociologists use to collect data: surveys, participant observation, secondary analysis, documents, unobtrusive measures, and experiments

validity the extent to which an operational definition measures what it was intended to measure

reliability the extent to which research produces consistent results

4. Formulating a Hypothesis

The fourth step is to formulate a **hypothesis,** a statement of what you expect to find according to predictions from a theory. A hypothesis predicts a relationship between or among **variables,** factors that change, or vary, from one person or situation to another. For example, the statement, "Men who are more socially isolated are more likely to abuse their wives than are men who are more socially integrated" is a hypothesis. Hypotheses need **operational definitions**—that is, precise ways to measure their variables. In this example, we would need operational definitions for three variables: social isolation, social integration, and spouse abuse.

In Chapter 4 (page 112), we noted that men and women patients reacted differently when a nurse touched them before surgery. Women felt soothed, and their blood pressure dropped. Men grew anxious, and their blood pressure went up (Thayer 1988). The experimenter's suggested explanation that the men found it harder than the women to acknowledge dependency and fear, and that the touch was a reminder of their vulnerability, is a hypothesis. It can be related to theories of gender and sex roles. To test this hypothesis, we would need operational definitions of anxiety, dependency, fear, and vulnerability.

5. Choosing a Research Method

The means by which sociologists collect data are called **research methods** (or research designs). Sociologists use six basic research methods, selecting the one that will best answer their particular questions. We'll examine these methods in the next section.

6. Collecting the Data

The next step is to gather the data. Sociologists take great care to assure both the validity and reliability of their data. **Validity** refers to whether the operational definitions really measure what they are intended to measure. For example, how should we measure social isolation and integration? Would it be enough to simply find out how often someone interacts with other people? That would be simple enough, but don't we also have to measure how much the individual identifies with others, or feels a part of a group? This would be a much more difficult matter, but isn't this part of integration? Even an operational definition for spouse abuse isn't simple to determine. For example, acts that are an accepted part of everyday life in some cultures and subcultures are viewed as abuse by people from other groups. Whose definition of abuse would we use? After grappling with such problems, our operational definitions must make sense *and* be so precise that no one has any question about what we are measuring.

The term **reliability** refers to the extent to which different studies come up with similar results. If one study shows that 10 percent of the women in a certain city have been the victims of spouse abuse, while another study finds that it is 1 percent, you can see why sociologists use the term "unreliable" to describe the findings. What hurts reliability are inadequate operational definitions and sampling (to be covered later). If these are adequate, two studies of domestic violence in the same city should show similar results (that is, be reliable).

7. Analyzing the Results

After the data are gathered, it is time to analyze them. To do this, sociologists use qualitative and quantitative techniques. *Qualitative* analysis is especially useful for data gathered by participant observation. Sociologists classify books, movies, television programs, and

A major concern of sociologists and other social scientists is that their research methods do not influence their findings. Respondents often change their behavior when they know they are being studied.

"Anthropologists! Anthropologists!"

people's conversations in order to identify the main themes. The goal is to faithfully reproduce the world of the people being studied. In my research on cabdrivers, for example, I (1967, 1993) tried to picture the world as cabbies see it so anyone reading the analysis would understand not just what cabbies do but also why they do it.

Quantitative analysis involves crunching numbers. This is especially useful for testing hypotheses, which is done at this stage. The computer, which has become an especially powerful tool for quantitative analysis, has four main values for sociologists. First, it allows sociologists to analyze huge amounts of information and identify basic patterns. Second, current software programs take much of the drudgery out of analyzing data. What used to take tedious hours, and even days or weeks of mathematical analysis can now be performed in an instant. Third, researchers can try various statistical tests to see which prove the most valuable for their data. Fourth, freed from the time-consuming tasks of number crunching, researchers can think more about what those numbers mean. The basic programs that sociologists, even many undergraduates, learn are Microcase and the Statistical Package for the Social Sciences (SPSS). Some software, such as the Methodologist's Toolchest, provides advice about collecting data, including sample size, and even about ethical issues.

8. Sharing the Results

After analyzing the data, it is time to wrap up the research (or, if it is a broad project, at least some part of it). In this step, the researchers write a report to share their findings with the scientific community. To help others evaluate the research, the report includes a review of these first steps. It also shows how their findings are related to the literature, reviews what has already been published on the topic, and shows how their findings support or refute the theories that apply to the topic.

When research is published, usually in a scientific journal or a book, it "belongs" to the scientific community. Table 5.1 on the next page is an example of published research. These findings are available for **replication**; that is, others can repeat the study to see if they come up with similar results. As finding is added to finding, scientific knowledge builds.

Let's look in greater detail at the fifth step to see what research methods sociologists use.

RESEARCH METHODS

To gather data, sociologists use six research methods (or "research designs"): surveys, participant observation, secondary analysis, documents, unobtrusive measures, and experiments. To understand these strategies, let's continue our example of spouse abuse. As we do so, note how the method we would choose depends on the questions we want to answer. Because researchers often want to know what "average" is so they can have a yardstick for comparison, we discuss three measures of average in Table 5.2 on page 131.

Surveys

Let's suppose that your goal is to know how many wives are abused each year. Some husbands are also abused, of course, but let's assume that you are going to focus on wives. An appropriate method for this purpose would be the **survey**, in which you would ask people a series of questions. Before using this method, however, you must deal with practical matters that face all researchers—selecting a sample, asking neutral questions, using questionnaires or interviews, and establishing rapport. Let's look at each of these practical problems.

Selecting a Sample   If you had your way, you might want to learn about all wives in the world. Obviously, however, your resources will not permit such a study, and you must narrow your **population**, the target group that you are going to study.

Let's assume that your resources (money, helpers, time) are very limited. They allow you to investigate wife abuse only on your college campus. Let's also suppose that your college

Table 5.1		

HOW TO READ A TABLE

Comparing Violent and Nonviolent Husbands

Based on interviews with 150 husbands and wives in a Midwestern city who were getting a divorce.

Husband's Achievement and Job Satisfaction	Violent Husbands $n = 25$	Nonviolent Husbands $n = 125$
He started but failed to complete high school or college.	44%	27%
He is very dissatisfied with his job.	44%	18%
His income is a source of constant conflict.	84%	24%
He has less education than his wife.	56%	14%
His job has less prestige than his father-in-law's.	37%	28%

Source: Modification of Table 1 in O'Brien 1975.

A table is a concise way of presenting information. Because sociological findings are often presented in tabular form, it is important to understand how to read a table. Tables contain six elements: title, headnote, headings, columns, rows, and source. When you understand how these elements work together, you know how to read a table.

1. The *title* states the topic of a table. It is located at the top of the table. What is the title of this table? Please determine your answer before looking at the correct answer below.

2. The *headnote* is not always included in a table. When it is, it is located just below the title. Its purpose is to give more detailed information about how the data were collected or how data are presented in the table. What are the first seven words of the headnote of this table?

3. The *headings* tell what kind of information is contained in the table. There are three headings in this table. What are they? In the second heading, what does $n = 25$ mean?

4. The *columns* present information arranged vertically. What is the fourth number in the second column and the second number in the third column?

5. The *rows* present information arranged horizontally. In the fourth row, which husbands are more likely to have less education than their wives?

6. The *source* of a table, usually listed at the bottom, provides information on where the data shown in the table originated. Often, as in this instance, the information is specific enough for you to consult the original source. What is the source for this table?

Some tables are much more complicated than this one, but all follow the same basic pattern. To apply these concepts to a table with more information, see page 339.

Answers

1. Comparing Violent and Nonviolent Husbands.
2. Based on interviews with 150 husbands and
3. Husband's Achievement and Job Satisfaction, Violent Husbands, Nonviolent Husbands. The *n* is an abbreviation for number, and *n* = 25 means there were 25 in the sample of violent husbands.
4. 56%, 18%.
5. Violent husbands.
6. A 1975 article by O'Brien (listed in the References section of this text).

---

sample the individuals intended to represent the population to be studied

random sample a sample in which everyone in the target population has the same chance of being included in the study

stratified random sample a sample of specific subgroups of the target population in which everyone in the subgroups has an equal chance of being included in the study

enrollment is large, so you won't be able to survey all the married women who are enrolled. To do your research, you must select a **sample**, individuals from among your target population. How you choose a sample is critical, for the choice will affect the results of your study. For example, if you surveyed only freshmen—or only seniors, or only those enrolled in introductory sociology or advanced physics classes—you would end up with skewed results.

To be able to generalize your findings to the entire campus, you must select a sample that represents the campus (called a "representative sample"). What kind of sample will allow you to do this?

The best is a **random sample**. This does *not* mean that you stand on some campus corner and ask questions of any woman who happens to walk by. *In a random sample, everyone in your population has the same chance of being included in the study.* In this case, since the population is every married woman enrolled in your college, all married women—whether first-year or graduate students, whether they are taking introductory

Table 5.2

THREE WAYS TO MEASURE "AVERAGE"

The Mean

The term *average* seems clear enough. As you learned in grade school, to find the average you add a group of numbers and then divide the total by the number of cases that were added. For example, assume that the following numbers represent men convicted of battering their wives:

321
229
57
289
136
57
1,795

The total is 2,884. Divided by 7 (the number of cases), the average is 412. Sociologists call this form of average the *mean*.

The mean can be deceptive because it is strongly influenced by extreme scores, either low or high. Note that six of the seven cases are less than the mean.

Two other ways to compute averages are the median and the mode.

The Median

To compute the second average, the *median,* first arrange the cases in order—either from the highest to the lowest or the lowest to the highest. In this example, that arrangement will produce the following distribution:

57
57
136
229
289
321
1,795

Then look for the middle case, the one that falls halfway between the top and the bottom. That figure is 229, for three numbers are lower and three numbers higher. When there is an even number of cases, the median is the halfway mark between the two middle cases.

The Mode

The third measure of average, the *mode* is simply the cases that occur the most often. In this instance the mode is 57, which is way off the mark. Because the mode is often deceptive, and only by chance comes close to either of the other two averages, sociologists seldom use it. In addition, it is obvious that not every distribution of cases has a mode. And if two or more different numbers appear with the same frequency, you can have more than one mode.

---

sociology or advanced physics—must have the same chance of being included in the sample. Equally, such factors as a woman's major, her age, grade point average, or whether she is a day or evening or full- or part-time student must not affect her chance of becoming part of your study.

How can you get a random sample? First, you need a list of all the married women enrolled in your college. You then would assign a number to each name on the list and, using a table of random numbers, determine which of these women become part of your sample. (Random numbers are available on tables in statistics books, or they can be generated by a computer.)

Because a random sample represents the population—in this case married women enrolled at your college—you can generalize your findings to all the married women students on your campus, whether they were included in the sample or not.

Social scientists have developed a variation of this sampling technique that you might want to consider. Suppose you want to compare the experiences of freshmen and seniors. If so, you could use a **stratified random sample.** You would first identify freshmen and seniors, and then use random numbers to select subsamples from each group.

Because sociologists usually cannot interview or observe every member of a group they wish to study, such as the spectators at this boxing match between heavyweight world champion Evander Holyfield and Mike Tyson, they must select a sample that will let them generalize to the entire group. The text explains how samples are selected.

Improperly worded question-naires steer respondents toward answers that are not their own, thus producing invalid results.

Doonesbury © 1989 G. B. Trudeau. Reprinted with permission of Universal Press Syndicate. All rights reserved.

Asking Neutral Questions   After you have decided on your population and sample, your next task is to make certain that your questions are neutral. You must allow respondents, people who respond to a survey, to express their own opinions. Otherwise, you will end up with biased answers—and biased findings are worthless. For example, if you were to ask, "Don't you agree that men who beat their wives should go to prison?" you would be

Sociology

Down-to-Earth

LOADING THE DICE: HOW *NOT* TO DO RESEARCH

The methods of science lend themselves to distortion, misrepresentation, and downright fraud. Consider the following information. Surveys show that

- *Americans overwhelmingly prefer Toyotas to Chryslers.*
- *Americans overwhelmingly prefer Chryslers to Toyotas.*
- *Americans think that cloth diapers are better for the environment than disposable diapers.*
- *Americans think that disposable diapers are better for the environment than cloth diapers.*

Obviously such opposites cannot both be true. In fact, *both* sets of findings are misrepresentations, although each does come from surveys conducted by so-called independent researchers. These researchers, however, are biased, not independent and objective.

It turns out that some consumer researchers load the dice. Hired by firms that have a vested interest in the outcome of the research, they deliver the results their clients

are looking for. There are six basic ways of loading the dice.

1. **Choose a biased sample.** For example, if you want to "prove" that Americans prefer Chryslers over Toyotas, interview unemployed union workers who trace their job loss to Japanese imports. The answer is predictable. You'll get what you're looking for.

2. **Ask biased questions.** Even if you choose an unbiased sample, you can phrase questions in such a way that most people see only one logical choice. When the disposable diaper industry paid for the survey cited above, the researchers used an excellent sample, but they worded the question this way: "It is estimated that disposable diapers account for less than 2 percent of the trash in today's landfills. In contrast, beverage containers, third-class mail and yard waste are estimated to account for about 21 percent. Given this, in your opinion, would it be fair to ban disposable diapers?"

Is it surprising, then, that 84 percent of the respondents said that disposable diapers are better for the environment than cloth diapers? Similarly, when the cloth diaper industry funded its survey, they worded the questions to load the dice in their favor.

Consider the following finding, which is every bit as factual as those just cited:

- *80 percent of Americans support foreign aid.*

It is difficult to get 80 percent of Americans to agree on anything, but as loaded as this question was it is surprising that there was *only* 80 percent agreement. Incredibly, the question was phrased this way: *"Should the U.S. share at least a small portion of its wealth with those in the world who are in great need?"*

This question is obviously designed to channel people's thinking toward a predetermined answer—quite contrary to the standards of scientific research.

tilting the answer toward agreement with that position. For other examples of flawed research, see the Down-to-Earth Sociology box below.

Questionnaires and Interviews   Even if you have a representative sample and neutral questions, you can still end up with biased findings. **Questionnaires,** the list of questions to be asked, can be administered in ways that are flawed. There are two basic techniques for administering questionnaires. The first is for the respondents to fill them out. These **self-administered** questionnaires allow a larger number of people to be sampled at a relatively low cost, but the researchers lose control. They don't know the conditions under which people answered the questions. For example, others could have influenced their answers.

The second technique is the **interview.** Researchers ask people questions, either face to face or by telephone. The advantage of this method is that they can ask each question in precisely the same way. The disadvantage is that this is more expensive and time-consuming, and they can complete fewer questionnaires. This also can create **interviewer bias;** that is, the presence of interviewers can affect what people say. For example, some people won't tell an interviewer what they really feel. Instead, they give "socially acceptable" answers. They may be willing to write their true opinions in an anonymous situation, but not to tell them to another person directly. Some even shade their answers to match what they think an interviewer wants to hear.

In some cases, **structured interviews** work best. This type of interview uses **closed-ended questions**—each question is followed by a list of possible answers. Structured interviews

questionnaires a list of questions to be asked

self-administered questionnaires questionnaires filled out by respondents

interview direct questioning of respondents

interviewer bias effects that interviewers have on respondents that lead to biased answers

structured interviews interviews that use closed-ended questions

closed-ended questions questions followed by a list of possible answers to be selected by the respondent

---

3. **List biased choices.** Another way to load the dice is to use closed-ended questions that push people into the answers you want. Consider this finding:

- *U.S. college students overwhelmingly prefer Levis 501 to the jeans of any competitor.*

Sound good? Before you rush out to buy Levis, note what the researchers for Levis did: In asking students which jeans would be the most popular in the coming year, their list of choices included *no other jeans* but Levis 501!

4. **Discard undesirable results.** Researchers can simply keep silent about results they find embarrassing, or they can even continue to survey samples until they find one that matches what they are looking for.

As stressed in this chapter, research must be objective if it is to be scientific. Obviously, none of

the preceding results qualifies. The underlying problem with the research cited here—and with so many surveys bandied about in the media as fact—is that survey research has become big business. Simply put, the vast sums of money offered by corporations have corrupted some researchers.

The beginning of the corruption is subtle. Paul Light, dean at the University of Minnesota, put it this way: "A funder will never come to an academic and say, 'I want you to produce finding *X,* and here's a million dollars to do it.' Rather, the subtext is that if the researchers produce the right finding, more work—and funding—will come their way." He adds, "Once you're on that treadmill, it's hard to get off."

The first four sources of bias are intentional, inexcusable fraud. The fifth and sixth sources of bias reflect sloppiness—which is also inexcusable in science.

5. **Misunderstand the subjects' world.** This route can lead to errors every bit as great as

those just cited. Even researchers who use an adequate sample, word their questions properly, and offer adequate choices can end up with skewed results. For example, surveys show that 80 percent of Americans are environmentalists. Most Americans, however, are probably embarrassed to tell a stranger otherwise. Today, that would be like going against the flag, motherhood, and apple pie.

6. **Analyze the data incorrectly.** Even when researchers strive for objectivity, the sample is good, the wording is neutral, and the respondents answer the questions honestly, the results can still be skewed—the researchers may make a mistake in their calculations, such as entering incorrect data into computers. This, too, of course, is inexcusable in science. ■

Sources: Based on Crossen 1991; Goleman 1993; Barnes 1995.

unstructured interviews interviews that use open-ended questions

open-ended questions questions that respondents are able to answer in their own words

rapport a feeling of trust between researchers and subjects

participant observation (or field-work) research in which the researcher participates in a research setting while observing what is happening in that setting

generalizability the extent to which the findings from one group (or sample) can be generalized or applied to other groups (or populations)

secondary analysis the analysis of data already collected by other researchers

documents in its narrow sense, written sources that provide data; in its extended sense, archival material of any sort, including photographs, movies, and so on

are faster to administer, and they make it easier to *code* (categorize) answers so they can be fed into a computer for analysis. Because the answers listed on the questionnaire may not include the respondent's opinions, however, some researchers prefer **unstructured interviews.** Here the interviewer asks **open-ended questions,** ones that people can answer in their own words. Although open-ended questions allow respondents to express the full range of their opinions, they make it difficult to compare people's answers. For example, how would you compare these answers to the question "What do you think causes men to abuse their wives?"

> "They're sick."
> "They haven't been raised right."
> "I think they must have had problems with their mother."
> "We ought to kill every one!"
> "They're just *·*·* bastards!"

Establishing Rapport   Research on spouse abuse also brings up another significant issue. You may have been wondering if your survey would be worth anything even if you rigorously followed scientific procedures. Will women who have been abused really give honest answers? Will they even admit their victimization to a stranger?

If you were to walk up to a woman on the street and ask if her husband had ever beaten her, there would be little basis for taking your findings seriously. Researchers have to establish **rapport** ("ruh-pour"), a feeling of trust, with their respondents, especially when it comes to sensitive topics, areas of their lives about which people feel embarrassment, shame, or other deep emotions.

We know that once rapport is gained (for example, by first asking nonsensitive questions), victims will talk to researchers about very personal, sensitive issues. A good example is rape. To go beyond police statistics, each year researchers conduct a national crime survey. They interview a random sample of 100,000 Americans, asking them if they have been victims of burglary, robbery, and so on. After gaining rapport, the researchers ask about rape. They find that rape victims will talk about their experiences. The national crime surveys show that rape is three times as high as the official statistics (*Statistical Abstract* 1999: page 212).

Sociologists who enter a research setting to discover information are following a research method known as participant observation. As discussed in the text, sociologists also conduct research in controversial settings. Can you identify the sociologist in this photo?

Participant Observation (Fieldwork)

In the second method, **participant observation,** the researcher *participates* in a research setting while *observing* what is happening in that setting. My research with the homeless, mentioned in Chapter 1, is an example of participant observation.

How is it possible to study spouse abuse by participant observation? Obviously, being present during the abuse and taking notes while it occurs is not feasible. Spouse abuse, however, is a broad topic, and many questions about abuse cannot be answered adequately by any method other than participant observation.

Let's suppose that your interest is in learning how spouse abuse affects wives. You may want to know how the abuse has changed their relationship with their husbands. How has it changed their hopes and dreams? Or their ideas about men? Certainly it has affected their self-concept as well. But how? Participant observation may be able to provide insight into such questions.

Let's go back to your campus again. Let's assume that it has a crisis intervention center that might lend itself to participant observation. Here you may be able to observe victims of spouse abuse from the time they first report the attack to the time they start attending counseling sessions. With good rapport, you may even be able to spend time with victims outside this setting, observing other aspects of their lives. Their statements and interaction with others may hold the keys that help you unlock answers about how the abuse has affected their lives. This, in turn, may allow you to make suggestions about how to improve college counseling services.

Participant observers face a problem with **generalizability,** being able to apply their findings to larger populations. Most of their studies are exploratory, documenting in detail the experiences of people in a particular setting. Although such research suggests that other people who face similar situations react in similar ways, it is difficult to know just how far the findings apply beyond their original setting. The results of participant observation, however, can stimulate hypotheses and theories and can be tested in other settings, using other research techniques.

Secondary Analysis

In **secondary analysis,** a third research method, researchers analyze data that have already been collected by others. For example, if you were to examine the original data from a study of women who had been abused by their husbands, you would be doing secondary analysis. Ordinarily, researchers prefer to gather their own data, but lack of resources, especially money, may make that impossible. In addition, existing data may contain a wealth of information that wasn't pertinent to the goals of the original researchers, which you can analyze for your own purposes.

Like the other methods, secondary analysis also poses its own problems. How can a researcher who did not carry out the research be sure that the data were systematically gathered and accurately recorded, and that biases were avoided? This problem plagues researchers who do secondary analysis, especially if the original data have been gathered by a team of researchers, not all of whom were equally qualified.

Domestic abuse is one of the most common forms of violence. Until recently, it was treated by the police as a private family matter. Shown here are police pulling a woman from her bathroom window, where she had fled from her armed husband, who was threatening to shoot her.

Documents

The fourth method sociologists use is the study of **documents,** written sources. To investigate social life, they examine such diverse documents as books, newspapers, diaries, bank records, police reports, immigration files, and records kept by various organizations.

To study spouse abuse, you might examine police reports and court records. These could reveal what proportion of complaints result in arrest and what proportion of the men arrested are charged, convicted, or put on probation. If these were your questions, police statistics would be valuable.

Sociologists use different methods of research to answer different questions. One method that can be used to study spouse abuse is to examine the documents kept by shelters for battered women, which log the number of calls and visits made by victims.

But for other questions, those records would be useless. If you want to know about the victim's social and emotional adjustment, for example, those records would tell you little. Other documents, however, might help answer this question. A crisis intervention center, for example, might have records that provide key information. Diaries kept by victims could yield insight into their reactions to abuse, showing how their attitudes and relationships change. If you couldn't locate such diaries, you might contact victims and ask them to keep diaries. Again, an intervention center might help you in this research. Their personnel might ask clients to keep diaries for you. To my knowledge, no sociologist has yet studied spouse abuse in this way.

Of course, I am presenting an ideal situation, a crisis intervention center that opens its arms to you. In actual fact, the center might not cooperate at all. It might refuse to ask victims to keep diaries, and it might not even let you near its records. *Access,* then, is another problem researchers face. Simply put, you can't study a topic unless you can gain access to it.

Unobtrusive Measures

The fifth method is **unobtrusive measures,** observing the behavior of people who do not know they are being studied. For example, social researchers studied the level of whisky consumption in a town that was officially "dry" by counting empty bottles in trash cans. To study the degree of fear induced by ghost stories, they measured the shrinking diameter of a circle of seated children (Webb 1966). To study gender differences, one of my graduate students recorded all the graffiti in every public rest room in two towns (Darnell 1971). Researchers have also gone high-tech in their unobtrusive measures. They have outfitted shopping carts with infrared surveillance equipment so they can trace customers' paths through stores. Retailers use these findings to move items in their stores to more strategic locations (McCarthy 1993).

If we wanted to use unobtrusive measures to study spouse abuse, we could go to a battered women's shelter. There we could secretly tape conversations among the women, as well as their telephone calls. Or we could use a one-way mirror to observe their interactions, and even surreptitiously videotape them. As may be obvious, although such unobtrusive measures might yield rich data, professional ethics would prohibit such a study.

Experiments

The sixth method, the **experiment,** is useful for determining cause and effect. Causation has three necessary conditions, which are discussed in Table 5.3 on the facing page.

Let's suppose you develop the hypothesis that the consumption of alcohol creates attitudes that favor wife beating. You can conduct an experiment to test this hypothesis. Your **independent variable** (something that causes a change in another variable) would be alcohol consumption. Your **dependent variable** (the variable that is changed) would be attitudes toward spouse abuse.

Let's also assume that you have access to a laboratory and to some male volunteers. You could randomly divide the men into two groups. The reason for doing this is that many of the men's characteristics will differ—their experiences, attitudes, perhaps even their "suggestibility." If you randomly divide the men—making certain that each man has an equal chance of becoming a member of either group—these unknown variables will be distributed among both groups.

As shown in Figure 5.2 on page 138, your next step is to measure the dependent variable, the men's attitudes toward spouse abuse. Then in one group, called the **experimental group,** you introduce the independent variable; that is, you give the men in this group a specified amount of alcohol. The other men, the **control group,** are not exposed to the independent variable; that is, they are not given alcohol. You then measure the dependent variable (attitudes toward spouse abuse) in both groups again. Because only the experimental group received the alcohol, you can assume that any change in the group's attitude is due to the alcohol.

There always are unknown third variables that complicate experiments. This is why you randomly divide your subjects (the people being studied) into two groups. These third variables, however, are not necessarily distributed evenly among the groups. Because of this, you must *replicate* (repeat) your experiment with other groups of men. When you do this,

unobtrusive measures various ways of observing people who do not know they are being studied

experiment the use of control groups and experimental groups and dependent and independent variables to test causation

independent variable a factor that causes a change in another variable, called the dependent variable

dependent variable a factor that is changed by an independent variable

experimental group the group of subjects exposed to the independent variable

control group the group of subjects not exposed to the independent variable

CAUSE, EFFECT, AND SPURIOUS CORRELATIONS

Causation means that a change in one variable is due to another variable. Three conditions are necessary for causation: correlation, temporal priority, and no spurious correlation. Let's apply each of these conditions to spouse abuse and alcohol abuse.

1. The first necessary condition is **correlation.**

   If two variables exist together, they are said to be correlated. If batterers have drunk alcohol, battering and alcohol abuse are correlated.

   Spouse Abuse **+** Alcohol Abuse

   People sometimes assume that correlation is causation. In this instance, they conclude that alcohol abuse causes spouse abuse.

   Alcohol Abuse ───────────▶ Spouse Abuse

   But *correlation never proves causation. Either* variable could be the cause of the other. Perhaps battering pushes men into getting drunk.

   Spouse Abuse ───────────▶ Alcohol Abuse

2. The second necessary condition is *temporal priority* (one variable must occur before the other).

   Temporal priority means that one thing happens before something else does. For a variable to be a cause (the *independent* variable), it must *precede* that which is changed (the *dependent* variable). If the men had not drunk alcohol until after they beat their wives, obviously alcohol abuse could not be the cause of the spouse abuse. Although the necessity of temporal priority is obvious, in many studies this is not easy to determine.

3. The third necessary condition is *no spurious correlation.*

   This is the necessary condition that really makes things difficult. Even if we identify correlation and can determine temporal priority, we still don't know that alcohol abuse is the cause. It is possible that we have a **spurious correlation;** that is, the cause may be some underlying third variable that is not easily visible. Some sociologists identify male culture as that underlying third variable.

   Male Culture ───────────▶ Spouse Abuse

   Socialized into dominance, some males learn to view women as objects on which to take out their frustration. In fact, this underlying third variable could be a cause of both spouse abuse and alcohol abuse.

But since only some men beat their wives, while all males are exposed to male culture, other variables must also be involved. Perhaps specific subcultures that promote violence and denigrate women lead to both spouse abuse and alcohol abuse.

If so, this does *not* mean that it is the only causal variable, for spouse abuse probably has many causes. Unlike the movement of amoebas or the action of heat on some object, human behavior is infinitely complicated. What is especially important is people's *definitions of the situation,* including their views of right and wrong. To explain spouse abuse, then, we need to add such variables as men's views of violence and their definitions of the relative rights of women and men. It is precisely to help unravel such complicating factors in human behavior that we need the experimental method.

More on Correlations

Correlation simply means that two or more variables are present together. The more often they are found together, the greater the strength of their relationship. To indicate their strength, sociologists use a number called a *correlation coefficient.* If two variables are *always* related, that is, they are always present together, they have what is called a *perfect positive correlation.* The number 1.0 represents this correlation coefficient. Nature has some 1.0's, such as the lack of water and the death of trees. 1.0's also apply to the human physical state, such as the absence of nutrients and the absence of life. But social life is much more complicated than physical conditions, and there are no 1.0's in human behavior.

Two variables can also have a *perfect negative correlation.* This means that when one variable is present, the other is always absent. The number −1.0 expresses this correlation coefficient.

Positive correlations of 0.1, 0.2, 0.3, and 0.4 mean that one variable is associated with another only 1 time out of 10, 2 times out of 10, 3 times out of 10, and 4 times out of 10. In other words, in most instances the first variable is *not* associated with the second, indicating a weak relationship.

The greater the correlation coefficient, the stronger the relationship. A strong relationship *may* indicate causation, but not necessarily. Testing the relationship between variables is the goal of some sociological research.

---

you may wish to give different amounts of alcohol to see if there is a threshold effect; that is, alcohol may affect the men's attitudes only after a certain amount has been consumed.

Some experiments are not conducted this rigorously, which increases the likelihood that variables will be confused. As described in the Down-to-Earth Sociology box on page 138, in the 1920s Elton Mayo did a set of famous experiments that uncovered a surprising third variable.

The experiment is best suited for precise measurements of small variables. Because most sociologists are interested in broad features of society, or in studying interaction as it naturally occurs, few use this classic method of the natural sciences. We could devise an experiment to study spouse abuse, however. We might even be able to come up with one that would prove beneficial for society. For example, the independent variable could be therapy.

Figure 5.2   **THE EXPERIMENT**

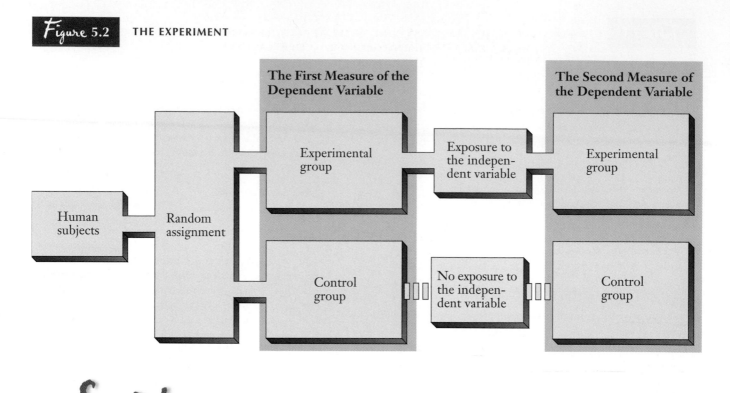

Sociology

THE HAWTHORNE EXPERIMENTS

Research from the 1920s, known as the Hawthorne experiments, became a classic in sociology. This research drives home how necessary it is to accurately identify independent and dependent variables.

The managers of the Hawthorne plant of the Western Electric Company near Chicago wanted to know if different levels of lighting would affect productivity. Several groups of women participated in what are known as the Relay Room Experiments. In the control room, the level of lighting was held constant, while in the experimental room the lighting was varied. To everyone's surprise, output increased in *both* locations. In the experimental room, productivity remained high even when the lights were dimmed to about the level of moonlight—so low that workers could barely see what they were doing!

To solve this mystery, management called in a team of researchers headed by Elton Mayo of the University of Chicago. This team tested thirteen different work conditions. When they changed the workers' pay from hourly wages to piecework (paying them at a set rate for each unit they produce), productivity increased. When they served refreshments, output again went up. When they added two 5-minute rest periods, productivity jumped. When they changed the rest periods to two 10-minute periods, again output increased. When they let the workers go home early, they found the same result. Confused, the researchers restored the original conditions, offering none of these added benefits. The result? Even higher productivity.

The situation grew even more confusing when they observed men workers in what is known as the Bank Wiring Room Study. Here, the researchers didn't change the work conditions at all. They simply observed the men while they worked and interviewed them after work. They expected no change in productivity. What happened was that productivity *dropped*.

None of this made sense. Finally, Mayo concluded that the changes in productivity were due to the research itself. The women, pleased at the attention being paid to them, responded by increasing their efforts. The men, in contrast, were suspicious about why the researchers were observing them. They feared that if they had higher productivity, they would be expected to produce more each day, or that higher productivity might even cost some of them their jobs. Consequently, they decreased their output.

The Hawthorne research is important—not for its findings on worker productivity, but for what it revealed about the research process itself. Today, researchers carefully monitor the *Hawthorne effect,* the change in behavior that occurs when people know they are being studied. ■

Sources: Based on Roethlisberger and Dickson 1939; Mayo 1966; Baron and Greenberg 1990.

We could randomly assign abusers to experimental and control groups to help assure that their individual characteristics (attitudes, number of arrests, length of abuse, severity of abuse, education, race, age, and so on) are distributed evenly among the groups. Then we could arrange for the experimental group to receive some form of therapy. The control group would not receive therapy. If the abuse (the dependent variable) *decreased* in the experimental group, we would assume that this was due to the therapy (the independent variable). If the abuse *increased,* which it could, we would assume that the therapy was also the cause. If there was no change in abuse, we would know that the therapy had no effect.

If we were to conduct such an experiment, ideally we would test different types of therapy. Perhaps only some work. We might even want to test self-therapy by assigning articles, books, and videos. Frankly, no one knows how to change a wife abuser into a loving husband, and such experiments are badly needed.

Deciding Which Method to Use

How do sociologists choose from among these methods? Four primary factors affect their choice. First, *resources* are crucial. Sociologists must match methods with available resources. For example, although they may want to conduct a survey, they may find that finances won't permit it, and instead they turn to the study of documents. The second significant factor is *access to subjects.* If the people who comprise a sample live in remote parts of the country, researchers may have to mail them questionnaires or conduct a telephone survey even if they would prefer face-to-face interviews. The third factor concerns the *purpose* of the research, the questions that the sociologist wishes to answer. Each method is better for answering some questions than for others. Participant observation, for example, is good for uncovering people's real attitudes, while experiments work better for resolving questions of cause and effect. Fourth, the researcher's *background or training* comes into play. In graduate school, sociologists study many methods, but they are able to practice only some of them. Consequently, after graduate school they generally use the methods in which they have had the most training.

Thus, sociologists who have been trained in **quantitative research methods,** which emphasize measurement, numbers, and statistics, are likely to use surveys. Sociologists who have been trained in **qualitative research methods,** which emphasize describing, observing, and interpreting people's behavior, lean toward participant observation. In the Down-to-Earth Sociology box below, you can see how applied sociologists use a combination of quantitative and qualitative methods.

Sociologists sometimes find themselves in the hot seat because of their research. Some poke into private areas of life, which upsets people. Others investigate public matters, but their findings threaten those who have a personal stake in the situation. From the homeless research discussed in the Thinking Critically section on the next page, you can see how significant the choice of research method is, and how using rigorous research methods can land sociologists in the midst of controversy.

quantitative research methods
research in which the emphasis is placed on precise measurement, the use of statistics and numbers

qualitative research methods
research in which the emphasis is placed on observing, describing, and interpreting people's behavior

Sociology

Down-to-Earth

APPLIED SOCIOLOGY: MARKETING RESEARCH AS A BLEND OF QUANTITATIVE AND QUALITATIVE METHODS

If a company is going to survive in the highly competitive business world, it must figure out what consumers need and want, and then supply it—or else convince people that what they need or want is what the company already is producing.

What Marketing Research Is

To increase sales, manufacturers try to improve the "position" of their products. "Position" is marketing jargon for how customers think about a product.

This is where marketing researchers come into play. They find out what customers want, how they select products, how they use them, and what images they hold of a product or service. They also assess how the public will react to a new product or to a change in an established product.

Continued

Sociology

Down-to-Earth

APPLIED SOCIOLOGY: MARKETING RESEARCH AS A BLEND OF QUANTITATIVE AND QUALITATIVE METHODS, Continued

Marketing researchers use a combination of qualitative and quantitative techniques. They use qualitative methods to help determine what questions they should include in surveys. They also use qualitative methods as their primary research technique. An example is "focus groups." Groups of about ten people are invited to discuss a product. A moderator leads a discussion while other team members observe or videotape the session from behind a one-way mirror. To control for regional variations, the researchers may hold other focus groups at the same time in other cities. Sociologist Roger Straus points out that his training in symbolic interactionism has been especially useful for interpreting these results.

Marketing researchers also use quantitative techniques. For example, they may conduct surveys to determine what the public thinks of a new product. They also gather sales data from the "bar codes" found on almost all products. They use statistics to analyze the data, and they prepare tables and graphics that summarize the findings for clients.

A Sociological Controversy

Marketing research occupies a controversial position in sociology. Most of the results of marketing research are proprietary (owned by the client) and are therefore confidential. This means that the findings do not appear in sociology journals and are not used to create social theory. In addition, clients are usually interested only in specific marketing problems, and they seldom commission research on important social issues. For such reasons, many sociologists do not consider marketing research a "legitimate" sociological activity. Some even scorn marketing researchers as wasting their sociological talents. They chide them for having "sold out," for using sociological methods to help corporations exploit the public by convincing them to purchase unneeded goods and services.

Marketing researchers, of course, do not see things this way. They argue that marketing research is a neutral activity, that there is no reason to be against it on principle. They add that they do more than just help sell beer and soft drinks. They point out that they have helped colleges attract students and communities assess public needs. They argue that the decision to do research on any topic involves the researcher's own values. This applies to studying how to reduce juvenile delinquency as well as investigating how to sell a particular product. It is unreasonable, they say, for anyone to pass judgment on marketing research—as though other research were morally superior. ■

Sources: Based on Straus 1991 and communication with Straus 1993.

Thinking *Critically*

DOING CONTROVERSIAL RESEARCH— COUNTING THE HOMELESS

What could be simpler, or less offensive, than counting the homeless? As sometimes happens, however, even basic research lands sociologists in the midst of controversy. This is what happened to sociologist Peter Rossi and his associates.

It happened this way. There was a dispute between advocates for the homeless and the federal government. The advocates claimed that 3 to 7 million Americans were homeless; the government claimed that only a quarter of a million people were homeless, just one-twelfth to one-twenty-eighth the number claimed by the advocates. Each side accused the other of gross distortion—the one to place undue pressure on Congress, the other to keep the public from knowing how bad the situation really was.

Only an accurate count could clear up the picture, for both sides were only guessing at the numbers. Peter Rossi and the National Opinion Research Center decided to carry out an accurate count. They had no vested interest in supporting one side or the other, only in answering this question honestly.

As discussed on this page, research sometimes lands sociologists in the midst of controversy. An example is a study conducted to determine how many homeless people there are in the United States. Homeless advocates were not pleased with the results.

The challenge was immense. The *population* was evident—the U.S. homeless. A *survey* would be appropriate, but how do you survey a *sample* of the homeless? No federal, state, county, or city has a list of the homeless, and only some of the homeless stay at shelters. As for *validity,* to make certain that they were counting only people who were really homeless the researchers needed a good *operational definition* of homelessness. To include people who weren't really homeless would destroy the study's *reliability.* The researchers wanted results that would be consistent if others were to *replicate,* or repeat, the study.

As an operational definition, the researchers used "literally homeless," people "who do not have access to a conventional dwelling and who would be homeless by any conceivable definition of the term." Because a national count would cost about $6 million, far beyond their resources, the researchers decided to count just the homeless in Chicago. By using a *stratified random sample,* they were able to *generalize* to the entire country. The cost was still high, however—about $600,000.

To be able to generalize about the homeless who sleep in shelters, the researchers used a stratified random sample of the city's shelters. For the homeless who sleep in the streets, vacant buildings, and so forth, they used a stratified random sample of the city's blocks. To make doubly certain that their count was accurate, the researchers conducted two surveys. At night, trained teams visited the shelters and searched the alleys, bridges, and vacant houses.

Many found the results startling. On an average night, Chicago has 2,722 homeless people. Because people move in and out of homelessness, between 5,000 and 7,000 are homeless at some point during the year. On warm nights, only two out of five sleep in the shelters, and even in winter only three out of four do so. The median age is 40; 75 percent are men, and 60 percent are African Americans. One in four is a former mental patient, one in five a former prisoner. A homeless person's income from all sources is less than $6 a day. Projecting these findings to the United States results in a national total of about 350,000 homeless people, a figure that is much closer to the government's estimate of 250,000 than it is to the advocates' estimate of 7 to 8 million.

The reactions were predictable. Government officials rubbed their hands in glee. The stunned homeless advocates denied the findings and began a sniping campaign at the researchers.

Remember that Rossi and his associates had no interest in proving which side in the debate was right, only in getting reliable figures. Using impeccable methods, this they did.

The researchers had no intention of minimizing the problem of homelessness. They stressed that 350,000 Americans are so poor that they slip through the welfare system, sleep in city streets, live in shelters, eat out of garbage cans, are malnourished, and suffer from severe health problems. In short, these people live hopeless, desperate lives.

It is good to *know* how many Americans are homeless. Guesses aren't worth much. Even though the number is far less than what the homeless advocates had estimated, this information can still serve their cause: Because there are fewer homeless people than many had thought, it makes the problem more manageable. It means that if we choose to do so, we can put our resources to work with greater certainty of success.

Nevertheless, as in this instance, people whose positions are not supported by research are not pleased, and they tend to take potshots at the researchers. This, of course, is one of the risks of doing sociological research, for sociologists never know whose toes they will step on. ■

Sources: Based on Anderson 1986; Rossi et al. 1986; Rossi et al. 1987; Coughlin 1988; Rossi 1989; Rossi 1991; De Parle 1994; Rossi 1999.

GENDER IN SOCIOLOGICAL RESEARCH

As you know, gender is significant in social life. It affects our orientations, our attitudes, and, especially, what happens to us in life. Researchers are aware that gender can also be a significant factor in social research, and they take steps to prevent gender from biasing their findings.

For example, two sociologists, Diana Scully and Joseph Marolla, interviewed convicted rapists in prison. Their gender could easily have led to *interviewer bias*. The prisoners might shift their answers, depending on whether they were talking to a man or a woman. They might share certain experiences or express certain attitudes to a man, but say something else to a woman. Scully and Marolla (1984, 1985) took this into account and, to prevent gender bias, each interviewed half the sample. Later in this chapter, we'll look at their research in detail.

Gender can also be a major impediment to doing research. In our imagined research on spouse abuse, for example, could a man even do participant observation of women who have been beaten by their husbands? Technically, the answer is yes. But because the research centers on women who have been victimized by men, the women might be less likely to share their experiences and feelings with men researchers. If so, women would be better suited to conduct this research, more likely to achieve valid results. Such a commonsense supposition regarding what these victims are likely to disclose to women versus men, however, is just that—a supposition. Research alone will verify or refute this assumption.

Gender is significant in other ways, too. As sociologists Chloe Bird and Patricia Rieker (1997) point out, it is a mistake to assume that what applies to one sex applies to the other. Women's and men's lives differ significantly, and if we do research on just half of humanity, our research will be vastly incomplete. With today's huge numbers of women sociologists, there is little risk of ignoring women in contemporary research. In the past, however, when almost all sociologists were men, women's lives were neglected.

Gender pops up in unexpected ways in sociological research. I vividly recall an incident in San Francisco. The streets were getting dark, and I was still looking for homeless people. When I saw someone lying down, huddled in a doorway, I approached the individual. As I got close, I began my opening research line, "Hi, I'm Dr. Henslin from. . . ." The individual began to scream and started to thrash wildly. Startled by this sudden, high-pitched scream and by the rapid movements, I quickly backed away. When I later analyzed what had happened, I concluded that I had intruded into a woman's bedroom.

Of course, one can draw another lesson from this incident. Researchers do their best, but they make mistakes. Sometimes these are minor, and even humorous. The woman sleeping in the doorway wasn't frightened. It was only just getting dark, and there were many people on the street. She was just assertively marking her territory and letting me know in no uncertain terms that I was an intruder. If we make a mistake in research, we pick up and go on. As we do so, we take ethical considerations into account, and this is the topic of our next section.

ETHICS IN SOCIOLOGAL RESEARCH

Sociologists cannot do just any type of research that they might desire. Their research must meet their profession's ethical criteria, which center on basic assumptions of science and morality (American Sociological Association 1997). Research ethics require openness (sharing findings with the scientific community), honesty, and truth. Ethics clearly forbid the falsification of results, as well as plagiarism—that is, stealing someone else's work. Another basic ethical guideline is that research subjects should not be harmed by the research. Ethics also require that sociologists protect the anonymity of people who provide information.

Ethics in social research are of vital concern to sociologists. As discussed in the text, sociologists may disagree on some of the issue's finer points, but none would approve of slipping LSD to unsuspecting subjects just "to see what would happen," as was done to U.S. servicemen in the 1960s under the guise of legitimate testing.

Sometimes they reveal things that are intimate, potentially embarrassing, or otherwise harmful to them. Finally, although not all sociologists are in agreement about this, it generally is considered unethical for researchers to misrepresent themselves.

Sociologists take these ethical criteria seriously. To illustrate the extent to which they will go to protect their respondents, consider the research conducted by Mario Brajuha.

Protecting the Subjects: The Brajuha Research

Mario Brajuha, a graduate student at the State University of New York at Stony Brook, was doing participant observation of restaurant work. He lost his job as a waiter when the restaurant where he was working burned down—due to a fire of "suspicious origin," as the police said. During their investigation, detectives learned that Brajuha had taken field notes (Brajuha and Hallowell 1986). They asked to see his notes, but Brajuha refused. When the district attorney subpoenaed the notes, Brajuha still refused to hand them over. The district attorney threatened to put Brajuha in jail. By this time, Brajuha's notes had become rather famous, and unsavory characters, perhaps those who had set the fire, also began to wonder what was in them. They, too, demanded to see them—accompanying their demands with threats of a different nature. Brajuha unexpectedly found himself in a very disturbing double bind.

For two years Brajuha refused to hand over his notes, even though he had to appear at numerous court hearings and was filled with anxiety. Finally, the district attorney dropped the subpoena. When the two men under investigation for setting the fire died, so did the threats to Brajuha, his wife, and his children.

Misleading the Subjects: The Humphreys Research

Sociologists agree on the necessity of protecting respondents, and they applaud the professional manner in which Brajuha handled himself. Although there is less agreement that researchers should not misrepresent themselves, sociologists who violate this norm can become embroiled in ethical controversy. Let's look at the case of Laud Humphreys, whose research forced sociologists to rethink and refine their ethical stance.

Laud Humphreys, a classmate of mine at Washington University in St. Louis, was an Episcopal priest who decided to become a sociologist. For his Ph.D. dissertation, Humphreys (1970, 1971, 1975) studied social interaction in "tearooms," public rest rooms where some men go for quick, anonymous oral sex with other men.

Humphreys found that some rest rooms in Forest Park, just across from our campus, were tearooms. He first began a participant observation study by hanging around these rest rooms. He found that in addition to the two men having sex, a third person—called a "watchqueen"—served as a lookout for police and other unwelcome strangers. Humphreys took on the role of watchqueen, not only watching for strangers but also watching what the men did. He recorded these encounters, and they became part of his dissertation.

Humphreys became curious about the regular lives of these men. Impersonal sex in tearooms was a fleeting encounter, and the men spent most of their time doing other things. What things? With whom? And what was the significance of the wedding rings that many of the men wore? Humphreys then hit on an ingenious technique. After observing a sexual encounter, he would leave the rest room and record the license number of the man's car. A friend in the St. Louis police department gave Humphreys each man's address. About a year later, Humphreys arranged for these men to be included in a medical survey conducted by some of the sociologists on our faculty. Disguising himself with a different hairstyle and clothing, and driving a different car, he visited these men at their homes. He then interviewed them, supposedly for the medical study.

Humphreys said that no one recognized him—and he did get the information he was looking for: the men's education, income, health, religion, and even the kind of relationship they had with their wives and children. He found that most of the men were in their mid-thirties and had at least some college education. Surprisingly, the majority were married, and a higher proportion than in the general population turned out to be Roman Catholic. Moreover, these men led very conventional lives. They voted, mowed their lawns, and took their kids to Little League games.

Humphreys also found that although most of the men were committed to their wives and families, their sex life was far from satisfactory. Many reported that their wives were not aroused sexually or were afraid of getting pregnant because their religion did not allow them to use birth control. Humphreys concluded that these were heterosexual men who were using the tearooms for an alternative form of sex, which, unlike affairs, was quick (taking no time away from their families), inexpensive (zero cost), and nonthreatening (the encounter required no emotional involvement that might compromise their commitment to their wives). If one of the wives had discovered her husband's secret sex life, of course, she would have been devastated. And today's tearoom encounters present a much more ominous threat, for Humphreys conducted his research before the arrival of AIDS. Anyone participating in tearooms today risks death—both for himself and, through transmission, also for any sexual partner, wife included.

This study stirred controversy among sociologists and nonsociologists alike (Goodwin et al. 1991). Humphreys was severely criticized by many sociologists, and a national columnist even wrote a scathing denunciation of "sociological snoopers" (Von Hoffman 1970). Concerned about protecting the identity of his respondents, Humphreys hid his master list in a safe deposit box. As the controversy grew more heated and a court case loomed, Humphreys feared that his list might be subpoenaed. He gave me a list to take from Missouri to Illinois, where I had begun teaching. (It could have been some other list of respondents; I was told not to examine it, and I did not.) When he called and asked me to destroy it, I burned it in my backyard. Humphreys had a contract to remain at Washington University as an assistant professor, but he was fired before he could begin teaching. (Although other reasons were involved, his research was a central issue. There was even an attempt by one professor to have his doctorate revoked.)

Was this research ethical? This question is not easily decided. Although many sociologists sided with Humphreys—and his book reporting the research won a highly acclaimed award—the criticisms mounted. At first Humphreys vigorously defended his position, but five years later, in a second edition of his book (1975), he stated that he should have identified himself as a researcher.

*H*OW RESEARCH AND THEORY WORK TOGETHER

As discussed, sociological research is based on the sociologist's interests, access to subjects, appropriate methods, and ethical considerations. But the value of research is also related to sociological theory. On the one hand, as sociologist C. Wright Mills (1959) so forcefully argued in a classic book, research without theory is of little value. It is simply a collection of unrelated "facts." On the other hand, if theory is unconnected to research, it is abstract and empty. It is unlikely to represent the way life really is.

Research and theory are both essential for sociology. Every theory that sociologists develop must be tested. Thus theory stimulates research. And as sociologists do research, they often come up with surprising findings. Those findings, in turn, stimulate the development of theory to explain them. Such findings may also stimulate more research, for they may indicate that different samples or better operational variables are necessary. As sociologists study social life, then, they combine research and theory.

The Real World: When the Ideal Meets the Real

Although we can list the ideals of research, real-life situations often force sociologists to settle for something that falls short of the ideal. Let's look at how two sociologists confronted the ideal and the real in the following Thinking Critically section.

Thinking Critically

ARE RAPISTS SICK? A CLOSE-UP VIEW OF RESEARCH

Two sociologists, Diana Scully and Joseph Marolla, were not satisfied with the typical explanation that rapists are "sick," psychologically disturbed, or different from other men. They developed the hypothesis that rape, like most behavior, is learned through interaction with others. That is, some men learn to think of rape as appropriate behavior.

To test this hypothesis, it would be best to interview a random sample of rapists. But this is impossible. There is no list of all rapists, so there is no way to give them all the same chance of being included in a sample. You can't even use prison populations to select a random sample, for many rapists have never been caught, some who were caught were found not guilty, and some who were found guilty were given probation. Some, too, who were convicted of rape are innocent. Consequently, Scully and Marolla confronted the classic dilemma of sociologists— either to not do the study or to do it under less than ideal conditions.

They chose to do the study. When they had the opportunity to interview convicted rapists in prison, they jumped at it. They knew that whatever they learned would be more than we already knew. They sent out 3,500 letters to men serving time in seven prisons in Virginia, the state where they were teaching. About 25 percent of the prisoners agreed to be interviewed. They matched these men on the basis of age, education, race, severity of offense, and previous criminal record. This resulted in a sample of 98 prisoners who were convicted of rape and a control sample of 75 nonrapists, men convicted of other offenses.

As noted earlier, the sex of the interviewer can bias research results. To avoid this, Marolla and Scully each interviewed half the sample. It took them 600 hours to gather information on the prisoners, including their psychological, criminal, and sexual history. To guard against lies, they did what is called a "validity check"; in this case, they checked what the individuals said against their institutional record. They used twelve scales to measure the men's attitudes about women, rape, and themselves. They also presented nine vignettes of forced sexual encounters to measure the circumstances under which the men defined a situation as rape or viewed the victim as responsible for the rape.

Scully and Marolla discovered something that goes against common sense—that most rapists are not sick, that they are not overwhelmed by uncontrollable urges. The psychological histories of the rapists and the nonrapists were similar. Rapists, they concluded, are emotionally average men who have learned to view rape as appropriate in certain situations. Some rape spontaneously, while others plan their rapes. For some, rape is a form of recreation, and they rape with friends on a regular basis, such as on weekends. Others use rape as a form of revenge, to get even with someone, not necessarily the woman.

Scully and Marolla also found support for what feminists had been pointing out for years, that power was a major element in rape. Here is what one man said:

Rape gave me the power to do what I wanted to do without feeling I had to please a partner or respond to a partner. I felt in control, dominant. Rape was the ability to have sex without caring about the woman's response. I was totally dominant.

To discover that most rape is calculated behavior—that rapists are not "sick"; that the motivating force is power, not passion; that the behavior stems from the criminal pursuit of pleasure, not from mental illness—is significant. It makes the sociological quest worthwhile.

In comparing their sample of rapists with their control group of nonrapists, Scully and Marolla also found something else significant. The rapists are more likely to believe "rape myths." They are more likely to believe that women cause their own rape by the way they act and the clothes they wear, that a woman who charges rape has simply changed her mind after participating in consensual sex, and that most men accused of rape are innocent.

Connecting Research and Theory

Such findings go far beyond simply adding to our storehouse of "facts." As indicated in Figure 5.1 on page 127, research stimulates both the development of theory and the need for more research. Scully and Marolla suggest that rape myths act as neutralizers, that they allow "potential rapists to turn off social prohibitions against injuring others."

This hypothesis, in turn, pinpoints the need to determine how such myths are transmitted. Which male subcultures perpetuate them? Do the mass media contribute to these myths? Do family, religion, and education create respect for females and help keep males from learning such myths? Or do they somehow contribute to these myths? If so, how?

At some point sociologists will build on this path-breaking research, which was done, as usual, under less than ideal conditions. The resulting theorizing and research may provide the basis for making changes that reduce rape in U.S. society. ■

Sources: Scully and Marolla 1984, 1985; Marolla and Scully 1986; Scully 1990; Foley et al. 1995.

This is exactly what sociology needs more of—imaginative and sometimes daring research conducted in an imperfect world under less than ideal conditions. This is really what sociology is all about. Sociologists study what people do—whether their behaviors are conforming or deviant, whether they please others or disgust them and arouse intense anger. No matter the behavior that is studied, systematic research methods and the application of social theory take us beyond common sense. They allow us to penetrate surface realities so we can better understand human behavior—and, in the ideal case, make changes to help improve social life.

SUMMARY AND REVIEW

■ What Is a Valid Sociological Topic?

Any human behavior is a valid sociological topic, even disreputable behavior. Spouse abuse is an example. Sociological research is based on the sociologist's interests, access to subjects, appropriate methods, and ethical considerations. P. 126.

■ Common Sense and the Need for Sociological Research

Why isn't common sense adequate?

Common sense doesn't provide reliable knowledge. When subjected to scientific research, commonsense ideas often are found to be very limited or false. P. 126.

■ A Research Model

What are the eight basic steps of scientific research?

1. Selecting a topic, 2. Defining the problem, 3. Reviewing the literature, 4. Formulating a hypothesis, 5. Choosing a research method, 6. Collecting the data, 7. Analyzing the results, 8. Sharing the results. These steps are explained in detail on Pp. 126–129

■ Six Research Methods

How do sociologists gather data?

To gather data, sociologists use six research methods (or research designs): surveys, participant observation, secondary analysis, documents, unobtrusive measures, and experiments. Pp. 129–139.

How do sociologists choose a research method?

Sociologists choose their research method based on questions to be answered, their access to potential subjects, the resources available, their training, and ethical considerations. P. 139

■ Gender in Sociological Research

What is the relationship between gender and research?

There are two aspects. First, sociologists used to ignore the world of women, but no longer. Second, in some kinds of research, such as studying rapists in prision, the gender of the researcher could affect findings. P. 142.

■ Ethics in Sociological Research

How important are ethics in sociological research?

Ethics are of fundamental concern to sociologists, who are committed to openness, honesty, truth, and protecting their subjects from harm. The Brajuha research on restaurants and the Humphreys research on "tearooms" were cited to illustrate ethical issues of concern to sociologists. Pp. 142–144.

■ How Research and Theory Work Together

What is the relationship between theory and research?

Research, in turn, helps to generate theory when findings don't match what is expected, indicating the need for new thinking. Although conducted in an imperfect world, social research stimulates sociological theory, leads to further research, and has the potential to effect changes that improve human life. Pp. 145–146.

Where can I read more on this topic?

Suggested readings for this chapter are listed at the back of this book.

All URLs listed are current as of the printing of this book. URLs often change. Please check our Web site, **http://www.abacon.com/ henslin,** for updates.

1. In this exercise you will use secondary analysis of 1990 census data to construct a table. Go to the 1990 Census lookup page at **http://www.census.gov/cdrom/lookup.** Under the heading "Choose a database to browse," select the database "STF3C-Part 1." At the "Choose an Option" page, click on the *submit* button. At the "Choose a Data Retrieval Option" page, click again on the *submit* button. At the page headed "Select the tables you wish to retrieve," scroll down to "P70-Sex by Employment Status," click on that option, and then scroll back up to the top of the page and click on the *submit* button. At the next "Data Retrieval Option" page, click on the *submit* button. You should see a table that shows the employment status of males and females. Depending on your Web browser, you can either save the table or print it. Use these data to construct a table. Notice that the Census table reports the number of men and women in each employment category; when you construct your own table, you may want to translate ths information into percentages. Apply the concepts presented in Table 5.1 on page 130, "How to Read a Table." Be sure to include all of the elements of a typical table in your final version.

2. As the text discusses, ethics are a fundamental concern of sociologists when they are conducting research. Let's examine some of the policies that govern sociological research. Go to the National Institute of Health (NIH) site at **http://grants.nih.gov/ grants/oprr/humansubjects/guideance/faqoprr.htm** to see the NIH regulations for conducting research on human subjects. Now look at the Code of Ethics of the American Sociological Association (ASA) at **http://www.asanet.org/asaethic.htm.** Write a brief overview of the principles, regulations, and policies that govern research involving human subjects. How are the NIH principles similar to those of the ASA? How are they different?

3. A new research model has been developed in recent years. This model stresses collaboration between academic researchers and community agencies. The Center of Urban Research and Learning at Loyola University of Chicago is engaged in such research. Go to **http://www.luc.edu/depts/curl** and read more about the Center, the collaborative research model, and some of the Center's on-going projects. What are the advantages of this model? What are some of its drawbacks? Write a paper in which you discuss how this new model attempts to bridge the gap between academic research and applied research.

4. As the Down-to-Earth Sociology box on pages 132–133 illustrates, doing sound survey research takes skill. Researchers must learn how to write good survey instruments. Before they can even write a good question, they must analyze factors that could influence the survey. Go to **http://hammock.ifas.ufl.edu/txt/ fairs/13457** and read about reliability, validity, and bias. What impact do these factors have on the design of surveys and survey questions? Continue on and learn more about the three techniques for constructing surveys. After studying Table 1, which compares the different techniques, design three research projects. Use each of the techniques, keeping in mind the issues of validity, reliability, and bias.

chapter

6

Societies to Social Networks

- **Social Groups and Societies**
- **The Transformation of Societies**
  Hunting and Gathering Societies
  Pastoral and Horticultural Societies
  Agricultural Societies
  Industrial Societies
  Postindustrial Societies
- **Groups Within Society**
  Primary Groups
  Secondary Groups
  In-Groups and Out-Groups

Reference Groups
Social Networks
A New Group: Electronic Communities
- **Group Dynamics**
  Effects of Group Size on Stability and Intimacy
  Effects of Group Size on Attitudes and Behavior
  Leadership
  The Power of Peer Pressure: The Asch
    Experiment
  Global Consequences of Group Dynamics
- **Summary and Review**

As soon as the ramp had been erected in the castle [in Chelmo, Poland], people started arriving in trucks . . . the people were told that they had to take a bath, that their clothes had to be disinfected, and that they could hand in any valuable items beforehand to be registered. . . .When they had

undressed they were sent to the cellar of the castle and then along a passageway on to the ramp and from there into the gas-van. In the castle there were signs marked "To the baths."

The gas-vans [had] . . . interior walls . . . lined with sheet metal. On the floor there was a wooden grille. The floor of the van had an opening which could be connected to the exhaust by means of a removable metal pipe. When the trucks were full of people the double doors at the back were closed. . . .

The Kommando member detailed as driver would start the engine straight away so that the people inside the truck were suffocated by the exhaust gases. . . . The van was driven to the camp in the woods where the bodies were unloaded. . . . I then drove the van back to the castle and parked it there. Here it would be cleaned of the excretions of the people that had died in it. Afterwards it would once again be used for gassings. . . .

I can no longer say today what I thought at the time or whether I thought of anything at all. ■

—Testimony of Walter Burmeister in Klee
et al., 1991:219–220.

149

As a society—the largest and most complex type of group—changes, so, too, do the groups, activities, and ultimately the types of people that form that society. The local garage used to be a central meeting place for men. Women felt unwelcome in this "men's territory" and stayed away as men conducted "their" business. The owner and workers would often stop work during the day to swap stories with friends and customers, as shown in this Norman Rockwell painting of a soldier's return from World War II. Our more impersonal *Gesellschaft* society, with its emphasis on "putting out work" at a huge charge per hour, makes such scenes a rarity.

group defined differently by various sociologists, but in a general sense, people who have something in common and who believe that what they have in common is significant; also called a social group

society people who share a culture and a territory

hunting and gathering society a human group dependent on hunting and gathering for its survival

shaman a priest (or intermediary with the spirit world) in a tribal society

Social Groups and Societies

Groups are the essence of life in society. We become who we are because of our membership in human groups. As we saw in Chapter 3, even our mind is a product of society, or, more accurately phrased, of the groups to which we belong.

In this chapter, we'll examine the various groups that make up society, and we'll consider the power that groups wield over us. Although none of us wants to think that we could participate in mass killings such as those recounted in our opening vignette, don't bet on it. You are going to read about some surprising aspects of groups in this chapter.

Sociologists define *group* in many ways. Albion Small (1905), who was mentioned in Chapter 1 as an early North American sociologist, used this term in a broad sense to mean people who have some sort of relationship, so that they are thought of as belonging together. Sociologists Michael Olmsted and Paul Hare (1978) said that the "essential feature of a **group** is that its members have something in common and that they believe what they have in common makes a difference." This will be our general definition of group.

The largest and most complex group that sociologists study is **society,** which consists of people who share a culture and a territory. The characteristics of a society, especially its values and beliefs, profoundly affect the groups within it. In the former Soviet Union, for example, underground artists formed hundreds of groups. They shared opposition to the Soviet state, which they found stifling, and they painted pictures that showed the difficulties of Soviet life. Not being sure that their friends or roommates weren't government spies, however, engendered suspicion and unhappiness among them.

The collapse of the Communist government—which had set up an extensive spy network—put out the spark that had given life to these groups. Today's protest artists focus on other problematic features of Soviet life—from inflation to insecurities brought about by the new capitalism. Thousands of other groups in the former Soviet Union are also adapting to the new conditions of their society. The sociological principle is this: *As a society changes, so do the nature and types of its groups.*

To understand groups, let's first look at the big picture. Let's examine how contemporary society came into being. For example, how did the United States become an industrialized nation with literally millions of groups?

The Transformation of Societies

To better understand this envelope that surrounds us and sets the stage for all our life experiences, let's trace the development of societies from their earliest beginnings. As we review this evolution, portrayed in Figure 6.1 on the facing page, note how changes in technology brought sweeping changes to society. Also picture yourself as a member of each society. Consider how your life would be different in each society—how even your thoughts and values would be different.

Hunting and Gathering Societies

Societies with the fewest social divisions are called **hunting and gathering societies.** As the name implies, these groups depend on hunting and gathering for their survival. In some,

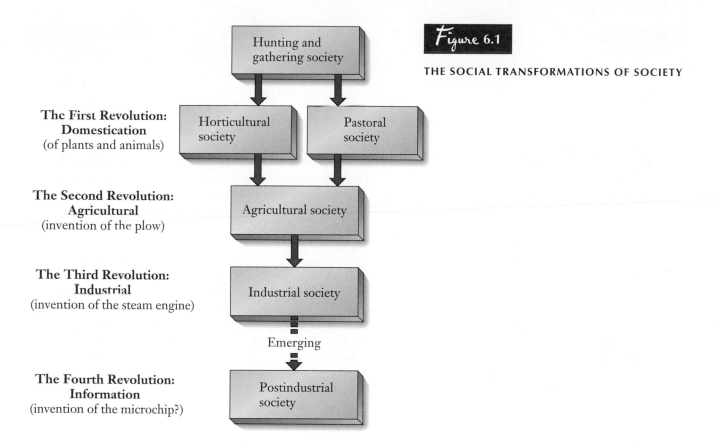

Figure 6.1

THE SOCIAL TRANSFORMATIONS OF SOCIETY

Hunting and gathering society

The First Revolution: Domestication (of plants and animals)

Horticultural society

Pastoral society

The Second Revolution: Agricultural (invention of the plow)

Agricultural society

The Third Revolution: Industrial (invention of the steam engine)

Industrial society

Emerging

The Fourth Revolution: Information (invention of the microchip?)

Postindustrial society

the men do the hunting (of animals), the women the gathering (of plants). In others, both men and women (and children) gather plants, the men hunt the large animals, and both men and women hunt small animals. Beyond this basic division of labor by sex, there are few social divisions. The groups usually have a **shaman,** an individual thought to be able to influence spiritual forces, but shamans, too, must help obtain food. Although these groups give greater prestige to the men hunters, the women gatherers contribute more food to the group, perhaps even four-fifths of their total food supply(Bernard 1992).

In addition to gender, the major unit of organization is the family. Most members are related by ancestry or marriage. Because the family is the only distinct social institution in these societies, it fulfills functions that are divided among many specialized institutions in modern societies. The family distributes food to its members, educates its children (especially in food skills), nurses the sick, and so on.

Because an area cannot support a large number of people who hunt animals and gather plants (they do not plant, only gather what is already there), hunting and gathering societies are small. They usually consist of only twenty-five to forty people. These groups are nomadic, moving from one place to another as the food supply of an area gives out. They place a high value on sharing food, which is essential to their survival. Some groups run a high risk of having their food supply destroyed—by disease, drought, famine, and pestilence. Members of hunting and gathering groups have only about a fifty-fifty chance of surviving childhood (Lenski and Lenski 1987).

Of all societies, hunters and gatherers are the most egalitarian. Because what they hunt and gather is perishable, the people can't accumulate possessions. Consequently, no one becomes wealthier than anyone else. There are no rulers, and most decisions are arrived at through discussion. Because their needs are basic and they do not accumulate material possessions, hunters and gatherers have the most leisure of all human groups (Sahlins 1972; Lorber 1994; Volti 1995).

All human groups were once hunters and gatherers, and until several hundred years ago such societies were common. Their demise came when other groups took over the areas

The simplest societies are called hunting and gathering societies. The members of these societies have adapted well to their environments. They have the most leisure of people in any type of society. The man shown here is a member of a hunting and gathering society in the Brazilian Amazon.

FUNDAMENTAL CONSEQUENCES OF ANIMAL HUSBANDRY AND PLANT CULTIVATION

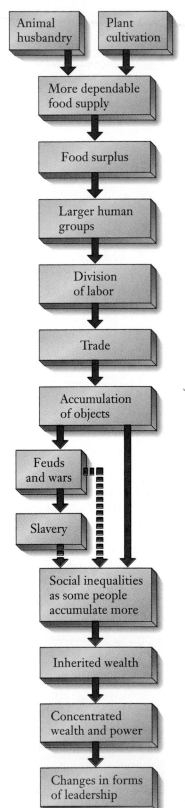

on which they depended for their food. Today, only a few remain, such as the pygmies of central Africa, the San of the Namibian desert, and the aborigines of Australia. These groups seem doomed to a similar fate, and it is likely that their way of life will soon disappear from the human scene (Lenski and Lenski 1987).

Pastoral and Horticultural Societies

About ten thousand to twelve thousand years ago, some groups found that they could tame and breed some of the animals they hunted—primarily goats, sheep, cattle, and camels. Others discovered that they could cultivate plants. As a result, hunting and gathering societies branched in one of two directions.

The key to understanding the first branching is the word *pasture;* **pastoral societies** are based on the *pasturing of animals.* Pastoral societies developed in arid regions, where lack of rainfall made it impractical to build life around crops. Groups that took this turn remained nomadic, for they followed their animals to fresh pasture. The key to understanding the second branching is the word *horticulture,* or plant cultivation. **Horticultural societies** are based on the *cultivation of plants by the use of hand tools.* Because they no longer had to abandon an area as the food supply gave out, these groups developed permanent settlements.

We can call the domestication of animals and plants the *first social revolution.* As shown in Figure 6.1, it transformed human society. Although the **domestication revolution** was extremely gradual, occurring over a period of thousands of years, it represented a fundamental break with the past and changed human history.

Horticulture may have begun independently in several areas of the globe, including the fertile areas of the Middle East and Central and South America. Primitive agricultural technology—which consisted of hoes and digging sticks (used to punch holes in the ground for seeds)—gradually spread to Europe and China. We don't know for certain if these techniques were independently invented in several parts of the world or if, due to contacts yet unknown to us, they spread through *cultural diffusion* (the dispersion of items from one culture to another).

The sociological significance of animal husbandry and plant cultivation is that they *transformed human society.* By creating a more dependable food supply, they ushered in a series of changes that altered almost every aspect of human life. Because a more dependable food supply was able to support more people, human groups became larger. With more food than was necessary for survival, not everyone had to produce food. This allowed groups to develop a specialized division of labor: Some people became full-time priests; others made jewelry, tools, weapons, and so on. This production of objects, in turn, stimulated trade. As groups traded with one another, they began to accumulate objects they considered valuable, such as gold, jewelry, and utensils.

As Figure 6.2 illustrates, these changes set the stage for social inequality, for now some families (or clans) acquired more goods than others. Feuds and wars erupted, for groups now possessed animals, pastures, croplands, jewelry, and other material goods to fight about. War, in turn, opened the door to slavery, for people found it convenient to let captives from their battles do their drudge work. Social stratification remained limited, however, for the surplus itself was limited. As individuals passed on their possessions to their descendants, wealth grew more concentrated and power more centralized. Forms of leadership then changed as chiefs emerged.

Note that the primary pattern that runs through this fundamental transformation of group life is the change *from fewer to more possessions and from greater to lesser equality.* Where people were located *within* a society came to be vital for determining what happened to them in life. Again, Figure 6.2 summarizes how these changes led to social inequality.

Agricultural Societies

About five to six thousand years ago, the invention of a new technology, the plow, changed social life forever. With the **agricultural revolution** came a new type of society. Compared with hoes and digging sticks, the use of animals to pull plows was immensely efficient. As the ground was turned up, more nutrients were returned to the soil, making the land more productive. The resulting food surplus was unlike anything ever seen in human history. It allowed even more people to engage in activities other than farming. In this new **agricultural society,** people developed cities and the things popularly known as "culture," such as philosophy, art, literature, and architecture. Accompanied by the inventions of the wheel, writing, and numbers, the changes during this period in history were so profound that they sometimes are referred to as "the dawn of civilization."

Though societies previously had shown a tendency toward social inequality, such inequality now became a fundamental feature of social life. Some people managed to gain control of the surplus resources. To protect their expanding privileges and power, this elite surrounded itself with armed men. They even levied taxes on others, who now had become their "subjects." As conflict theorists point out, this concentration of resources and power, along with the oppression of people not in power, was the forerunner of the state.

No one knows exactly how it happened, but sometime during this period females also became subjugated to males. Sociologist Elise Boulding (1976) theorizes that this change occurred because men were in charge of plowing and the cows. She suggests that when metals were developed, men took on the new job of attaching the metal as tips to the wooden plows and doing the plowing. As a result,

> the shift of the status of the woman farmer may have happened quite rapidly, once there were two male specializations relating to agriculture: plowing and the care of cattle. This situation left women with all the subsidiary tasks, including weeding and carrying water to the fields. The new fields were larger, so women had to work just as many hours as they did before, but now they worked at more secondary tasks. . . .This would contribute further to the erosion of the status of women.

This explanation, however, creates more questions than it answers. Why, for example, did men take over metal work and plowing? Why didn't women? Why did anyone? It also does not account for why men control societies in which women are in charge of the cattle. In short, we are left in the dark as to why and how men became dominant, a reason likely to remain lost in human history.

Industrial Societies

In the 1700s, the invention of another new technology again turned society upside down. In 1765 the steam engine was first used to run machinery in Britain, and this marked the start of the **Industrial Revolution.** Before this, people used a few machines (such as wind and water mills) to harness nature, but most machines had depended on human and animal power. This new source of energy led to the development of **industrial society,** defined by sociologist Herbert Blumer (1990) as a society in which goods are produced by machines powered by fuels, instead of by the brute force of humans or animals.

This new form of production was far more efficient than anything before it. Just as its surplus was greater, so were its effects on the human group. Again social inequality increased, especially during the first stage of industrialization. The individuals who first used the new technology accumulated such great wealth that in many instances their riches outran the imagination of kings. Gaining an early position in the markets, they were able not only to control the means of production (factories, machinery, tools), but also to dictate people's working conditions. The breakdown of feudal society made it even easier for them to control their workers. Masses of people were thrown off the lands that they and their ancestors had farmed as tenants for centuries. Having become homeless, these landless peasants moved to the cities. There they faced the choice of stealing, starving, or working for starvation wages (Chambliss 1964; Michalowski 1985).

Workers had no legal right to safety, or even to humane working conditions. They also had no right to unionize. The law considered employment to be a private contract between the employer and the individual worker. If workers banded together to improve some condition of their work or to ask for higher wages, they were fired. If they returned to the factory, they were arrested for trespassing on private property. Strikes were illegal, and strikers

pastoral society a society based on the pasturing of animals

horticultural society a society based on cultivating plants by the use of hand tools

domestication revolution the first social revolution, based on the domestication of plants and animals, which led to pastoral and horticultural societies

agricultural revolution the second social revolution, based on the invention of the plow, which led to agricultural society

agricultural society a society based on large-scale agriculture, dependent on plows drawn by animals

Industrial Revolution the third social revolution, occurring when machines powered by fuels replaced most animal and human power

industrial society a society based on the harnessing of machines powered by fuels

were savagely beaten by the employer's private security force. On some occasions, U.S. strikers were shot by private police, and even by the National Guard.

Against huge odds, workers gradually won their fight for better working conditions. Wealth then spread to ever larger segments of society. Eventually, home ownership became common, as did the ownership of automobiles and an incredible variety of consumer goods. Today's typical worker in advanced industrial societies enjoys a high standard of living in terms of material conditions, health care, longevity, and access to libraries and education. Such gains go far beyond what early social reformers could have imagined.

As industrialization progressed, then, it reversed the pattern set earlier, and equality increased. Indicators of greater equality include better housing and a vast increase in consumer goods, the abolition of slavery, the shift from monarchies to more representative political systems, the right to be tried by a jury of one's peers and to cross-examine witnesses, the right to vote, the right to travel, and greater rights for women and minorities.

It is difficult to overstate the sociological principle that the type of society we live in is the fundamental reason for why we become who we are. To see how industrial society affects your life, note that you would not be taking this course if it were not for industrialization. Clearly you would not have a computer, car, telephone, DVD player, television, or your type of clothing or home. You wouldn't even have electric lights. You would also be affected on a much deeper level than material items—you would not feel the same about life, or have your particular aspirations for the future. Actually, no aspect of your life would be the same; you would be locked into the attitudes and views that come with an agricultural or horticultural way of life.

Postindustrial Societies

If you were to choose one word that characterizes our society, what would it be? Of the many candidates, the word *change* would have to rank high among them. The primary source of the sweeping change that is transforming our lives is the new technology centering around the microchip. The change is so vast that sociologists say that a new type of society is emerging. They call it the **postindustrial society.**

What are the main characteristics of this new society? Unlike the industrial society from which we are emerging, its hallmark is not raw materials and manufacturing. Rather, its basic component is *information.* Teachers pass on knowledge to students, while lawyers, physicians, bankers, pilots, and interior decorators sell their specialized knowledge of law, the body, money, aerodynamics, and color schemes to clients. Unlike the factory workers in an industrial society, these workers don't *produce* anything. Rather, they transmit or use information to provide services that others are willing to pay for.

The United States was the first country to have more than 50 percent of its work force in service industries such as education, health, research, the government, counseling, banking, investments, insurance, sales, law, and the mass media. Australia, New Zealand, western Europe, and Japan soon followed. This basic trend away from manufacturing to selling information and services shows no sign of letting up.

The changes are so fundamental that we are undergoing a *fourth social revolution.* As we saw with preceding societies, new technology can transform established ways of life, uprooting old perspectives and replacing them with new ones. So it is with the microchip. This new invention allows people to work at home and to talk to others in distant cities and even in countries on the other side of the globe while driving in their automobiles. Because of it, we can peer farther into the remote recesses of space than ever before. Because of it, our buying patterns are changing as we spend billions of dollars on Internet purchases. And because of it, millions of children spend countless hours struggling against video enemies, at home and in the arcades. For a review of other changes, see the section on *the computer* in Chapter 22 (pages 646–649).

Although the full implications of the information explosion are still unknown, of this we can be certain: Just as the larger group called society has always exerted a fundamental force on people's thinking and behavior, so it will in its new form. As society is transformed,

postindustrial society a society based on information, services, and high technology, rather than on raw materials and manufacturing

we, too, shall be swept along with it. As history is our guide, the changes will be so extensive that they will transform even our attitudes about the self and life.

There is no "historical necessity" governing the transformation of societies. That is, there is no reason that all the world's societies must go through the same stages and become postindustrial. Whether any hunting and gathering societies will survive during the next decades, however, remains to be seen. In today's transition, many countries are "mixed" types. China, for example, is mostly agricultural, yet it has a large and growing industrial base. The Social Map below shows the world's divisions by type of society.

GROUPS WITHIN SOCIETY

One of the main concerns of sociologist Emile Durkheim (1933) was what prevents *anomie* (AN-uh-mee), that bewildering sense of not belonging. He found the answer in small groups, which he said stand as a buffer between the individual and the larger society. If it weren't for these groups, he said, we would feel oppressed by that huge, amorphous entity known as society. By establishing intimate relationships, small groups give us a sense of meaning and purpose, helping to prevent anomie.

Before we examine groups in more detail, we should distinguish some terms. Two terms sometimes confused with "group" are *aggregate* and *category*. An **aggregate** consists of individuals who temporarily share the same physical space but who do not see themselves as belonging together. People waiting in a checkout line or drivers parked at the same red light are an aggregate. A **category** consists of people who have similar characteristics, such as all college women who wear glasses or all men over 6 feet tall. Unlike groups, the individuals who make up a category neither interact with one another nor take one another into account.

aggregate individuals who temporarily share the same physical space but do not see themselves as belonging together

category people who have similar characteristics

Figure 6.3 **SOCIAL MAP: TYPES OF SOCIETIES IN TODAY'S WORLD**

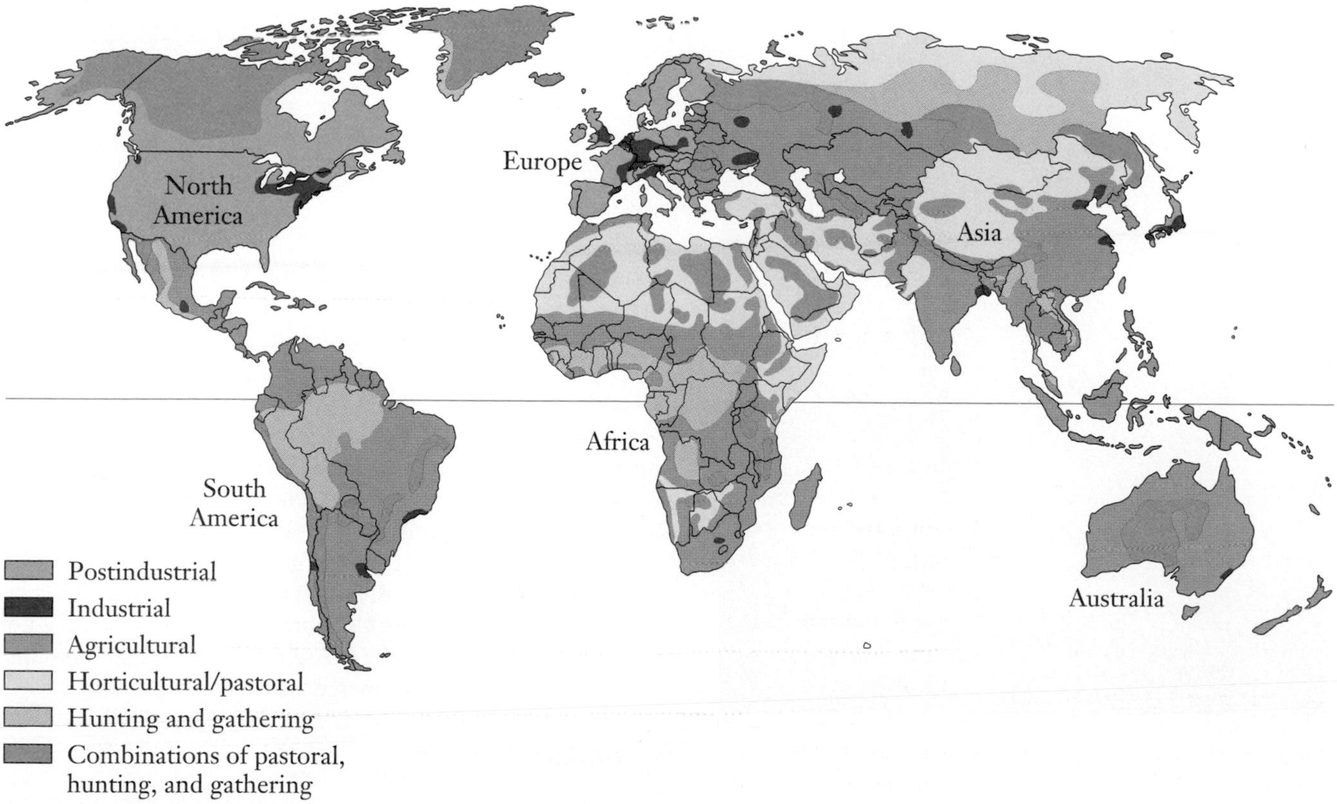

- Postindustrial
- Industrial
- Agricultural
- Horticultural/pastoral
- Hunting and gathering
- Combinations of pastoral, hunting, and gathering

Primary groups such as the family, a key focus of socio-logical investigation, play a key role in the develop-ment of the self. As a small group, the family also serves as a buffer from the often-threatening larger group known as society. The family has been of primary significance in forming the basic orientations of this Latino couple, as it will be for their daughter.

In contrast, the members of a *group* think of themselves as belonging together, and they interact with one another. To better understand this essential feature of social life, let's look at the types of groups that make up our society and at how they affect our lives.

Primary Groups

Our first group, the family, gives us our basic orientation to life. Later, among friends, we find more intimacy and an additional sense of belonging. These groups are what sociolo-gist Charles Cooley called **primary groups.** By providing intimate, face-to-face interaction, they give us an identity, a feeling of who we are. As Cooley (1909) put it,

> By primary groups I mean those characterized by intimate face-to-face association and cooper-ation. They are primary in several senses, but <u>chiefly in that they are fundamental in forming the social nature and ideals of the individual.</u>

primary group a group charac-terized by intimate, long-term, face-to-face association and cooperation

secondary group compared with a primary group, a larger, relatively temporary, more anonymous, formal, and im-personal group based on some interest or activity, whose mem-bers are likely to interact on the basis of specific roles

Producing a Mirror Within It is significant that Cooley calls primary groups the "springs of life." By this, he means that primary groups are essential to our emotional well-being—whether those groups be the family, friends, or even gangs. As humans, we have an intense need for face-to-face interaction that generates feelings of self-esteem. By offering a sense of be-longing, a feeling of being appreciated, and sometimes even loved, primary groups are uniquely equipped to meet this basic human need.

Primary groups are also so significant because their values and attitudes become fused into our identity. We internalize their views, which become the lenses through which we view life. Even as adults—no matter how far we may have come from our childhood roots—early primary groups remain "inside" us, where they continue to form part of the perspective from which we look out onto the world. Ultimately, then, it is difficult, if not impossible, for us to separate the self from our primary groups, for the self and our groups merge into a "we."

Relationships in secondary groups are more formal and temporary than those in primary groups. In order to satisfy basic emotional needs, members of secondary groups, such as members of the military, form smaller primary groups.

Secondary Groups

Compared with primary groups, **secondary groups** are larger, relatively temporary, more anonymous, more formal, and more impersonal. Secondary groups are based on some interest or activity, and their members are likely to interact on the basis of specific roles, such as president, manager, worker, or student. Examples are a college classroom, the American Sociological Association, a factory, or the Democratic party.

In hunting and gathering and horticultural societies, the entire society forms a primary group. In industrial and postindustrial societies, secondary groups have become essential to our welfare. They are part of the way we get our education, make our living, and spend our money and leisure time.

As necessary as secondary groups are for contemporary life, they often fail to satisfy our deep needs for intimate association. Consequently, *secondary groups tend to break down into primary groups*. For Walter Burmeister in our opening vignette, his police-army unit was a secondary group. The police-army buddies he drank with, though, formed a primary group. We, too, at school and work, form friendship cliques. Our interaction with them is so important to us that we sometimes feel that if it weren't for our friends, school or work "would drive us crazy." The primary groups we form within secondary groups, then, serve as a buffer between us and the demands that secondary groups place on us.

In-Groups and Out-Groups

Groups toward which we feel loyalty are called **in-groups**; those toward which we feel antagonisms, **out-groups**. For Walter Burmeister in our opening vignette, and the thousands like him, the police-army unit was an in-group, while the Jews and all others who were classified as "enemies of the state" were out-groups. That we make such a fundamental division of the world has far-reaching consequences for our lives.

Producing Loyalty and a Sense of Superiority Identification with a group can generate not only a sense of belonging, but also loyalty and feelings of superiority. These, in turn, often produce rivalries. Usually the rivalries are mild, such as sports rivalries between neighboring towns, and the most extreme act is likely to be the furtive invasion of the out-group's territory in order to steal a mascot, paint a rock, or uproot a goal post. The consequences

"So long, Bill. This is my club. You can't come in."

How our participation in social groups shapes our self-concept is a major focus of symbolic interactionists. In this process, knowing who we are *not* is as significant as knowing who we are.

in-groups groups toward which one feels loyalty

out-groups groups toward which one feels antagonisms

All of us have reference groups—the groups we refer to when we evaluate ourselves. Although the groups by which we evaluate our own attitudes and behaviors certainly differ from the reference groups of these members of the KKK who are demonstrating in Houston, Texas, both ours and theirs serve the same sociological functions.

of in-group membership also <u>can be discrimination</u>, <u>hatred</u>, and, as we saw in our opening vignette, even a willingness to participate in mass murder.

Implications for Social Diversity It is not surprising that in-group membership leads to discrimination, for, with our strong identifications and loyalties, we all favor members of our in-groups. This aspect of in- and out-groups is, of course, the basis of many problems in society. It underlies many gender and racial-ethnic divisions. As sociologist Robert Merton (1968) observed, one consequence is an interesting double standard. We view the traits of our in-group as virtues, while we see those *same* traits in out-groups as vices. The Nazis in our opening vignette saw themselves as intelligent men, the saviors of the human race. Instead of acknowledging a Jew as intelligent, however, they would say the individual was scheming or sly. Today, men may perceive an aggressive man as assertive, but an aggressive woman as pushy. A male employee who doesn't speak up may be thought of as "knowing when to keep his mouth shut," whereas a quiet woman may be perceived as too timid to make it in the business world.

To divide the world into "we" and "them" poses a severe danger for a pluralistic society. As the Jews did for the Nazis, an out-group can come to symbolize evil, arousing contempt and hatred. During times of economic insecurity, for example, *xenophobia,* or fear of strangers, may grow. For some, the out-group may represent jobs that have been "stolen" from their friends and family. The result may be attacks against immigrants, a national anti-immigration policy, or a resurgence of neo-Nazis or the Ku Klux Klan.

In short, to divide the world into in-groups and out-groups is a natural part of social life. But in addition to bringing about functional consequences, it can bring about some highly dysfunctional ones.

Reference Groups

Suppose you have just been offered a good job. It pays double what you hope to make even after you graduate from college. You have just three days to make up your mind. If you accept it, you will have to drop out of college. As you consider the matter, thoughts like this may go through your mind: "My friends will say I'm a fool if I don't take the job . . . but Dad and Mom will practically go crazy. They've made sacrifices for me, and they'd be crushed if I didn't finish college. They've always said I've got to get my education first, that good jobs will always be there. . . . But, then, I'd like to see the look on the faces of those neighbors who said I'd never amount to much!"

We all use reference groups to evaluate our accomplishments, failures, values, and attitudes. We compare what we see in ourselves with what we perceive as normative in these groups. As is evident in these two photos, the reference groups these youths are using are unlikely to lead them to the same social destination.

This is an example of how people use **reference groups,** the groups that embody the standards we use to evaluate ourselves. Your reference groups may include family, the Scouts, the members of a church or synagogue, your neighbors, teachers, classmates, and co-workers. Your reference group need not be one you actually belong to; it may include a group to which you aspire. For example, if you are thinking about going to graduate school, graduate students or members of the profession you want to join may form your reference group as you evaluate your grades or writing skills.

Providing a Yardstick Reference groups exert tremendous influence over our lives. For example, if you want to become a corporate executive, you might start to dress more formally, try to improve your vocabulary, read the *Wall Street Journal,* and change your major to business or law. In contrast, if you want to become a rock musician, you might wear three earrings in one ear, dress in ways your parents and many of your peers consider extreme, read *Rolling Stone,* drop out of college, and hang around clubs and rock groups.

Exposure to Contradictory Standards in a Socially Diverse Society From these examples, you can see that the yardsticks provided by reference groups operate as a form of social control. When we see ourselves as measuring up to the yardstick, there is no conflict. If our behavior, or even aspirations, do not match the standards held by a reference group, however, the mismatch can lead to inner turmoil. For example, to want to become a corporate officer would create no inner turmoil for most of us, but it would if we had grown up in an Amish home, for the Amish strongly disapprove of such activities for their children. They ban high school and college education, three-piece suits, and corporate employment. Similarly, if you wanted to become a soldier and your parents were dedicated pacifists, you likely would experience deep conflict, as your parents would hold quite different aspirations for you.

Given the social diversity of our society as well as our social mobility, many of us are exposed to contradictory ideas and standards from the many groups that become significant to us. The "internal recordings" that play contradictory messages from these reference groups, then, are one cost of social mobility.

Social Networks

If you are a member of a large group, there probably are a few people within that group with whom you regularly associate. In a sociology class I was teaching at a commuter campus, six women chose to work together on a project. They got along well, and they began to sit together. Eventually they planned a Christmas party at one of their homes. These clusters, or internal factions, are called **cliques.** The links between people—their cliques, as well as their family, friends, acquaintances, and even "friends of friends"—are called **social networks.** Think of a social network as ties that extend outward from yourself, gradually encompassing more and more people.

The Small World Phenomenon Although we live in a huge society, we don't experience social life as an ocean of nameless, strange faces. Instead, we interact within social networks that connect us to the larger society. Social scientists have wondered just how extensive the connections are between social networks. If you list everyone you know, and each of those individuals lists everyone he or she knows, and you keep doing this, would almost everyone in the United States eventually be included on those lists?

It would be too cumbersome to test this hypothesis by drawing up such lists, but psychologist Stanley Milgram (1967) hit on an ingenious way to find out just how interconnected our social networks are. In what has become a classic experiment known as "the small world phenomenon," he selected names at random from across the United States. Some he designated as "senders," others as "receivers." Milgram addressed letters to the receivers and asked the senders to mail the letters to someone they knew on a first-name basis who they thought might know the receiver. This person, in turn, was asked to mail the letter to someone he or she knew who might know the receiver, and so on. The question was, Would the letters ever get to the receivers? If so, how long would the chain be?

reference groups Herbert Hyman's term for the groups we use as standards to evaluate ourselves

clique a cluster of people within a larger group who choose to interact with one another; an internal faction

social network the social ties radiating outward from the self that link people together

Although personal abilities and efforts are vitally important for success in life, so are social characteristics. Among them are our social networks, which open and close doors of opportunity. A good example occurs at sociology conventions. Despite the official program, much of the "real" business centers around renewing and extending social networks.

Think of yourself as part of this experiment. What would you do if you were a sender, but the receiver lived in a state in which you know no one? You would send the letter to someone you knew who might know someone in that state. And this is just what happened. None of the senders knew the receivers, and in the resulting chains some links broke; that is, after receiving a letter, some people didn't send it on. Surprisingly, however, most letters did reach their intended receivers. Even more surprising, the average chain was made up of only *five* links.

Global Considerations Milgram's experiment shows just how small our world really is, and it gives us insight into why strangers from different parts of the country sometimes find they have a mutual acquaintance. If our social networks are so interrelated that almost everyone in the United States is connected by just five links, how many links connect us to everyone on earth? This experiment is yet to be done.

networking using one's social networks for some gain

Implications for Social Diversity One reason that overcoming social inequality (the subject of Chapters 9–13) is so difficult is that our own social networks contribute to inequality. This topic is explored in the Diversity box below.

PERSPECTIVES | Cultural Diversity in the United States

HOW OUR SOCIAL NETWORKS PERPETUATE SOCIAL INEQUALITY

Consider some of the principles we have reviewed. People tend to form in-groups with which they identify, they use reference groups to evaluate their attitudes and behavior, and they interact in social networks. Our in-groups, reference groups, and social networks are likely to consist of people whose backgrounds are similar to our own. This means that, for most of us, just as social inequality is built into society, so it is built into our own relationships. One consequence is that *we, too, tend to perpetuate social inequality.*

Consider social networks and jobs. Suppose that an outstanding job—great pay, interesting work, and opportunity for advancement—has just opened up where you work. Whom will you tell? Most likely it will be someone you know, someone for whom you would like to do a favor. And most likely your important social network is made up of people who look much like yourself—especially in terms of race, age, and social class. This tends to keep good jobs moving in the direction of people who have characteristics similar to those of the people already in an organization. Our social networks, then, are an essential part of social inequality. They both reflect the

inequality that characterizes our society and they help to perpetuate it.

One result is the "old boy network," white men who are established in an organization. As they learn of opportunities (jobs, investments, real estate development, and so on), they share this information with their networks. This helps keep opportunities and good jobs flowing to people who have characteristics similar to their own. Those who benefit from this information, in turn, reciprocate with similar information when they learn of it. This perpetuates the "old boys' " control and locks out others from opportunities— people who have different characteristics, women and minorities.

To overcome this barrier, women and minorities do **networking.** They develop and use their own social networks, usually for career advancement. Hoping to establish a circle of acquaintances who will prove valuable to them, like the "good old boys," they, too, go to parties, join clubs, churches, synagogues, and political parties. African-American leaders cultivate a network of African-American leaders, and women cultivate a network of women. Their networks are not limited to people like themselves, but, like the white men, their networks

tend to center around people who look like them. The network of African-American leaders is so tight that one-fifth of the entire national African-American leadership are personal acquaintances. Add some "friends of a friend," and *three-fourths* of the entire leadership belong to the same network (Taylor 1992). Women who reach top positions end up in a circle so tight that the term "new girl" network is now being used, especially in the field of law. Remembering those who helped them and sympathetic to those who are trying to get ahead, these women tend to steer their business to other women. Like the "good old boys" who preceded them, the new insiders also justify their exclusionary practice (Jacobs 1997). ■

For Your Consideration

The principles that tend to perpetuate social inequality are clear. They do not depend on gender or race-ethnicity. Just as white men do, women and minorities tend to favor people who look like them. What suggestions do you have for breaking this cycle? The key must center on creating diversity in social networks.

A New Group: Electronic Communities

In the 1990s, due to our new technology, an entirely new type of human group, the **electronic community,** made its appearance. On the Internet are hundreds of thousands of people who communicate electronically about almost any conceivable topic, from donkey racing and bird-watching to sociology and quantum physics. Most news groups provide only an interesting, new way of communicating. Some, however, meet our definition of *group:* people who interact with one another and who think of themselves as belonging together.

Some of these groups pride themselves on the distinctive nature of their interest and knowledge—factors that give them a common identity, bind them together, and distinguish them from others. This new form of group is explored in the Sociology and the New Technology box on the next page.

$\mathcal{G}$ROUP DYNAMICS

As you know from personal experience, the lively interaction *within* groups—who does what with whom—has profound consequences for how you adjust to life. Sociologists use the term **group dynamics** to refer to how groups affect us and how we affect groups. Let's consider the differences that the size of a group makes, and then examine leadership, conformity, and decision making.

Before doing this, we should see what sociologists mean by the term **small group.** This is a group small enough for everyone to interact directly with all the other members. Small groups can be either primary or secondary. A wife, husband, and children, as well as workers who take their breaks together, are examples of primary small groups, while bidders at an auction and passengers on a flight from Saint Louis to Minneapolis are examples of secondary small groups.

Effects of Group Size on Stability and Intimacy

Writing in the early 1900s, sociologist Georg Simmel (1858–1918) noted the significance of group size. He used the term **dyad** for the smallest possible group, which consists of two people. Dyads, which include marriages, love affairs, and close friendships, show two distinct qualities. First, they are the most intense or intimate of human groups. Because only two

electronic community individuals who more or less regularly interact with one another on the Internet

group dynamics the ways in which individuals affect groups and the ways in which groups influence individuals

small group a group small enough for everyone to interact directly with all the other members

dyad the smallest possible group, consisting of two people

Japanese who work for the same firm think of themselves more as a group or team, Americans more as individuals. Japanese corporations use many techniques to encourage group identity, such as making group exercise a part of the work day. Sociologically, similarity of appearance and activity helps to fuse group identity and company loyalty.

Sociology & the New Technology

ELECTRONIC COMMUNITIES: CYBERCOMMUNICATIONS AND OUR CHANGING CULTURE

As you have seen in this chapter, a new technology can change the way people relate to one another, and, sometimes, even transform the shape of society itself. This is what happened with the domestication of animals and the invention of the plow and the steam engine. Today's new technology, the microchip, is also changing human relationships, and it, too, may transform the face of society.

Through most of human history, "talk" meant face-to-face communication. With the invention of writing, people who were far apart could "talk" to one another—leaving a record of what they "said." Another transforming technology, the printing press, not only multiplied the power of "long-distance talk," but it even transformed religion and politics by putting literature in the hands of common people. By making Bibles available to the masses, the printing press broke the dominance of the Roman Catholic Church as the exclusive interpreter of God's Word. Political tracts, pouring off the press, encouraged independent thinking. Independent religious and political thinking undermined church and monarchy, helping to bring about constitutional forms of government and ushering in our wide variety of protestant religions.

If we think of the media as passive channels of information, as mere "holders" and "senders" of messages, we miss the sociological point. The media certainly do transmit messages, but they also shape our lives. Just as the new technology of the printing press changed people's ideas and undermined the power of church and government, so our new technology is not only bringing new forms of "talk" but is also changing our relationships. It, too, may transform our social institutions.

Consider how electronic communications, centering on the Internet,

In the days before television . . .

are extending the boundaries of our homes. While remaining home, we instantly "travel" electronically around the world. With global translating programs available online, even language barriers have been broken. We can share information with people we have never met, and develop friendships with people across the globe.

The result is the **electronic community,** a type of group that until now was unknown in human history, but which we already take for granted. Electronic communities center on any shared interest, whether it be antique cars, radical politics, or deviant sex. In most instances, these communities are like a circle of acquaintances. People share information with one another, but they also hold back many personal details. In some cases, these communities offer a form of support. People who suffer from cancer form online support groups. By sharing their experiences with pain, surgery, radiation, and chemotherapy, they break the depressing experience of isolation. People who suffer from other debilitating diseases do the same.

In some cases, people even form what we might call an "**electronic primary group.**" Here, as they regu-

larly interact with one another, they share more personal information, sometimes even of an intimate nature. They come to identify with one another, and they develop a sense of intimacy. Some people build their life around these groups. They eagerly get online the first thing each morning to read their latest e-mails from their Internet friends, and to go to exclusive "chat rooms" where they discuss the latest development in their "real" (not online) relationships. Only then do they get dressed and go to work. After work, they rush back to their online world. For them, the people they have "met" electronically are as real as their family—and sometimes have a greater impact on their lives.

The implications of cybercommunications for social relationships are tentative. An interesting aspect is that easy access to people in distant localities can separate us from people nearby (Meyrowitz 1995). For example, I may only wave to my next-door neighbor when I walk between my car and house—and only if we happen to be outside at the same time. Yet I contact my Net friends on a regular basis. I know more about events in their households than I do about what is happening to my next door neighbor.

It is likely that we are seeing a new form of social intimacy emerge. With the Net, people need never meet in order to identify on a personal, even intimate, basis. They experience closeness without permanence, and depth without commitment (Cerulo et al. 1992). It is too soon to know the ramifications of this changed sense of community, and at this point we can only identify some of its characteristics. The new electronic primary groups, however, seem bound to affect not only our social interactions, but also our culture, and even our sense of self. ■

people are involved, the interaction is focused on them. Second, because dyads require the active participation and commitment of both members, they are the most unstable of social groups. If one member loses interest, the dyad collapses. In larger groups, in contrast, even if one member withdraws, the group can continue, for its existence does not depend on any single member (Simmel 1950).

A **triad** is a group of three people. As Simmel noted, the addition of a third person fundamentally changes the group. For example, with the birth of a child hardly any aspect of a couple's relationship goes untouched. Their social life, conversations, even lovemaking, change. Despite difficulties that couples experience adjusting to their first child, their marriage is usually strengthened. Simmel's principle that groups larger than a dyad are inherently stronger helps explain why. Like dyads, triads are also intense, for interaction is shared by only three people; but because interaction is shared with an additional person, the intensity lessens.

Simmel also pointed out that triads, too, are inherently unstable. Because relationships among a group's members are seldom neatly balanced, **coalitions** tend to form; that is, some group members align themselves against others. In a triad, it is not uncommon for two members to feel stronger bonds with one another, leading them to act as a dyad and leaving the third person feeling hurt and excluded. In addition, triads sometimes produce an arbitrator or mediator, someone who tries to settle disagreements between the other two.

The general principle is this: *As a small group grows larger, it becomes more stable, but its intensity, or intimacy, decreases.* To see why, look at Figure 6.4. As each person comes into a group, the connections among people multiply. In a dyad, there is only 1 relationship; in a triad, 3; in a group of four, 6; in a group of five, 10. If we expand the group to six, we have 15 relationships; while a group of seven yields 21 relationships. If we continue adding members, we soon are unable to follow the connections: A group of eight has 28 possible relationships; a group of nine, 36 relationships; a group of ten 45; and so on.

It is not only the number of relationships that makes larger groups more stable. As groups grow, they tend to develop a more formal structure to accomplish their goals. For example, leaders emerge and more specialized roles come into play, often resulting in such

---

Figure 6.4   **THE EFFECTS OF GROUP SIZE ON RELATIONSHIPS**

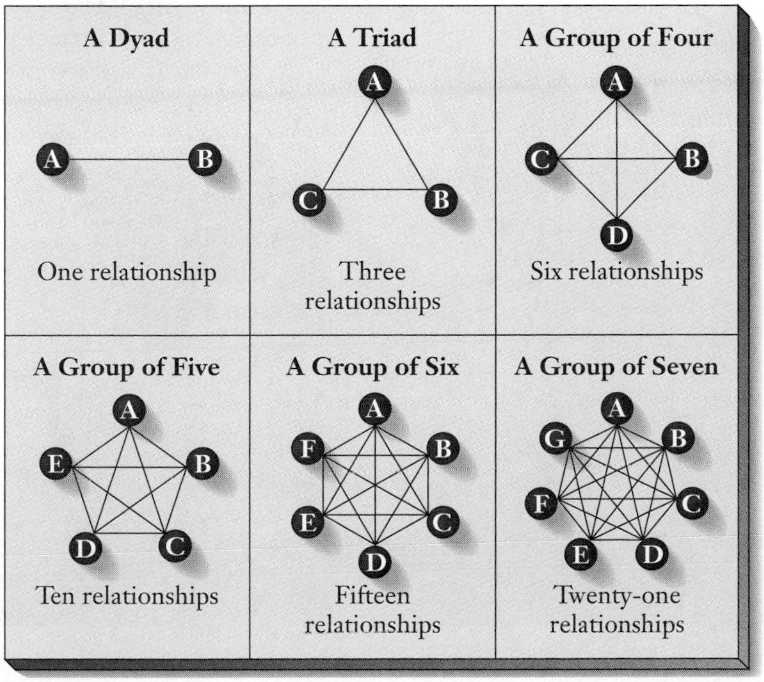

A Dyad	A Triad	A Group of Four
One relationship	Three relationships	Six relationships

A Group of Five	A Group of Six	A Group of Seven
Ten relationships	Fifteen relationships	Twenty-one relationships

---

"electronic primary group" individuals who regularly interact with one another on the Internet, who see themselves as a group, and who develop close ties with one another

triad a group of three people

coalition the alignment of some members of a group against others

familiar offices as president, secretary, and treasurer. This structure provides a framework that helps the group survive over time.

Effects of Group Size on Attitudes and Behavior

Imagine that your social psychology professors have asked you to join a few students to discuss your adjustment to college life. When you arrive, they tell you that to make the discussion anonymous they want you to sit unseen in a booth. You will participate in the discussion over an intercom, talking when your microphone comes on. The professors say they will not listen to the conversation, and they leave.

You find the format somewhat strange, to say the least, but you go along with it. You have not seen the other students in their booths, but when they begin to talk about their experiences, you find yourself becoming wrapped up in the problems they are sharing. One student even mentions how frightening he has found college because of his history of epileptic seizures. Later, this individual begins to breathe heavily into the microphone. Then he stammers and cries for help. A crashing noise follows, and you imagine him lying helpless on the floor. Nothing but an eerie silence follows. What do you do?

Your professors, John Darley and Bibb Latané (1968), staged the whole thing, but you don't know that. No one had a seizure. In fact, no students were even in the other booths. Everything, except your comments, was on tape.

Some participants were told they would be discussing the topic with just one other student, others with two, others with three, and so on. Darley and Latané found that all students who thought they were part of a dyad rushed out to help. If they thought they were part of a triad, only 80 percent went to help—and they were slower in leaving the booth. In six-person groups, only 60 percent went to see what was wrong—and they were even slower.

This experiment demonstrates how deeply group size influences our attitudes and behaviors—it even affects our willingness to help one another. Darley and Latané concluded that students in the dyad clearly knew it was up to them. The professor was gone, and if they didn't help there would be no help. In the triad, students felt less personal responsibility. In the larger groups, they felt *a diffusion of responsibility:* It was no more up to them than it was up to anyone else.

You probably have observed the second consequence of group size firsthand. When a group is small, its members are informal, but as the group grows, they lose their sense of intimacy and grow more formal. No longer can the members assume that the others are "insiders" in sympathy with what

Group size has a significant influence on how people interact. When a group changes from a dyad (two people) to a triad (three people), the relationships among the participants undergo a shift.

they say. Now they must take a "larger audience" into consideration, and instead of merely "talking," they begin to "address" the group. As their speech becomes more formal, their body language stiffens, too.

You probably have observed a third aspect of group dynamics, too. In the very early stages of a party, when only a few people are present, almost everyone talks with everyone else. But as others arrive, the guests break into smaller groups. The hosts, who may want all their guests to mix together, sometimes make a nuisance of themselves trying to achieve *their* idea of what a group should be like. The division into small groups is inevitable, however, for it follows the basic sociological principles we have just reviewed. Because the addition of each person rapidly increases connections (in this case, "talk lines"), it makes conversation more difficult. The guests then break into smaller groups where they can see each other and comfortably interact directly with one another.

Leadership

All groups, no matter what their size, have leaders, although they may not hold formal positions in the group. A **leader** is someone who influences the behaviors, opinions, or attitudes of others. Some people are leaders because of their personalities, but leadership involves much more than this, as we shall see.

Types of Leaders Groups have two types of leaders (Bales 1950, 1953; Cartwright and Zander 1968). The first is easy to recognize. This person, called an **instrumental leader** (or task-oriented leader), tries to keep the group moving toward its goals. These leaders try to keep group members from getting sidetracked, reminding them of what they are trying to accomplish. The **expressive leader** (or socioemotional leader), in contrast, is not usually recognized as a leader, but he or she certainly is. This person is likely to crack jokes, to offer sympathy, or to do other things that help lift the group's morale. Both types of leadership are essential: the one to keep the group on track, the other to increase harmony and minimize conflicts.

It is difficult for one person to be both an instrumental and an expressive leader, for these roles contradict one another. Because instrumental leaders are task oriented, they sometimes create friction as they prod the group to get on with the job. Their actions often cost them popularity. Expressive leaders, in contrast, being peacemakers who stimulate personal bonds and reduce friction, are usually more popular (Olmsted and Hare 1978).

Leadership Styles Let's suppose that the president of your college has asked you to head a task force to determine how the college can improve race relations on campus. Although this position requires you to be an instrumental leader, you can adopt a number of **leadership styles**, or ways of expressing yourself as a leader. The three basic styles are those of **authoritarian leader**, one who gives orders; **democratic leader**, one who tries to gain a consensus; and **laissez-faire leader**, one who is highly permissive. Which should you choose?

Social psychologists Ronald Lippitt and Ralph White (1958) carried out a classic study of these three leadership styles. Boys matched for IQ, popularity, physical energy, and leadership were assigned to "craft clubs" made up of five youngsters each. The experimenters trained adult men in the three leadership styles and rotated them among the clubs. As the researchers peered through peepholes, taking notes and making movies, each adult played all three styles to control possible effects of their individual personalities.

The *authoritarian* leaders assigned tasks to the boys and set the working conditions. They also praised or condemned their work arbitrarily, giving no explanation for why it was good or bad. The *democratic* leaders held group discussions and outlined the steps that were necessary for the group to reach its goals. They also suggested alternative approaches to these goals and let the children work at their own pace. When they evaluated the children's projects, they gave "facts" as the bases for their decisions. The *laissez-faire* leaders were passive, giving the boys almost total freedom to do as they wished. They stood ready to offer help when asked, but made few suggestions. They did not evaluate the children's projects, either positively or negatively.

leader someone who influences other people

instrumental leader an individual who tries to keep the group moving toward its goals; also known as a task-oriented leader

expressive leader an individual who increases harmony and minimizes conflict in a group; also known as a socioemotional leader

leadership styles ways in which people express their leadership

authoritarian leader a leader who leads by giving orders

democratic leader a leader who leads by trying to reach a consensus

laissez-faire leader an individual who leads by being highly permissive

The results? The boys who had authoritarian leaders grew dependent on their leader and showed a high degree of internal solidarity. They also became either aggressive or apathetic, with the aggressive boys growing hostile toward their leader. In contrast, the boys with democratic leaders were friendlier, more "group minded," and looked to one another for mutual approval. They did less scapegoating, and when the leader left the room they continued to work at a steadier pace. The boys with laissez-faire leaders asked more questions, but they made fewer decisions. They were notable for their lack of achievement. The researchers concluded that the democratic style of leadership worked best. Their conclusions, however, may have been biased, as the researchers preferred a democratic style of leadership, and they did the research during a highly charged political period (Olmsted and Hare 1978).

You may have noted that only males were involved in this experiment. It is interesting to speculate how the results might differ if we were to repeat the experiment with all-girl groups and with groups of both girls and boys, and if we used both men and women as leaders. Perhaps you will become the sociologist to study such variations of this classic experiment.

Adapting Leadership Styles to Changing Situations It is important to note that different situations require different styles of leadership. Suppose, for example, that you are leading a dozen backpackers in California's Sierra Madre mountains, and it is time to make dinner. A laissez-faire style would be appropriate if everyone had brought their own food—or perhaps a democratic style if the meal were to be communally prepared. Authoritarian leadership—you telling all the hikers how to prepare their meals—would create resentment. This, in turn, would likely interfere with meeting the primary goals of the group—in this case, to have a good time while enjoying nature.

Now assume the same group but a different situation: One of your party is lost, and a blizzard is on its way. This situation calls for you to take charge and be authoritarian. To simply shrug your shoulders and say, "You figure it out," would invite disaster.

Adolf Hitler was voted the most influential person of the Twentieth Century. He also was among the most evil. Why did so many people follow Hitler? That question stimulated the research discussed on these pages. Shown here is Hitler on his birthday, June 3, 1943, with Herman Goering, the commander of the Luftwaffe (air force).

Who Becomes a Leader? Are leaders born with characteristics that propel them to the forefront of a group? No sociologist would agree with such a premise. In general, people who become leaders are seen as strongly representing the group's values, or as able to lead a group out of a crisis (Trice and Beyer 1991). Leaders also tend to be more talkative and to express determination and self-confidence.

These findings may not be surprising, as such traits appear related to leadership. Researchers, however, have also discovered significant traits that seem to have no bearing whatsoever on ability to lead. For example, taller people and those judged better looking are more likely to become leaders (Stodgill 1974; Crosbie 1975). The taller and more attractive are also likely to earn more, but that is another story (Deck 1968; Feldman 1972; Katz 1999).

Many other factors underlie people's choice of leaders, most of which are quite subtle. A simple experiment performed by social psychologists Lloyd Howells and Selwyn Becker (1962) uncovered one of these factors. They formed groups of five people who did not know one another, seating them at a rectangular table, three on one side and two on the other. After discussing a topic for a set period of time, each group chose a leader. The findings are startling: Although only 40 percent of the people sat on the two-person side, 70 percent of the leaders emerged from that side. The explanation is that we tend to direct more interactions to people facing us than to people to the side of us.

The Power of Peer Pressure: The Asch Experiment

How influential are groups in our lives? To answer this, let's look first at conformity in the sense of going along with our peers. Our peers have no authority over us, only the influence that we allow.

Imagine that you are taking a course in social psychology with Dr. Solomon Asch and you have agreed to participate in an experiment. As you enter his laboratory, you see seven chairs, five of them already filled by other students. You are given the sixth. Soon the seventh person arrives. Dr. Asch stands at the front of the room next to a covered easel. He explains that he will first show a large card with a vertical line on it, then another card with three vertical lines. Each of you is to tell him which of the three lines is identical to the line on the first card (see Figure 6.5).

Dr. Asch then uncovers the first card with a single line and the comparison card with the three lines. The correct answer is easy, for two of the lines are obviously wrong, and one exactly right. Each person, in order, states his or her answer aloud. You all answer correctly. The second trial is just as easy, and you begin to wonder what the point of your being here is.

Then on the third trial something unexpected happens. Just as before, it is easy to tell which lines match. The first student, however, gives a wrong answer. The second gives the same incorrect answer. So do the third and the fourth. By now you are wondering what is wrong. How will the person next to you answer? You can hardly believe it when he, too, gives the same wrong answer. Then it is your turn, and you give what you know is the right answer. The seventh person also gives the same wrong answer.

On the next trial, the same thing happens. You know the choice of the other six is wrong, yet they give what to you are obviously wrong answers. You don't know what to think. Why aren't they seeing things the same way you are? Sometimes they do, but in twelve trials they don't. Something is seriously wrong, and you are no longer sure what to do.

When the eighteenth card is finished, you heave a sigh of relief. The experiment is finally over, and you are ready to bolt for the door. Dr. Asch walks over to you with a big smile on his face, thanks you for participating in the experiment, and then explains that you were the only real subject in the experiment! "The other six were stooges! I paid them to give those answers," he says. Now you feel real relief. Your eyes weren't playing tricks on you after all.

What were the results? Asch (1952) tested fifty people. One third (33 percent) gave in to the group half the time, giving what they knew to be wrong answers. Another two of five (40 percent) gave wrong answers, but not as often. One of four (25 percent) stuck to their guns and always gave the right answer. I don't know how I would do on this test (if I knew nothing about it in advance), but I like to think that I would be part of the 25 percent. You probably feel the same way about yourself. But why should we feel that we wouldn't be like *most* people?

The results are disturbing. In our "land of individualism," the group is so powerful that most people are willing to say things that they know do not match objective reality. And this was a group of strangers! How much more conformity can we expect when our group consists of friends, people we value highly and depend on for getting along in life? Again, perhaps you will become the sociologist to run that variation of Asch's experiment, perhaps using female subjects.

Even more disturbing are the results of the experiment described in the following Thinking Critically section.

Figure 6.5 ASCH'S CARDS

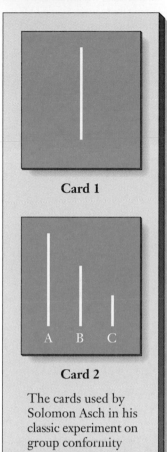

Card 1

Card 2

The cards used by Solomon Asch in his classic experiment on group conformity

Source: Asch 1952:452–453

Thinking Critically

IF HITLER ASKED YOU TO EXECUTE A STRANGER, WOULD YOU? THE MILGRAM EXPERIMENT

Imagine that you are taking a course with Dr. Stanley Milgram (1963, 1965), a former student of Dr. Asch's. Assume that you do not know about the Asch experiment and have no reason to be wary. You arrive at the laboratory to participate in a study on punishment and

In the 1960s, U.S. social psychologists ran a series of creative but controversial experiments. Among these were Stanley Milgram's experiments, described in the text. From this photo of the "learner" being prepared for the experiment, you can get an idea of how convincing the situation would be for the "teacher."

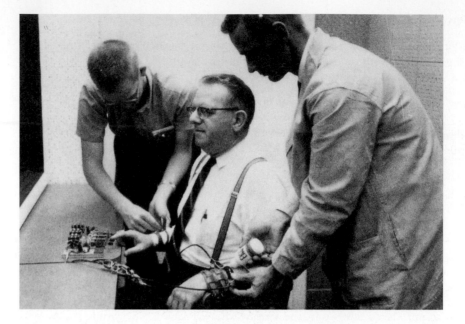

learning. You and a second student draw lots for the roles of "teacher" and "learner." You are to be the teacher. When you see that the learner's chair has protruding electrodes, you are glad that you are the teacher. Dr. Milgram shows you the machine you will run. You see that one side of the control panel is marked "Mild Shock, 15 volts," while the center says "Intense Shock, 350 Volts" and the far right side reads "DANGER: SEVERE SHOCK."

"As the teacher, you will read aloud a pair of words," explains Dr. Milgram. "Then you will repeat the first word, and the learner will reply with the second word. If the learner can't remember the word, you press this lever on the shock generator. The shock will serve as punishment, and we can then determine if punishment improves memory." You nod, now extremely relieved that you haven't been designated a learner.

"Every time the learner makes an error, increase the punishment by 15 volts," instructs Dr. Milgram. Then, seeing the look on your face, he adds, "The shocks can be extremely painful, but they won't cause any permanent tissue damage." He pauses, and then says, "I want you to see." You then follow him to the "electric chair," and Dr. Milgram gives you a shock of 45 volts. "There. That wasn't too bad, was it?" "No," you mumble.

The experiment begins. You hope for the learner's sake that he is bright, but unfortunately he turns out to be rather dull. He gets some answers right, but you have to keep turning up the dial. Each turn makes you more and more uncomfortable. You find yourself hoping that the learner won't miss another answer. But he does. When he received the first shocks, he let out some moans and groans, but now he is screaming in agony. He even protests that he suffers from a heart condition.

How far do you turn that dial?

By now, you probably have guessed that there was no electricity attached to the electrodes and the "learner" was a stooge who only pretended to feel pain. The purpose of the experiment, of course, was to find out at what point people refuse to participate. Does anyone actually turn the lever all the way to "DANGER: SEVERE SHOCK"?

Milgram wanted the answer because of the Nazi slaughter of Jews, gypsies, homosexuals, people with disabilities, and others whom they designated as "inferior." That millions of ordinary people did nothing to stop the deaths seemed bizarre, and Milgram wanted to see how ordinary, intelligent Americans might react in an analogous situation.

Milgram was upset by what he found. Many "teachers" broke into a sweat and protested to the experimenter that this was inhuman and should be stopped. But when the experimenter calmly replied that the experiment must go on, this assurance from an "authority" ("scientist, white coat, university laboratory") was enough for most "teachers" to continue, even though the learner screamed in agony. Even "teachers" who were "reduced to twitching, stuttering wrecks" continued to follow orders.

Milgram varied the experiments (Miller 1986). He used both men and women and put some "teachers" and "learners" in the same room, where the "teacher" could clearly see the suffering. He had some "learners" pound and kick the wall during the first shocks and then go silent. The results varied. When there was no verbal feedback from the "learner," 65 percent of the "teachers" pushed the lever all the way to 450 volts. Of those who could see the "learner," 40 percent turned the lever all the way. When Milgram added a second "teacher," a stooge who refused to go along with the experiment, only 5 percent of the "teachers" carried out the "severe shocking," a result that bears out some of Asch's findings.

A stormy discussion about research ethics erupted. Not only were researchers surprised and disturbed by what Milgram found, but they also were alarmed at his methods. Universities began to require that subjects be informed of the nature and purpose of social research. Researchers agreed that to reduce subjects to "twitching, stuttering wrecks" was unethical, and almost all deception was banned. ■

For Your Consideration

What is the connection between Milgram's experiment and the actions of Walter Burmeister in our opening vignette? Considering how significant these findings are, do you think that the scientific community overreacted to Milgram's experiments? Should we allow such research? Consider both the Asch and Milgram experiments, and use symbolic interactionism, functionalism, and conflict theory to explain why groups have such influence over us.

Global Consequences of Group Dynamics

In our era of nuclear weapons, one of the disturbing implications of the Asch and Milgram experiments is **groupthink.** Sociologist Irving Janis (1972) coined this term to refer to the collective tunnel vision that groups sometimes develop: Members think alike and any suggestion of alternatives is taken as a sign of disloyalty. Even moral judgments must be put aside, for the "team" is convinced that its welfare depends on a single course of action. Groupthink may lead to overconfidence and a disregard for the risks that the group is taking (Hart 1991).

Suppose you are a member of the president's inner circle. It is midnight, and the president has just called an emergency meeting to deal with a national crisis. At first, various options are presented. Eventually, these are narrowed to only a few choices, and at some point everyone seems to agree on what now seems "the only possible course of action." At that juncture, expressing doubts will bring you into conflict with *all* the other important people in the room, while criticism may mark you as not being a "team player." So you keep your mouth shut, with the result that each step commits you—and them—more and more to the "only" course of action.

We can choose from a variety of examples from around the globe, but, as Janis points out, U.S. history provides a fertile field for illustrating groupthink: the refusal of President Franklin D. Roosevelt and his chiefs of staff to believe that the Japanese might attack Pearl Harbor, and the subsequent decision to continue naval operations as usual; President Kennedy's invasion of Cuba; and U.S. policies in Vietnam. Watergate is especially noteworthy, for it plunged the United States into political crisis, and for the first time in history a U.S. president was forced to resign.

In each of these cases, options closed as officials committed themselves to a single course of action. To question this course would have marked one as disloyal, as not a "team player." Those in power plunged ahead, no longer able to see different perspectives, no longer even trying to objectively weigh evidence as it came in, but interpreting everything as supporting their one "correct" decision. Like Milgram's subjects, they became mired in actions that as individuals they would have considered unacceptable. In some cases, they found themselves pursuing policies that they otherwise might have considered morally repugnant.

Preventing Groupthink Groupthink is a danger that faces government leaders, who tend to surround themselves with an inner circle that closely reflects their own views. Isolated at the top, they can become cut off from information that does not support their own

groupthink Irving Janis' term for a narrowing of thought by a group of people, leading to the perception that there is only one correct answer, in which to even suggest alternatives becomes a sign of disloyalty

opinions. Perhaps the key to preventing the mental captivity and intellectual paralysis known as groupthink is the widest possible circulation—especially among a nation's top government officials—of research that has been freely conducted by social scientists and information that has been freely gathered by media reporters.

✳ If this conclusion comes across as an unabashed plug for sociological research and the free exchange of ideas, it is. Giving free rein to diverse opinions can effectively curb groupthink, which—if not prevented—can lead to the destruction of a society and, in today's world of sophisticated weapons, the obliteration of the earth's inhabitants.

SUMMARY AND REVIEW

■ Social Groups and Societies

What is a group?

Sociologists use many definitions of groups, but, in general, **groups** are people who have something in common and who believe that what they have in common is significant. **Societies** are the largest and most complex groups that sociologists study. P. 150.

■ The Transformation of Societies

What inventions are linked to the change from one type of society to another?

On their way to postindustrial society, humans passed through four types of societies, each due to a social revolution that was linked to new technology. The **domestication revolution,** which brought the pasturing of animals and the cultivation of plants, transformed **hunting and gathering societies** into **pastoral** and **horticultural societies.** Then the invention of the plow ushered in the **agricultural society,** while the **Industrial Revolution,** caused by machines that were powered by fuels, allowed the **industrial society** to develop. Today, the computer chip is leading to a new type of society called **postindustrial society.** Pp. 150–155.

How is social inequality linked to the transformation of societies?

Social equality was greatest in hunting and gathering societies, but over time social inequality grew. The root of the transition to social inequality was the accumulation of a food surplus, made possible through the domestication revolution. This surplus stimulated the division of labor, trade, accumulation of material goods, the subordination of females by males, the development of the state, and the rule by a few over many. Pp. 150–155.

■ Groups Within Society

How do sociologists classify groups?

Sociologists divide groups into primary, secondary, in-groups, outgroups, reference groups, and networks. The cooperative, intimate, long-term, face-to-face relationships provided by **primary groups** are fundamental to our sense of self. **Secondary groups** are larger, relatively temporary, more anonymous, more formal, and more impersonal than primary groups. **In-groups** provide members with a strong sense of identity and belonging, while **out-**

groups help create this identity by showing in-group members what they are not. **Reference groups** are groups whose standards we mentally refer to as we evaluate ourselves. **Social networks** consist of social ties that link people together. Changed technology has given birth to a new type of group, the **electronic community.** Pp. 155–161.

■ Group Dynamics

How does a group's size affect its dynamics?

The term **group dynamics** refers to how individuals affect groups and how groups influence individuals. In a **small group,** everyone can interact directly with everyone else. As a group grows larger, its intensity decreases and its stability increases. A **dyad,** consisting of two people, is the most unstable of human groups, but it provides the most intense or intimate relationships. The addition of a third person, forming a **triad,** fundamentally alters relationships. Triads are unstable, as **coalitions** tend to form (the alignment of some members of a group against others). Pp. 161–165

What characterizes a leader?

A **leader** is someone who influences others. **Instrumental leaders** try to keep a group moving toward its goals, even at the cost of causing friction and losing popularity. **Expressive leaders** focus on creating harmony and raising group morale. Both types are essential to the functioning of groups. P. 165.

What are the three main leadership styles?

Authoritarian leaders give orders, **democratic leaders** try to lead by consensus, and **laissez-faire leaders** are highly permissive. An authoritarian style appears to be more effective in emergency situations, a democratic style works best for most situations, and a laissez-faire style is usually ineffective. Pp. 165–166.

How do groups encourage conformity?

The Asch experiment was cited to illustrate the power of peer pressure, the Milgram experiment to illustrate the influence of authority. Both experiments demonstrate how easily we can succumb to **groupthink,** a kind of collective tunnel vision. Preventing groupthink requires the free circulation of contrasting ideas. Pp. 167–170.

Where can I read more on this topic?

Suggested readings for this chapter are at the back of this book.

Sociology & the Internet

All URLs listed are current as of the printing of this book. URLs often change. Please check our Web site, **http://www.abacon.com/henslin**, for updates.

1. The type of society in which we live sets boundaries around our lives. After reading the descriptions of the different types of societies, examine the !Kung San culture at one of these Web sites:

   http://www.lawrence.edu/dept/anthropology/Kungsan/Kungsan.html

   http://www.ucc.uconn.edu/~epsadm03/kung.html

   What type of society does the !Kung San best represent and why? What are some key characteristics of the !Kung San culture that help us determine which type of society it is? Focus your discussion on techniques for meeting the members' survival needs; ways the economy influences political decision making, spirituality, education; and interaction in the family. Write a paper describing what your life would be like if you lived in this culture.

2. A new type of human group called the electronic community emerged in the 1990s. Some Internet news groups merely provide an interesting way of communicating, but many meet our definition of a group. Some news groups have even taken on the characteristics we associate with primary groups. To learn more about news groups, go to **http://www.liszt.com/news/**. Click on "What are newsgroups?" and "How do I Use Them?" What are some of the topics that news groups tackle? Next, click on "alt" and scroll down until you reach the news group entitled "infertility." Click on the first "infertility" and read ten to fifteen postings from individuals. In what ways does this news group resemble a primary group? Return to the main page and click on "rec." Click on the second "collecting" and then on "sport." Finally, click on the sport of your choice and read ten to fifteen postings. Does this electronic community function like a group? If so, what kind of group does it represent? How do the two different news groups differ from one another? Write a brief paper in which you discuss what you have learned about the definition, function, and types of news groups.

3. Reference groups are the groups whose standards we use to evaluate ourselves. For someone studying to become a doctor or a lawyer, professional associations like the American Medical Association or the American Bar Association can serve as reference groups. You can learn more about these two organizations at their Web sites: **http://www.americanmedicalassociation.org** and **http://www.abanet.org**. Assume that you are beginning your professional career and are seeking direction as to how you should behave as a doctor or a lawyer. What kind of information could you obtain from these sites that could help you? Prepare a presentation to the class about professional associations as reference groups.

4. Collectors clubs exist for almost any kind of collectible you can think of. Let's focus on the Peanuts Collectors Club. Go to **http://www.peanutscollectorclub.com**. Using your sociological imagination, discuss why people join collectors' clubs. What kind of group would you say these clubs represent? What are their functions? Are you a collector? Search the Internet and see if there is a club devoted to your interests. Do you think you would be motivated to join a collectors club if you were involved in collecting? Why or why not?

chapter

7

Bureaucracy and Formal Organizations

Jean -Pierre Stora, Les Flaneurs, 1995

■ **The Rationalization of Society**
Why Did Society Change?
Marx: Capitalism Broke Tradition
Weber: Religion Broke Tradition

■ **Formal Organizations and Bureaucracy**
Formal Organizations
The Characteristics of Bureaucracies
"Ideal" Versus "Real" Bureaucracy
Dysfunctions of Bureaucracies
The Perpetuation of Bureaucracies
The Sociological Significance of Bureaucracies

■ **Voluntary Associations**
Functions of Voluntary Associations
Shared Interests
The Problem of Oligarchy

■ **Careers in Bureaucracies**
The "Hidden" Corporate Culture

■ **Humanizing the Corporate Culture**
Quality Circles
Employee Stock Ownership
Small Work Groups
Corporate Day Care
The Cooperative
The Conflict Perspective
Technology and the Control of Workers

■ **Myths and Realities of the Japanese Corporate Model**
Hiring and Promoting Teams
Lifetime Security
Almost Total Involvement
Broad Training
Decision Making by Consensus
The Myth Versus Reality

■ **Summary and Review**

This was the most exciting day Jennifer could remember. Her first day at college. So much had happened so quickly. Her senior year had ended with such pleasant memories: the prom, graduation—how proud she had felt at that moment. But best of all had been her SAT scores. Everyone, especially Jennifer, had been surprised at the results—she had outscored everyone in her class.

"Yes, they're valid," her advisor had assured her. "You can be anything you want to be."

Those words still echoed in Jennifer's mind. "Anything I want to be," she thought.

Then came the presidential scholarship! Full tuition for four years. It went beyond anything Jennifer had ever dreamed possible. She could hardly believe it, but it was really true.

"Your Social Security number, please!"

These abrupt words snapped Jennifer out of her reverie. After waiting in line for an hour, she had finally reached the registration desk. She quickly mumbled the nine digits that would identify her as an incoming student.

"What?" asked the clerk. Jennifer repeated the numbers more clearly.

"I can't give you a class card. You haven't paid your fees."

"What do you mean? I'm on scholarship."

"Evidently not, or else you'd be in the computer," replied the clerk, rolling her eyes.

"But I am."

"If you were, it would say so here."

"But I really am. Look," Jennifer said as she took the prized letter out of her purse.

"I can't help what it says there," replied the clerk. "The only thing that counts is what it says here," she said, gesturing toward the computer. "You'll have to go over to Forsyth Hall to clear it up." Then looking past Jennifer, she called to the next student: "Next!"

Jennifer felt thoroughly confused. Dejected, she crossed the quadrangle to Forsyth and joined a double line of students that stretched from the building to the courtyard.

No one told Jennifer that this was the line for deferring tuition. The "problems" line was the shorter one in the basement. ■

You can understand Jennifer's dismay. Things could have been clearer—a lot clearer. The problem is that many colleges must register thousands of students, most of whom are going to start classes on the same day. To make the job manageable, colleges have broken down the registration process into separate steps. Each step is an integrated part of the entire process. Computerized advance registration has facilitated this process, but as Jennifer found out, things don't always go as planned.

This chapter looks at how society is organized to "get its job done." As you read it, you may be able to trace the source of some of your frustrations to this social organization—as well as see how your welfare depends on it.

THE RATIONALIZATION OF SOCIETY

In the previous chapter, we discussed how over the course of history societies underwent transformations so extensive that whole new types of societies emerged. We also saw that we are now in the midst of one of those earth-shattering transformations. Underlying our emerging postindustrial society is a major change that has been unfolding for the past 150 years or so—**rationality,** the idea that the right way to approach human affairs is to focus on efficiency and practical results. Let's examine how this approach to life—which today we take for granted—came about.

Why Did Society Change?

Until recently, the world's groups and nations had been immersed in a **traditional orientation** to life—the idea that the past is the best guide for the present. In this view, what exists is good because it has passed the test of time. Customs—and relationships based on them—have served people well, and they should not be abandoned lightly. A central orientation of a traditional society is to protect the status quo. Change is viewed with suspicion and comes but slowly, if at all.

The traditional orientation to life stands in the way of industrialization. As Table 7.1 shows, the traditional orientation is based on personal relationships. Deep obligation and responsibility, which are often lifelong, permeate society. What counts in production is not who is best at doing something, but the relationships that people have to one another. Based on origins that are lost in history, everyone—even children—has an established role to play. The past is prized, and it rules the present.

Capitalism requires an entirely different way of looking at life. If a society is to industrialize, a deep-seated shift must occur in people's thinking. Tradition ("This is the way we've always done it")

rationality the acceptance of rules, efficiency, and practical results as the right way to approach human affairs

traditional orientation the idea, characteristic of tribal, peasant, and feudal societies, that the past is the best guide for the present

As college registration illustrates, bureaucracies break tasks down into their component parts and have specialists handle each part. The efficiency of this procedure is sometimes lost on the clientele being served.

Table 7.1	
A MODEL OF PRODUCTION IN TRADITIONAL AND NONTRADITIONAL SOCIETIES	
Traditional Societies (Horticultural, Agricultural)	**Nontraditional Societies (Industrial, Postindustrial)**
1. Production is done by family members and same-sex groups (men's and women's groups).	1. Production is done by workers hired for the job.
2. Production takes place in the home (or in fields and other areas adjacent to the home).	2. Production takes place in a centralized location set up for this purpose. (Some decentralization is occurring in the emerging postindustrial societies.)
3. Personal relationships determine who does what tasks (men, women, and children do specific tasks based on custom).	3. Agreements and training determine who does what tasks.
4. Relationships are based on history ("the way it's been").	4. Relationships are based on contract and current need.
5. Relationships are diffuse (vague, specific, covering many areas of life).	5. Relationships are specific; conditions are specified by contract (even if not written).
6. Relationships are long-term, often lifelong.	6. Relationships are short-term, for the length of the contract.
7. The "how" of production is not evaluated; production is based on the idea that "this is the way we've always done it."	7. The "how" of production is evaluated; the question is, "How can we make this more efficient?"
8. It is assumed that arrangements will continue indefinitely.	8. A decision to continue or to change arrangements is made periodically.
9. Evaluation is based on how well people perform according to the traditional expectations for their roles.	9. Evaluation is based on the "bottom line" (profits).

Note: This model is an ideal type. Rationality is never totally absent from any society, and no society (or organization) is based entirely on rationality. Even the most rational organizations (those that most carefully and even ruthlessly compute the "bottom line") have traditional components. To properly understand this table, consider these characteristics as being "more" or "less" present.

must be replaced with rationality ("Let's find the most efficient way to do it"). As Table 7.1 shows, personal relationships become replaced by impersonal, short-term contracts. The "bottom line" (results) becomes the primary concern, and rule-of-thumb methods give way to explicit ways of measuring results.

It is difficult to overstate the change from tradition to rationality, for it flies in the face of human history. Judging things from the bottom line instead of by personal relationships goes against the basic orientation of all human societies until recent times. It is like a wife saying to her husband, "I'll evaluate you in terms of how much you've contributed to the family budget and how much time you put in on household tasks—and I'll keep or replace you on that basis." How, then, did the **rationalization of society**—the widespread acceptance of rationality and a social organization largely built around this idea—come about?

Marx: Capitalism Broke Tradition

An early sociologist, Karl Marx (1818–1883), was one of the first to note how tradition had given way to rationality. As he thought about why this fundamental change had taken place, he concluded that capitalism had broken the bonds of tradition. As people who had money developed capitalism, they immediately saw that it was more efficient. They were impressed that it produced things they wanted in much greater abundance and paved the way for high profits. This encouraged their investment of capital into industry, and as capitalism spread, traditional thinking receded. Gradually, the traditional approach to life was replaced by the rationality of capitalism. Marx's equation: The change to capitalism changed the way people thought about life.

Weber: Religion Broke Tradition

To sociologist Max Weber (1864–1920), this problem was like an unsolved murder is to a detective. He wasn't satisfied with Marx's answer, and he kept searching for the solution. He

rationalization of society a widespread acceptance of rationality and a social organization largely built around this idea

capitalism the investment of capital with the goal of producing profits

found the clue when he noted that capitalism thrived only in certain parts of Europe. "There has be a reason for this," he mused. As Weber pursued the matter, he began to think that religion held the key. He noted that capitalism flourished in Protestant countries, while Roman Catholic countries held onto tradition and were relatively untouched by capitalism.

But why did Roman Catholics cling to the past, while Protestants embraced change? Why did only Protestants welcome the new emphasis on practical results? Weber's answer to this puzzle has been the source of controversy ever since he first proposed it in his highly influential book, *The Protestant Ethic and the Spirit of Capitalism* (1904–1905). Weber concluded that Roman Catholic doctrine emphasized the acceptance of present arrangements, not change: "God wants you where you are. You owe primary allegiance to the Church, to your family, to your community and country. Accept your lot in life and remain rooted." Weber argued that Protestant theology made its followers open to change. Weber was intimately familiar with Calvinism, his mother's religion. Calvinists (followers of the teachings of John Calvin, 1509–1564) believed that before birth people are destined to go either to heaven or to hell—and they do not know their destiny until after they have died. Weber believed that this teaching filled Calvinists with an anxiety that pervaded their lives. Salvation became their chief concern—they wanted to know *now* where they were going after death.

To resolve their spiritual dilemma, Calvinists hit upon an ingenious solution: God surely did not want those chosen for heaven to be ignorant of their destiny. Therefore, those who were in God's favor would know it—they would receive a sign from God. But what sign? The answer, claimed Calvinists, was found not in mystical, spiritual experiences, but in tangible achievements that people could see and measure. The sign of God's approval was success: Those whom God had predestined for heaven would be blessed with visible success in this life.

This idea transformed the lives of Calvinists, giving them a strong motivation to work hard. Because Calvinists also believed that thrift is a virtue, their dedication to work led to an accumulation of money. Calvinists could not spend the excess on themselves, however, for to purchase items beyond the basic necessities was considered sinful. **Capitalism,** the investment of capital in the hope of producing profit, became an outlet for their excess money. The success of those investments, in turn, became a further sign of God's approval. In this way, Calvinists transformed worldly success into a spiritual virtue. Other branches of Protestantism, although not in agreement with predestination, also adopted the creed of thrift and hard work. Consequently, said Weber, Protestant countries embraced capitalism.

In traditional society, religion was a dominant force. This painting, *The Church at East Gloucester* (Childe Hassma, 1919), reflects the power of the traditional way of life. As discussed in the text, Max Weber and Karl Marx disagreed about why society changed from a traditional orientation to one of rationality.

But what has this to do with rationalization? Simply put, capitalism demands rationalization, the careful calculation of practical results. If profits are your goal, you must compute income and expenses. You must calculate inventories and wages, the cost of producing goods and how much they bring in. You must determine "the bottom line." In such an arrangement of human affairs, efficiency, not tradition, becomes the drum to which you march. Traditional ways of doing things, if inefficient, are replaced, for what counts are the results. Weber's equation: a changed orientation to life produced capitalism.

Who is correct? Weber, who concluded that Protestantism produced rationality, which then paved the way for capitalism? Or Marx, who concluded that capitalism produced rationality? No analyst has yet reconciled these two opposing answers to the satisfaction of sociologists: The two views still remain side by side.

FORMAL ORGANIZATIONS AND BUREAUCRACY

Regardless of whether Marx or Weber was right about its cause, rationality was a totally different way of thinking that came to permeate society. This new orientation transformed the way in which society is organized. As a result, **formal organizations**, secondary groups designed to achieve explicit objectives, have become a central feature of contemporary society. Most of us are born within them, we are educated in them, we spend our working lives in them, and we are buried by them.

Formal Organizations

guilds

Prior to industrialization, only a few formal organizations existed. The guilds of western Europe during the twelfth century are an example. People who performed the same type of work organized to control their craft in a local area. They set prices and standards of workmanship (Bridgwater 1953; Volti 1995). Much like modern unions, guilds also prevented outsiders (nonmembers of the guild) from working at the particular craft. Another example of an early formal organization is the army, with its hierarchical structure of senior officers, junior officers, and ranks. Formal armies, of course, go back to early history.

With industrialization, secondary groups became common. Today we take their existence for granted and, beginning with grade school, all of us spend a good deal of time in them. Formal organizations tend to develop into bureaucracies, and in general, the larger the formal organization, the more likely it is to be bureaucratic.

The division of labor, a central characterisitic of formal organizations, is not new. Shown here are Incans planting their fields. The men are using the footplows, the woman is handing out the corn seeds, and the children are planting. This depiction is by Felipe Guaman Poma de Ayala (1583–1615).

The Characteristics of Bureaucracies

What do the Soviet army, the U.S. postal service, the Canadian government, the Mormon Church, General Motors, and your college have in common? The sociological answer is that they all are **bureaucracies**. As Weber (1913/1947) pointed out, bureaucracies have

1. *Clear-cut levels, with assignments flowing downward and accountability flowing upward.* Each level assigns responsibilities to the level beneath it, while each lower level is accountable to the level above for fulfilling those assignments. The bureaucratic structure of a typical university is shown in Figure 7.1 on the following page.

2. *A division of labor.* Each worker has a specific task to fulfill, and all of the tasks are then coordinated to accomplish the purpose of the organization. In a college, for example, a teacher does not run the heating system, the president does not teach, and a secretary does not evaluate textbooks. These tasks are distributed among people who have been trained to do them.

3. *Written rules.* In their attempt to become efficient, bureaucracies stress written procedures. In general, the longer a bureaucracy exists and the larger it grows, the more written rules it has. The rules of some bureaucracies cover just about every imaginable situation. In my university, for example, the rules are published in the form of handbooks: separate ones for faculty, students, administrators, civil service workers, and perhaps others that I do not even know exist. The guiding principle generally becomes, "If there isn't a written rule covering it, it is allowed."

formal organization a secondary group designed to achieve explicit objectives

bureaucracy a formal organization with a hierarchy of authority; a clear division of labor; emphasis on written rules, communications, and records; and impersonality of positions

Figure 7.1 **THE TYPICAL BUREAUCRATIC STRUCTURE OF A MEDIUM-SIZED UNIVERSITY**

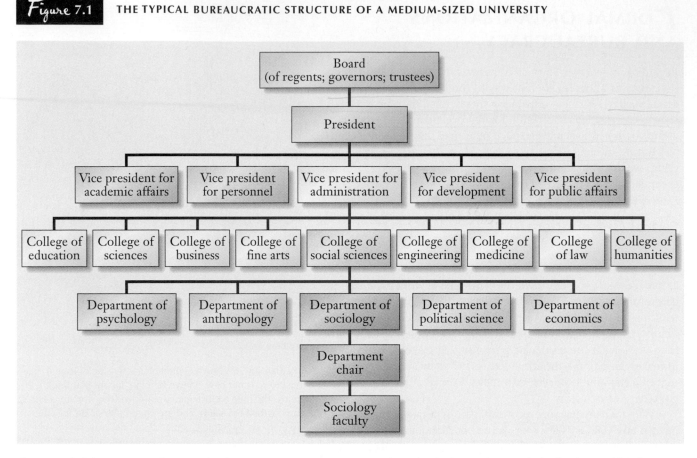

This is a scaled-down version of a university's bureaucratic structure. The actual lines of a university are likely to be much more complicated than those depicted here. A large university may have a chancellor and several presidents under the chancellor, with each president responsible for a particular campus. Although in this figure extensions of authority are shown only for the vice president for administration and the College of Social Sciences, each of the other vice presidents and colleges has similar positions. If the figure were to be extended, departmental secretaries would be shown, and eventually, somewhere, even students.

This 1907 photo indicates one way that technology has changed our lives. The little drawers that the women are searching contain customer records of the Metropolitan Life Insurance Company. Today, this entire bank of records could be stored on a personal computer. We also could use the computer to search or modify the records, infinitesimally faster—and certainly much easier on the legs—than standing on the ladder.

4. *Written communications and records.* Records are kept of much of what occurs in a bureaucracy. ("Fill that out in triplicate.") Consequently, workers in bureaucracies spend a fair amount of time sending memos back and forth. They also produce written reports detailing their activities. My university, for example, requires that each faculty member fill out quarterly reports summarizing the number of hours per week spent on specified activities as well as an annual report listing what was accomplished in teaching, research, and service—all accompanied by copies of publications, testimonies to service, and written teaching evaluations from each course. These materials go to committees whose task it is to evaluate the relative performance of each faculty member. With e-mail, the form of the memo is changing.

Today's armies, no matter what country they are from, are bureaucracies. They have a strict hierarchy of rank, division of labor, impersonality (an emphasis on the office, not the person holding it), and they stress written records, rules, and communications—essential characteristics identified by Max Weber. Though its outward appearance may differ from Western standards, this army in India, is no exception to this principle.

5. *Impersonality*. It is the office that is important, not the individual who holds the office. You work for the organization, not for the replaceable person who heads some post in the organization. Consequently, members of a bureaucracy owe allegiance to the office, not to particular people. If you work in a bureaucracy, you become a small cog in a large machine. Each worker is a replaceable unit, for many others are available to fulfill each particular function. For example, when a professor retires or dies, someone else is appointed to take his or her place.

These five characteristics not only help bureaucracies reach their goals but also allow them to grow and endure. One bureaucracy in the United States, the postal service, has become so large that one out of every 150 employed Americans works for it (*Statistical Abstract* 1999:Tables 678, 946). If the head of a bureaucracy dies, retires, or resigns, the organization continues without skipping a beat, for unlike a "mom and pop" operation, the functioning of a unit does not depend on the individual who heads it. The expansion (some would say domination) of bureaucracies in contemporary society is illustrated by the Down-to-Earth Sociology box on the following page.

"Ideal" Versus "Real" Bureaucracy

Just as people often act differently from the way the norms say they should, so it is with bureaucracies. The characteristics of bureaucracies identified by Weber are **ideal types;** that is, they are a composite of characteristics based on many specific examples. Think of the judges at a dog show. They have a mental image of how each particular breed of dog should look and behave, and they judge each individual dog according to that mental image. Each dog will rank high on some of these characteristics, and lower on others. In the same way, a particular organization will rank higher or lower on the traits of a bureaucracy, yet still qualify as a bureaucracy. (Instead of labeling a particular organization as a "bureaucracy" or "not a bureaucracy," it probably makes more sense to think in terms of the *extent* to which an organization is bureaucratized [Udy 1959; Hall 1963]).

As with culture, then, a bureaucracy often differs from its ideal image. The actual lines of authority ("going through channels"), for example, may be different from those portrayed on organizational charts such as the one shown in Figure 7.1. For example, suppose that before being promoted, the university president taught in the history department. As a result, friends from that department may have direct access to him or her. If they wish to provide "input" (ranging from opinions about how to solve problems to personal grievances or even gossip), these individuals may skip their chairperson or even the dean of their college, and go directly to the president.

ideal type a composite of characteristics based on many specific examples ("ideal" in this case means a description of the abstracted characteristics, not what one desires to exist)

179

Down-to-Earth *Sociology*

THE MCDONALDIZATION OF SOCIETY

The thousands of McDonald's restaurants that dot the U.S. landscape—and increasingly, the world—have a significance that goes far beyond the convenience of ready-made hamburgers and milk shakes. As sociologist George Ritzer (1993) says, our everyday lives are becoming rationalized. To refer to this, he coined the term **the McDonaldization of society.**

Ray Kroc, the founder of McDonald's, applied the assembly-line procedures developed by Henry Ford to the preparation and serving of food. Ritzer quotes from a 1958 manual:

It told operators exactly how to draw milk shakes, grill hamburgers, and fry potatoes. It specified precise cooking times for all products and temperature settings for all equipment. It fixed standard portions on every food item, down to the quarter ounce of onions placed on each hamburger patty and the thirty-two slices per pound of cheese. It specified that french fries be cut at nine-thirty-seconds of an inch thick. . . . Grill men . . . were instructed to put hamburgers down on the grill moving from left to right, creating six rows of six patties each. And because the first two rows were farthest from the heating element, they were instructed (and still are) to flip the third row first, then the fourth, fifth, and sixth before flipping the first two.

McDonald's in Tokyo, Japan

Ritzer stresses that "McDonaldization" does not refer just to the robotlike assembly of food. Rather, this process is occurring throughout society, and it is transforming our lives. Need to do some shopping? Shopping malls offer controlled environments that are designed to make shopping a one-stop experience. Everything—from the layout of the stores to the temperature of the air to the location of the food court—is designed to make your shopping experience as efficient as possible. Planning a trip? With prepackaged travel, no one need fear meeting a "real" native: Travel agencies transport middle-class Americans to ten European capitals in fourteen days, and all visitors experience the same hotels, restaurants, and other scheduled sites. Want to keep up on the world? *USA Today* spews out McNews—short, bland, unanalytic pieces that can be easily digested between gulps of the McShake or the McBurger.

Efficiency brings dependability. You can expect your burger and fries to taste the same whether you buy them in Los Angeles or Beijing. It also brings lower prices. But all this efficiency comes at a cost. It marks the loss of something that is difficult to define, an element of spontaneity that gets washed away by predictability, changing the quality of our lives. In my own travels, for example, had I taken packaged tours I never would have had the enjoyable, eye-opening experiences that have added so much to my appreciation of human diversity.

For good or bad, human experience is being McDonaldized, and the predictability of packaged settings seems to be our social destiny. When education is rationalized, our children will no longer have to put up with real professors, who insist on discussing ideas endlessly, never come to decisive answers, and come saddled with all manner of quirks and idiosyncrasies. Our preprogrammed society will eliminate the need for discussion, bringing us packaged solutions to social issues, definitive answers like those we find in mathematics and engineering. Computerized courses will teach the same answers to everyone—the approved, "politically correct" ways to think about social issues. Mass testing will assure that students can regurgitate the programmed responses. This will be efficient, of course. But it also will mean that we are functioning within the "iron cage" of bureaucracy that Weber warned would one day entrap us. ■

Dysfunctions of Bureaucracies

<u>Although in the long run no other form of social organization is more efficient</u>, as Weber recognized, bureaucracies also have a dark side. Let's look at some of <u>their dysfunctions</u>.

Red Tape: <u>A Rule Is a Rule</u> Bureaucracies can be so bound by <u>red tape that their pro</u>cedures impede the purpose of the organization. <u>Some rules (or "correct procedures" in bu</u>reaucratic jargon) are enough to try the patience of a saint.

the McDonaldization of society the process by which ordinary aspects of life are rationalized and efficiency comes to rule such things as food preparation

In the Bronx, Mother Teresa spotted a structurally sound abandoned building and wanted to turn it into a homeless shelter. But she ran head on into a rule: The building must have an elevator for the handicapped homeless. Not having the funds for the elevator, Mother Teresa struggled to get permission to bypass this rule. Two frustrating years later, she gave up. The abandoned building is still rotting away. (Tobias 1995)

Obviously this rule about elevators was not intended to stop Mother Teresa from ministering to the down and out. But, hey, rules is rules!

Lack of Communication Between Units Each unit within a bureaucracy performs specialized tasks, which are designed to contribute to the organization's overall goals. At times, units fail to communicate with one another and end up working at cross-purposes. In Granada, Spain, for example, the local government was concerned about the rundown appearance of buildings along one of its main streets. Consequently, one unit of the government fixed the fronts of these buildings, painting and repairing concrete, iron, and stonework. The results were impressive, and the unit was proud of what it had accomplished. The only problem was that another unit of the government had slated these same buildings for demolition (Arías 1993). Because neither unit of this bureaucracy knew what the other was doing, one beautified the buildings while the other made sure they ended up as a heap of rubble.

Bureaucracies are so powerful and overwhelming that even Mother Teresa, one of the most famous religious figures of the late twentieth century, was not able to overcome bureaucratic rules in order to help the U.S. homeless. She is shown here in a homeless shelter in New York City.

Bureaucratic Alienation Many workers find it disturbing to deal with others in terms of roles, rules, and functions rather than as individuals. Similarly, they may dislike writing memos instead of talking to people face to face. It is not surprising, then, that workers in large organizations sometimes feel more like objects than people, or, as Weber (1978) put it, "only a small cog in a ceaselessly moving mechanism which prescribes to [them] an endlessly fixed routine. . ." Because workers must deal with one another in such formal ways, and because they constantly perform routine tasks, some come to feel that no one cares about them and that they are misfits in their surroundings.

Marx termed these reactions **alienation**, which he said comes from being cut off from the finished product of one's labor. Although assigning workers to repetitive tasks makes for efficient production, Marx argued that it also reduces their satisfaction by limiting their creativity and sense of contribution to the finished product. Underlying alienation is the workers' loss of control over their work because they no longer own their own tools. Before industrialization, workers used their own tools to produce an entire product, such as a chair or table. Now the capitalists own the tools (machinery) and assign each worker only a single step or two in the entire production process. Relegated to repetitive tasks that seem remote from the final product, workers lose a sense of identity with what they produce. They come to feel estranged not only from their products but also from their whole work environment.

Resisting Alienation Because workers want to feel valued and want to have a sense of control over their work, they resist alienation. Forming primary groups at work is a major form of that resistance. Workers band together in informal settings—at lunch, around desks, or for a drink after work. There they give one another approval for jobs well done and express sympathy for the shared need to put up with cantankerous bosses, meaningless routines, and endless rules. There they relate to one another not just as workers, but as people who value one another. They flirt, laugh and tell jokes, and talk

alienation Marx's term for the experience of being cut off from the product of one's labor that results in a sense of powerlessness and normlessness

about their families, their frustrations, and their goals. Adding this dimension to their work relationships maintains their sense of being persons rather than mere cogs in a machine.

Consider a common sight. While visiting an office, you see work areas that are decorated with family and vacation photos. The sociological implication is that of workers striving to resist alienation. By staking a claim to individuality, the workers are rejecting an identity as mere machines that exist to perform functions.

The Alienated Bureaucrat Not all workers succeed in resisting alienation, however, and some become extremely alienated. They remain in the organization because they see no viable alternative or because they have "only so many years until retirement." They hate every minute of it, and it shows—in their attitudes toward clients, toward fellow workers, and especially toward authority in the organization. The alienated bureaucrat does not take initiative, will not do anything for the organization beyond what he or she is absolutely required to do, and uses rules to justify doing as little as possible. If Jennifer in this chapter's opening vignette had come across an alienated bureaucrat behind the registration window, she might have been asked, "What's the matter with you—can't you read? Everyone else manages to pay their fees on time, why can't you? I don't know what kind of students they're sending us nowadays." If the worker had been even more alienated, he or she might have denied knowledge of where to get the problem taken care of.

Despite poor attitude and performance, alienated workers often retain their jobs, either because they have seniority, or know the written rules backward and forward, or threaten expensive, time-consuming, and embarrassing legal action if anyone tries to fire them. Some alienated workers are shunted off into small bureaucratic corners, where they do trivial tasks and have little chance of coming in contact with the public. This treatment, of course, only alienates them further.

Bureaucratic Incompetence In a tongue-in-cheek analysis of bureaucracies, Laurence Peter proposed what has become known as the **Peter principle**: Each employee of a bureaucracy is promoted to his or her *level of incompetence* (Peter and Hull 1969). People who perform well in a bureaucracy come to the attention of those higher up the chain of command and are promoted. If they again perform well, they are again promoted. This process continues until they are finally promoted to a level at which they can no longer handle the responsibilities well; this is their level of incompetence. There they hide behind the work of others, taking credit for what those under their direction accomplish.

Although the Peter principle contains a grain of truth, if it were generally true, bureaucracies would be staffed entirely by incompetents, and none of these organizations could succeed. In reality, bureaucracies are remarkably successful. Sociologists Peter Evans and James Rauch (1999) examined the government bureaucracies of 35 developing countries. They found that prosperity comes to the countries that have central bureaucracies that hire workers on the basis of merit and offer them rewarding careers.

The Perpetuation of Bureaucracies

Bureaucracies sometimes take on a life of their own, adopting new goals in place of old ones. In this process, called **goal displacement**, even when the goal of the organization has been achieved and there is no longer any reason for the organization to continue, continue it does. A classic example is the National Foundation for the March of Dimes, organized in the 1930s to fight polio, a crippling disease that strikes without warning (Sills 1957). The origin of polio was a mystery to the medical profession, and the public was alarmed and fearful. Rumors about what caused this disease ran rampant. Everyone knew someone who had been crippled by polio. Overnight, a healthy child would be stricken. Parents lived in fear, because no one knew whose child would be next. They frantically washed the fruit they gave their children, suspecting that polio germs were lurking on the surface of apples and plums. The March of Dimes began to publicize individual cases. An especially effective strategy was

Peter principle a bureaucratic "law" according to which the members of an organization are promoted for good work until they reach their level of incompetence, the level at which they can no longer do good work

goal displacement a goal displaced by another; in this context, the adoption of new goals by an organization; also known as goal replacement

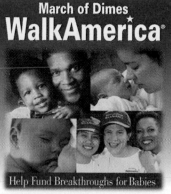

The March of Dimes was founded by President Franklin Roosevelt in the 1930s to fight polio. When a vaccine for polio was discovered in the 1950s, the organization did not declare victory and disband. Instead, it kept the organization intact by creating new goals—fighting birth defects. Sociologists use the term goal displacement to refer to this process of adopting new goals. "Fighting birth defects" is now being replaced by an even vaguer goal, "Breakthroughs for Babies." This new goal displacement may guarantee the organization's existence forever, for it is a goal so elusive it can never be reached. (Can we ever run out of the need for "breakthroughs"?)

placing posters of a child on crutches near cash registers in almost every store in the United States. The U.S. public took the campaign to heart and contributed heavily. The huge amount of money raised went beyond the organization's wildest dreams.

During the 1950s, Dr. Jonas Salk developed a vaccine for polio, and the threat of this disease was wiped out almost overnight. The public breathed a collective sigh of relief. What then? Did the organization fold? After all, its purpose had been fulfilled. But, as you know, the March of Dimes is still around. Faced with the loss of their jobs, the professional staff that ran the organization quickly found a way to keep the bureaucracy intact by pursuing a new enemy—birth defects. Their choice of enemy is particularly striking, for it is doubtful that we will ever run out of birth defects—and thus unlikely that these people will ever run out of jobs. Just in case, however, (because the mapping of human genes could possibly threaten its existence), the March of Dimes has adopted "Breakthroughs for Babies" as its slogan. This latest goal should ensure the organization's existence forever—for it is so vague that we are not likely to ever run out of the need for "breakthroughs."

The Sociological Significance of Bureaucracies

Perhaps the main sociological significance of bureaucracies is that they represent a fundamental change in how people relate to one another (see Table 7.1). When work is rooted in social relationships, much more is at stake than performing tasks efficiently and keeping an eye on the bottom line. Seeing that all family members are employed, or that everyone in the community has a chance to make a living, for example, were once the determining factors in making decisions. Bureaucracies, or the rationalization of society, changed all this (Volti 1995).

VOLUNTARY ASSOCIATIONS

Although bureaucracies have become the dominant form of organization for large, task-oriented groups, even more common are voluntary associations. Let's examine their characteristics.

Back in the 1830s, Alexis de Tocqueville, a Frenchman, traveled across the United States, observing the customs of this new nation. His report, *Democracy in America* (1835), became widely read in Europe and in the United States. It is still quoted for its insights into the American character. As an outsider, de Tocqueville could see patterns that were invisible to the people who were immersed in them. One of de Tocqueville's observations was that Americans joined a lot of **voluntary associations,** groups made up of volunteers who organize on the basis of some mutual interest.

Over the years, Americans have maintained this pattern and are extremely proud of it. A visitor entering any of the thousands of small towns that dot the U.S. landscape is greeted with a highway sign proclaiming some of the town's volunteer associations: Girl Scouts, Boy Scouts, Kiwanis, Lions, Elks, Eagles, Knights of Columbus, Chamber of Commerce, American Legion, Veterans of Foreign Wars, and perhaps a host of others. One form of voluntary association is so prevalent that a separate sign usually indicates which varieties are present in the town: Roman Catholic, Baptist, Lutheran, Methodist, Episcopalian, and so on. Not listed on these signs are many other voluntary associations, such as political parties, unions, health clubs, the National Right to Life, the National Organization for Women, Alcoholics Anonymous, Gamblers Anonymous, Association of Pinto Racers, and Citizens United For or Against This and That.

Americans love voluntary associations, using them to express a wide variety of interests, goals, opinions, and even dissatisfactions. Some groups are local, consisting of only a few volunteers; others are national, with a paid professional staff. Some are temporary and have been organized to accomplish a specific task, such as arranging for Fourth of July fireworks. Others, such as the Scouts and political parties, are permanent—large, secondary organizations with clear lines of command—and they are also bureaucracies.

Functions of Voluntary Associations

Whatever their form, voluntary associations are numerous because they meet people's basic needs. People do not *have* to belong to these organizations. They join because they obtain benefits from their participation. Functionalists have identified seven functions of voluntary associations.

1. Voluntary organizations advance the particular interests they represent. For example, adults who are concerned about children's welfare volunteer for the Scouts because they think kids are better off joining this group than hanging out on the street corner. In short, voluntary associations get things done, whether that means arranging for the fireworks to go off on time or making people familiar with the latest legislation affecting their occupation.

2. Voluntary groups also offer people an identity. For some, they even offer a sense of purpose in life. As in-groups, they provide their members with a feeling of togetherness, of belonging, and in many cases, of doing something worthwhile. This function is so important for some individuals that their participation in voluntary associations becomes the center of their lives.

3. Voluntary associations help govern the nation and maintain social order. Groups that help "get out the vote" or assist the Red Cross in coping with disasters are obvious examples.

Note that the first two functions apply to all voluntary associations. In a general sense, so does the third. Although few organizations are focused on politics and the social order, taken together, voluntary associations help to incorporate individuals into the general society. By allowing the expression of desire and dissent, they help prevent anomie.

Sociologist David Sills (1968) identified four other functions, which apply only to some voluntary groups.

4. Some voluntary groups mediate between the government and the individual. For example, some provide a way for people to put pressure on lawmakers.

5. By providing training in organizational skills, some groups help individuals climb the occupational ladder.

voluntary association a group made up of volunteers who have organized on the basis of some mutual interest

6. Some voluntary groups help bring people into the political mainstream. The National Association for the Advancement of Colored People (NAACP) is an example of such a group.

7. Finally, some voluntary groups pave the way to social change. Opposing society's definitions of "normal" and socially acceptable, some groups such as Greenpeace challenge society's established boundaries. Their activities often indicate the direction of social change.

Shared Interests

Voluntary associations, then, represent no single interest or purpose. They can be reactionary, resisting new ways of doing things, or they can be visionary, standing at the vanguard of social change. Despite their amazing diversity, however, a common thread runs through all voluntary associations. That thread is mutual interest. Although the particular interest varies from group to group, shared interest in some view or activity is the tie that binds their members together.

Although a group's members are united by shared interests, their motivations for joining the group differ widely. Some join because they have strong convictions concerning the stated purpose of the organization, others simply because membership gives them a chance to make contacts that will help them politically or professionally. Some even join to be closer to some special person of the opposite sex.

Because members have varied motivations for joining voluntary associations, and because the commitment of some is fleeting, these organizations often have a high turnover. Some people move in and out of groups almost as fast as they change clothes. Within each organization, however, is an inner core of individuals who stand firmly behind the group's goals, or at least are firmly committed to maintaining the organization itself. If this inner core loses commitment, the group is likely to fold.

The Problem of Oligarchy

This inner core often turns inward as its members become convinced that the regular members can't be counted on. They conclude that only the core group can be trusted to make the group's important decisions. To see this principle at work, let's look at the Veterans of Foreign Wars (VFW).

Sociologists Elaine Fox and George Arquitt (1985) studied three local posts of the VFW, a national organization of former U.S. soldiers who have served in foreign wars. They found that although the leaders are careful to conceal their attitudes from the other members, they view the rank and file as a bunch of ignorant boozers. Because the leaders can't stand the thought that such people might represent them to the community and at national meetings, a curious situation arises. Although the VFW constitution makes rank-and-file members fully eligible for top leadership positions, they never become leaders. In fact, the leaders are so effective in controlling these top positions that even before an election they can specify who is going to win. "You need to meet Jim," the sociologists were told. "He's the next post commander after Sam does his time."

At first, the researchers found this puzzling. The election hadn't been held yet. As they investigated further, they found that leadership is actually decided behind the scenes. The elected leaders appoint their favored people to chair the key committees. This makes the members aware of their accomplishments, and they elect them as leaders. The inner circle, then, maintains control over the entire organization simply by appointing members of their inner circle to highly visible positions.

Like the VFW, most organizations are run by only a few of their members (Cnaan 1991). Building on the term *oligarchy*, a system in which many are ruled by a few, sociologist Robert Michels (1876–1936) coined the term **the iron law of oligarchy** to refer to how formal organizations come to be dominated by a small, self-perpetuating elite. The majority of members are passive, and an elite inner group keeps itself in power by passing the leadership positions from one clique member to another.

the iron law of oligarchy
Robert Michels' phrase for the tendency of formal organizations to be dominated by a small, self-perpetuating elite

In a process called the iron law of oligarchy, a small, self-perpetuating elite tends to take control of formal organizations. Shown in this photo taken in St. Joseph, Missouri, is one of the organizations sociologists have studied.

What many find disturbing about the iron law of oligarchy is that people are excluded from leadership because they don't represent the inner circle's values, background, or even their images of themselves. This is true even of organizations that are strongly committed to democratic principles. U.S. political parties, for example—supposedly the backbone of the nation's representative government—have fallen prey to it. Run by an inner group that may or may not represent the community, they pass their leadership positions from one elite member to another. This principle is also demonstrated by the U.S. Senate. With their control of statewide political machinery, their access to free mailing, and even the free use of tax dollars to produce videos that can be sent via e-mail, about 90 percent of U.S. senators who choose to run are reelected (*Statistical Abstract* 1998:Table 468; Simpson 2000).

The iron law of oligarchy is not without its limitations, of course. Members of the inner group must remain attuned to the opinions of the other members, regardless of their personal feelings. If the oligarchy gets too far out of line, it runs the risk of a grassroots rebellion that would throw this elite group out of office. It is this threat that often softens the iron law of oligarchy by making the leadership responsive to the membership. In addition, because not all organizations become captive to an elite, this is a tendency, not an inevitability (Fisher 1994).

CAREERS IN BUREAUCRACIES

Since you are likely to end up working in a bureaucracy, let's look at how its characteristics may affect your career.

The "Hidden" Corporate Culture

Who gets ahead in a large corporation? Although we might like to think that success comes from intelligence and hard work, many factors other than merit underlie salary increases and promotions. As sociologist Rosabeth Moss Kanter (1977, 1983) stresses, the *corporate culture* contains "hidden values." These values create a self-fulfilling prophecy that affects people's corporate fate.

It works like this: The elite have ideas about who the best workers and colleagues are, and who is most likely to succeed. People who fit this mold are those who have backgrounds similar to the elite and who look like them. These people receive better access to information, networking, and "fast track" positions. They then perform better, become more committed to the organization, and become more successful—thus confirming the initial expectation. In contrast, those judged to be outsiders (for whom there are few expectations of success) find most opportunities closed to them. They tend to work at a level that is beneath their capacity. They come to think poorly of themselves, become less committed to the organization, and fail to succeed—thus confirming the initial expectation.

The hidden values that created this self-fulfilling prophecy remain invisible to most. What is visible are the promotions of people with superior performances and greater commitment to the company, not the low expectations and closed opportunities that produced these attitudes and accomplishments.

You can see how such hidden values contribute to the iron law of oligarchy. The corporate elite, the tight inner circle that heads a corporation, tends to reproduce itself by favoring people who "look" like its members, generally white and male. Because they are shown favor, these people develop a commitment to the company and climb the corporate ladder. Women and minorities, who don't match the stereotype, are often "showcased." That is, in order to demonstrate how progressive the company is, they are placed in highly visible positions—where they have little power. Because these positions are often "slow-track," their accomplishments seldom come to the attention of top management, and they fail to advance.

Kanter found that the level people reach in the organization also shapes their behavior, and even their attitudes toward themselves and others. In general, the higher people go, the higher their morale. "This is a good company," they say to themselves. "They recognize my abilities." With their greater satisfaction, people in higher office also tend to be more helpful to subordinates and more flexible in their style of leadership. In contrast, people who don't get very far in the organization are frustrated and tend to have lower morale. A less apparent result of their blocked opportunity, however, is that they are likely to be rigid supervisors and strong defenders of whatever privileges they have.

There is a significant hidden level in bureaucracies, then. Because the workers in a corporation tend to see only the level that is readily visible, they usually ascribe differences in behaviors and attitudes to people's personalities. Sociologists probe beneath this level, however, to examine how corporate culture shapes people's attitudes, and, by extension, the quality of their work.

One of the major changes in bureaucracies is the growing diversity in the work force, the topic of the Perspectives box on the following page.

Sociologist Rosabeth Moss Kanter has written extensively about corporations. Her works include such titles as *Men and Women of the Corporation, Innovation: Breakthrough Thinking,* and *World Class: Thriving Locally in the Global Economy.*

*H*UMANIZING THE CORPORATE CULTURE

Bureaucracies have transformed society by harnessing people's energies to specific goals and monitoring progress to those goals. Weber (1946) predicted that because bureaucracies were so efficient and had the capacity to replace themselves indefinitely, they would come to dominate social life. More than any prediction in sociology, this one has withstood the test of time (Rothschild and Whitt 1986; Perrow 1991).

Bureaucracies appear likely to remain our dominant form of social organization, and most of us, like it or not, are destined to spend our working lives in bureaucracies. Many people have become concerned about the negative side of bureaucracies, however, and would like to make them more humane. **Humanizing a work setting** means organizing work in such a way that it develops rather than impedes human potential. Such work settings offer access to opportunities on the basis of ability and contributions rather than on the basis of personal characteristics. They distribute power more equally and have fewer rigid rules and more open decision making. In short, more people are involved in making decisions, their contributions are more readily recognized, and individuals feel freer to participate.

Can bureaucracies adapt to such a model? Contrary to some popular images, not all bureaucracies are unyielding, unwieldy monoliths. There is nothing in the nature of bureaucracies that makes them *inherently* insensitive to people's needs or that prevents them from humanizing corporate culture.

humanizing a work setting
organizing a workplace in such a way that it develops rather than impedes human potential

---

PERSPECTIVES | Cultural Diversity in the United States

CHANGING TIMES: DIVERSITY IN THE CORPORATION

Times have changed. In San Jose, California, the *Nguyens* outnumber the *Joneses* by nearly 50 percent. More than half of U.S. workers are minorities, immigrants, and women. Diversity in the workplace is much more than skin color. Diversity includes ethnicity, gender, age, religion, social class, and sexual orientation.

In the past, the idea was for people to become like the dominant group. Today, with the huge successes of the civil rights and women's movements, people take more pride in their heritage and in being different from the dominant group. People who assimilate—are absorbed into the dominant culture—relinquish their distinctive cultural traits. In a reversal from the past, people today are more likely to prize their distinctive traits. Realizing that assimilation is probably not the wave of the future, three of four Fortune 500 companies have "diversity training." They hold lectures and workshops so employees can learn to work with colleagues of diverse cultures and racial-ethnic backgrounds.

Coors Brewery is a prime example of this change. Coors went into a finan-cial tailspin after one of the Coors brothers gave a racially charged speech in the 1980s. Today, Coors offers diversity workshops, has sponsored a gay dance, and has paid for a corporate-wide mammography program. The company even had rabbis certify its suds as kosher. Its proud new slogan: "Coors cares" (Cloud 1998). Now, that's quite a change.

What Coors cares about, of course, is the bottom line. It's the same with the other corporations. Blatant racism and sexism once made no difference to profitability. Today, they do. To promote profitability, companies must promote diversity—or at least pretend to. The sincerity of corporate heads is not what's important; diversity in the workplace is.

Diversity training has the potential to build bridges, but it can backfire. Its directors can be so incompetent that they create antagonisms and reinforce stereotypes. The directors of training sessions at the U.S. Department of Transportation, for example, used to have women grope men as the men ran by. They also encouraged blacks and whites to insult one another and call one another names (Reibstein 1996). Although their intentions may have been good (understanding the other through role reversal and getting hostilities "out in the open"), their approach was moronic. Instead of healing, such behaviors wounded and left scars.

The growing diversity in today's workplace provides a glimpse into our future. The white male is just now becoming a minority in the workplace—but he will remain dominant for some time in top management. By working together to meet goals that benefit them all, workers of dissimilar backgrounds and characteristics can develop an appreciative understanding of their differences. The potential exists for a society less divided by gender and race-ethnicity. Granted the severe divisions of our present society, any step that reduces these divisions is welcome. To be effective, diversity training must be built on encouraging and instilling mutual respect. If in the workplace we can develop this same mutual respect, we will have taken a giant step into the future. ■

But what about the cost of such changes? The United States is in intense economic competition with other nations, especially Japan and western Europe, and it would be difficult to afford costly changes. To humanize corporate culture, however, does not require huge expense. Sociologist Rosabeth Moss Kanter (1983) compared forty-seven companies that were rigidly bureaucratic with competitors of the same size that were more flexible. It turned out that the more flexible companies were also the more profitable—probably because their greater flexibility encouraged greater company loyalty, creativity, and productivity.

Quality Circles

In light of such findings, many corporations have taken steps to humanize their work settings. They are not motivated by any altruistic urge to make life better for their workers, but by the same motivation as always, the bottom line. It is in their self-interest to make their organizations more competitive. About two thousand U.S. companies—from the smallest to the largest—have experimented with changing their work organizations. Some have developed "quality circles," which consist of perhaps a dozen workers and a manager or two who meet regularly to try to improve the quality of both the work setting and the company's products. More than half of these companies, however, report that quality circles have yielded few benefits. Part of the reason may be that many companies are entrenched in their way of doing things and don't really take employee suggestions seriously; for many firms, changes such as quality circles are mere window dressing. Whatever the reason for the disappointing results, companies such as Whirlpool and GE have abandoned quality circles. Each company continues to solicit ideas from its employees, however. GE now uses town hall type meetings and rewards workers with cash and stock options (Naj 1993).

Employee Stock Ownership

Many companies offer an opportunity for their employees to purchase the firm's stock at a discount or as part of their salary, and about eight thousand U.S. companies are now partially owned by their employees. Because each employee typically owns only a tiny amount of stock in the company, such "ownership" is practically meaningless. In about a thousand of these companies, however, the employees own the majority of the stock. On average, companies with at least 10 percent of their stock owned by employees are more profitable than other firms, probably because the workers are more committed and the managers take a longer-term view (White 1991).

One might think that employee ownership of a company's stock would eliminate problems between workers and management. Profitability, however, not ownership, appears to be the key to reducing these problems. Unprofitable firms put more pressure on their employee-owners, creating tension between workers and managers, while profitable companies are quicker to resolve problems.

Small Work Groups

Pioneered in the computer industry to increase productivity and cut down on absenteeism, small work groups, or self-managed teams, are now used by one in five U.S. companies. Small work groups stimulate creative ideas and imaginative solutions to problems, and employees who work in them feel a greater sense of loyalty to the company, work harder, and have less absenteeism. Workers in these groups also react more quickly to threats posed by technological change and competitors' advances. No less a behemoth than IBM has found that people work more effectively in small groups than in a distant, centralized command structure (Drucker 1992).

The concepts we discussed in the last chapter help to explain these results. In small work groups, people form primary relationships, and their identities become tied up with their group. This reduces alienation, for rather than being lost in a bureaucratic maze, their individuality is appreciated, their contributions more readily recognized. The group's successes become the individual's successes—as do its failures—and these reflect positively or negatively on the individual. As a consequence of their expanded personal ties, workers make more of an effort. The results have been so good that, in what is known as "worker empowerment," some self-managed teams even replace bosses as the ones who control everything from schedules to hiring and firing (Lublin 1991).

Corporate Day Care

Another way to humanize the work setting is to set up day care facilities at work. This eases the strain on parents, especially on new mothers, who are able to go to work and still keep an eye on a baby or young child. Parents are also able to spend time with their children during breaks and lunch hours. Mothers can even nurse their children at these times.

Given the global competition that they face, can U.S. firms afford child care? Accountable to its stockholders, the Union Bank of Monterey, California, decided to measure the net cost of its day care. They found that the turnover of employees who used the center was only 2.2 percent, compared with 9.5 percent of those who did not use it. Users of the center also were absent from work less often (two fewer days per year) than the nonusers. Their maternity leaves were also shorter. The net cost? After subtracting the center's costs from these savings, the bank saved more than $200,000 (Solomon 1988).

Humanizing the work setting, an attempt to make working conditions better match human needs, has taken many forms. One (used by only a minority of corporations) is to offer on-site day care. Shown here are working parents dropping their daughter off at the company-run day care center in Los Angeles. Such services cost companies less than they appear to, for they reduce worker turnover.

Rather than offering no child care services whatsoever, some companies that don't provide on-site child care choose an option that falls somewhere in between: They offer emergency back-up child care. With this approach, parents use their own baby-sitter, but if the sitter can't make it, the center's backup services allow the parent to get to work—and to work without worry. Some of these centers are staffed by care givers who hold master's degrees in early childhood education (Narayan 1994).

With increasing numbers of women in management, it is likely that more and more U.S. firms will offer child care services as part of a benefits package designed to attract and hold capable workers.

The Cooperative

In the 1970s, many Americans, especially those opposed to capitalism and what they considered to be the deadening effects of bureaucracy, began to seek an alternative organizational form. They began to establish cooperatives, organizations owned by members who collectively make decisions, determine goals, evaluate resources, set salaries, and assign work tasks. These tasks are all carried out without a hierarchy of authority, for all members can participate in the decisions of the organization. Since the 1970s, about five thousand cooperatives have been established.

As sociologists Joyce Rothschild and Allen Whitt (1986) pointed out, cooperatives are not new; they were introduced into the United States during the 1840s. Cooperatives attempt to achieve some specific social good (such as lowering food prices and improving food quality) and to provide a high level of personal satisfaction for their members as they work toward that goal. Because all members can participate in decision making, cooperatives spend huge amounts of time in deciding even routine matters. The economic results of cooperatives are mixed. Many are less profitable than private organizations, others more so. A few have been so successful that they have been bought out by Wall Street firms.

The Conflict Perspective

Conflict theorists point out that the basic relationship between workers and owners is confrontational regardless of how the work organization is structured (Edwards 1979; Derber and Schwartz 1988). Each walks a different path in life, the one exploiting workers to extract a greater profit, the other trying to resist that exploitation. Because their basic interests are fundamentally opposed, these critics argue, employers' attempts to humanize the work setting (or to manage diversity) are mere window dressing, efforts to conceal their fundamental goal of exploiting workers. In fact, such actions may even be an attempt to manipulate workers into actively cooperating in their own exploitation. This analysis does not apply to cooperatives because they are owned by the workers.

Technology and the Control of Workers

As stressed in the previous chapter, the microchip is changing our lives. Many people rejoice over the computer's capacity to improve their quality of life. They are pleased with the quality control of manufactured goods and the reduction of drudgery. Records are much easier to keep, and we can type just one letter and let the computer print it out and address it to ten individuals—or to ten thousand. Working on my computer, I can modify this sentence, this paragraph, or any section of this book with ease.

Of course, the potential for abuse also exists. Computers may make it easier for governments to operate a police state by monitoring our every move. The Big Brother in Orwell's classic novel, *1984*, may turn out to be a computer.

Whether this happens or not, the computer does allow managers to achieve greater control over workers. Social psychologist Shoshana Zuboff (1991) reports how computers allow managers to increase surveillance without face-to-face supervision. They let managers know the number of keystrokes made on a word processor each minute or hour, and they tell supervisors how long each telephone operator takes per call. Operators who are "underperforming" are singled out for discipline. It does not matter that the slower operators may be more polite or more helpful, only that the computer reports slower performance.

As sociologist Gary Marx (1985, 1986, 1995) says, with computers able to measure motion, air currents, vibrations, odors, pressure changes, and voice stress, accompanied by video cameras that need only a pinhole through which to spy, we may be moving to a "maximum-security" workplace. To prevent employees from punching in someone else's time card, a leading hotel uses a device to scan their workers' eyes. It compares their retinas with computerized data on file. A truck driver at Safeway used to enjoy his job. He says, "No one was looking over your shoulder, and you felt like a human being." But now he says he feels "pushed around." A small computer in the dashboard of his truck (called, appropriately, a Tripmaster) keeps track of his speed, shifting, and excessive idling, and even reports when and how long he stops for lunch or a coffee break. The driver says he will retire early.

The maximum-security workplace seems an apt term for what some of us may be facing. Some fear that, with the computer's awesome capacities, the surveillance of the workplace may be just one aspect of a coming "maximum-security society" (Marx 1995). The Technology box on the following page illustrates a new way that computers are being used to monitor workers who think that their actions have gone unnoticed.

MYTHS AND REALITIES OF THE JAPANESE CORPORATE MODEL

How were the Japanese able to arise from the defeat of World War II—including the nuclear devastation of two of their main cities—to become a giant in today's global economy? Some analysts trace part of the answer to the way their corporations are organized. One of these analysts, William Ouchi (1981), pinpointed five ways in which Japanese corporations differ from those of the United States. You will be surprised at how different they are. But are these differences myth or reality?

Hiring and Promoting Teams

In *Japan,* teamwork is central. College graduates who join a corporation are all paid about the same starting salary. To learn the company's various levels, they are rotated as a team through the organization. They are also promoted as a team. They develop intense loyalty

Sociology & the New Technology

CYBERSLACKERS AND CYBERSLEUTHS: SURFING AT WORK

Few people work constantly at their jobs. Most of us take breaks and, at least once in a while, goof off. We meet fellow workers at the water cooler, and we talk in the hallway. Much of this interaction is good for the company, for it bonds us to fellow workers and ties us to our jobs.

Part of our workday may even cross over into our personal lives. Some of us make personal calls from the office. Bosses know that we need to check in with our child's preschool or make arrangements for a babysitter; they expect such calls. Some even wink as we call a friend to chat, make arrangements to have our car worked on, or set up a date. And most bosses make personal calls of their own from time to time. It's the abuse of this policy that bothers them, and they're likely to fire anyone who hangs on the phone all day for personal reasons.

Now comes *cyberslacking,* using computers at work for personal purposes. With almost every office equipped with at least one computer,

cyberslacking was bound to emerge. Perhaps most workers fritter away some of their workday online. Some play games, others shop online, and many send personal e-mail. Some Web sites even protect cyberslackers: They feature a panic button to be used in case the boss pokes her head in your office. You just click the button and a phony spreadsheet pops onto your screen while typing sounds emerge from your speakers.

Some cyberslackers operate their own private online businesses during office hours. Others can hardly wait to get to work so they can play games; many spend most of their "working" hours battling virtual enemies. (One computer programmer even became a national champion playing Starcraft at work.) Some spend a good part of their "working" hours downloading pornography. Xerox fired 40 employees for mixing their pornographic pleasure with business (Naughton 1999).

To combat cyberslacking, a new specialty, the cybersleuth, has

emerged. Using specialized software, cybersleuths examine everything employees have read online, everything they've written, and every Internet site they've visited. What some of us don't know (and what some of us forget) is that delete does not mean delete. Although we hit the delete button, our computers still contain a permanent record of what appears to be erased. Without knowing it, we have left behind a hidden diary of our computer activities. Just a few clicks on the cybersleuth software and this "deleted" information becomes visible, our personal diary exposed for anyone who wants to read it. ■

For Your Consideration

Do you think that cybersleuthing is an abuse of power? Or do employers have a right to check on what their employees are doing with the company computers on company time? Can you think of another solution to cyberslacking?

to one another and to their company, for the welfare of one represents the welfare of all. Only in later years are individuals singled out for recognition. When there is an opening in the firm, outsiders are not even considered.

In the *United States,* personal achievement is central. An employee is hired on the basis of what the firm thinks that individual can contribute. Employees try to outperform others, and they regard a higher salary and a promotion as signs of personal success. The individual's loyalty is to himself or herself, not to the company. Outsiders are considered for openings in the firm.

Lifetime Security

In *Japan,* lifetime security is taken for granted. Employees can expect to work for the same firm for the rest of their lives. In return for not being laid off or fired, they are expected to be loyal to the company, to stick with it through good and bad times. Employees do not go job shopping, for their careers—and many aspects of their lives—are wrapped up in this one firm.

In the *United States,* lifetime security is unusual. It is limited primarily to teachers, who receive what is called *tenure.* Companies lay off workers in slow times, and to become more competitive they reorganize and fire entire divisions. Workers "look out for number one." They seek better pay and opportunities elsewhere. Job shopping and job hopping are common.

Almost Total Involvement

In *Japan,* work is like a marriage: The employee and the company are committed to each other. The employee supports the company with loyalty and long hours at work, while the company supports its workers with lifetime security, health services, recreation, sports and social events, even a home mortgage. Involvement with the company does not stop when the workers leave the building. They join company study and exercise groups, and are likely to spend evenings with co-workers in bars and restaurants.

In the *United States,* work is a specific, often temporary contract. Employees are hired to do a certain job. When they have done that job, they have fulfilled their obligation to the company. Their after-work hours are their own. They are free to go home to their private lives, which usually are highly separate from the firm.

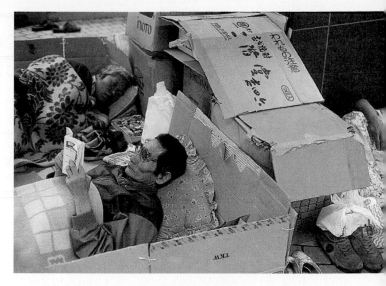

For a time, Americans stood in awe of the Japanese corporate model. Research (as well as the passage of time that revealed problems with competitiveness), however, have uncovered serious flaws. Lifetime job security, for example, is a myth. These homeless men are living in the Shinjuko train station in Tokyo. Note how they have followed the Japanese custom of placing their shoes outside before entering their "home."

Broad Training

In *Japan,* employees move from one job to another within the company. Not only are they not stuck doing the same thing for years on end, but they gain a broader picture of the corporation and how the specific jobs they are assigned fit into the bigger picture.

In the *United States,* employees are expected to perform one job, to do it well, and then to be promoted upward to a job with more responsibility. Their understanding of the company is largely tied to the particular corner they occupy, often making it difficult for them to see how their job fits into the overall picture.

Decision Making by Consensus

In *Japan,* decision making is broad and lengthy. Each person who will be affected by a decision is consulted. After lengthy deliberations, a consensus emerges, and everyone agrees on which suggestion is superior. Workers feel that they are an essential part of the organization, not simply cogs in a giant machine.

In the *United States,* decisions are made by whoever has responsibility for the unit to be affected. This person does as much consulting with others as he or she thinks necessary and then makes the decision.

The Myth Versus Reality

Peering beneath the surface reveals a reality that is quite different from the myth that has been promoted. Lifetime job security, for example, is elusive, and only about a third of Japanese workers find it. Japanese corporations have also found that paying the same wages to almost everyone in the same age group, regardless of their productivity, is expensive and makes them less able to compete in the global market. The myth makes management by consensus a centerpiece of the Japanese corporation. This was not how decisions were made at Sony, however, one of Japan's most successful corporations (Nathan 1999). Akio Morita, Sony's founder, was an entrepreneur from the same mold as Bill Gates. Morita didn't send memos up and down the line, as the myth would have you believe. Instead, he relied on his gut feeling about products, and he made quick decisions. Over lunch, he decided to buy CBS Records. The cost was $2 billion. When he thought up the Walkman, Morita didn't discuss it until consensus was reached. Instead, he simply ordered it to be manufactured. The Perspectives box on the following page, with which we close this chapter, explores other aspects of the Japanese myth.

PERSPECTIVES | Cultural Diversity Around the World

JAPANESE AND U.S. CORPORATIONS IN AN AGE OF GREED

Do you know which of these statements is false?

- The Japanese are more productive than Americans.

- The living standard of Americans has fallen behind that of the Japanese.

- All Japanese workers enjoy lifetime job security.

- The Japanese are paid less than Americans.

From what you just read, you know that the third one is false. So are the other three.

A while back, Japanese corporations seemed invincible. There was even talk that the United States had won World War II, but had lost the economic war. Impressed with the Japanese success, many nations, including the United States, sent executives to Japan to study the Japanese economic model. U.S. corporations then copied parts of that model.

Cracks in the facade soon appeared. Small at first, they grew, threatening to destroy some of Japan's major corporations. These companies had been built on personal relationships, on mutual obligations that transcend contracts. This had been a key to creating fierce loyalty. This corporate strength, however, turned out to be an Achilles heel. When Japan's economy went into a nosedive, these companies refused to lay off workers; such action was not part of their corporate culture. Their expenses continued while their profits disappeared, sinking them in a sea of red ink.

In a reverse move, Japan studied U.S. corporations to see why they were more efficient. Flying in the face of their tradition, Japanese corporations began to lay off workers and to offer merit pay. Toyota and Honda, for example, now give bonuses to managers who meet their goals, a standard U.S. practice, but unthinkable in Japan just a few years ago (Schlesinger and Sapsford 1993; Reitman and Suris 1994; Shirouzu and Williams 1995; Kanabayashi 1996).

One of the biggest surprises was Ford's takeover of Mazda. With Mazda teetering on the edge of bankruptcy, its creditors decided that Ford knew more about building and marketing cars than Mazda and invited Ford to manage the company. In true U.S. fashion, Ford laid off workers and renegotiated contracts with suppliers. With its work force slashed from 46,000 to 36,000, Mazda again became profitable. The process isn't over: After Ford turned Mazda around, Renault took over Nissan Motor (Shirouzu 2000). A much leaner, meaner Japanese production machine is emerging.

The real bottom line is that we live in a global marketplace—of ideas as well as products. The likely result of global competition will be that both the West and Japan will feed off each other. For certain, Japan will learn how to compete more effectively in capitalism's cutthroat production and marketing arenas. It must, if it is to survive the new reality of global capitalism. It is not as apparent, however, that the United States will learn the kind of cooperation that underlies the Japanese corporation. ■

SUMMARY AND REVIEW

■ The Rationalization of Society

How did the rationalization of society come about?

The term **rationalization of society** refers to a transformation in people's thinking and behaviors—one that shifts the focus from protecting time-honored ways to being efficient and producing results. Weber, who developed this term, traced the rationalization of society to Protestant theology, which he said brought about capitalism. Marx attributed rationalization to capitalism itself. Pp. 174–176.

■ Formal Organizations and Bureaucracy

What are formal organizations?

Formal organizations are secondary groups designed to achieve specific objectives. Their dominant form is the **bureaucracy,** which Weber characterized as consisting of a hierarchy, a division of labor, written rules, written communications, and impersonality of positions—characteristics that allow bureaucracies to be efficient and enduring. Pp. 177–180.

What dysfunctions are associated with bureaucracies?

The dysfunctions of bureaucracies include alienation, red tape, lack of communication between units, **goal displacement**, and incompetence (as seen in the **Peter principle**). In Weber's view, the impersonality of bureaucracies tends to produce **alienation** among workers—the feeling that no one cares about them and that they do not really fit in. Marx's view of alienation is somewhat different—workers are separated from the product of their labor because they participate in only a small part of the production process. Pp. 180–183.

■ Voluntary Associations

What are the functions of voluntary associations?

Voluntary associations are groups made up of volunteers who organize on the basis of common interests. These associations further mutual interests, provide a sense of identity and purpose, help to govern and maintain order, mediate between the government and the individual, give training in organizational skills, help provide access to political power, and pave the way for social change. Pp. 183–185.

What is "the iron law of oligarchy"?

Sociologist Robert Michels noted that formal organizations have a tendency to become controlled by a small group that limits leadership to its own inner circle. The dominance of a formal organization by an elite inner circle that keeps itself in power is called **the iron law of oligarchy.** Pp. 185–186.

■ Careers in Bureaucracies

How does the corporate culture affect workers?

The term **corporate culture** refers to an organization's traditions, values, and unwritten norms. Much of corporate culture, such as its hidden values, is not readily visible. Often, a self-fulfilling prophecy is at work: Those deemed likely to succeed (that is, people who match a corporation's hidden values) are put on tracks that enhance their chance of success, and they become successful; those deemed less likely to succeed (who do not match those values) are set on a course that minimizes their performance, and they become less successful. Pp. 186–187.

■ Humanizing the Corporate Culture

What does it mean to humanize the work setting?

Humanizing a work setting means to organize it in a way that develops rather than impedes human potential. Among the characteristics of more humane bureaucracies are expanded opportunities on the basis of ability and contributions rather than personal characteristics, a more even distribution of power, less rigid rules, and more open decision making. Attempts to modify bureaucracies include quality circles, small work groups, and self-management teams. Employee ownership plans give workers a greater stake in the outcomes of their work organizations. Cooperatives are an alternative to bureaucracies. Conflict theorists see attempts to humanize work as a way of manipulating workers. Pp. 187–191.

■ Myths and Realities of the Japanese Corporate Model

How do Japanese and U.S. corporations differ?

The Japanese corporate model contrasts sharply with the U.S. model in terms of hiring and promotion practices, lifetime security, worker involvement outside the work setting, broad training of workers, and collective decision making. Much of this model is a myth, an idealization of reality, and does not reflect Japanese corporate life today. Pp. 191–194.

Where can I read more on this topic?

Suggested readings for this chapter are at the back of this book.

All URLs listed are current as of the printing of this book. URLs often change. Please check our Web site, **http://www.abacon.com/henslin,** for updates.

1. The United States government is probably the largest and most complex bureaucracy in the world. You can explore a small portion of this bureaucracy at the Web site for the Department of Defense at **http://www.defenselink.mil.** Click on the button marked "Organization." On this page, you can begin to see how detailed the Department of Defense bureaucracy is. The different branches are identified along the side—the Office of the Secretary of Defense, Joint Chiefs of Staff, the Unified Combatant Commands, Defense Agencies, the Military Branches, and the Congressional Committees. The Secretary of Defense's immediate staff is also outlined on this page. If you click on any of the Undersecretaries' offices, you can see the staff that operates below this initial level of bureaucracy.

   Which of Weber's essential characteristics of bureaucracy are illustrated at this Web site? Draw an organizational chart of the Department of Defense. From what you have learned about bureaucracy, what advantages are created by organizing activities this way? What drawbacks can you see to this form of organization? Can you think of an alternative way of organizing the work of the Department of Defense?

2. In this chapter you read about the McDonaldization of society, which involves the rationalization of the routine tasks of everyday life. Although this trend may appear inevitable, there is opposition to it. You can read about the famous McLibel case at **http://www.mcspotlight.org,** the Web site maintained by the McInformation Network, an independent group of volunteers who distribute information about the policies and practices of the McDonald's Corporation. This group also highlights global campaigns in opposition to this multinational corporation. At this site you will find information about these campaigns, the McDonald's Corporation, and the wider impact of McDonaldization in various areas of our lives. You can read an interview with George Ritzer, the sociologist who first wrote about this trend (**http://www.mcspotlight.org/people/interviews/ritzer_george.html**). You can also read an excerpt from his book, The McDonaldization of Society (**http://www.mcspotlight.org/media/books/ritzer_excerpt.html**), in which he provides a number of suggestions about how to resist the forces of McDonaldization. Write a paper about whether or not we are destined to live in a McDonaldized world.

3. Examine the Alzheimer's Association web site at **http://www.alz.org/.** Is this a voluntary organization? How do you know? What are some of the functions of this organization? Does this association fulfill all seven of the functions of voluntary associations that are discussed in the text? If not, which functions are absent? Based on the information on this Web site, why do you think people join this group? Prepare a presentation to your class about the role of organizations like this one in our society.

4. This chapter discusses cooperatives as an alternative to bureaucratic structure. Go to the Coop America's site, **http://www.coopamerica.org,** and the National Cooperative Business Association's site, **http://www.cooperative.org**. What are the characteristics and types of cooperatives? What principles and values are at the heart of this type of organization? How would you start your own cooperative? Now go to the Web page that is maintained by the Small Business Association, **http://www.sba.gov/starting/indexsteps.html.** Read about the process of starting a small business; then compare and contrast this type of business organization with cooperatives. Which is more appealing to you? Why? Prepare a presentation for your class on cooperatives as alternatives to traditional business organization.

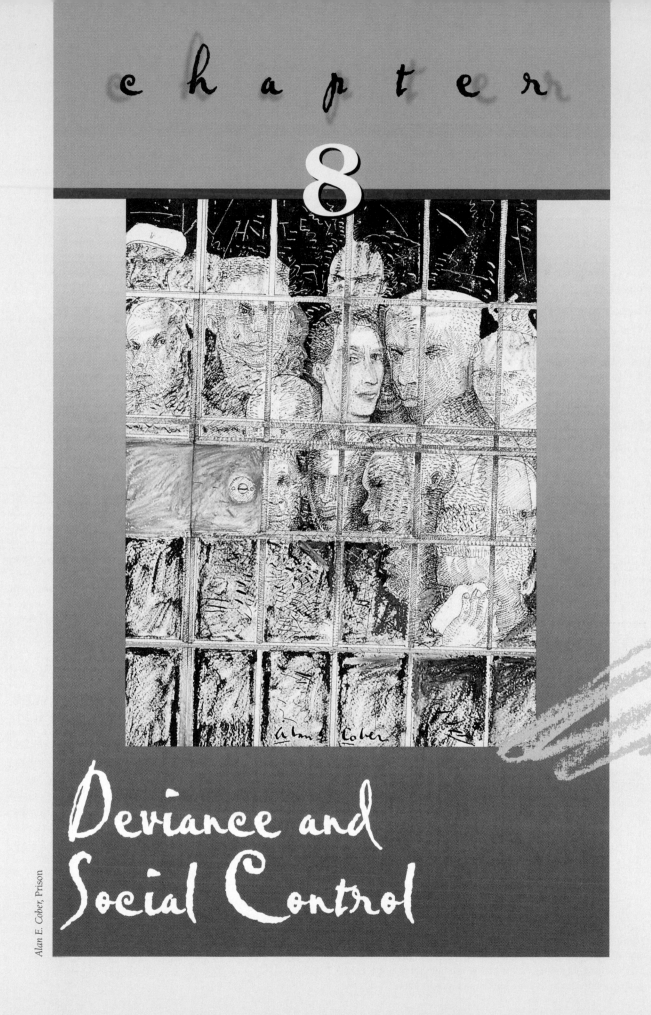

Deviance and Social Control

- **Gaining a Sociological Perspective on Deviance**
  The Relativity of Deviance
  Who Defines Deviance?
  How Norms Make Social Life Possible
  Comparing Biological, Psychological, and
      Sociological Explanations

- **The Symbolic Interactionist Perspective**
  Differential Association Theory
  Control Theory
  Labeling Theory

- **The Functionalist Perspective**
  How Deviance Is Functional for Society
  Strain Theory: How Social Values Produce
      Deviance
  Illegitimate Opportunity Theory: Explaining Social
      Class and Crime

- **The Conflict Perspective**
  Class, Crime, and the Criminal Justice System
  Power and Inequality
  The Law as an Instrument of Oppression

- **The Need for Multiple Theories**

- **Reactions to Deviance**
  Sanctions
  Degradation Ceremonies
  Imprisonment
  The Death Penalty
  New Legislation
  The Trouble with Official Statistics
  The Medicalization of Deviance: Mental Illness

- **The Need for a More Humane Approach**

- **Summary and Review**

In just a few moments I was to meet my first Yanomamo, my first primitive man. What would it be like? . . . I looked up (from my canoe) and gasped when I saw a dozen burly, naked, filthy, hideous men staring at us down the shafts of their drawn arrows. Immense wads of green tobacco were

stuck between their lower teeth and lips, making them look even more hideous, and strands of dark green slime dripped or hung from their noses. We arrived at the village while the men were blowing a hallucinogenic drug up their noses. One of the side effects of the drug is a runny nose. The mucus is always saturated with the green powder and the Indians usually let it run freely from their nostrils. . . . I just sat there holding my notebook, helpless and pathetic. . . .

The whole situation was depressing, and I wondered why I ever decided to switch from civil engineering to anthropology in the first place. . . .[Soon] I was covered with red pigment, the result of a dozen or so complete examinations. . . . These examinations capped an otherwise grim day. The Indians would blow their noses into their hands, flick as much of the mucus off that would separate in a snap of the wrist, wipe the residue into their hair, and then carefully examine my face, arms, legs, hair, and the contents of my pockets. I said (in their language), "Your hands are dirty"; my comments were met by the Indians in the following way: they would "clean" their hands by spitting a quantity of slimy tobacco juice into them, rub them together, and then proceed with the examination. ■

deviance the violation of rules or norms

stigma "blemishes" that discredit a person's claim to a "normal" identity

GAINING A SOCIOLOGICAL PERSPECTIVE ON DEVIANCE

So went Napoleon Chagnon's eye-opening introduction to the Yanomamo tribe of the rain forests of Brazil. His ensuing months of fieldwork continued to bring surprise after surprise, and often Chagnon (1977) could hardly believe his eyes—or his nose.

Where would we start if we were to list the deviant behaviors of these people? With the way they appear naked in public? Use hallucinogenic drugs? Let mucus hang from their noses? Or with the way they rub hands that are filled with mucus, spittle, and tobacco juice over a frightened stranger who doesn't dare to protest? Perhaps. But it isn't this simple, for, as we shall see, deviance is relative.

The Relativity of Deviance

Sociologists use the term **deviance** to refer to any violation of norms—whether the infraction is as minor as jaywalking, as serious as murder, or as humorous as Chagnon's encounter with the Yanomamo. This deceptively simple definition takes us to the heart of the sociological perspective of deviance, which sociologist Howard S. Becker (1966) identified this way: *It is not the act itself, but the reactions to the act, that make something deviant.* In other words, people's behaviors must be viewed from the framework of the culture in which they take place. To Chagnon, the behaviors were frighteningly deviant, but to the Yanomamo they represented normal, everyday life. What was deviant to Chagnon was *conformist* to the Yanomamo. From their viewpoint, you *should* check out strangers as they did, and nakedness is good, as are hallucinogenic drugs and letting mucus be "natural."

This Aymara Indian in Bolivia has just taken a pinch of coca leaves from the sack made for this purpose by his wife or mother. For centuries, the Indians of Bolivia and nearby countries have chewed coca leaves as a stimulant. It would be the deviant who would not participate in this custom, affirming the sociological point that deviance is relative.

Chagnon's abrupt introduction to the Yanomamo allows us to see the *relativity of deviance,* a major point made by symbolic interactionists. Because different groups have different norms, *what is deviant to some is not deviant to others.* This principle holds *within* a society as well as across cultures. Thus acts that are perfectly acceptable in one culture—or in one group within a society—may be considered deviant in another culture, or by another group within the same society. This idea is explored in the Perspectives box on the facing page.

Unlike the general public, sociologists use the term *deviance* nonjudgmentally, to refer to any act to which people respond negatively. When sociologists use this term, it does not mean that they agree that an act is bad, just that people judge it negatively. To sociologists, then, all of us are deviants of one sort or another, for we all violate norms from time to time.

To be considered deviant, a person may not even have to *do* anything. Sociologist Erving Goffman (1963) used the term **stigma** to refer to characteristics that discredit people. These include violations of norms of ability (blindness, deafness, mental handicaps) and violations of norms of appearance (a facial birthmark, obesity). They also include involuntary memberships, such as being the victim of AIDS or the brother of a rapist. The stigma becomes a person's master status, defining him or her as deviant. Recall from Chapter 4 that a master status cuts across all other statuses that a person occupies.

■ **In Sum** In sociology, the term *deviance* refers to all violations of social rules, regardless of their seriousness. The term is not a judgment about the behavior. Deviance is relative, for what is deviant in one group may be conformist in another. As symbolic interactionists stress, if we are to understand people, we must understand the meanings that they give to events. Consequently, we must consider deviance from *within* a group's own framework, for it is *their* meanings that underlie their behavior.

PERSPECTIVES | Cultural Diversity Around the World

SUICIDE AND SEXUAL BEHAVIOR IN CROSS-CULTURAL PERSPECTIVE

Anthropologist Robert Edgerton (1976) reports how differently human groups react to similar behaviors. Let's look at suicide and sexuality to illustrate how a group's *definition* of a behavior, not the behavior itself, determines whether or not it will be considered deviant.

Suicide

In some societies, suicide is seen not as a deviant behavior but as a positive act, at least under specified conditions. In traditional Japanese society, *hara-kiri,* a ritual disembowelment, was considered to be the proper course for disgraced noblemen or defeated military leaders. Similarly, kamikaze pilots in World War II who crashed their explosives-laden planes into U.S. warships were admired for their bravery and sacrifice. Traditional Eskimos approved of suicide for individuals who could no longer contribute their share to the group. Sometimes an aged father would hand his hunting knife to his son, asking him to drive it through his heart. For a

son to refuse this request would be considered deviant.

Sexuality

Norms of sexual behavior vary so widely around the world that what is considered normal in one society may be considered deviant in another. The Pokot people of northwestern Kenya, for example, place high emphasis on sexual pleasure and fully expect that both a husband and his wife will reach orgasm. If a husband does not satisfy his wife, he is in serious trouble. Pokot men often engage in adulterous affairs, and should a husband's failure to satisfy his wife be attributed to his adultery, his wife and her female friends will tie him up when he is asleep. The women will shout obscenities at him, beat him, and, as a final gesture of their utter contempt, slaughter and eat his favorite ox before releasing him. His hours of painful humiliation are intended to make him henceforth more dutiful concerning his wife's conjugal rights.

Ideal Versus Covert Norms

People can also become deviants for failing to understand that their group's ideal norms may not be its real norms. As with many groups, the Zapotec Indians of Mexico profess that sexual activity should take place exclusively between husband and wife. Yet the *only* person in one Zapotec community who had had no extramarital affairs was considered deviant. Evidently these people have a common understanding that married couples will engage in discreet extramarital affairs. Customarily, when a wife learns that her husband is having an affair, she does the same thing.

One Zapotec wife did not follow this covert norm. Instead, she would praise her own virtue to her husband—and then voice the familiar "headache" excuse. She also informed the other husbands and wives in the village whom their spouses were sleeping with. As a result, this virtuous woman was condemned by everyone in the village. Clearly, covert norms can conflict with formal norms—another illustration of the gap between ideal and real culture. ■

Who Defines Deviance?

If deviance does not lie in the act, but in definitions of the act, where do those definitions come from? To answer this question, let's look first at areas of agreement between functionalists and conflict theorists, then at how these views diverge.

Tribal Versus Industrial Societies Let's first consider groups that have no written language. Each of these groups, such as the Yanomamo, has passed through a unique history. Each has faced and solved a set of problems that threatened its survival. The solutions to these problems— of how to investigate strangers and protect itself from enemies—have become part of the group's norms and now are an essential part of its way of life. Agreement on how life should be lived is relatively simple, for the group is small and has strong social bonds.

Industrialized societies, in contrast, are made up of many competing groups. Each has its own history of problems, its own solutions, its own ideas about the way the world is and ought to be, and its own norms to uphold its ideas of right and wrong. Because these groups participate

Suicide is not inherently deviant: It is deviant only when that meaning is assigned to it. During World War II, some Japanese pilots were trained for kamikaze, or suicide, missions. Their planes were loaded with bombs, and their mission was to ram U.S. ships, killing themselves in the process. Shown here are six kamikaze pilots after their training.

in the same general culture, they agree on many things. Yet due to their separate histories, they may differ sharply on many aspects of life—to the extent that what one group considers right, another may consider wrong.

Regardless of how they define deviance, all groups, in order to enforce their version of what is good, set up techniques of **social control**. Up to this point in the analysis, functionalists and conflict theorists are in basic agreement about social control. But now they diverge.

Functionalism and Social Control Functionalists stress how the many groups that make up a pluralistic society coexist. Each enforces its own norms among its members, and the groups attain a more or less balanced state. Although tensions between groups may appear from time to time, the balancing of these tensions produces the whole that we call society. If some group threatens to upset the equilibrium, efforts are made to restore balance. For example, in a pluralistic society the central government often plays a mediating role between groups. In the United States, the executive, legislative, and judicial branches of the government mediate the demands of the various groups that make up society, preventing groups whose basic ideas deviate from those held by most members of society from taking political control (Riesman 1950). This view of mediation and balance among competing groups is broadly representative of what may be called the **pluralistic theory of social control.**

Conflict Theory and Social Control Conflict theorists, in contrast, stress that each society is dominated by a group of elite, powerful people, and that the basic purpose of social control is to maintain their power. Society does not consist of groups that work together in harmonious balance, but, rather, of groups that are uneasily held together under this dominant power. The group that holds power must fend off groups that desire to replace it and take over the society themselves. If another group does gain power, it, too, immediately tries to neutralize competing groups.

As they exercise power, some groups are more ruthless than others. At the same time as when the Nazis perpetrated the Holocaust, the Communists in the Soviet Union also systematically eliminated people—millions altogether—that they believed were a threat to their vision of the ideal society. In more recent years, the Khmer Rouge did the same in Cambodia. Even though other dominant groups may be less brutal than in these extreme examples, they, too, are committed to maintaining power.

Power in the United States is not as naked as it is in dictatorships, but conflict theorists note that an elite group of wealthy, largely white males maintains power by working behind the scenes to control the three branches of government (Domhoff 1990, 1997). These men make certain that their interests are served by the decisions of Congress, by the nominees to the U.S. Supreme Court, and by the presidential candidates of the two major political parties. Thus, the laws of society represent this group's views of capital and property, which form the basis of their power. This means that **official deviance**—the statistics on victims, lawbreakers, and criminal investigations and sentencing—reflects their interests.

Thus, say conflict theorists, the state's machinery of social control—lawmaking, police, and courts—represents the interests of the wealthy and powerful. It is this group that determines the laws, whose enforcement helps to keep the group in power. Other norms may derive from other sources, such as those that govern informal behavior (chewing with a closed mouth, appearing in public with combed hair, and so on), but they simply do not count for much. Although they influence everyday behavior, they do not determine who receives a prison sentence and who does not.

How Norms Make Social Life Possible

Regardless of which of these views is correct regarding the origin of a group's norms, or whose interests they represent, *norms make social life possible by making behavior predictable*. Consequently, every group within a society, and even human society itself, depends on norms for its existence. Only because we can count on most people most of the time to meet the expectations of others can social life as we know it exist.

social control a group's formal and informal means of enforcing its norms

pluralistic theory of social control the view that society is made up of many competing groups, whose interests manage to become balanced

official deviance a society's statistics on lawbreaking; its measures of crimes, victims, lawbreakers, and the outcomes of criminal investigations and sentencing

What would life be like if you could not predict what others would do? Imagine for a moment that you have gone to a store to purchase milk:

> Suppose the clerk says, "I won't sell you any milk. We're overstocked with soda, and I'm not going to sell anyone milk until our soda inventory is reduced."
>
> You don't like it, but you decide to buy a case of soda. At the checkout, the clerk says, "I hope you don't mind, but there's a $5 service charge on each fifteenth customer." You, of course, are the fifteenth.
>
> Just as you start to leave, another clerk stops you and says, "We're not working any more. We decided to have a party." Suddenly a stereo begins to blast, and everyone in the store begins to dance. "Oh, good, you've brought the soda," says one clerk, who takes your package and passes sodas all around.

But life is not like this. You can depend on grocery clerks to sell you milk. You also can depend on paying the same price as everyone else and not being forced to attend a party in the store. Why can you depend on this? Because we are socialized to follow norms, to play the basic roles society assigns to us.

Without norms, we would have social chaos. Norms lay out the basic guidelines for how we play our roles and how we interact with others. In short, norms bring about **social order,** a group's customary social arrangements. Our lives are based on these arrangements, which is why deviance is often seen as so threatening. It undermines predictability, the foundation of social life. Consequently, human groups develop a system of *social control,* formal and informal means of enforcing norms.

Comparing Biological, Psychological, and Sociological Explanations

Since norms are essential for society, why do people violate them? To better understand the reasons, it is useful to know how sociological explanations differ from biological and psychological ones.

Psychologists and *sociobiologists* explain deviance by looking for answers *within* individuals. They assume that something in the makeup of people leads them to become deviant. By contrast, sociologists look for answers in factors *outside* the individual. They assume that something in the environment influences people to become deviant.

Biological explanations focus on **genetic predispositions** to such deviance as juvenile delinquency and crime (Lombroso 1911; Sheldon 1949; Glueck and Glueck 1956; Wilson and Hernstein 1985; Rose 1986; Hauser et al. 1995). Biological explanations include (but are not restricted to) the following three theories: (1) intelligence—low intelligence leads to crime; (2) the "XYY" theory—an extra Y chromosome in males leads to crime; and (3) body type—people with "squarish, muscular" bodies are more likely to commit **street crime,** acts such as mugging, rape, and burglary.

How have these theories held up? Not very well. Most people with these supposedly "causal" characteristics do not become criminals. Some criminals are very intelligent, and most people of low intelligence do not commit crimes. Most men who commit crimes have the normal "XY" chromosome combination, and most men with the "XYY" combination do not become criminals. In addition, no women have this combination of genes, so this explanation can't be applied to female criminals. Criminals also exhibit the full range of body types, and most people with "squarish, muscular" bodies do not become street criminals. In short, these supposedly "causal" characteristics are even more common among the general population of people who do not commit crimes.

Still, we cannot rule out the possibility that biological factors influence deviance. Advances in biology have renewed interest in this issue, and some of the findings are intriguing. Psychiatrist Dorothy Lewis (1981), for example, compared the medical histories of delinquents and nondelinquents. She found that delinquents had significantly more head injuries. Then she matched the delinquents by the seriousness of their crimes. When she compared their medical histories, she found that the more violent delinquents—those in

social order a group's usual and customary social arrangements, on which its members depend and on which they base their lives

genetic predispositions inborn tendencies, in this context, to commit deviant acts

street crime crimes such as mugging, rape, and burglary

personality disorders the view that a personality disturbance of some sort causes an individual to violate social norms

crime the violation of norms that are written into law

prison for murder, assault, and rape—also had more head injuries than boys who were locked up for less violent acts such as fights and threats with weapons. Many of the injuries had occurred before the age of 2.

The answers, then, are not yet in, and we must await more research. Even if biological factors are involved in some forms of deviance, from a sociological perspective the causes of deviance cannot be answered by biology alone. Biological factors are always mediated through the social environment. That is, conditions of society channel different categories of people in different directions. For example, compared with females, U.S. males are expected to be braver, tougher, more independent, and less tolerant of insult. It should be obvious that this increases the likelihood that males will become involved in violence.

Psychologists focus on abnormalities *within* the individual, on what are called **personality disorders.** Their supposition is that deviating individuals have deviating personalities (Kalichman 1988; Stone 1989; Heilbrun 1990), that various unconscious devices drive people to deviance. No specific negative childhood experience, however, is invariably linked with deviance. For example, children who had "bad toilet training," "suffocating mothers," or "emotionally aloof fathers" may become embezzling bookkeepers—or good accountants. Just as students, teachers, and police officers represent a variety of bad—and good—childhood experiences, so do deviants. In short, there is no inevitable outcome of any particular childhood experiences, and deviance is not associated with any particular personality.

Sociologists, in contrast, search for factors *outside* the individual. They look for social influences that "recruit" some people rather than others to break norms. To account for why people commit crimes, for example, sociologists examine such external influences as socialization, subcultural membership, and social class. *Social class,* a concept discussed in depth in the next two chapters, refers to people's relative standing in terms of education, occupation, and especially income and wealth.

Knowing how relative deviance is, sociologists ask a critical question: "Why would anyone look for something constant within people to account for a behavior that is conforming in one society and deviant in another?" For example, because **crime** is the violation of norms that have been written into law, what a crime is varies from one human group to another. Why, then, should we expect to find anything constant within people to account for crime—or any other behavior that is conforming in one group but deviant in another?

To see how sociologists explain deviance, especially criminal behavior, let's contrast the three sociological perspectives—symbolic interactionism, functionalism, and conflict theory.

Unlike biology and psychology, which look *within* individuals for explanations of human behavior, sociological explanations focus on *external* experiences, such as people's associations or group memberships. Sociological explanations of human behavior have become widely accepted and now permeate society, as illustrated by this teenager, whom I photographed as we were exiting the Staten Island Ferry in New York City.

THE SYMBOLIC INTERACTIONIST PERSPECTIVE

As we examine symbolic interactionism, it will become more evident why sociologists are not satisfied with explanations rooted in biology or personality. A basic principle of symbolic interactionism is that each of us uses symbols to interpret life. We learn these symbols from the groups to which we belong. A different set of symbols leads to a different way of viewing life—and a different set of behaviors. Consider the contrasting views of life illustrated in the Perspectives box on the facing page.

Differential Association Theory

The Theory Contrary to theories built around biology and personality, sociologist Edwin Sutherland stressed that people *learn* deviance. He coined the term *differential association* to indicate that whether people learn to deviate or to conform to society's norms depends on the *different* groups they *associate* with (Sutherland 1924, 1947; Sutherland and Cressey 1974; Sutherland et al. 1992).

PERSPECTIVES | Cultural Diversity in the United States

IS IT RAPE OR IS IT MARRIAGE? A STUDY IN CULTURE CLASH

Surrounded by cornfields, Lincoln, Nebraska, is about as provincial as a state capital gets. Most of its residents have little experience with people from different ways of life. Their baptism into cultural diversity came as a shock.

The wedding was traditional and followed millennia-old Islamic practices (Annin and Hamilton 1996). A 39-year-old Iraqi refugee had arranged for his two eldest daughters, ages 13 and 14, to marry two fellow Iraqi refugees, ages 28 and 34. A Muslim cleric flew in from Ohio to perform the ceremony.

Nebraska went into shock. So did the refugees. What is marriage in Iraq is rape in Nebraska. The husbands were charged with rape, the girls' father with child abuse, and their mother with contributing to the delinquency of minors.

The event made front page news in Saudi Arabia, where people shook their heads in amazement at Americans. Ne-braskans shook their heads in amazement, too.

In Fresno, California, a young Hmong refugee took a group of friends to a local college campus. There they picked up the girl he had selected to be his wife (Sherman 1988; Lacayo 1993a). The young men brought her to his house, where he had sex with her. The young woman, however, was not in agreement with this plan.

The Hmong call it *zij poj niam,* marriage by capture. For them, this is an acceptable form of mate selection, one that mirrors Hmong courtship ideals of strong men and virtuous, resistant women. The Fresno District Attorney, however, called it kidnapping and rape. ■

For Your Consideration

To apply *symbolic interactionism* to these real-life dramas, ask how the per-spectives of the people involved explain why they did what they did. To apply *functionalism,* ask how the U.S. laws that were violated are "functional" (that is, what are their benefits, to whom?). To apply *conflict theory,* ask what groups are in conflict in these examples. (do not focus on the individuals involved, but on the groups to which they belong.)

Understanding events in terms of different theoretical perspectives does not tell us what reaction is "right" when cultures clash. Remember that science can analyze causes and consequences, but it cannot answer questions of "ought." Any "ought" that you feel about these cases comes from your system of values—which brings us, once again, to the initial issue—the relativity of deviance.

On the most obvious level, some boys and girls join the Scouts, while others join Satan's Servants. What they learn influences them toward or away from deviance.

Sutherland's theory is actually more complicated than this, but he basically said that deviance is learned. This goes directly against the view that deviance is biological or is due to deep personality needs. Sutherland stressed that the different groups to which we belong (our *differential* association) give us messages about conformity and deviance. We may receive mixed messages, but we end up with more of one than the other (an "excess of definitions," as Sutherland put it). The end result is an imbalance—attitudes that tilt us more in one direction than the other. Consequently, we conform or deviate.

Families Since the family is so important for teaching attitudes, does the family make a difference in whether children learn to conform to norms—or even to become criminals? Researchers have found that families involved in crime tend to set their children on a law-breaking path. Of all jail inmates across the United States, about half have a father, mother, brother, or sister who has served time (*Sourcebook of Criminal Justice Statistics* 1997:483). Delinquents are also more likely to come from families that get in trouble with the law. Researchers who studied the family history of 25,000 delinquents who were in high-security state institutions found that 25 percent had a father

To experience a sense of belonging is one of humanity's basic needs. Membership in groups, especially peer groups, is a primary way that people meet this need. Regardless of the group's orientation—whether it is to conformity or to deviance—the process is the same. Shown here are the Sons of Samoa, a group in west Los Angeles, flashing their gang signs, which help provide them with a vital sense of belonging.

who had been in prison, 25 percent a brother or sister, 9 percent a mother, and 13 percent some other relative (Beck et al. 1988).

Friends and Neighborhoods Friends are similarly important. If someone's friends are delinquent, that person is likely to be delinquent. In fact, the longer someone has delinquent friends, the more likely he or she is to be delinquent (Warr 1993). Much delinquency is clustered in certain neighborhoods, and children from those neighborhoods are likely to become delinquent (Miller 1958; Wolfgang and Farracuti 1967). This, of course, comes as no surprise to parents, who generally are eager to get their kids out of "bad" neighborhoods and away from "bad" friends. Although they may not know the term *differential association*, they know how it works.

Subcultures Subcultures work in the same way. Particular attitudes about deviance and conformity dominate each subculture, and its members learn those attitudes. In a lower-class Chicano neighborhood in Chicago, for example, the concept of "honor" helped propel its young men into deviance. Sociologist Ruth Horowitz (1983, 1987), who did participant observation in this neighborhood, reports that the formula was simple: "A man must have honor. An insult is a threat to one's honor. Therefore, not to stand up to someone is to be less than a real man."

Now suppose you were a young man growing up in this neighborhood. You likely would do a fair amount of fighting, for you would interpret many statements and acts as attacks on your honor. You might even carry a knife or a gun, for words and fists wouldn't always be sufficient. Along with members of your group, you would define fighting, knifing, and shooting quite differently from the way most people do.

For members of the Mafia, ideas of manliness are also intertwined with deviance. For them, *to kill is a measure of their manhood.* Not all killings are accorded the same respect, however, for "the more awesome and potent the victim, the more worthy and meritorious the killer" (Arlacchi 1980). Some killings are done to enforce norms. A member of the Mafia who gives information to the police, for example, has violated *omertá* (the Mafia vow of secrecy). Such an offense can never be tolerated, for it threatens the very existence of the group. This example further illustrates just how relative deviance is. Although killing is deviant to mainstream society, for the Mafia, *not* to kill after certain rules are broken—such as when someone "squeals" to the cops—is the deviant act.

The exhibit of deviants on *The Jerry Springer Show* offers viewers a sense of being participants in forbidden events. As Springer and others like him continue to parade deviants before the public, the shock and surprise wear off, making the deviance seem "more" normal. What is occurring is the *mainstreaming of deviance*—the disapproved moving into the mainstream, or becoming more socially acceptable.

Prison or Freedom? An issue that comes up over and over again in sociology is whether we are prisoners of socialization. Symbolic interactionists stress that we are not mere pawns in the hands of others. We are not destined by our group memberships to think and behave as our groups dictate. Rather, we *help produce our own orientations to* life. Our choice of membership (differential association), for example, helps to shape the self. For instance, one college student may join a feminist group that is trying to change the treatment of women in college; another may associate with a group of women who shoplift on weekends. Their choice of groups points them in two different directions. The one who associates with shoplifters may become even more oriented toward deviant activities, while the one who joins the feminist group may develop an even greater interest in producing social change.

Control Theory

Inside most of us, it seems, are strong desires to do things that would get us in trouble—inner drives, temptations, urges, hostilities, and so on. I'm sure you know what I'm talking about. Yet most of us stifle these desires most of the time. Why?

This is the basic question of **control theory,** which looks at deviance as a natural part of human nature. In order to have group life, commonly called society, the human group must restrain people's natural drives for self-gratification. Working against our tendencies to deviate, says sociologist Walter Reckless (1973), who developed control theory, are two control systems. Our *inner controls* include our internalized morality—conscience, religious principles, ideas of right and wrong. Inner controls also include fears of punishment, feelings of integrity, and the desire to be a "good" person (Hirschi 1969; Rogers 1977). Our *outer controls* consist of people—such as family, friends, and the police—who influence us not to deviate. Control theory is sometimes classified as a functional theory, because when our outer controls operate well, we conform to social norms and thereby do not threaten the status quo. Because symbols and meanings are central to this theory, however, it can also be classified as a symbolic interactionist theory.

As sociologist Travis Hirschi (1969) noted, the stronger our bonds with society, the more effective our inner controls. Bonds are based on *attachments* (feeling affection and respect for people who conform to society's norms), *commitments* (having a stake in society that you don't want to risk, such as a respected place in your family, a good standing at college, a good job), *involvements* (putting time and energy into approved activities), and *beliefs* (holding that certain actions are morally wrong).

The likelihood that we will deviate from social norms, for example, by committing a crime, depends on which is stronger—the two control systems or the pushes and pulls toward the deviance. If our control systems are weaker, we deviate. If they are strong enough, however, we do not commit the deviant act. This theory can be summarized as *self*-control, says Hirschi. The key to learning high self-control is socialization, especially in childhood. Parents help their children develop self-control by supervising them and punishing their deviant acts (Gottfredson and Hirschi 1990).

Labeling Theory

Symbolic interactionists have developed **labeling theory,** which focuses on the significance of the labels (names, reputations) that are given to people. Labels tend to become a part of the self-concept, which helps to set people on paths that propel them into or divert them from deviance. Let's look at how people react to society's labels—from "whore" and "pervert" to "cheat" and "slob."

Rejecting Labels: How People Neutralize Deviance Most people resist the labels that others try to pin on them. Some are so successful that even though they persist in deviance, they still consider themselves conformists. For example, even though they beat up people and vandalize property, some delinquents consider themselves conforming members of society. How do they do it?

Sociologists Gresham Sykes and David Matza (1988) studied boys who were in this exact situation. They found that they used five **techniques of neutralization** to deflect society's norms:

Denial of Responsibility The boys said, "I'm not responsible for what happened because . . . " and then were quite creative about the "becauses." Some said that what happened was an "accident." Others saw themselves as "victims" of society. What else could you expect? They were like billiard balls shot around the pool table of life.

Denial of Injury Another favorite explanation of the boys was "What I did wasn't wrong because no one got hurt." They would define vandalism as "mischief," gang fighting as a

control theory the idea that two control systems—inner controls and outer controls—work against our tendencies to deviate

labeling theory the view, developed by symbolic interactionists, that the labels people are given affect their own and others' perceptions of them, thus channeling their behavior either into deviance or into conformity

techniques of neutralization ways of thinking or rationalizing that help people deflect society's norms

"private quarrel," and stealing cars as "borrowing." They might acknowledge that what they did was illegal, but claim that they were "just having a little fun."

Denial of a Victim Sometimes the boys thought of themselves as avengers. Vandalizing a teacher's car was done to get revenge for an unfair grade, while shoplifting was done to even the score with "crooked" store owners. In short, if the boys did accept responsibility and even admit that someone did get hurt, they protected their self-concept by claiming that the people "deserved what they got."

Condemnation of the Condemners Another technique the boys used was to deny that others had the right to judge them. They might accuse people who pointed their fingers at them of being "a bunch of hypocrites": The police were "on the take," teachers had "pets," and parents cheated on their taxes. In short, they said, "Who are *they* to accuse *me* of something?"

Appeal to Higher Loyalties A final technique the boys used to justify their antisocial activities was to consider loyalty to the gang more important than following the norms of society. They might say, "I had to help my friends. That's why I got in the fight." They might even say that's why they *shot* two members of the rival group as well as a bystander!

■ **In Sum** These five techniques of neutralization have implications far beyond these boys, for it is not only delinquents who try to neutralize the norms of mainstream society. Look again at these five techniques: (1) "I couldn't help myself" (2) "Who really got hurt?" (3) "Don't you think she deserved that, after what *she* did?" (4) "Who are *you* to talk?" and (5) "I had to help my friends—wouldn't you have done the same thing?" Don't such statements have a familiar ring? All of us attempt to neutralize the moral demands of society, for such neutralizations help us sleep at night.

Three Stages in Self-Labeling: The Example of Prostitutes Sociologist Nanette Davis (1978), who interviewed young women to find out how they had become prostitutes, noted that they had moved gradually from sexual promiscuity to prostitution. Their first acts of selling sex were casual. One girl even "turned a few tricks" so she could have a few dollars to purchase a prom dress. At this point, the girls were in a stage of deviance that sociologist Edwin Lemert (1972) calls **primary deviance**—fleeting acts that do not become part of the self-concept. The young women did not think of themselves as prostitutes. As one girl said, "I never thought about it one way or another."

Girls who prostitute themselves for a longer time, however, must come to terms with their activities. They incorporate a deviant identity into their self-concept and come to think of themselves as prostitutes. When this occurs, they have entered **secondary deviance**.

The movement from primary to secondary deviance may be gradual. Through *self-labeling*, bit by bit the deviance becomes part of the self-concept. Often the reactions of others facilitate this transition. For example, if a young woman is arrested for prostitution, it is difficult for her to define her activities as "normal," as she might in primary deviance. A face-to-face confrontation with the law and being publicly labeled a sexual deviant challenges her self-definitions. (Self-jarring labels can also be informal, as indicated by such terms as "nut," "pervert," and "whore.") Such powerful labels tend to lock people out of conforming groups and push them into contact with other deviants.

There is yet another stage, one that few deviants reach. In **tertiary deviance**, deviant behavior is normalized by *relabeling* it as nondeviant (Kitsuse 1980; de Young 1989). Most people in this stage simply reject the judgment that the behavior is wrong, but some go so far as to relabel it a virtue. Although none of the women in Davis' sample had reached this stage, other prostitutes have. They have formed an organization called Coyote (Call Off Your Old Tired Ethics). This group takes the position that prostitutes perform a service to society. Therefore, prostitution is a reasonable occupational choice and legislation should allow prostitutes to operate without interference from the government.

primary deviance Edwin Lemert's term for acts of deviance that have little effect on the self-concept

secondary deviance Edwin Lemert's term for acts of deviance incorporated into the self-concept, around which an individual orients his or her behavior

tertiary deviance "normalizing" behavior considered deviant by mainstream society; relabeling behavior as nondeviant

Embracing Labels: The Example of Outlaw Bikers Although most of us resist attempts to label us as deviant, there are those who revel in a deviant identity. Some teenagers, for example, make certain by their clothing, choice of music, and hairstyles that no one misses their purposeful rejection of adult norms. Their status among fellow members of a subculture, within which they are almost obsessive conformists, is vastly more important than any status outside it.

One of the best examples of a group that embraces deviance is motorcycle gangs. Sociologist Mark Watson (1988) did participant observation with outlaw bikers. He rebuilt Harleys with them, hung around their bars and homes, and went on "runs" (trips) with them. He concluded that outlaw bikers see the world as "hostile, weak, and effeminate." They pride themselves on looking "dirty, mean, and generally undesirable" and take great pleasure in provoking shocked reactions to their appearance. Holding the conventional world in contempt, they also pride themselves on getting into trouble, laughing at death, and treating women as lesser beings whose primary value is to provide them with services—especially sex. Outlaw bikers also look at themselves as losers, a factor that becomes woven into their unusual embrace of deviance.

The Power of Labels: The Saints and the Roughnecks We can see how powerful labeling is by referring back to the study of the "Saints" and the "Roughnecks" cited in Chapter 4 on pages 121–122. As you recall, both groups of high school boys were "constantly occupied with truancy, drinking, wild parties, petty theft, and vandalism." Yet their teachers looked on the Saints as "headed for success" and the Roughnecks as "headed for trouble." By the time they finished high school, not one Saint had been arrested, while the Roughnecks had been in constant trouble with the police.

Why did the community see these boys so differently? Chambliss (1973/1999) concluded that this split vision was due to *social class*. As symbolic interactionists emphasize, social class vitally affects our perceptions and behavior. The Saints came from respectable, middle-class families; the Roughnecks came from less respectable, working-class families. These backgrounds led teachers and the authorities to expect good behavior from the

We perceive—and are perceived—not directly, but, rather, through intermediary concepts. This abstract principle of symbolic interactionists, which may seem obtuse, is really a down-to-earth principle of everyday life. In short, we tend to see people in terms of the labels we place on them. In these photos, what different sets of labels are we likely to apply? What consequence are these labels likely to have on how we "see" the people in these photos?

Saints but trouble from the Roughnecks. And like the rest of us, teachers and police saw what they expected to see.

The boys' social class also affected their visibility. The Saints had automobiles, and they did their drinking and vandalizing out of town. Without a car, the Roughnecks could not even make it to the edge of town. They hung around their own street corners, where their boisterous behavior drew the attention of police and confirmed the ideas that the community already had of them.

The boys' social class also equipped them with distinct *styles of interaction.* When police or teachers questioned the Saints, they were apologetic. Their show of respect for authority elicited a positive reaction from teachers and police, allowing them to escape school and legal problems. The Roughnecks, in contrast, were "almost the polar opposite." When questioned, they were hostile. Even when they tried to assume a respectful attitude, everyone could see through it. Consequently, while teachers and police let the Saints off with warnings, they came down hard on the Roughnecks.

Although what happens in life is not determined by labels alone, the Saints and Roughnecks did live up to the labels that the community gave them. As you recall, all but one of the Saints went on to college. One earned a doctorate, one became a lawyer, one a doctor, and the others business managers. In contrast, only two of the Roughnecks went to college. They earned athletic scholarships and became coaches. The other Roughnecks did not fare so well. Two of them dropped out of high school, later became involved in separate killings, and received long prison sentences. One became a local bookie, and no one knows the whereabouts of the other.

How do labels work? Although the matter is complex, because it involves the self-concept and reactions that vary from one individual to another, we can note that labels open and close the doors of opportunity. Unlike in sociology, the label "deviant" is judgmental in everyday usage. This label is so powerful that it can lock people out of conforming groups and push them into almost exclusive contact with people who have been similarly labeled.

■ **In Sum** Symbolic interactionists examine how people's definitions of the situation underlie their deviation from or conformance to social norms. They focus on group membership (differential association), how people balance pressures to conform and to deviate (control theory), and the significance of the labels that are given to people (labeling theory).

As is apparent from this discussion, the label deviant involves competing definitions and reactions to the same behavior. This central point of symbolic interactionism is explored in the Mass Media box on the facing page.

THE FUNCTIONALIST PERSPECTIVE

When we think of deviance, its dysfunctions are likely to come to mind. Functionalists, in contrast, are as likely to stress the functions of deviance as much as its dysfunctions.

How Deviance Is Functional for Society

Most of us are upset by deviance, especially crime, and assume that society would be better off without it. The classic functionalist theorist Emile Durkheim (1893/1933, 1893/1964), however, came to a surprising conclusion. Deviance, he said, including crime, is functional for society. Its three main functions are

1. *Deviance clarifies moral boundaries and affirms norms.* A group's ideas about how people should act and think mark its *moral boundaries.* Deviance challenges those boundaries. To call a deviant member into account, saying in effect, "You broke an important rule, and we cannot tolerate that," affirms the group's norms and clarifies the distinctions between conforming and deviating behavior. To punish deviants is to assert what it means to be a member of the group.

Mass Media in Social Life

PORNOGRAPHY ON THE INTERNET: FREEDOM VERSUS CENSORSHIP

Pornography vividly illustrates one of the sociological principles discussed in this chapter—the relativity of deviance. It is not the act, but the reaction to the act, that makes something deviant. Consider one of today's major issues, pornography on the Internet.

Web surfers have a wide choice of pornography. Some sites are even indexed: heterosexual or gay, single or group activity, teenagers, cheerleaders, and older women who "still think they have it." Some offer only photographs, others video. Live sites are also available, such as one that bills itself as "direct from Amsterdam." Sign on, and you can command your "model" to do anything your heart desires. Both male and female "models" are available, and the per minute charges are hefty.

What is the problem? Why can't people exchange nude photos electronically if they want to? Or watch others having sex online, if someone offers that service? Although some object to any kind of sex site, what disturbs many are the sites that feature bondage, torture, rape, and bestiality (humans having sex with animals). Judging from the number of these sites, many people derive sexual excitement from viewing such activities.

The Internet abounds with "news groups" (people who "meet" online to discuss some topic). No one is bothered by the news groups (or "chat rooms") that center on Roman architecture or rap music or turtle racing. But news groups that focus on

Pornography (literally, the "writings of harlots") goes far back in history. The ancient Greeks and Romans had pornographers, those who wrote stories and drew pictures for the purpose of sexually exciting others. Pornography keeps up with technological change, as witnessed by the proliferation of pornography on the Internet.

how to torture women are another matter. So are those that offer lessons on how to seduce grade school children—or that extol the delights of having sex with preschool children.

In response to demands to ban such sites, the state and federal governments have passed laws against child pornography on the Internet. The FBI seizes computers and searches them for illegal pictures. Fines and imprisonment are the punishment. It remains legal to exchange pictures of tortured and sexually abused women, however. Sites that feature these activities, as well as those that discuss having sex with children, also remain legal. ■

For Your Consideration

Some feel that no matter how much they may disagree with a point of view, or find it repugnant, communications about it (including photos) must be allowed. If we prohibit them, they say, then the government will censor other activities. What do you think? For example, do you think it should be legal to exchange photos of women being sexually abused or tortured? Should it be legal to discuss ways to seduce children? If not, on what basis should they be banned? If we should make these activities illegal, then what other activities should we prohibit? On what basis?

Assume that such photos and discussion groups remain legal. If so, should school and public libraries be allowed to install filters that screen out designated Internet sites? One side insists that this would violate the First Amendment's guarantee of free speech, the other that it is only a reasonable precaution to protect children. What do you think?

Finally, can you disprove the central point of the symbolic interactionists—that an activity is deviant only because people decide that it is deviant? You may use examples cited in this box, or any others that you wish. You cannot invoke God or moral absolutes in your argument, however, as they are outside the field of sociology. As you will recall from the first chapter of this book, sociology cannot decide moral issues. This applies to even extreme cases.

2. *Deviance promotes social unity.* To affirm the group's moral boundaries by punishing deviants fosters a "we" feeling among the group's members. In saying, "You can't get by with that," the group collectively affirms the rightness of its own ways.

3. *Deviance promotes social change.* Groups do not always agree on what to do with people who push beyond their acceptable ways of doing things. Some group members may even approve the rule-breaking behavior. Boundary violations that gain enough support become new, acceptable behaviors. Thus, deviance may force a group to rethink and redefine its moral boundaries, helping groups, and whole societies, to change their customary ways.

Strain Theory: How Social Values Produce Deviance

Functionalists argue that crime is a *natural* part of society, not an aberration or some alien element in our midst. Indeed, they say, some mainstream values actually generate crime. To understand what they mean, consider what sociologists Richard Cloward and Lloyd Ohlin (1960) identified as the crucial problem of the industrialized world: the need to locate and train the most talented people of every generation—whether they were born into wealth or into poverty—so that they can take over the key technical jobs of modern society. When children are born, no one knows which ones will have the abilities to become dentists, nuclear physicists, or engineers. To get the most talented people to compete with one another, society tries to motivate *everyone* to strive for success. It does this by arousing discontent—making people feel dissatisfied with what they have so they will try to "better" themselves.

Most people, then, end up with strong desires to reach **cultural goals,** such as wealth or high status, or to achieve whatever other objectives society holds out for them. Not everyone, however, has equal access to society's **institutionalized means,** the legitimate ways of achieving success. Some people, for example, find their path to education and good jobs blocked. These people experience *strain* or frustration, which may motivate them to take a deviant path.

This perspective, known as **strain theory,** was developed by sociologist Robert Merton (1956, 1968). People who experience strain, he said, are likely to feel *anomie,* a sense of normlessness. Because mainstream norms (work, education) don't seem to be getting them anywhere, they have a difficult time identifying with these norms. They may even feel wronged by the system, and its rules may seem illegitimate (Anderson 1978).

Merton's classic outline of how people react to cultural goals and institutionalized means is depicted in Table 8.1 below. The first reaction, which Merton said is the most common, is *conformity,* using socially acceptable means to strive to reach cultural goals. In industrialized societies most people try to get good jobs, a good education, and so on. If well-paid jobs are unavailable, they take less desirable jobs. If they are denied access to Harvard or Stanford, they go to a state university. Others take night classes and attend vocational schools. In short, most people take the socially acceptable road.

Four Deviant Paths The remaining four responses, which are deviant, represent reactions to anomie. Let's look at each. *Innovators* are people who accept the goals of society but use illegitimate means to try to reach them. Drug dealers, for instance, accept the goal of achieving wealth but reject the legitimate avenues for doing so. Other examples are embezzlers, robbers, and con artists.

The second deviant path is taken by people who become discouraged and give up on achieving cultural goals. Yet they still cling to conventional rules of conduct. Merton called this response *ritualism.* Although ritualists have given up on excelling and advancing in position, they survive by closely following the rules of their job. If they show up on time and go

---

cultural goals the legitimate objectives held out to the members of a society

institutionalized means approved ways of reaching cultural goals

strain theory Robert Merton's term for the strain engendered when a society socializes large numbers of people to desire a cultural goal (such as success) but withholds from many the approved means to reach that goal; one adaptation to the strain is crime, the choice of an innovative means (one outside the approved system) to attain the cultural goal

---

Table 8.1

HOW PEOPLE MATCH THEIR GOALS TO THEIR MEANS

Do They Feel the Strain That Leads to Anomie?	Mode of Adaptation	Cultural Goals	Institutionalized Means
No	Conformists	Accept	Accept
Yes	Innovators	Accept	Reject
	Ritualists	Reject	Accept
	Retreatists	Reject	Reject
	Rebels	Reject/Accept	Reject/Accept

through the motions, they can't be fired. Teachers whose idealism is shattered (who are said to suffer from "burnout"), for example, continue in the classroom, where they teach without enthusiasm. Their response is considered deviant because they cling to the job although they have abandoned the goal, such as stimulating young minds or making the world a better place.

People who choose the third deviant path, *retreatism,* reject both cultural goals and the institutionalized means of achieving them. Those who drop out of the pursuit of success by way of alcohol or drugs are retreatists. Unlike ritualists, they do not even try to appear as though they share the goals of their society.

The final type of deviant response is *rebellion.* Convinced that their society is corrupt, rebels, like retreatists, reject both society's goals and its institutionalized means. Unlike retreatists, however, they seek to replace existing goals with new ones. Revolutionaries are the most committed type of rebels.

Strain theory underscores the main sociological point about deviance, namely, that deviants are the product of society. Due to their social location, some people experience greater pressure to deviate from society's norms, others much less. Simply put, if a society emphasizes the goal of material success, groups deprived of access to this goal will be more involved in property crime. This is a good part of the reason that people join the gangs discussed in the Down-to-Earth Sociology box on the next page.

Illegitimate Opportunity Theory: Explaining Social Class and Crime

One of the more interesting sociological findings in the study of deviance is that the social classes have distinct styles of crime. Let's see how unequal access to the institutionalized means to success helps explain this.

Street Crime Functionalists point out that industrialized societies have no trouble socializing the poor into wanting to own things. Like others, they are bombarded with messages urging them to buy everything from designer jeans to DVD players and new cars. By their vivid images of the middle class enjoying luxurious lives, television and movies reinforce the myth that all full-fledged Americans can afford society's many goods and services. This bombardment of messages also instills the idea that they have a *right* to these items.

The school system, however, the most common route to success, fails the poor. It is run by the middle class, and there the children of the poor confront a bewildering world, one at odds with their background. Their grammar and nonstandard language may be liberally sprinkled with what the middle class considers obscene words and phrases. Their ideas of punctuality and neatness, as well as their lack of preparation in paper-and-pencil skills, are a mismatch with their new environment. Facing such barriers, the poor are more likely to drop out of school than their more privileged counterparts. Educational failure, in turn, closes the door on many legitimate avenues to financial success.

Often, however, a different door opens to the poor, one that sociologists Richard Cloward and Lloyd Ohlin (1960) called **illegitimate opportunity structures.** Woven into the texture of life in urban slums, for example, are robbery, burglary, drug dealing, prostitution, pimping, gambling, and other remunerative crimes, commonly called "hustles" (Liebow 1967/1997; Bourgois 1994; Anderson 1978, 1990, 1999). For many of the poor, the "hustler" is a role model—glamorous, in control, the image of "easy money," one of the few people in the area who comes close to the cultural goal of success. For such reasons, then, these activities attract disproportionate numbers of the poor.

White-Collar Crime The more privileged social classes are not crime-free, of course, but for them different illegitimate opportunities beckon. They find *other forms* of crime to be functional. Rather than mugging, pimping, and burglary, the more privileged encounter "opportunities" for evading income tax, bribing public officials, embezzling from employers, participating in fraud, and so on. Physicians, for example, never hold up cabbies, but many do cheat Medicare. Sociologist Edwin Sutherland (1949) coined the term **white-collar crime**

[handwritten margin note: Schools fail the poor]

illegitimate opportunity structures opportunities for crimes that are woven into the texture of life

white-collar crime Edwin Sutherland's term for crimes committed by people of respectable and high social status in the course of their occupations; for example, bribery of public officials, securities violations, embezzlement, false advertising, and price fixing

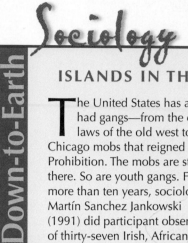

ISLANDS IN THE STREET: URBAN GANGS IN THE UNITED STATES

The United States has always had gangs—from the outlaws of the old west to the Chicago mobs that reigned during Prohibition. The mobs are still there. So are youth gangs. For more than ten years, sociologist Martín Sanchez Jankowski (1991) did participant observation of thirty-seven Irish, African-American, Puerto Rican, Chicano, Dominican, Jamaican, and Central American gangs in Boston, Los Angeles, and New York City. Jankowski ate, slept, and sometimes fought with the gangs. By mutual agreement, he did not participate in drugs or other illegal activities. He was seriously injured twice during the study.

Jankowski identified five main traits of gang members: competitiveness, mistrust, self-reliance, social isolation, and a drive for survival. Central to the lives of gang members, almost all of whom come from low-income neighborhoods, is the struggle to survive in a hostile world filled with predators.

Contrary to stereotypes, Jankowski did not find that the motive for joining was to escape from a broken home (there were as many members from intact homes) or to seek a substitute family (as many members said they were close to their families as said they were not). Rather, the boys joined to gain access to money, to find recreation (including girls and drugs), to obtain anonymity in committing crimes, to get protection, and to help the community. This last reason may sound surprising, but in some neighborhoods gangs help to protect residents from outsiders. The boys also saw the gang as an alternative to the dead-end—and deadening—jobs held by their parents.

The gangs earn money through gambling, arson, mugging, armed robbery, wholesaling drugs to pushers, and selling moonshine, guns, stolen car parts, and protection. Some gangs are involved in legal economic activities such as running "mom and pop" stores and renovating and renting abandoned apartment buildings—but this is unusual.

Jankowski witnessed much gang violence. When the members of a gang fight over drugs or women—or to test one another's *machismo*—gang rules and other members usually keep violence under control. Fights with rival gangs, in contrast, often escalate into serious violence. Similarly, the gangs don't attack residents of their own community unless someone insults them or threatens to turn them in to the police. Gang members will attack people outside the community, however—sometimes to test their strength, or even because they don't like the way someone looks.

Neighborhood residents are ambivalent about gangs. On the one hand, they don't like the violence. On the other hand, they may complain that the police use unnecessary force against gangs. Several reasons underlie the ambivalence: Many adults once belonged to gangs, gang members are the children of neighbors, and the gangs often provide better protection than do the police.

Particular gangs will come and go, but gangs will likely always be part of the city. As functionalists point out, gangs fulfill needs for poor youth who live on the margins of society. ■

For Your Consideration

What are the functions that gangs fulfill (the needs they meet)? If you were an urban planner, how might you make arrangements to meet those needs in ways that encourage adherence to cultural norms and minimize violence?

to refer to crimes that people of respectable and high social status commit in the course of their occupations.

Although the general public seems to think that the lower classes are more prone to crime, numerous studies show that white-collar workers also commit many crimes (Weisburd et al. 1991; Zey 1993). This difference in perception is largely based on visibility. While crimes committed by the poor are given much publicity, the crimes of the more privileged classes seldom make the evening news and go largely unnoticed. Yet, the dollar cost of "crime in the suites," which runs between $200 billion and $400 billion a year (Wells 1998), is much higher than "crime in the streets." This refers only to dollar costs. No one has yet figured out a way to compare, for example, the suffering experienced by a rape victim with the pain felt by an elderly couple who lose their life savings to white-collar fraud.

In terms of dollars, perhaps the most costly crime in U.S. history has been the plundering of the savings and loan industry. Corporate officers systematically looted these banks of billions of dollars. The total cost ran somewhere around $500 billion—a staggering $2,000 for every man, woman, and child in the entire country (Kettl 1991; Newdorf 1991). Of the thousands involved, the most infamous culprit is Neil Bush, son of George Bush, the former president of the United States. As an officer of Silverado, a Colorado savings and loan, Bush approved loans totaling $100 million to a company in which he secretly held interests, an act that helped to bankrupt his firm (Tolchin 1991).

Future generations will continue to suffer from the wholesale looting of this industry. The interest alone will be exorbitant (at 5 percent, a year's interest on an increase of $500 billion in the national debt would be $25 billion, at 10 percent $50 billion). Because the government does not pay its debt, but merely borrows more to pay the compounding interest, this extra $500 billion will double in just a few years. As the late Senator Everett Dirkson once said, "A billion here and a billion there, and pretty soon you're talking about real money."

Although white-collar crime is not as dramatic as street killings, abduction, or rape—and therefore is usually considered less newsworthy—it, too, can involve physical harm, sometimes even death. Unsafe working conditions, for example—many the result of executive decisions to put profits ahead of workers' safety—kill about 100,000 Americans each year. This is about *five* times the number of people killed by street criminals (Simon and Eitzen 1993). Nevertheless, the greatest concern of Americans is street crime, for they are fearful of an encounter with violence that could change their life forever. As the Social Map below shows, the chances of such an encounter actually happening depend on where you live.

Sociologists compute the costs of white-collar crime in dollar terms, but their analyses generally make it sound as though white-collar crime were a harmless nuisance. Perhaps most is. But some white-collar crime has horrible costs. Shown here is Alisha Parker, who, with three siblings was burned when the gas tank of her 1979 Chevrolet Malibu exploded after a rear-end collision. Outraged at the callousness of GM's conduct, the jury awarded these victims the staggering sum of $4.9 billion.

Gender and Crime As Table 8.2 shows, a major change in crime is the growing number of female offenders. As you can see, women are committing a larger proportion of almost all crimes—from drugs to burglary. The exceptions are murder and gambling. As more women have joined the professions and corporate world, they, too, have been enticed by its illegitimate opportunities, and their involvement in embezzlement, fraud, and forgery has increased.

Safer than average (87–336)
Average safety (345–590)
More dangerous than average (603–1024)

Figure 8.1

SOCIAL MAP: SOME STATES ARE SAFER: VIOLENT CRIME IN THE UNITED STATES

Violent crimes are murder, rape, robbery, and aggravated assault. The variation of violence among the states is incredible. Some states have a rate that is ten times higher than that of other states. With a rate of 87 per 100,000 people, North Dakota has the lowest rate of violence, while Florida, at 1,024, has the highest rate. The U.S. average rate is 424 (the total of the states' average rates of violence divided by 50). This total does not include Washington, D.C., whose rate is 2,024, 23 times as high as North Dakota and almost five times the national average.

Source: *Statistical Abstract* 1999:Table 344.

Table 8.2

MORE WOMEN ARE COMMITTING CRIME

Of those arrested, what percentage are women?

Crime	1987	1997	Change
Aggravated Assault	13.3	19.0	+49%
Burglary	7.9	11.8	+49%
Car Theft	9.7	14.5	+49%
Vandalism	10.6	14.7	+39%
Drunk in Public	9.2	12.4	+35%
Stolen Property (buying, possessing)	11.6	15.4	+33%
Drunken Driving	11.7	15.4	+32%
Robbery	8.1	9.8	+21%
Drugs	14.9	17.1	+15%
Weapons (carrying, concealing)	7.6	8.5	+12%
Larceny-Theft	31.1	34.4	+11%
Embezzlement	38.1	41.7	+9%
Arson	13.7	14.7	+7%
Forgery and Counterfeiting	34.4	36.6	+6%
Gambling	13.5	12.6	–7%
Murder	12.5	10.0	–20%

Sources: Statistical Abstract 1989:Table 293; 1999:Table 358.

■ **In Sum** Functionalists conclude that much street crime is the consequence of socializing everyone into equating success with material possessions, while denying the lower social classes the means to attain that success. People from higher social classes encounter different opportunity structures to commit crimes.

THE CONFLICT PERSPECTIVE

Class, Crime, and the Criminal Justice System

> The federal government accused two multinational corporations, Grumman and SmithKline, of fraud that cost the taxpayers millions of dollars. No executives went to jail. Instead, the corporations paid fines—and then were awarded more contracts by the federal government (Pasztor 1993; Tanouye 1997).

Contrast this event with stories you often read in newspapers about young men who steal automobiles and are sentenced to several years in prison. How can a legal system that is supposed to provide "justice for all" be so inconsistent? According to conflict theorists, this question is central to the analysis of crime and the **criminal justice system**—the police, courts, and prisons that deal with people who are accused of having committed crimes.

Power and Inequality

Conflict theorists look at power and social inequality as the primary characteristics of society. The most fundamental division in industrial society is that between the few who own the means of production and the many who do not, those who sell their labor and the privileged few who buy it. Those who buy labor and thereby control workers make up the **capitalist class;** those who sell their labor form the **working class.** Toward the most depressed

criminal justice system the system of police, courts, and prisons set up to deal with people who are accused of having committed a crime

capitalist class the wealthy who own the means of production and buy the labor of the working class

working class those who sell their labor to the capitalist class

end of the working class is the **marginal working class,** people with few skills, who are subject to unexpected layoffs, and whose jobs are low paying, part time, or seasonal. This class is marked by unemployment and poverty, and from its ranks come most of the prisoners in the United States. Desperate, these people commit street crimes, and because their crimes threaten the social order, they are severely punished.

The Law as an Instrument of Oppression

According to conflict theorists, the idea that the law is a social institution that operates impartially and administers a code that is shared by all is a cultural myth promoted by the capitalist class. These theorists see the law as an instrument of oppression, a tool designed to maintain the powerful in their privileged position (Spitzer 1975; Ritzer 1992; MacDonald 1995). Because the working class has the potential to rebel and overthrow the current social order, when its members get out of line, they are arrested, tried, and imprisoned.

This 1871 wood engraving depicts children as they are being paid for their day's work in a London brickyard. In early capitalism, most street criminals came from the marginal working class, as did these children. It is the same today.

For this reason, the criminal justice system does not focus on the owners of corporations and the harm they do to the masses through unsafe products, wanton pollution, and price manipulations. Instead, it directs its energies against violations committed by the working class (Gordon 1971; Platt 1978; Coleman 1989). The violations of the capitalist class cannot be totally ignored, however, for if they became too outrageous or oppressive, the working class might rise up in revolution. To prevent this, occasionally a flagrant violation by a member of the capitalist class is prosecuted. The publicity given to the case helps to stabilize the social system by providing visible evidence of the "fairness" of the criminal justice system.

Usually, however, the powerful are able to bypass the courts altogether, appearing instead before some agency that has no power to imprison (such as the Federal Trade Commission). These agencies are directed by people from wealthy backgrounds who sympathize with the problems of the members of their social class and understand the intricacies of the corporate world. This means that most cases of illegal sales of stocks and bonds, price fixing, trade restraint, collusion, and so on are handled by "gentlemen overseeing gentlemen." Is it surprising, then, that the typical sanction is a token fine? In contrast, the property crimes of the masses are handled by courts that do have the power to imprison. Burglary, armed robbery, and theft committed by the poor threaten not only the sanctity of private property but, ultimately, the positions of the powerful.

When groups that have been denied access to power gain that access, we can expect to see changes in the legal system. This is precisely what is occurring now. Racial-ethnic minorities and homosexuals, for example, have more political power today than ever before. In line with conflict theory, a new category of crime has been formulated. We analyze this change in the Thinking Critically box on page 221.

■ **In Sum** From the perspective of conflict theory, the small penalties imposed for crimes committed by the powerful are typical of a legal system that has been designed by the elite (capitalists) to control workers, and, ultimately, to stabilize the social order. From this perspective, law enforcement is a cultural device through which the capitalist class carries out self-protective and repressive policies.

marginal working class the most desperate members of the working class, who have few skills, little job security, and are often unemployed

THE NEED FOR MULTIPLE THEORIES

Few of us deviate seriously from cultural norms. Many of us may drink too much, lie, or cheat a little, but few of us rob or kill—even if robbing and killing are common in our neighborhood. If our access to good-paying jobs is blocked, we still are unlikely to commit these crimes. Why do so few of us do these things even though we have the opportunity and motive to do so?

Each of the theories we've examined has merit. Each focuses on some aspect of social life that helps to explain deviance. A key that unlocks the other theories is control theory. When we add control theory to the others, we have a better understanding of why people deviate—or conform. Differential association and illegitimate opportunity theories, for example, stress the circumstances that influence us. But circumstances are never enough. A lot of people face similar circumstances, but only some murder and rape, for example. Control theory indicates that people with stronger internal controls are better able to resist the allure of deviance.

Apparently, then, deviance is due to a *combination* of opportunities, motivations, and self-control (Smith and Brame 1994). Little, however, is known about this combination. When opportunity is strong (for example, drug dealing in the inner city), how much inner control does it take to avoid becoming a drug dealer? How much motivation *not* to participate? Reliable measurements of opportunity, motivation, and inner controls are yet to be made.

REACTIONS TO DEVIANCE

Whether it involves cheating on a sociology quiz or holding up a liquor store, any violation of norms invites reaction. Let's look first at the reactions of others, and then at how people react to their own deviance.

Sanctions

As discussed in Chapter 2, people do not strictly enforce folkways, but they become very upset when mores are broken. Disapproval of deviance, called **negative sanctions,** ranges from frowns and gossip for breaking folkways to imprisonment and capital punishment for breaking mores. **Positive sanctions,** in contrast—ranging from smiles to formal awards—are used to reward people for conforming to norms. Getting a raise is a positive sanction, being fired a negative sanction. Getting an *A* in basic sociology is a positive sanction, getting an *F* a negative one.

Most negative sanctions are informal. You probably will merely stare when someone dresses in what you consider to be inappropriate clothing, or just gossip if a married person spends the night with someone other than his or her spouse. Whether you consider the breaking of a norm simply an amusing matter that warrants no severe sanctions or a serious infraction that does, however, depends on your perspective. If a woman appears at your college graduation ceremonies in a swimsuit, you may stare and laugh, but if it is *your* mother you are likely to feel that different sanctions are appropriate. Similarly, if it is *your* father who spends the night with an 18-year-old college freshman, you are likely to do more than gossip.

Degradation Ceremonies

When someone seriously disregards a group's standards, the reaction is likely to be harsh. In some instances, the group may find some special way to mark the individual as a deviant and hold him or her up for all the world to see. In Nathaniel Hawthorne's *The Scarlet Letter,* for example, officials forced Hester Prynne to wear a dress that had a scarlet *A* sewn on it. The A stood for adulteress. Furthermore, the community expected her to wear this badge of shame every day for the rest of her life.

Sociologist Harold Garfinkel (1956) called such formal attempts to mark an individual with the status of an outsider **degradation ceremonies.** The individual is called to account

negative sanction a punishment or negative reaction for disapproved behavior, for deviance

positive sanction a reward or positive reaction for approved behavior, for conformity

degradation ceremonies rituals designed to strip an individual of his or her identity as a group member; for example, a court martial or the defrocking of a priest

Degradation ceremonies are intended to humiliate norm violators and mark them as "not members" of the group. This photo was taken by the U.S. army in 1945 after U.S. troops liberated Cherbourg, France. Members of the French resistance shaved the heads of these women, who had "collaborated" (had sexual contact with) the occupying Nazis. They then marched the shamed women down the streets of the city, while the public shouted insults and spat on them.

before the group; witnesses denounce him or her; the offender is pronounced guilty; and, most important in sociological terms, steps are taken to *strip the individual of his or her identity as a group member.* Following a court martial, for example, officers found guilty stand at attention before their peers while the insignia of rank are ripped from their uniforms. A priest may be defrocked before a congregation, a citizen forced to wear a prison uniform. These procedures indicate that the individual is no longer a member of the group— no longer able to command soldiers, to preach or offer sacraments, or to vote or move about freely. Although Hester Prynne was not banished from the group physically, her degradation ceremony proclaimed her a *moral* outcast from the community, the scarlet A marking her as "not one" of them.

Imprisonment

Today, we don't make people wear scarlet letters, but we do remove them from society and make them wear prison uniforms. And we still use degradation ceremonies, in this case, a public trial and the public pronouncement that the person is "unfit to live among decent, law-abiding people" for some specified period of time. Figure 8.2 illustrates the phenomenal growth in the U.S. prison population, and Table 8.3 summarizes major characteristics of those prisoners.

For the past dozen years or so, the United States has followed a "get tough" policy. "Three strikes and you're out" laws (life imprisonment upon conviction for a third felony) have become common. While few of us would feel sympathetic if a man who was convicted of a third rape (or a

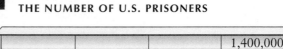

HOW MUCH IS ENOUGH? THE EXPLOSION IN THE NUMBER OF U.S. PRISONERS

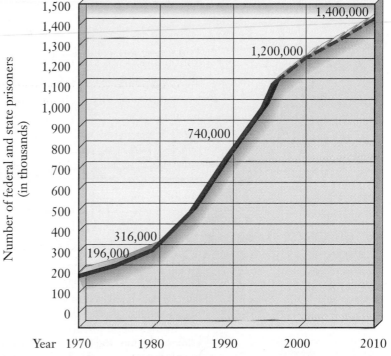

To better understand the significance of this growth, compare it with the change in the U.S. population. Between 1970 and 1997, the U.S. population grew 31 percent, while the prison population grew 635 percent, *20 times as fast.* If the prison population had increased at the same rate as the U.S. population, there would now be about 257,000 prisoners, between one-fourth and one-fifth of the actual number.
The dotted line indicates the author's projection.

Source: Statistical Abstract 1995:Table 349; 1999:Table 382.

Table 8.3

INMATES IN U.S. STATE PRISONS

Characteristics	Prisoners Percentage with These Characteristics	U.S. Population Percentage with These Characteristics
Age		
Under 18	0.6%	25.9%
18–24	21.3	10.2
25–34	45.7	16.6
35–44	22.7	15.7
45–54	6.5	10.7
55–64	2.4	8.2
65 and over	0.7	12.7
Race		
White[a]	47.8	83.4
African American	49.4	12.4
Other races	2.8	4.2
Sex		
Male	93.8	48.8
Female	6.2	51.2

[a]The category "white" includes Latinos.

Sources: Sourcebook of Criminal Justice Statistics 1998:Table 6.40; *Statistical Abstract* 1997:Tables 14, 18, 22, 356; 1999:Table 382.

third murder) was sent to prison for life, these laws have had severe unanticipated consequences. Let's look at those consequences in the Thinking Critically section.

Thinking *Critically*

"THREE STRIKES AND YOU'RE OUT!"
UNINTENDED CONSEQUENCES
OF WELL-INTENDED LAWS

In the 1980s, violent crime soared. Americans were fearful, and they demanded that their lawmakers do something. Politicians heard the message and responded by passing the "three strikes" law. Anyone convicted of a third felony receives an automatic mandatory sentence. Judges are not allowed to consider the circumstances. Some mandatory sentences carry life imprisonment.

In their haste to appease the public, the politicians did not limit these laws to *violent* crimes. And they did not consider that some minor crimes are considered felonies. As the functionalists would say, this has led to some unanticipated consequences.

Here are some actual cases (Cloud 1999).

- In Iowa, a man was sentenced to 10 years for stealing $30 worth of steaks from a grocery store.

- In California, a 21-year-old anthropology major was sentenced to 10 years for mailing sheets of LSD to her boyfriend.

- In Los Angeles, a 27-year-old man was sentenced to 25 years for stealing pizza.

- In Alabama, a husband, father, Vietnam veteran, and owner of a roofing business bought a pound of marijuana. Thirteen years earlier, he had been arrested for several petty crimes—crimes that didn't even carry a prison sentence. He was sentenced to life in prison without parole.

- In Atlanta, a man opened a garden store, where he sold hydroponic equipment for growing plants. His wife, who worked as a customer service agent for an insurance company, did occasional bookwork for the garden store. Some customers who purchased merchandise at the store used it to grow marijuana. When they were arrested, they were given reduced sentences for testifying that this husband and wife had given them advice on how to grow marijuana. The owner of the store and his wife were sentenced to 10 years in prison.

- In New York City, a man who was about to be sentenced for selling crack said to the judge, "I'm only 19. This is terrible." He then hurled himself out of a courtroom window, plunging to his death sixteen stories below. ■

For Your Consideration

Apply the symbolic interactionist, functionalist, and conflict perspectives to mandatory sentencing. For *symbolic interactionism,* what do these laws represent to the public? How does your answer differ depending on what part of "the public" you are referring to? For *functionalism,* who benefits from these laws? What are some of their dysfunctions? For the *conflict perspective,* what groups are in conflict? Who has the power to enforce their will on others?

One of the many problems with imprisonment is that prisons fail to teach their clients to stay away from crime. The **recidivism rate** (the percentage of people who are rearrested) runs as high as 85 to 90 percent (Blumstein and Cohen 1987). Three years after being given probation—released into the community under the court's supervision—62 to 64 percent have been arrested for a felony or had a disciplinary hearing for violating their parole (Langan and Cunniff 1992; Alter 1997).

Perhaps an underlying reason for this high recidivism rate is that Americans do not agree on *why* people should be put in prison. There appears to be widespread agreement that offenders should be imprisoned, but less agreement about the reasons for doing so. Let's examine the four primary reasons for imprisoning people.

Retribution The purpose of **retribution** is to right a wrong by making offenders suffer, or to pay back what they have stolen. The offense is thought to have upset a moral balance; the punishment is an attempt to restore that balance. Attempts to make the punishment "fit the crime," such as sentencing someone who has stolen from a widow to work a dozen weekends in a nursing home, are rooted in the idea of retribution.

Deterrence The purpose of **deterrence** is to create fear so that others won't break the law. The belief underlying deterrence is that if people know that they will be punished, they will refrain from committing the crime. Sociologist Ernest van den Haag (1975, 1983), a chief proponent of deterrence, believes, like many Americans, that the criminal justice system is too soft. He thinks juveniles who commit adult crimes should be tried as adults, and he advocates abolishing parole boards and forcing prisoners to work.

Does deterrence work? Evidence is mixed, but those who claim that it does not like to recall an example from the nineteenth century. When English law meted out the death penalty for pickpockets, other pickpockets looked forward to the hangings—for people whose attention was riveted on the gallows made easy victims (Hibbert 1963). At this point, no firm evidence resolves the issue.

Rehabilitation The purpose of **rehabilitation** is not to punish offenders, but to resocialize them so they can become conforming citizens. One example of rehabilitation is teaching

recidivism rate the proportion of people who are rearrested

retribution the punishment of offenders in order to restore the moral balance upset by the offense

deterrence creating fear so people will refrain from breaking the law

rehabilitation the resocialization of offenders so that they can become conforming citizens

Charles Manson, shown here, has been confined in a California maximum security prison
since ordering several murders, including one
in which the fetus was ripped out of a pregnant woman, Sharon Tate. Manson is an
example of why many people, despairing of
rehabilitation, call for retribution, deterrence,
and incapacitation. Manson is up for parole.

prisoners skills so they can support themselves after their release. Other examples include college courses in prison, encounter groups for prisoners, and *halfway
houses*—community support facilities where ex-prisoners supervise many aspects
of their own lives, such as household tasks, and still report to authorities.

Incapacitation Removing offenders from circulation is called **incapacitation.** "Nothing works," some say, "but we can at least keep them off the streets."
Criminologist James Wilson (1975, 1992; Kelling and Coles 1998) supports incapacitation, calling it the only policy that works. He proposes what he calls *added
incapacitation,* increasing an offender's sentence each time he or she is convicted
of a crime.

In the United States, the public is fearful of crime and despairing of solutions.
Increasing dependence on prisons may indicate that Americans are throwing up
their hands as far as criminals are concerned and are just trying to "keep them off
the streets." Our high rate of imprisonment may also be an attempt to seek retribution or achieve deterrence. It certainly does not indicate an effort to provide rehabilitation, for U.S. prisons are basically just holding tanks. Few offer programs
of rehabilitation.

The Death Penalty

Capital punishment, the death penalty, is the most extreme and controversial
measure the state takes. Its purpose is a mixture of retribution, deterrence, and
incapacitation. Apart from the moral and philosophical controversy surrounding
the death penalty, people object to its biases. The death penalty is not administered evenly. Consider geography: Where one commits a murder greatly affects
one's chances of being put to death by the state. The Social Map on the facing page shows
this unevenness.

The death penalty also shows gender, social class, and racial-ethnic bias. It is almost
unheard of for a woman or a rich person to be put to death by the state. It happens, but
rarely. About 1.5 percent of prisoners on death row are women (*Sourcebook of Criminal Justice Statistics* 1998:Table 6.77). Instead of bias in favor of women, however, these totals may
reflect the relative frequency and severity of their crimes.

The bias that once put an end to the death penalty, though, was flagrant. Donald Partington (1965), a lawyer, examined all executions for rape and attempted rape in Virginia
between 1908 and 1963. Convicted of these crimes were 2,798 men (56 percent were
whites and 44 percent blacks). Forty-one men were executed for rape and 13 for attempted
rape. *All* were black. *Not one* of the whites was executed.

After listening to evidence like this, in 1972 the Supreme Court ruled in *Furman v. Georgia* that the death penalty was unconstitutionally applied. The execution of prisoners
stopped—but not for long. The states wrote new laws, and in 1977 they again began to execute prisoners. Since then, 59 percent of those put to death have been white and 40 percent African American. Of the 3,064 prisoners now on death row, 48 percent are whites, 42
percent African Americans, 8 percent Latinos, 1 percent Native Americans, and 1 percent
Asian Americans (*Statistical Sourcebook* 1998:Table 6.78).

New Legislation

Did you know that it is a crime in Iran for women to wear makeup, a crime in Illinois for
merchants to sell meat before noon on Sundays, and a crime in all states but Texas for motorists to drink beer while driving? As stressed in this chapter, deviance, including the form
called crime, is relative. It varies from one society to another, and from group to group
within large, pluralistic societies. It also varies from one time period to another, as opinions
change or as different groups gain access to power.

Let's consider legal change.

incapacitation to take away
someone's capacity to commit
crimes, in this instance, by
putting the offender in prison

capital punishment the death
penalty

hate crime crimes to which
more severe penalties are
attached because they are
motivated by hatred (dislike,
animosity) of someone's
race–ethnicity, religion,
sexual orientation, or disability

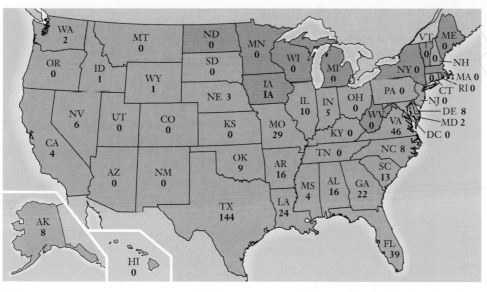

Figure 8.3

SOCIAL MAP: EXECUTIONS IN THE UNITED STATES

Executions since 1977, when the death penalty was reinstituted.

Source: Statistical Abstract 1999:Table 389.

☐ States with death penalty   ☐ States without death penalty

Thinking Critically

OUR CHANGING SOCIETY: THE SIGNIFICANCE OF HATE CRIMES

Because crime is whatever authorities decide will be called crime, new crimes emerge from time to time. A prime example is juvenile delinquency, which Illinois lawmakers designated a separate type of crime in 1899. Juveniles committed crimes prior to this time, of course, but these youths were not considered to be a separate type of lawbreaker. They were just young people who committed crimes, and they were treated the same as adults who committed the same crime. Some new crimes depend on the appearance of new technology. Motor vehicle theft, a separate crime in the United States, obviously did not exist before the automobile was invented. Nor did "theft by computer," a relatively recent crime, exist prior to the invention of computers.

In 1980s, another new crime was born when state governments developed the classification of **hate crime.** This is a crime that is motivated by bias (dislike, hatred) against someone's race-ethnicity, religion, sexual orientation, or disability. Prior to this, of course, people attacked others or destroyed their property out of these same motivations, but in those cases the motivation was not the issue. If someone injured or killed another person because of that person's race-ethnicity, religion, sexual orientation, or disability, he or she was charged with assault or murder. Today, motivation has become a central issue, and hate crimes carry more severe sentences than do crimes that involve the very same act but without hatred as the motive. Table 8.4 summarizes the victims of hate crimes.

We can be certain that the "evolution" of crime is not yet complete, that as society changes we will see more new types of crime. As different groups gain access to the seat of power, we can expect the definitions of crime to change accordingly. ■

For Your Consideration

Do you think there should be a separate classification called hate crime? How do you think your particular social location (race-ethnicity, age, gender, social class) affects your opinion?

Table 8.4

HATE CRIMES

Directed Against	Number of Victims
Race-Ethnicity	
African Americans	3,951
Whites	1,293
Latinos	649
Asian Americans	466
Native Americans	36
Religion	
Jews	1,247
Protestants	61
Catholics	32
Islamics	32
Sexual Orientation	
Male Homosexuals	927
Female Homosexuals	236
Homosexuals (general)	214
Heterosexuals	14
Disabilities	
Physical	9
Mental	3

Source: Statistical Abstract 1999: Table 351.

police discretion the practice of the police, in the normal course of their duties, to arrest someone for an offense or to overlook the matter

medicalization of deviance to make deviance a medical matter, a symptom of some underlying illness that needs to be treated by physicians

The Trouble with Official Statistics

Both the findings of symbolic interactionists (that authorities practice discretion when dealing with groups such as the Saints and the Roughnecks) and the conclusion of conflict theorists (that the criminal justice system exists to serve the ruling elite) demonstrate the need for caution in interpreting official statistics. Crime statistics are not irrefutable demonstrations of truth. They do not have an objective, independent existence, like oranges in a grocery store. Rather, they are a human creation, produced within a specific social and political context for some particular purpose.

According to official statistics, working-class boys are clearly more delinquent than middle-class boys. Yet, as we have seen, *who actually gets arrested for what* is affected by social class, a point that has far-reaching implications. As symbolic interactionists point out, the police follow a symbolic system as they enforce the law. Their ideas of "typical criminals" and "typical good citizens," for example, permeate their work. The more a suspect matches their "criminal profile," the more likely that person is to be arrested. **Police discretion**, the decision whether or not to arrest someone or even to ignore a matter, is a routine part of police work. Consequently, official crime statistics always reflect these and many other biases.

■ **In Sum** Reactions to deviants vary from such mild sanctions as frowns and stares to such severe responses as imprisonment and death. Some sanctions are formal—court hearings, for example—although most are informal, as when friends refuse to talk to each other. One sanction is to label someone a deviant, which can have powerful consequences for the person's life, especially if the label closes off conforming activities and opens deviant ones. The degradation ceremony, in which someone is publicly labeled "not one of us," is a powerful sanction. So is imprisonment. Official statistics must be viewed with caution, for they reflect social class bias.

The Medicalization of Deviance: Mental Illness

Another way in which society deals with deviance is to "medicalize" it. Let's look at what this entails.

People whose behaviors violate norms often are called mentally ill. "Why else would they do such things?" is a common response to deviant behaviors that we don't understand. Mental illness is a label that contains the assumption that there is something wrong "within" people that "causes" their disapproved behavior. Outlaw bikers reject such labels, and in an "in-your-face" approach replace them with their own labels of approval.

Neither Mental nor Illness? To *medicalize* something is to make it a medical matter, to classify it as a form of illness that properly belongs in the care of physicians. For the past hundred years or so, especially since the time of Sigmund Freud (1856–1939), the Viennese physician who founded psychoanalysis, there has been a growing tendency toward the **medicalization of deviance.** In this view, deviance, including crime, is a sign of mental sickness. Rape, murder, stealing, cheating, and so on are external symptoms of internal disorders, consequences of a confused or tortured mind.

Thomas Szasz (1986, 1996, 1998), a renegade in his profession of psychiatry, argues that *mental illnesses are neither mental nor illnesses. They are simply problem behaviors.* Some forms of so-called mental illnesses have organic causes; that is, they are *physical* illnesses that result in unusual perceptions and behavior. Some depression, for example, is caused by a chemical imbalance in the brain, which can be treated by drugs. The depression, however, may show itself as crying, long-term sadness, and lack of interest in anything, including work or school. When a person becomes deviant in ways that disturb others, and when these others cannot find a satisfying explanation for why the person is "like that," they conclude that a "sickness in the head" causes the inappropriate, unacceptable behavior.

All of us have troubles. Some of us face a constant barrage of problems as we go through life. Most of us continue the struggle, encouraged by relatives and friends, motivated by job, family responsibilities, and life goals. Even when the odds seem hopeless, we carry on, not perfectly, but as best we can.

Some people, however, fail to cope well with the challenges of daily life. Overwhelmed, they become depressed, uncooperative, or hostile. Some strike out at others, while some, in Merton's terms, become retreatists and withdraw into their apartments or homes, not wanting to come out. These are *behaviors, not mental illnesses,* stresses Szasz. They may be inappropriate coping devices, but they are coping devices, nevertheless, not mental illnesses. Thus, Szasz concludes that "mental illness" is a myth foisted on a naive public by a medical profession that uses pseudoscientific jargon in order to expand its area of control and force nonconforming people to accept society's definitions of "normal."

Szasz's extreme claim forces us to look anew at the forms of deviance we usually refer to as mental illness. To explain behavior that people find bizarre, Szasz directs our attention not to causes hidden deep within the "subconscious," but, instead, to the ways people learn such behaviors. Asking, "What is the origin of inappropriate or bizarre behavior?" then becomes similar to asking, "Why do some women steal?" "Why do some men rape?" "Why do some teenagers cuss their parents and stalk out of the room slamming doors?" *The answers depend on those people's particular experiences in life, not on an illness in their mind.* In short, some sociologists find Szasz's renegade analysis refreshing because it indicates that *social experiences,* not some illness of the mind, underlie bizarre behaviors—as well as deviance in general.

The Homeless Mentally Ill

Jamie was sitting on the low wall surrounding the landscaped courtyard of an exclusive restaurant. She appeared unaware of the stares that were elicited by her many layers of mismatched clothing, her dirty face, and the shopping cart that overflowed with her meager possessions.

Every once in a while Jamie would pause, concentrate, and point to the street, slowly moving her finger horizontally. I asked her what she was doing.

"I'm directing traffic," she replied. "I control where the cars go. Look, that one turned right there," she said, now withdrawing her finger.

"Really?" I said.

After a while she confided that her cart talked to her.

"Really?" I said again.

"Yes," she replied. "You can hear it, too." At that, she pushed the shopping cart a bit.

"Did you hear that?" she asked.

When I shook my head, she demonstrated again. Then it hit me. She was referring to the squeaking wheels!

I nodded.

When I left, Jamie was pointing to the sky, for, as she told me, she also controlled the flight of airplanes.

The homeless are located at the bottom of the U.S. social class ladder. One might even say that their status is so low that they occupy the space beneath its lowest rung. Why do you think a society as wealthy as the United States has homeless people?

To most of us, Jamie's behavior and thinking are bizarre. They simply do not match any reality we know. Could you or I become like Jamie?

Suppose for a bitter moment that you are homeless and have to live on the streets. You have no money, no place to sleep, no bathroom, do not know *if* you are going to eat, much less where, have no friends or anyone you can trust, and live in constant fear of rape and violence. Do you think this might be enough to drive you over the edge?

Consider just the problems involved in not having a place to bathe. (Shelters are often so dangerous that the homeless prefer to take their chances and sleep in public settings.) At first, you try to wash in the toilets of gas stations, bars, the bus station, or a shopping center. But you are dirty, and people stare when you enter and call the management when they see you wash your feet in the sink. You are thrown out and told in no uncertain terms never to come back. So you get dirtier and dirtier. Eventually you come to think of being dirty as a fact of life. Soon, maybe, you don't even care. The stares no longer bother you, at least not as much.

No one will talk to you, and you withdraw more and more into yourself. You begin to build a fantasy life. You talk openly to yourself. People stare, but so what? They stare anyway. Besides, they are no longer important to you.

Jamie might be mentally ill. Some organic problem, such as a chemical imbalance in her brain, might underlie her behavior. But perhaps not. How long would it take us to exhibit bizarre behaviors if we were homeless—and hopeless? The point is that *just being on the streets can cause mental illness*—or whatever we want to label socially inappropriate behaviors that we find difficult to classify. *Homelessness and mental illness are reciprocal:* Just as "mental illness" can cause homelessness, so the trials of being homeless, of living on cold, hostile streets, can lead to unusual and unacceptable thinking and behaviors.

THE NEED FOR A MORE HUMANE APPROACH

As Durkheim (1895/1964:68) pointed out, deviance is inevitable—even in a group of saints.

> Imagine a society of saints, a perfect cloister of exemplary individuals. Crimes, properly so called, will there be unknown; but faults which appear [invisible] to the layman will create there the same scandal that the ordinary offense does in ordinary [society].

With deviance an inevitable occurrence, one measure of a society is how it treats its deviants. Our prisons certainly don't say much that's good about U.S. society. Filled with the poor, they are warehouses of the unwanted, and they reflect patterns of broad discrimination in our larger society. White-collar criminals continue to get by with a slap on the wrist while street criminals are severely punished. Some deviants, who fail to meet current standards of admission to either prison or a mental hospital, take refuge in shelters and cardboard boxes in city streets. Although no one has *the* answer, it does not take much reflection to see that there are more humane approaches than these.

Because deviance is inevitable, the larger issues are to find ways to protect people from deviant behaviors that are harmful to themselves or others, to tolerate those that are not harmful, and to develop systems of fairer treatment for deviants. In the absence of the fundamental changes that would bring about a truly equitable social system, most efforts are, unfortunately, Band-Aid solutions. What we need is a more humane social system, one that would prevent the social inequalities that are the focus of the next five chapters.

SUMMARY AND REVIEW

■ **Gaining a Sociological Perspective on Deviance**

How do sociologists view deviance?

From a sociological perspective, **deviance** (the violation of norms) is relative. What people consider deviant varies from one culture to another and from group to group within the same society. Consequently, as symbolic interactionists stress, it is not the act itself but the reactions to the act that make something deviant. All groups develop systems of **social control** to punish **deviants**, those who violate its norms. Pp. 198–201.

How do sociological and individualistic explanations of deviance differ?

To explain why people deviate from norms, biologists and psychologists look for reasons *within* the individual, such as **genetic predispositions** or **personality disorders**. Sociologists, in contrast, look for explanations *outside* the individual, in social relations. Pp. 201–202.

■ **The Symbolic Interactionist Perspective**

How do symbolic interactionists explain deviance?

Symbolic interactionists have developed several theories to explain deviance such as **crime** (the violation of norms that have been written into law). According to **differential association theory,** people learn to deviate by associating with others. According to **control theory,** each of us is propelled toward deviance, but most of us conform because of an effective system of inner and outer controls. People who have less effective controls deviate. Pp. 202–208.

■ **The Functionalist Perspective**

How do functionalists explain deviance?

Functionalists point out that deviance, including criminal acts, is functional for society. Functions include affirming norms and promoting social unity and social change. According to **strain theory,** societies socialize their members into desiring **cultural goals.** Many people, however, are unable to achieve these goals in socially acceptable ways—that is, by **institutionalized means.** *Deviants,* then, are people who either give up on the goals or use deviant means to attain them. Merton identified five types of responses to cultural goals and institutionalized means: conformity, innovation, ritualism, retreatism, and rebellion. **Illegitimate opportunity theory** stresses that some people have easier access to illegal means of achieving goals. Pp. 208–214.

■ **The Conflict Perspective**

How do conflict theorists explain deviance?

Conflict theorists take the position that the group in power (the **capitalist class**) imposes its definitions of deviance on other groups (the **working class** and the **marginal working class**). From the conflict perspective, the law is an instrument of oppression used to maintain the power and privilege of the few over the many. The marginal working class has little income, is desperate, and commits highly visible property crimes. The ruling class directs the **criminal justice system,** using it to punish the crimes of the poor while diverting its own criminal activities away from this punitive system. Pp. 214–215.

■ Reactions to Deviance

How do societies react to deviance?

Deviance results in **negative sanctions**, acts of disapproval ranging from frowns to capital punishment. Some groups use **degradation ceremonies** to impress on their members that certain violations will not be tolerated. Imprisonment is motivated by the goals of **retribution, deterrence, rehabilitation,** and **incapacitation.** The death penalty is the most extreme action of the state against deviants. Bias in the death penalty is a major social issue. New laws are also passed as definitions of deviance and access to power change. Pp. 202–208.

Are official statistics on crime reliable?

The conclusions of both symbolic interactionists (that the police operate with a large measure of discretion) and conflict theorists (that the legal system is controlled by the capitalist class) indicate that we must be cautious when using crime statistics. Pp. 216–221.

What is the medicalization of deviance?

The medical profession has attempted to **medicalize** many forms of deviance, claiming that they represent mental illnesses. Thomas Szasz disagrees, claiming that they are just problem behaviors, not mental illnesses. Research on homeless people illustrates how problems in living can lead to bizarre behavior and thinking. Pp. 222–224.

■ The Need for a More Humane Approach

Deviance is inevitable, so the larger issues are to find ways to protect people from deviance that harms themselves and others, to tolerate deviance that is not harmful, and to develop systems of fairer treatment for deviants. P. 224.

Where can I read more on this topic?

Suggested readings for this chapter are at the back of this book.

All URLs listed are current as of the printing of this book. URLs often changed. Please check our Web site, **http://www.abacon.com/henslin**, for updates.

1. As new technologies emerge, so do new kinds of crime. How to avoid Internet fraud is discussed at **http://www.fraud.org/internet/intset.htm**. By understanding how to avoid this type of crime, you also can see how it occurs. Another crime that has emerged in recent years, also facilitated by the Internet and other new technology, is identity theft. Learn about this type of crime at: **http://www.privacyrights.org/identity.htm**. Discuss these new forms of deviance, including who might be behind scams and what aspects of our social structure may influence these behaviors. Be sure to apply the theories of deviance presented in the text. As you apply the functionalist perspective, discuss how Internet-based deviance may contribute to social order. As you review the victims' experiences with trying to "get justice," apply what Durkheim had to say about the functions of deviance.

2. The text discusses how hatred has been criminalized in the United States through the passage of hate crime laws. Go to the Web site maintained by the Anti-Defamation League (ADL) at **http://www.adl.org**. This organization, which has been fighting hatred and prejudice since 1913, provided Model hate crime legislation that has served as a foundation for our hate crime laws. Here you will find a wide range of information about hate crimes, including in-depth reports on organizations that promote hatred, ways to prevent these crimes, and strategies for responding to them. To read more about legislative efforts, go to **http://www.adl.org/frames/front_99hatecrime.html**. Another site that has information on hate crimes is **http://www.religioustolerance.org/hom_hat1/htm**. Use the different sociological theories of deviance to explain why hate crimes exist. Then analyze the reactions to hate crimes that are promoted by the ADL. Which of the reactions to deviance that are discussed in the text do you think the ADL stresses for dealing with hate crimes? Finally, prepare a presentation for your class in which you discuss the concept of hate crimes, the perpetrators of such crimes, and how our society reacts to them.

3. Gangs are found throughout our society, although they tend to operate more in poor urban neighborhoods than elsewhere. You can read a research report on Latino gangs in Los Angeles by accessing **http://www.CSUN.edu/~hcchs006/gang.html**. At the first page, click on "Table of Contents." Here you can click on different chapters and read about the research methodology, as well as about many of the findings and conclusions of this study. As you read the report, look for evidence to support differential association, control, illegitimate opportunity, and strain theory. Read the chapter on "Non-gang Affiliated Essay Excerpts" to learn why many young people who live in areas with high levels of gang activity do not get involved in gangs. Prepare a report for your class about gang membership and gang activity. Be sure to use a sociological perspective.

4. One argument for imprisoning those convicted of committing a crime is that criminals should be rehabilitated. This argument switches the focus from punishment to resocialization. Examine the following sites with regard to the issues involved in rehabilitation.

   http://www.soft.net.uk/turner/aftermath.htm

   http://users.aol.com/newpaths/page.htm

   http://detnews.com/menu/stories/28523.htm

   The first site provides information on a British program, while the other two sites relate to U.S. programs. After reading about these programs, answer these questions: What are the issues involved in rehabilitation? Who benefits from rehabilitation? Who should undergo rehabilitation? Finally, in what ways is the British program different from the two U.S. programs?

Global Stratification

- **What Is Social Stratification?**
- **Systems of Social Stratification**
  Slavery
  Caste
  Estate
  Class
  Global Stratification and the Status of Females

- **What Determines Social Class?**
  Karl Marx: The Means of Production
  Max Weber: Property, Prestige, and Power

- **Why Is Social Stratification Universal?**
  The Functionalist View of Davis and Moore:
    Motivating Qualified People
  Tumin: A Critical Response
  Mosca: A Forerunner of the Conflict Perspective
  The Conflict Perspective: Class Conflict and
    Scarce Resources
  Lenski's Synthesis

- **How Do Elites Maintain Stratification?**
  Ideology Versus Force

- **Comparative Social Stratification**
  Social Stratification in Great Britain
  Social Stratification in the Former Soviet Union

- **Global Stratification: Three Worlds**
  The Most Industrialized Nations
  The Industrializing Nations
  The Least Industrialized Nations
  Modifying the Model

- **How the World's Nations Became Stratified**
  Colonialism
  World System Theory
  Dependency Theory
  Culture of Poverty
  Evaluating the Theories

- **Maintaining Global Stratification**
  Neocolonialism
  Multinational Corporations
  Technology and Global Domination

- **A Concluding Note**

- **Summary and Review**

Let's contrast three "average" families from around the world: For Getu Mulleta, 33, and his wife, Zenebu, 28, of rural Ethiopia, life is a constant struggle to keep themselves and their seven children from starving. They live in a 320-square-foot manure-plastered hut with no electricity, gas, or running water. They have a radio, but the battery is dead. Surviving on $130 a year, the family farms teff, a cereal grain.

The Mulletas' poverty is not due to a lack of hard work. Getu works about 80 hours a week, while Zenebu puts in even more hours. "Housework" for Zenebu includes fetching water, making fuel pellets out of cow dung for the open fire over which she cooks the family's food, and cleaning animal stables. Like other Ethiopian women, she eats after the men.

In Ethiopia, the average male can expect to live to 48, the average female to 50.

The Mulletas' most valuable possession is their oxen. Their wishes for the future: more animals, better seed, and a second set of clothing.

In Guadalajara, Mexico, Ambrosio and Carmen Castillo Balderas and their five children, ages 2 to 10, live in a four-room house. They also have a walled courtyard, where the family spends a good deal of time. They even have a washing machine, which is hooked up to a garden hose that runs to a public water main several hundred yards away. Like most Mexicans, they do not have a telephone, nor do they own a car. Unlike many, however,

227

they own a refrigerator, a stereo, and a recent proud purchase that makes them the envy of their neighbors, a television.

Ambrosio, 29, works full time as a produce wholesale distributor. He also does welding on the side. The family's total annual income is $3,600. They spend 57 percent of their income on food. Carmen works about 60 hours a week taking care of their children and keeping their home spotless. The neatness of their home stands in stark contrast to the neighborhood, which is lined with littered dirt roads. As in many other Mexican neighborhoods, public utilities and road work do not keep pace with people's needs.

The average life expectancy for males in Mexico is 70. For females, it is 76.

The Castillo Balderas' most valued possessions are their refrigerator and television. Their wish for the future: a truck.

Springfield, Illinois, is home to the Kellys—Rick, 36, Patti, 34, Julie, 10, and Michael, 7. The Kellys live in a four-bedroom, 2,100-square-foot, carpeted ranch-style house, with central heating and air conditioning, a basement, and a two-car garage. Their home is equipped with a refrigerator, washing machine, clothes dryer, dishwasher, garbage

disposal, vacuum cleaner, food processor, microwave, and toaster. They also own three radios, a CD player, four telephones (one cellular), two televisions, a camcorder, VCR, DVD player, tape recorder, Gameboy, Nintendo, and a computer and printer, not to mention two blow dryers, an answering machine, a blender, an electric can opener, and an electric toothbrush. This doesn't count the stereo-radio-CD players in their pickup and car.

Rick works 40 hours a week as a cable splicer for the local telephone company. Patti teaches school part time. Together they make $44,568, plus benefits. The Kellys can choose from among dozens of superstocked supermarkets. They spend $4,101 for food they eat at home, and another $2,362 eating out, a total of 15 percent of their annual income.

In the United States, the average life expectancy is 73 for males, 80 for females.

On the Kellys' wish list are a new Bronco, a 20 gigabyte computer, a flat screen television, a digital camera, a fax machine, a scanner, a Palm Pilot, a boat, a camping trailer, an ATV, and, oh yes, further down the road, a vacation cabin. ■

Sources: Menzel 1994; Population Reference Bureau 1995; *Statistical Abstract* 1999:Tables 127, 739, 749.

What is Social Stratification?

Some of the world's nations are wealthy, others poor, and some in between. This layering of nations, and of groups of people within a nation, is called *social stratification*. Social stratification is one of the most significant topics we shall discuss in this book, for it affects our life chances—from our access to material possessions to the age at which we die.

Social stratification also affects our orientations to life. If you had been born into the Ethiopian family, for example, you would be illiterate and would expect your children to be the same. You also would expect hunger to be a part of life and would not be too surprised when people die young. If you had been born into either of the other two families, you also would have quite different views of the world.

Social stratification is a system in which groups of people are divided into layers according to their relative power, property, and prestige. It is important to emphasize that social stratification does not refer to individuals. It is a *way of ranking large groups of people in a hierarchy that shows their relative privileges.*

Let's examine how the nations of the world became so stratified that, as with these three families, it profoundly affects everyone's chances in life. But first let's review the major systems of social stratification.

social stratification the division of large numbers of people into layers according to their relative power, property, and prestige: applies to both nations and to people within a nation, society, or other group

"Worlds Apart" could be the title for these photos, which illustrate how life chances depend on global stratification. On the left is the Mulleta family of Ethiopia, featured in the opening vignette, standing in front of their home with all their material possessions. On the right is the Skeen family of Texas, surrounded by their possessions.

Systems of Social Stratification

Every society stratifies its members. Some, like agricultural societies, draw firm lines that separate group from group, while others, like hunting and gathering societies, show greater equality. Regardless of its forms, however, the existence of social stratification is universal. Let's look at four major systems of social stratification: slavery, caste, estate, and class.

Slavery

Slavery, whose essential characteristic is *ownership of some people by others,* has been common in world history. The Old Testament even lays out rules for how the Israelites should treat their slaves. So does the Koran. The Romans had slaves, as did the Africans and Greeks. In classical Greece and Rome, slaves did the work, freeing citizens to engage in politics and the arts. Slavery was least common among nomads, especially hunters and gatherers, and most common in agricultural societies (Landtman 1938/1968). As we examine the major causes and conditions of slavery, you will see how remarkably it has varied around the world.

Causes of Slavery Contrary to popular assumption, slavery was not usually based on racism, but on one of three other factors. The first was debt. In some cultures, an individual who could not pay a debt could be enslaved by the creditor. The second was crime. Instead of being killed, a murderer or thief might be enslaved by the family of the victim as compensation for their loss. The third was war and conquest. When one group of people conquered another, they often enslaved at least some of the vanquished (Starna and Watkins 1991). Historian Gerda Lerner (1986) notes that the first people enslaved through warfare were women. When premodern men raided a village or camp, they killed the men, raped the women, and then brought the women back as slaves. The women were valued for sexual purposes, for reproduction, and for extra labor.

Roughly twenty-five hundred years ago, when Greece was but a collection of city-states, slavery was common. A city that became powerful and conquered another city would enslave some of the vanquished. Both slaves and slaveholders were Greek. Similarly, when Rome became the supreme power of the Mediterranean area about two thousand years ago, following the custom of the time the Romans enslaved some of the Greeks they had conquered. More

slavery a form of social stratification in which some people own other people

Slavery is an age-old system of social stratification. This 1769 broadside from Charleston, South Carolina, reminds us that this form of stratification was once the custom in the United States.

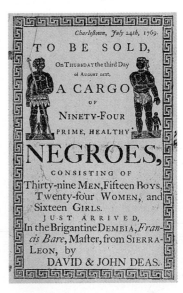

This little Pakastani boy does backbreaking work each day in the brick kilns in the village of Batapur. He is a bonded laborer, a status that is close to that of slave. He cannot quit work, for, like his family, he must work to pay off debt that passes from generation to generation.

indentured service a contractual system in which someone sells his or her body (services) for a specified period of time in an arrangement very close to slavery, except that it is voluntarily entered into

ideology beliefs about the way things ought to be that justify social arrangements

educated than their conquerors, some of these slaves served as tutors in Roman homes. Slavery, then, was a sign of defeat in battle, of crime, or of debt. It was not the sign of an inherently inferior status.

Conditions of Slavery The conditions of slavery have varied widely around the world. *In some cases, slavery was temporary.* After serving a set number of years, slaves were free to return to their home country. Slaves of the Israelites were set free in the year of jubilee, which occurred every fifty years. Roman slaves ordinarily had the right to buy themselves out of slavery. They knew what their purchase price was, and some were able to meet this price by striking a bargain with their owner and selling their services to others. Such was the case with some of the educated Greek slaves. In most instances, however, slavery was a lifelong condition. Some criminals, for example, became slaves when they were given life sentences as oarsmen on Roman war ships. There they served until death, which often came quickly to those in this exhausting service.

Slavery was not necessarily inheritable. In most places, the children of slaves were automatically slaves themselves. But in some instances, the child of a slave who served a rich family might even be adopted by that family, becoming an heir who bore the family name along with the other sons or daughters of the household. In ancient Mexico, the children of slaves were always free (Landtman 1938/ 1968:271).

Slaves were not necessarily powerless and poor. In almost all instances, slaves owned no property and had no power. Among some slaveholding groups, however, slaves could accumulate property and even rise to high positions in the community. Occasionally, a slave might even become wealthy, loan money to the master, and, while still a slave, own slaves himself or herself (Landtman 1938/ 1968). This, however, was rare.

Slavery in the New World Indentured service occupies a gray area between a contract and slavery (Main 1965; Elkins 1968). Many people who wanted to start a new life in the American colonies were unable to pay their passage. Ship captains would carry them on credit, and colonists would "buy their paper" when they arrived. This arrangement provided passage for the penniless, payment for the ship's captain, and servants for wealthier colonists for a set number of years. During that specified period, the servants were required by law to serve their master. If they ran away, they became outlaws and were captured and forcibly returned. At the end of the period of indenture, they became full citizens, able to live where they chose and free to sell their labor.

When the colonists found that there were not enough indentured servants to meet their growing need for labor, they tried to enslave Indians. This attempt, however, failed miserably. One reason was that when Indians escaped they knew how to survive in the wilderness and were able to make their way back to their tribe. The colonists then turned to Africans, who were being brought to North and South America by the Dutch, English, Portuguese, and Spanish.

Given this history, some analysts conclude that racism didn't lead to slavery, but, rather, slavery led to racism. Finding it profitable to make people slaves for life, U.S. slave owners developed an **ideology**, a system of beliefs that justifies social arrangements. Essential to an ideology that would justify lifelong slavery was the view that the slaves were inferior. Some said that they were locked into a childlike, helpless state, which meant that they needed to be taken care of by superior people—white colonists, of course. Others said that the slaves were not fully human. In short, the colonists developed elaborate justifications for slavery on the presumed superiority of their own race.

To make slavery even more profitable, slave states passed laws that made slavery *inheritable;* that is, the babies born to slaves became the property of the slave owners (Stampp 1956). These children could be sold, bartered, or traded. To strengthen their control, slave states passed laws making it illegal for slaves to hold meetings or to be away from the master's premises without carrying a pass (Lerner 1972). As sociologist W. E. B. Du Bois (1935/1966:12) noted, "gradually the entire white South became an armed camp to keep Negroes in slavery and to kill the black rebel."

Patterns of legal discrimination did not end after the Civil War. For example, until 1954 the states operated two separate school systems. Even until the 1950s, to keep the races from "mixing," it was illegal in Mississippi for a white and an African American to sit together on the same seat of a car! The reason there was no outright ban on both races being in the same car was to allow for African-American chauffeurs.

In a caste system, status is determined by birth and is lifelong. At birth, these women in India received not only membership in a lower caste but also, because of their gender, a predetermined position in that caste and in the division of labor.

Slavery Today   Slavery has again reared its ugly head, this time in Sudan, Mauritania, and Benin (Horwitz 1989; Liben 1995; Hentoff 1998; Jacobs 1999). This region has a long history of slavery, and it was not until 1980 that slavery was officially abolished in Mauritania, and not until 1987 in Sudan (Ayittey 1998). Although officially abolished, slavery continues. Enslavement of the Dinka tribe in southern Sudan is the topic of the Mass Media box on the next page.

Caste

The second system of social stratification is caste. In a **caste system,** status is determined by birth and is lifelong. Someone born into a low-status group will always have low status, no matter how much that person may accomplish in life. In sociological terms, the basis of a caste system is ascribed status (discussed on pages 99–100). Achieved status cannot change an individual's place in this system.

Societies with this form of stratification try to make certain that the boundaries between castes remain firm. They practice **endogamy,** marriage within one's own group, and prohibit intermarriage. To prevent contact between castes, they even develop elaborate rules about *ritual pollution,* teaching that contact with inferior castes contaminates the superior caste.

India   India provides the best example of a caste system. Based not on race but on religion, India's caste system has existed for almost three thousand years (Chandra 1993a, b). India's four main castes, or *varnas,* are depicted in Table 9.1. The four main castes are subdivided into thousands of specialized subcastes, or *jati,* with each *jati* working in a specific occupation. For example, knife sharpening is done only by members of a particular subcaste.

The lowest group listed on Table 9.1, the Harijan, is actually so low that it is beneath the caste system altogether. The Harijans, along with some of the Shudras, make up India's "untouchables." If they touch someone of a higher caste, that person becomes unclean. Even the shadow of an untouchable can contaminate. Early morning and late afternoons are especially risky, for the long shadows of these periods pose a danger to everyone higher up the caste system. Consequently, Harijans are not even allowed in some villages during these times. Anyone who becomes contaminated must follow *ablution,* or washing rituals, to restore purity (Lannoy 1975).

caste system   a form of social stratification in which one's status is determined by birth and is lifelong

Table 9.1

INDIA'S CASTE SYSTEM

Caste	Occupation
Brahman	Priests or scholars
Kshatriya	Nobles and warriors
Vaishva	Merchants and skilled artisans
Shudra	Common laborers
Harijan	The outcastes; degrading labor

Mass Media in Social Life

WHAT PRICE FREEDOM?
SLAVERY TODAY

Children of the Dinka tribe in rural Sudan don't go to school. They work. Their families depend on them to tend the cattle that are so important to their way of life. On the morning of the raid, ten-year-old Adhieu had been watching the cattle. "We were very happy because we would soon leave the cattle camps and return home to our parents. But in the morning, there was shooting. There was yelling and crying everywhere. My uncle grabbed me by the hand, and we ran. We swam across the river. I saw some children drowning. We hid behind a rock."

By morning's end, 500 children were either dead or enslaved. Their attackers were their fellow countrymen—Arabs from northern Sudan. The children who were captured were forced to march hundreds of miles north. Some escaped on the way. Others tried to—and were shot (Akol 1998).

Thousands—maybe tens of thousands—of Dinkas have been killed or enslaved since civil war broke out in the Sudan in the mid 1980s. Yet the Arab-led government—the powerful National Islamic Front—piously insists that slavery does not exist. It claims it is an invention of foreign politicians, Christian humanitarians, and hostile foreign media (Akol 1998). But there are too many witnesses, and there has been too much documentation by human rights groups. There also are some devastating accounts by journalists: Public television (PBS) has even run film footage of captive children in chains. And then there are the slaves who managed to survive, who recount their ordeal in horrifying detail. The

reasonable question is not whether slavery exists, but to what extent the Sudanese government encourages and supports this trafficking in human bodies.

The United States, which bombed Kosovo into submission for its crimes against humanity, has remained strangely silent and inactive in the face of this outrage. A cynic might say that Kosovo was located at a politically strategic spot in Europe, whereas the Sudan occupies a remote, less significant area of Africa; that outrages against black Africans are not as significant to the U.S. and European powers as those against white Europeans; and that these governments fear Arab retaliation, which might take the form of terrorism and oil embargoes.

Appalled by the lack of response shown by the world's most powerful governments, private groups have been spurred into action. Foremost among them is Christian Solidarity International (CSI), based in Zurich, Switzerland. The technique this human rights organization uses is controversial. Arab "retrievers" go to northern Sudan, where they either buy or abduct slaves. Walking by night and hiding by day, they elude security forces and bring the slaves south. There, CSI pays the retrievers $50 per slave (Mabry 1999).

As CBS news cameras rolled, the rescuer paid the slave trader $50,000 in Sudanese pounds. At $50 per person, the bundle of bills was enough to free 1,000 slaves. The liberated slaves, mostly women and children, were then free to return to their villages (Jacobs 1999).

CSI has been severely criticized. Some claim that buying slaves, even if it serves to set them free, encourages slavery; that it provides a strong motivation to enslave people in order to turn around and sell them. Fifty dollars is a lot of money in Sudan, where the average income for an entire year is $180.

That is a bogus argument, replies CSI. What is intolerable is to leave women and children in slavery where they are deprived of their freedom and families, and also are abused by brutal masters.

CSI claims to have purchased the freedom of about 10,000 slaves. No one knows how many remain in slavery. ■

For Your Consideration

What do you think about buying the freedom of slaves? Can you suggest a workable alternative? Why do you think the U.S. government has remained inactive about this issue for so long, when it invades other countries for human rights abuses? Do you think that, perhaps, its excursions into such places as Haiti and Kosovo were pretexts for political motives, and had little to do with human rights? If not, why the silence in the face of slavery?

The media coverage of this issue has motivated many Americans to become active in freeing slaves. High schools nationwide—and even some grade schools—are raising money to participate in slave buy-back programs (Schaefer 1999). If you were a principal of a high school, would you encourage or discourage this practice? Why or why not?

---

endogamy marriage within one's own group

Although the Indian government formally abolished the caste system in 1949, centuries-old practices cannot be so easily eliminated, and the caste system remains part of everyday life in India (Sharma 1994). The ceremonies people follow at births, marriages, and deaths,

As discussed in the text, slavery still exists. In this photo, a representative of the Liason Agency Network (on the left) is buying the freedom of the Sudanese slaves (in the background).

for example, are dictated by caste (Chandra 1993a). Entrenched in power, the upper castes fear the upward mobility of the untouchables. On occasion, they even resist it with violence and ritual suicide (Crosette 1996; Filkins 1997).

South Africa Until recently, South Africa provided another example of social stratification based on caste. Europeans of Dutch descent, a numerical minority called Afrikaaners, controlled the government, the police, and the military. They used these sources of power to enforce a system called **apartheid** (ah-PAR-tate), the separation of the races. Everyone was classified by law into one of four racial groups: Europeans (whites), Africans (blacks), Coloureds (mixed races), and Asians. One's classification determined where one could live, work, and go to school. It also established where one could swim or see movies—for by law whites and Africans were not allowed to mix socially.

After decades of trade sanctions, sports boycotts, and worldwide negative publicity, Afrikaaners reluctantly dismantled their caste system (Ford 1993; Melloan 1993a). No longer do Africans carry special passes, public facilities are integrated, and all races have the right to vote and to hold office. In 1994, in the country's first postapartheid election, Nelson Mandela, an African who had been imprisoned for nineteen years for revolutionary activities, was elected president of South Africa.

Although apartheid has been dismantled, its legacy haunts South Africa (Krog 1999). Whites still dominate the country's social institutions. Although the black middle class is growing, most blacks remain uneducated and poor. Many new rights—such as the right to higher education, to eat in restaurants, to go swimming, even to see a doctor—are of little use to people who can't afford them. Political violence has been replaced by old-fashioned crime. South Africa's murder rate, the highest in the world, runs *seven times* higher than the extraordinary U.S. rate and *50 times* higher than the murder rate of Great Britain (Hambler and Lewis 1998). Apartheid's legacy of prejudice, bitterness, and hatred is destined to fuel race relations for generations.

A U.S. Racial Caste System Before leaving the subject of caste, we should note that when slavery ended in the United States it was replaced by a *racial caste system,* in which a person was marked for life at birth (Berger 1963/1999). In this system, *all* whites, no matter if they were poor and uneducated, considered themselves to have a higher status than *all* African Americans. When any white met any African American on a southern sidewalk, for example, the African American had to move aside. And as in India and South Africa, the

apartheid the separation of races as was practiced in South Africa

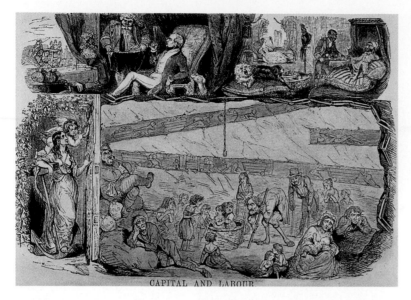

This cartoon of political protest appeared in London newspapers in 1843. It illustrates the severe exploitation of labor that occurred after the Estate System of social stratification broke down and peasants were forced to leave the land and find work elsewhere. Depicted here are the extremes of early capitalism. Scenes such as these stimulated Marx's analysis of social class.

upper caste, fearing pollution from the lower caste, insisted on separate schools, hotels, restaurants, and even toilets and drinking fountains in public facilities.

Estate

During the middle ages, Europe developed a unique system of stratification. The **estate** system, as it was known, consisted of three groups, or estates. The *first* estate was made up of the nobility, the wealthy and powerful families that ruled the country. They owned the land, which was the source of wealth at that time. The nobility did no farming themselves, or any "work," for that matter. Having an occupation was considered beneath their dignity, and "work" was done by servants. The nobility's responsibility was to administer their lands and fortunes, and to live "genteel" lives worthy of their high position.

The *second* estate consisted of the clergy. The Roman Catholic Church was a political power at this time. It owned vast tracts of lands and collected taxes from commoners (everyone who lived within the boundaries of a parish had to pay a set amount). The church also set its seal of approval on rulers: To be crowned, a king had to obtain the pope's permission.

Another intricate connection ran between the nobility and the church. To prevent its vast land holdings from being carved into smaller chunks, the nobility practiced *primogeniture,* allowing only the firstborn son to inherit land. The other sons had to look around for some way to support themselves. Joining the clergy was one of those ways. (Others were becoming an officer in the military or practicing law.) To become a priest was to take a lifetime position and to be guaranteed a comfortable living. The church at that time sold offices, and the wealthy could buy the position of bishop, for example, which guaranteed a high income.

The *third* estate consisted of the commoners. These were the farmers (known as serfs), the carpenters, the harnessmakers, the servants, and all the other people who made up society. Born into the third estate, and with practically no way to move out of it, they died there, too. The rare person who made it out of the third estate was a man who was knighted for performing an extraordinary feat for the king. Exceptional bravery in battle could lead to knighthood. But this was rare, and membership in this estate, as in the others, was lifelong.

Women in the Estate System Women belonged to the estate of their husbands. Women in the first estate had no occupation, for, like their husbands, work was considered beneath their dignity. Their responsibility was to administer the household, overseeing the servants. Women were not members of the second estate, as the Roman Catholic clergy did not marry. (They did join this estate—following King Henry the VIII's rebellion against the Roman Catholic Church in 1534. For a while, the estate system continued to exist, and the new Anglican clergy could marry.) Women of the third estate shared the hard life of their husbands, including physical labor and food shortages. In addition, they faced the real perils of childbirth and of rape by men of the first estate. A few commoners who caught the eye of men of the first estate did marry and join them in the first estate. This, however, was rare.

Class

As we have seen, stratification systems based on slavery, caste, and clan are rigid. The lines marking the divisions between people are so firm that there is little or no movement from

estate stratification system the stratification system of medieval Europe, consisting of three groups or estates: the nobility, clergy, and serfs (or peasants)

one group to another. A **class system,** in contrast, is much more open, for it is based primarily on money or material possessions. It, too, begins at birth, when individuals are ascribed the status of their parents, but, unlike with slavery, caste, and estate, one can change one's social class due to what one achieves (or fails to achieve) in life. In addition, no laws specify people's occupations on the basis of birth or prohibit marriage between the classes.

A major characteristic of this fourth system, then, is its relatively fluid boundaries. A class system allows **social mobility,** that is, movement up or down the class ladder. The potential for improving one's social circumstances, or class, is one of the major forces that drives people to go far in school and to work hard. In the extreme, the family background that an individual inherits at birth may present such obstacles that the child has little chance of climbing very far—or it may provide such privileges that it is almost impossible for the individual to fall down the class ladder.

Global Stratification and the Status of Females

In every society of the world, gender is a basis for social stratification. In no society is gender the sole basis for stratifying people, but gender cuts across *all* systems of social stratification—whether slavery, caste, estate, or class (Huber 1990). As we explored briefly in the estate system, on the basis of their gender, people are sorted into categories and given different access to the good things available in their society.

Apparently these distinctions always favor males. It is remarkable, for example, that in every society of the world men's earnings are higher than women's. Control of females by males is even more evident when we look at examples of child brides, child prostitution (see the box on page 251), and female circumcision (see the box on page 294). That most of the world's illiterate are females drives home the relative positions of males and females. Of the 885 million adults who are illiterate, two-thirds are women, while of the 13 million school-age children who receive no education, two-thirds are girls (Browne 1995). Because gender is so significant for what happens to us in life, we shall devote a separate chapter to this topic (Chapter 11).

WHAT DETERMINES SOCIAL CLASS?

In the early days of sociology, a disagreement arose about the meaning of social class in industrialized societies. Let's compare how Marx and Weber saw the matter.

Karl Marx: The Means of Production

As discussed in Chapter 1, Karl Marx (1818–1883) witnessed the effects of societies in upheaval. When the feudal system broke up, masses of peasants were displaced from their traditional lands and occupations. Fleeing to cities, they competed for the few available jobs. Offered only a pittance for their labor, they dressed in rags, went hungry, and slept under bridges and in shacks. In contrast, the factory owners built mansions, hired servants, and lived in the lap of luxury. Seeing this great disparity between owners and workers, Marx concluded that social class depends on a single factor—the **means of production**—the tools, factories, land, and investment capital used to produce wealth (Marx 1844/1964; Marx and Engels 1848/1967).

Marx argued that the things people use to distinguish among themselves—such as clothing, speech, education, paycheck, or, today, even the type of car they drive—are superficial matters. These things camouflage the only dividing line that counts. Modern society, said Marx, is made up of just two classes of people: the **bourgeoisie,** those who own the means of production, and the **proletariat,** those who work for the owners. In short, people's relationship to the means of production determines their social class.

Marx did recognize that other groups were part of industrial society: farmers and peasants; a *lumpenproletariat* (marginal people such as beggars, vagrants, and criminals); and a middle group of self-employed professionals. Marx did not consider these groups social

class system a form of social stratification based primarily on the possession of money or material possessions

social mobility movement up or down the social class ladder

means of production the tools, factories, land, and investment capital used to produce wealth

bourgeoisie Karl Marx's term for the people who own the means of production

proletariat Karl Marx's term for the people who work for those who own the means of production

Taken at the end of the 1800s, these photos illustrate the contrasting worlds of social classes produced by capitalism. The sleeping boys shown in this classic 1890 photo by Jacob Riis sold newspapers in London. They did not go to school, and they had no home. The children on the right, Cornelius and Gladys Vanderbilt, are shown in front of their parents' estate. They went to school and did not work. You can see how the life situations illustrated in these photos would have produced different orientations to life—and, therefore, politics, ideas about marriage, values, and so on—the stuff of which life is made.

class consciousness Karl Marx's term for awareness of a common identity based on one's position in the means of production

false consciousness Karl Marx's term to refer to workers identifying with the interests of capitalists

The text describes the many relationships among Weber's three components of social class: property, prestige, and power. Colin Powell is an example of power that was converted into prestige.

classes, however, for they lacked **class consciousness**—a common identity based on their position in the means of production. They did not see themselves as exploited workers whose plight could be solved by collective action. Consequently, Marx thought of these groups as insignificant in the coming workers' revolution that would overthrow capitalism.

As the bourgeoisie grow even wealthier, Marx said, hostilities will grow. When workers come to realize that capitalists are the source of their oppression, they will unite and throw off the chains of their oppressors. In a bloody revolution, they will seize the means of production and usher in a classless society, where no longer will the few grow rich at the expense of the many. What holds back the workers' unity and their revolution is **false consciousness**, workers mistakenly identifying with capitalists. For example, workers with a few dollars in the bank may forget that they are workers and instead see themselves as investors, or as capitalists who are about to launch a successful business.

The only distinction worth mentioning, then, is whether a person is an owner or a worker. This decides everything else, Marx stressed, for property determines people's lifestyles, shapes their ideas, and establishes their relationships with one another.

Max Weber: Property, Prestige, and Power

Max Weber (1864–1920) became an outspoken critic of Marx. Weber argued that property is only part of the picture. Social class, he said, is actually made up of three components—property, prestige, and power (Gerth and Mills 1958; Weber 1922/1968). Some call these the three P's of social class. (Although Weber used the terms *class, status,* and *power,* some sociologists find *property, prestige,* and *power* to be clearer terms. To make them even clearer, you may wish to substitute *wealth* for *property.*)

Property (or wealth), said Weber, is certainly significant in determining a person's standing in society. On that he agreed with Marx. But, added Weber, ownership is not the only significant aspect of property. For example, some powerful people, such as managers of corporations, *control* the means of production although they do not *own* them. If managers can control property for their own benefit—awarding themselves huge bonuses and magnificent perks—it makes no practical difference that they do not own the property that they so generously use for their own benefit.

Prestige, the second element in Weber's analysis, is often derived from property, for people tend to look up to the wealthy. Prestige, however, can also be based on other factors. Olympic gold medalists, for example, may not own property, yet they have very high prestige. Some are even able to exchange their prestige for property—such as when they are paid a small fortune for claiming that they start their day with "the breakfast of champions." In other words, property and prestige are not one-way streets: Although property can bring prestige, prestige can also bring property.

Power, the third element of social class, is the ability to control others, even over their objections. Weber agreed with Marx that property is a major source of power, but he added that it is not the only source. For example, prestige can be turned into power. Perhaps the best example is Ronald Reagan, an actor who became president of the most powerful country in the world. For other interrelationships of property, prestige, and power, see Figure 9.1.

■ **In Sum** For Marx, social class was based solely on a person's relationship to the means of production. One is either a member of the bourgeoisie or the proletariat. Weber argued that social class is a combination of property, prestige, and power.

WHY IS SOCIAL STRATIFICATION UNIVERSAL?

What is it about social life that makes all societies stratified? We shall first consider the explanation proposed by functionalists, which has aroused much controversy in sociology, then explanations proposed by conflict theorists.

The Functionalist View of Davis and Moore: Motivating Qualified People

Functionalists take the position that the patterns of behavior that characterize a society exist because they are functional for that society. (They conclude that because social inequality is universal, inequality helps societies survive.) Using this principle, sociologists Kingsley Davis and Wilbert Moore (1945, 1953) concluded that stratification is inevitable for the following reasons:

1. Society must make certain that its positions are filled.
2. Some positions are more important than others.
3. The more important positions must be filled by the more qualified people.
4. To motivate the more qualified people to fill these positions, society must offer them greater rewards.

Let's look at some examples to flesh out this functionalist argument. The position of college president is deemed much more important than that of a student because the president's decisions affect many more people. Any mistakes he or she makes carry implications for a large number of people, including many students. The same is true for the general of an army as opposed to a private in the army. The decisions of college presidents and generals affect careers, paychecks, and, in some cases, even determine life and death.

(Positions with greater responsibility also require greater accountability.) College presidents and army generals are accountable—to boards of trustees and to the leader of a country, respectively—for how they perform. How can society motivate highly qualified people to enter such high-pressure positions? What keeps people from avoiding them and seeking only less demanding jobs?

The answer, said Davis and Moore, is that society offers greater rewards for its more responsible, demanding, and accountable positions. If these jobs didn't offer greater prestige, salaries, and benefits, why would anyone strive for them? Thus, a salary of $2 million,

WEBER'S THREE COMPONENTS OF SOCIAL CLASS: INTERRELATIONSHIPS AMONG THEM

Property → Power, Prestige

(Bill Gates; the wealthy men who become presidents) (the wealthy in general)

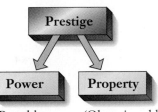

Prestige → Power, Property

(Ronald Reagan) (Olympic gold medalists who endorse products)

Power → Property, Prestige

(crooked politicians) (Abe Lincoln; Colin Powell)

country club membership, a private jet, and a chauffeured limousine may be necessary in order to get the most highly qualified people to compete with one another for a certain position, while a $30,000 salary without fringe benefits is enough to get hundreds of less qualified people to compete for less demanding positions. Higher rewards are also necessary in order to recruit more qualified people to positions that require rigorous training. If you can get the same pay with a high school education, why suffer through the many tests and term papers that college requires?

The functionalist argument is simple and clear. Society works better if its most qualified people hold its most important positions. For example, to get highly talented people to become surgeons—to undergo many years of rigorous training and then cope with life-and-death situations on a daily basis, as well as withstand the Sword of Damocles known as malpractice suits—society must provide a high payoff.

Tumin: A Critical Response

Note that the Davis-Moore thesis is an attempt to explain *why* social stratification is universal, not an attempt to *justify* social inequality. Note also that their view nevertheless makes many sociologists uncomfortable, for they see it as coming close to justifying the inequalities in society.

Melvin Tumin (1953) was the first sociologist to point out what he saw as major flaws in the functionalist position. Here are four of his arguments.

First, how do you measure the importance of a position? You can't measure importance by the rewards a position carries, for that argument is circular. You must have an independent measure of importance to test whether the more important positions actually carry higher rewards. For example, is a surgeon really more important to society than a garbage collector, since the garbage collector helps prevent contagious diseases?

Second, if stratification worked as Davis and Moore described it, society would be a **meritocracy**; that is, all positions would be awarded on the basis of merit. Ability, then, should predict who goes to college. Instead, the best predictor of college entrance is family income—the more a family earns, the more likely their children are to go to college. Similarly, while some people do get ahead through ability and hard work, others simply inherit wealth and the opportunities that go with it. Moreover, a stratification system that places most men above most women does not live up to the argument that talent and ability are the bases for holding important positions. In short, factors far beyond merit give people their relative positions in society.

Third, Davis and Moore place too much emphasis on money and fringe benefits. These aren't the only reasons people take jobs. An example is college teaching. If money were the main motivator, why would people spend four years in college, then average another six or seven years pursuing a Ph.D.—only to earn slightly more than someone who works in the post office? Obviously college teaching offers more than monetary rewards: high prestige (see Table 10.2, page 261), autonomy (college teachers have considerable discretion about how they do their jobs), rewarding social interaction (much of the job consists of talking to people), security (many college teachers get tenure, giving them a lifetime position), leisure, and the opportunity to travel (many professors work short days, enjoy several weeks of vacation during the school year, and have the entire summer off).

Fourth, if social stratification is so functional, it ought to benefit almost everyone. In actual fact, however, social stratification is *dysfunctional* for many. Think of the people who could have made invaluable contributions to society had they not been born in slums and had to drop out of school and take menial jobs to help support the family; or the many who, born female, are assigned "women's work," thus ensuring that they do not maximize their mental abilities.

Mosca: A Forerunner of the Conflict Perspective

In 1896, Italian sociologist Gaetano Mosca wrote an influential book entitled *The Ruling Class.* He argued that every society will be stratified by power, for three main reasons:

meritocracy a form of social stratification in which all positions are awarded on the basis of merit

1. A society cannot exist unless it is organized. This requires leadership of some sort in order to coordinate people's actions and get society's work done.

2. Leadership (or political organization) means inequalities of power: Some people take leadership positions, while others follow.

3. It is human nature to be self-centered. Therefore, people in positions of power will use their positions to bring greater rewards for themselves.

There is no way around these facts of life, said Mosca. Social stratification is inevitable, and every society will stratify itself along lines of power. Because the ruling class is well organized and enjoys easy communication among its relatively few members, it is difficult for the majority they govern to resist (Marger 1987). (Remember the *iron law of oligarchy* that we reviewed in Chapter 7.) Mosca's argument is a forerunner of explanations developed by conflict theorists.

The Conflict Perspective: Class Conflict and Scarce Resources

Conflict theorists don't just criticize details of the functionalist perspective. Rather, they say its basic premise is wrong. Conflict theorists stress that conflict, not function, is the basis of social stratification. They point out that in every society groups struggle with one another to gain a larger share of the society's limited resources. Whenever some group gains power, it uses that power to extract what it can from the groups beneath it. It also uses the social institutions to keep other groups weak and itself in power. Class conflict, then, is the key to understanding social stratification, for society is far from being a harmonious system that benevolently distributes greater resources to society's supposedly more qualified members.

All ruling groups—from slave masters to modern elites—develop an ideology to justify their position at the top. This ideology often seduces the oppressed into believing that their welfare depends on keeping society stable. Consequently, the oppressed may support laws that go against their own interests. They may even sacrifice their children, encouraging them to serve as soldiers in wars that are designed to enrich the bourgeoisie.

Marx predicted that the workers would revolt. The day will come, he said, when class consciousness will overcome ideology. When their eyes are opened, the workers will throw off their oppressors. At first, this struggle for control of the means of production may be covert, showing up as work slowdowns or industrial sabotage, but ultimately it will break out into open resistance. The struggle will be difficult, for the bourgeoisie control the police, the military, and even education (where they implant false consciousness in the workers' children).

Some sociologists have refocused conflict theory. C. Wright Mills (1956), Ralf Dahrendorf (1959), Randall Collins (1974, 1988), and James Schellenberg (1996), for example, stress that groups within the *same class* also compete for scarce resources—for power, wealth, education, housing, and even prestige—whatever benefits society has to offer. The result is conflict not only between labor unions and corporations, but also between the young and the old, women and men, and racial and ethnic groups. Unlike functionalists, then, conflict theorists hold that just beneath the surface of what may appear to be a tranquil society lies conflict that is barely held in check.

Lenski's Synthesis

Despite vast differences between the functionalist and conflict views, some analysts have tried to synthesize them. Sociologist Gerhard Lenski (1966), for example, used the development of surpluses as a basis for reconciling the two views. He said that the functionalists are right if you look at societies that have only basic resources and do not accumulate wealth. In hunting and gathering societies, the limited resources are channeled to people as rewards for taking on important responsibilities. When it comes to societies with a surplus, however, the conflict theorists are right. Because humans pursue self-interest, they struggle to control those surpluses, and a small elite emerges. To protect its position, the elite builds social inequality into the society, which results in a full-blown system of social stratification.

How DO ELITES MAINTAIN STRATIFICATION?

Suppose that you are part of the ruling elite of your society. What can you do to maintain your privileged position? The key lies in controlling ideas and information, in social networks, and in the least effective of all, the use of force.

Ideology Versus Force

Medieval Europe provides a good example of the power of ideology. In the estate system, only the nobility and clergy owned land, the primary source of wealth. With the exception of a few craftsmen who belonged to guilds (early unions), almost everyone was a peasant who worked for this small group of powerful landowners. The peasants farmed the land, took care of the livestock, and built the roads and bridges. Each year, they had to turn over a designated portion of their crops to their feudal lord. Year after year, for centuries, they did so. Why?

Controlling Ideas Why didn't the peasants rebel and take over the land themselves? There were many reasons, not the least of which was that the army was controlled by the nobility. Coercion, however, only goes so far, for it breeds hostility and nourishes rebellion. How much more effective it is to get the people to *want* to do what the ruling elite desires. This is where *ideology* comes into play, and the nobility and clergy used it to great effect. They developed an ideology known as the **divine right of kings**—the idea that the king's authority comes directly from God—which can be traced back several thousand years to the Old Testament. The king delegates authority to nobles, who as God's representatives must be obeyed. To disobey is a sin against God; to rebel means physical punishment on earth and eternal suffering in hell.

The control of ideas, then, can be remarkably more effective than brute force. Although this particular ideology no longer governs people's minds today, the elite in every society develops ideologies to justify its position at the top. For example, around the world schools teach that their country's form of government—*whatever form of government that may be*—is the best. Religious leaders teach that we owe obedience to authority, that laws are to be obeyed. To the degree that their ideologies are accepted by the masses, political arrangements are stable.

Controlling Information To maintain their positions of power, elites also try to control information. In dictatorships this is accomplished through the threat of force, for dic-

divine right of kings the idea that the king's authority comes directly from God

The divine right of kings was an ideology that made the king God's direct representative on earth—to administer justice and punish evildoers. This theological-political concept was supported by the Roman Catholic Church, whose representatives crowned the king. Depicted here is the coronation of Charlemagne by Pope Leo III on Christmas Day A.D. 800, thus establishing what became known as the Holy Roman Empire.

tators can—and do—imprison editors and reporters for printing critical reports, sometimes even for publishing information unflattering to them (Timerman 1981). The ruling elites of democracies, lacking such power, accomplish the same purpose by manipulating the media through the selective release of information, withholding what they desire "in the interest of national security." But just as coercion has its limits, so does the control of information—especially given the new technology of satellite communications, e-mail, and the Internet, a technology that pays no respect to international borders.

Technology The elite's desire to preserve its position is aided by recent developments in technology, especially monitoring devices. These devices—from "hot telephones," taps that turn your telephone into a microphone even when it is off the hook, to machines that can read the entire contents of your computer without leaving a trace—help the elite monitor citizens' activities without their even being aware that they are being shadowed. Dictatorships have few checks on how such technology will be employed, but in democracies, checks and balances, such as constitutional rights and the necessity of court orders, at least partially curb their use.

Social Networks Also crucial for maintaining stratification are social networks—the social ties that link people together (Higley et al. 1991). As discussed in Chapter 6, social networks—contacts that extend outward from the individual, gradually encompassing more and more people—supply valuable information and tend to perpetuate social inequality. In the Perspectives box on page 160, we discussed how even our own social networks help to perpetuate social stratification. Sociologist William Domhoff (1990, 1998) has documented how members of the elite move in a circle of power that multiplies their opportunities. Contacts with people of similar backgrounds, interests, and goals allow the elite to pass privileges from one generation to the next. In contrast, the social networks of the poor perpetuate poverty and powerlessness.

■ **In Sum** Underlying the maintenance of stratification is control of a society's institutions. In a dictatorship, the elite makes the laws. In a democracy, it influences the laws. In both, the legal establishment enforces the laws. The elite also commands the police and military and can give orders to crush a rebellion—or even to run the post office or air traffic control if workers strike. As noted, force has its limits, and a nation's elite generally finds it preferable to maintain its stratification system by peaceful means, especially by influencing the thinking of its people.

COMPARATIVE SOCIAL STRATIFICATION

Now that we have examined different systems of social stratification and considered why stratification is universal, let's compare social stratification in Great Britain and in the former Soviet Union.

Social Stratification in Great Britain

Great Britain is often called England by Americans, but England is only one of the countries that make up the island of Great Britain. The others are Scotland and Wales. In addition, Northern Ireland is part of the United Kingdom of Great Britain and Northern Ireland.

Like other industrialized countries, Great Britain has a class system that can be divided into a lower, middle, and upper class. A little over half the population is in the lower or working class, while close to half the population is in the nation's very large middle class. A tiny upper class, perhaps 1 percent of the population, is powerful, highly educated, and extremely wealthy.

Compared with Americans, the British are extremely class conscious. Like Americans, the British recognize class distinctions on the basis of the type of car a person drives, or the stores a person patronizes. But the most striking characteristics of the British class system are language and education. Differences in speech have a powerful impact on British life. Accent almost always betrays class, and as soon as someone speaks, the listener is aware of that person's class—and treats him or her accordingly (Sullivan 1998).

Education is the primary way by which the British perpetuate their class system from one generation to the next. Almost all children go to neighborhood schools, but the children of Great Britain's more privileged 5 percent—who own *half* the nation's wealth—attend exclusive private boarding schools (known as "public" schools), where they are trained in subjects considered "proper" for members of the ruling class. An astounding 50 percent of the students at Oxford and Cambridge, the country's most prestigious universities, come from this 5 percent of the population. To illustrate how powerfully this system of stratified education affects the national life of Great Britain, sociologist Ian Robertson (1987) says,

> [E]ighteen former pupils of the most exclusive of them, Eton, have become prime minister. Imagine the chances of a single American high school producing eighteen presidents!

Social Stratification in the Former Soviet Union

Vladimir Ilyich Lenin (1870–1924) and Leon Trotsky (1879–1940) heeded Karl Marx's call for a classless society. They led a revolution in Russia to bring this about. They, and the nations that followed their banner, never claimed to have achieved the ideal of communism, in which all contribute their labor to the common good and receive according to their needs. Instead, they used the term *socialism* to describe the intermediate step between capitalism and communism, in which social classes are abolished but some individual inequality remains.

The socialist nations often manipulated the world's mass media in order to tweak the nose of Uncle Sam, stressing the glaring inequalities of the United States. They, too, however, were marked by huge disparities in privilege—much more than they ever acknowledged to the outside world. Their major basis of stratification—membership in the Communist party—often was the determining factor in deciding who would gain admission to the better schools or obtain the more desirable jobs. The equally qualified son or daughter of a nonmember would be turned down, for such privileges came with demonstrated loyalty to the Party.

Divided into three layers, even the Communist party was highly stratified. Most members occupied a low level, having such assignments as spying on other workers. For their services, they might be given easier jobs in the factory or occasional access to special stores to purchase hard-to-find goods. A smaller number were mid-level bureaucrats with better than average access to resources and privileges. The top level consisted of a small elite: party members who enjoyed not only power but also limousines, imported delicacies, vacation homes, and even servants and hunting lodges. As with other stratification systems around the world, women held lower positions in the Party, as was readily evident in each year's May Day photos of the top members of the Party reviewing the weapons paraded in Moscow's Red Square. The top officials were always men. They still are.

Russia's recent reluctant embrace of capitalism has brought many changes. Advertising in order to create demand for products is one new development. The stark contrast now evident between the social classes is another.

Rather than eliminating social classes, then, the Communist revolution merely ushered in a different set of classes. An elite continued to rule from the top. Before the revolution this elite was based on lineage and inherited wealth; afterward it consisted of top party officials. Below this elite was a small middle class consisting of white-collar and other skilled workers. At the bottom was a mass of peasants and unskilled workers—just as there was before the revolution.

The leaders of the USSR grew frustrated as they saw the West thrive. They struggled with a bloated bureaucracy, the gross inefficiencies of central planning, workers who did the minimum because they could not be fired and they received no bonus for being efficient, and a military so costly that it spent one of every eight of the nation's rubles (*Statistical Abstract* 1993:1432). Their ideology did not call for their citizens to be deprived, and in an attempt to turn things around, the Soviet leadership initiated reforms. They sold the public huge chunks of state-owned businesses and allowed elections with more than one candidate for an office. (Prior to this, voters had a choice of one candidate per office!) With the transition to private investment and ownership, making a profit changed from being a crime to being a respectable goal.

The transition to capitalism has taken a bizarre twist. As authority broke down, some Russians saw a chance to gain wealth and power by forming criminal groups. These groups are headed by gangsters, corrupt government officials, and crooked businessmen. Many are advised by former KGB (Russian secret police) agents. This new Russian Mafia is ruthless; they assassinate heads of banks and other business leaders who refuse to cooperate with them (Bernstein 1994; Goble 1996; Finckenauer and Waring 1999). They have stolen vast amounts of state property and moved much of their wealth to offshore banks. Their enterprise and ruthlessness have propelled them to success, and they now control more than half of Russia's economy (Foster 1998). Russia's "wild west" days are bound to disappear as the central government reestablishes its authority. At that time, this group of organized criminals will likely take its place in Russia's new capitalist class.

GLOBAL STRATIFICATION: THREE WORLDS

As noted at the beginning of this chapter, just as the people within a nation are stratified by power, prestige, and property, so are the world's nations. Until recently, a simple model consisting of First, Second, and Third Worlds was used to depict global stratification. *First World* referred to the industrialized capitalist nations, *Second World* to the communist nations, and *Third World* to any nation that did not fit into the first two categories. After the Soviet Union broke up in 1989, these terms became outdated. In addition, although *first, second,* and *third* did not mean "best," "better," and "worst," they sounded like it. An alternative classification some now use—developed, developing, and undeveloped nations—has the same drawback. By calling ourselves "developed," it sounds as though we are mature, and the "undeveloped" nations somehow retarded.

Consequently, I have chosen more neutral, descriptive terms: *Most Industrialized, Industrializing,* and *Least Industrialized Nations.* One can measure industrialization, with no judgment implied as to whether a nation's industrialization represents "development," ranks it "first, "or is even desirable at all.

The intention is to depict on a global level social stratification's three primary dimensions: property, power, and prestige. The Most Industrialized Nations have much greater property (wealth), power (they do get their way in international relations), and prestige (rightly or wrongly, they are looked up to as world leaders and viewed as having something worthwhile to contribute to humanity). The three families sketched in the opening vignette illustrate the far-reaching effects of global stratification on the citizens of this world.

The Most Industrialized Nations

The Most Industrialized Nations are the United States and Canada in North America; Great Britain, France, Germany, Switzerland, and the other industrialized nations of western Europe; Japan in Asia; and Australia and New Zealand in the area of the world known as Oceania. Although there are variations in their economic systems, these nations are capitalistic. As Table 9.2 shows, although these nations have only 16 percent of the world's people, they have 31 percent of the earth's land. Their wealth is so enormous that even their poor live better and longer lives than do the average citizens of the Least Industrialized Nations. The Social Map on the next two pages shows the tremendous disparities in income among the world's nations.

The Industrializing Nations

The Industrializing Nations include most of the nations of the former Soviet Union and its former satellites in eastern Europe. As Table 9.2 shows, these nations account for 20 percent of the earth's land and 16 percent of its people.

Table 9.2

DISTRIBUTION OF THE WORLD'S LAND AND POPULATION

	Land	Population
Most Industrialized Nations	31%	16%
Industrializing Nations	20%	16%
Least Industrialized Nations	49%	68%

Sources: Computed from Kurian 1990, 1991, 1992.

The Most Industrialized Nations

	Nation	Income per Person
1	Switzerland	$43,060
2	Luxembourg	$41,200
3	Japan	$38,160
4	Norway	$36,100
5	Singapore	$32,810
6	United States	$29,080
7	Germany	$28,280
8	Austria	$27,920
9	Belgium	$26,730
10	France	$26,300
11	Sweden	$26,210
12	Netherlands	$25,830
13	Hong Kong	$25,200
14	Iceland	$25,000
15	Finland	$24,790
16	United Kingdom	$20,870
17	Australia	$20,650
18	Italy	$20,170
19	Canada	$19,640
20	Ireland	$17,790
21	Denmark	$16,637
22	Israel	$16,180
23	New Zealand	$15,830
24	Taiwan	$14,700

The Industrializing Nations

	Nation	Income per Person
25	Spain	$14,490
26	Greece	$11,640
27	Portugal	$11,010
28	South Korea	$10,550
29	Slovenia	$9,840
30	Malta	$9,330
31	Argentina	$8,950
32	Seychelles	$6,910
33	Colombia*	$6,200
34	Uruguay	$6,130
35	Czech Republic	$5,240
36	Chile	$4,820
37	Brazil	$4,790
38	Malaysia	$4,530
39	Hungary	$4,510
40	Mexico	$3,700
41	Slovakia	$3,680
42	Poland	$3,590
43	Venezuela	$3,480
44	South Africa	$3,210
45	Turkey	$3,130
46	Thailand	$2,740
47	Russia	$2,680

*Income listed for Colombia is so much greater than previous years that I assume it now includes the country's cocaine industry.

The Oil-Rich Nations

	Nation	Income per Person
164	United Arab Emirates	$23,800
165	Qatar	$21,300
166	Kuwait	$17,000
167	Bahrain	$13,000
168	Oman	$9,500
169	Saudi Arabia	$7,150
170	Libya	$6,570

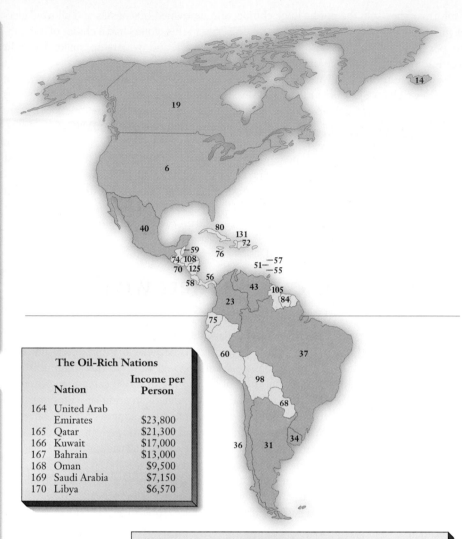

The Least Industrialized Nations

	Nation	Income per Person		Nation	Income per Person
48	Gabon	$4,120	68	Paraguay	$2,000
49	Croatia	$4,060	69	Fed. States of Micronesia	$1,920
50	Mauritius	$3,870	70	El Salvador	$1,810
51	Saint Lucia	$3,510	71	Iran	$1,780
52	Estonia	$3,360	72	Dominacan Republic	$1,750
53	Lebanon	$3,350	73	Marshall Islands	$1,610
54	Botswana	$3,310	74	Guatemala	$1,580
55	Grenada	$3,140	75	Ecuador	$1,570
56	Panama	$3,080	76	Jamaica	$1,550
57	Dominica	$3,040	77	Swaziland	$1,520
58	Costa Rica	$2,680	78	Jordan	$1,510
59	Belize	$2,670	79	Algeria	$1,500
60	Peru	$2,610	80	Cuba	$1,480
61	Fiji	$2,460	81	Romania	$1,410
62	Lativa	$2,430	82	Kazakstan	$1,350
63	Lithuania	$2,260	83	Vanuatu	$1,340
64	Belarus	$2,150	84	Suriname	$1,320
65	Namibia	$2,110	85	Philippines	$1,200
66	Tunisia	$2,110	86	Morocco	$1,260
67	Iraq	$2,000			

𝓕𝓲𝓰𝓾𝓻𝓮 9.2 **SOCIAL MAP: GLOBAL STRATIFICATION: INCOME* OF THE WORLDS' NATIONS**

*Income is the country's per capita gross national product measured in U.S. dollars. Since some totals vary widely from year to year, they must be taken as approximate.

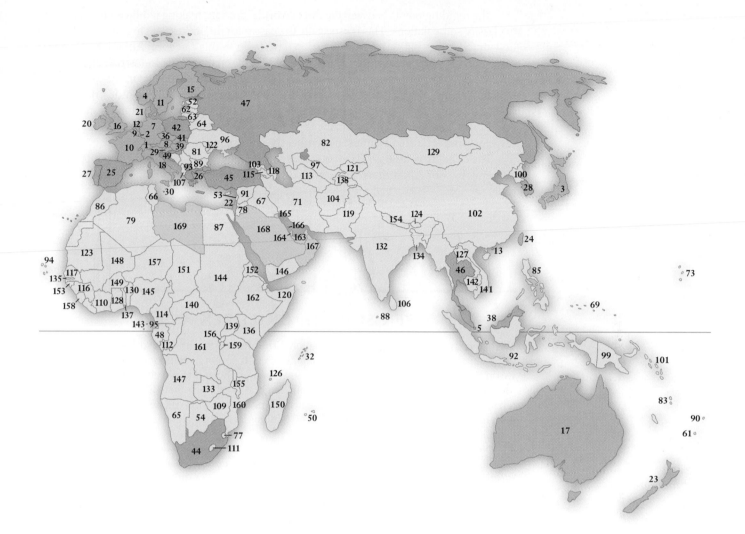

The Least Industrialized Nations

Nation	Income per Person	Nation	Income per Person	Nation	Income per Person	Nation	Income per Person
87 Egypt	$1,200	106 Sri Lanka	$800	127 Laos	$400	146 Yemen	$270
88 Maldives	$1,180	107 Albania	$760	128 Ghana	$390	147 Angola	$260
89 Bulgaria	$1,170	108 Honduras	$740	129 Mongolia	$390	148 Mali	$260
90 Western Samoa	$1,140	109 Zimbabwe	$720	130 Benin	$380	149 Burkina Faso	$250
91 Syria	$1,120	110 Cote d'Ivoire	$710	131 Haiti	$380	150 Madagascar	$250
92 Indonesia	$1,110	111 Lesotho	$680	132 India	$370	151 Chad	$230
93 Macedonia	$1,100	112 Congo	$670	133 Zambia	$370	152 Eritrea	$230
94 Cape Verde	$1,090	113 Turkmenistan	$640	134 Bangladesh	$360	153 Guinea-Bissau	$230
95 Equatorial Guinea	$1,060	114 Cameroon	$620	135 Gambia	$340	154 Nepal	$220
96 Ukraine	$1,040	115 Armenia	$560	136 Kenya	$340	155 Malawi	$210
97 Uzbekistan	$1,020	116 Guinea	$550	137 Togo	$340	156 Rwanda	$210
98 Bolivia	$970	117 Senegal	$540	138 Tajikistan	$330	157 Niger	$200
99 Papua-New Guinea	$930	118 Azerbaijan	$510	139 Uganda	$330	158 Sierra Leone	$170
100 North Korea	$900	119 Pakistan	$500	140 Central African Republic	$320	159 Burundi	$140
101 Solomon Islands	$870	120 Somalia	$500	141 Vietnam	$310	160 Mozambique	$140
102 China	$860	121 Kyrgystan	$480	142 Cambodia	$300	161 Congo, Democratic Republic of	$110
103 Georgia	$860	122 Moldova	$460	143 Sao Tome and Principe	$290	162 Ethiopia	$110
104 Afghanistan	$800	123 Mauritania	$440	144 Sudan	$290		
105 Guyana	$800	124 Bhutan	$430	145 Nigeria	$280		
		125 Nicaragua	$410				
		126 Comoros	$400				

Sources: Haub and Cornelius 1999 (except Famighetti 1999 for Afghanistan, Bahrain, Cuba, Iceland, Iraq, Libya, Luxembourg, North Korea, Oman, Qatar, Somalia, Taiwan, and the United Arab Emirates).

The dividing points between the three "worlds" are soft, making it difficult to know how to classify some nations. This is especially the case with the Industrializing Nations. Exactly how much industrialization must a nation have to be in this category? Although soft, these categories do pinpoint essential differences. Most inhabitants of the Industrializing Nations have much lower incomes and standards of living than people who live in the Most Industrialized Nations. Most, however, are better off than members of the Least Industrialized Nations. For example, on such measures as access to electricity, indoor plumbing, automobiles, telephones, and even food, citizens of the Industrializing Nations rank lower than those in the Most Industrialized Nations, but higher than those in the Least Industrialized Nations.

The benefits of industrialization are uneven. Large numbers of people are illiterate and desperately poor. Conditions can be gruesome, as discussed in the following Thinking Critically section.

Thinking *Critically*

OPEN SEASON: CHILDREN AS PREY

What is childhood like in the poor nations? The answer depends primarily on who your parents are. If you are the son or daughter of rich parents, childhood can be pleasant—a world filled with luxuries, and even servants. If you are born into poverty, but living in a rural area where there is plenty to eat, life can still be good—although there likely will be no books, television, and little education. If you live in a slum, however, life can be horrible—worse even than in the slums of the Most Industrialized Nations. Let's take a glance at what is happening to children in the slums of Brazil.

Not having enough food, this you would find no surprise—as well as broken homes, alcoholism, drug abuse, and a high crime rate. From your knowledge of slums in the Most Industrialized Nations, you would expect these things. What you may not expect, however, are the brutal conditions in which Brazilian slum *(favela)* children live.

Sociologist Martha Huggins (1993) reports that poverty is so deep that children and adults swarm over garbage dumps to try to find enough decaying food to keep them alive. And you

Poverty in the Least Industrialized Nations is so severe that some families survive by picking through garbage. This photo from Rio de Janeiro, Brazil, shows some of the 600 people whose survival depends on plucking from the city's dump any bit or piece that seems even remotely reusable.

might be surprised to discover that in Brazil the owners of these dumps hire armed guards to keep the poor out—so they can sell the garbage for pig food. And you might be shocked to learn that poor children are systematically killed. Each year, the Brazilian police and death squads murder about 2,000 children. Some associations of shop owners even put hit men on retainer and auction victims off to the lowest bidder! The going rate is half a month's salary—figured at the low Brazilian minimum wage.

Life is cheap in the poor nations—but death squads for children? To understand this, we must first note that Brazil has a long history of violence. Brazil also has a high rate of poverty, only a tiny middle class, and is controlled by a small group of families who, under a veneer of democracy, make the country's major decisions. Hordes of homeless children, with no schools or jobs, roam the streets. To survive, these street children wash windshields, shine shoes, beg, and steal. These children, part of the "dangerous classes," as they are known, threaten the status quo.

The "respectable" classes see these children as nothing but trouble. They hurt business, for customers feel uncomfortable or intimidated when they see a group of begging children clustered in front of stores. Some shoplift; others dare to sell items that place them in competition with the stores. With no social institutions to care for these children, one solution is to kill them. As Huggins notes, murder sends a clear message—especially if it is accompanied by ritual torture—gouging out the eyes, ripping open the chest, cutting off the genitals, raping the girls, and burning the victim's body.

Not all life is bad in the poor nations, but this is about as bad as it gets. ■

The extent and depth of poverty in the Least Industrialized Nations is stunning to someone who has grown up in a Most Industrialized Nation. Like millions of other people in Indonesia, this woman lives in a shack made of discarded materials. How do you think her chances of escaping from poverty compare with those of the U.S. poor? Why the difference?

For Your Consideration

Do you think there is anything the Most Industrialized Nations can do about this situation? Or is it any of their business? Is it, though unfortunate, just an "internal" affair that is up to the Brazilians to handle as they wish?

The Least Industrialized Nations

In the Least Industrialized Nations, most people are peasant farmers living on farms or in villages. These nations account for 49 percent of the earth's land and 68 percent of the world's people.

It is difficult to imagine the poverty that plagues the Least Industrialized Nations. In Luanda, the capital of Angola, for example, skinny street children live in sewers (McNeil 1999). Although wealthy nations have their pockets of poverty, *most* people in these nations live on less than $1,000 a year, in many cases considerably less. Most of them have no running water, indoor plumbing, central water supply, or access to trained physicians. Because modern medicine has cut infant mortality but not births, the population of most of these nations is growing quickly. This places even greater burdens on their limited facilities, causing them to fall farther behind each year. The twin specters of poverty and death at an early age stalk these countries.

Modifying the Model

This classification of nations into Most Industrialized, Industrializing, and Least Industrialized is helpful in that it pinpoints gross differences among them. But it also presents problems. As mentioned, just how much industrialization does a nation need in order to be classified as Most Industrialized or Industrializing? Also, in Chapter 6 we noted that several nations have become "postindustrial." Does this new stage require a separate classification?

Table 9.3

AN ALTERNATIVE MODEL OF GLOBAL STRATIFICATION

Four Worlds of Development

1. Most Industrialized Nations
2. Industrializing Nations
3. Least Industrialized Nations
4. Oil-rich, nonindustrialized nations

Finally, the oil-rich nations of the Middle East are not industrialized, but by providing the oil and gasoline that fuel the machinery of the Most Industrialized Nations, they have become immensely wealthy. Consequently, to classify them simply as Least Industrialized glosses over significant distinctions, such as their modern hospitals, extensive prenatal care, pure water systems, abundant food and shelter, high literacy, and even computerized banking (see the Social Map on pages 244–245).

Kuwait, on whose formal behalf the United States and other Most Industrialized Nations fought Iraq in the Gulf War, is an excellent example of the problem. Kuwait is so wealthy that almost none of its citizens are employed. The government simply pays them a generous annual salary just for being citizens. Migrant workers from the poor nations do most of the onerous chores that daily life requires, while highly skilled workers from the Most Industrialized Nations run the specialized systems that keep Kuwait's economy going— and, as with the Gulf War, apparently fight its wars for it as well. Table 9.3 reflects this significant distinction.

How the World's Nations Became Stratified

How did the globe become stratified into such distinct worlds of development? The obvious answer is that the poorer nations have fewer resources than the richer nations. As with so many other "obvious" answers, however, this one, too, falls short, for many of the Industrializing and Least Industrialized Nations are rich in natural resources, while one Most Industrialized Nation, Japan, has few. Four competing theories explain how global stratification came about.

Colonialism

The first theory, **colonialism,** focuses on how the nations that industrialized first got the jump on the rest of the world. Beginning in Great Britain about 1750, industrialization spread throughout western Europe. Plowing some of their immense profits into powerful armaments and fast ships, these nations invaded weaker nations, making colonies out of them (Harrison 1993). After subduing them, the more powerful nations left behind a controlling force in order to exploit their labor and natural resources. At one point, there was even a free-for-all among the industrialized European nations as they frantically rushed to divide up an entire continent. As Africa was sliced into pieces, even tiny Belgium got into the act and acquired the Congo, which was *seventy-five* times larger than itself.

Whereas the more powerful European nations would plant their national flags in a colony and send their representatives to run the government directly, the United States, after it industrialized, usually chose to plant corporate flags in a colony and let these corporations dominate the territory's government. Central and South America are prime examples of such U.S. "economic colonies." No matter what the form, and whether it was benevolent or harsh, the purpose was the same—to exploit the nation's people and resources for the benefit of the "mother" country.

Colonialism, then, shaped many of the Least Industrialized Nations. In some instances, the Most Industrialized Nations were so powerful that to divide their spoils, they drew lines across a map, creating new states without regard for tribal or cultural considerations (Kifner 1999). Britain and France did just this in North Africa and parts of the Middle East, which is why the national boundaries of Libya, Saudi Arabia, Kuwait, and other nations are so straight. This legacy of European conquests still erupts into tribal violence, because tribes with no history of national identity were arbitrarily incorporated into the same political boundaries.

World System Theory

To explain how global stratification developed, Immanuel Wallerstein (1974, 1979, 1984, 1990) proposed a **world system** theory. Since the 1500s, he said, the economic and polit-

colonialism the process by which one nation takes over another nation, usually for the purpose of exploiting its labor and natural resources

world system economic and political connections that tie the world's countries together

ical connections between nations have been expanding. Today, they tie most of the world's countries together.

Wallerstein identified four groups of interconnected nations. The first group is the *core nations*, those that industrialized first (Britain, France, Holland, and later Germany). These nations grew rich and powerful. The second group, the nations around the Mediterranean, are called the *semi-periphery*. Their economies stagnated because they grew dependent on trade with the core nations. The third group, the *periphery*, or fringe, consists of the eastern European countries. Because they mainly sold cash crops to the core nations, their economies developed even less. The fourth group, the *external area*, includes most of Africa and Asia. These nations were left out of the development of capitalism and had few economic connections with the core nations.

Capitalism's relentless expansion has given birth to a **capitalist world economy,** which is dominated by the Most Industrialized Nations. This economy is so all-encompassing that today even the nations in the external area are being drawn into its commercial web.

The world's people always have been part of an interconnected system of water and air, and, ultimately, part of a food chain. Now they also are interconnected by a global system of telecommunications. This photo was taken in Riyash, the capital of Saudi Arabia, at an Internet cafe called The Rendezvous.

Globalization This extensive movement of capital and ideas among the nations of the world ushered in by the expansion of capitalism is called **globalization** (Kanter 1997; Soysa and Oneal 1999). Although globalization has been under way for several hundred years, today's new forms of communication and transportation have greatly speeded it up. The interconnections have grown so extensive that events in remote parts of the world now affect us all—sometimes immediately, as when a revolution interrupts the flow of raw materials, or, perish the thought, if in Russia's unstable political climate terrorists manage to seize an arsenal of earth-destroying nuclear missiles. At other times, the effects arrive like a slow ripple, as when a government's policies impede its ability to compete in world markets. All of today's societies, then, no matter where they are located, are part of a global social system.

Dependency Theory

The third theory is sometimes difficult to distinguish from world system theory. **Dependency theory** stresses how the Least Industrialized Nations grew dependent on the Most Industrialized Nations (Cardoso 1972; Furtado 1984). According to this theory, the first nations to industrialize turned other nations into their plantations and mines, harvesting or extracting whatever they needed to meet their growing appetite for raw materials and exotic foods. As a result, many of the Least Industrialized Nations began to specialize in a single cash crop. Brazil became the Most Industrialized Nations' giant coffee plantation. Nicaragua and other Central American countries specialized in bananas (hence the term *banana* republic). Chile became the primary source of tin, while Zaire (then the Belgian Congo) was transformed into a rubber plantation. And the Mideast nations were turned into gigantic oil wells. A major point of dependency theory is that the domination of the Least Industrialized Nations rendered them unable to develop independent economies.

Culture of Poverty

An entirely different explanation of global stratification was proposed by economist John Kenneth Galbraith (1979), who claimed that it was the Least Industrialized Nations' own cultures that held them back. Building on the ideas of anthropologist Oscar Lewis (1966a, 1966b), Galbraith argued that some nations are crippled by a **culture of poverty,** a way of life that perpetuates poverty from one generation to the next. He explained it in this way: Most of the world's poor live in rural areas, where they barely eke out a living from the land. Their marginal life offers little room for error or risk, so they tend to stick closely to tried-and-true,

capitalist world economy the dominance of capitalism in the world along with the international interdependence that capitalism has created

globalization the extensive movement of capital and ideas among nations due to the expansion of capitalism

dependency theory the view that the Least Industrialized Nations have been unable to develop their economies because they grew dependent on the Most Industrialized Nations

culture of poverty a culture that perpetuates poverty from one generation to the next

traditional ways. Experimenting with new farming or manufacturing techniques could be a disaster, for if they fail they bring hunger and death. Their religion also reinforces traditionalism, for it teaches fatalism, the acceptance of their lot in life as God's will.

Evaluating the Theories

Most sociologists prefer colonialism, world system theory, and dependency theory. To them, an explanation based on a culture of poverty places blame on the victim, the poor nations themselves. It points to characteristics of the poor nations, rather than to international arrangements that benefit the Most Industrialized Nations at the expense of the poor nations. But even taken together, these theories yield only part of the picture, as becomes evident from the example of Japan. None of these theories would lead anyone to expect that after World War II, Japan—which had a religion that stressed fatalism, which had two major cities destroyed by atomic bombs, and which had been stripped of its colonies—would become an economic powerhouse able to turn the Western world on its head.

Each theory, then, yields but a partial explanation, and the grand theorist who will put the many pieces of this puzzle together has yet to appear.

*M*AINTAINING GLOBAL STRATIFICATION

Regardless of how the world's nations became stratified, why do the same countries remain rich year after year, while the rest stay poor? Let's look at two explanations of how global stratification is maintained.

Neocolonialism

Sociologist Michael Harrington (1977) argued that colonialism fell out of style and was replaced by **neocolonialism.** When World War II changed public sentiment about sending soldiers and colonists to weaker countries, the Most Industrialized Nations turned to the international markets as a way to control the Least Industrialized Nations. These powerful nations determine how much they will pay for tin from Bolivia, copper from Peru, coffee from Brazil, and so forth. They also move hazardous industries into the Least Industrialized Nations.

As many of us to our sorrow learn, owing a large debt and falling behind on payments puts us at the mercy of our creditors. So it is with neocolonialism. The *policy* of selling weapons and other manufactured goods to the Least Industrialized Nations on credit turns those countries into eternal debtors. The capital they need to develop their own industries goes instead to the debt, which becomes increasingly bloated with mounting interest. As debtors, these nations also are vulnerable to trading terms dictated by the neocolonialists (Tordoff 1992; Carrington 1993).

Thus, although the Least Industrialized Nations have their own governments—whether elected or dictatorships—they remain almost as dependent on the Most Industrialized Nations as they were when those nations occupied them. For an example of neocolonialism today, see the Perspectives box.

Multinational Corporations

Multinational corporations, companies that operate across many national boundaries, also help to maintain the global dominance of the Most Industrialized Nations. In some cases, multinational corporations exploit the Least Industrialized Nations directly. A prime example is the United Fruit Company, which for decades controlled national and local politics in Central America. It ran these nations as fiefdoms for the company's own profit while the U.S. Marines waited in the wings in case the company's interests needed to be backed up. Most commonly, however, multinational corporations help to maintain international stratification simply by doing business. A single multinational may do mining in several countries, do manufacturing in many others, and run transportation and marketing networks

neocolonialism the economic and political dominance of the Least Industrialized Nations by the Most Industrialized Nations

multinational corporations companies that operate across many national boundaries; also called transnational corporations

PERSPECTIVES | Cultural Diversity Around the World

SEX TOURISM AND THE PATRIOTIC PROSTITUTE

Holidays with the most beautiful women of the world. An exclusive tour by Life Travel. . . . You fly to Bangkok and then go to Pattaya. . . . Slim, sunburnt and sweet, they . . . are masters in the art of making love by nature, an art we European people do not know. . . . In Pattaya costs of living and loving are low. (from a Swiss pamphlet)

Some travel agencies promote sex tourism—travel for the purpose of exotic sex or for types of sex that are forbidden in the home country. Sex with children in Thailand and Tokyo is especially popular (Dickey 1996; Reitman 1996).

A related development is the "patriotic prostitute." These are young women who are encouraged by their governments to prostitute themselves to help their country's economy. Patriotic prostitution is one of the seediest aspects of global stratification. Some poor countries encourage prostitution to accumulate national income for industrial development and to help pay their national debts. A consequence is that perhaps 10 percent of all Thai women between the ages of 15 and 30 have become prostitutes. Bangkok alone reports 100,000 prostitutes—plus 200,000 "masséuses."

Government officials encourage prostitution as a service to their country. In South Korea, prostitutes are issued identification cards that serve as hotel passes. In orientation sessions, they are told, "Your carnal conversations [sic] with foreign tourists do not prostitute either yourself or the nation, but express your heroic patriotism." With such an official blessing, sex tourism has become big business. Travel agencies in Germany openly advertise "trips to Thailand with erotic pleasures included in the price." Japan Air Lines hands out brochures that advertise the "charming

attractions" of Kisaeng girls, advising men to fly JAL for a "night spent with a consummate Kisaeng girl dressed in a gorgeous Korean blouse and skirt."

What the enticing advertising fails to mention is the misery underlying this prostitution. Many of the prostitutes are held in bondage. Some are only children. Some have been sold by their families to pimps; others have been kidnapped. Some are kept under lock and key to keep them from escaping. The advertisements also fail to mention AIDS. Somewhere between 25 percent and 50 percent of Nairobi's 10,000 prostitutes appear to be infected.

Women's groups have protested this international sex trade, deploring its exploitation of the world's most impoverished and underprivileged women. Some changes are apparent, notably concerning sex with children. The United States has passed a law that U.S. citizens cannot have sex with children, even if it is tolerated in the host country. Europeans who are flying to Thailand now find something extra in their tickets: warning notices about the child sex trade.

What do you think should be done?

Sources: Based on Gay 1985; O'Malley 1988; Hornblower 1993; Son 1995; Seabrook 1997; Kempadoo 2000.

---

around the globe. No matter where the profits are made, or where they are reinvested, the primary beneficiaries are the Most Industrialized Nations, especially the one in which the multinational corporation has its world headquarters. As Michael Harrington (1977) stressed, the real profits are made in processing the products and in controlling their distribution—and these profits are withheld from the Least Industrialized Nations. For more on multinational corporations, see pages 400–404.

Multinational corporations try to work closely with the elite of the Least Industrialized Nations (Lipton 1979; Waldman 1995a). This elite, which lives a sophisticated upper-class life in the major cities of its home country, sends its children to Oxford, the Sorbonne, or Harvard to be educated. The multinational corporations funnel investments to this small circle of power, whose members favor projects such as building laboratories and computer centers in the capital city, projects that do not help the vast majority of their people, who live in poor, remote villages where they eke out meager livings on small plots of land.

The end result is an informal partnership between multinational corporations and the elite of the Least Industrialized Nations. To gain access to the country's raw materials, labor, and market, the corporations pay off the elite. (These are politely called "subsidies," not bribes.) The elite use their payoffs not only to maintain their genteel lifestyle, but also to purchase high-powered weapons from multinational corporations, which they use to oppress their people and maintain their dominance. Both elites and corporations benefit through political stability, which is necessary for keeping their diabolical partnership alive.

This, however, is not the full story. Multinational corporations also play a role in changing international stratification. This is an unintentional by-product of their worldwide search for cheap resources and labor. By moving manufacturing from the Most Industrialized Nations to the Least Industrialized Nations, they not only exploit cheap labor but in some cases also bring prosperity to those nations. Although workers in the Least Industrialized Nations are paid a pittance, it is more than they can earn elsewhere. With new factories come opportunities to develop new skills and a capital base. This does not occur in all nations, but the Pacific Rim nations, nicknamed the "Asian tigers," are a remarkable case in point. They have developed such a strong capital base that they have begun to rival the older capitalist nations. As became painfully apparent with a severe currency crisis and economic downturn in these countries, they also are subject to capitalism's infamous "boom and bust" cycles.

Technology and Global Domination

The race between the Most and Least Industrialized Nations to develop and apply the new information technologies is like a race between a marathon runner and a one-legged man. Can the outcome be in doubt? The vast profits piled up by the multinational corporations allow the Most Industrialized Nations to invest huge sums in the latest technology. Gillette, for example, spent $100 million simply to adjust its output "on an hourly basis" (Zachary 1995). These millions came from just one U.S. company. Many Least Industrialized Nations would love to have $100 million to invest in their entire economy, much less to use for fine-tuning the production of razor blades. In short, in the quest to maintain global domination, the new technologies pile up even more advantages for the Most Industrialized Nations.

A CONCLUDING NOTE

Let's go back to the three families in the chapter's opening vignette. Remember that these families represent distinct worlds of development, that is, global stratification. Their life chances—from access to material possessions to the opportunity for education and even the likely age at which they will die—are profoundly affected by the global stratification reviewed in this chapter. This division of the globe into interconnected units of nations with more or less wealth and more or less power and prestige, then, is much more than a matter of theoretical interest. In fact, it is *your* life we are talking about.

SUMMARY AND REVIEW

■ What Is Social Stratification?

The term **social stratification** refers to a hierarchy of relative privilege based on power, property, and prestige. Every society stratifies its members. P. 228.

■ Systems of Social Stratification

What are four major systems of social stratification?

Four major stratification systems are slavery, caste, estate, and class. The essential characteristic of **slavery** is that some people own other people. Initially, slavery was based not on race but on debt, punishment, or defeat in battle. Slavery could be temporary

or permanent, and was not necessarily passed on to one's children. North American slaves had no legal rights, and the system was gradually buttressed by a racist ideology. In a **caste system,** status is determined by birth and is lifelong. People marry within their own group and develop rules about ritual pollution. The **estate system** of feudal Europe consisted of the nobility, clergy, and commoners. A **class system** is much more open than these other systems, for it is based primarily on money or material possessions. Industrialization encourages the formation of class systems. Gender discrimination cuts across all forms of social stratification. Pp. 229–235.

■ What Determines Social Class?

Karl Marx argued that a single factor determines social class: If you own the **means of production,** you belong to the **bourgeoisie;** if you do not, you are one of the **proletariat.** Max Weber argued that three elements determine social class: *property, prestige,* and *power.* Pp. 235–237.

■ Why Is Social Stratification Universal?

To explain why stratification is universal, functionalists Kingsley Davis and Wilbert Moore argued that in order to attract the most capable people to fill its important positions, society must offer them higher rewards. Melvin Tumin criticized this view, arguing that if it were correct, society would be a **meritocracy,** with all positions awarded on the basis of merit. Gaetano Mosca argued that stratification is inevitable because every society must have leadership, which by definition means inequality. Conflict theorists argue that stratification comes about because resources are limited, and groups struggle against one another for them. Gerhard Lenski suggested a synthesis between the functionalist and conflict perspectives. Pp. 237–239.

■ How Do Elites Maintain Stratification?

To maintain social stratification within a nation, the ruling class uses an ideology that justifies current arrangements. It also controls information, and, when all else fails, depends on brute force. The social networks of the rich and poor also perpetuate social inequality. Pp. 240–241.

■ Comparative Social Stratification

What are some key characteristics of stratification systems in other nations?

The most striking features of the British class system are differences in speech and in educational patterns. In Britain, accent reveals class standing, and virtually all of the elite attend "public" schools (the equivalent of our private schools). In what is now the former Soviet Union, communism was supposed to abolish class distinctions. Instead, it merely ushered in a different set of classes. Pp. 241–243.

■ Global Stratification: Three Worlds

How are the world's nations stratified?

The model presented here divides the world's nations into three groups: the Most Industrialized, the Industrializing, and the Least Industrialized. This layering represents relative property, power, and prestige. The oil-rich nations are an exception. Pp. 243–248.

■ How the World's Nations Became Stratified

Why are some nations rich and others poor?

The main theories that seek to account for global stratification are **colonialism, world system theory, dependency theory,** and the **culture of poverty.** Pp. 248–250.

■ Maintaining Global Stratification

How is global stratification maintained?

There are two basic explanations for why nations remain stratified. **Neocolonialism** is the ongoing dominance of the Least Industrialized Nations by the Most Industrialized Nations. The second explanation points to the influence of **multinational corporations,** which operate across national boundaries. The new technology gives further advantage to the Most Industrialized Nations. Pp. 250–252.

Where can I read more on this topic?

Suggested readings for this chapter are at the end of this book.

All URLs listed are current as of the printing of this book. URLs often change. Please check our Web site, **http://www.abacon.com/ henslin,** for updates.

1. The text mentions slavery in the Sudan, Mauritania, and Benin. Examine the site created by the Coalition Against Slavery in Mauritania and Sudan at **http://members.aol.com/casmasalc.** The controversy surrounding the practice of purchasing the freedom of captives is discussed at **http://www.religioustolerance.org/ sla_sud.htm.** You can gain a picture of slavery worldwide by visiting **http://www.antislavery.org** and **http://www.channel1. com/~aasg.** What issues lie at the heart of modern slavery? Who is being enslaved? Why? What can be done to stop the slavery? Finally, discuss how modern slavery is different from and similar to historical slavery in the U.S.

2. Many people believe that the United States is a meritocracy. The Web site at **http://www2.theatlantic.com/atlantic/unbound/ aandc/trnscrpt/lemtest.htm** has an online conference with Nicholas Lemann about merit in our society. After reading this conference, answer these questions: Do you think we have a meritocracy? What are some of the problems associated with measuring merit and aptitude using standardized tests? How can we accurately measure merit and aptitude? What other issues are involved in the discussion about meritocracy?

3. You have read about the influence of multinational corporations on the maintenance of global stratification. Multinational corporations exploit the Least Industrialized Nations both directly and indirectly. Browse through this Web site: **http://www.essential. org/EI.html.** Founded by Ralph Nader, Essential Organization is a nonprofit, tax-exempt organization that is involved in projects designed to encourage citizens to become active in their communities, including the "Multinational Monitor" and the "Multinationals Resource Center." Describe the issues concerning multinational corporations. What are some of the global concerns about multinational corporations? How can citizens become involved in the fight against global stratification and multinational domination and exploitation?

c h a p t e r

10

Social Class in the United States

■ **What Is Social Class?**
Wealth
Power
Prestige
Status Inconsistency

■ **Sociological Models of Social Class**
Updating Marx
Updating Weber
Social Class in the Automobile Industry

■ **Consequences of Social Class**
Physical Health
Mental Health
Family Life
Education
Religion
Politics
Crime and the Criminal Justice System
The New Technology

■ **Social Mobility**
Three Types of Social Mobility
Women in Studies on Social Mobility
The New Technology and Fears of the Future
The Pain of Social Mobility

■ **Poverty**
Drawing the Poverty Line
Who Are the Poor?
Children of Poverty
The Dynamics of Poverty
Why Are People Poor?
Welfare Reform
Deferred Gratification
Where Is Horatio Alger? The Social Functions
   of a Myth

■ **Summary and Review**

Ah, New Orleans, that fabled city on the Gulf. Images from its rich past floated through my head—pirates, wealth, intrigue. Memories from a pleasant vacation stirred my thoughts—the exotic French Quarter with its enticing aroma of Creole food and sounds of earthy jazz drifting through the air.

The shelter for the homeless, however, forced me back to an unwelcome reality. The shelter was the same as those I had visited in the North, West, and East—only dirtier. The dirt, in fact, was the worst that I had encountered during my research, and this shelter was the only one to insist on payment in exchange for sleeping in one of its filthy beds.

The men looked the same—disheveled and haggard, wearing that unmistakable expression of despair—just like the homeless anywhere in the country. Except for the accent, you wouldn't know what region of the country you were in. Poverty wears the same tired face, I realized. The accent may differ, but the look remains the same.

The next morning, I felt indignation swell within me. I had grown used to the sights and smells of abject poverty. Those no longer surprised me. But now, just a block or so from the shelter, I was startled by a sight so out of step with the misery and despair I had just experienced that I stopped in midtrack.

I was confronted by life-size, full-color photos that were mounted on the transparent plastic shelter covering a bus stop. Staring back at me were finely dressed men and women proudly strutting about as they modeled elegant suits, dresses, diamonds, and furs.

A wave of disgust swept over me. "Something is cockeyed in this society," I thought, my mind refusing to stop juxtaposing these images with the suffering I had just witnessed. ■

O ccasionally the facts of social class hit home with brute force. This was one of those moments. The disjunction that I felt in New Orleans was triggered by the ads, but it was not the first time that I had experienced this sensation. Whenever my research abruptly transported me from the world of the homeless to one of another social class, I felt unfamiliar feelings of disjointed unreality. Each social class has its own way of being, and because these fundamental orientations to the world contrast so sharply, the classes do not mix well.

WHAT IS SOCIAL CLASS?

"There are the poor and the rich—and then there are you and I, neither poor nor rich." This is just about as far as most Americans' consciousness of social class goes. Let's try to flesh out this idea.

Our task is made somewhat difficult because sociologists have no clear-cut, agreed-on definition of social class. As noted in the last chapter, conflict sociologists (of the Marxist orientation) see only two social classes: those who own the means of production and those who do not. The problem with this view, say most sociologists, is that it lumps too many people together. Physicians and corporate executives with incomes of $400,000 a year are lumped together with hamburger flippers who work at McDonald's for $12,000 a year.

Most sociologists agree with Weber that there is more to social class than just a person's relationship to the means of production. Consequently, most sociologists use the components Weber identified and define **social class** as a large group of people who rank close to one another in wealth, power, and prestige. These three elements separate people into different lifestyles, give them different chances in life, and provide them with distinct ways of looking at the self and the world.

Let's look at how sociologists measure these three components of social class.

Wealth

The primary dimension of social class is wealth. **Wealth** consists of property and income. *Property* comes in many forms, such as buildings, land, animals, machinery, cars, stocks, bonds, businesses, and bank accounts. *Income* is money received as wages, rents, interest, royalties, or the proceeds from a business.

Distinction Between Wealth and Income Wealth and income are sometimes confused, but they are not the same. Some people have much wealth and little income. For example, a farmer may own much land (a form of wealth), but a little bad weather, combined with the high cost of fertilizers and machinery, can cause the income to disappear. Others have much income and little wealth. For example, an executive with a $200,000 annual income may be debt ridden. Below the surface prosperity—exotic vacations, country club membership, private schools for the children, fancy sports cars, and an elegant home in an exclusive suburb—he or she may be greatly overextended, the fancy cars in danger of being repossessed, and the mortgage payments "past due." Typically, however, wealth and income go together.

Who owns the wealth in the United States? One answer, of course, is "everyone." Although this statement has some merit, it overlooks how the nation's wealth is divided among "everyone." Let's look at how the two forms of wealth—property and income—are distributed among Americans.

Distribution of Property Overall, Americans are worth a hefty sum, about $25 trillion (*Statistical Abstract* 1999:Table 774). Most of this wealth is in the form of real estate,

social class according to Weber, a large group of people who rank closely to one another in wealth, power, and prestige; according to Marx, one of two groups: capitalists who own the means of production or workers who sell their labor

wealth property and income

In the United States, a mere 0.5 percent of the population owns over a quarter of the nation's wealth. Very few minorities are numbered among this 0.5 percent. An outstanding exception is Oprah Winfrey, whose ultra-successful career in entertainment, bringing her over $250 million a year, has made her one of the 400 richest Americans.

corporate stocks, bonds, and business assets. As Figure 10.1 shows, this wealth is highly concentrated. The vast majority, 68 percent, is owned by only *10 percent* of the nation's families.

The higher we go up the income ladder, the more concentrated that wealth becomes. As sociologist Leonard Beeghley (2000) observes, *the super-rich, the richest 1 percent of U.S. families, are worth more than the entire bottom 90 percent of Americans.*

Distribution of Income How is income distributed in the United States? Economist Paul Samuelson (1989:644) put it this way: "If we made an income pyramid out of a child's blocks, with each layer portraying $500 of income, the peak would be far higher than Mount Everest, but most people would be within a few feet of the ground."

Actually, if each block were 1½ inches tall, the typical American would be just *7 feet off the ground,* for the average per capita income in the United States is about $26,000 per year. (This is the average annual income of everyone in the population, even children.) The typical family climbs a little higher, for most families have more than one worker, and together they average about $45,000 a year. Yet compared with the Mount Everest incomes of a few, the average U.S. family would find itself only 11 feet off the ground (*Statistical Abstract* 1999:Tables 733, 752). Figure 10.2 on the next page portrays these differences.

The fact that some Americans enjoy the peaks of Mount Everest while most make it only 7 to 11 feet up the slope presents a striking image of income inequality in the United States. Another picture emerges if we divide the U.S. population into five equal groups and rank them from highest to lowest income. As Figure 10.3 on page 259 shows, the top 20 percent of the population receives *almost half* (47.2 percent) of all income in the United States. In contrast, the bottom 20 percent of Americans receives only 4.2 percent of the nation's income.

Two features of Figure 10.3 are outstanding. First, notice how remarkably consistent income inequality remains through the years. Second, the changes that do occur indicate *growing inequality. The richest 20 percent of U.S. families have grown richer, while the poorest 20 percent have grown poorer.* In spite of numerous antipoverty programs, the poorest 20 percent of Americans receive *less* of the nation's income today than they did in the 1940s (a drop from 5.4 percent to 4.2 percent). The richest 20 percent, in contrast, receive *more* than ever (an increase from about 41 percent to just over 47 percent).

The most affluent group in U.S. society is the chief executive officers (CEOs) of the nation's largest corporations. The *Wall Street Journal* surveyed the 350 largest U.S. companies to find out what they paid their CEOs ("Executive Pay," 1999). Their median compensation, including salaries, bonuses, and stock options, came to $3,093,000 a year. (Median means that half received more than this amount, and half less.) The CEOs' income—which does

Figure 10.1

DISTRIBUTION OF WEALTH OF AMERICANS

68% of the total net worth of all U.S. families...

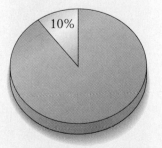

...is owned by just 10% of those families

Source: Beeghley 1996.

Figure 10.2   **INEQUALITY OF U.S. INCOME**

Some U.S. incomes are higher than Mt. Everest

29,028 feet

If a 1½-inch child's block equals $500 of income, the average American is only 7 feet off the ground, the average family just 11 feet, while the income of some families propels them past the top of Mount Everest.

7 feet   11 feet

Average   Average
American   U.S. Family

not include their interest, dividends, rents, and capital gains—is *100 times* higher than the average pay of U.S. workers (*Statistical Abstract* 1999:Table 700). Table 10.1 on the facing page lists the 8 highest paid executives.

Imagine how you could live with an income like this. And that is precisely the point. Beyond cold numbers lies a dynamic reality that profoundly affects people's lives. The difference in wealth between those at the top and those at the bottom of the U.S. class structure means vastly different lifestyles. For example, a colleague of mine who was teaching at an exclusive eastern university piqued his students' curiosity when he lectured on poverty in Latin America. That weekend, one of his students borrowed his parents' corporate jet and pilot, and in class the next Monday he and his friends related their personal observations on poverty in Latin America. Americans who are at the low end of the income ladder, in contrast, lack the funds to travel even to a neighboring town for the weekend; their choices revolve around whether to spend the little they have at the laundromat or on milk for the baby. In short, divisions of wealth represent not "mere" numbers, but choices that make vital differences in people's lives, a theme explored in the Down-to-Earth Sociology box on page 260.

Power

Like many people, you may have said to yourself, "Sure, I can vote, but somehow the big decisions are always made despite what I might think. Certainly *I* don't make the decision to send soldiers to Kuwait or Somalia. *I* don't launch missiles against the Sudan or Kosovo. *I* don't decide to raise taxes or interest rates. It isn't *I* who decides to change welfare benefits."

And then another part of you may say, "But I do participate in these decisions by writing my representatives in Congress, and by voting for president." True enough—as far as it goes. The trouble is, it just doesn't go far enough. Such views of being a participant in the nation's "big" decisions are a playback of the ideology we learn at an early age—an ideology that Marx said is put forward by the elites to both legitimate and perpetuate their power. Sociologists Daniel Hellinger and Dennis Judd (1991) call this the "democratic facade" that conceals the real source of power in the United States.

Back in the 1950s, sociologist C. Wright Mills (1956) was criticized for insisting that **power**—the ability to carry out your will despite resistance—was concentrated in the hands of the few, for his analysis contradicted the overpowering ideology of equality. As discussed

Bill Gates, a cofounder of Microsoft Corporation, is the wealthiest person in the world. His fortune of $70 billion continues to increase as his company develops new products. In his Seattle, Washington, home, which cost $50 million, Gates hung a $30 million painting in his living room. His fortune is so vast that in 2000 when the Dow Jones Industrial Average dropped, Gates lost $35 billion.

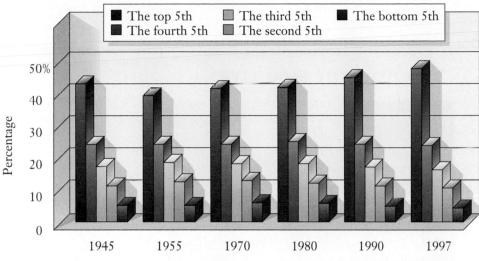

Figure 10.3

GROWING INEQUALITY: THE PERCENTAGE OF THE NATION'S INCOME RECEIVED BY EACH FIFTH OF U.S. FAMILIES SINCE WORLD WAR II

Source: Statisitical Abstract 1947; 1999:Table 751.

Note: The distribution of U.S. income—salaries, wages, and all other money received, except capital gains and government subsidies in the form of food stamps, health benefits, or subsidized housing.

in earlier chapters, Mills coined the term **power elite** to refer to those who make the big decisions in U.S. society.

Mills and others have stressed how wealth and power coalesce in a group of like-minded individuals who share ideologies and values. They belong to the same private clubs, vacation at the same exclusive resorts, and even hire the same bands for their daughters' debutante balls. These shared backgrounds and vested interests reinforce their view of the world and of their special place in it (Domhoff 1998, 1999). This elite wields extraordinary power in U.S. society. Although there are exceptions, *most* U.S. presidents have come from this group—millionaire white men from families with "old money" (Baltzell and Schneiderman 1988).

Continuing in the tradition of Mills, sociologist William Domhoff (1990,1998) argues that this group is so powerful that no major decision of the U.S. government is made without its approval. He analyzed how this group works behind the scenes with elected officials to determine both the nation's foreign and domestic policy—from establishing Social Security taxes to imposing trade tariffs. Although Domhoff's conclusions are controversial—and alarming—they certainly follow logically from the principle that wealth brings power, and extreme wealth brings extreme power.

Table 10.1

HIGHEST-PAID CEOS		
Executive	**Company**	**Annual Compensation**
1. Michael Eisner	Disney	$576 million
2. Sanford Weil	Citigroup	$167 million
3. Stephen Case	America Online	$159 million
4. John Welch	GE	$84 million
5. Douglas Ivester	Coca-Cola	$57 million
6. Charles Heimbold	Bristol-Myers	$56 million
7. Philip Purcell	Morgan Stanley	$53 million
8. Reuben Mark	Colgate-Palmolive	$53 million

Source: "Executive Pay," 1999.

power the ability to get your way despite the desires of other people

power elite C. Wright Mills' term for the top people in U.S. corporations, military, and politics who make the nation's major decisions

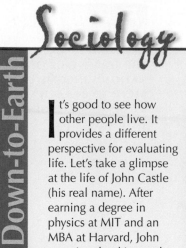

Sociology

HOW THE RICH LIVE

It's good to see how other people live. It provides a different perspective for evaluating life. Let's take a glimpse at the life of John Castle (his real name). After earning a degree in physics at MIT and an MBA at Harvard, John went into banking and securities, where he made more than $100 million (Lublin 1999).

Wanting to follow in the footsteps of someone famous, John bought President John F. Kennedy's "Winter White House," his oceanfront estate in Palm Beach, Florida. He spent $11 million to remodel the 13,000-square-foot house so it would be more to his liking, adding bathrooms numbers 14 and 15. He especially likes to show off the John F. Kennedy bed and also the dresser that has the drawer labeled "black underwear," carefully hand-lettered by Rose Kennedy.

If he gets bored at his beachfront estate, or tired of swimming in the Olympic-size pool where JFK swam the weekend before his assassination, John entertains him-

How do the rich live? The entrance to one of Sylvestor Stallone's homes, this one in Coconut Grove, Florida.

self by riding one of his thoroughbred horses at his nearby 10-acre ranch. If this fails to ease his boredom, he can relax aboard his custom-built 45-foot Hinckley yacht.

The yacht is a real source of diversion. He once boarded it for an around-the-world trip. He didn't stay on board, though—just joined the cruise from time to time. A captain and crew kept the vessel sailing in the right direction, and whenever he felt like it John would fly in and stay a few days. Then he would fly back to the States to direct his business. He did this about

a dozen times, flying perhaps 150,000 miles. An interesting way to go around the world.

How much does a custom-built Hinckley yacht cost? John can't tell you. As he says, "I don't want to know what anything costs. When you've got enough money, price doesn't make a difference. That's part of the freedom of being rich."

Right. And for John, being rich also meant paying $1,000,000 to charter a private jet to fly Spot, his Appaloosa horse, back and forth to the vet. John didn't want Spot to have to endure a long trailer ride. Oh, and of course, there was the cost of Spot's medical treatment, another $500,000.

Other wealthy people put John to shame. Wayne Huizenga, the CEO of AutoNation, owns a 2,000-acre country club, complete with an 18-hole golf course, a 55,000-square foot clubhouse, and 68 slips for visiting vessels. The club is so exclusive that its only members are Wayne and his wife. ■

Prestige

Occupations and Prestige What are you thinking about doing after college? Chances are you don't have the option of lolling under palm trees at the beach. Almost all of us have to choose an occupation and go to work. Look at Table 10.2 to see how the one you are considering stacks up in terms of **prestige** (respect or regard). Because we are moving toward a global society, this table also shows how the rankings given by Americans compare with those of the residents of sixty other countries.

Why do people give more prestige to some jobs than to others? If you look at Table 10.2, you will notice that the jobs at the top share four elements:

1. They pay more.
2. They require more education.
3. They entail more abstract thought.
4. They offer greater autonomy (freedom, or self-direction).

prestige respect or regard

Table 10.2

OCCUPATIONAL PRESTIGE: HOW THE UNITED STATES COMPARES WITH 60 COUNTRIES

Occupation	United States	Average of 60 Countries	Occupation	United States	Average of 60 Countries
Supreme court judge	85	82	Professional athlete	51	48
College president	82	86	Undertaker	51	34
Physician	82	78	Social worker	50	56
Astronaut	80	80	Electrician	49	44
College professor	78	78	Secretary	46	53
Lawyer	75	73	Real estate agent	44	49
Dentist	74	70	Farmer	44	47
Architect	71	72	Carpenter	43	37
Psychologist	71	66	Plumber	41	34
Airline pilot	70	66	Mail carrier	40	33
Electrical engineer	69	65	Jazz musician	37	38
Civil engineer	68	70	Bricklayer	36	34
Biologist	68	69	Barber	36	30
Clergy	67	60	Truck driver	31	33
Sociologist	65	67	Factory worker	29	29
Accountant	65	55	Store sales clerk	27	34
Banker	63	67	Bartender	25	23
High school teacher	63	64	Lives on public aid	25	16
Author	63	62	Bill collector	24	27
Registered nurse	62	54	Cab driver	22	28
Pharmacist	61	64	Gas station attendant	22	25
Chiropractor	60	62	Janitor	22	21
Veterinarian	60	61	Waiter or waitress	20	23
Classical musician	59	56	Bellhop	15	14
Police officer	59	40	Garbage collector	13	13
Actor or actress	55	52	Street sweeper	11	13
Athletic coach	53	50	Shoe shiner	9	12
Journalist	52	55			

Sources: Treiman 1977, Appendices A and D; Nakao and Treas 1991.

If we turn this around, we can see that people give less prestige to jobs that are low-paying, require less preparation or education, involve more physical labor, and are closely supervised. In short, the professions and white-collar jobs are ranked at the top of the list, blue-collar jobs at the bottom.

One of the more interesting aspects of these rankings is how consistent they are across countries and over time. For example, people in every country rank college professors higher than nurses, nurses higher than social workers, and social workers higher than janitors. Similarly, the occupations that were ranked high back in the 1970s still rank high today—and likely will rank high in the years to come.

Displaying Prestige To get a sense of payoff, people want others to acknowledge their prestige. In times past, in some countries only the emperor and his family could wear purple. In France, only the nobility could wear lace. In England, no one could sit while the king was on his throne. Some kings and queens required that subjects walk backward as they left the room—so no one would "turn their back" on the "royal presence."

Concern with displaying prestige has not let up—for some, it is almost an obsession. Western kings and queens expect commoners to curtsy and bow, while their Eastern counterparts expect their subjects to touch their faces to the ground. The U.S. president enters a room only after others are present (to show that *he* isn't the one waiting for *them*). Military officers surround themselves with elaborate rules about who must salute whom, while bailiffs, sometimes armed, make certain that everyone stands when the judge enters.

Acceptable display of prestige and high social position varies over time and from one culture to another. Shown here is Elisabeth d'Autriche, queen of France from 1554 to 1592. It certainly would be difficult to outdress her at a party.

The display of prestige permeates society. In Los Angeles, some people list their address as Beverly Hills and then add their correct ZIP code. When the town of East Detroit changed its name to East Pointe to play off its proximity to swank Grosse Pointe, property values shot up (Fletcher 1997). Many willingly pay more for clothing that bears a "designer" label. For many, prestige is a primary factor in deciding which college to attend. Everyone knows how the prestige of a generic sheepskin from Regional State College compares with a degree from Harvard, Princeton, Yale, or Stanford.

Interestingly, status symbols vary with social class. Clearly, only the wealthy can afford certain items, such as yachts. But beyond affordability lies a class-based preference in status symbols. For example, Yuppies (young upwardly mobile professionals) are quick to flaunt labels and other material symbols to show that they have "arrived," while the rich, who are more secure in their status, often downplay such images. The wealthy see designer labels of the more "common" classes as cheap and showy. They, of course, flaunt their own status symbols, such as $30,000 Rolex watches.

Status Inconsistency

Ordinarily a person has a similar rank on all three dimensions of social class—wealth, power, and prestige. The homeless men in the opening vignette are an example. Such people are **status consistent**. Sometimes the match is not there, however, and someone has a mixture of high and low ranks, a condition called **status inconsistency**. This leads to some interesting situations.

Sociologist Gerhard Lenski (1954, 1966) pointed out that each of us tries to maximize our **status**, our social ranking. Thus individuals who rank high on one dimension of social class but lower on others expect people to judge them on the basis of their highest status. Others, however, trying to maximize their own position, may respond to them according to their lowest status.

A classic study of status inconsistency was done by sociologist Ray Gold (1952). He found that after apartment-house janitors unionized, they made more money than some of

Status discrepancy is common for lottery winners, whose new wealth is vastly greater than their education and occupational status. Shown here are John and Sandy Jarrell of Chicago, after they learned that they were one of 13 families to share a $295 million jackpot. How do you think their $22 million will affect their lives?

the people whose garbage they carried out. Tenants became upset when they saw their janitors driving more expensive cars than they did. Some attempted to "put the janitor in his place" by making "snotty" remarks to him. For their part, the janitors took secret pride in knowing "dirty" secrets about the tenants, gleaned from their garbage.

Individuals with status inconsistency, then, are likely to confront one frustrating situation after another. They claim the higher status, but are handed the lower. The sociological significance of this condition, said Lenski, is that such people tend to be more politically radical. An example is college professors. Their prestige is very high, as we saw in Table 10.2, but their incomes are relatively low. Hardly anyone in U.S. society is more educated, and yet college professors don't even come close to the top of the income pyramid. In line with Lenski's prediction, the politics of most college professors are left of center. This hypothesis may also hold true *among* academic departments; that is, the higher a department's pay, the less radical are its politics. Teachers in departments of business and medicine, for example, are among the most highly paid in the university—and they also are the most politically conservative.

SOCIOLOGICAL MODELS OF SOCIAL CLASS

The question of how many social classes there are is a matter of debate. Sociologists have proposed various models, but no model has gained universal support. There are two main models: one that builds on Marx, the other on Weber.

Updating Marx

Marx argued that there are just two classes—capitalists and workers—with membership based solely on a person's relationship to the means of production. Sociologists have criticized this view because these categories are too broad. For example, executives, managers, and supervisors are technically workers because they do not own the means of production. But what do they have in common with assembly-line workers? Similarly, the category of "capitalist" takes in too many types. For example, the decisions of someone who employs a thousand workers directly affect a thousand families. Compare this with a man I know in Godfrey, Illinois. Working on cars out of his own back yard, he gained a following, quit his regular job, and in a few years put up a building with five bays and an office. This mechanic is now a capitalist, for he employs five or six other mechanics and owns the tools and the building (the "means of production"). But what does he have in common with a factory owner who controls the lives of one thousand workers? Not only is his work different, but so are his lifestyle and the way he looks at the world.

Sociologist Erik Wright (1985) resolved this problem by regarding some people as members of more than one class at the same time. They have what he called **contradictory class locations.** By this Wright means that people's position in the class structure can generate contradictory interests. For example, the automobile mechanic-turned-business owner may want his mechanics to have higher wages since he, too, has experienced their working conditions. At the same time, his current interests—making profits and remaining competitive with other repair shops—lead him to resist pressures to raise wages.

Because of such contradictory class locations, Wright modified Marx's model. As summarized in Table 10.3, Wright identified four classes: (1) *capitalists,* business owners who employ many workers, (2) *petty bourgeoisie,* small business owners, (3) *managers,* who sell their own labor but also exercise authority over other employees; and (4) *workers,* who simply sell their labor to others. As you can see, this model allows finer divisions than the one Marx proposed, yet it maintains the primary distinction between employer and worker.

Updating Weber

Sociologists Dennis Gilbert and Joseph Kahl (1993; Gilbert 1997) developed a six-class model to portray the class structure of the United States and other capitalist countries. Think of their model, illustrated in Figure 10.4 on the following page, as a ladder. Our discussion will start with the highest rung and move downward. In line with Weber, on each lower rung you find less wealth, less power, and less prestige. Note that in this model education is also a primary criterion of class.

The Capitalist Class The super-rich who occupy the top rung of the class ladder make up only about 1 percent of the population. As mentioned, this 1 percent is so wealthy that its members are worth more than the entire bottom 90 percent of the nation. Their power is so great that their decisions open or close jobs for millions of people. Through their ownership of newspapers, magazines, and radio and television stations, together with their access to politicians,

---

status consistency ranking high or low on all three dimensions of social class

status inconsistency (or status discrepancy) ranking high on some dimensions of social class and low on others

status social ranking

contradictory class location Erik Wright's term for a position in the class structure that generates contradictory interests

---

Table **10.3**

SOCIAL CLASS AND THE MEANS OF PRODUCTION

Marx's Class Model (based on the means of production)

1. Capitalists (bourgeoisie)
2. Workers (proletariat)

Wright's Modification of Marx's Class Model (to account for contradictory class locations)

1. Capitalists
2. Petty bourgeoisie
3. Managers
4. Workers

 **THE U.S. SOCIAL CLASS LADDER**

Social Class	Education	Occupation	Income	Percentage of Population
Capitalist	Prestigious university	Investors and heirs, a few top executives	$500,000+	1%
Upper Middle	College or university, often with postgraduate study	Professionals and upper managers	$100,000+	15%
Lower Middle	At least high school; perhaps some college or apprenticeship	Semiprofessionals and lower managers, craftspeople, foremen	About $40,000	32%
Working Class	High school	Factory workers, clerical workers, low-paid retail sales, and craftspeople	About $30,000	32%
Working Poor	Some high school	Laborers, service workers, low-paid salespeople	About $16,000	16%
Underclass	Some high school	Unemployed and part-time, on welfare	Under $10,000	4%

Source: Based on Gilbert and Kahl 1997 and Gilbert 1997; income estimates are modified from Duff 1995.

this elite class even helps to shape the consciousness of the nation. Its members perpetuate themselves by passing on to their children their assets and influential social networks.

The capitalist class can be divided into "old" and "new" money (Aldrich 1989). Those with "new money" are also called the *nouveau riche*. The longer that wealth has been in a family, the more it adds to the family's prestige. To accumulate their wealth, many people who join the capitalist class cut at least a few moral corners. In some instances, the money comes from illegal activities. The original source of the Kennedy fortune, for example, was bootlegging. This "taint" to the money disappears with time, and the later generations of Kennedys, Rockefellers, Vanderbilts, Mellons, Du Ponts, Chryslers, Fords, Morgans, Nashes, and so on are considered to have "clean" money simply by virtue of the passage of time. Because they are able to be philanthropic as well as rich, they establish foundations and support charitable causes. Subsequent generations attend prestigious prep schools and universities, and heirs are likely to study business or enter the field of law. These old-money capitalists wield vast power as they use extensive political connections to protect their huge economic empires (Persell et al. 1992; Domhoff 1990, 1999).

Those at the lower end of the capitalist class also possess vast sums of money and power, but it is new, and therefore suspect. Although these people may have made fortunes in business, the stock market, inventions, entertainment, or sports, they have not attended the right schools, and they lack the influential social networks that come with old money. Donald Trump, for example, is not listed in the *Social Register,* the "White Pages" of the blue-bloods that lists the most prestigious and wealthy one-tenth of 1 percent of the U.S. population.

Trump says he "doesn't care," but he reveals his true feelings by adding that his heirs will be in it (Kaufman 1996). He probably is right, for the children of the new-monied can ascend into this top part of the capitalist class if they go to the right schools *and* marry old money.

The Upper Middle Class Of all the classes, the upper middle class is the one most shaped by education. Almost all members of this class have at least a bachelor's degree, and many have postgraduate degrees in business, management, law, or medicine. These people manage the corporations owned by the capitalist class or else operate their own business or profession. As Gilbert and Kahl (1982) say, these positions

> may not grant prestige equivalent to a title of nobility in the Germany of Max Weber, but they certainly represent the sign of having "made it" in contemporary America. . . . Their income is sufficient to purchase houses and cars and travel that become public symbols for all to see and for advertisers to portray with words and pictures that connote success, glamour, and high style.

Consequently, parents and teachers push children to prepare themselves for upper-middle-class jobs. About 15 percent of the population belong to this class.

The Lower Middle Class About 32 percent of the population belong to the lower middle class. Members of this class have jobs that call for them to follow orders given by those who have upper-middle-class credentials. Their technical and lower-level management positions bring them a good living—albeit one constantly threatened by taxes and inflation—and they enjoy a generally comfortable, mainstream lifestyle. They usually feel secure in their positions and anticipate being able to move up the social class ladder.

The distinctions between the lower middle class and the working class on the next lower rung are more blurred than those between other classes. In general, however, members of the lower middle class work at jobs that have slightly more prestige, and their incomes are generally higher.

The Working Class About 32 percent of the U.S. population belong to this class of relatively unskilled blue-collar and white-collar workers. Compared with the lower middle class, they have less education and lower incomes. Their jobs are also less secure, more routine, and more closely supervised. One of their greatest fears is being laid off during a recession. With only a high school diploma, the average member of the working class has little hope of climbing up the class ladder. Job changes are usually "more of the same," so most concentrate on getting ahead by achieving seniority on the job rather than by changing their type of work.

The Working Poor Members of this class, about 16 percent of the population, work at unskilled, low-paying, temporary and seasonal jobs, such as sharecropping, migrant farm work, housecleaning, and day labor. Most are high school dropouts. Many are functionally illiterate, finding it difficult to read even the want ads. They are not likely to vote (Gilbert and Kahl 1993), for they feel that no matter what party is elected to office their situation won't change.

About 6 million of the working poor work full time (O'Hare 1996b), but still must depend on help such as food stamps to supplement their meager incomes. It is easy to see how you can work full time and still be poor. Suppose that you are married and have a baby 3 months old and another child 3 years old. Your spouse stays home to care for them, so earning the income is up to you. But as a high-school dropout, all you can get is a minimum wage job. At $5.25 an hour, you earn $210 for 40 hours. In a year, this comes to $10,920—before deductions. Your nagging fear—and daily nightmare—is of ending up "on the streets."

The Underclass On the lowest rung, and with next to no chance of climbing anywhere, is the **underclass**. Concentrated in the inner city, this group has little or no connection with the job market. Those who are employed, and some are, do menial, low-paying, temporary

underclass a group of people for whom poverty persists year after year and across generations

work. Welfare, if it is available, along with food stamps and food pantries, are their main support. Most members of other classes consider these people the ne'er-do-wells of society. Life is the toughest in this class, and it is filled with despair. About 4 percent of the population fall into this class.

The homeless men described in the opening vignette of this chapter, and the women and children like them, are part of the underclass. These are the people whom most Americans wish would just go away. Their presence on our city streets bothers passersby from the more privileged social classes—which includes just about everyone. "What are those obnoxious, dirty, foul-smelling people doing here, cluttering up my city?" appears to be a common response. Some people respond with sympathy and a desire to do something. But what? Almost all of us just shrug our shoulders and look the other way, despairing of a solution and somewhat intimidated by their presence.

The homeless are the "fallout" of industrialization, especially our developing postindustrial economy. In another era, they would have had plenty of work. They would have tended horses, worked on farms, dug ditches, shoveled coal, and run the factory looms. Some would have explored and settled the West. Others would have been lured to California, Alaska, and Australia by the prospect of gold. Today, however, with no frontiers to settle, factory jobs scarce, and farms that are becoming technological marvels, we have little need for unskilled labor.

Social Class in the Automobile Industry

The automobile industry illustrates the social class ladder. The Fords, for example, own and control a manufacturing and financial empire whose net worth is truly staggering. Their power matches their wealth, for through their multinational corporation their decisions affect production and employment in many countries. The family's vast accumulation of money, and its accrued power, are now several generations old. Consequently, Ford children go to the "right" schools, know how to spend money in the "right" way, and can be trusted to make family and class interests paramount in life. They are without question at the top level of the *capitalist* class.

Next in line come top Ford executives. Although they may have an income of several hundred thousand dollars a year (and some, with stock options and bonuses, earn several million annually), most are new to wealth and power. Consequently, they would be classified at the lower end of the capitalist class.

A husband and wife who own a Ford agency are members of the *upper middle class*. Their income clearly sets them apart from the majority of Americans, and their reputation in the community is enviable. More than likely they also exert greater-than-average influence in their community, but their capacity to wield power is limited.

A Ford salesperson, as well as people who work in the dealership office, belongs to the *lower middle class*. Although there are some exceptional salespeople, even a few who make a lot of money selling prestigious, expensive cars to the capitalist class, salespeople at a run-of-the-mill local Ford agency are lower middle class. Compared with the owners of the agency, their income is less, their education is likely to be less, and their work is less prestigious.

Mechanics who repair customers' cars are members of the *working class*. A mechanic who is promoted to supervise the repair shop joins the lower middle class.

Those who "detail" used cars (making them appear newer by washing and polishing the car, painting the tires, spraying "new car scent" into the interior, and so on) belong to the *working poor*. Their income and education are low, the prestige accorded their work minimal. They are laid off when selling slows down.

Ordinarily, the *underclass* is not represented in the automobile industry. It is conceivable, however, that the agency might hire a member of the underclass to do a specific job such as raking the grass or cleaning up the used car lot. In general, however, personnel at the agency do not trust members of the underclass and do not want to associate with them—even for a few hours. They prefer to hire someone from the working poor for such jobs.

A husband and wife in their Virginia family estate and the migrant worker are both shown "at home." From the contrast evident in these photos, you can easily infer consequences of social class: from life chances to health, from family life to education. It also should be apparent why these people are not likely to view politics in quite the same way.

CONSEQUENCES OF SOCIAL CLASS

Each social class can be thought of as a broad subculture with distinct approaches to life. Of the many ways that social class affects people's lives, we will briefly review health, family life, education, religion, politics, crime and the criminal justice system, and the new technology.

Physical Health

Social class even affects our chances of living and dying. The principle is simple: The lower a person's class, the more likely that individual is to die before the expected age. This principle holds true at all ages. Infants born to the poor are more likely than other infants to die before their first birthday. In old age—whether 70 or 90—a larger proportion of the poor die each year than do the wealthy. Part of the reason for these death rates is unequal access to medical care. Consider this example:

> Terry Takewell (his real name) was a 21-year-old diabetic who lived in a small trailer park in Somerville, Tennessee. When Zettie Mae Hill, Takewell's neighbor, found the unemployed carpenter drenched with sweat from a fever, she called an ambulance. Takewell was rushed to nearby Methodist Hospital, where, it turned out, he had an outstanding bill of $9,400. A notice posted in the emergency room told staff members to alert supervisors if Takewell ever returned.
>
> When the hospital administrator was informed of the admission, Takewell was already in a hospital bed. The administrator went to Takewell's room, helped him to his feet, and escorted him to the parking lot. There, neighbors found him under a tree and took him home.
>
> Takewell died about twelve hours later.
>
> Zettie Mae Hill is still torn up about it. She wonders if Takewell would be alive today if she had directed his ambulance to a different hospital. She said, "I didn't think a hospital would just let a person die like that for lack of money." (Based on Ansberry 1988)

Why was Terry Takewell denied medical treatment and his life cut short? The fundamental reason is that in the United States health care is not a citizen's right, but a commodity for sale. The result is a two-tier system of medical care—superior care for those who can afford the cost, and inferior care for those who cannot. Unlike the middle and upper classes, few poor people have a personal physician, and they usually must spend hours waiting in

In general, the time and activities of the rich are considered to be more valuable than those of the poor. One consequence is that the length of time that people wait is inversely related to social class. In other words, in most situations the poor wait longer than the rich. This principle is evident in "waiting rooms," such as this one in Los Angeles, California, where AFDC recipients fill out forms for the Department of Public Social Services.

crowded public health clinics. After waiting most of a day, some don't even get to see a doctor; instead, they are told to come back the next day (Fialka 1993). And when the poor are hospitalized, they are likely to find themselves in understaffed and underfunded public hospitals, where they are treated by rotating interns who do not know them and cannot follow up on their progress.

Mental Health

Social class also affects our mental health. From the 1930s until now, sociologists have found that the mental health of the lower classes is worse than that of the higher classes (Faris and Dunham 1939; Srole et al. 1978; Lundberg 1991; Miller 1994). Greater mental problems are part of a stress package that comes with poverty. Compared with middle- and upper-class Americans, the poor have less job security, lower wages, more unpaid bills, more divorce, more alcoholism, greater vulnerability to crime, more physical illnesses—all accompanied by the threat of eviction, which always hangs over their heads. Such conditions deal severe blows to people's emotional well-being.

People higher up the social class ladder experience stress, of course, but their stress is generally less and their coping resources greater. Not only can they afford vacations, psychiatrists, and counselors, but *their class position gives them greater control over their lives, a key to good mental health.*

Family Life

Social class plays an especially significant role in family life. Of its many consequences in this vital area, let's look at choice of spouse, divorce, and child rearing.

Choice of Husband or Wife The capitalist class strongly emphasizes family tradition. They stress the family's ancestors, history, and even a sense of purpose or destiny in life (Baltzell 1979; Aldrich 1989). Children of this class learn that their choice of husband or wife affects not just themselves but the entire family, that their spouse will have an impact on the "family line." Because of these background expectations, the field of "eligible" marriage partners is much narrower than it is for the children of any other social class. In effect, parents in this class play a strong role in their children's mate selection.

Divorce The more difficult life of the lower social classes, especially the many tensions that come from insecure jobs and inadequate incomes, leads to high marital friction and a greater likelihood of divorce. Consequently, the children of the poor are more likely to grow up in broken homes.

Child Rearing As discussed on pages 79–80, sociologist Melvin Kohn (1977) found significant class differences in child rearing. Lower-class parents were more concerned that their children conform to conventional norms and obey authority figures. Middle-class parents, in contrast, encouraged their children to be more creative and independent, and tolerated a wider range of behaviors (except in speech, where they were less tolerant of bad grammar and curse words).

Kohn concluded that lower- and middle-class parents rear their children differently because their occupations give them different visions of their children's futures. Lower-class parents are closely supervised in their jobs, and they anticipate that their children will work at similar jobs. Consequently, they try to teach their children to defer to authority. In contrast, parents from the more privileged classes enjoy greater creativity and self-expression at work. Anticipating similar work for their children, they encourage them to express greater freedom. Out of these contrasting orientations also arise different ways of enforcing discipline; lower-class parents are more likely to use the stick, while the middle classes rely more on verbal persuasion.

Education

As we saw in Figure 10.4, education increases as one goes up the social class ladder. It is not just the amount of education that changes, but also the type of education. Children of the capitalist class bypass public schools. They attend exclusive private schools where they are trained to take a commanding role in society. Prep schools such as Phillips Exeter Academy, Groton School, and Woodberry Forest School teach upper-class values and prepare their students for prestigious universities (Beeghley 2000). Aspiring members of the upper middle class, aware of the significance of this private school system, attempt to gain their children's entry into prestigious preschools by eliciting letters of recommendation for their 2- and 3-year-olds. Such differences in parental expectations and resources are a major reason why children from the more privileged classes do better in school and are more likely to enter and to graduate from college.

Religion

One area of social life that we might think would be unaffected by social class is religion. ("People are just religious, or they are not. What does social class have to do with it?") As we shall see in Chapter 18, however, the classes tend to cluster in different denominations. Episcopalians, for example, are much more likely to recruit from the middle and upper classes. Baptists draw heavily from the lower classes, and Methodists are more middle class. Patterns of worship also follow class lines: Religions that attract the lower classes have more spontaneous worship services and louder music, while the middle and upper classes prefer more "subdued" worship.

Politics

As has been stressed throughout this text, symbolic interactionists emphasize that people see events from their own corner in life. Political views are no exception to this principle, and the rich and the poor walk different political paths. The working class, which feels much more strongly than the classes above it that government should intervene in the economy to make citizens financially secure, is more likely to vote Democrat. The higher people are on the social class ladder, the more likely they are to vote Republican. Although the working class is more liberal on *economic* issues (those that favor government spending), it is more conservative on *social* issues (such as opposing abortion and the Equal Rights Amendment) (Lipset 1959; Houtman 1995). People toward the bottom of the class structure are also less likely to be politically active—to campaign for candidates, or even to vote (Gans 1991a; Gilbert and Kahl 1993; Beeghley 2000).

Crime and the Criminal Justice System

If justice is supposed to be blind, it certainly is not when it comes to one's chances of being arrested (Henslin 2000). In Chapter 8 (pages 211–213) we discussed how the upper and lower social classes have different styles of crime. The white-collar crimes of the more privileged classes are more likely to be dealt with outside the criminal justice system, while the street crimes of the lower classes are dealt with by the police. One consequence of this class standard is that members of the lower classes are more likely to be in prison, on probation, or on parole. In addition, since people tend to commit crimes in or near their own neighborhoods, the lower classes are more likely to be robbed, burglarized, or murdered.

The New Technology

Effects of the new technology also follow social class lines. The higher one goes up the social class ladder, the more this technology is a benefit. For the capitalist class, the new technology is a dream come true: By minimizing the obstacle of national boundaries, capitalists can locate factories in countries with cheap labor and maximize global profits through global integration. A product's components can be produced in several countries, assembled in another country, and the product then marketed throughout the world. The new technology also benefits the upper middle class, for their education prepares them to take a leading role in managing this global system for the capitalist class, or for using the new technology to advance in their chosen professions.

Below these two classes, however, the new technology adds to the uncertainty of life, with the insecurity becoming greater the farther one moves down the ladder. As the new technology transforms the workplace, it eliminates jobs and causes workers' skills to become outdated. People in lower management can transfer their skills from one job to another, although in shifting job markets the times between periods of employment can create a precarious situation. Those who work at specialized crafts are even less secure, for their training is more specific and the new technology can reduce and even eliminate the need for their narrower, more specialized skills.

From this middle point on the ladder down, people are hit the hardest. The working class is ill prepared for the changes ushered in by the new technology, and they are haunted by the specter of unemployment. The low technical skills of the working poor make them even more vulnerable, for they have even less to offer in the new job market. As unskilled jobs dry up, more and more of the working poor are consigned to the industrial garbage bin. The underclass, of course, with no technical skills, is bypassed entirely.

The playing field is far from level. Some even fear that current trends in exporting U.S. jobs mean that U.S. workers are becoming an expendable luxury, destined to be replaced by low-paid, nonunionized—and more compliant—workers in Mexico and on other continents. In short, as discussed in the New Technology box on the facing page, the new technology opens and closes opportunities for people largely by virtue of where they are located on the social class ladder.

$\int$OCIAL MOBILITY

No aspect of life, then—from marriage to politics—goes untouched by social class. Because life is so much more satisfying in the more privileged classes, people strive to climb the social class ladder. What affects their chances?

Sociology & the New Technology

CLOSING THE DIGITAL DIVIDE: THE TECHNOLOGY GAP FACING THE POOR AND MINORITIES

Digital divide refers to the technology gap between the poor and the middle and upper classes. It also has a race-ethnic component. Because a larger proportion of minorities are poor, compared with whites, a smaller percentage of African Americans, Latinos, and Native Americans have access to computers and the Internet (Meeks 1999).

Sociologists focus on the *structural* basis of wealth and poverty. That is, they examine how advantage and disadvantage are *built into society*. This does not mean that no one born into poverty can overcome this disadvantage. A lot of people do. In fact, the opportunities of this country are why so many people want to live in the United States. But because of structural reasons, some people face many obstacles because of their birth, while others face few.

The question, then, is not how we can destroy the advantages that some have, but, rather, how we can reduce the disadvantages that others face. What can we do to increase opportunities for those who are born into a world of huge obstacles? Or, at the very least, how can we prevent those obstacles from growing?

These questions take us to the digital divide. If the children who live in poverty have less access to computers and the Internet, their disadvantage in our new technological world will grow. If computers were only for playing cyber games, this would not be an issue. But the Internet has become a major source of information. Think of the Internet as a gigantic library that spans the globe. As a practical example, in writing this text I used to make frequent trips to libraries. Now I do most of my research on the Internet. I have not only instant access to the latest government reports, but also instant e-mail connections with people around the world who can help me track down bits of arcane data.

Using the Internet to access information is a skill, much of it learned by

trial and error. If children in poverty have less access to computers and the Internet, their skills in this vital area will be weak—and this will affect their future economic well-being. That disadvantage will be one more hurdle to keep them from advancing economically. No one wants middle- and upper-class children to relinquish this skill—the issue is how to level the playing field by enabling the children of the poor to increase their skills. ■

For Your Consideration

What do you think can be done to overcome this problem? For example, do you think the government should pay to connect every U.S. home to the Internet and buy a computer for every child, beginning in kindergarten? Why or why not?

Let's look at the problem this way: Would we ever allow libraries to grant entrance to white Americans and ban some minorities? Let in the wealthy, but close the door on some people because they are poor? Is it fair to draw this analogy, given that libraries are funded by tax dollars and computers and Internet access are paid for by individuals?

Three Types of Social Mobility

There are three basic types of social mobility: intergenerational, structural, and exchange. **Intergenerational mobility** refers to a change that occurs between generations—when adult children end up on a different rung of the social class ladder from the one their parents occupy. If the child of someone who sells used cars graduates from college and buys a Toyota dealership, that person experiences **upward social mobility.** Conversely, if a child of the dealer's owner parties too much, drops out of college, and ends up selling cars, he or she experiences **downward social mobility.**

We like to think that individual efforts are the reason people move up the class ladder—and individual faults the reason they move down. In these examples, we can identify hard work, sacrifice, and ambition on the one hand, versus indolence and alcohol abuse on the

intergenerational mobility the change that family members make in social class from one generation to the next

upward social mobility movement up the social class ladder

downward social mobility movement down the social class ladder

The term structural mobility refers to changes in society that push large numbers of people either up or down the social class ladder. A remarkable example was the stock market crash of 1929, when thousands of people suddenly lost immense amounts of wealth. People who once "had it made" found themselves standing on street corners selling apples or, as depicted here, selling their possessions at fire-sale prices.

other. Although individual factors such as these do underlie social mobility, sociologists consider **structural mobility** to be the crucial factor. This second basic type of mobility refers to changes in society that cause large numbers of people to move up or down the class ladder.

To better understand structural mobility, think of how opportunities opened when computers were invented. New types of jobs appeared overnight. Huge numbers of people took workshops and crash courses, switching from blue-collar to white-collar work. Although individual effort certainly was involved—for some seized the opportunity while others did not—the underlying cause was a change in the *structure* of work. Consider the opposite—how opportunities close during a depression, and millions of people are forced downward on the class ladder. In this instance, too, their changed status is due less to individual behavior than to *structural* changes in society.

The third type of social mobility, **exchange mobility,** occurs when large numbers of people move up and down the social class ladder, but, on balance, the proportions of the social classes remain about the same. Suppose that a million or so working-class people are trained in computers, and they move up the class ladder. Suppose also that there is a vast surge in imports and about a million skilled workers have to take lower-status jobs. Although millions of people change their social class, there is in effect an *exchange* among them. The net result more or less balances out, and the class system remains basically untouched.

Women in Studies on Social Mobility

The United States is known worldwide for its intergenerational mobility. That children can pass up their parents on the social class ladder is one of the attractions of this country. To find out how extensive this mobility is, sociologists used to study only men. In classic studies, they concluded that about half of sons passed their fathers; about one-third stayed at the same level, and only about one-sixth fell down the class ladder (Blau and Duncan 1967; Featherman and Hauser 1978; Featherman 1979).

Fathers and sons? How about the other half of the population? Feminists pointed out this obvious omission (Davis and Robinson 1988). They also objected to the assumption that women had no class position of their own and were simply assigned the class of their husbands. The defense was that too few women were in the labor force to make a difference.

With the large numbers of women now working for pay, more recent studies include women (Breen and Whelan 1995; Beeghley 2000). Sociologists Elizabeth Higginbotham and Lynn Weber (1992), for example, studied 200 women from working-class backgrounds who became professionals, managers, and administrators in Memphis. They found that almost without exception, the women's parents had encouraged them while they were still little girls to postpone marriage and get an education. This study confirms findings that the family is of utmost importance in the socialization process and that the primary entry to the upper middle class is a college education. At the same time, note that if there had not been a *structural* change in society, the millions of new positions that women occupy would not exist.

The New Technology and Fears of the Future

The ladder also leads down, of course, and that is precisely what strikes fear in the hearts of many workers. If the United States does not keep pace with global change and remain highly competitive by producing low-cost, quality goods, its economic position will decline. The result will be shrinking opportunities, with U.S. workers facing fewer good jobs and lower incomes.

structural mobility movement up or down the social class ladder that is attributable to changes in the structure of society, not to individual efforts

exchange mobility about the same numbers of people moving up and down the social class ladder, such that, on balance, the social class system shows little change

To compete in this global economic race, the United States is incorporating advanced technology in all spheres of life. While this means good jobs for many, it also means that the technologically illiterate are being left behind, and their future looks grim. This point was driven home to me when I saw the homeless sitting dejected in the shelters. There were our school dropouts, our technological know-nothings. Of what value are they to this new society that is now undergoing its piercing birth pains? They simply have no productive place. Their base of social belonging and self-esteem has been pulled out from under them.

Certainly one of the goals of most Americans is to better their lot in life. In sociological terms, this means that most Americans want a chance at upward social mobility. This heartfelt desire is so common around the world that it drives millions of people to uproot themselves from their native lands and move to the United States.

The Pain of Social Mobility

You know that to be knocked down the social class ladder is painful, but did you know that climbing it also brings pain? Sociologists Richard Sennett and Jonathan Cobb (1972/1988) studied working-class men and women in Boston who had made deep sacrifices so their children could finish high school and go to college. The fathers worked long hours and were seldom home, while the mothers did without things. The parents expected their children to appreciate their sacrifices. Instead, and to their dismay, they found estrangement and lack of communication. With the fathers seldom home, the children grew aloof. The children's education also contributed to the gap between them and their parents, since it was so remote from their parents' world. As the parents confronted this divide, bitterness set in. They felt betrayed: Instead of receiving appreciation for their sacrifice, they found aloofness and ingratitude.

In short, social class separates people into worlds so distinct that communication and mutual understanding become difficult. To change one's social class, then, is to tear oneself from one's roots. As you may recall, Richard Rodriguez, featured in the Perspectives box on page 82, found that his climb up the social class ladder brought some wrenching costs. In the Down-to-Earth Sociology box on pages 274–275, we explore this theme further.

*P*OVERTY

Many Americans find the "limitless possibilities" on which the American dream is based to be rather elusive. As illustrated in Figure 10.4 on page 264, the working poor and underclass together form about one-fifth of the U.S. population. This translates into a huge number, about 55 million people. Who are these people?

Drawing the Poverty Line

A good definition of **poverty** is the lack of resources to meet your basic needs, including food, clothing, shelter, and health. Because this definition is too vague to use in determining eligibility for poverty programs, the U.S. government uses a measure called the **poverty line**. It assumes that poor families spend one-third of their income on food and then multiplies a low-cost food budget by three. Those whose incomes are less than this amount are classified as below the poverty line.

As sociologists observe, this definition is unrealistic. It misjudges both income and expenses. On the one hand, it does not count as income benefits that the government gives poor people, such as food stamps and rent assistance. On the other hand, it does not subtract from income the expenses necessary to produce income, especially the amount working parents pay for child care. The poverty line is also the same amount across the nation, even though the cost of living is much higher in some states (Michael 1995; Corbett 1999). Nevertheless, this is how the government draws the line that separates the poor from the nonpoor.

It is part of the magical sleight-of-hand of modern bureaucracy that a change in this official measure of poverty instantly adds—or subtracts—millions of people from this category.

poverty lacking resources to meet your basic needs

poverty line the official measure of poverty; calculated to include those whose incomes are less than three times a low-cost food budget

Sociology

LIVING IN TWO WORLDS:
UPWARD MOBILITY ON THE SOCIAL CLASS LADDER

I want to begin this Down-to-Earth Sociology feature on a personal note. As you will read in the Down-to-Earth Sociology box on page 282, I was born in poverty. Education was my way out; it opened up a new world for me and led to the writing of this textbook. I was touched when I read sociologist David Croteau's account of his change in social class. Like myself, Croteau was born into a blue-collar family and was the first in his family to attend college. He describes his experience of upward social mobility as only someone who has gone through it could. What he says resonates, matching what I experienced so well that I want to share his account with you.

After brief periods as a logger and as a shipworker, my father worked in a paper mill. . . .My mother, after stints as a domestic and factory worker, toiled at home raising four children. . . .

That paper mill played a central role in my life, not only because my father and other family members worked there, but because it served as a source of motivation for me. As long as I can remember, I was determined not to work in the mill. . . .

Neither of my parents had attended high school, let alone college, so I was left rudderless in choosing schools. The two part-time guidance counselors at my regional high school of more than seven hundred students were not helpful. One had suggested to me that perhaps, despite my excellent grades, welding would be more "practical" for someone with my "background." After applying to what in retrospect was an eclectic collection of schools, I made the only logical choice: the one that offered me the most scholarship money. It was an elite private college in the Boston area.

From the very first day, my college education brought with it a new awareness of how different cultures could be. I have a vivid memory of the awkwardness and discom-

fort on my parents' faces when they met my assigned roommate and his obviously wealthy parents (both doctors) in the totally alien environment of a college dorm. (I was not feeling any better.) Cultures rarely confront each other so poignantly.

I shared my parents' discomfort as I learned lessons that would make it increasingly difficult for me to return to my working-class community. In both my formal and informal education, I was immersed in middle-class culture. Employment expectations ("careers," not jobs), food ("ethnic," not meat-and-potatoes), dress (natural fibers, not synthetic), music (folk and progressive/alternative rock, not heavy metal), entertainment and leisure (something other than television and hockey)—it was all different from what I was accustomed to.

Perhaps the most striking difference I encountered was the sense of entitlement shared by other students. For

How poverty is defined has serious practical consequences, because the government uses the poverty line to decide who will receive help and who will not. Using this official definition of poverty, let's see who is poor. Before we do this, though, compare your ideas of the poor with the myths that are explored in the Down-to-Earth Sociology box on page 276.

Who Are the Poor?

Geography As you can see from the Social Map on page 276, the poor are not evenly distributed among the states. This map also shows a clustering of poverty in the South, a pattern that has persisted for the past 100 years or longer.

A second aspect of geography is also significant. About 56 million Americans live in rural areas. Of these, 9 million are poor. At 16 percent, this is higher than the national average of 13 percent. The rural poor are less likely to be single parents, and more likely to be married and to have jobs. Compared with urban Americans, the rural poor are less skilled and less educated, and the jobs available to them pay less than similar jobs in urban areas (Dudenhefer 1993).

most of my middle-class peers, college seemed to be little more than a nuisance and an unexceptional part of their lives. Often choreographed by their parents, college was an expected step towards a larger world of broad opportunity. But for me school always seemed a luxury, and I had a strange sense that one day I would be told some terrible administrative error had been made and I would be sent packing back home to serve my time in the mill where I *really* belonged. (Years later, when I was a graduate student on a full scholarship, the feeling still lingered.)

On the whole, my experiences confirmed my earlier sense of the vast distance between "ordinary" people and the more privileged classes with whom I now interacted. Having strayed further and further from home, I saw and felt class differences more sharply than ever. The feelings were often unpleasant. During my first disorienting year at school

I found solace by making friends with local working-class "townies" and frequently drinking to excess. . . .

But as I was learning to better analyze and understand the world in which I lived, I was drifting away from the world from which I had come. My education had equipped me with middle-class skills and had introduced me to middle-class values, attitudes, and ways of thinking. . . .

In a study of social mobility, David Karp has commented that "Class background does not fall away like a snake's old skin once professional status is achieved." The image is a good one and it holds true for my travels to the middle-class Left. I found myself straddling a fence. I had a full set of middle-class educational credentials and was part of a middle-class movement ["peace-and-justice" organizations], but I still had strong attachments to my roots and to my working-class family

and friends. I had a foot in each world but was completely comfortable in neither of them. Having been socialized into two different classes, I was constantly aware—sometimes painfully so—of the differences between these cultures. . . .

I was confronted with the undeniable reality of a class divide that separated the cultures of the working-class world from which I had come from that of the middle-class, political Left to which I had traveled. . . . Such a confrontation of cultures is fertile ground for sociological analysis. That is what my professional training has taught me. My lived experience of this class divide has, for me, made it more than an academic question. ■

Source: David Croteau. *Politics and the Class Divide: Working People and the Middle-Class Left.* Philadelphia: Temple University Press, 1995: xxiv–xxviii.

The greatest predictor of whether Americans are poor is not geography, however; the most significant factors are race-ethnicity, education, and the sex of the person who heads the family. Let's look at each.

Race-Ethnicity One of the strongest factors in poverty is race-ethnicity. As Figure 10.6 on page 277 shows, only 11 percent of white Americans are poor, but 27 percent of African Americans and Latinos live in poverty. Although white Americans are less likely to be poor than are most racial-ethnic groups, because there are so many more white Americans, most poor people are white.

Education and Poverty As you know, education is also a vital factor in poverty, but you may not have known just how powerful it is. From Figure 10.7 on page 278, you can see that only 2 percent of people who finish college end up in poverty, but one of every four people who drop out of high school is poor. As you can see, the chances of someone being poor decrease with each higher level of education. Although this principle applies regardless

Sociology

Down-to-Earth

EXPLORING MYTHS ABOUT THE POOR

Myth 1: Most poor people are lazy. They are poor because they do not want to work.

Half of the poor are either too old or too young to work. About 40 percent are under age 18, and another 10 percent are age 65 or older. About 30 percent of the working-age poor work at least half the year.

Myth 2: Poor people are trapped in a cycle of poverty that few escape.

The U.S. poverty population is *dynamic*. Most poverty lasts less than a year (Gottschalk et al. 1994). Only 12 percent of the poor remain in poverty for five or more consecutive years (O'Hare 1996a). Most children who are born in poverty are not poor as adults (Ruggles 1989).

Myth 3: Most of the poor are African Americans and Latinos.

As shown on Figure 10.6, the poverty rates of African Americans and Latinos are much higher than that of whites. Because there are so many more whites in the population, however, *most poor people are white*. Fifty-six percent of the poor are white, 21 percent African American, 19 percent Latino, 3 percent Asian American, and 1 percent Native American (*Statistical Abstract* 1999:Tables 54, 760).

Myth 4: Most of the poor are single mothers and their children.

Although about 38 percent of the poor do match this stereotype, 34 percent of the poor live in married-couple families, 22 percent live alone or with nonrelatives, and 6 percent live in other settings.

Myth 5: Most of the poor live in the inner city.

This one is close to fact, as about 42 percent do live in the inner city. But 36 percent live in the suburbs, and 22 percent live in small towns and rural areas.

Myth 6: The poor live on welfare.

About half of the income of poor adults comes from wages and pensions, about 25 percent from welfare, and about 22 percent from Social Security. ■

Sources: Primarily O'Hare 1996a and O'Hare 1996b, but other sources as indicated.

Figure 10.5

SOCIAL MAP: PATTERNS OF POVERTY

Source: Statistical Abstract 1999:Table 765.

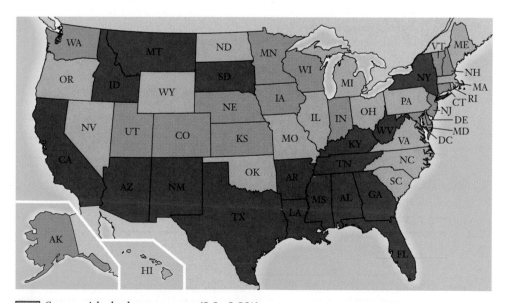

 States with the least poverty (8.0–9.9%)

States with average poverty (10.0–13.9%)

States with the most poverty (14.0–21.8%)

of race-ethnicity, you can see how race-ethnicity retains its impact at every level of education.

The Feminization of Poverty The other major predictor of poverty is the sex of the person who heads the family. Compared with men, women are more likely to be poor (*Statistical Abstract* 1999:Tables 756, 766). Women who head families average only two-thirds the income of men who head families (*Statistical Abstract* 1999:Table 754). Consequently, most poor families are headed by women. The three major causes of this phenomenon, called the **feminization of poverty**, are divorce, births to single women, and the lower wages paid to women.

Old Age As Figure 10.6 shows, the elderly are less likely than the general population to be poor. It used to be that growing old increased people's chances of being poor, but government policies to redistribute wealth— Social Security and subsidized housing, food, and medical care—have cut the rate of poverty among the elderly. As you can see from this figure, the prevailing racial-ethnic patterns carry over into old age; an elderly African American or Latino is almost three times as likely to be poor than is an elderly white person.

Children of Poverty

Children are more likely to live in poverty than are adults or the elderly. This holds true regardless of race-ethnicity, but as Figure 10.6 shows, poverty is much greater among Latino and African-American children. That about 15 million U.S. children are reared in poverty is shocking when one considers the wealth of this country and the supposed concern for the well-being of children. This tragic aspect of poverty is the topic of the following Thinking Critically section.

Beyond the awareness of most Americans are the rural poor, such as this family in Louisiana. This family is typical of the rural poor: white and headed by a woman. What do you think the future holds for these children?

feminization of poverty a trend in U.S. poverty whereby most poor families are headed by women

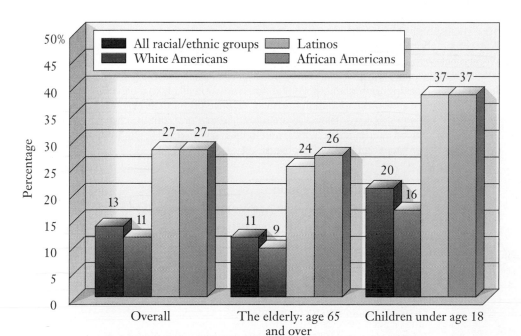

Figure 10.6

POVERTY IN THE UNITED STATES, BY AGE AND RACE-ETHNICITY

Source: Statistical Abstract 1999: Tables 760, 763.

Note: The poverty line on which this figure is based is $16,400 for a family of four.

Figure 10.7

EDUCATION AND POVERTY

Source: Statistical Abstract 1999:Table 769.

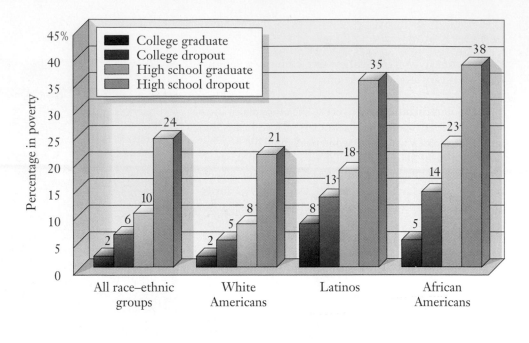

A disturbing aspect of poverty is that, of all U.S. age groups, children are the most likely to be poor. Explanations for this troubling change are given in the text. What do you think the future holds for these young people in North Philadelphia?

THE NATION'S SHAME: CHILDREN IN POVERTY

One of the most startling statistics in sociology is shown in Figure 10.6: One of every five U.S. children lives in poverty. One of six white children and one of three Latino and African-American children are poor. These figures translate into incredible numbers—approximately *14 million* children live in poverty: 6 million white children, 4 million Latino children, and 4 million African-American children.

According to sociologist and U.S. Senator Daniel Moynihan, this high rate of child poverty is due primarily to a general breakdown of the U.S. family. He pointed his finger at the sharp increase in births outside marriage. In 1960, only one of twenty U.S. children was born to an unmarried mother. Today that figure is *six times higher,* and single women now account for one of three (32 percent) of all U.S. births. The relationship to social class is striking, for as Table 10.4 shows, births to unmarried mothers are not distributed evenly across the social classes. For women above the poverty line, only 6 percent of births are to single mothers, while for women below the poverty line this rate jumps to 44 percent.

Regardless of the causes of childhood poverty—and there are many—what is most significant is its far-reaching consequences. Poor children are more likely to die in infancy, to go hungry and to become malnourished, to develop more slowly, and to have more health problems. They also are more likely to drop out of school, to become involved in criminal activities, and to have children while still in their teens—thus perpetuating the cycle of poverty. ■

For Your Consideration

Many social analysts—liberals and conservatives alike—are alarmed at this increase in child poverty. They emphasize that it is time to stop blaming the victim, and instead to focus on the structural factors that underlie child poverty. To relieve the problem, they say, we must take immediate steps to establish national programs of child nutrition and health care. Solutions will require at least these fundamental changes: (1) removing obstacles to employment; (2) improving education; and (3) strengthening the family. To achieve these changes, what specific programs would *you* recommend?

Sources: Moynihan 1991; Murray 1993; Sandefur 1995; *Statistical Abstract* 1997:Table 1338; 1999:Tables 22, 92, 760, 763.

The Dynamics of Poverty

In the 1960s, Michael Harrington (1962) and Oscar Lewis (1966a) suggested that the poor tend to get trapped in a **culture of poverty**. They assumed that the values and behaviors of the poor "make them fundamentally different from other Americans, and that these factors are largely responsible for their continued long-term poverty" (Ruggles 1989:7).

Lurking behind this concept is the idea that the poor are lazy people who bring poverty on themselves. Certainly some individuals and families match this stereotype—many of us have known them. But is a self-perpetuating culture—one that is transmitted across generations and that locks people in poverty—the basic reason for U.S. poverty?

Researchers who followed 5,000 U.S. families since 1968 uncovered some rather surprising findings. Contrary to common stereotypes, most poverty is short, lasting only a year or less. Most poverty comes about because of a dramatic life change such as divorce, sudden unemployment, or even the birth of a child (O'Hare 1996a). As Figure 10.8 shows, only 12 percent of poverty lasts five years or longer. Contrary to the stereotype of lazy people content to live off the government, the vast majority of poor people don't like poverty, and they do what they can to *not* be poor.

Yet from one year to the next the number of poor people remains about the same. This means that the people who move out of poverty are replaced by people who move *into* poverty. The vast majority of these newly poor also will move out of poverty within a year. Some people even bounce back and forth, never quite making it securely out of poverty. This means that poverty is dynamic, touching a lot more people than the official figures indicate. Although 13 percent of Americans may be poor at any one time, about one-fourth of the U.S. population is or has been poor for at least a year.

Why Are People Poor?

Two explanations for poverty compete for our attention. The first, which sociologists adopt, focuses on *social structure*. Sociologists stress that *features of society* deny some people access to education or learning job skills. They emphasize racial, ethnic, age, and gender discrimination, as well as changes in the job market—the closing of plants, drying up of unskilled jobs, and an increase in marginal jobs that pay poverty wages.

A competing explanation focuses on the *characteristics of individuals* that are assumed to contribute to poverty. Individualistic explanations that sociologists reject outright as worthless stereotypes are laziness and lack of intelligence. Individualistic explanations that sociologists reluctantly acknowledge include dropping out of school, bearing children at younger ages, and averaging more children than women in the other social classes. Most sociologists are reluctant to speak of such factors in this context, for they appear to blame the victim, something that sociologists bend over backward not to do.

The tension between these competing explanations is of more than just theoretical interest. These explanations affect our perception and have practical consequences, as is illustrated in the following Thinking Critically section.

THE WELFARE DEBATE: THE DESERVING AND THE UNDESERVING POOR

Throughout U.S. history, Americans have divided the poor into two types: the deserving and the undeserving. The deserving poor are people who, in the public mind, are poor through no fault of their own. Most of the working poor, such as the Lewises, are considered deserving

Nancy and Ted Lewis are married, in their late 30s, with two children. Ted works three part-time jobs; Nancy takes care of the children and house. Their total income is $12,000 a year

Table 10.4

U.S. BIRTHS TO SINGLE AND MARRIED WOMEN

Births to Women Above the Poverty Line

Married	Single
94%	6%

Births to Women Below the Poverty Line

Married	Single
56%	44%

Note: Figures were available only for white women.

Source: Murray 1993.

culture of poverty the assumption that the values and behaviors of the poor make them fundamentally different from other people, that these factors are largely responsible for their poverty, and that parents perpetuate poverty across generations by passing these characteristics to their children

Figure 10.8

HOW LONG DOES POVERTY LAST?

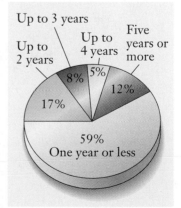

Source: Gottschalk et al. 1994:89.

To make ends meet, the Lewises rely on food stamps, Medicaid, and housing subsidies. (Milbank 1995b)

The undeserving poor, in contrast, are viewed as having brought on their own poverty. They are freeloaders who waste their lives in sloth, alcohol and drug abuse, and unwed motherhood. They don't deserve help, and, if given anything, will waste it on their dissolute lifestyles. Some would see Joan as an example:

Joan's grandmother and her six children were supported by welfare. Joan's parents are alcoholics—and on welfare. Joan started having sex at 13, bore her first child at 15, and, now at 23, is expecting her fourth child. Her first two children have the same father, the third a different father, and Joan isn't sure who fathered her coming child. Joan parties most nights, using both alcohol and whatever drugs are available. Her house is filthy, and social workers have threatened to take away her children.

This division of the poor into deserving and undeserving underlies the heated debate about welfare. "Why should we use *our* hard-earned money to help *them*? They are just going to waste it. Of course, there are those who want to get on their feet, and helping them is okay." ■

For Your Consideration

Of what use is such a division of the poor into deserving and undeserving? Should we let some people starve because they "brought poverty upon themselves"? Should we let children go hungry because their parents are unmarried and uneducated? Does "unworthy" mean that we should not offer assistance to people who "squander" the help they are given?

Try to go beyond such a simplistic division and use the sociological perspective to explain poverty without blaming the victim. What *social* conditions (conditions of society) create poverty? What *social* conditions produce the lifestyles of which the middle class so vehemently disapproves?

Welfare Reform

After decades of criticism, U.S. welfare was restructured in 1996. A federal law—the Personal Responsibility and Work Opportunity Reconciliation Act—required states to place a lifetime cap on welfare assistance and to require welfare recipients to look for work and to take available jobs. The maximum length someone can collect welfare is two years. Many states made it shorter. They also required unmarried teen parents to attend school and live at home or in some other adult-supervised setting.

This law set off a storm of criticism, with some calling it an attack on the poor. Defenders said that the new rules would rescue people from poverty—transforming them into self-supporting and hard-working citizens—and reduce welfare costs (Cohen 1997). Many states put up new signs, changing "Welfare Center" to "Job Placement Center." Welfare rolls plummeted, in Wisconsin by 90 percent. Overall, national welfare rolls dropped by 44 percent (Dervarics 1998; Associated Press 1999; DeParle 1999). This is only the rosy part of the picture, however. Apparently, about one-fifth to one-sixth of former welfare recipients have no job, and, having used up their allotted time to collect welfare, are worse off than before (Goldberg 1999; DeParle 1999).

Conflict theorists point out that the welfare system has a different purpose than we ordinarily realize—to maintain an army of reserve workers. It is designed to keep the unemployed alive during economic downturns until they are needed during the next economic boom. Reducing the welfare rolls through the 1996 law does fit this model, as it occurred during the longest economic boom in U.S. history. During our next recession, which is inevitable, unemployment will surge. In line with conflict theory, we can predict that welfare rules will be softened—in order to keep the reserve army of the unemployed ready for the next time they are needed.

Deferred Gratification

One consequence of a life of deprivation punctuated by emergencies—*and of seeing the future as more of the same*—is a lack of **deferred gratification**, giving up things in the present for the sake of greater gains in the future. It is difficult to practice this middle-class virtue if one does not have a middle-class surplus—or middle-class hope.

Back in 1967, sociologist Elliot Liebow noted this precise problem among African-American street-corner men. Their jobs were low-paying and insecure, their lives pitted with emergencies. With the future looking exactly like the present, and any savings they did manage gobbled up by emergencies—either theirs or their friends' and relatives'—saving for the future was pointless. The only thing that made sense from their perspective was to enjoy what they could at the moment. Immediate gratification, then, was not the cause of their poverty, but its consequence. Cause and consequence loop together, however, for their immediate gratification helped perpetuate their poverty. For another look at this "looping," see the Down-to-Earth Sociology box on the next page, in which I share my personal experiences with poverty.

If both causes are at work, why do sociologists emphasize the structural explanation? Reverse the situation for a moment. Suppose that members of the middle class drove old cars that ran only half the time, faced threats from the utility company to shut off the electricity and heat, and had to make a choice between buying medicine and food and diapers or paying the rent. How long would they practice deferred gratification? Their orientations to life would likely make a sharp U-turn.

Sociologists, then, do not view the behaviors of the poor as the cause of their poverty, but, rather, as the result of their poverty. Poor people would welcome the middle-class opportunities that would allow them the chance to practice the middle-class virtue of deferred gratification. Without those opportunities, though, they just can't afford it.

Where Is Horatio Alger? The Social Functions of a Myth

In the early 1900s, Horatio Alger was one of the country's most talked-about fictional heroes. The rags-to-riches exploits of this national character, and his startling successes in overcoming severe odds, motivated thousands of boys of that period. Although he has disappeared from U.S. literature, Horatio Alger remains alive and well in the psyche of Americans. From abundant, real-life examples of people from humble origins who climbed far up the social class ladder, Americans know that anyone can get ahead by really trying. In fact, they believe that most Americans, including minorities and the working poor, have an average or better than average chance of getting ahead—obviously a statistical impossibility (Kluegel and Smith 1986).

The accuracy of the **Horatio Alger myth** is less important than the belief that limitless possibilities exist for everyone. Functionalists would stress that this belief is functional for society. On the one hand, it encourages people to compete for higher positions, or, as the song says, "to reach for the highest star." On the other hand, it places blame for failure squarely on the individual. If you don't make it—in the face of ample opportunities to get ahead—the fault must be your own. The Horatio Alger myth helps to stabilize society, then, for since the fault is viewed as the individual's, not society's, current social arrangements can be regarded as satisfactory. This reduces pressures to change the system.

As Marx and Weber pointed out, social class penetrates our consciousness, shaping our ideas of life and our "proper" place in society. When the rich look at the world around them, they sense superiority and anticipate control over their own destiny. When the poor look around them, they sense defeat, and anticipate that their lives will be buffeted by unpredictable forces. Each knows the dominant ideology, that their particular niche in life is due to their own efforts, that the reasons for success—or failure—lie solely with the self. Like the fish that don't notice the water, people tend not to perceive the effects of social class on their own lives.

deferred gratification forgoing something in the present in the hope of achieving greater gains in the future

Horatio Alger myth the belief that due to limitless possibilities anyone can get ahead if he or she tries hard enough

A culture's dominant ideology is reinforced in many ways, including in its literature. As discussed in the text, Horatio Alger was the inspirational hero for thousands of boys. The central theme of these many novels, immensely popular in their time, was rags to riches. Through rugged determination and self-sacrifice, a boy could overcome seemingly insurmountable obstacles to reach the pinnacle of success.

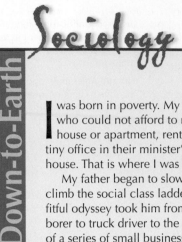

POVERTY: A PERSONAL JOURNEY

I was born in poverty. My parents, who could not afford to rent a house or apartment, rented the tiny office in their minister's house. That is where I was born.

My father began to slowly climb the social class ladder. His fitful odyssey took him from laborer to truck driver to the owner of a series of small businesses (tire shop, bar, hotel), then to vacuum cleaner salesman, and back to bar owner. He converted a garage into a house. Although it had no indoor plumbing or insulation (in northern Minnesota!), it was a start. Later, he bought a house, and then he built a new home. After that we moved into a trailer, and then back to a house. My father's seventh grade education was always an obstacle. Although he never became wealthy, poverty did become a distant memory for him.

My social class took a leap—from working to upper middle—when, after attending college and graduate school, I became a university professor. I entered a world that was unknown to my parents, a world much more pampered and privileged. I had opportunities to do research, to publish, and to travel to exotic places. My reading

centered on sociological research, and I read books in Spanish as well as in English. My father, in contrast, never read a book in his life, and my mother read only detective stories and romance paperbacks. One set of experiences isn't "better" than the other, just significantly different in determining what windows of perception it opens onto the world.

My interest in poverty, which was rooted in my own childhood experiences, stayed with me. I traveled to a dozen or so skid rows across the United States and Canada, talking to the homeless and staying in their shelters. In my own town, I spent considerable time with people on welfare, observing how they lived. I constantly marveled at the connections between *structural* causes of poverty (low-level education and skills, few unskilled jobs, the lack of transportation) and its *personal* causes (the *culture of poverty*—alcohol and drug abuse, multiple out-of-wedlock children, frivolous spending, all-night partying, and a seeming incapacity to keep appointments—except to pick up the welfare check).

Sociologists haven't unraveled this connection, and as much as we might *like* for only the structural causes to apply, clearly *both* are at work. The situation can be illustrated by looking at the perennial health problems I observed among the poor—the constant colds, runny noses, back aches, and injuries. The health problems stemmed from the *social structure* (little access to medical treatment, lesser trained or less capable physicians, drafty houses, lack of education regarding nutrition, and more dangerous jobs). At the same time, *personal* characteristics—hygiene, eating habits, and overdrinking—caused health problems. Which was the cause and which the effect? Both, of course, for one fed into the other. The medical problems (which were based on both personal and structural causes) fed into the poverty these people experienced, making them less able to perform their jobs successfully—or even to show up at work regularly.

What an intricate puzzle for sociologists! ■

SUMMARY AND REVIEW

■ What Is Social Class?

What is social class?

Most sociologists have adopted Weber's definition of **social class** as a large group of people who rank close to one another in terms of wealth, power, and prestige. **Wealth**, consisting of property and income, is concentrated in the upper classes. The distribution of wealth in the United States has changed little since World War II, but the changes that have occurred have been toward greater inequality. **Power** is the ability to carry out one's will, even over the

resistance of others. C. Wright Mills coined the term **power elite** to refer to the small group that holds the reins of power in business, government, and the military. **Prestige** is often linked to occupational status. Pp. 256–260.

People's rankings of occupational prestige have changed little over the decades and are similar from country to country. Globally, occupations that pay more, require more education and abstract thought, and offer greater autonomy are accorded greater prestige. Pp. 260–262.

What is meant by the term status inconsistency?

Status is social ranking. Most people are **status consistent**; that is, they rank high or low on all three dimensions of social class. People who rank higher on some dimensions than on others are status inconsistent. The frustrations of **status inconsistency** tend to produce political radicalism. P. 262.

■ Sociological Models of Social Class

What models are used to portray the social classes?

Two models that portray the social classes were described. Erik Wright developed a four-class model based on Marx: (1) capitalists or owners; (2) petty bourgeoisie or small business owners; (3) managers; and (4) workers. Gilbert and Kahl developed a six-class model based on Weber. At the top is the capitalist class. In descending order are the upper middle class, the lower middle class, the working class, the working poor, and the **underclass.** Pp. 263–266.

■ Consequences of Social Class

How does social class affect people's lives?

Social class leaves no aspect of life untouched. It affects people's chances of benefitting from the new technology, dying early, becoming ill, receiving good health care, and getting divorced. Class membership also affects child rearing, educational attainment, religious affiliation, political participation, and contact with the criminal justice system. Pp. 267–270.

■ Social Mobility

What are the three types of social mobility?

The term **intergenerational mobility** refers to changes in social class from one generation to the next. **Exchange mobility** is the movement of large numbers of people from one class to another, with the net result that the relative proportions of the population in the classes remain about the same. The term **structural mobility** refers to changes in society that affect the social class membership of large numbers of people. Pp. 270–273.

■ Poverty

Who are the poor?

Poverty is unequally distributed in the United States. Latinos, African Americans, Native Americans, children, women-headed households, and rural Americans are more likely than others to be poor. The poverty rate of the elderly is less than that of the general population. Pp. 273–279.

What are individual and structural explanations of poverty?

Some social analysts believe that characteristics of *individuals,* such as the desire for immediate gratification, cause poverty. Sociologists, in contrast, examine *structural* features of society, such as employment opportunities, to find the causes of poverty. Sociologists generally conclude that life orientations are a consequence, not the cause, of people's position in the social class structure. Pp. 279–281, 282.

How is the Horatio Alger myth functional for society?

The **Horatio Alger myth**—the belief that anyone can get ahead if only he or she tries hard enough—encourages people to strive to get ahead. It also deflects blame for failure from society to the individual. P. 281.

Where can I read more on this topic?

Suggested readings for this chapter are at the end of this book.

Sociology & the Internet

All URLs listed are current as of the printing of this book. URLs often change. Please check our Web site, **http://www.abacon.com/henslin,** for updates.

1. After reading the "Thinking Critically About Social Controversy" section on children living in poverty, go to the National Center for Children in Poverty Web site at **http://cpmcnet.columbia.edu/dept/nccp.** As you browse this site, notice the range of policy and research activities that are carried out at the Center. The author of your text suggests that the solutions to childhood poverty involve (1) removing obstacles to employment, (2) improving education, and (3) strengthening families. Drawing on what you've learned at this site about poverty and social policy, create recommendations for improving education, providing greater employment opportunities, and strengthening families. Present them as part of a panel discussion for your sociology class.

2. People want others to acknowledge their prestige. They use status symbols to display their position in the social hierarchy: They buy cars not only for transportation but also for prestige. Take a look at the Car Pricing Guide at **http://www.carprices.com/.** How are cars a status symbol? How does the variety of cars suggest inequality in the U.S. class system? According to your text, status symbols vary by social class. Which kinds of cars would the lower class be able to afford? (Be sure to include the cost of insurance.) How do these cars differ from the cars that are available to the upper class? Is it simply a matter of luxury or does safety also cost more?

   Find the Chevrolet that is the most luxurious and has the most safety features. How does it compare with the least expensive Mercedes? How does the most expensive Saturn compare in features with the least expensive BMW? What does this suggest about the role of inequality in car ownership?

3. If you are doing these exercises, it means that you have access to a computer and also some basic knowledge about how to use it and how to navigate around the Internet. In this chapter, you read about the technology gap facing the poor and minorities: Poor children, on average, have less access to these new technologies. At **http://www.benton.org/Library/Low-Income/home.html** there is a report on barriers to closing the digital gap, social policy, and programs designed to bring computers and the Internet to low-income communities. Write a paper about why the gap between the technology haves and have-nots exists and how it can be closed.

Sex and Gender

Wendy Seller, Dissension, 1993

■ **Issues of Sex and Gender**
Biology or Culture? The Continuing Controversy
The Dominant Position in Sociology
Opening the Door to Biology

■ **Gender Inequality in Global Perspective**
Sex Typing of Work
Prestige of Work
Other Areas of Global Discrimination

■ **How Females Became a Minority Group**
The Origins of Patriarchy

■ **Gender Inequality in the United States**
Fighting Back: The Rise of Feminism
Gender Inequality in Education
Gender Inequality in Everyday Life

■ **Gender Inequality in the Workplace**
The Pay Gap
The Glass Ceiling and the Glass Escalator
The "Mommy Track"
Sexual Harassment

■ **Gender and Violence**
Feminism and Gendered Violence
Solutions

■ **The Changing Face of Politics**

■ **Glimpsing the Future—With Hope**

■ **Summary and Review**

In Tunis, the capital of Tunisia, on Africa's northern coast, I met some U.S. college students, with whom I spent a couple of days. When they said that they wanted to see Tunis' red light district, I wondered if it would be worth the trip. I already had seen other red light districts, including

the unusual one in Amsterdam where the state licenses the women, requires medical checkups (certificates must be posted so customers can check them), sets the prices, and pays the prostitutes social security benefits upon retirement. The women sit behind lighted picture windows while customers who are strolling along the canalside streets browse from the outside.

This time the sight turned my stomach.

We ended up on a wharf that extended into the Mediterranean. Each side was lined with a row of one-room wooden shacks, each one crowded up against the next, their walls practically touching. In front of each open door stood a young woman. Peering from outside into the dark interiors, I could see that each door led to a tiny room with a well-worn bed.

The wharf was crowded with men who were eyeing the women. Many of them wore sailor uniforms from countries that I couldn't identify.

As I looked more closely, I could see that some of the women had runny sores on their legs. Incredibly, with such visible evidence of their disease, customers still entered. Evidently the low price (at that time $2) was too much to resist.

With a sickening feeling in my stomach and the desire to vomit, I kept a good distance between myself and the beckoning women. One tour of the two-block area was more than sufficient.

Out of sight, I knew, was a group of men whose wealth derived from exploiting these women who were condemned to live short lives punctuated by fear and misery. ■

I
n this chapter, we examine **gender stratification**—males' and females' unequal access to power, prestige, and property on the basis of sex. Gender is especially significant because it is a *master status;* that is, it cuts across *all* aspects of social life. No matter what our social class, age, race-ethnicity, or what we attain in life, we are labeled *male* or *female.* These labels carry images and expectations about how we should act. They not only guide our behavior but also serve as the basis of power and privilege.

In this chapter's fascinating journey, we shall look at inequality between the sexes around the world and in the United States. We shall explore whether it is biology or culture that makes us the way we are, and review sexual harassment, unequal pay, and violence against women. This excursion will provide a good context for understanding the power differences between men and women that lead to events such as the one just described in the vignette. It should also give you insight into your own experiences with gender.

*I*SSUES OF SEX AND GENDER

When we consider how females and males differ, the first thing that usually comes to mind is **sex,** the *biological* characteristics that distinguish males and females. *Primary sex characteristics* consist of a vagina or a penis and other organs related to reproduction; *secondary sex characteristics* are the physical distinctions between males and females that are not directly connected with reproduction. Secondary sex characteristics become clearly evident at puberty when males develop more muscles, a lower voice, and more hair and height while females form more fatty tissue, broader hips, and larger breasts.

Gender, in contrast, is a *social,* not a biological characteristic. Gender consists of whatever a group considers proper for its males and females. Consequently, gender varies from one society to another. Whereas *sex* refers to male or female, *gender* refers to masculinity or femininity. In short, you inherit your sex, but you learn your gender as you are socialized into specific behaviors and attitudes thought appropriate for your sex. Those expectations of gender vary around the world, as illustrated in the photo montage on the next page.

The sociological significance of gender is that it is a device by which society controls its members. Gender sorts us, on the basis of sex, into different life experiences. It opens and closes doors to power, property, and even prestige. Like social class, gender is a structural feature of society.

Before examining inequalities of gender, let's consider why the behaviors of men and women differ.

Biology or Culture?
The Continuing Controversy

Why are most males more aggressive than most females? Why do women enter "nurturing" occupations such as nursing in such far greater numbers than men? To answer such questions, many people respond with some variation of "They're just born that way."

Is this the correct answer? Certainly biology plays a significant role in our lives. Each of us begins as a fertilized egg. The egg, or ovum, is contributed by our mother, the sperm that fertilizes the egg by our father. At the very moment the egg is fertilized our sex is determined. Each of us receives twenty-three pairs of chromosomes from the ovum and twenty-three from the sperm. The egg has an X chromosome. If the sperm that fertilizes the egg also

gender stratification males' and females' unequal access to power, prestige, and property on the basis of their sex

sex biological characteristics that distinguish females and males, consisting of primary and secondary sex characteristics

gender the social characteristics that a society considers proper for its males and females; masculinity or femininity

Standards of beauty vary so greatly from one culture to another that what one group finds attractive, another may not. Yet, in its ethnocentrism, each group thinks that its standards are the best—that its preferences reflect what beauty "really" is. As indicated here, around the world men and women aspire to their group's standards of gender. To make themselves appealing to others, they make certain that their appearance reflects those standards.

India

Brazil

Mexico

Republic of Georgia

Kenya

Peru

Ivory Coast

Tibet

has an X chromosome, we become female (XX). If the sperm has a Y chromosome, we become male (XY).

That's the biology. Now, the sociological question is, Does this biological difference control our behavior? Does it, for example, make females more nurturing and submissive and males more aggressive and domineering? Almost all sociologists take the side of "nurture" in this "nature versus nurture" controversy, but a few do not, as you can see from the Thinking Critically sections on the next two pages.

Cynthia Fuchs Epstein, whose position in the ongoing "nature versus nurture" debate is summarized here.

Thinking *Critically*

BIOLOGY VERSUS CULTURE— CULTURE IS THE ANSWER

For sociologist Cynthia Fuchs Epstein (1986, 1988, 1989), differences between males' and females' behavior are solely the result of social factors—specifically, socialization and social control. Her argument is as follows:

1. A reexamination of the anthropological record shows greater equality between the sexes in the past than we had thought. In earlier societies, women, as well as men, hunted small game, made tools for hunting and gathering, and gathered food. Studies of today's hunting and gathering societies show that "both women's and men's roles have been broader and less rigid than those created by stereotypes. For example, the Agta and Mbuti are clearly egalitarian and thus prove that hunting and gathering societies exist in which women are not subordinate to men. Anthropologists who study them claim that there is a separate but equal status of women at this level of development."

2. The types of work that men and women perform in each society are determined not by biology but by social arrangements. Few people, whether male or female, can escape these arrangements and almost everyone works within his or her allotted narrow range. This gender inequality of work, which serves the interests of men, is enforced by informal customs and formal laws. When these socially constructed barriers are removed, women's work habits are similar to those of men.

3. The human behaviors that biology "causes" are limited to those involving reproduction or differences in body structure. These differences are relevant for only a few activities, such as playing basketball or "crawling through a small space."

4. Female crime rates, which are rising in many parts of the world, indicate that aggression, often considered a biologically dictated male behavior, is related instead to social factors. When social conditions permit, such as when women become lawyers, they also exhibit "adversarial, assertive, and dominant behavior." Not incidentally, this "dominant behavior" also appears in scholarly female challenges to the biased views about human nature that have been proposed by male scholars.

In short, rather than "women's incompetence or inability to read a legal brief, perform brain surgery, [or] to predict a bull market," social factors—socialization, gender discrimination, and other forms of social control—are responsible for gender differences in behavior. Arguments that assign "an evolutionary and genetic basis" to explain differences in sex status are simplistic. They "rest on a dubious structure of inappropriate, highly selective, and poor data, oversimplification in logic and in inappropriate inferences by use of analogy." ■

The Dominant Position in Sociology

The dominant sociological position is that social factors, not biology, are the reasons we do what we do. The visible differences of sex do not have any built-in meanings. Rather, each human group makes its own interpretation of these physical differences and on that basis assigns males and females to separate groups. There, people learn contrasting expectations of life and, on the basis of their sex, are given different access to their society's privileges.

Most sociologists find the argument compelling that if biology were the principal factor in human behavior, all around the world we would find women to be one sort of person and men another. In fact, however, ideas of gender vary greatly from one culture to another—and, as a result, so do male-female behaviors. The Tahitians in the South Pacific stand in remarkable contrast to our usual expectations of gender. They don't give their children names that are identifiable as male or female, and they don't divide their labor on the basis of gender. They expect *both* men and women to be passive, yielding, and to ignore slights. Neither males nor females are competitive in trying to attain material possessions (Gilmore 1990).

Thinking *Critically*

BIOLOGY VERSUS CULTURE—
BIOLOGY IS THE ANSWER

Steven Goldberg, whose position in the ongoing "nature versus nurture" debate is summarized here.

Sociologist Steven Goldberg (1974, 1986, 1993) finds it astonishing that anyone should doubt "the presence of core-deep differences in males and females, differences of temperament and emotion we call masculinity and femininity." Goldberg's argument—that it is not environment but inborn differences that "give masculine and feminine direction to the emotions and behaviors of men and women"—is as follows:

1. The anthropological record shows that all societies for which evidence exists are (or were) **patriarchies** (societies in which men dominate women). Stories about long-lost **matriarchies** (societies in which women dominate men) are myths.

2. In all societies, past and present, the highest statuses are associated with males. In every society, politics is ruled by "hierarchies overwhelmingly dominated by men."

3. The reason why men dominate societies is that they "have a lower threshold for the elicitation of dominance behavior . . . a greater tendency to exhibit whatever behavior is necessary in any environment to attain dominance in hierarchies and male-female encounters and relationships." Men are more willing "to sacrifice the rewards of other motivations—the desire for affection, health, family life, safety, relaxation, vacation and the like—in order to attain dominance and status."

4. Just as a 6-foot woman does not prove the social basis of height, so exceptional individuals, such as a highly achieving and dominant woman, do not refute "the physiological roots of behavior."

In short, only one interpretation of why every society from that of the Pygmy to that of the Swede associates dominance and attainment with males is valid. Male dominance of society is "an inevitable resolution of the psychophysiological reality." Socialization and social institutions merely *reflect*—and sometimes exaggerate—inborn tendencies. Any interpretation other than inborn differences is "wrongheaded, ignorant, tendentious, internally illogical, discordant with the evidence, and implausible in the extreme." The argument that males are more aggressive because they have been socialized that way is the equivalent of a claim that men can grow moustaches because boys have been socialized that way.

To acknowledge this reality is *not* to defend discrimination against women. Whether or not one approves what societies have done with these basic biological differences is not the point. The point is that biology leads males and females to different behaviors and attitudes—regardless of how we feel about this or wish it were different. ■

Opening the Door to Biology

The matter of "nature versus nurture" is not so easily settled, however, and some sociologists who take the "nurture" side still acknowledge that biological factors may be involved in some human behavior other than reproduction and childbearing. Alice Rossi, for example, a feminist sociologist and former president of the American Sociological Association, has suggested that women are better prepared biologically for "mothering" than are men. She (1977, 1984) says that women are more sensitive to the infant's soft skin and to their nonverbal communications. Her basic point is that the issue is not either biology or society. It is that nature provides biological predispositions, which are then overlaid with culture.

To see why the door to biology is opening, just slightly, in sociology, let's consider a medical accident and a study of Vietnam veterans.

A Medical Accident The drama began in 1963, when 7-month-old identical twins were taken to a doctor to be circumcised (Money and Ehrhardt 1972). The inept physician, who was using electrocautery (a heated needle), turned the electric current too high and

patriarchy a society in which men dominate women

matriarchy a society in which women dominate men

accidentally burned off the penis of one of the boys. You can imagine the parents' reaction of disbelief, followed by horror, as the truth sank in.

What can be done in a situation like this? The damage was irreversible. The parents were told that the child could never have sexual relations. After months of soul-searching and tearful consultations with experts, the parents decided that their son should have a sex change operation. When he was 17 months old, surgeons castrated the boy, using the skin to construct a vagina. The parents then gave the child a girl's name, dressed him in frilly clothing, let his hair grow long, and began to treat him as a girl. Later, physicians gave the child female steroids to promote female pubertal growth.

At first the results were promising. When the twins were 4½ years old, the mother said (remember that the children are biologically identical):

> One thing that really amazes me is that she is so feminine. I've never seen a little girl so neat and tidy. . . . She likes for me to wipe her face. She doesn't like to be dirty, and yet my son is quite different. I can't wash his face for anything. . . . She is very proud of herself, when she puts on a new dress, or I set her hair. . . . She seems to be daintier. (Money and Ehrhardt 1972)

About a year later, the mother described how their daughter imitated her while their son copied his father:

> I found that my son, he chose very masculine things like a fireman or a policeman. . . . He wanted to do what daddy does, work where daddy does, and carry a lunch kit. . . . And [my daughter] didn't want any of those things. She wants to be a doctor or a teacher. . . . But none of the things that she ever wanted to be were like a policeman or a fireman, and that sort of thing never appealed to her. (Money and Ehrhardt 1972)

If the matter were this clear-cut, we could use this case to conclude that gender is entirely up to nurture. Seldom are things in life so simple, however, and a twist occurs in this story. Despite this promising start and her parents' coaching, the twin whose sex had been reassigned did not adapt well to femininity. She preferred to mimic her father shaving, rather than her mother putting on makeup. She rejected dolls, preferring guns and her brother's toys. She liked rough and tumble games and insisted on urinating standing up. Classmates teased her and called her a "caveman" because she walked like a boy. At age 14, she was expelled from school for beating up a girl who teased her. Despite estrogen treatment, she was not attracted to boys, and, and at age 14, in despair over her inner turmoil, she was thinking of suicide. In a tearful confrontation, her father told her about the accident and her sex change.

"All of a sudden everything clicked. For the first time things made sense and I understood who and what I was," is what this twin says of this revelation. He then requested male hormone shots, and later had surgery to partially reconstruct a penis. At age 25, he married a woman and adopted her children (Diamond and Sigmundson 1997).

The Vietnam Veterans Study In various studies, researchers have found that boys and men who have higher levels of testosterone tend to be more aggressive. Some of the findings are intriguing. In one study, researchers compared the testosterone levels of college men in a "rowdy" fraternity with those of men in a fraternity that had a reputation for academic success and social responsibility. Men in the "rowdy" fraternity had higher levels of testosterone (Dabbs et al. 1996). In another study, researchers compared the levels of testosterone in prisoners who had committed property crimes with those of prisoners who had committed sex crimes and acts of violence against people. Those who had committed the crimes of sex and violence had higher levels of testosterone (Dabbs et al. 1995). The samples, though intriguing, were always small.

Then in 1985, the U.S. government began a health study of Vietnam veterans. To be certain the study was representative, the researchers chose a random sample of 4,462 men. Among the data they collected was a measurement of testosterone for each veteran. Until this time, research on testosterone and human behavior was based on small samples. Now, unexpectedly, sociologists had a large random sample available, and the sample is turning out to hold surprising clues about human behavior.

This sample supports earlier studies showing that men who have higher levels of testosterone tend to be more aggressive and to have more problems as a consequence. When the veterans with higher testosterone were boys, they were more likely to get in trouble with parents and teachers and to become delinquents. As adults, they are more likely to use hard drugs, to get into fights, to end up in lower-status jobs, and to have more sexual partners. Knowing this, you probably won't find it surprising to learn that they also are less likely to marry. Certainly their low-paying jobs and trouble with authorities make them less appealing candidates for marriage. Those who do marry are less likely to share problems with their wives. They also are more likely to have affairs, to hit their wives, and to get divorced (Dabbs and Morris 1990; Booth and Dabbs 1993).

Fortunately for us sociologists, the Vietnam veterans study does not leave us with biology as the sole basis for behavior. Not all men with high testosterone get in trouble with the law, do poorly in school, or mistreat their wives. A chief difference, in fact, is social class. High-testosterone men from higher social classes are less likely to be involved in anti-social behaviors than are high-testosterone men from lower social classes (Dabbs and Morris 1990). *Social* factors (socialization, life goals, self-definitions), then, also must play a part. Uncovering the social factors and discovering how they work in combination with testosterone will be of high sociological interest.

Sociologists stress the social factors that underlie human behavior, the experiences that mold us, funneling us into different directions in life. The study of Vietnam veterans discussed in the text is one indication of how the sociological door is slowly opening to also consider biological factors in human behavior. Shown here are men of the 173rd Airborne Brigade in a "search and destroy" patrol in Tuy Province, Vietnam, in June 1966.

■ **In Sum** We shall have to await further studies, but the initial findings are intriguing. They indicate that some behavior that we sociologists usually assume to be due entirely to socialization is, in fact, also influenced by biology. The findings are preliminary, but extremely significant. In the years to come, this should prove to be an exciting—and controversial—area of sociological research. One level of research will be to determine if there are behaviors that are due only to biology. The second level will be to discover how social factors modify biology. The third level will be, in sociologist Janet Chafetz's (1990:30) phrase, to determine how "different" becomes translated into "unequal."

$\mathcal{G}$ENDER INEQUALITY IN GLOBAL PERSPECTIVE

Some analysts speculate that in hunting and gathering societies women and men were social equals (Leacock 1981; Hendrix 1994). Apparently horticultural societies also had less gender discrimination than does our contemporary world (Collins et al. 1993). In these societies, women may have contributed about 60 percent of the group's total food. Yet, after reviewing the historical record, historian and feminist Gerda Lerner (1986) concluded that "there is not a single society known where women-as-a-group have decision-making power over men (as a group)."

Let's take a brief overview of some of this global inequality.

Sex Typing of Work

Anthropologist George Murdock (1937) surveyed 324 premodern societies around the world. He found that in all of them activities are **sex typed.** In other words, every society associates activities with one sex or the other. He also found that activities that are considered "female"

sex typing the association of behaviors with one sex or the other

Anthropologist George Murdock surveyed 324 traditional societies world-wide. He found that all of them considered some work "men's" and other work "women's." An example of sex typing of work is shown in this photo of Navajo women cooking lunch for their family during sheep sheering at Monument Valley, Arizona. Almost universally, cooking is considered women's work.

in one society may be considered "male" in another. In some groups, for example, taking care of cattle is women's work, while other groups assign this task to men.

Metalworking was the exception; it was considered men's work in all the societies Murdock examined. Three other pursuits—making weapons, pursuing sea mammals, and hunting—were almost universally the domain of men. In a few societies, however, women participated in these activities. Although Murdock found no specific work that was universally assigned to women, he did find that making clothing, cooking, carrying water, and grinding grain were almost always female tasks. In a few societies, however, such activities were regarded as men's work.

From Murdock's cross-cultural survey, we can conclude that nothing about biology requires men and women to be assigned different work. Anatomy does not have to equal destiny when it comes to occupations, for as we have seen, pursuits that are considered feminine in one society may be deemed masculine in another, and vice versa.

Prestige of Work

You might ask whether this division of labor really illustrates social inequality. Does it perhaps simply represent arbitrary forms of dividing up labor, not gender discrimination?

That could be the case, except for this finding: *Universally, greater prestige is given to male activities—regardless of what those activities are* (Linton 1936; Rosaldo 1974). If taking care of goats is men's work, then the care of goats is considered important and carries high prestige, but if it is women's work, it is considered less important and given less prestige. Or, to take an example closer to home, when delivering babies was "women's work" and was done by midwives, it was given low prestige. But when men took over this task, its prestige increased sharply (Ehrenreich and English 1973). In short, it is not the work that provides the prestige, but the sex with which the work is associated.

Other Areas of Global Discrimination

Let's briefly consider four additional areas of global gender discrimination. Later, when we focus on the United States, we shall examine these areas in greater detail.

Education Two figures illustrate how extensively females are discriminated against in education: Approximately 1 billion adults around the world cannot read; two-thirds are women. About 130 million children are not enrolled in grade school; 70 percent are girls (Ashford 1995). Table 11.1 illustrates this point further. From this table, you can see that females usually are less literate than males—but not always. In four of the countries listed, females and males have identical literacy rates, and in one their rate is slightly higher.

Politics That women lack equal access to national decision making can be illustrated by this global fact: No national legislature in the entire world has as many women as men. Women come closest to having equal representation in Norway, where 40 percent of the legislators are women, but in some countries, such as South Korea, the figure is only 1 percent (Riley 1997). In Kuwait and United Arab Emirates, women can't even vote (Crossette 1995a, b). In most nations, as in the United States, women hold about 10 percent of national legislative seats (Ashford 1995).

The Pay Gap In every nation, women average less pay than men. For manufacturing jobs, U.S. women earn about two-thirds of what men are paid, while in South Korea women make only half of what men earn (Ashford 1995).

Violence Against Women A global human rights issue is violence against women (Crossman 1995). Perhaps the most infamous historical examples are foot binding in China, *suttee* (burning the living widow with her dead husband's body) in India, and witch burning in Europe. In addition to rape, wife beating, forced prostitution (as was likely the case in our opening vignette), and female infanticide, the most notorious current example is female circumcision, the topic of the Perspectives box on the next page.

Throughout history, women have been denied the right to pursue various occupations on the basis of presumed biological characteristics. As society—and sex roles—have changed, women have increasingly entered occupations traditionally reserved for men.

Table 11.1	LITERACY AND GENDER: LITERACY RATES IN LEAST INDUSTRIALIZED AND INDUSTRIALIZING NATIONS							
Country	Women	Men	Country	Women	Men	Country	Women	Men
Nepal	14%	41%	Laos	44%	69%	Zimbabwe	80%	90%
Sierra Leone	18%	45%	Iraq	45%	71%	Dominican Republic	82%	82%
Mali	23%	39%	Nigeria	47%	67%	South Africa	82%	82%
Mozambique	23%	58%	Guatemala	49%	62%	Venezuela	90%	92%
Ethiopia	25%	46%	Gabon	53%	74%	Lebanon	90%	95%
Bangladesh	26%	49%	Ghana	54%	76%	Colombia	91%	91%
Morocco	31%	57%	Papua New Guinea	63%	81%	Thailand	92%	96%
Sudan	35%	58%	Kenya	70%	86%	Costa Rica	95%	95%
India	36%	66%	Turkey	72%	92%	Cuba	95%	96%
Egypt	39%	64%	Indonesia	78%	90%	Uruguay	98%	97%

Source: UNESCO: Institute for Statistics, 2000.

PERSPECTIVES | Cultural Diversity Around the World

FEMALE CIRCUMCISION

Female circumcision is common in parts of Muslim Africa and in some parts of Malaysia and Indonesia. This custom, often called female genital mutilation (FGM) by Westerners, is also known as clitoral excision, clitoridectomy, infibulation, and labiadectomy, depending largely on how much of the tissue is removed. Worldwide, between 100 million and 200 million females have been circumcised.

In some cultures only the girl's clitoris is cut off, in others the clitoris and both the labia majora and the labia minora. The Nubia in the Sudan cut away most of the girl's genitalia, then sew together the remaining outer edges with silk or catgut. The girl's legs are bound from ankles to waist for several weeks while scar tissue closes up the vagina almost completely. They leave a small opening the size of a matchstick or a pencil for the passage of urine and menstrual fluids. In East Africa the vaginal opening is not sutured shut, but the clitoris and both sets of labia are cut off.

Among most groups, the surgery takes place between the ages of 4 and 8. In some cultures it occurs seven to ten days after birth. In others, such as the Sabiny of Uganda, it is not performed until girls reach adolescence. Because the surgery is often done without anesthesia, the pain is so excruciating that adults must hold the girl down. In urban areas, the operation is sometimes performed by physicians; in rural areas, it is usually performed by a neighborhood woman.

Some of the risks are shock, extensive bleeding, infection, infertility, and death. Ongoing complications include vaginal spasms, painful intercourse, and lack of orgasms. The tiny opening makes urination and menstruation difficult. Frequent urinary tract infections result from urine and menstrual flow building up behind the little opening.

When the woman marries, the opening is cut wider to permit sexual intercourse. In some groups, this is the husband's responsibility. Before a woman gives birth, the opening is enlarged further. After birth, the vagina is again sutured shut, a cycle of surgically closing and opening that begins anew with each birth.

One woman, circumcised at 12, described it this way:

"Lie down there," the excisor suddenly said to me, pointing to a mat stretched out on the ground. No sooner had I laid down than I felt my frail, thin legs tightly grasped by heavy hands and pulled wide apart. I lifted my head. Two women on each side of me pinned me to the ground. My arms were also immobilized. Suddenly I felt some strange substance being spread over my genital area. . . . It was supposed to facilitate the excision. . . . I would have given anything at that moment to be a thousand miles away; then a shooting pain brought me back to reality. . . . I underwent the ablation of the labia minor and then of the clitoris. The operation seemed to go on forever . . . I was in the throes of agony, torn apart both physically and psychologically. It was the rule that girls of my age did not weep in this situation. I broke the rule. I reacted immediately with tears and screams of pain. . . . Never have I felt such excruciating pain!

[After the operation] they forced me, not only to walk back to join the other girls who had already been excised, but to dance with them . . . I was doing my best . . . then I fainted. . . . It was a month before I was completely healed. . . . When I was better, everyone mocked me, as I hadn't been brave, they said. (Walker and Parmar 1993: 107–108)

What are the reasons for this custom? Some groups believe that it reduces female sexual desire, thus making it more likely that a woman will be a virgin at marriage, and, afterward, will remain faithful to her husband. Others believe that it enhances female fertility, prevents the clitoris from getting infected, and enhances vaginal cleanliness.

Feminists, who call female circumcision a form of ritual torture to control female sexuality, point out that the societies that practice it are male dominated. Mothers cooperate with the circumcision because in these societies an unmarried woman has virtually no rights, and an uncircumcised woman is considered impure and is not allowed to marry. Grandmothers insist that the custom continue out of concern that their granddaughters marry well.

Some immigrants to the United States have taken their daughters back to the homeland for the operation, while others have pooled their money and flown in an excisor who performed the surgery on several girls. In 1997, the United States passed a law that makes arranging or performing female circumcision punishable by up to five years in prison. ■

For Your Consideration

Do you think that Western nations should try to make African nations stop this custom? Or would this be ethnocentric, the imposition of Western values on other cultures? As one Somali woman said, "The Somali woman doesn't need an alien woman telling her how to treat her private parts." What legitimate basis do you think there is for members of one culture to interfere with another?

Sources: Based on Mahran 1978, 1981; Ebomoyi 1987; Lightfoot-Klein 1989; Merwine 1993; Walker and Parmar 1993; Welsh 1995; "Egipto . . . " 1996; Chalkley 1997.

How Females Became a Minority Group

Around the world, gender is *the* primary division between people. Each society sets up barriers to provide unequal access to power, property, and prestige on the basis of sex. Consequently, sociologists classify females as a **minority group.** Because females outnumber males, you may think this strange, but because this term refers to people who are discriminated against on the basis of physical or cultural characteristics, this concept applies to females (Hacker 1951). For an overview of gender discrimination in a changing society, see the Perspectives box below.

Have females always been a minority group? As we just saw, some analysts speculate that in the horticultural and hunting and gathering societies women and men may have been social equals—or that at least there was much less gender discrimination than there is in our contemporary world. How did it happen, then, that around the world women came to be systematically discriminated against? Let's consider the primary theory that has been developed.

The Origins of Patriarchy

This theory points to social consequences of the biology of human reproduction (Lerner 1986; Friedl 1990). In early human history, life was short, and in order to reproduce the human group many children had to be born. Because only females get pregnant, carry a child

> **minority group** a group that is discriminated against on the basis of its members' physical or cultural characteristics

---

PERSPECTIVES | Cultural Diversity Around the World

"PSSST. YOU WANNA BUY A BRIDE?" CHINA IN TRANSITION

Nguyen Thi Hoan, age 22, thanked her lucky stars. A Vietnamese country girl, she had just arrived in Hanoi to look for work, and while she was still at the bus station a woman offered her a job in a candy factory.

It was a trap. After Nguyen had loaded a few sacks of sugar, the woman took her into the country to "get supplies." There some men took her to China, which was only 100 miles away. Nguyen was put up for sale at an auction, along with a 16-year-old Vietnamese girl. Each brought $350, a small fortune in China. Nguyen was traded from one bride dealer to another until she was taken to a Chinese village. There she was introduced to her new husband, who had paid $700 for her (Marshall 1999).

What's behind this kidnapping and sale of brides? Apparently two factors. First, there is a centuries-long tradition of bride selling in this part of China. Although the practice was stamped out under Communist rule and is illegal, it is now coming back. Second, China has a shortage of women. The government enforces a "one couple-one child" policy. Since sons are preferred, this has led to female infanticide (a topic explored on page 585), which, in turn, has created a shortage of women of marriageable age.

Actually, Nguyen was lucky. Many kidnapped women are sold to brothel owners.

As you might infer from these practices, the status of women in China is not high. Although the situation of women apparently improved under Communist rule, it is deteriorating under embryonic capitalism. Factory managers used to be assigned production goals and then given the resources to meet those goals. Profit was not a factor. Now it is. Maternity leaves, child care centers, and rooms for nursing mothers—all requirements under Chinese law—make women workers more expensive than men. Consequently, women have become the last hired and first fired.

Women are encouraged to enter "traditional" women's occupations. As an official with the Buding Labor Bureau said, being "nurses, nursery school teachers, grade school teachers, and street sweepers is more appropriate for women." Because these are among the least skilled of occupations, they pay little.

Women's bodies are being "westernized," too. A new cosmetic surgery industry has sprung up to give Chinese women Western-looking eyes, stenciled eyebrows, and bigger breasts. And advertising has begun to follow a Western model: Scantily clad women now perch on top of sports cars (Sun 1993; Chen 1995).

China in transition . . . It is a country that is bringing back the old, bride selling, and moving toward the new, a Westernized idea of beauty. In both the old and new, women are commodities for the consumption of men. ■

One theory about the origin of patriarchy is that because of childbirth women assumed tasks associated with home and child care, while men hunted and performed other tasks requiring greater strength, speed, and absence from home. Shown here is a woman in Mozambique as she tills her field.

for nine months, give birth, and nurse, women were limited in their activities for a considerable part of their lives. To survive, an infant needed a nursing mother. With a child at her breast or in her uterus, or one carried on her hip or on her back, women were physically encumbered. Consequently, around the world women assumed tasks that were associated with the home and child care, while men took over the hunting of large animals and other tasks that required greater speed and absence from the base camp for longer periods of time (Huber 1990).

As a consequence, males became dominant. It was the men who left camp to hunt animals, who made contact with other tribes, who traded with these other groups, and who quarreled and waged war with them. It was also men who made and controlled the instruments of death, the weapons used for hunting and warfare. It was they who accumulated possessions in trade, and gained prestige by triumphantly returning with prisoners of war or with large animals to feed the tribe. In contrast, little prestige was given to the ordinary, routine, taken-for-granted activities of women—who were not seen as risking their lives for the group. Eventually, men took over society. Their weapons, items of trade, and knowledge gained from contact with other groups became sources of power. Women became second-class citizens, subject to men's decisions.

Is this theory correct? Remember that the answer lies buried in human history, and there is no way of testing it. Male dominance may be due to some entirely different cause. For example, anthropologist Marvin Harris proposed that because most men are stronger than most women and hand-to-hand combat was necessary in tribal groups, men became the warriors and women the reward to entice them to do battle. Frederick Engels proposed that patriarchy (male dominance of a society) developed with the origin of private property (Lerner 1986). He could not explain why private property should have produced patriarchy, however. Gerda Lerner (1986) suggests that patriarchy may even have had different origins in different places. And, of course, we cannot rule out biology altogether.

Whatever its origins, a circular system of thought evolved. Men developed notions of their own inherent superiority—based on the evidence of their dominant position in society. They surrounded many of their activities with secrecy, and constructed elaborate rules and rituals to avoid "contamination" by females, whom they now openly deemed inferior. Even today, patriarchy is always accompanied by cultural supports designed to justify male dominance.

As tribal societies developed into larger groups, men, who enjoyed their power and privileges, maintained their dominance. Long after hunting and hand-to-hand combat ceased to be routine, and even after large numbers of children were no longer needed in order to reproduce the human group, males held onto their power. Male dominance in contemporary societies, then, is a continuation of a millennia-old pattern whose origin is lost in history.

GENDER INEQUALITY IN THE UNITED STATES

Gender inequality is not some accidental, hit-or-miss affair. Rather, the institutions of each society work together to maintain the group's particular forms of inequality. Customs, often venerated throughout history, both justify and maintain these arrangements. Although men have resisted sharing their privileged positions with women, change has come.

Fighting Back: The Rise of Feminism

To see how far we have come, it is useful to see where we used to be. In early U.S. society, the second-class status of women was taken for granted. A husband and wife were legally one person—him (Chafetz and Dworkin 1986). Women could not serve on juries, nor could they vote, make legal contracts, or hold property in their own name. How could times have changed so much that these examples sound like fiction?

A central lesson of conflict theory is that power yields privilege; like a magnet, it draws to the elite the best resources available. Because men held tenaciously onto their privileges and used social institutions to maintain their position, basic rights for women came only through prolonged and bitter struggle.

Feminism, the view that biology is not destiny, and, therefore, stratification by gender is wrong and should be resisted, met with strong opposition—both by men who had privilege to lose and by women who accepted their status as morally correct. In 1916, feminists, then known as suffragists, founded the National Women's Party. In January 1917, they formed a picket line around the White House. After picketing continuously for six months, the picketers were arrested. Hundreds went to prison, including Lucy Burns and Alice Paul, two leaders of the National Women's Party. The extent to which these women had threatened male prerogatives is demonstrated by their treatment in prison.

> Two men brought in Dorothy Day [the editor of a periodical that espoused women's rights], twisting her arms above her head. Suddenly they lifted her and brought her body down twice over the back of an iron bench. . . . They had been there a few minutes when Mrs. Lewis, all doubled over like a sack of flour, was thrown in. Her head struck the iron bed and she fell to the floor senseless. As for Lucy Burns, they handcuffed her wrists and fastened the handcuffs over [her] head to the cell door. (Cowley 1969)

This "first wave" of the women's movement had a radical branch that wanted to reform all the institutions of society, and a conservative branch that concentrated on winning the vote for women (Chafetz and Dworkin 1986). The conservative branch dominated, and after the vote was won in 1920 the movement basically dissolved.

The "second wave" began in the 1960s. Sociologist Janet Chafetz (1990) points out that up to this time most women thought of work as a temporary activity intended to fill the time between completing school and getting married. As more women took jobs, however, and many began to think of them as careers, they started to compare their working conditions with those of men. This shift in their reference group radically changed how they viewed their working conditions. The result was a "second wave" of protest and struggle against

Foot binding, a form of violence against women, was practiced in China. This photo of a woman in Canton, China, is from the early 1900s. The woman's tiny feet, which made it difficult for her to walk, were a "marker" of status, indicating that her husband was wealthy and did not need her labor.

feminism the philosophy that men and women should be politically, economically, and socially equal, and organized activity on behalf of this principle

The worldwide women's struggle for equal rights has been long and hard. Shown here is a 1919 photo from the "first wave" of the U.S. women's movement. Today's primary focus in this ongoing fight for justice is the workplace.

gender inequalities. The goals of this second wave (which continues today) are broad—they range from changing women's work roles to changing policies on violence against women.

This second wave of the women's movement also has its liberal and conservative branches. Although each holds a different view of what gender equality should look like, the two share several goals, including equality in job opportunities and pay. Both liberals and conservatives have a radical wing. The radicals on the liberal side call for hostility toward men; radicals on the conservative side espouse a return to traditional family roles. All factions—whether radical or conservative—claim to represent the "real" needs of today's women. It is from these claims and counterclaims that the women's movement will continue to take shape and affect public policy.

Although women enjoy fundamental rights today, gender inequality continues to play a central role in social life. In some instances, it can even be a life-and-death matter, as with the medical situations discussed in the Down-to-Earth Sociology box. Let's look at gender relations in education and everyday life, and then, in greater detail, at discrimination in the world of work.

Sociology

Down-to-Earth

MAKING THE INVISIBLE VISIBLE— THE DEADLY EFFECTS OF SEXISM

Medical researchers were perplexed. Reports were coming in from all over the country indicating that women were twice as likely as men to die after coronary bypass surgery. Researchers at Cedars-Sinai Medical Center in Los Angeles checked their own hospital's records. They found that of almost 2,300 coronary bypass patients, 4.6 percent of the women died as a result of the surgery, compared with only 2.6 percent of the men.

These findings presented a sociological puzzle. To solve it, medical researchers first turned to an explanation that was based on biology (Bishop 1990). In coronary bypass surgery, a blood vessel is taken from one part of the body and stitched to a coronary artery on the surface of the heart. Perhaps this operation was more difficult to perform on women because of

their smaller coronary arteries. To find out, researchers measured the amount of time that surgeons kept patients on the heart-lung machine while they operated. They were surprised to learn that women spent less time on the machine than men, indicating that the operation was not more difficult to perform on women.

As the researchers probed, a surprising answer unfolded—unintended gender discrimination. Referring physicians had not taken the chest pains of their women patients as seriously as they took the complaints of their men patients. Physicians, it turned out, were ten times more likely to give men exercise stress tests and radioactive heart scans. They also sent men to surgery on the basis of abnormal stress tests, but waited until women showed clear-cut symptoms of coronary heart disease before sending them to surgery. Being referred for surgery after

the disease is further along decreases the chances of survival.

Other researchers wondered if the sex of the physician mattered when it came to ordering Pap smears and mammography (Lurie et al. 1993). They examined the records of 98,000 patients and found that it did make a difference—women physicians were much more likely to order these screening tests. ■

For Your Consideration

In short, gender bias is so pervasive that it operates beneath our level of awareness and so severe that it can become a matter of life or death. It is important to note that the doctors in these studies were unaware that they were discriminating. They had no intention of doing so. In what ways does gender bias affect your own perceptions and behavior?

Gender Inequality in Education

In education, too, a glimpse of the past sheds light on the present. About a century ago, leading educators claimed that women's wombs dominated their minds, and higher education put a burden on women's frail capacities. Dr. Edward Clarke, of Harvard University's medical faculty, expressed the dominant sentiment this way:

> A girl upon whom Nature, for a limited period and for a definite purpose, imposes so great a physiological task, will not have as much power left for the tasks of school, as the boy of whom Nature requires less at the corresponding epoch. (Andersen 1988)

Because women were so much weaker, Clarke urged them to study only one-third as much as young men—and not to study at all during menstruation.

Over the years, such ideas were discarded. Until recently, however, college was seen as more valuable for men, and fewer women went to college. This created an educational gap between men and women that remains: Overall in the United States, 27 percent of men have completed college compared to 22 percent of women (*Statistical Abstract* 1999:Table 264.) This gap, however, is closing fast. More women than men are now enrolled in U.S. colleges and universities, and women earn 56 percent of all bachelor's degrees (*Statistical Abstract* 1999:Tables 328, 331). As Figure 11.1 shows, women also complete their bachelor's degrees faster than men. If this continues, it won't be long until the gap is reversed.

Another gap that is closing is illustrated on Figure 11.2 on the next page. As this figure illustrates, the proportion of professional degrees earned by women has increased sharply. The greatest change is in dentistry: In 1970 across the entire United States, only 34 women earned this degree. Today that annual total is about 1,300 (*Statistical Abstract* 1999:Table 333).

Women earning more degrees than men, graduating from college faster, and entering the professions in larger numbers is certainly a major break with the past. If we probe beneath the surface, however, we find old practices. Women's sports, for example, are often underfunded because they are not considered as important as men's sports. And whenever I attend a high school football or basketball game, I still see a group of girls in short, brightly colored skirts wildly cheering the boys from the sidelines—but no such group of boys leading organized cheers for the girls when they play *their* sports.

Then there is the matter of *gender tracking;* that is, degrees tend to follow gender, thus reinforcing male-female distinctions. Here are two extremes: Men earn 84 percent of

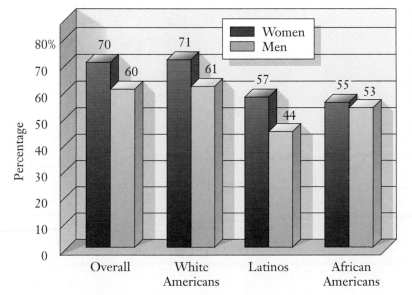

Figure 11.1

OF THOSE WHO GO TO COLLEGE, HOW MANY RECEIVE A BACHELOR'S DEGREE WITHIN 5 YEARS?

Source: Statistical Abstract 1999: Table 328.

**GENDER CHANGES IN
PROFESSIONAL DEGREES**

Source: *Statistical Abstract*
1999:Table 333.

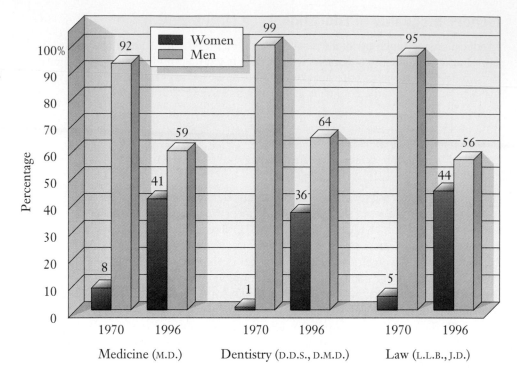

bachelor's degrees in the "masculine" field of engineering, while women are awarded 86 percent of bachelor's degrees in the "feminine" field of library "science" (*Statistical Abstract* 1999:Table 331). Because gender socialization gives men and women different orientations to life, they enter college with gender-linked aspirations. It is their socialization—rather than their innate characteristics—that channels men and women into different educational paths.

If we follow students into graduate school, we see that with each passing year the proportion of women decreases. Table 11.2 gives us a snapshot of doctoral programs in the sciences. Note how aspirations (enrollment) and accomplishments (doctorates earned) are sex

Table 11.2

DOCTORATES IN SCIENCE, BY SEX

Field	Students Enrolled		Doctorates Conferred		Completion Ratio* (Higher or Lower Than Expected)	
	Women	Men	Women	Men	Women	Men
Computer sciences	27%	73%	16%	84%	−41	+15
Engineering	19%	81%	12%	88%	−37	+9
Agriculture	38%	62%	26%	74%	−32	+19
Mathematics	34%	66%	23%	77%	−32	+17
Physical sciences	28%	72%	22%	78%	−21	+8
Social sciences	49%	51%	39%	61%	−20	+20
Biological sciences	50%	50%	43%	57%	−14	+12
Psychology	69%	31%	67%	33%	−3	+6

*The formula for the completion ratio is X minus Y divided by X, where X is the proportion enrolled in a program and Y is the proportion granted doctorates.

Source: *Statistical Abstract* 1999:Tables 1002, 1004.

Shown here are members of Team USA, the Women's World Cup victors at the Rose Bowl in Pasadena, California. On July 10, 1999, they beat Team China by the hair-raising score of 5–4. The winning goal was scored on the fifth shot of a penalty kick shoot-out. Women's sports in high school and college are often underfunded.

linked. In six of these doctoral programs, men outnumber women, in one they are even, and in one, women outnumber men. In *all* of them, women are less likely to complete the doctorate.

If we follow those who earn doctoral degrees into their teaching careers at colleges and universities, we find gender stratification in rank and pay. Throughout the United States, women are less likely to be awarded the rank of full professor, the highest, most prestigious rank. Professors are paid more than the lower ranks (instructor, assistant professor, and associate professor). In both private and public colleges, professors average more than twice the salary of instructors (*Statistical Abstract* 1999:Table 320). To see the extent of the stratification, we can note that even when women are full professors, they average less pay than men who are full professors (DePalma 1993).

Gender Inequality in Everyday Life

Of the many aspects of gender discrimination in everyday life that could be examined, we have space to look only at two: the general devaluation of femininity in U.S. society, and male dominance of conversation.

General Devaluation of Things Feminine

Leaning against the water cooler, two men—both minor executives—are nursing their cups of coffee, discussing last Sunday's Giants game, postponing for as long as possible the moment when work must finally be faced.

A [man] vice president walks by and hears them talking about sports. Does he stop and send them back to their desks? Does he frown? Probably not. Being a man, he is far more likely to pause and join in the conversation, anxious to prove that he, too, is "one of the boys," feigning an interest in football that he may very well not share at all. These men—all the men in the office—are his troops, his comrades-in-arms.

Now, let's assume that two women are standing by the water cooler discussing whatever you please: women's liberation, clothes, work, any subject—except football, of course. The vice president walks by, sees them, and moves down the hall in a fury, cursing and wondering whether it is worth the trouble to complain—but to whom?—about all those bitches standing around gabbing when they should be working. "Don't they know," he will ask, in the words of a million men, "that this is an office?" (Korda 1973:20–21)

As indicated in this scenario, women's capacities, interests, attitudes, and contributions are not taken as seriously as those of men. Masculinity is valued more highly, for it represents strength and success; femininity is devalued, for it is perceived as weakness and even failure (Schur 1984).

During World War II, sociologist Samuel Stouffer noted the general devaluation of things feminine. In his classic study of combat soldiers, *The American Soldier,* Stouffer reported that officers used feminine terms as insults to motivate soldiers (Stouffer et al. 1949). To show less-than-expected courage or endurance was to risk the charge of not being a man. An officer might say, "Whatsa matter, Bud—got lace on your drawers?" A generation later, accusations of femininity were still used as motivating insults to prepare soldiers to fight in Vietnam. Drill sergeants would mock their troops by saying, "Can't hack it, little girls?" (Eisenhart 1975). The practice continues. Male soldiers who show hesitation during maneuvers are mocked by others, who call them girls (Miller 1999). In the Marines, the worst insult that can be made to male recruits is to compare their performance to a woman's (Gilham 1989).

The same phenomenon occurs in sports. Sociologist Douglas Foley (1999) notes that football coaches insult boys who don't play well by saying that they are "wearing skirts," and sociologist Donna Eder (1995) notes that junior high boys call one another "girl" if they don't hit hard enough in football. Sociologists Jean Stockard and Miriam Johnson (1980), who observed boys playing basketball, heard boys who missed a basket being called a "woman." In professional hockey, players who are not rough enough on the ice are called "girls" (Gallmeier 1988:227).

This name-calling is sociologically significant. As Stockard and Johnson (1980:12) point out, such insults embody a generalized devaluation of females. As they noted, "There is no comparable phenomenon among women, for young girls do not insult each other by calling each other 'man.'"

Gender Inequality in Conversation You may have noticed that men are more likely to interrupt a conversation. If so, your observation is correct. In their studies of how men and women talk, sociologists not only confirm this but also report that men are more likely to control changes in topics. They note that talk between a man and a woman is often more like talk between an employer and an employee than between social equals (Hall 1984; West and Garcia 1988; Smith-Lovin and Brody 1989; Tannen 1990, 1999). Even in college classes, men interrupt their instructors more often than do women. This is especially true if the instructor is a woman (Brooks 1982). In short, conversations between men and women mirror their relative positions of power in society.

Derogatory terms and conversation represent only the tip of the iceberg, for underlying these aspects of everyday life is a structural inequality based on gender that runs throughout society. Let's examine that structural feature in the workplace.

GENDER INEQUALITY IN THE WORKPLACE

To examine the work setting is to make visible basic relations between men and women. Let's begin with one of the most remarkable areas of gender inequality at work, the pay gap.

The Pay Gap

One of the chief characteristics of the U.S. work force is a steady increase in the numbers of women who work outside the home for wages. Figure 11.3 shows that in 1890 about one of every five workers was a woman. By 1940, this ratio had grown to one of four, by 1960 to one of three, and today it is almost one of two.

Women who work for wages are not evenly distributed throughout the United States, and where a woman lives makes a difference in how likely she is to work outside the home.

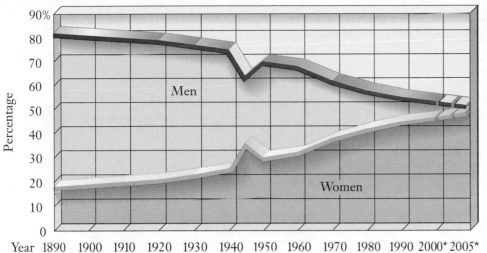

WOMEN'S AND MEN'S PROPORTION OF THE U.S. LABOR FORCE

Sources: 1969 Handbook on Women Workers, 1969:10; Manpower Report to the President, 1971:203, 205; Mills and Palumbo, 1980:6, 45; Statistical Abstract 1999: Table 652.

Note: Pre 1940 totals include women 14 and over: totals for 1940 and after are for women 16 and over. Broken lines are the author's projections.

From the Social Map below, you can see the geographical patterns. These apparently represent regional-subcultural differences of which we currently have little understanding.

Chances are, you are going to go to work after you complete college. (You might like to sit under a palm tree and drink piña coladas instead, but chances are you won't be able to retire right after college.) Assuming, then, that you're going to work, how would you like to earn an extra $950,000 on the job? If this sounds appealing, read on. I'm going to reveal to you how you can make an extra $2,000 a month between the ages of 25 and 65.

Is this hard to do? Actually, it is very simple for some, but impossible for others. All you have to do is be born a male and graduate from college. If we compare full-time workers, this is how much more the *average male* college graduate earns over the course of his

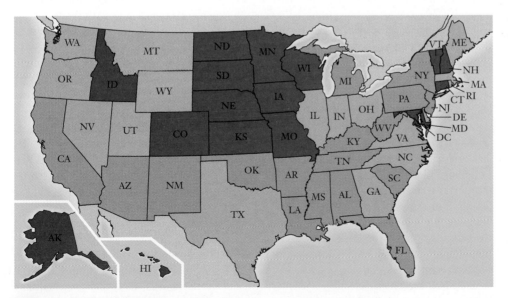

Figure 11.4

SOCIAL MAP: HOW LIKELY IS A WOMAN TO WORK FOR WAGES?

Note: The state with the lowest percentage of women in the work force is West Virginia (47.8%); the state with the highest percentage of women in the work force is Wisconsin (69.7%). This refers to women who are 16 years old and over who are in the civilian labor force, commonly called the *labor force participation rate.*

Sources: Statistical Abstract 1999: Table 654.

Less than average: 47% to 60% of women are in the work force
Average: 60% to 63% of women are in the work force
More than average: 63% to 76% of women are in the work force

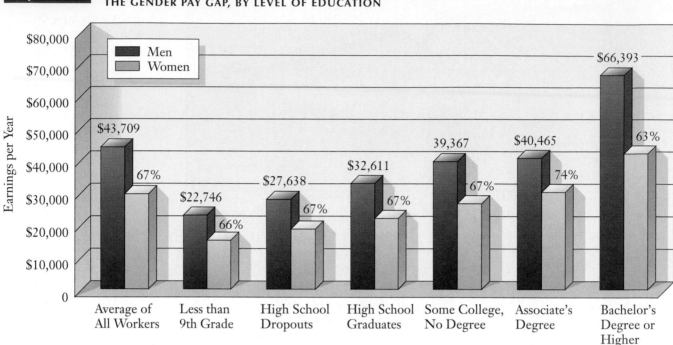

Figure 11.5   WHAT PERCENTAGE OF MEN'S EARNINGS DO WOMEN EARN?
THE GENDER PAY GAP, BY LEVEL OF EDUCATION

Source: Statistical Abstract 1999:Table 266.

career. Hardly any single factor pinpoints gender discrimination better than this total. From Figure 11.5, you can see that the pay gap shows up at all levels of education.

The pay gap is so great that women who work full time average only two-thirds (67 percent) of what men are paid. As Figure 11.6 shows, the pay gap used to be even worse. And it does not occur only in the United States. A gender gap in pay characterizes all industrialized nations, but only in Japan is the gap larger than in the United States (Blau and Kahn 1992).

What logic underlies the gender pay gap? Earlier we saw that college degrees are gender linked, so perhaps this gap is due to career choices. Maybe women are more likely to choose lower-paying jobs, such as grade school teaching, whereas men are more likely to go into better-paying fields, such as business, law, and engineering. Actually, this is true, and researchers have found that about *half* the pay gap is due to such factors. The balance, however, is due to gender discrimination (Kemp 1990).

Depending on your sex, then, you are likely either to benefit from gender discrimination—or to be its victim. Because the pay gap will be so important in your own work life, let's follow some college graduates to see how it actually comes about. Economists Rex Fuller and Richard Schoenberger (1991) examined the starting salaries of the business majors at the University of Wisconsin, of whom 47 percent were women. They found that the women's starting salaries averaged 11 percent ($1,737) less than the men's.

You might be able to think of valid reasons for this initial pay gap. For example, the women might have been less qualified. Perhaps their grades were lower. Or maybe they completed fewer internships. If so, they would deserve lower salaries. To find out, Fuller and Schoenberger reviewed the students' college records. To their surprise, they found that the women had *higher* grades and *more* internships. In other words, if women were equally qualified, they were offered lower salaries—and if they were more highly qualified, they were offered lower salaries—a classic lose-lose situation.

Figure 11.6   WHAT PERCENTAGE OF MEN'S INCOME DO WOMEN EARN? THE GENDER GAP OVER TIME

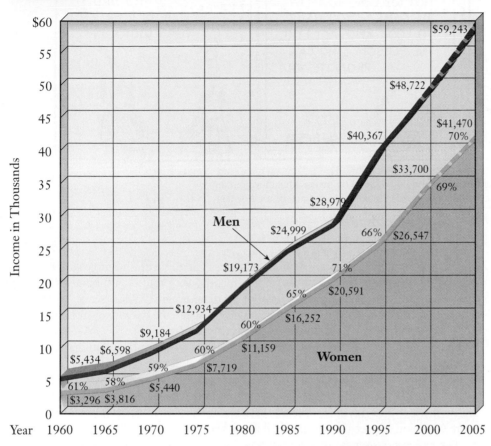

Note: The income jump from 1990 to 1995 is probably due to a statistical procedure. The 1995 source (for 1990 income) uses "median income," while the 1997 source (for 1995 income) merely says "average earnings." How the "average" is computed is not stated. For a review of this distinction, see Table 5.2. Broken lines indicate the author's estimates.

Source: Beeghley 1989:239; *Statistical Abstract* 1995:Table 739; 1999:Table 758.

What happened after these graduates had been on the job a while? Did things tend to even out, so that after a few years the women and men earned about the same? Fuller and Schoenberger checked their salaries five years later. Instead of narrowing, the pay gap had grown even wider. By this time, the women earned 14 percent ($3,615) less than the men.

As a final indication of the extent of the U.S. gender pay gap, consider this. I examined the names of the CEOs of the 350 largest U.S. corporations, and *not one of them is a woman.* Your best chance to reach the top is to be named (in this order) John, Robert, James, William, or Charles. Edward, Lawrence, and Richard are also advantageous. Amber, Katherine, Leticia, and Maria, however, apparently draw a severe penalty.

The Glass Ceiling and the Glass Escalator

What keeps women from breaking through the *glass ceiling,* the mostly invisible barrier that keeps women from reaching the executive suite? Researchers have identified a "pipeline" that leads to the top—the marketing, sales, and production positions that directly affect the corporate bottom line (Reich 1995). Stereotyped as being better at "support," women tend to

One of the frustrations felt by many women in the labor force is that no matter what they do, they hit a glass ceiling. Another is that to succeed they feel forced to abandon characteristics they feel are essential to their self.

be steered into human resources or public relations. There, successful projects are not appreciated in the same way as those that bring in corporate profits—and bonuses for their managers. Felice Schwartz, founder of Catalyst, an organization that focuses on women's issues in the workplace, put it this way: Men, who dominate the executive suite, stereotype potential leaders as people who look like themselves (Lopez 1992).

Another reason the glass ceiling is so powerful is that women lack mentors, successful executives who take an interest in them and teach them the ropes. Some men executives fear that gossip and sexual harassment charges may result if they get close to a woman in a subordinate position. Others don't mentor women because they stereotype women as being weak (Lancaster 1995; Reich 1995). Lack of a mentor is no trivial matter, for supposedly all top executives have had a coach or mentor (Lancaster 1995).

The glass ceiling is cracking, however, and more women are reaching the executive suite (Parker-Pope 1998). A look at women who've broken through the glass ceiling reveals highly motivated women with a fierce competitive spirit who are willing to give up sleep and recreation for the sake of career advancement. They also learn to play by "men's rules," developing a style that makes men comfortable. In the background of about three-fourths of these women is a supportive husband who shares household duties and adapts his career to the needs of his executive wife (Lublin 1996).

Sociologist Christine Williams (1995) interviewed men and women who worked as nurses, elementary school teachers, librarians, and social workers. She found that the men in these traditionally women's occupations, instead of bumping into a glass ceiling, had climbed aboard a *glass escalator*. That is, compared with women, the men were accelerated into higher-level positions, given more desirable work assignments, and paid higher salaries. The motor that drives the glass escalator is gender—the stereotype that because someone is male he is more capable.

Shown here is Martha Stewart, an entrepreneur. In 1999, Stewart went public with her company, Omnimedia Inc., a provider of household products and services. This initial public offering on the New York Stock exchange brought in $315 million.

The "Mommy Track"

Most employed wives face greater role conflict than do their husbands. They are more likely to be the caretakers of the marriage, to nurture it through the hard times. They also tend to spend more time in maintaining family ties (such as sending greeting cards). Most wives, even though employed full time, also spend more time taking care of the children and doing housework.

To help resolve this conflict, Felice Schwartz (1989) suggested that corporations offer women a choice of two parallel career paths. The "fast track" consists of the high-powered, demanding positions that may require sixty or seventy hours of work per week—regular responsibilities, emergencies, out-of-town meetings, and a briefcase jammed with work that has to be done at night and on weekends. With such limited time outside of work, family life often suffers. Women can choose this "fast track" if they wish. Or, instead, they may choose a "mommy track," which would emphasize both career and family. Less would be expected of a woman on the "mommy track," for her commitment to the firm would be lower and her commitment to her family higher.

That, of course, say critics, is exactly what is wrong with this proposal. A "mommy track" will encourage women to be satisfied with lower aspirations and fewer promotions and will confirm men's stereotypes of women executives. Because there is no "daddy track," it also assumes that child rearing is primarily women's work (Starrels 1992). Encouraging women to slow up in the race to climb the corporate ladder would perpetuate, or even increase, the executive pay gap. The "mommy track," critics conclude, would keep men in executive power and relegate women to an inferior position in corporate life.

Schwartz replied that what she was really proposing was a "zigzag track" (Shellenbarger 1995b). "In my ideal world," she said, "people, including men, would slow down during a period when their kids were small. Later they would be readmitted to the mainstream. If you choose this intermittent route upward, you would make it to the top more slowly than someone equally able who took the straight vertical route. The goal," she added, "is to balance family and career."

Critics suggest that a better way to confront the conflict between work and family is for husbands to take on greater responsibilities at home and for firms to provide on-site day care, flexible work schedules, and parental leave without loss of benefits (Auerbach 1990; Galinsky and Stein 1990). Others maintain that the choice between family and career is artificial, that there are ample role models of family-oriented, highly successful women, from Sandra Day O'Connor and Ruth Bader Ginsberg, Justices of the U.S. Supreme Court, to Ann Fisher, astronaut and physician (Ferguson and Dunphy 1991).

Sexual Harassment

Sexual harassment—unwelcome sexual attention that affects a person's job performance or creates a hostile work environment—wasn't recognized as a problem until the 1970s. Before this, women considered unwanted sexual comments, touches, looks, and pressure to have sex to be a personal matter.

Then in 1979, Catharine MacKinnon, a lawyer, published a book that forever changed our way of thinking. MacKinnon stressed that unwanted sexual advances at work are a structural problem; that is, they are built into the social structure. It is not a case of men doing obnoxious things because they are attracted to women: Rather, it is a case of men abusing their positions of authority in order to force unwanted sexual activities on women. Today, since women have moved into positions of authority, they, too, have become sexual harassers (Lawlor 1994).

As symbolic interactionists stress, the terms we use to describe things affect our perceptions. So it is with the term *sexual harassment*. Because we have this term, we now see the same behaviors in a different light from the way our predecessors saw them. The meaning

sexual harassment the abuse of one's position of authority to force unwanted sexual demands on someone

of this term is vague, however, and only through court cases is it being determined what it does and does not include. Originally, sexual desire was an essential element of sexual harassment, but this is no longer true in a legal sense. The Supreme Court considered the case of a homosexual who, while he was living on an oil rig, was tormented by his supervisors and fellow workers. The Court ruled that sexual harassment laws also apply to homosexuals who are harassed by heterosexuals on the job (Felsenthal 1998). The Court also added that we have to use common sense in interpreting what sexual harassment is. A football coach patting his players on the butt as they go onto the field is not sexually harassing, while the same man doing the same thing to his secretary (of either sex, I presume) is.

Central to sexual harassment is the abuse of power, a topic that is explored in the following Thinking Critically section.

Thinking *Critically*

SEXUAL HARASSMENT OF WOMEN IN THE MILITARY

The news spread like wildfire across the United States. Several male Army sergeants at Aberdeen Proving Ground in Maryland were accused of sexually abusing their female trainees (McIntyre 1997). The female recruits, many in their late teens, had been entrusted to the care of severe, demanding drill sergeants. There's nothing new about this; the Army uses rugged training to socialize *all* its recruits. What was new, however, were widespread accusations of sexual harassment, of using power—including intimidation and threats—to force unwanted sex on unwilling recruits. The accused drill sergeants, who said the sex was consensual, were tried and found guilty of rape. One married sergeant, who had pleaded guilty to having consensual sex with 11 trainees (adultery is a crime in the Army), was convicted of raping another 6 trainees a total of 18 times and was sentenced to 25 years in prison.

Some took an "I told you so" attitude. Their view was, you can't have coed dormitories unless you're looking for trouble. These are red-blooded men in the prime of their life, and the recruits are young, desirable, and, in some cases, naive. It is absolutely stupid to have them sleep under the same roof. If we are going to prepare women for combat, they need to be trained in separate military camps under the supervision of women. If men are brought in to assist, they should leave at the end of the day or sleep in separate barracks.

Others, who were also shocked by the rapes, took the attitude that the system was fine, but a few sergeants had gone bad. Training men and women together is the only way to assure equality, they insisted. Training must involve all phases of military life. To prevent such problems, however, we must instill greater controls over those in charge. From those whom we charge with great responsibility, we can demand total accountability. Recruits need to be told to report immediately all violations of touching or even of seductive language.

Then another bombshell hit. After the recruits made their accusations, the Army appointed a blue-ribbon panel to investigate sexual harassment in its ranks. When Sgt. Major Gene McKinney, the highest-ranking of the Army's 410,000 noncommissioned officers, was appointed to this committee, former subordinates accused him of sexual harassment (Shenon 1997). McKinney was relieved of duties and court-martialed. He was found not guilty of sexual harassment, but guilty of obstruction of justice. McKinney was reprimanded and demoted. His embittered accusers claimed the Army had sacrificed them for McKinney.

Marine recruits at basic training in Parris Island, South Carolina.

A civilian panel investigated. It recommended that the services remain integrated, but that platoons (the smallest units, with fifty soldiers) be segregated by sex (Mersereau 1998). The Navy didn't like this recommendation and said it wanted men and women to work together and to sleep in the same building, as they would on a ship. The Army and Navy continued as they were. The Marines did, too, but their practice has always been to keep men and women almost completely separate (Ricks 1998). ■

For Your Consideration

How can we set up a structure to minimize sexual harassment in the military? Can we do this and still train men and women together? Can we do this and still have them sleep in the same barracks? Be specific about the structure you would establish.

GENDER AND VIOLENCE

The high rate of violence in the United States shocks foreigners and frightens many Americans. Only a couple of generations ago, many Americans left their homes and cars unlocked. Today, fearful of carjackings, they lock their cars while driving, and, fearful of rape and kidnappings, they escort their children to school. Lurking behind these fears is gender inequality of violence—the fact that females are much more likely to be victims of males, not the other way around. Let's briefly review this almost one-way street in gender violence.

On pages 294 and 295, we examined violence against women in other cultures, and in Chapter 16 we shall review violence in the home. Here, due to space limitations, we can review only briefly the primary features of violence against U.S. women.

Forcible Rape Being raped is a common fear of U.S. women. And that fear is far from groundless. Rape has become so common that each year between 2 and 3 of every 1,000 females 12 years of age and over in the entire United States are raped. The official rate is 8.4 per 10,000. Surveys of crime victims, however, show that only one-third (32 percent) of rapes are reported, giving us a real rate of 25 per 10,000. Although females of all ages are victims, the typical victim is 16 to 19 years old. Rapists, too, span the age spectrum from early teens to over 65, but the typical rapist is under age 30. Contrary to stereotypes, most rape victims know their assailant; only ⅓ of rapes are committed by strangers. (*Statistical Abstract* 1999:Tables 349, 354, 355, 358, and page 212).

Date Rape What has shocked so many about date rape (also known as acquaintance rape) is studies showing that it does not consist of a few isolated events. For example, in a survey of the introductory psychology courses at Texas A&M University, about 21 percent of the women students reported that they had been forced to have sexual intercourse. (Keep in mind what we reviewed on sampling in Chapter 1. Students taking a specific course at a particular university are not representative of college students in general. We obviously need better studies.) Apparently, date rape most commonly occurs not between relative strangers on first dates, but between couples who have known each other about a year (Muehlenhard and Linton 1987). Most date rapes go unreported. Those that are reported are difficult to prosecute, for juries tend to believe that if a woman knows the accused she wasn't "really" raped.

Murder Table 11.3 summarizes U.S. patterns of murder and gender. Note that although females make up about 51 percent of the U.S. population, they don't even come close to making up 51 percent of the nation's killers. Note also that almost one-fourth of all murder victims are female—and nine times out of ten the killer is a male.

Table 11.3

KILLERS AND THEIR VICTIMS

The Victims

Male	Female
77%	23%

The Killers

Male	Female
89%	11%

Source: *FBI Uniform Crime Reports* 1998:Table 33; *Statistical Abstract* 1999:Table 347.

Violence against females is a global problem. Seldom does it capture the public's attention as it did with the death of Jon Benét Ramsey, whose killer, is still unknown as this book goes to press.

Violence in the Home Women are also the typical victims of family violence. Spouse battering, marital rape, and incest are discussed in Chapter 16, pages 469–471. A particular form of violence against women, genital circumcision, is the focus of the Perspectives box on page 294.

Women in the Criminal Justice System There is another side to gender and violence. Although women are much less likely to kill, when they do kill judges are more likely to be more lenient with them. As Table 11.4 shows, women are more likely than men to be given probation for murder (as well as for robbery, burglary, aggravated assault, larceny, and fraud). It is possible that sexual stereotypes underlie these decisions—such as the idea that women are less of a menace than men and should be given another chance. It is also possible that women defendants have less of a criminal history ("rap sheet") when they are charged with crimes. We need research on this topic.

Feminism and Gendered Violence

Feminist sociologists have been especially effective in bringing violence against women to the public's attention. Some use symbolic interactionism, pointing out that to associate strength and virility with violence—as is done in so many areas of U.S. culture—is to promote violence. Others use conflict theory. They argue that as gender relations change males are losing power, and that some males become violent against females as a way to reassert their declining power and status. Perhaps this is the underlying reason for the violence featured in the Mass Media box on the next page.

Solutions

There is no magic bullet for this problem, but to be effective any solution must break the connection between violence and masculinity. This would require an educational program that incorporates school, churches, homes, and the media. Given the gun-slinging heroes

Table 11.4

GOING EASIER ON WOMEN: WOMEN IN THE CRIMINAL JUSTICE SYSTEM
When Men and Women Are Convicted of the Same Crime, Who Gets Off Easier?*

Crime	Prison		Probation	
	Men	Women	Men	Women
Murder	97%	89%	1%	5%
Robbery	78%	67%	9%	13%
Burglary	55%	43%	19%	23%
Aggravated Assault	54%	30%	18%	26%
Larceny	42%	28%	24%	34%
Fraud	39%	31%	28%	41%
Drug Dealing	50%	37%	20%	26%
Weapons	49%	28%	22%	30%

*This table examines the extremes of sentencing; totals do not add to 100 because of jail sentences and unspecified "other" dispositions.

Source: Sourcebook of Criminal Justice Statistics 1997:Table 5.50.

Mass Media in Social Life

BEAUTY AND PAIN
HOW MUCH IS AN AD WORTH?

The studio audience at *Super Jockey*, a popular television program in Japan, waits expectantly. They've seen it before, and they can't get enough. A young woman, clad in a revealing bikini, walks onto the stage. Cringing with fear, she is lowered into a glass tank of scalding hot water.

The studio audience eagerly watches the woman through the glass. The national audience watches at home. Both break into laughter as the girl writhes in pain.

To make sure the young woman gets the full treatment, a man standing behind the tank ladles hot water over the woman's breasts—just as though he were basting a chicken. As her flesh quickly reddens, the television camera zooms in for a close-up shot of her breasts.

Most women last only three or four seconds.

The camera follows as the young woman climbs out of the tub, where she jumps up and down in pain and rubs ice all over her body.

The audience howls with glee.

Why do the women do it? For every second they stay in the hot water, they get one second on the program to advertise any product they wish. Most advertise their place of employment (Strauss 1998).

It is often difficult to understand other cultures. *Super Jockey* wouldn't be tolerated in the United States. If some television company tried to air a U.S. version, protests would erupt. The studio would be picketed, its sponsors boycotted.

Instead of trying to explain the intricacies of a culture that finds such behavior amusing ("Super Jockey" is a comedy show), we might wish to turn the focus onto our own culture. Why do we find the rape of women a source of entertainment? How can I say that we do? It is apparent from *our* television. I'm not talking about some dry, historical documentary on Public Television. I'm referring to TV "dramas," police shows, detective shows, and other programs in which the story line centers on women who are raped. Some of these programs focus on serial rapists, others on rape victims. Of course, in order to make sure

this kind of entertainment gets a seal of approval, producers see to it that the rapist is apprehended and punished. As further evidence that this kind of meritorious entertainment carries an honorable message, the rapist may commit suicide, get shot by the police, or get run down by a car as he tries to escape into his netherworld.

Our society also finds the murder of women to be highly entertaining. The Halloween shocker-thriller-slasher films serve as outstanding examples. Audiences that are simultaneously thrilled and terror-stricken watch, riveted, as crazed, masked killers hunt down college coeds with knives, axes, even chain saws. Audiences seem to find the screams of the victims especially entertaining. And the prettier, shapelier, and more skimpily clad the victim, the higher the entertainment value.

It is difficult to understand cultures, especially to explain why people find certain things amusing or entertaining. Why would Japanese and Americans find the victimization of women to be a scintillating source of entertainment? ■

of the Wild West and other American icons, as well as the violent messages so prevalent in today's mass media, it is difficult to be optimistic that a change will come any time soon.

Our next topic, women in politics, however, gives us much more reason for optimism.

THE CHANGING FACE OF POLITICS

What do these nations have in common?

Canada in North America

Argentina, Bolivia, and Nicaragua in Latin America

Britain, France, Ireland, and Portugal in western Europe

The Philippines in Asia

Israel in the Mideast

Poland in eastern Europe

India, Pakistan, and Sri Lanka on the subcontinent

The answer is that all have had a woman president or prime minister. To this list we can add even such bastions of male chauvinism as Haiti, Turkey, and Bangladesh (Harwood and Brooks 1993).

Then why not the United States? Why don't women, who outnumber men, take political control of the nation? Eight million more women than men are of voting age, and more women than men vote in U.S. national elections. As Table 11.5 shows, however, women are greatly outnumbered by men in political office. Despite the gains women have made in recent elections, since 1789 about 1,800 men have served in the U.S. Senate, but only 24 women have served, including the 9 current senators. Not until 1992 was the first African-American woman (Carol Moseley-Braun) elected to the U.S. Senate (National Women's Political Caucus 1998; *Statistical Abstract* 1999:Table 473).

Why are women underrepresented in U.S. politics? First, women are still underrepresented in law and business, the careers from which most politicians come. Further, most women do not perceive themselves as belonging to a class of people who need to organize politically in order to overcome domination. Most women also find that the irregular hours kept by those who run for office are incompatible with their role as mother. Fathers, in contrast, whose ordinary roles are more likely to take them away from home, do not feel this same conflict. Women are also less likely to have a supportive spouse who is willing to play an unassuming background role while providing solace, encouragement, child care, and voter appeal. Finally, preferring to hold on tightly to their positions of power, men have been reluctant to incorporate women into centers of decision making or to present them as viable candidates.

These factors are changing, however, and we can expect more women to seek and gain political office. As we saw in Figure 11.2 (on page 300), more women are going into law. The same is true for business. There they are doing more traveling and making statewide and national contacts. Increasingly, child care is seen as a mutual responsibility of both mother and father. And in some areas, such as my own political district, party heads are

Table 11.5	U.S. WOMEN IN POLITICAL OFFICE*, 1995–1999	
	Percentage of Offices Held by Women	**Number of Offices Held by Women**
National Office		
U.S. Senate	9%	9
U.S. House of Representatives	13%	56
State Office		
Governors	6%	3
Lt. Governors	38%	19
Attorneys general	22%	11
Secretaries of state	28%	14
Treasurers	32%	16
State auditors	8%	4
State legislators	22%	1,617
Local Office		
Mayors[a]	18%	177

*Does not include women elected to the judiciary, women appointed to state cabinet-level positions, women elected to executive posts by the legislature, or members of a university board of trustees.

[a] Of cities with a population over 30,000.

Source: National Women's Political Caucus 1998; *Statistical Abstract* 1999:Tables 473, 478, 482.

searching for qualified candidates (read "people with voter appeal and without skeletons in their closets") without regard to sex. The primary concern in at least some areas today is not gender, but the ability to win. This generation, then, is likely to mark a fundamental change in women's political participation, and it appears to be only a matter of time until a woman occupies the Oval Office.

$\mathcal{G}$LIMPSING THE FUTURE—WITH HOPE

By playing a fuller role in the decision-making processes of our social institutions, women are going against the stereotypes and role models that lock males into exclusively male activities and push females into roles that are considered feminine. As structural barriers fall and more activities are degendered, both males and females will be free to pursue activities that are more compatible with their abilities and desires as individuals.

As sociologists Janet Chafetz (1974), Janet Giele (1978), and Judith Lorber (1994) have pointed out, the ultimate possibility is a new conception of the human personality. At present, structural obstacles, accompanied by supporting socialization and stereotypes, cast most males and females into fairly rigid molds that are dictated by culture. Overcoming these obstacles and abandoning traditional stereotypes will give males and females new perceptions of themselves and one another. Both females and males will then be free to feel and to express needs and emotions that present social arrangements deny them. Females will be likely to perceive themselves as more in control of their environment and to explore this aspect of the human personality. Males will be likely to feel and to express more emotional sensitivity—to be warmer, more affectionate and tender, and to give greater expression to anxieties and stresses that their gender now forces them to suppress. In the future we may discover that such "greater wholeness" of males and females entails many other dimensions of the human personality.

As females and males develop a new consciousness of themselves and of their own potential, the relationships between them will change. Certainly distinctions between the sexes will not disappear. There is no reason, however, for biological differences to be translated into social inequalities. The reasonable goal is to have an appreciation of sexual differences coupled with equality of opportunity—which may well lead to a transformed society (Gilman 1911/1971; Offen 1990). If this happens, as sociologist Alison Jaggar (1990) observed, gender equality can become less a goal than a background condition for living in society.

$\mathcal{S}$UMMARY AND $\mathcal{R}$EVIEW

■ Issues of Sex and Gender

What is gender stratification?

The term **gender stratification** refers to unequal access to power, prestige, and property on the basis of sex. Each society establishes a structure that, on the basis of sex and gender, opens and closes doors to its privileges. P. 286.

How do sex and gender differ?

Sex refers to biological distinctions between males and females. It consists of both primary and secondary sex characteristics. **Gender,** in contrast, is what a society considers proper behaviors and attitudes for its male and female members. Sex physically distinguishes males from females; gender defines what is "masculine" and "feminine." P. 286.

Why do the behaviors of males and females differ?

The "nature versus nurture" debate refers to whether differences in the behaviors of males and females are caused by inherited (biological) or learned (cultural) characteristics. Almost all sociologists take the side of nurture. In recent years, however, sociologists have begun to cautiously open the door to biology. Pp. 286–291.

■ Gender Inequality in Global Perspective

Is gender stratification universal?

George Murdock surveyed information on premodern societies and found not only that all of them have sex-linked activities, but also that all of them give greater prestige to male activities. **Patriarchy,** or male dominance, does appear to be universal. Besides work, other areas of discrimination include education, politics, and violence. Pp. 291–294.

■ How Females Became a Minority Group

How did females become a minority group?

The main theory that attempts to explain how females became a minority group in their own societies focuses on the physical limitations imposed by childbirth. The origins of this discrimination, however, are lost in history, and no one knows for sure how this discrimination began. Pp. 295–297.

■ Gender Inequality in the United States

Is the feminist movement new?

In what is called the "first wave," feminists made political demands for change in the early 1900s—and were met with hostility, and even violence. The "second wave" began in the 1960s and continues today. Pp. 297–298.

What forms does gender stratification in education take?

Although more women than men attend college, each tends to select "feminine" or "masculine" fields. Women are underrepresented in most doctoral programs in science, and they are less likely to complete these programs. Fundamental change is indicated by the growing numbers of women in law and medicine. Pp. 299–301.

Is there gender inequality in everyday life?

Two indications of gender inequality in everyday life are the general devaluation of femininity and the male dominance of conversation. Pp. 301–302.

■ Gender Inequality in the Workplace

What gender inequality is present in the workplace?

Over the last century, women have made up an increasing proportion of the work force. Nonetheless, all occupations show a gender gap in pay. For college graduates, the lifetime pay gap runs almost a million dollars in favor of men. **Sexual harassment** also continues to be a reality of the workplace. Pp. 302–309.

■ Gender and Violence

What forms does violence against women take?

The victims of battering, rape, incest, and murder overwhelmingly are females. Female circumcision is a special case of violence against females. Conflict theorists point out that men use violence to maintain their power and privilege. Pp. 309–311.

■ The Changing Face of Politics

What is the trend in gender inequality in politics?

A traditional division of gender roles—women as child care providers and homemakers, men as workers outside the home—used to keep women out of politics. Women continue to be underrepresented in politics, but the trend toward greater political equality is firmly in place. Pp. 311–313.

■ Glimpsing the Future—With Hope

How might changes in gender roles and stereotypes affect out lives?

In the United States, women are playing a fuller role in the decision-making processes of our social institutions. Men, too, are reexamining their traditional roles. A new conception of the human personality may develop, one that allows both males and females to pursue their individual interests unfettered by gender. P. 313.

Where can I read more on this topic?

Suggested Readings for this chapter are found at the back of this book.

All URLs listed are current as of the printing of this book. URLs often change. Please check our Web site, **http://www.abacon.com/henslin,** for updates.

1. The key to understanding gender differences between men and women is to identify how they are socialized. This exercise will help you recognize some of the differences in their socialization. At **http://www.girltech.com/Mentors/MN_research.html,** read about the behavioral differences between boys and girls. Then browse some of the links at **http://www.girlscount.org** and **http://www.academic.org.** What recommendations at these sites are made to parents, teachers, and others for how to change the socialization of girls? Which gender expectations do you think these recommendations challenge? How do you think boys would be affected if these recommendations were adopted?

2. A global human rights issue is violence against women. One form of violence against women is female genital mutilation (FGM).

After reading the Perspectives box on page 294, examine these Web sites:

http://www.hollyfeld.org/fgm/index.html

http://www.fgm.org

http://www.religioustolerance.org/fem_cirm.htm

http://www.amnesty.org/ailib/intcam/femgen/fgm1.htm

Based on the information at these sites, write a short paper. (If several students are interested in this subject, you could also organize a panel discussion, with each of you presenting one aspect of the issue.) For example, you could cover: (1) what female genital mutilation is, (2) how it differs from male circumcision, (3) the reasons for the practice, (4) how widespread it is, (5) what countries engage in this practice, (6) the health risks, (7) how international organizations and groups have responded, and (8)) whether or not these groups have a right (and responsibility) to campaign against it.

3. The text states that, overwhelmingly, men are the aggressors and women the victims of violence. To study date rape, it is essential to look at the more general category of acquaintance rape. At **http://www.cs.utk.edu/~bartley/acquaint/acquaintRape.html** read the report on "friends" raping friends. Write a flyer or pamphlet on the incidence and characteristics of acquaintance rape, and on the strategies to use to avoid becoming a victim of acquaintance rape. You might include information on resources available on your campus or in your community for victims of acquaintance rape.

4. The text discusses some of the barriers that block women's election to public office, and states that change is occurring and it is only a matter of time before there is a woman in the White House. The White House Project, **http://www.thewhitehouse-project.org,** is a nonpartisan organization working to change the political climate so that women can launch successful campaigns for the White House. Go to that site and learn more about the activities of this group. The National Women's Political Caucus also recruits, trains, and supports women who run for and hold public office. You can learn more about this organization at **http://www.nwpc.org** Which of the barriers discussed in the text is this organization trying to overcome? What is the measure of the group's success?

Race and Ethnicity

- **Laying the Sociological Foundation**
  Race: Myth and Reality
  Ethnic Groups
  Minority Groups and Dominant Groups
  How People Construct Their Racial-Ethnic Identity
  Prejudice and Discrimination
  Individual and Institutional Discrimination

- **Theories of Prejudice**
  Psychological Perspectives
  Sociological Perspectives

- **Global Patterns of Intergroup Relations**
  Genocide
  Population Transfer
  Internal Colonialism
  Segregation

  Assimilation
  Multiculturalism (Pluralism)

- **Race and Ethnic Relations in the United States**
  White Europeans
  African Americans
  Latinos
  Asian Americans
  Native Americans

- **Looking Toward the Future**
  The Immigration Debate
  Affirmative Action
  Toward a True Multicultural Society

- **Summary and Review**

M y brother-in-law was a religious man," said Edmond. "When the militia came for him, he asked if he could pray first. They let him pray. After his prayers, he said he didn't want his family dismembered. They said he could throw his children down the latrine holes instead. He did. Then the militia threw him and my sister on top."

Shining a flashlight into the 40-foot-deep hole, Edmond said, "Look. You can still see the bones."

Between 800,000 and 1 million Rwandans died in the slaughter. Although the killings were low-tech—most were done with machetes— it took just 100 days in the summer of 1994 to complete the state-sanctioned massacres (Gourevitch 1995; 1998). Seven hundred thousand children were left orphans.

Rwanda has two major ethnic groups. The Hutus outnumber the Tutsis 6 to 1. Hutus are stocky and round-faced, dark-skinned, flat-nosed, and thick-lipped. The Tutsis are lankier and longer-faced, lighter-skinned, narrow-nosed, and thin-lipped. But the two groups, who speak the same language, have intermarried for so long that they have difficulty telling Hutu from Tutsi. National identity cards, originally issued by the Belgians when Rwanda was its colony, used to help people make the distinction.

During the genocide, a Tutsi card was a passport to death.

The Hutus, who controlled the government, called on all Hutus to kill all Tutsis. It was a national duty, said the Hutu leaders. Obediently, neighbors hacked neighbors to death in their homes. Colleagues hacked colleagues to death at work. Even teachers killed their students.

Local officials opened stadiums and churches, offering refuge to Tutsis. It was there that the largest massacres occurred, supervised by these same local officials.

While radio announcers urged their listeners to disembowel pregnant Tutsi women, the

317

government passed out machetes, guns, and alcohol—and bused men from massacre to massacre. Many Tutsis fled to neighboring Congo. There, in refugee camps, another 100,000 died at the hands of Hutus (Gourevitch 1998).

Nkongoli, a Tutsi who is now the vice-president of the National Assembly, says,

"One expected to die. Not by machete, one hoped, but with a bullet. If you were willing to pay for it, you could ask for a bullet. Death was more or less normal, a resignation. You lose the will to fight" (Gourevitch 1995). ■

At the end of World War II, the world was aghast at revelations of the Nazi slaughter of Jews, Slavs, gypsies, and homosexuals. Dark images of gas ovens and emaciated bodies stacked like cordwood haunted the world's nations. At Nüremberg, the Allies, flush with victory, put the top Nazis on trial, exposing their heinous deeds to a shocked world. Their public executions, everyone assumed, marked the end of genocide, a shameful aberration of history.

That such a thing could never happen again was the general consensus. Yet mass slaughters did occur. By far, the worst was the Khmer Rouge's killing spree in the 1970s. This communist group slaughtered 2 million Cambodians, one-fourth the entire population (Markusen 1995). This was purely political killing, however; the ruthless regime and its victims were of the same race and ethnicity.

Then in the 1990s reports of "ethnic cleansing"—merely a new term for an old act—seeped out of the former Yugoslavia (now Bosnia, Croatia, and Herzegovena). The reports, which originated with rebel forces, turned out to be exaggerated, but they were enough to alarm Western governments, and they were one factor in the decision to intervene militarily.

Although recent killings lacked swastikas and SS uniforms, and in some cases machetes may have replaced poison gas and ovens, the goal was the same. Hatred underlies **genocide**—the attempt to annihilate a people because of their presumed race or ethnicity. There are other reasons for these slaughters, of course. There always are. The Jews made good scapegoats for Germany's economic and political decline after World War I. In Bosnia, Muslim rebels were fighting the Serbian government. In Rwanda, the Hutus felt threatened by a Tutsi rebel group (twenty years earlier, the Tutsis had killed 100,000 Hutus). For our purposes, the political particulars and histories of these animosities matter little. What is significant is that these events occurred, even after the world vowed "Never Again" in 1945.

LAYING THE SOCIOLOGICAL FOUNDATION

Seldom do race and ethnic relations degenerate to the brutal extent that they did in Nazi Germany and Rwanda, but in our own society troubled race relations constantly confront us in newspaper headlines and TV news. Sociology can contribute greatly to our understanding of this aspect of social life. To begin, let's consider to what extent race itself is a myth.

Race: Myth and Reality

With its 6 billion people, the world offers a fascinating variety of human shapes and colors. People see one another as black, white, red, yellow, and brown. Eyes come in various shades of blue, brown, and green. Lips are thick and thin. Hair is straight, curly, kinky, black, white, and red—and, of course, all shades of brown.

As humans spread throughout the world, their adaptations to diverse climate and other living conditions resulted in this profusion of complexions, colors, and shapes. Genetic mutations added distinct characteristics to the peoples of the globe. In this sense the concept of **race**, a group with inherited physical characteristics that distinguish it from another group, is a reality. Humans do, indeed, come in a variety of colors and shapes.

genocide the systematic annihilation or attempted annihilation of a people based on their presumed race or ethnicity

race inherited physical characteristics that distinguish one group from another

Common Sense Versus Sociology At the beginning of this text (pages 8–10), I mentioned that common sense and sociology often conflict. This is especially so when it comes to race. According to common sense, our racial classifications represent biological differences between people. Sociologists, however, stress that what we call races are *social* classifications, not biological categories.

Sociologists point out that *our "race" depends more on the society in which we live than on our biological characteristics*. The racial categories common in the United States, for example, constitute merely one of *numerous* ways that people around the world classify physical appearances. Although groups around the world use different categories, each group assumes that its categories are natural, merely a response to visible biology.

To better understand this essential sociological point—that race is more social than it is biological—consider this: In the United States, children born to the same parents are all of the same race. "What could be more natural?" Americans assume. But in Brazil, children born to the same parents may be of different races—if their appearances differ. "What could be more natural?" assume Brazilians.

Or consider how Americans often classify a child born to a "black" mother and a "white" father as "black." Wouldn't it be equally as logical to classify the child as "white"? Similarly, if a child's grandmother is "black," but all her other ancestors are "white," the child is often considered "black," not "white." Yet she has much more "white blood" than "black blood." Why, then, is she considered "black"? Certainly not because of biology. Rather, such thinking is a legacy of slavery, when white masters tried to preserve the "purity" of their "race" by classifying anyone with even a "drop of black blood" as "not white." To accommodate changing thought, some now use the category "multiracial" to classify these children.

This sounds ridiculous, but *even a plane trip can change a person's race*. In the city of Salvador in Brazil, people classify one another by color of skin and eyes, breadth of nose and lips, and color and curliness of hair. They use at least seven terms for what we call white and black. Consider again a U.S. child who has "white" and "black" parents. If she flies to Brazil, she is no longer "black"; she now belongs to one of their several "whiter" categories (Fish 1995).

Has her "race" actually changed? Yes, it has. Our common sense revolts at this, I know. We want to argue that because her biological characteristics remain unchanged, her race remains unchanged. This is because we think of race as biological, when it *really is a label we use to describe perceived biological characteristics*. Simply put, the race we "are" depends on *where* we are.

But what about the biology? The biological differences are real, regardless of how we categorize them, aren't they? It is true that we humans have numerous physical differences. But if biology were the main element, biologists, of all people, would agree on the numbers and characteristics of human races.

But they do not. Human physical differences are so numerous that biologists cannot even agree on how *many* races there are, much less their characteristics. Biologists—and anthropologists, too—have drawn up many lists, each containing a different number of "races." Even trying to classify large groupings of people on the basis of blood type and gene frequencies does not clarify "race." Ashley Montagu (1964), a physical anthropologist, pointed out that some scientists have classified humans into only two races while others have identified as many as two thousand. Montagu (1960) himself classified humans into forty racial groups.

■ In Sum

Race, then, lies in the eye of the beholder. Humans show such a mixture of physical characteristics—in skin color, hair texture, nose shape, head shape, eye color, and so on—that there is no inevitable, much less universal, way to classify our many biological differences. Instead of falling into distinct types clearly separate from one another, human characteristics flow endlessly together. As with Tiger Woods (discussed in the Cultural Diversity box on page 320), these minute gradations make any attempt to draw firm lines purely arbitrary. Because racial classifications are arbitrary, the categories people use differ from one society to another, and they change over time. In this sense, then, race is a myth.

PERSPECTIVES | Cultural Diversity in the United States

TIGER WOODS AND THE EMERGING MULTIRACIAL IDENTITY: MAPPING NEW ETHNIC TERRAIN

Tiger Woods, one of the top golfers of all time, calls himself Cablinasian (Leland and Beals 1997). Woods invented this term as a boy to try to explain to himself just who he was—a combination of Caucasian, Black, Indian, and Asian. Woods wants to embrace both sides of his family. To be known by a racial identity that applies to just one of his parents is to deny the other parent.

Like many of us, Tiger Woods' racial-ethnic heritage is difficult to specify. Some, who like to count things mathematically, put Woods at one-quarter Thai, one-quarter Chinese, one quarter white, an eighth Native American, and an eighth African American. From this chapter, you know how ridiculous such computations are, but the sociological question is why many consider Tiger Woods an African American. The U.S. racial scene is indeed complex, but a good part of the reason is simply that this is the label the media chose. "Everyone has to fit somewhere" seems to be our attitude. If they don't, we grow uncomfortable. And for Tiger Woods, the media chose African American.

The "color line" used to be a firm barrier to marriage. It was unusual for anyone to marry outside his or her racial-ethnic group, and such couples brought stares wherever they went. Today, such marriages are common (Pollard and O'Hare 1999). In their struggle to establish a racial-ethnic identity, the children of these marriages often find support by associating with persons who have similar characteristics. At several campuses, students have formed Interracial Students Organizations. Harvard even has two, one just for students who have one African-American parent (Leland and Beals 1997).

Tiger Woods, after hitting a hole-in-one on the fourteenth hole of the Greater Milwaukee Open.

As we march into unfamiliar ethnic terrain, our ordinary classifications begin to burst at the seams. Kwame Anthony Appiah, of Harvard's Departments of Philosophy and Afro-American Studies, says, "My mother is English; my father is Ghanaian. My sisters are married to a Nigerian and a Norwegian. I have nephews who range from blond-haired kids to very black kids. They are all first cousins. Now according to the American scheme of things, they're all black—even the guy with blond hair who skis in Oslo" (Wright 1994).

Until recently, the U.S. census, which is taken every ten years, offered only the following categories: Caucasian, Negro, Indian, and Oriental. Everyone was carefully sliced and diced, and packed into one of these restrictive classifications.

After years of complaints from the public, the list was expanded. In the year 2000 census, everyone had to declare that they were or were not "Spanish/Hispanic/Latino." Then they had to mark "one or more races" that they "considered themselves to be." They could choose from White; Black, African American, or Negro; American Indian or Alaska Native; Asian Indian, Chinese, Filipino, Japanese, Korean, Vietnamese, Native Hawaiian, Guamanian or Chamorrro, Samoan, and other Pacific Islander. Finally, if these didn't do it, you could check a box called "Some Other Race" and then write whatever you wanted.

Perhaps the census should list Cablinasian. Of course, there should be GASH for the German-African-Swedish-Hispanic Americans, BITE for those of Botswanan-Indonesian-Turkish-English descent, and STUDY for the Swedish-Turkish-Uruguan-Danish-Yugoslavian Americans. As you read farther in this chapter, you will see why these terms make as much sense as the categories we currently use. ■

For Your Consideration

Just why do we count people by "race" anyway? Why not eliminate race from the U.S. census? (Race became a factor in the census during slavery, when five blacks were counted the same as three whites to determine how many representatives a state could send to Congress!) Why is race so important to some people? Perhaps you can use the materials in this chapter to answer these questions.

Racial Superiority The myth of race, however, remains a powerful force in social life. People are ethnocentric, and they are inclined to think that their own "race" is superior to others. Logic is lost in emotional ethnocentrism, and the idea of racial superiority haunts humanity.

Adolf Hitler believed that a super-race, the Aryan, was responsible for the cultural achievements of Europe. These tall, fair-skinned blonds, a supposed "master race," possessed the genetic stuff that made them inherently superior. (Never mind that Hitler was not a blond!) He believed that the Aryans were destined to establish an even higher culture and institute a new world order. This destiny required all Aryans to avoid the "racial contamination" that would come from breeding with inferior races. It also meant they should isolate or destroy races that might endanger Aryan culture.

Even many scientists of the time (not only in Germany but also in Europe and the United States) espoused the idea of racial superiority. Not surprisingly, they considered themselves members of the supposedly superior race.

The Power of the Myth The idea of racial superiority continues to persist even today. As one of the most significant elements of U.S. culture, it makes an impact on our everyday lives. That race is an arbitrary classification makes little difference to common thinking. "I know what I see, and you can't tell me any different" seems to be the common attitude. "I know what *they* are like. *They* are (fill in common responses you hear)." For most people, race is not myth, but reality.

As noted in Chapter 4, sociologist W. I. Thomas observed that "if people define situations as real, they are real in their consequences." That even experts can't decide how to classify people biologically into races is not what counts. What makes a difference for social life is what people believe, for *people act on beliefs, not facts.* Ideas of race are firmly embedded in our culture, and it is these, not remote scientific facts, that influence people's attitudes and behavior. As you read this chapter, perhaps you will examine some of the racial ideas that you learned as you were socialized in your culture.

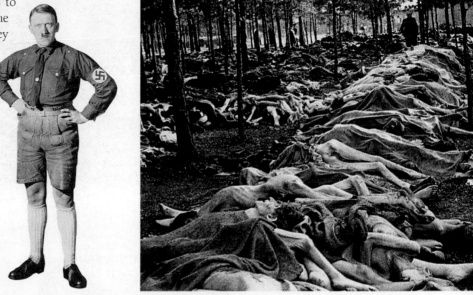

Although this strange-looking person could be a cartoon character, this is a serious photo of Adolf Hitler taken in 1924. Hitler is wearing lederhosen, traditional clothing of Bavaria, Germany.

The reason I selected this photo is to illustrate how seriously we must take all preaching of hatred and of racial supremacy, even though it seems to come from harmless or even humorous sources. This comical-appearing man caused the horrific scene on the right, which greeted the British army when it liberated the concentration camp in Bergen, Germany. They found 60,000 people dying of starvation and diseases amidst piles of rotting corpses awaiting mass burial.

Ethnic Groups

Whereas people use the term *race* to refer to supposed biological characteristics that distinguish one people from another, **ethnicity** and **ethnic** apply to cultural characteristics. Derived from the word *ethnos* (a Greek word meaning "people" or "nation"), ethnicity and ethnic refer to people who identify with one another on the basis of common ancestry and cultural heritage. Their sense of belonging may center on their nation of origin, distinctive foods, dress, language, music, religion, or family names and relationships.

People often confuse the terms *race* and *ethnic group*. For example, many people, including many Jews, consider the Jews a race. Jews, however, are more properly considered an ethnic group, for it is their cultural characteristics, especially their religion, that bind them together. Wherever Jews have lived in the world, they have intermarried. Consequently, Jews in China may look mongoloid, while some Swedish Jews are blue-eyed blonds. This matter is strikingly illustrated in the photo on the next page. Ethiopian Jews look so different from European Jews that when they immigrated to Israel many European Jews felt that they could not *really* be Jews.

Minority Groups and Dominant Groups

Sociologist Louis Wirth (1945) defined a **minority group** as people who are singled out for unequal treatment *and* who regard themselves as objects of collective discrimination. Either physical (racial) or cultural (ethnic) differences can serve as the basis of the unequal treatment. Wirth added that the discrimination excludes minorities from full participation in the life of their society.

ethnic (and **ethnicity**) having distinctive cultural characteristics

minority group people who are singled out for unequal treatment, and who regard themselves as objects of collective discrimination

Because ideas of race and ethnicity are such a significant part of society, all of us are classified according to those ideas. This photo illustrates the difficulty such assumptions posed for Israel. The Ethiopians, shown here as they arrived in Israel, although claiming to be Jews, looked so different from other Jews that it took several years for Israeli authorities to acknowledge this group's "true Jewishness."

Surprisingly, a minority group is not necessarily a *numerical* minority. For example, before India's independence in 1947, a handful of British colonial rulers discriminated against millions of Indians. Similarly, when South Africa practiced apartheid, a small group of Dutch discriminated against the black majority. And all over the world, females are a minority group. Accordingly, sociologists refer to those who do the discriminating not as the *majority*, but, rather, as the **dominant group**, for they have greater power, privileges, and social status.

Possessing political power and unified by shared physical and cultural traits, the dominant group uses its position to discriminate against those with different—and supposedly inferior—traits. The dominant group almost always considers its privileged position to be due to its own innate superiority.

Emergence of Minority Groups A group becomes a minority in one of two ways. The *first* is through the expansion of political boundaries. With the exception of females, tribal societies contain no minority groups; everyone shares the same culture, including the same language, and belongs to the same physical stock. When a group expands its political boundaries, however, it produces minority groups if it incorporates people with different customs, languages, values, and physical characteristics into the same political entity. For example, after defeating Mexico in war, the United States annexed the Southwest. The Mexicans living there, who had been the dominant group, were transformed into a minority group, a master status that has influenced their lives ever since. Referring to his ancestors, one Latino said, "We didn't move across the border—the border moved across us."

A *second* way in which a group becomes a minority is through migration. This can be voluntary, as with the millions of people who have chosen to move from Mexico to the United States, or involuntary, as with the millions of Africans who were brought in chains to the United States. (The way females became a minority group represents a third way, but, as reviewed in the previous chapter, no one knows just how this occurred.)

Shared Characteristics Anthropologists Charles Wagley and Marvin Harris (1958) noted that minorities, no matter where they are in the world, share these five characteristics:

1. Membership in a minority group is an ascribed status; that is, it is not voluntary, but comes through birth.

dominant group the group with the most power, greatest privileges, and highest social status

2. The physical or cultural traits that distinguish minorities are held in low esteem by the dominant group.

3. Minorities are unequally treated by the dominant group.

4. Minorities tend to marry within their own group.

5. Minorities tend to feel strong group solidarity (a sense of "we-ness").

These conditions—especially when combined with collective discrimination—tend to create a shared sense of identity among minorities, and, in many instances, even a sense of common destiny (Chandra 1993b).

How People Construct Their Racial-Ethnic Identity

Some of us have a greater sense of ethnicity than others. Some of us feel firm boundaries between "us" and "them." Others have assimilated so extensively into the mainstream culture that they are only vaguely aware of their ethnic origins. With extensive interethnic marrying, some do not even know the countries from which their families originated—nor do they care. If asked to identify themselves ethnically, they respond with something like "I'm Heinz 57—German and Irish, with a little Italian and French thrown in—and I think someone said something about being one-sixteenth Indian, too."

Why do some people feel an intense sense of ethnic identity, while others feel hardly any? Figure 12.1 portrays four factors, identified by sociologist Ashley Doane (1993), that heighten or reduce our sense of ethnic identity. From this figure, you can see that the keys are relative size, power, appearance, and discrimination. If your group is relatively small, has little power, looks different from most people in society, and is an object of discrimination, you will have a heightened sense of ethnic identity. In contrast, if you belong to the dominant group that holds most of the power, look like most people in the society, and feel no discrimination, you are likely to experience a sense of "belonging"—and wonder why ethnic identity is such a big deal.

We can use the term **ethnic work** to refer to how people construct their ethnicity. For people who have a strong ethnic identity, this term refers to how they enhance and maintain their group's distinctions—from clothing, food, and language to religion and holidays. For people whose ethnic identity is not as firm, it refers to attempts to recover their ethnic heritage, such as trying to trace family lines. Millions of Americans are engaged in ethnic work, which has confounded the experts who thought that the United States would be a **melting pot,** with most of its groups quietly blending into a sort of ethnic stew. In recent

Figure 12.1   A SENSE OF ETHNICITY

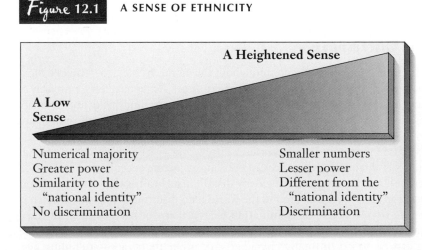

A Low Sense		A Heightened Sense
Numerical majority		Smaller numbers
Greater power		Lesser power
Similarity to the "national identity"		Different from the "national identity"
No discrimination		Discrimination

Source: Based on Doane 1993.

ethnic work activities designed to discover, enhance, or maintain ethnic and racial identification

melting pot the view that Americans of various backgrounds would blend into a sort of ethnic stew

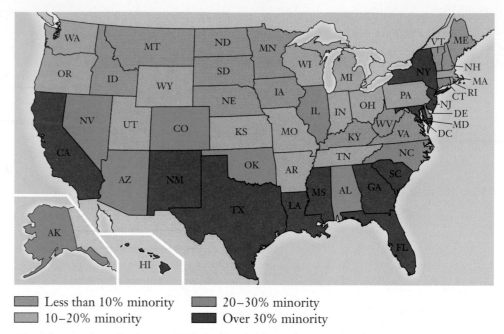

Figure 12.2

SOCIAL MAP: THE DISTRIBUTION OF DOMINANT AND MINORITY GROUPS IN THE UNITED STATES

Source: Statistical Abstract 1999:Tables 37, 38.

▨ Less than 10% minority ▨ 20–30% minority
▨ 10–20% minority ▨ Over 30% minority

Note: These totals are for the year 2000. As this map shows, the states' distribution of dominant and minority groups seldom comes close to the national average. Only 10 states are within 5 points of the national average (North Carolina, Arizona, Nevada, Alabama, Illinois, Alaska, Florida, New Jersey, South Carolina, and Georgia.)

years, however, Americans have become fascinated with their "roots," increasingly proud of their ethnic backgrounds, and, some, very assertive of their ethnicity (Karnow and Yoshihara 1992; Wei 1993). Consequently, some analysts think the term "tossed salad" is more appropriate than "melting pot."

Whites make up 72 percent of the U.S. population, minorities (African Americans, Asian Americans, Latinos, and Native Americans) 28 percent. As the Social Map above shows, the distribution of dominant and minority groups among the states seldom comes close to the national average. This is because minority groups tend to be clustered in regions. The extreme distributions are represented by Maine, which has only 2 percent minority, and by Hawaii, where the national average is reversed and minorities outnumber Anglos 71 percent to 29 percent.

Prejudice and Discrimination

Prejudice and discrimination are common throughout the world. In Mexico, Hispanic Mexicans discriminate against Native-American Mexicans; in Israel, Ashkenazi Jews, primarily of European descent, discriminate against Sephardi Jews from the Muslim world; and in Japan, the Japanese discriminate against just about anyone who isn't Japanese, especially immigrant Koreans and the descendants of the Eta caste. The Eta, now renamed the Burakumin, still bear a stigma because they used to do the society's dirty work—working with dead animals (stripping the hides and tanning the leather) and serving as Japan's executioners and prison guards (Mander 1992). In some places the elderly discriminate against the young, in others the young against the elderly. And all around the world men discriminate against women.

As you can see from this list, **discrimination** is an *action*—unfair treatment directed against someone. When the basis of discrimination is race, it is known as **racism**, but discrimination can be based on many characteristics other than race—including age,

discrimination an *act* of unfair treatment directed against an individual or a group

racism prejudice and discrimination on the basis of race

sex, height, weight, income, education, marital status, sexual orientation, disease, disability, religion, and politics. Discrimination is often the result of an *attitude* called **prejudice**—a prejudging of some sort, usually in a negative way. There is also positive prejudice, which exaggerates the virtues of a group, as when people think that some group (usually their own) is more capable than others. Most prejudice, however, is negative and involves prejudging a group as inferior.

The Extent of Prejudice You may not be prejudiced, but sociologists have found that ethnocentrism is so common that each racial or ethnic group views other groups as inferior in at least some ways. In a random sample of adults in the Detroit area, sociologists Maria Krysan and Reynolds Farley (1993) found that whites and African Americans tend to judge Latinos as less intelligent than themselves. Using a probability sample (from which we can generalize), sociologists Lawrence Bobo and James Kluegel (1991) found that older and less educated whites are not as willing to have close, sustained interaction with other groups as are younger and more educated whites. Details of their findings are shown in Figure 12.3. We must await matching studies to test the prejudices of Latinos, Asian Americans, and Native Americans.

Not everyone of the same age and education has the same amount of prejudice, of course. At the University of Alabama, sociologist Donald Muir (1991) measured racial attitudes of white students who belonged to fraternities and sororities and compared them to those of nonmembers. He asked a variety of questions—from their ideas about dating African Americans to their view on attending classes together. On all measures, fraternity members were more prejudiced than the nonfrats. Research on other campuses supports this finding (Morris 1991). Let's take a closer look at race relations on U.S. campuses.

Segregation in the South was not only a custom, but was also required by law. This photo, taken in South Carolina in 1950, shows a common sight of the time.

prejudice an *attitude* or prejudging, usually in a negative way

---

𝓕𝓲𝓰𝓾𝓻𝓮 12.3   **A MEASURE OF PREFERRED SOCIAL DISTANCE**

Percentage of white Americans, by education, who believe that different races should live in segregated housing

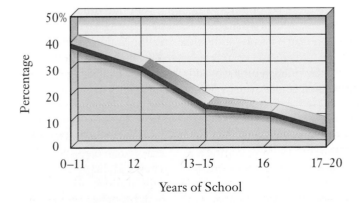

Years of School

Percentage of white Americans, by age, who believe that we should ban interracial marriage

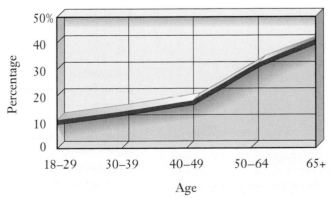

Age

Source: Bobo and Kluegel 1991.

Thinking Critically

SELF-SEGREGATION: HELP OR HINDRANCE FOR RACE RELATIONS ON CAMPUS?

Only after a long, bitter, and violent struggle was federal civil rights legislation prohibiting racial segregation on college campuses passed in the 1960s. These laws did not mark the end of self-segregation, however; certain practices continued, such as one area of a cafeteria or lounge being used almost exclusively by a particular group. In recent years, minority students have requested separate dormitories and campus centers. At Brown University, an Ivy League school located in Providence, Rhode Island, the old rows of fraternity and sorority houses have been replaced by Harambee House (for African Americans), Hispanic House, Slavic House, East Asian House, and German House. Cornell University offers "theme dorms" for African Americans, Hispanics, and Native Americans.

Intense controversy surrounds this self-segregation of racial-ethnic groups. On one side is William H. Gray III, the head of the United Negro College Fund. Both African-American and Latino students drop out of college at a much higher rate, Gray says, so colleges should do everything they can to make minority students feel welcome and accepted.

Critics call the trend toward separate housing a "separatist movement" that divides students into "small enclaves." Administrators at the University of Pennsylvania appointed a commission to study campus life. The committee concluded that when students self-segregate, they lose opportunities for wider interaction with diverse groups of students. Since students tend to socialize with the people they live with, separate housing inhibits the mixing of different groups, depriving students of the rich experiences that come through intercultural contacts.

Joshua Lehrer, a Brown University student who is white, says that various racial and ethnic groups "are separating themselves from everybody else, yet complain when society separates them. Can you really have it both ways?" he asks. ■

For Your Consideration

Compare separate racial-ethnic housing on college campuses with three patterns discussed in this chapter: segregation, assimilation, and multiculturalism. Is self-segregation permissible if minority students desire it, but not if white students desire it? Explain your position.

Sources: Bernstein 1993; Jordon 1996.

Individual and Institutional Discrimination

Sociologists stress that we need to move beyond thinking in terms of **individual discrimination,** the negative treatment of one person by another. Although such behavior certainly creates problems, it is primarily a matter of one individual treating another badly. With their focus on the broader picture, sociologists encourage us to examine **institutional discrimination,** that is, to see how discrimination is woven into the fabric of society to such an extent that it becomes routine, sometimes even a matter of social policy. Let's look at two examples.

Home Mortgages Mortgage lending provides an excellent illustration. As shown in Figure 12.4, race-ethnicity is a significant factor in getting a mortgage. When bankers looked at the statistics shown in this figure, however, they cried foul. They said that it might *look* like discrimination, but the truth was that whites had better credit histories. To see if this was true, researchers went over the data again, comparing the credit histories of applicants.

individual discrimination
the negative treatment of one person by another on the basis of that person's perceived characteristics

institutional discrimination
negative treatment of a minority group that is built into a society's institutions; also called *systemic discrimination*

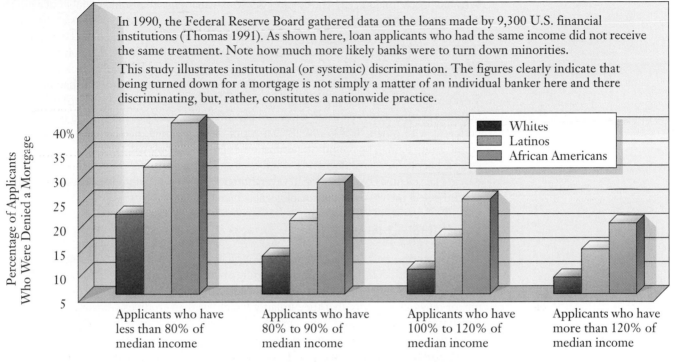

Figure 12.4 RACE-ETHNICITY AND MORTGAGES:
AN EXAMPLE OF INSTITUTIONAL DISCRIMINATION

In 1990, the Federal Reserve Board gathered data on the loans made by 9,300 U.S. financial institutions (Thomas 1991). As shown here, loan applicants who had the same income did not receive the same treatment. Note how much more likely banks were to turn down minorities.

This study illustrates institutional (or systemic) discrimination. The figures clearly indicate that being turned down for a mortgage is not simply a matter of an individual banker here and there discriminating, but, rather, constitutes a nationwide practice.

Percentage of Applicants Who Were Denied a Mortgage

Whites
Latinos
African Americans

Applicants who have less than 80% of median income

Applicants who have 80% to 90% of median income

Applicants who have 100% to 120% of median income

Applicants who have more than 120% of median income

Note: The totals refer to applicants for conventional mortgages. Although applicants for government-backed mortgages had lower overall rates of rejection, the identical pattern showed up for all income groups. Median income is the income of each bank's local area.

Not only did they check for late payments, but they also compared the applicants' debts, loan size relative to income, and even characteristics of the property they wanted to buy. The lending gap did narrow, but the bottom line was that even when two mortgage applicants were identical in all these areas, African Americans and Latinos were *60 percent* more likely to be rejected than whites (Thomas 1992; Passell 1996). In short, the results do not show that a banker here or there is discriminating; rather, they show that discrimination is built into the country's financial institutions.

Health Care Discrimination does not have to be deliberate. It can occur without the awareness of either the person doing the discriminating or those being discriminated against. An example is coronary bypass surgery. Physicians Mark Wenneker and Arnold Epstein (1989) studied all patients admitted to Massachusetts hospitals for circulatory diseases or chest pain. After comparing their age, sex, race, and income, they found that whites were 89 percent more likely to be given coronary bypass surgery. A national study of Medicare patients showed an even higher discrepancy—that whites were three times as likely as African Americans to receive this surgery (Winslow 1992).

The particular interracial dynamics that cause medical decisions to be made on the basis of race are unknown at present. It is likely that physicians *do not intend* to discriminate, but that in ways we do not yet fully understand discrimination is built into the medical delivery system. Race apparently works like gender. Just as women's higher death rates in bypass surgery can be traced to attitudes about gender (see page 298), so race serves as a subconscious motivation for giving or denying access to advanced medical procedures.

THEORIES OF PREJUDICE

Why are people prejudiced? The commonsense explanation is that some member of a group has done something negative to them or to someone they know, and they transfer their feelings to other members of the group. In some cases, this may be true, but as a classic piece of research by psychologist Eugene Hartley (1946) showed, much more is involved. Hartley asked people how they felt about various racial and ethnic groups. Besides blacks, Jews, and so on, his list included the Wallonians, Pireneans, and Danireans—names he had made up. Most people who expressed dislike for Jews and blacks also expressed dislike for these three fictitious groups. Hartley's study shows us that prejudice does not depend on negative experiences with others. It also reveals that people who are prejudiced against one racial or ethnic group tend to be prejudiced against other groups. People can be, and are, prejudiced against people they have never met—and even against groups that do not exist!

Social scientists have developed several theories to explain prejudice. Let's look first at psychological theories, then at sociological explanations.

Psychological Perspectives

Frustration and Scapegoats In 1939, psychologist John Dollard suggested that prejudice is the result of frustration. People who are unable to strike out at the real source of their frustration (such as low wages) find someone to blame. This **scapegoat**—often a racial, ethnic, or religious minority that they unfairly blame for their troubles—becomes a target on which they vent their frustrations. Gender and age are also common bases for scapegoating.

Even mild frustration can increase prejudice. In an ingenious experiment, psychologists Emory Cowen, Judah Landes, and Donald Schaet (1959) first measured the prejudice of a sample of students. Then they gave the students two puzzles to solve, making sure they did not have enough time to solve them. After the students had worked furiously on the puzzles, the experimenters shook their heads in disgust and said they couldn't believe they hadn't been able to finish such simple tasks. They then retested the students. Their scores on prejudice had increased. The students had directed their frustrations outward, onto people who had nothing to do with their problem.

The Authoritarian Personality Have you ever wondered if personality is a cause of prejudice—if some people are more inclined to be prejudiced, and others more fair-minded? For psychologist Theodor Adorno, who had escaped from the Nazis, this was no idle speculation. With the horrors he had observed still fresh in his mind, Adorno wondered whether there was a certain type of individual who was more likely to fall for the racist utterances and policies of people like Hitler, Mussolini, and the Ku Klux Klan.

To find out, Adorno (1950) tested about two thousand people, ranging from college professors to prison inmates. He used tests he had developed to measure ethnocentrism, anti-Semitism, and support for strong, authoritarian leaders. Adorno found that people who scored high on one test also scored high on the other two. For example, people who agreed with anti-Semitic statements also agreed that government should be authoritarian and that foreign ways of life posed a threat to the "American" way.

Adorno concluded that highly prejudiced people are insecure, are highly conformist, have deep respect for authority, and are highly submissive to superiors. He termed this the **authoritarian personality.** These people believe that things are *either* right *or* wrong. Ambiguity disturbs them, especially in matters of religion or sex. They become anxious when they confront norms and values that differ from their own. They define people who are different from themselves as inferior, for this assures them that their own positions are right.

Adorno's research stirred the scientific community, stimulating more than a thousand research studies. In general, the researchers found that people who are older, less educated, less intelligent, and from a lower social class are more likely to be authoritarian. Critics say that this doesn't indicate a particular personality, authoritarian or anything

scapegoat an individual or group unfairly blamed for someone else's troubles

authoritarian personality Theodor Adorno's term for people who are prejudiced and rank high on scales of conformity, intolerance, insecurity, respect for authority, and submissiveness to superiors

else, just that the less educated are more prejudiced—which we already knew (Yinger 1965; Ray 1991).

Sociological Perspectives

Sociologists find psychological explanations inadequate. They stress that the key to understanding prejudice is not an individual's *internal* state, but factors *outside* the individual. Thus, sociological theories focus on how some environments foster prejudice, while others discourage it. This topic is explored in the Mass Media box. With this

Mass Media in Social Life

PREACHING HATRED:
CRIME OR INALIENABLE RIGHT?

The Internet is a marvelous source of information. I am now able to do sociological research when I visit other countries. Worldwide, libraries and newspapers lie at my fingertips, waiting to be accessed through the marvels of satellites and fiber optic telephone lines.

The Internet is also a remarkable source of misinformation. Anyone can put up a Web site and fill it with distortions of truth or with outright lies. People of all ages, from all walks of life, can nurse grudges, seek revenge for perceived wrongs, and fan hatred.

Such negative communications are upsetting, especially those that champion hatred. Consider these statements:

> Civil Rights come out of the barrel of a gun, and we mean to give the niggers and Jews all the civil rights they can handle. . . . Our security team will see that no live targets escape from the range. Any who refuse to run or can't for any reason will be fed to the dogs. The dogs appreciate a good feed as much as we do.
> —An invitation to a summer conference held by the Aryan Nations at Hayden Lake, Idaho. The group's founder, Richard Butler, is a former Lockheed executive. (Statements quoted in Murphy 1999)

> Who's pimping the world? The hairy hands of the Zionist. . . .

The so-called Jew claims that there were six million in Nazi Germany. I am here today to tell you that there is absolutely no . . . evidence to substantiate, to prove that six million so-called Jews lost their lives in Nazi Germany. . . . Don't let no hooked-nose, bagel-eating, lox-eating, perpetrating-a-fraud so-called Jew who just crawled out of the ghettoes of Europe just a few days ago . . .
> —Statements of Khalid Abdul Muhammad, as quoted in Herbert 1998.

Hatred knows no racial-ethnic boundaries; the first statement was made by a white, the second by an African American.

The issue of what to do about hate speech is perplexing. Some want to ban it, while others say that censorship of any kind of speech threatens the free speech of us all. Canada has taken action. Ingrid Rimland of San Diego runs a Web site on which she sells anti-Semitic literature and publicizes the views of Ernst Zundel. Zundel, an immigrant from Germany who has lived in Canada for forty years, denies the Holocaust took place and preaches anti-Semitism. Canadian authorities accused Zundel of controlling the San Diego Web site and charged him under laws that prohibit the use of telephone lines to spread hate messages based on race, religion,

or ethnic origin ("Canada Tries to . . . " 1998).

The technological solution may be at hand. The Anti-Defamation League, a human rights group, has developed a "hate filter" (Mendels 1998). When it's installed on a computer, the software blocks access to Web sites that promote intolerance: the Ku Klux Klan, skinheads, and neo-Nazis, as well as those that spew hatred for homosexuals or other groups. ■

For Your Consideration

Should we ban statements of hate from the mass media? Should we perhaps make such statements illegal and punish their authors for breaking the law? Or should we allow the promotion of hatred in the mass media, regardless of its inflammatory nature, regardless of how it twists the facts and incites prejudice and hatred? Is there a middle ground, perhaps installing hate filters in grade and middle schools?

Do you think that censorship of this one type of speech can threaten free speech itself? Could it be one step toward banning other kinds of speech? Once we prohibit a specific kind of speech, what is to stop the government, for example, from censoring criticism of its leadership, claiming it is a threat to "national security"?

background, let's compare functionalist, conflict, and symbolic interactionist perspectives on prejudice.

Functionalism In a telling scene from a television documentary, journalist Bill Moyers interviewed Fritz Hippler, a Nazi intellectual who at age 29 was put in charge of the entire German film industry. Hippler said that when Hitler came to power the Germans were no more anti-Semitic than the French, probably less so. He was told to create anti-Semitism, which he did by producing movies that contained vivid scenes comparing Jews to rats whose breeding threatened to infest the population.

Why was Hippler told to create hatred? Prejudice and discrimination were functional for the Nazis; they helped the Nazis come to power. The Jews provided a convenient scapegoat, a common enemy against which the Nazis could unite a Germany weakened by defeat in World War I and bled by war reparations and rampant inflation. In addition, the Jews had businesses, bank accounts, and other property that could be confiscated. They also held key positions (as university professors, reporters, judges, and so on), which the Nazis could fill with their own flunkies. In the end hatred also showed its dysfunctional side, as the Nazi officials who were sentenced to death at Nüremberg discovered.

When state machinery is harnessed to hatred, as it was by the Nazis—who used the schools, police, courts, mass media, military, and almost all aspects of the government—prejudice becomes hard to resist. Recall the identical twins featured in the Down-to-Earth Sociology box on page 65. Oskar and Jack had been separated as babies. Jack was brought up as a Jew in Trinidad, while Oskar was reared as a Catholic in Czechoslovakia. Under the Nazi regime, Oskar learned to hate Jews, although, unknown to himself, he was a Jew.

That prejudice is functional and is shaped by the social environment was dramatically demonstrated by psychologists Muzafer and Carolyn Sherif (1953) in a simple but ingenious experiment. In a boys' summer camp, they assigned friends to different cabins and then had the cabins compete in sports. In just a few days, strong in-groups had formed, and even former lifelong friends were calling one another "crybaby" and "sissy" and showing intense dislike for one another.

Sherif's study illustrates four major points. First, we can arrange the social environment to generate either positive or negative feelings about people. Second, prejudice can be produced by pitting group against group in an "I win, you lose" situation. Third, prejudice is functional in that it creates in-group solidarity. Fourth, prejudice is dysfunctional in that it destroys human relationships.

Conflict Theory Conflict theorists stress that the capitalist class systematically pits group against group. If workers are united, they will demand higher wages and better working conditions. In contrast, groups that fear and distrust one another will work against one another. Reducing worker solidarity, then, weakens their bargaining power, drives down costs, and increases profits. Thus the capitalist class exploits racial and ethnic strife to produce a **split labor market** (also called a *dual labor market*), workers who are divided along racial, ethnic, and gender lines (Du Bois 1935/1992; Reich 1972; Lind 1995).

Unemployment is a useful weapon for helping to maintain a split labor market. If everyone were employed, the high demand for labor would put workers in a position to demand pay increases and better working conditions. Keeping some people unemployed, however, provides a **reserve labor force** from which owners can draw when they need to expand production. When the economy contracts, these workers are released to rejoin the ranks of the unemployed. Minority workers are especially useful for this manipulative goal, for white workers tend to see them as a threat (Willhelm 1980).

split-labor market workers split along racial, ethnic, gender, age, or any other lines; this split is exploited by owners to weaken the bargaining power of workers

reserve labor force the unemployed; unemployed workers are thought of as being "in reserve"—capitalists take them "out of reserve" (put them back to work) during times of high production and then lay them off (put them back in reserve) when they are no longer needed

The consequences are devastating, say conflict theorists. Just like the boys in the Sherif summer camp, African Americans, Latinos, whites, and so on see themselves as able to make gains only at one another's expense. This rivalry shows up along even finer racial-ethnic lines, such as that between Miami's Haitians and Miami's African Americans, who distrust each other as competitors. Divisions among workers cause anger and hostility to be deflected away from the capitalists and directed instead toward other racial and ethnic groups. Instead of recognizing their common class interests and working for their mutual welfare, workers learn to fear and distrust one another (Blackwelder 1993).

Symbolic Interactionism Where conflict theorists focus on the role of the capitalist class in exploiting racial and ethnic inequalities, symbolic interactionists examine how labels affect perception and produce prejudice.

How Labels Create Prejudice "What's in a name?" asked Juliet. In answer she declared, "That which we call a rose / By any other name would smell as sweet." This may be true of roses, but it does not apply to human relations. Words are not simply meaningless labels. Rather, *the labels we learn color the way we see people.*

the labels we learn color the way we see people

Symbolic interactionists stress that labels are an essential ingredient of prejudice. Labels cause **selective perception**; that is, they lead us to see certain things and blind us to others. If we apply a label to a group, we tend to see its members as all alike. We shake off evidence that doesn't fit. As sociologists George Simpson and Milton Yinger (1972) put it, "New experiences are fitted into old categories by selecting only those cues that harmonize with the prejudgment or stereotype."

Racial and ethnic labels are especially powerful. They are shorthand for emotionally laden stereotypes. The term *nigger,* for example, is not a neutral term. Nor are *honky, spic, mick, kike, limey, kraut, dago,* or any of the other scornful words people use to belittle ethnic groups. Such words overpower us with emotions, blocking out rational thought about the people to whom they refer (Allport 1954).

Stereotypes and Discrimination: The Self-Fulfilling Prophecy The stereotypes that we learn not only justify prejudice and discrimination but also can produce the behavior depicted in the stereotype. Let's consider Group X. Negative stereotypes characterize this group as lazy. If they are lazy, they don't deserve good jobs. ("They are lazy and undependable and wouldn't do well.") This attitude creates a *self-fulfilling prophecy:* Because they are denied jobs that require high dedication and energy, most members of Group X are limited to doing "dirty work," the kind of work that is thought appropriate for "that kind" of people. Since much dirty work is sporadic, members of Group X can often be seen standing around street corners. The sight of their idleness reinforces the original stereotype of laziness. The discrimination that created the "laziness" in the first place passes unnoticed.

Symbolic interactionists stress that we are not born with prejudices. Instead, we learn our prejudices through our interaction with others. At birth each of us joins some particular family and racial or ethnic group, where we learn beliefs and values. There, as part of our basic orientations to the world, we learn to like—or dislike—members of other groups and to perceive them positively or negatively. If discrimination is the common practice, we learn to practice it routinely. Just as we learn any other attitudes and customs, then, so we learn prejudice and discrimination.

One aspect of racism that has gained attention and concern from citizens and government alike is the rise of neo-Nazi and Ku Klux Klan organizations. To understand the racist mind—and the appeal it has to some—see the Down-to-Earth Sociology box on the next page.

selective perception seeing certain features of an object or situation, but remaining blind to others

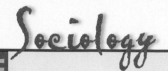

THE RACIST MIND

Sociologist Raphael Ezekiel wanted to get a close look at the racist mind. As a Jew, he faced a unique problem. The best way to examine racism from the inside is to do participant observation (see pp. 134–135). Would this be possible for him? Openly identifying himself as a Jew, Ezekiel asked Ku Klux Klan and neo-Nazi leaders if he could interview them and attend their meetings. Surprisingly, they agreed. Ezekiel published his pathbreaking research in a book, *The Racist Mind* (1995). Here are some of the insights he gained during his fascinating sociological adventure:

[The leader] builds on mass anxiety about economic insecurity and on popular tenden-

cies to see an Establishment as the cause of economic threat; he hopes to teach people to identify that Establishment as the puppets of a conspiracy of Jews. [He has a] belief in exclusive categories. For the white racist leader, it is profoundly true . . . that the socially defined collections we call races represent fundamental categories. A man is black or a man is white; there are no in-betweens. Every human belongs to a racial category, and all the members of one category are radically different from all the members of other categories. Moreover, race represents the essence *of* the person. A truck is a truck, a car is a car, a cat is a cat, a dog is a dog, a black is a black, a white

is a white. . . . These axioms have a rock-hard quality in the leaders' minds; *the world is made up of racial groups*. That is what exists for them.

Two further beliefs play a major role in the minds of leaders. First, life is war. The world is made of distinct racial groups; life is about the war between these groups. Second, events have secret causes, are never what they seem superficially. Events are caused by the complex scheming of tricksters. . . . Any myth is plausible, as long as it involves intricate plotting. . . . It does not matter to him what others say. . . . He lives in his ideas and in the little world he has created where they are taken seriously. . . . Gold can

GLOBAL PATTERNS OF INTERGROUP RELATIONS

Sociologists have studied racial-ethnic relations around the world. They have found that in any society that contains minorities, basic patterns of behavior develop between the dominant group and the minorities. These patterns are shown in Figure 12.5. Let's look at each.

Genocide

Stereotypes (or labels) powerfully influence human behavior. Symbolic interactionists point out that labels are so powerful they can even persuade people who believe that hurting others, much less killing them, is wrong, to participate in mass murder.

Last century's most notorious examples of genocide were Hitler's attempt to destroy all Jews and, as depicted in our opening vignette, the Hutus' attempt to destroy all Tutsis. One of the horrifying aspects of these slaughters was that those who participated did not crawl out from under a rock someplace. Rather, they were ordinary citizens—whose participation was facilitated by labels that singled out the victims as enemies worthy of death (Huttenbach 1991; Browning 1993; Simmons 1998).

To better understand how ordinary people can participate in genocide, let's focus on an example from the 1800s. The U.S. government and white settlers chose the label "savages" to refer to Native Americans. To define the Native Americans as less than human made it easier to justify killing them in order to take over their resources, and to slaughter those who resisted their advance toward the West. Most Native Americans, however, died not from bullets but from diseases that the whites brought with them. The Native Americans had no immunity against these diseases, such as measles and the flu (Dobyns 1983; Schaefer 2000).

be made from the tongues of frogs; Yahweh's call can be heard in the flapping swastika banner. (pp. 66–67)

Who is attracted to the neo-Nazis and Ku Klux Klan? Here is what Ezekiel discovered:

[There is a] ready pool of whites who will respond to the racist signal. . . . This population [is] always hungry for activity—or for the talk of activity—that promises dignity and meaning to lives that are working poorly in a highly competitive world . . . Much as I don't want to believe it, [this] movement brings a sense of meaning—at least for a while—to some of the discontented. To struggle in a cause that transcends the individual lends meaning to life, no matter how ill-founded or narrowing the cause. For the young men in the neo-Nazi group . . . membership was an alternative to atomization and drift; within the group they worked for a cause and took direct risks in the company of comrades. . . .

When interviewing the young neo-Nazis in Detroit, I often found myself driving with them past the closed factories, the idled plants of our shrinking manufacturing base. The fewer and fewer plants that remain can demand better education and more highly skilled workers. These fatherless Nazi youths, these high-school dropouts, will find little place in the emerging economy . . . a permanently underemployed white underclass is taking its place alongside the permanent black underclass. The struggle over race merely diverts youth from confronting the real issues of their lives. Not many seats are left on the train, and the train is leaving the station. (pp. 32–33) ■

For Your Consideration

Use functionalism, conflict theory, and symbolic interaction to explain (1) why some people are attracted to the message of hate, and (2) how the leaders and followers of these hate groups view the world.

The settlers also ruthlessly destroyed the Native Americans' food supply (buffalos, crops). As a result, about 95 *percent* of Native Americans died (Garbarino 1976; Thornton 1987).

The same thing was happening in other places. In South Africa, the Boers, or Dutch settlers, viewed the native Hottentots as jungle animals, and, following a policy of genocide, they totally wiped them out. In Tasmania, the British settlers stalked the local aboriginal population, hunting them for sport and sometimes even for dog food.

Figure 12.5   GLOBAL PATTERNS OF INTERGROUP RELATIONS: A CONTINUUM

Inhumanity → Humanity

Rejection → Acceptance

Genocide	Population Transfer	Internal Colonialism	Segregation	Assimilation	Multiculturalism (Pluralism)
The dominant group tries to destroy the minority (e.g., Germany and Rwanda)	The dominant group expels the minority (e.g., reservations for Native Americans)	The dominant group exploits the minority (e.g., low-paid, menial work)	The dominant group structures the social institutions to maintain minimal contact with the minority (e.g., the U.S. South before the 1960s)	The dominant group absorbs the minority (e.g., American Czechoslovakians)	The dominant group encourages racial and ethnic variation; when fully successful, there is no longer a dominant group (e.g., Switzerland)

Labels are powerful forces in human life. Labels that dehumanize others help people to **compartmentalize**—to separate their acts from their morality. If a group is less than human, treating them inhumanely is okay. If people don't compartmentalize their acts and their morality, their self-concept will be threatened, and it will be difficult for them to participate in killing (Bernard et al. 1971; Markusen 1995). Thus, *genocide is facilitated by labeling the targeted group as less than fully human.*

Population Transfer

Population transfer is of two types, indirect and direct. *Indirect* population transfer is achieved by making life so unbearable for members of a minority that they leave "voluntarily." Under the bitter conditions of czarist Russia, for example, millions of Jews made this "choice." *Direct transfer* occurs when a dominant group expels a minority. Examples include the relocation of Native Americans to reservations and the transfer of Americans of Japanese descent to relocation camps during World War II.

In the 1990s, population transfer occurred in Bosnia, a part of the former Yugoslavia. A hatred that had been carefully nurtured for centuries was kept under wraps during Tito's iron-fisted rule. After the breakup of communism, Yugoslavia split into warring factions, and these suppressed, smoldering hatreds broke to the surface. When the Serbs gained power, Muslims rebelled and began engaging in guerilla warfare. The Serbs vented their hatred by what they termed **ethnic cleansing**; they terrorized villages with killing and rape, forcing survivors to flee in fear.

Internal Colonialism

In Chapter 9, the term *colonialism* was used to refer to one way that the Most Industrialized Nations exploit the Least Industrialized Nations (pp. 248 and 250). Conflict theorists use the term **internal colonialism** to refer to how a country's dominant group exploits minority groups for its economic advantage. The dominant group manipulates the social institutions to suppress minorities and deny them access to the society's benefits. Slavery, reviewed in Chapter 9, is an extreme example of internal colonialism, as was the South African system of *apartheid*. Although the dominant Afrikaaners despised the minority, they found its presence necessary. As Simpson and Yinger (1972) put it, who else would do all the hard work?

Segregation

Internal colonialism is often accompanied by **segregation**—the formal separation of racial or ethnic groups. Segregation allows the dominant group to maintain social distance from the minority and yet to exploit their labor as cooks, cleaners, chauffeurs, housekeepers, nannies, factory workers, and so on. In the U.S. South until the 1960s, by law African Americans and whites had to use separate public facilities such as hotels, schools, swimming pools, bathrooms, and even drinking fountains. In thirty-eight states, laws prohibited marriage between blacks and whites. Violators could be sent to prison (Mahoney and Kooistra 1995). In Israel, Palestinians who worked for the dominant Israelis had to carry passes and go through armed checkpoints in the morning and return to their own areas at the end of the day.

Assimilation

Assimilation is the process by which a minority is absorbed into the mainstream culture. There are two types. In *forced assimilation* the dominant group refuses to allow the minority to practice its religion, speak its language, or follow its customs. Prior to the fall of the Soviet Union, for example, the dominant group, the Russians, required that Armenian children attend schools where they were taught in Russian. Armenians could honor only Russian, not Armenian, holidays. *Permissible assimilation,* in contrast, permits the minority to adopt the dominant group's patterns in its own way and at its own speed. In Brazil, for ex-

compartmentalize to separate acts from feelings or attitudes

population transfer involuntary movement of a minority group

ethnic cleansing a policy of population elimination, including forcible expulsion and genocide. The term emerged in 1992 among the Serbians during their planned policy of expelling Croats and Muslims from territories claimed by them during the Yugoslav wars

internal colonialism the policy of economically exploiting minority groups

segregation the policy of keeping racial or ethnic groups apart

assimilation the process of being absorbed into the mainstream culture

PERSPECTIVES | Cultural Diversity in the United States

HAITIAN ASSIMILATION

Phede came to the United States from Haiti when he was 12 years old. He quickly assimilated, hiding his Haitian identity by Americanizing his name to Fred. In high school he became an honors student, worked at McDonald's full time, and sang in the church choir. One day his girlfriend, an African American, came to talk to Fred during his break at McDonald's. While they were talking, Fred's sister arrived. She addressed Fred in Haitian Creole, the national language of Haiti. Fred became furious. She had blown his cover, and he screamed at her to never speak Creole to him again. He did not want to be known as Haitian. Four days later, Fred bought a .22 caliber revolver for $50, drove to an empty lot near his home, and put a bullet through his chest.

Six years later, Herve stood before his classmates at the same high school that Phede had attended. Herve, or Herb as he now called himself, tapped out a beat with his fists, shuffled a few dance steps, and rapped:

My name is Herb and I'm not poor…

I'm the Herbie that you're lookin' for,

like Pepsi,

a new generation

of Haitian education and determination…

I'm the Herb that you're lookin' for.

Fred and Herb embody two extreme reactions to a single problem, the integration of Haitians into the United States. Integration into U.S. society is especially difficult for immigrants who are black. During the 1970s and 1980s, no other immigrant group suffered more prejudice and discrimination than Haitians. The U.S. Coast Guard attempted to intercept boats of Haitians before they left Haitian waters; many undocumented Haitians who made it to U.S. shores were jailed; and Haitians were more likely to be denied political asylum than any other national group. Florida and U.S. officials announced that Haitians were a health threat: The Centers for Disease Control first said that tuberculosis was endemic among Haitians; then they announced that Haitians were at risk for AIDS. Even after Haitians were removed from that list, hospitals refused to accept donated blood from those of Haitian descent.

These realities create a tortured identity for Haitian adolescents. To avoid prejudice, like Phede, many Haitian youth cover up their Haitian roots and quickly assimilate to U.S. culture, specifically to African-American culture. They exemplify *segmentary assimilation,* assimilation not to a mainstream culture, but to a particular segment of a culture. Fred believed that covering up was the path to acceptance in the African-American neighborhood where he lived and attended school. Herb, in contrast, celebrated his Haitian culture. He resolved the tension by adopting an African-American style, the rap song, while expressing an immigrant belief, even driving force, in success.

Segmentary assimilation, in this case adopting an African-American expression of the self, is a viable option for Haitian immigrants. While some realize their dreams of success in the United States, prejudice and discrimination destroy the best intentions of others. ■

Alex Stepick
Florida International University

Pride against Prejudice: Haitian Refugees in the U.S., Allyn and Bacon (1996)

Haitian-American teenager in Belle Glade, Florida.

ample, an ideolgy favoring the eventual blending of the country's diverse racial types into a "Brazilian stock" encourages the racial and ethnic groups to intermarry. Difficulties of assimilation are discussed in the Perspective box above.

Multiculturalism (Pluralism)

A policy of **multiculturalism,** also called **pluralism,** permits or even encourages racial and ethnic variation. Minority groups are able to maintain their separate identities, yet freely participate in their country's social institutions, from education to politics. Switzerland provides an outstanding example of multiculturalism. The Swiss are made up of three separate groups—French, Italians, and Germans—who have kept their own languages, and who live peacefully in political and economic unity. Multiculturalism has been so successful that none of these groups can properly be called a minority.

multiculturalism (also called **pluralism)** a philosophy or political policy that permits or encourages ethnic variation

RACE AND ETHNIC RELATIONS IN THE UNITED STATES

As I have stressed, racial classifications are arbitrary and changing. Nevertheless, as a part of everyday life, we classify one another as belonging to distinct racial-ethnic groups (see Figure 12.6). Most of us also have strong racial-ethnic self-identities. Let's explore some of the consequences of that membership and identity.

U.S. RACIAL AND ETHNIC GROUPS

[a] To compute percentages, the population totals of the individual groups listed in the source were added, and the groups' totals were divided by this sum. To obtain the groups' population, these percentages were multiplied by the official U.S. population count.

[b] Includes "British."

[c] Includes "Scottish-Irish."

[d] Most Latinos trace at least part of their ancestry to Europe.

[e] In descending order, the largest six groups of Asian Americans are Chinese, Filipinos, Japanese, Asian Indians, Koreans, and Vietnamese.

[f] Includes Native American, Eskimo, and Aleut.

Source: Statistical Abstract 1999: Tables 19, 23, 32, 59.

		Number	Percentage
Americans of European Descent 205,266,000 73.3%	German	57,947,000	20.7%
	Irish	38,736,000	13.8%
	English[a]	33,751,000	12.0%
	Italian	14,665,000	5.2%
	Scottish[b]	11,012,000	3.9%
	French	10,321,000	3.7%
	Polish	9,366,000	3.3%
	Dutch	6,227,000	2.2%
	Swedish	4,681,000	1.7%
	Norwegian	3,869,000	1.4%
	Russian	2,953,000	1.1%
	Welsh	2,034,000	0.7%
	Slovak	1,883,000	0.7%
	Danish	1,635,000	0.6%
	Hungarian	1,582,000	0.6%
	Czech	1,296,000	0.5%
	Portuguese	1,153,000	0.4%
	Greek	1,110,000	0.4%
	Swiss	1,045,000	0.4%
Americans of African, Asian, and North, Central, and South American Descent 74,859,000 26.7%	African American	32,718,000	11.7%
	Latino[c]	30,250,000	10.8%
	Asian American[d]	9,890,000	3.5%
	Native American[e]	2,001,000	0.7%

Percentage of Americans

White Europeans

The term **WASP** stands for White Anglo-Saxon Protestant. In its narrow meaning, WASP refers to Protestant Americans whose ancestors came from England. These early immigrants did not consider all WASPs to be equal, and class distinctions quickly developed. Lacking an official royalty, and somewhat envious of European royal courts, in 1890 some WASPs established the Society of Mayflower Descendants to certify which families possessed the right "bloodlines." Membership was limited to those who could trace their ancestry to the immigrants who arrived on the *Mayflower*. Around this same time, the *Social Register* began to be published. To be listed in this book is to be deemed a member of the upper-upper class, for only people with "old" money are included. Such rules help organizations to insulate their members from the more "common" folk (Baltzell 1964).

The WASP colonists were highly ethnocentric, and they viewed white Europeans from countries other than England as inferior. They greeted **white ethnics**—immigrants from Europe whose language and other customs differed from theirs—with negative stereotypes. They viewed the Irish as dirty, lazy drunkards, and they painted Germans, Poles, Jews, Italians, and so on with similarly broad brush strokes.

Due to the cultural and political dominance of the WASPs, these immigrants felt pressure to blend into the mainstream culture. Their children embraced the new way of life and quickly came to think of themselves as Americans rather than as Germans, French, Hungarians, and so on. They dropped their distinctive customs, especially their language, often viewing them as symbols of shame. This second generation of immigrants was sandwiched between two worlds, however: the customs of their parents from the "old country" and the customs of their peers in the "new world." Their children, the third generation, had an easier adjustment, for they had fewer customs to discard. As immigrants from other parts of Europe assimilated into this Anglo culture, the meaning of WASP expanded to include people of this descent.

■ **In Sum** Because the English settled the Colonies, it was they who established the culture to which later immigrants had to conform—from the dominant language to the dominant religion and patterns of marriage. Highly ethnocentric, they considered the customs of any group that differed from theirs to be inferior. In short, it was the European colonists who, taking power and determining the national agenda, controlled the destiny of the nation and dominated and exploited other ethnic groups. Throughout the years, other ethnic groups have had to react to this institutional and cultural dominance of western Europeans, which still sets the stage for current ethnic relations.

African Americans

After slavery was abolished, in a practice known as *Jim Crow*, laws were passed in the South to segregate blacks and whites. In 1896, the Supreme Court ruled in *Plessy v. Ferguson* that state laws requiring "separate but equal" accommodations for blacks were a reasonable use of state power. Whites used this ruling to strip blacks of the political power they had gained after the Civil War: They prohibited blacks from voting in "white" primaries. It was not until 1944 that the Supreme Court ruled that African Americans could vote in Southern primaries, and not until 1954 that they had the legal right to attend the same public schools as whites (Schaefer 2000). Well into the 1960s, the South was openly—and legally—practicing segregation.

JUST SO.

Hoodlum. "'Tain't their color I mind s'much—(hic) it's their (hic) habits I 'bject to."

Almost all racial-ethnic groups, including white ethnics, have experienced prejudice and discrimination. The objects of scorn in this cartoon, which appeared in U.S. newspapers in 1879, are Irish immigrants. The Irish were despised at the time, and were often depicted drunk. In a surprising twist, the chinese immigrants in this cartoon are portrayed positively as hard workers.

WASP a White Anglo-Saxon Protestant; narrowly, an American of English descent; broadly, an American of western European ancestry

white ethnics white immigrants to the United States whose culture differs from that of WASPs

Until the 1960s, the South's public facilities were racially segregated. Some were reserved for whites only, others for blacks only. This apartheid was broken by blacks and whites who worked together and risked their lives to bring about a fairer society. Shown here is a 1963 sit-in at a Woolworth's lunch counter in Jackson, Mississippi. Sugar, ketchup, and mustard are being poured over the heads of the demonstrators.

The Struggle for Civil Rights

It was 1955, in Montgomery, Alabama. As specified by law, whites took the front seats of the bus, while blacks went to the back. As the bus filled up, blacks had to give up their seats to whites.

When Rosa Parks, a 42-year-old African-American woman and secretary of the Montgomery NAACP, was told she would have to stand so white folks could sit, she refused (Bray 1995). She stubbornly sat there while the bus driver raged and whites fumed with indignation. Her arrest touched off mass demonstrations, led fifty thousand blacks to boycott the city's buses for a year, and thrust an otherwise unknown preacher into a historic role.

Rev. Martin Luther King, Jr., who had majored in sociology at Morehouse College in Atlanta, Georgia, took control. He organized car pools and preached nonviolence. Incensed by the actions of this radical organizer and by the stirrings in the normally compliant black community, segregationists also put their beliefs into practice—by bombing homes and blowing up churches.

Rising Expectations and Civil Strife The barriers came down, but they came down slowly. Not until 1964 did Congress pass the Civil Rights Act, making it illegal to discriminate in restaurants, hotels, theaters, and other public places. Then in 1965, Congress passed the Voting Rights Act, banning the fraudulent literacy tests that the South had used to keep African Americans from voting.

Encouraged by such gains, African Americans experienced what sociologists call **rising expectations;** that is, they believed better conditions would soon follow. The lives of the poor among them, however, changed little, if at all. Frustrations built, finally exploding in Watts in 1965, when people living in that African-American ghetto of central Los Angeles took to the streets in the first of what have been termed "the urban revolts." When King was assassinated by a white supremacist on April 4, 1968, ghettos across the nation again erupted in fiery violence. Under threat of the destruction of U.S. cities, Congress passed the sweeping Civil Rights Act of 1968.

Continued Gains Since then, African Americans have made remarkable political, educational, and economic gains. At 9 percent, African Americans have *quadrupled* their membership in the U.S. House of Representatives in the past twenty-five years (Rich 1986; *Statistical Abstract* 1999:Table 473). College enrollment increased, and the middle class ex-

rising expectations the sense that better conditions are soon to follow, which, if unfulfilled, creates mounting frustration

panded. Today, one of every four African-American families makes more than $50,000 a year (one of ten makes more than $75,000) (*Statistical Abstract* 1999:Table 749).

The extent of African-American political prominence was highlighted when Jesse Jackson (another sociology major) competed for the Democratic presidential nomination in 1984 and 1988. In 1989, this progress was further confirmed when L. Douglas Wilder of Virginia became the nation's first elected African-American governor. The political prominence of African Americans came to the nation's attention again in 2000 when Alan Keyes competed for the Republican presidential nomination.

Current Losses Despite these gains, African Americans continue to lag behind in politics, economics, and education. No U.S. senators are African American, when by ratio in the population we would expect 12. As Table 12.1 shows, African Americans average only 61 percent of white income, have much more unemployment and poverty, and are much less likely to own their home. As Table 12.2 on the next page shows, only 15 percent have graduated from college.

That one of four African-American families makes more than $50,000 a year is only part of the story. The other part is that one of every six African-American families makes less than $10,000 a year (*Statistical Abstract* 1999:Table 749). Two worlds of African-American experience have developed—one educated and affluent, the other uneducated and ultra-poor. Concentrated among the poor are those with the least hope, the highest despair, and the violence that so often dominates the evening news. African-American males are *seven* times as likely to be homicide victims as are white males, and African-American females are more than *four* times as likely as white females to be murdered (*Statistical Abstract* 1999:Table 348). Homicide is now the leading cause of death for African-American males ages 15 to 24. Each year, more African-American males are killed by other African Americans than died in the entire nine years of the war in Vietnam.

Race or Social Class? A Sociological Debate This division of African Americans into "haves" and "have-nots" has fueled a sociological controversy. Sociologist William Wilson

Table 12.1								
RACE-ETHNICITY AND COMPARATIVE WELL-BEING								
	Median Family Income	Percentage of White Income	Percentage Unemployed	Percentage of White Unemployment	Percentage Below Poverty Line	Percentage of White Poverty	Percentage Owning Their Homes	Percentage of White Home Ownership
White Americans	$46,754	—	2.6%	—	11.0%	—	70%	—
African Americans	$28,602	61%	5.9%	227%	26.5%	241%	46%	66%
Latinos	$28,141	60%	4.9%	188%	27.1%	246%	45%	64%
Country of origin								
Mexico	$27,088	58%	5.0%	192%	27.9%	254%	49%	70%
Puerto Rico	$23,729	51%	5.0%	192%	34.2%	311%	34%	49%
Cuba	$37,537	80%	3.7%	142%	19.6%	178%	56%	80%
Central and South America	$32,030	69%	4.4%	169%	21.5%	195%	32%	46%
Asian Americans[a]	$51,850	111%	3.1%	119%	14.0%	127%	53%	76%
Native Americans	$25,000[b]	53%	NA[c]	NA	29.0%	264%	NA	NA

Note: The racial and ethnic groups are listed from largest to smallest.

[a] Includes Pacific Islanders.

[b] Author's estimate, based on the changes made by the other groups between 1990 and 1998.

[c] Not available.

Source: Statistical Abstract 1999:Tables 51, 52, 54, 55.

Table 12.2

EDUCATION AND RACE-ETHNICITY

	Less than High School Education	High School Education	1–3 Years of College	College Graduate	Number of Doctorates Awarded	Percentage of all Doctorates Awarded
White Americans	16%	34%	25%	25%	23,860	78%
African Americans	24%	36%	25%	15%	1,530	5%
Latinos	34%[a]	55%	NA	11%	1,224	4%
Asian Americans	15%	23%	20%	42%	3,060	10%
Native Americans	22%[a,b]	68%	NA	10%	306	1%

Note: NA = Not Available. Totals except for doctorates refer to persons 25 years and over.
[a]Totals for Latinos and Native Americans are not listed in the same way in the source as they are for other groups.
[b]Author's estimate, based on the changes made by the other groups between 1990 and 1998.
Source: Statistical Abstract 1999: Tables 51, 54, 55, 1004.

(1978, 1987) argues that social class is more important than race in determining the life chances of African Americans. Prior to civil rights legislation, he says, the African-American experience was dominated by race. Throughout the United States, African Americans were systematically excluded from avenues of economic advancement—from good schools and good jobs. When civil rights legislation opened new opportunities, middle-class African Americans seized them. Following the path taken by other ethnic groups, as they advanced economically, they, too, moved out of the inner city. Unfortunately, just as legal remedies began to open doors to African Americans, opportunities for unskilled labor declined: Manufacturing jobs dried up, and many other blue-collar jobs were moved to the suburbs. As a result, although better-educated African Americans were able to obtain middle-class, white-collar jobs, a large group of African Americans—those with poor education and lack of skills—was left behind, trapped in poverty in the inner city.

The result, says Wilson, is two worlds of African-American experience. One group is stuck in the inner city, lives in poverty, confronts violent crime daily, attends underfunded schools, faces dead-end jobs or welfare, and is filled with hopelessness and despair, combined with apathy or hostility. In contrast, those who have moved up the social class ladder live in good housing in secure neighborhoods, work at well-paid jobs that offer advancement, and send their children to good schools. Their middle-class experiences and lifestyle have changed their views on life. Their aspirations and values no longer have much in common with African Americans who remain poor. According to Wilson, social class—not race—is now the most significant factor in the lives of African Americans.

Many sociologists point out that this analysis overlooks the discrimination that continues to underlie the relative impoverishment of African Americans (Massey and Denton 1993; Feagin 1999). Sociologist Charles Willie (1991), for example, notes that even when they do the same work, whites average higher pay than do African Americans. This, he argues, points to racial discrimination, not to social class.

What is the answer to this debate? Wilson would reply that it is not an either-or question. My book is titled *The **Declining** Significance of Race,* he would say, not *The **Absence** of Race.* Certainly racism is still a reality in U.S. life, but today social class is *more* central to the African-American experience than is racial discrimination. The answer, then, is simple—provide jobs—for the availability of work offers hope, and work provides an anchor to a responsible life (Wilson 1996).

Continued Discrimination and Social Class African Americans who occupy higher statuses and enjoy greater opportunities apparently face less discrimination. What they do face, however, is no less painful. Many middle-class and

As discussed in the text, sociologists disagree about the relative significance of race and social class in determining social and economic conditions of African Americans. William Julius Wilson, shown here, is an avid proponent of the social class side of this debate.

wealthy African Americans report being pulled over in traffic by police who assume their expensive cars must be stolen. Christopher Darden (1996:110), an African-American prosecutor in the O. J. Simpson case, says that the police stop him about five times a year:

> I [know] the rules of the game, and I put them to work instinctively. Don't move. Don't turn around. Don't give some rookie an excuse to shoot you. Don't ask questions, no matter how badly you might want to know the answer to "Why are you stopping us, but no other cars on this street? Why aren't you stopping any of those white people?"

> "You've got a bad taillight," the cop would say. Or, "You were weaving a little." But you knew what the real crime was: suspicion of being black. (p. 97)

The Down-to-Earth Sociology box below reports on the racism experienced by middle-class African Americans.

Down-to-Earth Sociology

NO CROSS BURNING ALLOWED, BUT . . .
THE CONTINUING SIGNIFICANCE OF RACE IN EVERYDAY LIFE

Racism is much more subtle than it used to be. Burning crosses, midnight visits, beatings and lynchings—such things once got the message across. Authorities used to turn a blind eye, in some cases even to murder. Not only was housing discrimination legal—it was *illegal* to integrate a neighborhood. Separate schools, restaurants, hotels, swimming pools, bus and train station waiting areas, even drinking fountains—all were a part of everyday life in the United States. The races were not intended to mix, or else God would have made everyone the same color—white, of course.

Such conditions are now a distant memory, something that haunts us from another era. Occasionally today, someone does burn a cross, but the matter makes the evening news, and authorities investigate and make an arrest. If they don't, the FBI does. No hotel or restaurant refuses service on the basis of race-ethnicity. Blatant expressions of hatred have become a criminal matter. With times so changed, some may think that racism is a matter of the past. Although overt racism has been relegated to the back shelves, minorities still experience racism as part of their everyday lives. Joe Feagin (1999), a sociologist, asked middle-class African Americans about their experiences. His respondents told him about being stopped by cops, being followed around in stores, being given the worst rooms in hotels, and being ignored in restaurants while whites were served.

Feagin learned that the significance of racism extends far beyond any particular incident. If it consisted of only the incident, that incident, though unpleasant, could be shrugged off. Rather, racism permeates the everyday life of its victims, clutching at their souls. Here is how one man put it:

> Every day that you live as a black person you're reminded how you're perceived in society. . . . I've seen white couples and individuals dart in front of cars to not be on the same side of the street. Just the other day, I was walking down the street, and this white female with a child, I saw her pass a young white male about 20 yards ahead. When she saw me, she quickly dragged the child and herself across the busy street . . . [When I pass], white men tighten their grip on their women . . .

Racism also engenders deep fears and resentment. As one woman said:

One problem with being black in America is that you have to spend so much time thinking about stuff that most white people just don't even have to think about. I worry when I get pulled over by a cop. . . . I worry what some white cop is going to think when he walks over to our car, because he's holding on to a gun. And I'm very aware of how many black folks accidentally get shot by cops. I worry when I walk into a store, that someone's going to think I'm in there shoplifting. . . . And so, that thing that's supposed to be guaranteed to all Americans, the freedom to just be yourself, is a fallacious idea. And I get resentful that I have to think about things that a lot of people, even my very close white friends whose politics are similar to mine, simply don't have to worry about.

Perhaps the most succinct summary of how racism permeates life is this statement made by a student:

> You're just a person, but you're a black person perceived in an unblack world (Feagin 1999:395). ■

Afrocentrism In response to ongoing discrimination, many African Americans embrace **Afrocentrism**—an emphasis on uniquely African-American traditions and concerns. The Afrocentric movement has encouraged the establishment of black studies courses and has led to the creation of the holiday Kwanzaa, observed the week after Christmas. Afrocentrism is a modified form of *black nationalism,* which originally appeared in the mid-1800s (Lemann 1991). At that time, some African Americans perceived moving to Africa as the reasonable response to the conditions they faced in white America. Afrocentrism's emphasis today is not emigration but, rather, encouraging African-American culture and improving the status of African Americans.

Latinos

A Note on Terms To write on race-ethnicity is like stepping into a minefield: One never knows where to expect the next explosion. Even basic terms are controversial. Some, for example, prefer the term *Hispanic Americans,* while others reject it, saying that it ignores the Indian side of their heritage. Similarly, although the term *Chicanos* is commonly used to refer to Americans from Mexico, some would limit this term to Americans from Mexico who have a sense of oppression and ethnic unity; they would not use it to refer to those who have assimilated. Keep in mind as you read this section that *Latino* and *Hispanic* do not refer to a race, but to ethnic groups. Latinos may identify themselves racially as black, white, or Native American.

Numbers, Origins, and Location When birds still nestled in the trees from which the *Mayflower* was made, Latinos had already established settlements in Florida and New Mexico (Bretos 1994). Today, Latinos are the second-largest minority group in the United States. As shown in Figure 12.7, about 20 million people trace their origin to Mexico, 3 million to Puerto Rico, 1 million to Cuba, and 4 million to Central or South America, primarily Venezuela and Colombia. Officially tallied at 30 million, the actual number of Latinos is considerably higher, perhaps 35 million. No one knows for certain because, although most Latinos are legal residents, large numbers have entered the country illegally. Not surprisingly,

Afrocentrism an emphasis on African-American traditions and concerns

When the U.S. government took control of what is now the southwestern United States, Mexicans living there were transformed from the dominant group into a minority group. These children in Austin, Texas, dancing at a Cinco de Mayo festival, are learning to appreciate their ethnic identity, with its rich cultural heritage.

they avoid contact with both public officials and census forms. Each year more than 1 million people are apprehended at the border or at points inland and are deported to Mexico (*Statistical Abstract* 1999:Table 362), but perhaps another million or so manage to enter the United States. Most migrate for temporary work and then return to their homes and families.

To gain an understanding of these numbers, note that there are as many Latinos living in the United States as there are Canadians living in Canada (30 million). To midwesterners, such a comparison often comes as a surprise, for Latinos are absent from vast stretches of mid-America. As shown in Figure 12.8, 70 percent are concentrated in just four states: California, Texas, New York, and Florida. Latinos are the largest minority group in several major cities, including Los Angeles, San Antonio, Miami, and Houston. The federal government projects that in the year 2004 Latinos will become the largest minority group in the United States (*Statistical Abstract* 1999:Table 19).

Spanish Language The Spanish language distinguishes most Latinos from other U.S. ethnic minorities. With 17 million people speaking Spanish at home, the United States has become one of the largest Spanish-speaking nations in the world (*Statistical Abstract* 1999:Table 60). Because about half of Latinos are unable to speak English, or can do so only with difficulty, many face a major obstacle to getting good jobs.

The growing use of Spanish has become a matter of controversy. Perceiving the prevalence of Spanish as a threat, Senator S. I. Hayakawa of California initiated an "English only" movement in 1981. The constitutional amendment he sponsored never got off the ground, but 23 states have passed a law declaring English their official language (Schaefer 2000).

Diversity For Latinos, country of origin is highly significant. Those from Puerto Rico, for example, feel they have little in common with people from Mexico, Venezuela, or El Salvador—just as earlier immigrants from Germany, Sweden, and England felt they had little in common with one another. A sign of these divisions is the preference many have to refer to themselves in terms of their country of origin, such as Puerto Rican or Cuban American, rather than as Latino or Hispanic.

As with other ethnic groups, Latinos, too, are separated by social class. The half-million Cubans who fled Castro's rise to power in 1959, for example, were mostly well-educated, well-to-do professionals or businesspeople. In contrast, the 100,000 "boat people" from Cuba who fled in 1980 were mostly lower-class refugees, people with whom the earlier arrivals would not have associated in Cuba—and did not associate with here. The earlier arrivals, who are firmly established in Florida and who are in control of many businesses and financial institutions, distance themselves from the more recent immigrants.

These divisions of national origin and social class are a major obstacle to political unity. One consequence is an underrepresentation of Latinos in politics. Although Latinos make up 11 percent of the U.S. population, they hold only 4 percent of the seats in the U.S. Congress and 1 percent of the elected local offices (*Statistical Abstract* 1999:Tables 473, 481).

Fragmented among themselves, Latinos also find that a huge gulf separates them from African Americans. With highly distinct histories and cultures, these two minorities often avoid each other. As Latinos have become more visible in U.S. society and more vocal in their demands for equality, they have come face to face with African Americans who fear that Latino gains in jobs and at the ballot box will come at their expense (Chavez 1990).

Figure 12.7 COUNTRY OF ORIGIN OF U.S. LATINOS

Other countries 2,079,000
Cuba 1,307,000
Puerto Rico 3,117,000
Central and South America 4,437,000
Mexico 19,834,000

Source: Statistical Abstract 1999:Table 55.

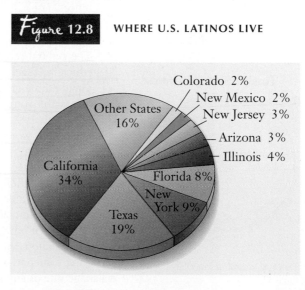

Figure 12.8 WHERE U.S. LATINOS LIVE

Colorado 2%
New Mexico 2%
New Jersey 3%
Arizona 3%
Illinois 4%
Other States 16%
California 34%
Florida 8%
New York 9%
Texas 19%

Source: Statistical Abstract 1999:Table 38.

Figure 12.9   **THE ETHNIC BACKGROUND OF ASIAN AMERICANS**

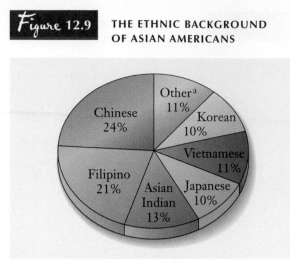

Source: Lee 1998.

Figure 12.10

RESIDENCE OF ASIAN AMERICANS

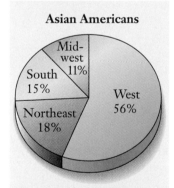

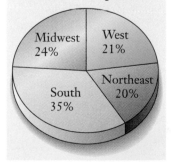

Source: Statistical Abstract 1999: Table 32.

Comparative Conditions   Table 12.1 on page 339 shows how Latinos compare with other groups. You can see that compared with European Americans and with Asian Americans, Latinos are worse off on all the indicators of well-being shown in this table. Their rankings on these indicators are similar to those of African Americans. This table also illustrates the significance of country of origin. You can see that Cuban Americans score higher on these indicators of well-being, while Puerto Rican Americans score far worse. Table 12.2 on page 340 shows that almost half of Latinos do not complete high school, and only 11 percent graduate from college. In a postindustrial society that increasingly requires advanced skills, these figures indicate that a large number of people will be left behind.

Asian Americans

I have stressed in this chapter that our race-ethnic categories are based more on social considerations than biological ones. This point is especially obvious when we examine the category Asian American. As Figure 12.9 shows, those who are called Asian Americans are diverse peoples who came to the United States from many nations. With no unifying culture or "race," why should they ever be clustered together in a single category? Think about it. What culture or race-ethnicity do Samoans and Vietnamese have in common? Or Laotians and Pakistanis? Or Native Hawaiians and Chinese? Or people from India and those from Guam? Yet all these groups—and more—are lumped together in this single category. Apparently the U.S. government is not satisfied until it is able to pigeonhole everyone into a race-ethnic category.

Since Asian American is a standard term, let's look at the characteristics of the 10 million people who are lumped together and assigned this label. Asian Americans are the fastest-growing minority in the United States. As can be seen in Figure 12.10, most live in the western states—two of five in California and one of ten in New York. With 7 percent, Hawaii comes a close third. Asian Americans of Chinese, Filipino, and Japanese descent are concentrated in Los Angeles, San Francisco, New York City, and Honolulu. Seven of every ten residents of Honolulu are Asian Americans (*Statistical Abstract* 1999:Tables 37, 48).

From Table 12.1 on page 339, you can see that Asian Americans have a higher annual income than any other racial-ethnic group listed on this table, including whites. This has led to the stereotype that all Asian Americans are successful, a stereotype that masks huge differences. Look at the poverty rate of Asian Americans shown on this table. Although 14 percent is much less than that of other minority groups, it means that about one and a half million Asian Americans live in poverty.

The general economic success of Asian Americans is due to three main factors: family life, educational achievement, and assimilation into the mainstream culture.

Of all ethnic groups, including whites, Asian-American children are the most likely to grow up with two parents and the least likely to be born to a single mother (Lee 1998; *Statistical Abstract* 1999:Table 99). Most grow up in close-knit families that stress self-discipline, thrift, and hard work (Suzuki 1985; Bell 1991). This early socialization provides strong impetus for the next two factors.

The second factor is educational achievement. Most Asian Americans get better grades in school than other groups, and they go farther in school than the rest of the population (Lee 1998). As Table 12.2 on page 340 shows, 42 percent of Asian Americans have completed college. To realize how stunning this is, compare this will all other groups shown on this table. Their educational attainment, in turn, opens doors to economic success.

Assimilation, the third factor, is indicated by several measures. With about two of five marrying someone of another race-ethnic group, Asian Americans have the highest intermarriage rate of any minority. They also are the most likely to live in integrated neighborhoods (Lee 1998). Japanese Americans, the financially most successful of Asian Americans, are the most assimilated (Bell 1991; Schaefer 2000). About 75 percent say that their best friend is not a Japanese American.

Asian Americans are becoming more prominent in politics. With 63 percent of its citizens being Asian American, Hawaii has elected Asian-American governors and sent several Asian-American senators to Washington (Lee 1998; *Statistical Abstract* 1999:Table 34). The first Asian-American governor outside of Hawaii is Gary Locke, who in 1996 was elected governor of Washington, a state in which Asian Americans make up less than 6 percent of the population.

Let's look at some of the groups that make up this broad category.

Chinese Americans Lured by gold strikes in the West and a vast need for unskilled workers, 200,000 Chinese immigrated to the United States between 1850 and 1880. Feeling threatened by competing cheap labor, Anglo mobs and vigilantes intimidated these new immigrants. Although 90 percent of the Central Pacific's labor force was Chinese, when the famous golden spike was driven at Promontory, Utah, in 1869 to mark the joining of the Union Pacific and the Central Pacific railroads, white workers prevented the Chinese from being present (Hsu 1971).

As fears of "alien genes and germs" grew, U.S. legislators passed anti-Chinese laws (Schrieke 1936). An 1850 California law, for example, required Chinese (and Latino) miners to pay a fee of $20 a month—at a time when wages were only $1 a day. The California Supreme Court even ruled that Chinese testimony against whites was inadmissible in court (Carlson and Colburn 1972). In 1882 Congress passed the Chinese Exclusion Act, suspending all Chinese immigration for ten years. Four years later, the Statue of Liberty was dedicated. The tired, the poor, and the huddled masses it was intended to welcome were obviously not Chinese.

Largely excluded from Anglo life, Chinese immigrants formed segregated communities called "Chinatowns." As discrimination lessened, the affluent moved out into integrated neighborhoods. Today, new immigrants and the poor are clustered in the Chinatowns, where they work in restaurants and sweatshops, often at jobs that pay below the minimum wage. The problems that often cluster around poverty, including gangs, are swept under the rug. No one wants to jeopardize tourism (Schaefer 2000).

Filipino Americans In 1899, the United States fought a war with Spain. As victor, part of its booty was the Philippine Islands. In 1934, the Philippines gained commonwealth status, giving Filipinos the unrestricted right to immigrate to the United States. They lost this right in 1948, when the Islands gained their independence.

Despite their numbers, about 2 million, and common country of origin, Filipino Americans have remained almost invisible, and most Americans are unaware of their presence. Little research has been done on Filipino Americans, and little has been written about them. They tend to maintain a strong loyalty to their families and to the Roman Catholic Church. Outside the church, their participation in organizations is primarily limited to clubs within their own culture. Consequently, Filipino Americans have not been politically active as a group, and they have not presented a united voice to other Americans (Schaefer 2000).

Japanese Americans

It was December 7, 1941, a quiet Sunday morning destined to "live in infamy," as President Roosevelt described it. At dawn, wave after wave of Japanese bombers began to attack Pearl Harbor, an American naval station in Oahu, Hawaii. To their surprise, Japanese pilots found the Pacific fleet anchored and unprepared for battle. The Americans were sitting ducks.

By propelling the United States into World War II, the attack on Pearl Harbor changed the world political order. As the nation readied for war, no American was untouched. Millions left home to go to battle overseas. Additional millions left the farm to work in factories that supported the war effort. Everyone lived with the rationing of food, gasoline, coffee, sugar, meat, and other essentials.

Amid hysterical fears that Japanese Americans were "enemies within" who would sabotage industrial and military installations on the West Coast, in the early days of World War II Japanese Americans were transferred to "relocation camps." Many returned home after the war to find that their property had been vandalized.

Just as waves of Japanese aircraft rolled over Pearl Harbor, so waves of suspicion and hostility rolled over the 110,000 Japanese Americans who called the United States their home. U.S. authorities feared that Japan would invade the United States and that the Japanese Americans would fight on Japan's side (Daniels 1975). They also feared that Japanese Americans would sabotage military installations on the West Coast.

Although no Japanese American had been involved in even a single act of sabotage, on February 1, 1942, President Franklin D. Roosevelt signed Executive Order 9066, authorizing the removal of everyone on the West Coast who was *one-eighth Japanese or more*. (One-eighth means the individual had one great grandparent who was Japanese.) Though they were never charged with any crime, these people were sent to what were termed "relocation camps." There were no indictments, no trials. Japanese ancestry was sufficient cause for being imprisoned.

After the war, as they continued to face prejudice and discrimination, Japanese Americans continued cultural traditions that helped them become upwardly mobile: high respect for authority, low crime and delinquency, a strong work ethic, and a low rate of divorce. As prejudice and discrimination against them gradually let up, Japanese Americans assimilated at a high rate. Today, they show little indication of wanting to maintain a separate culture. Their intermarriage rate is so high that two-thirds of all children born to Japanese Americans have a parent who is not Japanese American (Schaefer 2000).

Vietnamese Americans In 1975, after the United States was defeated in Vietnam, 135,000 Vietnamese, who had sided with the United States and who now feared for their lives, were evacuated. Scattered to various locations across the United States, they were denied an ethnic community, a primary means of adjustment used by previous immigrant groups to help them adjust to their new life. On their own, however, most Vietnamese moved to California and Texas, where they established such communities.

Another group of Vietnamese arrived later. Termed "the boat people" by the media and the public, this group, too, barely escaped with their lives. Fleeing Vietnam in leaky boats, they were attacked by pirates who robbed them and raped the women. Although no one knows the exact number, it is estimated that 200,000 drowned (McLemore 1994). About a half million, who were joined by refugees from Laos and Cambodia, made it to the United States (Schaefer 2000).

Despite their trauma and a huge language barrier, these immigrants adjusted well. With their parents placing an emphasis on education, the children have done well in school. Three-fourths have earned overall GPAs of A's and B's, and more than 60 percent score in the top half on the standardized California Achievement Test (McLemore 1994). Their high rate of interracial marriage is an indication of their assimilation: 35 percent of Vietnamese Americans born in the United States marry non-Asian Americans (Lee and Yamanaka 1990). Now that the United States and Vietnam have restored diplomatic relations, many Vietnamese Americans are visiting Vietnam. This will help them keep their Vietnamese culture alive (Schaefer 2000).

Native Americans

Diversity Thanks to countless grade-B Westerns, many Americans have stereotyped views of the Native Americans who lived on the frontier. They see them as a single people— wild, uncivilized savages. The European immigrants to the Colonies, however, encountered diverse groups of people with a variety of cultures. There were hundreds of tribes; altogether, they spoke 700 different languages (Schaefer 2000). Some were nomads, hunters and gatherers who moved from place to place in search of game and other food. Others were farmers who lived in wooden houses in agricultural communities. Each group had its own norms and values—and the usual ethnocentric pride in its own culture. Consider what happened in 1744 when the colonists of Virginia offered college scholarships for "savage lads." They were somewhat taken aback when the Iroquois replied:

> "Several of our young people were formerly brought up at the colleges of Northern Provinces. They were instructed in all your sciences. But when they came back to us, they were bad runners, ignorant of every means of living in the woods, unable to bear either cold or hunger, knew neither how to build a cabin, take a deer, or kill an enemy. . . . They were totally good for nothing."
>
> They added, "If the English gentlemen would send a dozen or two of their children to Onondaga, the great Council would take care of their education, bring them up in really what was the best manner and make men of them" (Nash 1974 in McLemore 1994).

As stated, the Native Americans, who numbered somewhere between 5 and 10 million, had no immunity to the diseases the Europeans brought with them. With deaths due to disease—and warfare, a much lesser cause—their number was reduced to about *one-twentieth* its original size, reaching a low point of about a half million a hundred years ago. Native Americans, who now number about 2 million (see Figure 12.6 on page 336), still represent diverse groups. Like Latinos and Asian Americans, Native Americans—who today speak 150 different languages—do not think of themselves as a single people that justifies a single label (McLemore 1994).

From Treaties to Genocide and Population Transfer At first, relations between the European settlers and the Native Americans were by and large peaceful. The Native Americans accommodated the strangers, as there was plenty of land for both. As wave after wave of settlers continued to arrive, however, Pontiac, an Ottawa chief, saw the future—and didn't like it. He convinced several tribes to unite in an effort to push the Europeans into the sea. He almost succeeded, but failed when the English were reinforced by fresh troops (McLemore 1994).

A pattern developed. The U.S. government would make treaties to buy some of a tribe's land, with the promise to honor forever the tribe's right to what it had not sold. European immigrants who continued to pour into the United States would disregard those boundaries. The tribes would resist, with death tolls on both sides. Washington would then intervene— not to enforce the treaty but to force the tribe off its lands. In its relentless drive westward, the U.S. government embarked on a policy of genocide. The U.S. Cavalry was assigned the task of "pacification," which translates as slaughtering Native Americans who "stood in the way" of this territorial expansion.

Of all the oppressive acts perpetrated against the Native Americans by the dominant Anglos, the Trail of Tears was certainly one of the most brutal. This painting presents a sanitized version of events; most victims walked (some were barefoot, although it was winter), and dead bodies were left strewn along the trail. Also, it is unlikely that any Native American was allowed to possess a rifle.

The acts of cruelty perpetrated by the Europeans against Native Americans appear endless, but two were especially grisly. The first was when the Europeans distributed blankets that were contaminated with smallpox—under the guise of a peace offering. The second was the Trail of Tears, a forced march of a thousand miles from the Carolinas and Georgia to Oklahoma. Conditions were so bad that of the 15,000 Cherokees who were forced to make this midwinter march in light clothing, 4,000 died. The symbolic end to Native American resistance came in 1890 with the massacre at Wounded Knee, South Dakota. Of 350 men, women, and children, the U.S. cavalry gunned down 300 (Thornton 1987; Lind 1995; Johnson 1998). These acts took place after the U.S. government changed its policy from genocide to population transfer and began to confine Native Americans to specified areas called *reservations.*

The Invisible Minority and Self-Determination Native Americans can truly be called the invisible minority. Because about 50 percent live in rural areas and one-third in just three states—Oklahoma, California, and Arizona—most other Americans are hardly conscious of a Native American presence in the United States. The isolation of one of every two Native Americans on reservations further reduces their visibility (*Statistical Abstract* 1999:Table 53).

The systematic attempts of European Americans to destroy the Native Americans' way of life and force their resettlement onto reservations continue to have deleterious effects. Of all U.S. minorities, Native Americans are the worst off. As Table 12.1 on page 339 shows, the poverty rate of Native Americans is high. In addition, their life expectancy is lower than that of the nation as a whole, and their rates of suicide and alcoholism are higher (U.S. Department of Health and Human Services 1990; Lester 1997). As Table 12.2 on page 340 shows, their education lags behind the nation and only 10 percent graduate from college.

These negative conditions are the consequence of Anglo domination. In the 1800s, U.S. courts determined that Native Americans did not own the land on which they had been settled and had no right to develop their resources. Native Americans were made wards of the state and were treated like children by the Bureau of Indian Affairs (Mohawk 1991). Then, in the 1960s, Native Americans won a series of legal victories that restored their control over the land and their right to determine economic policy. As a result, several Native

American tribes have opened businesses on their lands— ranging from industrial parks serving major metropolitan areas to fish canneries.

It is the casinos, though, that have attracted the most attention. In 1988, the federal government passed a law allowing Native Americans to operate gambling establishments on reservations. Tribal gambling has created 120,000 jobs, bringing a taste of prosperity to more than 200 tribes (McLemore 1994; Johnson 1999). And some tribes have struck it rich. The Mdewakanton Dakota in Minnesota, which has just 270 members, owns a casino that nets more than $600,000 a year for each man, woman, and child (Farney 1998). The most successful, however, are the Pequots of Connecticut. With only 310 members, they bring in more than $2 million a day (Zielbauer 1999).

A highly controversial issue is *separatism.* Because Native Americans were independent peoples when the Europeans arrived, and because they never willingly joined the United States, many tribes maintain the right to remain separate from the U.S. government and from U.S. society. The chief of the Onondaga tribe in New York, a member of the Iroquois Federation, summarizes the issue this way:

> For the whole history of the Iroquois we have maintained that we are a separate nation. We have never lost a war. Our government still operates. We have refused the U.S. government's reorganization plans for us. We have kept our language and our traditions, and when we fly to Geneva to UN meetings, we carry Hau de no sau nee passports. We made some treaties that lost some land, but that also confirmed our separate-nation status. That the U.S. denies all this doesn't make it any less the case. (Mander 1992)

One of the most significant changes is **pan-Indianism.** This emphasis on common elements that run through Native American cultures is an attempt to develop an identity that goes beyond the tribe. Whether Native Americans wish to work together as in pan-Indianism, or to stress separatism and to identify solely with their own tribes; to assimilate into the dominant culture or to remain apart from it; to move to cities or to remain on reservations; to operate casinos or to engage only in traditional activities—"Such decisions must be ours," say the Native Americans. "We are sovereign, and we will not take orders from the victors of the last centuries' wars."

*L*OOKING TOWARD THE FUTURE

Back in 1903, sociologist W.E.B. Du Bois said, "The problem of the twentieth century is the problem of the color line—the relation of the darker to the lighter races of men." It's now a hundred years since Du Bois made his observation, and the color line is still with us. It is weaker, to be sure, but the color of people's skin still affects human relationships.

During our new century, will the color line vanish? Or in a hundred years, will another sociologist repeat Du Bois' statement and lament that the color line still divides the nation? At this point, it is impossible to say for certain, but, granted the past, it seems that although racial walls will crumble here and there, the color line is not likely to disappear.

Certainly at this point in our history, race and ethnic relations remains one of the most volatile topics facing the United States. Two issues we are grappling with are immigration and affirmative action.

The Immigration Debate

Throughout its history, the United States has both welcomed immigration and feared its consequences. The gates opened wide for a massive wave of immigrants who arrived in the late nineteenth and early twentieth centuries, even though the welcome they received was not always a warm one. During the past 15 years, a second great wave of immigration has brought about a million new residents to the United States each year (*Statistical Abstract* 1999:Table 4). Unlike the first wave, which was almost exclusively from western Europe,

pan-Indianism a movement that focuses on common elements in Native-American culture in order to develop a mutual self-identity and to work toward the welfare of all Native Americans

PROJECTIONS OF THE RACIAL-ETHNIC MAKEUP OF THE U.S. POPULATION

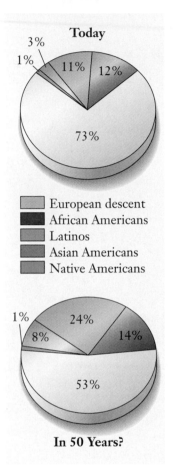

Today

3%
1%
11% 12%
73%

■ European descent
■ African Americans
■ Latinos
■ Asian Americans
■ Native Americans

1%
24%
8% 14%
53%

In 50 Years?

Source: Statistical Abstract 1999:
Tables 19, 23, 59.

this second wave has brought with it much greater variety. In fact, it is changing the U.S. racial-ethnic mix. If current trends in immigration (and birth) persist, somewhere between the years 2056 and 2080 the "average" American will trace his or her ancestry to Africa, Asia, South America, the Pacific Islands, the Middle East—to almost anywhere but white Europe. See Figure 12.11.

In some states, the future is arriving much more quickly than this. California is the first state in which ethnic and racial minorities together constitute the majority. California has 17 million minorities and 16 million whites (*Statistical Abstract* 1999:Table 38). Californians who request new telephone service from Pacific Bell can speak to customer service representatives in English, Spanish, Korean, Vietnamese, Mandarin, or Cantonese.

As in the past, there is concern that "too many" immigrants will alter the character of the United States. "Throughout the history of American immigration," write sociologists Alejandro Portés and Ruben Rumbaut (1990), "a consistent thread has been the fear that the 'alien element' would somehow undermine the institutions of the country and would lead it down the path of disintegration and decay." A widespread fear held by native-born European Americans in the early 1900s was that European immigrants would subvert the democratic system in favor of communism. Today, some fear that immigration threatens the primacy of the English language. In addition, the age-old fear that immigrants will take jobs away from native-born Americans remains strong. Finally, minority groups that struggled for political representation fear that newer groups will gain political power at their expense.

Affirmative Action

The role of affirmative action in our multicultural society lies at the center of a national debate about race and ethnic relations. In this policy, initiated by President Kennedy in 1961, goals based on race (and sex) are used in hiring, promotion, and college admission. Sociologist Barbara Reskin (1998) examined the results of affirmative action. In agreement with earlier studies (Badgett and Hartmann 1995), she concluded that, although it is difficult to separate the results of affirmative action from economic booms and busts and the increased numbers of women in the work force, affirmative action has had a modest impact.

The results may have been modest, but the reaction to this program has been anything but modest. Affirmative action has been the source of intense controversy for more than a generation. Liberals, both white and minority, say that this program is the most direct way to level the playing field of economic opportunity. If whites are passed over, this is an unfortunate cost we must pay if we are to make up for past discrimination. Conservatives, in contrast, both white and minority, agree that opportunity should be open to all, but claim that putting race (or sex) ahead of people's training and ability to perform a job is reverse discrimination. Because of their race (or sex), qualified people who had nothing to do with past discrimination are discriminated against. They add that affirmative action stigmatizes the people who benefit from it, because it suggests that they hold their jobs because of race (or sex), rather than merit.

This national debate crystallized with a series of controversial rulings during the 1990s. Perhaps the most significant was *Proposition 209,* an amendment to the California state constitution that banned preferences to minorities and women in hiring, promotion, and college admission. Despite appeals by a coalition of civil rights groups, the U.S. Supreme Court upheld the California law. The issue of the proper role of affirmative action in a multicultural society is likely to remain center stage for quite some time.

Toward a True Multicultural Society

The potential is for the United States to become a society in which different racial-ethnic groups not only coexist, but also respect one another and work for mutually beneficial goals. The idea of a multicultural society is for the minority groups that make up the United States to participate fully in the social institutions of the country while maintaining their cultural integrity. At present, however, this is only a potential. If we are to reach this goal, groups with different histories and cultures must *accept* one another. Among other things, this means that U.S. citizens—especially those who belong to the group that has taken its dominance for granted since the founding of the nation—must grapple with their traditional beliefs and national symbols. For example, does the Alamo represent the heroic action of dedicated Americans struggling against overwhelming odds—or the death of extremists bent on wresting territory from Mexico? Was the West settled by individuals who were seeking economic opportunity and freedom from oppression—or was it a savage conquest, another brutal expression of white imperialism? Such issues are the focus of the Thinking Critically section that concludes this chapter.

Thinking Critically

WHOSE HISTORY?
SEARCHING FOR TRUTH ABOUT THE
RELATIONSHIPS BETWEEN ETHNIC GROUPS

As symbolic interactionists stress, the events of life do not come with built-in meaning. Instead, we give them meaning by placing them within frameworks that lend a certain interpretation. It is no wonder, then, that the victors and the vanquished look at the same events in remarkably different ways.

The victors have the advantage of writing the textbooks that recount those events.

In Israel, schoolchildren are taught about the 1948 War of Independence, in which Israel defeated five Arab nations. The textbooks used to portray the early Zionists as peace-loving pioneers who fell victim to Arab hatred. Now, as Israel and the Palestinians are coming to terms, Israel is reexamining events and rewriting its texts. Consider the following two accounts of the same event, both from official Israeli history textbooks for ninth graders (Bronner 1999):

The old text: The Jewish community numbered 650,000. The Arab states together came to 40 million. The chances of success were doubtful, and the Jewish community had to draft every possible fighter for the defense of the community.

The new text: On nearly every front and in nearly every battle, the Jewish side had the advantage over the Arabs in terms of planning, organization, operation of equipment and also in the number of trained fighters who participated in the battle.

Such a drastic change does not come without resistance. Says one Israeli, a well-known novelist: "This is an act of moral suicide that deprives our children of everything that makes people proud of Israel. Why not just translate the Palestinian books for our children and be done with it?"

Consider the Battle of Little Bighorn. Children's history books usually recount the massacre of an outnumbered, brave band of cavalrymen, with Gen. George Custer going down to a sad but somehow glorious defeat. When Joe Marshall, a Lakota Sioux, heard this version as a fourth-grader, he mustered all the courage he could, raised his hand, and told the class the version he had heard as he was growing up among descendants of survivors of the battle. This version describes an armed group of soldiers who invade Native American lands (Charlier 1992). When the young boy finished, his teacher smiled indulgently and said, "That's nice, but we'll stick to the real story."

This issue of perspective underlies the current global controversy surrounding the teaching of history. How should Hitler be presented in German texts? As a mad butcher? Should some of his domestic policies, which stopped inflation and restored the middle class, be praised? Should Japanese textbooks present the traditional view of Emperor Hirohito as a revered descendant of the gods, or should they describe him as a warlord who directed an invasion and orchestrated the slaughter of millions of Chinese? How close to the truth is any of these statements?

In U.S. schools, the question of *what* should be taught used to be a moot point, for the school boards, teachers, and textbook writers were united by a background of shared assumptions. It was assumed, for example, that George Washington was the general-hero-founder of the nation. No question was raised about whether school curricula should mention that he owned slaves. Thomas Jefferson was presented as the primary architect of the Declaration of Independence, not as a slave master of a southern plantation. Most white boards, teachers, and textbook writers were ignorant of such facts. If they learned of them, they thought them irrelevant.

But no longer. Information is more available than it used to be, and the issue now is one of balance. How do we make certain that the accomplishments of both genders and of our many racial-ethnic groups are included? This issue, called *multiculturalism,* presents teachers, administrators, school boards, and publishers with a slew of difficult questions. How much space should be given to Harriet Tubman versus George Washington? Is enough attention paid to discrimination against Asian Americans? Against Latinos? Is the attempted genocide of Native Americans sufficiently acknowledged? What about the contributions of women to U.S. society? How about those of white ethnics—Jews, Poles, Russians, and so on?

And there are other issues. Thomas Jefferson is thought to have fathered children by his slave, Sally Hemings. At first, Jefferson's white descendants vigorously denied this accusation. Then came DNA tests and the finding that Hemings' pregnancies coincided with Jefferson's returns to Monticello and that at his death Jefferson freed Hemings and her children—but no other slaves. In the face of this evidence, the white descendants acknowledged that the Hemings, too, are Jefferson's descendants (Breaux 2000). What place should this play in our history texts?

No one yet knows the answers to such questions. As meaning is given to past events, we will construct new images of history. Like the images that preceded them, they, too, will be made up of a flowing, winding, sometimes twisted progression of myth making. ■

SUMMARY AND REVIEW

■ Laying the Sociological Foundation

How is race both a reality and a myth?

In the sense that different groups inherit distinctive physical traits, race is a reality. There is, however, no agreement regarding what constitutes a particular race, or of how many races there are. In the sense of one race being superior to another and of there being pure races, however, race is a myth. The *idea* of race is powerful, shaping basic relationships among people. Pp. 318–321.

How do race and ethnicity differ?

Race refers to inherited biological characteristics; **ethnicity,** to cultural ones. Members of ethnic groups identify with one another on the basis of common ancestry and cultural heritage. P. 321.

What are minority and dominant groups?

Minority groups are people singled out for unequal treatment by members of the **dominant group,** the group with more power, privileges, and social status. Minorities originate with the expansion of political boundaries or migration. Pp. 321–323.

What heightens ethnic identity, and what is "ethnic work"?

A group's size, power, physical characteristics, and amount of discrimination heighten or reduce ethnic identity. **Ethnic work** is the process of constructing an ethnic identity. For people with strong ties to their culture of origin, ethnic work involves enhancing and maintaining group distinctions. For those without a firm ethnic identity, ethnic work is an attempt to recover one's ethnic heritage. Pp. 323–324.

Are prejudice and discrimination the same thing?

Prejudice is an attitude, **discrimination,** an act. Some people who are prejudiced do not discriminate, while others who are not prejudiced do. Pp. 324–326.

How do individual and institutional discrimination differ?

Individual discrimination is the negative treatment of one person by another, while **institutional discrimination** is discrimination built into a society's social institutions. Institutional discrimination often occurs without the awareness of either the perpetrator or the object of discrimination. Referral rates for coronary bypass surgery are one example. Pp. 326–328.

■ Theories of Prejudice

How do psychologists explain prejudice?

Psychological theories of prejudice stress **authoritarian personalities** and frustration displaced toward **scapegoats.** Pp. 328–329.

How do sociologists explain prejudice?

Sociological theories focus on how different social environments increase or decrease prejudice. Functionalists stress the benefits and costs that come from discrimination. Conflict theorists look at how the groups in power exploit racial and ethnic divisions in order to hold down wages and otherwise maintain power. Symbolic interactionists stress how labels create **selective perception** and self-fulfilling prophecies. Pp. 329–332.

■ Global Patterns of Intergroup Relations

What are the major patterns of minority and dominant group relations?

Beginning with the least humane, they are **genocide, population transfer, internal colonialism, segregation, assimilation,** and **multiculturalism (pluralism).** Pp. 332–335.

■ Race and Ethnic Relations in the United States

What are the major ethnic groups in the United States?

From largest to smallest, the major ethnic groups are European Americans, African Americans, Latinos, Asian Americans, and Native Americans. P. 336.

What are some issues in race-ethnic relations and characteristics of minority groups today?

African Americans are increasingly divided into middle and lower classes, with two sharply contrasting worlds of experience. Latinos are divided by country of origin. On many measures, Asian Americans are better off than white Americans, but their well-being varies with country of origin. For Native Americans, the primary issues are poverty, nationhood, and settling treaty obligations. The overarching issue for minorities is overcoming discrimination. Pp. 337–349.

■ Looking Toward the Future

What main issues dominate race-ethnic relations?

The main issues are immigration, affirmative action, and how to develop a true multicultural society. The answers affect our future. Pp. 349–352.

Where can I read more on this topic?

Suggested Readings for this chapter are at the back of this book.

All URLs listed are current as of the printing of this book. URLs often change. Please check our Web site, **http://www.abacon.com/henslin,** for updates.

1. The Perspectives box in this chapter notes that our society's increasing diversity makes it difficult for many of us to specify our racial-ethnic heritage. Multiracial identity is discussed at **http://www.multiracial.com,** the Web site for *The Multiracial Activist.* This Web journal covers issues related to the civil rights of biracial and multiracial individuals and interracial couples and families. Scroll down until you reach "Hot Issues—Abolition of Racial Categorization." Browse through some of the articles at this site. What is at the heart of the debate? Why do we continue to count race? Do you think race will still be an important category in ten or twenty years? Write a paper in which you defend the current practice of "checking a box" or argue for its elimination.

2. In the Down-to-Earth Sociology box on page 341 you read about the continuing significance of race in everyday life. Controversy surrounds racial profiling, the police practice of singling out minority drivers. Some African Americans refer to this as "DWB," or "Driving While Black." The American Civil Liberties Union (ACLU) is challenging this policy. To learn more about this controversy and the work of the ACLU, go to **http://www.aclu.org/profiling.** Read firsthand accounts of minority motorists who were stopped, read an ACLU report, and read about legislative and legal campaigns to fight this practice. Prepare a report to your class on this issue; explain how it relates to the topics of prejudice and discrimination. As you do so, keep in mind that Alan Keyes, an African-American presidential candidate, said that if any group is more likely to commit a certain crime, it makes sense to profile that group for that type of crime.

3. Another controversy involves the use of Native American names and images for team logos and mascots in sports. Go to **http://pages.prodigy.net/munson/index.htm** and **http://members.tripod.com/earnestman/1indexpage.htm.** Why do Native Americans equate such practices with racism? Why do you think we continue to use these symbols? Did your high school or does your college or university use such logos or mascots? What do you think should be done?

4. In this exercise, you'll look at both sides of the argument concerning immigration. The Federation for American Immigration Reform (FAIR) argues that the current rate of immigration has a negative impact on our society. FAIR wants a new immigration policy. To learn more about this group's position, go to **http://www.fairus.org.** What was the impact of the 1965 immigration reform? How does immigration today differ from immigration that occurred in the past? What are the economic and social effects of immigration? Why should future immigration be restricted?

Now examine the views of The National Immigration Forum (NIR) at **http://www.immigrationforum.org.** Click on the opening graphic to go to NIR's home page. Read their criticisms of the 1996 legislation by clicking on "FIX '96." For information on several immigration-related issues, click on "Immigration Facts." You may also find the article on the history of nativism in our country interesting.

Drawing on your research, define the issues, problems, and solutions to the immigration debate advocated by each side. Which group do you think is right? Why? How does your position in society affect your opinion?

13

The Elderly

Phoebe Beasley, Holding Court, 1989

- **Aging in Global Perspective**
  The Social Construction of Aging
  Effects of Industrialization
  The Graying of America

- **The Symbolic Interactionist Perspective**
  Labeling and the Onset of Old Age
  The Meaning of Old Age:
      Cross-Cultural Comparisons
  U.S. Society: Changing Perceptions
  The Mass Media: Powerful Source of Symbols

- **The Functionalist Perspective**
  Disengagement Theory
  Activity Theory

- **The Conflict Perspective**
  Social Security Legislation

Intergenerational Conflict
Fighting Back: Elderly Empowerment

- **Problems of Dependency**
  Isolation and Gender
  Nursing Homes
  Elder Abuse
  The Elderly Poor

- **The Sociology of Death and Dying**
  Effects of Industrialization and the
      New Technology
  Death as a Process
  Hospices
  Suicide and the Elderly

- **Looking Toward the Future**

- **Summary and Review**

In 1928, Charles Hart, who was working on his Ph.D. in anthropology, did fieldwork with the Tiwi, who lived on an island off the northern coast of Australia. Because every Tiwi belonged to a clan, they assigned Hart to the bird (Jabijabui) clan and told him that a particular woman was his mother.

Hart described the woman as "toothless, almost blind, withered." He added that she was "physically quite revolting and mentally rather senile." He then recounted this remarkable event:

> [T]oward the end of my time on the islands an incident occurred that surprised me because it suggested that some of them had been taking my presence in the kinship system much more seriously than I had thought. I was approached by a group of about eight or nine senior men, all of whom I knew. They were all senior members of the Jabijabui clan and they had decided among themselves that the time had come to get rid of the decrepit old woman who had first called me son and whom I now called mother. As I knew, they said, it was Tiwi custom, when an old woman became too feeble to look after herself, to "cover her up." This could only be done by her sons and brothers and all of them had to

agree beforehand, since once it was done, they did not want any dissension among the brothers or clansmen, as that might lead to a feud. My "mother" was now completely blind, she was constantly falling over logs or into fires, and they, her senior clansmen, were in agreement that she would be better out of the way. Did I agree?

> I already knew about "covering up." The Tiwi, like many other hunting and gathering peoples, sometimes got rid of their ancient and decrepit females. The method was to dig a hole in the ground in some lonely place, put the old woman in the hole and fill it in with earth until only her head was showing. Everybody went away for a day or two and then went back to the hole to discover to their surprise, that the old woman was dead, having been too feeble to raise her arms from the earth. Nobody had "killed" her; her death in Tiwi eyes was a natural one. She had been alive when her relatives last saw her. I had

355

never seen it done, though I knew it was the custom, so I asked my brothers if it was necessary for me to attend the "covering up."

They said no and that they would do it, but only after they had my agreement. Of course I agreed, and a week or two later we heard in our camp that my "mother" was dead, and we wailed and put on the trimmings of mourning. (Hart and Pilling 1970:154) ■

$\mathcal{A}$ging in Global Perspective

We won't deal with the question of whether it was moral or ethical for Hart to agree that the old woman should be "covered up" (Hart seemed to be more concerned about not having to watch the act than he was about acquiescing to it). What is of interest for our purposes is how the Tiwi treated their frail elderly—or, more specifically, their frail *female* elderly. You probably noticed that the Tiwi "covered up" only old women. As noted in Chapter 11, females are discriminated against throughout the world. As this case makes evident, in some places that discrimination extends even to death.

Every society must deal with the problem of people growing old, and of some becoming very frail. Although few societies choose to bury old people alive, all societies must decide how to allocate limited resources among their citizens. As the proportion of the population that is old increases, as is happening in many nations, those decisions become more complex, and they generate tensions between the generations.

The Social Construction of Aging

The way the Tiwi treated frail elderly women reflects one extreme of how societies cope with aging. Another extreme, one that reflects an entirely different attitude, is illustrated by the Abkhasians, an agricultural people who live in a mountainous region of Georgia, a republic of the former Soviet Union. Rather than "covering up" their elderly, the Abkhasians pay them high respect and look to them for guidance. They would no more dispense with one of their elderly in this manner than we would "cover up" a sick child.

The Abkhasians may be the longest-lived people on earth. Many claim to live past 100—some beyond 120 and even 130 (Benet 1971). Although it is difficult to document

This Abkhasian man says he is 115 years old. Reasons for the Abkhasians' apparent longevity are explained in the text. Because birth records in this society do not reach back to the 1800s, however, we cannot be certain of the claims made by the Abkhasians.

Central to a group's culture are ways of viewing reality. Living for centuries in isolation on Bathurst and Melville Islands off the northern coast of Australia, the Tiwi, featured in the opening vignette, developed a unique culture. Shown here is Wurarbuti prior to leading a funeral dance. To be certain that his late uncle's ghost will not recognize him, Wurarbuti is wearing a "shirt" painted with ocher and clay, a topknot of cockatoo feathers, and a beard of goose feathers.

the accuracy of these claims (Haslick 1974; Harris 1990), government records indicate that an extraordinary number of Abkhasians do live to a very old age.

Three main factors appear to account for their long lives. The first is their diet, which consists of little meat, much fresh fruit, vegetables, garlic, goat cheese, cornmeal, buttermilk, and wine. The second is their lifelong physical activity. They do slow down after age 80, but even after the age of 100 they still work about four hours a day. The third factor—a highly developed sense of community—goes to the very heart of the Abkhasian culture. From childhood, each individual is highly integrated into a primary group, and remains so throughout life. There is no such thing as a nursing home, nor do the elderly live alone. Because they continue to work and contribute to the group's welfare, the elderly aren't a burden to anyone. They don't vegetate, nor do they feel the need to "fill time" with bingo and shuffleboard. In short, the elderly feel no sudden rupture between what they "were" and what they "are."

The examples of the Tiwi and the Abkhasians reveal an important sociological principle—that aging is *socially constructed.* That is, nothing in the nature of aging summons forth any particular set of attitudes. Rather, attitudes toward the aged are rooted in society and, therefore, differ from one social group to another. As we shall also see, even the age at which people are considered old depends not on biology, but on culture.

Effects of Industrialization

As noted in previous chapters, industrialization is a worldwide trend. Along with a higher standard of living, industrialization also brings more food, better public health measures (especially a purer water supply), and more effective ways of fighting the diseases that kill people at younger ages. Consequently, when a country industrializes, more of its people reach older ages. The Social Map below shows the percentage of elderly in the world's nations. The range is broad, from just 1 of 45 citizens in Cote d'Ivoire to 1 of 6 in Italy. You can see that almost all the countries that have the highest percentage of elderly are industrialized. No industrialized country is among the nations with the lowest percentage of elderly.

As a nation's elderly population increases, so, too, does the bill its younger citizens pay to provide for their needs. In the Most Industrialized Nations, this bill has become a major social issue. Although Americans commonly complain that Social Security taxes are too high, Table 13.1 shows that the U.S. rate of 14 percent is comparatively low. French workers are hit the hardest; they pay 43 percent of their wages into social security. People in the Least Industrialized Nations pay no social security taxes. There, families are expected to take care of their own elderly.

With industrialization continuing without letup and with the proportion of the elderly population continuing to increase, future liabilities for care of the elderly have alarmed analysts. An outstanding case is Germany, where by the year 2020 about 30 percent of the population will be over the age of 60. In order to continue to furnish the high level of care that is now provided, Germany will have to tax nearly *all* the income of its future workers (Wessel 1995). Obviously, this is impossible, but no one has yet come up with a workable solution to the problem. As you can see from Table 13.1, in several other countries the elderly make up an even larger proportion of the population. Although the percentages vary, the elderly are increasing throughout the world.

The Graying of America

The United States is no exception to this global trend. Figure 13.2 on page 360 shows how U.S. **life expectancy,** the number of years people can expect to live, increased since 1900.

SOCIAL MAP: THE GRAYING OF THE GLOBE

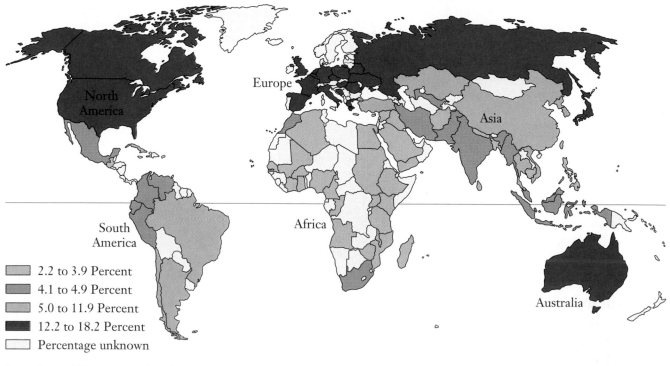

- 2.2 to 3.9 Percent
- 4.1 to 4.9 Percent
- 5.0 to 11.9 Percent
- 12.2 to 18.2 Percent
- Percentage unknown

Source: Statistical Abstract 1999:Table 1350.

Table 13.1

PAYROLL TAXES AND THE ELDERLY

Country	Total Population	Percentage over 65	Number over 65	Percentage of Payroll Paid in Taxes to Support the Elderly[a]
France	59,000,000	16.1	9,500,000	43
Hungary	10,000,000	14.6	1,500,000	40
Holland	16,000,000	13.7	2,200,000	39
Italy	57,000,000	18.2	10,400,000	39
Belgium	10,000,000	17.1	1,700,000	36
Czech Republic	10,000,000	13.8	1,400,000	35
Germany	82,000,000	16.5	13,500,000	34
Greece	11,000,000	17.2	1,900,000	34
Poland	39,000,000	12.2	4,800,000	33
Spain	39,000,000	16.8	6,600,000	29
Mexico	102,000,000	4.3	4,400,000	21
Great Britain	59,000,000	15.7	9,200,000	17
Turkey	67,000,000	6.0	4,000,000	16
Japan	126,000,000	17.0	21,400,000	14
United States	275,000,000	12.6	34,700,000	14
Canada	31,000,000	12.6	3,900,000	11
South Korea	47,000,000	6.9	3,200,000	4
Australia	19,000,000	12.6	2,400,000	2
China	1,256,000,000	7.0	87,900,000	N/A
Indonesia	219,000,000	4.3	9,400,000	N/A
Nigeria	117,000,000	3.0	3,500,000	N/A
Egypt	69,000,000	3.7	2,600,000	N/A
Kenya	29,000,000	2.8	800,000	N/A

[a] All countries for which the source lists the percentage of labor costs paid in social security taxes, plus five larger countries for comparison

Source: Statistical Abstract 1999:Tables 1349, 1350, 1384.

To me, and perhaps to you, it is startling to realize that a hundred years ago the average American could not even expect to see age 50. Since then, we've gradually added about *30* years to our life expectancy, and Americans born today can expect to live into their 70s or 80s.

The term **graying of America** has been coined to refer to this increasing percentage of older people in the U.S. population. As Figure 13.3 on the next page shows, in 1900 only 4 percent of Americans were age 65 and older. Today almost 13 percent are. The average 65-year-old can expect to live another eighteen years (*Statistical Abstract* 1999:Table 129). U.S. society has become so "gray" that the median age has *doubled* since 1850, and today there are almost seven million *more* elderly Americans than there are teenagers (*Statistical*

life expectancy the number of years that an average newborn can expect to live

graying of America a term that refers to the rising proportion of older people as a percentage of the U.S. population

Figure 13.2 U.S. LIFE EXPECTANCY BY YEAR OF BIRTH

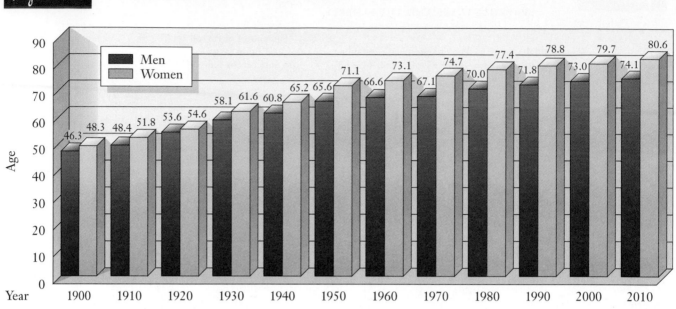

Sources: *Historical Statistics of the United States, Colonial Times to 1970,* Bicentennial Edition, Part I, Series B, 107–115; *Statistical Abstract* 1999:Table 127.

Abstract 1999:Table 22). Despite this change, as Table 13.2 shows, on a global scale Americans rank just seventeenth in life expectancy.

As anyone who has ever visited Florida has noticed, the elderly population is not evenly distributed around the country. (As Jerry Seinfeld sardonically noted, "There's a law that when you get old you've got to move to Florida.") The Social Map on the next page shows how uneven this distribution is expected to be in a couple of decades or so.

It is important to keep in mind that the maximum length of life possible, the **life span,** has not increased. Experts disagree, however, on what that maximum is. Certainly it is at

life span The maximum length of life of a species

Figure 13.3 THE GRAYING OF AMERICA

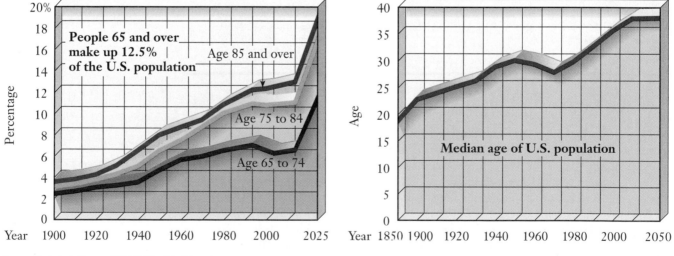

Source: *Statistical Abstract* 1999:Tables 13, 24.

Table 13.2

U.S. LIFE EXPECTANCY IN GLOBAL PERSPECTIVE

World Rank	Country	Life Expectancy at Birth
1	Hong Kong	82.4
2	Australia	80.4
3	Japan	80.2
4	Canada	79.6
5	France	78.8
6	Greece	78.6
7	Italy	78.6
8	Holland	78.3
9	Sweden	78.2
10	Taiwan	78.2
11	Spain	77.9
12	Switzerland	77.8
13	Belgium	77.7
14	Great Britain	77.5
15	Germany	77.3
16	Austria	76.7
17	United States	76.3

Source: Statistical Abstract 1997:Table 1336; 1999:Table 1352.

least 122, for this was the well-documented age of Jeanne Louise Calment of France at her death. If the reports on the Abkhasians are correct (and this is a matter of controversy), the human life span may exceed even this number by a comfortable margin.

Race-Ethnicity and Aging The U.S. racial-ethnic groups have different proportions of elderly. As you can see from Table 13.3, white Americans have a larger proportion of people age 65 and older than does any other group. Latinos have the smallest proportion of el-

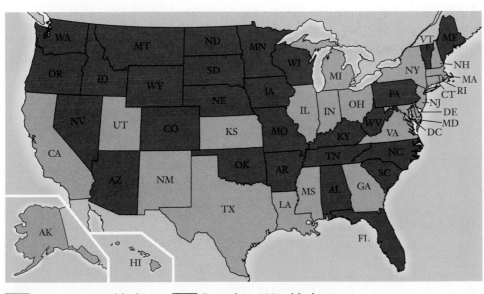

Figure 13.4

SOCIAL MAP: AS FLORIDA GOES, SO GOES THE NATION: THE YEAR 2025

Note: The growing proportion of the elderly in the U.S. population is destined to have profound effects on U.S. society. By the year 2025, one-fifth of the population of 27 states is expected to be 65 or older. Today, at 19 percent, only Florida comes close to this.

Source: U.S. Bureau of the Census, 1996, U.S. Department of Commerce, PPL-47.

■ 20% or more elderly   □ Less than 20% elderly

Table 13.3

RACE-ETHNICITY AND AGING
What Percentage of These Groups Are Elderly?

	Age			
	65–74	75–84	85 +	Total 65 and Over
Whites	7.8%	5.3%	1.8%	14.9%
African Americans	4.8%	2.6%	0.9%	8.3%
Asian Americans	4.6%	2.2%	0.6%	7.4%
Native Americans	4.0%	2.2%	0.9%	7.1%
Latinos	3.5%	1.7%	0.6%	5.8%
U.S. Average	6.8%	4.4%	1.5%	12.7%

Source: Statistical Abstract 1999:Table 23.

derly. The difference is so great that the proportion of elderly whites (14.9 percent) is more than twice that of Latinos (5.8 percent).

Of all the U.S. elderly, only about 10 percent are minorities. As we saw in Chapter 12, minorities are growing faster than whites. As a consequence, their representation among the U.S. elderly is also increasing. In a generation, the overall total of elderly who are minority will increase to 15 percent. In California, which attracts large numbers of minorities, this percentage will reach 40 percent (Wray 1991). Differences in cultural attitudes about aging, family relationships, work histories, and health practices will be important areas of sociological investigation in coming years.

THE SYMBOLIC INTERACTIONIST PERSPECTIVE

To study how aging is socially constructed, symbolic interactionists examine how the symbols associated with age affect our perceptions. Let's look at how culture underlies our ideas of when a person becomes "old," and also at how negative stereotypes and the mass media affect our perceptions of aging.

Eva Morris of Stone in Straffordshire, England, age 114, is the world's oldest living person whose age can be authenticated. She was born on November 18, 1885. The world's record for age that has been authenticated by a birth certificate was held by Jeanne Calment of France, who died in 1997 at the age of 122.

Labeling and the Onset of Old Age

You probably can remember when you thought a 12-year-old was "old"—and anyone older than that, beyond reckoning. You probably were 5 or 6 at the time. Similarly, to a 12-year-old, someone of 21 seems "old." To someone who is 21, 30 may mark the point at which one is no longer "young," and 40 may seem very old. And so it keeps on going, with "old" gradually receding further and further away from the self. To people who turn 40, 50 seems old; at 50, the late 60s look old (not the early 60s, for the passing of years seems to accelerate as we age, and at 50 the 60s don't seem too far away).

At some point, of course, an individual must apply the label "old" to himself or herself. Often, cultural definitions of age force this label on people sooner than they are ready to accept it. In the typical case, the individual has become used to what he or she sees in the mirror. The changes have taken place very gradually, and each change, if it has not exactly been taken in stride, has been accommodated. (Consequently, it comes as a shock, when meeting a friend one has not seen in years, to see how much that person has changed. At class reunions, *each* person can hardly believe how much older *the others* appear!)

If there is no single point at which people automatically cross a magical line and become "old," what, then, makes someone "old"? We can point to several factors that spur people to apply the label of old to themselves.

The first factor is *biology.* One person may experience "signs" of aging much earlier than another: wrinkles, balding, aches, difficulty in doing some things that he or she used to take for granted. Consequently, one person will feel "old" at an earlier or later age than others, and will only at that time *adopt the role of an "old person,"* that is, begin to act in ways old people in that particular society are thought to act.

Personal history or biography is a second factor that influences when people consider themselves old. An accident that limits mobility may make one person feel old sooner than others. Or a woman who gave birth at 16 may have a daughter who in turn has a child at 18, making the woman a biological grandmother at age 34. It is most unlikely that she will begin to play any stereotypical role—spending the day in a rocking chair, for example—but *knowing* that she is a grandmother has an impact on her self-concept. At a minimum, she must *deny* that she is old.

A third factor in determining when people label themselves old is **gender age,** the relative value that a culture places on men's and women's ages. For example, around the world, compared to most women most men are able to marry much younger spouses. Similarly, on men graying hair and even some wrinkles may be seen as signs of "maturing," while on women those same features are likely to be interpreted as signs of being "old." "Mature" and "old," of course, carry quite different meanings in Western cultures; the first attribute is desired, the second is shunned.

Many individuals, of course, are exceptions to these patterns. Maria, for example, may marry Bill, who is fourteen years younger than she. But in most marriages in which there is a fourteen-year age gap between husband and wife, around the world the odds greatly favor the wife being the younger of the pair. Biology, of course, has nothing to do with this socially constructed reality.

The fourth factor is *timetables,* the signals societies use to inform their members that they are old. Since there is no automatic age at which people become "old," these timetables vary around the world. One group may choose a particular birthday, such as the 60th or 65th, to signal the onset of old age. Other groups may not even have birthdays, making such numbers meaningless. Other than birthdays, can you think of other timetables used in U.S. society to designate "old"?

When does old age begin? Because biology doesn't determine the onset of old age, each culture develops and follows its own norms for when old age begins and for age-appropriate behavior. Due to longer lives and medical enhancements, those norms in U.S. culture are much less firm than they used to be. Shown here is Goldie Hawn at age 54, with Kurt Russell, age 48, with whom she has 1 child.

The Meaning of Old Age: Cross-Cultural Comparisons

To help pinpoint the extent to which people's experience of old age involves factors beyond biology, let's look at three cross-cultural examples.

The first example is from the United States. The statement I just made about some groups not celebrating birthdays may have sounded like an exaggeration. Only after they

gender age the relative values of men's and women's ages in a particular culture

moved to reservations, however, did Native Americans adopt the white custom of counting birthdays. For traditional Native Americans today, the signal for old age remains more the inability to perform productive social roles than any particular birthday. Consequently, those unable to continue in these roles tend to think of themselves as old, regardless of their age. In one survey, for instance, a Native American woman with many disabilities described herself as elderly. She was 37 (Kramer 1992).

Consider this fictionalized conversation between two Tiwi men:

> Bashti looked in envy at Masta. Masta strutted just a bit as he noticed Bashti glance his way. He knew what Bashti was thinking. Had he not thought the same just twenty years earlier? Then he had no wife; now he had three. Then he had no grand hut. Now he did, plus one for each wife. Then he had no respect, no power, no wealth. Now he was looked up to by everyone. "Ah, the marvels and beauty of gray hair," Masta thought.
>
> Bashti hung his head as he slouched toward the fringe of the group. "But my turn will come. I, too, will grow old," he thought, finding some comfort in his low status.

Why would a Tiwi man look forward to growing old, something that few people in the United States do? Traditional Tiwi society was a **gerontocracy,** a society run by the elderly. The old men held the power and controlled everything. Their power was so inclusive that the old men married *all* the women—both young and old—leaving none for the young men. Only at the age of 40 or so was a man able to marry (Hart and Pilling 1970). (In Tiwi society, females were the pawns, and aging was of no advantage to a woman. Indeed, in the opening vignette, we saw one of the disadvantages that old age brought to Tiwi women.)

Traditional Eskimo society also provides a rich contrast to an industrialized society such as the United States.

> Shantu and Wishta fondly kissed their children and grandchildren farewell. Then, sadly, but with resignation at the sacrifice they knew they had to make for their family, they slowly climbed onto the ice floe. The painful goodbyes were made as the large slab of ice inched into the ocean currents. Shantu and Wishta would now starve. But they were old, and their death was necessary, for it reduced the demand on the small group's scarce food supply.
>
> As the younger relatives watched Shantu and Wishta recede into the distance, each knew that their turn to make this sacrifice would come. Each hoped that they would face it as courageously.

Growing old in traditional Eskimo society meant a "voluntary" death. Survival in their harsh environment was so precarious that all, except very young children, had to pull their own weight. The food supply was so limited that nothing was left over to give to anyone who could not participate in the closely integrated tasks required for survival.

■ **In Sum** Symbolic interactionists stress that, by itself, old age has no particular meaning. There is nothing about old age that automatically summons forth responses of honor and respect (as with the Abkhasians), envy (as with the Tiwi), or resignation (as with the traditional Eskimo). This perspective helps us see the role of culture in how we view the process of growing old—how the social modifies the biological.

U.S. Society: Changing Perceptions

At first, the audience sat quietly as the developers explained their plans for a high-rise apartment building. After a while, people began to shift uncomfortably in their seats. Now they were showing open hostility.

gerontocracy a society (or some other group) run by the elderly

"That's too much money to spend on those people," said one.

"You even want them to have a swimming pool?" asked another incredulously.

Finally, one young woman put it all in a nutshell when she asked, "Who wants all those old people around?"

When physician Robert Butler (1975/1980) heard these responses to plans to construct an apartment building for senior citizens, he began to realize how deep feelings against the elderly can run. He coined the term **ageism** to refer to prejudice, discrimination, and hostility directed against people because of their age. Let's see how ageism developed in U.S. society.

Shifting Meanings As we have seen, there is nothing inherent in old age to summon forth negative attitudes. Some researchers even suggest that in early U.S. society old age had positive meanings (Cottin 1979; Kart 1990; Clair et al. 1993). Due to high death rates, they point out, not many people made it to old age. Consequently, growing old was seen as an accomplishment, and the younger generation listened to the elderly's advice about how to live a long life. With no pensions (this was before industrialization), the elderly continued to work at jobs that changed little over time. They were viewed as storehouses of knowledge about work skills.

The coming of industrialization, however, eroded these bases of respect. With improved sanitation and medical care, more people reached old age, and being elderly was no longer a distinction. New forms of mass production made young workers as productive as the elderly. This development, along with mass education, stripped away the elderly's possession of superior knowledge (Cowgill 1974). For a look at a similar process that is occurring in China, see the Perspectives box below.

> **ageism** prejudice, discrimination, and hostility directed against people because of their age; can be directed against any age group, including youth

---

PERSPECTIVES | Cultural Diversity Around the World
CHINA: CHANGING SENTIMENT ABOUT THE ELDERLY

As she contemplates her future, Zhao Chunlan, a 71-year-old widow, smiles shyly, but with evident satisfaction. She has heard about sons abandoning their aged parents. She has even heard whispering about brutality.

But Zhao has no such fears.

It is not that her son is such an exceptionally devoted man that he would never swerve from his traditional duty to his mother. Instead, it is a piece of paper that puts Zhao's mind at ease. Her 51-year-old son has signed a support agreement: He will cook her special meals, take her to regular medical checkups, even give her the largest room in his house and put the family's color television in it (Sun 1990).

The elderly have always occupied a high status in China. The story is well known: The elderly are considered a source of wisdom, given honored seating at both family and public gatherings, even venerated after death in ancestor worship.

Although this outline may represent more ideal than real culture, it appears to generally hold true. As China industrializes, however, the bonds between generations are weakening. Contributing to this change are a longer life expectancy and a national birth policy that allows each married couple only one child. With fewer young people, the percentage of the population that is over 65 is mushrooming. Numbering about 88 million, 7 percent of the population,

the percentage of elderly may soar to 40 percent in just fifty years (Kinsella and Taeuber 1993; *Statistical Abstract* 1999:Tables 1349, 1350).

Because China has no national social security system, it is essential that children provide for their elders. To make sure this happens, many local officials, alarmed by signs that parent-child bonds are weakening, insist that adult children sign support agreements for their aged parents. One province has hit on an ingenious device: In order to get a marriage license, a couple must sign a contract pledging to support their parents after they reach 60 (Sun 1990).

"I'm sure he would do right by me, anyway," says Zhao, "but this way I know he will." ■

PEANUTS® by Charles M. Schulz

Stereotypes, which play such a profound role in social life, are a basic area of sociological investigation. In contemporary society, the mass media are a major source
of stereotypes.

We have seen a basic principle of symbolic interactionism—that people perceive both
themselves and others according to the symbols of their culture. Thus, as the meaning of
old age was transformed—from an asset to a liability, from a sign of wisdom to a sign of
foolishness—not only did younger people see the elderly differently, but the elderly, who
also internalized the same cultural symbols, came to see themselves in a new light. A sign
of this shift in meanings is a change in how people lie about their age: They used to claim
they were older than they were, but now they say they are younger than they are (Clair et
al. 1993).

Because most U.S. elderly can take care of themselves financially—and many are well-
off—the meaning of old age is changing once again. In addition, the baby boom generation,
the first of whom are now in their 50s, has begun to confront the realities of aging. With
their vast numbers and better health and finances, they are destined to positively affect our
images of the elderly. The next step in this symbolic change, now in process, is to celebrate
old age as a time of renewal—not simply as a period that precedes death, but, rather, as another stage of growth.

The Mass Media:
Powerful Source of Symbols

In Chapter 3 (page 78), we noted that the mass media help to shape our ideas about gender and about relationships between men and women. As a powerful source of symbols, the
media also influence our ideas of the elderly, a topic that is discussed in the following Mass
Media box.

Mass Media in *Social Life*

SHAPING THE WAY WE LOOK AT THE WORLD:
THE MASS MEDIA AND OUR PERCEPTIONS OF THE ELDERLY

The mass media profoundly influence our lives. What we hear and see on television and in the movies, the songs we listen to, the books and magazines we read—all become part of our world view. Without our knowing it, the media shape our images of people—of minorities, of the dominant group, of men, women, children, of disabled people, and of people from other cultures. These images influence our perceptions and attitudes and, through them, our behaviors. The media similarly influence our images of the elderly and, along with them, our attitudes and behaviors.

The shaping is subtle, so much so that we are usually unaware of it. The media, for example, reflect and reinforce stereotypes of gender age. Older male news anchors are likely to be retained, while female anchors who turn the same age are more likely to be transferred to less visible positions. Similarly, in movies older men are more likely to play romantic leads—and opposite much younger rising stars.

Like women, the elderly are underrepresented on television, in advertisements, and in most popular magazines. Their underrepresentation implies a lack of social value. The covert message is that the elderly are of little consequence and can be safely ignored. This message is not

As emphasized in the text, age is much more than biology. The point at which old age begins, for example, differs from one culture to another. In some cultures, Tom Selleck, at age 50, would be considered an old man, but on the popular television show *Friends* he portrayed the romantic lead opposite Courteney Cox, age 31.

lost on viewers, who internalize the media's negative symbols. As people add years, they go to great lengths to deny that they are growing old. Advertisers exploit people's fears of losing their youth so that they can sell hair dyes, skin creams, and other

products that supposedly conceal even the appearance of old age (Vernon et al. 1990; Vasil and Wass 1993; Ryan and Wentworth 1999).

The American Association of Retired Persons (AARP) complains that television advertising is a major source of negative stereotypes of the elderly. The AARP points out that television often depicts the elderly as being feeble or foolish, or as passing their time in rocking chairs (Goldman 1993). The reason for this, claims the AARP, is that younger people dominate advertising firms, and their ads reflect their negative images of older people. They pick out the "worst traits of the group, making everyone believe that old is something you don't want to be." Because the mass media are so influential in shaping our perceptions, the AARP has zeroed in on a significant matter.

As discussed in the text, the elderly's affluence is growing. Their greater affluence translates into economic power, something that advertisers and producers must take into consideration. It is inevitable, then, that the media's images of the elderly will change. An indication of that change is shown in the photo in this box. We might also note the sexism that clings to these changing images—the primary depiction is that of older men and younger women. ■

THE FUNCTIONALIST PERSPECTIVE

Functionalists examine how the parts of society work together. We can consider an **age cohort,** people who were born at roughly the same time and who pass through the life course together, as a component of society. This component affects other parts. For example, if the age cohort nearing retirement is large (a "baby boom" generation), many jobs will

age cohort people born at roughly the same time who pass through the life course together

As the numbers of U.S. elderly grow, a new emphasis is being placed on their well-being. Researchers are exploring the elderly's mental and social development, as well as the causes of physical well-being. As research progresses, do you think we will reach the point where the average old person will be in this man's physical condition?

open at roughly the same time. If it is small (a "baby bust" generation), fewer jobs will open. For large numbers of people to retire, an adjustment must occur among the different parts of society.

Disengagement theory and activity theory, which we shall now examine, focus on the mutual adjustments that must be made by those who are retiring and by society's other components.

Disengagement Theory

Elaine Cumming and William Henry (1961) developed **disengagement theory** to explain how society prevents disruption when the elderly leave (or disengage from) their positions of responsibility. It would be disruptive if the elderly left their positions only when they died or became incompetent. Consequently, societies use pensions to entice the elderly to hand over their positions to younger people. Thus, disengagement is a mutually beneficial agreement between two parts of society; it facilitates a smooth transition between the generations.

Cumming (1976) also examined disengagement from the individual's perspective. She pointed out that disengagement begins during middle age, long before retirement, when someone senses that the end of life is closer than its start. The individual does not immediately disengage, however, but, realizing that time is limited, begins to assign priority to goals and tasks. Disengagement begins in earnest when children leave home, then increases with retirement and eventually widowhood.

disengagement theory the view that society prevents disruption by having the elderly vacate (or disengage from) their positions of responsibility so the younger generation can step into their shoes

Evaluation of the Theory Disengagement theory has come under attack. Anthropologist Dorothy Jerrome (1992) points out that it contains an implicit bias against older people—assumptions that the elderly disengage from productive social roles, and then sort of sink into oblivion. Her own research shows that, instead of disengaging, the elderly *exchange* one set of roles for another. The new roles, which center around friendship, are no less satisfying than the earlier roles—although they are less visible to researchers, who tend to have a youthful orientation, and who show their bias by assuming that productivity is the measure of self-worth.

Activity Theory

Are retired people less satisfied with life? Are intimate activities more satisfying than formal ones? Such questions are the focus of activity theory, in which the central hypothesis is that the more activities elderly people engage in, the more they find life satisfying. Although we could consider this theory under other perspectives, because its focus is how disengagement is functional or dysfunctional, it, too, can be considered from the functionalist perspective.

Evaluation of the Theory The research results are mixed. In general, research supports the central hypothesis that more active people are more satisfied. But not always. For example, a study of retired people in France found that some people are happier when they are very active, others when they are less involved (Keith 1982). Similarly, most people find informal, intimate activities, such as spending time with friends, to be more satisfying than formal activities. But not everyone. In one study, 2,000 retired U.S. men reported formal activities to be as important as informal ones. Even solitary activities, such as doing home repairs, had about the same impact as intimate activities on these men's life satisfaction (Beck and Page 1988).

With such mixed results, researchers need to search for key variables that underlie people's activities. I suggest three: finances, health, and individual orientations. Finances are likely a chief factor, for older people with adequate finances are usually more satisfied with life (Atchley 1975; Krause 1993). The second centers on health: Healthier people are more active (Jerrome 1992; Johnson and Barer 1992). The third factor, individual orientations, appears to undergird everything else. You saw how significant it was in the U.S. and French studies just mentioned. Just as some people are happier doing less, others feel satisfied only if they are highly involved. Similarly, some people prefer formal activities, while others derive more satisfaction from informal ones. To simply count people's activities, then, is far from adequate, and these three variables may unlock the relationship between disengagement, activity, and life satisfaction.

*T*HE CONFLICT PERSPECTIVE

From the conflict perspective, the guiding principles of social life are competition, disequilibrium, and change. So it is with society's age groups. Whether the young and old recognize it or not, they are part of a basic struggle that threatens to throw society into turmoil. The passage of Social Security legislation is an example of this struggle.

Social Security Legislation

In the 1920s, before Social Security provided an income for the aged, two-thirds of all citizens over 65 had no savings and could not support themselves (Holtzman 1963; Hudson 1978). The Great Depression made matters even worse, and in 1930 Francis Townsend, a physician, started a movement to rally older citizens. He soon had one-third of all Americans

activity theory the view that satisfaction during old age is related to a person's level and quality of activity

over 65 enrolled in his Townsend clubs, and he demanded that the federal government impose a national sales tax of 2 percent to provide $200 a month for every person over 65—the equivalent of more than $2,000 a month today. In 1934, the Townsend Plan went before Congress. Because it called for such high payments and many were afraid that it would destroy people's incentive to save for the future, Congress looked for a way to reject the plan without appearing to oppose old age pensions. When President Roosevelt announced his own, more modest Social Security plan in 1934, Congress embraced it (Schottland 1963; Amenta et al. 1997).

This legislation required that workers retire at 65. It did not matter how well people did their work, nor how much they needed an income. For decades, the elderly protested. Finally, in 1978 Congress raised the mandatory retirement age to 70, and in 1986 eliminated it altogether. Today, almost 90 percent of Americans retire by age 65, but they do so voluntarily. No longer can they be forced out of their jobs simply because of their age.

Conflict theorists point out that Social Security did not come about because members of Congress had generous hearts. Social Security, rather, emerged from a struggle between competing interest groups. As conflict theorists stress, equilibrium is only a temporary balancing of social forces, one that can be upset at any time. Perhaps, then, more direct conflict will emerge in the future. Let's consider that possibility.

Intergenerational Conflict

Will the future bring conflict between the elderly and the young? Although violence is not likely, the grumbling is increasing—complaints that the elderly are getting more than their share of society's resources (Brownstein and Rosenblatt 1999). The huge costs of Social Security and Medicare have become a national concern. These two programs alone account for one of every three tax dollars (*Statistical Abstract* 1999:Table 548). As Figure 13.5 shows, Social Security taxes were only $781 million in 1950; now they run about *500* times higher.

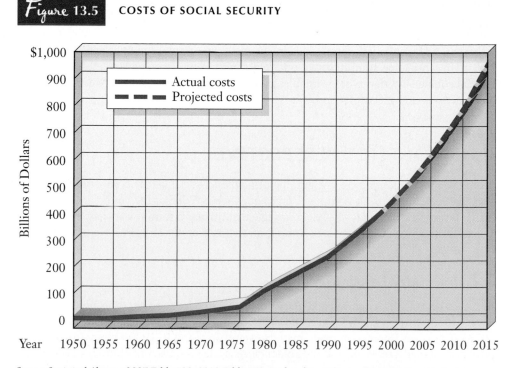

Figure 13.5 **COSTS OF SOCIAL SECURITY**

Source: Statistical Abstract 1997:Table 518; 1999:Table 543. Broken line indicates the author's projections.

Sociology

CHANGING SENTIMENT ABOUT THE U.S. ELDERLY

There used to be widespread concern about poverty among the elderly. As noted in the text, Congress took effective measures, and the elderly's rate of poverty dropped dramatically. Is this leading to a new sentiment about the elderly?

There are indications that it is. Senator Alan Simpson called the elderly "greedy geezers," "oldsters in Bermuda shorts teeing off near their second homes in Florida" and at the same time demanded government handouts (Duff 1995). Teresa Anderson (1985) felt resentful when she had to pay more than her parents for an identical room in the same motel. She said, "My parents work and own several pieces of property. Something is wrong when people are automatically entitled to a 'senior citizen discount' regardless of need."

Some even argue that we should ration medical care for the elderly (Perrin 1994). Considering costs, asks Daniel Callahan (1987), why should we perform open-heart surgery on people in their 80s, which might prolong life only two or three years? Doesn't it make more sense to use those same resources to give a kidney transplant to a child, whose life might be prolonged by fifty years?

Robert Samuelson (1988) proposes that we eliminate tax breaks for the elderly, such as

their extra standard deduction on federal income tax forms. He also suggests that we reduce the cost-of-living adjustments in Social Security. He accuses the elderly's powerful lobby, the American Association of Retired Persons (AARP), of using misleading stereotypes. He says, "In the real world, the stereotypes of the elderly as sedentary, decrepit, and poor have long vanished, but in politics the cliché is promoted and perpetuated." He accuses the AARP of outright hypocrisy: "They insist (rightfully) that age alone doesn't rob them of vitality and independence, while also arguing (wrongfully) that age alone entitles them to special treatment." They can't have it both ways, he says. ■

For Your Consideration

Use materials in this chapter to analyze why perceptions of the elderly are changing. In doing so, note two sides of the coin. On one side: Today's elderly have higher living standards than any 65-plus generation in U.S. history; one in three golfers is over 65, as are 60 percent of cruise va-

Attitudes toward the elderly have undergone major shifts during the short history of the United States. As the economic circumstances of the elderly improve, attitudes are changing once again.

cationers. On the other side: Twenty-one percent of the unmarried, 26 percent of African Americans, 24 percent of Latinos, 12 percent of Asian Americans, and 9 percent of whites live in poverty (*Statistical Abstract* 1999:Table 764). Note also the contrasting images—on one hand "blood-sucking vultures" and on the other hand, "pathetic creatures saving pennies to buy the best meal they can afford—dog food."

The Down-to-Earth Sociology box examines stirrings of resentment that may become widespread.

Some form of conflict seems inevitable. The graying of the United States leaves proportionately fewer working people to pay for the benefits received by the increasing millions who collect Social Security. This and other problems are discussed in the following Thinking Critically section.

Thinking *Critically*

EXPLODING THE MYTH OF U.S. BUDGET SURPLUSES: CAN WE PAY THE ELDERLY'S SOCIAL SECURITY OUT OF THIN AIR?

Each month the Social Security Administration mails checks to 44 million people. Across the country, 179 million U.S. workers pay into the Social Security system, looking to it to provide for their basic necessities—and even a little more than that—in their old age.

How dependable is Social Security? The short answer is "Don't bet your old age on it."

The first problem is well known. Social Security is not a bank account. The money taken from our checks is not deposited into our individual accounts. No money in the Social Security system is attached to anyone's name. At retirement, we don't withdraw our own Social Security money. Instead, the government writes checks on money that it collects from current workers. When these workers retire, they, too, will be paid, not from their own savings, but from money collected from others who are still working.

The Social Security system is like a giant chain letter—it works as long as enough new people join the chain. If you join early enough, you'll collect much more than you paid in—but if you join toward the end, you're simply out of luck. And, say some conflict theorists, we are nearing the end of the chain. The shift in the **dependency ratio,** the number of people collecting Social Security compared with the number of workers contributing to it, is especially troubling. As Figure 13.6 shows, sixteen workers used to support each person who was drawing Social Security. Now the dependency ratio has dropped to four. When it hits two, Social Security taxes could become so high that they stifle the country's economy. To prevent this, Social Security taxes were raised in 1977 and again in 1983. The increased revenues were intended to build a Social Security trust fund of trillions of dollars—a surplus that would guarantee payments to the retired and ease the burden on future workers.

The second problem with Social Security takes us to the root of the crisis, or, some say, fraud. In 1965 President Lyndon Johnson was bogged down in a war in Vietnam. To conceal the war's costs from the public, he hit on an ingenious solution—to prohibit the Social Security Administration from investing in anything but U.S. Treasury bonds—a form of government IOUs. This put the money collected for Social Security into the general fund, where he could

FEWER WORKERS SUPPORTING A LARGER NUMBER OF RETIREES

Source: Social Security Administration; *Statistical Abstract* 1999:Tables 614, 616.

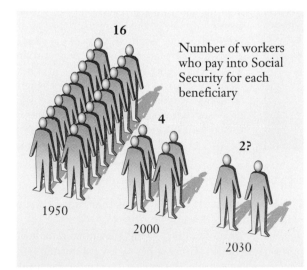

dependency ratio the number of workers required to support dependent persons—those 65 and older and those 15 and under

use it to finance the war. The amount owed Social Security was called "off budget," which was another way of saying it was not counted as part of the debt. The politicians still do this.

Suppose that you buy a $10,000 U.S. Treasury bond. The government takes your $10,000 and hands you a document that says it owes you $10,000 plus interest. This is how Social Security works. The Social Security Administration (SSA) collects the money from workers, pays the retired, disabled, and survivors of deceased workers, and then hands the excess over to the U.S. government. The government, in turn, gives SSA gigantic IOUs in the form of U.S. Treasury bonds. The government spends the money on whatever it wants—whether that means building roads and schools or subsidizing tobacco crops.

The government now boasts of huge budget surpluses. *There are none.* These so-called budget surpluses are a sleight-of-hand manipulation of money. The government spends billions more than it takes in. By putting the Social Security money in the general account, it looks like there is more income than expenditures. But there isn't. Many people don't believe that politicians would try to pull the wool over our eyes in such a gigantic way, and that the media would support them, but so it is. A glance at *Statistical Abstract of the United States,* available in your library, will clarify the government's magical bookkeeping. Table 542 in the 1999 edition reports a federal government surplus of $79 billion for 1999. Yet the *same* table shows that between 1998 and 1999 the federal government's debt increased by $136 billion.

Think of it this way: Suppose you were spending more money than you make—but to hide it you dip into Aunt Mary's bank account and put some of her money in your own account. If you don't count what you owe Aunt Mary, you have a surplus. The government simply does not count those huge IOUs it owes the elderly—and it reports a fraudulent surplus to the public.

Each month the government wipes the Social Security trust fund clean. Washington grabs the money and hands out the IOUs. The federal government now owes the fund about $15 trillion, which means that the national debt is *several times* its official total.

This arrangement is a politician's dream. The Gramm-Rudman law, which was designed to limit the amount of federal debt, does *not* count funds "borrowed" from Social Security (in their terms, it is "off budget"). It is as though this government spending does not exist—and to politicians it doesn't. To them, Social Security is a gigantic machine that produces billions from thin air. Those are just numbers on paper, not money that has been confiscated from workers. ■

For Your Consideration

Here are three proposals to solve this problem.

1. Raise the retirement age to 70.
2. Use the excess Social Security taxes to pay off the national debt. The debt could be paid off before the dependency ratio drops much further, making the money spent on interest (now $227 billion a year) available for Social Security payments. For this to work, the government could not increase its spending, something that is almost an impossibility for politicians.
3. Change the entire system. Put what workers pay as Social Security taxes into their own individual retirement accounts. A board, independent of the government, would select money managers to invest these accounts in real estate, stocks, and bonds. The board would retain the money managers that do the best job. All investment results would be published and would be available for public inspection.

Think in terms of your own Social Security. Do you prefer to retain the current Social Security system? Do you prefer one of these three proposals? None is perfect. What problems might each have? Can you think of a better alternative?

Sources: Smith 1986; Smith 1987; Hardy 1991; Genetski 1993; Stevenson 1998, *Remnant Review,* a private newsletter, *Statistical Abstract* 1999. Government publications that list Social Security receipts as deficits can be found in *Monthly Treasury Statement of Receipts and Outlays,* the *Winter Treasury Bulletin,* and the *Statement of Liabilities and Other Financial Commitments of the United States Government.*

HEALTH CARE COSTS FOR THE ELDERLY AND DISABLED

Source: Statistical Abstract, various years, and 1999:Tables 177, 181.

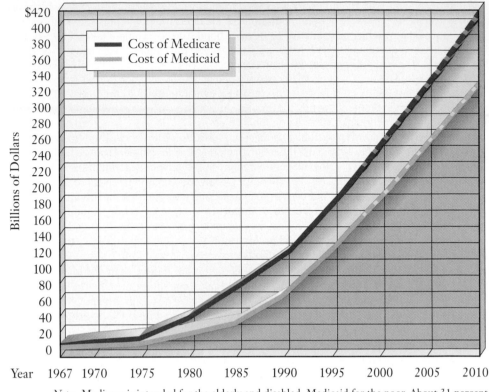

Note: Medicare is intended for the elderly and disabled, Medicaid for the poor. About 31 percent of Medicaid payments ($38 billion) goes to the elderly (*Statistical Abstract* 1999:Table:179). Broken lines indicate the author's projections.

As Figure 13.7 shows, medical costs for the elderly have also soared. Because of this, some fear that children's health care is being shortchanged and that Congress will be forced to "choose between old people and kids." What especially alarms some are the data shown in Figure 13.8. As the condition of the elderly has improved, that of children has worsened. Although critics are pleased that the elderly are better off than they were, they are bothered that this improvement has come at the cost of the nation's children.

TRENDS IN POVERTY

Source: Congressional Research Service, *Statistical Abstract* 1999:Table 763.

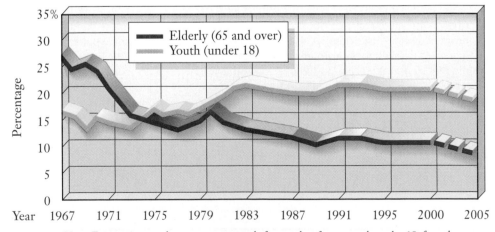

Note: For some years the government totals for youth refer to people under 18, for other years to people under 16 or 15. Broken lines indicate the author's projections.

But has it really? Conflict sociologists Meredith Minkler and Ann Robertson (1991) say that while the figures themselves are true, the comparison is misleading. The money that went to the elderly did *not* come from the children. Would anyone say that the money the government gives to flood victims comes from the children? Of course not. The government makes choices about where to spend money, and it could very well have decided to increase spending on *both* the elderly and children. It simply has not done so. Framing the issue as a case of money going to one group at the expense of the other group is an attempt to divide the working class. If the working class can be made to think that it must choose between pathetic children and suffering old folks, it will be divided and unable to work together to change U.S. society.

Fighting Back: Elderly Empowerment

Some organizations work to protect the hard-won gains of the elderly. Let's consider two.

The Gray Panthers The Gray Panthers are aware of the danger of dividing the working class along age lines. This organization, founded in the 1960s by Margaret Kuhn (1905–1995), encourages people of all ages to work for the welfare of both the old and the young. On the micro level, the goal is to develop positive self-concepts (Kuhn 1990). On the macro level, the goal is to build a base so broad that it can challenge institutions that oppress the poor, whatever their age—and to fight attempts to pit people against one another along age lines. One indication of their effectiveness is that Gray Panthers frequently testify before congressional committees concerning pending legislation.

The American Association of Retired Persons The AARP also combats negative images of the elderly. This 33-million member organization is politically powerful (Clark 1994). It monitors proposed federal and state legislation and mobilizes its members to act on issues affecting their welfare. The AARP can command tens of thousands of telephone calls, telegrams, and letters from irate elderly citizens. To protect their chances of reelection, politicians know better than to cross swords with the AARP. As you can expect, critics claim that the organization is too powerful, that it is able to muster forces to claim greater than its share of the nation's resources.

All this helps prove our point, say conflict theorists. Age groups are just one of society's many groups that are struggling for scarce resources, with conflict the inevitable result.

Before we close this chapter, let's look at problems of dependency and the sociology of death and dying.

PROBLEMS OF DEPENDENCY

"When I get old, will I be able to take care of myself? Will I become frail and not be able to get around? Will I end up poor and in some nursing home somewhere, in the hands of strangers who don't care about me?" These are common concerns. Let's examine the dependency of the elderly: isolation, nursing homes, abuse, and poverty.

Isolation and Gender

Contrary to some stereotypes, most U.S. elderly are *not* isolated. Because most women live longer than most men, however, women are more likely than men to lose their spouse and to experience isolation. As you can see from Figure 13.9, 73 percent of elderly men live with their wives, but only 41 percent of elderly women live with their husbands. The intense feelings of isolation that widowhood brings, then, are more likely to be experienced by women. This difference in mortality also means that women are much more likely to take care of frail husbands than husbands are to care for frail wives.

WHERE DO THE U.S. ELDERLY LIVE?

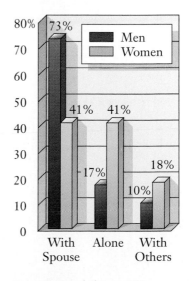

Source: Statistical Abstract 1999: Table 50.

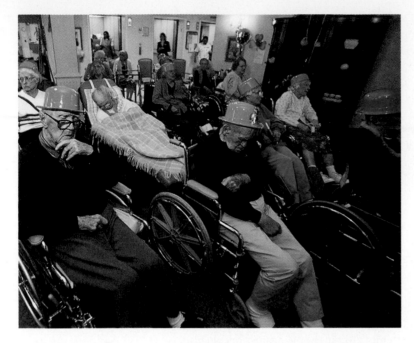

Nursing home residents are not typical of the elderly. They are in worse health and generally more isolated. Shown here are residents of a nursing home in Morristown, New Jersey, preparing to celebrate St. Patrick's Day.

Nursing Homes

Each year, about 13 percent of all U.S. citizens age 65 and older are admitted to nursing homes. Turnover is high, and at any one time, only about 4 percent of the U.S. elderly are nursing home residents (*Statistical Abstract* 1999:Tables 16, 220). The percentage of elderly people in nursing homes used to be higher, but home health care services financed by the government are now an alternative for many. Some nursing home residents return home after only a few weeks or a few months. Others die after a short stay. Overall, about one half of elderly women and one-third of elderly men spend at least some time in a nursing home.

Nursing home residents are *not typical* of the elderly. Most are age 80 or older (40 percent are 85 and older) (*Statistical Abstract* 1999:Table 220). They are likely to be widowed, or to never have married and therefore be without family to take care of them. More than half are incontinent (unable to control their urine), and two-thirds are disorientated or have memory loss (Treas 1995).

It is difficult to say good things about such health conditions or about nursing homes. Nursing care is so expensive that 70 percent of residents without family go broke within just three months (Ruffenbach 1988; Treas 1995). The literature, both popular and scientific, is filled with horror stories—reports of patients who have been neglected, beaten, and otherwise maltreated (Ellis 1991; Brink 1993). Of course, not all nursing homes are like that. On the contrary, most are probably at least halfway decent. Some even provide a pleasant decor and aides that care about their patients, but they still fall far short of being home (Butterworth 1992). Even the better ones have a tendency to strip away human dignity, as sociologist Sharon Curtin found (1976):

> Miss Larson entered Montcliffe the last week of October. . . . Shortly after her admission, I arrived at 7 a.m. to find the night nurse indignant and angry. Miss Larson had climbed over the side rails during the night, and had been found in the bathroom. "She didn't ring or call out," said the nurse. . . . "Why, she might have been hurt, and she is so confused. I want the doctor to order me more sedation. We can't have her carrying on, and disturbing all the other patients."
>
> I walked in the room and Miss Larson was in restraints. . . ." Get me out of these!" she ordered. "How dare they try to stop me from getting out of bed. I always have to relieve myself at night; and they never answer my bell."
>
> Miss Larson was not confused; but in a place where all the patients are so sedated that they scarcely move a muscle during the night, she was counted a nuisance. I did not want them to increase her sedation; barbiturates frequently make old people confused and disoriented. Even if she was a pain in the neck, I like her better awake and making some sense. The problem was she had no rights. She was old, sick, feeble. Therefore she must shut up, lie still, take what little was offered and be grateful. And if she did that, she would be a "good girl."

The elderly resent being treated like children—in an institution or anywhere else. They resist, as did Miss Larson, but resistance is usually fruitless.

Not everything about nursing homes is bad, of course. They do serve vital functions; they provide care for the elderly who have no families, or who are so sick that their families can no longer care for them. Sometimes nursing homes even help family relationships. A study of a well-run, middle-class nursing home showed that 70 percent of residents who were parents either grew closer to their family or maintained an already close relationship. Thirty percent continued to be alienated from their children. Often, affection between the aged parent and adult children had been strained by the parent's physical or mental condition. With professional care, the condition of patients improved, and many adult children felt free to again provide emotional support to the parent (Smith and Bengston 1979).

After numerous complaints about nursing home abuses and after much prodding by the AARP to change nursing homes from warehouses of bodies to places of treatment and human care, in 1987 Congress passed the Nursing Home Reform Amendments. This law provides a bill of rights for nursing home residents. It gives them the right to privacy, to be informed about their treatment and to refuse it, to keep personal belongings, to review medical records, to complain without reprisal, and to be unfettered—not tied to a chair or a bed as Miss Larson was. As with any other law, of course, this one, too, is only as good as its enforcement. For an example of an excellent system of institutionalized care, see the Perspectives box below.

PERSPECTIVES | Cultural Diversity Around the World

ALZHEIMER DISEASE: LESSONS FROM SWEDEN

"I'm ready," shouted Clay from the bedroom.

"That was fast," thought Virginia, his wife of forty-eight years. "He never gets ready for church that fast."

Virginia walked into the bedroom, and there, smiling and ready to leave for church, stood Clay—absolutely naked except for three watches strapped to his left wrist. Virginia told me this story later that morning when I asked her how things were going.

As people age, among their fears is that of "losing their mind." By this they mean senility, or, more technically, Alzheimer disease.

How do we care for people when they get like Clay?

Clay is in good hands. His wife is still healthy, and she lovingly makes certain that he eats nourishing meals, is included in social events—and wears clothes when he goes out.

But what about the many who don't have close, caring relatives? For them, senility means institutionalization—which, even if it does not mirror the horror stories we all have heard, is certainly

a far cry from the tender loving care that someone like Virginia gives.

Institutionalization, however, does not have to be a bad experience. To see the potential for positive care, we can turn to Sweden, which since the 1980s has been pioneering group homes for victims of Alzheimer disease (Malmberg and Sundström 1996). The group homes consist of six to eight small apartments fanning outward from a shared kitchen and living room. Residents have their own accommodations, but a trained and well-paid care staff is available around the clock. The goal is to mirror a supportive home environment in which residents are lovingly cared for, where they are treated as individuals, and where they participate in everyday activities. The benefits go far beyond personalized care; secondary problems associated with Alzheimer—depression, restlessness, and anxiety—apparently decrease. ■

For Your Consideration

The group home model pioneered by Sweden is exemplary, but expensive. In the United States, what chance do you think we have of providing similar group

Former president Ronald Reagan suffers from Alzheimer disease. This disease devastates the thinking process, making its victims unable to carry out the ordinary routines on which everyday life depends. As the percentage of the aged in our society increases, so will the number of people who suffer from this disease—and the caregiving that will become necessary.

homes for victims of Alzheimer disease? Suppose that we did provide such homes, but could not afford them for all Alzheimer victims—how should they be rationed?

Technology and Nursing Homes It is a challenging goal to reduce isolation, depression, and *anomie,* conditions that promote mental and physical deterioration. Some residents of nursing homes find that the computer and Internet help them overcome this debility. Sending and receiving e-mail is turning out to be especially valuable. It can help the elderly (institutionalized or not) to keep in contact with relatives and friends, who may be dispersed throughout the country, and, in our emerging global society, throughout the world.

Apparently, learning how to send e-mail reduces depression, loneliness, and boredom. To see why, imagine yourself in advanced age, in declining health and confined to a nursing home, your spouse and friends deceased, and your children living several states away. Then imagine how encouraged you would feel if you received this message from your granddaughter (an actual message received by a woman in her 90s, who took a course in e-mail offered in her nursing home): "Dear Grandma, I can't believe you just sent me e-mail. You're the coolest grandma in California" (Crary 1999).

Elder Abuse

Stories of elder abuse abound—and so does the abuse itself. In interviews with a random sample of nursing home staff, 40 percent admitted that during the preceding year they had abused patients psychologically. Ten percent admitted to abusing patients physically (Pillemer and Hudson 1993). Most abuse of the elderly, however, takes place not in nursing homes but at home. Most abusers are not paid staff, but family members, who hit, verbally and emotionally abuse, or financially exploit their aged relatives (Pillemer and Wolf 1987). Spouses are most likely to be the abusers (Nachman 1991; Pillemer and Suitor 1993).

Why do spouses, children, and other relatives abuse their own elderly? Sociologists Karl Pillemer and Jill Suitor (1993) interviewed more than 200 people who were caring for family members who suffered from Alzheimer disease. One husband told them,

> Frustration reaches a point where patience gives out. I've never struck her, but sometimes I wonder if I can control myself. . . . This is . . . the part of her care that causes me the frustration and the loss of patience. What I tell her, she doesn't register. Like when I tell her, "You're my wife." "You're crazy," she says.

Apparently, the precipitating cause of this form of abuse is stress from caring for a person who is dependent, demanding, and in some cases violent (Pillemer and Suitor 1993; Korbin et al. 1994). Since most people who care for the elderly undergo stress, however, but are not violent toward those they care for, we do not have the answer to why some caregivers become violent. For this, we must await future research.

This is not the only type of abuse of the elderly, of course. Consider, for example, that some elderly women are raped in nursing homes, and many nursing home residents have their possessions stolen. Underlying each of these abuses are complex reasons. More important than understanding the causes, however, is preventing nursing home residents from being abused in the first place. An important step in this direction is laws that require background checks of nursing home workers. At a minimum we can screen out people who have been convicted of such crimes as rape. This is similar to requiring background checks of nursery school workers in order to screen out people who have been convicted of molesting children. Most states have passed such laws.

The Elderly Poor

Many elderly live in nagging fear of poverty. Since they do not know how long they will live, nor what the rate of inflation will be, they fear that they will outlive their savings. How realistic is this fear? Although we cannot speak to any individual case, we can look at the elderly as a group.

Gender and Poverty As reviewed in Chapter 11, during their working years most women have lower incomes than men. As Figure 13.10 shows, this pattern follows women and men into their old age. As you can see, women are almost twice as likely as men to be poor.

GENDER AND POVERTY IN OLD AGE

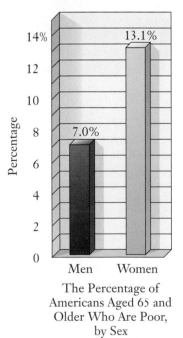

The Percentage of Americans Aged 65 and Older Who Are Poor, by Sex

Source: Statistical Abstract 1999: Table 50.

In old age, as in other stages in the life course, having enough money for one's needs and desires makes life more pleasant and satisfying. This elderly woman, who must live out of her car, is not likely to find this time of her life satisfying. Income, however, is hardly the sole determiner of satisfaction during old age. As indicated in the text, integration in a community in which one is respected is a crucial factor. Thus, these elderly men in Miami's "Little Havana," although poor, are likely to find this time of life much more satisfying than the isolated homeless woman.

Race—Ethnicity and Poverty The elderly also reflect the basic racial and ethnic patterns of the general society. As Figure 13.11 shows, elderly whites are the least likely to be poor. As you can see, elderly African Americans and Latinos are almost *three* times as likely as whites to be poor. For elderly Asian Americans, the gap is not as large, yet their poverty runs a third higher than whites.

A Decline in Poverty Poverty among the elderly was once (in the 1960s) so high that one of every three elderly Americans lived below the poverty line. The public was upset, and the federal government established anti-poverty programs and fattened Social Security checks. This led to one of the few success stories in the government's campaign against poverty. As Figure 13.12 on the next page shows, this campaign has been so successful that today's elderly are less likely than the average American to be poor.

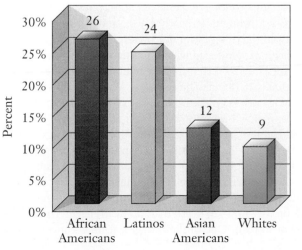

 13.11

POVERTY AND RACE-ETHNICITY

Source: Statistical Abstract 1999: Table 764.

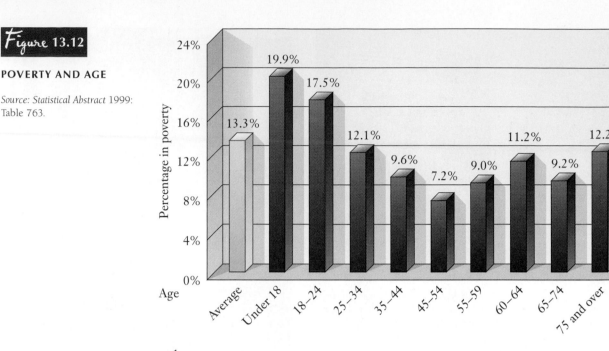

Figure 13.12

POVERTY AND AGE

Source: Statistical Abstract 1999: Table 763.

THE SOCIOLOGY OF DEATH AND DYING

In a fascinating subfield of sociology, death and dying, sociologists stress how death, like old age, is much more than a biological event. They examine how culture shapes the ways that people experience death. Let's look at some of their findings.

Effects of Industrialization and the New Technology

In preindustrial societies, the sick were taken care of at home, and they died at home. Because life was short, most children saw a sibling or parent die (Blauner 1966). As noted in Chapter 1 (page 29), the family even prepared corpses for burial.

Industrialization radically altered the circumstances of dying. With modern medicine, dying has been transformed into an event that is managed by professionals in hospitals. Consequently, today most Americans have never seen anyone die. Fictional deaths on television are the closest most come to witnessing death. In effect, dying has become an event that takes place behind closed doors—isolated, disconnected, remote.

This has made the process of dying something strange and alien to us. To help put on a mask of immortality, we hide from the fact of death. We have developed elaborate ways to refer to death without using the word itself, which uncomfortably reminds us of our human destiny. We carefully construct a language of avoidance, using terms such as "gone," "passed on," "no longer with us," "passed through the pearly gates," and "at peace now."

New technologies not only removed the dying from our presence, but also are bringing us a new experience of death. They have produced what sociologists Karen Cerulo and Janet Ruane (1996) call *technological lifespace*. By this term, they refer to a form of existence that is neither life nor death as we usually define it. The self of a "brain dead" person, for example, is gone—dead—yet technology can keep the body alive. What used to be firm—the boundary between life and death—is now becoming murky, for technological lifespace is a kind of bridge between life and death. (The Sociology & the New Technology box in Chapter 19, page 557, explores some aspects of technological lifespace.)

As people grow older, the reality of death becomes more real. With each passing year, the elderly see more of their friends and relatives die. Much of their talk may center on those persons—how they miss them, and how she "went" so suddenly, or how he lingered on. Fears about dying often focus more on the "how" of death than on death itself. The elderly are especially fearful of dying alone or in pain. One of their biggest fears is cancer, which seems to strike out of the blue.

Death as a Process

Psychologist Elisabeth Kübler-Ross (1969/1981) became curious about how people adjust to the knowledge that they will die soon. After interviewing people who had been informed that they had an incurable disease, she concluded that people who come face to face with their own death go through a similar process. She identified five stages in this process:

1. *Denial.* At first, people cannot believe that they are going to die. ("The doctor must have made a mistake. Those test results can't be right.") They avoid the topic of death and situations that might remind them of it.
2. *Anger.* After a while, they acknowledge that they are going to die, but they see their death as unjust. ("I didn't do anything to deserve this. So-and-so is much worse than I am, and he's in good health. It isn't right that I should die.")
3. *Negotiation.* Next, the individual tries to get around death by making a bargain with God, with fate, or even with the disease itself. ("I need one more Christmas with my family. I never appreciated them as much as I should have. Don't take me until after Christmas, and then I'll be ready.")
4. *Depression.* In this stage, people are resigned to their death, but they grieve because their life is about to end, and they have no power to change the course of events.
5. *Acceptance.* In this final stage, people come to terms with their impending death. They put their affairs in order—make wills, pay bills, instruct their children to take care of the surviving parent. They also express regret at not having done certain things when they had the chance. Devout Christians are likely to talk about the hope of salvation and their desire to be in heaven with Jesus.

Dying is more individualized than Kübler-Ross's model indicates. Not everyone, for example, tries to make bargains. What is important sociologically is that death is a process, not just an event. People who know they are going to die face a different reality from the one experienced by those of us who think we will be alive years from now. That reality of impending death powerfully affects their thinking and behavior.

When my mother was informed that she had inoperable cancer, she immediately went into a vivid stage of denial. If she later went through anger or negotiation, she kept it to herself. After a short depression, she experienced a longer period of questioning why this was happening to her. She then moved quickly into stage 5, which occurred very much as Kübler-Ross described it. After her funeral, my two brothers and I went to her apartment, as she had instructed us. There, to our surprise, attached to each item in every room—from the bed and the television to the boxes of dishes and knickknacks—was a piece of masking tape with one of our names on it. At first we found this strange. We knew she was an orderly person, but to this extent? As we sorted through her things, reflecting on why she had given certain items to whom, we began to appreciate the "closure" she had given to this aspect of her material life.

Hospices

In earlier generations, when few people made it to age 65 or beyond, death at an early age was taken for granted—much as people take it for granted today that most people *will* see 65. In fact, due to advances in medical technology, *most* deaths in the United States (about 75 percent) occur after age 65. Now that medical technology has reduced the swift deaths that come from infectious diseases and has given us earlier detection of fatal illnesses, often even before symptoms are felt, the time before "dying" has been lengthened (Levy 1994).

Such technological effects on disease and dying have led to a greater concern about the *how* of dying. Few elderly want to burden their children with their own death. They also want to die with dignity, surrounded with the comforting presence of friends and relatives. Hospitals, to put the matter bluntly, are awkward places in which to die. There people experience what sociologists call *institutional death*—they are surrounded by strangers in formal garb, in an organization that puts its routines ahead of patients' needs.

Hospices emerged as a solution to these problems, including the great expense of hospitalization. Hospices attempt to reduce the emotional and physical burden on the dying person and his or her friends and relatives and to lower costs. A central idea of hospices is that the

hospice a place, or services brought into someone's home, for the purpose of bringing comfort and dignity to a dying person

control of dying belongs to the people who are dying and their families. The term **hospice** originally referred to a place, but increasingly it refers to services that are brought into a dying person's home. Those services range from counseling to such down-to-earth help as providing baby sitters or driving the person to a doctor or lawyer (Levy 1994). At any one time, about 60,000 people are in hospice care in the United States (*Sociological Abstract* 1999:Table 216).

Whereas hospitals are dedicated to prolonging life, hospices are dedicated to providing dignity in death and to make people comfortable in what Kübler-Ross (1989) called the *living-dying interval,* that period between discovering that death is imminent and death itself. In the hospital, the focus is on the patient; in the hospice, the focus switches to both the dying person and his or her friends and family. In the hospital, the goal is to make the patient well; in the hospice, it is to relieve pain and suffering. In the hospital, the primary concern is the individual's physical welfare; in the hospice, although medical needs are met, the primary concern is the individual's social—and in some instances, spiritual—well-being.

Suicide and the Elderly

We noted in Chapter 1 how Durkheim stressed that suicide has a *social* base. Suicide, he said, is much more than an individual act. Each country, for example, has its own suicide rate, which remains quite stable year after year. In the United States, for example, we can predict with almost certainty that 31,000 people will commit suicide this year. If we are off by more than 500, it would be a surprise. We can also predict with certainty that firearms will be the most common way that Americans will kill themselves, and that hanging will come in second. It is this way, year after year. Look at Figure 13.13, and you will see that this predictability applies to both African Americans and whites (data are unavailable for other racial-ethnic groups).

This same stability can be seen in the age, sex, and race-ethnicity of people who kill themselves. Look at the striking patterns shown in Figure 13.14. At all ages, whites are more likely to kill themselves, and at all ages males are more likely to take their lives. It is this way year after year.

Statistics often fly in the face of the impressions we get from the mass media, and here we have such an example. Although the suicides of young people are given high publicity, such deaths are relatively rare. Note that with the exceptions of African-American men age 45 to 74 and African-American women age 75 and older, the suicide rate of adolescents is *lower* than all

Figure 13.13

HOW AMERICANS COMMIT SUICIDE

Source: Statistical Abstract 1999: Table 149.

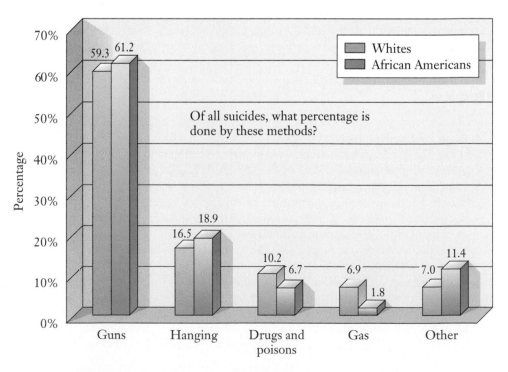

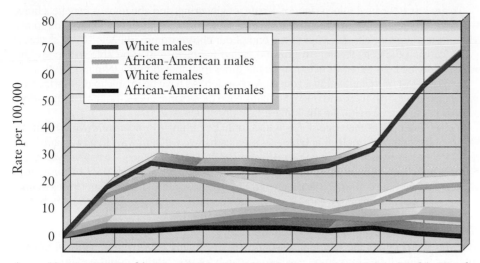

Figure 13.14

A PROFILE OF SUICIDE

Source: Statistical Abstract 1995:
Table 136; 1999:Table 149.

Note: The source contains data only for whites and African Americans. Data are from 1992, except 1990 for African-American women 65–74, and 1980 for African-American girls age 10–14, women 75 and over, and men 85 and over.

other ages. Because adolescents have such a low death rate, however, suicide does rank as their third leading cause of death—after accidents and homicide (*Statistical Abstract* 1999:Table 13.

What is also striking about Figure 13.14 is the sharp rise in the suicide rate of white men when they reach their middle 60s. No one has a good explanation for this, but from a symbolic interactionist viewpoint it may indicate that white men experience aging differently from the other groups shown in this figure. Because white men generally enjoy greater power and status in U.S. society, it could be that aging for them represents a relatively greater loss of privilege. As noted, however, no one knows the explanation—nor, for that matter, has anyone been able to adequately explain why year after year the suicide rate of African Americans is lower than that of white Americans.

These findings on suicide are an example of the primary sociological point stressed throughout this text: Recurring patterns of human behavior—whether education, marriage, work, crime, use of the Internet, or even suicide—represent underlying social forces. Consequently, if no basic changes take place in the social conditions under which the groups that make up U.S. society live, you can expect their suicide rates to be little changed five to ten years from now.

*L*OOKING TOWARD THE FUTURE

We have reviewed several key issues in aging—from the social construction of "old" to problems with nursing homes. We also caught a glimpse of what society would be like if it had much larger numbers of elderly. To close the chapter, I would like you to reflect on some exciting and, perhaps, disturbing scientific breakthroughs that may have a direct impact on your life.

Thinking *Critically*

HOW LONG DO YOU WANT TO LIVE?
PUSHING PAST THE LIMITS OF BIOLOGY

How would you like to live to 150? To 200?

Such a question may sound absurd. But with our new and still developing technology, science may stretch the life span to limits unheard of since biblical days.

We are just at the beginning stages of genetic engineering, and ahead of us may lie a brave new world. Predictions are that technicians will be able to snip out our bad DNA and replace it with more compliant bits. The caps at the end of our chromosomes, the telomeres, shrink as we age, causing the cells to die. An enzyme called telomerase may be able to modify this process, allowing cells to reproduce many more times than they do now (Nuland 1999).

Already—just by manipulating a gene or two—scientists have been able to double the normal life span of worms, flies, and mice. Humans have these same genes (Kolata 1999). A doubled human life span would take the longest living people past 200.

And we are only at the edge of the future, only beginning to understand what might be possible. Some optimistic molecular biologists predict that we will find ways to grow spare body parts. From the same stem cells we will grow livers, hearts, kidneys, fingers—whatever you need.

Spare body parts? Apparently they're on the way. If the growing of body parts becomes routine, I can envision the day when the organ and limb salespeople take over. Can't you just hear it now? "Such a deal! I got a new kidney coming in Tuesday. Everybody's gonna want it, but for some reason I like you, and I'm gonna give you a special price."

Back in grade school, my teachers told me stories about Ponce de León, an explorer from Spain who searched for the fountain of youth. He eventually "discovered" Florida, but the fountain of youth eluded him. In our perpetual search for immortality, could we, finally, have found what eluded Ponce de León? ■

For Your Consideration

Let's assume that biomedical science does stretch the human life span, that living to be 200 or so becomes common. What do you think life would be like? Consider this, which may be the basic flaw in this brave new scenario: Even with new body parts, the world would not be filled with 200-year-olds who functioned as though they were 25. They would be old people, subject to the diseases and debilities that come with advancing age. How would you answer this question (Nuland 1999): Is the real issue how we can live longer, or how we can live better?

SUMMARY AND REVIEW

■ Aging in Global Perspective

How are the elderly treated around the world?

No single set of attitudes, beliefs, or policies regarding the aged characterizes the world's nations. Rather, they vary from exclusion and killing, to integration and honor. The global trend is for more people to live longer. Pp. 356–358.

What does the term "graying of America" mean?

The phrase **graying of America** refers to the growing proportion of Americans who reach old age. With the costs of Social Security and health care for the elderly having become a social issue, sentiment about the elderly seems to be shifting. Pp. 358–362.

■ The Symbolic Interactionist Perspective

What factors influence perceptions of aging?

Symbolic interactionists stress that, by itself, reaching any particular age has no meaning. They identify four factors that influence when people label themselves as "old": biological changes, biographical events, **gender age**, and cultural timetables. Cross-cultural comparisons—for example, the traditional Native Americans, Tiwi, and Eskimos—demonstrate the role of culture in determining how individuals experience aging. **Ageism**, negative reactions to the elderly, is based on stereotypes, which, in turn, are influenced by the mass media. Pp. 362–367.

■ The Functionalist Perspective

How is retirement functional for society?

Functionalists focus on how the withdrawal of the elderly from positions of responsibility benefits society. **Disengagement theory** examines retirement as a device for ensuring that a society's positions of responsibility will be passed smoothly from one generation to the next. **Activity theory** examines how people adjust when they disengage from productive roles. Pp. 367–369

■ The Conflict Perspective

Is there conflict among different age groups?

Social Security legislation is an example of one generation making demands on another generation for limited resources. As the **dependency ratio**, the number of workers who support one retired person, decreases, workers may become resentful. The Social Security Trust Fund may be a gigantic fraud perpetrated by the power elite on the nation's elderly. The argument that benefits to the elderly come at the cost of benefits to children is fallacious. Organizations such as the Gray Panthers and the AARP recognize the potential for conflict between age groups. Pp. 369–375.

■ Problems of Dependency

What are some of the problems that today's elderly face?

Women are more likely to live alone and to be poor. At any one time, about 4 percent of the elderly live in nursing homes. Because of widespread abuse, the U.S. Congress passed a bill of rights to protect nursing home residents. The most common abusers of the elderly, however, are members of their own family. Poverty in old age, greatly reduced through government programs, reflects the gender and racial-ethnic patterns of poverty in the general society. Pp. 375–379.

■ The Sociology of Death and Dying

How does culture affect the meaning—and experience—of death and dying?

Like old age, death is much more than a biological event. Industrialization, for example, brought modern medicine, hospitals, and the custom of dying in a formal setting surrounded by strangers. Kübler-Ross identified five stages in the dying process, which, though insightful, do not characterize all people. **Hospices** are a cultural device designed to overcome the negative aspects of dying in hospitals. Suicide shows distinct patterns by age, sex, race-ethnicity, and method. It is possible that science will increase the human **life span.** Pp. 380–384.

Where can I read more on this topic?

Suggested Readings for this chapter are at the back of this book.

Sociology & the Internet

All URLs listed are current as of the printing of this book. URLs often change. Please check our Web site, **http://www.abacon.com/henslin**, for updates.

1. This exercise calls for you to create a profile of yourself as a senior citizen. You must be at least 65 years old and living in the United States. Now, how old are you going to be? What is your gender and marital status? What city and state do you reside in? Do you own your own home? How is your health? Do you have any close relatives? Are you working or retired? If you are retired, what kind of work did you do? What is your income level? Do you have any savings? What are your interests and hobbies? (If you are having trouble with some of these criteria, ask a parent or grandparent for some guidance.)

   Now go to **http://www.yahoo.com**. Select "Society and Culture," then "Cultures and Groups," and then "Seniors." To find the information you need, given your personal attributes, begin by scrolling through the list of Web sites on this page. Click on some of the links. For instance, if you are in bad health or your spouse has Alzheimer disease, click on "Health" to find information on health care or support services. If you are in good health and have enough money, you might plan a dream trip (click on "Travel") or a move into a luxury retirement community (click on "Retirement Communities"). You get the idea. See how far you can go toward meeting your needs. You might think of varying some of the attributes to see how social characteristics affect opportunities and life chances. In other words, see how life would be different depending on whether you were male or female, rich or poor, white or minority. Outline what you find out and share your findings with the class.

2. Every society must deal with the problem of aging. One of the problems our society faces today is elder abuse. To better understand this problem, go to the Elder Abuse Prevention Information and Resource Guide at **http://www.oaktrees.org/elder/** and the National Center for Elder Abuse at **http://www.gwjapan.com/NCEA/**. Drawing on the information available at these two sites and on the discussion of aging and elder abuse in your text, write an informational pamphlet about elder abuse. In your pamphlet, answer these questions: What is elder abuse? How widespread is this problem? Who is most often the abuser? What are the legal consequences of abusing an elderly person? How can elder abuse be detected and prevented? How have changes in our society—particularly the shifting meanings of old age, the effects of industrialization and new technology, and the graying of the United States—contributed to this form of abuse?

3. Your text identifies *ageism* as prejudice, discrimination, and hostility directed against people because of their age. Let's explore this more deeply. Browse Linda M. Woolf's ageism Web site at **http://www.webster.edu/~woolfflm/ageism.html.** How does ageism differ from sexism and racism? How does it affect men and women differently? What are some cross-cultural differences? You can read the results of a study on ageism done by Professor Woolf at **http://www.geriatricspt.org.** For an article on ageism published by the Gray Panthers (see your text for a discussion of this organization), click on "Section Publications & Journals," then on "To Gerinotes Table of Contents," then on "September 1996—Vol. 3, No. 3," and finally on "Ageism: What is It?" Read about the different types of ageists and about what we, as a society, can do to combat ageism. Prepare a presentation for your class on this problem. Include examples of ageism from cartoons, magazine ads or greeting cards.

4. How we die depends on our culture and our society. In the 1960s, hospices emerged in response to the impersonal experience of dying in a hospital. As your text notes, *hospice* originally referred to a place, but today it describes an approach to caring for the terminally ill that allows them to die with dignity, surrounded by caring family. You can learn more about hospice at the following sites:

   http://www.hospicenet.org
   http://www.teleport.com/~hospice
   http://www.hospicefoundation.org

   Browse through the answers to questions frequently asked about hospice, discover the reality behind the myths surrounding hospice, and read stories and messages posted by family and friends who experienced the services of hospice in caring for a dying family member. Write a paper about hospice. Discuss the history and functions of hospice, the services offered by hospice, and the differences between a hospice and a hospital. Also, consider why elderly people and their families might feel more comfortable living out their final days in hospice care instead of in a hospital bed.

The Economy

- **The Transformation of Economic Systems**
  Preindustrial Societies: The Birth of Inequality
  Industrial Societies: The Birth of the Machine
  Postindustrial Societies: The Birth of the
    Information Age

- **The Transformation of the Medium of Exchange**
  Earliest Mediums of Exchange
  Medium of Exchange in Agricultural Societies
  Medium of Exchange in Industrial Societies
  Medium of Exchange in Postindustrial Societies

- **World Economic Systems**
  Capitalism
  Socialism
  Ideologies of Capitalism and Socialism
  Criticisms of Capitalism and Socialism
  Changes in Capitalism and Socialism

- **The Functionalist View of the Globalization
  of Capitalism**
  The New Global Division of Labor
  Ownership and the Management of Corporations
  Functions on a Global Scale

- **The Conflict View of the Globalization
  of Capitalism**
  The Inner Circle and Corporate Capitalism
  Interlocking Directorates
  Global Investing

- **Work in U.S. Society**
  The Decline of Agriculture and the Transition to
    Postindustrial Society
  Women and Work
  The Underground Economy
  Shrinking Paychecks
  Patterns of Work and Leisure

- **The Future: Facing the Consequences of
  Global Capitalism**
  Expanding Global Trade
  New Technologies and Downsizing:
    Utopia or Nightmare?

- **Summary and Review**

The sound of her alarm rang in Kim's ears. "Not Monday already," she groaned. "There must be a better way of starting the week." She pressed the snooze button on the clock (from Germany) to sneak another ten minutes of sleep. In what seemed just thirty seconds, the alarm shrilly insisted she get up and face the week.

Still bleary-eyed after her shower, Kim peered into her closet and picked out a silk blouse (from China), a plaid wool skirt (from Scotland), and leather shoes (from India). She nodded, satisfied, as she added a pair of simulated pearls (from Taiwan). Running late, she hurriedly ran a brush (from Mexico) through her hair. As Kim wolfed down a bowl of cereal (from the United States), topped with milk (from the United States), bananas (from Costa Rica), and sugar (from the Dominican Republic), she turned on her kitchen television (from Korea) to listen to the weather forecast.

Gulping the last of her coffee (from Brazil), Kim grabbed her briefcase (from Wales), purse (from Spain), and jacket (from Malaysia), and quickly climbed into her car (from Japan). As she glanced at her watch (from Switzerland), she hoped the traffic would be in her favor. She muttered to herself as she pulled up at a street light (from Great Britain) and eyed her gas gauge. She muttered again when she pulled into a station and paid for gas (from Saudi Arabia), for the price had risen over the weekend. "My check never keeps up with prices," she moaned.

When Kim arrived at work, she found the office abuzz. Six months ago, New York headquarters had put the company up for sale, but there had been no takers. The big news this Monday was that both a German and a Canadian corporation had put in bids over the weekend. No one got much work done that day, as the whole office speculated about how things might change.

As Kim walked to the parking lot after work, she saw a tattered "Buy American" bumper sticker on the car next to hers. "That's right," she said to herself. "If people were more like me, this country would be in better shape." ■

Although this vignette may be slightly exaggerated, many of us are like Kim—we use a multitude of products from around the world, and yet we're concerned about our country's ability to compete in global markets. In terms of trade, the world has grown much smaller in recent years. We live in a global economy, and this chapter focuses on the consequences of this fact for the future of the United States—and for our own lives.

THE TRANSFORMATION OF ECONOMIC SYSTEMS

In Mexico, the market is a bustling scene. Farmers sell fruits and vegetables, as well as poultry, goats, and caged songbirds; others sell homemade blankets, serapes, huaraches, pottery, belts. Women bend over open fires cooking tacos, which their waiting customers wolf down with soft drinks. The market is a combined business and social occasion, as people make their purchases and catch each other up on the latest gossip. Such scenes used to characterize the world, but now they are limited primarily to the Least Industrialized Nations. The closest people come in the United States is a flea market, a farmer's market, or a street fair.

Although the term market now refers to the mechanisms by which people establish value so they can exchange goods and services, its original meaning referred to a direct exchange of goods, as shown in this photo of a market in Chiapas, Mexico. In peasant societies, where such markets are still a regular part of everyday life, people find the social interaction every bit as rewarding as the goods and money that they exchange.

Today, the term *market* means much more than such settings and activities. Market has kept its original meaning of buying and selling, but it now refers to things much more impersonal. The **market,** a system of producing and distributing goods and services, today means the Dow Jones Industrial Average in New York City, and the Nikkei Index in Tokyo. Market also means the movement of vast amounts of goods across international borders, even across oceans and continents. Market means brokers taking orders for GE, speculators trading international currencies, and futures traders making huge bets on whether oil, wheat, and pork bellies will go up or down—and, of course, it also refers to making a purchase at the local food store.

People's lives have always been affected by the dynamics of the market, or as sociologists prefer to call it, the **economy.** Today, the economy, which many sociologists believe is the most important of our social institutions, differs radically from all but our most recent past. Economic systems have become impersonal and global. The products mentioned in our opening vignette, which Kim uses, make it apparent that today's economy knows no national boundaries. The economy is essential to our welfare, for it means inflation or deflation, high or low interest rates, high or low unemployment, economic recession or economic boom. The economy affects our chances of going to college, of buying a new home, of having to work at a dead-end job, or of being on a fast track in an up-and-coming company.

To better understand how global forces affect the U.S. economy, let's begin with a review of sweeping historical changes. (Pages 150–155 go into these changes in greater detail.)

Preindustrial Societies: The Birth of Inequality

The earliest human groups, *hunting and gathering societies,* had a **subsistence economy.** Groups of perhaps twenty-five to forty people lived off the land. They gathered what they could find and moved from place to place as their food supply ran low. Because there was little or no excess food or other items, they did little trading with other groups. With no excess to accumulate, everybody possessed about the same as everyone else.

Then people discovered how to breed animals and cultivate plants. This produced a surplus and ushered in social inequality. Due to the more dependable food supply in *pastoral and horticultural societies,* humans settled down in a single place. Their groups grew larger, and for the first time some individuals could devote their energies to tasks other than producing food. Some people became leather workers, others weapon makers, and so on. This new division of labor produced a surplus, and groups traded items with one another. The primary sociological significance of surplus and trade is this: They fostered *social inequality,* for some people accumulated more possessions than others. The effects of that change remain with us today.

The invention of the plow brought the next major change. The plow made land much more productive and allowed *agricultural societies* to develop. Even more people were freed from food production, and more division of labor followed. Trade expanded, and trading centers developed. As trading centers turned into cities, power passed from the heads of families and clans to a ruling elite. The result was even greater social, political, and economic inequality.

Industrial Societies: The Birth of the Machine

The steam engine, invented in 1765, ushered in *industrial societies.* Based on machines powered by fuels, these societies created a surplus unlike anything the world had seen. This, too, stimulated trade among nations and brought greater inequality. A handful of individuals opened factories, exploiting the labor of many. As they became wealthy, these owners were able to manipulate the political machinery for their own purposes. This set the stage for the bloody battles that occurred when workers unionized to improve their working conditions.

As machines improved, surpluses grew even greater, and the emphasis changed from producing goods to consuming them. In 1912, sociologist Thorstein Veblen used the term **conspicuous consumption** to describe this fundamental change in people's orientations.

market any process of buying and selling; on a more formal level, the mechanism that establishes values for the exchange of goods and services

economy a system of distribution of goods and services

subsistence economy a type of economy in which human groups live off the land with little or no surplus

conspicuous consumption Thorstein Veblen's term for a change from the Protestant ethic to an eagerness to show off wealth by the elaborate consumption of goods

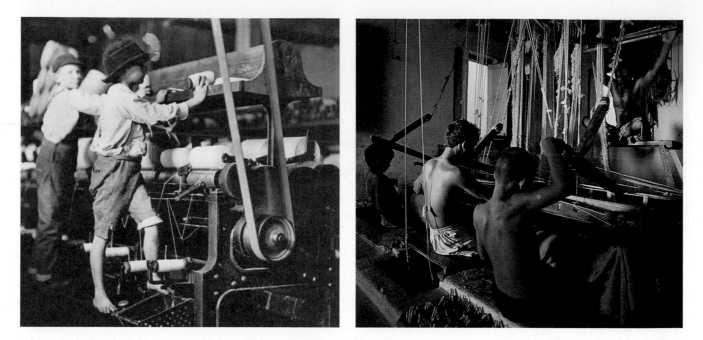

One of the negative consequences of early industrialization in the West was the use of child labor. In the photo on the left, of the U.S. textile industry in the 1800s, you can see spindle boys at work in a Georgia cotton mill. Today's Least Industrialized Nations are experiencing the same negative consequence as they industrialize. The photo on the right shows boys at work in a contemporary textile factory in Varanas, India. About the only improvement is that the child workers in India are able to sit down as they exhaust their childhood.

Veblen noted that the Protestant ethic identified by Weber—an emphasis on hard work, savings, and a concern for salvation (discussed on pages 175–176)—was being replaced by an eagerness to show off wealth by the "elaborate consumption of goods."

Postindustrial Societies: The Birth of the Information Age

In 1973, sociologist Daniel Bell noted that *a new type of society was emerging*. To refer to it, he coined the term *postindustrial society*. He identified six characteristics of the postindustrial society: (1) a service sector so large that it employs most workers; (2) an even greater surplus of goods; (3) even more extensive trade among nations; (4) a wider variety of goods available to the average person; (5) an "information explosion"; and (6) a "global village"(that is, the globe becomes linked by faster communications, transportation, and trade).

A key element of the postindustrial society is the information explosion. You and I are participating in this change directly, for almost all of us who graduate from college do some form of "knowledge work"—managing information and designing and servicing products. With more efficient agriculture and manufacturing techniques, however, fewer people work in farming and other blue-collar jobs.

To understand the implications of the global village, think of the globe as divided into three large neighborhoods—the three worlds of industrialization, which we reviewed in Chapter 9. Due to political and economic arrangements, some nations are located in the poor part of the village. Their citizens barely eke out a living from menial work. Some even starve to death—while fellow villagers in the rich neighborhood feast on the best that the globe has to offer. Inequalities also show up within the three neighborhoods; in all three live citizens who are well off and those who are poor.

The preceding five chapters focused on social inequality—from global stratification to inequalities of social class, gender, race-ethnicity, and age. There is little to add to that extensive presentation, but an overall snapshot of how the income of the United States is distributed may be useful.

THE INVERTED INCOME PYRAMID: THE PROPORTION OF INCOME RECEIVED BY EACH FIFTH OF THE U.S. POPULATION

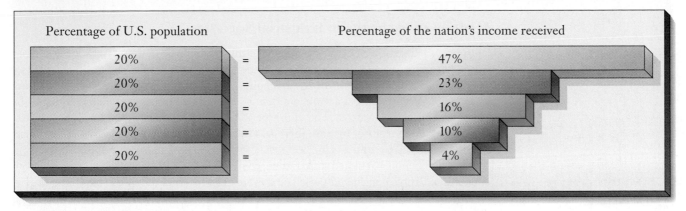

Source: Statistical Abstract 1999:Table 751.

The inverted pyramid shown in Figure 14.1 is that snapshot. Each rectangle represents a fifth of the U.S. population. At the top of the inverted pyramid is the proportion of the nation's income that goes to the wealthiest fifth, at the bottom the proportion going to the poorest fifth. Note that *47 percent* of the whole country's income goes to just one-fifth of Americans, while only *4 percent* goes to the poorest fifth. Rather than bringing equality, then, the postindustrial society has perpetuated the income inequalities of the industrial society.

THE TRANSFORMATION OF THE MEDIUM OF EXCHANGE

As each type of economy evolved, so, too, did the **medium of exchange,** the means by which people value and exchange goods and services. As we review this transformation, you'll see how the medium of exchange not only reflects the state of a country's development but also contributes to it.

Earliest Mediums of Exchange

As noted, the lack of surplus in hunting and gathering and pastoral and horticultural societies meant that there was little to trade. Whatever trading did occur was by **barter,** the direct exchange of one item for another. The surplus that stimulated trade in later societies led to different ways of valuing goods and services for the purpose of exchange. Let's look at how the medium of exchange was transformed.

Medium of Exchange in Agricultural Societies

Although bartering continued in agricultural societies, people increasingly came to use **money,** a medium of exchange by which items are valued. In most places, money consisted of gold and silver coins, their weight and purity determining the amount of goods or services they could purchase. In some places people made purchases with **deposit receipts,** receipts that transferred ownership to a specified number of ounces of gold or bushels of grain, or to a specified amount of other goods that were on deposit in a warehouse or bank. Toward the end of the agricultural period, deposit receipts became formalized into **currency** (paper money). Each piece of paper represented a specific amount of gold or silver on deposit in a warehouse. Thus currency (and deposit receipts) represented **stored value,** and no more currency could be issued than the amount of gold or silver represented

medium of exchange the means by which people value goods and services in order to make an exchange, for example, currency, gold, and silver

barter the direct exchange of one item for another

money any item (from seashells to gold) that serves as a medium of exchange; today, currency is the most common form

deposit receipts a receipt stating that a certain amount of goods is on deposit in a warehouse or bank; the receipt is used as a form of money

currency paper money

stored value the backing of a currency by goods that are stored and held in reserve by the currency. Gold and silver coins continued to circulate alongside the deposit receipts and currency.

Medium of Exchange in Industrial Societies

With but few exceptions, bartering became a thing of the past in industrial societies. Gold was replaced by paper currencies, which, in the United States, could be exchanged for a set amount of gold stored at Fort Knox. This policy was called the **gold standard,** and as long as each dollar represented a specified amount of gold the number of dollars that could be issued was limited. Toward the end of this period, U.S. paper money could no longer be exchanged for gold or silver. Instead, there was **fiat money,** currency issued by a government that is not backed by stored value.

When fiat money replaced stored value, coins made of precious metals disappeared from circulation. People considered these coins more valuable, and they were unwilling to part with them. Gold coins disappeared first, followed by the largest silver coin, the dollar. Then, as inferior metals (copper, zinc, and nickel) replaced the smaller silver coins, people began to hoard these silver coins, and they, too, disappeared from circulation.

Even without a gold standard that restrains the issuing of currency to stored value, governments have a practical limit on the amount of paper money they can issue. In general, prices increase if a government issues currency at a rate higher than the growth of its **gross domestic product (GDP),** the total goods and services that a country produces. This condition, **inflation,** means that each unit of currency will purchase fewer goods and services. Governments try to control inflation, for it is a destabilizing influence.

As you can see from Figure 14.2, as long as the gold standard limited the amount of currency, the purchasing power of the dollar remained relatively stable. When the United States departed from the gold standard in 1937, the dollar no longer represented stored value, and it plunged in value. Today, the dollar is but a shadow of its former self, retaining only about 9 percent of its original purchasing power.

In industrial societies, checking accounts held in banks became common. A *check* is actually a type of deposit receipt, for it is a promise that the writer of the check has enough currency on deposit to cover the check. The latter part of the industrial period saw the invention of the **credit card,** a device that allows its owner, who has been preapproved for a specified amount of credit, to purchase goods without an immediate exchange of money—either metal or currency. The credit card owner is billed for the purchases.

gold standard paper money backed by gold

fiat money currency issued by a government that is not backed by stored value

gross national product (GNP) the amount of goods and services produced by a nation

inflation an increase in prices

credit card a device that allows its owner to purchase goods but to be billed later

DECLINING VALUE OF THE U.S. DOLLAR

Source: Modified from "Alternative Investment Market Letter," November 1991.

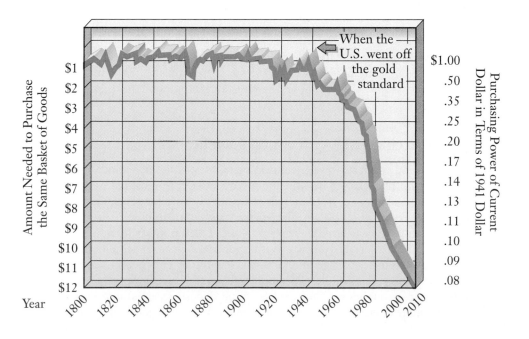

Medium of Exchange in Postindustrial Societies

During the first part of the postindustrial society, paper money circulated freely. It then became less common as it was gradually replaced by checks and credit cards. The next development was the **debit card**, a device by which a purchase is charged against its owner's bank account. Like the check, the debit card is a type of deposit receipt, for it serves as a guarantee that its user has enough currency on deposit to cover the purchase.

The latest and perhaps final phase in the evolution of money is e-cash. **E-cash** consists of digital money that is stored on the user's local computer. E-cash can even be encoded in e-mail and sent over the Internet. In effect, the new medium of exchange is itself a part of the information explosion.

WORLD ECONOMIC SYSTEMS

Now that we have outlined the main economic changes in history, let's compare capitalism and socialism, the two main economic systems in force today. Table 14.1 presents a summary of this discussion.

Capitalism

People who live in a capitalist society may not understand its basic tenets, though they see them reflected in their local shopping malls and fast-food chains. If we distill the businesses of the United States to their basic components, however, we see that **capitalism** has three essential features: (1) **private ownership of the means of production** (individuals own the land, machines, and factories, and decide what shall be produced); (2) the pursuit of *profit* (selling something for more than it costs); and (3) **market competition** (an exchange of items between willing buyers and sellers).

Many people believe that the United States is an example of pure capitalism. Pure capitalism, however, known as **laissez-faire capitalism** (literally meaning "hands off"), means that the government doesn't interfere in the market. Such is not the case in the United States, where the government has set up many restraints to capitalism. The current form of U.S. capitalism is **welfare** or **state capitalism.** Private citizens own the means of production and pursue profits, but they do so within a vast system of laws designed to protect the welfare of the population.

Suppose that you have discovered what you think is a miracle tonic: It will grow hair, erase wrinkles, and dissolve excess fat. If your product works, you will become an overnight sensation—not only a multimillionaire, but also the toast of television talk shows.

Before you count your money—and your fame—however, you must reckon with **market restraints,** the laws and regulations of welfare capitalism that limit your capacity to sell what you produce. First, you must comply with local and state rules. You must obtain a business license and a state tax number that allows you to buy your ingredients without paying

debit card a device that allows its owner to charge purchases against his or her bank account

e–cash digital money that is stored on computers

capitalism an economic system characterized by the private ownership of the means of production, the pursuit of profit, and market competition

private ownership of the means of production the ownership of machines and factories by individuals, who decide what shall be produced

market competition the exchange of items between willing buyers and sellers

laissez-faire capitalism unrestrained manufacture and trade (literally, "hands off" capitalism)

welfare (state) capitalism an economic system in which individuals own the means of production, but the state regulates many economic activities for the welfare of the population

market restraints laws and regulations that limit the capacity to manufacture and sell products

Table 14.1

COMPARING SOCIALISM AND CAPITALISM

Socialism	Capitalism
1. The public owns the means of production.	1. Individuals own the means of production.
2. Central committes plan production.	2. The owners (often through management) determine production.
3. There is no competition.	3. Production is based on competition.
4. No profit motive in the distribution of goods and services.	4. The pursuit of profit is the reason for distributing goods and services.

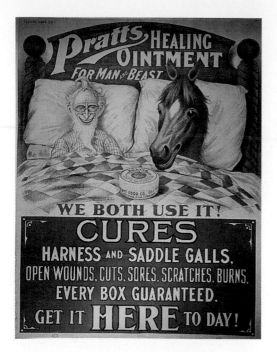

This advertisement from 1885 represents an earlier stage of capitalism, when individuals were free to manufacture and market products with little or no interference from the government. Today, the production and marketing of goods take place under detailed, complicated government regulations.

sales taxes. Then come the federal regulations. You cannot simply take your item to local stores and ask them to sell it; you must first get approval from federal agencies that monitor compliance with the Pure Food and Drug Act. This means you must prove that your product will not cause harm to the public. In addition, you must be able to substantiate your claims—or else face being shut down by state and federal agencies that monitor the market for fraud. Your manufacturing process is also subject to state and local laws concerning cleanliness and to state and federal rules for the disposal of hazardous wastes.

Suppose that you overcome these obstacles, and your business prospers. Other federal agencies will monitor your compliance with regulations concerning racial, sexual, and disability discrimination, the payment of minimum wages, and the remittance of Social Security taxes. State agencies will examine your records to see if you have paid unemployment taxes and sales taxes. Finally, the Internal Revenue Service will look over your shoulder and demand a healthy share of the profits (up to 39.6 percent, if you do well). In short, the highly regulated U.S. economic system is far from an example of laissez-faire capitalism.

To see how welfare or state capitalism developed in the United States, let's go back to an earlier era when capitalism was considerably less restrained. In the 1800s, you could have made your "magic" potion at home and sold it at any outlet willing to handle it. You could have advertised that it cured baldness, erased wrinkles, and dissolved fat, for no agency existed to monitor your product or your claims. (See the 1885 poster on this page.) In fact, that is precisely what thousands of individuals did at that time. They produced numerous "elixirs" with whimsical names such as "Grandma's Miracle Medicine" and "Elixir of Health and Happiness." A single product could claim that it restored sexual potency, purged the intestines, and made people more intelligent. These tonics often made people feel better, for many elixirs were braced with alcohol—and even cocaine (Ashley 1975). (Coca-Cola was a "pick me up" during this period, for until 1903 it contained cocaine.) To protect the public's health, in 1906 the federal government passed the Pure Food and Drug Act and began to regulate products.

John D. Rockefeller's remarkable success in unregulated markets helps explain why the government began to regulate capitalism. After a ruthless drive to eliminate competition, Rockefeller managed to corner the U.S. oil and gasoline market. He would reduce prices and then double them after driving out the competition. He would even sabotage competitors' pipelines and refineries (Josephson 1949). With his competitors crippled or eliminated, his company, Standard Oil, was able to dictate prices to the entire nation. Rockefeller had achieved the capitalist's dream, a **monopoly,** the control of an entire industry by a single company.

Rockefeller had played the capitalist game too well, however, for he had wiped out one of its essential components, competition. Consequently, to protect this cornerstone of capitalism, the federal government passed antimonopoly legislation and broke up Standard Oil. Today, the top firms in each industry—such as Ford Motors in automobiles and General Electric in household appliances—must obtain federal approval before acquiring another company in the same industry. If the government determines that one firm dominates a market, it can force that company to **divest** (sell off) some of its businesses.

Another characteristic of welfare capitalism is that although the government supports competition, it establishes its own monopoly over "common good" items—those items presumed essential for the common good of the citizens, such as soldiers, war supplies, highways, and sewers.

monopoly the control of an entire industry by a single company

divest to sell off

■ In Sum As currently practiced, capitalism is far from the classical laissez-faire model. The U.S. economic system encourages the first two components of capitalism, the private

ownership of the means of production and the pursuit of profit. But a vast system of government regulations both protects and restricts the third component, market competition. The government also controls "common good" items.

Socialism

Socialism also has three essential components: (1) the public ownership of the means of production; (2) central planning; and (3) distribution of goods without a profit motive.

In socialist economies, the government owns the means of production—not only the factories, but also the land, railroads, oil wells, and gold mines. Unlike capitalism, in which **market forces**—supply and demand—determine what will be produced and the prices that will be charged, in socialism central committees decide that the country needs X number of toothbrushes, Y toilets, and Z shoes. The committees decide how many of each shall be produced, which factories will produce them, what price will be charged for the items, and where they will be distributed.

Socialism is designed to eliminate competition, for goods are sold at predetermined prices regardless of demand for an item or the cost to produce it. Profit is not the goal, nor is encouraging consumption of goods in low demand (by lowering the price), nor limiting the consumption of hard-to-get goods (by raising the price). Rather, the goal is to produce goods for the general welfare and to distribute them according to people's needs, not their ability to pay.

In a socialist economy *everyone* in the economic chain works for the government. The members of the central committee who set production goals are government employees, as are the supervisors who implement those goals, the factory workers who produce the merchandise, the truck drivers who move it, and the clerks who sell it. Those who purchase the items may work at different jobs—in offices, on farms, in day care centers—but they, too, are government employees.

Just as capitalism does not exist in a pure form, neither does socialism. Although the ideology of socialism calls for resources to be distributed according to need and not position, in line with the functionalist argument of social stratification presented in Chapter 9 (pages 237–238), socialist countries found it necessary to offer higher salaries for some jobs in order to entice people to take greater responsibilities. For example, in socialist countries factory managers always earned more than factory workers. By narrowing the huge pay gaps that characterize capitalist nations, however, socialist nations established considerably greater equality of income.

Dissatisfied with the greed and exploitation of capitalism and the lack of freedom and individuality of socialism, Sweden and Denmark developed **democratic socialism** (also called welfare socialism). In this form of socialism, both the state and individuals produce and distribute goods and services. The government owns and runs the steel, mining, forestry, and energy concerns, as well as the country's telephones, television stations, and airlines; remaining in private hands are the retail stores, farms, manufacturing concerns, and most service industries.

Ideologies of Capitalism and Socialism

Not only do capitalism and socialism have different approaches to producing and distributing goods, but also they represent distinct ideologies.

socialism an economic system characterized by the public ownership of the means of production, central planning, and the distribution of goods without a profit motive

market forces the law of supply and demand

democratic socialism a hybrid economic system in which capitalism is mixed with state ownership

Throughout most of the twentieth century, capitalism and communism were pitted against one another in a deadly struggle. Each thought of itself as the correct economic form, and each viewed the other as an evil obstacle to be eradicated. In support of this view of essential goodness and evil, proponents of each system launched global propaganda campaigns. Shown here is a painting of Wladimir Lenin, leader of the worldwide workers' revolution. This 1930 painting by Alexander Gerassimow (1881–1963) hangs in the Tretyakov Gallery in Moscow.

The slogan of the Cuban revolution is "Socialism or Death." In spite of an invasion, a long embargo, and efforts by the CIA to assassinate him, Castro has remained in power. Many wonder when the animosity between the U.S. government and Castro will finally come to a close, and if the two political-economic systems can accommodate one another.

Capitalists believe that greed is good. Market forces should underlie society, determining both products and prices. It is healthy for people to strive after profits, for this stimulates them to develop and produce new products. Capitalists also believe that money should motivate workers; this makes people work hard to make as much money as possible in order to purchase more goods. The Mass Media box on the next page examines how capitalists *create* demand for their products.

Socialists, in contrast, believe that profit is immoral. Profit is the *excess value* that has been withheld from workers. Karl Marx said that an item's value is based on the work that has gone into it. The only way there can be profit is by paying workers less than the value of their labor. Socialists believe that the government should protect workers from this exploitation. To do so, it should own the means of production, using them not for profit, but to produce and distribute items according to people's needs rather than according to their ability to pay.

■ **In Sum** These two ideologies paint each other in such stark colors that *each sees the other as a system of exploitation.* Capitalists see socialists as violating basic human rights of freedom of decision and opportunity, while socialists see capitalists as violating basic human rights of freedom from poverty. With each side claiming moral superiority while viewing the other as a threat to its very existence, the last century witnessed the world split into two main blocs. The West armed itself to defend capitalism, the East to defend socialism.

Criticisms of Capitalism and Socialism

The primary criticism leveled against capitalism is that it leads to social inequality. Capitalism, say its critics, produces a tiny top layer of wealthy, powerful people, who exploit a vast bottom layer of poorly paid workers. Many of these workers are unemployed and underemployed (**underemployment** is having to work at a job beneath one's training and abilities or being able to find only part-time work). Another major criticism is that the tiny top layer wields vast political power. Those few who own the means of production reap huge profits, accrue power, and get legislation passed that goes against the public good.

The primary criticism leveled against socialism is that it does not respect individual rights (Berger 1991). Others (in the form of some government body) control people's lives. They decide where people will live, where they will go to school, where they will work, how much they will be paid. In the case of China, they even decide how many children women may bear (Mosher 1983). Critics also argue that central planning is grossly inefficient (Kennedy 1993) and that socialism is not capable of producing much wealth. They say that its greater equality really amounts to giving almost everyone an equal chance to be poor.

Changes in Capitalism and Socialism

Let's look at the fundamental changes that have taken place in these two economic systems.

Changes in Capitalism Over the years, the United States has adopted the socialist principle of the government extracting money from some to pay for benefits it gives to others. Examples include unemployment compensation (taxes paid by workers are distributed to those who no longer produce a profit); subsidized housing (shelter, paid for by the many, is given to the poor and elderly, with no motive of profit); welfare (taxes from the many are distributed to the needy); a minimum wage (the government, not the employer, determines the minimum that a worker will be paid); and Social Security (the retired do not receive what they pay into the system; rather, they receive money taken from current workers).

underemployment the condition of having to work at a job beneath one's level of training and abilities, or of being able to find only part-time work

Mass Media in Social Life

GREED IS GOOD—SELLING THE AMERICAN DREAM

Advertising is such an integral part of our lives that being deluged with ads almost appears to be our natural state. We open a newspaper or magazine and expect to find pages that proclaim the virtues of products and firms. We turn on the television and are assailed with commercials for about ten minutes of every half hour. Some social analysts even claim that the purpose of television is to round up an audience to watch the commercials, that the programs are mere diversions from the medium's real objective of selling products!

Advertising is so powerful that it can produce a desire to consume products for which we previously felt no need whatsoever. U.S. kitchens, filled with gadgets that slice and dice, attest to this power.

Advertising's power to make people gluttons goes beyond kitchen gadgets that are soon consigned to back drawers and garage sales. Many Americans would not think of going out in public without first shampooing, rinsing, conditioning, and blow-drying their hair. Many feel the need to apply an underarm deodorant so powerful that it overcomes the body's natural need to sweat. For many women, public appearance also demands the application of foundation, lipstick, eye shadow, mascara, rouge, powder, and perfume. For many men, after-shave lotion is essential. And only after covering the body with clothing bearing suitable designer labels do Americans feel that they are presentable to the public.

Advertising influences not only what we put on our bodies, what we eat, and what we do for recreation, but also how we feel about ourselves. Our ideas of whether we are too fat, too skinny, too hippy, too buxom, whether our hair is too oily or too dry, our body too hairy, or our skin too rough are largely a consequence of advertising. As we weigh our self-image against the idealized pictures that bombard us in our daily fare of commercials, we conclude that we are lacking something. Advertising assures us that there is salvation—some new product that promises to deliver exactly what we lack.

The approach is ingenious: Create constant discontent by presenting ideal images that are impossible to attain. And it works. Dissatisfied with ourselves, we strive to consume more of the never-ending products that the corporations offer us and that they have decided we need.

The American Dream . . . built on greed, discontent, and enticing images. Of course, dreams can produce strange realities. ■

Each program was viewed with alarm when it was first proposed. Now that it has become a part of the U.S. capitalist system, its socialist base has become almost invisible. There is an "of course" sense about these programs—they just seem to "belong" to capitalism.

Changes in Socialism In 1989 the Soviet Union, which headed an eastern European bloc of nations (East Germany, Czechoslovakia, and Hungary, among others), concluded that its system of central planning had failed. Suffering from shoddy goods and plagued by shortages, its standard of living severely lagged behind the West. Consequently, leaders of the former Soviet Union began to reinstate market forces. Making a profit, which had been a crime punishable by prison, was encouraged. Private ownership of property became respectable, and state industries were auctioned off. Even their former arch-enemies against whom they had uttered ten thousand curses, Western corporations, were

Although most people under communist rule lived in poverty, they were assured jobs that provided basic food and shelter. With today's erratic transition to capitalism, citizens of the former Soviet Union no longer have that assurance. Shown here is a scene in Kiev, the capital of Ukraine, where people are learning capitalism, that is, to buy and sell for profit.

PERSPECTIVES | Cultural Diversity Around the World

NO CASH? NO PROBLEM! BARTER IN THE FORMER SOVIET UNION

About 50 miles from the town of Bila Tserkva, you'll see a few tires piled alongside the highway. By the time you get to Bila Tserkva, the stacks of black tires have grown thicker and higher until they seem to line both sides of the road like thick rubber walls (Brzezinski 1997).

Welcome to Russia's transition to capitalism. This is payday at the tire plant in Bila Tserkva. With cash in short supply, workers are paid in tires. In other towns, workers get paid in airplanes, televisions, clothing, even tombstones, sex toys, and toilet bowls. Some laid-off workers get their unemployment benefits in manure (Paddock 1998;

Schmemann 1998; Powell 1999). In Volgograd, workers are paid in brassieres. So many brassieres will get you into the latest Sylvester Stallone movie—or buy you a hat, a pair of shoes, an ice cream cone. . . .

And in the cash-strapped former Soviet Union, it's not just individuals who conduct transactions using goods instead of cash. In Smolensk, the cannery pays its taxes in canned beef. It also uses canned meat to pay for the cows and pigs it slaughters; aluminum to make the cans; equipment to can the meat; electricity to run the equipment; and cardboard boxes to ship the cans (Paddock 1998).

Barter chains have developed. Ukraine's electric utility company receives payment in goods ranging from military uniforms to steel tubing. The company, in turn, passes these goods on to the Russian company that supplies it with electricity, which, in turn, uses the tubing in its pipelines. The uniforms? It gives these to Russia's Ministry of Defense in lieu of taxes.

When city workers in Tatarstan arrived at city hall, they found 600 new trucks parked on the front lawn. The trucks were payment on the local truck maker's tax bill. The workers were lucky—they might have been greeted with piles of tires or brassieres. ■

---

invited to open up shop. For a glimpse of Russia's transition to capitalism, see the Perspectives box above.

The second major socialist power, China, watched in dismay as its one-time mentor abandoned the basic principles of socialism (Szelenyi 1987). In 1989, at the cost of many lives and despite world opposition, Chinese authorities, in what is called the Tiananmen Square massacre, stood firm. They slaughtered thousands of students and workers who were demanding greater freedom and economic reform. Soon after, however, China, too, began to endorse capitalism. Its leaders also solicited Western investments. They allowed the use of credit cards and approved a stock market. They even permitted bits of that symbol of China itself, the Great Wall, to be sold as souvenirs—for profit (McGregor 1992). While still proclaiming Marxist-Leninist-Maoist principles, the Communist party—under the slogan "One China, two systems"—is trying to make Shanghai the financial center of East Asia (McGregor 1993; Schlesinger 1994). One consequence—besides Avon ladies swarming through the cities and Head & Shoulders climbing to the top of the charts in shampoo sales—is a rapidly rising standard of living (Kahn 1995; Ikels 1996).

Coming from behind with a vengeance, China has successfully arm-twisted multinational corporations to deliver breakthrough technology and to train Chinese workers to administer it. They are now building the base from which China will launch itself as a top competitor in world markets ("Price of Entry," 1995).

Convergence Theory The socialist nations, then, have embraced profit while the capitalist nations have adopted socialistic programs designed to redistribute wealth. Will the two systems continue to adopt features of the other until they converge, creating a sort of hybrid economic system? This, at least, is the bare bones outline of the prediction made by **convergency theory** (Form 1979; Kerr 1960, 1983; Inkeles 1998).

Evidence for this theory is impressive. The pursuit of profits introduced by socialist leaders in China has already begun to produce wealth and a higher standard of living. (In Russia, the experiment has had a fitful start.) This will make it almost impossible to erase profits from their economic system. Similarly, the citizens of capitalist nations have become so used to socialist features that they cannot imagine a government that does not protect the un-

convergence theory the view that as capitalist and socialist economic systems each adopt features of the other, a hybrid (or mixed) economic system will emerge

employed, guarantee a minimum wage, and so on. Leaders and citizens of both systems may deny it, or they may quarrel about the details, but they have embraced the opposing principles.

The matter, however, is not this simple. That each has adopted features of the other is only part of the picture. The systems remain far from "converged." Although it is considerably muted compared to what it was in the heady days of the cold war, the struggle between the systems continues. Russian and Polish citizens, for example, longing for greater stability, have voted Communists back into top government positions. In the United States, Republicans try to roll back socialistic measures and return to a purer capitalism, while Democrats resist. Meanwhile, the Chinese, longing to transform themselves into the world's number one capitalist nation, await the death of the elderly rulers who are barricaded in their "Kremlin" fortress.

■ **In Sum** At this historical point, with the pullback of socialism around the world, we can note that capitalism, if not on its way to total victory, has a strong lead. We also must note that there is no pure capitalism (and likely never was). Today, then, as it expands across the globe, capitalism speaks in a variety of accents, with the versions in China, Russia, Great Britain, Japan, Germany, Sweden, and the United States differing from one another.

*T*HE FUNCTIONALIST VIEW OF THE GLOBALIZATION OF CAPITALISM

> **mechanical solidarity**
> Durkheim's term for the unity that comes from being involved in similar occupations or activities

- Sun Microsystems uses a single phone number to offer round-the-globe, round-the-clock technical service. The number is staffed by teams in California, England, and Australia. They electronically hand work off as a team from another country comes on line.

- When the Turkish economy plunged, Goodyear Tire & Rubber didn't let its Turkish plant sit idle. Instead, thanks to flexible new tire-making technology, Goodyear swiftly regeared its tire models and redirected output to the rest of Europe (Zachary 1995).

The globalization of capitalism may be the most significant economic change in the past 100 years. Its impact on our lives may rival that of the Industrial Revolution itself. As Louis Gallambos, a historian of business, says, "This new global business system will change the way everyone lives and works" (Zachary 1995).

In their march toward globalization, multinational companies locate their corporate headquarters in one country, manufacture basic components in another country, assemble the items in still another, and sell them throughout the world. This photo was taken in Zhongshan, China.

The New Global Division of Labor

To view the globalization of capitalism from the perspective of functionalism, we must first step back a moment and look at work itself. Work is functional for society. It is only because people work that we have electricity, hospitals, schools, automobiles, and homes. Beyond this obvious point, however, lies a basic sociological principle: *Work binds us together.* As you may recall from Chapter 4, Emile Durkheim noted that in preindustrial societies people do similar work and directly share most aspects of life. Because of this, they look at the world in similar ways. Durkheim used the term **mechanical solidarity** to refer to the sense of unity that comes from doing similar activities.

Durkheim also noted that a fundamental change occurs when a society industrializes. A division of labor develops, and people work at different occupations. Because they don't share the same

PERSPECTIVES | Cultural Diversity Around the World

DOING BUSINESS IN THE GLOBAL VILLAGE

The globalization of capitalism means that businesspeople face cultural hurdles as they sell products in other cultures. At times, even experienced firms don't manage to break through cultural barriers. General Motors, for example, was successful in marketing its automobile, the Nova, in the United States. When GM tried to export that success south of the border, Mexicans snickered, and few would buy the car. Finally, someone let the company in on the secret: In Spanish, *"No va"* is an entire sentence that means "It doesn't go" or "It doesn't work."

Many U.S. companies are trying to market to Mexico's growing middle class and to the millions of Spanish-speaking Americans. Some of them have stumbled over their Spanish. When Parker Pen tried to translate "It won't leak in your pocket and embarrass you," it came out, "It won't leak in your pocket and make you pregnant." Frank Perdue's cute chicken slogan, "It takes a strong man to

make a tender chicken" didn't fare any better. It came out: "It takes an aroused man to make a chicken affectionate."

Some businesspeople have made the cultural leap without such problems. They have seized profit opportunities in cultural differences. For example, Japanese women are embarrassed by the sounds they make in public toilets. To drown out the offensive sounds, they flush the toilet an average of 2.7 times a visit (Iori 1988). This wastes a lot of water, of course, and a U.S. entrepreneur saw this cultural trait as an opportunity. He developed a battery-powered device that is mounted next to the toilet. When a woman activates the device, it emits a 25-second flushing sound. Although a toilet-sound duplicator may be useless in our culture, the Japanese have bought thousands of them.

Let's suppose that you decide to publish a magazine in Japan. Your market research shows that a magazine about sports heroes would be popular. It

wouldn't surprise you to know that your readers expect you to chronicle their idol's career, height, and hobbies. But you would miss something essential if you didn't learn that the Japanese also expect to read about their hero's blood type. They view it as a sort of zodiac birth sign (Ono 1993). And you might learn that Japanese mothers save their baby's umbilical cord in a wooden box. If you could get hold of a sports hero's umbilical cord, you could make a small fortune (Shirouzu 1995).

If you ran a golf course, you would need to understand why Japanese golfers fear shooting a hole-in-one. This obligates them to buy expensive gifts for their fellow players, to throw a drinking party, and to plant a commemorative tree to mark their "joy." Entrepreneurs have seized this cultural opportunity, too. To ward off such a catastrophe, they sell policies that for $100 provide $5,000 hole-in-one insurance (Hardy 1993a). ■

---

activity, they feel less solidarity with one another. Grape growers in California, for example, may feel they have little in common with manufacturers of aircraft in Missouri. Yet, each is part of the same economic system. *Like the separate organs in our body,* each performs a specific function and contributes to the welfare of the others. Durkheim called this economic interdependence **organic solidarity.**

Durkheim had observed the beginning of what turned out to be a global process. Today, organic solidarity engulfs the world. We now have a *global division of labor.* Like Kim, in our opening vignette, we, too, depend on workers around the globe. People who live in California or New York—or even Michigan—depend on workers in Tokyo to produce cars. Tokyo workers, in turn, depend on Saudi Arabian workers for oil, South American workers to operate ships, and workers in South Africa for palladium for their catalytic converters. Although we do not feel a sense of unity with one another—in fact, we sometimes feel threatened and hostile—interdependence links us all in the same economic web. This process does not occur without some cultural hurdles, of course, a topic of the Perspectives box above.

Ownership and the Management of Corporations

organic solidarity Durkheim's term for the interdependence that results from people needing others to fulfill their jobs

corporation the joint ownership of a business enterprise, whose liabilities and obligations are separate from those of its owners

The dominance of capitalism, which is driving this global interdependence, is rooted in a social invention called the corporation. A **corporation** is a business that is treated in law as a person. Its liabilities and obligations are separate from those of its owners. For example, each shareholder of General Motors—whether the owner of one or 100,000 shares—owns a portion of the company. General Motors is a legal entity and can buy and sell, sue and be sued, make contracts, and incur debts. The corporation, however, not the individual owner, is responsible for the firm's liabilities—such as paying its debts and fulfilling its contracts.

One of the most surprising, but functional, aspects of corporations is the *separation of ownership and management*. Unlike most businesses, the owners, those who own the company's stock, do not run the day-to-day affairs of the company. Instead, managers run the corporation, and they are able to treat it *as though it were their own* (Cohen 1990; Zampa and McCormick 1991). The result is the "ownership of wealth without appreciable control, and control of wealth without appreciable ownership" (Berle and Means 1932). Sociologist Michael Useem (1984) put it this way:

> When few owners held all or most of a corporation's stock, they readily dominated its board of directors, which in turn selected top management and ran the corporation. Now that a firm's stock [is] dispersed among many unrelated owners, each holding a tiny fraction of the total equity, the resulting power vacuum allow[s] management to select the board of directors; thus management [becomes] self-perpetuating and thereby acquire[s] de facto control over the corporation.
>
> Management determines its own salaries, sets goals and awards itself bonuses for meeting them, authorizes market surveys, hires advertising agencies, determines marketing strategies, and negotiates with unions. The management's primary responsibility to the owners is to produce profits.

What makes this separation of ownership and management functional is profits. With stock options and bonuses tied to the company's performance, managers are highly motivated to make profits. At the annual stockholders' meeting, the owners consider broad company matters, including the selection of a board of directors and a firm to audit the company's books. As long as the managers report a handsome profit, the stockholders rubber-stamp their recommendations. It is so unusual for this not to happen, that when it doesn't the outcome is called a **stockholders' revolt.** The irony of this term is generally lost, but remember that in such cases it is not the workers but the owners who are rebelling!

stockholders' revolt the refusal of a corporation's stockholders to rubber-stamp decisions made by its managers

Functions on a Global Scale

The globalization of capitalism is leading to the division of the world's nations into three primary trading blocks: North and South America, dominated by the United States, Europe, dominated by Germany, and Asia, dominated by Japan. Functionalists stress not only how the multinational corporate giants benefit from this new world structure, but also how it benefits the citizens of the world.

Consider free trade. Putting free trade into practice leads to greater competition, which drives the search for greater productivity. This lowers prices and brings a higher standard of living. Free trade also has dysfunctions. As production moves to countries where labor costs are lower, millions of high-paid U.S., U.K., French, and German workers lose their jobs. Functionalists point out that this is merely a temporary dislocation. As the Most Industrialized Nations lose production jobs, their workers shift into service and high-tech jobs. Meanwhile, the unemployed of the poor nations are given work, and the chance for a better life.

A primary sociological significance of global capitalism is that the giant multinational corporations owe allegiance to profits and market share, not to any nation. As a U.S. executive said, "The United States does not have an automatic call on our resources. There is no mind-set that puts the country first" (Kennedy 1993). This fundamental shift in orientation is so new that its implications

The globalization of capitalism means the dominance of markets by the main capitalist countries. Mattell, a United States corporation ships Barbie and Ken around the world. Along with these dolls goes a reflection of U.S. culture, in this case an image of a way of life, one destined to shape people's thinking and aspirations.

are unknown at present. Certainly there are dysfunctions, as the millions of workers whose jobs have been pulled out from under them know. But this shift may also yield one of the greatest functions the world has ever seen. Removed from tribal loyalties and national boundaries these corporations' global interconnections may be a force for peace. It also could create a New World Order dominated by a handful of corporate leaders, a topic discussed in the next chapter.

THE CONFLICT VIEW OF THE GLOBALIZATION OF CAPITALISM

Conflict theorists say that to place the focus on global interdependence, which, without doubt, is occurring, is to miss the central point—how the wealthy benefit at the expense of workers. Let's see what they mean by this.

The Inner Circle and Corporate Capitalism

The multinational corporations are headed by a group that Michael Useem (1984) calls the *inner circle*. Members of this inner circle, though in competition with one another, are united by a mutual interest in preserving capitalism (Mizruchi and Koenig 1991). Within their own country, they consult with high-level politicians, promote legislation favorable to big business, and serve as trustees for foundations and universities. They also promote political candidates who stand firmly for the private ownership of property. On a global level, they promote the ideology of capitalism and move capital from one nation—or region—to another in their search for greater and more immediate profits.

Table 14.2 illustrates how the United States dominates world trade. After World War II, with Germany destroyed and France in shambles, the United States eclipsed Great Britain and became the major player in international business. Of the world's twenty-five largest corporations, the United States holds the lead with twenty. Japan follows at a distant second with two.

If the giant corporations cannot attain a monopoly, they strive for an **oligopoly**—several large companies that dominate a single industry, such as gasoline, breakfast cereal, or light bulbs. If they attain this, they can set pricing, dictate the quality of their products, and protect their markets. Oligopolies also cultivate political connections to pass legislation that gives them special tax breaks. Corporations have so changed capitalism that the term **corporate capitalism** is used to indicate that giant corporations dominate the economic system. To gain global markets, giant corporations based in one nation are merging with those based in other nations.

To consolidate their power, the inner circle looks for cooperative politicians and develops a cozy relationship with them. If they find hostility, some are not above plotting murder and overthrowing governments. In 1973, a U.S. multinational, the International Telephone & Telegraph Company (ITT), joined the CIA in a plot to unseat Chile's elected government. They first attempted to bring about the economic collapse of Chile. When this failed, they then plotted a coup d'état. This led to the assassination of the Chilean president, Salvador Allende (Coleman 1995).

In the United States, economic power is so integrated with politics that the inner circle can even get the U.S. president to pitch their products. If this sounds like an exaggeration, consider this dispatch from the Associated Press (October 29, 1995):

> The White House celebrated Saudi Arabia's $6 billion purchase of U.S.-made airplanes Thursday, calling it a victory for both American manufacturers and the Clinton administration. . . . President Clinton helped broker the sale. . . . Prince Bandar bin Sultan, [Saudi Arabia's] minister of defense and aviation, credited Clinton for closing the purchase. *Clinton personally pitched the quality of the U.S. planes to Saudi King Fahd.* (Italics added)

oligopoly the control of an entire industry by several large companies

corporate capitalism the domination of the economic system by giant corporations

Table 14.2

THE WORLD'S LARGEST CORPORATIONS*

Rank	Name	Country	Market Value	Profit
1	Microsoft	U.S.	$460 billion	$7.8 billion
2	GE	U.S.	$371 billion	$9.3 billion
3	IBM	U.S.	$234 billion	$6.3 billion
4	Wal-Mart	U.S.	$215 billion	$4.4 billion
5	Cisco Systems	U.S.	$206 billion	$1.4 billion
6	Lucent Technologies	U.S.	$206 billion	$1.0 billion
7	Shell	Holland	$201 billion	$0.4 billion
8	Intel	U.S.	$198 billion	$6.1 billion
9	Exxon	U.S.	$187 billion	$6.4 billion
10	Nippon Telephone	Japan	$187 billion	$5.3 billion
11	AT&T	U.S.	$178 billion	$6.4 billion
12	Merck	U.S.	$175 billion	$5.3 billion
13	Amoco	U.K.	$174 billion	$3.3 billion
14	Citigroup	U.S.	$171 billion	$5.8 billion
15	MCI	U.S.	$160 billion	$2.7 billion
16	Coca Cola	U.S.	$153 billion	$3.5 billion
17	American International	U.S.	$145 billion	$4.3 billion
18	Pfizer	U.S.	$142 billion	$3.4 billion
19	Bristol-Myers	U.S.	$140 billion	$3.1 billion
20	Johnson & Johnson	U.S.	$132 billion	$3.1 billion
21	Deutsche Telekom	Germany	$127 billion	$2.6 billion
22	Bank of America	U.S.	$126 billion	$5.2 billion
23	Toyota	Japan	$119 billion	$3.1 billion
24	Proctor & Gamble	U.S.	$119 billion	$3.8 billion
25	America Online	U.S.	$118 billion	$0.8 billion

*For the year 1998.

Source: "The Global Giants" 1999.

> . . . (T)he Clinton Administration worked this sale awfully damn hard because of the president's commitment to promoting U.S. business abroad. . . . He has done that routinely, instructed his ambassadors and his diplomats to put the economic interests of Americans forward as they conduct their diplomacy.

Although the president wasn't selling toothpaste, it was the same principle.

In short, the interests of the heads of the multinational corporations and the top political leaders usually converge. Much of the activity of top government leaders is dedicated to promoting the economic interests of the country's economic leaders. Together, they form a power elite—a topic to which we shall return in the next chapter.

Interlocking Directorates

Conflict theorists stress how the powerful use **interlocking directorates** (Mizruchi and Koenig 1991). The elite serve as directors of several companies. Their fellow members on those boards also sit on the boards of other companies, and so on. Like a spider's web that starts at the center and then fans out in all directions, eventually the top companies in the country are interlocked into a network (Mintz and Schwartz 1985). The chief executive

interlocking directorates the same people serving on the board of directors of several companies

officer of a firm in Great Britain, who also sits on the board of directors of half a dozen other companies, said:

> If you serve on, say, six outside boards, each of which has, say, ten directors, and let's say out of the ten directors, five are experts in one or another subject, you have a built-in panel of thirty friends who are experts who you meet regularly, automatically each month, and you really have great access to ideas and information. You're joining a club, a very good club. (Useem 1984)

The resulting concentration of power minimizes competition, for a director is not going to approve a plan that will be harmful to another company in which he or she (mostly he) has a stake. The top executives of the top U.S. companies are part of the powerful capitalist class described on pages 263–265. They even get together in recreational settings, where they renew their sense of solidarity, purpose, and destiny (Domhoff 1997).

Global Investing

Central to the globalization of capitalism is the practice of making investments around the globe. Look at the Social Maps on these two pages. The one below shows the percentage of U.S. businesses that are owned by foreign corporations. The global map shows the investments U.S. corporations have made in other countries. Outgrowing national boundaries, the giant corporations have become more and more detached from the interests and values of their country of origin. They move investments and production from one part of the globe to another—with no concern for consequences other than profits. How their adding—or withdrawing—investments affects workers is of no concern to them. Their dollars simply follow the path of greatest profit (Kennedy 1993).

Multinational corporations are becoming a primary political force in the world. They are reshaping the globe as no political or military force has been able to do. All of our lives are touched by these global giants. Although we already have started to take this for granted—this is new to the world scene. If a New World Order comes about, we all may find ourselves at the mercy of a global elite, one directed by the heads of the world's corporate giants.

SOCIAL MAP: THE GLOBALIZATION OF CAPITALISM: FOREIGN OWNERSHIP OF U.S. BUSINESS

Source: Statistical Abstract 1999: Table 1314.

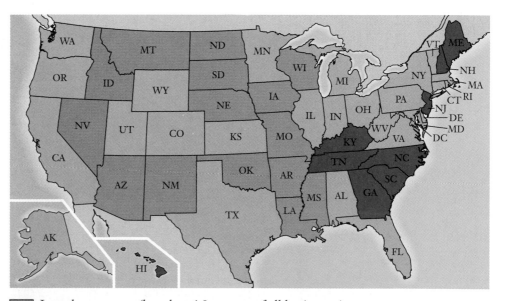

▢ Less than average (less than 4.0 percent of all businesses)
▢ Average (4.0–5.9 percent of all businesses)
▪ More than average (6 percent or more of all businesses)

SOCIAL MAP: THE GLOBALIZATION OF CAPITALISM: U.S. OWNERSHIP IN OTHER COUNTRIES

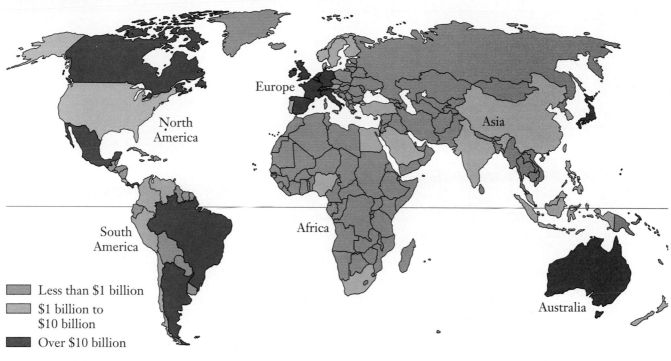

Less than $1 billion

$1 billion to $10 billion

Over $10 billion

Source: Statistical Abstract 1999:Table 1317.

Work in U.S. Society

With this broad, even global, background, let's turn our focus on work in U.S. society.

The Decline of Agriculture and the Transition to Postindustrial Society

At various times in this text, I have used the term postindustrial society to describe the United States. Figure 14.5 illustrates why this term is appropriate. This figure shows a change that is without parallel in human history. In the 1800s most U.S. workers were farmers. Today, farmers make up just over 2 percent of the work force. With the technology of the 1800s, a typical farmer produced enough food for only five people. With today's powerful machinery and hybrid seeds, he or she now feeds about eighty. In 1940, about half of U.S. workers wore a blue collar; then changing technology shrank the market for blue-collar jobs. White-collar work continued its ascent, reaching the dominant position it holds today. This figure illustrates nothing less than the transition to a new society. Because of this change, your life is different—not just your work activities—but also your attitudes and even the way you view the world.

THE REVOLUTIONARY CHANGE IN THE U.S. WORK FORCE

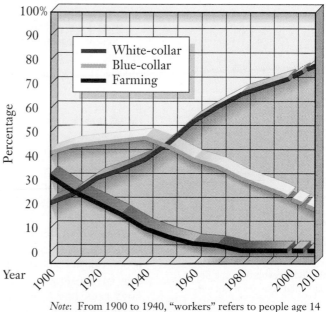

Note: From 1900 to 1940, "workers" refers to people age 14 and over, from 1970 to people age 16 and over. Broken lines are the author's projections.

Source: Statistical Abstract, various years, and 1999:Table 677.

14.6 WOMEN MAKE UP WHAT PERCENTAGE OF THE LABOR FORCE IN THE MOST INDUSTRIALIZED NATIONS?

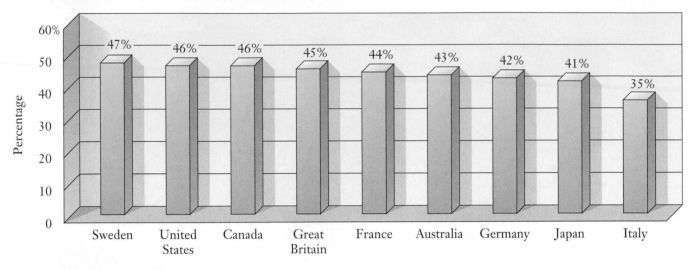

Source: *Statistical Abstract* 1999:Table 1376.

Women and Work

One of the chief characteristics of the U.S. work force has been a steady increase in the numbers of women who work outside the home for wages. Over the past century, the number steadily increased, and today almost one of two U.S. workers is a woman. As you can see from Figure 14.6, this ratio is one of the highest in the industrialized world.

How likely it is that a woman is in the labor force depends on several factors. Figure 14.7a shows how working for wages increases with each level of education. This is probably because as one ascends the educational ladder work is more satisfying and the pay much better. Figure 14.7b shows the influence of marital status. You can see that single women are the most likely to work for wages, married women follow closely behind, and divorced, widowed, and separated women are the least likely to be in the work force. From Figure 14.7c, you can see that race-ethnicity makes little difference.

Researchers have found distinctions between women and men in the world of work. For one, women tend to be more concerned than men with maintaining a balance between their work and family lives (Statham et al. 1988). For another, men and women tend to follow different models for success: Men tend to emphasize individualism, power, and competition, while women are more likely to stress collaboration, persuasion, and helping (Miller-Loessi 1992). A primary concern of many women is the extent to which they must adopt the male model of leadership in order to be successful in their careers. You should note that these findings represent tendencies. Although they characterize the average woman or man, many people diverge from them.

As discussed in Chapter 11, women face discrimination at work. The Down-to-Earth Sociology box on page 408 explores how some women cope with this discrimination.

the quiet revolution the fundamental changes in society that occur as a result of vast numbers of women entering the work force

The Quiet Revolution Because its changes are so gradual but its implications so profound, sociologists use the term "**quiet revolution**" to refer to the continually increasing proportions of women who have joined the ranks of paid labor. This means a transformation of consumer patterns, relations at work, self-concepts, and relationships with boyfriends, husbands, and children. One of the most significant aspects of the quiet revolution is indicated by Figure 14.7d. Note that since 1960 the proportion of married women who work for wages and have preschool children has tripled. It now equals the average of all U.S. women. We discuss implications of these changes in Chapter 16.

14.7 PERCENTAGE OF WOMEN IN THE U.S. LABOR FORCE

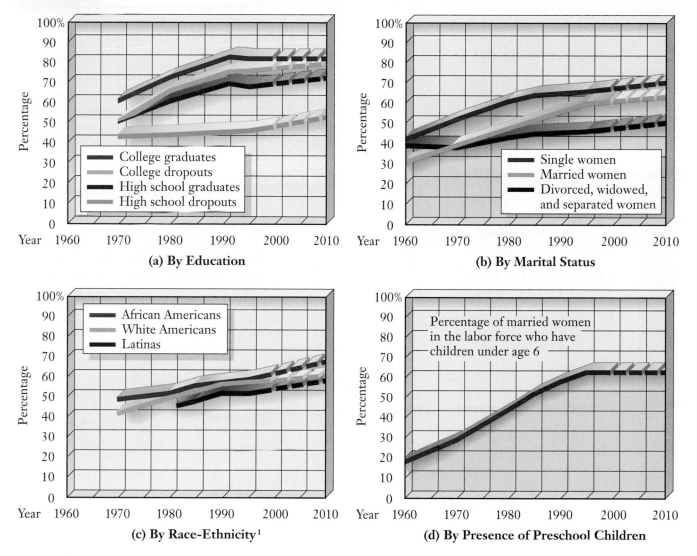

(a) By Education

(b) By Marital Status

(c) By Race-Ethnicity[1]

(d) By Presence of Preschool Children

[1]Data for other racial-ethnic groups unavailable in the source; no data for Latinas for 1970–1980.

Source: Statistical Abstract 1995:Tables 627, 629, 637, 639; 1999:Tables 650, 653, 657, 659. Broken lines indicate author's projections.

The Underground Economy

The underground economy. It has a sinister ring—suggestive of dope deals struck in alleys and wads of dollar bills hastily exchanged. The underground economy is this, but it is a lot more—and it is usually a lot more innocent. If you pay the plumber with a check made out to "cash," if you purchase a pair of sunglasses from a street vendor or a kitchen gadget at a yard sale, if you so much as hand a neighbor's kid a $20 bill to mow the lawn or to baby sit (or if you accept such a check), you are participating in the underground economy. (Pennar and Farrell 1993)

Also known as the informal economy and the off-the-books economy, the **underground economy** consists of economic activities—whether legal or illegal—that people don't report to the government. What interests most of us is not unreported baby-sitting money, but the illegal

underground economy
exchanges of goods and services that are not reported to the government and thereby escape taxation

Sociology

MANEUVERING THE HIDDEN CORPORATE CULTURE: WOMEN SURVIVING THE MALE-DOMINATED BUSINESS WORLD

I work for a large insurance company. Of its twenty-five hundred employees, about 75 percent are women. Only 5 percent of the upper management positions, however, are held by women.

I am one of the more fortunate women, for I hold a position in middle management. I am also a member of the twelve-member junior board of directors, of whom nine are men and three are women.

Recently one of the female members of the board suggested that the company become involved in Horizons for Tomorrow, a program designed to provide internships for disadvantaged youth. Two other women and I spent many days developing a proposal for our participation.

The problem was how to sell the proposal to the company president. From past experiences, we knew that if he saw it as a "woman's project" it would be shelved into the second tier of "maybes." He hates what he calls "aggressive bitches."

We three decided, reluctantly, that the proposal had a chance only if it were presented by a man. We decided that Bill was the logical choice. We also knew that we had to "stroke" Bill if we were going to get his cooperation.

We first asked Bill if he would "show us how to present our proposal." (It is ridiculous to have to play the role of the "less capable female" in the 1990s, but, unfortunately, the corporate culture sometimes dictates this strategy.) To clinch matters, we puffed up Bill even more by saying, "You're the logical choice for the next chairmanship of the board."

Bill, of course, came to our next planning session, where we "prepped" *him* on what to say.

At our meeting with the president, we had Bill give the basic presentation. We then backed *him* up, providing the background and rationale for why the president should endorse the project. As we answered the president's questions, we carefully deferred to Bill.

The president's response? "An excellent proposal," he concluded, "an appropriate project for our company."

To be successful, we had to maneuver through the treacherous waters of the "hidden culture" (actually not so "hidden" to women who have been in the company for a while). The proposal was not sufficient on its merits, for the "who" behind a proposal is at least as significant as the proposal itself.

"We shouldn't have to play these games," Laura said, summarizing our feelings.

But we all know that we have no choice. To become labeled "pushy" is to commit "corporate suicide"—and we're no fools. ■

Source: Written by an insurance executive in the author's introductory sociology class who, out of fear of retaliation at work, chooses to remain anonymous.

activities that people cannot report even if they want to. As a 20-year-old child care worker who also works as a prostitute two or three nights a week told me, "Why do I do this? For the money! Where else can I make this kind of money in a few hours? And it's all tax free." Drug dealing is perhaps the largest single source of illegal income, for billions of dollars flow from users to sellers and their networks of growers, importers, processors, transporters, dealers, and enforcers. These particular networks are so huge that each year the police arrest more than a million Americans for illegal drug activities (*Statistical Abstract* 1999:Table 358).

The million or so illegal immigrants who enter the United States each year, a topic mentioned in Chapter 12, are also part of the underground economy. Often called *undocumented workers* (referred to as *los sin documentos* in Spanish), they work for employers who don't pay attention to their forged documents, or for those who pay them in cash and don't ask to see Social Security cards. Some enter on their own, but smugglers bring in many (Henslin 2000:275). The undocumented workers from China work primarily in Chinese restaurants and in New York's garment industry. Many from India and Pakistan work in fast food restaurants (Rosenbaum 1998). Those from Mexico and Central and South America are concentrated in California and Texas, but they disperse throughout the country. They work on farms and in factories, in restaurants and auto shops, and at a variety of other low-paying and dirty jobs that, for the most part, U.S. citizens avoid. The rest of us benefit from the labor of undocumented workers, for they bring us cheaper goods.

Because of its subterranean nature, no one knows the exact size of the underground economy, but it probably runs 10 to 15 percent of the regular economy (Pennar and Farrell 1993). Since the official gross domestic product of the United States is about $9 trillion (*Statistical Abstract* 1999:Table 721), the underground economy probably runs about $1 trillion. It is so huge that it distorts the official statistics of the country's gross national product, and the IRS loses more than $100 billion a year in taxes.

Shrinking Paychecks

U.S. workers are some of the most productive in the world (*Statistical Abstract* 1999:Table 1382), and as we saw on Table 14.2 (page 403), U.S. multinational corporations make gigantic profits. One might think, therefore, that the pay of U.S. workers would be increasing. This brings us to a disturbing trend.

Until about 1970, gains in productivity did translate into paychecks that allowed workers to buy more goods. But how things have changed. Look at Figure 14.8 on the next page. The gold bars show current dollars, the dollars the average worker finds in his or her paycheck. From this, it appears that U.S. workers are making a lot more than they used to. They bring home *four* times as many dollars than they did in 1970. Back in 1970, workers averaged only a little over $3 an hour, and now it is over $13. The green bars, which show the *buying power* of these paychecks, strip away the illusion. They show that inflation has whittled away the value of those dollars. Today's workers can't buy as much with their $13 as workers in 1970 could with their "measly" $3 an hour. The question is not "How could you live on just $3 back in 1970?" but, rather, "How can you live on just $13 an hour today?"

Some workers, however, can't bring home even these shrinking paychecks. The Perspectives box on page 411 presents an overview of who is unemployed—and explains why these figures are deceptive.

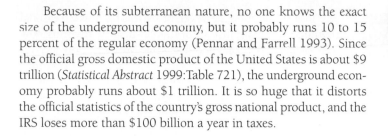

AVERAGE HOURLY EARNINGS OF U.S. WORKERS IN CURRENT AND CONSTANT (1982) DOLLARS

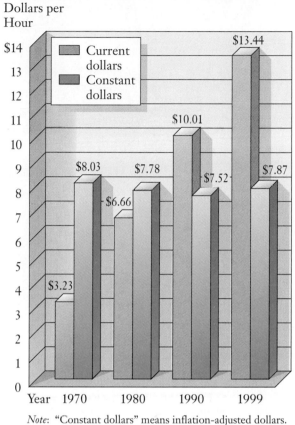

Note: "Constant dollars" means inflation-adjusted dollars.

Source: *Statistical Abstract* 1999:Table 698; Bureau of Labor Statistics 2000:Table B4.

Patterns of Work and Leisure

Suppose that it is 1860 and you work for a textile company in Lowell, Massachusetts. When you arrive at work one day, you find that the boss has posted a new work rule: All workers will have to come in at the same time and remain until quitting time. Like the other workers, you feel outrage. You join them as they shout, "This is slavery!" and march out on strike, indignant at such a preposterous rule (Zuboff 1991). This did happen. The workers were angry because up to then they had been able to come and go when they wanted. Let's consider how patterns of work and leisure are related to the transformation of economies.

Effects of Industrialization Hunting and gathering societies provided tremendous amounts of leisure. Assuming they didn't live in a barren place or have to deal with some unusual event, such as drought or pestilence, it did not take long for them to hunt and gather what they needed for the day. In fact, *most of their time was leisure,* and the rhythms of nature were an essential part of their lives. Agricultural economies also allowed much leisure, for, at least in the western hemisphere, work peaked with the spring planting, let up in the summer, and then peaked again with the fall harvest. During the winter work again receded, for by this time the harvest was in, animals had been slaughtered, food had been canned and stored, and a wood supply had been laid up.

The term underground economy has a sinister ring to it. Part of the underground economy does consist of drug deals furtively transacted in back alleys, but the term refers to any unreported, untaxed commercial transaction. Most are as innocuous, and common, as that depicted in this photo.

LEISURE AND THE LIFE COURSE: THE "U" CURVE OF LEISURE

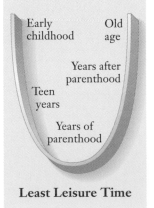

Industrialization, however, broke this harness to seasonal rhythms. Going against all of human history, rhythms now were dictated by bosses and machines. Workers, however, resisted, and insisted on moving to their traditional rhythms. After working for several weeks, a worker would disappear, only to reappear when money ran out. For most, enjoying leisure was considerably more important than amassing money (Weber 1958/1904–1905). Bosses, wanting to profit from regular, efficient production, began to insist that all workers start work at the same time. To workers, that seemed like slavery. Today, in contrast, work patterns that are artificially imposed on us have become part of our culture and are taken for granted.

Trends in Leisure Leisure is time not taken up by work or required activities such as eating and sleeping. It is not the activity itself that makes something leisure, but the purpose for which it is done. Consider driving a car. If you do it for pleasure, it is leisure, but if you are an on-duty police officer or if you must commute to the office, it is work. If done for enjoyment, horseback riding and reading a book are leisure—but these activities are work for jockeys and students.

Patterns of leisure change with the life course, following the U-curve shown on Figure 14.9. Young children enjoy the most leisure, but teenagers still have considerably more leisure than their parents. Parents with small children have the least leisure, but after the children leave home, leisure picks up again. After the age of 60 or so, the amount of leisure for adults peaks.

Compared with early industrialization, workers today have far more leisure. A hundred years ago the work week was half again as long as today's, for then workers had to be at their machines 60 hours a week. When workers unionized, they demanded a shorter work week. Over the years, the work week has gradually shrunk. In Germany the work week is 35 hours, with Friday afternoons usually off. Volkswagen was the world's first global corporation to adopt a 30-hour work week (Rifkin 1995). In addition, German workers get six weeks of paid vacation a year. Unlike western Europe, in the United States this trend toward more leisure reversed course during the 1960s (Schor 1991; Rifkin 1995). U.S. workers now average 1,948 hours of work a year, matched only by workers in Great Britain. They are soundly beaten, however, by Japanese workers, who average 2,120 hours a year (Ono and Schlesinger 1992; MacShane 1993).

The Alternative Office Technology always affects work. Just as the Industrial Revolution took workers away from home-based production to factories, so today the technological revolution is returning millions of workers to the home. In order to save money on real estate, many companies encourage their employees to remain home and commute electronically. Some companies even buy their employees laptop computers and office furniture to use at home, in what is called the *alternative office.*

The alternative office saves companies money, and its unsupervised nature does not seem to hurt productivity. Workers gain more than a paycheck from work, however, and many who work at home miss the camaraderie of their work companions. E-mail isn't quite the same. Here is what a student who read this text reported:

My husband is still working as a software engineer. His company "wired" most of their employees for home offices. So he now works from home and has a boss in another state whom he rarely sees in person. He misses his "community" at the office and often, out of the blue,

WHO IS UNEMPLOYED?

It is hard to believe that Amy and Peter are not officially part of the unemployed. After all, they have no jobs. In fact, they have no home. They are among the many homeless and jobless Americans sleeping in alleys and shelters for the destitute. That, however, is *not* enough to count them as unemployed.

To see how the calculation works, let's suppose that you lose your job. After a frustrating six months of searching for work, you become so discouraged that you stay home and stare blankly at the television. Amazingly, you are no longer counted as unemployed. As far as official statistics are concerned, to be unemployed you must be *actively seeking work*. If not, the government leaves you out of its figures. People without jobs who are so discouraged that they have not looked for work during the previous four weeks are dropped from the government's unemployment figures.

Now, suppose that you do keep on looking for work. You remain part of the government's count. But if your neighbor pays you to clean out her garage and rake the leaves, and if you put in fifteen hours and report them, you won't be counted, for the government figures that you have a job. Now assume that you stop raking leaves, keep on looking for work, but can't pay your telephone bill. Again, you won't show up in the totals, for the Bureau of Labor Statistics counts only people it reaches in a random telephone survey. To get an accurate idea of how many are unemployed, then, we need to add about 3 percent to the official unemployment rate (Myers 1992). If the Labor Department says it is 7 percent, the true rate runs about 10 percent—a difference of about *8 million people*.

Granted these problems, certain patterns do show up year after year. As you can see from Table 14.3, unemployment varies by sex, marital status, presence of preschool children, race-ethnicity, and education. African Americans and Latinos are more likely to be unemployed than are whites and Asian American. You won't be surprised to see that people with less education are more likely to be unemployed, but you might be surprised to see that single workers are more likely to be without work than either divorced or married people. Although the percentages fluctuate with changing economic conditions, these general patterns remain fairly constant. ■

Table 14.3

THE OFFICIAL U.S. UNEMPLOYMENT RATE

Category	Percentage	Category	Percentage	Category	Percentage	Category	Percentage
Sex		**Race/Ethnicity**		**Ethnic Background of Latinos**		**Education**	
Male	4.1%	African Americans		Puerto Rican		High school dropouts	
Female	3.9	Men	8.3%	Men	8.5%	Men	8.0%
Marital Status of Women[a]		Women	7.0	Women	8.2	Women	9.3
Married	3.2	Latinos		Mexican		High school graduates	
Single	7.5	Men	6.4	Men	6.5	Men	5.1
Divorced, widowed,		Women	8.2	Women	8.6	Women	4.1
and separated	5.0	Whites		Cuban		1–3 years of college	
Women with Preschool Children[a]		Men	3.5	Men	4.1	Men	3.7
Married	4.5	Women	3.4	Women	8.6	Women	3.5
Single	17.5	Asian Americans[b]		Other[c]		College graduates	
Divorced, widowed,		Men	4.6	Men	5.4	Men	1.7
and separated	10.6	Women	4.6	Women	7.0	Women	1.9

[a]Source does not list totals for men.

[b]Source does not list employment of Asian Americans by sex, and this is the overall total listed for both men and women.

[c]Refers primarily to people from Central or South America.

Source: Statistical Abstract 1999:Tables 52, 55, 651, 659, 684. Bureau of Labor Statistics 2000: Table B4.

---

will just go in for a few hours for no good reason. He's usually disappointed, though, because most everyone else works at home, and he finds few people to chat with. His company recognizes this as a big problem. It's hard to keep the team spirit, so they have tried to gently "mandate" once a week togetherness lunches. But it's not the same as everyday contact.

As capitalism globalizes, it is not just the products but also the cultures of the dominant capitalist nations that are exported around the world. As the premier producer and exporter of images, Hollywood makes a global impact. Shown here in Xian, China, is what has become a global icon.

THE FUTURE: FACING THE CONSEQUENCES OF GLOBAL CAPITALISM

The best way to catch a glimpse of the future is to look at two trends that are firmly in place: global trade and the new technology.

Expanding Global Trade

With the giant multinational corporations carving up the world into major trading blocs and pushing for the drastic reduction or elimination of tariffs, trade among nations will increase beyond anything we have ever seen. The United States will be at the forefront of this expanding global trade, for world markets have become crucial for the success of many U.S. corporations. For example, with the huge costs of making movies (the average movie now runs $50 million), the U.S. movie industry would go broke if it weren't for global distribution.

Not all nations will benefit equally, of course, and some nations will not benefit at all. There is no reason to assume that the Most Industrialized Nations (even though in a postindustrial phase) will not continue to garner the lion's share of the world's wealth, nor that their exploitation of the poorer nations will not continue.

New Technologies and Downsizing: Utopia or Nightmare?

Computer-driven production will continue to reduce the number of workers needed to make the goods we use. As I wrote back in 1975,

> Although it may sound as though it is taken from some utopian scheme, it has been estimated that the day will come when only 2 percent of the population will be needed to produce all the manufactured goods our total population needs. That day may not be far off as Ford Motor Company now takes only six workers to produce a single car while it took 104 workers for the same task in 1910 . . . it is possible that a single plant with but a single worker can produce all the bread needed in southern California. . . . Whether such changes represent a utopian dream come true or not, for displaced workers it can well be a nightmare. (p. 341)

Utopia or a nightmare? From a symbolic interactionist standpoint, it all depends on your point of view. As conflict theorists stress, that point of view depends on where you stand in the production process. The jobs the new technology destroys are not located at the top levels of the multinationals, nor are they held by the capitalists who own huge blocs of stock. For the most part, these people are immune from such disruptions. Although they must modify their investment strategies to match changing situations, by lowering production costs the new technology increases profits and fattens their dividend checks. The people who bear the brunt of the change are low-level workers who live from paycheck to paycheck. It is they who suffer the ravages of uncertainty, the devastation of job loss, and, often, the wrenching adjustments that come from being forced from their jobs.

Let's close this chapter, then, with a Thinking Critically section that focuses on the far-reaching implications of this global transformation of our economy.

Thinking *Critically*

NEW TECHNOLOGY AND THE RESTRUCTURING OF WORK: WHAT TYPE OF NEW SOCIETY?

Many workers fear that they will be automated out of their jobs. They have seen machines displace people who once worked at their side. Neighbors with a solid work history have had to join the lines of the unemployed. Friends who were forced to take "early retirement" are now wondering how they will support themselves in their old age.

But does technology actually take away jobs? This is a complicated question. On the one hand, there is no doubt that technology destroys job after job. On this score, the workers' fears are not irrational. In recent years, the number of workers at U.S. Steel dropped from 120,000 to just 20,000—yet production remained the same. If each telephone operator handled the number of calls she or he did in the 1920s, today's telephone traffic would require 50 million operators! (Volti 1995) Computerization will continue to erase millions of U.S. manufacturing jobs.

But there is another side to the story, for technology also creates jobs. The automobile industry, for example, wiped out the livelihood of many bicycle workers and stable hands, but it put tens of thousands more to work in the new steel and gasoline industries. These jobs are in addition to mechanics, salespeople, advertisers, as well as the work done in the body shops that dot our landscape.

Each new technology, then, both destroys old jobs and creates new ones. Some of these jobs, as with the gasoline stations required by automobiles, are readily visible. Others are less evident. The technology that went into airplanes, for example, not only spawned pilots, mechanics, and reservation clerks, but also stimulated global tourism. To put this in a nutshell: *Most of us work at jobs that did not even exist a hundred years ago.*

And the future? This we can take for granted: There will be more new technologies—and they will make millions of our current jobs obsolete. The basic question is whether the new technologies will destroy jobs faster than they create them. For the millions of workers who find their jobs pulled out from under them, this question is of much more than theoretical interest.

Consider two futures (Rifkin 1995). The one is a technoparadise of abundance and leisure. With few workers needed, work is spread around, and the work week is only 10 or 15 hours. Yet everyone is able to possess goods in abundance. Having restored the leisure that humans used to enjoy in their early days as hunters and gatherers, creative leisure becomes a chief characteristic of the new society. Some spend time in intellectual pursuits, studying the sciences, philosophy, languages. Some follow the arts—painting, poetry, the theater. Many travel. Parents spend much more time with their children. Others, of course, just watch more soap operas, play more video games, or sit transfixed, with beer in one hand and remote in the other, through more hours of televised sports.

The second future is a divided society. A smaller, affluent group forms a country inside a country of impoverished workers and those dispossessed from the work force. Millions, surviving in hopelessness, accept meager welfare handouts that are grudgingly given. Displaced from job opportunities, the nation's youth produce a violent criminal subculture. Frightened and confused at the increasing violence, the affluent lock themselves behind gated communities.

We can't turn back the clock. New technology is here to stay, and it will continue to change the

As conflict theorists stress, in order to keep labor costs low and profits high, capitalist economies need a reserve labor force that pits one worker against another. This poorly paid gold miner in South Africa, working under the debilitating conditions you see in this photo, is an expendable part of the profit system that drives the economic machinery called capitalism. If this worker protests his working conditions, he will be fired immediately, for waiting in the wings are thousands of unemployed workers eager to take his place.

shape of work. The basic issue, then, is how we, as a society, react. In other words, the transformation of work is inevitable, but the consequences of that restructuring are not. ■

For Your Consideration

Which of these futures appears to be more likely? In answering this, refer to the discussion in this chapter about the effects of the new technologies on work, the globalization of capitalism, and the growing power of multinational corporations.

SUMMARY AND REVIEW

■ The Transformation of Economic Systems

How are economic systems linked to types of societies?

The earliest societies, hunting and gathering, were **subsistence economies:** Small groups lived off the land and produced little or no surplus. Economic systems grew more complex as people discovered how to domesticate and cultivate (pastoral and horticultural societies), farm (agricultural societies), and manufacture (industrial societies). Each of these methods allowed people to produce a *surplus,* which fostered trade. Trade, in turn, brought social inequality as some people began to accumulate more than others. Pp. 388–391.

■ The Transformation of the Medium of Exchange

How has the medium of exchange evolved?

A **medium of exchange** is any means by which people exchange goods and services. In hunting and gathering and pastoral and horticultural societies, people **bartered** goods and services. In agricultural societies, **money** came into use, which evolved into **currency,** or paper, representing a specific amount of gold or silver. Postindustrial societies rely increasingly on electronic transfer of funds in the form of **credit cards, debit cards,** and **e-cash.** Pp. 391–393.

■ World Economic Systems

How do the major economic systems differ?

The world's two major economic systems are capitalism and socialism. In **capitalism,** private citizens own the means of production and pursue profits. In **socialism,** the state owns the means of production and determines production with no goal of profit. Adherents of each have developed ideologies that defend their own systems and paint the other as harmful. Following **convergence theory,** in recent years each system has adopted features of the other. Pp. 393–399.

■ The Functionalist View of the Globalization of Capitalism

From the functionalist perspective, work is a basis of social solidarity. Preindustrial societies have **mechanical solidarity;** people perform similar tasks and identify with one another. Industrialization brings **organic solidarity,** economic interdependence based on the division of labor. This process has continued, and we now are developing a global division of labor. Corporations, with their separation of ownership and management, underlie the success of capitalism. Pp. 399–402.

■ The Conflict View of the Globalization of Capitalism

Conflict theorists, who focus on power, note how global capitalism is another means by which capitalists exploit workers. At the top of the major corporations is an inner circle, whose mutual interests make certain that corporate capitalism is protected. Workers lose jobs to automation, while the inner circle maintains its political power and profits from these changes. The term **corporate capitalism** indicates that giant corporations dominate capitalism today. Pp. 402–404.

■ Work in U.S. Society

How has the workforce changed?

The United States is making a transition to a postindustrial society. The number of farm workers has plummeted, blue-collar work is decreasing, and almost everyone works at service jobs. The proportion of women in the labor force is almost one in two, one of the highest ratios in the industrialized world. Pp. 405–406.

What is the underground economy?

The **underground economy** consists of any economic activity not reported to the government, from babysitting to prostitution. The size of the underground economy runs perhaps 10 to 15 percent of the regular economy. Pp. 407–409.

How have patterns of work and leisure changed?

In hunting and gathering societies, most time was leisure. In agricultural societies, work was dictated by the seasons. Industrialization reduced workers' leisure. Workers have gained some leisure back. Among the industrialized nations, only the Japanese work more hours per year than do U.S. workers. Pp. 409–411.

■ The Future: Facing the Consequences of Global Capitalism

Expanding global trade, new technologies, and downsizing will continue to force a restructuring of work. Choices made now can lead to a better society or to a nightmare. Pp. 412–413.

Where can I read more on this topic?

Suggested Readings for this chapter are at the back of this book.

Sociology & the Internet

All URLs listed are current as of the printing of this book. URLs often change. Please check our Web site, **http://www.abacon.com/ henslin,** for updates.

1. Bartering, the direct exchange of one item for another, is the earliest medium of exchange. The Perspectives box on page 398 in this chapter describes the bartering that has developed in the former Soviet Union among cash-strapped individuals and businesses. Another place where bartering has become common is on the Internet. On these sites—**http://www.traderewards.com, http://www.wearsthebaby.com/mamabaarter.html,** and **http:// ubarter.com** you can see how bartering is being applied to the e-commerce economy.

   Prepare a report to your class about this new development. What gets exchanged? How is it managed? What types of individuals or businesses are likely to barter? In what ways do these Web sites reflect different types of bartering arrangements? What is it about the Internet that makes this a particularly appropriate place for the exchange of goods and services?

2. No doubt one of the reasons you are in college is so that you can get a good job after you graduate. In order to improve your chances in the job search, it would be wise to investigate the direction society and the economy are headed. In particular, what will tomorrow's jobs look like? Go to **http://stats.bls.gov/oco/ oco2003.htm** and read a report issued by the Bureau of Labor Statistics on employment trends. By clicking on the blue-colored text, you can view graphs of the forecasted changes in employment and study the composition of the labor force. Which occupations are expected to grow the fastest? Which are expected to decline? In what ways is the labor force expected to change? Using what you learned in this chapter, describe the social forces that are responsible for these changes. How are you likely to be affected?

3. Under capitalism, workers organize into labor unions in order to demand better pay and working conditions. Today, unions in this country face a number of critical issues. Traditionally, unions were most heavily concentrated in the manufacturing sector. As the manufacturing sector declined, so did union membership. In order to survive, unions have had to turn their attention to workers in those occupations that are growing. They have also had to find ways to address the concerns of new types of workers. Additionally, unions have had to try to protect their membership against the globalization of production by multinational corporations.

   To learn more about the contemporary union movement, go to **http://www.aflcio.org/home.htm,** the Web site for the American Federation of Labor-Congress of Industrial Organization, and **http://www.labornet.org,** the Web site for Labornet, a democratic communications network working to revitalize and rebuild the labor movement. Select two or three topics listed on these sites and browse through them. Write a paper in which you discuss the impact of recent changes—especially the growth of global capitalism—on workers today. Describe how unions are responding to this new stage of capitalism.

4. In this chapter, you read that in the early stages of industrialization the labor of children was common. In the United States in the nineteenth century, children were routinely employed in the mines and mills. Today, children in the Least Industrialized Nations often work in factories and fields. To learn more about the history of child labor in the United States, go to **http://www. historyplace.com/unitedstates/childlabor/index.html,** where you can view pictures of children employed in a wide range of industries and read brief descriptions of their activities. To learn more about child labor today, examine the reports written by the International Child Labor Program at **http://www.dol.gov/dol/ ilab/public/media/reports/main.htm.**

   In a report for your class, compare and contrast child labor in the United States with child labor in the Least Industrialized Nations. What countries and industries exploit children? Under what conditions do children work on farms and in the apparel industry? Why are children used in these capacities? An international organization working to end this practice is the Global March Against Child Labor, whose Web site can be accessed at **http://www.globalmarch.org.** What activities does this group support? Is child labor today due to global capitalism? How are multinational corporations responsible for child labor in the Least Industrialized Nations today?

Franklin McMahon, Visitors Viewing the United States Constitution and Bill of Rights

Politics

- **Micropolitics and Macropolitics**

- **Power, Authority, and Violence**
  Authority and Legitimate Violence
  Traditional Authority
  Rational-Legal Authority
  Charismatic Authority
  Authority as Ideal Type
  The Transfer of Authority

- **Types of Government**
  Monarchies: The Rise of the State
  Democracies: Citizenship as a Revolutionary Idea
  Dictatorships and Oligarchies: The Seizure
    of Power

- **The U.S. Political System**
  Political Parties and Elections
  Democratic Systems in Europe
  Voting Patterns
  Lobbyists and Special-Interest Groups
  PACs in U.S. Politics

- **Who Rules the United States?**
  The Functionalist Perspective: Pluralism
  The Conflict Perspective: The Power Elite, or
    Ruling Class
  Which View Is Right?

- **War and Terrorism: Means to Implement
  Political Objectives**
  Is War Universal?
  How Common Is War?
  Why Nations Go to War
  Costs of War
  Sowing the Seeds of Future Wars
  Nuclear, Biological, and Chemical Terrorism
  War and Dehumanization

- **A New World Order?**

- **Summary and Review**

I

In 1949, George Orwell wrote *1984,* a book about a future in which the government, known as "Big Brother," dominates society, dictating almost every aspect of each individual's life. Even to love someone is considered a sinister activity, a betrayal of the supreme love and total

allegiance that all citizens owe Big Brother.

Despite the danger, Winston and Julia fall in love. They meet furtively, always with the threat of discovery hanging over their heads. When informers turn them in, expert interrogators separate Julia and Winston, and proceed swiftly to quash their affection in order to restore their loyalty to Big Brother.

Then follows a remarkable account of Winston and his tormentor, O'Brien. Winston is strapped into a chair so tightly that he can't even move his head. O'Brien explains that although the infliction of pain is not always enough to break a person's will, everyone has a breaking point, some worst fear that will push that person over the edge.

O'Brien tells Winston that he has discovered his worst fear. He then sets a cage with two giant, starving sewer rats on the table next to Winston. O'Brien picks up a hood connected to the door of the cage and places it over Winston's head. In a quiet voice, he explains that when he presses the lever, the door of the cage will slide up, and the rats will shoot out like bullets and bore straight into Winston's face. Winston's eyes, the only part of his body that he can move, dart back and forth, revealing his terror. Speaking so quietly that Winston has to strain to hear him, O'Brien adds that the rats sometimes attack the eyes first, but sometimes they burrow through the cheeks and devour the

417

tongue. When O'Brien places his hand on the lever, Winston realizes that the only way out is for someone else to take his place. But who? Then he hears his own voice screaming, "Do it to Julia! . . . Tear her face off! Strip her to the bones. Not me! Julia! Not me!"

Orwell does not describe Julia's interrogation, but when Julia and Winston see each other later they realize that each has betrayed the other. Their love is gone. Big Brother has won.

Winston's misplaced loyalty had made him a political heretic, for it was the obligation of every citizen to place the state above all else in life. To preserve the state's dominance over the individual, Winston's allegiance had to be taken away from Julia. As you see, it was. ■

Although seldom this dramatic, politics is always about power and authority, the focus of this chapter.

MICROPOLITICS AND MACROPOLITICS

The images that come to mind when we think of politics are those of government—kings, queens, coups, dictatorships, running for office, voting. Politics, however, refers to power relations, and is a part of everyday life. As Weber (1922/1968) said, **power** is the ability to get your way even over the resistance of others. In every group, large or small, some individuals have power over others. Several employees trying to impress the new boss—who is going to decide which one of them will be promoted to manager—is an example of jockeying for power. So are parents' efforts to enforce a curfew despite protests from a reluctant daughter or son. Even the struggle over the TV remote control is an attempt to gain power. *Every group, then, is political, for in every group there is a power struggle of some sort.* Symbolic interactionists use the term **micropolitics** to refer to the exercise of power in everyday life (Schwartz 1990).

In contrast, **macropolitics**—the focus of this chapter—refers to the exercise of large-scale power over a large group. Governments, whether the dictatorship faced by Winston or the elected forms in the United States and Canada, are examples of macropolitics. Let's turn, then, to macropolitics, considering first the matter of authority.

POWER, AUTHORITY, AND VIOLENCE

power the ability to carry out one's will, even over the resistance of others

micropolitics the exercise of power in everyday life, such as deciding who is going to do the housework

macropolitics the exercise of large-scale power, the government being the most common example

authority power that people accept as rightly exercised over them; also called *legitimate power*

coercion power that people do not accept as rightly exercised over them; also called *illegitimate power*

To exist, every society must have a system of leadership. Some people must have power over others. As Max Weber (1913/1947) pointed out, however, we perceive power as legitimate or illegitimate. Legitimate power is called **authority**. This is power that people accept as right. In contrast, illegitimate power—called **coercion**—is power that people do not accept as just.

Imagine that you are on your way to buy a DVD player on sale for $250. As you are on your way to the store, a man jumps out of an alley and shoves a gun in your face. He demands your money. Frightened for your life, you hand over the $250. After filing a police report, you head back to college to take a sociology exam. You are running late, so you step on the gas. As the needle hits 85, you see flashing blue and red lights in your rear-view mirror. Your explanation about the robbery doesn't faze the officer—nor the judge who hears your case a few weeks later. She first lectures you on safety and then orders you to pay $50 in court costs plus $10 for every mile an hour over 65. You pay the $250.

The mugger, the police officer, and the judge—each has power, and in each case you part with $250. What, then, is the difference? The difference is that the mugger has no authority. His power is illegitimate—he has no *right* to do what he did. In contrast, you acknowledge that the officer has the right to stop you and that the judge has the right to fine you. They have authority, or legitimate power.

Authority and Legitimate Violence

As sociologist Peter Berger observed, it makes little difference whether you willingly pay the fine that the judge levies against you, or refuse to pay it. The court will get its money one way or another.

> There may be innumerable steps before its application [violence], in the way of warnings and reprimands. But if all the warnings are disregarded, even in so slight a matter as paying a traffic ticket, the last thing that will happen is that a couple of cops show up at the door with handcuffs and a Black Maria (billy club). Even the moderately courteous cop who hands out the initial traffic ticket is likely to wear a gun—just in case. (Berger 1963)

The *government,* then, also called the **state,** claims a monopoly on legitimate force or violence. This point, made by Max Weber (1946, 1922/1968)—that the state claims the exclusive right to use violence and the right to punish everyone else who does—is crucial to our understanding of politics. If someone owes you a debt, you cannot imprison that person or even forcibly take the money. The state, however, can. The ultimate proof of the state's authority is that you cannot kill someone because he or she has done something that you consider absolutely horrible—but the state can. As Berger (1963) summarized this matter, *"Violence is the ultimate foundation of any political order."*

Before we explore the origins of the modern state, let's first look at a situation in which the state loses legitimacy.

The Collapse of Authority Sometimes the state oppresses its people, and they resist their government just as they do a mugger. The people cooperate reluctantly—with a smile if that is what is required—while they eye the gun in the hand of the government's representatives. But, as they do with a mugger, if they are able they take up arms to free themselves. **Revolution,** armed resistance with the intent to overthrow a government, is not only a people's rejection of a government's claim to rule over them but also a rejection of its monopoly on violence. In a revolution, people claim that right for themselves. If successful, they establish a new state in which they claim the right to monopolize violence.

What some see as coercion, however, others see as authority. Consequently, while some people are ready to take up arms against a government, others remain loyal to it, willingly defend it, and perhaps even die for it. *The more that its power is seen as legitimate, then, the more stable a government is.*

But just why do people accept power as legitimate? Max Weber (1922/1968) identified three sources of authority: traditional, rational-legal, and charismatic. Let's examine each.

Traditional Authority

Throughout history, the most common basis for authority has been tradition. **Traditional authority,** which is based on custom, is the hallmark of preliterate groups. In these societies, custom dictates basic relationships. For example, birth makes a particular individual the chief, king, or queen. As far as members of that society are concerned, this is the right way to determine who shall rule because "We've always done it this way."

Gender relations in most human groups are an example of traditional authority, for they are based on custom. For example, in the villages of Spain widows are expected to wear only

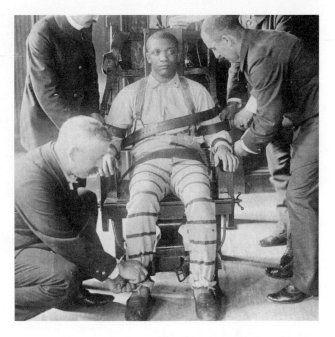

The ultimate foundation of any political order is violence. At no time is this more starkly demonstrated than when a government takes human life. Shown in this 1910 photo from Sing Sing Prison is a man about to be executed.

state a political entity that claims monopoly on the use of violence in some particular territory; commonly known as a country

revolution armed resistance designed to overthrow a government

traditional authority authority based on custom

For centuries, widows in the Mediterranean area were expected to dress in black for the rest of their lives. Widows conformed to this expression of lifetime sorrow for their deceased husband not because of law, but because of custom. As industrialization erodes traditional authority, fewer widows follow this practice.

black until they remarry. See the photo at the left. This generally means that they wear black for the rest of their lives. By law, a widow is free to wear any color she wishes, but not by tradition. Tradition, decreeing black, is so strong that if a widow were to violate this dress code, she would be seen as having profaned the memory of her deceased husband and would be ostracized by the community.

When a traditional society changes, it undermines traditional authority. For example, as a society industrializes, people have new experiences. This opens up new perspectives on life, and no longer does traditional authority go unchallenged. Thus, in Spain you can still see old women dressed in black from head to toe—and you immediately know their marital status. Younger widows, however, are likely to be indistinguishable from other women.

Traditional authority declines with industrialization, but it never dies out. In postindustrial societies, for example, parents exercise authority over their children *because* parents always have had such authority. From generations past, we inherit the idea that parents should discipline their children, choose their doctors and schools, and teach them religion and morality.

Rational-Legal Authority

The second type of authority, **rational-legal authority,** is not based on custom but on written rules. *Rational* means reasonable, and *legal* means part of law. Thus *rational-legal* refers to matters agreed to by reasonable people and written into law (or regulations of some sort). The matters agreed to may be as broad as a constitution that specifies the rights of all members of a society or as narrow as a contract between two individuals. Because bureaucracies are based on written rules, rational-legal authority is also called *bureaucratic authority.*

Rational-legal authority comes from the position that an individual holds, not from the person who holds the position. In a democracy, for example, the president's authority comes from the office, as specified in a written constitution, not from custom or the individual's personal characteristics. In rational-legal authority, everyone—no matter how high the office—is subject to the organization's written rules. In governments based on traditional authority, the ruler's word may be law, but in those based on rational-legal authority, the ruler's word is subject to the law.

Charismatic Authority

A few centuries back, in 1429, the English controlled large parts of France. When they prevented the coronation of a new French king, a farmer's daughter heard a voice telling her that God had a special assignment for her—that she should put on men's clothing, recruit an army, and go to war against the English. Inspired, Joan of Arc raised an army, conquered cities, and vanquished the English. Later that year, her visions were fulfilled as she stood next to Charles VII while he was crowned king of France. (Bridgwater 1953)

Joan of Arc is an example of **charismatic authority,** the third type of authority Weber identified. (*Charisma* is a Greek word that means a gift freely and graciously given [Arndt and Gingrich 1957].) A charismatic individual is someone to whom people are drawn because they believe that person has been touched by God or has been endowed by nature with exceptional qualities (Lipset 1993). The armies did not follow Joan of Arc because it was the custom to do so, as in traditional authority. Nor did they risk their lives alongside her because she held a position defined by written rules, as in rational-legal authority. Instead, peo-

rational-legal authority authority based on law or written rules and regulations; also called *bureaucratic authority*

charismatic authority authority based on an individual's outstanding traits, which attract followers

One of the best examples of charismatic authority is Joan of Arc, shown here at the coronation of Charles VII, whom she was instrumental in making king. Uncomfortable at portraying Joan of Arc wearing only a man's coat of armor, the artist has made certain she is wearing plenty of makeup, and also has added a ludicrous skirt.

ple followed her because they were drawn to her outstanding traits. They saw her as a messenger of God, fighting on the side of justice, and they accepted her leadership because of these appealing qualities.

The Threat Posed by Charismatic Leaders A king owes allegiance to tradition, and a president to written laws. To what, however, does a charismatic leader owe allegiance? Because their authority is based only on their personal ability to attract followers, charismatic leaders pose a threat to the established political system. They lead followers according to personal inclination, not according to the paths of tradition or the regulations of law. Accordingly, they can inspire followers to disregard—or even to overthrow—traditional and rational-legal authorities.

This means that charismatic leaders pose a threat to the established order. Consequently, traditional and rational-legal authorities are often quick to oppose charismatic figures. If they are not careful, however, their opposition may arouse even higher sentiment in favor of the charismatic leader, causing him or her to be viewed as a martyr. Occasionally the Roman Catholic church faces such a threat, as when a priest claims miraculous powers that appear to be accompanied by amazing healings. As people flock to this individual, they bypass parish priests and the formal ecclesiastical structure. This transfer of allegiance from the organization to an individual threatens the church bureaucracy. Consequently, the church hierarchy may encourage the priest to withdraw from the public eye, perhaps to a monastery, to rethink matters. Thus the threat is defused, rational-legal authority reasserted, and the stability of the organization maintained.

Charismatic authorities can be of any morality, from the saintly to the most bitterly evil. Like Joan of Arc, Adolf Hitler attracted throngs of people, providing the stuff of dreams and arousing them from disillusionment to hope. This poster from the 1930s, entitled *Es Lebe Deutschland* ("Long Live Germany"), illustrates the qualities of leadership that Germans of that period saw in Hitler.

Authority as Ideal Type

Weber's classifications—traditional, rational-legal, and charismatic—represent ideal types of authority. As noted on page 179, ideal type does not refer to what is ideal or desirable, but to a composite of characteristics found in many real-life examples. A particular leader, then, may show a combination of characteristics.

An example is John F. Kennedy, who combined rational-legal and charismatic authority. As the elected head of the U.S. government, Kennedy represented rational-legal authority. Yet his mass appeal was so great that his public speeches aroused large numbers of people to action. When in his inaugural address Kennedy said, "Ask not what your country can do for you, ask what you can do for your country," millions of Americans were touched. When Kennedy proposed a Peace Corps to help poorer countries, thousands of idealistic young people volunteered for challenging foreign service.

Charismatic and traditional authority can also overlap. The Ayatollah Khomeini of Iran, for example, was a religious leader, holding the traditional position of ayatollah. His embodiment of the Iranian people's dreams, however, as well as his austere life and devotion to principles of the Koran, gave him such mass appeal that he was also a charismatic leader. Khomeini's followers were convinced that he had been chosen by God, and his speeches could arouse tens of thousands of followers to action.

In rare instances, then, traditional and rational-legal leaders possess charismatic traits. This is unusual, however, and most authority is clearly one type or another.

The Transfer of Authority

The orderly transfer of authority from one leader to another is crucial for social stability. Under traditional authority, people know who is next in line. Under rational-legal authority, people may not know who the next leader will be, but they do know how that person will be selected. South Africa provides a remarkable example of the orderly transfer of authority under a rational-legal organization. Despite this country being ripped apart by decades of racial strife, accompanied not only by deep suspicions and hatreds but also by many murders committed by each side, by maintaining its rational-legal authority the country was able to peacefully transfer power from the dominant group led by President de Klerk to the minority group led by Nelson Mandela.

Charismatic authority, however, has no such rules of succession, which makes it inherently less stable than either traditional or rational-legal authority. Because charismatic au-

Crucial for society is the orderly transfer of power. One of the most remarkable transfers occurred in South Africa. Under this country's constitutional system, power was transferred from the white dominated government headed by Fredrik Willem De Klerk (on the right) to Nelson Mandela (on the left).

thority is built around a single individual, the death or incapacitation of a charismatic leader can mean a bitter struggle for succession. Consequently, some charismatic leaders make arrangements for an orderly transition of power by appointing a successor. This does not guarantee orderly succession, of course, for the followers may not perceive the designated heir in the same way as they did the charismatic leader. A second strategy is for the charismatic leader to build an organization, which then develops a system of rules or regulations, thus transforming itself into a rational-legal leadership. Weber used the term the **routinization of charisma** to refer to this transition of authority from a charismatic leader to either traditional or rational-legal authority.

TYPES OF GOVERNMENT

How do the various types of government—monarchies, democracies, dictatorships, and oligarchies—differ? As we compare them, let's also look at how the institution of the state arose, and how the idea of citizenship was revolutionary.

Monarchies: The Rise of the State

Early societies were small and needed no extensive political system. They operated more like an extended family, with decisions being made as they became necessary. As surpluses developed and societies grew larger, cities evolved—perhaps about 3500 B.C. (Fischer 1976). **City-states** then came into being, with power radiating outward from a city like a spider's web. Although the city controlled the immediate area around it, the areas between cities remained in dispute. Each city-state had its own **monarchy**, a king or queen whose right to rule was passed on to the children. If you drive through Spain, France, or Germany, you can still see evidence of former city-states. In the countryside, you will see only scattered villages. Farther on, your eye will be drawn to the outline of a castle on a faraway hill. As you get closer, you will see that the castle is surrounded by a city. Several miles farther, you will see another city, also dominated by a castle. Each city, with its castle, was once a center of power.

City-states often quarreled, and wars were common. The victorious ones extended their rule, and eventually a single city-state was able to wield power over an entire region. As the size of these regions grew, the people slowly developed an identity with the larger region. That is, they began to see distant inhabitants as "we" instead of "they." What we call the *state*—the political entity that claims a monopoly on the use of violence within a territory—came into being.

Democracies: Citizenship as a Revolutionary Idea

The United States had no city-states. Each colony, however, like a city-state, was small and independent. After the American Revolution, the colonies united. With the greater strength and resources that came from political unity, they conquered almost all of North America, bringing it under the power of a central government.

The government formed in this new country was called a **democracy.** (Derived from two Greek words—*kratos* [power], and *demos* [common people]—*democracy* literally means "power to the people.") Because of the bitter antagonisms associated with the revolution against the British king, the founders of the new country were distrustful of monarchies. They wanted to put political decisions into the hands of the people. This was not the first democracy the world had seen, but such a system had been tried before only with smaller groups. Athens, a city-state of Greece, practiced democracy two thousand years ago, with each free male above a certain age having the right to be heard and to vote. Members of some Native American tribes also were able to elect a chief, and in some, women were able to vote and to hold the office of chief. (The Incas and Aztecs of Mexico and Central America had monarchies.)

routinization of charisma the transfer of authority from a charismatic figure to either a traditional or a rational-legal form of authority

city-state an independent city whose power radiates outward, bringing the adjacent area under its rule

monarchy a form of government headed by a king or queen

democracy a system of government in which authority derives from the people; the term comes from two Greek words that translate literally as "power to the people"

Democracy was a heritage left by the British rule of India. The people take elections seriously, and the government transfers power peacefully from one party and candidate to another. Shown here are elephants as they carry ballot boxes to remote areas of the northern Indian state of Assam.

direct democracy a form of democracy in which the eligible voters meet together to discuss issues and make their decisions

representative democracy a form of democracy in which voters elect representatives to govern and make decisions on their behalf

citizenship the concept that birth (and residence) in a country impart basic rights

universal citizenship the idea that everyone has the same basic rights by virtue of being born in a country (or by immigrating and becoming a naturalized citizen)

dictatorship a form of government in which power is seized by an individual

oligarchy a form of government in which power is held by a small group of individuals; the rule of the many by the few

Because of their small size, tribes and cities were able to practice **direct democracy.** That is, they were small enough for the eligible voters to meet together, express their opinions, and then vote publicly—much like a town hall meeting today. As populous and spread out as the United States was, however, direct democracy was impossible, and **representative democracy** was invented. Certain citizens (at first only male white landowners) voted for men to represent them in Washington. Later the vote was extended to nonowners of property, to African-American men, then to women, and to others. Our new communications technologies, which make "electronic town meetings" possible, may also allow a new form of direct democracy. This issue is explored in the Mass Media box.

Today we take the idea of citizenship for granted. What is not evident to us is that the idea had to be conceived in the first place. There is nothing natural about citizenship—it is simply one way in which people choose to define themselves. Throughout most of human history, people were thought to *belong* to a clan, to a tribe, or even to a ruler. The idea of **citizenship**—that by virtue of birth and residence people have basic rights—is quite new to the human scene (Turner 1990).

The concept of representative democracy based on citizenship, perhaps the greatest gift the United States has given to the world, was revolutionary. Power was to be vested in the people themselves, and government was to flow from the people. That this concept was revolutionary is generally forgotten, but its implementation meant *the reversal of traditional ideas, for the government was to be responsive to the people's wishes, instead of the people being responsive to the wishes of the government.* To keep the government responsive to the needs of its citizens, people had not only the right, but the obligation, to express dissent. In a widely quoted statement, Thomas Jefferson observed that

> a little rebellion now and then is a good thing. . . . It is a medicine necessary for the sound health of government. . . . God forbid that we should ever be twenty years without such a rebellion. . . . The tree of liberty must be refreshed from time to time with the blood of patriots and tyrants. It is its natural manure. (In Hellinger and Judd 1991)

The idea of **universal citizenship**—of *everyone* having the same basic rights by virtue of being born in a country (or by immigrating and becoming a naturalized citizen)—flowered very slowly, and came into practice only through fierce struggle. When the United States was founded, for example, this idea was still in its infancy. Today it seems inconceivable to us that anyone should be denied the right to vote, hold office, make a contract, testify in court, or own property on the basis of gender or race-ethnicity. For earlier generations of Americans, however, it seemed just as inconceivable that women, African Americans, Native Americans, Asian Americans, and the poor should be allowed such rights.

Over the years, then, rights have been extended, and in the United States citizenship and its privileges now apply to all. No longer does property, sex, or race determine the right to vote, to testify in court, and so on. These characteristics, however, do influence whether or not one votes, as we shall see in a later section on voting patterns.

Dictatorships and Oligarchies: The Seizure of Power

If an individual seizes power and then dictates his will onto the people, the government is known as a **dictatorship.** If a small group seizes power, the government is called an **oligarchy.** The frequent coups in Central and South America, in which a few military leaders seize control of a country, are examples of oligarchies. Although one individual may be named president, it often is a group of high-ranking military officers, working behind the scenes, that makes the decisions. If their designated president becomes uncooperative, they remove him from office and designate another.

Mass Media in Social Life

POLITICS AND DEMOCRACY IN A TECHNOLOGICAL SOCIETY

"Politics is just like show business."—RONALD REAGAN

Is the new technology a threat to democracy? Politicians use computers, telephone link-ups, faxes, e-mail, and Web sites to take the pulse of the public—and to convey their platforms and their biases. Instead of tuning in and passively listening to a politician's speech, we now can interact with—talk back to—candidates and leaders via chat rooms, "electronic town meetings," and call-in radio and TV talk shows.

This shift to interactive communication lies at the heart of a debate over the health and future of our democracy. Critics charge that when officials use the new technology to constantly "take the public's temperature," they give more attention to minute shifts in public opinion than they do to the business of governing. Politicians use poll results to "fine tune" their public posturing—they take stands on issues without having any personal conviction about what is right. In other words, politicians now campaign nonstop.

A major issue is voting on the Internet. It may be possible for "televoting" to replace our representational democracy with a form of direct democracy. The people will be able to decide a wide variety of issues that politicians now decide for them. Voters will be able to sign petitions with digital signatures, and even go online to make laws.

Some fear that the Internet isn't safe for voting. There are no poll watchers, for example, so undue influence (threats, promises, or gifts in return for votes) would go undetected. Others raise a much more fundamental issue: Direct democracy might detour the U.S. Constitution's careful system of checks and balances, which was designed to safeguard us from the "tyranny of the majority." To determine from a poll that 51 percent of adults hold a certain opinion on an issue is one thing—that information can guide our leaders. But to have 51 percent of televoters determine a law or an issue is not the same as having elected representatives publicly argue a proposed law or an issue and then try to balance the interests of the many groups that make up their constituents.

Some point with alarm to the election of Jesse Ventura as governor of Minnesota. He ran as an independent, and for much of his campaign Ventura had no physical headquarters. Ventura fans used e-mail extensively, sending notes to friends and encouraging them to pass on the message. Even two-thirds of Ventura's fund-raising pledges arrived by e-mail. ■

For Your Consideration

Emphasizing visual image over substance, replacing reasoned leadership with nonstop campaigning,

Crucial for society is the orderly transfer of power. Under its constitutional system, the United States is remarkably stable: Power is transferred peacefully—even when someone of an unusual background wins an election. Jesse Ventura, shown here, is now governor of Minnesota.

fundamentally changing our current form of democracy—do you think these are real issues? Do you think direct democracy would be superior to representational democracy? Is an e-mail campaign any worse than 30-second "sound bites"? How do you think the mass media could be used to *improve* government? Do you think Ventura's election breathed some fresh air into the stale world of politics, or was it an indication that the Internet poses a danger to U.S. politics? Or was it something else entirely?

Sources: "Democracy and Technology" 1995; Diamond and Silverman 1995; Grossman 1995; Fineman 1999; Raney 1999; Seib 2000.

Monarchies, dictatorships, and oligarchies vary in the amount of control they exert over their people. **Totalitarianism** is almost *total* control of a people by the government. As our opening vignette demonstrated, totalitarian regimes tolerate no opposing opinion. In Nazi Germany, for example, Hitler organized a ruthless secret police force, the Gestapo, which searched for any sign of dissent. Spies even watched moviegoers' reactions to newsreels, reporting those who did not respond "appropriately" (Hippler 1987).

In totalitarian regimes, the names of those who rule may change, but the techniques of control remain similar. Threats and terror force citizen compliance and allow the dictator to remain in power. Privacy is viewed as a threat to the regime, and the police may keep a dossier

totalitarianism a form of government that exerts almost total control over the people

on each citizen. A description of Nazi Germany could just as well be applied to the Soviet Union under Stalin or Iraq under Saddam Hussein. The police, courts, armed forces, and entire government bureaucracy are directly accountable to the dictator. Individual rights, if they existed prior to the dictator, simply disappear, while if individuals dissent, they disappear.

People around the world find the ideas of citizenship and representative democracy appealing. Those who have no say in their government's decisions, or who face prison for expressing dissent, find in these ideas the hope for a brighter future. With today's electronic communications, people no longer remain ignorant of whether they are more or less privileged politically than others. This knowledge produces pressure for greater citizen participation in government. As electronic communications develop further, this pressure will increase.

THE U.S. POLITICAL SYSTEM

With this global background, let's examine the U.S. political system. We shall consider the two major political parties and elections, compare the U.S. political system with other democratic systems, and examine voting patterns and the role of lobbyists and PACs.

Political Parties and Elections

After the founding of the United States, numerous political parties emerged, but by the time of the Civil War, two parties dominated U.S. politics (Burnham 1983): the Democrats, who in the public mind are associated with the working class, and the Republicans, who are associated with wealthier people. Each party nominates candidates, and in pre-elections, called *primaries,* the voters decide which candidates will represent their party. Each candidate then campaigns, trying to appeal to the most voters. Figure 15.1 on page 428 shows how Americans align themselves with political parties.

Although the Democrats and Republicans represent different philosophical principles, each party appeals to such a broad membership that it is difficult to distinguish a conservative Democrat from a liberal Republican. The extremes, however, are easy to discern. Deeply committed Democrats support legislation that transfers income from one group to another or that controls wages, working conditions, and competition. Dyed-in-the-wool Republicans oppose such legislation.

Those elected to Congress may cross party lines. That is, some Democrats vote for legislation proposed by Republicans, and *vice versa.* This happens because officeholders support their party's philosophy but not necessarily its specific proposals. Thus, when it comes to a specific bill, such as raising the minimum wage, some conservative Democrats may view the measure as unfair to small employers, or too costly, and vote with the Republicans against the bill. At the same time, liberal Republicans—feeling that the proposal is just, or sensing a dominant sentiment in voters back home—may side with its Democratic backers.

Regardless of their differences, however, the Democrats and Republicans represent *different slices of the center.* Although each may ridicule its opposition and promote different legislation, each party firmly supports such fundamentals of U.S. political philosophy as free public education, a strong military, freedom of religion, speech, assembly, and, of course, capitalism—especially the private ownership of property.

Third parties also play a role in U.S. politics, but to have any influence they, too, must support these centrist themes. Any party that advocated their radical change is doomed to a short life of little political consequence. Because most Americans consider a vote for a third party a waste, third parties do notoriously poorly at the polls. Two exceptions are Theodore Roosevelt's Bull Moose party, which won more votes in 1912 than Taft, the Republican presidential candidate, and the United We

As a quarterback at the University of Oklahoma, J. C. Watts guided the Sooners to two Orange Bowl victories. Now, as a Republican and a leader in the House of Representatives, Watts is pushing the Republican party to support more social spending. Because the Democrats and Republicans represent different slices of the center of political thought, Watts is difficult to distinguish from a conservative Democrat.

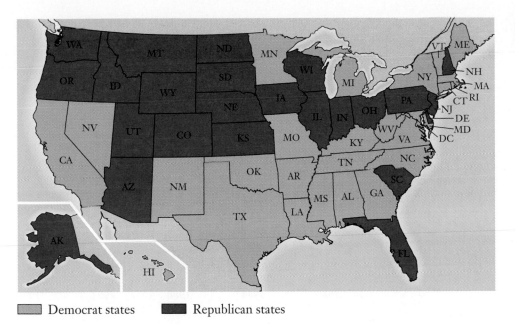

Democrat states   Republican states

Figure 15.1

SOCIAL MAP: POLITICAL PARTIES IN THE UNITED STATES

Which party dominates, Democrat or Republican?

Note: Based on the composition of the state legislatures. In the case of Delaware, Nevada, New York, N. Carolina, S. Carolina, and Texas, whose lower and upper houses are dominated by different parties, the percentage of the legislators was used. For Nebraska, whose legislators are elected with no party designation, percentage vote for president was used. The most recent available data in the source is 1996.

Source: Statistical Abstract 1999: Table 479.

Stand (now Reform) party, headed by billionaire political hopeful Ross Perot, which won 19 percent of the vote in 1992, but only 8 percent in 1996 (Bridgwater 1953; *Statistical Abstract* 1995:Table 437; 1999:Table 466).

Democratic Systems in Europe

We tend to take our political system for granted and assume that any other democracy looks like ours—even down to having two major parties. Such is not the case. To gain a comparative understanding, let's look at the European system.

Although both theirs and ours are democracies, there are fundamental distinctions between the two (Domhoff 1979, 1983; Lind 1995). First, elections in most of Europe are not winner-take-all. In the United States, elections are determined by a simple majority. For example, if a Democrat wins 51 percent of the votes cast in an electoral district, he or she takes office. The Republican candidate, who may have won 49 percent, loses everything. In contrast, most European countries base their elections on a system of **proportional representation;** that is, the seats in the national legislature are divided according to the proportion of votes each political party receives. If one party wins 51 percent of the vote, for example, that party is awarded 51 percent of the seats; while a party with 49 percent of the votes receives 49 percent of the seats.

Second, proportional representation encourages minority parties, while the winner-take-all system discourages them. As we saw, the U.S. system pushes parties to the center as they strive to obtain the broadest possible support they need to win elections. For this reason, the United States has **centrist parties.** The proportional representation followed in most European countries means that if a party gets 10 percent of the voters to support its candidate, it will get 10 percent of the seats. This system encourages the formation of **noncentrist parties,** those that propose less popular or even offbeat ideas. For example, a party may make its central platform a return to the gold standard, or the retirement of nuclear weapons and the shutting down of nuclear power reactors.

Three main results follow from being able to win even just a few seats in the national legislature. First, if a minority party has officeholders, it gains access to the media throughout the year, receiving publicity that helps keep its issues alive. Second, small parties gain power beyond their numbers. Because many parties compete in the elections, no single party is likely to gain a majority of the seats in the national legislature. To muster the required votes to make national decisions, the party with the most seats must align itself with one or more of the smaller parties and form a **coalition government.** A party with only

proportional representation an electoral system in which seats in a legislature are divided according to the proportion of votes each political party receives

centrist party a political party that represents the center of political opinion

noncentrist party a political party that represents marginal ideas

coalition government a government in which a country's largest party aligns itself with one or more smaller parties

10 or 15 percent of the seats, then, may be able to trade its vote on some issues for the larger party's support on others. Third, because coalitions break down, the governments tend to be less stable. Italy, for example, has had fifty-seven different governments since World War II, compared with the United States, which has had ten presidents since then. To add greater stability, the Italians have voted that three-fourths of their Senate seats will be decided on the winner-take-all system (Melloan 1993b; "Italy's Revolving-Door Prime Minister" 1999).

Voting Patterns

Let's examine the major voting patterns in the U.S., and then consider reasons for them.

Year after year, Americans show consistent voting patterns. From Table 15.1, you can see that the percentage of people who vote increases with age. The exception is those ages 21 to

Table 15.1

WHO VOTES IN U.S. PRESIDENTIAL ELECTIONS?

	1980	1984	1988	1992	1996
Overall					
Americans Who Vote	59%	60%	57%	61%	54%
Age					
18–20	36	37	33	39	31
21–24	38	44	46	33	24
25–34	55	58	48	53	43
35–44	64	64	61	64	55
45–64	69	70	68	70	64
65 and up	65	68	69	70	67
Sex					
Male	59	59	56	60	53
Female	59	61	58	62	56
Race/Ethnicity[a]					
Whites	61	61	59	64	56
African Americans	51	56	52	54	51
Latinos	30	33	29	29	27
Education					
Grade school only	43	43	37	35	28
High school dropout	46	44	41	41	34
High school graduate	59	59	55	58	49
College dropout	67	68	65	69	61
College graduate	80	79	78	81	73
Labor Force					
Employed	62	62	58	64	55
Unemployed	41	44	39	46	37
Income					
Under $5,000	38	39	35	NA	NA
$5,000 to $9,999	46	49	41	NA	NA
$10,000 to $14,999	54	55	48	NA	NA
$15,000 to $19,999	57	60	54	NA	NA
$20,000 to $24,999	61	67	58	NA	NA
$25,000 to $34,999	67	74	64	NA	NA
$35,000 and over	74	74	70[b]	NA	NA

[a]Other race-ethnic groups are not listed in the sources.

[b]For 1988, the percentage is an average of $35,000 to $49,900 and over $50,000.

Sources: Statistical Abstract 1991:Table 450; 1997:Table 462; *Current Population Reports,* Series P-20, vols. 440, 446, 504.

PERSPECTIVES | Cultural Diversity in the United States

THE POLITICS OF IMMIGRANTS: POWER, ETHNICITY, AND SOCIAL CLASS

That the United States is the land of immigrants is a truism; every schoolchild knows that since the English Pilgrims first landed on Plymouth Rock, successive groups—among them Germans, Scandinavians, Italians, Poles, and Greeks—crossed the Atlantic Ocean to reach U.S. shores.

Some, such as the Irish immigrants in the late 1800s and early 1900s, left to escape brutal poverty and famine. Others, such as the Jews of czarist Russia, fled a government that singled them out for persecution. Some were seeking refuge or asylum from lands ravaged by war. Others, called *entrepreneurial immigrants,* sought economic opportunities that were absent in their native lands. Still others came as *sojourners* who planned to return home after a temporary stay. Some, not usually called immigrants, came in chains, held in bondage by early immigrants.

Today, the United States witnesses its second large wave of immigration. The first, in the early 1900s, consisted largely of Europeans. Those immigrants came to account for 13 percent of the U.S. population. Today, the mix of immigrants—currently about 8 percent of the population—is far more diverse. Most are from Asia, Mexico, the Caribbean, and South and Central America. More

than twice as many immigrants come from Asia than from Europe. Since 1980, more than 11 million legal immigrants have settled in the United States. Another 5 million are here illegally.

In the last century, U.S.-born Americans feared that immigrants would subvert the democratic system in favor of socialism or communism. Today some fear that the millions of immigrants from Spanish-speaking countries threaten the primacy of the English language. As in the last century, the fear that immigrants will take jobs away from U.S.-born Americans remains strong. In addition, minority groups that struggled for political participation fear that newer groups will gain political power at their expense.

What route to political participation do immigrants take? In general, they first organize as a group on the basis of *ethnicity* rather than *class.* In response to common problems, especially discrimination and adapting to a new way of life, they reaffirm their cultural identity. "This represents the first effective step in their social and political incorporation," note sociologists Alejandro Portes and Ruben Rumbaut. "By mobilizing the collective vote and by electing their own to office, immigrant minorities have learned the rules of the democratic

game and absorbed its values in the process."

Irish immigrants to Boston illustrate this pattern of banding together on the basis of ethnicity. They built a power base that put the Irish in political control of the city and, ultimately, saw John F. Kennedy, one of their own, sworn in as president of the United States.

As Portes and Rumbaut observe, "Assimilation as the rapid transformation of immigrants into Americans 'as everyone else' has never happened." Instead, all immigrant groups began by fighting for their own interests as Irish, Italians, and so on. Only when they had attained enough political power to overcome discrimination did they become "like everyone else"—that is, like others who had power.

Thus, only when a certain level of political power is achieved, when groups gain political representation somewhat proportionate to their numbers, does social class become more significant than race-ethnicity. This, then, is the path that immigrants follow in their socialization into the U.S. political system. ■

Sources: Portes and Rumbaut 1990; Salholz 1990; Prud'Homme 1991; James 1993; *Statistical Abstract* 1999:Tables 8, 10, 56.

24. This table also shows the significance of race-ethnicity. Non-Hispanic whites are more likely to vote than are African Americans, while Latinos are the least likely to vote. The significance of race-ethnicity is so great that non-Hispanic whites are more than twice as likely to vote as are Latinos. A crucial aspect of the socialization of newcomers to the United States is to learn the U.S. political system, the topic of the Perspectives box above.

Table 15.1 also shows that voting increases with education. College graduates are more than twice as likely to vote as those who don't complete high school. Employment and income are also significant. People who make more than $35,000 a year are twice as likely to vote as those who make less than $5,000. Finally, note that women are slightly more likely to vote than men.

Social Integration How can we explain the voting patterns shown in Table 15.1? The people most likely to vote are older, more educated, affluent, employed whites, while those least likely to vote are poor, younger, ill-educated, unemployed Latinos. From these patterns, we can draw this principle: *The more that people feel they have a stake in the political system,*

the more likely they are to vote. They have more to protect, and feel that voting can make a difference. In effect, people who have been rewarded by the political system feel more socially integrated. They vote because they perceive that elections directly affect their own lives and the type of society in which they and their children live.

Alienation and Apathy   In contrast, those who gain less from the system—in terms of education, income, and jobs—are more likely to feel alienated from politics. Looking at themselves as outsiders, many feel hostile to the government. Some feel betrayed, believing that politicians have sold out to special interest groups. They are convinced that "all politicians are liers." Minorities who feel the U.S. political system is a "white" system are less likely to vote.

From Table 15.1, we see that many highly educated people with good incomes also stay away from the polls. Many people do not vote because of **voter apathy,** or indifference. Their view is that "next year will just bring more of the same, regardless of who is president." A common attitude of those who are apathetic is "What difference will my one vote make when there are millions of voters?" Many see little difference between the two major political parties.

Alienation and apathy are so common that *half* of the eligible voters do not vote for president, and only *one-third* of the nation's eligible voters bother to vote for candidates for Congress (*Statistical Abstract* 1999:Table 490).

How People Vote   Historically, men and women have voted the same way. Now when they go to the ballot box, however, they are somewhat more likely to vote for different presidential candidates. This *gender gap in politics,* which has just appeared, is illustrated in Table 15.2. This table also shows the older and much larger racial-ethnic gap in politics. Note how few African Americans vote for a Republican presidential candidate.

Voting patterns reflect life experiences, especially economic circumstances. On average, women and African Americans earn less than men and whites, and at this point in history women and African Americans tend to look more favorably on government programs that redistribute income (Seib 1996).

voter apathy indifference and inaction on the part of individuals or groups with respect to the political process

special-interest group a group of people who have a particular issue in common who can be mobilized for political action

lobbyists people who influence legislation on behalf of their clients

Lobbyists and Special-Interest Groups

Suppose that you are president of the United States, and you want to make milk and bread more affordable for the poor. As you check into the matter, you find that one reason prices are high is because the government is paying farmers millions of dollars a year in price supports (*Statistical Abstract* 1996:Table 1091; 1999:Tables 1109, 1110). You therefore propose to eliminate these subsidies.

Immediately, large numbers of people leap into action. They send telegrams and e-mail to your office, contact their senators and representatives, and call reporters for news conferences. The Associated Press distributes pictures of a farm family—their Holsteins grazing contentedly in the background—and informs readers how this hard-working, healthy, happy family of good Americans who are struggling to make a living will be destroyed by your harsh proposal. President or not, you have little chance of getting your legislation passed.

What happened? The dairy industry went to work to protect its special interests. A **special-interest group** consists of people who think alike on a particular issue and who can be mobilized for political action. The dairy industry is just one of thousands of such groups that employ **lobbyists,** people who are paid to influence legislation on behalf of their clients. Special-

Table 15.2

HOW THE TWO-PARTY PRESIDENTIAL VOTE IS SPLIT

	1988	1992	1996
Women			
Democrat	50%	61%	65%
Republican	50%	39%	35%
Men			
Democrat	44%	55%	50%
Republican	56%	45%	50%
African Americans			
Democrat	92%	94%	99%
Republican	8%	6%	1%
Whites			
Democrat	41%	53%	54%
Republican	59%	47%	46%

Note: 1996 is the latest year reported in the 1999 source.

Source: Statistical Abstract 1999:Table 464.

interest groups and lobbyists have become a major force in U.S. politics. Members of Congress who want to be re-elected must pay attention to them, for they represent blocs of voters who have a vital interest in the outcome of specific bills. Well financed and able to contribute huge sums, lobbyists can deliver votes to you—or to your opponent.

Because so much money was being passed under the table from special-interest groups to members of Congress, in the 1970s Congress passed legislation to limit the amount that any individual, corporation, or special-interest group can give a candidate, and to require all contributions over $1,000 to be reported. Special-interest groups immediately did an end sweep around the new laws by forming **political action committees (PACs)**, organizations that solicit contributions from many donors—each contribution being within the allowable limit—and then use the large total to influence legislation.

PACs are powerful, for they bankroll lobbyists and legislators. To influence politics, about 4,000 PACs shell out $220 million a year directly to their candidates (*Statistical Abstract* 1999:Table 499). They also contribute millions in indirect ways, such as by giving "honorariums" to Senators who agree to say a few words at a breakfast. A few PACs represent broad social interests such as environmental protection, but most stand for narrow financial concerns, such as the dairy, oil, banking, and construction industries. Those PACs with the most clout in terms of money and votes gain the ear of Congress. To politicians, the sound of money talking apparently sounds like the voice of the people.

> **political action committee (PAC)**
> an organization formed by one or more special-interest groups to solicit and spend funds for the purpose of influencing legislation

PACs in U.S. Politics

Suppose that you want to run for the Senate. To have a chance of winning, you must not only shake hands around the state, be photographed hugging babies, and eat a lot of chicken dinners at local civic organizations, but you must also send out hundreds of thousands of pieces of mail to solicit votes and financial support. During the home stretch, television ads may run $700,000 a week (Harwood 1994). If you are an *average* candidate for the Senate, you will spend $5 million on your campaign. To run for the House will cost a paltry one half million dollars (*Statistical Abstract* 1999:Tables 472, 498).

Now suppose that it is only a few weeks from the election, the polls show you and your opponent neck and neck, and your war chest is empty. The representatives of a couple of PACs pay you a visit. One says that his organization will pay for a mailing, while the other offers to buy television and radio ads. You feel somewhat favorable toward their positions anyway, and you accept. Once elected, you owe them. When legislation that affects their interests comes up for vote, their representatives call you—at your unlisted number at home—and tell you how they want you to vote. It would be political folly to double-cross them.

It is said that the first duty of a politician is to get elected—and the second duty is to get reelected. If you are an average senator, to finance your reelection campaign you must raise $2,300 *every single day* of your six-year term. It is no wonder that money has been dubbed the "mother's milk of politics."

Criticism of Lobbyists and PACs The major criticism leveled against lobbyists and PACs is that their money, in effect, buys votes. Rather than representing the people who elected them, legislators support the special interests of groups that have the ability to help them stay in power. The influence of foreign lobbyists has been a target of especially harsh criticism. As shown in Figure 15.2 the top ten foreign lobbyists spend $163 million annually to influence votes. Japan has hired more than 100 former U.S. government officials to pressure members of Congress to reduce quotas and duties on imports of its products. During election years, Japan contributes to *both* presidential candidates. Critics argue that the playing field is not level, for Japan has made it a crime for foreigners to influence its legislation (Judis 1990; Duffy 1992).

Even if the United States were to outlaw PACs, special-interest groups would not disappear from the U.S. political scene. Lobbyists walked the corridors of the Senate long before PACs, and since the time of Alexander Graham Bell they have carried the unlisted numbers of members of Congress. For good or ill, lobbyists play an essential role in the U.S. political system.

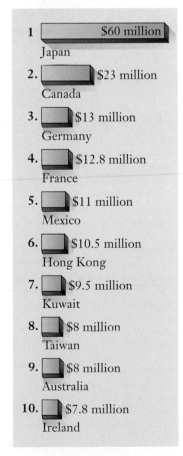

Figure 15.2

FOREIGN LOBBYISTS: THE TOP 10 SPENDERS

1. $60 million — Japan
2. $23 million — Canada
3. $13 million — Germany
4. $12.8 million — France
5. $11 million — Mexico
6. $10.5 million — Hong Kong
7. $9.5 million — Kuwait
8. $8 million — Taiwan
9. $8 million — Australia
10. $7.8 million — Ireland

Source: Engelberg and Tolchin 1993.

The Great Depression transformed Americans' attitudes about government intervention in economic matters. Shown here is a 1939 poster that was displayed in post offices and other public buildings throughout the country.

anarchy a condition of lawlessness or political disorder caused by the absence or collapse of governmental authority

pluralism the diffusion of power among many interest groups, preventing any single group from gaining control of the government

checks and balances the separation of powers among the three branches of U.S. government—legislative, executive, and judicial—so that each is able to nullify the actions of the other two, thus preventing the domination of any single branch

power elite C. Wright Mills's term for those who rule the United States: the top people in the leading corporations, the most powerful generals and admirals of the armed forces, and certain elite politicians

Who Rules the United States?

With lobbyists and PACs so influential, just whom do U.S. senators and representatives really represent? This question has led to a lively debate among sociologists.

The Functionalist Perspective: Pluralism

Functionalists view the state as having arisen out of the basic needs of the social group. To protect themselves from oppressors, people formed a government and gave it the monopoly on violence. The risk is that the state can turn that force against its own citizens. To return to the example used earlier, states have a tendency to become muggers. Thus, people must find a balance between having no government—which would lead to **anarchy,** a condition of disorder and violence—and having a government that protects them from violence, but that also may itself turn against them. When functioning well, then, the state is a balanced system that protects its citizens—from one another *and* from government.

What keeps the U.S. government from turning against its citizens? Functionalists say that **pluralism,** a diffusion of power among many interest groups, prevents any one group from gaining control of the government and using it to oppress the people (Polsby 1959; Huber and Form 1973; Dahl 1961, 1982). To keep the government from coming under the control of any one group, the founders of the United States set up three branches of government: the executive branch (the president), the judiciary branch (the courts), and the legislative branch (the Senate and House of Representatives). Each is sworn to uphold the Constitution, which guarantees rights to citizens, and each can nullify the actions of the other two. This system, known as **checks and balances,** was designed to ensure that power remains distributed and that no one branch of government dominates.

Women, men, race-ethnic groups, farmers, factory and office workers, religious groups, bankers, bosses, the unemployed, coal miners, the retired, as well as the broader categories of the rich, middle class, and poor, are all parts of our pluralist society. Because each has political muscle to flex at the polls, to be reelected politicians must take them into consideration. Thus, as each group pursues its own interests, it is balanced by other groups pursuing theirs. As special-interest groups negotiate with one another and reach compromises, conflict is minimized, and the resulting policies gain wide support. Consequently, say functionalists, no one group rules, and the political system is responsive to the people.

The Conflict Perspective: The Power Elite, or Ruling Class

Conflict theorists disagree. If you focus on the lobbyists scurrying around Washington, they say, you get a blurred image of superficial activities. What really counts is the big picture, not its fragments. The important question is who holds the power that determines the overarching policies of the United States. For example, who determines how many Americans will be out of work by raising or lowering interest rates? Who sets policies that transfer jobs from the United States to countries with low-cost labor? And the ultimate question of power: Who is behind decisions to go to war?

Sociologist C. Wright Mills (1956) took the position that the country's most important matters are not decided by lobbyists or even by Congress. Rather, the decisions that have the greatest impact on the lives of Americans—and people across the face of the globe—are made by a *power elite.* The **power elite** consists of a coalition of individuals who have similar interests and access to the center of U.S. political power. As depicted in Figure 15.3 on the next page, the power elite consists of the top leaders of the largest corporations, the most powerful generals and admirals of the armed forces, and certain elite politicians—the president, his cabinet, and select senior members of Congress who chair the major committees. It is they who wield power, who make the decisions that direct the country and shake the world (Hellinger and Judd 1991; Ferguson 1995).

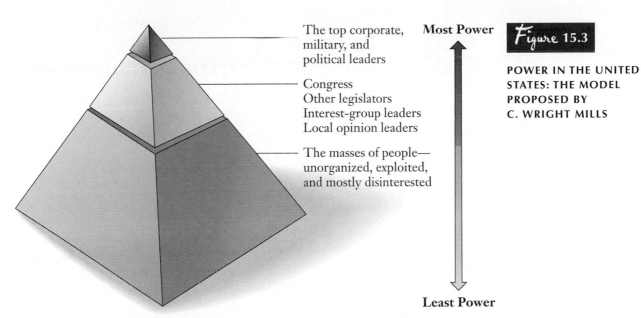

Most Power

The top corporate, military, and political leaders

Congress
Other legislators
Interest-group leaders
Local opinion leaders

The masses of people—unorganized, exploited, and mostly disinterested

Least Power

Figure 15.3

POWER IN THE UNITED STATES: THE MODEL PROPOSED BY C. WRIGHT MILLS

Source: Based on Mills 1956.

Are the three groups that make up the power elite—the top corporate, political, and military leaders—equal in power? Mills said they were not, and he pointed not to the president and his staff or even to the generals and admirals as the most dominant group, but, instead, to the corporate heads. Because all three segments of the power elite view capitalism as essential to the welfare of the country, business interests, he said, come foremost in setting national policy. (Remember the incident mentioned in the previous chapter (pages 402–403) of the U.S. president selling airplanes.)

Sociologist William Domhoff (1967, 1990) uses the term **ruling class** to refer to the power elite. He focuses on the 1 percent of Americans who belong to the super rich, the powerful capitalist class studied in Chapter 10 (pages 263–265). Members of this class control our top corporations and foundations, even the boards that oversee our major universities. It is no accident, says Domhoff, that from this group the president chooses most members of his cabinet and appoints the top ambassadors to the most powerful countries of the world.

Conflict theorists point out that we should not think of the power elite (or ruling class) as a group that meets together in order to agree on specific matters. Rather, it consists of people whose backgrounds and orientations to life are so similar—they attend prestigious private schools, belong to exclusive private clubs, and are millionaires many times over—that they share the same values and goals. Their behavior stems not from some grand conspiracy to control the country, but, instead, from a mutual interest in solving the problems that face big business (Useem 1984). With their political connections extending to the top centers of power, this elite determines the economic and political conditions under which the rest of the country operates (Domhoff 1990, 1998). We shall return to this line of inquiry later.

Which View Is Right?

The functionalist and conflict views of power in U.S. society cannot be reconciled. Either competing interests block the dominance of any single group, as functionalists assert, or a power elite oversees the major decisions of the United States, as conflict theorists maintain. Perhaps at the middle level of Mills' model, depicted in Figure 15.3, the competing interest groups do keep each other at bay, and none is able to dominate. If so, the functionalist view would apply to this middle level, as well as the lowest level of power. Perhaps functionalists have not looked high enough, however, and activities at the peak remain invisible to them. If so, on that level lies the key to U.S. power, the dominance by an elite whose members are following their mutual interests.

The answer, however, is not yet conclusive. For that, we must await more research.

ruling class another term for the power elite

WAR AND TERRORISM: MEANS TO IMPLEMENT POLITICAL OBJECTIVES

As we have noted, an essential characteristic of the state is that it claims a monopoly on violence. At times, a state may direct that violence against other nations. **War**, armed conflict between nations (or politically distinct groups), is often part of national policy. Let's look at this aspect of politics.

Is War Universal?

Although human aggression and individual killing characterize all human groups, war does not. War is simply *one option* that groups may choose for dealing with disagreements; but not all societies choose this option. The Mission Indians of North America, the Arunta of Australia, the Andaman Islanders of the South Pacific, and the Eskimos of the Arctic, for example, had procedures to handle aggression and quarrels, but they did not have organized battles that pitted one tribe or group against another. These groups do not even have a word for war (Lesser 1968).

How Common Is War?

One of the contradictions of humanity is that people long for peace while at the same time they glorify war. The glorification of war can be seen by noting how major battles hog the center of a country's retelling of its history and how monuments to generals, patriots, and battles are scattered throughout the land. From May Day parades in Moscow's Red Square to the Fourth of July celebrations in the United States and the Cinco de Mayo victory marches in Mexico, war and revolution are interwoven into the fabric of daily life.

To find out how often war occurred in European history, sociologist Pitirim Sorokin (1937) counted the wars from 500 B.C. to A.D. 1925. He documented 967 wars, an average of one war every two to three years. Counting years or parts of a year in which a country was at war, at 28 percent Germany had the lowest record of warfare, while Spain's 67 percent gave it the dubious distinction of being the most war-prone. Sorokin found that Russia, the land of his birth, had experienced only one peaceful quarter-century during the entire previous thousand years. Since the time of William the Conqueror, who took power in 1066, England was at war an average of 56 out of each 100 years. Spain fought even more often. It is worth noting the history of the United States in this regard: Since 1850, it has intervened militarily around the world more than 150 times, an average of *more than once a year* (Kohn 1988). With Grenada, Panama, Kuwait, Somalia, Haiti, Bosnia, and Kosovo, the pattern continues.

Why Nations Go to War

Why do nations choose war to handle disputes? Sociologists answer this question by focusing not on factors *within* humans, such as aggressive impulses, but by looking for *social causes*—conditions in society that encourage or discourage combat between nations.

Sociologist Nicholas Timasheff (1965) identified three essential conditions of war. The first is a cultural tradition of war. Because their nation has fought wars in the past, the leaders of a group see war as an option for dealing with serious disagreements with other nations. The second is an antagonistic situation in which two or more states confront incompatible objectives. For example, each may want the same land or resources. The third is a "fuel" that heats the antagonistic situation to a boiling point, so that people cross the line from thinking about war to actually engaging in it. Timasheff identified seven such "fuels." He found that war is likely if a country's leaders see the antagonistic situation as an opportunity to achieve one of the following objectives:

1. Gain revenge or settle "old scores" from previous conflicts
2. Dictate their will to a weaker nation
3. Enhance the nation's prestige, or save the nation's "honor"

war armed conflict between nations or politically distinct groups

4. Unite rival groups within their country

5. Protect or exalt their own position

6. Satisfy the national aspirations of ethnic groups, bringing under their rule "our people" who are living in another country

7. Forcibly convert others to religious and ideological beliefs

Costs of War

One side effect of the new technologies stressed in this text has been a growing capacity to inflict death. During World War I, bombs claimed fewer than 3 of every 100,000 people in England and Germany. During World War II, the combatants fought with more powerful airplanes and bombs. Their sense of it being wrong to kill noncombatants diminished, and this figure increased a hundredfold, to 300 of every 100,000 civilians (Hart 1957). As you know, further technological advances in human destruction have so increased our killing capacity that if a war were fought with nuclear bombs the death rate could run 100 percent.

War is also costly in terms of money. As shown in Table 15.3, the United States has spent $4 trillion on nine major wars. Despite its massive cost in lives and property, warfare continues as a common technique for pursuing political objectives. For about seven years, the United States fought in Vietnam—at a cost of 59,000 American and about 2 million Vietnamese lives (Herring 1989; Hellinger and Judd 1991). For nine years, the Soviet Union waged war in Afghanistan—with a death toll of about 1 million Afghanistani and perhaps 20,000 Soviet soldiers (Armitage 1989). An eight-year war between Iran and Iraq cost about 400,000 lives. The total exacted by Cuban mercenaries in Africa and South America is unknown. Also unknown is the number of lives—almost exclusively Iraqi—lost in "Desert Storm," a brief war against Iraq by international forces led by the United States. The figure of 100,000 losses on the Iraqi side has been suggested by media reports. Not even counting the slaughter in Rwanda, the topic of the opening vignette of Chapter 12, civil wars in Africa, Asia, and South America have claimed hundreds of thousands of lives, mostly civilian noncombatants. Colombia, Egypt, India, Indonesia, Israel, Peru, Sierra Leone, Sudan, Turkey, Uganda—the list grows, with more names added yearly.

Sowing the Seeds of Future Wars

The hypocrisy is incredible. The Most Industrialized Nations lament the regional conflicts that can escalate into larger wars, yet they zealously pursue profits by selling advanced war technology to the Least Industrialized Nations. When one Least Industrialized Nation buys high-tech weapons, its neighbors get nervous, sparking an arms race among them (Cole and Lubman 1994; Ricks 1994). Table 15.4 shows that the United States is the chief merchant of death. Great Britain and France place a distant second and third. This table also shows the major customers in the business of death. Two matters are of interest. First, Egypt, a country so poor that it can hardly keep its people from starving, is one of the biggest spenders. Either its power elite is drastically insecure (and seeks to bolster its power through these tremendous expenditures), or else it is incredibly secure because of the weapons it has purchased. Second,

Table 15.3

WHAT U.S. WARS COST	
War of 1812	$615,000,000
Mexican War	$1,076,000,000
American Revolution	$1,918,000,000
Spanish-American War	$5,961,000,000
Civil War	$45,990,000,000
Korean War	$262,062,000,000
World War I	$369,580,000,000
Vietnam War	$553,088,000,000
World War II	$2,953,716,000,000
Total	$4,194,006,000,000

Note: In the source, the costs are listed in 1967 dollars. To account for inflation, I increased these amounts by 350 percent, and added the costs of service-connected benefits. Where a range was listed, the mean was used.

The costs of the many "military interventions" such as in Grenada, Panama, Somalia, and Haiti, are not listed in the source, nor is the more expensive "military intervention" on behalf of Kuwait. These costs do *not* include interest payments on war loans, nor are they reduced by the financial benefits to the United States, such as the acquisition of California and Texas in the Mexican War. Also not included are ongoing "national defense" expenditures, currently about $320 billion a year.

Source: Statistical Abstract 1993:Table 553; 1999:Table 574.

Table 15.4

THE BUSINESS OF DEATH	
The 5 Largest Arms Sellers	
United States	$23.5 billion
Great Britain	$6.1 billion
France	$3.2 billion
Germany	$0.8 billion
China	$0.6 billion
The 10 Largest Consumers	
Saudi Arabia	$9.8 billion
Japan	$2.4 billion
Egypt	$1.8 billion
Kuwait	$1.7 billion
Great Britain	$1.5 billion
Turkey	$1.4 billion
Australia	$1.3 billion
United States	$1.1 billion
South Korea	$1.1 billion
Israel	$0.9 billion

Source: Statistical Abstract 1999:Table 582. Russia used to be listed in the source as a top exporter of arms, but it no longer appears on this list. Either Russia no longer exports many arms, or it is excluded for some other reason.

War takes many forms, only one of which is armed conflict officially declared between countries. More common is terrorism. This photo was taken outside the Greek Embassy in London following protests over the arrest of Abdullah Ocalan (a Kurdish guerrilla). The girl engulfed in flames is 15-year-old Nijla Coskun.

the purchases of arms by Saudi Arabia and Kuwait indicate that U.S. dollars spent on oil tend to return to the United States. There is, in reality, an exchange of arms and oil.

The seeds of future wars are also sown by nuclear proliferation. Several Least Industrialized Nations, such as India and China, already have nuclear weapons. Iran, Iraq, Libya, and North Korea are furiously trying to develop their own nuclear arsenals. In the hands of a dictator who uses them to settle personal or nationalistic grudges, these weapons, always a threat to the world's safety, can mean nuclear blackmail or nuclear attack.

On the positive side, with the cold war over, the United States and Russia have announced that they no longer aim their nuclear missiles at the other's cities. Nonetheless, these countries continue to eye each other suspiciously, neither of them wholly convinced that the other has truly peaceful intentions. G-7 is especially concerned that Russia's democratic reform movement may be undermined by inflation, currency collapse, and organized crime, that reactionary politicians will attempt to recapture Russia's faded glory through military might, and that, with its nuclear arsenal, it may threaten the global coalitions now being worked out. As a consequence, despite Russia's weakened and near chaotic state, Russia is invited to G-7 summits.

Nuclear, Biological, and Chemical Terrorism

With hatreds that span generations and with opposing groups escalating hostilities by endlessly chronicling the atrocities committed by the archenemy, terrorism is an unmitigated danger on the world scene. One of the few options open to a weaker group that seeks to retaliate against a powerful enemy is suicide terrorism. Use of this tactic shocks the world and captures headlines, as it did when Libyan insurgents used it against U.S. marines, and as it does time after time when Palestinian liberationists use it against Israel. The tools that have been used, however, have been relatively weak—a hijacked plane, or car bombs that blow up only a few people at a time.

The real danger lies elsewhere: in nuclear, chemical, and biological weapons, which could be unleashed against a civilian population. As discussed in the Down-to-Earth sociology box on the next page, the United States is ripe for such an attack. Its armed interventions around the world have stimulated hatred and a burning desire for revenge. The availability of nuclear, chemical, and biological weapons due to the breakup of the Soviet empire makes terrorism on U.S. soil a chilling possibility. In my estimation, it is only a matter of time until such attacks are launched against major U.S. cities.

War and Dehumanization

> Proud of his techniques, the U.S. trainer was demonstrating to the South American soldiers how to torture a prisoner. As the victim screamed in anguish, the trainer was interrupted by a phone call from his wife. His students could hear him say, "A dinner and a movie sound nice. I'll see you right after work." Hanging up the phone, he then continued the lesson. (Stockwell 1989)

War exacts many costs in addition to killing people and destroying property. One is its effect on morality. Exposure to brutality and killing often causes **dehumanization**, the process of reducing people to objects that do not deserve to be treated as humans.

As we review findings on dehumanization and see how it breeds callousness and cruelty, perhaps we can better understand how O'Brien in the opening vignette could have unleashed rats into someone's face. Consider the four characteristics of dehumanization (Bernard et al. 1971):

1. *Increased emotional distance from others.* People stop identifying with others, no longer seeing them as having qualities similar to themselves. Instead of people, they come to be seen as subhumans, "the enemy," or objects of some sort.

dehumanization the act or process of reducing people to objects that do not deserve the treatment accorded humans

Sociology

Down-to-Earth

THINKING THE UNTHINKABLE:
BIOLOGICAL TERRORISM IN THE TWENTY-FIRST CENTURY

Consider this scenario:

Over a period of years, agents of a nation whose leader hates the United States and has a grudge to settle quietly infiltrate the United States. Most are admitted as students at universities around the country. All have been highly trained by their country's secret police. On a predetermined day, at a specified hour, they release anthrax and smallpox into the air of 20 major cities. Within days, a third of Americans are dead.

This scenario haunts U.S. officials. Some think that such an attack has already been planned and may soon be carried out. There will be no warning, no attempt to hold the United States hostage in order to extort billions of dollars. Money is not the goal. The motive is revenge for humiliation suffered at U.S. hands. The goal will be no less than to wipe out the United States itself.

U.S. officials are scared. The White House conducted a secret exercise to play out what would happen if terrorists, armed with genetically modified germs, decided to strike. The president and other officials were alarmed at how easily such an attack could be carried out and at the millions who would die (Broad and Miller 1998). The seriousness with which they regard this threat is indicated by the federal budget: More than $1 billion is earmarked for civil defense in the event of a terrorist attack (Richter 1999). Government officials have stockpiled vaccines around the country and have trained emergency medical teams in major cities (Broad and Miller 1998). All 2.4 million military personnel, including National Guard and reserve units, are being vaccinated against anthrax. All military personnel who refuse to be vaccinated are punished and discharged (Myers 1999).

The president has issued secret directives. The plans are not to evacuate populations, but to block roads and stop people at gunpoint from fleeing cities and spreading the disease. The president wants Congress to approve a military takeover of state and local governments in order to fight the chaos that would result from such an attack (Miller and Broad 1999). Reading between the lines, it is certain that the secret directives include Pentagon control of the continental United States.

An ancient Chinese proverb says: "May you live in exciting times." This seemingly innocuous saying is actually a curse; it expresses the hope that an enemy's life will be upset. We live in exciting times. Let's hope that the curse that envelops us—proliferating nuclear, chemical, and biological weapons, interstate rivalries and domination, aspiring nationalistic goals, and the growing threat of terrorism—does not mean our destruction. ■

2. *An emphasis on following procedures.* Regulations are not questioned, for they are seen as a means to an end. People are likely to say, "I don't like doing this, but it is necessary to follow procedures," or "We all have to die some day. What difference does it make if these people die now?"

3. *Inability to resist pressures.* Fears of losing one's job, losing the respect of one's peers, or having one's integrity and loyalty questioned take precedence over individual moral decisions.

4. *A diminished sense of personal responsibility.* People come to see themselves as only small cogs in a large machine. They are not responsible for what they do, for they are simply following orders. The higher-ups who give the orders are thought to have more complete or even secret information that justifies what is being done. They think, "The higher-ups are in a position to judge what is right and wrong, but in my humble place, who am I to question these acts?"

A Vietnam vet who read this section remarked, "You missed the major one we used. We killed kids. Our dehumanizing technique was a saying, 'The little ones are the soldiers of tomorrow.'"

Dehumanization numbs the conscience. As in the little vignette that opened this section, even acts of torture become dissociated from one's "normal self." Brutality and killing, though regrettable, become means that help to accomplish a job. Torturing and killing somehow fit into the larger scheme of things—and someone has to do such "dirty work." The individual clothes such acts in patriotic language: They are "the soldier's duty." Those who make the decisions are the ones who are responsible—soldiers simply follow orders.

As sociologist Tamotsu Shibutani (1970) stressed, dehumanization is aided by the tendency for prolonged conflicts to be transformed into a struggle between good and evil. The enemy, of course, represents evil in the equation. To fight against absolute evil sometimes requires the suspension of moral standards—for one is dealing with an abnormal situation, opposing an enemy that is less than human, and fighting for the precarious survival of good (Markhusen 1995). War, then, exalts treachery, cruelty, and killing—and medals are given to glorify actions that would be condemned in every other context of social life.

As soldiers participate in acts that they, too, would normally condemn, they neutralize their morality. This insulates them from acknowledging their behaviors as evil, which would threaten their self-concept and mental adjustment. Surgeons, highly sensitive to patients' needs in ordinary medical situations, become capable of mentally removing an individual's humanity. By thinking of Jews as "people who are going to die anyway," German surgeons during World War II were able to mutilate them just to study the results.

Dehumanization does not always insulate the self from guilt, however, and its failure to do so can bring severe personal consequences. During the war, while soldiers are surrounded by army buddies who agree that the enemy is less than human and deserves inhuman treatment, such definitions ordinarily remain intact. After returning home, however, the dehumanizing definitions more easily break down. Many soldiers then find themselves seriously disturbed by what they did during the war. Although most eventually adjust, some cannot, such as this soldier from California who wrote this note before putting a bullet through his brain (Smith 1980):

> I can't sleep anymore. When I was in Vietnam, we came across a North Vietnamese soldier with a man, a woman, and a three-or four-year-old girl. We had to shoot them all. I can't get the little girl's face out of my mind. I hope that God will forgive me . . . I can't.

nationalism a strong identity with a nation, accompanied by the desire for that nation to be dominant

A NEW WORLD ORDER?

The globalization of capitalism, accompanied by the worldwide flow of information, capital, and goods discussed in the previous chapter, is little affected by national boundaries. The United States, Canada, and Mexico have formed a North American Free-Trade Association (NAFTA), to which all of South America will eventually belong. Argentina and other countries have even adopted the dollar as an official currency, even as their national currency coexists alongside it. Transcending their national boundaries, most European countries have formed an economic and political unit (the European Union, or EU). They, too, have adopted a cross-national currency, the Euro. The EU has also established a "rapid reaction force" of 60,000 troops under a unified command (Krauthammer 1999). Transcending national borders, the United Nations has sent out "peace keeping" troops—to Korea in 1950, Iraq in 1990, and on a smaller scale, Somalia in 1993, Bosnia in 1994 and 1997, and Kosovo in 1999.

Will this process continue until there is but one state or empire that envelops the earth itself? This is a distinct possibility, deriving perhaps not only from these historical trends but also from a push by a powerful group of capitalists who profit from global free trade (Domhoff 1990). Although the trend is in full tilt, we are unlikely to see its conclusion during our lifetimes, for national boundaries and national patriotism die only a hard death. As borders shift, as occurred with the breakup of the Soviet Union, previously unincorporated nations such as Lithuania and Azerbaijan demand their independence and the right to full statehood. The following Perspectives box explores this tension between nations and states.

Nationalism is showing up all over the world. In Myanmar, a children's crusade is being waged against the government. In a case of truth being stranger than fiction, the revolution is led by 12-year old twin brothers, Johnny and Luther Htoo, who believe they have divine inspiration. The children shown here are armed with M-16s. Johnny is the child in the center.

PERSPECTIVES | Cultural Diversity Around the World

ROADBLOCKS IN THE PATH TO THE NEW WORLD ORDER: THE GLOBALIZATION OF CAPITALISM VERSUS THE RESURGENCE OF NATIONALISM

The world has about five thousand nations. What makes each a *nation* is that its people share a language, culture, territory, and political organization. A *state,* in contrast, claims a monopoly on violence over a territory. A state may contain many nations. The Kayapo Indians are but one nation within the state called Brazil. The Chippewa and Sioux are two nations within the state called the United States. The world's five thousand nations have existed for hundreds, some even for thousands, of years. In contrast, most of the world's 194 states have been around only since World War II.

Most modern states are empires; that is, they have incorporated nations into their boundaries—usually by conquest. Some states have far better records than others, but overall, no ideology, left or right, religious or sectarian, has protected nations or promoted pluralism much better or worse than any other. The last century probably saw more genocides and *ethnocides* (the destruction of an ethnic group) than any other.

For nation peoples, group identity transcends political affiliation. Clearly, the Palestinians who live within Israel's borders do not identify themselves as Israelis. But did you know that the Oromos in Ethiopia have more members than do three-quarters of the states in the United Nations, and that they do not think of themselves as Ethiopians? The 22 million Kurds don't consider themselves first and foremost to be Iranians, Iraqis, Syrians, or Turks. There are about 450 nations in Nigeria, 350 in India, 180 in Brazil, 130 in the former USSR, and 90 in Ethiopia. That nations are squeezed into states with which they don't identify is the nub of the problem.

In most states, power resides in the hands of an elite that operates by a simple credo: Winner take all. The elite control foreign investment and aid, and use both to reinforce their power. They set

Shown here are Russian troops in what remains of downtown Grozny, the capital of Chechnya. Russia bombed the city in order to stop the independence of its former colony.

local commodity prices, control exports, levy taxes—and buy the weapons. They confiscate the resources of the nations, whether those take the form of Native American land in North and South America or oil from the Kurds in Iraq. When nations resist, the result is open conflict—and sometimes genocide.

About half of the debt of the least industrialized states and nearly all debt in Africa comes from the purchase of weapons, which the states use to suppress their own citizens. Most of the world's 12 million refugees are victims of such conflicts, as are most of the 100 million internally displaced people who have been uprooted from their homelands.

A vicious cycle forms. The appropriation of a nation's resources leads to conflict, conflict leads to insecurity and the purchase of weapons, weapons purchases lead to debt, and debt leads to the appropriation of more resources. This self-feeding cycle helps to ensure that elites of the least industrialized states will cooperate with G7, which supplies the arms, as it divides the globe's resources among its members.

G7's march to a New World Order has met a serious obstacle, the resur-

gence of **nationalism**—identity with and loyalty to a nation. Because it promotes loyalty to small groups instead of to the regional divisions into which G7 wants to carve the globe, nationalism threatens the evolving New World Order. The shooting wars increase—fought over issues and animosities that are rooted in history. Not only are such events only faintly understood by those who are not a party to them, but also they have been kept vividly alive in the folklore and collective memory of these nations. These wars threaten the fragile coalitions that G7 is building as it divides up the world's resources.

Consequently, we should not be surprised to see the United States and its allies maintain silence as the Soviets oppress the nations under their dominance; and we should expect Russia to be silent as the United States and certain European powers put out their own nationalistic brushfires.[a]

G7 will continue to divide the globe into regional trading blocs, and we will continue to witness this oppositional struggle. We will see seemingly contradictory outcomes: the formation of global coalitions matched by the simultaneous outbreak of small-scale shooting wars as nations struggle for independence.

The end result? It is sufficient to note how greatly the scales are tipped in favor of the most industrialized states and the multinational corporations. David is not likely to defeat Goliath this time.

[a] I first wrote this paragraph in 1996. The silence of the United States in the face of the Russian slaughter in Chechnya, including the torture of combatants and civilians and the destruction of Grozny, the capital city, bears out the prediction. ■

Sources: Clay 1990; Ohmae 1995; Jáuregui 1996; Marcus 1996; Alter 2000.

If global political and economic unity does come about, it is fascinating to speculate on what type of government will result. If Hitler had had his way, his conquests would have resulted in world domination by a single dictator, and in a world totalitarian regime based on racial identification. If our current trend continues—and it is a big "if"—and if a world order does emerge, the potential for human welfare is tremendous. There could be almost global peace. And if a benevolent government arises, there could be highly satisfying participation in politics. If we end up with totalitarianism, however, and the world's resources and people come under the control of a dictatorship or an oligarchy, the future for humanity could be bleak, perhaps like that of Winston and Julia in our opening vignette.

$\int$UMMARY AND $\int$EVIEW

■ Micropolitics and Macropolitics

What is the difference between micropolitics and macropolitics?

The essential nature of politics is **power,** and every group is political. The term **micropolitics** refers to the exercise of power in everyday life, **macropolitics** to large-scale power, such as governing a nation. P. 418.

■ Power, Authority, and Violence

How are authority and coercion related to power?

Authority is power that people view as legitimately exercised over them, while **coercion** is power they consider unjust. The **state** is a political entity that claims a monopoly on violence over some territory. If enough people consider a state's power illegitimate, **revolution** is possible. Pp. 418–419.

What kinds of authority are there?

Max Weber identified three types of authority. Power in **traditional authority** derives from custom—patterns set down in the past are rules for the present. Power in **rational legal authority** (also called *bureaucratic authority*) is based on law and written procedures. In **charismatic authority** power is based on loyalty to an individual to whom people are attracted. Charismatic authority, which undermines traditional and rational-legal authority, has built-in problems in transferring authority to a new leader. Pp. 419–423.

■ Types of Government

How are the types of government related to power?

In a **monarchy,** power is based on hereditary rule; in a **democracy,** power is given to the ruler by citizens; and in a **dictatorship,** power is seized by an individual or small group. Pp. 423–426.

■ The U.S. Political System

What are the main characteristics of the U.S. political system?

The United States has a "winner take all" system, in which elections are determined by a simple majority. Most European democracies, in contrast, have **proportional representation,** with legislative seats divided among political parties according to the percentage of votes each receives. If no single party is in power, proportional representation creates the need of a **coalition government.** Pp. 426–428.

Voter turnout is higher among people who are more socially integrated, those who sense a greater stake in the outcome of elections, such as the more educated and well-to-do. **Lobbyists** and **special-interest groups,** such as **political action committees** (PACs), play a significant role in U.S. politics. Pp. 428–432.

■ Who Rules the United States?

Is the United States controlled by a ruling class?

In a view known as **pluralism,** functionalists say that no one group holds power, that the country's many competing interest groups balance one another. Conflict theorists, who focus on the top level of power, say that the United States is governed by a **power elite,** a **ruling class** made up of the top corporate, political, and military leaders. At this point, the matter is not settled. Pp. 432–433.

■ War and Terrorism: Means to Implement Political Objectives

How is war related to politics—and what are its costs?

War, which has been common throughout human history, is a means of attempting to reach political objectives. Because of technological advances in killing, the costs of war in terms of human lives have escalated. The Least Industrialized Nations, which can least afford it, spend huge amounts on technologically advanced weapons. Another cost is **dehumanization,** whereby people no longer see others as worthy of human treatment. This paves the way for torture and killing. Pp. 434–438.

■ A New World Order?

Is humanity headed toward a one-world political order?

The global expansion of communications, transportation, and trade, the widespread adoption of capitalism, the retreat of socialism, and the trend toward regional economic and political unions may indicate that a world political system is developing. The oppositional trend is a fierce **nationalism.** If a New World Order develops, the possible consequences for human welfare range from excellent to calamitous. Pp. 438–440.

Where can I read more on this topic?

Suggested Readings for this chapter are at the back of this book.

Sociology & the Internet

All URLs listed are current as of the printing of this book. URLs often change. Please check our Web site, **http://www.abacon.com/henslin**, for updates.

1. As noted in this chapter's Mass Media box, new technologies like the Internet make televoting possible. The Democratic Party of Arizona became the first U.S. political party to use televoting in its 2000 primary elections. Almost 40,000 people voted online over a one-week period in an election managed by a company called Election.com. You can learn more about this company and the election services it offers to associations, nonprofit organizations, trade unions, and school districts, as well as to governments and political parties around the world, by going to **http://www.votation.com/services/internet.htm**. Why would this service be attractive to organizations? To voters? Is this a solution to the problems of low voter turnout and voter apathy? Using your sociological imagination, write a paper in which you present both sides of the argument—in favor of this new development and against it.

2. Several firms are trying to draw swing voters into the political process by promoting public discourse on political issues through the Internet. These companies hope to make a profit by selling their services to political candidates and political parties. At these sites—**http://www.voter.com, http://www.grassroots.com** and **http://www.speakout.com**—you will find links to candidates for public office as well as to those currently in office. You'll also find commentaries by writers whose views range across the political spectrum, and information on current issues and advocacy groups. Visitors can write e-mails to public representatives, take part in surveys, join a group, and get involved in chat rooms. After you have browsed around these sites, take a look at the Web site for the Democratic Party, **http://www.democrats.org/index.html**, and the one for the Republican Party, **http://www.rnc.org**. How are the sites for the political parties different from those you looked at first? Which are more likely to attract citizens to the political process? Why? Make a presentation to your class about the democratic process on the Internet.

3. It is often difficult to keep track of changes and developments in politics because they occur so fast and at each level of society. Let's see if we can grasp this wide range of political activity in the U.S. To start, go to the National Political Index at **http://www.politicalindex.com**. This Web site provides political information for voters, activists, constituents, lobbyists, politicians, academics, and the media. Click on areas that reflect the different levels of political organization—international, national, state, and local—or that reflect different expressions of political activity. Identify and briefly discuss what you have found out about the contemporary U.S. political scene.

4. Voter apathy, which you have read about in your text, is just one problem that results from the U.S. system of electing public officials. Examine the following links for proposals for alternative voting systems:

http://www.alumni.caltech.edu/~croft/research/government/approval/voting.html

http://www.mtholyoke.edu/acad/polit/damy/prlib.htm

http://www.prairienet.org/icpr

http://www.igc.apc.org/cvd/

What changes are discussed at these sites? What problems in the current system do they hope to counteract? If adopted, what problems could these new systems create? How do you feel about these alternatives?

The Family

- **Marriage and Family in Global Perspective**
  Defining Family
  Common Cultural Themes
- **Marriage and Family in Theoretical Perspective**
  The Functionalist Perspective:
      Functions and Dysfunctions
  The Conflict Perspective: Gender and Power
  The Symbolic Interactionist Perspective: Gender
      and the Meanings of Marriage
- **The Family Life Cycle**
  Love and Courtship in Global Perspective
  Marriage
  Childbirth
  Child Rearing
  The Family in Later Life
- **Diversity in U.S. Families**
  African-American Families
  Latino Families
  Asian-American Families
  Native-American Families
  One-Parent Families
  Families Without Children

  Blended Families
  Gay and Lesbian Families
- **Trends in U.S. Families**
  Postponing Marriage
  Cohabitation
  Unmarried Mothers
  The Sandwich Generation and Elder Care
- **Divorce and Remarriage**
  Problems in Measuring Divorce
  Children of Divorce
  The Absent Father and Serial Fatherhood
  The Ex-Spouses
  Remarriage
- **Two Sides of Family Life**
  The Dark Side of Family Life: Battering, Child
      Abuse, Marital Rape, and Incest
  The Bright Side of Family Life:
      Successful Marriages
- **The Future of Marriage and Family**
- **Summary and Review**

old still. We're going to be late," said Sharon as she tried to put shoes on 2-year-old Michael, who kept squirming away.

Finally succeeding with the shoes, Sharon turned to 4-year-old Brittany, who was trying to pull a brush through her hair. "It's stuck, Mom," Brittany said.

"Well, no wonder. Just how did you get gum in your hair? I don't have time for this, Brittany. We've got to leave."

Getting to the van fifteen minutes behind schedule, Sharon strapped the kids in, and then herself. Just as she was about to pull away, she remembered that she had not checked the fridge for messages.

"Just a minute, kids. I'll be right back."

Running into the house, she frantically searched for a message from Tom. She vaguely remembered him mumbling something about being held over at work. She grabbed the Post-It and ran back to the van.

"He's picking on me," complained Brittany when her mother climbed back in.

"Oh, shut up, Brittany," Sharon said. "He's only 2. He can't pick on you."

"Yes, he did," Brittany said, crossing her arms defiantly as she stretched out her foot to kick her brother's seat.

"Oh, no! How did Mikey get that smudge on his face? Did you do that, Brit?"

Brittany crossed her arms again, pushing out her lips in her classic pouting pose.

As Sharon drove to the day care center, she tried to calm herself. "Only two more days of work this week, and then the weekend. Then

I can catch up on housework and have a little relaxed time with the kids. And Tom can finally cut the lawn and buy the groceries," she thought. "And maybe we'll even have time to make love. Boy, that's been a long time."

At a traffic light, Sharon found time to read Tom's note. "Oh, no. That's what he meant. He has to work Saturday. Well, there go those plans."

What Sharon didn't know was that her boss also had made plans for Sharon's Saturday. And that their emergency Saturday baby-sitter wouldn't be available. And that the van would break down on the way home from work. That Michael was coming down with chicken pox. That Brittany would follow next. That... ■

T hat there isn't enough time to get everything done is a common complaint of most of us. But it is especially true for working parents of young children, who find themselves without the support services taken for granted just a generation ago: stay-at-home moms who were the center of the neighborhood, a husband whose sole income was enough to support a wife and several children, a safe neighborhood where even small children could play outside, and a grandma who could pitch in during emergencies.

Those days are gone forever. Today, more and more families are like Sharon's and Tom's. They are harried, pressured, working more and seemingly making less, and, certainly, having less time for one another—and for their children. In this chapter, we shall try to understand what is happening to the U.S. family, and to families worldwide.

Often one of the strongest family bonds is that of mother–daughter. The young artist, an eleventh grader, wrote: "This painting expresses the way I feel about my future with my child. I want my child to be happy and I want her to love me the same way I love her. In that way we will have a good relationship so that nobody will be able to take us apart. I wanted this picture to be alive, that is why I used a lot of bright colors."

MARRIAGE AND FAMILY IN GLOBAL PERSPECTIVE

To better understand U.S. patterns of marriage and family, let's first sketch a cross-cultural portrait. The perspective it yields will give us a context for interpreting our own experience in this vital social institution.

Defining Family

"What is a family, anyway?" asked William Sayres (1992) at the beginning of an article on this topic. By this question he meant that although the family is so significant to humanity that it is universal—every human group in the world organizes its members in families—the world's cultures display so much variety that the term *family* is difficult to define. For example, although the Western world regards a family as a husband, wife, and children, other groups have family forms in which men have more than one wife (polygyny) or women more than one husband (polyandry). To try to define the family as the approved group into which children are born overlooks the Banaro of New Guinea. In this group a young woman must give birth before she can marry, and she *cannot* marry the father of her child (Murdock 1949).

And so it goes. For just about every element you might consider essential to marriage or family, some group has a different custom. Even the sex of the bride and groom may not be what you expect. Although in almost every instance the bride and groom are female and male, there are rare exceptions. In some Native American tribes, for example, a man or woman who wanted to be a member of the opposite sex went through a ceremony (*berdache*) and was *declared* a member of the opposite sex. From then on, not only did the "new" man or woman do the tasks associated with his or her new sex, but also the individual was allowed to marry. In this instance, the husband and wife were of the same biological sex. In the contemporary world, Denmark (in 1989), Norway (in 1993), Sweden (in 1995), and Holland (in 1998) have legalized same-sex marriages.

Even to say that the family is the unit in which children are disciplined and that parents are responsible for their material needs is not universally true. Among the Trobriand Islanders, the wife's eldest brother is responsible for making certain that his sister's children have food and for disciplining them when they get out of line (Malinowski 1927). Finally, even sexual relationships don't universally characterize a husband and wife. The Nayar of Malabar never allow a bride and groom to have sex. After a three-day celebration of the marriage, they send the groom packing—and never allow him to see his bride again (La Barre 1954). (In case you're wondering, the groom comes from another tribe, and Nayar women are allowed to have sex, but only with approved lovers—who can never be the husband. This system keeps family property intact—along matrilineal lines.)

Such remarkable variety means settling for a very broad definition. A **family** consists of two or more people who consider themselves related by blood, marriage, or adoption. A **household,** in contrast, consists of people who occupy the same housing unit—a house, apartment, or other living quarters.

We can classify families as **nuclear** (husband, wife, and children) and **extended** (including people such as grandparents, aunts, uncles, and cousins in addition to the nuclear unit). Sociologists also refer to the **family of orientation** (the family in which an individual grows up) and the **family of procreation** (the family formed when a couple have their first child). Finally, regardless of its form, **marriage** can be viewed as a group's approved mating arrangements—usually marked out by a ritual of some sort (the wedding) to indicate the couple's new public status.

Common Cultural Themes

Despite this diversity, several common themes do run through marriage and family. As Table 16.1 below illustrates, all societies use marriage and family to establish patterns of mate selection, descent, inheritance, and authority. Let's look at these patterns.

family two or more people who consider themselves related by blood, marriage, or adoption

household people who occupy the same housing unit

nuclear family a family consisting of a husband, wife, and child(ren)

extended family a nuclear family plus other relatives, such as grandparents, uncles and aunts, who live together

family of orientation the family in which a person grows up

family of procreation the family formed when a couple's first child is born

marriage a group's approved mating arrangements, usually marked by a ritual of some sort

Table 16.1

COMMON CULTURAL THEMES: MARRIAGE IN TRADITIONAL AND INDUSTRIALIZED SOCIETIES

Characteristic	Traditional Societies	Industrialized (and Postindustrialized) Societies
What is the structure of marriage?	*Extended* (marriage embeds spouses in a large kinship network of explicit obligations)	*Nuclear* (marriage brings fewer obligations toward the spouse's relatives)
What are the functions of marriage?	Encompassing (see the six functions listed on p. 447)	More limited (many functions are fulfilled by other social institutions)
Who holds authority?	Highly *patriarchal* (authority is held by males)	Although some patriarchal features remain, authority is more evenly divided
How many spouses at one time?	Most have one spouse (*monogamy*), while some have several (*polygamy*)	One spouse
Who selects the spouse?	The spouse is selected by the parents, usually the father	Individuals choose their own spouse
Where does the couple live?	Couples most commonly reside with the groom's family (*patrilocal residence*), less commonly with the bride's family (*matrilocal residence*)	Couples establish a new home (*neolocal residence*)
How is descent figured?	Most commonly figured from male ancestors (*patrilineal* kinship), less commonly from female ancestors (*matrilineal* kinship)	Figured from male and female ancestor equally (*bilateral kinship*)
How is inheritance figured?	Rigid system of rules; usually patrilineal, but may be matrilineal	Highly individualistic; usually bilateral

Norms of Mate Selection Each human group establishes norms to govern who marries whom. Norms of **endogamy** specify that people should marry within their own group. Groups may prohibit interracial marriages, for example. In contrast, norms of **exogamy** specify that people must marry outside their group. The best example is the *incest taboo,* which prohibits sex and marriage among designated relatives.

In some societies, norms of mate selection are written into law, but in most cases they are informal. For example, in the United States most whites marry whites and most African Americans marry African Americans, not because of any laws but because of informal norms.

Reckoning Patterns of Descent How are you related to your father's father or to your mother's mother? The explanation is found in your society's **system of descent,** the way people trace kinship over generations. To us, a **bilateral** system seems logical—and natural— for we think of ourselves as related to both our mother's and our father's side of the family. "Doesn't everyone?" you might ask. Interestingly, this is only one logical way to reckon descent. In a **patrilineal** system, descent is traced only on the father's side, and children are not considered related to their mother's relatives. In a **matrilineal** system, descent is figured only on the mother's side, and children are not considered related to their father's relatives.

Rights of Inheritance Marriage and family—in whatever form is customary in a society—are also used to compute rights of inheritance. In the bilateral system, property is passed to both males and females, in the patrilineal system only to males, and in the matrilineal system (the rarest form) only to females. Each system matches a people's ideas of justice and logic.

Patterns of Authority Some form of **patriarchy,** a social system in which men dominate women, has formed a thread running through all societies. As noted in Chapter 11, there are no historical records of a true **matriarchy,** a social system in which women as a group dominate men as a group. Our marriage and family customs, then, developed within a framework of patriarchy. Although U.S. family patterns are becoming more **egalitarian,** or equal, many customs practiced today point to their patriarchal origin. Naming patterns, for example, reflect patriarchy. Despite recent trends, the typical bride still takes the groom's last name; children, too, are usually given the father's last name. For information on a society that systematically promotes equality in marriage, see the Perspectives box on the next page.

MARRIAGE AND FAMILY IN THEORETICAL PERSPECTIVE

A global perspective reveals that human groups have chosen many forms of mate selection, ways to trace descent, and so on. Although these patterns are arbitrary, each group sees its own forms of marriage and family as natural. Now let's see what picture emerges when we apply the three sociological perspectives.

The Functionalist Perspective: Functions and Dysfunctions

Functionalists stress that to survive, a society must meet certain basic needs, or functions. When functionalists look at family, they examine how it is related to other parts of society, especially how it contributes to the well-being of society.

Why the Family Is Universal Functionalists note that although the form of the family varies from one human group to another, the family is universal because it fulfills six needs that are basic to every society's well-being. As described on pages 27–29, these needs, or func-

endogamy the practice of marrying within one's own group

exogamy the practice of marrying outside one's group

system of descent how kinship is traced over the generations

bilateral (system of descent): a system of reckoning descent that counts both the mother's and the father's side

patrilineal (system of descent): a system of reckoning descent that counts only the father's side

matrilineal (system of descent): a system of reckoning descent that counts only the mother's side

patriarchy authority vested in males; male control of a society or group

matriarchy authority vested in females; female control of a society or group

egalitarian authority more or less equally divided between people or groups, in this instance between husband and wife

PERSPECTIVES | Cultural Diversity Around the World

FAMILY LIFE IN SWEDEN

Swedish lawmakers hold a strong image of what good family life is. That image centers on equality in marriage and on the welfare of children. Lawmakers bolster this image with laws designed to put women and men on equal footing in marriage, to give mothers and fathers equal responsibility for the home and children, and to protect the financially weaker party in the event of divorce.

At the center of family laws is the welfare of children. Health care for mothers and children, for example, is free. This includes obstetric care and all health care during pregnancy. Maternity centers offer free health checks and courses in preparation for childbirth. Fathers are encouraged to attend the childbirth classes.

When a child is born, the parents are eligible for fifteen months' leave of absence with pay. Both cannot receive compensation at the same time; the parents decide how they will split the leave between them. For the first twelve months the state pays 90 percent of gross income, and then a generous fixed rate for the remaining three months. The paid leave does not have to be taken all at once, but can be spread over eight years. The parents can stay at home full time, or they can work part time for a longer period. Because most mothers take all the leave, the law now includes a "father's month," one month that cannot be transferred to the mother.

The government also guarantees other benefits. All fathers are entitled to ten days leave of absence with full pay when a child is born. When a child is sick, either parent can care for the child and receive full pay for missed work—up to sixty days a year per child. Moreover, by law local governments must offer child care. And if a husband becomes violent or threatens his wife, the woman can have a security alarm installed in their home free of charge.

The divorce laws have been drawn up with an eye to what is best for the child. Local governments are required to provide free counseling to any parent who requests it. If both parties agree and if they have no children under the age of 16, a couple is automatically entitled to a divorce. Otherwise the law requires a six-month cooling-off period so parents can more calmly consider what is best for their children. Joint custody of children is automatic, unless one of the parents opposes it. The children must live with only one of the parents. The parent who does not live with the children is required to pay child support in proportion to his or her finances. If the parent fails to do so, the social security system makes the payments. ■

For Your Consideration

How does the Swedish system compare with that of the United States? What "system" for watching out for the welfare of children does the United States have, anyway?

Sources: Based on The Swedish Institute 1992; Froman 1994.

---

tions, are (1) economic production, (2) socialization of children, (3) care of the sick and aged, (4) recreation, (5) sexual control, and (6) reproduction. To make certain that these functions are performed, every human group has found it necessary to adopt some form of the family.

Functions of the Incest Taboo Functionalists note that the incest taboo helps families avoid *role confusion*. This, in turn, facilitates the socialization of children. For example, if father-daughter incest were allowed, how should a wife treat her daughter—as a daughter, as a subservient second wife, or even as a rival? Should the daughter act toward her mother as a mother or as a rival? Would her father be a father or a lover? And would the wife be the husband's main wife, a secondary wife—or even "the mother of the other wife" (whatever role that might be)? Maternal incest would also lead to complications every bit as confusing as these.

Another function of the incest taboo is to force people to look outside the family for marriage partners. Anthropologists theorize that exogamy was especially functional in tribal societies, for it forged alliances between tribes that otherwise might have killed each other off. Today, exogamy extends a bride's and groom's social networks beyond the nuclear family by building relationships with the spouses' families.

Isolation and Emotional Overload Functionalists also analyze the dysfunctions that arise from the relative isolation of the nuclear family. Unlike extended families, which are enmeshed in kinship networks, members of nuclear families can count on fewer people for material and emotional support. This makes nuclear families vulnerable to "emotional overload." That is, the stress that comes with crises such as the loss of a job—or even the routine pressures of a harried life, as depicted in our opening vignette—is spread among fewer people. This places greater strain on each family member. In addition, the relative isolation of the nuclear family makes it vulnerable to a "dark side"—incest and various other forms of abuse, matters we examine later in this chapter.

The Conflict Perspective: Gender and Power

As you recall, central to conflict theory is the struggle over scarce resources. The recurring struggle over who does housework is actually a struggle over scarce resources—time, energy, and the leisure to pursue interesting activities.

The Power Struggle Over Housework   Most men resist doing housework. As Figure 16.1 shows, even wives who work outside the home full time end up doing most of it. The lesser effort that husbands make seems so great to them, however, that even when his wife does almost all the cooking and cleaning, the husband is likely to see himself as splitting the work fifty-fifty (Galinsky et al. 1993). Things are so one-sided that wives are *eight* times more likely than husbands to feel that the division of housework is unfair (Sanchez 1994).

And no wonder. Wives who put in an eight-hour day of working for wages average eleven hours more child care and housework each week than their husbands do (Bianchi and Spain 1996). *Incredibly, this is the equivalent of twenty-four 24-hour days a year.* Sociologist Arlie Hochschild (1989) calls this the working wife's "second shift." To stress the one-sided nature of the second shift, she quotes this satire by Garry Trudeau in the Doonesbury comic strip:

> A "liberated" father is sitting at his word processor writing a book about raising his child. He types: "Today I wake up with a heavy day of work ahead of me. As Joannie gets Jeffry ready for day care, I ask her if I can be relieved of my usual household responsibilities for the day. Joannie says, 'Sure, I'll make up the five minutes somewhere.' "

Not surprisingly, the burden of the second shift creates deep discontent among wives (Risman 1998). These problems, as well as how wives and husbands cope with them, are discussed in the following Thinking Critically section.

Figure 16.1

IN TWO-PAYCHECK MARRIAGES, WHO HAS MORE RESPONSIBILITY FOR HOUSEWORK?

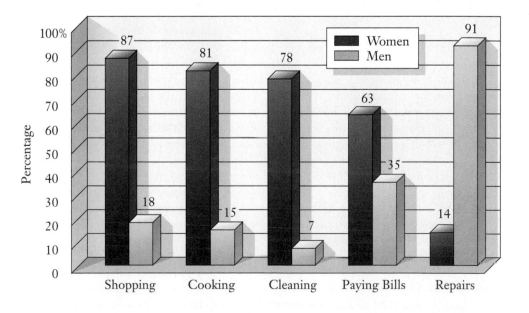

Thinking Critically

THE SECOND SHIFT—STRAINS AND STRATEGIES

To find out what life is like in two-paycheck marriages, for nine years sociologist Arlie Hochschild (1989) and her research associates interviewed and reinterviewed fifty-some families. Hochschild also did participant observation with a dozen of them. She "shopped with them, visited friends, watched television, ate with them, and came along when they took their children to day care."

Hochschild notes that women have no more time in a day now than when they stayed home, but that now there is twice as much to get done. Most wives and husbands in her sample felt that the *second shift*—the household duties that follow the day's work for pay— is the wife's responsibility. But as they cook, clean, and take care of the children after their job at the office or factory, many wives feel tired, emotionally drained, and resentful. Not uncommonly, these feelings show up in the bedroom, where the wives show a lack of interest in sex.

It isn't that men do nothing around the house. But since they see household responsibilities as the wife's duty, they "help out" when they feel like it—or when they get nagged into it. And since most of us prefer to tend to our children than to clean house, men are more likely to "help out" on the second shift by taking children to do "fun" things—to see movies, or to go for outings in the park. In contrast, the woman's time with the children is more likely to be "maintenance"—feeding and bathing them, taking them to the doctor, and so on.

The strains from working the second shift affect not only the marital relationship, but also the wife's self-concept. Here is how one woman tried to buoy her flagging self-esteem:

> After taking time off for her first baby, Carol Alston felt depressed, "fat," and that she was "just a housewife." For a while she became the supermarket shopper who wanted to call down the aisles, "I'm an MBA! I'm an MBA!"

Most wives feel strongly that the second shift should be shared, but many feel that it is hopeless to try to get their husbands to change. They work the second shift, but they resent it. Others have a "showdown" with their husbands. Some even give the ultimatum, "It's share the second shift, or it's divorce." Still others try to be the "supermom" who can do it all.

Some men cooperate and cut down on their commitment to a career. Others cut back on movies, seeing friends, doing hobbies. Most men, however, engage in what Hochschild describes as "strategies of resistance." She identified the following:

- *Waiting it out.* Many men never volunteer to do household chores. Since many wives dislike asking, because it feels like "begging," this strategy often works. Some men make this strategy even more effective by showing irritation or becoming glum when they are asked, which discourages the wife from asking again.

- *Playing dumb.* When they do housework, some men become incompetent. They can't cook rice without burning it; when they go to the store, they forget grocery lists; they can never remember where the broiler pan is. Hochschild did not claim that husbands do these things on purpose, but, rather, that by withdrawing their mental attention from the task, they "get credit for trying and being a good sport"—but in such a way that they are not chosen next time.

- *Needs reduction.* An example of this strategy is a father of two who explained that he never shopped because he didn't "need anything." He didn't need to iron his clothes because he "[didn't] mind wearing a wrinkled shirt." He didn't need to cook because "cereal is fine." As Hochschild observed, "Through his reduction of needs, this man created a great void into which his wife stepped with her 'greater need' to see him wear an ironed shirt . . . and cook his dinner."

- *Substitute offerings.* Expressing appreciation to the wife for being so organized that she can handle both work for wages and the second shift at home can be a substitute for helping—and a subtle encouragement for her to keep on working the second shift. ■

ARLO & JANIS ® by Jimmy Johnson

The cartoonist has beautifully captured the reduction of needs strategy discussed by Hochschild.

For Your Consideration

Hochschild (1991) is confident that such problems can be solved. Based on the materials just presented,

1. Identify the underlying *structural* causes of the problem of the second shift.
2. Based on your answer to number 1, identify *structural* solutions to this problem.
3. Determine how a working wife and husband might best reconcile this problem.

The Symbolic Interactionist Perspective: Gender and the Meanings of Marriage

As noted in Chapter 1, symbolic interactionists focus on the meanings that people give to their lives. Let's apply this perspective to some surprising findings about husbands and housework.

The first finding is probably what you expect—the closer a husband's and wife's earnings, the more likely they are to share housework. Although husbands in such marriages don't share housework equally, they do more than other husbands. This finding, however, may be surprising: When husbands get laid off, most *decrease* their housework. *And husbands who earn less than their wives do the least housework.*

How can we explain this? It would seem that husbands who get laid off or who earn less than their wives would want to balance things out by doing more around the house, not less. Researchers suggest that the key is gender role. If a wife earns more than her husband, it threatens his masculinity—he takes it as a sign that he has failed in his traditional gender role of provider. To do housework—"women's work" in his eyes—threatens it even further. By avoiding housework, he "reclaims" his masculinity (Hochschild 1989; Brines 1994).

Two Marriages in One Another interesting finding of symbolic interactionists is how husbands and wives perceive their marriage. When asked how much housework each does, they give different answers. They even disagree about whether or not they fight over doing housework (Sanchez 1994). Sociologist Jessie Bernard, who studied this marital gulf, noted in a classic work (1972) that when researchers

> ask husbands and wives identical questions about the union they often get quite different replies. There is usually agreement on the number of children they have and a few other such verifiable items, although not, for example, on length of premarital acquaintance and of engagement, on age at marriage and interval between marriage and birth of first child. Indeed, with respect to even such basic components of the marriage as frequency of sexual relations, social interaction, household tasks, and decision making, they seem to be reporting on different marriages.

Why don't husbands and wives agree on basic matters such as how frequently they have sex? The answer lies in differing *perceptions* of lovemaking. It appears that in the typical marriage the wife desires greater emotional involvement from her husband, while the husband's desire is for more sex (Komter 1989; Barbeau 1992). When questioned about sex, then, the husband, feeling deprived, tends to underestimate it, while the wife, who is more reluctant to participate in sex because of unsatisfied intimacy needs, overestimates it (Bernard 1972).

Symbolic interactionists conclude that because husbands and wives hold down such different corners in marriage they perceive marriage differently. Their experiences contrast so sharply that *every marriage contains two separate marriages—his and hers.*

THE FAMILY LIFE CYCLE

Thus far we have seen that the forms of marriage and family vary widely, and we have examined marriage and family from the three sociological perspectives. Now let's discuss love, courtship, and the family life cycle.

Love and Courtship in Global Perspective

Until recently, social scientists thought that romantic love originated in western Europe during the medieval period (Mount 1992). When anthropologists William Jankowiak and Edward Fischer (1992) surveyed the data available on 166 societies around the world, they found that this was not so. **Romantic love**—people being sexually attracted to one another and idealizing the other—showed up in 88 percent (147) of these groups. The role of love, however, differs sharply from one society to another. As the Perspectives box on the next page details, for example, Indians don't expect love to occur until *after* marriage—if then.

Because love plays such a significant role in Western life—and often is thought to be the *only* proper basis for marriage—social scientists have probed this concept with the tools of the trade: laboratory experiments, questionnaires, interviews, and systematic observations. One of the more interesting experiments was conducted by psychologists Donald Dutton and Arthur Aron, who discovered that fear breeds love (Rubin 1985). Across a rocky gorge, about 230 feet above the Capilano River in North Vancouver, a rickety footbridge sways in the wind. Another footbridge, a solid structure, crosses only ten feet above a shallow stream. An attractive woman approached men who were crossing these bridges, and told them she was studying "the effects of exposure to scenic attractions on creative expression." She showed them a picture, and they wrote down their associations. The sexual imagery in their stories showed that the men on the unsteady, frightening bridge were more sexually aroused than the men on the solid bridge. More of these men also called the young woman afterward—supposedly to get more information about the study.

This research, of course, was really about sexual attraction, not love. The point, however, is that romantic love usually begins with sexual attraction. We find ourselves sexually attracted to someone and spend time with that person. If we discover mutual interests, we may label our feelings "love." Apparently, then, romantic love has two components. The first is emotional, a feeling of sexual attraction. The second is cognitive, a label that we attach to our feelings. If we do attach this label, we describe ourselves as being "in love."

romantic love feelings of erotic attraction accompanied by an idealization of the other

Romantic love reaches far back into history, as illustrated by this Etruscan sarcophagus. The Etruscans, reaching their peak of civilization in 500 B.C. in what is now Italy, were vanquished by Rome about one hundred years later. The artist has portrayed the couple's mutual affection and satisfaction.

PERSPECTIVES | Cultural Diversity Around the World

EAST IS EAST AND WEST IS WEST . . .
LOVE AND ARRANGED MARRIAGE IN INDIA

After Arun Bharat Ram returned home with a degree from the University of Michigan, his mother announced that she wanted to find him a wife. Arun would be a good "catch" anywhere: 27 years old, educated, well mannered, intelligent, handsome—and, not incidentally, heir to a huge fortune.

Arun's mother already had someone in mind. Manju came from a solid, middle-class family and was also a college graduate. Arun and Manju met in a coffee shop in a luxury hotel—along with both sets of parents. He found her pretty and quiet. He liked that. She was impressed that he didn't boast about his background.

After four more meetings, one where the two young people met by themselves, the parents asked their children if they were willing to marry. Neither had any major objections.

The Prime Minister of India and fifteen hundred other guests came to the wedding.

"I didn't love him," Manju says. "But when we talked, we had a lot of things in common." She then adds, "But now I couldn't live without him. I've never thought of another man since I met him."

Although India has undergone extensive social change, Indian sociologists estimate that about 95 percent of marriages are still arranged by the parents. Today, however, as with Arun and Manju, couples have veto power over their parents' selection. Another innovation is that the couple are allowed to talk to each other before the wedding—unheard of just a generation ago.

The fact that arranged marriages are the norm in India does not mean that this ancient land is without a tradition of passion and love. Far from it. The *Kama-sutra* is world-renowned for its explicit details about lovemaking, and the erotic sculptures at Khajuraho still startle Westerners today. Indian mythology extols the copulations of gods, and every Indian schoolchild knows the love story of the god Krishna and Radha, the beautiful milkmaid he found irresistible.

Why, then, aren't love and passion the basis of marriage in India? Why does it have arranged marriages? And why does this practice persist today, even among the educated and upper classes? We can also ask why the United States has such an individualistic approach to marriage.

To answer these questions takes us to a basic sociological principle: *A group's marriage practices match its values and its patterns of social stratification.* Individual mate selection matches U.S. values of individuality and independence, while arranged marriages match Indian values of children deferring to parental authority. In addition, arranged marriages reaffirm caste lines by channeling marriage within the same caste.

To Indians, to practice unrestricted dating would be to trust important matters to inexperienced young people. It would encourage premarital sex, which, in turn, would break down family lines (virginity at marriage assures the upper castes that they know the fatherhood of the children). Consequently, Indian young people are socialized to think that parents have cooler heads and superior wisdom in these matters. In the United States, family lines are much less important, and caste is an alien concept.

Even ideas of love differ. For Indians, love is a peaceful emotion, based on long-term commitment and devotion to family. Indians also think of love as something that can be "created" between two people. To do so, one needs to arrange the right conditions. Marriage is one of those right conditions.

Thus, Indian and U.S. cultures have produced different approaches to love and marriage. For Indians, marriage produces love—while for Americans, love produces marriage. Americans see love as having a mysterious element, a passion that suddenly seizes an individual. Indians see love as a peaceful feeling that develops when a man and a woman are united in intimacy and share common interests and goals in life. ■

Sources: Based on Cooley 1962; Gupta 1979; Weintraub 1988; Bumiller 1992; Sprecher and Chandak 1992; Whyte 1992; Dugger 1998.

Marriage

In the typical case, marriage in the United States is preceded by "love," but, contrary to folklore, whatever love is, it certainly is not blind. That is, love does not hit people willy-nilly, as if Cupid had shot darts blindly into a crowd. If it did, marital patterns would be unpredictable. An examination of who marries whom, however, reveals that love is socially channeled.

The Social Channels of Love and Marriage When we marry, we generally think that we have freely chosen our spouse. With few exceptions, however, our choices follow highly predictable social channels, especially age, education, social class, race, and religion (Tucker and Mitchell-Kerman 1990; Kalmijn 1991). For example, a Latina with a college degree whose parents are both physicians is likely to fall in love and marry a Latino slightly older than herself who has graduated from college. Similarly, a female high school dropout whose parents are on welfare is likely to fall in love with and marry a man who comes from a background similar to hers.

Sociologists use the term **homogamy** to refer to the tendency of people with similar characteristics to marry one another. Homogamy occurs largely as a result of *propinquity,* or spatial nearness. That is, we tend to "fall in love" and marry people who live near us or whom we meet at school, church, or work. The people with whom we associate are far from a random sample of the population, for social filters produce neighborhoods, schools, and churches that follow racial-ethnic and social class lines.

As with all social patterns, there are exceptions. Although 94 percent of Americans who marry choose someone of their same race, 6 percent do not. Because there are 55 million married couples in the United States, those 6 percent add up, totaling three and a half million couples.

One of the more dramatic changes in U.S. marriage is a sharp increase in interracial marriages. We can trace this change back to the norm-shattering 1960s. Among the many changes ushered in during this period was a breaking of the "color line" in courtship. As you can see from Figure 16.2, interracial marriages also show distinct subpatterns.

Childbirth

The popular image is that the arrival of a baby makes a couple deliriously happy. The facts are somewhat different.

Marital Satisfaction Sociologist Martin Whyte (1992), who interviewed wives in the Detroit area, found that marital satisfaction usually *decreases* with the birth of a child (Whyte 1992; Bird 1997). To understand why, recall from Chapter 6 that a dyad (just two persons) provides greater intimacy than a triad (after adding a third person, interaction must be shared). To move from the theoretical to the practical, think about the implications for marriage of coping with a fragile newborn's 24-hour-a-day needs of being fed, soothed, and diapered, while having less free time, heavier expenses, and less sleep.

Social Class Sociologist Lillian Rubin (1976, 1992b) compared fifty working-class couples with twenty-five middle-class couples. She found that social class made a significant difference in how couples adjusted to the arrival of children. For the average working-class couple, the first baby arrived just nine months after marriage. They hardly had time to adjust to being husband and wife before they were thrust into the demanding roles of mother and father. The result was financial problems, bickering, and interference from in-laws. The young husbands weren't ready to "settle down" and resented getting less attention from their wives. A working-class husband who became a father just five months after getting married made a telling remark to Rubin when he said, "There I was, just a kid myself, and I finally had someone to take care of me. Then suddenly, I had to take care of a kid, and she was too busy with him *to take care of me*" (italics added).

In contrast, the middle-class couples postponed the birth of their first child, which gave them more time to adjust to each other. On average, their first baby arrived three years after marriage. Their greater financial resources also worked in their favor, making life a lot easier and marriage more pleasant.

Child Rearing

Who's minding the kids while the parents are at work? A while back such a question would have been ridiculous, for the mother was at home taking care of the children. As with Sharon in our opening vignette, however, that assumption no longer holds. With three of five U.S. mothers working for wages, who is taking care of the children?

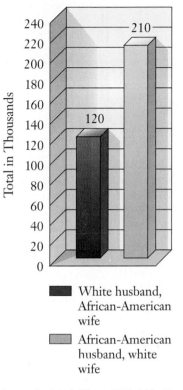

THE RACIAL BACKGROUND OF HUSBANDS AND WIVES IN MARRIAGES BETWEEN WHITES AND AFRICAN AMERICANS

■ White husband, African-American wife

□ African-American husband, white wife

Source: Statistical Abstract 1999:Table 65.

homogamy the tendency of people with similar characteristics to marry one another

Married Couples and Single Mothers Figure 16.3 compares the child care arrangements of married couples and single mothers. As you can see, their overall child care arrangements are similar. For each group, about one of three preschoolers is cared for in the child's home. The main difference is the role of the child's father while the mother is at work. For married couples, almost one of four children is cared for by the father, while for single mothers that figure plummets to only one of fourteen. As you can see, grandparents step in to help fill the gap left by the absent father.

Day Care As Figure 16.3 shows, about one of six children is in day care. The broad conclusions of research on day care were reported in Chapter 3 (pages 80–81). Apparently

Figure 16.3

WHO TAKES CARE OF PRESCHOOLERS WHILE THEIR MOTHERS ARE AT WORK?

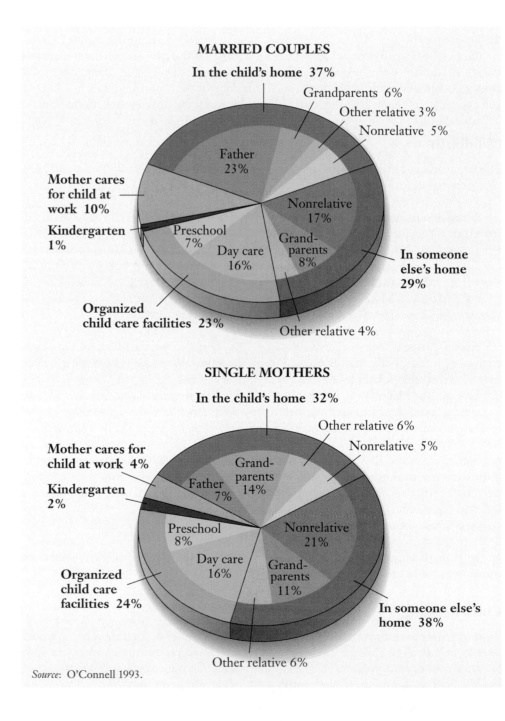

MARRIED COUPLES

In the child's home 37%

Grandparents 6%

Other relative 3%

Nonrelative 5%

Father 23%

Nonrelative 17%

Mother cares for child at work 10%

Kindergarten 1%

Preschool 7%

Day care 16%

Grandparents 8%

In someone else's home 29%

Organized child care facilities 23%

Other relative 4%

SINGLE MOTHERS

In the child's home 32%

Other relative 6%

Nonrelative 5%

Mother cares for child at work 4%

Kindergarten 2%

Father 7%

Grandparents 14%

Preschool 8%

Nonrelative 21%

Day care 16%

Grandparents 11%

Organized child care facilities 24%

In someone else's home 38%

Other relative 6%

Source: O'Connell 1993.

only a minority of U.S. day care centers offer high quality care as measured by stimulating learning activities, safety, and emotional warmth and support (Bergmann 1995). A primary reason for this dismal situation is the abysmal salaries paid day care workers, which average less than $10,000 a year (Casper and O'Connell 1997).

It is difficult for parents to judge the quality of day care, since they don't know what takes place when they are not there. The Internet is providing an innovative solution to parents' nagging fears that their children might be neglected or even abused. Closed circuit television cameras pipe images onto the Web. Parents at work can visit via cyberspace each room of the day care center, monitoring their toddler's activities and care (Rabinovitz 1998).

Nannies   For upper-middle-class parents, nannies have become popular. Part of their attraction is one-on-one care. Another is in-home care, which reduces the chances of a child catching illnesses and eliminates the need to transport the child to an unfamiliar environment. A recurring problem is tensions between the parents and the nanny: jealousy that the nanny may be the one to see the first step or hear the first word or is sometimes called mommy; different discipline styles; disdain on the part of the nanny that the mother isn't staying home with her child; the child crying when the nanny leaves, but not when the mother goes to work (Ansberry 1993).

Social Class   Social class is highly significant in child rearing. As noted on pages 79–80, sociologist Melvin Kohn found that parents socialize their children into the norms of their work worlds. Because members of the working class are more closely supervised and are expected to follow explicit rules laid down for them by others, their concern is less with their children's motivation and more with outward conformity. They are more apt to use physical punishment. In contrast, middle-class parents, who are expected to take more initiative on the job, are more concerned that their children develop curiosity, self-expression, and self-control. They also are more likely to withdraw privileges or affection than they are to use physical punishment.

Birth Order   Birth order is also important. Parents tend to discipline their firstborns more than their later children, and to give them more attention. When the second child arrives, the firstborn competes to maintain the attention. Researchers suggest that this instills in firstborns a greater drive for success, which is why they are more likely than their siblings to earn higher grades in school, to go to college, and to go further in college. Firstborns are even more likely to become astronauts, to appear on the cover of *Time* magazine, and to become president of the United States. Although subsequent children may not go as far, most are less anxious about being successful, and more relaxed in their relationships (Snow et al. 1981; Goleman 1985). Firstborns are also more likely to defend the status quo and to support conservative causes, later-borns to upset the apple cart and to support liberal causes (Sulloway 1997).

Although such tendencies are strong, they are only that—tendencies. Some first-borns, for example, are conservative on some issues, but liberal on others (Freese et al. 1999). *There are no inevitable outcomes of birth order, social class, or any other social characteristic.*

The Family in Later Life

The later stages of family life bring their own pleasures to be savored and problems to be solved. Let's look at the empty nest, retirement, and widowhood.

The Empty Nest   When the last child leaves home, the husband and wife are left, as at the beginning of their marriage, "alone together." This situation, sometimes called the **empty nest,** is thought to signal a difficult time of adjustment for women, because they have devoted so much energy to a child-rearing role that is now gone. Sociologist Lillian Rubin (1992a), who interviewed both career women and homemakers, found that this picture is largely a myth. Contrary to the stereotype, she found that women's satisfaction generally

empty nest a married couple's domestic situation after the last child has left home

A type of "not-so-empty nest" consists of older women who bear children. Shown here is an unusual situation: Aracelia Garcia, a 54-year-old mother of eight (who also has thirteen grandchildren) as she awaited the birth of triplets. The triplets were born in good health. Mrs. Garcia will be 72 when her youngest children enter college.

increases when the last child leaves home. A typical statement was made by a 45-year-old woman, who leaned forward in her chair as though to tell Rubin a secret:

> To tell you the truth, most of the time it's a big relief to be free of them, finally. I suppose that's awful to say. But you know what, most of the women I know feel the same way. It's just that they're uncomfortable saying it because there's all this talk about how sad mothers are supposed to be when the kids leave home.

Similar findings have come from other researchers, who report that most mothers feel relieved at being able to spend more time on themselves. Many couples also report a renewed sense of intimacy at this time (Mackey and O'Brien 1995). This closeness appears to stem from four causes: The couple is free of the many responsibilities of child rearing, they have more leisure, their income is at its highest, and they have fewer financial obligations.

The Not-So-Empty Nest An interesting twist on leaving home has taken place in recent years. With prolonged education and the higher cost of establishing a household, U.S. children are leaving home later. In addition, many who strike out on their own find the cost or responsibility too great and return to the home nest. As a result, 53 percent of all U.S. 18- to 24-year-olds live with their parents, and one of eight 25- to 34-year-olds is still living at home (*Statistical Abstract* 1997:Table 65).

Widowhood Women are more likely than men to become widowed and to have to face the wrenching problems this entails. Not only does the average wife live longer than her husband, but also she is married to a man who is older than she. The death of a spouse tears at the self, clawing at identities that had merged through the years (DiGiulio 1992). Now that the one who had become an essential part of the self is gone, the survivor, as in adolescence, is forced once again to wrestle with the perplexing question "Who am I?"

When death is unexpected, the adjustment is more difficult (Hiltz 1989). Survivors who know that death is impending make preparations that smooth the transition—from arranging finances to psychologically preparing themselves for being alone. Saying goodbye and cultivating treasured last memories help them to adjust to the death of an intimate companion.

DIVERSITY IN U.S. FAMILIES

It is important to note that there is no such thing as *the* American family. Rather, family life varies widely throughout the United States. The significance of social class, noted earlier, will continue to be evident as we examine diversity in U.S. families.

African-American Families

Note that the heading reads African-American *families,* not *The* African-American family. There is no such thing as *the* African-American family any more than there is *the* white family or *the* Latino family. The primary distinction is not between African Americans and other groups, but between social classes. Because African Americans who are members of the upper class follow the class interests reviewed in Chapter 10—preservation of privilege and family fortune—they are especially concerned about the family background of those whom their children marry (Gatewood 1990). To them, marriage is viewed as a merger of family lines. Children of this class marry later than children of other classes.

Middle-class African-American families focus on achievement and respectability. Both husband and wife are likely to work outside the home. Their concerns are that the family stay intact and that their children go to college, get good jobs, and marry well—that is, marry people like themselves, respectable and hardworking, who want to get ahead in school and pursue a successful career.

African-American families in poverty face all the problems that cluster around poverty (Franklin 1994). Because the men are likely to have few skills and to be unemployed, it is difficult for them to fulfill the cultural roles of husband and father. Consequently, these families are likely to be headed by a woman and to have a high rate of unwed motherhood. Divorce and desertion also are more common than among other classes. Sharing scarce resources and broadening the notion of kinship are primary survival mechanisms. That is, people who have helped out in hard times are considered brothers, sisters, or cousins to whom one owes obligations as though they were blood relatives (Stack 1974). Sociologists use the term *fictive kin* to refer to this stretching of kinship.

From Figure 16.4, you can see that, compared with other groups, African-American families are less

There is no such thing as *the* African-American family, any more than there is *the* Native-American, Asian-American, Latino, or Irish-American family. Rather, each racial-ethnic group has different types of families, with the primary determinant being social class.

This African-American family is observing Kwanzaa. This new festival, observed from December 26 to January 1, celebrates African heritage. Can you explain how Kwanzaa is an example of ethnic work, a concept introduced in Chapter 9?

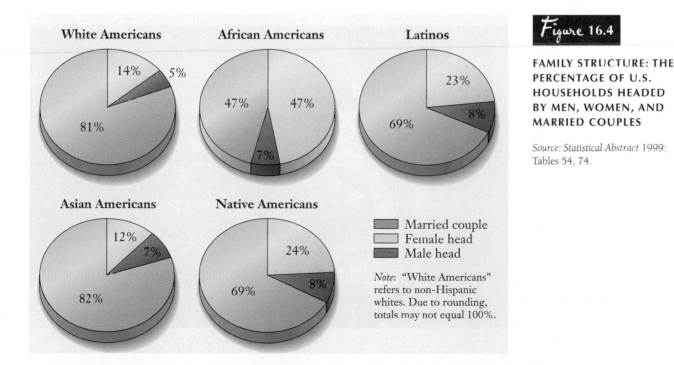

Figure 16.4

FAMILY STRUCTURE: THE PERCENTAGE OF U.S. HOUSEHOLDS HEADED BY MEN, WOMEN, AND MARRIED COUPLES

Source: Statistical Abstract 1999: Tables 54, 74.

White Americans — 14%, 5%, 81%

African Americans — 47%, 47%, 7%

Latinos — 23%, 8%, 69%

Asian Americans — 12%, 7%, 82%

Native Americans — 24%, 8%, 69%

Legend:
■ Married couple
□ Female head
■ Male head

Note: "White Americans" refers to non-Hispanic whites. Due to rounding, totals may not equal 100%.

likely to be headed by married couples and more likely to be headed by women. Because of a **marriage squeeze**—an imbalance in the sex ratio, in this instance fewer unmarried men per 100 unmarried women—African-American women are more likely than other racial-ethnic groups to marry men who are less educated than themselves, who are unemployed, or who are divorced (South 1991).

Latino Families

As Figure 16.4 shows, the proportion of Latino families headed by married couples and women falls in between whites and African Americans. The effects of social class on families, which I just sketched, also apply to Latinos. In addition, families differ by country of origin. Families from Cuba, for example, are more likely to be headed by a married couple than are families from Puerto Rico (*Statistical Abstract* 1999:Table 55).

What really distinguishes Latino families, however, is culture—especially the Spanish language, the Roman Catholic religion, and a strong family orientation coupled with a disapproval of divorce. Although there is some debate among the experts, another characteristic seems to be **machismo**—an emphasis on male strength and dominance. In Chicano families (those originating from Mexico), the husband-father plays a stronger role than in either white or African-American families (Vega 1990). Machismo apparently decreases with each generation in the United States (Hurtado et al. 1992). In general, however, the wife-mother makes most of the day-to-day decisions for the family and does the routine disciplining of the children. She is usually more family centered than her husband, displaying more warmth and affection for her children.

Generalizations have limits, of course, and as with other ethnic groups individual Latino families vary considerably from one to another (Baca Zinn 1994; Carrasquillo 1994).

Asian-American Families

As you can see from Figure 16.4, the structure of Asian-American families is almost identical to that of white families. Apart from this broad characteristic, because Asian Americans come from twenty countries, their family life varies considerably, reflecting their many cultures. In addition, as with Latino families, the more recent their immigration, the closer their family life reflects the family life of their country of origin (Kibria 1993; Glenn 1994).

marriage squeeze the difficulty a group of men or women have in finding marriage partners, due to an imbalanced sex ratio

machismo an emphasis on male strength and dominance

Although there is no such thing as *the* Latino family, in general, Latinos place high emphasis on extended family relaitonships.

Despite such differences, sociologist Bob Suzuki (1985), who studied Chinese-American and Japanese-American families, identified several distinctive characteristics. Although Asian Americans have adopted the nuclear family, they have retained Confucian values that provide a distinct framework for family life: humanism, collectivity, self-discipline, hierarchy, respect for the elderly, moderation, and obligation. Obligation means that each individual owes respect to other family members and is responsible for never bringing shame on the family. Asian Americans tend to be more permissive than Anglos in child rearing and more likely to use shame and guilt rather than physical punishment to control their children's behavior.

Native-American Families

Perhaps the single most significant issue that Native-American families face is whether to follow traditional values or to assimilate (Yellowbird and Snipp 1994). This primary distinction makes for vast differences among families. The traditionals speak native languages and emphasize distinctive Native-American values and beliefs. Those that have assimilated into the broader culture do not.

Figure 16.4 depicts the structure of Native-American families. You can see how it is almost identical to that of Latinos. In general, Native-American parents are permissive with their children and avoid physical punishment. Elders play a much more active role in their children's families than they do in most U.S. families: They not only provide child care, but also teach and discipline children. Like others, Native-American families differ by social class.

To search for *the* Native-American family would be fruitless. There are rural, urban, single-parent, extended, nuclear, rich, poor, traditional, and assimilated Native-American families, to name just a few. Shown here is an Inupiat family in Kotzebue, Alaska.

■ **In Sum** From this brief review, you can see that race-ethnicity signifies little for understanding family life. Rather, social class and culture hold the keys. The more resources a family has, the more it assumes the characteristics of a middle-class nuclear family. Compared with the poor, middle-class families have fewer children, have fewer unmarried mothers, and place greater emphasis on educational achievement and deferred gratification.

One-Parent Families

One-parent families have become a matter of general concern. They are discussed by TV talk show hosts and government officials alike. The increase in the number of one-parent families is no myth. Since 1970, the number of one-parent families has tripled, while the number of two-parent families has decreased by 200,000 (*Statistical Abstract* 1995:Table 71; 1999:Table 77). Two primary reasons underlie this change. The first is the high divorce rate, which each year forces a million children from two-parent homes to one-parent homes (*Statistical Abstract* 1999:Table 159). The second is the increase in births to women who are not married. Overall, 32 percent of U.S. children are born to unmarried women (*Statistical Abstract* 1995:Table 94; 1999:Table 99).

The primary reason for the concern, however, may have less to do with children being reared by one parent and more to do with most one-parent families being poor. The poverty is not a coincidence. Most one-parent families are headed by women. Although 90 percent of children of divorce live with their mothers, most divorced women earn less than their former husbands. And most mothers who have never married have little education and few marketable skills, which condemns them to bouncing from one minimum-wage job to another, with welfare sandwiched in between.

To understand the typical one-parent family, then, we need to view it through the lens of poverty, for that is its primary source of strain. The results are serious, not just for these

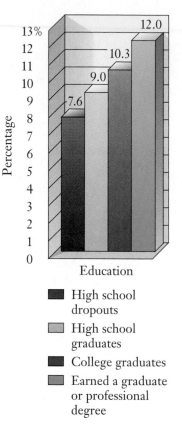

Education

■ High school dropouts

□ High school graduates

■ College graduates

■ Earned a graduate or professional degree

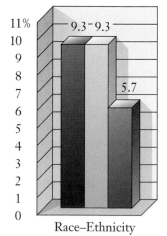

Race–Ethnicity

■ White Americans

□ African Americans

■ Latinas

Note: Only these three groups are in the source.

Source: *Statistical Abstract* 1997:Table 107.

parents and their children, but for society as a whole. Children from single-parent families are more likely to drop out of school, to get arrested, to have emotional problems, and to get divorced (McLanahan and Sandefur 1994; Menaghan et al. 1997). If female, they are more likely as teenagers to bear children and more likely to bear children outside marriage. The cycle of poverty is so powerful that *nearly half* of all welfare recipients are current or former teenage parents (Corbett 1995).

Families Without Children

Overall, about 14 percent of U.S. married couples never have children (*Statistical Abstract* 1999:Table 109). The percentage differs by education. As Figure 16.5 shows, the more education a woman has, the more likely she is to expect to bear no children. This figure shows that race-ethnicity is also significant. As you can see, Latinas are much less likely to expect to remain childless than are white and African-American women.

Why do some couples choose not to have children? Sociologist Kathleen Gerson (1985) found that some women see their marriage as too fragile to withstand the strains a child would bring. Other women believe they would be stuck at home—bored, lonely, and with diminishing career opportunities. Perhaps the most common reason, though, is summarized by this statement in a newsletter:

> We are DINKS (dual incomes, no kids). We are happily married. I am 43, my wife is 42. We have been married for almost twenty years. . . . Our investment strategy has a lot to do with our personal philosophy: "You can have kids . . . Or you can have everything else!"

With trends firmly in place—more education and careers for women; technological advances in contraception; abortion; the high cost of rearing children; and an emphasis on possessing more and more materials things—the proportion of women who never bear children is likely to increase.

Many childless couples, however, are not childless by choice. Some adopt, while a few turn to the solutions featured in the Sociology and New Technology box.

Blended Families

An increasingly significant type of family in the United States is the **blended family,** one whose members were once part of other families. Two divorced people who marry and each bring their children into a new family unit become a blended family. With divorce common, millions of children spend some of their childhood in blended families. One result is more complicated family relationships. This is exemplified by the following description written by one of my students:

> I live with my dad. I should say that I live with my dad, my brother (whose mother and father are also my mother and father), my half sister (whose father is my dad, but whose mother is my father's last wife), and two stepbrothers and stepsisters (children of my father's current wife). My father's wife (my current stepmother, not to be confused with his second wife who, I guess, is no longer my stepmother) is pregnant, and soon we all will have a new brother or sister. Or will it be a half brother or half sister?
>
> If you can't figure this out, I don't blame you. I have trouble myself. It gets very complicated around Christmas. Should we all stay together? Split up and go to several other homes? Who do we buy gifts for, anyway?

Gay and Lesbian Families

In 1989, Denmark was the first country to legalize marriage between people of the same sex. Since then, Holland, Norway, and Sweden have made same-sex marriages legal. In no U.S. state are same-sex marriages legal, but that is changing. In 2000, Vermont became the

Sociology & the New Technology

THE BRAVE NEW WORLD OF HIGH-TECH REPRODUCTION: WHERE TECHNOLOGY OUTPACES LAW AND SOMETIMES COMMON SENSE

Jaycee has five parents—or none, depending on how you look at it. The story goes like this. Luanne and John Buzzanca were infertile. Although they spent more than $100,000 on treatments, nothing worked. Then, a fertility clinic took an egg that had been surgically removed from another woman, placed it in a laboratory dish, and mixed it with sperm from another man. They implanted the fertilized egg in Pamela Snell, who delivered Jaycee (Davis 1998a; Foote 1998).

Her job as surrogate mother completed, Pamela handed Jaycee over to Luanne, who was waiting at her bedside. John would have been there, but he had filed for divorce just a month before. When Luanne asked John for child support, John refused. Luanne sued. The judge ruled that John didn't have to pay. Because Jaycee had been conceived in a petri dish with an egg and sperm from anonymous donors, John wasn't the baby's father. The judge added that Luanne wasn't the baby's mother either.

Five parents—or none? Welcome to the brave—and very real—new world of high-tech reproduction. Although most children conceived with the aid of high-tech procedures claim only two parents, reproductive technologies have made such scenarios a nightmare for the unsuspecting. ■

For Your Consideration

In our new, high-tech world, what's a mother? Is Pamela Snell,

The McCaughey septuplets of Carlisle, Iowa, with their parents, Bobby and Kenny, and their three-year-old sister, Mikayla.

who carried Jaycee, a mother? Strangely, although she gave birth, she is not. Is the donor of the egg a mother? Biologically, yes, but legally, no. Is Luanne a mother? Fortunately, for Jaycee's sake, a higher court ruled that she is.

What's a father? Consider this case. Elizabeth Higgins of Jacksonville, Indiana, had difficulty conceiving. She gave eggs to Memorial Hospital. Her husband gave sperm. A hospital technician mistakenly mixed someone else's sperm with Mrs. Higgins' eggs. The fertilized eggs were implanted in Mrs. Higgins, who gave birth to twin girls. Mrs. Higgins is white, her husband black. Mr. Higgins was bothered because the girls had only Caucasian features, and he

couldn't bond with them. Mr. and Mrs. Higgins separated. They sued the hospital for child support, arguing that the hospital, not Mr. Higgins, is the father (Davis 1998b).

What's a grandparent in this brave new world? A man in New Orleans donated sperm to a fertility clinic. He died, and his girlfriend decided to be artificially inseminated with his sperm. The grieved parents of the man were upset that their son, although dead, could still father children. They also feared that those children, who would be their grandchildren, would have a legal claim to their estate (Davis 1998b).

With same-sex marriages now legal in several European countries, how long will it be until they are legal in the United States? Shown here are Ninia Baehr and Genora Dancel, who challenged Hawaii's right to limit marriage to opposite-sex couples.

first state to legalize what they call "gay unions." Except for the name, "gay unions" are marriages. By retaining the term "marriage" for heterosexual couples, Vermont softened criticism of its pathbreaking law. It seems inevitable that other states will follow, and that some will use the term marriage to refer to same-sex unions.

What are gay marriages like? As with everything else in life, same-sex couples cannot be painted with a single brush stroke (Allen and Demo 1995). As with opposite-sex couples, social class is highly significant, and orientations to life differ according to education, occupation, and income. Sociologists Blumstein and Schwartz (1985) interviewed same-sex couples and found their main struggles to be housework, money, careers, problems with relatives, and sexual adjustment—the same problems that face heterosexual couples. Same-sex couples are more likely to break up, however, and one argument for legalizing gay marriages is that they will become more stable.

*T*RENDS IN U.S. FAMILIES

As is apparent from this discussion, patterns of marriage and family life in the United States are undergoing a fundamental shift. Other indicators of this change, which we shall now examine, include the postponement of marriage, cohabitation, single motherhood, divorce, and remarriage.

Postponing Marriage

blended family a family whose members were once part of other families

Figure 16.6 illustrates one of the most significant trends in U.S. marriage. As you can see, the average age of first-time brides and grooms declined from 1890 to about 1950. In 1890 the typical first-time bride was 22, but by 1950 she had just left her teens. For about twenty years, there was little change. Then in 1970 the average age started to increase sharply. *To-*

Figure 16.6

THE MEDIAN AGE AT WHICH AMERICANS MARRY FOR THE FIRST TIME

Source: Statistical Abstract 1999:Table 158.

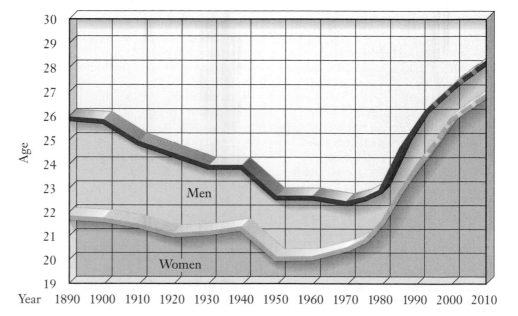

day the average first-time bride is older than at any time in U.S. history. The average age of first-time grooms is back to where it was in 1890.

Since postponing marriage is today's norm, it may come as a surprise to many readers to learn that *most* U.S. women used to marry before they turned 25. Look at Figure 16.7. You can see that the proportion of younger Americans who have not married has soared. The percentage of unmarried women is now *double* what it was in 1970.

Why did this change occur? As sociologist Larry Bumpass points out, if we were to count cohabitation, we would find that this average age has changed little (Bumpass et al. 1991). Although Americans have postponed the age at which they first marry, they have *not* postponed the age at which they first set up housekeeping with someone of the opposite sex. Let's look at this trend in cohabitation.

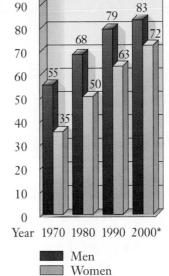

Figure 16.7

AMERICANS AGES 20–24 WHO HAVE NEVER MARRIED

Source: Statistical Abstract 1993:Table 60; 1999:Table 63.

Cohabitation

Figure 16.8 shows the remarkable increase in **cohabitation**, adults living together in a sexual relationship without being married. *Eight times* more Americans are cohabiting today than did so twenty-five years ago. Forty-one percent of U.S. women have cohabited (*Statistical Abstract* 1999:Table 66). (Although the source does not give totals for men, it must be similar.) With this change in behavior have come changed attitudes. For example, when hiring executives, some corporations now pay for live-in partners to attend orientation sessions.

cohabitation unmarried couples living together in a sexual relationship

Commitment is the essential difference between cohabitation and marriage. Whereas the assumption of marriage is permanence, cohabiting couples agree to remain together for "as long as it works out." Marriage requires public vows—and a judge to authorize its termination. Cohabitation requires only that a couple move in together; if the relationship sours, they can move out. Sociologists have found that couples who cohabit before marriage are more likely to divorce than couples who do not first cohabit (Bennett et al. 1988; Whyte 1992). The reason, they conclude, is that cohabiting couples have a weaker commitment to marriage and to relationships.

Unmarried Mothers

Earlier we discussed the steady increase in births to unmarried U.S. mothers. To better understand this trend, we can place it in global perspective. As Figure 16.9 on the next page shows, the United States is not alone in this increase. Of the ten industrialized nations for which we have data, all except Japan have experienced sharp increases in births to unmarried mothers. The U.S. rate is far from the highest; it falls in the middle third of these nations.

From this figure, it seems fair to conclude that industrialization sets in motion social forces that encourage

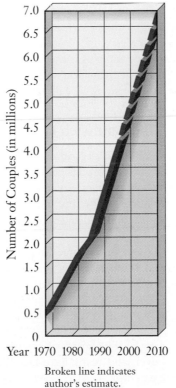

Figure 16.8

COHABITATION IN THE UNITED STATES

Source: Statistical Abstract 1995:Table 60; 1999:Table 68.

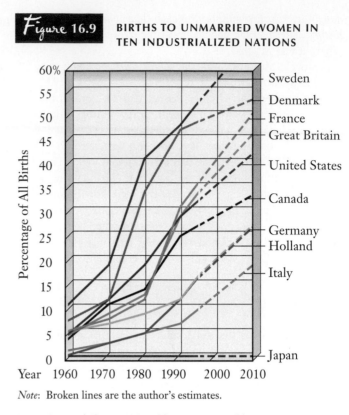

Figure 16.9 **BIRTHS TO UNMARRIED WOMEN IN TEN INDUSTRIALIZED NATIONS**

Note: Broken lines are the author's estimates.

Source: Statistical Abstract 1993:Table 1380; 1998:Table 1347.

out-of-wedlock births. There are several problems with this conclusion, however. Why was the rate so low in 1960? Industrialization had been in process for many decades prior to that time. Why are the rates in the bottom four nations only a fraction of those in the top two nations? Why does Japan's rate remain so consistently low? Why are Sweden's and Denmark's so high? With but a couple of minor exceptions, the ranking of these nations today is the same as it was in 1960. By itself, then, industrialization is too simple an answer. A fuller explanation must focus on customs and values embedded within these cultures. For that answer, we will have to await further research.

The Sandwich Generation and Elder Care

The *sandwich generation* refers to people who find themselves sandwiched between two generations, responsible both for their children and for their own aging parents. Typically between the ages of 40 and 55, these people find themselves pulled in two strongly compelling directions. Feeling responsible both for their children and their parents, they are plagued with guilt and anger because they can be in only one place at a time (Shellenbarger 1994a).

Concerns about elder care have gained the attention of the corporate world, and about 25 percent of large companies offer some kind of elder care assistance to their employees (Hewitt Associates 1995). This assistance includes seminars, referral services, and flexible work schedules designed to help employees meet their responsibilities without missing so much work (Shellenbarger 1994b). Some experts believe that companies may respond more positively to the issue of elder care than to child day care. Why? Most CEOs are older men whose wives stayed home to take care of their children, so they lack an understanding of the stresses of balancing work and child care. Nearly all have aging parents, however, and many have faced the turmoil of trying to cope with work, family, and aging parents.

With people living longer, this issue is likely to become increasingly urgent.

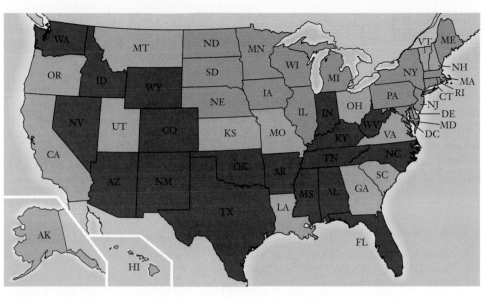

Figure 16.10

SOCIAL MAP: THE "WHERE" OF U.S. DIVORCE

Source: Statistical Abstract 1999: Table 162.

■ Lower than average (2.6 to 3.9 annual divorces per 1,000 population)
■ Average (4.0–4.9 annual divorces per 1,000 population)
■ Higher than average (5.0 to 10.4 annual divorces per 1,000 population)

DIVORCE AND REMARRIAGE

The topic of family life would not be complete without considering divorce. Let's first try to determine how much divorce there really is.

Problems in Measuring Divorce

You probably have heard that the U.S. divorce rate is 50 percent, a figure that is popular with reporters. The statistic is true in the sense that each year about half as many divorces are granted as there are marriages performed. In 1998, for example, 2,244,000 U.S. couples married and 1,135,000 couples divorced ("Population Today" 2000).

With these statistics, what is wrong with saying that the divorce rate is 50 percent? The real question is why these two totals should be compared in the first place. The couples who divorced do not—with rare exceptions—come from the group that married that year. The one set of figures has *nothing* to do with the other, so these statistics in no way establish the divorce rate.

What figures should we compare, then? Couples who divorce are drawn from the entire group of married people in the country. Since the United States has 55,000,000 married couples, and only 1,135,000 of them obtained divorces in 1998, the divorce rate is 2.1 percent, not 50 percent. A couple's chances of still being married at the end of a year are 98 percent—not bad odds—and certainly much better odds than the mass media would have us believe. As the Social Map above shows, however, the "odds," if we want to call them that, change depending on where you live.

Over time, of course, those annual 2.1 percentages add up. A third way of measuring divorce, then, is to ask, "Of all U.S. adults, what percentage are divorced?" Figure 16.11 shows the

Figure 16.11   **WHAT PERCENTAGE OF AMERICANS ARE DIVORCED?**

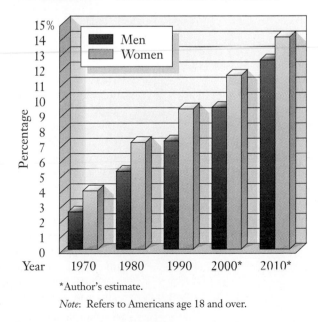

*Author's estimate.

Note: Refers to Americans age 18 and over.

Source: Statistical Abstract 1995:Table 58; 1999:Table 62.

Table 16.2

DIVORCE RATES IN TEN INDUSTRIALIZED NATIONS

	1960	1970	1980	1990	1995
United States	10	15	23	21	20
Denmark	6	8	11	13	12
Canada	2	6	10	11	11
Great Britain	2	5	12	13	13
Sweden	5	7	11	12	14
Germany	4	5	6	8	9
France	3	3	6	8	9
Netherlands	2	3	8	8	10
Japan	4	4	5	5	6
Italy	NA	1	1	2	2

Note: Rates are per 1,000 women. Strangely, this is the only way the source presents them.
Source: Statistical Abstract 1992:Table 1364; 1998:Table 1346.

increase. Again, a cross-cultural comparison helps to place U.S. statistics in perspective—but the news is not good. As Table 16.2 illustrates, the United States has—by far—the highest divorce rate in the industrialized world. If current trends persist, it is likely that half or even more of all U.S. marriages will end in divorce (Milbank 1996).

Although this could occur, Table 16.2 also shows that the U.S. divorce rate has declined since peaking around 1980. The Down-to-Earth Sociology box on pages 467–468 reports some "curious" findings about divorce, while factors that make marriage successful are summarized at the end of this chapter.

Children of Divorce

Each year, more than 1 million U.S. children learn that their parents are divorcing (*Statistical Abstract* 1999:Table 159). Most divorcing parents become so wrapped up in their own problems that they are unable to prepare their children for the divorce—even if they knew how to do so. When the break comes, children become confused and insecure. For security, many cling to the unrealistic idea that their parents will be reunited (Wallerstein and Kelly 1992). To help resolve the conflict, they may side with one parent and reject the other.

What are the effects of divorce on children? This common concern of divorcing parents is not easily answered. Studies show that these children have more hostility, anxiety, and nightmares, and that they don't do as well in school (Guidubaldi et al. 1987). One problem with these studies, which compare the children of divorce with children from average homes, is that children whose parents divorce don't come from average homes. They come from conflict-ridden homes. The real question is how they compare with children whose parents have high conflict but who remain married. Sociologist Susan Jekielek (1998), who made such a comparison, found that both conflict and divorce make children anxious and depressed. Children whose parents divorce, however, generally do slightly better emotionally than children who must live with their parents' conflict (Jekielek 1998).

What helps children adjust to divorce? Adjustment is better if (1) both parents show understanding and affection; (2) the child lives with a parent who is making a good adjustment; (3) family routines are consistent; (4) the family has adequate money for its needs; and (5) at least according to preliminary studies, the child lives with the parent of the same sex (Lamb 1977; Clingempeel and Reppucci 1982; Peterson and Zill 1986; Wallerstein and Kelly 1992). Sociologists have found that children adjust better if there is a second adult who can be counted on for support (Hayashi and Strickland 1998). Urie Bronfenbrenner

It is difficult to capture the anguish of the children of divorce, but when I read these lines by the fourth-grader who drew these two pictures, my heart was touched:

Me alone in the park . . .
All alone in the park.
My Dad and Mom are divorced
that's why I'm all alone.

This is me in the picture with my son.
We are taking a walk in the park.
I will never be like my father.
I will never divorce my wife and kid.

(1992a) says this person makes the third leg of a stool, giving stability to the smaller family unit.

Divorce follows people into adulthood. Grown-up children of divorced parents have less contact with either their father or their mother (Webster and Herzog 1995). They also are more likely to divorce (Diekmann and Engelhardt 1999). Their apparently greater difficulty in romance depends more on how they were reared, however, than it does on their parents' divorce. Those who have the most difficulty are those whose mothers did not remarry, who remarried and then divorced again, or who interfered with their relationship with their father. In line with Bronfenbrenner's analysis, those whose mothers established a single, stable relationship after the divorce are more secure in their intimate relationships

Sociology Down-to-Earth

YOU BE THE SOCIOLOGIST: CURIOUS DIVORCE PATTERNS

Sociologists Alex Heckert, Thomas Nowak, and Kay Snyder (1995) did secondary analysis (see page 135) of data gathered from a nationally representative sample of 5,000 U.S. households. Here are three of their findings:

1. If a wife earns more than her husband, the chances of divorce increase; if a husband earns more than his wife, divorce is less likely.

2. If the wife's health is poorer than her husband's, the marriage is more likely to break up; if the husband's health is poorer than his wife's, divorce is less likely.

3. The more housework a wife does, the less likely a couple is to divorce.

You be the sociologist. Can you explain these findings? Please develop your own explanations before looking at the box on the next page. ■

YOU BE THE SOCIOLOGIST: CURIOUS DIVORCE PATTERNS *(continued)*

What do the findings mean? Heckert, Nowak, and Snyder suggest these explanations:

1. A wife who earns more than her husband has more alternatives to an unsatisfying mar-

riage; a wife who earns less is more dependent.

2. Social pressure is greater for a wife to take care of a husband in poor health than it is for a husband to take care of a wife in poor health.

3. Who does the most housework is an indication of a husband's and wife's relative bargaining power. Wives with the most bargaining power are the least likely to put up with unsatisfying marriages. ■

(Bolgar et al. 1995). For a controversial solution to divorce, see the Down-to-Earth Sociology box below.

serial fatherhood a pattern of parenting in which a father, after divorce, reduces contact with his own children, serves as a father to the children of the woman he marries or lives with, then ignores them after moving in with or marrying another woman; this pattern repeats

The Absent Father and Serial Fatherhood

With divorce common and with mothers usually granted custody of the children, a new fathering pattern has emerged. In this pattern, known as **serial fatherhood,** a divorced father tends to maintain high contact with his children during the first year or two after the divorce. As the man develops a relationship with another woman, he begins to play a fathering role with the woman's children and reduces contact with his own children. With another breakup, this pattern may repeat. Only about one-sixth of children who live apart from

SHALL WE TIGHTEN THE TIES THAT BIND? ROLLING BACK NO-FAULT DIVORCE

It is not divorce, but the children of divorce, that bother people. What can you do about such a huge problem, a million kids a year? How about making it difficult to get a divorce? In 1997, the Louisiana legislature decided to take this direct approach, and passed a law that created "covenant marriages." In a covenant marriage, vows are to be taken more seriously, and they can be broken only because of extreme circumstances.

Following symbolic interactionist principles, people's reactions have depended on their orientations. Conservatives applaud

covenant marriages as a step in the right direction. The disintegration of the family, they point out, is at the root of what ails our society: crime, violence, even poor national test scores. Having children should mean pledging to remain together as husband/wife, mother/father, in order to nurture those children. Children deserve that kind of commitment. Personal goals, other relationships, even personal happiness, need to be put aside for the welfare of the children. If you want "Marriage Lite," then don't choose the covenant marriage. Otherwise, be prepared to follow through. It's your choice.

Liberals, in contrast, view covenant marriage through a different lens. They see it as a step backward, as a way of shackling women to their husbands. Covenant marriages will reduce women's choices and bind them to the home. Abuse and betrayal aren't the only signs of a bad marriage, and people—men as well as women—need the right to leave bad marriages. If someone is unhappy, he or she should be able to seek happiness elsewhere.

What do you think about covenant marriages? Can you explain what lens you are using to come to your conclusions? ■

their fathers see their dad as often as every week. Actually *most* divorced fathers stop seeing their children altogether (Ahlburg and De Vita 1992; Furstenberg and Harris 1992; Seltzer 1994). Apparently, for many men fatherhood has become a short-term commitment.

The Ex-Spouses

Anger, depression, and anxiety are common feelings at divorce. But so is relief. Women are more likely than men to feel that the divorce is giving them a "new chance" in life. A few couples manage to remain friends through it all—but they are the exception. The spouse who initiates the divorce usually gets over it sooner (Stark 1989; Kelly 1992).

Divorce does not necessarily mean the end of a couple's relationship. Some divorced couples maintain contact because of their children. For others, the "continuities," as sociologists call them, represent lingering attachments (Vaughan 1985; Masheter 1991). The former husband may help his former wife hang a picture and move furniture, for example, or she may invite him over for a meal. Some couples even continue to make love after their divorce.

After divorce, a couple's cost of living increases—two homes, two utility bills, and so forth. But the financial impact is different for men and for women. Divorce often spells economic hardship for women (Smock et al. 1999). This is especially true for mothers of small children, whose standard of living drops about 37 percent (Seltzer 1994). In contrast, the former husband's standard of living is likely to increase (Weitzman 1985). The higher a woman's education, the better prepared she is to survive financially after the divorce (Dixon and Rettig 1994).

Remarriage

Despite the number of people who emerge from the divorce court swearing "Never again!" most do get married again. But they aren't remarrying as quickly as they used to. In the 1960s, the average woman remarried in about two years. Today she waits five years to remarry (*Statistical Abstract* 1999:Table 160). Comparable data are not available for men.

As Figure 16.12 shows, most divorced people marry other divorced people. You may be surprised that the women most likely to remarry are young mothers and those who have not graduated from high school (Glick and Lin 1986). Apparently women who are more educated and more independent (no children) can afford to be more selective. Men are more likely than women to remarry, perhaps because they have a larger pool of potential mates from which to select.

How do remarriages work out? The divorce rate of remarried people *without* children is the same as that of first marriages. Those who bring children into a new marriage, however, are more likely to divorce again (MacDonald and DeMaris 1995). As sociologist Andrew Cherlin (1989) notes, we have not developed adequate norms for remarriages. For example, we lack satisfactory names for stepmothers, stepfathers, stepbrothers, stepsisters, stepaunts, stepuncles, stepcousins, and stepgrandparents. At the very least, these are awkward terms to use, but they also represent ill-defined relationships. To understand the dynamics of remarriages, we need further research.

TWO SIDES OF FAMILY LIFE

Let's first look at situations in which marriage and family have gone seriously wrong and then try to answer the question of what makes marriage work.

The Dark Side of Family Life:
Battering, Child Abuse, Marital Rape, and Incest

The dark side of family life involves events that people would rather keep in the dark. We shall look at battering, child abuse, rape, and incest.

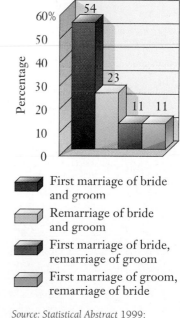

THE MARITAL HISTORY OF
U.S. BRIDES AND GROOMS

First marriage of bride and groom

Remarriage of bride and groom

First marriage of bride, remarriage of groom

First marriage of groom, remarriage of bride

Source: Statistical Abstract 1999:
Table 156.

With spouse battering a focus of national attention, a publicity-educational campaign is being run to try to break what is often called the cycle of violence. Shown here is one of the attention-getting posters used in this campaign.

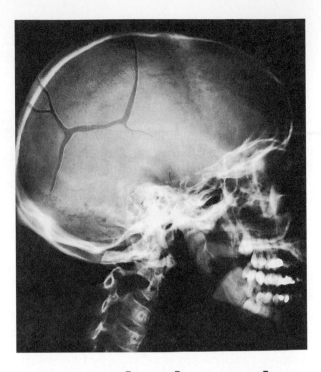

Some men break more than their girlfriends' hearts.

A bad relationship can hurt more than your feelings.

Battering To determine the amount and types of violence in U.S. homes, sociologists have interviewed nationally representative samples of U.S. couples (Straus 1980; Straus, Gelles, and Steinmetz 1980; Straus and Gelles 1988; Straus 1992). Although not all sociologists agree (Dobash et al. 1992, 1993; Pagelow 1992), Murray Straus concludes that husbands and wives are about equally likely to attack one another. When it comes to the effects of violence, however, gender equality vanishes (Gelles 1980; Straus 1980, 1992). As Straus points out, even though *she* may throw the coffeepot first, it is generally *he* who lands the last and most damaging blow. Consequently, many more wives than husbands seek medical attention because of marital violence. A good part of the reason, of course, is that most husbands are bigger and stronger than their wives, putting women at a disadvantage in this literal battle of the sexes.

Violence against women is related to the sexist structure of society, which we reviewed in Chapter 11, and to the socialization we reviewed in Chapter 3. Because they grew up with norms that encouraged aggression and the use of violence, many men feel it is their right to control women. When frustrated in a relationship—or even by causes outside it—many men turn violent toward their wives and lovers. The basic sociological question is how to socialize males to handle frustration and disagreements without resorting to violence (Rieker et al. 1997). We do not yet have this answer.

Child Abuse

My wife and I answered an ad about a house in a middle-class neighborhood that was for sale by owner. As the woman showed us through the house, which was immaculate, we were surprised to see a plywood box in the youngest child's bedroom. About 3 feet high, 3 feet wide, and 6 feet long, the box was perforated with holes and had a little door with a padlock. Curious, I asked what it was. The woman replied matter-of-factly that her son had a behavior problem, and this was where they locked him for "time out." She added that other times they would tie him to a float, attach a line to the dock, and put him in the lake.

We left as soon as we could. With thoughts of a terrorized child filling my head, I called the state child abuse hotline.

As you can tell, what I saw upset me. Most of us are bothered by child abuse—the victimization of helpless children by their own parents, the adults who are supposed to love, protect, and nurture them. The most gruesome of these cases make the evening news: The 4-year-old girl who was beaten and raped by her mother's boyfriend, who passed into a coma and then three days later passed out of this life; the 6- to 10-year-old children whose stepfather videotaped them engaging in sex acts. Unlike these cases, which made headlines in my area, most child abuse is never brought to our attention: the children who live in filth, who are neglected, who are left alone for hours or even days at a time, or who are beaten with extension cords. Cases like the little boy I learned about on my house-hunting expedition.

We do know that child abuse is extensive. Each year, about 3 million U.S. children are reported to the authorities as victims of abuse or neglect. About 1 million of these cases are substantiated (*Statistical Abstract* 1999:Table 379).

Marital Rape Sociologists have found that marital rape is more common than is usually supposed. For example, between one-third and one-half of women who seek help at shelters for battered women are victims of marital rape (Bergen 1996). But these women make up a special group; they are not representative of U.S. women. To get a better answer, sociologist Diana Russell (1990) used a sampling technique that allows generalization. She found that 14 percent of married women report that their husbands have raped them. Similarly, 10 percent of a representative sample of Boston women interviewed by sociologists David Finkelhor and Kersti Yllo (1985, 1989) reported that their husbands had used physical force to compel them to have sex.

Finkelhor's and Yllo's in-depth interviews with fifty victims showed that marital rape most commonly occurs during separation or during the breakup of a marriage. They found three types of marital rape.

■ *Nonbattering rape* (40 percent). The husband forces his wife to have sex but has no intention of hurting her physically. These instances generally involve conflict over sex, such as when the husband feels insulted because his wife refuses to have sex.

■ *Battering rape* (48 percent). In addition to sexually assaulting his wife, the husband intentionally inflicts physical pain to retaliate for some supposed wrongdoing on her part.

■ *Perverted rape* (6 percent). These husbands, who apparently are sexually aroused by the violent elements of rape, force their wives to submit to unusual sexual acts. Anger and hostility can also motivate this type of rape. (The remaining 6 percent are mixed, containing elements of more than one type.)

Incest Sexual relations between relatives (for example, between brothers and sisters or between parents and children) constitute **incest.** Incest is most likely to occur in families that are socially isolated (Smith 1992). As with marital rape, sociological research has destroyed assumptions that incest is not common. Sociologist Diana Russell (n.d.) found that incest victims who experience the most difficulty are those who were victimized the most often, over longer periods of time, and whose incest was "more intrusive," for example, sexual intercourse as opposed to sexual touching.

Who are the offenders? Russell found that uncles are the most common offenders, followed by first cousins, fathers (stepfathers especially), brothers, and, finally, relatives ranging from brothers-in-law to stepgrandfathers. Other researchers report that brother-sister incest is several times more common than father-child incest (Canavan et al. 1992). Incest between mothers and sons is rare.

incest sexual relations between specified relatives, such as brothers and sisters or parents and children

The Bright Side of Family Life: Successful Marriages

Successful Marriages After examining divorce and family abuse, one could easily conclude that marriages seldom work out. That would be far from the truth, however, for about two of every three married Americans report that they are "very happy" with their marriages (Cherlin and Furstenberg 1988; Whyte 1992). To find out what makes marriage successful, sociologists Jeanette and Robert Lauer (1992) interviewed 351 couples who had been married fifteen years or longer. Fifty-one of these marriages were unhappy, but the couples stayed together for religious reasons, family tradition, or "for the sake of the children." Of the others, the 300 happy couples, all:

1. Think of their spouse as their best friend
2. Like their spouse as a person
3. Think of marriage as a long-term commitment
4. Believe that marriage is sacred
5. Agree with their spouse on aims and goals
6. Believe that their spouse has grown more interesting over the years
7. Strongly want the relationship to succeed
8. Laugh together

Sociologist Nicholas Stinnett (1992) used interviews and questionnaires to study 660 families from all regions of the United States and parts of South America. He found that happy families:

1. Spend a lot of time together
2. Are quick to express appreciation
3. Are committed to promoting one another's welfare
4. Do a lot of talking and listening to one another
5. Are religious
6. Deal with crises in a positive manner

Symbolic Interactionism and the Misuse of Statistics Many of my students express concerns about their own marital future, a wariness born out of the divorce of their parents, friends, neighbors, relatives—even their pastors and rabbis. They wonder what chance they really have. Because sociology is not just about abstract ideas, but is really about our lives, it is valuable to stress that we are individuals, not statistics. That is, if the divorce rate were 33 percent or 50 percent, this would *not* mean that if we marry our chances of getting divorced are 33 percent or 50 percent. That is a misuse of statistics, and a very common one at that. Divorce statistics represent all marriages, and have absolutely *nothing* to do with any individual marriage. Our own chances depend on our own situation—especially the way we approach marriage.

To make this point clearer, let's apply symbolic interactionism. From a symbolic interactionist perspective, we create our own worlds. That is, experiences don't come with built-in meanings. Rather, we interpret our experiences, and act accordingly. Simply put, if we think of our marriage as likely to fail, we increase the likelihood that it will fail; if we think that our marriage will work out well, the chances of a good marriage increase. In other words, we tend to act according to our ideas, creating a sort of self-fulfilling prophecy. The folk saying "There are no guarantees in life" is certainly true, but it does help to have a vision that a good marriage is possible and that it is worth achieving.

*T*HE FUTURE OF MARRIAGE AND FAMILY

What can we expect of marriage and family in the future? Despite its many problems, marriage is in no danger of becoming a relic of the past. Marriage is so functional that it exists in every society. Consequently, the vast majority of Americans will continue to find marriage vital to their welfare.

Certain trends are firmly in place. Cohabitation, births to single women, and age at first marriage will increase. More married women will join the work force, and they will continue to gain marital power. Equality in marriage, however, is not even on the horizon. The number of elderly will continue to increase, and more couples will find themselves sandwiched between caring for their parents and their own children. The reduction in our divorce rate is another matter entirely. At this point we don't know if it is the prelude to a long-term decline, or if it merely signals a lull, out of which an even higher rate will be launched.

Finally, our culture will continue to be haunted by distorted images of marriage and family: the bleak ones portrayed in the mass media and the rosy ones painted by cultural myths. Sociological research can help correct these distortions and allow us to see how our own family experiences fit into the patterns of our culture. Sociological research also can help to answer the big question of how to formulate social policy that will support and enhance family life.

SUMMARY AND REVIEW

■ Marriage and Family in Global Perspective

What is a family—and what themes are universal?

Family is difficult to define. For just about every element one might consider essential, there are exceptions. Consequently, **family** is defined broadly—as two or more people who consider themselves related by blood, marriage, or adoption. Sociologists and anthropologists have documented extensive variation in family customs—from cultures in which babies are married to those in which husbands and wives refrain from sexual relations for years at a time. Universally, **marriage** and family are mechanisms for governing mate selection, reckoning descent, and establishing inheritance and authority. Pp. 444–446.

■ Marriage and Family in Theoretical Perspective

What is the functionalist perspective on marriage and family?

Functionalists examine the functions and dysfunctions of family life. Examples include the **incest taboo** and the ways in which weakening family functions increase divorce. Pp. 446–448.

What is the conflict perspective on marriage and family?

Conflict theorists examine how marriage and family help perpetuate inequalities, especially the subservience of women. Power struggles in marriage, such as those over housework, are an example. Pp. 448–450.

What is a symbolic interactionist perspective on marriage and family?

Symbolic interactionists examine how the contrasting experiences and perspectives of men and women are played out in marriage. They stress that only by grasping the perspectives of wives and husbands can we understand their behavior. Pp. 450–451.

■ The Family Life Cycle

What are the major elements of the family life cycle?

The major elements are love and courtship, marriage, childbirth, child rearing, and the family in later life. Most mate selection follows predictable patterns of age, social class, race, and religion. Childbirth and child-rearing patterns also vary by social class. Pp. 451–456.

■ Diversity in U.S. Families

How significant are race and ethnicity in family life?

The primary distinction is social class, not race or ethnicity. Families of the same social class are likely to be similar, regardless of their racial or ethnic makeup. Pp. 456–459.

What other diversity in U.S. families is there?

Also discussed were one-parent, childless, **blended**, and gay families. Although each has its own unique characteristics, social class is also significant in determining primary characteristics. Poverty is especially significant for one-parent families, most of which are headed by women. Pp. 459–462.

■ Trends in U.S. Families

What major changes characterize U.S. families?

Two changes are postponement of first marriage and an increase in **cohabitation**. With more people living longer, many middle-aged couples find themselves sandwiched between caring for their own children and caring for their own parents. Pp. 462–464.

■ Divorce and Remarriage

What is the current divorce rate?

Depending on what figures you choose to compare, you can produce almost any rate you wish, from 75 percent to just 2.1 percent. However you figure it, the U.S. divorce rate is higher than any other industrialized nation. P. 465–466.

How do children and their parents adjust to divorce?

Divorce is especially difficult for children, whose adjustment problems often continue into adulthood. Most divorced fathers do not maintain ongoing relationships with their children. Financial problems are usually greater for the former wives. Although most divorced people remarry, their rate of remarriage has slowed considerably. Pp. 466–469.

■ **Two Sides of Family Life**

What are the two sides of family life?

The dark side is family abuse—spouse battering, child abuse, marital rape, and incest, activities that revolve around the misuse of family power. The bright side is families that produce intense satisfaction for spouses and their children. Pp. 469–472.

■ **The Future of Marriage and Family**

What is the likely future of marriage and family?

We can expect cohabitation, births to unmarried mothers, and age at marriage to increase. The growing numbers of women in the work force will likely continue to shift the marital balance of power. Pp. 472–473.

Where can I read more on this topic?

Suggested Readings for this chapter are at the back of this book.

All URLs listed are current as of the printing of this book. URLs often change. Please check our Web site, **http://www.abacon.com/ henslin,** for updates.

1. Although the rate of teen pregnancy in the United States has declined recently, births to teen mothers remain a social problem. To learn about the risks and realities of early childbearing, go to the site maintained by the National Campaign to Prevent Teen Pregnancy at **http://www.teenpregnancy.org/factstats.htm.** Scroll down and read the section on "General Facts and Statistics." How extensive is this problem? How does teen pregnancy affect both the mother and the child? What factors are associated with a lower teen pregnancy? Which groups have the highest rates of teen pregnancy and early childbearing? What accounts for these higher rates? After you are finished, go to the top of the page and click on the national data on birth rates and pregnancy rates. Which states have rates that are higher than the national average? Which have lower rates? How does your state compare to the national average? How can the state-by-state variations be explained?

    Since both your text and the information on this Web site suggest that teen pregnancy has many negative consequences, consider the strategies and programs promoted by Advocates for Youth at **http://www.advocatesforyouth.org/TPP.htm.** Click on "Local Programs" and "Model Programs." To review pregnancy prevention programs of some European countries go to **http:// www/advocatesforyouth.org/factsheet/FSEST.htm.** Can solutions presented by Advocates for Youth be applied globally or only to the U.S. population? Would some of the European initiatives work here?

2. As we begin the twenty-first century, our definition of the family is changing. One recent consideration is whether to include same-sex couples in the definition. Since the early 1990s, a campaign for same-sex marriages has centered on legal initiatives. A landmark ruling in Hawaii, Baehr v. Lewin, opened the door to same-sex marriages. You can read more about the history of this case, which ushered in legislative initiatives in other states, at **http://www.hawaiilawyer.com/same_sex/samesex.htm.** To learn more about recent legislative activities, go to **http://www. grasshopperdesign.com/gay_marriage.** Can same-sex partners legally marry in any state? Based on the information you have read in your text and on these Web sites, do you think same-sex marriages will soon be legalized? Why or why not? Create a panel of students from your sociology class to debate the pros and cons of same-sex marriage.

3. As the number of single-parent families and two-career families has increased, the way we rear children has changed. Your text discusses types of child care arrangements for preschool children. But have you ever wondered what school-age children are doing when they are not in school? Who's keeping an eye on them? To find out more about the lives of our children, go to the Web page for the National Institute on Out-of-School Time at Wellesley College's Center for Research on Women, located at **http://www. wellesley.edu/WCW/CRW/SAC/index.html.** Scroll down to "News & Notes" and click on "NIOST Fact Sheet, January 2000." According to the information published at this site, how many children regularly spend time without adult supervision? How do school-age children spend their time after school hours? In what ways have their activities changed since 1981? As a society, should we be concerned about what children are doing when they are not in school? What types of before- and after-school arrangements do parents use? How can school age children benefit from organized childcare programs?

4. As family roles have changed, a small but growing number of men have become "stay-at-home" dads. Two Web sites for learning about these men who are challenging traditional family roles are **http://www.slowlane.com** and **http://www.daddyshome. com.** Browse through both. At SLOWLANE. COM check out the Discussion Forum; begin by clicking on "Online Chats, Listserves, Email loops & Web rings." On the next page, click on "Online Discussion Forums." When the Online Discussion Fo-

rum page comes up, click on a topic. Read some of the postings by stay-at-home dads. What concerns do these men have? Are their concerns related to their gender or to their role as caregiver for their children? In other words, how are their concerns the same as those of stay-at-home moms? How are they different? The DADDYSHOME. COM site has articles related to men as caregivers. What problems do men who stay home and take care of their children face? Do you think men can do the same job caring for their children that women do? Why or why not? What do men, women, and children gain or lose by this arrangement? Write a paper in which you defend or attack this new development.

c h a p t e r

17

Phoebe Beasley, *Training Ground #2*, 1989

Education

- **The Development of Modern Education**
  Education in Earlier Societies
  Democracy, Industrialization, and
    Universal Education

- **Education in Global Perspective**
  Education in the Most Industrialized Nations:
    Japan
  Education in the Industrializing Nations:
    Russia
  Education in the Least Industrialized Nations:
    Egypt

- **The Functionalist Perspective:
  Education's Social Benefits**
  Teaching Knowledge and Skills
  Cultural Transmission of Values
  Social Integration
  Gatekeeping
  Promoting Personal Change
  Promoting Social Change
  Replacing Family Functions
  Other Functions

- **The Conflict Perspective: How Education
  Reproduces the Social Class Structure**
  The Hidden Curriculum
  Tilting the Tests: Discrimination by IQ
  Stacking the Deck: Unequal Funding
  The Correspondence Principle
  The Bottom Line: Family Background and the
    Educational System

- **The Symbolic Interactionist Perspective:
  Teacher Expectations and the
  Self-Fulfilling Prophecy**
  The Rist Research
  The Rosenthal-Jacobson Experiment
  How Do Teacher Expectations Work?

- **Problems in U.S. Education—and Their Solutions**
  Problems: Mediocrity, Teen Pregnancy,
    and Violence
  Solutions: Retention, Standards, Safety, and
    Other Reforms

- **Summary and Review**

There wasn't much for teenagers to do in Littleton, Colorado. Not much happened in this quiet town of 35,000, a middle-class suburb southwest of Denver. Some of the high school kids liked to draw attention to themselves by wearing black trenchcoats and black shirts with swastikas. They called themselves the Trenchcoat Mafia and tossed around a few phrases in German.

"Just kids. They'll grow out of it," was the typical adult response. "We all went through something ourselves."

The Trenchcoat Mafia had their own table in the cafeteria and their group picture in the yearbook. The caption: "Who says we're different? Insanity's healthy. . . . Stay alive, stay different, stay crazy! Oh, and stay away from CREAM SODA!!"

Just another high school group: jocks, Goths, stoners, deadbeats, geeks, preppies. Every school has some.

The jocks despised the Trenchcoat Mafia. They threw them into lockers and called them scumbags, faggots, and inbreeds. They threw rocks and bottles at them from moving cars.

Two seniors, Eric Harris and Dylan Klebold, honors students and members of the Trenchcoat Mafia, talked and dreamed about killing their classmates, especially the jocks. Eric even had his own Web page, where he described whom he wanted to kill and how he wanted to do it. As a class project, Eric and Dylan made a video in which they pretended to kill the classmates they didn't like. Just talk. But as the killing on *Doom,* the video game they loved, no longer satisfied, the boys hatched a plan for real killing. It was risky. Maybe they would survive, maybe not. But if not, they would go out in a blaze of glory. Hitler's birthday would be perfect.

The carnage left Columbine High School seared into the national memory. TV viewers switched on their sets and found that a quiet Tuesday afternoon had been interrupted by stunning events. The drama was high as SWAT teams moved in and cautiously began to assess the situation. Bodies lay strewn on sidewalks. No one knew how many were dead inside the school. The nation watched transfixed as events unfolded.

As bombs went off and shots rang out, students ran in terror, cowering in closets and under tables. Harris and Klebold went from room to room in search of victims. In the library, they found students hiding under a table. "Do you believe in God?" asked one of the shooters. "Yes," replied Cassie Bernall. "There is no God," the gunman retorted, as he placed a gun against her head and squeezed the trigger.

The boys killed twelve of their fellow students and one teacher before they turned their guns on themselves. They wounded twenty-three students.

Once again, the nation shook its head in collective disbelief. ■

—Based on Bai 1999; Gibbs 1999.

The mass killings in today's schools have confused just about everybody. No one has the full explanation for why they are occurring, or what we can do to prevent them. When we return to this topic, we are going to find a surprise. But, first, let's look at how our educational system developed.

THE DEVELOPMENT OF MODERN EDUCATION

We shall first look at education in earlier societies, and then trace the development of universal education.

Education in Earlier Societies

In earlier societies, there was no separate social institution called education. There were no special buildings called schools, and no people who earned their living as teachers. Rather, as an integral part of growing up children learned what was necessary to get along in life. If hunting or cooking were the essential skills, then people who already possessed those skills taught them. *Education was synonymous with* **acculturation,** learning a culture. It still is in today's tribal groups.

In some societies, when a sufficient surplus developed—as in Arabia, China, North Africa, and classical Greece—a separate institution developed. Some people then devoted themselves to teaching, while those who had the leisure—the children of the wealthy—became their students. In ancient China, for example, Confucius taught a few select pupils, while in Greece, Aristotle, Plato, and Socrates taught science and philosophy to upper-class boys. **Education,** then, came to be something quite distinct from informal acculturation; education is a group's *formal* system of teaching knowledge, values, and skills. Such instruction stood in marked contrast to the learning of traditional skills such as farming or hunting, for it was clearly intended to develop the mind.

The flourishing of education during the period roughly marked by the birth of Christ, however, slowly died out. During the Dark Ages of Europe, the candle of enlightenment was kept burning by monks, who, except for a handful of the wealthy and nobility, were the only ones who could read and write. Although they delved into philosophy, the intellectual ac-

acculturation the transmission of culture from one generation to the next

education a formal system of teaching knowledge, values, and skills

In hunting and gathering societies, there is no separate social institution called education. As with this 4-year-old Kalahari boy in South Africa, children learn their adult economic roles from their parents and other kin.

tivities of the monks centered on learning Greek, Latin, and Hebrew so that they could read early texts of the Bible and writings of the church fathers. Similarly, Jews kept formal learning alive as they studied the Torah.

Formal education, however, remained limited to those who had the leisure to pursue it. (In fact *school* comes from the Greek word σχωλή *[scholē]* meaning "leisure.") Industrialization transformed this approach to learning, for the new machinery and new types of jobs meant that workers had to be able to read, to write, and to work accurately with figures—the classic three R's of the nineteenth century (Reading, 'Riting, and 'Rithmetic).

Democracy, Industrialization, and Universal Education

The development of universal education is linked to industrialization. Let's see how the United States pioneered free, universal education.

In the years following the American Revolution, the founders of the new republic felt that formal education should be the principal mechanism for creating a uniform national culture out of its many nationalities and religions. Thomas Jefferson and Noah Webster proposed a universal system of schooling based on standardized texts that would instill patriotism and teach the principles of republican government (Hellinger and Judd 1991). They reasoned that if the American political experiment was to succeed, it needed educated voters who were capable of making sound decisions. Several decades later, in the early 1800s, the country remained politically fragmented, with many of its states still thinking of themselves as near-sovereign nations.

Education reflected this political situation. The United States had no comprehensive school system, just a hodgepodge of independent schools administered by separate localities, with no coordination among them. Most public schools were supported by tuition, with a few poor children being allowed to attend free. Parochial schools were run by Lutherans, Presbyterians, Congregationalists, and Roman Catholics (Hellinger and Judd 1991). Children of the rich attended private schools. Most children of the lower classes—and all slaves—received no formal education at all. Only the wealthy could afford to send their children to high school. College, too, was beyond the reach of almost everyone.

Horace Mann, an educator from Massachusetts, found it deplorable that the average family could not afford to send its children even to grade school. In 1837 he proposed that "common schools," supported through taxes, be established throughout his state. Mann's

This 1893 photo of a school in Hecla, Montana, taught by Miss Blanche Lamont, provides a glimpse into the past, when free public education, pioneered in the United States, was still in its infancy. In these one-room rural schools, a single teacher had charge of grades 1 to 8. Children were assigned a grade not by age but by mastery of subject matter. Occasionally, adults who wished to learn to read, to write, or to do mathematics would join the class. Attendance was sporadic, for the family's economic survival came first.

mandatory education laws laws that require all children to attend school until a specified age or until they complete a minimum grade in school

idea spread throughout the country, and state after state began to support free public education. It is no coincidence that universal education and industrialization occurred simultaneously. Seeing that the economy was undergoing fundamental change, political and civic leaders recognized the need for an educated work force. They also feared the influx of foreign values and looked on public education as a way to "Americanize" immigrants (Hellinger and Judd 1991).

Over time, the amount of education considered necessary continued to expand. By 1918, all U.S. states had **mandatory education laws** requiring children to attend school, usually until they had completed the eighth grade or turned 16, whichever came first. In the early 1900s, graduation from the eighth grade marked the end of education for most people. "Dropouts" at that time were students who did not complete grade school. *High* school, as its name implies, was viewed as a form of "higher" education.

As industrialization progressed and as fewer people made their living from agriculture, formal education came to be thought of as essential to the well-being of society. As you can see from Figure 17.1 below, college graduation in the United States is now more common than high school graduation used to be. Sixty-seven percent of all high school graduates now enter college, the highest rate of any nation (*Statistical Abstract* 1999:Table 307).

One-fourth of Americans still don't make it through high school, however, condemning most of them to a difficult economic life. As you can see from the Social Map on the next page, the rate of high school graduation is far from evenly distributed across the states. You may wish to compare the clustering of states on this Social Map with the one on page 276 that shows the distribution of poverty.

 17.1   **EDUCATIONAL ACHIEVEMENT IN THE UNITED STATES**

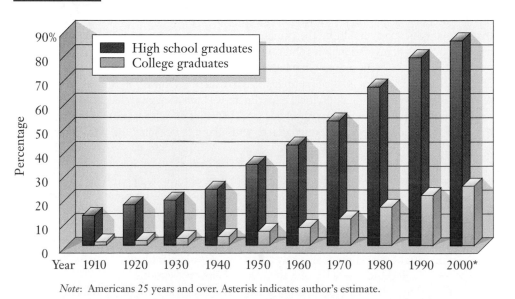

Note: Americans 25 years and over. Asterisk indicates author's estimate.

Source: National Center for Education Statistics, 1991:Table 8; *Statistical Abstract* 1999:Table 263.

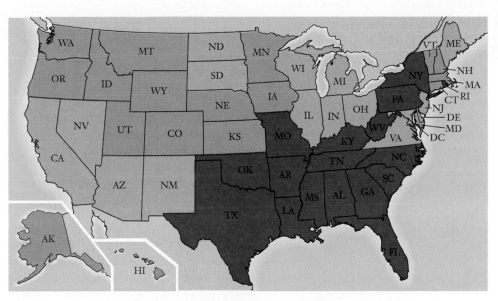

Figure 17.2

SOCIAL MAP: NOT MAKING IT: DROPPING OUT OF HIGH SCHOOL

Source: Statistical Abstract 1999: Table 267.

What percentage of a state's residents age 25 and over are high school dropouts?

▭ Less than 21% ▭ 22%–25% ■ Over 25%

EDUCATION IN GLOBAL PERSPECTIVE

To gain an idea of the variety of education around the world, and to see how education is directly related to a nation's economy, let's look at education in three countries. Keep in mind that these are just examples, that no single nation represents the wide variety of educational approaches that characterizes these three levels of industrialization.

Education in the Most Industrialized Nations: Japan

A central sociological principle of education is that a nation's education reflects its culture. Because a core Japanese value is solidarity with the group, competition among individuals is downgraded. For example, people who are hired by a company together work as a team and are promoted as a group (Ouchi 1993). Japanese education reflects this group-centered ethic. Children in grade school work as a group, all mastering the same skills and materials. Teachers stress cooperation and respect for elders and others in positions of authority. By law, Japanese schools even use the same textbooks (Haynes and Chalker 1997).

College admission procedures in Japan and the U.S. also differ (Cooper 1991). Like the Scholastic Assessment Test (SAT) required of U.S. college-bound high school seniors, Japanese seniors who want to attend college must take a national test. Only the top scorers in Japan, however—rich and poor alike—are admitted to college. In contrast, even U.S. high school graduates who perform poorly on these tests can find some college to attend—as long as their parents can pay the tuition.

This Japanese practice poses a fascinating cultural contradiction. Although cooperation is a

The poverty of some of the Least Industrialized Nations defies the imagination of most people who have been reared in the industrialized world. Their educational systems are similarly marked by poverty. This photo depicts rural education in Eritrea, a former Italian colony on the Red Sea in Northeast Africa.

core Japanese value, students are admitted to college only on the basis of intense competition. Because this make-or-break process affects their entire lives, each day after high school and on weekends about half of those who plan to go to college attend cram schools (*juku*). Affluent parents hire tutors for their children (Stevenson and Baker 1994). The annual college admission tests have become a national obsession. Families and friends nervously stand on college campuses at midnight awaiting the outcome that seals their fate. The results are posted on flood-lit bulletin boards. Families shout in joy—or hide their faces in shame and disappointment—while reporters photograph the results and rush back to their papers with the news. The next day, entire neighborhoods are abuzz about the results (Rohen 1983).

Education in the Industrializing Nations: Russia

After the Revolution of 1917, the Soviet Communist party attempted to upgrade the nation's educational system. At that time, as in most other countries, education was limited to the elite. The revolution, which was meant to usher in social equality, was also intended to make education accessible to all. Just as the new central government directed the economy, so it directed the country's education. Following the sociological principle that education reflects culture, the government made certain that socialist values dominated its schools, for it saw education as a means to undergird the new political system. As a result, schoolchildren were taught that capitalism was evil and that communism was the salvation of the world.

With the country still largely agricultural, education remained spotty for the next two decades. The Nazi invasion of the Soviet Union during World War II dealt a severe blow to the attempt to provide universal education, as military service disrupted the education of hundreds of thousands of young people. Even by 1950, only about half of Soviet young people were in school, and most of these came from the more privileged strata (children of the more educated and of party members) rather than from workers and peasants (Bell 1973; Grant 1979; Ballantine 1983; Matthews 1983).

Eyeing the gains of the West, the Soviet leadership continued to struggle toward universal education, seeing education as a key to becoming a world power. Education, including college, was free. Mathematics and the natural sciences were stressed, and few courses in the social sciences were taught (Taylor and Mechitov 1994). Although the Soviet Union never succeeded in becoming a world industrial power—its power was based on military threat, not industrial might—its educational success did challenge the West. The launching of *Sputnik*, the first satellite, in the 1950s caught Western leaders by surprise. They were forced to acknowledge how effective Soviet education had become.

The breakup of the Soviet empire in 1989 again caught Western experts by surprise, but this time they were surprised at the backwardness of Soviet education. Many schools lacked such basics as heat and indoor plumbing. To control ideas, education was centralized, with orders issued out of a remote educational bureaucracy in Moscow. Schools throughout the country followed the same state-prescribed curriculum, and all students in the same grade used the same textbooks. Students memorized the materials and were discouraged from discussing them (Bridgman 1994).

Since the breakup of their empire, Russians have had to try to "reinvent" education. For the first time, private, religious, and even foreign-run schools were allowed, and teachers were faced with the foreign idea of asking students to question and to think for themselves. Not only did they have to retrain tens of thousands of teachers who were used to teaching pat political answers, but also school budgets shrank while inflation spiralled upward. Urban teachers stampeded out of education into fields that, with the new capitalism, paid many times the going rate for teachers.

Because it is true of education everywhere, we can safely predict that the educational system Russia finally designs will reflect its culture. Like others, the system will glorify its historical exploits and reinforce its values and world views. One difficulty for Russians at this point is that their values and world views are changing rapidly. Due to the transition to capitalism, basic ideas about profit and private property are being transformed—and the Russian educational system is destined to reflect those changed values.

Education in the Least Industrialized Nations: Egypt

Education in the Least Industrialized Nations stands in sharp contrast to the industrialized world. Even if the Least Industrialized Nations have mandatory attendance laws, they are not enforced. Because most of their people work the land or take care of families, they find little need for education. In addition, most of these nations cannot afford extensive formal education. As we saw in Figure 12.2 (on pages 244–245), most people in the Least Industrialized Nations live on less than $1,000 a year. Consequently, in many nations most children do not go to school beyond the first couple of grades. Figure 17.3 contrasts education in China and the United States. As was once common around the globe, it is primarily the wealthy in the Least Industrialized Nations who have the means and the leisure for formal education—especially anything beyond the basics. As an example, let's look at education in Egypt.

Several centuries before the birth of Christ, Egypt's world-renowned centers of learning produced such acclaimed scientists as Archimedes and Eukleides. The primary areas of study during this classic period were physics, astronomy, geometry, geography, mathematics, philosophy, and medicine. The largest library in the world was at Alexandria. Fragments from the papyrus manuscripts of this library, which burned to the ground, have been invaluable in deciphering ancient manuscripts. After defeat in war, however, education declined, never again to rise to its former prominence.

Although the Egyptian constitution makes five years of grade school free and compulsory for all children, as in most of the Least Industrialized Nations qualified teachers are few, classrooms are crowded, and education is limited. Many poor children go uneducated, while others receive but rudimentary instruction in numbers and basic reading. Only 39 percent of women and 64 percent of men can read and write ("Egypt," 1998). Three years of preparatory school follow the five of grade school, and high school lasts for three years. During the first two years, all students take the same required courses, but during the third year they specialize in arts, science, or mathematics. Examinations are held monthly, and a national exam is given at the end of the senior year. The Egyptian government specifies the manifest functions of higher education: to prepare graduates for the world of work, to develop scientific research, and to help solve

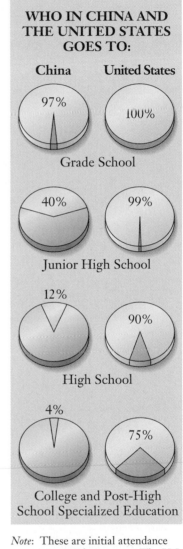

Figure 17.3

EDUCATION IN A MOST INDUSTRIALIZED (POSTINDUSTRIAL) NATION AND A LEAST INDUSTRIALIZED NATION

WHO IN CHINA AND THE UNITED STATES GOES TO:

China | United States

97% | 100%

Grade School

40% | 99%

Junior High School

12% | 90%

High School

4% | 75%

College and Post-High School Specialized Education

Note: These are initial attendance rates, not completion rates. The U.S. junior high school total is the author's estimate.

Source: Brauchli 1994.

Education is costly, and financing education is a burden on the Least Industrialized Nations. Consequently, their schools are minimal, their teachers are undereducated, and attendance is sporadic. Shown here is an Egyptian school in Hellwan, near Cairo.

the economic and social problems that confront Egypt's development (El-Meligi 1992). Although education is free at all levels, including college, children of the wealthy are several times as likely to get a college education.

THE FUNCTIONALIST PERSPECTIVE: EDUCATION'S SOCIAL BENEFITS

A central position of functionalism is that when the parts of society are working properly, each contributes to the well-being or stability of society. The positive things that people intend their actions to accomplish are known as **manifest functions;** the positive consequences that they did not intend are called **latent functions.** Let's look at these functions.

Teaching Knowledge and Skills

Education's most obvious manifest function is to teach knowledge and skills—whether the traditional three R's or their more contemporary counterparts, such as computer literacy. Each society must train the next generation to fulfill its significant positions. Because our postindustrial society needs highly educated people, the schools supply them.

Often what counts is not the learning, but the *certification* of learning. Sociologist Randall Collins (1979) observed that we have become a **credential society.** By this, he means that employers use diplomas and degrees as *sorting* devices. Because our society is so large, urbanized, and anonymous, employers aren't likely to know potential workers personally or even by reputation. By hiring college graduates, employers assume that the individuals are responsible people; for evidently they have shown up on time for numerous classes, have turned in scores of assignments, and have demonstrated basic writing and thinking skills. The specific job skills that a position requires can then be grafted onto this base, which has been certified by the college.

In some cases, specific job skills must be mastered before an individual is allowed to do certain work. With our more complex technology and knowledge, simple on-the-job training will not do for physicians, engineers, and airline pilots. That is precisely why doctors display their credentials so prominently. Their framed degrees declare that they have been certified by institutions of higher learning, that they have completed a rigorous training program, and that they are qualified to work on our bodies.

Cultural Transmission of Values

Another manifest function of education is the **cultural transmission** of values, a process by which schools pass a society's core values from one generation to the next. As discussed in Chapter 2, values lie at the center of every culture (see pages 50–55 for a summary of values that characterize U.S. culture). In addition to responding to the demands of the economy, the need to produce an informed electorate, and the desire to "Americanize" immigrants, how else does the U.S. educational system reflect—and transmit—cultural values?

Schools are such an essential part of U.S. culture that it is difficult even to know where to begin. For example, the fact that instruction takes place almost exclusively in English, the dominant language of the society, reflects an intimate evolution from British institutions. Similarly, the architecture of school buildings themselves reflects Western culture. Unlike the thatched-roof schools of some tropical societies, the distinctive appearance of U.S. schools identifies them as schools on sight.

Americans value "bigness," and this value is reflected in the U.S. educational system. With 53 million students attending grade and high schools, and another 15 million enrolled in college, U.S. education has become big business. Primary and secondary schools provide employment for 2½ million teachers, while another 900,000 people teach in colleges and universities (*Statistical Abstract* 1999:Tables 253, 281, 322). Millions more work as support

manifest functions intended beneficial consequences of people's actions

latent functions unintended beneficial consequences of people's actions

credential society the use of diplomas and degrees to determine who is eligible for jobs, even though the diploma or degree may be irrelevant to the actual work

cultural transmission in reference to education, the ways in which schools transmit a society's culture, especially its core values

personnel—aides, administrators, bus drivers, janitors, and secretaries. Another several million earn their living in industries that service schools—from building schools to manufacturing pencils, paper, and desks. Overall, the United States spends $320 billion a year on its elementary and secondary schools, and another $200 billion on its colleges and universities (*Statistical Abstract* 1999:Tables 286, 315).

To better understand the connection between education and values, let's look at how the educational system transmits individualism, competition, and patriotism.

Individualism Individualism is a thread that runs throughout the U.S. educational system. Unlike their Japanese counterparts, U.S. teachers and students seldom focus on teamwork. Where Japanese schools stress that the individual is only one part of a larger, integrated whole, U.S. students learn that the individual is on his or her own. Pervasive but often subtle, such instruction begins in the early grades when teachers point out the success of a particular student. They might say, for example, "Everyone should be like José," or, "Why can't you be like María, who got all the answers right?" By such seemingly innocuous comments, teachers thrust one child ahead of the rest, holding the individual up for praise.

Competition Competitive games in the classroom and the schoolyard provide an apt illustration of how schools transmit this core value. In the classroom, a teacher may divide the class into competitive groups for a spelling bee, while on the playground children are encouraged to play hard-driving competitive games and sports. The school's formal sports program—baseball, football, basketball, soccer, hockey, volleyball, and so on—pits team against team in head-to-head confrontations, driving home the lesson that the competitive spirit is highly valued. Although organized sports stress teamwork, the individual is held up for praise. The custom of nominating an "outstanding player" (emphasizing which of these persons is *the* best) reinforces the related lesson of individualism.

Patriotism Finally, as in schools around the world, U.S. schools teach patriotism. U.S. students are taught that the United States is the best country in the world; Russians learn that no country is better than Russia; and French, German, British, Spanish, Japanese, Chinese, Afghani, and Egyptian students all learn the same about their respective countries. To instill patriotism, grade school teachers in every country extol the virtues of the society's founders, their struggle for freedom from oppression, and the goodness of the country's basic social institutions.

In the United States, grade school teachers wax eloquent when it comes to the exploits of George Washington—whether real or mythical (and each society tends to develop myths about its own early heroes). Hearing about how Washington threw a silver dollar across the Potomac and chopped down a cherry tree creates vivid memories that many adults carry with them from their childhood classrooms. Any suspicions about whether throwing away the silver dollar was a waste of money or how such a good person could have chopped down a valued tree are hushed by the teacher, who stresses Washington's virtues: strength and accuracy in throwing the silver dollar, and honesty about what he did to the cherry tree.

Among the major functions of education is the cultural transmission of values such as patriotism and good citizenship. Another function of education, social integration, also is apparent from this photo, for the students are learning that despite their individual identities, they all are Americans.

Social Integration

Schools also perform the function of *social integration,* helping to mold students into a more cohesive unit. Indeed, as we just saw, forging a national identity by integrating immigrants into a common cultural heritage was one of the manifest functions of establishing a publicly funded system of education in the United States (Hellinger and Judd 1991). When children enter school, they come from many different backgrounds. Their particular family and social class may have taught them speech patterns, dress, and other behaviors or attitudes that differ from those generally recognized as desirable or acceptable. In the classroom and on the playground, those backgrounds take new shape. The end result is that schools help socialize students into the mainstream culture.

Peer culture is especially significant, for most students are eager to fit in. From their peers, they learn ideas and norms that go beyond their family and little corner of the world. Guided by today's powerful mass media, students in all parts of the country choose to look alike by wearing, for example, the same brands and styles of jeans, shirts, skirts, blouses, sneakers, hats, and jackets. Parental influence rapidly declines as the peer culture molds not only the youths' appearance but even their ideas, speech patterns, and interaction with the opposite sex (Thorne and Luria 1993).

The classroom itself helps to produce social integration. As students salute the flag and sing the national anthem, for example, they become aware of the "greater government," and their sense of national identity grows. One of the best indicators of how education promotes political integration is the millions of immigrants who have attended U.S. schools, learned mainstream ideas, and given up their earlier national and cultural identities as they became Americans (Violas 1978; Rodriguez 1995).

How significant is this integrative function of education? It goes far beyond similarities of appearance or speech. *To forge a national identity is to stabilize the political system.* If people identify with a society's social institutions and *perceive them as the basis of their welfare,* they have no reason to rebel. This function is especially significant when it comes to the lower social classes, from which most social revolutionaries are drawn. The wealthy already have a vested interest in maintaining the status quo, but to get the lower classes to identify with the social system *as it is* goes a long way to preserving the system as it is.

People with disabilities often have found themselves out of the mainstream of society. To overcome this, U.S. schools have added a new manifest function, **mainstreaming**, or inclusion. This means that schools try to incorporate these students into regular social activities. As a matter of routine policy, students with disabilities used to be placed in special

In recent years, social integration, a traditional function of public education, has been extended. In a process called mainstreaming (also known as inclusion by educators), children who used to be sent to special schools now attend regular schools. Shown here is a science class in a school in California.

mainstreaming helping people to become part of the mainstream of society

schools. Educators, however, concluded that in these settings such students learned to adjust only to a world of the disabled, leaving them ill prepared to cope with the dominant world. The educational philosophy then changed to one that encourages or even requires students with disabilities to attend regular schools.

Mainstreaming is easiest for students whose disabilities are minor, of course, for they fit more easily into regular schools. For people who cannot walk, schools and other public facilities have been required to build wheelchair ramps; for those who cannot hear, "signers" (interpreters who use their hands) may attend classes with them. Most students who are blind attend special schools, as do people with severe learning disabilities. Overall, one half of students with disabilities now attend school in regular classrooms ("State of American Education," 2000).

Gatekeeping

Gatekeeping, or determining which people will enter what occupations, is another major function of education. One type of gatekeeping is *credentialing*—using diplomas and degrees to determine who is eligible for a job—which, of course, open and close doors of opportunity.

Gatekeeping is often accomplished by **tracking**, sorting students into different educational programs on the basis of real or perceived abilities. Tests are used to determine which students should be directed into "college prep" programs, while others are put onto a vocational track. The impact is lifelong, with opportunities for jobs, raises, and promotions opening or closing on the basis of education.

Tracking begins in grade school, where on the basis of test results most students take regular courses, but some are placed in advanced sections of English and mathematics. In high school, tracking becomes more elaborate. In many schools, students are funneled into one of three tracks: general, college prep, or honors. All students who complete their sequence of courses receive a high school diploma and are eligible to go on to college. Those in the lowest track, however, are most likely to go to work after high school or perhaps to take a vocational course at a community college; those in the highest track enter the more prestigious colleges around the country; and those in between most often attend a local college or regional state university.

Gatekeeping sorts people on the basis of merit, say functionalists. Sociologists Talcott Parsons (1940), Kingsley Davis, and Wilbert Moore (1945), who pioneered this view, also known as **social placement,** argue that a major task of society is to fill its positions with capable people. Some positions, such as that of physician, require high intelligence and many years of advanced education. Consequently, to motivate capable people to postpone immediate gratification and to submit to many years of rigorous education, high income and prestige are held out as rewards. Other jobs require fewer skills and can be performed by people of lesser intelligence. Thus, functionalists look on education as a system that, to the benefit of society, sorts people according to their abilities.

Promoting Personal Change

Learning critical thinking skills helps to promote personal change. Schools teach students to "think for themselves"—to critically evaluate ideas and social life. One consequence is that the further people go in school, the more open they tend to be to new ways of thinking and doing things. People with more education tend to hold more liberal ideas, while those with less education tend to be more conservative.

Promoting Social Change

The educational institution also contributes to social change by sponsoring research. Most university professors, for example, are given time off from teaching so that they can do research. Their findings become part of a body of accumulated knowledge that stimulates social change. Sociologists, for example, presented conclusions from sociological research

gatekeeping the process by which education opens and closes doors of opportunity; another term for the **social placement** function of education

tracking the sorting of students into different educational programs on the basis of real or perceived abilities

social placement a function of education that funnels people into a society's various positions

Education has replaced several functions of the family. In most areas, parents have quietly acquiesced. Sex education, however, has remained a source of continuing controversy. Many parents object to the schools usurping their role, as well as to their children being taught values that violate their own.

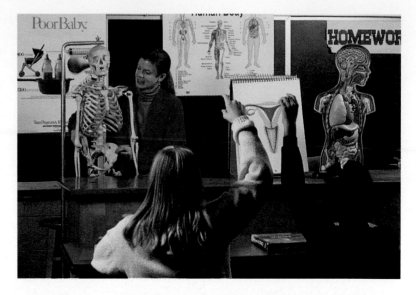

before the U.S. Supreme Court that helped bring about the 1954 decision to desegregate U.S. schools. Some academic research has had an explosive impact on society—literally, in the case of the atomic and hydrogen weapons that were developed in part from university research. Nobody remains untouched by this function of education. For example, medical research conducted in universities throughout the world is partially responsible for making it likely that you will reach old age.

Replacing Family Functions

Over the years, the functions of U.S. schools have expanded, and they now rival some family functions. Child care is an example. Grade schools do double duty as baby-sitters for parents who both work, or for single mothers in the work force. Child care always has been a latent function of formal education, for it was an unintended consequence of schooling. Now, however, because most families have two wage earners, child care has become a manifest function. Some schools even offer child care both before and after formal classes. Another school function is sex education and birth control advice, which has stirred controversy, for some families resent this function being taken from them.

Other Functions

Education also fulfills many other functions. For example, because most students are unmarried, high schools and colleges effectively serve as *matchmaking* institutions. It is here that many young people find their future spouses. The sociological significance of this function of schools is that they funnel people into marriages with mates of similar background, interests, and education. Schools also establish *social networks*. Some older adults maintain friendship networks from high school and college, while others become part of business or professional networks that prove highly beneficial to their careers. Finally, schools also help to *stabilize employment*. The Most Industrialized Nations have little use for unskilled individuals. To keep millions in school and out of the labor market keeps positions open for older workers.

*T*HE CONFLICT PERSPECTIVE: HOW EDUCATION REPRODUCES THE SOCIAL CLASS STRUCTURE

Unlike functionalists, who see education as a social institution that performs functions for the benefit of society, conflict theorists see the educational system as a tool used by the elite to maintain their dominance. Education, they stress, *reproduces the social class structure.* By this, they mean that education perpetuates a society's social divisions. For example, regardless of children's abilities, the more well-to-do are likely to be placed in college-bound tracks, the poor into vocational tracks, and both to inherit the corresponding life opportunities laid down before they were born.

Let's look at ways by which this occurs.

The Hidden Curriculum

The term **hidden curriculum** refers to the unwritten rules of behavior and attitudes, such as obedience to authority and conformity to cultural norms, that are taught in the schools in addition to the formal curriculum (Gillborn 1992). Conflict theorists note how this hidden curriculum helps to perpetuate social inequalities.

To better understand this central point, consider the values and work habits that students are taught in school: obedience to the teacher, punctuality, and turning in neat work on time. These traits are desired by employers, who want dependable, docile, subordinate workers. Or consider just the emphasis on "proper" English. Members of the elite need people to run their business empires, and they are more comfortable if their managers possess the "refined" language and manners that they themselves are used to. Consequently, middle-class schools, whose teachers know where their pupils are headed, stress "proper" English and "good" manners. In contrast, because few children from inner city schools will occupy managerial positions, their teachers allow ethnic and street language in the classroom.

To reproduce the social class structure, then, means to prepare students to work in positions similar to those of their parents. Some children, socially destined for higher positions, need to learn "refined" speech and manners. Others simply need to be taught to obey rules so they can take their place in the closely supervised, low-status positions for which they are socially destined (Bowles and Gintis 1976; Olneck and Bills 1980). "Refined" speech and manners would be wasted on them. From this conflict perspective, even kindergarten has a hidden curriculum, as the Down-to-Earth Sociology box on the next page illustrates.

Conflict theorists stress that education reproduces a country's social class system. To support this position, they point out that the U.S. social classes attend different schools, where they are taught by teachers of different backgrounds, and where they learn contrasting perspectives of the world and their place in it. Shown here are students lunching with their teacher at St. Alban's School in Washington, D.C., obviously not a school for the poor.

Tilting the Tests: Discrimination by IQ

Even intelligence tests play their part in keeping the social class system intact. For example, how would you answer the following question?

A symphony is to a composer as a book is to a(n) _____.

_____ paper _____ sculptor _____ musician _____ author _____ man

You probably had no difficulty coming up with "author" as your choice. Wouldn't any intelligent person have done so?

In point of fact, this question raises a central issue in intelligence testing. Not all intelligent people would know the answer, because this question contains *cultural biases*. In other words, children from some backgrounds are more familiar with the concepts of symphonies, composers, sculptors, and musicians than are other children. Consequently, the test is tilted in their favor (Turner 1972; Ashe 1992).

Perhaps asking a different question will make the bias clearer. How would you answer this question?

If you throw dice and "7" is showing on the top, what is facing down?

_____ seven _____ snake eyes _____ box cars _____ little Joes _____ eleven

This question, suggested by Adrian Dove (n.d.), a social worker in Watts, is slanted toward a lower-class experience. It surely is obvious that this *particular* cultural bias tilts the test so that children from some social backgrounds will perform better than others.

hidden curriculum the unwritten goals of schools, such as obedience to authority and conformity to cultural norms

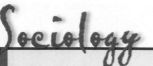

KINDERGARTEN AS BOOT CAMP

Sociologist Harry Gracey (1999), who did participant observation in a kindergarten, concluded that kindergarten is a sort of boot camp for the entire educational system. Here, tender students are drilled in the behaviors and attitudes deemed appropriate for the "student role," which, he argued, is to follow classroom routines. The goal of kindergarten is to mold many individuals from diverse backgrounds into a compliant group that will, on command, unthinkingly follow classroom routines.

Kindergarten's famous "show and tell," for example, does more than allow children to be expressive. It also teaches them to talk only when they are asked to speak. ("It's your turn, Jarmay.") The format also teaches children to request permission to talk ("Who knows what Letitia has?") by raising a hand and being acknowledged. Finally, the whole ritual teaches children to acknowledge the teacher's ideas as superior. She is the one who has the capacity to evaluate students' activities and ideas.

Gracey found a similar hidden curriculum in the other activities he observed. Whether students were engaged in drawing pictures, listening to records, snack time, or rest time, the teachers would quiet talkative students, scolding them at times and giving approval for conforming behaviors. In short, the message conveyed is that the teacher—and, by inference, the entire school system— is the authority.

The purpose of kindergarten, Gracey concluded, is to teach children to "follow orders with unquestioning obedience." To accomplish this, kindergarten teachers "create and enforce a rigid social structure in the classroom through which they effectively control the behavior of most of the children for most of the school day." This produces three kinds of students: (1) "good" students, those who submit to school-imposed discipline and come to identify with it; (2) "adequate" students, those who submit to the school's discipline but do not identify with it; and (3) "bad" students, those who refuse to submit to school routines. Children who fall into the third category are also known as "problem children." To bring them into line, a tougher drill sergeant, the school psychologist, is called in. Even kindergarten students are given Ritalin and other drugs to make them docile.

Learning the student role prepares children for grade school, where they "will be asked to submit to systems and routines imposed by the teachers and the curriculum. The days will be much like those of kindergarten, except that academic subjects will be substituted."

Gracey adds that these lessons extend well beyond the classroom. They prepare students for the routines of the work world, both on the assembly line and at the office. Mastering the student role prepares them to follow unquestioningly the routines imposed by "the company." ■

It is no different with IQ (intelligence quotient) tests that use such words as *composer* and *symphony*. A lower-class child may have heard about rap, rock, hip hop, or jazz but not about symphonies. In other words, IQ tests measure not only intelligence but also culturally acquired knowledge. Whatever else we can say, the cultural bias built into the IQ tests used in schools is clearly *not* tilted in favor of the lower classes.

A second inadequacy of IQ tests is that they focus on mathematical, spatial, symbolic, and linguistic abilities. Intelligence, however, consists of more than these components. The ability to compose music, to be empathetic to the feelings of others, or to be humorous or persuasive are also components of intelligence.

The significance of these factors, say conflict theorists, is that culturally biased IQ tests favor the middle classes and discriminate against students from lower-class backgrounds. These tests, which are used to assign students to tracks, place disproportionate numbers of minorities and the poor in noncollege tracks (Kershaw 1992). This outcome, as we have seen, destines them for lower-paying jobs in adult life. Thus, conflict theorists view IQ tests as another weapon in an arsenal designed to maintain the social class structure across the generations (Postman 1992).

Stacking the Deck: Unequal Funding

Conflict theorists also stress that how we fund education stacks the deck against the poor. Money is a scarce resource, unequally distributed among rich and poor school districts and states. The geographical inequality becomes readily visible when we look at Table 17.1 below. You can see that for each of their students Alaska and New Jersey spend more than two times what Utah and Oklahoma spend on their students. If you divide the list in the middle, you can see that all of the eastern states rank in the top half, while all but two of the southern states fall in the bottom half.

Higher spending, often thought to be the key to high educational quality, does not guarantee quality education. Students from North Dakota, for example, which ranks only forty-fifth in spending, score the highest on the SAT test. But this figure, too, is misleading, for compared with some other states a smaller proportion of North Dakota students take the test. Table 17.2 on the next page shows spending and results on an international level. Although Switzerland spends the most per student and gets the best test results, the United States is the third highest spender but gets the worst test results.

Table 17.1

WHAT STATES SPEND ON EDUCATION, PER STUDENT

1.	$10,650	Alaska	26.	$6,283	Kentucky
2.	$10,427	New Jersey	27.	$6,237	Montana
3.	$9,812	New York	28.	$6,177	Georgia
4.	$9,218	Connecticut	29.	$6,137	Florida
5.	$8,576	Delaware	30.	$6,127	Hawaii
6.	$8,429	Rhode Island	31.	$5,865	New Mexico
7.	$7,925	Vermont	32.	$5,846	Nebraska
8.	$7,861	Massachusetts	33.	$5,830	North Carolina
9.	$7,752	Pennsylvania	34.	$5,713	Iowa
10.	$7,673	Michigan	35.	$5,704	Colorado
11.	$7,375	Maryland	36.	$5,601	Nevada
12.	$7,272	Wisconsin	37.	$5,597	Missouri
13.	$7,110	West Virginia	38.	$5,591	Tennessee
14.	$7,107	Maine	39.	$5,555	South Carolina
15.	$6,727	Minnesota	40.	$5,345	California
16.	$6,719	Oregon	41.	$5,222	Arkansas
17.	$6,642	Indiana	42.	$5,194	Louisiana
18.	$6,569	Virginia	43.	$5,166	South Dakota
19.	$6,556	New Hampshire	44.	$5,110	Alabama
20.	$6,539	Ohio	45.	$4,978	North Dakota
21.	$6,188	Washington	46.	$4,973	Idaho
22.	$6,363	Illinois	47.	$4,937	Arizona
23.	$6,348	Kansas	48.	$4,732	Mississippi
24.	$6,312	Wyoming	49.	$4,634	Oklahoma
25.	$6,291	Texas	50.	$3,900	Utah

Note: These are 1998 totals. They refer to the amount spent per student in grade school and high school.

Source: Statistical Abstract 1999:Table 286.

Table 17.2

EDUCATIONAL EXPENDITURES AND STUDENT SCORES

Rank by Student Performance	Country	Math Scores (percentage correct)	Science Scores (percentage correct)	Money Spent per Student	Rank by Money Spent per Student
1.	Switzerland	71%	74%	$6,815	1.
2.	Italy	64	70	4,470	4.
3.	France	64	69	4,380	5.
4.	Canada	62	69	6,191	2.
5.	Ireland	61	63	2,240	7.
6.	Spain	55	68	2,500	6.
7.	United States	55	67	6,103	3.

Note: These are the only countries in the source for which both expenditures and test scores are given. These are the latest data available in the source. U.S. expenditure is now $6,360, but to keep the data comparable, the lower total is retained. Based on testing of 13-year-olds. Expenditures are for 1991 and 1992, test scores for 1991.

Source: Statistical Abstract 1992:Table 1369; 1994:Table 1362; 1995:Table 1370; 1999:Table 280.

Conflict theorists go beyond this observation, however. They stress that in each state the deck is stacked against the poor. Because public schools are largely supported by local property taxes, the richer communities (where property values are higher) have more to spend on their children, while the poorer communities end up with much less. Consequently, the richer communities are able to offer higher salaries (and take their pick of the most highly qualified and motivated teachers), afford the latest textbooks and computers, teach additional courses in foreign language, music, and so on. Because U.S. schools so closely reflect the U.S. social class system, then, the children of the privileged emerge from grade school best equipped for success in high school. In turn, they come out of high school best equipped for success in college. Their greater likelihood of success in college, in turn, serves to maintain their dominance.

The Correspondence Principle

Conflict sociologists Samuel Bowles and Herbert Gintis (1976) used the term **correspondence principle** to refer to the ways in which schools reflect the social structure of society. This term means that what is taught in a nation's schools *corresponds* to the characteristics of that society. Thus education helps to perpetuate a society's social inequalities. The following list provides some examples.

Characteristics of Society	Characteristics of Schools
1. Capitalism	1. Promote competition
2. Social inequality	2. Provide unequal funding of schools; funnel the poor into job training programs
3. Racial-ethnic prejudice	3. Make minorities feel inferior; funnel minorities into job training programs
4. Bureaucratic structure of corporation	4. Provide a model of authority in the classroom
5. Need for submissive workers	5. Make students submissive
6. Need for dependable workers	6. Promote punctuality
7. Need to maintain armed forces	7. Promote patriotism (to fight for capitalism)

correspondence principle
the sociological principle that schools correspond to (or reflect) the social structure of society

Thus, conclude conflict theorists, the U.S. educational system is designed to produce dependable workers who will not question their bosses, as well as some individuals who will go on to be innovators in thought and action but can still be counted on to be loyal to the social system as it exists (Olneck and Bills 1980).

The Bottom Line:
Family Background and the Educational System

The end result of unequal funding, IQ tests, and so on is that family background proves more important than test scores in predicting who attends college. Back in 1977, sociologist Samuel Bowles compared the college attendance of the brightest 25 percent of high school students with the intellectually weakest 25 percent. Figure 17.4 shows the results. Of the *brightest* 25 percent of high school students, 90 percent of those from affluent homes went to college, while only half of those from low-income homes did so. Of the *weakest* students, 26 percent from affluent homes went to college, while only 6 percent from poorer homes did so. And today? This same general relationship still holds. If you rank families from the poorest to the richest, as the income increases the likelihood that the children will attend college also increases (Manski 1992–1993).

Conflict theorists point out that the educational system not only reproduces the wealth-poverty gulf of the U.S. social class structure, but also its divisions of race and ethnicity. From Figure 17.5, you can see that, compared with whites, African Americans and Latinos are less likely to complete high school, less likely to go to college, and, if they go to college, less likely to graduate. Those without college degrees have less access to jobs with better pay and the potential for advancement. Then, too, we can look at what types of colleges different groups are likely to attend. As Table 17.3 on the next page shows, whites are more likely than other racial-ethnic groups to attend private and four-year colleges.

The *purpose* of the educational system, stress conflict theorists, is to *reproduce inequality,* to help keep the social class structure intact from one generation to the next. Consequently, most children of the less privileged are funneled into community college job training programs, while children of the middle classes attend state universities and small private colleges. The offspring of the elite, in contrast, attend exclusive boarding high schools, where their learning environment includes small classes and well-paid teachers (Persell et al. 1992). Here they inherit a cozy social network that encompasses the school's college advisers and the admissions officers of the nation's most elite colleges. Some of these networks are so efficient that half of these private schools' graduating classes are admitted to Harvard, Yale, and Princeton (Persell and Cookson 1986).

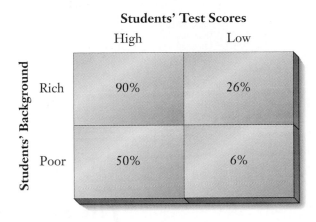

Figure 17.4 WHO GOES TO COLLEGE? THE ROLE OF SOCIAL CLASS AND PERSONAL ABILITY IN DETERMINING COLLEGE ATTENDANCE

Source: Bowles 1977.

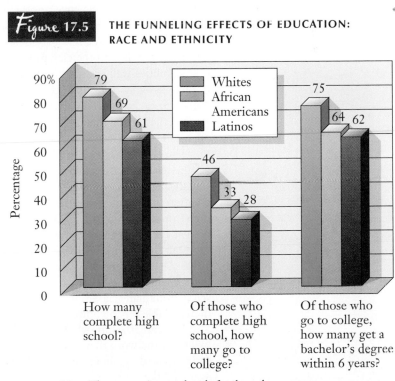

Figure 17.5 THE FUNNELING EFFECTS OF EDUCATION: RACE AND ETHNICITY

Note: The source gives totals only for these three groups.

Source: Statistical Abstract 1999:Tables 304, 328.

Table 17.3	OF THOSE WHO GO TO COLLEGE, WHAT PERCENTAGE ATTENDS EACH TYPE OF COLLEGE?			
Racial-Ethnic Group	Public College	Private College	2-Year College	4-Year College
Whites	77%	23%	37%	63%
African Americans	79%	21%	39%	61%
Asian Americans	80%	20%	42%	58%
Latinos	86%	14%	50%	50%
Native Americans	87%	13%	56%	44%

Source: Statistical Abstract 1999:Table 309.

*T*HE SYMBOLIC INTERACTIONIST PERSPECTIVE: TEACHER EXPECTATIONS AND THE SELF-FULFILLING PROPHECY

Whereas functionalists look at how education benefits society and conflict theorists examine how education perpetuates social inequality, symbolic interactionists study face-to-face interactions inside the classroom. They have found that the expectations of teachers have profound consequences for their students.

The Rist Research

Symbolic interactionists have uncovered some of the dynamics of educational tracking. In what has become a classic study, sociologist Ray Rist did participant observation in an African-American grade school with an African-American faculty. Rist (1970) found that after only eight days in the classroom, the kindergarten teacher felt that she knew the children's abilities well enough to assign them to three separate worktables. To Table 1, Mrs. Caplow assigned those she considered to be "fast learners." They sat at the front of the room, closest to her. Those whom she saw as "slow learners," she assigned to Table 3, located at the back of the classroom. She placed "average" students at Table 2, in between the other tables.

This seemed strange to Rist. He knew that the children had not been tested for ability, yet the teacher was certain that she could differentiate between bright and slow children. Investigating further, Rist found that social class was the underlying basis for assigning the children to the different tables. Middle-class students were separated out for Table 1, children from poorer homes to Tables 2 and 3. The teacher paid the most attention to the children at Table 1, who were closest to her, less to Table 2, and the least to Table 3. As the year went on, children from Table 1 perceived that they were treated better and came to see themselves as smarter. They became the leaders in class activities and even ridiculed children at the other tables, calling them "dumb." Eventually, the children at Table 3 disengaged themselves from many classroom activities. Not surprisingly, at the end of the year only the children at Table 1 had completed the lessons that prepared them for reading.

This early tracking stuck. When these students entered the first grade, their new teacher looked at the work they had accomplished and placed students from Table 1 at her Table 1. She treated her tables much as the kindergarten teacher had, and the children at Table 1 again led the class.

The children's reputations continued to follow them. The second-grade teacher reviewed their scores and also divided her class into three groups. The first she named the

"Tigers" and, befitting their name, gave them challenging readers. Not surprisingly, the Tigers came from the original Table 1 in kindergarten. The second group she called the "Cardinals." They came from the original Tables 2 and 3. Her third group consisted of children she had failed the previous year, whom she called the "Clowns." The Cardinals and Clowns were given less advanced readers.

Rist concluded that *the child's journey through school was determined at the eighth day of kindergarten!* What had occurred was a **self-fulfilling prophecy,** a term coined by sociologist Robert Merton (1949) to refer to an originally false assumption of what is going to happen that comes true simply because it was predicted. For example, if people believe an unfounded rumor that a bank is in trouble and assume that they won't be able to get their money out, they all rush to the bank to demand their money. The prediction—*although originally false*—is now likely to be true.

In this case, of course, we are dealing with something more important than money, the welfare of little children. As with the story of the Saints and Roughnecks, reported in Chapter 4 (pages 121–122), this research demonstrates the power of labels. They can set people on courses of action that affect the rest of their lives. This, of course, is the significance of Rist's observations of these grade school children.

The Rosenthal-Jacobson Experiment

During the course of our education, most of us have seen teacher expectations at work. We know that if our teacher expects higher standards, then we must perform at a higher level to earn good grades. Teacher expectations, however, also work subtly but effectively in ways that we don't perceive. In what has become a classic experiment, social psychologists Robert Rosenthal and Lenore Jacobson (1968) tried out a new test in a San Francisco grade school. They tested the children's abilities and then told the teachers which students would probably "spurt" ahead during the year. They instructed the teachers to watch these students' progress, but not to let the students or their parents know about the test results. At the end of the year, they tested the students again and found that the IQs of the predicted "spurters" had jumped ten to fifteen points higher than those of the other children.

You might think that Rosenthal and Jacobson then became famous for developing such an impressive scholastic aptitude test. Actually, however, this "test" was another of those covert experiments. Rosenthal and Jacobson had simply given routine IQ tests to the children and had then *randomly* chosen 20 percent of the students as "spurters." These students were *no* different from the others in the classroom. A self-fulfilling prophecy had taken place: The teachers expected more of those particular students, and the students responded. In short, expect dumb and you get dumb. Expect smart, and you get smart.

Although attempts to replicate this experiment have had mixed results (Pilling and Pringle 1978), a good deal of research confirms that students who are expected to do better generally do (Seaver 1973; Snyder 1993).

How Do Teacher Expectations Work?

Just as teacher expectations operate in the early grades, so they continue throughout school. A research team led by sociologist George Farkas (1990a, 1990b, 1996) became interested in how teacher expectations affect students' grades. A fascinating finding emerged from their stratified sample of students in a large school district in Texas: *Even though they had the same test scores,* girls and Asian Americans averaged higher course grades than did boys, African Americans, Latinos, and whites.

Why should this be? Discrimination doesn't seem to provide an answer. Look who the victims are. It is most unlikely that the teachers would be prejudiced against boys and whites. To interpret these unexpected results, the Farkas team used symbolic interactionism. They observed that some students "signal" to their teachers that they are "good students." They show an eagerness to cooperate, and they quickly agree with what the teacher says. They also show that they are trying hard. The teachers pick up these signals and

self-fulfilling prophecy Robert Merton's term for an originally false assertion that becomes true simply because it was predicted

Sociology & the New Technology

INTERNET UNIVERSITY:
NO WALLS, NO IVY, NO KEG PARTIES

Distance learning, courses taught to students who are not physically present with their instructor, is not new. For decades, we have had correspondence courses.

Today, however, distance learning refers to something much more than this. Joe Martin, a 41-year-old executive in Indianapolis, is enrolled in Duke University's MBA program. On his lunch hour or at night in his bedroom, Martin logs on to the Internet and does homework assigned by a professor in another state whom he has never met. He also listens to lectures on the Internet and chats with classmates in China and Brazil (Hamilton and Miller 1997).

Telecommunications—satellites, computers, television, and CD-ROMs—are changing the face of education. With computer link-ups, students in remote parts of Alaska earn B.A.s from their state university. This practice is rapidly gaining in popularity,

and cybercolleges soon may be part of mainstream education. Already about 400 colleges and universities offer virtual degrees.

In the past, distance learning often meant a TV screen that replaced a live teacher in a classroom. Consequently, some critics say that the only real change has been an increased capacity to bore: Instead of a live teacher boring a few students in a single classroom, that person's image bores thousands simultaneously (Thornburg 1994). Certainly until now most distance learning has been either slow (a correspondence course) or one-way (students passively receiving instruction, usually providing feedback only through tests). The new technology, such as teleconferencing, however, permits students and teachers to see one another, to talk with one another, and to share documents worldwide.

The potential is staggering, and it may soon become reality. One of the

new silicone valley billionaires has put up $400 million to fund a full-fledged Internet University (Loose 2000).

Why, indeed, should our learning be limited to walled classrooms? When studying human culture, for example, wouldn't it be intriguing to be able to compare notes on eating, dating, or burial customs with fellow students in Thailand, Iceland, South Africa, Germany, Egypt, China, and Australia? Or even to write a joint paper comparing your cross-cultural experiences with those described in the text, and then submitting that paper to your mutual instructor?

Will we eventually go from kindergarten to grad school, proceeding at our own pace, with classmates from around the world? While this may sound intriguing, no walls also means no flirting after class, no joking in the hallway or dorm, no keg parties. . . . ■

reward these "good students" with better grades. Girls and Asian Americans, the researchers concluded, are better at displaying these characteristics so coveted by teachers.

We do not have enough information on how teachers form their expectations or how they communicate them to students. Nor do we know much about how students "signal" messages to teachers. (As discussed in the Sociology and New Technology box above, technology is producing new forms of student-teacher interaction and "signaling.") Perhaps you will become the educational sociologist who will shed more light on these significant everyday aspects of human behavior.

PROBLEMS IN U.S. EDUCATION— AND THEIR SOLUTIONS

To conclude this chapter, let's examine some of the major problems facing U.S. education today. Let's also consider their potential solutions.

Problems: Mediocrity, Teen Pregnancy, and Violence

The Rising Tide of Mediocrity All Arizona high school sophomores took a math test. It covered the math that sophomores should know. One of ten passed. Meanwhile, in New

York, to get its students to graduate, the state had to lower its passing grade to 55 out of 100 (Steinberg 1999). Perhaps nothing so captures what is wrong with U.S. schools than this event, reported by sociologist Thomas Sowell (1993b):

> [A]n international study of 13-year-olds . . . found that Koreans ranked first in mathematics and Americans last. When asked if they thought they were "good at mathematics," only 23 percent of the Korean youngsters said "yes"—compared to 68 percent of American 13-year-olds. The American educational dogma that students should "feel good about themselves" was a success in its own terms—though not in any other terms.

In 1983, a blue-ribbon presidential panel gave a grim assessment of U.S. education. This panel warned that a "rising tide of mediocrity threatens our very future as a nation and as a people." Even the title of the report, *A Nation at Risk,* sounded an alarm. What especially upset panel members was a decline in scores on the Scholastic Assessment Test (SAT). As Figure 17.6 shows, the math scores have recovered a good amount of lost ground. The verbal scores, however, are still low, and holding steady. Both are lower than they were thirty years ago.

The president of the American Federation of Teachers came up with a unique defense of the decline in SAT scores: The low test scores, he said, mean that teachers are doing a *better* job! They are getting more students to stay in high school and to go on to college. Students from poorer academic backgrounds, who used to drop out of high school, now become part of the test results (Sowell 1993b). Perhaps this is the reason. But if it is, it indicates not success, but a severe underlying problem—teachers giving inferior education to disadvantaged students (Murray and Hernstein 1992).

Others suggest that SAT scores have declined because children find television and video games more appealing than reading (Rigdon and Swasy 1990). Students who read little acquire a smaller vocabulary and less rigor in thought and verbal expression. Sociologists Donald Hayes and Loreen Wolfer (1993a, b) are convinced that the culprit is the "dummied down" textbooks that pervade U.S. schools. Some point their fingers at other low standards: "frill" courses, less homework, fewer term papers, grade inflation, and burned-out teachers who are more interested in collecting paychecks than in educating their students. Some of the examples they offer are startling, such as the college freshman who couldn't understand why she was doing poorly in college since she had placed third in her Chicago high school graduating class. Testing showed that she ranked in the lowest 2 percent of the nation's high school graduates (Kotlowitz 1992).

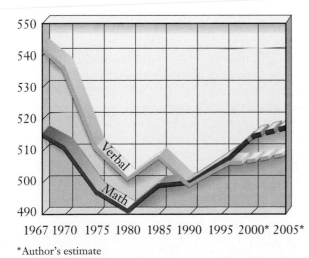

Figure 17.6

NATIONAL RESULTS OF THE SCHOLASTIC ASSESSMENT TEST (SAT)

Source: Statistical Abstract 1999: Table 296.

*Author's estimate

How to Cheat on the SATs If you receive poor grades this semester, wouldn't you like to use a magic marker to, presto!, change them into better grades? I suppose every student would. Now imagine that you had that power. Would you use it?

Some people in authority apparently have found such a magic marker, and they are using it to raise our embarrassingly low national SAT scores. Table 274 of the 1996 edition of the *Statistical Abstract of the United States* says that in 1995 only 8.3 percent of students earned 600 or more on the verbal portion of the SAT test. The very next edition, in 1997, however, holds a pleasant surprise. Table 276 tells us that it was really 21.9 percent of students who scored 600 or higher in 1995. Future editions of this source retain the higher figure. What a magic marker!

In the twinkle of an eye, we get another bonus. Somehow, between 1996 and 1997 the scores of *everyone* who took the test in previous years improved. Now that's the kind of power we all would like to have. Students, grab your report cards. Workers, change those numbers on your paycheck.

While all the explanations for this sleight-of-hand are not in, we do know that it is easier to make a test simpler than to do better teaching. And this is what the authorities have done to the SAT. The test is now shorter, students have more time to answer fewer questions, and the verbal part was made easier by dropping the antonym portion (Manno 1995; Stecklow 1995). This "dummying down" of the SAT is yet another form of grade inflation, the topic to which we shall now turn.

Grade Inflation, Social Promotion, and Functional Illiteracy In the 1960s, high school teachers gave out about twice as many *C*'s as *A*'s, but now there are more *A*'s than *C*'s. Keep in mind that this happened while learning went down! Another sign of **grade inflation** is that *one-third* of all entering college freshmen have an overall high school grade point average of A. This is *twice* what it was in 1970 (*Statistical Abstract* 1999:Table 324).

Grade inflation in the face of declining standards has been accompanied by **social promotion,** the practice of passing students from one grade to the next even though they have not mastered basic materials. One result is **functional illiteracy,** people having difficulty with reading and writing even though they have graduated from high school. Some high school graduates cannot fill out job applications; others can't figure out if they are given the right change at the grocery store.

Peer Groups A team of two psychologists and a sociologist studied 20,000 high school students in California and Wisconsin (Steinberg et al. 1996). They found that the peer group was the most important of all the influences affecting these teenagers. Simply put: Those who hang out with good students tend to do well; those who hang out with friends who do poorly in school do poorly. The subcultures that students develop include informal norms about educational achievement; some groups set up norms of classroom excellence, while others sneer at getting good grades. The applied question that arises from this research, of course, is how to build educational achievement into student culture.

Teenage Pregnancy Students who lack a high school diploma face a severe handicap in life. At several points in this text, I have mentioned the negative consequences that often follow single motherhood, especially the cycle of poverty (see pages 278 and 459–460). Those consequences are especially stark for teenage mothers. Not only do these young women, some still girls, have the expense and responsibility of caring for a child, but also they are unlikely to complete high school, thus perpetuating a cycle of poverty and interrupted education.

Violence in Schools Violence in schools has captured the public's attention, and that of worried parents across the nation. Many U.S. schools have deteriorated to the point that safety is an issue. In some of our schools, uniformed guards, unknown of a few years ago, have become a routine fixture. To get into some schools, students must pass through metal detectors. Some grade schools even supplement their traditional fire drills with "drive-by shooting drills" (Toch 1993; Grossman 1995).

And the school shootings? For a surprising analysis, read the following Mass Media box.

grade inflation higher grades given for the same work; a general rise in student grades without a corresponding increase in learning or test scores

social promotion passing students to the next grade even though they have not mastered basic materials

functional illiterate a high school graduate who has difficulty with basic reading and math

Mass Media in Social Life

SCHOOL SHOOTINGS:
WHEN MYTH GIVES WAY TO PANIC

Understandably, school shootings have captured media attention. Sprinkling their reports with such dramatic phrases as "alarming proportions, "outbreak of violence," and "out of control," the mass media convey the impression that schools all over the nation are set to erupt in gunfire. The public views the shootings as convincing evidence that something is seriously wrong with society, or with our schools. Parents used to consider schools safe havens, but no longer. Those naive thoughts have been shattered by the bullets that have sprayed our schools—or at least by the media's portrayal of increasing danger and violence in our schools.

Have our schools really become war zones, as the mass media would have us believe? Certainly events such as those at Columbine High School are extremely disturbing, but we need to probe deeper than newspaper headlines and televised images in order to understand their social significance.

When we do, we find that the media's sensationalist reporting has created a myth. Contrary to "what everyone knows," *there is no trend toward greater school violence.* Without doubt, violence in schools is a problem for which we must find a solution. But despite the many dramatic school shootings of recent years, as Table 17.4 shows, shooting deaths at schools remain within the usual range. As you can see, even during the 1998–1999 school year, when the Columbine killers went on their lethal rampage, the number of shooting deaths at

U.S. schools was *below* the average for the 1990s. And the number that year was *half* what it had been six years earlier.

This is not to say that school shootings are not a serious problem. Even one student being wounded or killed in a shooting is one too many. But, contrary to the impression fostered by the media, we are *not* seeing an escalation of school shooting deaths.

This is why we need sociology: to quietly, dispassionately search for facts so we can understand the true social significance of the events that shape our lives. The first requirement for solving any problem is accurate data, for we do not want to create solutions based on hysteria. The information presented in this box may not make for sensational headlines, but it does serve to explode the myth that the media promulgate. ■

This picture was taken when Drew Golden was 6 years old. Five years later, when Drew was 11, he teamed up with 13-year-old Mitch Johnson. Together, they ambushed their middle school teachers and classmates in Jonesboro, Arkansas. They wounded nine students and one teacher and killed four girls and one teacher.

Table 17.4

EXPLODING A MYTH:
DEATHS AT U.S. SCHOOLS[a]

School Year	Shooting Deaths	Other Homicides[b]	Total by Gender		Total
			Boys	Girls	
1992–1993	43	11	47	7	54
1993–1994	39	12	41	10	51
1994–1995	15	5	17	3	20
1995–1996	28	7	25	10	35
1996–1997	15	10	18	7	25
1997–1998	35	8	26	17	43
1998–1999	21	5	21	5	26
Mean, 1992–1999	28	8.3	27.9	8.4	36.3

[a] Includes all school-related homicides, even those that occurred on the way to or from school; includes suicides; includes school personnel killed at school by other adults; includes adults who had nothing to do with the school but who were found dead on school property.

[b] Beating, hanging, jumping, stabbing, and strangling.

Source: National School Safety Center, 2000.

Solutions: Retention, Standards, Safety, and Other Reforms

It is one thing to identify problems, and quite another to find solutions for them. Let' s begin by looking at a program designed to help pregnant teenagers complete high school, as described in the following Thinking Critically section. Then let's consider solutions to the other problems we have just reviewed.

Thinking *Critically*

HIGH SCHOOLS AND TEEN PREGNANCY: A PROGRAM THAT WORKS

To improve the high school graduation rates of teenage mothers, researchers in Ohio designed a program called LEAP—Learning, Earning, and Parenting. They made it tough for themselves by singling out teenage mothers on welfare, the group of teenage mothers that has the least chance of completing high school. The researchers randomly selected twelve of Ohio's eighty-eight counties, which included rural, suburban, and urban counties. All teens who were receiving Aid to Families with Dependent Children (AFDC), 7,000 individuals, became part of LEAP. They were required to stay in school or to return to school if they had dropped out—either to high school or to an Adult Basic Education program leading to a high school diploma.

The teens were randomly assigned to one of two groups. Those in the *experimental group* received a $62 bonus in their welfare check for providing evidence that they were enrolled in school and attending an assessment interview. Teens who did not comply had $62 deducted from their check. For each month they were absent no more than four times, the mothers received an additional $62 on their check, while those absent more than four times had $62 deducted from theirs. Because the monthly AFDC grant was $274, receiving a check with a bonus ($336) or a check reduced by the penalty ($212) made a considerable difference. Mothers who enrolled in school were also eligible for assistance with child care and transportation to attend school. In contrast, teens assigned to the *control group* were treated as usual—no school attendance requirements, no child care or transportation, no bonuses, and no deductions.

The program design is simple and straightforward, and, as discussed in Chapter 5 (pages 136-139), random assignment to control and experimental groups allows us to separate cause and effect. What, then, were the results? These are shown in Figure 17.7.

As you can see, teen mothers are like the rest of us—we all desire rewards and try to avoid punishments. Because of the random assignment to the groups, we know that the higher rates of staying in school and returning to school were due to the experimental variable. Beyond its effectiveness, what is also good about the program is its cost. There is little additional bureaucracy to feed, nor are there expensive educational programs to design and administer. There is little administrative work involved—simply identifying the teens and adjusting welfare checks on the basis of attendance data. In addition, a good part of the cost is covered by an internal transfer of money: For every two teens who received bonuses, one teen received penalties. ■

Figure 17.7

LEAP'S IMPACT ON HIGH SCHOOL RETENTION AND DROPOUTS

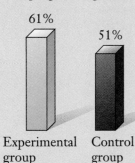

Teens who stayed in school
(students who were enrolled in school when the program began)

61%
51%

Experimental group

Control group

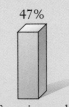

Dropouts who returned to school
(students who had dropped out of school before the program began)

47%
33%

Experimental group

Control group

For Your Consideration

If you were in charge of this program, how might you modify it to improve the results? Although the program had positive results, two of five teens in the experimental group still dropped out. Suppose that you were the head of Ohio's schools; would you recommend that the program be continued? Do you think this program should be applied nationally? Why or why not?

Source: Based on Bloom et al. 1993.

A Secure Learning Environment The first criterion for a good education is security, to guarantee students' physical safety and freedom from fear (Shanker 1995). With the high rate of violence in U.S. society, we can expect some violence to spill over into the schools. To minimize that spillover, school administrators can expel all students who threaten the welfare of others. They also can refuse to tolerate threats, violence, and weapons (Toby 1992). A zero tolerance policy for guns on school property is not unreasonable.

Higher Standards Within a secure learning environment, then, steps can be taken to improve the quality of education. There are many ways of measuring that quality, including the SAT test results we've reviewed. Another consideration is to realize that our schools compete with private industry for the same pool of college students. If the starting salary in other fields is higher than it is in education, those fields will have a better pick of brighter, more energetic graduates. Figure 17.8 shows the abysmal job we are doing in this competition.

A study by sociologists James Coleman and Thomas Hoffer (1987) provides helpful guidelines for improving the quality of education. They wanted to see why the test scores of students in Roman Catholic schools average 15 to 20 percent higher than those of students in public schools. Is it because Catholic schools attract better students, while public schools have to put up with everyone? To find out, Coleman and Hoffer tested 15,000 students in public and Catholic high schools.

Their findings? From their sophomore through their senior years, students at Catholic schools pull ahead of public school students by a full grade in verbal and math skills. The superior test performance of students in Catholic schools, they concluded, is due not to better students, but to higher standards. Catholic schools have not watered down their curricula as have public schools. The researchers also found another significant factor, parental involvement. Parents and teachers in Catholic schools reinforce each other's commitment to learning.

These findings support the basic principle reviewed earlier about teacher expectations: Students perform better when they are expected to do well. To this, you might want to

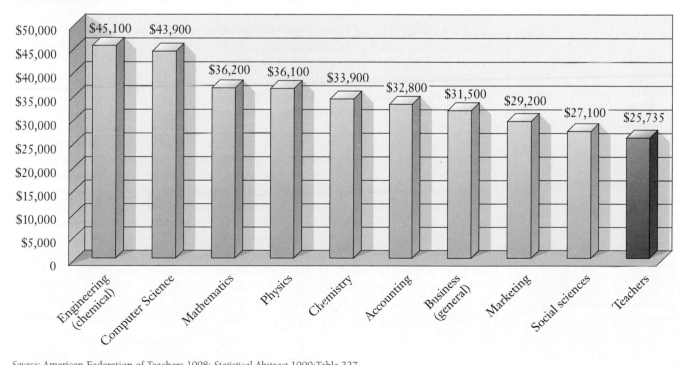

Figure 17.8 STARTING SALARIES OF U.S. COLLEGE GRADUATES: PUBLIC SCHOOL TEACHERS COMPARED WITH PRIVATE INDUSTRY

Source: American Federation of Teachers 1998; *Statistical Abstract* 1999:Table 327.

On average, students in Roman Catholic schools do better academically than students in public schools. Is it because Roman Catholic schools have better students, or because they do better teaching? The text reports the sociological findings.

reply, "Of course. I knew that. Who wouldn't?" Somehow, however, this basic principle seems to be lost on many teachers, who end up teaching at a low level—and lost on most school administrators, who accept low student performance. The reason, actually, is probably not their lack of awareness of such basics, but, rather, the constraints in which they find themselves organizationally, the bureaucracies in which ritual often replaces performance. To understand this point better, you may wish to review Chapter 7.

Ultimately, then, we must expect more not only of students, but also of teachers and administrators. They, too, must be held accountable to higher standards. One way to do this is to peg their salaries, or at least bonuses, to the performance of their students. This may be the single most effective step we could take to improve student performance.

Other Reforms—From School Choice to Site-Based Management There is no lack of proposals for improving schools, but perhaps the one that has gained the most media attention—both because it is so controversial and because it holds such potential—is **school choice**. The state would give the parents of each school-age child a voucher to be spent on the school of the parents' choice. As you can see from Table 17.1 (page 491), the states have a great deal of money to work with, and the amount available per pupil would be large. Public and private schools—even those operated by individuals and business firms—would compete for the vouchers. With each school's test results published in local newspapers and available online, parents would be able to shop around for the school they like best.

Although many applaud this proposal, others fear that vouchers would mean the end of public schools, as vouchers would drain away their resources. Proponents of the proposal reply that public schools should compete in the marketplace. Vouchers should stimulate them to produce better results. Schools that can't produce should fold.

Public school teachers and administrators are especially fearful of this proposal, for it threatens their jobs. In the face of widespread dissatisfaction with the performance of public schools and a demand for reform, administrators and teachers have developed proposals designed to keep public education out of private hands. The main counterproposal is *site-based management*; that is, schools would design their own reforms (Dunleavey 1994). It is difficult for those at the center of a problem to reform themselves, but not impossible. True reforms, however, (as opposed to mere window dressing) would require accountability—that students meet high academic standards and that teachers teach at a high level.

school choice parents being able to choose the school their child will attend; often used in the context of expecting for-profit schools to compete for vouchers issued by the state

Reform in anything needs a guiding principle. I suggest that this serve as the guiding principle in reforming education: The problem is not the ability of the students, but, rather, the educational system. That this principle is true becomes apparent when we consider the results reported in the following Thinking Critically section, with which we close this chapter.

Thinking *Critically*

BREAKING THROUGH THE BARRIERS: THE JAIME ESCALANTE APPROACH TO RESTRUCTURING THE CLASSROOM

Called "the best teacher in America," Jaime Escalante taught in an East Los Angeles inner-city school that was plagued with poverty, crime, drugs, gangs, and the usual miserably low student scores. In this desolate environment, he taught calculus. Escalante's students scored so high on national tests that test officials, suspecting cheating, asked his students to retake the test. They did. Again they passed—this time with even higher scores.

Escalante's school ranks fourth in the nation in the number of students who have taken and passed the Advanced Placement SAT Calculus examination. For students to even take the test, they must complete Algebra I, Geometry, Algebra II, Trigonometry or Math Analysis, and Calculus for first-year college and/or Calculus for second-year college.

How did Escalante overcome such odds? His success is *not* due to a recruitment of the brightest students. Students' poor academic performance did not stand in the way of being admitted to the math program. The *only* requirement was an interest in math. What did Escalante do right, and what can we learn from his approach?

"Success starts with attitude" could be Escalante's motto. He noted that few Latino students were taking math. Most were tracked into craft classes, where they learned to make jewelry and birdhouses. "Our kids are just as talented as anyone else. They just need the opportunity to show it. And for that, they must be motivated," he said. "They just don't think about becoming scientists or engineers."

Here are the keys to what Escalante accomplished. First, teaching and learning can't take place unless there is discipline. For that the teachers, not gangs, must control the classroom. Second, the students must believe in themselves. The teacher must inspire students with the idea that they *can* learn (remember teacher expectations). Third, the students must be motivated to perform, in this case to see learning as a way out of the barrio, and as the path to good jobs.

Escalante used a team approach. He had his students think of themselves as a team, with him as the coach and the national exams as a sort of Olympics for which they were preparing. To stimulate team identity, the students wore team jackets, caps, and T-shirts with logos that identified them as part of the team. Before class, his students did "warm-ups" (hand clapping and foot stomping to a rock song).

His team had practice schedules as rigorous as a championship football team. Students had to sign a contract that bound them to participate in the summer program he developed, to complete the daily homework, and to attend Saturday morning and after-school study sessions. To get in his class, even the student's parents had to sign the contract. To make sure his students were mindful of the principle that self-discipline pays off, Escalante covered his room with posters of sports figures in action—Michael Jordan, Babe Ruth, Jackie Joyner-Kersie, and Scottie Pippin.

To say that today's schoolchildren can't learn as well as previous schoolchildren is a case of blaming the victim. As discussed in the text, Jaime Escalante (shown here) demonstrated that teachers can motivate even highly deprived students to study hard and to excel in learning. His experience challenges us to rethink our approach to education.

"How have I been successful with students from such backgrounds?" he asks. "Very simple. I use a time-honored tradition—hard work, lots of it, for teacher and student alike."

Here's how Escalante challenged his students to think of what is possible in life, instead of focusing on obstacles that make achievement seem impossible:

> The first day when these kids walk into my room, I have a bunch of names of schools and colleges on the chalkboard. I ask each student to memorize one. The next day I pick one kid and ask, "What school did you pick?" He says USC or UCLA or Stanford, MIT, Colgate, and so on. So I say, "Okay, keep that in mind. I'm going to bring in somebody who'll be talking about the schools."

Escalante then had a college adviser talk to the class. But more than this, he also arranged for foundation money to help the students attend the colleges of their choice.

The sociological point is that the problem was *not* the ability of the students. Their failure to do well in school was not due to something *within* them. The problem was what we sociologists call *social structure*—the *system,* the way classroom instruction is arranged. When Escalante changed the structure—the system of instruction—both attitudes and performance changed. Escalante makes this very point—that student performance does not depend on the charismatic personality of a single person, but on how we structure the learning setting. ■

For Your Consideration

What principles discussed in this or earlier chapters did Escalante apply? Do you think we could bring about similar results all over the country? If so, what changes would we have to make?

Sources: Based on Barry 1989; Meek 1989; Escalante and Dirmann 1990; Hilliard 1991.

$\int$UMMARY AND $\mathcal{R}$EVIEW

■ The Development of Modern Education

How did modern education develop?

In most of human history, **education** consisted of informal learning, equivalent to **acculturation**. In some earlier societies, centers of formal education did develop, such as among the Arabians, Chinese, Greeks, and Egyptians. Because modern education came about in response to industrialization, formal education is much less common in the Least Industrialized Nations. Pp. 478–480.

■ Education in Global Perspective

How does education compare among the Most Industrialized, Industrializing, and Least Industrialized Nations?

In general, formal education reflects a nation's economy. Consequently, education is extensive in the Most Industrialized Nations, undergoing vast change in the Industrializing Nations, and spotty in the Least Industrialized Nations. Japan, Russia, and Egypt provide examples of education in countries at three levels of industrialization. Pp. 481–484.

■ The Functionalist Perspective: Education's Social Benefits

What is the functionalist perspective on education?

Among the functions of education are the teaching of knowledge and skills, providing credentials for employers, **cultural transmission** of values, social integration, **gatekeeping**, promoting personal and social change, and **mainstreaming.** Functionalists also note that education has replaced some traditional family functions. Pp. 484–488.

■ The Conflict Perspective: How Education Reproduces the Social Class Structure

What is the conflict perspective on education?

The basic view of conflict theorists is that education *reproduces the social class structure;* that is, through such mechanisms as unequal funding and operating different schools for the elite and for the masses, education reinforces a society's basic social inequalities. Pp. 488–493.

■ The Symbolic Interactionist Perspective: Teacher Expectations and the Self-Fulfilling Prophecy

What is the symbolic interactionist perspective on education?

Symbolic interactionists focus on face-to-face interaction. In examining what occurs in the classroom, they have found a **self-fulfilling prophecy**—student performance tends to conform to teacher expectations, whether they are high or low. Pp. 494–496.

■ Problems in U.S. Education—and Their Solutions

What are the chief problems that face U.S. education?

The major problems are low achievement (as shown in low SAT scores), **grade inflation, social promotion, functional illiteracy,** teen pregnancy, and violence. Pp. 496–499.

What are the potential solutions to these problems?
The primary solution is to restore high educational standards, which can be done only after providing a safe learning environment. Specific problems, such as the high dropout rate of pregnant teenagers, must have specific solutions, one of which is detailed in the text. Any solution for improving quality must be based on rais-ing standards and expecting more of students and teachers alike. Pp. 500–504.

Where can I read more on this topic?
Suggested Readings for this chapter are found at the back of this book.

All URLs listed are current as of the printing of this book. URLs often change. Please check our Web site, **http://www.abacon.com/ henslin,** for updates.

1. As you read in the Sociology and the New Technology box entitled "Internet University: No Walls, No Ivy, No Keg Parties," college courses are no longer restricted to the classroom. This project gives you the opportunity to explore online instruction, which is on the cutting edge of "Distance learning." First, go to Penn State University's World Campus Web site at **http://www.worldcampus.psu.edu/pub/index.shtml** and click on "Learn More about the World Campus." What are its mission and goals? When you are finished, click on "World Campus 101." This is a free orientation course designed to acquaint you with online teaching and learning; you can take either the quick tour or a more in-depth look. After you are through, return to the home page and check out "Programs and Courses." What types of courses and programs are available? What are the requirements for enrolling in a particular program or course of study?

    You can read profiles of students who have participated in distance learning at **http://www.outreach.psu.edu/DE/Catalog/ Profiles.** When you have finished browsing through these pages, use your sociological imagination to answer these questions: Why do you think colleges and universities are developing these new ways of instruction? To whom do they appeal? Would you be attracted to such courses? Why or why not? What do you think is gained when learning is taken out of the classroom? What is lost?

2. In recent years, many parents have opted to home school their children. Perhaps you know someone who was home schooled. A major reason why parents choose to home school their children is because of problems in the public schools. Explore the information posted at **http://www.home-ed-magazine.com, http://www.nhen.org,** and **http://www.n-h-a.org.** Think about both the advantages and disadvantages of this arrangement. Which functions of education are still fulfilled when children learn at home? Which are not? Write a paper in which you apply the functionalist, conflict, and symbolic interactionist perspectives to this development in education.

3. As your text notes, one of the problems that schools today must confront is violence. This exercise will provide you with more knowledge about violence in schools. To start, go to the Social Statistics Briefing Room of the White House at **http://www.whitehouse.gov/fsbr/ssbr.html** and click on "Education Statistics." Scroll down and then click on the words "Guns in School." This will take you to a report on school crime. Browse through the "Table of Contents," clicking on and then reading about activities that could jeopardize students' safety—physical attacks, availability of drugs, the presence of both gangs and guns. In what ways did the situation change between the time periods compared at this site? Which students in our society are most likely to encounter school crime? Write a short paper in which you summarize the information you gathered at this site and compare it with the information in the Mass Media box on page 499.

4. As you have discovered from reading this chapter, U. S education faces many problems. In this project, you will analyze the views of supporters of educational reform. Go to the Center for Educational Reform at **http://www.edreform.com.** Click on "Reform Overview." What problems in education are examined at this site? What solutions does the Center for Educational Reform offer? School choice is often seen as a solution. After reading about school choice in your text, examine the Center's information on school choice at **http://www.edreform.com/school_choice.** What is school choice? Why is it controversial? What problems in the U.S. school system does this proposal hope to solve? How is the idea of school choice being implemented? Write a paper in which you explain school choice and discuss the degree to which it might solve the problems facing schools today.

Religion

- **What Is Religion?**

- **The Functionalist Perspective**
  Functions of Religion
  Functional Equivalents of Religion
  Dysfunctions of Religion

- **The Symbolic Interactionist Perspective**
  Religious Symbols
  Rituals
  Beliefs
  Religious Experience
  Community

- **The Conflict Perspective**
  Opium of the People
  A Reflection of Social Inequalities
  A Legitimation of Social Inequalities

- **Religion and the Spirit of Capitalism**

- **The World's Major Religions**
  Judaism
  Christianity

  Islam
  Hinduism
  Buddhism
  Confucianism

- **Types of Religious Groups**
  Cult
  Sect
  Church
  Ecclesia
  Variations in Patterns
  When Religion and Culture Conflict

- **Characteristics of Religion in the United States**
  Characteristics of Members
  Characteristics of Religious Groups
  Secularization of Religion and Culture

- **The Future of Religion**

- **Summary and Review**

The first report was stunning. About a hundred armed agents of the Bureau of Alcohol, Tobacco, and Firearms (ATF) attacked the compound of the Branch Davidians, an obscure religious group in Waco, Texas. Four of the agents were shot to death. So were six men who tried to defend the compound.

Then came a fifty-one-day standoff, televised to the U.S. public, in which the ATF and FBI did such strange things as bombarding the compound with loud music day and night. At 6 A.M. on the fifty-first day of the siege, following on-again, off-again negotiations with David Koresh, the 33-year-old leader of the group, a tank rammed the compound's main building. It pumped in gas consisting of chemicals that, by international law, the U.S. military was unable to use against Iraqi soldiers. As a second tank punched holes in the walls, the women and children fled to the second floor. The men shot futilely at the tanks. An explosion rocked the compound, and the buildings burst into flames. Eighty men, women, and children were burned to death. Some of the charred bodies of the twenty-five children were found huddled next to their mothers. The government removed the bodies, sealed off the area, and bulldozed the charred remains of the buildings. Survivors claimed that the government had set the fire. The government said the Branch Davidians had set it; they had committed suicide by fire, they said. ■

507

sacred Durkheim's term for things set apart or forbidden, that inspire fear, awe, reverence, or deep respect

profane Durkheim's term for common elements of everyday life

religion according to Durkheim, beliefs and practices that separate the profane from the sacred and unite its adherents into a moral community

church according to Durkheim, one of the three essential elements of religion—a moral community of believers; a second definition is the type of religious organization described on page 523, a large, highly organized group with formal, sedate worship services and little emphasis on personal conversion

W e will return to this interesting event later in the chapter. But first, let's turn to a sociological analysis of religion.

What is Religion?

All human societies are organized by some form of the family, as well as by some kind of economic system and political order. As we have seen, these key social institutions touch on aspects of life that are essential to human welfare. This chapter examines religion, another universal social institution.

Sociologists who do research on religion analyze the relationship between society and religion and study the role that religion plays in people's lives. They do not seek to make value judgments about religious beliefs. Nor is their goal to verify or disprove anyone's faith. As mentioned in Chapter 1, sociologists have no tools for deciding that one course of action is more moral than another, much less that one religion is "the" correct one. Religion is a matter of faith; sociologists deal with empirical matters, things they can observe or measure. Thus sociologists can measure the effects of religious beliefs and practices on people's lives and how religion is organized. They can also analyze how religion matches a culture, or, as in our opening vignette, how religion comes in conflict with it. Unlike theologians, however, they cannot evaluate the truth of a religion's teachings.

In 1912 Emile Durkheim published an influential book, *The Elementary Forms of the Religious Life,* in which he tried to identify the elements common to all religions. After surveying religions around the world, Durkheim concluded that there is no specific belief or practice shared by all religions. He did find, however, that all religions separate the sacred from the profane. By **sacred,** Durkheim referred to aspects of life having to do with the supernatural that inspire awe, reverence, deep respect, even fear. By **profane,** he meant aspects of life that are not concerned with religion or religious purposes but, instead, are part of the ordinary aspects of everyday life. Durkheim also found that all religions develop a community around their practices and beliefs. He (1912/1965) concluded:

> A religion is a unified system of beliefs and practices relative to sacred things, that is to say, things set apart and forbidden—beliefs and practices which unite into one single moral community called a Church, all those who adhere to them.

Thus, he argued, a **religion** is defined by three elements:

1. *Beliefs* that some things are sacred (forbidden, set off from the profane)
2. *Practices* (rituals) centering around the things considered sacred
3. *A moral community* (a church) resulting from a group's beliefs and practices

Durkheim used the word **church** in an unusual sense, to refer to any "moral community" centered on beliefs and practices regarding the sacred. In Durkheim's sense, *church* refers to Buddhists bowing before a shrine, Hindus dipping in the Ganges River, and Confucianists offering food to their ancestors. Similarly, the term *moral community* does not imply morality in the sense familiar to most of us. A moral community is simply people united by their religious practices—and that would include sixteenth-century Aztec priests who each day gathered around an altar to pluck out the beating heart of a virgin.

To better understand the sociological approach to religion, let's see what pictures emerge when we apply the three theoretical perspectives.

From his review of world religions, Durkheim concluded that all religions have beliefs, practices, and a moral community. Part of Hindu belief is that the Ganges is a holy river and bathing in it imparts spiritual benefits. Each year, millions of Hindus participate in this rite of ablution (purification).

THE FUNCTIONALIST PERSPECTIVE

Functionalists stress that religion is universal because it meets basic human needs. What are some of the functions—and dysfunctions—of religion?

Functions of Religion

Questions About Ultimate Meaning Around the world, religions provide answers to perplexing questions about ultimate meaning—such as the purpose of life, the reason people suffer, and the existence of an afterlife. Those answers give people a sense of purpose. Instead of seeing themselves buffeted by random events in an aimless existence, religious believers see their lives as fitting into a divine plan.

Emotional Comfort The answers that religion provides about ultimate meaning also comfort people by assuring them that there is a purpose to life, even to suffering. Similarly, religious rituals that enshroud critical events such as illness and death provide emotional comfort at times of crisis. The individual knows that others care and can find consolation in following familiar rituals.

Social Solidarity Religious teachings and practices unite believers into a community that shares values and perspectives ("we Jews," "we Christians," "we Muslims"). The religious rituals that surround marriage, for example, link the bride and groom with a broader community that wishes them well. So do other religious rituals, such as those that celebrate birth and mourn death.

Guidelines for Everyday Life The teachings of religion are not only abstract. They also apply to people's everyday lives. For example, four of the Ten Commandments delivered by Moses to the Israelites concern God, but the other six contain instructions on how to live everyday life, from how to get along with parents, employers, and neighbors to warnings about lying, stealing, and having affairs.

Social Control Religion not only provides guidelines for everyday life, but it also controls people's behaviors. Most norms of a religious group apply only to its members, but some set limits on nonmembers also. An example is religious teachings that are incorporated into criminal law. In the United States, for example, blasphemy and adultery were once crimes for which people could be arrested, tried, and sentenced. Laws that prohibit the sale of alcohol before noon on Sunday—or, in some places, the sale of any "nonessential items"—are another example.

Adaptation Religion can help people adapt to new environments. For example, it isn't easy for immigrants to adjust to the confusing customs of a new land. By keeping their native language alive and preserving familiar rituals and teachings, religion provides continuity with the immigrants' cultural past.

The handful of German immigrants who settled in Perry County, Missouri, in the 1800s, for example, even brought their Lutheran minister with them. Their sermons and hymns continued to be in German, and their children attended a school in which the minister conducted classes in German. Out of this small group grew the Lutheran Church-Missouri Synod, which, despite its name, is an international denomination that numbers about 2.5 million members. Little by little, this group's descendants and converts entered mainstream U.S. culture. Today, except for Luther's basic teachings and a few church practices, little remains of the past, for just as it helped the immigrants adapt to a new environment, so the religion itself changed to reflect that same environment.

Support for the Government Most religions provide support for the government. An obvious example is the way many churches so prominently display the U.S. flag. For their

Religion can promote social change, as was evident in the U.S. civil rights movement. Dr. Martin Luther King, Jr., a Baptist minister, shown here in his famous "I have a dream" speech, was the foremost leader of this movement.

part, governments reciprocate by supporting God—as witnessed by the way U.S. presidents, whether they are believers or not, invariably ask God to bless the nation in their inaugural speeches.

Some governments sponsor a particular religion, ban all others, provide financial support for building churches and seminaries, and even pay salaries to the clergy. These religions are known as **state religions.** During the sixteenth and seventeenth centuries in Sweden, the government sponsored Lutheranism; in Switzerland, Calvinism; and in Italy, Roman Catholicism. In other instances, even though the government sponsors no particular religion, religious beliefs are so established in a nation's life that the country's history and social institutions are sanctified by being associated with God. For example, U.S. officials—even those who do not belong to any particular religion—take office by swearing that they will, in the name of God, fulfill their duty. Similarly, Congress opens each session with a prayer led by its own chaplain, schoolchildren recite the pledge of allegiance daily (including the phrase "one nation under God"), and coins bear the inscription "In God We Trust." Sociologist Robert Bellah (1970) referred to this phenomenon as **civil religion.**

Social Change Although religion is often so bound up with the prevailing social order that it resists social change, occasionally religion spearheads change. In the 1960s, for example, the civil rights movement, which fought to desegregate public facilities and abolish racial discrimination at southern polls, was led by religious leaders, especially leaders of African-American churches such as Martin Luther King, Jr. Churches also served as centers at which demonstrators were trained and rallies were organized.

Functional Equivalents of Religion

These functions can also be fulfilled by other components of society. If some other component answers questions about ultimate meaning, provides emotional comfort and guidelines for daily life, and so on, sociologists call it a **functional equivalent** of religion. Thus, for some people, Alcoholics Anonymous is a functional equivalent of religion (Chalfant 1992). For others, psychotherapy, humanism, transcendental meditation, or even a political party performs similar functions.

Some functional equivalents are difficult to distinguish from a religion (Brinton 1965; Luke 1985). For example, communism had its prophets (Marx and Lenin), sacred writings (everything written by Marx, Engels, and Lenin, but especially the *Communist Manifesto*), high priests (the heads of the Communist party), sacred buildings (the Kremlin), shrines (Lenin's body on display in Red Square), rituals (the annual May Day parade in Red Square), and even martyrs (Cuba's Che Guevara). Soviet communism was avowedly atheistic and tried to wipe out all traces of Christianity, Judaism, and Islam from its midst. It even tried to replace baptisms and circumcisions with state-sponsored rituals that dedicated the child to the state. The Communist party also composed its own rituals for weddings and funerals.

As sociologist Ian Robertson (1987) pointed out, however, there is a fundamental distinction between a religion and its functional equivalent. Although the substitute may perform similar functions, its activities are not directed toward God, gods, or the supernatural.

Dysfunctions of Religion

Functionalists also examine ways in which religion is *dysfunctional,* that is, how it can bring harmful results. Two main dysfunctions are war and religious persecution.

War History is filled with wars based on religion—commingled with politics. Between the eleventh and fourteenth centuries, for example, Christian monarchs conducted nine

state religion a government-sponsored religion

civil religion Robert Bellah's term for religion that is such an established feature of a country's life that its history and social institutions become sanctified by being associated with God

functional equivalent in this context, a substitute that serves the same functions (or meets the same needs) as religion, for example, psychotherapy

Woodcuts (prints made from engraved blocks of wood coated with ink to leave an impression on paper) were used to illustrate books shortly after the printing press was invented. This woodcut commemorates a dysfunction of religion, the burning of witches at the stake. This particular event occurred at Derneburg, Germany, in 1555.

bloody Crusades in an attempt to wrest control of the Holy Land from the Muslims. Unfortunately, such wars are not just a relic of the past. Even in recent years we have seen Protestants and Catholics kill one another in Northern Ireland, while Jews and Muslims in Israel and Christians and Muslims in Bosnia have done the same thing.

Religion as Justification for Persecution Beginning in the 1200s and continuing into the 1800s, in what has become known as the Inquisition, special commissions of the Roman Catholic church tortured women to elicit confessions that they were witches, and then burned them at the stake. In 1692, Protestant leaders in Salem, Massachusetts, drowned women who were accused of being witches. (The last execution for witchcraft was in Scotland in 1722 [Bridgwater 1953].) Similarly, it seems fair to say that the Aztec religion had its dysfunctions—at least for the virgins who were offered to appease angry gods. In short, religion has been used to justify oppression and any number of brutal acts.

THE SYMBOLIC INTERACTIONIST PERSPECTIVE

Symbolic interactionists focus on the meanings that people give their experiences, especially how they use symbols. Let's apply this perspective to religious symbols, rituals, and beliefs to see how they help to forge a community of like-minded people.

Religious Symbols

Suppose that it is about two thousand years ago and you have just joined a new religion. You have come to believe that a recently crucified Jew named Jesus is the Messiah, the Lamb of God offered for your sins. The Roman leaders are persecuting the followers of Jesus. They hate your religion because you and your fellow believers will not acknowledge Caesar as God.

Christians are few in number, and you are eager to have fellowship with other believers. But how can you tell who is a believer? Spies are all over. The government has sworn to destroy this new religion, and you do not relish the thought of being fed to lions in the Coliseum.

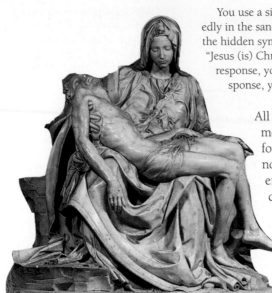

You use a simple technique. While talking with a stranger, as though doodling absentmindedly in the sand or dust, you casually trace the outline of a fish. Only fellow believers know the hidden symbolism—that, taken together, the first letter of the words in the Greek sentence "Jesus (is) Christ the Son of God" spell the Greek word for *fish*. If the other person gives no response, you rub out the outline and continue the interaction as usual. If there is a response, you eagerly talk about your new faith.

All religions use symbols to provide identity and social solidarity for their members. For Muslims, the primary symbol is the crescent moon and star; for Jews the Star of David; for Christians the cross. For members, these are not ordinary symbols, but sacred symbols that evoke feelings of awe and reverence. In Durkheim's terms, religions use symbols to specify what is sacred and to separate the sacred from the profane.

A symbol is a condensed way of communicating. Worn by a fundamentalist Christian, for example, the cross says, "I am a follower of Jesus Christ. I believe that He is the Messiah, the promised Son of God, that He loves me, that He died to take away my sins, that He rose from the dead and is going to return to earth, and that through Him I will receive eternal life."

Symbolic interactionists stress that a basic characteristic of humans is that they attach meaning to objects and events and then use representations of those objects or events to communicate with one another. Some religious symbols are used to communicate feelings of awe and reverence. Michaelangelo's Pietà, depicting Mary tenderly holding her son, Jesus, after his crucifixion, is one of the most acclaimed symbols in the Western world, admired for its beauty by believers and nonbelivers alike.

That is a lot to pack into one symbol—and it is only part of what the symbol means to a fundamentalist believer. To people in other traditions of Christianity, the cross conveys somewhat different meanings—but to all Christians, the cross is a shorthand way of expressing many meanings. So it is with the Star of David, the crescent moon and star, the cow (expressing to Hindus the unity of all living things), and the various symbols of the world's many other religions.

Rituals

Rituals, ceremonies or repetitive practices, are also symbols that help unite people into a moral community. Some rituals, such as the bar mitzvah of Jewish boys and the Holy Communion of Christians, are designed to create in the devout a feeling of closeness with God and unity with one another. Rituals include kneeling and praying at set times, bowing, crossing oneself, singing, lighting candles and incense, scripture readings, processions, baptisms, weddings, funerals, and so on.

Beliefs

Symbols, including ritual, develop from beliefs. The belief may be vague ("God is") or highly specific ("God wants us to prostrate ourselves and face Mecca five times each day"). Religious beliefs include not only *values* (what is considered good and desirable in life—how we ought to live) but also a **cosmology,** a unified picture of the world. For example, the Jewish, Christian, and Muslim belief that there is only one God, the Creator of the universe, who is concerned about the actions of humans and who will hold us accountable for what we do, is a cosmology. It presents a unifying picture of the universe.

Religious Experience

The term **religious experience** refers to a sudden awareness of the supernatural or a feeling of coming in contact with God. Some people undergo a mild version, such as feeling closer to God when they look at a mountain or listen to a certain piece of music. Others report a life-transforming experience; for example, St. Francis of Assisi tells of how he became aware of God's presence in every living thing.

Some Protestants use the term **born again** to describe people who have undergone such a life-transforming religious experience. These people say they came to the realization that they had sinned, that Jesus had died for their sins, and that God wants them to live a

rituals ceremonies or repetitive practices; in this context, religious observances or rites, often intended to evoke a sense of awe of the sacred

cosmology teachings or ideas that provide a unified picture of the world

religious experience a sudden awareness of the supernatural or a feeling of coming in contact with God

born again a term describing Christians who have undergone a life-transforming religious experience so radical that they feel they have become new persons

new life. Their worlds become transformed. They look forward to the Resurrection and to a new life in heaven, and they see relationships with spouses, parents, children, and even bosses in a new light. They also report a need to make changes in how they interact with others so that their lives reflect their new, personal commitment to Jesus as their "Savior and Lord." They describe a feeling of beginning life anew, hence the term *born again.*

Community

Finally, the shared meanings that come through symbols, rituals, and beliefs (and for some, a religious experience) unite people into a moral community. People in a moral community feel a bond with one another, for their beliefs and rituals bind them together while at the same time separating them from those who do not share their unique

One of the functions of religion is to create community. An example is the Promise Keepers, a fundamentalist movement for men founded by Bill McCartney, the former head football coach of the University of Colorado Buffaloes. Controversy surrounds the Promise Keepers' position on the roles of men and women.

symbolic world. Mormons, for example, feel a "kindred spirit" (as it is often known) with other Mormons. Baptists, Jews, Jehovah's Witnesses, and Muslims feel the same toward members of their respective faiths.

As a symbol of their unity, members of some religious groups address one another as "brother" or "sister." "Sister Luby, we are going to meet at Brother and Sister Maher's on Wednesday" is a common way of expressing a message. The terms *brother* and *sister* are intended to symbolize a relationship so close that the individuals consider themselves members of the same family.

Community is powerful, not only because it provides the basis for mutual identity, but also because it establishes norms that govern the behavior of its members. Members either conform, or they lose their membership. In Christian churches, for example, an individual whose adultery becomes known, and who refuses to ask forgiveness, may be banned from the Church. He or she may be formally excommunicated, as in the Catholic tradition, or more informally "stricken from the rolls," as is the usual Protestant practice.

Removal from the community is a serious matter for people whose identity is bound up in the community. Sociologists John Hostetler (1980), William Kephart, and William Zellner (1994) describe the Amish practice of *shunning*—ignoring an offender in all situations. Persons who are shunned are treated as though they do not exist (for if they do not repent by expressing sorrow for their act they have ceased to exist as members of the community). The shunning is so thorough that even family members, who themselves remain in good standing in the congregation, are not allowed to talk to the person being shunned. This obviously makes for some interesting meals.

THE CONFLICT PERSPECTIVE

The conflict perspective has an entirely different focus. Conflict theorists examine how religion supports the status quo and helps to maintain social inequalities.

Opium of the People

In general, conflict theorists are highly critical of religion. Karl Marx, an avowed atheist who believed that the existence of God was an impossibility, set the tone for conflict theorists with his most famous statement on this subject: "Religion is the sigh of the oppressed creature, the sentiment of a heartless world . . . It is the opium of the people" (Marx 1844/1964). By this statement, Marx meant that oppressed workers, longing for release from their suffering, escape into religion. For them, religion is like a drug that helps them forget their misery. By diverting their thoughts to future happiness in a coming world, religion takes their eyes off their suffering in this one, thereby greatly reducing the possibility that they will rebel against their oppressors.

A Reflection of Social Inequalities

Conflict theorists stress that religious teachings and practices are a mirror of a society's inequalities. Gender inequality illustrates this point. When men completely dominated U.S. society, U.S. churches and synagogues ordained only men, limiting women to such activities as teaching children Sunday school or preparing meals for congregational get-togethers—things that were considered appropriate "feminine" activities. As women's roles in the broader society changed, however, religion reflected those changes. First, many religious groups allowed women to vote. Then, as women attained prominent positions in the business world and professions, some Protestant and Jewish groups allowed women to be ordained. Similarly, just as women still face barriers in secular society, so some congregations still refuse to ordain women. In some congregations the barriers remain so high that women are still not allowed to vote.

A Legitimation of Social Inequalities

Conflict theorists say that religion not only mirrors the social inequalities of the larger society, but also legitimates them. By this, they mean that by reflecting the interests of those in power, religion teaches that the existing social arrangements of a society represent what God desires. For example, during the Middle Ages Christian theologians decreed the "divine right of kings." This doctrine meant that God determined who would become king, and set him on the throne. The king ruled in God's place, and it was the duty of a king's subjects to be loyal to him (and to pay their taxes). To disobey the king was to disobey God.

In what was perhaps the supreme technique of legitimating the social order (and one that went even a step further than the "divine right of kings"), the religion of ancient Egypt held that the Pharaoh was a god. The Emperor of Japan was similarly declared divine. If this were so, who could even question his decisions? Today's politicians would give their right arm for such a religious teaching. Deification endorsed by religion!

Conflict theorists point to many other examples of how religion legitimates the social order. In India, Hinduism supports the caste system by teaching that an individual who tries to change caste will come back in the next life as a member of a lower caste—or even as an animal. One of the more remarkable examples took place in the decades before the American Civil War. Southern ministers used scripture to defend slavery, saying that it was God's will—while northern ministers legitimated *their* region's social structure by using scripture to denounce slavery as evil (Ernst 1988; Nauta 1993; White 1995).

RELIGION AND THE SPIRIT OF CAPITALISM

Max Weber disagreed with the conflict perspective that religion merely reflects and legitimates the social order, and that religion impedes social change by encouraging people to focus on the afterlife. In contrast, Weber saw religion's focus on the afterlife as a source of profound social change.

Like Marx, Weber observed the industrialization of European countries. Weber was intrigued with the question of why some societies embraced capitalism while others clung to their traditional ways. Tradition is strong and tends to hold people in check, yet some societies had been transformed by capitalism, while others remained untouched. As he explored this problem, Weber concluded that religion held the key to **modernization**—the transformation of traditional societies to industrial societies.

To explain his conclusions, Weber wrote *The Protestant Ethic and the Spirit of Capitalism* (1904–1905/1958). Because Weber's argument was presented in Chapter 7 (pages 175–176), it is only summarized here.

modernization the transformation of traditional societies into industrial societies

1. Capitalism is not just a superficial change. Rather, capitalism represents a fundamentally different way of thinking about work and money. *Traditionally, people worked just enough to meet their basic needs, not so that they could have a surplus to invest.* To accumulate money (capital) as an end in itself, not just to spend it, was a radical departure from traditional thinking. People even came to consider it a duty to invest money in order to make profits, which, in turn, they reinvested to make more profits. Weber called this new approach to work and money the **spirit of capitalism.**

2. Why did the spirit of capitalism develop in Europe, and not, for example, in China or India, where the people had similar intelligence, material resources, education, and so on? According to Weber, *religion was the key.* The religions of China and India, and indeed Roman Catholicism in Europe, encouraged a traditional approach to life, not thrift and investment. Capitalism appeared when Protestantism came on the scene.

3. What was different about Protestantism, especially Calvinism? John Calvin taught that God had predestined some people to heaven, others to hell. Neither church membership nor feelings about your relationship with God could assure you that you were saved. You wouldn't know your fate until after you died.

4. This doctrine created intense anxiety among Calvin's followers: "Am I predestined to hell or to heaven?" they wondered. As Calvinists wrestled with this question, they concluded that church members have a duty to prove that they are one of God's elect, and to live as though they are predestined to heaven—for good works are a demonstration of salvation.

5. This conclusion motivated Calvinists to lead highly moral lives *and* to work hard, to not waste time, and to be frugal—for idleness and needless spending were signs of worldliness. Weber called this self-denying approach to life the **Protestant ethic.**

6. As people worked hard and spent money only on necessities (a pair of earrings or a second pair of dress shoes would have been defined as sinful luxuries), they accumulated money. Because it couldn't be spent, this capital, in turn, was invested—which led to a surge in production.

7. Thus, a change in religion (from Catholicism to Protestantism, especially Calvinism) led to a fundamental change in thought and behavior (the *Protestant ethic*). The result was the *spirit of capitalism.* Thus capitalism originated in Europe, and not in places where religion did not encourage capitalism's essential elements: the accumulation of capital and its investment and reinvestment.

Although Weber's analysis has been influential, it has not lacked critics (Marshall 1982). Hundreds of scholars have attacked it, some for overlooking the lack of capitalism in Scotland (a Calvinist country), others for failing to explain why the Industrial Revolution was born in England (not a Calvinist country). Hundreds of other scholars have defended Weber's argument. There is currently no historical evidence that can definitively prove or disprove Weber's thesis.

At this point in history, the Protestant ethic and the spirit of capitalism are not confined to any specific religion or even to any one part of the world. Rather, they have become cultural traits that have spread to societies around the world (Greeley 1964; Yinger 1970). U.S. Catholics have about the same approach to life as do U.S. Protestants. In addition, Hong Kong, Japan, Malaysia, Singapore, South Korea, and Taiwan—not exactly Protestant countries—have embraced capitalism (Levy 1992).

THE WORLD'S MAJOR RELIGIONS

The largest of the thousands of religions in the world are listed in Table 18.1. Let's briefly review six of them.

spirit of capitalism Weber's term for the desire to accumulate capital as a duty—not to spend it, but as an end in itself—and to constantly reinvest it

Protestant ethic Weber's term to describe the ideal of a self-denying, highly moral life, accompanied by hard work and frugality

Table 18.1
THE WORLD'S LARGEST RELIGIONS[a]

Religion	Number of Followers
Christians	1,900,000,000
Muslims	1,200,000,000
Hindus	762,000,000
Chinese folk religions	379,000,000
Buddhists	354,000,000
Sikhs	22,000,000
Jews	14,000,000
Spiritualists	12,000,000
Baha'is	7,000,000
Confucians	6,000,000
Jains	4,000,000
Shintoists	3,000,000

[a] *Note:* The classification of religions is often confusing. Animists, for example, although numerous, are not listed as a separate group in the source, while an amorphous classification of "new religions" is. It is often difficult to tell what groups are encompassed in what categories.

Source: Statistical Abstract 1999:Table 1348.

monotheism the belief that there is only one God

polytheism the belief that there are many gods

animism the belief that all objects in the world have spirits, some of which are dangerous and must be outwitted

anti-Semitism prejudice, discrimination, and persecution directed against Jews

Judaism

The origin of Judaism is traced to Abraham, who lived about four thousand years ago in Mesopotamia. Jews believe that God (Jahweh) made a covenant with Abraham, selecting his descendants as a chosen people and promising to make them "as numerous as the sands of the seashore" and to give them a special land that would be theirs forever. The sign of this covenant was the circumcision of males, which was to be performed when a boy was eight days old. Descent is traced through Abraham and his wife, Sarah, their son Isaac, and their grandson Jacob (also called Israel).

Joseph, a son of Jacob, was sold by his brothers into slavery and taken to Egypt. Following a series of hair-raising adventures, Joseph became Pharaoh's right-hand man. When a severe famine hit Canaan, where Jacob's family was living, Jacob and his eleven other sons fled to Egypt. Under Joseph's leadership, they were welcome. A subsequent Pharaoh, however, enslaved the Israelites. After about four hundred years, Moses, an Israelite who had been adopted by Pharaoh's daughter, confronted Pharaoh. He persuaded Pharaoh to release the slaves, which at that time numbered about 2 million. Moses led them out of Egypt, but before they reached their Promised Land the Israelites spent forty years wandering in the desert. Sometime during those years, Moses delivered the Ten Commandments from Mount Sinai. Abraham, Isaac, Jacob, and Moses hold revered positions in Judaism. The events of their lives and the recounting of the early history of the Israelites are contained in the first five books of the Bible, called the Torah.

The founding of Judaism marked a fundamental change in religion, for it was the first religion based on **monotheism,** the belief that there is only one God. Prior to Judaism, religions were based on **polytheism,** the belief that there are many gods. In Greek religion, for example, Zeus was the god of heaven and earth, Poseidon the god of the sea, and Athena the goddess of wisdom. Other groups followed **animism,** believing that all objects in the world have spirits, some of which are dangerous and must be outwitted.

Contemporary Judaism in the United States comprises three main branches: Orthodox, Reform, and Conservative. Orthodox Jews adhere to the laws espoused by Moses. They eat only foods prepared in a designated manner (kosher), observe the Sabbath in a traditional way, and segregate males and females in their religious services. During the 1800s, a group that wanted to make their practices more compatible with U.S. culture broke from this tradition. This liberal group, known as Reform Judaism, mostly uses English in its religious ceremonies and has reduced much of the ritual. The third branch, Conservative Judaism, falls somewhere between the other two. No branch has continued polygyny (allowing a husband to have more than one wife), the original marriage custom of the Jews, which was outlawed by rabbinic decree about a thousand years ago.

The history of Judaism is marked by conflict and persecution. The Israelites were conquered by Babylon, and were again made slaves. After returning to Israel and rebuilding the temple, they were later conquered by Rome, and after their rebellion at Masada in A.D. 70 failed, they were exiled for almost two thousand years into other nations. During those centuries, they faced prejudice, discrimination, and persecution (called **anti-Semitism**) by many peoples and rulers. The most horrendous example was Hitler's attempt to eliminate the Jews as a people in the Nazi Holocaust of World War II. Under the Nazi occupation of Europe and North Africa, about 6 million Jews were slaughtered. Many died in gas ovens that were constructed for just this purpose.

Central to Jewish teaching is the requirement to love God and do good deeds. Good deeds begin in the family, where each member has an obligation toward the others. Sin is a conscious choice to do evil, and must be atoned for by prayers and good works. Jews consider Jerusalem their holiest city and believe that the Messiah will one day appear there, bringing redemption for them all.

Christianity

Christianity, which developed out of Judaism, is also monotheistic. Christians believe that Jesus Christ is the Messiah whom God promised the Jews.

Jesus was born in poverty, and traditional Christians believe he was born to a virgin. Within two years of his birth, Herod, named king of Palestine by Caesar, who had conquered Israel, was informed that people were saying a new king had

been born. When Herod sent soldiers to kill Jesus, Jesus' parents fled with him to Egypt. After Herod died, they returned, settling in the small town of Nazareth.

At about the age of 30, Jesus began a preaching and healing ministry. His teachings challenged the contemporary religious establishment, and as his popularity grew the religious leaders plotted to have him killed by the Romans. Christians interpret the death of Jesus as a blood sacrifice made to atone for their sins. They believe that through his death they have peace with God and will inherit eternal life.

The twelve main followers of Jesus, called *apostles,* believed that Jesus rose from the dead. They preached the need to be "born again," that is, to accept Jesus as Savior, give up selfish ways, and live a devout life. The new religion spread rapidly, and after an initial period of hostility on the part of imperial Rome—during which time believers were fed to the lions in the Coliseum—in A.D. 317 Christianity became the empire's official religion.

During the first thousand years of Christianity, there was only one church organization, directed from Rome. During the eleventh century, after disagreement over doctrine and politics, Greek Orthodoxy was established. It was headquartered in Constantinople (now Istanbul, Turkey). During the Middle Ages, the Roman Catholic church, which was aligned with the political establishment, grew corrupt. Some Church offices, such as that of bishop, were sold for a set price, and, in a situation that touched off the Reformation led by Martin Luther in the sixteenth century, the forgiveness of sins (including those not yet committed) could be purchased by buying an "indulgence."

Although Martin Luther's original goal was to reform the Church, not divide it, the Reformation began a splintering of Christianity. It coincided with the breakup of feudalism, and as the ancient political structure came apart, people clamored for independence not only in political but also in religious thought. Today, Christianity is the most popular religion in the world, with about 2 billion adherents. Christians are divided into hundreds of groups, some with doctrinal differences so slight that only members of the group can appreciate the extremely fine distinctions that, they feel, significantly separate them from others. The Social Map on the next page shows how some of these groups are distributed in the United States.

Islam

Islam, whose followers are known as Muslims, began in the same part of the world as Judaism and Christianity. Islam, the world's third monotheistic religion, has over a billion followers. It was founded by Muhammad, who was born in Mecca (now in Saudi Arabia) in about A.D. 570. Muhammad married Khadija, a wealthy widow. About the age of 40, he reported that he had had visions from God. These, and his teachings, were later written down in a book called the Koran. Few paid attention to Muhammad, although Ali, his son-in-law, believed him. When he found out that there was a plot to murder him, Muhammad fled to

Religion, which provides subculture, community, and self-identification, is passed from the older to the younger. Shown here are older orthodox Jews in Miami Beach as they bind prayers around the arms of adolescent boys, who, in turn, will replace their elders and transmit their religion to the next generation.

SOCIAL MAP: CHURCH MEMBERSHIP: DOMINANT RELIGION, BY COUNTY

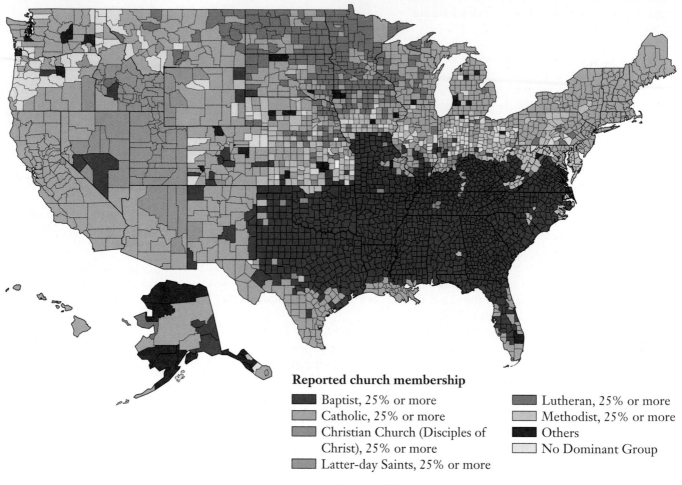

Reported church membership

- Baptist, 25% or more
- Catholic, 25% or more
- Christian Church (Disciples of Christ), 25% or more
- Latter-day Saints, 25% or more
- Lutheran, 25% or more
- Methodist, 25% or more
- Others
- No Dominant Group

Source: Bradley et al. 1992.

Medina, where he found a more receptive audience. There he established a *theocracy* (a government based on the principle that God is the ruler, his laws the statutes of the land, and priests his earthly administrators) and founded the Muslim empire. In A.D. 630 he returned to Mecca, this time as a conqueror (Bridgwater 1953).

After Muhammad's death, a struggle for control over the empire he had founded split Islam into two branches that remain today, the Sunni and the Shi'ite. The Shi'ites, who believe that the *imam* (the religious leader) is inspired as he interprets the Koran, are generally more conservative and are inclined to **fundamentalism**, the belief that modernism threatens religion and that the faith as it was originally practiced should be restored. The Sunni, who do not share this belief, are generally more liberal.

Like the Jews, Muslims trace their ancestry to Abraham. Abraham fathered a son, Ishmael, by Hagar, his wife Sarah's Egyptian maid (Genesis 25:12). Ishmael had twelve sons, from whom a good portion of today's Arab world is descended. For them also, Jerusalem is a holy city. The Muslims consider the Bibles of the Jews and the Christians to be sacred but take the Koran as the final word. They believe that the followers of Abraham and Moses (Jews) and Jesus (Christians) changed the original teachings and that Muhammad restored their purity. It is the duty of each Muslim to make a pilgrimage to Mecca during his or her lifetime. Unlike the Jews, the Muslims continue to practice polygyny. They limit a man, however, to four wives.

fundamentalism the belief that true religion is threatened by modernism and that the faith as it was originally practiced should be restored

PERSPECTIVES | Cultural Diversity in the United States

THE NEW NEIGHBOR: ISLAM IN THE UNITED STATES

It is Sunday morning, and across the nation Americans are on their way to worship. Instead of going into a Baptist or a Roman Catholic church (or into a synagogue on Saturday), many Americans now enter mosques. In a scene that is growing increasingly familiar, they take off their shoes, face Mecca, and kneel with their faces to the floor.

Called by some the fastest growing religion in the United States, Islam is making its presence felt. Islam's growth is fueled by two main sources. The primary source is the millions of immigrants from the Middle East and Asia who have arrived in the United States since the 1980s. Like the immigrants before them, these refugees from Muslim countries brought along their religion as part of their culture. The second source is African Americans. Although believers represent a cross-section of African Americans, the call of Islam is heard most loudly in the inner city (Peart 1993). Overall, U.S. Muslims are about 42 percent African American, 25 percent South Asian, 12 percent Arab, and the remainder from a mix of backgrounds (Power 1998).

The appeal of Islam to African Americans is the message of black pride, self-improvement, and black power. Although U.S. Muslims are divided among about twenty groups, the appeal is similar: moral-ity (no drugs, crime, or extramarital sex), respect for women, and black empowerment. Among all groups, modest clothing is required. Among some, ultraconservative codes govern behavior: Men and women sit apart in public, women wear robes that cover them from head to toe, and one-on-one dating is prohibited (Tapia 1994). Many men embrace the authority that Islam ascribes to them. For many, both men and women, Islam is a way to connect with African roots.

For many Americans, Louis Farrakhan is synonymous with U.S. Islam. Although he is the most visible and vocal Muslim leader, the group he heads, the Nation of Islam, has only about 10,000 members (Brooke 1995). The Chicago-based Muslim American Society, headed by W. Dean Mohammed, has 200,000 members (Miller 1999).

Just as their organizations are diverse, so their opinions are wide-ranging. With regard to race, for example, some believe the races are equal; others believe African Americans are superior and whites are devils. Similarly, some groups stress black separatism, while others emphasize the need to start businesses and run for office (Miller 1999).

Alarmed that Islam has gained so many converts, some African-American Christians are counterattacking. They hold Muslim Awareness seminars in order to warn Christians away from Islam (Tapia 1994). A former Black Muslim who is now a Christian evangelist and who sees it as his duty to counter Islam, says the difference is grace. "Islam is a works-oriented religion, but Christianity is built on God's grace in Jesus."

"His is just a slave religion," retort some Muslims.

Despite tension and confrontation, it is apparent that the Muslim presence is not temporary, that the face of U.S. religion is being fundamentally altered. Mosques are taking their place in the midst of churches and synagogues, a sign of a maturing multicultural society. ■

Universally, children are socialized into the religion of their group. The kindergarten students shown here at the Al-Ghazaly Islamic school in Jersey City, New Jersey, are learning how to pray.

Because of immigration from the Mideast and conversions of African Americans, Islam has grown rapidly in the past few decades in the United States. This topic is explored in the Perspectives box above.

Hinduism

Unlike the other religions described, Hinduism has no specific founder. Going back about four thousand years, Hinduism is the chief religion of India. The term *Hinduism*, however, is Western, and in India the closest term is *dharma* (law). Unlike Judaism, Christianity, and Islam, Hinduism has no canonical scripture, that is, no texts thought to be inspired by God. Instead, several books, including the *Brahmanas*, *Bhagavad-Gita*, and *Upanishads*, expound on moral qualities that people should strive to develop. They also delineate the sacrifices people should make to the gods.

This marble statue of the Buddha is in the Chuang-Yen Monastery in Carmel, New York. At 37 feet tall, it is the second largest indoor statue of the Buddha in the world.

Hindus are *polytheists;* that is, they believe that there are many gods. They believe that one of these gods, Brahma, created the universe. Brahma, along with Shiva (the Destroyer) and Vishnu (the Preserver), form a triad that is at the center of modern Hinduism. A central belief is *karma,* spiritual progress. There is no final judgment, but, instead, **reincarnation,** a cycle of life, death, and rebirth. Death involves only the body, and each person's soul comes back in a form that matches the individual's moral progress in the previous life (which centers on proper conduct in following the rules of one's caste). If an individual reaches spiritual perfection, he or she has attained *nirvana.* This marks the end of the cycle of death and rebirth, when the soul is reunited with the universal soul. When this occurs, *maya,* the illusion of time and space, has been conquered.

Some Hindu practices have been modified as a consequence of social protest—especially child marriage and *suttee,* the practice of cremating a surviving widow along with her deceased husband (Bridgwater 1953). Other ancient rituals remain unchanged, such as *kumbh mela,* a purifying washing in the Ganges River, which takes place every twelve years, and in which many millions participate.

Buddhism

In about 600 B.C., Siddhartha Gautama founded Buddhism. (Buddha means the "enlightened one," a term Gautama was given by his disciples.) Gautama was the son of an upper-caste Hindu ruler in an area north of Benares, India. At the age of 29, he renounced his life of luxury and became an ascetic. Through meditation, he discovered the "four noble truths," which emphasize self-denial and compassion.

1. Existence is suffering.
2. The origin of suffering is desire.
3. Suffering ceases when desire ceases.
4. The way to end desire is to follow the "noble eightfold path."

The noble eightfold path consists of

1. Right belief
2. Right resolve (to renounce carnal pleasure and to harm no living creature)
3. Right speech
4. Right conduct
5. Right occupation or living
6. Right effort
7. Right-mindedness (or contemplation)
8. Right ecstasy

The central symbol of Bhuddism is the eight-spoked wheel. Each spoke represents one aspect of the path. As with Hinduism, the ultimate goal of Buddhism is the cessation of rebirth and thereby of suffering. Buddhists teach that all things are temporary, even the self. Because all things are destined to pass away, there is no soul (Reat 1994).

Buddhism spread rapidly. In the third century B.C., the ruler of India adopted Buddhism and sent missionaries throughout Asia to spread the new teaching (Bridgwater 1953). By the fifth century A.D., Buddhism reached the height of its popularity in India, after which it died out. Buddhism, however, had been adopted in Ceylon, Burma, Tibet, Laos, Cambodia, Thailand, China, Korea, and Japan, where it flourishes today. Vigorous communities of Buddhists have also developed in the United States.

reincarnation in Hinduism and Buddhism, the return of the self after death in a different form

Confucianism

About the time that Gautama lived, K'ung Fu-tsu (551–479 B. C.) was born in China. Confucius (his name strung together in English), a public official, was distressed by the corruption that he saw in government. Unlike Gautama, who urged withdrawal from social activities, Confucius urged social reform and developed a system of morality based on peace, justice, and universal order. His teachings were incorporated into writings called the *Analects*.

The basic moral principle of Confucianism is to maintain *jen*, sympathy or concern for other humans. The key to jen is to maintain right relationships—being loyal and placing morality above self-interest. In what is called the "Confucian Golden Rule," Confucius stated a basic principle for jen: to treat those who are subordinate to you as you would like to be treated by people superior to yourself. Confucius taught that right relationships within the family (loyalty, respect) should be the model for society. He also taught the "middle way," an avoidance of extremes.

Confucianism was originally atheistic, simply a set of moral teachings without reference to the supernatural. As the centuries passed, however, local gods were added to the teachings, and Confucius himself was declared a god. Confucius' teachings became the basis for the government of China. About A.D. 1000, the emphasis on meditation gave way to a stress on improvement through acquiring knowledge. This emphasis remained dominant until the twentieth century, by which time the government had become rigid, with approval of the existing order having replaced respectful relationships (Bridgwater 1953). Following the Communist revolution of 1949, political leaders attempted to weaken the people's ties with Confucianism.

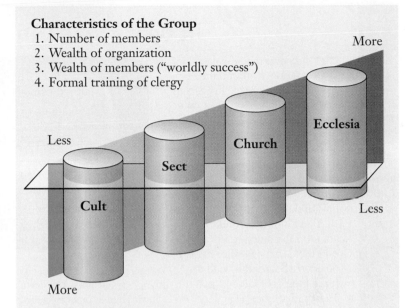

Figure 18.2 A CULT-SECT-CHURCH-ECCLESIA CONTINUUM

Characteristics of the Group
1. Number of members
2. Wealth of organization
3. Wealth of members ("worldly success")
4. Formal training of clergy

The Group Emphasizes
1. The need to reject society
   (the culture is a threat to true religion)
2. That it is rejected by society (the group feels hostility)
3. Hostility toward other religions
4. Hostility from other religions
5. Personal salvation
6. Emotional expression of religious beliefs
7. Revelation (God speaks directly to people)
8. God's direct intervention in people's lives
   (such as providing guidance or healing)
9. A duty to spread the message (evangelism)
10. A literal interpretation of scripture
11. A literal heaven and hell
12. That a conversion experience is necessary

Note: Any religious organization can be placed somewhere on this continuum, based on its having "more" or "less" of these characteristics.

Sources: Based on Troeltsch 1931; Pope 1942; and Johnson 1963.

TYPES OF RELIGIOUS GROUPS

Sociologists have identified four types of religious groups: cult, church, sect, and ecclesia. The summary presented here is a modification of analyses by sociologists Ernst Troeltsch (1931), Liston Pope (1942), and Benton Johnson (1963). Figure 18.2 illustrates the relationship between each of these four types of groups.

Cult

The word *cult* conjures up bizarre images—shaven heads, weird music, brainwashing—even ritual suicide may come to mind. Cults sometimes make instant headlines around the world, as did the one described in the Down-to-Earth Sociology box on the next page. Cults, however, are not necessarily weird, and few practice "brainwashing" or bizarre rituals. In fact, *all religions began as cults* (Stark 1989). A **cult** is simply a new or different religion whose teach-

cult a new religion with few followers, whose teachings and practices put it at odds with the dominant culture and religion

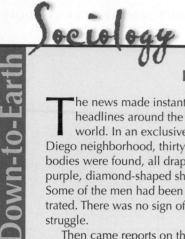

Sociology

HEAVEN'S GATE AND OTHER CULTS

The news made instant headlines around the world. In an exclusive San Diego neighborhood, thirty-nine bodies were found, all draped in purple, diamond-shaped shrouds. Some of the men had been castrated. There was no sign of a struggle.

Then came reports on the beliefs of those who died. A spaceship was hiding behind the Hale-Bopp comet, ready to transport them to a new life. To be beamed aboard, they had to leave their "containers" behind: They had to commit suicide. For their space travels, each cult member put on new Nike sneakers. Each also packed a bag with clothing, $5 bills and quarters—and a passport.

Then there is the garbage-eating Brotherhood led by an ex-Marine who claims he is Jesus. His long-haired followers rummage through dumpsters, removing the mold before dining on rotting scraps of the material world they so disdain. They blame their stomachaches on Satan (O'Neill 1997).

Other Messiahs have been just as influential. In the 1970s, hundreds of Americans followed Jim Jones to Guyana. More than 900 committed suicide—or were murdered. In the 1990s, 74 members of the Solar Temple in Canada,

Marshal Applewhite, pictured here, was able to persuade 38 men to commit suicide with him in order to be beamed aboard a spaceship. The text explains how such bizarre events can occur.

France, and Switzerland arranged themselves in the shape of a cross and set themselves afire. They believed they would be transported to the star Sirius (Lacayo 1997). In Uganda, a group called Movement for the Restoration of the Ten Commandments of God believed that the world would end as the clock struck midnight on December 31, 1999. It didn't. Three months later, in March of 2000, the group's leaders murdered their 1,000 or so followers. They strangled some, but most died by fire when the church in which they were praising God was set ablaze (Robinson 2000).

Why would anyone fall for such "obvious" deceptions? At the center of religion is finding *meaning* in life. Those who accept a cult learn its teachings among people who satisfy deep needs of belonging, who provide a life-enhancing sense of community. Newcomers are isolated, cut off from family and friends who would provide a balancing perspective on reality. Gradually, the bizarreness of the beliefs wears off as the group's views are confirmed by people the new member has come to like and respect. Cult members come to think of themselves as "insiders" who are privy to secret messages that lie beyond the grasp of ordinary people.

Heaven's Gate, and its many counterparts throughout the world, matches the public's image of cults—bizarre people with strange teachings whose followers act in repugnant ways. As this chapter stresses, however, the *sociological* meaning of *cult* is different. All new religions begin as cults. Some grow and become sects. Others even develop into churches and ecclesias.

None that do so, however, include mass suicide as part of their message. That sort of eliminates the possibility of moving up the continuum illustrated on the previous page. ■

---

ings and practices put it at odds with the dominant culture and religion. Because the term cult arouses such negative meanings in the public mind, however, some scholars prefer to use "new religion" instead.

Cults often begin with the appearance of a **charismatic leader,** an individual who inspires people because he or she seems to have extraordinary qualities. **Charisma** refers to an outstanding gift or to some exceptional quality. Finding something highly appealing about the individual—in some instances, almost a magnetic charm—people feel drawn to both the person and the message.

The most popular religion in the world began as a cult. Its handful of followers believed that an unschooled carpenter who preached in remote villages in a backwater country was the Son of God, that he was killed and came back to life. Those beliefs made the early Christians a cult and set them apart from the rest of their society. Persecuted by both religious and political authorities, these early believers clung to one another for support. Many cut off associations with their friends, who didn't accept the new message. To others, the early Christians must have seemed deluded and brainwashed.

So it was with Islam. When Muhammad revealed his visions and said that God's name was really Allah, only a few people believed him. To others, he must have seemed crazy, deranged.

Each cult (or new religion) is met with rejection on the part of society. Its message is considered bizarre, its approach to life strange. Its members antagonize the majority, who are convinced that they have a monopoly on the truth. The new message may claim revelation, visions, visits from God and angels, some form of enlightenment, or seeing the true way to God. The cult demands intense commitment, and its followers, who are confronting a hostile world, pull together in a tight circle, separating themselves from nonbelievers.

Most cults fail. Not many people believe the new message, and the cult fades into obscurity. Some, however, succeed and make history. Over time, large numbers of people may come to accept the message, and become followers of the religion. If this happens, the new religion changes from a cult to a sect.

Sect

A **sect** is larger than a cult, but its members still feel tension with the prevailing beliefs and values of the broader society. A sect may even be hostile to its society. At the very least, its members remain uncomfortable with many of the emphases of the dominant culture, and nonmembers, in turn, tend to be uncomfortable with members of the sect.

Ordinarily, sects are loosely organized and fairly small. They emphasize personal salvation and an emotional expression of one's relationship with God. Clapping, shouting, dancing, and extemporaneous prayers are hallmarks of sects. Like cults, sects also stress **evangelism,** the active recruitment of new members.

If a sect grows, its members tend to gradually make peace with the rest of society. To appeal to its new, broader base, the sect shifts some of its doctrines, redefining matters to remove some of the rough edges that created tension between it and the rest of society. As the members become more respectable in the eyes of the society, they feel less hostility and little, if any, isolation. If a sect follows this course, as it grows and becomes more integrated into society, it changes into a church.

Church

At this point, the religious group is highly bureaucratized—probably with national and international headquarters that give directions to the local congregations, enforce rules about who can be ordained, and control finances. The relationship with God becomes less intense. The group is likely to have less emphasis on personal salvation and emotional expression. Worship service is likely to have grown more sedate, with sermons more formal, and written prayers read before the congregation. Rather than being recruited from the outside by fervent, personal evangelism, most new members now come from within, from children born to existing members. Rather than joining through conversion—seeing the new truth—children may be baptized, circumcised, or dedicated in some other way. At some designated age, children may be asked to affirm the group's beliefs in a confirmation or bar mitzvah ceremony.

Ecclesia

Finally, some groups become so well integrated into a culture, and so strongly allied with their government, that it is difficult to tell where one leaves off and the other takes over. In these *state religions,* also called **ecclesia,** the government and religion work together to try to shape society. There is no recruitment of members, for citizenship makes everyone a

sect a group larger than a cult that still feels substantial hostility from and toward society

evangelism an attempt to win converts

ecclesia a religious group so integrated into the dominant culture that it is difficult to tell where the one begins and the other leaves off; also called a *state religion*

Americans are a religious people, and one cannot understand them or their history unless one takes this into account. Most Americans consider religion to be a private matter, but some violate this background assumption and take to the streets with their message. As you can see, these urban dwellers are numb to such displays.

member. The majority of the society, however, may belong to the religion in name only. The religion is part of a cultural identification, not an eye-opening experience. How extensively religion and government intertwine in an ecclesia is illustrated by Sweden; in the 1860s all citizens had to memorize Luther's *Small Catechism* and be tested on it yearly (Anderson 1995). Today, Lutheranism is still the state religion, but most Swedes come to church only for baptisms, marriages, and funerals.

Where cults and sects see God as personally involved and concerned with an individual's life, requiring an intense and direct response, ecclesias envision God as more impersonal and remote. Church services reflect this view of the supernatural, for they tend to be highly formal, directed by ministers or priests who, after undergoing rigorous training in approved schools or seminaries, follow prescribed rituals.

Examples of ecclesia include the Church of England (whose very name expresses alignment between church and state), the Lutheran church in Sweden and Denmark, Islam in Iran and Iraq, and, during the time of the Holy Roman Empire, the Roman Catholic church, which was the official religion for what is today Europe.

Variations in Patterns

Obviously, not all religious groups go through all these stages—from cult to sect to church to ecclesia. Some die out because they fail to attract enough members. Others, such as the Amish, remain sects. And, as is evident from the few countries that have state religions, very few religions ever become ecclesias.

In addition, these classifications are not perfectly matched in the real world. For example, although the Amish are a sect, they place little or no emphasis on recruiting others. The early Quakers, another sect, shied away from emotional expressions of their beliefs. They would quietly meditate in church, with no one speaking, until God gave someone a message to share with others. Finally, some groups that become churches may retain a few characteristics of sects, such as an emphasis on evangelism or a personal relationship with God.

Although all religions began as cults, not all varieties of a particular religion begin that way. For example, some **denominations**—"brand names" within a major religion, such as Methodism or Reform Judaism—may begin as splinter groups. A group within a church may disagree with *some* aspects of the church's teachings (not its major message) and break away to form its own organization. An example is the Southern Baptist Convention, which was formed in 1845 to defend the right to own slaves.

When Religion and Culture Conflict

As we have seen, cults and sects represent a break with the past. Consequently, they challenge the social order. Three major patterns of adaptation occur when religion and the culture in which it is embedded find themselves in conflict.

First, the members of a religion may reject the dominant culture and have as little as possible to do with nonmembers of their religion. Like the Amish, they may withdraw into closed communities. As noted in the Perspectives box on page 109, the Amish broke away from Swiss-German Mennonites in 1693. They try to preserve the culture of their ancestors, who lived in a simpler time when life was not contaminated by television, movies, au-

denomination a "brand name" within a major religion, for example, Methodist or Baptist

tomobiles, or even electricity. To do so, they emphasize family life and traditional male and female roles. They continue to wear the style of clothing that their ancestors wore three hundred years ago, to light their homes with oil lamps, and to speak German at home and in church. They also continue to reject radio, television, motorized vehicles, and education beyond the eighth grade. They do mingle with non-Amish when they shop in town—where they are readily distinguishable by their form of transportation (horse-drawn carriages), clothing, and speech.

In the *second* pattern, a cult or sect rejects only specific elements of the prevailing culture. For example, religious teachings may dictate that immodest clothing—short skirts, swimsuits, low-cut dresses, and so on—is immoral, or that wearing makeup or going to the movies is wrong. Most elements of the main culture, however, are accepted. Although specific activities are forbidden, members of the religion are able to participate in most aspects of the broader society. They resolve this mild tension either by adhering to the religion or by "sneaking," doing the forbidden acts on the sly.

In the *third* pattern, the society rejects the religious group. In the extreme, as with the early Christians, leaders may even try to destroy it. The Roman emperor declared the followers of Jesus to be enemies of Rome and ordered them to be hunted down and destroyed. The Mormons provide another example. Their rejection of Roman Catholicism and Protestantism as corrupt, along with their belief in polygyny, led to their persecution. In 1831, they left Palmyra, New York, and moved first to Kirtland, Ohio, and subsequently to Independence, Missouri. When the persecution continued, they moved to Nauvoo, Illinois. There a mob murdered the founder of the religion, Joseph Smith, and his brother Hyrum. The Mormons decided to escape the dominant culture altogether by founding a community in the wilderness. In 1847, they settled in the Great Salt Lake Valley of what is today the state of Utah (Bridgwater 1953).

Our opening vignette focused on another example. Let's return to it.

HOW TO DESTROY A CULT: THE U.S. GOVERNMENT VERSUS THE BRANCH DAVIDIANS

After the killing of Koresh and eighty or so of his followers at Waco, rumors persisted that federal agents had used flammable devices to burn down the compound. For six years, the FBI denied the rumors. Journalists continued to track down leads, and in 1999, the Texas Rangers revealed that federal agents had used incendiary devices. They also revealed that the U.S. Army's supersecret Delta Force had been involved in the attack.

What crimes could have justified this lethal assault against the Branch Davidians? The government first said that it took action because the group had violated firearms laws. Later, agents changed their story to make saving the children their primary goal. Was the death of those children—and their parents—just an ironic twist of events that marked the stunning end to a strange group? Or was it part of a conspiracy by U.S. government agencies to put an end to groups that dare to challenge their authority?

Koresh's teachings certainly were bizarre. He taught that he was Jesus Christ returned to earth. Many have made this same claim, but Koresh's twist was that he had returned in sinful form so he could better understand sinners. As a sinner, Koresh had a voracious sexual appetite. He demanded—and received—sex from the men's wives, while insisting that the men remain celibate. Some reports, perhaps sponsored by the government, indicate that he also had sex with their daughters, some as young as 12 and 13 years old. Koresh also taught that Armageddon was on its way, that one day the government would attack them. About this, he was right.

Since the official version has been published in the mass media, let's consider the case for the other side. This analysis is written from the conflict perspective. It assumes a conspiracy on the part of the elite to destroy a group that posed a threat to its power.

On April 19, 1993, the U.S. Bureau of Alcohol, Tobacco, and Firearms attacked the Branch Davidian compound in Waco, Texas. The leader of the cult and over 80 followers, including children, died in this fire.

First, Koresh was no recluse. He drove around the area, shopped in stores, and ate in restaurants. The government could have arrested him in public, with no confrontation. Second, after the government's first assault, Koresh let anyone leave who wanted to go. Some parents and twenty-one children did leave. After studying these children, the worst the government could come up with was that some children had been spanked for disobedience. They also learned that the children had been taught Bible stories and songs. Third, the accounts of the survivors don't support government claims. Sheila Martin, whose husband, a Harvard-trained attorney, died in the fire along with four of their children, says that people don't know how nice it was to live there. "Those were the happiest days of my life," she said.

On the other hand, there may have been child abuse. But does child abuse explain an armed attack by government agents? Unlikely. Rather, the ATF's first accounts that the Branch Davidians had stockpiled weapons is the key to explain the government's desire to annihilate the group. In the months before their destruction, the Branch Davidians had purchased thousands of dollars of guns and ammunition. Their purchases were legal, but the government became concerned about reports of a heavily armed strange group, holed up in a compound. Who knows what such a group might do? The solution was to destroy it. ■

For Your Consideration

If this analysis is correct, what groups might be targeted next? How about the militant Islamic groups, which government agents have already infiltrated? Other candidates are the survivalist groups that believe the U.S. government is the Antichrist and reject the government's authority. Like the Branch Davidians, some have armed themselves and retreated into compounds. The Prophet's Church Universal and Triumphant, for example, under the leadership of Elizabeth Clare, has built underground shelters near Yellowstone National Park—and is rumored to have stockpiled arms. Dozens of other groups, which teach that society is about to collapse, have, like Koresh, stockpiled weapons in order to defend themselves.

Can we expect more Wacos? It is difficult to see how the government can sit idly by while groups with paramilitary structures arm themselves, denounce the government as the Antichrist—and perhaps refuse to pay taxes. With the public outcry over the death of the Waco children, however, future attacks may be more restrained—and they probably won't be televised.

Sources: Barkun 1993; Chua-Eoan 1993; Corbin 1993; Dillin 1993; Lacayo 1993b; Pressley 1993; Tye 1993; Gotschall 1994; Paul 1994; "Faddish Justice" 1995; Isikoff 1999; Kuntz 1999.

CHARACTERISTICS OF RELIGION IN THE UNITED STATES

With its hundreds of denominations and sects, how can we generalize about religion in the United States? What do these many religious groups have in common? It certainly isn't doctrine, but doctrine is not the focus of sociology. Sociologists, rather, are interested in the relationship between society and religion, and the role that religion plays in people's lives. To better understand religion in U.S. society, then, we shall focus first on characteristics of members of religious groups, and then on the groups themselves.

Characteristics of Members

About 70 percent of Americans belong to a church or synagogue. Let's look at the characteristics of people who hold formal membership in a religion.

Region Membership is not evenly distributed around the country. As Table 18.2 shows, membership is highest in the South and Midwest, and not much lower in the East. Why is membership in the West so much lower? This may be due to the West being the newest region in the nation and having the highest net migration. If so, when its residents have put down firmer roots, the West's proportion of religious membership will increase.

Social Class Religion in the United States is stratified by social class. As can be seen from Figure 18.3 below, each religious group draws members from all social classes, but some are "top-heavy" and others "bottom-heavy." The most top-heavy are the Episcopalians and Jews, the most bottom-heavy the Baptists and Evangelicals. This figure is further confirmation that churchlike groups tend to appeal more to the successful, while the more sectlike groups appeal to the less successful.

Americans have a tendency to change their religion. About 40 percent of Americans belong to a denomination that is different from the one in which they were reared (Sherkat and Wilson 1991). People who change their social class are also likely to change their denomination. Upwardly mobile people are likely to seek a religion that draws more people from their new social class. An upwardly mobile Baptist, for example, may become a Methodist or a Presbyterian. For Roman Catholics, the situation is somewhat different. Because each parish is a geographical unit, an upwardly mobile individual who moves into a more affluent neighborhood is likely to automatically transfer into a congregation that has a larger proportion of affluent members.

Race and Ethnicity It is common for religions around the world to be associated with race and ethnicity: Islam with Arabs, Judaism with Jews, Hinduism with Indians, and Confucianism with Chinese. Sometimes, as with Hinduism and Confucianism, a religion and a

Table 18.2

CHURCH OR SYNAGOGUE MEMBERSHIP
Percentage of Population, by Region

Region	Membership
South	73%
Midwest	73%
East	70%
West	51%

Source: Statistical Abstract 1999:Table 89.

Figure 18.3   INCOME AND RELIGIOUS AFFILIATION

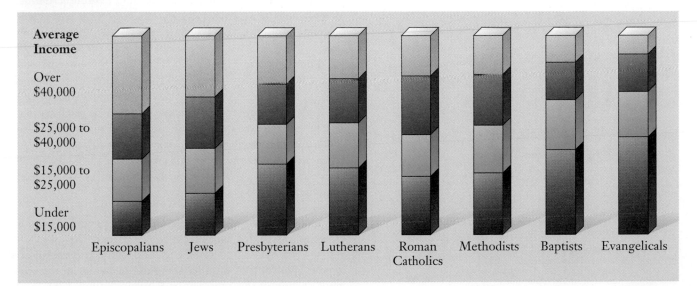

Source: Compiled from data in *Gallup Opinion Index*, 1987:20–27, 29.

Table 18.3

CHURCH OR SYNAGOGUE MEMBERSHIP
Percentage of Population, by Age

Age	Membership
18–29	63%
30–49	66%
50–64	71%
65+	75%

Source: Statistical Abstract 1999:Table 89.

Table 18.4

THE LARGEST U.S. CHURCHES[a]

1. Roman Catholic	61,200,000
2. Baptist	36,500,000
3. Pentecostal	10,200,000
4. Methodist	9,300,000
5. Lutheran	8,200,000
6. African (and Christian) Methodist Episcopal	5,500,000
7. Mormon	5,200,000
8. Churches of Christ	4,300,000
9. Eastern Orthodox	4,200,000
10. Presbyterian	4,000,000
11. Jews	3,100,000
12. Episcopal Church	2,400,000
14. Christian Churches	1,200,000
15. Jehovah's Witnesses	1,000,000
16. Seventh Day Adventist	800,000
17. Armenian Church	600,000
18. Church of the Nazarene	600,000
19. Islamic[b]	500,000
20. Reformed Churches	500,000
21. Salvation Army	500,000
22. Unitarian Universalist	500,000
23. Buddhist	400,000
24. Christian and Missionary Alliance	300,000
25. Community Churches	300,000
26. Evangelical Church	300,000
27. Brethren	200,000
28. Congregationalist	200,000
29. Hindu	200,000
30. Mennonite	200,000

[a]All totals must be taken as approximate. Some groups ignore reporting forms; others exaggerate. Totals are also rounded to the nearest 100,000.

[b]Some popular sources list U.S. Muslims at 6 million. The actual number must fall between these extremes.

*Source: Statistical Abstract:*1999:Table 88.

particular country are almost synonymous. Christianity is not associated with any one country, although it is associated primarily with Western culture.

In the United States, all major religious groups draw from the nation's many racial and ethnic groups. Like social class, however, race and ethnicity tend to cluster. People of Latino or Irish descent are likely to be Roman Catholics, those of Greek origin to belong to the Greek Orthodox church. African Americans are likely to be Protestants, more specifically Baptists, or to belong to fundamentalist sects.

Although many churches are integrated, it is with good reason that Sunday morning between 10 and 11 A.M. has been called "the most segregated hour in the United States." African Americans tend to belong to African-American churches, while most whites see only whites in theirs. The segregation of churches is based not on law, but on custom.

Age As shown in Table 18.3, the chances that an American belongs to a church or synagogue increase with age. Possibly this is because people become more concerned about an afterlife as they age. A different explanation for the increase at ages 30 to 49 is the assumption of adult roles: Along with marriage, parenthood, and becoming established often comes religious affiliation. A possible—and intriguing—explanation for the large increase at ages 50 to 64 and the still larger increase among people over 65 is that religious people outlive those who do not affiliate with a church or synagogue. Each year, as alcohol abuse and other forms of unhealthy lifestyles take their toll, a larger percentage of church members—whose lifestyles are more sedate, more conforming—remain. Perhaps some reader of this text will become the sociologist who will test these three hypotheses.

Characteristics of Religious Groups

Let's examine the major features of religious groups in the United States.

Diversity With its 350,000 congregations and hundreds of denominations, no religious group even comes close to being a dominant religion in the United States (*Statistical Abstract* 1999:Table 88). Table 18.4 illustrates some of this remarkable diversity, as did the box on U.S. Islam on page 519.

Pluralism and Freedom It is the U.S. government's policy not to interfere with religions. The government's position is that its obligation is to ensure an environment in which people can worship as they see fit. Religious freedom is so extensive that anyone can start his or her own church and proclaim himself or herself a minister, revelator, or any other desired term. At times, however, the government grossly violates its hands-off policy, as we discussed in the Thinking Critically section on pages 525-526.

Competition and Recruitment The many religious groups of the United States compete for clients. They even advertise in the Yellow Pages of the telephone directory and insert appealing advertising—under the guise of news—in the religious section of the Saturday or Sunday edition of the local newspapers. Because of this intense competition, some groups

PEANUTS® by Charles M. Schulz

In its technical sense, to evangelize means to "announce the Good News" (that Jesus is the Savior). In its more common usage, to evangelize means to make converts. As *Peanuts* so humorously picks up, evangelization is sometimes accomplished through means other than pronouncements.

modify their message, making it closer to what their successful competitors are offering (Greeley and Hout 1999).

Commitment Americans are a deeply religious people, as demonstrated by the high proportion who believe in God and attend religious services. They back up their commitment with generous support for religion and its charities. Each year Americans donate about $75 billion to religious causes (*Statistical Abstract* 1999:Table 646). To appreciate the significance of this huge figure, keep in mind that, unlike a country in which there is an ecclesia, those billions of dollars are not taxes but voluntary contributions.

Toleration The general religious toleration can be illustrated by three prevailing attitudes: (1) "All religions have a right to exist—as long as they don't try to brainwash anyone or bother me." (2) "With all the religions to choose from, how can anyone tell which one—if any—is true?" (3) "Each of us may be convinced about the truth of our religion—and that is good—but to try to convert others is a violation of the individual's dignity."

Fundamentalist Revival The fundamentalist Christian churches are undergoing a revival. They teach that the Bible is literally true and that salvation comes only through a personal relationship with Jesus Christ. They also decry what they see as the permissiveness of U.S. culture: sex on television, in movies, and in videos, abortion, corruption in public office, premarital sex, cohabitation, and drugs. Their answer to these problems is firm, simple, and direct: People whose hearts are changed through religious conversion will change their lives. The mainstream churches, which offer a more remote God and a corresponding reduction in emotional involvement, fail to meet the basic religious needs of large numbers of Americans. Consequently, mainstream churches are losing members while the fundamentalists are gaining. Figure 18.4 on the next page depicts this change. The exception is the Roman Catholic church, whose growth is due primarily to heavy immigration from Mexico and other Catholic countries.

The Electronic Church What began as a ministry to shut-ins and those who do not belong to a church has blossomed into its own type of church. Its preachers, called "televangelists," reach millions of viewers and raise millions of dollars. Some of its most famous ministries are those of Robert Schuler (the "Crystal Cathedral") and Pat Robertson (the 700 Club).

Many local ministers view the electronic church as a competitor. They complain that it competes for the attention and dollars of their members. The electronic church replies that its money goes to good causes and that through its conversions it feeds members into the local churches, strengthening, not weakening them.

The Internet and Religion As with so many aspects of life, the Internet has begun to have an impact on religion. We will focus on this change in the concluding section.

Figure 18.4 U.S. CHURCHES: GAINS AND LOSSES IN TEN YEARS

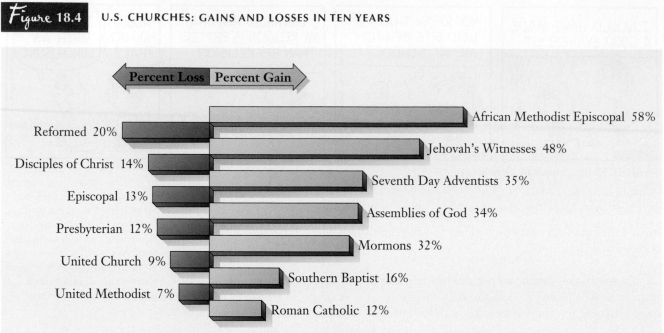

Percent Loss | Percent Gain

African Methodist Episcopal 58%
Reformed 20%
Jehovah's Witnesses 48%
Disciples of Christ 14%
Seventh Day Adventists 35%
Episcopal 13%
Assemblies of God 34%
Presbyterian 12%
Mormons 32%
United Church 9%
Southern Baptist 16%
United Methodist 7%
Roman Catholic 12%

Note: Mergers are excluded. Inconsistent reporting and classifications make it difficult to compare membership over time, making these totals only approximate.

Sources: Yearbook of American and Canadian Churches 1993:Table 2; *Statistical Abstract* 1985:Table 74; 1995:Table 84.

Secularization of Religion and Culture

The term **secularization** refers to the process by which worldly affairs replace spiritual interests. (The term **secular** means "belonging to the world and its affairs.") As we shall see, both religions and cultures can become secularized.

The Secularization of Religion

As the model, fashionably slender, paused before the head table of African-American community leaders, her gold necklace glimmering above the low-cut bodice of her emerald-green dress, the hostess, a member of the Church of God in Christ, said, "It's now OK to wear more revealing clothes—as long as it's done in good taste." Then she added, "You couldn't do this when I was a girl, but now it's OK—and you can still worship God." (Author's files)

When I heard these words, I grabbed a napkin and quickly jotted them down, my sociological imagination stirred by their deep implications. As strange as it may seem, this simple event pinpoints the essence of why the Christian churches in the United States have splintered. Let's see how that could possibly be.

The simplest answer to why Christians don't have just one church, or at most several, instead of the hundreds of sects and denominations that dot the U.S. landscape, is disagreements about doctrine (church teaching). As theologian and sociologist Richard Niebuhr pointed out, however, there are many ways of settling doctrinal disputes beside splintering off and forming another religious organization. Niebuhr (1929) suggested that the answer lies more in *social* change than it does in *religious* conflict.

The explanation goes like this. As noted earlier, when a sect becomes more churchlike, tension between it and the surrounding culture lessens. Quite likely, when a sect is first established, its founders and first members are poor, or at least not too successful in worldly pursuits. Feeling like strangers in the mainstream culture, they derive a good part of their identity from their religion. Their services and customs stress differences between their values and those of the dominant culture. Typically, their religion also stresses the joys of the coming afterlife, when they will be able to escape from their present pain.

secularization the process by which spiritual concerns are replaced by worldly concerns

secular belonging to the world and its affairs

As time passes, the group's values—such as frugality and the avoidance of gambling, alcohol, and drugs—help later generations become successful. As they attain more education and become more middle class, the group's members grow more respectable in the eyes of society. They no longer experience the alienation that was felt by the founders of their group. Life's burdens don't seem as heavy, and the need for relief through an afterlife doesn't seem as pressing. Similarly, the pleasures of the world no longer appear as threatening to the "true" belief. As illustrated by the woman at the fashion show, what follows is an attempt to harmonize religious beliefs with their changing ideas about the culture.

This process is called the **secularization of religion**—shifting the focus from spiritual matters to the affairs of this world. Anyone familiar with today's ultra-mainstream Methodists, for example, would be surprised to know they once were a sect. Methodists used to ban playing cards, dancing, and theater attendance. They even considered circuses to be sinful. As Methodists grew more middle-class, however, they began to change their views on sin. They then began to dismantle the barriers that they had constructed between themselves and the outside world (Finke and Stark 1992).

Secularization leads to a splintering of the group, for accommodation with the secular culture displeases some of the group's members, especially those who have had less worldly success. These people still feel a gulf between themselves and the broader culture. For them, tension and hostility continue to be realities of everyday life. They see secularization as a desertion of the group's fundamental truths, a "selling out" to the secular world. (The Down-to-Earth Sociology box on the next page describes another group whose needs are not met by mainstream religious groups.)

After futile attempts by die-hards to bring the group back to its senses, the group splinters. Those who protested the secularization of Methodism, for example, were kicked out— even though *they* represented the values around which the group had organized in the first place. The dissatisfied—who by now are viewed as complainers—then form a sect that continues to stress its differences from the world, the need for more personal, emotional religious experiences, and salvation from the pain of living in this world. As time passes, the same process—adjustment to the dominant culture by some, and continued dissatisfaction by others—occurs among this group, and the cycle repeats itself.

The Secularization of Culture Just as religion can be secularized, so can culture. Sociologists use the term **secularization of culture** to refer to a culture that, though it was once heavily influenced by religion, loses much of its religious influence. The United States provides an example.

Despite attempts to reinterpret history, the Pilgrims and most of the Founding Fathers of the United States were highly religious people. The Pilgrims were even convinced that God had guided them to found a new land, while many of the Founding Fathers felt that God had guided them to develop a new form of government.

The clause in the Constitution that mandates the separation of church and state was *not* an attempt to keep religion out of government, but a (successful) device to avoid the establishment of a state religion like that in England. Here, people were to have the freedom to worship as they wished. The assumption of the founders was even more specific—that Protestantism represented the true religion.

The phrase in the Declaration of Independence, "All men are created equal," refers to a central belief in God as the creator of humanity. A member of the clergy opened Congress with prayer. Many colonial laws were based on principles derived explicitly from the Old and New Testaments. In some colonies, blasphemy was a crime, as was failing to observe the Sabbath. Similarly, adultery was a crime; in some places it even carried the death penalty. Even public kissing between husband and wife was considered an offense, punishable by placement in the public stocks (Frumkin 1967). In other words, religion permeated U.S. culture. It was part and parcel of how the Colonists saw life. Their lives, laws, and other aspects of the culture reflected their religious beliefs.

Today, however, U.S. culture has been secularized; that is, the influence of religion on public affairs has greatly lessened. No longer are laws based on religious principles. In

secularization of religion the replacement of a religion's "other-worldly" concerns with concerns about "this world"

secularization of culture the process by which a culture becomes less influenced by religion

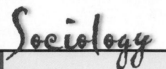

BIKERS AND BIBLES

The Bible Belt churchgoers in Eureka Springs, Arkansas, stare as Herbie Shreve, unshaven, his hair hanging over the collar of his denim vest, roars into town on his Harley Davidson. With hundreds of other bikers in town, it is going to be a wild weekend of drinking, nudity, and fights.

But not for Herbie. After pitching his tent, he sets up a table at which he offers other bikers free ice water and religious tracts. "No hard sell. They seek us out when it's the right time," says Herbie.

The ministry began when Herbie's father, a pastor, took up motorcycling to draw closer to his rebellious teen-age son. As the pair rode around the heartland of America, they often were snubbed by fellow Christians when they tried to attend church. So Herbie's father hatched plans for a motorcycle ministry. "Jesus said, 'Go out to the highways and hedges,' and that always stuck with me," says the elder Shreve. "I felt churches ought to be wherever the people are."

They founded the Christian Motorcyclists Association (CMA), headquartered in Hatfield, Arkansas. It now has 33,000 members in more than 300 chapters in the United States and Canada. Members of the CMA call themselves "weekend warriors."

"Riding for the Son" is emblazoned on their T-shirts and jackets—something that would make them stand out almost anywhere, but especially in the midst of the nudity and drunkenness.

Some Christian groups make evangelism, the conversion of others, a primary goal. One such group is the Christian Motorcyclists' Association, discussed in this box. Another is the Full Gospel Motorcycle Association, shown here joining hands in prayer before setting out to change tires, help stranded motorists, and preach the gospel. The bikers strike up conversations about their motorcycles, then change the topic to "how to reverse direction from the highway to hell to the highway to heaven."

No CMA member has ever been harmed by a biker. But they have come close. In the early days, bikers at a rally surrounded Herbie's tent and threatened to burn it down. "Some of those same people are friends of mine today," says the elder Shreve.

Stepping over a biker who has passed out in front of his tent, Herbie goes through the campground urging last night's carousers to join them by a lake for a Sunday service. Four years ago no one took him up on it. Today twenty bikers straggle down to the dock.

Herbie's brief sermon is plainspoken. He touches on the biker's alienation—the unpaid bills, the oppressive bosses, the righteous church ladies "who are always mad and always right." He tells them that Jesus loves them, and that they can call him anytime. "I'll help fix your life," he says.

CMA has several conversions this weekend. "You just stay at it. You don't know when their hearts are touched. Look at these guys," Herbie says, pointing to fellow CMA members. "They were all bikers headed for hell, too. Now they follow the Son."

Herbie gets on his Harley. In town, the traditional churchgoers stare as he roars past, his long hair sweeping behind him. ■

Sources: Based on Graham 1990; Shreve 1991.

general, ideas of what is "generally good" have replaced religion as an organizing principle for the culture.

The major cause for the secularization of a culture is *modernization*, a term that refers to a society industrializing, urbanizing, developing mass education, and adopting science and advanced technology. The significance of modernization goes far beyond these surface changes. Science and advanced technology bring with them a secular view of the world that begins to permeate society. They provide explanations for many aspects of life that people traditionally attributed to God. As a consequence, people come to depend much less on religion to explain life events. Its satisfactions and problems—from births to deaths—are attributed to natural causes. When a society has secularized thoroughly, even religious leaders may turn to answers provided by biology, philosophy, psychology, sociology, and so on.

Although the secularization of its culture means that religion has become less important in U.S. public life, *personal* religious involvement among Americans has not diminished. Instead, it has *increased*. Ninety-four percent believe there is a God, 77 percent believe there is a heaven, and 70 percent claim membership in a church or synagogue. On any given weekend, 40 percent of all Americans report that they attended a church or synagogue (Woodward 1989; Gallup 1990; *Statistical Abstract* 1999:Table 89).

Table 18.5 underscores the paradox of how religious participation has increased while the culture has secularized. The proportion of Americans who belong to a church or synagogue is now *four* times higher than it was when the country was founded. Church membership, of course, is only a rough indicator of how significant religion is in people's lives, for some church members are not particularly religious, while many intensely religious people—Lincoln, for one—never join a church.

Table 18.5

GROWTH IN RELIGIOUS MEMBERSHIP: THE PERCENTAGE OF AMERICANS WHO BELONG TO A CHURCH OR SYNAGOGUE

Year	Percentage Who Claim Membership
1776	17%
1860	37%
1890	45%
1926	58%
1975	71%
1998	70%

Sources: Finke and Stark 1992; *Statistical Abstract* 1999: Table 89.

THE FUTURE OF RELIGION

Marx was convinced that religion would crumble when the workers threw off their chains of oppression. When the workers usher in a new society based on justice, he argued, there will no longer be a need for religion, for religion is the refuge of the miserable, and people will no longer be miserable. Religion will wither away, for people will see that thoughts about an afterlife are misdirected. In its place, they will put their energies into developing a workers' paradise here on earth (De George 1968).

After communist countries were established, however, people continued to be religious. At first, the leaders thought this was simply a remnant of the past that would eventually dwindle to nothing. Old people might cling to the past, but the young would give it up, and with the coming generation religion would cease to exist.

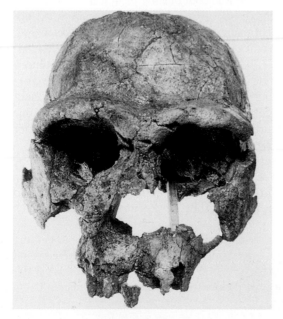

A basic principle of symbolic interactionism is that meaning is not inherent in an object or event, but is determined by people as they interpret the object or event. Old bones and fossils are an excellent illustration of this principle. Does this skull of homo erectus "prove" evolution? Does it "disprove" creation? Such "proof" and "disproof" lie in the eye of the beholder, as evidenced by the recent rise of "scientific creationism," now gaining adherents in the U.S. universities.

Table 18.6

RELIGIOUS BELIEF IN RUSSIA
Percentage of Russians
Who Believe In . . .

God	74%
Life after death	40%
Miracles	33%
Heaven	33%
Hell	30%

Source: Greeley 1994.

The new Marxist states, avowing atheism, were not content to allow this withering to occur on its own, and they tried to eradicate religion from their midst. (Keep in mind that Marx said that he was not a Marxist. He did not advocate the persecution of religion, for he felt that religion would crumble on its own.) The Communist government in the Soviet Union confiscated church buildings and turned them into museums or government offices. The school curriculum was designed to ridicule religion, and, as noted, a civil marriage ceremony was substituted for the religious ceremony (complete with an altar and a bust of Lenin), while a ceremony dedicating newborns to the state was substituted for baptism. Ministers and priests were jailed as enemies of the state. Parents who dared to teach religion to their children were imprisoned or fired from their jobs, their children taken from them to be reared by the state, under whose guardianship they would learn the "truth."

Despite severe, extended persecution, religion remained strong, even among many of the youth. Table 18.6 shows results of the first scientific sampling of the Russian population since the collapse of the Soviet Union. Three of four Russians believe there is a God, and one of three believes there is a heaven.

Another group of thinkers, who placed their faith not in socialism or communism but in science, foresaw a similar end to religion. As science advanced, it would explain everything. Science would transform human thought and replace religion, which was merely mistaken prescientific thinking. For example, in 1966 Anthony Wallace, one of the world's best-known anthropologists at the time, made the following observation:

> The evolutionary future of religion is extinction. Belief in supernatural beings . . . will become only an interesting historical memory. . . . doomed to die out, all over the world, as a result of the increasing adequacy and diffusion of scientific knowledge.

Marx, Wallace, and the many other social analysts who took this position were wrong. Religion thrives in the most advanced scientific nations, in capitalist and in socialist countries. It is evident that these analysts did not understand the fundamental significance of religion in people's lives.

Humans are inquiring creatures. They are aware that they have a past, a present, and a future. They reflect on their experiences to try to make sense out of them. One of the questions people develop as they reflect on life concerns the purpose of it all. Why are we born? Is there an afterlife? If so, where are we going, and what will it be like when we get there? Out of these concerns arises this question: If there is a God, what does God want of us in this life? Does God have a preference about how we should live?

Science, including sociology, cannot answer such questions. By its very nature, science cannot tell us about four main concerns that many people have: (1) the existence of God; (2) the purpose of life; (3) morality; and (4) the existence of an afterlife. About the first, science has nothing to say (no test tube has either isolated God or refuted God's existence). For the second, although science can provide a definition of life and can describe the characteristics of living organisms, it has nothing to say about ultimate purpose. For the third, science can demonstrate the consequences of behavior but not the moral superiority of one action compared with another. For the fourth, again science can offer no information, for it has no tests that it can use to prove or disprove a "hereafter."

Science simply cannot replace religion. Nor can political systems, as demonstrated by the experience of socialist and communist countries. Science cannot even prove that loving your family and neighbor is superior to hurting and killing them. It can describe death and compute consequences, but it cannot dictate the *moral* superiority of any action, even in such an extreme example.

There is no doubt that religion will last as long as humanity lasts—or until humans develop adequate functional alternatives. And even though such alternatives may come, would they not be religion under a different name?

To glimpse the cutting edge of change, we'll close with a look at the online marketing of religion.

Mass Media in Social Life

GOD ON THE NET:
THE ONLINE MARKETING OF RELIGION

Muslims in France download sermons and join an invisible community of worshippers at virtual mosques. Jews in Sweden type messages that fellow believers in Jerusalem download and insert in the Western Wall. Christians in California make digital donations to the Crystal Cathedral. Buddhists in Japan seek enlightenment online. The Internet helps to level the pulpit: On the Net, the leader of a pagan group can compete directly with the Pope.

The Internet is making religious rebellion easier, too. And it has become harder for organizations to punish those who do rebel. Jacques Gaillot is a French bishop who is critical of the Roman Catholic church. The church hierarchy exiled him to the Saharan desert of North Africa, a strategy that used to work. Instead of being silenced in his remote outpost, however, Gaillot logged onto the Internet, where he now preaches to a virtual congregation via Real Audio (Huffstutter 1998).

No one knows the outcome, but the times, they are a'changin'. Some say that we are on the edge of a religious reformation as big as the one set off by Gutenberg's invention of the printing press (Huffstutter 1998).

Could be. Here are some of the developments in religion made possible by the Internet:

- New churches that exist only in cyberspace
- Online counseling for spiritual matters
- Chat rooms directed by rabbis
- Video and audio feeds of sermons
- Easy-to-use forms for making donations by credit card
- Online stores that sell religious books and trinkets
- Mailing lists for those devoted to witchcraft

Will virtual religion satisfy? Will it prove to be an adequate replacement for the warm embrace of a fellow believer? Will it bring comfort to someone in mourning the way a sympathetic touch can? For some, not at all. For others, yes. We are gazing into the future. To what extent this new medium will affect our religious lives—and perhaps even alter the face of religion—remains to be seen. ■

SUMMARY AND REVIEW

■ What Is Religion?
Durkheim identified three essential characteristics of **religion**: beliefs that set the **sacred** apart from the **profane, rituals,** and a moral community (a **church**). P. 508.

■ The Functionalist Perspective
What are the functions and dysfunctions of religion?
Among the functions of religion are answering questions about ultimate meaning, providing emotional comfort, social solidarity, guidelines for everyday life, social control, adaptation, support for the government, and fostering social change. Groups or activities that provide these same functions are called **functional equivalents** of religion. Among the dysfunctions of religion are war and religious persecution. Pp. 509–511.

■ The Symbolic Interactionist Perspective
What aspects of religion do symbolic interactionists study?
Symbolic interactionists focus on the meanings of religion for its followers. They examine religious symbols, **rituals,** beliefs, **religious experiences,** and the sense of community provided by religion. Pp. 511–513.

■ The Conflict Perspective
What aspects of religion do conflict theorists study?
Conflict theorists examine the relationship of religion to social inequalities, especially how religion reinforces a society's social stratification. Pp. 513–514.

■ Religion and the Spirit of Capitalism
What does the spirit of capitalism have to do with religion?
Max Weber disagreed with Marx's conclusion that religion impedes social change. In contrast, Weber saw religion as a primary source of social change. He analyzed how Protestantism gave rise to **the Protestant ethic,** which stimulated what he called **the spirit of capitalism.** The result was capitalism, which transformed society. Pp. 514–515.

■ The World's Major Religions

What are the world's major religions?

Judaism, Christianity, and Islam, all **monotheistic** religions, can be traced to the same Old Testament roots. Hinduism, the chief religion of India, has no specific founder, as do Judaism (Abraham), Christianity (Jesus), Islam (Muhammad), Buddhism (Gautama), and Confucianism (K'ung Fu-tsu). Specific teachings and history of these six religions are given in the text. Pp. 515–521.

■ Types of Religious Groups

What types of religious groups are there?

Sociologists divide religious groups into cults, sects, churches, and ecclesias. All religions began as **cults.** Those that survive tend to develop into **sects** and eventually into **churches.** Sects, often led by **charismatic leaders,** are unstable. Some are perceived as threats and are persecuted by the state. **Ecclesias,** or state religions, are rare. Pp. 521–526.

■ Characteristics of Religion in the United States

What are the main characteristics of religion in the United States?

Membership varies by region, social class, age, and race or ethnicity. The major characteristics are diversity, pluralism and freedom, competition, commitment, toleration, a fundamentalist revival, and the electronic church. Pp. 526–529.

What is the connection between secularization of religion and the splintering of churches?

Secularization of religion, a change in a religion's focus from spiritual matters to concerns of "this world," is the key to understanding why churches divide. Basically, as a cult or sect changes to accommodate its members' upward social class mobility, it changes into a church. Left dissatisfied, members who are not upwardly mobile tend to splinter off and form a new cult or sect, and the cycle repeats itself. Cultures permeated by religion also secularize. This, too, leaves many dissatisfied and promotes social change. Pp. 529-533.

■ The Future of Religion

Although industrialization led to the **secularization of culture,** this did not spell the end of religion, as many social analysts assumed it would. Because science and education cannot answer questions about ultimate meaning, the existence of God or an afterlife, or provide guidelines for morality, the need for religion will remain. In any foreseeable future, religion—or its functional equivalents—will prosper. The Internet is likely to have far-reaching consequences on religion. Pp. 533–535.

Where can I read more on this topic?

Suggested Readings for this chapter are found at the back of this book.

Sociology & the Internet

All URLs listed are current as of the printing of this book. URLs often change. Please check our Web site, **http://www.abacon.com/henslin** for updates.

1. Why do people get involved in a church? To get a sense of what a church offers its members, go to **http://www.willownet.com.** This is the Web site for Willow Creek Community Church, an independent Christian church located in Barrington, Illinois, which weekly draws 16,000 to 17,000 worshippers to its several weekend services. Begin by clicking on "More about Willow Creek." How did this church begin? What type of person is drawn to this church? In what ways does the church attempt to draw people into its congregation? You can learn more about the many programs, or ministries, offered at Willow Creek by clicking on "Getting Connected." Select the category that best describes yourself and click on it. What kinds of special ministries does the church offer for people like you? Go back and look at some of the other groups listed. How are the various ministries related to each group's special concerns? Prepare a report for your class in which you discuss the appeal of churches like Willow Creek. In your presentation, consider the functions of religion that were presented in this chapter. How does Willow Creek fulfill these functions?

2. This exercise will introduce you to humanism, which could be considered a functional equivalent of religion. The American Humanist Association represents both the religious and secular branches of humanism. You can learn more about this system of beliefs at **http://www.humanist.net.** Begin by reading about how humanism is defined. Then browse through the section on the "Philosophy of Humanism." What is humanism? How does it deal with traditional religious beliefs? What ceremonies does religious humanism have? There are many types of humanism. Click on "Humanist and Freethought Websites." Select a few of the varieties and learn more about them. What differentiates them? What unites them under the banner of humanism? Finally, explore humanists' views on different social issues. When you are through, write a paper about how this movement represents a functional equivalent to religion. In what ways does it meet the definition of a church, as specified by Emile Durkheim? How does it fulfill the functions of religion?

3. Begin this exercise by jotting down the names of as many different religious groups as you can. What do members of each religious group believe? Now go to the Web site for the Pluralism Project at Harvard University, **http://www.fas.harvard.edu/~pluralism.** Why was this project started? What are its goals? As you read through this page, you will come to a list of publications; click on a few of them and read more about religious pluralism. Then return to the home page and click on "World Religions in Boston." After reading the Introduction, click on some of the different religions to learn more about their histories and belief sys-

tems. When you are finished, go back to the home page and click on "Public Square." This will take you to a list of groups that are engaged in public debate and discussion on topics reflecting the religious diversity of our society. Select a few links from among the categories listed and learn more about their views. Finally, return to the home page for the Pluralism Project and click on "Selected Links." Here you will find a list of many different religions. Compare this list with the one you originally generated; then search the links for a few of the religions that are on your list. Make a note of anything new you discover about these religions. Return to the Pluralism Project's list of religious links. Pick two or three religions that you had not heard of before doing this exercise, and explore those links. What did you discover about them? Use your sociological imagination to write a paper in which you explore both the wide range of beliefs and the consequences of this diversity for our social life.

4. The text includes a discussion of cults. You can learn more about cults at **http://www.religioustolerance.org/cultmenu.htm.** Explore how individuals and organizations apply widely different meanings to the word *cult*. In the section on "General Information about Cults," you can read more about the differences between cults, sects, and denominations. You may be surprised to learn that there are positive, neutral, and negative characteristics of cults. To learn about "brainwashing," browse through the section on academic studies of new religions, and explore the issues surrounding cult member recruitment. In the section on "Negative Aspects of Dangerous New Religious Groups," identify the warning signs of destructive cults, especially doomsday cults. There are also sections on organizations that harass new religions, as well as sections on some of the new religions that are targeted for harassment. Prepare a report for your class in which you discuss what a cult is, why people join cults, why some cults can be dangerous, and how society reacts to cults.

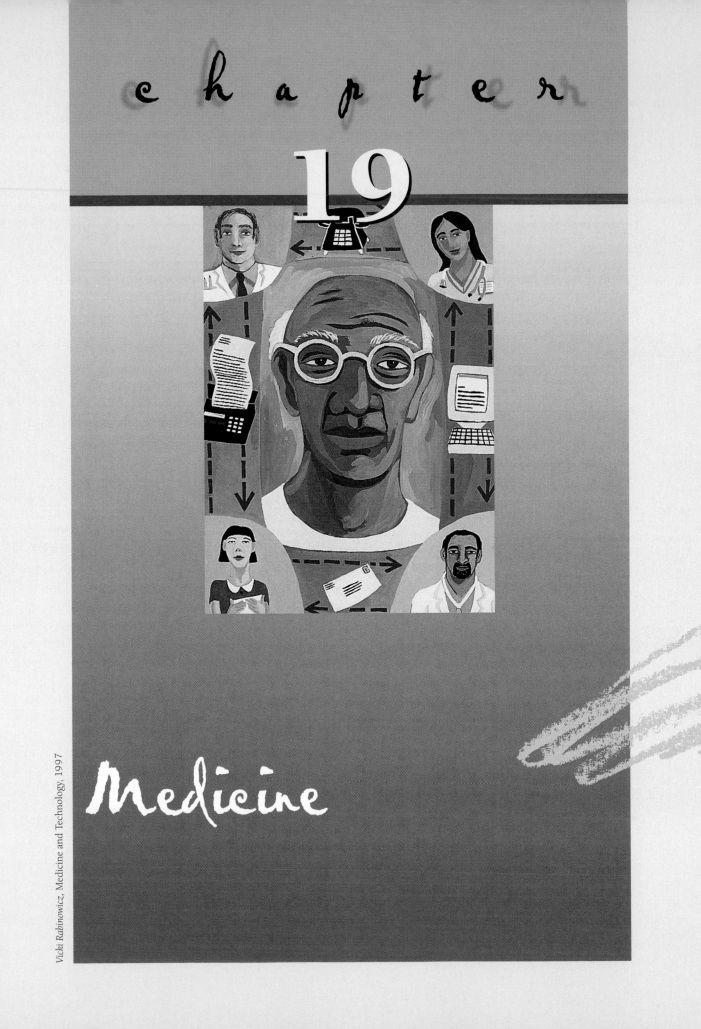

Medicine

- **Sociology and the Study of Medicine**
- **The Symbolic Interactionist Perspective**
  The Role of Culture in Defining Health and Illness
  The Components of Health
- **The Functionalist Perspective**
  The Sick Role
- **The Conflict Perspective**
  Effects of Global Stratification on Health Care
  Establishing a Monopoly on U.S. Health Care
- **Historical Patterns of Health**
  Physical Health
  Mental Health
- **Issues in Health Care**
  Medical Care: A Right or a Commodity?
  Social Inequality
  Malpractice Suits and Defensive Medicine
  Medical Incompetence

Depersonalization: The Medical Cash Machine
Conflict of Interest
Medical Fraud
Sexism in Medicine
The Medicalization of Society
Medically Assisted Suicide
Curbing Costs: Issues in Private and National
    Health Insurance
- **Threats to Health**
  AIDS
  The Globalization of Disease
  Drugs: Alcohol and Nicotine
  Disabling Environments
  Misguided, Foolish, and Callous Experiments
- **The Search for Alternatives**
  Treatment or Prevention?
  Health Care in Global Perspective
- **Summary and Review**

I had decided that it was not enough to just study the homeless—I had to help them. I learned that a homeless shelter in St. Louis was planning to help poor people save on utilities by installing free wood stoves in their homes. This would help keep them from being forced onto the streets. It wasn't exactly applied sociology, but I volunteered.

I was a little anxious about the coming training session on how to install stoves, as I had never done anything like this. As I entered the homeless shelter on that Saturday morning, I found the building in semi-darkness. "They must be saving on electricity," I thought to myself. Then I was greeted with an unnerving sight. A nude man was running through the halls being chased by two police officers. They caught him. I watched as the elderly man, looking confused, struggled to put on his clothing. From the police I learned that he had ripped the wires out of the shelter's main electrical box; that was why there were no lights on.

I asked the officers where they were going to take the man, and they replied, "To Malcolm Bliss" (the state hospital). When I said, "I guess he'll be in there for quite a while," they replied, "Probably just a day or two. We picked him up last week—he was crawling under cars at a traffic light—and they let him out in two days."

The police then explained that one must be a danger to others or to oneself in order to be admitted to the hospital as a long-term patient. Visualizing this old man crawling under stopped cars at an intersection, and considering how he had risked electrocution by ripping out the electrical wires with his bare hands, I marveled at the definition of "danger" that the psychiatrists must be using. ■

SOCIOLOGY AND THE STUDY OF MEDICINE

This incident points to a severe problem with U.S. medical care. In this chapter, we will examine why the poor often receive second-rate medical care and, in some instances, abysmal treatment. We'll also look at how skyrocketing costs have created such dilemmas as whether or not medical care should be rationed.

As we consider these issues, the role of sociology in studying **medicine**—a society's standard ways of dealing with illness and injury—will become apparent. For example, because U.S. medicine is a profession, a bureaucracy, and a big business, sociologists study how it is influenced by self-regulation, the bureaucratic structure, and the profit motive. Sociologists also study how illness and health are much more than biological matters—how, for example, they are related to cultural beliefs, lifestyle, and social class. Because of these emphases, the sociology of medicine is one of the applied fields of sociology, and many medical schools and even hospitals have sociologists on their staffs.

THE SYMBOLIC INTERACTIONIST PERSPECTIVE

Let's begin, then, by examining how culture influences health and illness. This takes us to the heart of the symbolic interactionist perspective.

The Role of Culture in Defining Health and Illness

Suppose that one morning you look in the mirror and see strange blotches covering your face and chest. Hoping against hope that it is not serious, you rush to a doctor. If the doctor said that you had "dyschromic spirochetosis," your fears would be confirmed.

Now, wouldn't everyone around the world draw the conclusion that your spots are symptoms of a disease? No, not everybody. In one South American tribe this skin condition is so common that the few individuals who *aren't* spotted are seen as the unhealthy ones. They are even excluded from marriage because they are "sick" (Ackernecht 1947; Zola 1983).

Consider mental "illness" and mental "health." People aren't automatically "crazy" because they do certain things. Rather, they are defined as "crazy" or "normal" according to cultural guidelines. If an American talks aloud to spirits that no one else can see, and takes direction from them, he or she is likely to be defined as insane—and, for everyone's good, locked up. In some tribal societies, in contrast, someone who talks to invisible spirits might be honored for being in close contact with the spiritual world—and, for everyone's good, be declared a **shaman,** or spiritual intermediary, who would then diagnose and treat medical problems.

"Sickness" and "health," then, are not absolutes, as we might suppose. Rather, they are matters of definition. Around the world, each culture provides guidelines that its people use to determine whether they are "healthy" or "sick." This is another example of how the social construction of reality plays a vital role in our lives.

The Components of Health

Back in 1941, international "health experts" identified three components of **health:** physical, mental, and social (World Health Organization 1946). They missed the focus of our pre-

---

medicine one of the major social institutions that sociologists study; a society's organized ways of dealing with sickness and injury

shaman the healing specialist of tribal groups who attempts to control the spirits thought to cause a disease or injury; commonly called a witch doctor

health a human condition measured by four components: physical, mental, social, and spiritual

---

Health practices vary around the world. Gray Squirrel, a Native-American shaman in New Mexico, is following a traditional ceremony designed to maintain harmony between spiritual forces and human activities. He also performs healing ceremonies based on this underlying principle.

vious chapter, however, and I have added a spiritual component to Figure 19.1. Even the dimensions of health, then, are subject to debate.

If we were to agree on the components of health, we would still be left with the question of what makes someone physically, mentally, socially, or spiritually "healthy." Again, as symbolic interactionists stress, these are not objective matters but, rather, matters whose definitions vary from culture to culture. In a pluralistic society, they even differ from one group to another.

As with religion in the previous chapter, then, the concern of sociologists is not to define "true" health or "true" illness. Instead, it is to analyze the effects that people's ideas of health and illness have on their lives, and even the ways in which people determine that they are sick.

THE FUNCTIONALIST PERSPECTIVE

Functionalists begin with an obvious point: If society is to function well, its people need to be healthy enough to perform their normal roles. This means that societies must set up ways to control sickness. One way they do this is to develop a system of medical care. But another way is to make rules to keep too many people from "being sick." Let's look at how this works.

The Sick Role

Do you remember when your throat began to hurt and when your mom or dad took your temperature the thermometer registered 102°F? Your parents took you to the doctor, and despite your protests that tomorrow was the first day of summer vacation, you had to spend the next three days in bed taking medicine. You were forced to play what sociologists call the "sick role." What do they mean by this term?

Elements of the Sick Role Talcott Parsons, the functionalist who first analyzed the **sick role,** pointed out that it has four elements—that you are not held responsible for being sick, that you are exempt from normal responsibilities, that you don't like the role, and that you will get competent help so you can return to your routines. If people don't seek competent help, they are considered responsible for being sick. They are denied the right to claim sympathy from others and to be excused from their normal routines. People who seek help are given sympathy and encouragement, the others are given the cold shoulder for wrongfully claiming the sick role.

Ambiguity in the Sick Role Instead of a fever of 102°F, suppose the thermometer registers 99.5°F. Do you then "become" sick or not? That is, do you decide to claim the sick role? Because most instances of illness are not as clear-cut as, say, a heart attack or a limb fracture, decisions to claim the sick role often are based more on social considerations than they are on physical conditions. Let's also suppose that you are facing a midterm, you are unprepared for it, and you are allowed to make it up. The more you think about the test, the worse you are likely to feel—which makes the need to claim the sick role seem more legitimate. Now assume that the thermometer still shows 99.5, but you have no test and your friends are coming over to take you out to celebrate your twenty-first birthday. You are not likely to play the sick role. Note that in both cases your physical condition is the same.

Gatekeepers to the Sick Role Parents and physicians are the primary gatekeepers to the sick role. That is, they mediate between children's feelings of illness and their claim to being sick. Before parents call the school to excuse a child's absence, they decide whether the child is faking or has genuine symptoms that are serious enough to warrant keeping the child home from school. For adults, physicians are gatekeepers of the sick role. If employers and teachers receive a "doctor's excuse" (official permission for someone to play the sick role), they have no need to pass judgment on the individual's claim.

A CONTINUUM OF HEALTH AND ILLNESS

Health
Excellent Functioning

PHYSICAL | MENTAL | SOCIAL | SPIRITUAL

Poor Functioning
Illness

sick role a social role that excuses people from normal obligations because they are sick or injured, while at the same time expecting them to seek competent help and cooperate in getting well

Gender Differences in the Sick Role   Try to figure out this riddle. On average, females are healthier than males, and they live longer lives. Yet they also are sick more often and go to doctors more frequently (*Statistical Abstract* 1999:Tables 199, 222). How can both statements be true? Testing college students from working-class backgrounds, researchers Elizabeth Klonoff and Hope Landrine (1992) found a simple answer—women are more willing than men to claim the sick role when they don't feel well. They identified two primary reasons for this. Because fewer women are employed, they experience less role conflict in claiming the sick role. They also are socialized to be more dependent and to more freely share their feelings. And, as you know, the sick role does not match the *macho* image that boys and men try to project.

This research helps us understand how social factors underlie the sick role. Gender roles—ideas of what is properly feminine or masculine—vary from one culture to another. An ideal that men should be strong, keep their pain to themselves, and "tough it out"—while women should share their feelings and seek help from others—underlies this riddle of why women can be healthier than men and yet be sick and go to doctors more often.

*T*HE CONFLICT PERSPECTIVE

As stressed in earlier chapters, the primary focus of conflict theorists is how people struggle over scarce resources. Since medical treatment is one of those resources, let's examine this competition in global perspective and then see how one group developed a monopoly on U.S. health care.

Effects of Global Stratification on Health Care

In Chapter 9 (pages 248–250), we saw how the nations that industrialized obtained the economic and military power that brought them riches and allowed them to dominate the globe. This has also led to global stratification of medical care, which is a matter of life and death.

Many of us know people who have had their lives saved by open heart surgery, a high-tech operation that has become routine. The Least Industrialized Nations, however, cannot even begin to afford the technology that these surgeries require. Victims of AIDS in the United States and other rich nations have had their lives extended by new medicines, but those medicines are expensive, and people with AIDS in the Least Industrialized Nations can't afford them. They die from their illness.

Global stratification in health care is starkly contrased in these two photos. It is difficult to believe, but the photo on the left is a hospital scene. It was taken in Ruhengeri Hospital in Rwanda, one of the poorest countries in the world. The photo on the right, of a heart transplant in New York City, illustrates the kind of medical treatment available in the Most Industrialized Nations. As discussed in the text, stratification within nations yields unequal access to this technology.

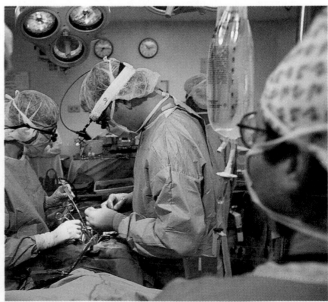

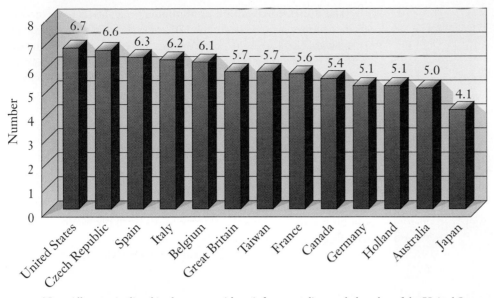

HOW MANY BABIES DIE BEFORE THEIR FIRST BIRTHDAY?

Source: Statistical Abstract 1999: Table 1352.

Note: All countries listed in the source with an infant mortality rate below that of the United States. That this is not a complete list is evident from Austria, Switzerland, Hong Kong, and Sweden being dropped from the source, all of which had lower rates in the 1997 edition. Infant mortality is defined as the number of babies that die before their first birthday, per 1,000 live births.

Life expectancy tells the story. Whereas most people in the industrialized world can expect to live to about 75, *most* people in Afghanistan, Cambodia, Congo, and Ethiopia die before they reach 50. In Zimbabwe, the average person won't even see his or her 40th birthday. Figure 19.2 lists the countries where fewer than 7 of every 1,000 babies die before they are a year old. All of them are industrialized nations. The contrast is stark—of every 1,000 babies born in Afghanistan, 138 never reach their first birthday (*Statistical Abstract* 1999:Table 1352).

Global stratification even helps to determine what diseases we get. Suppose that you had been born in a Least Industrialized Nation located in the tropics. During your much shorter life, you would face illness and death from four major sources: malaria (from mosquitos), internal parasites (from contaminated water), diarrhea (from food and soil contaminated with human feces), and malnutrition. You would not face heart disease and cancer, for they are "luxury" diseases; that is, they characterize the industrialized world where people live long enough to get them. As nations industrialize, their people live longer; they trade in the things that used to be their primary killers and begin to worry about cancer and heart attacks instead.

There is also the matter of social stratification *within* these poorer countries. Many diseases that ravage people in these countries could be brought under control if more funds were spent on public health. Cheap drugs can prevent malaria, while safer water supplies and higher food production would go a long way toward eliminating the other major killers. The meager funds that these countries have at their disposal, however, are not spent this way. Instead, having garnered the lion's share of the country's resources, the elite lavish it on themselves. They also send a few students to top medical schools in the West. This gives the elite access to advanced technology—from X rays to life support systems—while the poor of these nations go without even basic medical services and continue to die at an early age.

Establishing a Monopoly on U.S. Health Care

Let's turn our focus onto medicine in the Unites States. How did medicine become the largest business in the country? How did it become the only legal monopoly in the United States? To find the answers, we need to understand how medicine became professionalized.

As hard as it is to believe, doctors used to be available at the beck and call of patients. They would come to a patient's home, diagnose the illness, prescribe medication, and even sit up all night with the critically ill—all for a modest fee. This photo is from the 1950s.

professionalization of medicine the development of medicine into a field in which education becomes rigorous, and in which physicians claim a theoretical understanding of illness, regulate themselves, claim to be doing a service to society (rather than just following self-interest), and take authority over clients

The Professionalization of Medicine Imagine that you are living in the American colonies in the 1700s and that you want to become a physician. There are no required courses. No entrance exams. In fact, there are no medical schools. You won't have to have *any* education at all. You'll simply ask a physician to train you. In return for the opportunity to learn, you'll be his assistant and will help him with menial tasks. When *you* think that you have learned enough, you'll hang out a shingle and proclaim yourself a doctor. The process is much the same as what an automobile mechanic goes through today. In fact, you can even skip the apprenticeship if you wish, and simply hang out your shingle—just like a mechanic. If you can convince people you are good, you'll make a living. If not, you'll turn to something else.

Let's consider what developed in the 1800s. A few medical schools opened, and there was some licensing of physicians. Medical schools, however, were like religions are today; they competed for clients and made different claims to the truth. That is, one medical school would have a particular idea about what caused illness and how to treat it, while another medical school would disagree and would teach different ideas about these vital matters. Training was short (often, not even a high school diploma was required). There was no clinical training, and lectures went unchanged from year to year. Even the medical school at Harvard University took only two school years to complete—and the school year lasted only four months (Starr 1982; Rosenberg 1987; Riessman 1994).

Then came the 1900s. In 1906, there were 160 medical schools in the United States. The American Medical Association (AMA) evaluated them and found 82 of them to be acceptable (Starr 1982). The Carnegie Foundation asked Abraham Flexner, a renowned educator, to visit these schools. Even the most inadequate institutions opened their doors to him, for they thought that gifts from the Carnegie Foundation would follow (Rodash 1982). Flexner found glaring problems. In some schools, the laboratories consisted only of "a few vagrant test tubes squirreled away in a cigar box." Other schools had libraries with no books. Flexner (1910) recommended that admissions and teaching standards be raised and that philanthropies fund the most promising schools. Those schools that were funded upgraded their facilities and were able to attract more capable faculty and students. Most of the other schools, left with inadequate funds and few students, had to close their doors.

The Flexner report led to the **professionalization of medicine.** When sociologists use the term *profession,* they mean something quite specific. What happened was that physicians began to (1) undergo a rigorous education; (2) claim a theoretical understanding of illness; (3) regulate themselves; (4) claim that they were performing a service for society (rather than just following self-interest); and (5) take authority over clients (Goode 1960).

The Monopoly of Medicine When medicine became a profession, it also became a monopoly, and this is the key to understanding our current situation. The group that gained control over U.S. medicine set itself up as *the* medical establishment. This group was able to get laws passed to restrict medical licensing to graduates of approved schools. By controlling the education and licensing of physicians, the medical establishment silenced most competing philosophies of medicine. The WASP males who took control also either refused to admit women and minorities to medical schools or severly limited their enrollment.

Eliminating the competition paved the way for medicine to become big business. The monoploy was so thorough that by law only a select group of men—a sort of priesthood of medicine—were allowed to diagnose and treat medical problems. Only they knew what was right for people's health. Only they could scribble the secret language (Latin) on special pieces of parchment (prescription forms) for translators (pharmacists) to decipher (Miner 1995). This select group was able to shape itself into the most lucrative profession in the country—for its members set their own fees and had little competition. This group of men became so powerful that it was even able to take childbirth away from midwives—the focus of the following Down-to-Earth sociology box.

Sociology

Down-to-Earth

TO ESTABLISH A MONOPOLY, ELIMINATE YOUR COMPETITION: HOW PHYSICIANS DEFEATED MIDWIVES

Midwifery helps us understand the professionalization of medicine and provides insight into the founding of the U.S. medical establishment. In the United States, as in Europe and elsewhere, pregnancy and childbirth were considered natural events, and women were thought best equipped to help other women deal with them. Consequently, midwives delivered babies. Some midwives were trained; others were simply neighborhood women who had experience in childbirth. In many European countries, midwives were licensed by the state—as they still are.

As medicine professionalized, physicians wanted to expand their business. Their desire for expansion, however, ran up against two major problems. First, they didn't know anything about delivering babies. It was considered indecent for a man to know much about pregnancy, much less to help a woman give birth. Second, childbirth was controlled by midwives, whom physicians came to see as business competitors.

They solved these problems. They bribed midwives so they could sneak into the bedrooms where women were giving birth. To say "sneaked" is no exaggeration, for some physicians crawled on their hands and knees so that the mother-to-be wouldn't know a man was present. Many midwives refused to let them in, however, and most physicians had to train with mannequins. Gradually, physicians gained admission to childbirth, but a veil of indecency persisted; doctors had to fumble blindly under a sheet in a dark room, their head decorously turned aside.

As physicians grew more powerful politically, they launched a ruthless campaign against their

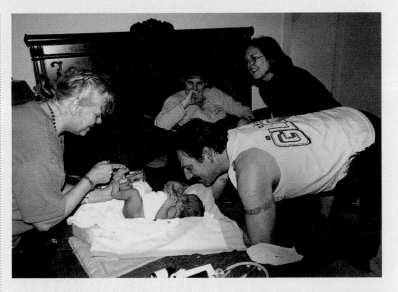

The text discusses how physicians were able to eliminate their competition in delivering babies. In some states, midwives have made a comeback. Shown here is a midwife after she delivers a baby at the parent's home.

competitors. They attacked midwives as "dirty, ignorant, and incompetent," even calling them a "menace to the health of the community." Using their new political clout in the AMA, physicians succeeded in persuading many states to pass laws that made it illegal for anyone but a physician to deliver babies. Some states, however, continued to allow nurse-midwives to practice. The struggle is not yet over, and nurse-midwives and physicians still clash over who has the right to deliver babies.

Conflict theorists emphasize that this was a gender struggle— men sought to take control over what had been women's work. They stress that political power was central to how physicians expanded their domain. Symbolic interactionists, without denying the political aspect, stress the so-

cial construction of reality. The key, they say, is how pregnancy and childbirth were redefined so that it was no longer a natural event but a medical condition. To eliminate midwives, physicians launched a campaign of images, stressing that pregnancy and childbirth were not normal conditions. Their new definition, which flew in the face of the millennia-old tradition of women helping women to have babies, transformed pregnancy and childbirth from a natural process to a "medical condition" that required the assistance of an able man. When this new definition made childbirth "men's work," the prestige of the work went up—and so did the price. ■

Sources: Wertz and Wertz 1981; Rodash 1982; Danzi 1989; Rothman 1994.

fee-for-service payment to a physician to diagnose and treat a patient's medical problems

epidemiology the study of disease and disability patterns in a population

Figure 19.3

THE TOP TEN CAUSES OF DEATH IN THE UNITED STATES, 1900 AND 1996

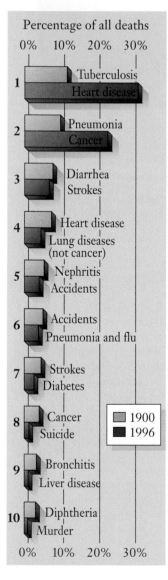

Percentage of all deaths

	1900	1996
1	Tuberculosis	Heart disease
2	Pneumonia	Cancer
3	Diarrhea	Strokes
4	Heart disease	Lung diseases (not cancer)
5	Nephritis	Accidents
6	Accidents	Pneumonia and flu
7	Strokes	Diabetes
8	Cancer	Suicide
9	Bronchitis	Liver disease
10	Diphtheria	Murder

Source: Statistical Abstract 1999: Table 139.

This approach, **fee-for-service** (payment to a physician in exchange for diagnosis and treatment)—which made medicine a *business*—usually went unquestioned. Then, as monopolies do, the medical monopoly drove up the price of health care. This led to a public outcry: Because the poor can't afford medical treatment, the government should pay for it. The AMA fought every proposal for the government to fund medical treatment. Physicians were convinced that government funding would "socialize" medicine, that it would eliminate the fee for service and turn them into government employees.

In the 1960s, proponents of government funding won out. *Medicaid* (government-paid medical care for the poor) and *Medicare* (government-sponsored medical insurance for the elderly) were begun. Physicians' fears proved groundless. Instead of leading to the socialization of medicine, these programs gave physicians millions of additional customers. People who previously could not afford medical services now had their medical expenses covered by the government. As Figure 13.5 on page 370 illustrates, these programs have become extremely expensive—and they put millions of dollars into physicians' pockets.

From its humble origins, medicine has grown into the largest business in the United States. This business consists not only of physicians, but also of nurses, physician extenders, hospital personnel, pharmacists, the manufacturers and sales forces of medical technology, insurance and pharmaceutical companies, and Wall Street corporations that own hospitals and nursing homes. The medical monopoly is so powerful that it not only wages national advertising campaigns to drum up customers but also lobbies all the state legislatures and the U.S. Congress. Like sports, some hospitals even pay million-dollar sign-up bonuses to lure big-name surgeons (McCartney 1993).

HISTORICAL PATTERNS OF HEALTH

Let's look at how health and illness in the United States have changed. This will take us into the field of **epidemiology,** the study of how medical disorders are distributed throughout a population.

Physical Health

Leading Causes of Death One way to see how the physical health of Americans has changed is to compare the leading causes of death in two time periods. To get an idea of how dramatic this change is, look at Figure 19.3. Note that half of the leading causes of death in 1900 don't even appear on today's list. Heart disease and cancer, which placed fourth and eighth in 1900, have now jumped to the top of the list, while tuberculosis and diarrhea, which were the number one and number three killers in 1900 don't even show up in today's top ten. Similarly, murder and suicide didn't make the top ten in 1900, but they do now. These shifts indicate that extensive changes have occurred in society. Disease, then, is not only a biological event. It is also *social,* following the contours of social change.

Were Americans Healthier in the Past? A second way to see how the physical health of Americans has changed is to ask if they are healthier—or sicker—than they used to be. This question brings us face to face with the definitional problem discussed earlier. "Healthy" by whose standards? An additional problem is that many of today's diseases went unrecognized in the past. One way around these problems is to look at mortality. If Americans used to live longer, we can assume they were healthier. Because most people today live longer than their ancestors, however, we can conclude that contemporary Americans are healthier.

Some may think this conclusion flies in the face of abundant evidence to the contrary: polluted air and water, and the high rates of heart disease and cancer shown in Figure 19.3. And it does. Sometimes older people say, "When I was a kid, cancer wasn't even around. I never knew anyone who died from cancer, and now it seems everyone does." What they overlook is that most cancers strike older people, and when life expectancy is shorter there is less chance that people will die from cancer. Also, in the past most cancer went unrecognized. People were simply said to have died of "old age" or "heart failure."

Mental Health

When it comes to mental health, we have no way to make good comparisons. We may picture a past in which the elderly had lower suicide rates, less mental illness, and so on, but we need solid measures of mental illness or mental health, not anecdotes. The idyllic past—where everyone grew up in a happy home with two loving parents, married for life, and lived in harmony with the rest of the world—never existed. All groups have their share of mental problems—and commonsense beliefs that mental illness is worse today represent a perception, not measured reality. Such perceptions may be true, of course, but the *opposite* could also be true. Since we don't even know how extensive mental illness is today (Miller 1993), we certainly can't judge how much there was in the past.

*I*SSUES IN HEALTH CARE

Let's turn to issues in health care in the United States.

Medical Care: A Right or a Commodity?

A primary controversy in the United States is whether or not medical care is a right or a privilege. If it is a right, then all citizens should have easy access to good medical care. If it is a privilege, then, as with automobiles, clothing, and other commodities, the rich will have access to one type of care, the poor to another. Currently, medical care is not the right of citizens, but a commodity to be sold at the highest price. Those with the money can buy better quality, while the poor and uninsured must go without—or wait for handouts. This is the concern that underlies what have until now been futile attempts to institute national medical care.

Related to this issue is the skyrocketing cost of medical care, shown in Figure 19.4. In 1960, the average American spent just $150 a year on health care. Today that figure is $4,000. In 1960, a 17-inch black-and-white television also cost about $150. If television prices had risen at the same rate as health care, a 17-inch *black-and-white* television would now cost about $4,000. Several factors have fueled medical costs, including a larger segment of the population that is elderly, and the new, expensive high technology. Because health care is considered a commodity, the result is a *two-tier system of medical care*—superior care for those who can afford the cost, and inferior care for those who cannot.

Social Inequality

The opening vignette, which described the nude man in the homeless shelter who was being taken to the state mental hospital, lays bare the two-tier system of medical care. A middle-class or rich person who had mental problems would go to a private psychiatrist, not to a state mental hospital.

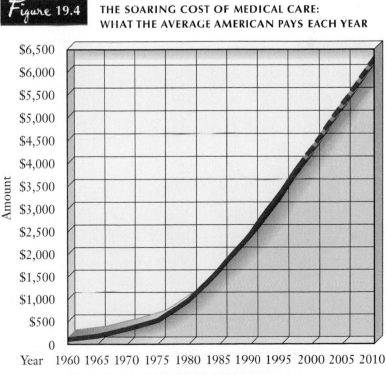

Figure 19.4 THE SOARING COST OF MEDICAL CARE: WHAT THE AVERAGE AMERICAN PAYS EACH YEAR

The broken line is the author's estimate.

Source: Statistical Abstract 1999:Table 165 (and earlier years).

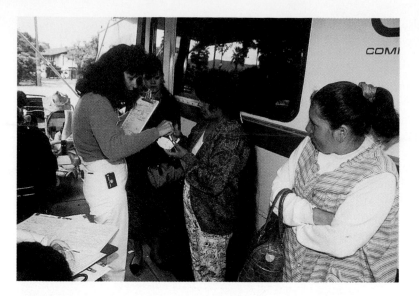

Because the U.S. medical system often bypasses the poor, some cities send mobile medical vans to poverty areas. This Los Angeles nurse is giving out birth control information.

deinstitutionalization the release of patients from mental hospitals into the community, supposedly while receiving treatment within a network of outpatient services

Figure 19.5 NUMBER OF DAYS SICK

Note: Number of days people were so sick or injured that they cut down on their usual activities for more than half a day; includes days off work and school.

Source: Statistical Abstract 1999:Table 222.

Of course, he or she would not have been in that shelter in the first place.

Since 1939, sociologists have found an inverse correlation between mental problems and social class. In other words, the lower the social class, the higher the proportion of serious mental problems. This finding has been confirmed in numerous studies (Faris and Dunham 1939; Hudson 1988; Ortega and Corzine 1990; Ross and Willigen 1997). Sociologists have little difficulty understanding why people in the lower social classes have greater mental problems, for these people bear the stresses that come with poverty. Compared with middle- and upper-class Americans, the poor have less job security, lower wages, more unpaid bills and insistent bill collectors, more divorce, greater vulnerability to crime, more alcoholism, more violence, and more physical illness. Such conditions deal severe blows to people's emotional well-being.

In the 1960s, politicians and psychiatrists came up with a policy called **deinstitutionalization.** The plan was to open the locked wards of state mental hospitals, release the patients, and provide them with community-based services—counseling and medications—so they could adjust to life outside the mental hospital. The patients were released, but the outpatient services were not put in place. As a result, U.S. streets were flooded with former mental patients who had no income and nowhere to go. The streets became their home.

Needless to say, these were poor people. Members of the middle and upper classes who had mental problems were counseled by private psychiatrists and, if hospitalized, went to expensive private mental hospitals. The rich were treated with "talk" therapy (various forms of psychotherapy), while the poor were given "medicinal straitjackets" (medication to sedate them).

When it comes to physical illnesses, we find similar inequalities among the social classes. As Figure 19.5 shows, the poor are more likely to become ill. Unlike the middle and upper classes, however, few poor people have a personal physician, and they are likely to spend hours waiting in crowded public health clinics. After waiting most of a day, some don't even get to see a doctor; they are simply told to come back the next day (Fialka 1993). Finally, when hospitalized, the poor are likely to find themselves in understaffed and underfunded public hospitals, where they are treated by rotating interns who do not know them and cannot follow up on their progress.

Malpractice Suits and Defensive Medicine

Some analysts have observed that physicians used to kill more patients than they cured. Given that physicians didn't know about germs and didn't wash before surgery or childbirth, this may be true. In the 1800s, doctors thought that sickness was caused by "bad fluids," and they had four techniques for getting rid of these fluids: (1) bleeding (cutting a vein and draining out bad blood); (2) blistering (making the bad pus come to the surface by applying packs so hot they burned the skin); (3) vomiting (feeding patients liquids that made them vomit up the bad fluids); and

(4) purging (feeding patients substances that caused diarrhea).

In light of today's vastly superior technology and treatment, one might think malpractice suits would be a thing of the past. The opposite, however, is true. Back then, the law didn't allow patients to recover damages. "People make mistakes" was the thinking, and that included doctors. Today, in contrast, physicians are held to much higher standards—some say to impossible ones. Damage awards are high, and doctors are anxious. One physician told me, "I'm looking for something else to do, because medicine is no longer fun. Every time I treat a patient, I wonder if this is the one who is going to turn around and sue me."

To protect themselves, physicians practice **defensive medicine**. They consult with colleagues and order lab tests not because the patient needs them but because they want to leave a paper trail in case they are sued. These consultations and tests—done for the doctor's benefit, not the patient's—add several billion dollars to the nation's annual medical bill (Volti 1995). To reduce the costs of defensive medicine, the state of Maine has instituted physician checklists. If doctors follow them, malpractice suits are dismissed (Felsenthal 1993). Although physicians complain about a "paint-by-numbers" or cookbook approach to medicine, many prefer this to the threat of lawsuits.

What cigarette do you smoke, Doctor?

If you were to follow a doctor on his rounds, you'd have a busy time keeping up with him!

He's accustomed to being called out in the middle of the night. His days are often 24 hours long!

So, time out for doctors often means just long enough to enjoy a cigarette! And doctors, too, are particular about the brand they choose!

In a nationwide survey, 113,597 doctors were asked, "What cigarette do you smoke, Doctor?" The brand named most was Camel!

Repeated Nationwide Surveys Show:

More Doctors Smoke Camels
than any other cigarette!

"WHAT cigarette do you smoke?" 113,597 doctors were asked that question a few years ago. The brand named most was Camel. Since then, repeated cross-sectional surveys have been made and *every time* Camel has been first choice!

Smoke the cigarette so many doctors enjoy! Smoke only Camels for 30 days and see how much you enjoy Camel's rich flavor . . . see how well Camels agree with your throat, week after week!

START YOUR OWN 30-DAY TEST TODAY

Medical Incompetence

We've probably all heard stories about surgeons who removed the wrong leg or breast. Do such things really happen? Although not an everyday event, they do happen. And when they do, doctors and hospitals, to preserve their reputations, do their best to hush up the matter. They settle quietly—and generously—out of court, with the stipulation that the matter will not be publicized.

Are some malpractice suits unfair? Certainly. Some doctors are sued for trivial matters, others for matters over which they have no control. Yet, despite the rigors of medical education, medical incompetence is extensive and fatal. The Institute of Medicine, a branch of the National Academy of Sciences, reports that each year between 44,000 and 98,000 Americans die at the hands of doctors. *If the number of Americans killed by medical errors were an official classification of death, it would rank as one of the top ten leading causes of death* (Bazell 1999; Lemonick 1999).

Many proposals have been made to reduce these needless deaths (what the medical profession calls "adverse events"). One is that the patient and doctor sign their names in ink at the point where an incision is to be made, so no doctor will lop off the wrong arm, leg, or breast. Because many patients die from cross-reactions of prescription drugs, some suggest that doctors enter all prescriptions online. A computer program would check patient records, causing the monitor to flash a warning if a doctor tries to prescribe a drug that will interfere with other medications.

These proposals have merit, but perhaps the proposal that gets at the heart of the matter is the one made by the Institute of Medicine. It recommends that we establish a federal

Although this ad strikes us as strange, in the 1950s newspapers and magazines were filled with testimonials about how cigarettes were good for people's health. They were even said to "soothe the throat." The health hazards of smoking were not unknown at this time. Today's cigarette advertising may be more subtle, but it has the same intent—to seduce the young into smoking, and to assure current smokers that it is all right to continue.

defensive medicine medical practices done not for the patient's benefit but in order to protect a physician from malpractice suits

Center for Patient Safety. All medical deaths and injuries would be reported to the Center. Just as the Federal Aviation Agency investigates each plane crash, the Center would investigate each medical injury and death. Based on the cause it pinpointed, it would set up guidelines designed to reduce the number of similar events.

Depersonalization: The Medical Cash Machine

One of the main criticisms leveled against the medical profession is **depersonalization**, the practice of dealing with people as though they were cases and diseases, not individuals. Many patients have the impression that they are being treated by a cash machine—a physician who, while talking to them, is impatiently counting minutes and tabulating dollars so that he or she can move on to the next customer and make more dollars. After all, extra time spent with a patient is money down the drain.

Sociologist Sue Fisher (1986), who was examined for an ovarian mass, gives this account:

> On my initial visit a nurse called me into an examination room, asked me to undress, gave me a paper gown to put on and told me the doctor would be with me soon. I was stunned. Was I not even to see the doctor before undressing? . . . How could I present myself as a competent, knowledgeable person sitting undressed on the examining table? But I had a potentially cancerous growth, so I did as I had been told.
>
> In a few minutes the nurse returned and said, "Lie down. The doctor is coming." Again I complied. The doctor entered the examining room, nodded in my direction while reading my chart, and proceeded to examine me without ever having spoken to me.

Participant observation of medical students at McMaster University in Canada by sociologists Jack Haas and William Shaffir (1993) provides insight into how physicians learn to depersonalize patients. Haas and Shaffir found that students begin medical school wanting to "treat the whole person." As vast amounts of material are thrown at them, their feelings for patients are overpowered by the need to be efficient. This student's statement illustrates the change in attitude:

> Somebody will say, "Listen to Mrs. Jones's heart. It's just a little thing flubbing on the table." And *you forget about the rest of her* . . . and it helps in learning in the sense that you can go in to a patient, put your stethoscope on the heart, listen to it, and walk out. . . . The advantage is that *you can go in a short time and see a patient, get the important things out of the patient, and leave* (italics added).

Another student's statement illustrates the extent to which patients become objects.

> You don't know the people that are under anesthesia—just practice putting the tube in, and the person wakes up with a sore throat, and well, it's just sort of a part of the procedure. . . . Someone comes in who has croaked (and you say), "Well, come on. Here is a chance to practice your intubation" (inserting a tube in the throat).

Conflict of Interest

As part of her treatment for cancer, Julia Lippman needed intravenous feeding at home. Her doctor told her to cancel the arrangements she had made with a company that provided such services and to use a company called T^2 instead. If she didn't, he added, he would not be responsible for her treatment. It turned out that he had invested in T^2 (Rodwin 1993).

The medical cash machine generates conflicts of interest. A physician may make hidden income by choosing one course of treatment instead of another or by referring a patient to a hospital, pharmacy, or medical supply company of which he or she is part owner. Some drug companies pay for physicians to go on golf outings and river cruises. Others award doctors all-expense-paid trips to conferences (Zuger 1999). Such conflicts of inter-

depersonalization dealing with people as though they were objects; in the case of medical care, as though patients were merely cases and diseases, not persons

est make it difficult to know if a doctor has based a course of treatment on the patient's best interest or on the best interest of the doctor's bank account.

Medical Fraud

With 2 million Medicare claims filed every day, a physician with Medicare patients is not likely to be audited. Many physicians have not been able to resist the temptation to cheat. The following are not isolated incidents—they are just some of the most outrageous.

> . . . [D]octors have been caught billing for services on persons who were dead. . . . [A] psychiatrist in California charged Medicaid for sexual liaisons with a patient. . . . Another doctor billed for abortions on women who were not pregnant, including one who had a hysterectomy. . . . (He even claimed he performed) two abortions within a month on the same patient. . . . (Another doctor billed Medicare for) treating a 22-year-old for diaper rash (Geis et al. 1995:248).

Medical suppliers have also been guilty of outrageous fraud. A wheelchair van service, for example, billed Medicare $62,000 for just one patient, who supposedly made a $260 trip every two days for sixteen months. But worse yet is medical fraud that endangers people's lives, as was the case with the pharmacists who sold expired pacemakers (Schatz 1995) and the ophthalmologist who, in an attempt to pocket an extra $14,000, performed unnecessary eye operations that left fourteen people with impaired vision (Geis et al. 1995).

Sexism in Medicine

Although usually quite subtle (often, people are not even aware it exists), sexism in medicine can carry serious consequences. As we saw in the Down-to-Earth Sociology box on page 298, physicians don't take women's health complaints as seriously as they do men's. As a result, women with heart disease are operated on at a later stage, making it more likely that they will die from their surgery.

Bias *against* women's reproductive organs has also been reported. Sue Fisher (1986), whose encounter with depersonalized medicine was cited earlier, did participant observation in a hospital. When she heard doctors recommend total hysterectomy (removal of both the uterus and the ovaries) although no cancer was present, she asked why. The doctors explained that the uterus and ovaries are "potentially disease-producing" organs. Also, they said, they are unnecessary after the childbearing years, so why not remove them?

Since few women feel the same way, in order to make money surgeons have to "sell" the operation. Here is how one resident explained it to sociologist Diana Scully (1994):

> You have to look for your surgical procedures; you have to go after patients. Because no one is crazy enough to come and say, "Hey, here I am. I want you to operate on me." You have to sometimes convince the patient that she is really sick—if she is, of course [laughs], and that she is better off with a surgical procedure.

To "convince" a woman to have this surgery, the doctor tells her that, unfortunately, the examination has turned up fibroids in her uterus—and they *might* turn into cancer. This statement is often sufficient, for it frightens women, who picture themselves becoming terminally ill. To clinch the sale, the surgeon withholds the rest of the truth—that the fibroids probably will not turn into cancer and that there are a variety of nonsurgical alternatives.

Underlying this sexism is male dominance of medicine in the United States. This is not a worldwide phenomenon. For example, while only one of four U.S. physicians is a woman, in the former Soviet Union three out of four physicians are women (Knaus 1981; *Statistical Abstract* 1999:Table 675). The sex ratio is changing. In 1970, only 8 percent of U.S. medical degrees went to women. Today it is 41 percent (*Statistical Abstract* 1999:Table 333). This change should reduce sexism in medical practice, including that described in the Down-to-Earth Sociology box on the next page.

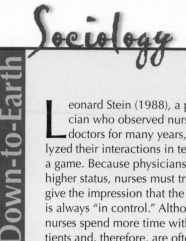

Sociology

THE DOCTOR-NURSE GAME

Leonard Stein (1988), a physician who observed nurses and doctors for many years, analyzed their interactions in terms of a game. Because physicians have higher status, nurses must try to give the impression that the doctor is always "in control." Although nurses spend more time with patients and, therefore, are often more familiar with their needs, nurses can never be perceived as making recommendations to a doctor. Consequently, nurses disguise their recommendations. Consider the following dialog between a nurse and a resident physician whom the nurse has called at 1 A.M. The rotating resident does not know the patient.

"This is Dr. Jones." (*an open and direct communication*)

"Dr. Jones, this is Nurse Smith on 2W. Mrs. Brown learned today that her father died, and she is unable to fall asleep." (*This apparently direct, open communication of factual information—that the*

patient is unable to sleep and has learned of a death in the family— *contains a hidden recommendation. The nurse has diagnosed the cause of the sleeplessness and is suggesting that a sedative be prescribed.*)

The conversation continues: "What sleeping medication has been helpful to Mrs. Brown in the past?" (*This communication, supposedly a mere request for facts, is actually a request for a recommendation of what to prescribe.*)

"Pentobarbital, 100 milligrams, was quite effective the night before last." (*This is actually a specific recommendation from the nurse to the physician, but it comes disguised in the form of factual information.*)

"Pentobarbital, 100 milligrams before bedtime, as needed for sleep. Got it?" (*This communication is spoken with audible authority—a little louder, a little firmer.*)

"Yes, I have, and thank you very much, doctor."

The two have successfully played the doctor-nurse game. The lower-status person has made a recommendation to the higher-status person in a covert manner that required neither of them to acknowledge what really occurred and that did not threaten their relative statuses.

When I interviewed Stein, he said that the doctor-nurse game is breaking down because of the larger number of men in nursing, because of the feminist movement, which is challenging male authority, and because of the growing number of women physicians. As a consequence, nurses are less subservient, and physicians are less able to exert unquestioned authority.

Some version of the game will continue to be played, however, as long as status differences remain. The rules will simply be modified to meet changing circumstances. ■

The Medicalization of Society

As we have seen, childbirth and women's reproductive organs have come to be defined as medical matters. Sociologists use the term **medicalization** to refer to the process of turning something that was not previously considered a medical issue into a medical matter. Examples include acne, anxiety, balding, depression, sagging buttocks and chins, small breasts, weight, and wrinkles. The most notable example of recent years is "penile dysfunction," the subject of the Mass Media box on the next page.

Symbolic interactionists would stress that there is nothing inherently medical in such human conditions. People used to define them as normal problems of life, yet now we tend to consider it natural for them to be viewed as medical concerns. Functionalists would stress that medicalization helps the medical establishment by broadening its customer base. They also would point out that medicalization provides people with someone who will listen to their problems, and that sometimes they are helped by this. Conflict sociologists would argue that this process is another indication of the growing power of the medical establishment: The more conditions of life that physicians can medicalize, the greater their profits and power.

Medically Assisted Suicide

I started the intravenous dripper, which released a salt solution through a needle into her vein, and I kept her arm tied down so she wouldn't jerk it. This was difficult as her veins were fragile.

medicalization the transformation of something into a matter to be treated by physicians

Mass Media in Social Life

VIAGRA ON THE INTERNET

The event made the six o'clock news, was headlined around the world, and became the topic of countless talk shows. Probably only a cure for cancer would have garnered this much attention. In a short time, almost everyone, even schoolchildren, knew about Viagra, the marvel of technology designed to help men with erectile problems. Viagra also quickly became an abused drug. It gained a reputation as a recreational aphrodisiac for men who had no erectile dysfunction, one that would enable them to prolong lovemaking.

Obtaining Viagra legally requires a physician's prescription, which can be purchased for between $35 and $50, the price of an office visit. This has made Viagra a gold mine for doctors. A few of the more venturesome ones have even found out how to use the new technology to expand their profitable pill pushing: They offer on-line services. To see how it works, go on the Internet and search for "Viagra." Several sites will appear that offer this legal drug. First you'll be asked to answer yes or no to just 4 questions. (Who knows? An online physician may even read what you put down on your questionnaire.) Then you'll pay $75 for the doctor's "consulting" fee (this keeps it legal), plus you'll pay a prescription fee. *You* will pick your dosage and the number of pills you want. You may have to lie and say that you have erectile dysfunction, but as long as you have a valid credit card, for another $37.50 to $427.50 (plus delivery fee) UPS will deliver Viagra right to your front door.

As ads continue to tout the benefits of this drug, the profits pile up. They are so great that Pfizer, the company that produces Viagra, has been able to hire former vice president and presidential candidate Bob Dole to pitch the drug. ■

For Your Consideration

What is your opinion about physicians offering Viagara on the Internet to people they have never seen? Do you think we should allow all prescription drugs to be sold this way? If not, which ones should we allow? Why?

And then once she decided she was ready to go, she just hit the switch and the device cut off the saline drip and through the needle released a solution of thiopental that put her to sleep in ten to fifteen seconds. A minute later, through the needle flowed a lethal solution of potassium chloride. (Jack Kevorkian, as quoted in Denzin 1992)

The topic of suicide fascinates the U.S. public. A how-to book on suicide, *Final Exit,* sold more than a half million copies. The Hemlock Society, a group that advocates voluntary **euthanasia** (mercy killing) for terminally ill people, has grown to eighty chapters. Oregon passed a law allowing medically assisted suicide, which opponents call legalized murder (Smith 1999).

With new technology that can keep the body alive even after the heart, lungs, and other vital organs no longer function on their own, a burning question that has yet to be answered is, "Who has the right to pull the plug?" Should someone's body be kept alive for years even though his or her mind is no longer functioning? To resolve this issue, some people sign a **living will**—a declaration, made while they are still in good health, about what they want medical personnel to do in case they become dependent on artificial life support systems.

Our technology and the acts of Kevorkian have brought us face to face with matters of death that are both disturbing and unresolved. Should "medically assisted suicide" be legal? Few find this medical-ethical issue easy to resolve. The following Thinking Critically section explores these issues.

> **euthanasia** mercy killing
>
> **living will** a statement people in good health sign that clearly expresses their feelings about being kept alive on artificial life support systems

Shown here is Dr. Jack Kevorkian at one of his trials in Michigan. Because of the deaths he assisted, Kevorkian became the most controversial M.D. in the United States. He also became known as "Dr. Death."

Thinking Critically

SHOULD DOCTORS BE ALLOWED TO KILL PATIENTS?

Euthanasia is a hot topic among both medical professionals and the lay public. Articles on euthanasia regularly appear in the print media and on television, designed, some say, to provide information, or, as others claim, to subtly condition the U.S. public to accept the practice. Except for the name, this is a true story:

> Bill Simpson, who was in his seventies, had battled leukemia for years. After doctors removed his spleen, he developed an abdominal abscess. It took another operation to drain it. A week later, the abscess filled, and Bill required more surgery. Again the abscess returned. Simpson began to drift in and out of consciousness. His brother-in-law suggested euthanasia. The surgeon injected a lethal dose of morphine into Simpson's intravenous feeding tubes.

At a medical conference in which euthanasia was discussed, a cancer specialist (oncologist) who had treated thousands of end-stage patients, announced that he had kept count of the patients who had asked him to help them die. "There were 127 men and women," he said. Then he added, "And I saw to it that 25 of them got their wish." Thousands of other physicians have done the same (Nuland 1995).

To end a patient's life by taking active measures such as injecting a lethal drug is called *active euthanasia*. To withhold life support (nutrients or liquids) is called *passive euthanasia*. To remove life support by, for instance, disconnecting a patient's oxygen supply, often falls somewhere in between. The end result, of course, is the same.

The public seems to hold two dominant images of people who undergo euthanasia. One image is of an individual who is devastated by chronic pain being assisted by a doctor who mercifully helps to end that pain by performing euthanasia. The second is of a brain-dead individual—a human vegetable—who lies in a hospital bed, alone, with no possible future, kept alive only by machines. How accurate are these images?

In Holland euthanasia remains illegal, but it is practiced openly. In 1984, the Royal Dutch Medical Association set standards for euthanasia, and the government honors those standards.

The results have been studied thoroughly (Shapiro 1997). Although physicians must report the deaths in which they assist, two of three go unreported (Keown and van der Wal 1999). In a study of 3,200 physician-assisted deaths, one-fifth took place without the patient's consent. Most of these patients were in a coma, but in one case a physician ended the life of a patient with breast cancer who said that she did not want euthanasia. In the doctor's words, "It could have taken another week before she died. I needed this bed" (Hendin et al. 1997).

Some Dutch, concerned that if they have a medical emergency they may be euthanized, carry "passports" that instruct medical personnel that they wish to live. Most Dutch support euthanasia, however, and more carry another "passport," one that instructs medical personnel to carry out euthanasia (Shapiro 1997).

In the United States, Oregon made assisted suicide legal in 1997. The next year, doctors helped only fifteen people commit suicide. Not one was suffering from intractable pain. Instead, these individuals felt that they would become dependent in the future, and they chose death rather than future dependence (Smith 1999).

Dr. Jack Kevorkian, the author of the quote that opened this section, was a Michigan pathologist (he didn't treat patients; he studied diseased tissues). Kevorkian decided that regardless of the laws, doctors had the right to help people commit suicide. He did—120 times. He provided the poison as well as a machine to administer it, and watched while the patient pulled the lever. But he never touched that lever. He left bodies in motels and in vans, and dropped them off at hospitals.

Michigan prosecutors tried Kevorkian for murder four times but couldn't get a jury to convict him. Then, in 1998 Kevorkian played a videotape on national television, showing him giving a lethal injection to a man who was dying from Lou Gehrig's disease. Prosecutors impounded the tape and put Kevorkian on trial again. Kevorkian was convicted of second degree murder and was sentenced to 10 to 25 years in prison. ■

For Your Consideration

If Kevorkian had lived in Oregon, he could have legally killed people any time they asked him to do so. But he couldn't have done so in Michigan—or in any of the other states. Do you think Michigan or Oregon is right? Why? Do you think the rest of the nation will follow Oregon's path? Do the findings concerning doctor-assisted deaths in Holland and Oregon justify medically assisted suicide?

Finally, as is evident in Holland, physician-assisted deaths have a way of expanding. In addition to what is reported here, Dutch doctors also kill newborn babies that have serious birth defects (Smith 1999). Their justification is "quality of life." What do you think?

Sources: Gomez 1991; Markson 1992; Angell 1996; Smith 1999.

Curbing Costs: Issues in Private and National Health Insurance

We have seen some of the reasons why the price of medical care in the United States has soared: advanced—and expensive—technology for diagnosis and treatment, a growing elderly population, tests performed as defensive measures rather than for medical reasons, and health care that is regarded as a commodity to be sold to the highest bidder. As long as these conditions are in place, the price of medical care will continue to outpace inflation. Let's look at some attempts to reduce costs.

HMOs **Health maintenance organizations,** or **HMOs,** are medical companies that negotiate an annual fee in exchange for providing medical care for a corporation's employees. Whatever is left over at the end of the year is the HMO's profit. If they bid too low, they lose money. While this arrangement eliminates unnecessary medical treatment, it also puts pressure on doctors to reduce *necessary* treatment.

The results are anything but pretty. Over her doctor's strenuous objections, a friend of mine was discharged from the hospital even though she was still bleeding and running a fever. Her HMO representative said he would not authorize another day in the hospital. A lung specialist in Washington Heights, New York, fought with his HMO for three hours to get permission to do a procedure on a woman who was coughing up life-threatening amounts of blood (Steinhauer 1999). After a heart attack, a man in Kansas City, Missouri, needed surgery that could be performed only at Barnes Hospital in St. Louis, Missouri. The HMO said, "Too bad. That hospital is out of our service area." The man died while appealing the HMO decision (Spragins 1996).

The basic question, of course, is: At what human cost do we reduce spending on medical treatment?

Diagnosis-Related Groups To curb spiraling costs, the federal government has classified all illnesses into 468 diagnosis-related-groups (DRGs) and has specified the amount that it will pay for the treatment of each illness. Hospitals make a profit only if they move patients through the system quickly. If patients are discharged before the hospital has spent

health maintenance organization (HMO) a health care organization that provides medical treatment to its members for a fixed annual cost

FRANK & ERNEST by ® Bob Thaves

The cartoonist has captured an unfortunate reality of U.S. medicine.

the allotted amount, the hospital makes money. One consequence is that some patients are discharged before they are fully ready to go home. Others are refused admittance because they appear to have a "worse than average" case of a particular illness. In other words, they would cost the hospital money instead of making it a profit (Easterbrook 1987; Feinglass 1987).

National Health Insurance

A young woman who was five months pregnant was taken to a hospital complaining of stomach pains. The hospital refused to admit her, because she had no money or credit. As they were about to transfer her to a hospital for the poor, she gave birth. The baby was stillborn. The hospital went ahead and transferred the woman—dead baby, umbilical cord, and all.

In Somerville, Tennessee, Terry Takewell, drenched with sweat from a fever, was rushed to Methodist Hospital. It turned out he had an outstanding bill of $9,400. The hospital administrator went to Takewell's room, helped him to his feet, and escorted him to the parking lot. Neighbors found him under a tree and took him home. Takewell died about twelve hours later. (Ansberry 1988)

Dumping, the practice of refusing to treat unprofitable patients and sending them to public hospitals, is one consequence of a system that focuses on turning a profit on patient care. Most cases are less dramatic than that of the woman and her stillborn baby or that of Takewell's needless death, but the same principle applies. With 43 million Americans—primarily the poor—uninsured (*Statistical Abstract* 1999:Table 185), pressure has grown for the government to provide national health insurance. The Social Map below shows how the uninsured are distributed among the states.

Advocates point out that national health insurance will reduce costs by allowing for centralized, large-scale purchases of medical and hospital supplies. They also cite the inadequacy of medical care for the poor. Such horror stories as those just told make their point. Opponents of national health insurance stress the red tape such plans would require. They ask if federal agencies—such as those that run the postal service—inspire so much confidence that they should be entrusted with administering something so vital as the nation's health care. This debate is not new, and even if some form of national health insurance is adopted the argument is likely to continue.

Rationing Medical Care The most controversial suggestion for how to reduce medical costs is to ration medical care. We cannot afford to provide all the available technology to everyone, goes the argument. No easy answer has been found for this pressing matter,

dumping the practice of sending unprofitable patients to public hospitals

Figure 19.6

SOCIAL MAP: WHO LACKS MEDICAL INSURANCE?

Note: The range is broad, from a low of 7.5% who lack medical insurance in Hawaii to a high of 24.5 percent in Arizona and Texas.

Source: Statistical Abstract 1999: Table 190.

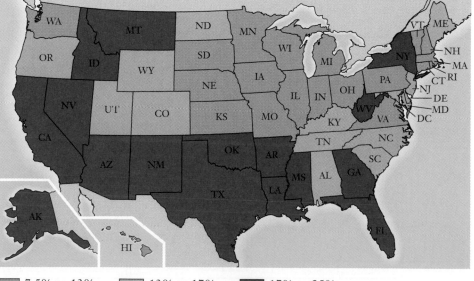

■ 7.5% to 13%   ■ 13% to 17%   ■ 17% to 25%

Sociology & the New Technology

WHO SHOULD LIVE, AND WHO SHOULD DIE?
TECHNOLOGY AND THE DILEMMA OF MEDICAL RATIONING

Visiting a doctor or a hospital is not without risk. We have seen that doctors kill thousands of patients a year. But the risk is small compared to that of earlier times, when physicians bled and purged their patients in an effort to cure them. Today's physicians are well trained, and medical care is based on scientific studies. Our new technology even allows us to cure medical conditions that just a short time ago doomed people to premature deaths. In other instances, the medical condition can't be cured, but the patient is able to live a long and satisfying life.

And therein lies the rub. Some kinds of technology are available only on a limited basis; there isn't enough to go around to everyone who needs it. Other kinds of technology are so costly that it could bankrupt society if they were made available to everyone who had a particular condition. Who, then, should receive the benefits of our new medical technology?

Consider dialysis, the use of machines to cleanse the blood of people suffering from kidney disease. Currently, dialysis is available to anyone who needs it, and the cost runs several billion dollars a year. Four percent of all Medicare goes to pay for the dialysis of just one-fourth of 1 percent of Medicare patients. Great Britain, which faces this same problem, rations dialysis to people under the age of 55 (Volti 1995).

Open heart surgery is a technological wonder, but its costs are astounding. One percent of all the money the nation spends on its medical bills goes to pay for the bypass surgeries of just four-hundredths of 1 percent of the population.

The cost of medical technology that is used at the end of people's lives helps us understand the issue. Of all Medicare money, about one-fourth is spent to maintain patients during just the last year of their lives. Almost a third of this amount is spent during just the last month of life (Volti 1995).

At the heart of this issue of how to spend limited resources lie questions not only of cost, but also of fairness, of how to distribute the benefits of advanced medical technology in an equitable manner. ■

For Your Consideration

The dilemma is harsh: If we ration medical treatment, many sick people will die. If we don't, we may go bankrupt. But how should we decide who should receive and who should be denied? In more specific terms: Should a baseball icon be given a liver transplant even though there is little chance that it will substantially prolong his life? (This is what happened to Mickey Mantle, whose liver had been ravaged by years of hard drinking, by hepatitis C, and by cancer, which had spread to other parts of his body. Mantle waited just 2 days for a new liver. He died less than 3 months after receiving it.) Use ideas, concepts, and principles from this and other chapters to develop a proposal for solving this pressing issue. Also note how this dilemma changes shape if you view it from the contrasting perspectives of conflict, functionalism, and symbolic interactionism.

---

which is becoming the center of a national debate. This dilemma is the focus of the Sociology and the New Technology box above.

THREATS TO HEALTH

Let's look at four threats to health both in the United States and wordwide: disease; drugs; disabling environments; and misguided, foolish, and callous experiments.

AIDS

Perhaps the most pressing health issue in the United States—and globally—is AIDS (acquired immune deficiency syndrome). Since the first case of this virus that attacks the human immune system was documented in 1981, more than 700,000 Americans have been diagnosed with the disease. Almost 500,000 have died from it (see Figure 19.7 on the next page). The average cost to treat a U.S. AIDS patient is $20,000 a year, making the nation's AIDS medical bill about $7 billion a year (Maugh 1998).

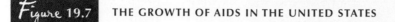

Figure 19.7   THE GROWTH OF AIDS IN THE UNITED STATES

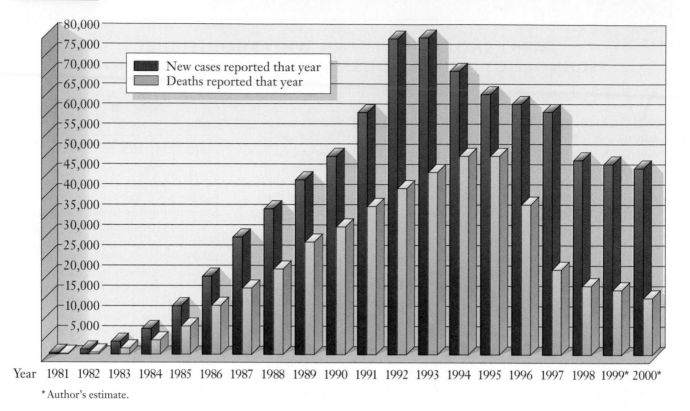

Year   1981   1982   1983   1984   1985   1986   1987   1988   1989   1990   1991   1992   1993   1994   1995   1996   1997   1998   1999*   2000*

*Author's estimate.

Source: Centers for Disease Control 1999:Tables 5, 26 (and earlier years).

Globally, about 35 million people have AIDS. The hardest-hit region in the world is sub-Saharan Africa, where about two-thirds of all the world's AIDS victims live (see Figure 19.8). Worldwide, each minute 11 people are infected with HIV, the virus that causes AIDS. Ten of them are in sub-Saharan Africa (Will 2000). About 2 million Africans die from AIDS a year, making it the leading cause of death among Africans (Waldholz 1999). Let's look at some of the major characteristics of this disease.

Origin   The question of how AIDS originated, which baffled scientists for two decades, appears to be solved (Altman 1999; Kalb 1999). Apparently, the virus was present in chimpanzees in Africa and was then transmitted to humans. How this occurred is not known, but the best guess is that hunters were exposed to the animals' blood as they slaughtered them for meat. Others suggest that the virus was transmitted during the 1920s and 1950s, when, in a peculiar experiment for malaria, people were inoculated with blood from monkeys and chimpanzees. The blood may unknowingly have been infected with viral ancestors of HIV (Rathus and Nevid 1993).

The Transmission of AIDS   The only way a person can become infected with AIDS is if bodily fluids pass from one person to another. AIDS is known to be transmitted through the exchange of blood and semen, and it can be transmitted to newborns and infants in mother's milk. Since the AIDS virus is present in all bodily fluids (including sweat, tears, spittle, and urine), some people think that AIDS can also be transmitted in these forms. The U.S. Centers for Disease Control, however, say that AIDS cannot be transmitted by casual contact in which traces of these fluids would be exchanged (Edgar 1994). One case in which AIDS was transmitted by deep kissing has been documented, but both of the individuals involved had gum disease (Altman 1997).

Patterns of transmission vary from one society to another. In some, for example, AIDS is transmitted almost entirely by heterosexual sex, while in others a larger percentage of AIDS victims contract the disease from homosexual sex. Patterns are also different for men and women within the same society. Figure 19.9 compares the patterns for men and women in the United States.

Gender, Race-Ethnicity, and AIDS Although many people think of AIDS as a man's disease, in parts of Africa AIDS strikes males and females equally. In the United States, each year women make up a larger proportion of new cases. In 1982, only 6 percent of AIDS cases were women, but today 23 percent of all new AIDS cases are women (Centers for Disease Control 1997:Tables 3, 10; 1999:Table 5). AIDS is the fourth leading cause of death of U.S. women ages 25 to 44, while it is the second main cause of death for U.S. men in this age bracket (*Statistical Abstract* 1999:Table 140).

As shown in Table 19.1 on the next page, the risk of AIDS is also related to race-ethnicity. The reason for this is not genetic; that is, no racial-ethnic group is more susceptible to AIDS because of biological factors. Rather, risks differ because of *social* factors, such as rates of intravenous drug use and the use of condoms.

The Stigma of Aids One of the most significant sociological aspects of AIDS is the stigma it carries. This provides another example of how social factors are essential to health and illness. Some people refuse even to be tested because they fear the stigma they would bear if they tested HIV-positive. One unfortunate consequence is the continuing spread of AIDS by people who "don't want to know." If this disease is to be brought under control, its stigma must be overcome: AIDS must be viewed like any other lethal disease—as the work of a destructive biological organism.

Is There a Cure for AIDS? Figure 19.7 shows how AIDS in the United States increased dramatically, peaked, and then declined. After rising sharply, the number of new U.S. AIDS cases peaked in 1993; the number of deaths peaked in 1994. Since then, the decline has been rapid. Have we found a cure for AIDS?

With thousands of scientists searching for a cure, the media have heralded each new breakthrough in research as a possible cure. The most promising treatment to date, the one

Figure 19.8

AIDS: A GLOBAL GLIMPSE

How many people get infected with HIV/AIDS per year?

Sub-Saharan Africa 3.8 million
Asia 1.5 million
South America 150,000
Caribbean 57,000
North America 45,000
Western Europe 30,000
North Africa 19,000
Australia 500

Source: World Health Organization.

Figure 19.9 **HOW AMERICANS GET AIDS**

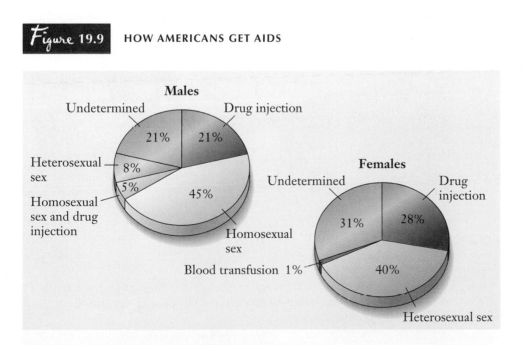

Males
Undetermined 21%
Drug injection 21%
Heterosexual sex 8%
Homosexual sex and drug injection 5%
Homosexual sex 45%

Females
Undetermined 31%
Drug injection 28%
Homosexual sex —
Blood transfusion 1%
Heterosexual sex 40%

Source: Centers for Disease Control 1999:Table 5.

Table 19.1

AIDS AND RACE-ETHNICITY

	Percentage of U.S. Population	Percentage of AIDS Cases
Whites	73.3%	43.8%
African Americans	11.7%	36.9%
Latinos	10.8%	18.2%
Asian Americans	3.5%	0.7%
Native Americans	0.7%	0.3%

Source: Centers for Disease Control, 1999:Table 7, and Figure 12.6 on page 336 of this text.

that lies behind the reduction in deaths, was spearheaded by David Ho, a virologist (virus researcher). If patients in the very early stages of the disease take a "cocktail" of drugs (a combination of protease inhibitors, AZT, and 3TC), all signs of the virus can be erased from their bodies. Their immune systems then rebound (Gorman 1997). No one is yet calling this a cure, however. Apparently, the virus lingers undetected, ready to flourish if the drugs are withdrawn (Cowley 1998).

While most praise this new treatment, some researchers have issued a dire warning (Rotello 1996). They suggest that the cocktail may become this decade's penicillin. When penicillin was introduced, everyone was ecstatic about its effectiveness. But over the years the microbes it targets mutated, producing "super germs" against which we have no protection. If this is the case with AIDS, then a new, "super-AIDS" virus may hit the world with more fury than the first devastating wave.

The Globalization of Disease

The year was 1918. Men and women who were seemingly healthy the day before collapsed and quickly died. In the morning, men wheeled open carts down the streets to pick up corpses that were left on porches like last night's trash. In a matter of months, a half million Americans died. Worldwide, the death toll reached between 20 million and 40 million. (Phillips 1998)

What was the killer? The flu. For some reason, still unknown, a particularly lethal variety of the flu bug suddenly appeared.

Medical researchers fear that something like this will happen again. This time, however, global travel will have destroyed the natural frontiers that used to contain diseases. In a matter of hours, the disease will spread around the world via commercial airlines. Because older diseases have mutated and have produced "super bugs" that are immune to antibiotics, the resulting number of deaths could make the 1918 death toll seem puny by comparison.

A new controversy surrounding AIDS is the "semilegal" marijuana clubs in San Francisco. Here marijuana is sold openly to people seeking to combat the side effects of AIDS treatments.

Such are the fears. Twenty-eight new diseases have recently appeared on the world scene. Antibiotics are ineffective against many of them. Because some of these new diseases are lethal, we may have to resort to an old remedy—isolating people in asylums. When the ebola virus appeared on the scene in 1976, with its particularly hideous form of death, the only way it could be contained was to isolate an entire region in Zaire (Olshansky 1997).

One disease that is particularly feared is drug-resistant tuberculosis. It was once thought that the battle against TB had been won, but this disease has had a resurgence and is now the leading cause of infectious deaths among adults worldwide. Today more people die globally from TB than died before the microbe was discovered (Garrett 1999). Drug-resistant strains of TB are common in Russian prisoners. From there, they are likely to spread (Harpaz 1999). Already, to treat patients who have TB that does not respond to drugs, U.S. surgeons are turning again to a technique that they they abandoned decades ago, removing lungs and other infected body parts (Belkin 1999).

Drugs: Alcohol and Nicotine

Let's examine some of the health consequences of alcohol and nicotine, the most frequently used drugs in the United States.

Alcohol Alcohol is the standard recreational drug of Americans. The *average* adult American consumes 36 gallons of alcoholic beverages per year—almost 32 gallons of beer, 2½ gallons of wine, and 2 gallons of whiskey, vodka, or other distilled spirits. Alcohol is so popular that Americans drink more beer than they do milk, coffee, tea, or fruit juices (*Statistical Abstract* 1999:Table 252).

Despite laws banning alcohol consumption before the age of 21, underage drinking is common. During the past year, about three out of four high school seniors drank alcohol. For college students, the figure is almost nine out of ten (see Table 19.2 and Table 19.3). As Table 19.2 also shows, more than half of all high school seniors have been drunk during the past year, one-third during just the past month. Drinking alcohol is directly related to college grades, as Table 19.4 on the next page makes evident: The more college students drink, the worse they do in their classes.

Is alcohol bad for health? This beverage cuts both ways. About two drinks a day for men and one drink a day for women reduces the risk of heart attacks and strokes (Greenberg 1999; Kazman 1999). (Women weigh less on average and produce fewer enzymes that metabolize alcohol.) Beyond these amounts, however, alcohol increases the risk of a variety of diseases, from cancer to stroke. It also increases the likelihood of birth defects. Each year, more than 600,000 Americans seek treatment for alcohol problems; about 20,000 die from alcohol abuse (*Statistical Abstract* 1999:Tables 153, 237).

Nicotine By far, nicotine is the most lethal of all recreational drugs. Sociologist Erich Goode (1989) points out that, compared with nonsmokers, smokers are three times as likely to die before reaching the age of 65. Smokers in their thirties are *six* times as likely to have heart attacks as are nonsmokers of the same age (Winslow 1995). Smoking doubles the risk of blindness in old age (Lagnado 1996). Smoking also causes progressive emphysema and several types of cancer that kill about 390,000 Americans each year.

An antitobacco campaign that stresses the health hazards of smoking is being waged successfully in Europe and North America.

Table 19.2

WHAT DRUGS HAVE HIGH SCHOOL SENIORS USED . . .

	In the Past Year?	In the Past Month?
Alcohol	73.8%	51.0%
Nicotine (cigarettes)	NA	34.6%
Marijuana	37.8%	23.1%
Hallucinogens	9.4%	3.5%
LSD	8.1%	2.7%
Cocaine	6.2%	2.6%
Barbiturates	5.8%	2.6%
Heroin	1.1%	0.5%
. . .		
How many have been drunk?	53.2%	32.9%

Source: Johnston et al. 2000:Table 2.

Table 19.3

WHAT DRUGS HAVE FULL-TIME COLLEGE STUDENTS USED IN THE PAST YEAR?

	Men	Women
Alcohol	86.9%	86.3%
Nicotine (cigarettes)	38.0%	39.3%
Marijuana	30.0%	26.2%
LSD	7.1%	3.6%
Cocaine	3.7%	1.9%
Barbiturates	2.2%	1.0%
Heroin	0.1%	0.1%

Source: Johnston et al. 1995:Table 19.

Table 19.4

GRADE-POINT AVERAGE (GPA) AND DRINKING HABITS OF COLLEGE STUDENTS

GPA	Number of Drinks per Week	
	Men	Women
A	5	2
B	7	3
C	9	4

Source: Presley et al. 1993.

Table 19.5

PERCENTAGE OF AMERICANS WHO SMOKE CIGARETTES

	1965	1985	1995
Men	52%	33%	27%
Women	34%	28%	23%

Source: Statistical Abstract 1993:Table 210; 1999:Table 239.

It has ended smoking on U.S. airlines and has resulted in legislation that requires restaurants and offices to establish nonsmoking zones. It is even illegal to light up in a bar in California. Table 19.5 shows how this antismoking message has hit home. In less than two decades, cigarette smoking has been cut in *half* among U.S. men, and has dropped by a third among U.S. women.

Yet many people continue to smoke. Why, when it is so destructive to their health? The two major reasons are addiction and advertising. Nicotine may be as addictive as heroin (Tolchin 1988). While this may sound far-fetched, consider Buerger's disease:

> In this disease, the blood vessels, especially those supplying the legs, become so constricted that circulation is impaired whenever nicotine enters the bloodstream. If a patient continues to smoke, gangrene may eventually set in. First a toe may have to be amputated, then the foot at the ankle, then the leg at the knee, and ultimately at the hip. . . . Patients are informed that if they will only stop smoking, it is virtually certain that the otherwise inexorable march of gangrene up the legs will be curbed. Yet surgeons report that some patients with Buerger's disease vigorously puff away in their hospital beds following a second or third amputation (Brecher et al. 1972).

The second reason is advertising. Even though cigarette ads were banned from television in the 1980s, cigarettes continue to be heavily advertised on billboards and in print. The tobacco industry has a huge advertising budget, spending $5 billion a year to encourage people to smoke (Federal Trade Commission 1996). The industry targets youth, often by associating cigarette smoking with success, high fashion, and independence. With the tobacco industry's political clout and with 40,000 Americans depending on it for their livelihood, attempts to stop cigarette advertising have failed (*Statistical Abstract* 1999:Table 679). Joe Camel, however, the industry's most blatant attempt to lure youthful smokers, has been banned. (See the photo below.)

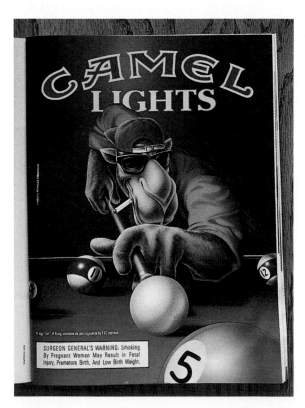

Do you think this magazine ad is designed to make cigarettes appealing to male youth? Although tobacco industry officials denied that they were trying to entice youth to smoke, the evidence such as this ad is overwhelmingly against them. After pressure from the U.S. Congress, Camel stopped its Joe Camel ads.

In my opinion, it is not an exaggeration to call the U.S. tobacco industry criminal. At its feet must be laid countless painful deaths. Among those torturous deaths, I count those of my mother and my only sister.

Awareness of disabling environments has grown—from air pollution to asbestos and harmful food additives. Coping mechanisms also are taking many forms, from reducing auto emissions and eating organically grown foods to that depicted here—Tokyo shoppers "stopping off for a quick one," in this case, a hit of pure oxygen.

Disabling Environments

A **disabling environment** is one that is harmful to people's health. The health risk of some occupations is evident: Lumberjacking, riding rodeo bulls, and taming lions are obvious examples. In many occupations, however, people become aware of the risk only years after they worked at jobs they thought were safe. For example, several million people worked with asbestos during and after World War II. The federal government estimates that one-quarter of them will die of cancer from having breathed asbestos dust. It is likely that many other substances that we have not yet identified also cause slowly developing cancers—including, ironically, some asbestos substitutes (Meier 1987).

Industrialization increased the world's standard of living and brought better health to hundreds of millions of people. Ironically, it also threatens to disable the basic environment of the human race, posing what may be the greatest health hazard of all time. The burning of vast amounts of carbon fuels is leading to the *greenhouse effect,* a warming of the earth that may change the globe's climate, melt its polar ice caps, and flood the earth's coastal shores. Use of fluorocarbon gases in refrigerators and air conditioners is threatening the *ozone shield,* the protective layer of the earth's upper stratosphere that screens out a high proportion of the sun's ultraviolet rays. High-intensity ultraviolet radiation is harmful to most forms of life. In humans, it causes skin cancer. The pollution of land, air, and water, especially through nuclear waste, pesticides, herbicides, and other chemicals, poses additional risks to life on our planet.

Identifying environmental threats to world health is only the first step. The second is to introduce short- and long-term policies to reduce such problems. The sociology of the environment is discussed on pages 649–656.

Misguided, Foolish, and Callous Experiments

At times, physicians and government officials behave so arrogantly that they callously disregard the health of the people they are sworn to protect. Let's look at two notorious instances.

The Tuskegee Syphilis Experiment Imagine that you are living in Macon County, Alabama, during the Depression years. You are dirt poor. You live in a little country shack with a dirt floor and no electricity or running water. You never finished grade school, and you

> **disabling environment** an environment that is harmful to health

make a living, such as it is, by doing odd jobs. You haven't been feeling quite right lately, but you can't afford a doctor.

Then you rub your eyes in disbelief. It is just like winning the lottery. You've been offered free physical examinations at Tuskegee University—free rides to and from the clinic, hot meals on examination days, and free treatment for minor ailments. Your survivors are even guaranteed a burial payment. You eagerly accept.

You have just become part of what is surely slated to go down in history as one of the most callous experiments of all time, outside of the infamous Nazi experiments. With heartless disregard for human life, the U.S. Public Health Service told 399 African-American men that they had joined a social club and burial society called "Miss Rivers' Lodge." They also told them that they had "bad blood," and if they went to a private doctor they would lose their benefits.

What the men were *not* told was that they had syphilis. For forty years, the "Public Health Service" let their disease go untreated just "to observe what happened." There was even a control group of 201 men free of the disease (Jones 1993).

By the way, there was one further benefit for the men—free autopsies to determine the ravages of syphilis on their bodies.

The Cold War Experiments   Now assume that you are a soldier stationed in Nevada, and the U.S. Army orders your platoon to march through an area in which an atomic bomb has just been detonated. Because you are a soldier, you obey. Nobody knows much about radiation, and you don't know that the army is using you as a guinea pig: It wants to see if you'll be able to withstand the fallout—without any radiation equipment. Or suppose you are a patient at the University of Rochester in 1946, and your doctor, whom you trust implicitly, says he is going to give you something "to help you." You are pleased. But the injection, it turns out, is uranium (Noah 1994). He and a team of other doctors are conducting an experiment to find out how much uranium it will take to damage your kidneys ("U.S. Department of Energy, Advisory Committee").

Like the Tuskegee experiment, radiation experiments like these were conducted on unsuspecting subjects simply because government officials wanted information. There were others, too; some soldiers were given LSD. And in Palmetto, Florida, officials released whooping cough viruses into the air, killing a dozen innocent children (Conahan 1994).

Playing God   To most of us, it is incredible that government officials and medical personnel would so callously disregard human life, but it obviously happens. Those in official positions sometimes reach a point where they think they can play God and determine who shall live and who shall die. And, obviously, the most expendable citizens are the poor and powerless. It is inconceivable that an experiment such as the syphilis study would be forced on the wealthy and powerful. The elite are protected from such callous disregard of human rights and life. The only way the poor can be protected against such gross abuse of professional positions is if we publicize each known instance of abuse and insist on vigorous prosecution of those who direct and carry out such experiments.

THE SEARCH FOR ALTERNATIVES

What alternatives are there to the way U.S. medicine is usually practiced? One suggestion is to shift the emphasis from the treatment of disease to the prevention of disease. After considering this approach to medical care, we will look at the health care systems of other countries. Perhaps these two closing topics will suggest new ideas for you to follow, or to avoid.

Treatment or Prevention?

Effects of Values and Lifestyles.   The impact of values and lifestyle on health becomes apparent if we contrast Utah (home of the Mormons, who disapprove of alcohol, coffee, cokes, and tobacco) with its adjacent state of Nevada (home of the gambling industry). Although these two states have similar climates and similar levels of income, education, medical care, and urbanization (Fuchs 1981), Nevada's overall death rate is 50 percent higher than Utah's. Nevadans are 50 percent more likely to commit suicide, twice as likely to die from lung disease, and three times as likely to be murdered or to die from AIDS (*Statistical Abstract* 1998:Table 143; 1999:Table 141). The difference in their statistics is due to how people in each state live their lives. In short, many threats to health are preventable.

Prevention implies both an individual and a group responsibility. On the individual level, exercising regularly, eating nutritious food, maintaining sexual monogamy, and avoiding smoking and alcohol abuse go a long way toward preventing disease. Following these guidelines can add years to your life—and can make those years healthy and enjoyable ones.

On the group level, one alternative is preventive medicine. Instead of focusing on treating disease, U.S. medicine could have "wellness" as its goal. What would implementing a national policy of "prevention, not intervention" require? First, the medical establishment would have to change its basic philosophy, not an easy task to accomplish. Essentially, physicians, nurses, and hospitals would have to be convinced that prevention is profitable. One possibility is that a group of doctors and a hospital could be paid an annual fee for keeping people well (Cooper 1993). Second, the public's attitude

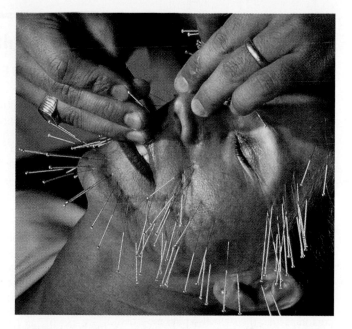

Each culture makes basic assumptions about the causes and cures of health problems. The traditional assumptions of Eastern medical practitioners, usually ridiculed by Western physicians, are now being taken seriously by some. Acupuncture, for example, is gradually gaining acceptance in the West, although it does not fit Western assumptions of cause and cure.

would have to be turned around so they, too, could see the benefits of "wellness." This would require educational programs in the schools, and the media would need to show how healthy living habits—good nutrition, exercise, safe sex, and drug avoidance—lead to better health and a longer life. For example, diet is a significant factor in many types of cancer, and an educational program to replace fatty, low-fiber foods with a diet rich in fruits, green tea, and leafy, green vegetables would go a long way in saving lives. Unfortunately, rather than making such basic changes, most Americans seem to prefer that their doctors prescribe drugs.

On a broader scale, we could focus on comprehensive prevention—eliminating disabling environments and the use of harmful drugs. Some businesses continue to spew industrial waste into the air and to use rivers and oceans as industrial sewers, while others use advertising to seduce youths to use harmful drugs. These acts are unconscionable. Finally, since we now live in a global village, the creation and maintenance of a health-producing environment requires international controls and cooperation.

Health Care in Global Perspective

The search for alternatives also leads us to examine health care in other nations. Consequently, we shall close this chapter with a comparison of health care in the three worlds of industrialization. As with education (see pages 481–484), no one country can adequately illustrate the varieties of medicine that are practiced in nations in a particular stage of industrialization. Nevertheless, the countries highlighted in the Perspectives box do illustrate major characteristics of health care around the world. The following materials, then, help us place both positive and negative aspects of the U.S. health care system in cultural perspective.

PERSPECTIVES | Cultural Diversity Around the World
HEALTH CARE IN SWEDEN, RUSSIA, AND CHINA

Health Care in the Most Industrialized Nations: Sweden

Sweden has the most comprehensive health care system in the world. National health insurance, which is financed by contributions from the state and from employers, covers all Swedish citizens and alien residents. The government pays most physicians a salary to treat patients, but 5 percent work full time in private practice (Swedish Institute 1990). Except for a small consultation fee, medical and dental treatment by these government-paid doctors is free. The state also pays most of the charges of private physicians. The government reimburses travel expenses for patients and for the parents of a hospitalized child. Only minimal fees are charged for prescriptions and hospitalization.

Medical treatment is just one component of Sweden's broad system of social welfare. For example, people who are sick or who must stay home with sick children receive 90 percent of their salaries. Swedes are given parental leave upon the birth of a child, and are guaranteed a pension.

Sweden's socialized medicine is inefficient. Swedes have not solved the twin problems of eliminating waiting lines and getting physicians to "get down to work." Because salaries of medical personnel are guaranteed, regardless of how many patients they see, the system has poor productivity. When reporters visited Sweden's largest hospital on a weekday morning, when 80 of 120 surgeons were on duty, they found 19 of 24 operating rooms idle. Their photos of empty operating rooms—at a time when there was a one- to two-year waiting period for hip replacements and cataract operations—provoked a public outcry (Bergström 1992). Due to public pressure and renewed emphasis on accountability, efficiency is improving (Hakansson 1994).

Health Care in the Industrializing Nations: Russia

As I write this in 2000, Russia is in disarray. Its economic and political system is on the verge of collapse. It can't

pay its debts, and it is just barely being kept afloat by emergency loans from the World Bank—and this only because the Most Industrialized Nations fear a nuclear holocaust should Russia dissolve into anarchy.

Russia's health care system is similarly in tatters. Under the communists, Russia had established a system that made health care available to most. Like the rest of the nation's systems of production, the health care system was centralized. The state owned the medical schools and determined how many doctors would be trained in what specialties. The state paid medical salaries, which it set, and determined where doctors would practice.

Under Russia's fitful, torturous transition to capitalism, its health care system has fallen apart, and the health of the population has declined. An example is Moscow's ambulance system. It used to be efficient—dial 03 and an ambulance would arrive within minutes. Now an ambulance sometimes takes eight to twelve hours to arrive, because drivers are using the ambulances as free-lance cabs, and they keep emergency cases waiting (Field 1998).

The only hospitals comparable to those in the United States are reserved for the elite (Light 1992). In the rest, conditions are deplorable. Patients must bring their own linens, medicines, and syringes with them to the hospital. Some hospitals do not even have a doctor on staff. Surgical scalpels are resharpened until they break. Sometimes even razor blades are used for surgery (Donelson 1992). Outdated and broken equipment is not replaced. Doctors are paid about $35 a month and may go unpaid for six months at a time (Paddock 1999). Some doctors face the choice of operating without anesthetic or not operating at all (Paddock 1999).

Perhaps no event more pinpoints the disarray than this: Three patients lay unconscious in the intensive care unit, kept alive only by the Siberian hospital's life support system. Two were elderly; one was 39.

On Wednesday, the hospital received a telegram from the local

power company: "You haven't paid your bill for five years. You owe us $94,931. Pay up, or we'll shut off your electricity." The next morning, at 6 A.M., the company shut off the power. Forty minutes later, all three patients were dead. (Paddock 1999)

The years of environmental degradation under the communists have also taken their toll. Serious birth defects have jumped to four times the U.S. rate. A likely culprit is radiation pollution from decades of nuclear irresponsibility (Specter 1995). Perhaps the single best indicator of the deterioration of health is the drop in life expectancy that began in the 1960s and continues today (Cockerham 1997). See Table 19.6.

Health Care in the Least Industrialized Nations: China

Because this nation of 1.2 billion people has a vast shortage of trained physicians, hospitals, and medicine, most Chinese see "barefoot doctors," people who have only a basic knowledge of medicine, are paid low wages, and travel from village to village. With its emphases on medicinal herbs and acupuncture, Chinese medicine differs from that of the West. Although Westerners have scoffed at the Chinese approach, some have found reason to change their minds. For example, one of the herbs that the Chinese have used for a thousand years or more to treat liver disease has been tested by Western societies; it reduces liver cancer (Tanouye 1995).

Recent changes include payment for medical treatment. Treatment used to be free, but now a hospital stay can cost several hundred yuan; the average monthly wage is 200 yuan. Physician salaries are as low as $7.25 a month (Chu 1998). Some physicians take extra jobs because they cannot survive on their salaries. Some medical personnel demand payment before they will give medical treatment, as with the surgeons who, arms scrubbed and held high in the air, refused to enter the operating room until the patient's relatives had stuffed their pockets with cash (Sampson 1992). ■

For Your Consideration

No nation has discovered the perfect medical system, and each country faces a medical crisis of "too much demand at too great a cost" (Moore and Winslow 1993). How would you say that the U.S. medical system is superior—and inferior—to each of these systems? Is there one that you would pick over the U.S. system? Why? Short of instituting socialized medicine, which goes against the value system of Americans, how do you think the U.S. medical system can overcome the deficiencies reviewed in this chapter—and maintain its strengths?

Table 19.6

INDICATORS OF HEALTH

	Sweden	United States	Russia	China
Life expectancy	79.2 years	76.3 years	65.3 years	70.3 years
Infant mortality[a]	3.9	6.7	22.7	41.1
Birth rate[b]	11.7	14.2	9.7	14.6
Death rate[b]	10.8	8.8	15.0	7.0
Health costs as a percent of Gross Domestic Product	8.6	14.0	2.3	NA

[a]Per 1,000 live births.
[b]Per 1,000 population.

Source: Field 1998; Statistical Abstract 1998:Tables 1345, 1348; 1999:Tables 1352, 1355.

SUMMARY AND REVIEW

■ Sociology and the Study of Medicine

What is the role of sociology in the study of medicine?

Sociologists study medicine as a social institution. As practiced in the United States, three of its primary characteristics are professionalization, bureaucracy, and the profit motive. P. 540.

What is the symbolic interactionist perspective on health and illness?

Health is not only a biological matter; it also is intimately related to society. Illness is also far from an objective matter, for illness is always viewed from the framework of culture, and such definitions vary from one group to another. Pp. 540–541.

What is the functionalist perspective on health and illness?

Functionalists stress that in return for being excused from their usual, responsible activities, people have to accept the **sick role**. They must assume responsibility for seeking competent medical help and cooperate in getting well so they can quickly resume normal activities. Pp. 541–542.

What is the conflict perspective on health and illness?

Health care is one of the scarce resources over which groups compete. On an international level, health care follows the global stratification that we studied in Chapter 9, with the best health care available in the dominant nations and the worst in the dependent nations.

In the American colonies, no training or licensing was necessary if one wanted to call oneself a doctor. Even until the early 1900s, medical training was a hit-or-miss affair. In 1910, the education of physicians came under the control of a group of men who eliminated most of their competition and turned medicine into the largest business in the United States. Pp. 542–546.

■ Historical Patterns of Health

How have health patterns changed over time?

Patterns of disease in the United States have changed so extensively that of today's top ten killers five did not even show up on the 1900 top ten list. Because most Americans live longer than their ancestors did, we can conclude that contemporary Americans are healthier. For mental illness, we have no idea how today compares with the past, for we have no baselines from which to make comparisons. Pp. 546–547.

■ Issues in Health Care

How does treating health care as a commodity lead to social inequalities?

Because medical care is a commodity to be sold to the highest bidder, the United States has a two-tier system of medical care in which the poor receive inferior health care for both their mental and physical illnesses. Pp. 547–548.

What are some other problems in U.S. health care?

One problem is **defensive medicine**, which refers to medical procedures that are done for the physician's benefit, not for the benefit of the patient. Intended to protect physicians from lawsuits, these tests and consultations add huge amounts to the nation's medical bill. Other problems are **depersonalization**, incompetence, conflict of interest, and medical fraud. Another is sexism, which leads to tests on females being done too late and to much unnecessary surgery. Pp. 548–552.

Why is medically assisted suicide an issue now?

Due to advanced technology, people can be kept technically alive even when they have no brain waves. Physicians who openly assist in suicides have come under severe criticism. Research findings on **euthanasia** in Holland have fueled this controversy. Pp. 552–555.

What attempts have been made to cut medical costs?
Health maintenance organizations (HMOs) and diagnosis-related groups are among the measures that have been taken to reduce medical costs. National health insurance, which has run into immense opposition, has been proposed as another solution. Pp. 555–557.

■ **Threats to Health**

What are some threats to the health of Americans?
Discussed here are AIDS, which is declining in the United States but rapidly increasing in many nations, especially in Africa; alcohol and nicotine, the most lethal drugs used by Americans; **disabling environments**, environments that are harmful to health, such as work-related diseases or pollution of air and water; and unethical ex-

periments, of which the Tuskegee syphilis experiments and the radiation experiments are two examples. P. 557–564.

■ **The Search for Alternatives**

Are there alternatives to our current health care system?
The primary alternative discussed here is a change in focus from treatment to prevention. Other alternatives may be found by examining health care systems in other countries. Both positive and negative characteristics of health care in Sweden, Russia, and China were reviewed. Pp. 564–567.

Where can I read more on this topic?
Suggested Readings for this chapter are found at the back of this book.

All URLs listed are current as of the printing of this book. URLs often change. Please check our Web site, **http://www.abacon.com/henslin,** for updates.

1. In this chapter's Down-to-Earth Sociology box, you read about how physicians defeated midwives and claimed control of the birthing process. This struggle continues today. Many states now recognize the right of nurse-midwives to deliver babies, but only if they are certified to do so. They must also be affiliated with a physician before they are allowed to practice. The certified nurse-midwife is considered a specialist within the profession of nursing. You can learn more about this field of nursing at the Web site for the American College of Nurse-Midwives, **http://www.acnm. org.** Scroll down to the bottom of the page and click on "About ACNM." In what ways was the group's philosophy shaped by the struggles midwives had with doctors? Return to the home page and click on "Midwifery Education." What are the educational and licensing requirements for nurse-midwives? What extra training is required before a nurse can become a midwife? Return to the home page and click on a report on the birth outcomes for midwife-attended deliveries. What does this suggest about the physicians' claim to control the birth process? Finally, go back to the home page, and click on "Political Action." Examine some of the issues that concern the ACNM. If you click on "Fact Sheets," you will find a discussion of barriers to midwifery. Write a paper in which you discuss the professional development of nurse-midwives and how they continue to struggle with physicians over who should assist in births.

2. Among the medical issues facing our society are euthanasia and physician-assisted suicide. This chapter includes a discussion of whether or not doctors should be allowed to kill patients. Explore both sides of these issues at **http://www.religioustolerance. org/euthanas.htm** and **http://www.euthanasia.com.** How do euthanasia and physician-assisted suicide differ? What are the opposing arguments on these issues? What are the ethical and re-

ligious aspects of euthanasia? What is the legal status of euthanasia and physician-assisted suicide in the United States and around the globe? Some suggest that a living will is a solution to many of the issues raised by euthanasia and physician-assisted suicide. You can learn more about living wills at **http://www. euthanasia.com.** Is this the answer? Why or why not? Write a paper in which you apply the sociological perspective in evaluating both sides of these issues. Should our society support these? Why or why not?

3. AIDS is among the many health topics covered in this chapter. The continent of Africa has been particularly affected by this epidemic. This exercise provides you with the opportunity to explore the AIDS epidemic in Africa in greater depth. Go to **http://www.aids.africa.com** and read the introduction. You will see an interactive map of the continent, which shows changes in the level of AIDS cases since 1982. Where is the epidemic most heavily concentrated? Click on "Statistics." How do the statistics differ between sub-Saharan Africa and North Africa/Middle East? Next, click on "AIDS in Africa." What impact has the epidemic had on families, the economy, and society? Why are women and children at greatest risk of contracting the disease? Finally, click on "Views." From the list of articles and statements, select some to read in more detail. Write a paper in which you explore the dimensions of AIDS—who gets the disease and how the disease affects individuals and society.

4. Look again at Table 19.6 on page 567. Note how life expectancy at birth and infant mortality vary from one nation to another. In this exercise, you will use these variables to test the hypothesis that the greater a nation's industrial development, the poorer its health care. First, go to the two-page map of global stratification on pages 244–245. Pick out ten countries from each of the three categories: "Most Industrialized Nations," "Industrializing Nations," and "Least Industrialized Nations." List these thirty countries in the left column, grouped according to their level of

industrial development. Then make two more columns with the headings "Life Expectancy" and "Infant Mortality." Now go to the CIA home page at **http://cia.gov.** Click on the "World Factbook." At the Factbook home page, select "Country Listing." You should see the alphabet listed across the top of the page; choose a nation from your list and select its initial. (For example, if you want to look for Japan, click on "J.") In the list that appears, click on your country. At the next screen, click on "People." You will see information regarding that country's population. Write the coun-

try's life expectancy and infant mortality on your table. Repeat this procedure for each country on your list. Doing this will create a table that shows how the life expectancy and infant mortality vary for each level of industrial development. Calculate the mean to get an average for each category. (Check Table 5.1 on page 130 if you don't recall how to calculate the mean.) Now write a report in which you state your hypothesis, explain your methodology, and discuss your findings.

chapter

20

Population and Urbanization

Population in Global Perspective

■ **A Planet with No Space for Enjoying Life?**
The New Malthusians
The Anti-Malthusians
Who Is Correct?
Why Are People Starving?

■ **Population Growth**
Why Do the Least Industrialized Nations Have
   So Many Children?
Implications of Different Rates of Growth
The Three Demographic Variables
Problems in Forecasting Population Growth

Urbanization

■ **The Development of Cities**
The Industrial Revolution and the Size
   of Cities
Urbanization, Metropolises,
   and Megalopolises
U.S. Urban Patterns

■ **Models of Urban Growth**
The Concentric Zone Model
The Sector Model
The Multiple-Nuclei Model
The Peripheral Model
Critique of the Models

■ **City Life**
Alienation
Community
Types of Urban Dwellers
Urban Sentiment: Finding a Familiar World
The Norm of Noninvolvement and the Diffusion
   of Responsibility

■ **Urban Problems and Social Policy**
Suburbanization
Disinvestment and Deindustrialization
The Rural Rebound
The Potential of Urban Revitalization

■ **Summary and Review**

Τhe image still haunts me. There stood Celia, age 30, her distended stomach visible proof that her thirteenth child was on its way. Her oldest was only 14 years old! A mere boy by our standards, he had already gone as far in school as he ever would. Each morning, he joined the men to work in the fields.

Each evening around twilight, we saw him return home, exhausted from hard labor in the subtropical sun.

My wife and I, who were living in Colima, Mexico, had eaten dinner in Celia and Angel's home, which clearly reflected the family's poverty. A thatched hut consisting of only a single room served as home for all fourteen members of the family. At night, the parents and younger children crowded into a double bed, while the eldest boy slept in a hammock. As in many other homes in the village, the others slept on mats spread on the dirt floor.

The home was meagerly furnished. It had only a gas stove, a table, and a cabinet where Celia stored her few cooking utensils and clay dishes. There were no closets; clothes were hung on pegs in the walls. There also were no chairs, not even one. We were used to the poverty in this village, but this really startled us. The family was so poor that they could not afford even a single chair.

Celia beamed as she told us how much she looked forward to the birth of her next child. Could she really mean it? It was hard to imagine that any woman would want to be in her situation.

Yet Celia meant every word. She was as full of delightful anticipation as she had been with her first child—and with all the others in between. ■

571

ow could Celia have wanted so many children—especially when she lived in such poverty? That question bothered me. I couldn't let it go until I had the solution. This chapter helps provide an answer.

POPULATION IN GLOBAL PERSPECTIVE

Celia's story takes us into the heart of **demography,** the study of the size, composition, growth, and distribution of human populations. It brings us face to face with the question of whether we are doomed to live in a world so filled with people that there will be practically no space for anybody. Will our planet be able to support its growing population? Or are chronic famine and mass starvation the sorry fate of most earthlings? Let's look at how this concern began, and then at what today's demographers say about it.

A PLANET WITH NO SPACE FOR ENJOYING LIFE?

The story begins with the lowly potato. When the Spanish Conquistadors found that people in the Andes ate this vegetable, which was unknown in Europe, they brought it home with them. Europeans viewed it suspiciously, but gradually the potato became the main food of the lower classes. With more abundant food, fertility increased, the death rate dropped, and Europe's population soared, almost doubling during the 1700s (McKeown 1977).

Thomas Malthus (1766–1834), an English economist, saw this growth as a sign of doom. In 1798, he wrote a book that became world famous, *An Essay on the Principle of Population.* In it, Malthus proposed what became known as the **Malthus theorem.** He argued that while population grows geometrically (from 2 to 4 to 8 to 16 and so forth), the food supply increases only arithmetically (from 1 to 2 to 3 to 4 and so on). This meant, he claimed, that if births go unchecked, the population of a country, or even of the world, will outstrip its food supply.

demography the study of the size, composition, growth, and distribution of human populations

Malthus theorem an observation by Thomas Malthus that although the food supply increases only arithmetically (from 1 to 2 to 3 to 4 and so on), population grows geometrically (from 2 to 4 to 8 to 16 and so forth)

In earlier generations, large farm families were common. (My own father came from a Minnesota farm family of ten children.) Having many children was functional—there were many hands to help with crops, food production, and food preparation. As the country industrialized and urbanized, this changed to a dysfunction—children became expensive and nonproducing. Consequently, the size of families shrank as we entered Stage 3 of the demographic transition, and today U.S. families of this size are practically nonexistent.

Figure 20.1 HOW FAST IS THE WORLD'S POPULATION GROWING?

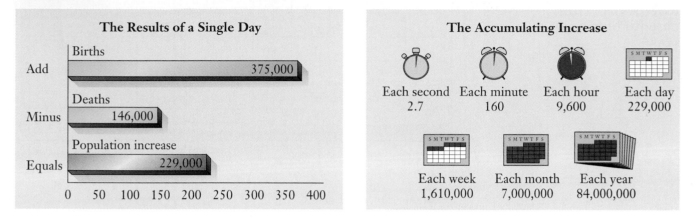

Source: "Population Update" 2000.

The New Malthusians

Was Malthus right? This question became a matter of heated debate among demographers. One group, which can be called the "New Malthusians," is convinced that today's situation is at least as grim, if not grimmer, than anything Malthus ever imagined. For example, *the world's population is growing so fast that in just the time it takes you to read this chapter, another fifteen thousand to twenty thousand babies will be born!* By this time tomorrow, the earth will have an additional quarter of a million people to feed. This increase goes on hour after hour, day after day, without letup. For a picture of this growth, see Figure 20.1.

The New Malthusians point out that the world's population is following an **exponential growth curve.** In other words, if growth doubles during approximately equal intervals of time, it suddenly accelerates. To illustrate the far-reaching implications of exponential growth, sociologist William Faunce (1981) told a parable about a man who saved a rich man's life. The rich man was grateful and said that he wanted to reward the man for his heroic deed.

> The man replied he would like his reward to be spread out over a four-week period, with each day's amount being twice what he received on the preceding day. He also said he would be happy to receive only one penny on the first day. The rich man immediately handed over the penny and congratulated himself on how cheaply he had gotten by. At the end of the first week, the rich man checked to see how much he owed and was pleased to find that the total was only $1.27. By the end of the second week he owed only $163.83. On the twenty-first day, however, the rich man was surprised to find that the total had grown to $20,971.51. When the twenty-eighth day arrived the rich man was shocked to discover that he owed $1,342,177.28 for that day alone and that the total reward had jumped to $2,684,354.56!

This is precisely what alarms the New Malthusians. They claim that humanity has just entered the "fourth week" of an exponential growth curve. Figure 20.2 on the next page shows why they think the day of reckoning is just around the corner. They point out that it took all of human history for the world's population to reach its first billion around 1800. It then took about one hundred thirty years (until 1930) to add the second billion. Just thirty years later (1960), the world population hit 3 billion. The time needed to reach the fourth billion was cut in half, to only fifteen years (1975). It then took just twelve more years (1987) for the total to hit 5 billion, and another twelve for it to reach 6 billion (in 1999).

To illustrate this increase, the New Malthusians have come up with some mind-boggling statistics. They note that before the Industrial Revolution, it took 1,600 years for the world's population to double, but the most recent doubling took just forty years—*forty* times as fast (Cohen 1996). They also point out that between 8000 B.C. and A.D. 1750 the world added

exponential growth curve a pattern of growth in which numbers double during approximately equal intervals, thus accelerating in the latter stages

Figure 20.2

**WORLD POPULATION
GROWTH OVER 2,000
YEARS**

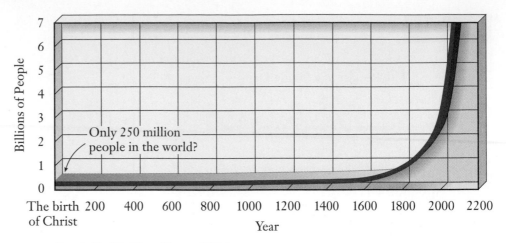

Only 250 million
people in the world?

Source: Modified from Piotrow 1973:4.

an average of only 67,000 people a year—but now that many people are being added *every seven hours* (Weeks 1994).

It is obvious, claim the New Malthusians, that there is going to be less and less for more and more.

The Anti-Malthusians

This does seem obvious, and no one wants to live shoulder-to-shoulder and fight for scraps. How, then, can anyone argue with the New Malthusians?

A much more optimistic group of demographers, whom we can call the "Anti-Malthusians," believe that Europe's **demographic transition** provides a more accurate picture of the future. This transition is diagrammed in Figure 20.3. During most of its history, Europe was in stage 1. High birth rates offset by high death rates led to a fairly stable population.

demographic transition a three-stage historical process of population growth: first, high birth rates and high death rates; second, high birth rates and low death rates; and third, low birth rates and low death rates; a fourth stage has begun to appear in the Most Industrialized Nations, as depicted in Figure 20.3.

Figure 20.3   **THE DEMOGRAPHIC TRANSITION**

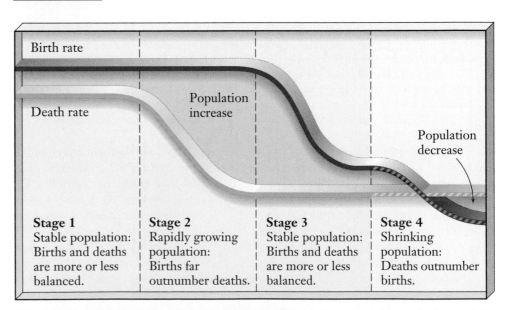

Note: The standard demographic transition is depicted by Stages 1–3.
Stage 4 has recently been suggested by some Anti–Malthusians.

Then came stage 2, the "population explosion" that so upset Malthus. Europe's population surged because birth rates remained high, while death rates went down. Finally, Europe made the transition to stage 3—the population stabilized as people brought their birth rates into line with their lower death rates.

This, say the Anti-Malthusians, is precisely what will happen in the Least Industrialized Nations. Their current surge in growth simply indicates that they have reached stage 2 of the demographic transition. Hybrid seed and Western medicine have cut their death rates, but their birth rates remain high. When they move into stage 3, as surely they will, we will wonder what all the fuss was about.

Who Is Correct?

As you can see, both the New Malthusians and the Anti-Malthusians have looked at historical trends and projected them onto the future. The New Malthusians project continued world growth and are alarmed. The Anti-Malthusians project stage 3 of the demographic transition onto the Least Industrialized Nations and are reassured.

There is no question that the Least Industrialized Nations are in stage 2 of the demographic transition. The question is, will these nations enter stage 3? After World War II, the West exported its hybrid seeds, herbicides, medicine, and techniques of public hygiene around the globe. Death rates plummeted in the Least Industrialized Nations as their food supply increased and health improved. Their birth rates stayed high, however, and their populations mushroomed. Just as Malthus had done 200 years before, demographers predicted worldwide catastrophe if something was not done immediately to halt the population explosion (Ehrlich and Ehrlich 1972, 1978).

We can use the conflict perspective to understand what happened when this message reached the leaders of the industrialized world. They saw the mushrooming populations of the Least Industrialized Nations as a threat to the balance of power they had so carefully worked out. With swollen populations, the poorer countries might demand a larger share of the earth's resources. The leaders found the United Nations to be a willing tool, and they used it to spearhead efforts to reduce world population growth. The results have been remarkable. The birth rates of the Least Industrialized Nations have dropped from an average of 2.1 percent a year in the 1960s to 1.4 percent today (Haub and Yinger 1994; Haub and Cornelius 1999).

The New Malthusians and Anti-Malthusians have greeted this news with significantly different interpretations. The New Malthusians stressed that the populations of the Least Industrialized Nations had not stopped growing—their growth had just slowed. A slower growth rate still spells catastrophe—it just takes a little longer for it to hit (Ehrlich and Ehrlich 1997). For the Anti-Malthusians, however, this slowing of growth was the signal they had been waiting for—stage 3 of the demographic transition was arriving. First the death rate in the Least Industrialized Nations fell—now, just as we predicted, they said, their birth rates are also falling.

The Anti-Malthusians also argue that our future will be the opposite of what the New Malthusians worry about: There will be too few children in the world, not too many. The world's problem will not be a population explosion, but **population shrinkage**—populations getting smaller. They point out that births in 65 of the world's nations have dropped so low that these countries no longer produce enough children to maintain their populations. Table 20.1 lists ten of those nations. As you look at those numbers, keep in mind that it takes an average of 2.1 children per couple to reproduce a population. (The extra .1 child makes up for those who die and fail to reproduce.) Due to immigration or to low death rates, these countries are continuing to grow slowly—but already Germany and Italy fill more coffins than cradles.

Some Anti-Malthusians even predict a "demographic free fall" (Mosher 1997). As more nations enter stage 4 of the demographic transition, the world's population will peak at about 7 or 8 billion, then begin to grow smaller. Two hundred years from now, they say, we will have a lot fewer people on earth.

Table 20.1

EXTREMES IN CHILDBIRTH

Where Do Women Give Birth to the Fewest Children?

Country	Number of Children
1. Bulgaria	1.1
2. Latvia	1.1
3. Czech Republic	1.2
4. Estonia	1.2
5. Italy	1.2
6. Macao	1.2
7. Russia	1.2
8. San Marino	1.2
9. Slovenia	1.2
10. Spain	1.2

Where Do Women Give Birth to the Most Children?

Country	Number of Children
1. Niger	7.5
2. Oman	7.1
3. Ethiopia	7.0
4. Gaza	7.0
5. Uganda	6.9
6. Angola	6.8
7. Somalia	6.8
8. Western Sahara	6.8
9. Mali	6.7
10. Yemen	6.7

Note: The primary source also lists a fertility rate of 6.7 for Burkina Faso and the Marshall Islands. The secondary source listed these two countries as having a lower rate, so I have not included them in this table.

Sources: Primary, Haub and Cornelius 1999; Secondary, *Statistical Abstract* 1999:Table 1352.

population shrinkage the process by which a country's population becomes smaller because its birth rate and immigration are too low to replace those who die and emigrate

Who is right? It simply is too early to tell. Like the proverbial pessimists who see the glass of water half empty, the New Malthusians interpret changes in world population growth negatively. And like the optimists who see the same glass half full, the Anti-Malthusians view the figures positively.

Why Are People Starving?

Pictures of starving children gnaw at our conscience. We live in such abundance, while these children and their parents starve before our very eyes. Why don't they have enough food? Is it because there are too many of them, or simply that the abundant food produced around the world does not reach them?

The Anti-Malthusians make a point that seems irrefutable. As Figure 20.4 shows, *the amount of food produced for each person in the world is now much more than it was in 1950.* Although the world's population has more than doubled during this time, improved seeds and fertilization have made more food available for *each* person on earth. And even more food is on the way, for chemists have discovered how to split nitrogen molecules. Since the earth's atmosphere is 78 percent nitrogen, one day we may be able to produce chemical compounds—including fertilizers—out of thin air (Naj 1995).

Then why do people die of hunger? From Figure 20.4, we can conclude that starvation does not occur because the earth produces too little food, but because particular places lack food. Some countries produce more food than their people can consume, others less than they need for survival. At the same time as widespread famine ravishes West Africa, the U.S. government pays farmers to *reduce* their crops. The United States' problem is too much food, *theirs* too little.

The New Malthusians counter with the argument that the world's population is continuing to grow and that we do not know how long the earth will continue to produce enough food. They remind us of the penny doubling each day. It is only a matter of time, they say, until the earth no longer produces enough food—not "if," but "when."

Both the New Malthusians and the Anti-Malthusians have contributed significant ideas, but theories will not eliminate famines. Starving children are going to continue to peer out at us from our televisions and magazines, their tiny, shriveled bodies and bloated stomachs nagging at our conscience and calling for us to do something. Regardless of the underlying

Photos of starving people, such as this mother and her child, haunt Americans and other members of the Most Industrialized Nations. Many of us wonder why, when some are starving, we should live in the midst of such abundance, often overeating and even casually scraping excess food into the garbage. The text discusses reasons for such unconscionable disparities.

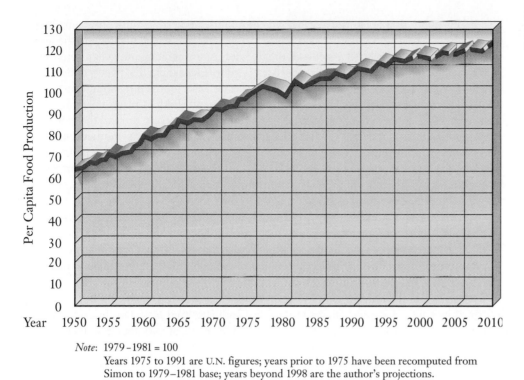

Figure 20.4

HOW MUCH FOOD DOES THE WORLD PRODUCE PER PERSON?

Sources: Simon 1981:58; United Nations Statistical Yearbook: 1985–1986: Table 7; and 1990–1991:Table 4, *Statistical Abstract* 1999:Table 1394, and earlier years.

Note: 1979–1981 = 100

Years 1975 to 1991 are U.N. figures; years prior to 1975 have been recomputed from Simon to 1979–1981 base; years beyond 1998 are the author's projections.

cause of this human misery, it can be alleviated by transferring food from nations that have a surplus.

The pictures of starving Africans leave the impression that Africa is overpopulated. Why else would all those people be starving? The truth, however, is far different. Africa has 22 percent of the earth's land surface, but only 10.5 percent of the earth's population (Nsamenang 1992). The reason for famines in Africa, then, can *not* be too many people living on too little land. In fact, Africa contains some of the world's largest untapped land suitable for agriculture (Bender and Smith 1997). Rather, these famines are due to three primary causes: drought, inefficient farming techniques, and wars that disrupt harvests and food distribution.

POPULATION GROWTH

Even if famines are due to a maldistribution of food rather than to world overpopulation, the fact remains that the Least Industrialized Nations are growing *fifteen times faster* than the Most Industrialized Nations—1.7 percent a year compared with 0.1 percent. (This looks like seventeen times faster because of rounding.) At these rates, it will take 583 years for the average Most Industrialized Nation to double its population, but just 40 years for the average Least Industrialized Nation to do so (Haub and Cornelius 1999). Figure 20.5 puts the matter in stark perspective. Why do those who can least afford it have so many children?

Why Do the Least Industrialized Nations Have So Many Children?

To understand why the population is growing so much faster in the Least Industrialized Nations, let's figure out why Celia

Figure 20.5 **WORLD POPULATION GROWTH, 1750–2150**

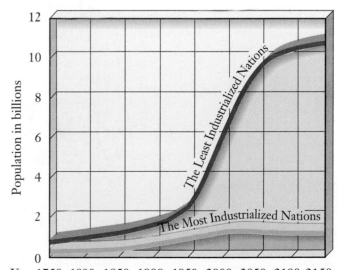

Source: "The World of the Child 6 Billion," 2000.

is so happy about having her thirteenth child. To do this, we need to apply the symbolic interactionist perspective. We need to take the role of the other so we can understand the world of Celia and Angel as *they* see it. As our culture does for us, their culture provides a perspective on life that guides their choices. Celia's and Angel's culture tells them that twelve children are *not* enough, that they ought to have a thirteenth—as well as a fourteenth and fifteenth. How can this be? Let's consider three reasons why bearing many children plays a central role in their lives—and in the lives of millions upon millions of poor people around the world.

First is the status of parenthood. In the Least Industrialized Nations, motherhood is the most prized status a woman can achieve. The more children a woman bears, the more she is thought to have achieved the purpose for which she was born. Similarly, a man proves his manhood by fathering children. The more children he fathers, especially sons, the better—for through them his name lives on.

Second, the community supports this view. Celia and those like her live in *Gemeinschaft* communities, where people share values and closely identify with one another. Here children are seen as a sign of God's blessing. Accordingly, a couple should have many children. By producing children, people reflect the values of the community and achieve status. The barren woman, not the woman with a dozen children, is to be pitied.

These factors certainly provide strong motivations for bearing many children. Yet, there is a third incentive. For poor people in the Least Industrialized Nations, children are economic assets. These people have no Social Security or medical and unemployment insurance. This motivates them to bear *more* children, not fewer, for when parents become sick or too old to work—or when no work is to be found—they rely on their families to take care of them. The more children they have, the broader their base of support. Moreover, like the eldest son of Celia and Angel, children begin contributing to the family income at a young age. See Figure 20.6.

To those of us who live in the Most Industrialized Nations, it seems irrational to have many children. And *for us it would be.* Understanding life from the framework of people who

WHY THE POOR NEED CHILDREN

Surviving children are an economic asset in the Least Industrialized Nations. Based on a survey in Indonesia, this figure shows that boys and girls can be net income earners for their families by the age of 9 or 10.

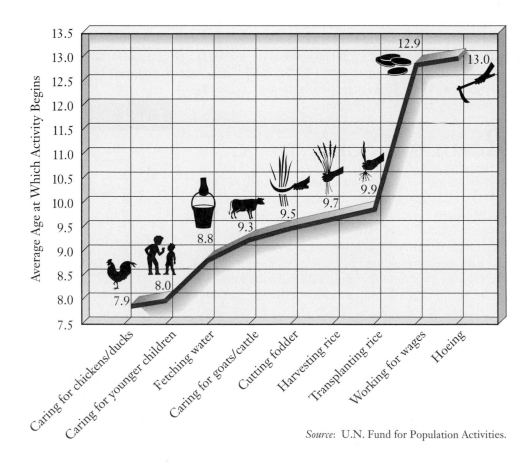

Source: U.N. Fund for Population Activities.

are living it, however—the essence of the symbolic interactionist perspective—reveals how it makes perfect sense to have many children. For example, consider the following incident, reported by a government worker in India:

> Thaman Singh (a very poor man, a water carrier) . . . welcomed me inside his home, gave me a cup of tea (with milk and "market" sugar, as he proudly pointed out later), and said: "You were trying to convince me in 1960 that I shouldn't have any more sons. Now, you see, I have six sons and two daughters and I sit at home in leisure. They are grown up and they bring me money. One even works outside the village as a laborer. *You told me I was a poor man and couldn't support a large family. Now, you see, because of my large family I am a rich man.*" (Mamdani 1973, italics added)

Conflict theorists offer a different view of why women in the poor nations bear so many children. They would argue that Celia has internalized values that support male dominance. In Latin America, *machismo*—an emphasis on male virility and dominance—is common. To father many children, especially sons, demonstrates virility, giving a man valued status in the community. From a conflict perspective, then, the reason poor people have so many children is that men control women's reproductive choices.

Implications of Different Rates of Growth

The result of Celia's and Angel's desire for many children—and of the many millions of Celias and Angels like them—is that Mexico's population will double in thirty-two years. In contrast, Austria is growing so slowly that it will take more than 2,000 years to double (Haub and Cornelius 1999). To illustrate population dynamics, demographers use **population pyramids.** These depict a country's population by age and sex. Figure 20.7 compares the population pyramids of the United States, Mexico, and the world.

You can see how important age structure is. If by some miracle Mexico were transformed overnight into a nation as industrialized as the United States, and the average number of children per woman dropped to 2.0, the same as in the United States, the population of Mexico would continue to grow much faster—simply because a much higher percentage of Mexican women are in their childbearing years.

The implications of a doubling population are mind-boggling. *Just to stay even,* within thirty-two years Mexico must double its jobs, food production, and factories; hospitals and

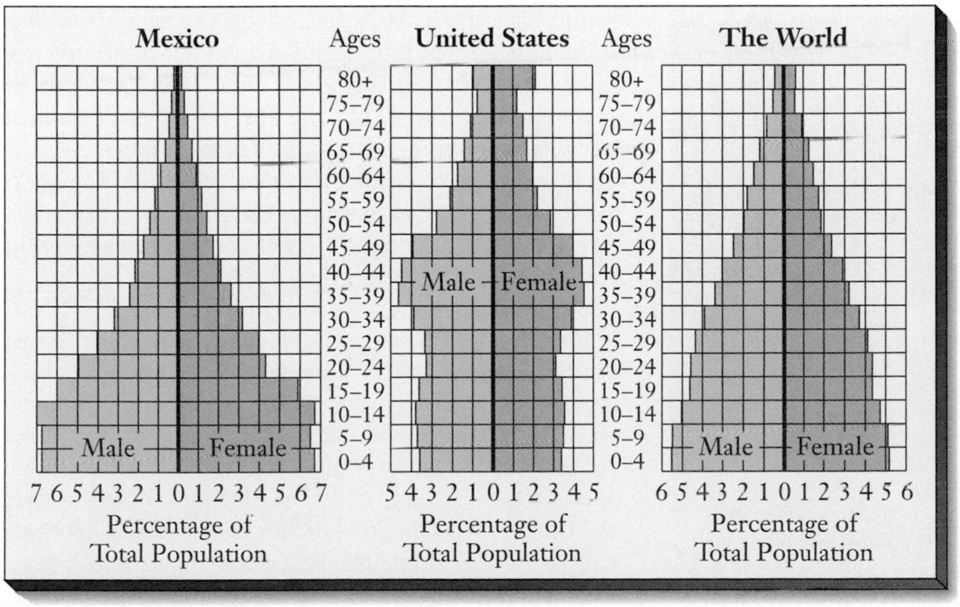

population pyramid a graphic representation of a population, divided into age and sex

Figure 20.7

THREE POPULATION PYRAMIDS

Source: Population Today, 26, 9, September 1998:4, 5.

schools; transportation, communication, water, gas, sewer, and electrical systems; housing, churches, civic buildings, theaters, stores, and parks. If Mexico fails to double them, its already meager standard of living will drop even further.

Conflict theorists point out that a declining standard of living poses the threat of political instability—protests, riots, even revolution, and, in response, repression by the government. Political instability in one country can spill over into others, threatening an entire region's balance of power. Consequently, leaders of the Most Industrialized Nations use the United Nations to direct a campaign of worldwide birth control. With one hand they give agricultural aid, IUDs, and condoms to the masses in the Least Industrialized Nations—while, with the other, they sell weapons to the elites. Both actions, say conflict theorists, serve the same purpose of promoting political stability and the dominance of the Most Industrialized Nations in global stratification.

The Three Demographic Variables

How many people will live in the United States fifty years from now? What will the world's population be then? These are important questions. Educators want to know how many schools to build. Manufacturers want to anticipate changes in demand for their products. The government needs to know how many doctors, engineers, and executives to train. Politicians want to know how many people will be paying taxes—and how many young people will be available to fight a war.

To project the future of populations, demographers use three **demographic variables:** fertility, mortality, and migration. Let's look at each.

Fertility The **fertility rate** is the number of children the average woman bears. A term sometimes confused with fertility is **fecundity,** the number of children women are *capable* of bearing. The fecundity of women around the world is around twenty children each. Their fertility rate, however (the actual number of children they bear), is much lower. The world's overall fertility rate is 2.9, which means that the average woman in the world bears 2.9 children during her lifetime. At 2.0, the fertility rate of U.S. women is considerably less.

The region of the world that has the highest fertility rate is sub-Saharan Africa, where the average woman gives birth to 5.8 children; the lowest is Europe, where the average woman bears only 1.4 children. As you can see from Table 20.1 on page 575, Bulgaria and Latvia tie for the world's lowest fertility rate. There, the average woman gives birth to only 1.1 children. Niger in Western Africa holds the record for the world's highest rate. There the average woman gives birth to 7.5 children, *seven* times as many children as the average woman in Bulgaria or Latvia.

To compute the fertility rate of a country, demographers analyze the government's records of births. From these, they figure the country's **crude birth rate,** the annual number of live births per 1,000 population. There may be considerable slippage here, of course. The birth records in many of the Least Industrialized Nations are haphazard.

Mortality The second demographic variable, **crude death rate,** refers to the number of deaths per 1,000 population. It, too, varies widely around the world. The highest death rate is 24, a record held by Niger in West Africa, the country that also has the world's highest birth rate. At 2, three oil rich countries in the Mideast—Kuwait, Qatar, and United Arab Emirates—tie for the world's lowest death rate (Haub and Cornelius 1999). Recall Figure 9.2 on pages 244–245 for the incredible difference in standards of living and quality of life that underlie these death rates.

demographic variables the three factors that influence population growth: fertility, mortality, and net migration

fertility rate the number of children that the average woman bears

fecundity the number of children that women are capable of bearing

crude birth rate the annual number of live births per 1,000 population

crude death rate the annual number of deaths per 1,000 population

Although all humans face mortality (the second demographic variable), the conditions of death vary from one culture to another. In the Most Industrialized Nations, the death of a child is rare, whereas in the Least Industrialized Nations it is common. Shown here are mourners at the death of a child in South America.

Between 1892 and 1954, New York's Ellis Island was the port of entry for most immigrants to the United States. The photo on the left shows the inspection that customs officials gave to immigrants in order to weed out those who had obvious medical problems. The photo on the right depicts a more unusual scene, a group of women from Guadelupe in the West Indies after their arrival at Ellis Island.

Migration The third major demographic variable is *migration,* the movement of people from one area to another. There are two types of migration. The first type is illustrated by the Social Map below, people moving from one region to another in the same country. Although there is two-way movement among U.S. regions, as shown on this map, at the end of the year each region has a net loss or gain. A few years ago, the pattern was simple—a net migration from the North and East to the West and South. Now it is more complicated. The Northeast still shows a loss to the other three regions, but the West, which used to have a net gain from the other regions, now has a loss to the Midwest and South. We do not know why the pattern changed.

The second type of migration is people moving from one country to another. Demographers use the term **net migration rate** to refer to the difference between the number of *immigrants* (people moving in) and *emigrants* (people moving out) per 1,000 population. Unlike fertility and mortality rates, migration does not affect the global population, for people are simply shifting their residence from one country or region to another.

As you know, immigrants are seeking a better life. These are a special people. They are willing to give up the security of their family and friends to move to a country with a strange

net migration rate the difference between the number of immigrants and emigrants per 1,000 population

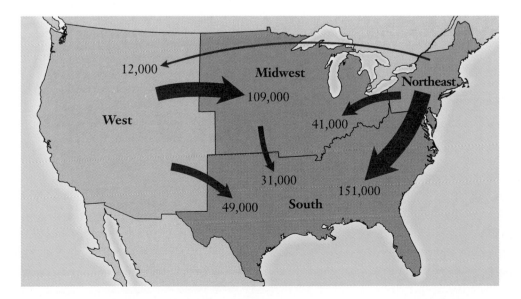

Figure 20.8

SOCIAL MAP: NET MIGRATION FLOWS BETWEEN REGIONS, 1997–1998

Source: Statistical Abstract 1999: Table 28.

language and unfamiliar customs. What motivates people to embark on such a venture? To understand immigration, we need to look at both *push* and *pull* factors. The push factors are the things that people want to escape—poverty, the lack of religious and political freedoms, political persecution. The pull factors are the magnets that draw people to a new land, such as a chance for higher wages and better jobs.

Around the world, the flow of migration is from the Least Industrialized Nations to the industrialized countries. After "migrant paths" are established, immigration often accelerates as networks of kin and friends become additional magnets that attract more people from the same nation—and even from the same villages (Kalish 1994). As discussed in the Perspectives box below, immigration is contributing to a shifting U.S. racial-ethnic mix.

PERSPECTIVES | Cultural Diversity in the United States

GLIMPSING THE FUTURE: THE SHIFTING U.S. RACIAL-ETHNIC MIX

During the next twenty-five years, the population of the United States is expected to grow by about 22 percent. To see what the U.S. population will look like in 25 years, can we simply multiply the current racial-ethnic mix by 22 percent? The answer is a resounding no. As you can see from the figure below, some groups will grow much more than others, giving us a different-looking United States. Some of the changes in the U.S. racial-ethnic mix will be dramatic. In twenty-five years, one of every seventeen Americans is expected to have an Asian background, and one of every six a Latino background.

The basic cause of this shift is immigration. Because the racial-ethnic groups have different rates of immigration, their proportions of the U.S. population will change. As you can see, the proportion of non-Hispanic whites is expected to shrink, that of Native Americans to remain the same. Little immigration is expected from Africa, but because African Americans have a higher than average birth rate, their proportion of the overall population is expected to increase. Due to vast immigration, in twenty-five years Latinos will be, by far, the largest minority group, outnumbering African Americans by 16 million people. ■

For Your Consideration

This shifting racial-ethnic mix is one of the most significant events occurring in the United States. To better understand its implications, apply the three theoretical perspectives.

Use the conflict perspective to identify the groups most likely to be threatened by this change. Over what resources are struggles likely to develop? What impact do you think this changing mix might have on European Americans? On African Americans? What changes in immigration laws (or their enforcement) can you anticipate?

To apply the symbolic interactionist perspective, consider how groups might perceive one another differently as their proportion of the population changes. Do you think the growing number of interracial marriages will affect the way the government classifies people by race-ethnicity? How?

To apply the functionalist perspective, try to determine how the various racial-ethnic groups will benefit from this changing mix. How will other groups (such as businesses) benefit? What dysfunctions can you anticipate?

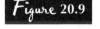 **20.9** **LOOKING TOWARD THE FUTURE**

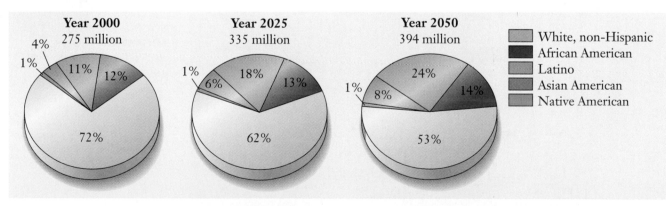

Source: U.S. Bureau of the Census. *Current Population Reports* P25–1130, 1996.

Table 20.2

PLACE OF BIRTH OF IMMIGRANTS TO THE UNITED STATES, BY REGION AND COUNTRY, 1981–1997

North America	6,173,000	Central and South America	1,698,000
Mexico	3,451,000	El Salvador	380,000
Dominican Republic	512,000	Colombia	219,000
Jamaica	341,000	Guatemala	167,000
Cuba	288,000	Guyana	159,000
Haiti	270,000	Peru	143,000
Canada	222,000	Ecuador	110,000
Trinidad and Tobago	88,000	Nicaragua	101,000
		Honduras	97,000
Asia	**5,025,000**	Brazil	62,000
		Panama	49,000
Philippines	893,000	Argentina	45,000
Vietnam	757,000	Venezuela	38,000
China	699,000	Chile	37,000
India	537,000		
Korea	467,000	**Europe**	**1,701,000**
Iran	243,000	Former Soviet Union	487,000
Laos	186,000	Great Britain	248,000
Pakistan	145,000	Poland	240,000
Cambodia	130,000	Germany	120,000
Hong Kong	124,000	Ireland	89,000
Thailand	105,000	Romania	79,000
Taiwan	90,000	Yugoslavia	63,000
Japan	89,000	Portugal	60,000
Lebanon	76,000	Italy	50,000
Israel	62,000	France	43,000
Jordan	62,000	Greece	41,000
Iraq	52,000		
Bangladesh	45,000	**Africa**	**453,000**
Afghanistan	42,000	Nigeria	83,000
Syria	40,000	Egypt	66,000
Turkey	40,000	Ethiopia	65,000
		Ghana	40,000

Note: Because only the countries with the largest emigration are listed, the total for an entire region is larger than the total of the countries from that region. When 1997 data was missing, 1996 data was doubled.

Source: Statistical Abstract 1999:Table 8.

By far, the United States is the world's number one choice of immigrants. The United States admits more immigrants each year than all the other nations of the world combined. Twenty million—one of every twelve Americans—were born in another country. Table 20.2 above shows where U.S. immigrants were born. To escape grinding poverty, such as that which surrounds Celia and Angel, people also enter the United States illegally. The U.S. government puts their number at 5 million. Most of them have come from Central and South America, especially Mexico (*Statistical Abstract* 1999:Table 10).

Experts cannot agree whether immigrants are a net contributor to or a drain on the U.S. economy. Economist Julian Simon (1986, 1993) claimed that the net results benefit the country. After subtracting what immigrants collect in welfare and adding what they produce in jobs and taxes, he concluded that immigrants make an overall positive contribution to the U.S. economy. Other economists such as Donald Huddle (1993) produce figures showing that immigrants are a drain on taxpayers. The fairest conclusion seems to be that the more educated immigrants produce more than they cost, while the less educated cost more than they produce. The cost is also unevenly distributed. Native-born Americans who have less than a high school education find that their incomes decline because they compete for jobs with low-educated immigrants ("Immigration's Costs" 1997).

Problems in Forecasting Population Growth

The total of the three demographic variables—fertility, mortality, and net migration—gives us a country's **growth rate,** the net change after people have been added to and subtracted from a population. What demographers call the **basic demographic equation** is quite simple:

$$\text{Growth rate} = \text{births} - \text{deaths} + \text{net migration}$$

With such a simple equation, it might seem that it would be a simple matter to project a country's future population. To try to forecast population growth, however, is to invite yourself to be wrong. Consider the following event.

> During the depression of the late 1920s and early 1930s, birth rates plunged as unemployment reached unprecedented heights. Demographers issued warnings about the dangers of depopulation almost as alarmist as some of today's forecasts of overpopulation. Because each year fewer and fewer females would enter the childbearing years, they felt that the population of countries such as Great Britain would shrink. (Waddington 1978)

What actually happened? The Great Depression ended, but World War II broke out, and the birth rate stayed low. After the war, however, the birth rate jumped, bringing a "baby boom" (from 1946 to 1965) to both the United States and Europe.

If population increase depended only on biology, the demographer's job would be simple. But social factors—wars, economic booms and busts, plagues, and famines—push rates up or down. As shown in the Perspectives box on the next page, even infanticide can affect population growth. A government's efforts to influence a country's growth rate also complicate the demographer's task of projecting future populations. Some governments take steps to get women to bear more children. When Hitler decided that Germany needed more "Aryans," the German government outlawed abortion and offered cash bonuses for women who gave birth. The population increased.

Other countries take steps to reduce the number of children. None has been so draconian as China. As you read these details, recall the Big Brother vignette that opened Chapter 15.

growth rate the net change in a population after adding births, subtracting deaths, and either adding or subtracting net migration

basic demographic equation growth rate = births – deaths + net migration

Due to the Chinese government's policy of "one couple, one child," the birth rate of China has dropped sharply. As discussed in the text, this policy is carried out ruthlessly, including forcing abortions on protesting women.

PERSPECTIVES | Cultural Diversity Around the World

KILLING LITTLE GIRLS: AN ANCIENT AND THRIVING PRACTICE

"The Mysterious Case of the Missing Girls" could have been the title of this box. Around the globe, for every 100 girls born about 105 boys are born. In China, however, for every 100 girl babies, there are 111 boy babies. Given China's huge population, this means China has about 400,000 fewer baby girls than it should have. What is the explanation for this?

The answer is rooted in sexism— the preference for boy babies. For millennia, people have experimented with a variety of folk techniques designed to ensure the birth of boy babies. None has worked. Only in recent years, with the development of technology that separates X and Y chromosomes in semen, has a technique become available that is 80 percent effective. China, however, is not technologically advanced; this isn't the reason for its shortage of girl babies. Might the Chinese have stumbled on an effective folk technique?

The answer points in a different direction—to the ancient practice of *female infanticide,* the killing of girl babies. When a Chinese woman goes into labor, village midwives sometimes grab a bucket of water. If the newborn is a girl, she is plunged into the water before she can draw her first breath.

At the root of China's infanticide is economics. The people are poor, and they have no pensions. When parents can no longer work, sons support them. In contrast, a daughter must be married off, at great expense, and at that point her obligations transfer to her husband and his family.

In the past few years, the percentage of boy babies has grown. The reason, again, is economics, but this time it has a new twist. As China opened the door to capitalism, travel and trade opened up—but primarily to men, for it is not thought appropriate for women to travel alone. Thus men find themselves in a better position to bring profits home to the family—and one more reason for parents to desire male children.

Female infanticide is not limited to China. Although the British banned this practice in India in 1870, it continues there. Western technology even plays a part. Many Indian women use amniocentesis to learn the sex of their child, and then decide whether or not to abort. In 99.9 percent of these abortions, the fetus is female.

One case in which amniocentesis was used for sex selection led to a public outcry in India. The outrage was not about female infanticide, however; nor was it due to an antiabortion movement. Rather, the public became incensed when a physician mistakenly gave the parents wrong information and aborted a *male* baby!

It is likely that the preference for boys, and the resulting female infanticide, will not disappear until the social structures that perpetuate sexism are dismantled. This will not take place until women hold as much power as men, a development that, should it ever occur, apparently lies far in the future. ■

Sources: Lagaipa 1990; McGowan 1991; Polumbaum 1992; Renteln 1992; Greenhalgh and Li 1995.

What occurs in China goes beyond even Orwell's fertile imagination. China's "One couple, one child" national policy is well known, but few know how ruthlessly it is carried out. Steven Mosher, an anthropologist who did fieldwork in China, revealed that—whether she wants it or not—after the birth of her first child, each woman is fitted with an IUD (intrauterine device). If a woman has a second child, she is sterilized. If a woman gets pregnant without permission (yes, you read that right), she is aborted. If she does not consent to an abortion, one is performed on her anyway—even if she is nine months pregnant (Erik 1982). The government even has its agents check sanitary napkins to make sure that women are having their menstrual periods and are not pregnant.

Industrialization is extremely significant. *In every country that industrializes, the growth rate declines.* Not only does industrialization open up economic opportunities, but it also makes children more expensive. They require more education and remain dependent longer. Significantly, the basis for conferring status also changes—from having children to attaining education and displaying material wealth. People like Celia and Angel begin to see life differently, and their motivation to have many children drops sharply. Although this principle is solid, demographers don't know how rapidly industrialization will progress, or how quickly changes in values and reproductive behavior will follow.

Because of these many complications, demographers play it safe by making several projections of population growth. For example, what will the U.S. population be in the year 2050? Will we be at **zero population growth**, with every 1,000 women giving birth to 2,100 children? (The extra 100 children make up for those who do not survive.) Will a larger proportion of women go to college? (The more education women have, the fewer children

zero population growth a demographic condition in which women bear only enough children to reproduce the population

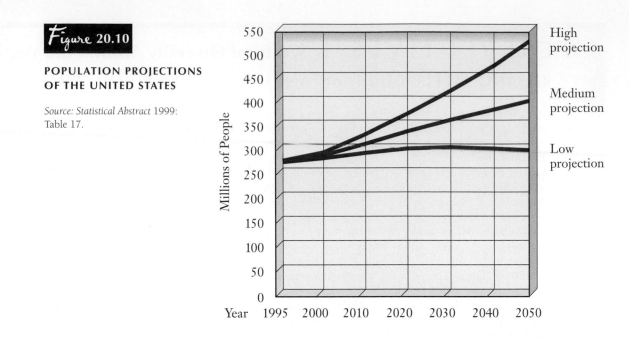

Figure 20.10

POPULATION PROJECTIONS OF THE UNITED STATES

Source: Statistical Abstract 1999: Table 17.

they bear.) How will immigration change during the coming years? Will AIDS rage out of control? Will some other devastating disease appear? What will happen to the new global economy? With such huge variables, it is easy to see why demographers make the three projections of the U.S. population shown in Figure 20.10.

Let's look at a different aspect of population, where people live. Since the world is rapidly becoming urban, we shall concentrate on urban trends and urban life.

URBANIZATION

The transformation of the San Francisco streets was as intriguing as it was unexpected. I'd been interviewing the homeless for longer than I had planned, and dusk had begun to settle in. Heading back to my fleabag hotel, I spotted a 20-year-old man carrying a backpack. Trying for one more interview, I sat on the sidewalk with my back against a building— a self-protective position that let me feel more secure—and started asking questions. In the middle of an answer to one of my questions, the man suddenly stopped mid-sentence, stared at me intently, and, in a voice so low I had to concentrate to hear what he was saying, said very slowly, "I know why you're here."

Somewhat taken back, I said, "What?"

He replied, "I know why you're here."

In measured tones, I said that I had already explained to him that I was doing sociological interviews.

"No," he said, not taking his eyes off mine. "I know why you're here." He paused, then said, "You're here to help me. I can tell because of the way you move your hands."

I felt a tingling go up my spine as the man leaned closer, as though he was about to reveal some secret. He then began to mutter that the FBI was after him.

Not taking my eyes off him, I looked past him to seek out an escape route—just in case.

The man fell silent. He continued to stare intensely at me. Then, as I uttered a silent prayer, he scooped up his knapsack and walked briskly off into the falling darkness.

Ordinarily I would have felt bad about losing an interview. Not this time.

I had begun to take too much for granted in my homeless research; this experience put me on guard once again. I was forced to develop a keener awareness of the city. With dusk gently falling on the city streets, I looked for my hotel and saw the area change.

The men and women in business dress, who had been scurrying around these streets carrying their briefcases, and the fashionably dressed shoppers who had been going in and out of the stores were now replaced by people whose clothing and hairstyles were remarkably different. The orange and blue hair especially stood out. A woman with a tattoo on her left breast, mostly exposed by her half-zipped leather jacket and absence of bra or blouse, leaned against a building. A man on roller skates, wearing a white jump suit with the zipper opened to his navel, rhythmically moved his feet back and forth to a beat only he heard, never leaving the tiny space he had claimed. Women in short, tight skirts strolled slowly on the outside of the sidewalk, keenly eyeing passing cars.

And there was the couple who rode by on a Harley hog; their image is forever emblazoned in my memory. The man, who must have been in his forties, was shirtless but wore an open denim vest. Other than his flowing beard and long, unkempt hair, his most pronounced characteristic was the huge beer gut that kept his vest from closing. On the back of his motorcycle, her arms tightly clutched about him, but not quite able to reach around his stomach, sat a skinny blonde who couldn't have been more than 16. ■

This transformation took place in San Francisco. But if I had been in New Orleans or Atlanta in the South, New York or Boston in the East, or Chicago in the Midwest, the scene would have been similar. This is a distinctly *urban* phenomenon. That is, cities have specific characteristics that give them their unique "flavor." Their "urbanness" comes not only from their size, but also from the anonymity they provide, which allows people to both blend in and stand out at the same time.

Such a scene as the one I just described whets the sociological imagination. Earlier (pages 106–107), we reviewed Emile Durkheim's conclusions about organic and mechanical solidarity and Ferdinand Tönnies' contrasts of rural and urban life (*Gemeinschaft* and *Gesellschaft*). In the 1920s, Chicago was a vivid mosaic of immigrants, gangsters, prostitutes, the homeless, the rich and the poor—much as it is today. Sociologists at the University of Chicago began to study these contrasting ways of life. From what became known as the Chicago School of Sociology emerged stunning studies of city life—from hobos (Anderson 1923) and gangs (Thrasher 1927) to the contrasting lives of the poor and the rich (Zorbaugh 1929). Today, sociologists still study why and how some people find the city a place of refuge, while others find it a threatening, foreboding sort of place.

To better understand urban life, let's first find out how the city itself came about.

Early cities were small economic centers surrounded by walls designed to keep out enemies. These cities, built like fortresses, were constantly threatened by armed, roving tribesmen and by the leaders of nearby city-states who raised armies in an effort to enlarge their domain and enrich their coffers by sacking neighboring cities. Pictured here is Carcasonne, a restored medieval city in southern France.

$\mathcal{T}$HE DEVELOPMENT OF CITIES

Cities are not new to the world scene. Perhaps as early as seven to ten thousand years ago people built small cities with massive defensive walls, such as Catal Hüyük (Schwendinger and Schwendinger 1983) and biblically famous Jericho (Homblin 1973). Cities on a larger scale originated about 3500 B.C., about the same time writing was invented (Chandler and Fox 1974; Hawley 1981). At that time, cities appeared in several parts of the world—first in Mesopotamia (Iran) and later in the Nile, Indus, and Yellow River valleys, in West Africa, around the Mediterranean, in Central America, and in the Andes (Fischer 1976; Flanagan 1990).

The key to the origin of cities is the development of more efficient agriculture (Lenski and Lenski 1987). Only when farming produces a surplus can some people stop being food producers and gather in cities to spend time in other pursuits. A **city,** in fact, can be defined as a place in which a large number of people are permanently based and do not produce their own food. The invention of the plow between five and six thousand years ago created widespread agricultural surpluses, stimulating the development of towns and cities (Curwin and Hart 1961). (For a review of the sweeping historical changes that laid the organizational groundwork for the rise and expansion of cities, see pages 150–155.)

The Industrial Revolution and the Size of Cities

Most early cities were tiny by comparison with those of today, merely a collection of a few thousand people in agricultural centers or on major trade routes. The most notable exceptions are two cities that reached 1 million for a brief period of time before they declined—Changan in China about A.D. 800 and Baghdad in Persia about A.D. 900 (Chandler and Fox 1974). Even Athens at the peak of its power in the fifth century B.C. had less than 200,000 inhabitants. Rome, at its peak, may have had a million or more (Flanagan 1990).

Even 200 years ago, the only city in the world that had a population of more than a million was Peking (now Beijing), China (Chandler and Fox 1974). Then in just 100 years, by 1900, the number of such cities jumped to sixteen. The reason was the Industrial Revolution, which drew people to cities by providing work. The Industrial Revolution also stimulated rapid transportation and communication, and allowed people, resources, and products

city a place in which a large number of people are permanently based and do not produce their own food

to be moved efficiently—all essential factors (called *infrastructure*) on which large cities depend. Today about 300 cities have a million or more people (Frisbie and Kasarda 1988).

Urbanization, Metropolises, and Megalopolises

Although cities are not new to the world scene, urbanization is. **Urbanization** refers to masses of people moving to cities, and to these cities being a growing influence on society. Urbanization is worldwide. In 1800, only 3 percent of the world's population lived in cities (Hauser and Schnore 1965). Today 45 percent do: 75 percent of people in the industrialized world and 37 percent of those who live in the Least Industrialized Nations (Haub and Cornelius 1999). Soon most people will live in cities. Without the Industrial Revolution this remarkable growth could not have taken place, for an extensive infrastructure is needed to support hundreds of thousands and even millions of people in a relatively small area.

To understand the city's attraction, we need to consider the "pulls" of urban life. Due to its exquisite division of labor, the city offers incredible variety—music ranging from rock and blues to country and classic, diets for vegetarians and diabetics as well as imported delicacies from around the world for everyone else. Cities also offer anonymity, which so many find refreshing in light of the much tighter controls of village and small-town life. And, of course, the city offers work.

Some cities have grown so large and have so much influence over a region that the term *city* is no longer adequate to describe them. The term **metropolis** is used instead. This term refers to a central city surrounded by smaller cities and their suburbs. They are linked by transportation and communication and connected economically, and sometimes politically, through county boards and regional governing bodies.

St. Louis is an example. Although this name, St. Louis, properly refers to a city of fewer than than 400,000 people in Missouri, it also refers to another 2 million people living in more than a hundred separate towns in both Missouri and Illinois. Altogether the region is known as the "St. Louis or Bi-State Area." Although these towns are independent politically, they form an economic unit. They are linked by work (many people in the smaller towns work in St. Louis, or are served by industries from St. Louis), by communications (they share the same area newspaper and radio and television stations), and by transportation (they use the same interstate highways, "Bi-State Bus" system, and international airport). As symbolic interactionists would note, a common identity also arises from the area's shared symbols (the Arch, the Mississippi River, Busch Brewery, the Cardinals, the Rams, the Blues—both the hockey team and the music). Most of the towns run into one another, and if you were to drive through this metropolis you would not know you were leaving one town and entering another—unless you had lived there for some time and were aware of the fierce small-town identifications and rivalries that exist side by side with this larger identification.

Some metropolises have grown so large and influential that the term **megalopolis** is used to describe them. This term refers to an overlapping area consisting of at least two metropolises and their many suburbs. Of the twenty or so megalopolises in the United States, the three largest are the Eastern seaboard running from Maine to Virginia, the area in Florida between Miami, Orlando, and Tampa, and California's coastal area between San Francisco and San Diego. This California megalopolis extends into Mexico and includes Tijuana and its southern suburbs.

This process of urban areas turning into a metropolis, and a metropolis developing into a megalopolis occurs worldwide. Figure 20.11 on the next page shows the ten largest cities in the world. Note that most of them are located in the Least Industrialized Nations.

U.S. Urban Patterns

In its early years, the United States was almost exclusively rural. In 1790, only about 5 of every 100 Americans lived in cities. By 1920, this figure had jumped to 1 of 2. Urbanization

urbanization the process by which an increasing proportion of a population lives in cities

metropolis a central city surrounded by smaller cities and their suburbs

megalopolis an urban area consisting of at least two metropolises and their many suburbs

Figure 20.11 THE URBAN GIANTS: THE WORLD'S TEN LARGEST CITIES (POPULATION IN MILLIONS)

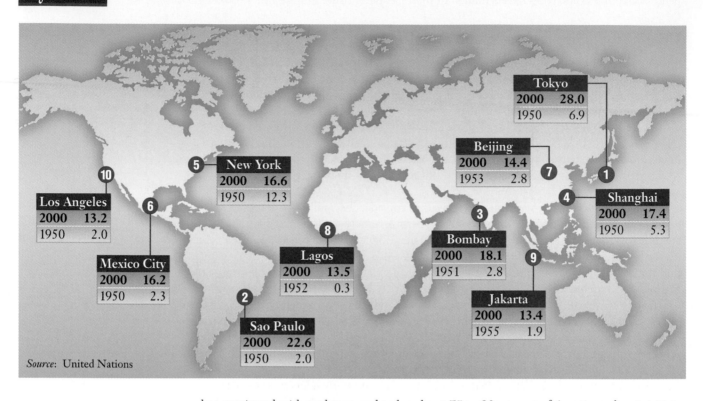

Tokyo	
2000	28.0
1950	6.9

Beijing	
2000	14.4
1953	2.8

New York	
2000	16.6
1950	12.3

Los Angeles	
2000	13.2
1950	2.0

Shanghai	
2000	17.4
1950	5.3

Mexico City	
2000	16.2
1950	2.3

Bombay	
2000	18.1
1951	2.8

Lagos	
2000	13.5
1952	0.3

Jakarta	
2000	13.4
1955	1.9

Sao Paulo	
2000	22.6
1950	2.0

Source: United Nations

metropolitan statistical area (MSA) a central city and the urbanized counties adjacent to it

has continued without letup, and today about 75 to 80 percent of Americans live in cities. As you can see from Figure 20.12, like our other social patterns, urbanization is uneven across the United States.

The U.S. Census Bureau has divided the country into 284 **metropolitan statistical areas (MSAs).** Each MSA consists of a central city of at least 50,000 people and the ur-

Figure 20.12

SOCIAL MAP: HOW URBAN IS YOUR STATE? THE RURAL-URBAN MAKEUP OF THE UNITED STATES

Source: Statistical Abstract 1999: Table 46.

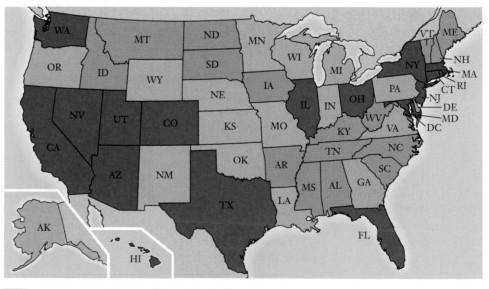

■ The most rural states, 32%–61% urban
■ Average states, 63%–73% urban
■ The most urban states, 74%–93% urban

Note: The most rural state is Vermont, where 2 of 3 residents (68 percent) live in rural areas. The most urban state is California, where only 1 of 14 residents (7 percent) lives in rural areas.

banized areas linked to it. As Table 20.3 shows, about three of every five Americans live in just fifty or so MSAs.

As Americans migrate in search of work and better lifestyles, some cities gain population while others shrink. Table 20.4 below compares the fastest growing U.S. cities with those that are losing people. As you can see, ten of the fastest growing cities are in the West; two are in the South. Of the declining cities, ten are in the Northeast, while the South and West have one each.

As Americans migrate, **edge cities** have developed. This term refers to clusters of shopping malls, hotels, office parks, and residential areas that are located near the intersection of major highways. Although these clusters may overlap the boundaries of several cities or towns, they provide a sense of place to those who live, work, or shop there.

Table 20.3	METROPOLITAN AREAS LARGER THAN 1 MILLION PEOPLE		
Year	Number of Areas	Population (millions)	Percentage of U.S. Population
1950	14	45	30%
1960	22	64	36%
1970	31	84	41%
1980	35	104	46%
1990	40	133	53%
1996	47	148	56%
2000[a]	51	159	58%

[a]Author's estimate.

Sources: Census Bureau 1991:2; Statistical Abstract 1999:Tables 26, 41.

Another major U.S. urban pattern is **gentrification,** the movement of middle-class people into rundown areas of a city. They are attracted by the low prices for quality housing that, though deteriorated, can be restored. One consequence is an improvement in the appearance of some urban neighborhoods—freshly painted buildings, well-groomed lawns, and the absence of boarded-up windows. Another consequence is that the poor residents are displaced as the more well-to-do newcomers move in and drive up prices. Tension often arises between these groups (Anderson 1990, 1997).

A common pattern is for the gentrifiers to be whites and the displaced to be minorities. As discussed in the Down-to-Earth Sociology box on the following page, in Harlem, New York, both the gentrifiers and the displaced are African Americans. As middle-class and professional African Americans reclaim this and other urban areas, an infrastructure—which includes everything from Starbucks coffee houses to dentists—follows. So do soaring real estate prices.

| Table 20.4 | THE FASTEST-GROWING AND FASTEST-SHRINKING U.S. CITIES |

The Fastest-Growing Cities	The Fastest-Shrinking Cities
1. 40.9% Las Vegas, NV	1. −4.7% Salinas, CA
2. 29.2% McAllen-Edinburg-Mission, TX	2. −4.5% Utica-Rome, NY
3. 25.9% Boise City, ID	3. −3.9% Birmingham, NY
4. 23.7% Fayetteville-Springdale-Rogers, AR	4. −2.3% Charleston, SC
5. 23.1% Austin-San Marcos, TX	5. −1.9% Springfield MA
6. 22.7% Phoenix-Mesa, AZ	6. −1.6% Scranton-Wilkes Barre, PA
7. 22.2% Olympia, WA	7. −1.5% Vineland-Millville-Bridgeton, NJ
8. 22.1% Bremerton, WA	8. −1.4% New London-Norwich, CT
9. 21.3% Provo-Orem, UT	9. 1.2% Buffalo-Niagara Falls, NY
10. 21.1% Brownsville-Harlingen-San Benito, TX	10. −1.2% New Haven-Meriden, CT
11. 19.4% Raleigh-Durham-Chapel Hill, NC	11. −1.1% Hartford, CT
12. 19.1% Colorado Springs, CO	12. −0.9% Providence, RI

Note: Figures indicate the percentage of population change from 1990–1996. A minus sign indicates a loss of population.

Source: Statistical Abstract 1999:Table 43.

edge city a large clustering of service facilities and residential areas near highway intersections that provides a sense of place to people who live, shop, and work there

gentrification the displacement of the poor by the relatively affluent, who purchase and renovate the former's homes

Down-to-Earth

Sociology

RECLAIMING HARLEM: "IT FEEDS MY SOUL"

The story is well known. The inner city is filled with crack, crime, and corruption. It stinks from foul, festering garbage strewn on the streets and piled up around burned-out buildings. Only those who have no other choice live in this desolate, abandoned environment where danger lurks around every corner.

What is not so well known is that affluent African Americans are reclaiming some of these areas.

Howard Sanders was living the American Dream. After earning a degree from Harvard Business School, he took a position with a Manhattan investment firm. He lived in an apartment on Central Park West, but he missed Harlem, where he had grown up. He moved back, along with his wife and daughter.

African-American lawyers, doctors, professors, and bankers are doing the same.

What's the attraction? The first is nostalgia, a cultural identification with the Harlem of legend and folklore. It was here that black writers and artists lived in the 1920s, here that the blues and jazz attracted young and accomplished musicians.

The second reason is a more practical one. Harlem offers housing value. Five bedroom homes with 6,000 square feet are available. Some feature Honduran mahogany. Some brownstones are only shells, and have to be renovated; others are in perfect condition. With the influx of the new professionals, prices have risen. A shell sells for $80,000; a house in mint condition goes for $450,000.

What is happening is the rebuilding of a community. People who "made" it want to be role models. They want children to see them going to

and returning from work in their communities.

When the middle class moved out of Harlem, so did the amenities. Now that young professionals are moving back in, the amenities are returning. There were no coffee shops, restaurants, jazz clubs, florists, copy centers, optometrist offices, art galleries—the types of things urbanites take for granted. Now there are.

The same thing is happening on Chicago's West Side and in other U.S. cities.

The drive to find community—to make a connection with others and with one's roots—is strong. As one migrant to Harlem, an investment banker, said, "It feeds my soul." ■

Source: Based on Cose 1999; McCormick 1999.

MODELS OF URBAN GROWTH

Sociologist Robert Park coined the term **human ecology** to describe how people adapt to their environment (Park and Burgess 1921a; Park 1936). (This concept is also known as *urban ecology*.) The process of urban growth is of special interest to human ecologists. Let's look at the four main models they developed.

The Concentric Zone Model

To explain how cities expand, sociologist Ernest Burgess (1925) proposed a *concentric-zone model*. As shown in segment A of Figure 20.13, Burgess noted that a city expands outward from its center. Zone I is the central business district. Zone II, which encircles the downtown area, is a zone in transition. It contains deteriorating housing and rooming houses, which Burgess said breed poverty, disease, and vice. Zone III is the area to which thrifty workers have moved in order to escape the zone in transition and yet maintain easy access to their work. The wealthy live in Zone IV, which contains exclusive areas of expensive apartments, residential hotels, and single-family homes. Commuters live in Zone V, which consists of suburbs or satellite cities that have developed around rapid transit routes.

Burgess intended this model to represent "the tendencies of any town or city to expand radially from its central business district." He noted, however, that no "city fits perfectly this

human ecology Robert Park's term for the relationship between people and their environment (natural resources such as land)

Figure 20.13 HOW CITIES DEVELOP: MODELS OF URBAN GROWTH

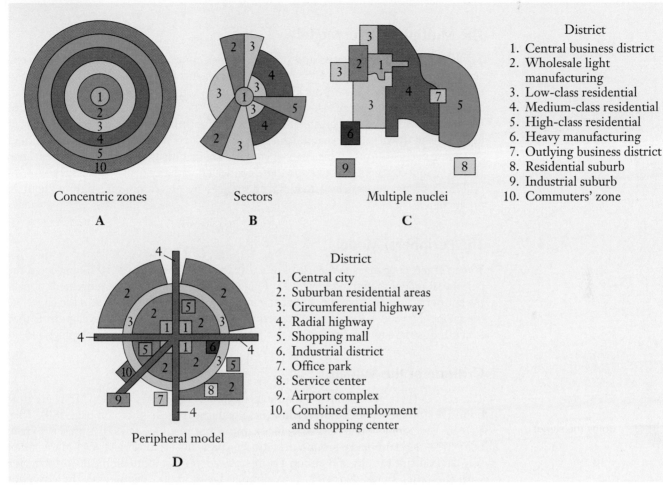

Concentric zones
A

Sectors
B

Multiple nuclei
C

District
1. Central business district
2. Wholesale light manufacturing
3. Low-class residential
4. Medium-class residential
5. High-class residential
6. Heavy manufacturing
7. Outlying business district
8. Residential suburb
9. Industrial suburb
10. Commuters' zone

Peripheral model
D

District
1. Central city
2. Suburban residential areas
3. Circumferential highway
4. Radial highway
5. Shopping mall
6. Industrial district
7. Office park
8. Service center
9. Airport complex
10. Combined employment and shopping center

Source: Cousins and Nagpaul 1970; Harris 1997.

ideal scheme." Some cities have physical obstacles such as a lake, river, or railroad, which cause their expansion to depart from the model. Burgess also noted that businesses had begun to deviate from the model by locating in outlying zones. This was in 1925, and Burgess was seeing the first stage of a major shift that led businesses away from downtown areas and brought them to suburban shopping malls. Today, these malls account for most of the country's retail sales.

The Sector Model

Sociologist Homer Hoyt (1939, 1971) noted that a city's concentric zones do not form a complete circle, and he modified Burgess' model of urban growth. As shown in segment B of Figure 20.13, a concentric zone can contain several sectors—one of working-class housing, another of expensive homes, a third of businesses, and so on—all competing for the same land.

What sociologists call an **invasion-succession cycle** is an example of this dynamic competition of urban life. When poor immigrants or rural migrants enter a city, they settle in the lowest-rent area they can find. As their numbers swell, they spill over into adjacent areas. Upset by their presence, the middle class moves out, thus expanding the

> **invasion-succession cycle** the process of one group of people displacing a group whose racial-ethnic or social class characteristics differ from their own

sector of low-cost housing. The invasion-succession cycle is never complete, for later another group will replace this earlier one. It may also be gentrified, a topic to which we will return.

The Multiple-Nuclei Model

Geographers Chauncey Harris and Edward Ullman noted that some cities have several centers or nuclei (Harris and Ullman 1945; Ullman and Harris 1970). As shown in segment C of Figure 20.13, each nucleus is the focus of some specialized activity. A familiar example is the clustering of fast-food restaurants in one area and automobile dealerships in another. Sometimes similar activities are grouped together because they profit from cohesion; retail districts, for example, draw more customers if there are more stores. Other clustering occurs because some types of land use are incompatible with one another, such as those connected with factories and those connected with expensive homes. Thus, push-pull factors separate areas by activities, and services are not evenly spread throughout an urban area.

The Peripheral Model

To depict recent changes in the use of urban space, Chauncey Harris (1997) proposed the peripheral model shown in segment D of Figure 20.13. It portrays the movement of people and services away from the central city into the periphery, or outskirts of the city. Note the radial highways, which now characterize many U.S. cities, and the developments they foster. Industrial and office parks are also recent and significant urban developments.

Critique of the Models

These models are very limited in their explanation of how cities develop. They are time bound, for medieval cities didn't follow these patterns (see the photo on page 588). They also are geography bound. England, for example, has planning laws that preserve green belts (trees and farmlands) around the city. This prevents urban sprawl: Wal-Mart cannot buy land outside the city and put up a store; instead, it must locate in the downtown area with the other stores. Norwich, for example, has 250,000 people; yet the city ends abruptly, and on its green belt pheasants skitter across plowed fields while sheep graze in verdant meadows (Milbank 1995b). The models, then, do not account for urban planning policies.

The models also fall short when it comes to the cities of the Least Industrialized Nations. U.S. visitors are often surprised when they visit one of these cities. The wealthy often claim the inner city, where fine restaurants and other services are readily accessible. Tucked behind tall walls and protected from public scrutiny, they enjoy luxurious homes and gardens. In contrast, the poor, especially rural migrants, settle in areas outside the city. This topic is discussed in the Perspectives box on the facing page.

CITY LIFE

Cities are intended to be solutions to problems. They are the result of human endeavors that seek to improve life collectively, to develop a way of life that transcends the limitations of farm and village. Cities hold out the hope of jobs, education, and other advantages. The perception of opportunity underlies mass migration to cities throughout the world.

Just as cities provide opportunities, however, they also create problems. Humans have not only physical needs—food, shelter, and safety—but also a need for **community**, a feeling of belonging—the sense that others care what happens to us, and that we can depend on the people around us. Some people find this sense of community in the city; others find

community a place people identify with, where they sense that they belong and that others care what happens to them

PERSPECTIVES | Cultural Diversity Around the World

WHY CITY SLUMS ARE BETTER THAN THE COUNTRY: URBANIZATION IN THE LEAST INDUSTRIALIZED NATIONS

Images of the Least Industrialized Nations that portray serene pastoral scenes distort today's reality. In these nations, poor rural people have flocked to the cities in such numbers that, as we saw in Figure 20.11 (page 590), these nations now contain most of the world's largest cities. Each year the cities of the Least Industrialized Nations grow by 62 million people (Annez 1998). That's more than all the Italians who live in Italy, the equivalent of adding twice the population of Canada every year. In the Most Industrialized Nations, industrialization usually preceded urbanization, but here *urbanization is preceding industrialization.*

The settlement patterns are also different. When rural migrants and immigrants move to U.S. cities, they usually settle in deteriorating housing near the city's center. The wealthy reside in suburbs and luxurious city enclaves. Migrants to cities of the Least Industrialized Nations, in contrast, establish illegal squatter settlements outside the city. There they build shacks from scrap board, cardboard, and bits of corrugated metal. Even flattened tin cans are used for building material. The squatters enjoy no city facilities—roads, public transportation, water, sewers, or garbage pickup. After thousands of squatters have settled an area, the city acknowledges their right to live there and adds bus service and minimal water lines. Hundreds of people use a single spigot. About *5 million* of Mexico City's residents live in such conditions, with hundreds of thousands more pouring in each year.

This story is repeated throughout South America, Africa, India, and the rest of the so-called undeveloped world. Why this vast rush to live in the city under such miserable conditions? The explanation lies in the many "push" factors that arise from the breakdown of traditional rural life. With the importation of modern medicine, a safer water supply, and better transportation and distribution of food, the death rate has dropped, and the rural populations are multiplying. There is not enough land for every-

The Least Industrialized Nations are facing massive upheaval as they rapidly urbanize, resulting in disparities such as those depicted here. Lacking the infrastructure to support their many newcomers, cities in the Least Industrialized Nations, already steeped in poverty, face the daunting task of developing jobs, housing, sewage and electrical systems, roads, schools, and so on.

one, and rural life can no longer support so many people. "Pull" factors also draw people to the cities—the hope of jobs, education, better housing, and even a more stimulating life.

> At the bottom of a ravine near Mexico City is a dismal bunch of shacks. Some of the families living in them have 14 children.
>
> "We used to live up there," Señora Gonzalez gestured toward the mountain, "in those caves. Our only hope was one day to have a place to live. And now we do." She smiled with pride at the jerry-built shacks . . . each one had a collection of flowers planted in tin cans. "One day, we hope to extend the water pipes and drainage—perhaps even pave. . . ."
>
> And what was the name of her community? Señora Gonzalez beamed. "Esperanza!" (McDowell 1984:172)

Esperanza is the Spanish word for hope. This is what lies behind the rush to

these cities—the hope of a better life. And this is why the rush won't slow down. In 1930, only one Latin American city had more than a million people—now fifty do! The world's cities are growing by one million people each week (Brockerhoff 1996).

Will the Least Industrialized Nations adjust to this vast, unwanted migration? They have no choice. Authorities in Brazil, Guatemala, Venezuela, and other countries have sent in the police and the army to evict the settlers. It doesn't work. It just leads to violence, and the settlers keep streaming in. The adjustment will be painful. The infrastructure (roads, water, sewers, electricity, and so on) must be built, but these poor countries don't have the resources to build them. As the desperate flock to the cities, the problems will worsen. ■

For Your Consideration

What solutions do you see?

its opposite, *alienation,* a sense of not belonging, and a feeling that no one cares what happens to you. Let's look at these two aspects of city life.

Alienation

> Twenty-eight-year-old Catherine Genovese, who was called Kitty by almost everyone in her Queens neighborhood, was returning home from work. After she had parked her car, a man grabbed her. She screamed, "Oh my God, he stabbed me! Help me! Please help me!"
>
> For more than half an hour, thirty-eight respectable, law-abiding citizens looked out their windows and watched as the killer stalked and stabbed Kitty in three separate attacks. Twice the sudden glow from their bedroom lights interrupted him and frightened him off. Each time he returned, sought her out, and stabbed her again. Not one person telephoned the police during the assault. (*New York Times,* March 26, 1964)

When the police interviewed them, some witnesses said, "I didn't want to get involved." Others said, "We thought it was a lovers' quarrel." Some just said they didn't know. People throughout the country were shocked. It was as though Americans awoke one morning to discover that the country had changed overnight. They took this event as a sign that people could no longer trust one another, that the city was a cold, lonely place.

Why should the city be alienating? In a classic essay, "Urbanism as a Way of Life," sociologist Louis Wirth (1938) argued that the city undermines kinship and neighborhood, which are the traditional sources of social control and social solidarity. Urban dwellers live in anonymity. As they go from one superficial encounter with strangers to another, they grow aloof from one another and indifferent to other people's problems—as did the neighbors of Kitty Genovese. In short, the personal freedom that the city provides comes at the cost of alienation.

Wirth built on some of the ideas discussed on pages 106–107. As a country industrializes, *Gemeinschaft,* the sense of community that comes from everyone knowing everyone else, is ripped apart. What emerges is a new society based on *Gesellschaft,* secondary, impersonal relationships. Lacking identification with one another, people develop the attitude, "It's simply none of *my* business." Their alienation can grow so deep that people can just sit by while someone else is being murdered.

Community

The city, however, is more than a mosaic of strangers who feel disconnected and distrustful of one another. It also consists of a series of smaller worlds, within which people find community. People don't live in a city in some abstract sense. Rather, they come to know the smaller areas of the city where they live, work, shop, and play. Even slums, which to outsiders seem so threatening, can provide a sense of belonging. In a classic study, sociologist Herbert Gans noted,

> After a few weeks of living in the West End (of Boston), my observations—and my perceptions of the area—changed drastically. The search for an apartment quickly indicated that the individual units were usually in much better condition than the outside or the hallways of the buildings. Subsequently, in wandering through the West End, and in using it as a resident, I developed a kind of selective perception, in which my eye focused only on those parts of the area that were actually being used by people. Vacant buildings and boarded-up stores were no longer so visible, and the totally deserted alleys or streets were outside the set of paths normally traversed, either by myself or by the West Enders. . . .
>
> Since much of the area's life took place on the street, faces became familiar very quickly. I met my neighbors on the stairs and in front of my building. And, once a shopping pattern developed, I saw the same storekeepers frequently, as well as the area's "characters" who wandered through the streets every day on a fairly regular route and schedule. In short, the exotic quality of the stores and the residents also wore off as I became used to seeing them.

As he lived in the West End, Gans gradually gained an insider's view of the area. Despite the narrow streets, substandard buildings, and even piled-up garbage, most West End-

The city dwellers whom Gans identified as ethnic villagers find community in the city. Living in tightly knit neighborhoods, they know many other residents. Some first-generation immigrants have even come from the same village in the "old country."

ers had chosen to live there: *To them, the West End was a low-rent district, not a slum.* Within this deteriorated area was a community, people who visited back and forth with relatives and were involved in extensive networks of friendships and acquaintances. Gans therefore titled his book *The Urban Villagers* (1962).

Then came well-intentioned urban planners, who drew up urban renewal plans to get rid of the "slum." The residents of the West End were upset when they heard about the plans, and distrustful that the improvements would benefit them. Their distrust proved well founded, for the urban renewal brought with it another invasion-succession cycle. Along with the gleaming new buildings came people with more money who took over the area. The former residents were dispossessed, their intimate patterns destroyed.

Types of Urban Dwellers

Whether you find alienation or community in the city largely depends on who you are, for the city offers both. People from different backgrounds experience the city differently. Gans (1962, 1968, 1991a) identified five types of people who live in the city. The first three types live in the city by choice, for they find a sense of community.

The Cosmopolites The cosmopolites are the city's students, intellectuals, professionals, musicians, artists, and entertainers. They have been drawn to the city because of its conveniences and cultural benefits.

The Singles Young, unmarried people come to the city seeking jobs and entertainment. Businesses and services such as singles bars, singles apartment complexes, and computer dating companies cater to their needs. Their stay in the city often reflects a temporary stage in their life course, for most move to the suburbs after they marry and have children.

The Ethnic Villagers United by race-ethnicity and social class, these people live in tightly knit neighborhoods that resemble villages and small towns. Moving within a close circle of family and friends, the ethnic villagers try to isolate themselves from what they view as the harmful effects of city life.

The next two groups, the deprived and the trapped, have little choice about where they live. Alienated outcasts of industrial society, they are always skirting the edge of disaster.

The Deprived The deprived live in blighted neighborhoods that are more like urban jungles than urban villages. Consisting of the very poor and the emotionally disturbed, the

Men like this one, who has just drunk himself into a stupor, are not an unfamiliar sight in some parts of U.S. cities. The text describes various types of urban dwellers. What type is this man?

deprived represent the bottom of society in terms of income, education, social status, and work skills. Some of them stalk their jungle in search of prey; their victims are usually deprived people like themselves. Their future holds little chance for anything better in life, either for themselves or for their children.

The Trapped The trapped can find no escape either. They consist of people who could not afford to move when their neighborhood was "invaded" by another ethnic group, elderly people who are not wanted elsewhere, alcoholics and other drug addicts, and the downwardly mobile, people who have fallen from a higher social class. Like the deprived, the trapped also suffer high rates of assault, mugging, robbery, and rape.

Gans' typology provides insight into the great variety of ways in which urban dwellers experience the city. Recall my observations of San Francisco. Some find the streets a stimulating source of cultural contrasts. For others, however, these same events pose a constant threat as they try to survive in what for them amounts to an urban jungle.

Urban Sentiment: Finding a Familiar World

Sociologists note that *the city is divided into little worlds* that people come to know down to their smallest details. City people create a sense of intimacy by *personalizing* their shopping (Stone 1954; Gans 1970). They shop in the same stores, and after a period of time customers and clerks greet each other by name. Particular bars, restaurants, and shops are more than just buildings in which they purchase items and services. They become places where neighborhood residents build social relationships with one another, where they share informal news about the community.

Spectator sports also help urban dwellers find a familiar world in the city (Hudson 1991). When Mark McGwire of the Cardinals hit the 61st home run that broke Roger Maris' longstanding record, fans around the world celebrated, but in the St. Louis area the celebration was special: It was for "our" man on "our" team—even though fewer than one in seven of the area's 2.5 million people live in the city. Sociologists David Karp and William Yoels (1990) note that such identification is so intense that long after moving to other parts of the country, many people maintain an emotional allegiance to the sports teams of the city in which they grew up.

The Norm of Noninvolvement and the Diffusion of Responsibility

Urban dwellers try to avoid intrusions from strangers. As they traverse everyday life in the city, they follow a *norm of noninvolvement*.

> To do this, we sometimes use props such as newspapers to shield ourselves from others and to indicate our inaccessibility for interaction. In effect, we learn to "tune others out." In this regard, we might see the Walkman as the quintessential urban prop in that it allows us to be tuned in and tuned out at the same time. It is a device that allows us to enter our own private world and thereby effectively to close off encounters with others. The use of such devices protects our "personal space," along with our body demeanor and facial expression (the passive "mask" or even scowl that persons adopt on subways). (Karp et al. 1991)

Recall Kitty Genovese, whose story was recounted on page 596. Her story troubled social psychologists John Darley and Bibb Latané (1968), who ran the series of experiments featured in Chapter 6 (see pages 164–165). Darley and Latané uncovered a *diffusion of responsibility*. They found that the *more* bystanders there are, the *less* likely they are to help. As a group grows, people's sense of responsibility becomes diffused, with each person assuming that *another* will do the responsible thing. "With these other people here, it is not *my* responsibility," they reason.

The diffusion of responsibility, along with the norm of noninvolvement, helps explain the response to Kitty Genovese's murder. The bystanders at her death were *not* uncaring people. They *did* care that a woman was being attacked. They simply were abiding by an urban norm—one that was helpful for getting them through everyday city life, but, unfortunately, dysfunctional in some critical situations. This norm, combined with killings, rapes, carjackings, muggings, and the generalized fear that the city now engenders in many Americans, underlies a desire to retreat to a safe haven. This topic is discussed in the Down-to-Earth Sociology box below.

Sociology

Down-to-Earth

URBAN FEAR AND THE GATED FORTRESS

Gated neighborhoods— where wrought-iron gates open and close to allow or prevent access to a neighborhood—are not new. They always have been available to the rich. What is new is the upper middle class's rush to towns where residents pay heavy taxes to keep all of the town's facilities, including its streets, private.

Towns cannot discriminate on the basis of religion or ethnicity-race, but they can—and do—discriminate on the basis of social class. Klahanie, Washington, is an excellent example. Begun in 1985, it was supposed to take twenty years to develop. With its safe

streets and 300 acres of open space—and with its ban on satellite dishes, flagpoles, and even basketball hoops on garages—demand for the $300,000-plus homes nestled by a lake in this private community exceeded supply (Egan 1995).

The future will bring many more such private towns as the upper middle class flees urban areas and attempts to build a bucolic dream. A strong sign of the future is Celebration, a planned town of 20,000 people built by the Walt Disney Company just south of Orlando, Florida. With our new technology, the residents of private communities such as these will be able to communicate with the out-

side world while remaining securely locked within their gated fortresses. ■

For Your Consideration

Community always involves a sense of togetherness, a sense of identity with one another. Can you explain how this concept also contains the idea of separateness from others (not just in the example of gated communities, but in general)? What will our future be if we become a nation of gated communities, where middle-class homeowners withdraw into private domains, separating themselves from the rest of the nation?

The U.S. economic system has proven highly beneficial to most citizens, but it also has left many in poverty. To protect themselves, primarily from the poor, the upper middle class increasingly seeks sanctuary behind gated residential enclaves.

A fundamental drama being played out in various areas of the United States is the struggle between the haves and the have-nots. As much as possible, the haves segregate themselves from the have-nots. Urban life, however, sometimes makes their paths cross, at least momentarily, as captured in this photo.

URBAN PROBLEMS AND SOCIAL POLICY

The primary problems of urban life today are poverty, decay, and a general decline of quality of life in U.S. cities. Let's examine underlying reasons for these conditions and consider how to develop social policy to solve urban problems.

Suburbanization

Suburbanization, which refers to people moving from cities to **suburbs,** the communities located just outside a city, is not new. Many dream of a place of their own with green grass, a few trees, and kids playing in the yard. For the past hundred years or so, as transportation grew more efficient, especially with the development of automobiles, people have moved to small towns near the cities in which they work. Minorities joined this movement about 1970. The extent to which people have left the city in search of their dreams is remarkable. In 1957, only 37 million Americans lived in the suburbs (Karp et al. 1991); today, over half of all Americans live in them (Rybczynski 1999).

The U.S. city has been the loser in this transition. As people moved out of the city, businesses and jobs followed. Now about two-thirds of people who live in the suburbs also work there (Gans 1991b). As the city's tax base shrank, it left a budget squeeze that not only affected parks, zoos, libraries, and museums, but also the city's basic services—its schools, streets, sewer and water systems, and police and fire departments.

This shift in population and resources bypassed people who had no choice but to stay in the city. The net result, observed sociologist William Wilson, was to transform the inner city into a ghetto. Left behind were highly disadvantaged

> families that have experienced long-term spells of poverty and/or welfare dependency, individuals who lack training and skills and have either experienced periods of persistent unemployment or have dropped out of the labor force altogether, and individuals who are frequently involved in street criminal activity. The term ghetto . . . suggests that a fundamental social transformation has taken place . . . that groups represented by this term are collectively different from and much more socially isolated from those that lived in these communities in earlier years. (quoted in Karp et al. 1991)

City Versus Suburb Having made the move out of the city—or having been born in a suburb and preferring to live there—suburbanites want the city to keep its problems to

suburbanization the movement from the city to the suburbs

suburb the communities adjacent to the political boundaries of a city

redlining the officers of a financial institution deciding not to make loans in a particular area

disinvestment the withdrawal of investments by financial institutions, which seals the fate of an urban area

itself. They reject proposals to share suburbia's revenues with the city and oppose measures that would allow urban and suburban governments joint control over what has become a contiguous mass of people and businesses. Suburban leaders generally see it as in their best interests to remain politically, economically, and socially separate from their nearby city. They do not mind going to the city to work, or venturing there on weekends for the diversions it offers, but they do not want to help shoulder the city's burdens.

It is likely that the mounting bill will come due ultimately, however, and that suburbanites will have to pay for their uncaring attitude toward the urban disadvantaged. Karp et al. (1991) put it this way:

> It may be that suburbs can insulate themselves from the problems of central cities, at least for the time being. In the long run, though, there will be a steep price to pay for the failure of those better off to care compassionately for those at the bottom of society.

Our occasional urban riots may be part of that bill—perhaps just the down payment.

Suburban Flight For some, the bill is coming due quickly. As they age, some suburbs are becoming a mirror image of the city their residents so despise, with rising crime, increased flight of the middle class, a shrinking tax base, and eroding services. This, in turn, creates a spiraling sense of insecurity, more middle-class flight, and a further reduction of property values. Figure 20.14 illustrates this process, which is new to the urban-suburban scene.

Disinvestment and Deindustrialization

As the movement out of cities to suburbs eroded the cities' tax base, services declined—from garbage pickup to education. Buildings deteriorated, and banks began **redlining**: Afraid of loans going bad, loan officers drew a line on a map around a problem area and refused to make loans for housing or businesses there. The **disinvestment** (withdrawal of investment) pushed these areas into even faster decline. Youth gangs, murders, and muggings are high in these areas, while education, employment, and income are low—factors that are not unconnected to this process of disinvestment.

Globalization has also left a heavy mark on U.S. cities. As sociologist Victor Rodriguez (1994) points out, to compete in the global market many U.S. industries abandoned local communities and moved their factories to places where labor costs were lower. Although this made U.S. industries more competitive, it also eliminated millions of manufacturing jobs. Lacking training in the new information technologies, poor people are locked out of the postindustrial economy that is engulfing the United States. Left behind in the inner cities, many live in despair.

The Rural Rebound

The United States is now undergoing a trend that is without precedent in its history. In the 1970s, people began to move out of cities and suburbs and into rural areas. During the 1990s, seven of every ten U.S. rural counties grew in population. The only losses occurred in the Great Plains and the Mississippi Delta (Johnson 1999). Little farming towns are making a comeback, their boarded-up stores and schools once again open for business and learning.

The "push" factors for this fundamental shift are fears of urban crime and violence. The "pull" factors are safety, lower cost of living, recreation, and more space. Facilitating this movement are improvements in transportation and communication. Interstate highways make airports—and the city itself—accessible from longer distances. With satellite communications, mobile phones, fax machines, and the Internet, people can be connected with others in the city—and around the world—even though they live in what just a short time ago were remote areas.

Figure 20.14

URBAN GROWTH AND URBAN FLIGHT

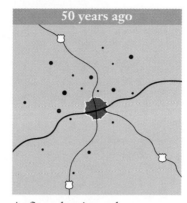

At first, the city and surrounding villages grew independently.

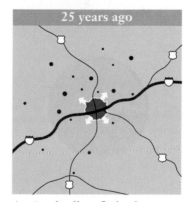

As city dwellers fled urban decay, they created a ring of suburbs.

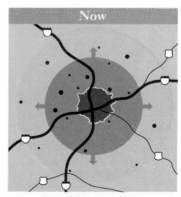

As middle-class flight continues outward, urban problems are arriving in the outer rings.

Listen to the wife of a former student of mine describe why she and her husband moved to a rural area, three hours from the international airport that they fly out of each week:

> I work for a Canadian company. Paul works for a French company, with headquarters in Paris. He flies around the country doing computer consulting. I give motivational seminars to businesses. When we can, we drive to the airport together, but we often leave on different days. I try to go with my husband to Paris once a year.
>
> We almost always are home together on the weekends. We often arrange three- and four-day weekends, because I can plan seminars at home, and Paul does some of his consulting from here.
>
> Sometimes shopping is inconvenient, but we don't have to lock our car doors when we drive, and the new Wal-Mart superstore has most of what we need. E-commerce is a big part of it. I just type in www.—whatever, and they ship it right to my door. I get make-up and books on-line. I even bought a part for my stove.
>
> Why do we live here? Look at the lake. It's beautiful. We enjoy boating and swimming. We love to walk in this parklike setting. We see deer and wild turkeys. We love the sunsets over the lake. (author's files)

She added, "I think we're ahead of the learning curve," referring to the idea that their lifestyle is a wave of the future.

The Potential of Urban Revitalization

Social policy usually takes one of two forms. The first involves efforts to tear down and re-build—something that is fancifully termed **urban renewal.** The result is the renewal of an area—but *not* for the benefit of its inhabitants. Stadiums, high-rise condos, luxury hotels, and expensive shops replace run-down, cheap housing. Outpriced, the area's inhabitants are displaced into adjacent areas.

The second is the establishment of some sort of **enterprise zone.** The government offers economic incentives, such as reduced taxes, that are intended to encourage businesses to move into the area. Although the intention is good, failure is usually the result. Most businesses refuse to locate in high-crime areas. Those that do pay high prices for additional security and may end up suffering losses because of crime. If workers are hired from within the problem area, and the jobs pay a decent wage, which most do not, the workers move to better neighborhoods, frustrating the purpose of establishing an enterprise zone (Lemann 1994). After all, who chooses to live with the fear of violence?

Although urban renewal and enterprise zones have failed to solve the problems facing U.S. cities, a "nothing works" mentality will indeed solve nothing. U.S. cities can be revitalized and made into safe and decent places to live. There is nothing in the nature of cities that turns them into dangerous, deteriorating slums. Most European cities, for example, are both safe and pleasant. If U.S. cities are to change, they must become top agenda items of the U.S. government, with adequate resources in terms of money and human talents focused on overcoming urban woes.

Given the deplorable condition of many U.S. cities, and the flight of the middle classes—both whites and minorities—to greener pastures, an *urban Manhattan Project* seems in order. During World War II the United States and the Allies faced a triumphant Hitler in Europe and a victorious Tojo in Asia. The United States gathered its top scientific minds and challenged them to produce the atomic bomb. "Manhattan Project" was the code name for that effort. It involved 37 installations throughout the country, at least 37 university laboratories, and more than 100,000 people, including several Nobel prize-winning physicists. Today, similar resources may be required to triumph over urban ills.

Sociologist William Flanagan (1990) suggests three guiding principles for revitalizing our cities.

urban renewal the rehabilitation of a rundown area, which usually results in the displacement of the poor who are living in that area

enterprise zone the use of economic incentives in a designated area with the intention of encouraging investment there

Like the phoenix that rose from the ashes, luxury hotels and apartments, along with exclusive restaurants and shops, have sprung from the ruins of urban decay. Urban renewal, a benefit for the privileged, has displaced the poor, often shoving them into adjacent areas every bit as bad as those in which they previously lived.

Scale. Regional and national planning is necessary. Local jurisdictions, with their many rivalries, competing goals, and limited resources, tend to implement a hodgepodge of mostly unworkable solutions. A positive example of regional planning is Portland, Oregon, where a regional government prohibits urban sprawl and ensures a greenbelt (Ortega 1995).

Livability. Cities must be appealing and meet human needs, especially the need of community we discussed earlier. This will attract the middle classes into the city and increase its tax base. In turn, this will finance the services that make the city more livable.

Social justice. In the final analysis, social policy must be evaluated by how it affects people. For example, "urban renewal" programs that displace the poor for the benefit of the middle class and wealthy do not pass this standard. The same would apply to solutions that create "livability" for select groups but neglect the poor and the homeless.

Unless we address the *root* causes of urban problems—poverty, housing, education, and jobs—any solutions we come up with will be, at best, only Band-Aids that cover up problems. Such fixes will be window dressings for politicians who want to *appear* as though they are doing something constructive about the problems that affect our quality of life.

SUMMARY AND REVIEW

■ A Planet with No Space for Enjoying Life?

What debate did Thomas Malthus initiate?

In 1798, Thomas Malthus analyzed the surge in Europe's population. His conclusion, called the **Malthus theorem**, was that because the population grows geometrically but food only arithmetically, the world will outstrip its food supply. The debate between today's New Malthusians and those who disagree, the Anti-Malthusians, continues. Pp. 572–576.

Why are people starving?

Starvation is not due to a lack of food in the world, for there is now more food for each person in the entire world than there was fifty years ago. Starvation, rather, is due to a maldistribution of food, which is primarily due to drought and civil war. Pp. 576–577.

■ Population Growth

Why do the poor nations have so many children?

In the Least Industrialized Nations, children generally are viewed as gifts from God, cost little to rear, contribute to the family income at an early age, and represent the parents' social security. Consequently, people are motivated to have large families. Pp. 577–580.

What are the three demographic variables?

To compute population growth, demographers use *fertility, mortality,* and *migration.* The **basic demographic equation** is births minus deaths plus net migration equals growth rate. Pp. 580–584.

Why is forecasting population difficult?

A nation's growth rate is affected by unanticipated variables—from economic conditions, wars, and famines to industrialization and government policies. Pp. 584–586.

■ Urbanization

What is the relationship of cities to farming?

Cities can develop only if there is a large agricultural surplus, which frees people from food production. The primary impetus to the development of cities was the invention of the plow about five or six thousand years ago. Pp. 586–588.

How did the Industrial Revolution affect the size of cities?

Almost without exception, throughout history cities have been small. After the Industrial Revolution stimulated rapid transportation and communication, cities grew quickly and became much larger. Pp. 588–589.

What are metropolises and megalopolises?

Urbanization is so extensive that some cities have become **metropolises,** dominating the area adjacent to them. The areas of influence of some metropolises have merged, forming a **megalopolis.** Pp. 589–592.

■ Models of Urban Growth

What models of urban growth have been proposed?

The primary models are concentric zone, sector, multiple-nuclei, and peripheral. These models fail to account for medieval cities, many European cities, and those in the Least Industrialized Nations. Pp. 592–594.

■ City Life

Is the city inherently alienating?

Although some people experience alienation in the city, others find community in it. Five types of people who live in cities are cosmopolites, singles, ethnic villagers, the deprived, and the trapped. Pp. 594–599.

■ Urban Problems and Social Policy

Why have U.S. cities declined?

Three primary reasons for their decline are **suburbanization** (as people moved to the suburbs, the tax base of cities eroded and services deteriorated), **disinvestment** (banks withdrawing their financing), and **deindustrialization** (which has caused a loss of jobs). Pp. 600–601.

What is the rural rebound?

As people flee cities and suburbs, the population of most U.S. rural counties is growing. This is a fundamental departure from a trend that has been in place for a couple of hundred years. Pp. 601–602.

What social policy can salvage U.S. cities?

A Manhattan Project on Urban Problems could likely produce workable solutions. Three guiding principles for developing social policy are scale, livability, and social justice. Pp. 602–603.

Where can I read more on this topic?

Suggested Readings for this chapter are at the back of this book.

All URLs listed are current as of the printing of this book. URLs often change. Please check our Web site, **http://www.abacon.com/henslin,** for updates.

1. Population growth is an important issue for every society. Go to **http://www.popexpo.net/eMain.html** and examine the current world population. This site will help you understand the problems of population growth. Answer the questions that come up on the screen. As you work through them, you will see how your actions and decisions affect the overall size of the population. After you have explored the factors that contribute to population growth, look at the arguments presented by the Zero Population Growth organization at **http://www.zpg.org/About_ZPG/policies.html** and by the Negative Population Growth organization at **http://www.npg.org/whatsnpg.htm.** Compare and contrast the views taken toward population growth by both organizations. How are they similar? What are the main differences? Which viewpoint do you think describes the correct way to curb population growth? Why? Along with some fellow classmates, organize a panel for your sociology class. Discuss the dynamics of population growth and what can be done to slow down the growth.

This exercise assumes that population growth is negative and that the position of the New Malthusians is correct. You may wish to argue the position of the Anti-Malthusians. If so, search the Internet for arguments that either support continued population growth or that explain why population growth is already coming under control. You may want to focus on the fourth stage of the demographic transition, especially the shrinking native populations of Europe.

2. For this exercise on world hunger, you will compare two sites, each of which is dedicated to the elimination of starvation around the world. Go to "The 30-Hour Famine" page at **http://30hour-famine** and browse the site. What is this organization and how is it responding to world hunger? Then go to the Hunger Web site at **http://www.brown.edu/Departments/World_Hunger_ Program.** To learn more about world hunger, click on "World Hunger Education Service" and read some of the articles in the current issue of Hunger Notes. When you are through, go back to the main page and click on "Introduction" to find out more about the myths and realities of hunger and what you can do about it. Returning to the home page, click on "Advocacy and Policy" and explore some of the different advocacy groups that are fighting hunger. When you are finished, write a brief paper in which you explain the efforts to solve the problem as described in the sites you have visited. Do their basic assumptions seem to be New Malthusian or Anti-Malthusian? Explain your answer.

3. This chapter discusses global trends in urbanization. Look at Figure 20.11 on page 590. Have you ever visited or lived in any of these cities? In this exercise you will have the opportunity to tour some of them by way of the Internet. Begin by going to **http://www.netscout.net/oneworld/bigcities.htm.** You will find a list of the largest cities in the world. Select one city and click on it. This should take you to that city's Web site. Here you can learn more about what it is like to live and work in this city. Keep a journal of your impressions as you travel around each of the ten largest global cities. After you have completed your world tour, prepare a presentation to your class about your trip. Share with them your thoughts on city life in different societies. In what ways are these cities similar? In what ways are they different?

4. In the Down-to-Earth Sociology box on page 599 there is a brief reference to Celebration, Florida, a planned community of 20,000 people built by the Walt Disney Company. Here is your chance to look more closely at this community. Go to **http://www.celebrationfl.com.** Read about the philosophy behind Celebration, take a look at the choice of residential arrangements, check out what the community has to offer, and explore the commercial opportunities. In the "Press Room" you can read articles about Celebration and find answers to frequently asked questions. When you have completed your tour, write a paper in which you discuss what people find appealing about Celebration. What problems of modern life is Celebration trying to address? Would you want to live there? Why or why not?

Collective Behavior and Social Movements

COLLECTIVE BEHAVIOR

■ **Early Explanations: The Transformation of the Individual**
Charles Mackay, Gustave LeBon, and Robert Park: How the Crowd Transfoms the Individual
Herbert Blumer: The Acting Crowd

■ **The Contemporary View: The Rationality of the Crowd**
Richard Berk: The Minimax Strategy
Ralph Turner and Lewis Killian: Emergent Norms

■ **Forms of Collective Behavior**
Riots
Panics
Moral Panics
Rumors
Fads and Fashions
Urban Legends

SOCIAL MOVEMENTS

■ **Types and Tactics of Social Movements**
Types of Social Movements
Tactics of Social Movements
The Mass Media: Gatekeepers to Social Movements

■ **Why People Join Social Movements**
Mass Society Theory
Deprivation Theory
Moral Issues and Ideological Commitment
A Special Case: The Agent Provocateur

■ **On the Success and Failure of Social Movements**
The Stages of Social Movements
The Difficult Road to Success

■ **Summary and Review**

The news spread like wildfire. A police officer had been killed. In just twenty minutes, the white population was armed and heading for the cabin. Men and mere boys, some not more than 12 years old, carried rifles, shotguns, and pistols.

The mob, now about four hundred, surrounded the log cabin. Tying a rope around the man's neck, they dragged him to the center of town. While the men argued about the best way to kill him, the women and children shouted their advice—some to hang him, others to burn him alive.

Someone pulled a large wooden box out of a store and placed it in the center of the street. Others filled it with straw. Then they lifted the man, the rope still around his neck, and shoved him head first into the box. One of the men poured oil over him. Another lit a match.

As the flames shot upward, the man managed to lift himself out of the box, his body a mass of flames. Trying to shield his face and eyes from the fire, he ran the length of the rope, about twenty feet, when someone yelled, "Shoot!" In an instant, dozens of shots rang out. Men and boys walked to the lifeless body and emptied their guns into it.

They dragged the man's body back to the burning box, then piled on more boxes from the stores, and poured oil over them. Each time someone threw more oil onto the flames, the crowd roared shouts of approval.

Standing about seventy-five feet away, I could smell the poor man's burning flesh. No one tried to hide their identity. I could clearly see town officials help in the burning. The inquest, dutifully held by the coroner, concluded that the man met death "at the hands of an enraged mob unknown to the jury." What else could he conclude? Any jury from this town would include men who had participated in the man's death.

They dug a little hole at the edge of the street, and dumped in it the man's ashes and what was left of his body.

The man's name was Sam Pettie, known by everybody to be quiet and unoffensive. I can't mention my name. If I did, I would be committing suicide. ■

(Based on a May 1914 letter to *The Crisis*)

COLLECTIVE BEHAVIOR

Why did the people in this little town "go mad"? These men—and the women who watched in agreement—were ordinary, law-abiding citizens. Even some of the "pillars of the community" joined in the vicious killing of Sam Pettie, who may have been innocent.

Lynching is a form of **collective behavior,** actions by a group of people who bypass the usual norms governing their behavior and do something unusual (Turner and Killian 1987; Lofland 1993). Collective behavior is a broad term. It includes not only such violent acts as lynchings and riots, but also panics, rumors, fads, and fashions. Before examining its specific forms, let's look at theories that seek to explain collective behavior.

collective behavior extraordinary activities carried out by groups of people; includes lynchings, rumors, panics, urban legends, and fads and fashions

ℰARLY EXPLANATIONS: THE TRANSFORMATION OF THE INDIVIDUAL

When people can't figure something out, they often resort to using "madness" as an explanation. People may say, "She went 'off her rocker'—that's why she drove her car off the bridge." "He must have 'gone nuts,' or he wouldn't have shot into the crowd." Early explanations of collective behavior were tied in to such assumptions. Let's look at how these ideas developed.

U.S. race relations have gone through many stages, some of them very tense. They sometimes have exploded into violence, as with the lynchings in the 1920s and 1930s. This gruesome photo was taken on August 7, 1930, in Marion, Indiana. The victims, Thomas Shipp and Abram Smith, were accused of rape.

Charles Mackay, Gustave LeBon, and Robert Park: How the Crowd Transforms the Individual

The field of collective behavior began when Charles Mackay (1814–1889), a British journalist, noticed that "country folks," who ordinarily are reasonable sorts of people, sometimes "went mad" and did "disgraceful and violent things" when they formed a crowd. The best explanation Mackay (1852) could come up with was that people had a "herd mentality"—they were like a herd of cows that suddenly stampede.

About fifty years later, Gustave LeBon (1841–1931), a French psychologist, built on this initial idea. In an 1895 book, LeBon stressed how people feel anonymous in crowds, less accountable for what they do. Some even develop feelings of invincibility and come to think that they can do almost anything. A **collective mind** develops, he said, and people are swept up by almost any suggestion. Then contagion, something like mass hypnosis, takes over, releasing the destructive instincts that society has so carefully repressed.

Robert Park (1864–1944), a U.S. sociologist who studied in Germany and wrote a 1904 dissertation on the crowd, was influenced by LeBon (McPhail 1991). After Park joined the faculty at the University of Chicago, he added the ideas of social unrest and circular reaction. He said,

> Social unrest . . . is transmitted from one individual to another . . . so that the manifestations of discontent in A [are] communicated to B, and from B reflected back to A. (Park and Burgess 1921a)

Park used the term **circular reaction** to refer to this back-and-forth communication. Circular reaction, he said, creates a "collective impulse" that comes to "dominate all members of the crowd." If "collective impulse" sounds just like LeBon's "collective mind," that's because it really is. As noted, Park was influenced by LeBon, and his slightly different term did not change the basic idea at all.

Herbert Blumer: The Acting Crowd

Herbert Blumer (1900–1987), who studied under Park, synthesized LeBon's and Park's ideas. As you can see from Figure 21.1, Blumer (1939) identified five stages that precede what he called an **acting crowd**, an excited group that moves toward a goal. This model

collective mind Gustave LeBon's term for the tendency of people in a crowd to feel, think, and act in extraordinary ways

circular reaction Robert Park's term for a back-and-forth communication between the members of a crowd whereby a "collective impulse" is transmitted

acting crowd Herbert Blumer's term for an excited group that collectively moves toward a goal

Figure 21.1 **BLUMER'S MODEL OF HOW AN ACTING CROWD DEVELOPS**

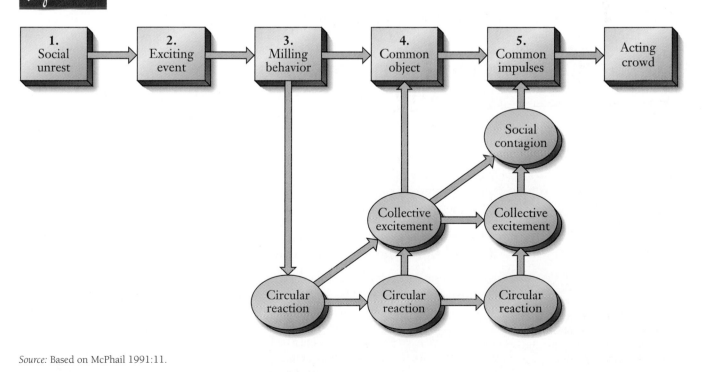

Source: Based on McPhail 1991:11.

still dominates today's police manuals on crowd behavior (McPhail 1989). Let's apply it to the lynching of Sam Pettie.

1. *Tension or unrest.* At the root of collective behavior is a background condition of tension or unrest. Disturbed about some condition of society, people are apprehensive. This makes them vulnerable to rumors and suggestions. Sam Pettie was lynched during the early 1900s. At this time, traditional southern life was in upheaval. Due to industrialization, millions of Americans were moving from farm to city in search of jobs, and from South to North. Left behind were many poor, rural southerners, white and black, who faced a bleak future. In addition, African Americans were questioning the legitimacy of their low status and deprivation.

2. *Exciting event.* An exciting event occurs, one so startling that people become preoccupied with it. In this instance, that event was the killing of a police officer.

3. *Milling.* Next comes **milling**, people standing or walking around, talking about the exciting event. A circular reaction then sets in. As people pick up cues as to the "right" way of thinking and feeling, they reinforce them in one another. During the short period in which Sam Pettie's lynch mob milled, the white residents of this small town became increasingly agitated as they discussed the officer's death.

4. *A common object of attention.* In this stage, people's attention becomes riveted on some aspect of the event. They get caught up in the collective excitement. In this case, people's attention turned to Sam Pettie. Someone may have said that he had been talking to the officer or that they had been arguing.

5. *Common impulses.* A sense of collective agreement about what should be done emerges. These common impulses are stimulated by *social contagion,* a sense of excitement that is passed from one person to another. In this instance, people concluded that only an immediate, public death of the killer would be adequate vengeance—as well as a powerful warning for other African Americans who might even think about getting "out of line."

Acting crowds aren't always negative or destructive, as this one was. Some involve spontaneous demonstrations directed against oppression. Nor are they all serious, for students engaging in food fights are also acting crowds.

*T*HE CONTEMPORARY VIEW: THE RATIONALITY OF THE CROWD

If we were to see a lynching—or a screaming mob or a prison riot—most of us might agree with LeBon that some sort of "madness" had swept over the crowd. Sociologists today, however, point out that beneath the surface, crowds are actually quite rational. They point out that crowds take deliberate steps to reach some desired goal. As sociologist Clark McPhail (1991) says, even a lynch mob is cooperative—someone gets the rope while others hold the victim, some tie the knot, and others hoist the body.

Richard Berk: The Minimax Strategy

milling a crowd standing or walking around as they talk excitedly about some event

minimax strategy Richard Berk's term for the effort people make to minimize their costs and maximize their rewards

A general principle of human behavior is that we try to minimize our costs and maximize our rewards. Sociologist Richard Berk (1974) called this a **minimax strategy.** The fewer costs and the more rewards we anticipate from something, the more likely we are to do it. For example, if we believe that others will approve an act, the likelihood increases that we will do it. Whether yelling for the referee's blood following a bad call in a football game, or shouting for real blood as a member of a lynch mob, this principle applies. In short, whether people are playing cards with a few friends or are part of a mob, the principles of human behavior remain the same.

Ralph Turner and Lewis Killian: Emergent Norms

Since collective behavior is unusual behavior, however, could it also involve unusual norms? Sociologists Ralph Turner and Lewis Killian (1987) use the term **emergent norms** to express this idea. They point out that life usually goes much as we expect, and our usual norms are adequate. If some unusual event disrupts our usual ways of doing things, however, our ordinary norms may not cover the new situation. People then may develop *new* norms to deal with the new situation. Sometimes they even produce new definitions of right and wrong that *under the new circumstances* justify actions that they would otherwise consider wrong.

To understand how new norms emerge, we need to keep in mind that not everyone in a crowd shares the same point of view (Snow et al. 1993; Rodríguez 1994). As Turner and Killian (1987) point out, there are at least five kinds of crowd participants:

1. The *ego-involved* feel a personal stake in the unusual event.

2. The *concerned* also have a personal interest in the event, but less so than the ego-involved.

3. The *insecure* care little about the matter, but they join the crowd because it gives them a sense of power and security.

4. The *curious spectators* also care little about the issue, but they are inquisitive about what is going on.

5. The *exploiters* don't care about the event, but they use it for their own purposes, such as hawking food or T-shirts.

The different attitudes, motives, and emotions of these participants influence the emergence of new norms. The most important role goes to the "ego-involved": Some make suggestions about what should be done, while others take action. As the "concerned" join in, they, too, help to set the crowd on a particular course of action. The "insecure" and the "curious spectators" may then join in. Although the "exploiters" are unlikely to participate, they do lend the crowd passive support. A common mood completes the stage for new norms to emerge: Activities that are "not OK" in everyday life may now seem "OK"—whether they involve throwing bottles at the cops or shouting obscenities at the college president.

emergent norms Ralph Turner's and Lewis Killian's term for the development of new norms to cope with a new situation, especially among crowds

Elián Gonzalez, whose mother died as she fled from Cuba, became a political pawn. Staunch anti-Castro members of the Cuban exile community garnered publicity and rallied anti-Castro supporters, while Castro held his own rallies in Cuba. Invectives flew in both directions—all, supposedly, for "the boy's sake." Elián's uncle's home in the Little Havana section of Miami became a center of protest. The home was surrounded by crowds day and night, even at 5 A.M., when agents of the Immigration and Naturalization Service seized Elián at gunpoint.

This analysis of emergent norms helps us see that collective behavior is *rational*. The crowd, for example, does not consider all suggestions made by the ego-involved to be equal: To be acceptable, suggestions must match predispositions that the crowd already has. This analysis, then, is a far cry from earlier interpretations that people were so transformed by a crowd that they went out of their minds.

FORMS OF COLLECTIVE BEHAVIOR

Sociologists, then, analyze collective behavior the same way they do other forms of behavior (Turner and Killian 1987; Lofland 1993; Turner 1993). They view it as ordinary people responding to extraordinary situations (Rodríguez 1994). They ask their usual questions about interaction, such as, How do people influence one another? What is the significance of the members' age, gender, race-ethnicity, and social class? What role do preexisting attitudes play? How do people's perceptions get translated into action?

In addition to lynchings, collective behavior includes riots, panics, moral panics, rumors, fads, fashions, and urban legends. Let's look at each.

riot violent crowd behavior aimed against people and property

Riots

The nation watched in horror. White Los Angeles police officers had been caught on videotape beating an African-American traffic violator with their nightsticks. The videotape showed the officers savagely bringing their nightsticks down on a man prostrate at their feet. Television stations around the United States—and the world—broadcast the pictures to stunned audiences.

The evidence was vivid and irrefutable. When the officers went on trial for beating the man identified as Rodney King, how could the verdict be anything but guilty? Yet a jury consisting of eleven whites and one Asian American found the officers innocent of using excessive force. The result was a **riot**—violent crowd behavior aimed against people and property. Within minutes of the verdict, angry crowds began to gather in Los Angeles. That night, mobs set fire to businesses in south-central Los Angeles, and looting and arson began in earnest. The rioting spread to other cities, including Atlanta, Georgia, Tampa, Florida, and even Madison, Wisconsin, and Las Vegas, Nevada. Whites and Koreans were favorite targets of violence.

Again Americans sat transfixed before their television sets as they saw parts of Los Angeles go up in flames and looters carrying television sets and lugging sofas in full view of the Los Angeles Police Department, which took no steps to stop them. Seared into the public's collective consciousness was the sight of Reginald Denny, a 36-year-old white truck driver who had been pulled from his truck in the riot area. As he sat dazed in the street, Damian Williams, laughing, broke Denny's skull with a piece of concrete.

On the third night, after 4,000 fires had been set and more than 30 people killed, President George Bush announced on national television that the U.S. Justice Department had appointed prosecutors to investigate possible federal charges against the police officers for violating the civil rights of Rodney King. The president stated that he had ordered the Seventh Infantry, SWAT teams, and the FBI into Los Angeles. He also federalized the California National Guard and placed it under the command of Gen. Colin Powell, the chairman of the Joint Chiefs of Staff. Even Rodney King went on television and tearfully pleaded for peace.

As mentioned in Chapter 15, violence is the foundation of the political order. As in the photograph on the preceding page, when the government is challenged it may remove the velvet glove that conceals its iron fist—or its automatic weapons, as the case may be. This photo was taken at a demonstration against the World Trade Organization in Seattle in 1999. When the police moved against the demonstrators, the protest turned into a riot.

The Los Angeles riot was the bloodiest since the U.S. Civil War. Before it was over, 54 people lost their lives, 2,328 people were treated in hospital emergency rooms, thousands of small businesses were burned, and about $1 billion of property was destroyed. Two of the police officers were later sentenced to 2½ years in prison on federal charges, and King was awarded several million dollars in damages. (Rose 1992; Stevens and Lubman 1992; Holden and Rose 1993; Cannon 1998)

The background conditions of urban riots are frustration and anger brought on by feelings of deprivation. In people who are kept out of mainstream society—limited to a meager education and denied jobs and justice—frustration and anger simmer. Then a precipitating event brings those pent-up feelings to a boiling point, and they erupt in collective violence. All these conditions existed in the Los Angeles riot, with the jury's verdict being the precipitating event.

Sociologists have found that it is not only the deprived who participate in riots. After the assassination of Dr. Martin Luther King, Jr., in 1968, when many U.S. cities erupted in riots, even people with good jobs participated (McPhail 1991). In the L. A. riots, the first outbursts didn't come from the poorest neighborhoods but from the most stable neighborhoods. Why would middle-class people participate in riots? The answer, says sociologist Victor Rodríguez (1994), is a sense of frustration that many minorities feel when they perceive that they are treated as second-class citizens even though they are gainfully employed and living stable lives.

The event that precipitates a riot is less important than the riot's general context. The precipitating event is only the match that lights the fuel. The fuel is the background of tension and unrest—feeling that injustice is being ignored, or even condoned and encouraged by officials. Just beneath the surface is seething rage that erupts following incidents such as the Rodney King verdict. Because this rage is felt not only by the poor but also by those who are materially better off, both groups participate. There also are opportunists—people who participate not out of rage, or even because they are particularly concerned about the precipitating event, but because the riot provides an opportunity for looting.

Panics

In 1938, on the night before Halloween, a radio program of dance music was interrupted with a report that explosions had been observed on the surface of Mars. The announcer breathlessly added that a cylinder of unknown origin had been discovered embedded in the ground on a farm in New Jersey. The radio station then switched to the farm, where an alarmed reporter gave details of horrible-looking Martians coming out of the cylinder. Their death-ray weapons had destructive powers unknown to humans. An interview with an astronomer confirmed that Martians had invaded the Earth.

Perhaps six million Americans heard this broadcast. About one million were frightened by it. Thousands panicked, grabbed their weapons, and hid in their basements or ran into the streets. Hundreds bundled up their families and jumped into their cars, jamming the roads as they headed to who knows where.

Of course, there was no invasion. This was simply a dramatization of H. G. Wells' *War of the Worlds,* starring Orson Welles. There had been an announcement at the beginning of the program and somewhere in the middle that the account was fictional, but apparently many people missed it. Although the panic reactions to this radio program may appear humorous to us, to anyone who is in a panic the situation is far from humorous. **Panic** occurs when people become so fearful that they cannot function normally, and may even flee.

Why did people panic in this instance? Psychologist Hadley Cantril (1941) attributed the reaction to widespread anxiety about world conditions. The Nazis were marching in Europe, and millions of Americans (correctly, as it turned out) were afraid that the United States would get involved. War jitters, he said, created fertile ground for the broadcast to touch off a panic.

panic the condition of being so fearful that one cannot function normally, and may even flee

Natural disasters often provide examples of collective behavior. A primary finding of disaster research is that people act rationally. Emergency personnel remain on the job. Others first check on the safety of their loved ones, then organize to overcome the effects of the disaster. Although this woman is dazed, she likely will participate in organized efforts to recover from the tornado that destroyed her home.

Contemporary analysts, however, question whether there even was a panic. Sociologist William Bainbridge (1989) acknowledges that some people did become frightened, and that a few actually did get in their cars and drive like maniacs. But he says that most of this famous panic was an invention of the news media. Reporters found a good story and milked it, exaggerating as they went along.

Bainbridge points to a 1973 event in Sweden. To dramatize the dangers of atomic power, Swedish Radio broadcast a play about an accident at a nuclear power plant. Knowing about the 1938 broadcast in the United States, Swedish sociologists were waiting to see what would happen. Might some people fail to realize that it was a dramatization and panic at the threat of ruptured reactors spewing out radioactivity? The sociologists found no panic. A few people did become frightened. Some telephoned family members and the police; others shut windows to keep out the radioactivity—reasonable responses, considering what they thought had occurred.

The Swedish media, however, reported a panic! Apparently, a reporter had telephoned two police departments and learned that each had received calls from concerned citizens. With a deadline hanging over his head, the reporter decided to gamble. He reported that police and fire stations were jammed with citizens, that people were flocking to the shelters, and that others were fleeing south (Bainbridge 1989).

Panics do occur, of course—which is why nobody has the right to shout "Fire!" in a public building when no such danger exists—for if people fear immediate death, they will lunge toward the nearest exit in a frantic effort to escape. Such a panic occurred on Memorial Day weekend in 1977 at the Beverly Hills Supper Club in Southgate, Kentucky. About half the 2,500 patrons were crowded into the Cabaret Room, awaiting the appearance of singer John Davidson. A fire, which began in a small banquet room near the front of the building, burned undetected until it was beyond control. When employees discovered the fire, they warned patrons. People began to exit in orderly fashion, but when flames rushed in the result was panic. Patrons trampled one another in a furious attempt to reach the exits, which were immediately blocked by masses of screaming people trying to push their way through all at once. The writhing bodies at the exits created further panic among the remainder, who pushed even harder to force their way through the bottlenecks. One hundred sixty-five people died. All but two were within thirty feet of two exits in the Cabaret Room.

Sociologists who studied this panic found what other researchers have discovered in analyzing other disasters. *Not everyone panics.* In disturbances, many people continue to act responsibly. Especially important are primary group bonds. Parents help their children, for example (Morrow 1995). Gender roles also persist, and more men help women than women help men (Johnson 1993). Even work roles continue to guide some behavior. Sociologists Drue Johnston and Norris Johnson (1989) found that only 29 percent of the employees of the Beverly Hills Supper Club left when they learned of the fire. As noted in Table 21.1,

Table 21.1

EMPLOYEES' FIRST ACTION
AFTER LEARNING OF THE FIRE

Action	Percentage
Left	29%
Helped others to leave	41%
Fought or reported the fire	17%
Continued routine activities	7%
Others (e.g., looked for a friend or relative)	5%

Note: These figures are based on interviews with 95 of the 160 employees present at the time of the fire: 48 males and 47 females, ranging in age from 15 to 59.

Source: Based on Johnston and Johnson 1989.

41 percent helped customers, 17 percent reported or fought the fire, 7 percent simply went about their routines, and 5 percent did such things as search for friends and relatives.

Sociologists use the term **role extension** to describe the actions of most of the employees. By this, they mean that the employees incorporated other activities into their occupational roles. For example, servers extended their role to include helping people to safety. How do we know that giving help was an extension of the occupational role, not simply a general act of helping? Johnston and Johnson found that servers who were away from their assigned stations returned to them in order to help *their* customers.

Moral Panics

Moral panics occur when large numbers of people become intensely concerned, even fearful, about some behavior that they believe threatens morality, and when the fear is out of proportion to any supposed danger (Cauthen and Jasper 1994; Goode and Ben-Yehuda 1994). The threat is seen as enormous, and hostility builds toward those deemed responsible. The most famous moral panic was the fear of witches in Europe between 1400 and 1650. It resulted in the Inquisition—investigations, torture, and burning at the stake of people accused of witchcraft.

Today, moral panics are fueled by the mass media. During the 1980s, the fear that children would be sexually abused in day care centers spread across the United States. The media reported bizarre rituals with devil worshippers and naked priests and weird sex. The situation grew so bad that almost every day care worker became suspect in someone's eyes. Only fearfully did parents leave their children in day care centers. Although sexual abuse at day care centers has occurred, the stories of children subjected to bizarre rituals were never substantiated. Since this time, the hysteria has died down.

Like other panics, moral panics center around a sense of danger. The supposed thousands of U.S. children who are snatched by strangers from playgrounds, city streets, and their own backyards are part of a moral panic. Parents are fearful, and others are perplexed at how U.S. society could go to hell in a handbasket. This moral panic is destined to meet the same fate as others. The fear and hysteria will subside, and people will feel less fear as they drop children off at school or let them play outside. The actual number of stranger kidnappings per year is between 200 and 300 (Bromely 1991).

Moral panics are fed by **rumor,** information for which there is no discernible source and which is usually unfounded. In the 1990s, a rumor swept the country that some of these supposedly thousands of missing children were being sold to Satanists who abused them sexually and then ritually murdered them. This rumor was fueled by people who claimed to have been involved in such sacrifices. The police investigated but uncovered no evidence to substantiate the rumor.

Moral panics thrive on uncertainty and anxiety. Today's changing family gives rise to a great deal of anxiety. Concerns that children are receiving inadequate care because so many mothers have joined the work force have become linked with thoughts that dangers to children are lurking almost everywhere.

Rumors

In *Aladdin*, the handsome young title character murmurs, "All good children, take off your clothes." In *The Lion King*, Simba, the cuddly lion star, stirs up a cloud of dust that, floating off the screen, spells S-E-X. Then there is the bishop in *The Little Mermaid*, who, presiding over a wedding, becomes noticeably aroused.

Ann Runge, a mother of eight who owned stacks of animated Disney films, said she felt betrayed when she heard that the Magic Kingdom was sending obscene, subliminal messages. "I felt as though I had entrusted my kids to pedophiles," she said (Bannon 1995).

role extension the incorporation of additional activities into a role

moral panic a fear that grips large numbers of people that some evil group or behavior threatens the well-being of society, followed by intense hostility, sometimes violence, toward those thought responsible

rumor unfounded information spread among people

Rumors have swirled around the Magic Kingdom's supposed plots to undermine the morality of youth. Could Mickey Mouse be a dark force, and these children his victims? As humorous as this may be, some have taken these rumors seriously.

Thriving in conditions of ambiguity, rumors function to fill in missing information (Turner 1964; Shibutani 1966). In response to the rumor, Disney reported that Aladdin really says, "Scat, good tiger, take off and go." The line is hard to understand, however, leaving enough ambiguity for others to continue to hear what they want to hear, and even to insist that the line is an invitation to a teenage orgy. Similar ambiguity remains with Simba's dust and the aroused bishop.

Most rumors are short-lived. They arise in a situation of ambiguity, only to dissipate when they are replaced by factual information—or by another rumor. Occasionally, however, a rumor has a long life. In the eighteenth and nineteenth centuries, for no known reason, healthy people would grow weak and slowly waste away. No one understood the cause and people said they had *consumption* (now called tuberculosis). People were terrified as they saw their loved ones wither into shells of their former selves. With no one knowing when the disease would strike, or who its next victim would be, the rumor began that some of the dead weren't really dead. What had happened, people said, was that they had turned into vampire-like beings, and at night they were coming back from the grave and draining the life out of the living. The evidence was irrefutable—loved ones who wasted away before their very eyes. To kill these ghoulish "undead," people began to sneak into graveyards. They would dig up a grave, remove the leg bones and place them on the skeleton's chest, then lay the skull at the feet, forming a skull and crossbones. Having thus killed the "undead," they would rebury the remains. These rumors and the resulting mutilations of the dead continued off and on in New England until the 1890s (Associated Press, November 30, 1993).

Why do people believe rumors? Three main factors have been identified. Rumors deal with a subject that is important to an individual, and they replace ambiguity with some form of certainty. They also are attributed to a credible source. An office rumor may be preceded by "Jane has it on good authority that . . . " or "Bill overheard the boss say that . . . "

Ambiguity or uncertainty help give life to rumors. Surrounded by unexplained illnesses and deaths, the New Englanders speculated about why people slowly died. Their rather bizarre conclusions gave them certainty in the face of bewildering events. The uncertainty that sparked the Disney rumor may have been feelings among some that the moral fabric of modern society is decaying. If one believes this, perhaps it is not too far a stretch to believe that a conspiracy may underlie the decay. Perhaps even the Magic Kingdom . . .

fad a temporary pattern of behavior that catches people's attention

Fads and Fashions

A **fad** is a novel form of behavior that briefly catches people's attention. The new behavior appears suddenly and spreads by imitation and identification with people already involved in the fad. As the mass media report on the fad, they help to spread it. After a short life, the fad fades into oblivion, although it may reappear from time to time (Aguirre et al. 1993).

Sociologist John Lofland (1985) identified four types of fads. First are object fads, such as the Hula Hoop of the 1950s, pet rocks of the 1970s, the Rubik's Cube and Cabbage Patch dolls of the 1980s, pogs and beanie babies of the 1990s, and Pokemon in this decade. Second are activity fads, such as eating goldfish in the 1920s, bungee jumping in the 1990s, and body piercing today. Third are idea fads, such as astrology. Fourth are personality fads, such as Elvis Presley, Princess Diana, and Michael Jordan.

Some fads are very short-lived, such as "streaking" (running naked in a public place), which lasted only a couple of months in 1974. Some fads involve millions of people but die just as quickly as they appeared. In the 1950s the Hula Hoop sold so quickly that stores couldn't keep them in stock. Children cried and pleaded for these brightly colored plastic hoops. Across

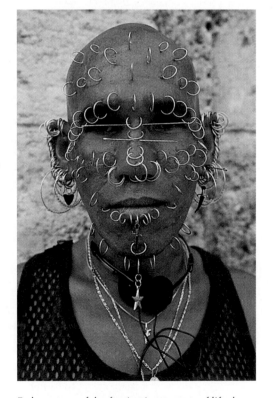

Fads are one of the fascinating aspects of life that sociologists study. Body piercing, whose origins reach back into antiquity, has become popular in the Western world. It is unlikely, however, that body piercing will enter the mainstream culture. Certainly its extremes won't.

the nation, children, and some adults, held contests to see who could keep the hoops up the longest or who could rotate the most hoops at one time. Then, in a matter of months it was over, and parents wondered what to do with the abandoned items, which seemed useless for any other purpose.

When a fad lasts, it is called a **fashion.** Some fashions, as with clothing and furniture, are the result of a coordinated international marketing system that includes designers, manufacturers, advertisers, and retailers. By manipulating the tastes of the public, they sell billions of dollars of products. Fashion, however, also refers to hairstyles, and even to the design and colors of buildings. Sociologist John Lofland (1985) pointed out that fashion also applies to language, as demonstrated by these roughly comparable terms: "Neat!" in the 1950s, "Right on!" in the 1960s, "Really!" in the 1970s, "Awesome!" in the 1980s, "Bad!" in the early 1990s, and, recurringly, "Cool."

Urban Legends

> Did you hear about Katie and Paul? They were parked at Echo Bay, listening to the radio, when the music was interrupted by an announcement that a rapist-killer had escaped from prison. Instead of a right hand, he had a hook. Katie said they should leave, but Paul laughed and said there wasn't any reason to go. When they heard a strange noise, Paul agreed to take her home. When Katie opened the door, she heard something clink. It was a hook hanging on the door handle!

For decades, some version of "The Hook" story has circulated among Americans. It has appeared as a "genuine" letter in "Dear Abby," and some of my students heard it in grade school. **Urban legends** are stories with an ironic twist that sound realistic but are false. Although untrue, they usually are told by people who believe that they happened.

Another urban legend that has made the rounds is the "Kentucky Fried Rat."

> One night, a woman didn't have anything ready for supper, so she and her husband went to the drive-through at Kentucky Fried Chicken. While they were eating in their car, the wife said, "My chicken tastes funny."
>
> Her husband said, "You're always complaining about something." When she insisted that the chicken didn't taste right, he put on the light. She was holding fried rat—crispy style. The woman went into shock and was rushed to the hospital.
>
> A lawyer from the company offered them $100,000 if they would sign a release and not tell anyone. This was the second time this happened.

Folklorist Jan Brunvand (1981, 1984, 1986) reported that urban legends are passed on by people who think that the event happened just one or two people down the line of transmission, often to a "friend of a friend." The story has strong appeal and gains credibility from naming specific people or local places. Brunvand views urban legends as "modern morality stories", each one teaches a moral lesson about life.

If we apply Brunvand's analysis to these two urban legends, three major points emerge. First, these morals serve as warnings. "The Hook" warns young people that they should be careful about where they go, with whom they go, and what they do. The world is an unsafe place, and "messing around" is risky. "The Kentucky Fried Rat" contains a different moral: Do you *really* know what you are eating when you buy food from a fast-food outlet? Maybe you should eat at home, where you know what you are getting.

Second, each story is related to social change: "The Hook" to changing sexual morality, the "Kentucky Fried Rat" to changing male-female relationships, especially to changing sex roles at home. Third, each is calculated to instill guilt and fear: guilt—the wife failed in her traditional role of cooking supper, and she was punished; and fear—we should all be afraid of the dangerous unknown, whether it lurks in the dark countryside or inside our bucket of chicken. The ultimate moral of these stories is that we should not abandon traditional roles or the safety of the home.

fashion a pattern of behavior that catches people's attention and lasts longer than a fad

urban legend a story with an ironic twist that sounds realistic but is false

These principles can be applied to an urban legend that made the rounds in the late 1980s. I heard several versions of this one; each narrator swore that it had just happened to a friend of a friend.

> Jerry (or whoever) went to a nightclub last weekend. He met a good-looking woman, and they hit it off. They spent the night in a motel. When he got up the next morning, the woman was gone. When he went into the bathroom, he saw a message scrawled on the mirror in lipstick: "Welcome to the wonderful world of AIDS."

SOCIAL MOVEMENTS

When the Nazis, a small group of malcontents in Bavaria, first appeared on the scene in the 1920s, their ideas appeared to the world to be laughable. They believed that the Germans were a race of supermen (*Übermenschen*) who would launch a Third Reich (rule or nation) that would control the world for a thousand years. Their race destined them for greatness; lesser races were meant for their service and exploitation.

They started as a little band of comic characters who looked as though they had stepped out of a grade B movie (see the photo on page 321.) From this inauspicious start, the Nazis gained such power that they threatened the existence of Western civilization. How could a little man with a grotesque moustache, surrounded by a few sycophants in brown shirts, ever come to threaten the world? Such things don't happen in real life—only in novels or movies. They are the deranged nightmare of some imaginative author. Only this was real life. The Nazis' appearance on the human scene caused the deaths of millions of people and changed the course of world history. ■

social movement a large group of people who are organized to promote or resist social change

proactive social movement a social movement that promotes some social change

reactive social movement a social movement that resists some social change

social movement organization an organization developed to further the goals of a social movement

Social movements, the second major topic of this chapter, hold the answer to Hitler's rise to power. **Social movements** consist of large numbers of people who organize to promote or resist social change. Members of social movements hold strong ideas about what is wrong with the world—or some part of it—and how to make things right. Examples include the abolitionist (anti-slavery) crusade, the civil rights movement, the white supremacist movement, the women's movement, the animal rights movement, the nuclear freeze movement, and the environmental movement.

At the heart of social movements lies a sense of injustice (Klandermans 1997). Some find a condition of society intolerable, and their goal is to *promote* social change. Theirs is called a **proactive social movement.** Others, in contrast, feel threatened because some condition of society is changing, and they organize to *resist* that change. Theirs is a **reactive social movement.**

To further their goals, people develop **social movement organizations.** Those whose goal is to promote social change develop such organizations as the National Organization for Women (NOW) and the National Association for the Advancement of Colored People (NAACP). In contrast, those who are trying to resist these particular changes form the Stop-ERA and the Ku Klux Klan. To recruit followers and publicize their grievances, leaders of social movements use attention-getting devices, from marches and protest rallies to sit-ins and boycotts. Some stage "media events," sometimes quite effectively (see the Perspectives box).

PERSPECTIVES | Cultural Diversity in the United States

THE MILLION-MAN MARCH:
ANOTHER STEP IN AN UNFINISHED SOCIAL MOVEMENT

The Civil Rights Movement of the 1950s and 1960s brought huge gains: integrated public facilities, schools, voting booths, housing, and workplaces. Or, rather, the movement affirmed that all Americans have the *right* to such aspects of social life, for the gains have always seemed to be elusive, to somehow disappear just when they seemed on the verge of being realized. Today, the inner city, with all of its ills, from unemployment to violent crime, has become the single most powerful symbol that this social movement is unfinished.

The Million-Man March—which consisted of several hundred thousand African-American males from all over the country who gathered on the Mall in Washington, D.C., in the fall of 1995—picked up where this movement stalled. It had two essential features. The first was directed outward: protest at continued obstacles; insistence that the walls of racism come down; voter registration drives; a sense of optimism and determination that good can be accomplished. The second, and overriding, feature was more inwardly directed: a sense of black unity arising from twin sources—

shared pain and a glimpse of a promising future.

This first feature is a direct reflection of the old Civil Rights Movement.

The second feature, an inward turning, is a redirecting of the Civil Rights Movement. It is a conservative, proactive stance by African Americans who desire to make changes in the African-American community. As the organizers of the march stressed, this feature underscores the need to build greater respect between men and women, to reduce spouse abuse, and to assume the obligations of fatherhood—including marriage, nurturing and supporting one's children, and giving them a positive role model of responsible masculinity (Whetstone 1996).

This desire for inward change that is manifested in personal relationships reflects the religious orientation of the march's organizers. The emphases are on repentance, atonement, and changed behavior. Although the Civil Rights Movement has always had a religious orientation—a dedication to religious principles motivated by moral outrage over grievous wrongs—this focus on inner change is new.

The Million-Man March did not begin with a march to Washington, nor did it end with the departure of the buses. There may be other marches—a Million Youth March, a Million Young Women March, and so forth. These specifics are not what is relevant. The march is but one facet of a continuing social movement. The movement is destined to stay with us, for grievances remain and its goals have been only partially reached. ■

For Your Consideration

What are these marches intended to accomplish? What do you think they accomplish? What other techniques might be more effective? What symbols did the organizers use? What messages are these marches intended to communicate? Who are the intended audiences? Look at Figure 21.2 on page 620; is this an alterative, redemptive, reformative, or transformative social movement? Look at Figure 21.3 on page 621; identify the three memberships and three publics involved in these demonstrations.

Social movements are like a rolling sea, says sociologist Mayer Zald (1992). During one period, few social movements may appear, but shortly afterward a wave of them rolls in, each competing for the public's attention. Zald suggests that a *cultural crisis* can give birth to a wave of social movements. By this, he means that there are times when a society's institutions fail to keep up with social change, when many people's needs go unfulfilled, and when massive unrest follows. Social movements spring into action to bridge this gap.

TYPES AND TACTICS OF SOCIAL MOVEMENTS

Let's see what types of social movements there are and then examine their tactics.

Types of Social Movements

Since social change is their goal, we can classify social movements according to their *target* and the *amount of change* they seek. Figure 21.2 on the next page summarizes the classification developed by sociologist David Aberle (1966). If you read across, you will see that the target of the first two types of social movements is *individuals*. **Alterative social movements**

alterative social movement a social movement that seeks to alter only particular aspects of people

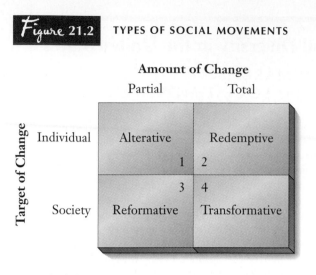

Figure 21.2   **TYPES OF SOCIAL MOVEMENTS**

Amount of Change

	Partial	Total
Individual	Alterative 1	Redemptive 2
Society	Reformative 3	Transformative 4

Target of Change

Source: Aberle 1966.

seek only to *alter* some particular behavior of people. An example is the Women's Christian Temperance Union, a powerful social movement of the early 1900s. Its goal was to get people to stop drinking alcohol. Its members were convinced that if they could close the saloons such problems as poverty and wife abuse would go away. **Redemptive social movements** also target individuals, but here the aim is for *total* change. An example is a religious social movement that stresses conversion. In fundamentalist Christianity, for example, when someone converts to Christ, the entire person is supposed to change, not just some specific behavior. Self-centered acts are to be replaced by loving behaviors toward others as the convert becomes, in their terms, a "new creation."

The target of the next two types of social movements is *society*. **Reformative social movements** seek to *reform* some specific aspect of society. The environmental movement, for example, seeks to reform the ways society treats the environment, from its disposal of garbage and nuclear wastes to its use of land and water. **Transformative social movements,** in contrast, seek to *transform* the social order itself. Its members want to replace it with their version of the good society. Revolutions, such as those in the American colonies, France, Russia, and Cuba, are examples.

One of the more interesting examples of transformative social movements is **millenarian movements,** which are based on prophecies of coming calamity. Of particular interest is a type of millenarian movement called a **cargo cult** (Worsley 1957). About one hundred years ago, Europeans colonized the Melanesian Islands of the South Pacific. Ships from the home countries of the colonizers arrived one after another, each loaded with items the Melanesians had never seen. As the Melanesians watched the cargo being unloaded, they expected some of it to go to them. They noted, however, that it all went to the Europeans. Melanesian prophets then revealed the secret of this exotic merchandise. Their own ancestors were manufacturing and sending the cargos to them, but the colonists were intercepting the merchandise. Since the colonists were too strong to fight, and too selfish to share the cargo, there was little the Melanesians could do.

Then came a remarkable self-fulfilling prophecy. Melanesian prophets revealed that if the people would destroy their crops and food and build harbors, their ancestors would see their sincerity and send the cargo directly to them. The Melanesians did so. When the colo-

redemptive social movement
a social movement that seeks to change people totally

reformative social movement
a social movement that seeks to change only particular aspects of society

transformative social movement
a social movement that seeks to change society totally

millenarian movement a social movement based on the prophecy of coming social upheaval

cargo cult a social movement in which South Pacific islanders destroyed their possessions in the anticipation that their ancestors would send items by ship

Social movements involve large numbers of people who, upset about some condition in society, organize to do something about it. Shown here is Carrie Nation, a temperance leader who in 1900 began to break up saloons with a hatchet. Her social movement eventually became so popular that it resulted in Prohibition.

nial administrators of the island saw that the natives had destroyed their crops and were just sitting in the hills waiting for the cargo ships to arrive, they informed the home government. The prospect of thousands of islanders patiently starving to death was too horrifying to allow. The British government fulfilled the prophecy by sending ships to the islands with cargo earmarked for the Melanesians.

Some social movements have developed a global orientation. As with many aspects of life today, numerous issues that bother people know no national boundaries. Participants of what are called **new social movements** have a goal to change some condition not just in their society, but throughout the world. The social movements often center on improving the quality of life (Melucci 1989). The women's movement, environmental movement, and animal rights movements are examples (McAdam et al. 1988).

Figure 21.3 THE MEMBERSHIP AND PUBLICS OF SOCIAL MOVEMENTS

6. Indifferent and unaware public
5. Hostile public
4. Sympathetic public
3. The less committed
2. The committed
1. The inner core

Tactics of Social Movements

The leaders of a social movement can choose from a variety of tactics. Should they peacefully boycott, march, or hold an all-night candlelight vigil? Or should they bomb a building, blow up an airplane, or assassinate a key figure? To understand why the leaders of social movements choose their tactics, we need to examine a group's levels of membership, the publics it addresses, and its relationship to authorities.

Levels of Membership Figure 21.3 shows the composition of social movements. Beginning at the center and moving outward are three levels of membership. At the center is the inner core, those most committed to the movement. The inner core sets the group's goals, timetables, strategies, and inspires the other members. People at the second level are also committed to the movement, but somewhat less so than the inner core. They can be counted on to show up for demonstrations and to do the grunt work—coordinate mailings, pass out petitions and leaflets, make telephone calls. The third level consists of a wider circle of people who are less committed and less dependable. Their participation depends on convenience—if an activity doesn't interfere with something else they want to do, they participate.

new social movements social movements with a new emphasis on some condition in the world, instead of on a condition in a specific country

Activists in social movements become committed to "the cause." The social movement around abortion, currently one of the most dynamic in the United States, has split Americans, is highly visible, and has articulate spokespeople on both sides.

What tactics are chosen largely depends on the predispositions and backgrounds of the inner core. Because of their differing backgrounds, some members of the inner core may be predisposed to use peaceful means. Others may be more confrontational, while still others prefer violence. Tactics also depend on the number of committed members. Different tactics are called for depending on whether the inner core can count on seven hundred—or only seven—committed members to show up.

The Publics Outside the group's membership is the **public,** a dispersed group of people who may have an interest in the issue. As you can see from Figure 21.3, there are three types of publics. Just outside the third circle of members, and blending into it, is the sympathetic public. Although their sympathies lie with the movement, these people have no commitment to it. Their sympathies with the movement's goals, however, make them fertile ground for recruiting new members. The second public is hostile. It is aware of the group's goals and wants to stop the social movement, for the movement's values go against its own. The third public consists of disinterested people. They are either unaware of the social movement or, if aware, are indifferent to it.

In selecting tactics, the leadership pays attention to these publics. The sympathetic public is especially significant, because it is the source of new members and support at the ballot box. Leaders avoid tactics that appear likely to alienate the sympathetic public and choose those they think will elicit even more sympathy from this group. The leadership may even force a confrontation with the hostile public, trying to make itself appear a victim, a group whose rights are being trampled on. Tactics directed toward the unaware or indifferent public are designed to neutralize their indifference and increase their awareness.

Relationship to Authorities The movement's relationship to authorities is also significant in determining tactics—especially in choosing peaceful or violent tactics. If a social movement is *institutionalized,* accepted by authorities, violence will not be directed against the authorities, for they are on the same side. This, however, does not rule out violence directed against the opposition. If authorities are hostile to a social movement, aggressive or even violent tactics are more likely. For example, because the goal of a transformative (rev-

public a dispersed group of people who usually have an interest in the issue on which a social movement focuses; the sympathetic and hostile publics have such an interest, but a third public is either unaware of the issue or indifferent to it

The social movement to stop violence against women has had a major impact on our thinking about gender relations, laws, and law enforcement. Discussed in the text are social factors that underlie the choice of tactics used by women's centers. Shown here are the Purple Berets in Santa Rosa, California, who are protesting against county officials for wanting to treat spouse abuse as a counseling problem instead of a criminal problem.

olutionary) social movement is to replace the government, the movement and the government are clearly on a collision course.

Other Factors Sociologist Ellen Scott (1993), who studied the movement to stop rape, discovered that friendship, race, and even size of town are important in determining tactics. Women in Santa Cruz, California, chose to directly confront accused rapists, to publicly humiliate them. In a town of 41,000, the tactic worked. In Washington, D.C., women rejected confrontation as ineffective because of the anonymity that comes with a city of 640,000. Another factor was race. Both groups of women were white, but in Santa Cruz it was white women confronting white men, while in Washington, D.C., it would have been white women confronting black men. Friendships were also important. Public confrontations require a closely working team of people who will back each other up. In Santa Cruz, the women had lived together for years, while the group in Washington, D.C., was a more formal organization.

Movement leaders try to avoid tactics that may backfire. An error may be fatal. Women from the Santa Cruz center hung pictures of a man accused of rape all around town. He sued. The long litigation that followed sapped the women's energy, and the Santa Cruz center folded.

The Mass Media: Gatekeepers to Social Movements

As they choose tactics, the leaders of social movements keep the mass media in mind (Zald 1992). Their goal is to influence **public opinion,** how people think about some issue. The right kind of publicity enables them to arouse the sympathetic public and to lay the groundwork for recruiting more members. Pictures of bloodied, dead baby seals, for example, go a long way toward getting the group's message across.

A key to understanding social movements, then, is **propaganda.** Although this word often evokes negative images, it actually is a neutral term. Propaganda is simply the presentation of information in the attempt to influence people. Its original meaning was positive. *Propaganda* referred to a committee of cardinals of the Roman Catholic church whose assignment was the care of foreign missions. (They were to *propagate* the faith.) The term

public opinion how people think about some issue

propaganda in its broad sense, the presentation of information in the attempt to influence people; in its narrow sense, one-sided information used to try to influence people

The use of propaganda is popular among those committed to the goals of a social movement. They can see only one side to the social issue about which they are so upset. Do you think there is another side to this social issue?

has traveled a long way since then, however, and today it usually refers to a one-sided presentation of information that distorts reality.

Propaganda, in the sense of organized attempts to manipulate public opinion, is a regular part of modern life. Advertisements, for example, are a form of propaganda, for they present a one-sided version of reality. Underlying effective propaganda are seven basic techniques, discussed in the Down-to-Earth Sociology box below. Perhaps by understanding

Down-to-Earth *Sociology*

"TRICKS OF THE TRADE"—
THE FINE ART OF PROPAGANDA

Sociologists Alfred and Elizabeth Lee (1939) found that propaganda relies on seven basic techniques, which they termed "tricks of the trade." To be effective, the techniques should be subtle, with the audience unaware that their mind and emotions are being manipulated. If propaganda is effective, people will not know why they support something, only that they do—and they'll fervently defend it.

1. *Name calling.* This technique aims to arouse opposition to the competing product, candidate, or policy by associating it with a negative image. By comparison, one's own product, candidate, or policy is attractive. Political candidates who call an opponent "soft on crime" are using this technique.

2. *Glittering generality.* Essentially the opposite of the first technique, this one surrounds the product, candidate, or policy with phrases that arouse positive feelings. "She's a *real* Democrat" has little meaning, but it makes the audience feel that something has been said. "He stands for individualism" is so general that it is meaningless, yet the audience thinks that it has heard a specific message about the candidate.

3. *Transfer.* In its positive form, this technique associates the product, candidate, or policy with something the public respects or approves.

You might not be able to get by with saying, "Coors is patriotic," but surround a beer with images of the U.S. flag, and beer drinkers will get the idea that it is more patriotic to drink this brand of beer than to drink any other kind. In its negative form, this technique associates the product, candidate, or policy with something the public disapproves.

4. *Testimonials.* Famous and admired individuals are used to endorse a product, candidate, or policy. Michael Jordan lends his name to cologne, Nike products, and even underwear, while Cindy Crawford does the same for Revlon. Candidates for political office solicit the endorsement of movie stars who may know next to nothing about the candidate, or who may not even be interested in politics. In the negative form of this technique, a despised person is associated with the competing product. If propagandists (called "spin docters" in politics) could get by with it, they would show Saddam Hussein announcing support for an opposing candidate.

5. *Plain folks.* Sometimes it pays to associate the product, candidate, or policy with "just plain folks." "If Mary or John Q. Public likes it, you will, too." A political candidate who kisses babies, puts on a hard hat, and has lunch at McDonald's while photogra-

phers "catch him (or her) in the act"—is using the "plain folks" strategy. "I'm just a regular person" is the message of the presidential candidate who poses for photographers in jeans and a work shirt—while making certain that the chauffeur-driven Mercedes does not show up in the background.

6. *Card stacking.* The aim of this technique is to present only positive information about what a person or group supports, and only negative information about what the person or group opposes. The intent is to make it sound as though there is only one conclusion that a rational person can draw. Falsehoods, distortions, and illogical statements can be used if necessary.

7. *Bandwagon.* "Everyone is doing it" is the idea behind this technique. Emphasizing how many others buy the product or support the candidate or policy conveys the message that anyone who doesn't join in is on the wrong track. After all, "20 million Frenchmen can't be wrong," can they?

The Lees (1939) added, "Once we know that a speaker or writer is using one of these propaganda devices in an attempt to convince us of an idea, we can separate the device from the idea and see what the idea amounts to on its own merits." ■

these techniques, you will be able to resist one-sided appeals—whether they come from social movements or from hawkers of some new product.

The mass media play such a crucial role in social movements that we can say they are the gatekeepers to social movements. If those who control and work in the mass media—from owners to reporters—are sympathetic to some particular "cause," you can be sure that it will receive sympathetic treatment. If the social movement goes against their own views, it will be ignored or will receive unfavorable treatment. If you ever get the impression that the media are trying to manipulate your opinions and attitudes on some particular social movement—or some social issue—you probably are right. Far from doing unbiased reporting, the media are under the control and influence of people who have an agenda to get across. To the materials in the Down-to-Earth Sociology box on propaganda, then, we need to add the biases of the media establishment, the issues to which it chooses to give publicity, those it chooses to ignore, and its favorable and unfavorable treatment of issues and movements.

Sociology can be a liberating discipline (Berger 1963/1999). It sensitizes us to the existence of *multiple realities;* that is, for any single point of view on some topic, there are competing points of view, which some find equally as compelling. Each represents reality as people see it, but different experiences lead to different perceptions. Consequently, although the committed members of a social movement are sincere and perhaps even make sacrifices for "the cause," theirs is but one view of the way the world is. If other sides were presented, the issue would look quite different.

Why People Join Social Movements

As we have seen, social movements are fed by a sense of injustice. They stem from widespread, deeply felt discontent, the conviction that some condition of society is no longer tolerable. However, not everyone who feels strongly dissatisfied with an issue joins a social movement. Let's look at three explanations for why some people join social movements.

Mass Society Theory

To explain why people are attracted to social movements, sociologist William Kornhauser (1959) proposed **mass society theory.** Kornhauser argued that **mass society**—an impersonal, industrialized, highly bureaucratized society—makes many people feel isolated. Social movements fill a void by offering them a sense of belonging. In geographical areas where social ties are supposedly weaker, such as the western United States, one would expect to find more social movements than one would find in areas where traditional ties are supposedly stronger, such as in the Midwest and South.

This theory seems to match commonsense observations. Certainly, social movements seem to proliferate on the West Coast. But sociologist Doug McAdam (1988), who interviewed people who had risked their lives in the civil rights movement, found that these people were firmly rooted in families and communities. It was their strong desire to right wrongs and to overcome injustices, not their isolation, that motivated their participation. Even the Nazis attracted many people who were firmly rooted in their communities (Oberschall 1973). Finally, those most isolated of all, the homeless, generally do not join anything—except food lines.

Deprivation Theory

A second explanation to account for why people join social movements is *deprivation theory.* According to this theory, people who are deprived of things deemed valuable in society—whether it is money, justice, status, or privilege—join social movements with the hope of redressing their grievances. This theory may seem so obvious as to need no evidence. Don't the thousands of African Americans who participated in the civil rights movement of the 1950s and the World War I soldiers who marched on Washington after

mass society theory an explanation for participation in social movements based on the assumption that such movements offer a sense of belonging to people who have weak social ties

mass society industrialized, highly bureaucratized, impersonal society

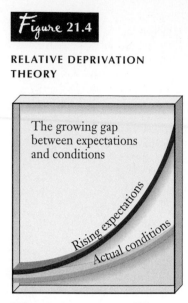

RELATIVE DEPRIVATION THEORY

The growing gap between expectations and conditions

Rising expectations

Actual conditions

Time 1   Time 2

Congress refused to pay their promised bonuses provide ample evidence that the theory is true?

Deprivation theory does provide a starting point. But there is more to the matter than this. We must also pay attention to what Alexis de Tocqueville (1856/1955) noted almost 150 years ago. The peasants of Germany were worse off than the peasants of France, and according to deprivation theory we would expect that the Germans would have rebelled and overthrown their king. Revolution, however, occurred in France, not Germany. The reason this did not occur, said de Tocqueville, is *relative* deprivation. French peasants had experienced improving living conditions, and could imagine even better conditions, while German peasants, having never experienced anything but depressed conditions, had no comparative basis for feeling deprived.

According to **relative deprivation theory,** then, it is not people's actual deprivation that matters. Rather, the key to participation is *relative* deprivation—that is, what people *think* they should have relative to what others have, or relative to their own past or perceived future. This theory, which has provided excellent insight into revolutions, also holds a surprise. Because improving conditions fuel human desires for even better conditions, in some instances *improving* conditions can spark revolutions. As Figure 21.4 shows, this occurs when people's expectations outstrip actual change.

Relative deprivation also explains an interesting aspect of the civil rights movement. At the center of the sit-ins and other protests in the South during the 1950s and 1960s were relatively well-off African Americans—college students and church leaders who went to restaurants and lunch counters that were reserved for whites. When refused service, they sat peacefully while abuse and food were heaped on them (Morris 1993). Why did they subject themselves to such treatment? Remember that what is significant is not what we have or don't have, but whom we compare ourselves with. The sit-ins were a form of rebellion against the white establishment: Compared with whites, the African-American demonstrators saw themselves as deprived.

But why did white, middle-class college students from the North risk their lives and join these Southern protesters? Relative deprivation theory doesn't help us here. Although their own personal welfare was not at stake, they became active for *moral* reasons (McAdam 1988; Fendrich and Lovoy 1993). Let's consider that motivation in social movements.

Moral Issues and Ideological Commitment

As sociologists James Jasper and Dorothy Nelkin (1992) point out, we would miss the basic reason for many people's involvement in social movements if we overlooked the moral issue. Some people join because of *moral shock*—a sense of outrage at finding out what is "really" going on (Jasper and Poulsen 1995). For people who see a social movement in moral terms, great issues hang in the balance. They feel they must choose sides and do what they can to make a difference. As sociologists put it, they join because of *ideological commitment* to the movement. Many members on both sides of the abortion issue see their involvement in such terms. Similarly, most activists in the animal rights movement are convinced that there can be no justification for making animals suffer in order to make safer products for humans. Some see nuclear weapons and power in similar moral terms, and they risk arrest and ridicule for their participation in demonstrations. For others, matters of the environment are moral issues, and to not act would be an inexcusable betrayal of future generations. The *moral* component of a social movement, then, is a primary reason for some people's involvement.

A Special Case: The Agent Provocateur

A unique type of social movement participant is the **agent provocateur,** an agent of the government or even of a rival social movement whose job is to spy on the leadership and perhaps to sabotage its activities. Some are recruited from the membership itself; such people

relative deprivation theory in this context, the belief that people join social movements based on their evaluations of what they think they should have compared with what others have

agent provocateur someone who joins a group in order to spy on it and to sabotage it by *provoking* its members to commit illegal acts

Militias—citizens who arm themselves and form paramilitary organizations—have sprung up across the United States. This photo was taken of a militia in Shingleton, California. Although all the theories discussed in the text may apply to members of these militias, those that deal with moral issues and ideological commitment are especially relevant.

are willing to become traitors to the organization for a few Judas dollars. Others are members of the police or members of a rival group who go underground and join the movement.

Because the social change that some social movements represent is radical and threatens the power elite, the use of agent provocateurs is not surprising. What may be surprising, however, is that some agents convert to the social movement on which they are spying. Sociologist Gary Marx (1993) explains that to be credible, agents must share at least some of the class, age, gender, racial-ethnic, or religious characteristics of the group. This, however, makes the agents more likely to sympathize with the movement's goals and to become disenchanted with trying to harm the group. Also, to be effective, agents must work their way into the center of the group. This requires frequent interaction with the group's committed members; following a basic sociological principle, this tends to produce liking. In addition, while they build trust with the rival group, they may be cut off from their own group. This allows the point of view they represent to recede, and concerns about betraying and deceiving people who now trust them begin to creep in.

What also may be surprising is how far some agents go. During the 1960s, when a wave of militant social movements rolled across the United States, the FBI and other police recruited agent provocateurs to sabotage groups. These agents provoked illegal activities that otherwise would not have occurred: They set the leadership up for arrest and, in some instances, set them up for death. Two examples will let us see how agent provocateurs operate (Marx 1993). One of the four men involved in a plot to blow up the Statue of Liberty by a group called the Black Liberation Front was an undercover agent. It was he who drew up the plans and even provided funds to pay for the dynamite and rent the car. In another instance, the FBI paid $36,500 to two members of the White Knights of the Ku Klux Klan to arrange for other Klansmen to bomb a Jewish businessman's home. A trap was set in which one Klansman was killed and another was arrested in the unsuccessful attempt.

■ **In Sum** Recruitment generally follows channels of social networks, and people most commonly join a social movement because they have friends and acquaintances already in it (McCarthy and Wolfson 1992; Snow et al. 1993). Motivations are mixed. Some join because of moral convictions, others to further their own careers, because they find a valued identity, or even because it is fun. Some participate even though they *don't want to*. The Cuban government, for example, compels people to turn out for mass demonstrations to show support of the Communist regime (Aguirre 1993). As we just saw, police agents may join social movements in order to spy on them and sabotage their activities. In no social movement, then, is there a single cause for people joining. As in all other activities in life, people remain a complex bundle of motivations—and this provides a challenge for sociologists to unravel.

On THE SUCCESS AND FAILURE OF SOCIAL MOVEMENTS

Large industrial societies give rise to the discontent that spawns social movements, but most social movements are not successful. Let's look at the reasons for their success or failure.

The Stages of Social Movements

Social movements go through several stages as they grow and mature. Sociologists have identified these five stages (Lang and Lang 1961; Mauss 1975; Spector and Kitsuse 1977; Tilly 1978; Jasper 1991):

1. *Initial unrest and agitation.* During this first stage, people are upset about some condition in society and want to change it. Leaders emerge who verbalize people's feelings and crystallize issues. Most social movements fail at this stage. Unable to gain enough support, after a brief flurry of activity they quietly die.

2. *Resource mobilization.* The crucial factor that enables social movements to make it past the first stage is **resource mobilization.** By this term, sociologists mean the mobilization of resources—time, money, people's skills, and the ability to get the attention of the mass media (Oliver and Marwell 1992; Buechler 1993). Technology and mailing lists are key resources: direct mailing, faxing, and e-mailing. Increasingly, international resources are becoming important.

   In some cases, an indigenous leadership arises to mobilize available resources. Other groups, having no capable leadership of their own, turn to outsiders, "specialists for hire." As sociologists John McCarthy and Mayer Zald (1977; Zald and McCarthy 1987) point out, even though large numbers of people may be upset over some condition of society—as is often the case—without resource mobilization they remain a group of upset people; they do not constitute a social movement.

3. *Organization.* A division of labor is set up. The leadership makes policy decisions, and the rank and file carry out the daily tasks necessary for keeping the movement alive. There is still much collective excitement about the issue, the movement's focal point.

4. *Institutionalization.* At this stage, the movement has developed a bureaucracy, the type of formal hierarchy described in Chapter 7. The collective excitement is gone, and control lies in the hands of career officers, who may care more about their own position in the organization than the movement for which the organization's initial leaders made sacrifices. They may move the group's headquarters to a "good" location, for example, furnish it with expensive furniture and art work, and take pains to be seen with the "right" people in the "right" places.

5. *Organizational decline and possible resurgence.* At this point, the organization may decline. Instead of working on the issues, the leadership may waste its energies on managing a bureaucracy. Or, a change in public sentiment may so dominate the society that most members jump ship, leaving the leaders with few to lead. With no strong, committed group united by a common cause, the movement may wither away and finally disappear. Its diehards always linger, grasping at any straw in the hope that there may be a resurgence.

resource mobilization a theory that social movements succeed or fail based on their ability to mobilize resources such as time, money, and people's skills

And appearances can be deceiving. Even if most participants desert and those most committed flounder with little support, this does not necessarily mean the end of a movement. After suffragists won the right to vote in 1920 (discussed on pages 297–298), their movement declined until nothing but a shell remained. During a period researchers call *abeyance*, only a handful of committed organizers were left, and the best they could do was to keep a small flame burning. Yet, fifty years later the women's movement was reenergized and was again thrust into national prominence (Taylor 1997). The following Thinking Critically section discusses another social movement that has undergone resurgence.

WHICH SIDE OF THE BARRICADES? PROCHOICE AND PROLIFE AS A SOCIAL MOVEMENT

No issue so divides Americans as abortion does. Although most Americans take a more moderate view, on one side are some who feel that abortion should be permitted under any circumstances, even during the last month of pregnancy. They are matched by some on the other side who are convinced that abortion should never be allowed for any circumstances, not even during the first month of pregnancy. This polarization constantly breathes new life into the movement.

When the U.S. Supreme Court determined in its 1973 decision, *Roe v. Wade,* that states could not restrict abortion, the prochoice side relaxed. Victory was theirs, and they thought their opponents would quietly disappear. Instead, large numbers of Americans were disturbed by what they saw as the legal right to murder unborn children.

The views of the two sides could not be more incompatible. Those who favor choice view the nearly 1.5 million abortions performed annually in the United States as examples of women exercising their basic reproductive rights. Those who gather under the prolife banner see these acts as legalized murder. To the prochoice side, those who oppose abortion are blocking women's rights, forcing women to continue pregnancies they desire to terminate. To the prolife forces, those who advocate choice are seen as condoning murder, as putting their own desires for school, career, or convenience ahead of the lives of their unborn children.

There is no way to reconcile such contrary views. Each side sees the other as unreasonable and extremist. And each uses propaganda by focusing on worst-case scenarios: prochoice images of young women raped at gunpoint, forced to bear the children of rapists; prolife images of women who are eight months pregnant killing their babies instead of nurturing them.

With no middle ground, these views are in permanent conflict. As each side fights for what it considers basic rights, it invigorates the other. When in 1989 the U.S. Supreme Court decided in *Webster v. Reproductive Services* that states could restrict abortion, one side mourned it as a defeat, the other hailed it as a victory. Seeing the political battle going against them, the prochoice side regrouped for a determined struggle. The prolife side, sensing judicial victory within its grasp, gathered forces to push for a complete overthrow of *Roe v. Wade.*

This goal of the prolife side came close to becoming reality in *Casey v. Planned Parenthood.* On June 30, 1992, in a 6-to-3 decision the Supreme Court upheld the right of states to require women to wait 24 hours between the confirmation of pregnancy and abortion; to require girls under 18 to obtain the consent of one parent; and to require that women be informed about alternatives to abortion and that they be given materials that describe the fetus. In the same case, by a 5-to-4 decision, the Court ruled that a wife does not have to inform her husband if she intends to have an abortion.

Because the two sides do not see the same reality, this social movement cannot end unless the vast majority of Americans commit to one side or the other. Otherwise, all legislative and judicial outcomes—including such extremes as a constitutional amendment that declares abortion to be either murder or a woman's right—are victories to one and defeats to the other. To committed activists, then, no battle is ever complete. Rather, each action is only one small part of a hard-fought, bitter, moral struggle. ■

For Your Consideration

Typically, the last stage of a social movement is decline. Why does this last stage not apply to this social movement? Under what conditions will this social movement decline?

The longer the pregnancy in question, the smaller the proportion of Americans who approve abortion. Does your opinion about abortion change depending on the length of pregnancy? For example, how do you feel about abortion during the second month versus the eighth month? What do you think of abortion in cases of rape and incest? Or partial-birth abortion? Can you identify some of the *social* reasons that underlie your opinions?

Sources: Neikirk and Elsasser 1992; McKenna 1995; Williams 1995; Beckman and Harvey 1998; *Statistical Abstract* 1999:Table 124; Henslin 2000.

The Difficult Road to Success

Despite their significance in contemporary society, social movements seldom solve social problems. Resource mobilization helps to explain why. To mobilize resources, a movement must appeal to a broad constituency. This means that the group must focus on things that a lot of people are concerned about. For example, if workers at one particular plant are upset about their working conditions, their discontent is not adequate for recruiting the broad support necessary for a social movement. At best, it will result in local agitation. Unsafe working conditions of millions of workers, however, have a chance of becoming the focal point of a social movement.

Such broad problems, however, are deeply embedded in society, which makes them extremely difficult to solve. Minor tinkering will never be adequate. Just as the problem touches many interrelated components of society, so the solutions must be all-encompassing. With no quick fix available, the social movement must stay around. But longevity brings its own danger of failure, for, as noted, social movements tend to become bureaucratized, to turn inward, and to focus their energies on running the organization.

Many social movements, however, do vitally affect society. Some, such as the civil rights movement, become powerful forces for social change. They highlight problems and turn the society on a path that leads toward solutions. Others become powerful forces for resisting the social change that its members—and the public it is able to mobilize—consider undesirable. In either case, social movements are highly significant for contemporary society, and we can anticipate that new ones will be a regular feature of our social landscape.

$\mathcal{S}$UMMARY AND $\mathcal{R}$EVIEW

■ **Early Explanations of Collective Behavior**

How did early theorists explain the effects of crowds on individuals?

Early theorists of **collected behavior** argued that crowds transform individuals. Charles Mackay used the term *herd mentality* to explain why people did wild things when they were in crowds. Gustave LeBon said that a **collective mind** develops, and people are swept away by suggestions. Robert Park said that collective unrest develops, which, fed by a **circular reaction**, leads to collective impulses. Pp. 608–609.

What are the five stages of crowd behavior?

Herbert Blumer identified five stages that crowds go through before they become an **acting crowd**: social unrest, an exciting event, **milling**, a common object of attention, and common impulses. Pp. 609–610.

■ **The Contemporary View of Collective Behavior**

What is the current view of crowd behavior?

Current theorists view crowds as rational. Richard Berk stresses a **minimax strategy**; that is, people try to minimize their costs and maximize their rewards, whether or not they are in crowds. Ralph Turner and Lewis Killian analyze how new norms emerge that allow people to do things in crowds that they otherwise would not do. Pp. 610–612.

■ **Forms of Collective Behavior**

What forms of collective behavior are there?

Forms of collective behavior include **lynchings, riots, panics, moral panics, rumors, fads, fashions,** and **urban legends.** Conditions of discontent or uncertainty provide fertile ground for collective behavior, and each form provides a way of dealing with these conditions. Pp. 612–618.

■ Types and Tactics of Social Movements

What types of social movements are there?

Social movements consist of large numbers of people who organize to promote or resist social change. Depending on their target (individuals or society) and the amount of social change desired (partial or complete), social movements can be classified as **alterative, redemptive, reformative,** and **transformative.** Pp. 618–621.

How do social movements select their tactics?

Leaders choose tactics on the basis of a group's levels of membership, its **publics,** and its relationship to authorities. The three levels of membership are *the inner core, the committed,* and *the less committed.* The predispositions of the inner core are crucial in choosing tactics, but so is the public they wish to address. If relationships with authorities are bad, the chances of aggressive or violent tactics increase. Friendship, size of city, and the race of movement participants and their targets may also be significant. Pp. 621–623.

How are the mass media related to social movements?

The mass media are gatekeepers for social movements. Because the media's favorable or unfavorable coverage affects **public opinion,** leaders choose tactics with the media in mind. Social movements also make use of **propaganda** to further their cause. Pp. 623–625.

■ Why People Join Social Movements

Why do people join social movements?

There is no single, overriding reason why people join social movements. According to **mass society theory,** social movements relieve feelings of isolation created by an impersonal, bureaucratized society. According to **relative deprivation theory,** people join movements in order to address their grievances. A sense of justice, morality, values, and ideological commitment also motivates people to join social movements. The **agent provocateur** illustrates that even people who hate a cause may participate in it. Pp. 625–628.

■ On the Success and Failure of Social Movements

Why do social movements succeed or fail?

Social movements go through several stages—initial unrest and agitation, mobilization, organization, institutionalization, and, finally, decline. Resurgence is also possible. Groups that appeal to few people cannot succeed. But to appeal broadly in order to accomplish **resource mobilization,** the movement must focus on broad concerns. These are embedded deeply in society, which makes success difficult. Pp. 628–630.

Where can I read more on this topic?

Suggested Readings for this chapter are at the back of this book.

Sociology & the Internet

All URLs listed are current as of the printing of this book. URLs often change. Please check our Web site, **http://www.abacon.com/henslin,** for updates.

1. Tulsa, Oklahoma, was the site of one of the worst race riots in the history of the United States. Over a 24-hour period beginning on May 31, 1921, white residents of Tulsa burned and looted the local black community. About 300 people were killed. Read more about the history of this riot at the following Web sites: **http://www.tulsalibrary.org/aarc/Riot/raceriot.htm, http://www.tulsahistory.org/riot.html,** and **http://www.ok-history.mus.ok.us/trrc/trrc.htm.** Write a paper in which you explain how and why this riot happened by applying one or more of the theories of collective behavior discussed in your text.

2. One form of collective behavior is the urban legend. You can read more about urban legends at the Web site maintained by the Urban Legends Research Center, **http://www.ulrc.com.au.** Choose from a list of recently added legends, or view the full list of topics by going to the UL Library or the Ghost Legends Archives. When you are finished, give a presentation on urban legends to your sociology class. Be sure to explain what urban legends are, where they come from, why people spread urban legends, and why people believe them.

3. In this chapter you studied four different types of social movements, each with a different goal. You can use the Internet to learn more about social movements that reflect these four types. For an example of alterative social movements, which seek to change some specific behavior, go to **http://www.tobacco.org.** For an example of redemptive social movements, which stress near-to-tal personal change, you may want to go to **http://www.watchtower.org.** For an example of reformative social movements, which attempt to change some specific aspect of society, go to **http://www.greenpeace.org.** An example of transformative social movements, which focus on changing the entire social order, is provided by the Rastafarians at either **http://www.africana.com/tt_010.htm** or **http://www.cwrl.utexas.edu/~bill/e309m/students/marley/history/rastafar/index.html.** Write a paper in which you compare these four movements in terms of goals, membership, sympathetic publics outside the movement, and relationships with authorities. Discuss evidence of how each social movement attempts to mold public opinion. Why do you think each of these social movements has had its particular success?

4. In recent years some social movements have developed a global orientation. As the text notes, the goal of these *new social movements* is to change some condition both in their own society and throughout the world. An example of such a social movement is the Women's Environment and Development Organization (WEDO), whose Web site is at **http://www.wedo.org.** WEDO is an international advocacy network working to transform society. Read more about the values and vision of WEDO, as well as a summary of its program objectives and projects, by clicking on "About WEDO." Browse through some of its areas of activity—monitoring U.N. Conference Agreements, Women & The Environment, Advocacy at the U.N., and Women & the Global Economy—by clicking on the icons. When you have gathered enough information, discuss the group's goals and tactics. Whom does it see as its sympathetic publics? What kind of relationships does it have with those in power? What evidence is there of success?

Social Change and the Environment

- **How Social Change Transforms Society**
  The Four Social Revolutions
  From *Gemeinschaft* to *Gesellschaft*
  Capitalism, Modernization, and Industrialization
  Social Movements
  Geopolitics and Ethnic Conflicts

- **Theories and Processes of Social Change**
  Cultural Evolution
  Natural Cycles
  Conflict Over Power
  Ogburn's Theory

- **How Technology Changes Society**
  Types of Transformation

  The Impact of the Automobile
  The Impact of the Computer
  Cyberspace and Social Inequality

- **The Growth Machine Versus the Earth**
  Environmental Problems in the Most
    Industrialized Nations
  Environmental Problems in the Industrializing
    and Least Industrialized Nations
  The Environmental Movement
  Environmental Sociology

- **Summary and Review**

T he morning of January 28, 1986, dawned clear but cold, with near freezing temperature—strange weather for subtropical Florida. At the Kennedy Space Center, launch pad 39B was lined with 3 inches of ice. Icicles 6 to 12 inches long hung like stalactites from the pad's service structure.

Shortly after 8 A.M., the crew took the elevator to the white room, where they entered the crew module. By 8:36 A.M., the seven members of the crew were strapped in their seats. They were understandably disappointed when liftoff, scheduled for 9:38 A.M., was delayed because of the ice.

Due to a strong public relations campaign, public interest in the flight ran high. Attention focused on Christa McAuliffe, a 37-year-old high school teacher from Concord, New Hampshire, the first private citizen to fly aboard a space shuttle. Across the nation, schoolchildren watched with great anticipation, for Mrs. McAuliffe, who had been selected from thousands of applicants (including the author of this text), was to give a televised lesson during the flight about life aboard a spacecraft.

At the viewing site, thousands of spectators had joined the families and friends of the crew awaiting the launch. After two hours of delays, they were delighted to see *Challenger's* two solid-fuel boosters ignite, and they broke into cheers when this product of technical innovation thundered majestically into space. The time was 11:38 A.M.

Seventy-three seconds later, the *Challenger* was 7 miles from the launch site, racing skyward at 2,900 feet per second, when suddenly a brilliant glow appeared on one side of the external tank. In seconds, the glow blossomed into a gigantic fireball. Screams of horror arose from the crowd as the *Challenger,* now 19 miles away, exploded, and bits of debris began to fall from the sky.

In classrooms across the country, children burst into tears. Adults stared at their televisions in stunned disbelief. ■

Sources: Based on Broad 1986; Magnuson 1986; Lewis 1988; Maier 1993.

The Protestant reformation ushered in not only religious change but also, as Max Weber analyzed, fundamental social-economic change. This painting by Hans Holbein, the Younger, shows the new prosperity of the merchant class. Previously, only the nobility could afford such possessions.

 If any characteristic describes social life today, it is rapid social change. As we shall see in this chapter, technology, such as that which made the *Challenger* first a reality and then a disaster, is a driving force behind this change. To understand social change is to better understand today's society—and our own lives.

HOW SOCIAL CHANGE TRANSFORMS SOCIETY

Social change, a shift in the characteristics of culture and society, is such a vital part of our lives that it has been a theme throughout this book. To make this theme more explicit, let's review the main points about social change made in the preceding chapters.

The Four Social Revolutions

The rapid, far-reaching social change that the world is currently experiencing did not "just happen." Rather, it is the result of forces that were set in motion thousands of years ago, beginning with the domestication of plants and animals. This first social revolution allowed hunting and gathering societies to develop into horticultural and pastoral societies (see pages 150–155). The plow brought about the second social revolution, from which agricultural societies emerged. Then the invention of the steam engine ushered in the Indus-

social change the alteration of culture and societies over time trial Revolution, and now we are witnessing the fourth social revolution, stimulated by the invention of the microchip.

From *Gemeinschaft* to *Gesellschaft*

Although our lives are being vitally affected by this fourth revolution, at this point we are seeing only the tip of the iceberg. By the time this social revolution is full-blown, little of our way of life will have been left untouched. We can assume this because that is how it was with the first three social revolutions. For example, the change from agricultural to industrial society meant not only that people moved from villages to cities but also that intimate, lifelong relationships were replaced by impersonal, short-term associations. Paid work, contracts, and especially money replaced the reciprocal obligations required by kinship, social status, and friendship. As reviewed on pages 107–108, sociologists use the terms *Gemeinschaft* and *Gesellschaft* to indicate this fundamental shift in society.

Traditional, or *Gemeinschaft,* societies are small, rural, and slow-changing. They are dominated by men, and have firm divisions between the sexes. People look to the past for guidelines to the present. They live in extended families, have little formal education, and treat most illnesses at home. They tend to see life and morals in absolute terms. Modern, or *Gesellschaft,* societies, in contrast, are large, more urbanized, and fast changing. Divisions between the sexes are more fluid. People stress formal education, and are more future-oriented. In the third stage of the demographic transition, they have smaller families and low rates of infant mortality. They live longer lives, have higher incomes, and have vastly more material possessions.

Capitalism, Modernization, and Industrialization

Just why did societies change from *Gemeinschaft* to *Gesellschaft?* Karl Marx pointed to a social invention called *capitalism*. He analyzed how the breakup of feudal society threw people off the land, creating a surplus of labor. These masses moved to the cities and were exploited by the owners of the means of production (factories, machinery, tools), setting in motion antagonistic relationships between capitalists and workers that remain today.

Max Weber traced capitalism to the Protestant Reformation (see pages 175–176). He noted that the Reformation stripped Protestants of the assurance that church membership would save them from eternal damnation. As they agonized over heaven and hell, they concluded that God did not want the elect to live in uncertainty. He would give a sign to let people know that they were predestined to heaven. That sign, they decided, was prosperity. An

Social change comes in many forms. Shown here is a Chinese peasant in 1911, whose pigtail is being cut off by the revolutionary army. To retain the custom of never cutting one's hair was considered a sign of allegiance to warlords and of resistance to the new regime.

Table 22.1

COMPARING TRADITIONAL AND MODERN SOCIETIES

Characteristics	*Traditional Societies*	*Modern Societies*
General Characteristics		
Social change	Slow	Rapid
Size of group	Small	Large
Religious orientation	More	Less
Formal education	No	Yes
Place of residence	Rural	Urban
Demographic transition	First stage	Third stage (or Fourth)
Family size	Larger	Smaller
Infant mortality	High	Low
Life expectancy	Short	Long
Health care	Home	Hospital
Temporal orientation	Past	Future
Material Relations		
Industrialized	No	Yes
Technology	Simple	Complex
Division of labor	Simple	Complex
Income	Low	High
Material possessions	Few	Many
Social Relationships		
Basic organization	*Gemeinschaft*	*Gesellschaft*
Families	Extended	Nuclear
Respect for elders	More	Less
Social stratification	Rigid	More open
Statuses	More ascribed	More achieved
Gender equality	Less	More
Norms		
View of reality, life, and morals	Absolute	Relativistic
Social control	Informal	Formal
Tolerance of differences	Less	More

modernization the process by which a *Gemeinschaft* society is transformed into a *Gesellschaft* society

unexpected consequence of the Reformation, then, was to make Protestants work hard and be thrifty. The result was an economic surplus. This stimulated capitalism, laying the groundwork for the Industrial Revolution that transformed the world.

The term given to the sweeping changes ushered in by the Industrial Revolution is **modernization**. Table 22.1 reviews these changes. The features listed in this table are *ideal types* in Weber's sense of the term, for no society exemplifies to the maximum degree all the traits listed here. In addition, technology has created great unevenness. The elite in Uganda, for example, now have computers. Thus the characteristics shown in Table 22.1 should be interpreted as "more" or "less" rather than "either-or."

As technology from the industrialized world is introduced into traditional societies, we are able to witness how far-reaching the changes are. Take modern medicine as an example. Its introduction into the Least Industrialized Nations helped to usher in the second stage of the demographic transition. Death rates dropped, birth rates remained high, and the population exploded. This brought hunger, starvation, and mass migration to the industrialized nations. It also led to mass migration from country to cities in the Least Industrialized Nations. As discussed in the Perspectives box on page 595 this is creating a host of problems yet to be solved.

Social Movements

Social movements reveal the cutting edge of change in society. People band together to express their feelings about something that upsets them. They organize to demand change, or to resist some change they don't like. Because social movements form around issues that bother large numbers of people, they indicate areas of society in which there is the greatest pressure for change. With globalization, these issues increasingly cut across international boundaries, indicating areas of discontent and sweeping change that affect many millions of people (see pages 618–630).

Geopolitics and Ethnic Conflicts

One of the most significant areas of change is the interrelationship of power among nations. Already, during the sixteenth century, today's global divisions had begun to emerge. Trade alliances, forged by the nations that had the most advanced technology of the time (the swiftest ships and the most powerful armaments), created a division into rich and poor nations. Then, according to *dependency theory,* as capitalism emerged the nations that industrialized exploited the resources of those that did not. This made the nonindustrialized nations dependent, and they did not develop their own resources (see pages 248–249).

Today's information revolution will also have far-reaching consequences for global stratification. Those nations that make the fastest, most significant advances in computerized technology (sometimes called taking the fast lane on the information superhighway), primarily the Most Industrialized Nations, are destined to dominate in the coming generation.

The *Rulers of the World* could be the caption of this photo. These ordinary looking men are heads of G7, the seven most powerful nations of the world. They are shown here in Cologne, Germany, at their annual summit, at which they evaluate their progress in ruling the world. As explained in the text, because others are fearful of its nuclear arsenal, Russia is an honorary member of this exclusive group. (The man who is second from the right is president of the European Commission.)

Since World War II, the realignment of national and regional powers (called *geopolitics*) has resulted in a triadic division of the world: a Japan-centered East, a Germany-centered Europe, and a United States-centered western hemisphere. These three global powers, along with four lesser ones—Canada, France, Great Britain, and Italy—dominate today's globe. Known as G7 (meaning the "Group of Seven"), these industrial giants hold annual meetings at which they decide how to divide up the world's markets and regulate global economic policy, such as interest rates, tariffs, and currency exchanges. Their goal is to perpetuate their global dominance, which includes keeping prices down on the raw materials they buy from the Least Industrialized Nations. Cheap oil is essential for this goal, which requires the domination of the Mideast, whether that is accomplished through peaceful means or by a joint war effort of the United Nations. Because of Russia's nuclear arsenal, G7 has courted Russia—giving Russia observer status at its annual summits and providing loans and expertise to help Russia's transition to capitalism. The breakup of the Soviet Union has been a central consideration in G7's plans for a new world order. Events in Russia and throughout its former satellite nations will help determine the shape of future global stratification.

Despite the vast social change occurring around the globe, race remains a fundamental distinction among human groups. Shown here is a Ukrainian being measured to see if he is really "full lipped" enough to be called a Tartar.

Threatening the global divisions so carefully constructed by G7 is the resurgence of ethnic conflicts (see page 439). The breakup of the Soviet empire lifted the cover that had held in check the centuries-old hatreds and frustrated nationalistic ambitions of many ethnic groups. With the Soviet military and the KGB in disarray, these groups turned violently on one another. In Africa, similar hatreds rose to the surface, and warfare erupted among groups that had been superficially bound together in political boundaries. In Europe, the former Yugoslavia divided, with some parts self-destructing as pent-up fury was unleashed. Ethnic conflicts threaten to erupt in Germany, France, Italy, the United States, and Mexico. At what point these resentments and hatreds will play themselves out (if they ever do) is unknown.

For the most part, the Most Industrialized Nations care little if the entire continent of Africa self-destructs in ethnic slaughter. They cannot tolerate interethnic warfare in Europe, however. If the fighting in Bosnia and Kosovo, for example, had spread, an inferno could have engulfed Europe. For global control, G7 must be able to depend on political and economic stability in its own neighborhood as well as in those countries that provide the essential raw materials for its industrial machine. G7 may camouflage its military interventions by saying that its intentions are humanitarian, but you can be certain that geopolitical stability and dominance are the underlying reasons.

*T*HEORIES AND PROCESSES OF SOCIAL CHANGE

Social change has fascinated theorists. We shall consider just four of the many explanations for why societies change: cultural evolution, cycles, conflict theory, and the pioneering views of sociologist William Ogburn.

Cultural Evolution

Evolutionary theories can be classified into three basic types: unilinear, multilinear, and natural cycles. Let's consider each.

Unilinear Evolution *Unilinear* evolutionary theories assume that all societies follow the same path. Each society evolves from simpler to more complex forms, and each goes through uniform sequences (Barnes 1935). Of the many versions of this theory, the one proposed by Lewis Morgan (1877) once dominated Western thought. Morgan said that all societies go through three stages: savagery, barbarism, and civilization. In Morgan's eyes, England, his society, was the epitome of civilization, and all others were destined to follow it.

The basic assumption of this theory, that all non-literate groups have the same form of social organization, has been found to be untrue, and unilinear evolution has been discredited. In addition, to see one's own society as the peak of cultural evolution is now considered unacceptably ethnocentric.

Multilinear Evolution *Multilinear* views of evolution have replaced unilinear theories. Instead of assuming that all societies follow the same sequence, multilinear theorists propose that different routes lead to the same stage of development. Although the path leads to industrialization, societies need not pass through the same sequence of stages on this journey (Sahlins and Service 1960; Lenski and Lenski 1987).

Evaluating Evolutionary Theories Central to evolutionary theories, whether unilinear or multilinear, is the assumption that cultural evolution represents *progress*. According to these theories, non-literate or tribal societies have a primitive form of human culture. As these simpler cultures evolve, they eventually reach a higher state—the advanced and superior form that characterizes modern societies.

Growing appreciation of the rich diversity—and complexity—of traditional cultures has discredited this idea. In addition, Western culture is now in crisis (poverty, racism, discrimination, war, terrorism, alienation, sexual assaults, unsafe streets), and it is no longer regarded as the apex of human development, that which holds the answers to human happiness. Consequently, the idea of cultural progress has been cast aside, and evolutionary theories have been rejected (Eder 1990; Smart 1990).

Natural Cycles

Theories of natural cycles attempt to account for the rise of entire civilizations, not for the rise of a particular society. Why, for example, did Egypt, Greece, and Rome wield such power and influence, only to crest and fall into a decline? Cyclical theories assume that civilizations are like organisms: They are born, see an exuberant youth, come to maturity, then decline as they reach old age, and finally die (Hughes 1962).

To explain this pattern, historian Arnold Toynbee (1946) proposed that each time a civilization successfully meets a challenge, oppositional forces are set up. At its peak, when a civilization has become an empire, the ruling elite loses its capacity to keep the masses in line "by charm rather than by force." Oppositional forces are set loose, which rip apart the fabric of society. Although force may hold the empire together for hundreds of years, the civilization is doomed.

In a book that provoked widespread controversy, *The Decline of the West* (1926–1928), Oswald Spengler, a high school teacher in Germany, proposed that Western civilization had passed its peak and was in decline. Although the West succeeded in overcoming the crises provoked by Hitler and Mussolini, as Toynbee noted, civilizations do not end in a sudden collapse. Because the decline can last hundreds of years, perhaps the crisis in Western civilization mentioned earlier (poverty, rape, murder, and so on) indicates that Spengler was right.

Conflict Over Power

Long before Toynbee, Marx identified a recurring process in human history. He said that each *thesis* (a current arrangement of power) contains its own *antithesis* (contradiction or opposition). A struggle develops between the thesis and its antithesis, leading to a *synthesis* (a new arrangement of power). This new social order, in turn, becomes a thesis that will be challenged by its own antithesis, and so on. Figure 22.1 gives a visual summary of this process.

According to Marx's view (called a **dialectical process** of history), each ruling group sows the seeds of its own destruction. Consider capitalism. Marx said that capitalism (the thesis) is built on the exploitation of workers (an antithesis, or built-in opposition). With workers and owners on a collision course, the dialectical process will not stop until workers establish a classless state (the synthesis).

The analysis of G7 on pages 637–638 follows conflict theory. G7's current division of the globe's resources and markets is a thesis. Resentment on the part of have-not nations is an antithesis. If one of the Least Industrialized Nations gains in military power, that nation will press for a redistribution of resources. China, India, and Pakistan, with their nuclear weapons, fit this scenario. Any new arrangement, or synthesis, will contain its own antitheses, such as ethnic hostilities or the desire of a country for more resources and greater status. These antitheses will haunt the arrangement of power and must at some point be resolved into a synthesis. The process repeats itself.

Ogburn's Theory

Sociologist William Ogburn (1922, 1961, 1964) proposed a view of social change based on technology. Technology, he said, changes society by invention, discovery, and diffusion. Let's look at these three processes of social change.

Invention Ogburn defined **invention** as a combining of existing elements and materials to form new ones. We usually think of inventions as being only material, such as computers, but there also are *social inventions*. We have considered three social inventions in this text: capitalism (pages 174–176), bureaucracy (pages 177–183), and the corporation (pages 186–194, 399–402). As we saw in these instances, social inventions can have far-reaching consequences for a society. In this chapter, we will examine how two other inventions, the automobile and the computer, have transformed society.

Discovery Ogburn identified **discovery**, a new way of seeing reality, as a second process of change. The reality is already present, but people now see it for the first time. An example is Columbus' "discovery" of North America, which had consequences so huge that they altered the course of history. This example also illustrates another principle: A discov-

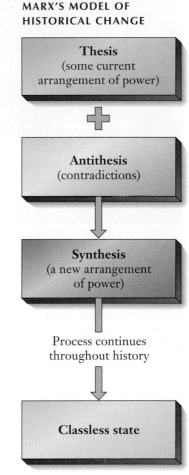

Figure 22.1

MARX'S MODEL OF HISTORICAL CHANGE

Thesis (some current arrangement of power) + Antithesis (contradictions) → Synthesis (a new arrangement of power)

Process continues throughout history

Classless state

dialectical process each arrangement, or thesis, contains contradictions, or antitheses, which must be resolved; the new arrangement, or synthesis, contains its own contradictions, and so on

invention the combination of existing elements and materials to form new ones; identified by William Ogburn as the first of three processes of social change

discovery a new way of seeing reality; identified by William Ogburn as the second of three processes of social change

Culture contact is the source of diffusion, the spread of an invention or discovery from one area to another. Shown here are two children of the Huli tribe in Papua New Guinea. They are amused by a Polaroid photo of themselves.

ery brings extensive change only when it comes at the right time. Other groups, such as the Vikings, had already "discovered" America in the sense of learning that a new land existed. Obviously, to the Native Americans who already lived there, this was no "discovery." Viking settlements disappeared into history, and Norse culture was left untouched by the discovery.

Diffusion Ogburn stressed how **diffusion,** the spread of an invention or discovery from one area to another, can have extensive effects on people's lives. Consider a simple object such as the axe. When missionaries introduced steel axes to the Aborigines of Australia, it upset their whole society. Before this, the men controlled axe-making. They used a special stone, available only in a remote region, and they passed axe-making skills from father to son. Women had to request permission to use the axe. When steel axes became common, women also possessed them, and the men lost both status and power (Sharp 1995).

Diffusion also includes the spread of ideas. As we saw in Chapter 11, the idea of citizenship changed political structure around the world. It removed monarchs as an unquestioned source of authority. The concept of gender equality is now circling the globe. Although taken for granted in a few parts of the world, the idea that it is wrong to withhold rights on the basis of someone's sex is revolutionary. Like citizenship, it is destined to transform basic human relationships and entire societies.

Cultural Lag Ogburn coined the term **cultural lag** to refer to how some elements of a culture lag behind the changes that come from invention and discovery. Technology, he suggested, usually changes first, with culture lagging behind. In other words, we play catch-up with changing technology, adapting our customs and ways of life to meet its needs.

Evaluation of Ogburn's Theory Some find Ogburn's analysis too one-directional, saying that it makes technology the cause of almost all social change. They point out that how people adapt to technology is only one part of the story. The other part consists of how people take control over technology. People develop the technology they need, and they selectively use it. Some groups, such as the Amish (see page 109), even reject technologies they perceive as threatening to their culture. Other resistance to technology is discussed in the Sociology and the New Technology box on the next page.

Technology and social change actually form a two-way street: Just as technology leads to social change, so social change leads to technology. For example, a major social change is the growing number of elderly in our society. Their needs have stimulated new medical technologies, such as those used to treat Alzheimer disease. Another example is our changing ideas about the role the disabled should have in society. This has stimulated the development of new types of wheelchairs that allow people who cannot move their legs to play basketball, participate in the Special Olympics, and enter downhill races.

In fairness to Ogburn, we must note that he never said technology is the only force for social change. He did not assert that people are passive pawns in the face of overwhelming technological forces. He did stress, though, that the material culture (technology) usually changes first, and the symbolic culture (people's ideas and ways of life) follows. This direction still holds, as you can see with the many changes that are following on the heels of the development of computers.

Let's consider, then, how technology changes society.

diffusion the spread of invention or discovery from one area to another; identified by William Ogburn as the final of three processes of social change

cultural lag Ogburn's term for human behavior lagging behind technological innovations

Sociology & the New Technology

FROM THE LUDDITES TO THE UNABOMBER: OPPOSITION TO TECHNOLOGY

In the early 1800s in Great Britain, a machine was invented that could make stockings. The owners of the stocking-making factories were delighted. The workers were not. Seeing their livelihood, such as it was, jerked from beneath them, they picked up axes and hammers and smashed the machines to bits. The local police were ineffective against this uprising, and the government called out twelve thousand troops to restore order. Some of the workers were executed. Others were shipped off to Australia.

One of the apprentice stocking makers who destroyed his machine was Ned Ludlum. Since this time, people who oppose new technology have been called *Luddites* (Volti 1995).

New technology always poses threats and creates fears. Because every new technology replaces some existing technology, it always threatens someone. Opposition to new technology, then, is common. Opposition is usually directed at a specific new technology, but it may serve as a protest against technology in general.

Jacques Ellul (1965), a French sociologist, became upset at technological change. He warned that technology was destroying traditional values. He feared that humans were becoming "a single tightly integrated and articulated component" of technology. He said that technology is producing a monolithic world culture

Ted Kaczynski after his arrest in Helena, Montana.

in which "variety is mere appearance." Ellul's message, and that of others, such as Neil Postman (1992), garnered the attention of only a few intellectuals who discussed the matter in faculty seminars and wrote obscure papers on the subject.

The Unabomber's message, in contrast, came thundering into our consciousness. His warning signals took the form not of books and articles, but of air-mail explosives that maimed and killed their unsuspecting recipients. For seventeen years, the man sent bombs to addresses in states from Michigan to Utah to California. There was no apparent message behind his seemingly random attacks. Then unexpectedly, in 1995, he delivered a verbal message, promising to stop his terror if his 35,000-word essay against technology were published. The *New York Times* and the *Washington Post* duly printed it. His message, in its essence, was similar to Ellul's: Technology is destroying us. A recluse in the mountains of Montana was eventually identified as the Unabomber. Ted Kaczynski, who had an undergraduate degree from Harvard and a Ph.D. from the University of Michigan, was arrested and found guilty. ■

For Your Consideration

What do the Luddites, Jacques Ellul, and the Unabomber have in common? Use concepts presented in this and earlier chapters to analyze the effects of technology on society. Given your conclusions, should we fear new technologies?

How TECHNOLOGY CHANGES SOCIETY

As you may recall from Chapter 2, **technology** has a double meaning. It refers both to *tools*, the items used to accomplish tasks, and to the skills or procedures needed to make and use those tools. This broad concept includes tools as simple as a comb as well as those as complicated as a computer. Technology's second meaning—the skills or procedures needed to make and use tools—refers in this case not only to the procedures used to manufacture combs and computers but also to those required to "produce" an acceptable hairdo or to gain access to the Internet. Apart from its particulars, technology always refers to *artificial means of extending human abilities*.

All human groups make and use technology, but the chief characteristic of postindustrial societies (also called **postmodern societies**) is technology that greatly extends our abilities to

technology often defined as the applications of science, but can be conceptualized as tools, items used to accomplish tasks, along with the skills or procedures necessary to make and use those tools

postmodern society another term for postindustrial society; its chief characteristic is the use of tools that extend the human abilities to gather and analyze information, to communicate, and to travel

Technology, which drives much social change, is at the forefront of our information revolution. This revolution, based on the computer chip, allows reality to cross with fantasy, a merging that sometimes makes it difficult to tell where one ends and the other begins. Shown here is an example of "performance animation," or "morphing," in the David Byrnes video "She's Mad."

analyze information, to communicate, and to travel. These *new technologies,* as they are called, allow us to do what had never been done in history: to probe space, to communicate almost instantaneously anywhere on the globe, to travel greater distances faster, and to store, retrieve, and analyze vast amounts of information.

Types of Transformation

This level of accomplishment, although impressive, is really superficial. Of much greater sociological significance is a deeper issue, how technology changes our way of life. *Technology is much more than the apparatus.* When a technology is introduced into a society, it forces other parts of society to give way. In fact, *a new technology can reshape an entire society.* Let's look at five ways that technology changes society.

Transformation of Existing Technologies As the stocking makers in Great Britain found, when technology changes, people who are working with the old technology feel the first impact. Telephone operators, for example, saw their jobs change when rotary dial telephones replaced manual connections. Rotary dial telephones, in turn, were replaced by touchtone telephones. Eventually, devices into which we simply speak the number we want will replace touchtone telephones. Similarly, IBM electric typewriters, "state of the art" equipment a few years ago, have been rendered obsolete by the desktop computer. Desktop computers, in turn, are giving way to laptops—and some laptops are being replaced by hand-held devices.

Changes in Social Organization Technology also changes social organization. As discussed in Chapter 6, machine technology gave birth to the factory. Prior to machine technology, most workers labored at home, but power-driven machinery required people to gather in one place to do their work. Then it was discovered that workers could produce more items if each did a specialized task. Instead of each worker making an entire item, as

Technology varies greatly from one culture to another, and at least part of each culture is built around its technology. Shown here is a very basic technology used in Dazuo, China. It is of primary sociological interest to note that the people carrying these 1,100-pound slabs of granite are women.

had been the practice, each individual worked on only part of an item. One worker would hammer on a single part, or turn so many bolts, and then someone else would take the item and do some other repetitive task before a third person took over, and so on. Henry Ford built on this innovation by developing the assembly line: Instead of workers moving to the parts, a machine moved the parts to the workers. In addition, the parts were made interchangeable and easy to attach (Womack et al. 1991).

Changes in Ideology Technology also spurs ideology. Karl Marx saw the factory system as a source of **alienation.** He noted that workers who did repetitive tasks on just a small part of a product no longer felt connected to the finished product and could therefore no longer take pride in it. They became alienated from the product of their labor, Marx said, which bred dissatisfaction and unrest.

Marx also noted that, like machines and tools, workers, too, had become replaceable parts. Before factories came on the scene, workers owned their tools and were essentially independent. If they didn't like their work situation, they could pack up their hammers and saws and leave. Others would hire them to build a wagon or make a harness. In the factory, however, the capitalists owned the tools and machinery, and with this came power over the workers. They used the power that came with ownership to extract every ounce of sweat and blood they could. The workers had to submit, for if they left, other workers took their place. The result, said Marx, will be more social change, for only a workers' revolution will change this exploitation. When the workers realize the common basis of their exploitation, they will take over the means of production and establish a workers' state.

Note how the new technology that led to the factory stimulated new ideologies. First, defenders of capitalism developed an ideology to support the principle of maximizing profits. Then, followers of Marx built theories of socialism to attack capitalism. As we shall see shortly, just as changes in technology stimulated the development of communism, changes in technology have been crucial in bringing about its end.

Transformation of Values Just as ideology follows technology, so do values. If technology is limited to clubbing animals, then strength and cunning are valued. So are animal skins. No doubt primitive men and women who wore the skins of some especially unusual or dangerous animal walked with their heads held high—while their neighbors, wearing the same old sheepskins, looked on in envy. Today's technology, in contrast, produces an abundance of synthetic fabrics. Americans brag about cars, boats, hot tubs, and jacuzzis—and make certain that their jeans have the right labels prominently displayed. In short, while jealousy, envy, and pride may be basic to human nature, the particular emphasis on materialism depends on the state of technology.

Transformation of Social Relationships Technology also changes social relationships. When men left their homes to work in factories, family relationships changed. No longer home on a daily basis, the husband-father grew isolated from many of the day-to-day affairs of the family. As husbands became relative strangers to their wives and children, one consequence was more divorce. Current technology is drawing more women from the home to offices and factories, and the consequences are similar—greater isolation from husbands and children, and one more impetus toward fragile marriages. A counter-trend, however, is also in force. Because of the new technology, millions of workers are able to do their work at home. One consequence may be a strengthening of families.

To get a better idea of how our way of life has been affected by inventions, let's look in detail at the changes ushered in by automobiles and the computer.

The Impact of the Automobile

If we try to pick the single item that has had the greatest impact on social life in the past 100 years, the automobile stands out. Let's look at some of the ways in which it has changed U.S. society.

alienation Marx's term for workers' lack of connection to the product of their labor; caused by their being assigned repetitive tasks on a small part of a product

In this 1905 photo, Henry Ford sits in the driver's seat of his latest model car. As is apparent, especially from the spokes on the car's wheels, new technology builds on existing technology. Only after supporting technology was developed, such as graveled and paved roads, did the automobile become a serious contender with other forms of transportation. At the time this photo was taken, who could have imagined that this vehicle would transform society?

Displacement of Existing Technology In a process that began in earnest when Henry Ford began to mass-produce the Model T in 1908, the automobile gradually pushed aside the old technology. People found automobiles to be cleaner, safer, more reliable, and more economical than horses (Flink 1990). People even thought that cars would lower their taxes, for no longer would the public have to pay to clean up the tons of horse manure that accumulated on city streets each day. Humorous as it sounds now, they also thought that automobiles would eliminate the cities' parking problems, for an automobile took up only half as much space as a horse and buggy.

The automobile also replaced a second technology. The United States had developed a vast system of urban transit, with electric streetcar lines radiating outward from the center of the city. As the automobile became more affordable and dependable, Americans found it to be more convenient than public transportation. Instead of walking to the streetcar and waiting for it in the cold and rain, people were able to travel directly from home on their own schedules.

Effects on Cities The decline in the use of streetcars changed the shape of U.S. cities. U.S. cities had been web-shaped, for residences and businesses had located along the streetcar lines. When automobiles freed people from having to live so close to the tracks, they filled in the areas between the "webs."

The automobile also stimulated mass suburbanization. By the 1920s, Americans had begun to leave the city. They found that they could commute to work in the city from outlying areas where they enjoyed more space and lower taxes (Preston 1979). Eventually, this exodus to the suburbs reduced the cities' tax base, contributing, as discussed in Chapter 20, to many of the problems that U.S. cities experience today.

Effects on Farm Life and Villages The automobile had a profound impact on farm life and villages. Before the 1920s, most farmers were isolated from the city. Because using horses for a trip to town was slow and cumbersome, they made such trips infrequently. By the 1920s, however, the popularity and low price of the Model T made the "Saturday trip to town" a standard event. There, farmers would market products, shop, and visit with friends. This changed farm life. Mail-order catalogs stopped being the primary source of shopping, and access to better medical care and education improved (Flink 1990). Farmers also began to travel to bigger towns, where they found more variety of goods. As farmers began to use the nearby villages only for immediate needs, these flourishing centers of social and commercial life dried up.

Changes in Architecture The automobile's effects on commercial architecture are clear—from the huge parking lots that surround shopping malls to the drive-up windows at banks and fast food restaurants. Not so apparent is how the automobile altered the architecture of U.S. homes (Flink 1990). Before the car, each home had a stable in the back where the family kept its horse and buggy. As first, people parked their cars here, as it required no change in architecture. Then, in three steps, architectural change occurred. First, new homes were built with a detached garage. It was located, like the stable, at the back of the home. As the automobile became more essential to the U.S. family, the garage was incorporated into the home. It was moved from the backyard to the side of the house, and was connected by a breezeway. In the final step the breezeway was removed, and the garage was integrated into the home. This allowed people to enter their automobiles without even going outside.

Changed Courtship Customs and Sexual Norms By the 1920s, the automobile was used extensively for dating. This removed children from the watchful eye of parents and undermined parental authority. The police began to receive complaints about "night riders" who parked their cars along country lanes, "doused their lights, and indulged in orgies" (Brilliant 1964). Automobiles became so popular for courtship that by the 1960s about 40 percent of marriage proposals took place in them (Flink 1990).

In 1925 Jewett introduced cars with a foldout bed, as did Nash in 1937. The Nash version became known as "the young man's model" (Flink 1990). Since the 1970s, mobile love-making has declined, primarily because changed sexual norms made bedrooms more accessible.

Effects on Women's Roles The automobile may also lie at the heart of the changed role of women in U.S. society. To see how, we first need to see what a woman's life was like before the automobile. Historian James Flink (1990) described it this way:

> Until the automobile revolution, in upper-middle-class households groceries were either ordered by phone and delivered to the door or picked up by domestic servants or the husband on his way home from work. Iceboxes provided only very limited space for the storage of perishable foods, so shopping at markets within walking distance of the home was a daily chore. The garden provided vegetables and fruits in season, which were home-canned for winter consumption. Bread, cakes, cookies, and pies were home-baked. Wardrobes contained many home-sewn garments.

> Mother supervised the household help and worked alongside them preparing meals, washing and ironing, and housecleaning. In her spare time she mended clothes, did decorative needlework, puttered in her flower garden, and pampered a brood of children. Generally, she made few family decisions and few forays alone outside the yard. She had little knowledge of family finances and the family budget. The role of the lower-middle-class housewife differed primarily in that far less of the household work was done by hired help, so that she was less a manager of other people's work, more herself a maid-of-all-work around the house.

Because automobiles required skill rather than strength, women were able to drive as well as men. This new mobility freed women physically from the narrow confines of the home. As Flink (1990) observed, the automobile changed women "from producers of food and clothing into consumers of national-brand canned goods, prepared foods, and ready-made clothes. The automobile permitted shopping at self-serve supermarkets outside the neighborhood and in combination with the electric refrigerator made buying food a weekly rather than a daily activity." When women began to do the shopping, they gained greater control over the family budget, and as their horizons extended beyond the confines of the home, they also gained different views of life.

In short, the automobile changed women's roles at home, including their relationship with their husbands. It altered their attitudes, transformed their opportunities, and stimulated them to participate in areas of social life not connected with the home.

■ **In Sum** With changes this extensive, it would not be inaccurate to say that the automobile also shifted basic values and changed the way we look at life. Because they were no longer isolated, women, teenagers, and farmers began to see the world differently. So did husbands and wives, whose marital relationship had also been altered. The automobile even transformed views of courtship, sexuality, and gender relations.

No one attributes such fundamental changes solely to the automobile, of course, for many historical events, as well as many other technological changes, occurred during this same period, and each made its own contribution to social change. Even this brief overview of the social effects of the automobile, however, illustrates that technology is not merely an isolated tool but exerts a profound influence on social life.

The second candidate for bringing about the greatest social change is that technological marvel, the computer. Let's consider its impact on society.

Most of us take computers for granted, but they are new to the world scene—as are their effects on our lives. This photo captures a significant change in the evolution of computers. The laptop held by the superimposed model has *more* power than the room-size ENIAC of 1946.

The Impact of the Computer

The ominous wail seemed too close for comfort. Sally looked in her rear-view mirror and realized that the flashing red lights and screaming siren might be for her. She felt confused. "I'm just on my way to Soc," she thought. "I'm not speeding or anything." After she pulled over, an angry voice over a loudspeaker ordered her out of the car.

As she got out, someone barked the command, "Back up with your hands in the air!" Bewildered, Sally stood frozen for a moment. "Put 'em up now! Right now!" She did as she was told.

The officer crouched behind his open door, his gun drawn. When Sally reached the police car—still backing up—the officer grabbed her, threw her to the ground, and handcuffed her hands behind her back. She heard words she would never forget, "You are under arrest for murder. You have the right to remain silent. Anything you say can and will be used against you in a court of law. You have the right to an attorney. If you cannot afford one, one will be provided for you."

Traces of alarm still flicker across Sally's face when she recalls her arrest. She had never even had a traffic ticket, much less been arrested for anything. The nightmare that Sally experienced happened because of a "computer error." With the inversion of two numbers, her car's license number had been entered into the police databank instead of the number belonging to a woman wanted for a brutal killing earlier that day.

None of us is untouched by the computer, but it is unlikely that many of us have felt its power as directly and dramatically as Sally did. For most of us, the computer's control lies quietly behind the scenes. Although the computer has intruded into our daily lives, most of us never think about it. Our grades are computerized, and our paychecks probably are as well. When we buy groceries, a computer scans our purchases and presents a printout of the name, price, and quantity of each item.

Many people rejoice over the computer's capacity to improve their quality of life. They are pleased with the quality control of manufactured goods and with the reduction of drudgery. Records are much easier to keep, and we can type just one letter and let the computer print and address it to ten individuals—or to ten thousand. If we use e-mail, those letters can be delivered in seconds.

Some people, however, worry about errors that can creep into computerized records. They are aware that something similar to Sally's misfortune could happen to them. Others fear that confidentiality of computerized data will be abused, in the way that Orwell's Big Brother used information to achieve total control. Others are concerned about how easily computerized records can be manipulated to accomplish "identity theft." These are legitimate concerns, but space does not permit us to pursue them further.

At this point, let's consider how the computer is changing medicine, education, and the workplace. We'll then consider its likely effects on social inequality.

Computers in Medicine

The patient's symptoms were mystifying. After exercise, one side of his face and part of his body turned deep red, the other chalky white. He looked as though someone had taken a ruler and drawn a line down the middle of his body.

Stumped, the patient's physician consulted a medical librarian, who punched a few words into a personal computer to search for clues in the world's medical literature. Soon, the likely answer flashed on the screen: Harlequin's disease. (Winslow 1994)

The computer was right, and a neurosurgeon was able to correct the patient's nervous system. With computers, physicians can peer within the body's hidden recesses to determine how its parts are functioning or to see if surgery is necessary. Surgeons can operate on unborn babies and on previously inaccessible parts of the brain. In a few years, tiny devices—smaller than the diameter of a single human hair—will be inserted into the bloodstream to detect cancer cells (Kalb 2000).

As the future rushes in, the microchip is bringing even more technological wonders. In what is called *telemedicine,* doctors use stethoscopes to check the heart and lungs of patients who are hundreds of miles away. The data are transmitted by fiber-optic cable (Richards 1996). Soon a surgeon in Boston or San Francisco, using a remote-controlled robot and images relayed via satellite to computers, will be able to operate on a wounded soldier in a battlefield hospital on the other side of the world (Associated Press 1995).

Will the computer lead to "doctorless" medical offices? Will we perhaps one day feed vital information about ourselves into a computer and receive a printout of what is wrong with us (and, of course, a prescription)? Although computers do outperform physicians in their ability to make an accurate diagnosis (Waldholz 1991), they are likely to replace doctors only in some futurist's fanciful imagination. Like Great Britain's stocking makers, physicians will vigorously resist any technological onslaught on their expertise. Many patients are also likely to resist, for they would miss interacting with their doctors, especially the assurances and other emotional support that good physicians provide. (Somehow, "Take two aspirins and key me in the morning" doesn't sound comforting.) It is likely, then, that the computer will remain a diagnostic tool for physicians, not a replacement for them.

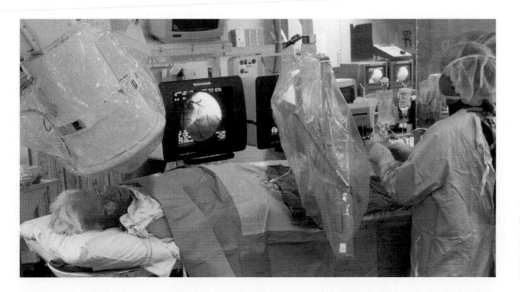

Because of the computer, some surgery that was previously impossible to perform has become routine. An example is the coronary intervention balloon angioplasty shown here.

Computers in Education   Almost every grade school in the United States introduces its students to the computer. Children learn how to type on it, as well as how to use mathematics and science software. Successful educational programs use a gamelike format that makes students forget they are "studying." Classrooms are wired to the Internet. Students in schools that have no teachers knowledgeable in foreign languages are able to take courses in Russian, German, and Spanish. Even though they have no sociology instructors, they can take course in the sociology of sports or gender and race.

The unequal funding we discussed in Chapter 13 is significant in this context. Schools that can afford the latest in computer technology are able to better prepare their students for the future. That advantage, of course, goes to students of private schools and to the richest public school districts, thus helping to perpetuate the social inequalities that arise from the chance of birth. At one point in our history, some schools could not afford textbooks. It is likely that, eventually, education's digital divide will also become a distant memory.

The computer will transform the college of the future. Each office and dormitory room and off-campus residence will be connected by fiber-optic cable. Professors will be able to transmit entire books directly from their office to a student's room, or back the other way, in *less* time than it took to read this sentence. To help students and professors do research or prepare reports, computers will search millions of pages of text. Digital textbooks will replace printed versions such as this one. You will be able to key in the terms *social interaction* and *gender,* select your preference of historical period and geographical area—and the computer will spew out text, maps, moving images, and sounds. You will be able to do the same with any topic: riots and Los Angeles, sexual discrimination in the military, or even the price of marijuana and cocaine. If you wish, the computer will give you a test—geared to the level of difficulty you choose—so you can check your mastery of the material.

Computers in the Workplace   The computer is also transforming the workplace. At the simplest level, it affects how we do work. For example, I wrote the first two editions of this book on a computer, which commanded a printer to produce a copy of the manuscript. Then, even in this electronic age, a series of archaic, precomputer processes followed: I sent the printed copy via the postal service to an editor, who physically handled the manuscript and sent it to others who did the same. The manuscript, marked up in red pencil, was then returned to me via the postal service. I then returned a corrected copy by mail. The transmission was a rather primitive process, much the same as what would have occurred in Benjamin Franklin's day.

Practice is finally catching up with potential. My editors and I now zap text back and forth electronically. I may be in the United States or in Spain, and they in Oregon and Massachusetts. It makes no difference. I print nothing, and send no papers. Although the distances are greater, the time lapse has shortened. For me, the process is marvelous testimony of our changing world—and unsettling confirmation of our steady steps into a brave new world.

The computer is also changing things on a deeper level, for it alters social relationships. For example, I no longer have to bring my manuscript to a university secretary, wait several days for her to type it, and then retrieve it. Because I make the corrections directly at the computer, the secretary is bypassed entirely. In this instance, the computer enhanced social relationships, for I made fewer demands on the department secretary. This new process also eliminated the necessity of excuses when a manuscript was not ready on time—and the tensions in the relationship that this brought.

On the negative side are increased surveillance of workers and depersonalization. As a telephone information operator said,

> The computer knows everything. It records the minute I punch in, it knows how long I take for each call. . . . I am supposed to average under eighteen seconds per call. . . . Everything I do is reported to my supervisor on his computer, and if I've missed my numbers I get a written warning. I rarely see the guy. . . . It's intense. It's me and the computer all day. I'm telling you, at the end of the day I'm wiped out. *Working with computers is the coal mining of the nineties.* (Mander 1992:57, italics added)

Computers in Business and Finance   It wasn't long ago that the advanced technology of businesses consisted of cash registers and adding machines. Connection to the outside world was by telephone. Today, those same businesses are electronically "wired" to suppliers, salespeople, and clients around the country—and around the world. Computers record changes in inventory and set in motion the process of reordering and restocking. They produce detailed reports of sales that alert managers to changes in their customers' tastes or preferences.

National boundaries have become meaningless as computers instantaneously transfer billions of dollars from one country to another. No "cash" changes hands in these transactions. The "cash" consists of digits in computer memory banks, which update the accounts of businesses around the world. Governments are concerned. In a single day, this new type of digitized money can be transferred from the United States to Switzerland, from there to the Grand Cayman Islands, and then to the Isle of Mann, leaving few traces for government sleuths to follow. "Where's my share?" governments around the world are moaning, as they consider how to control—and tax—this new technology.

■ **In Sum** A change in technology inevitably leads to a change in culture. To some, such changes are threatening, for, always, established ways of life must be modified. Consequently, while some welcome new technology, others resist it.

Cyberspace and Social Inequality

The term *information superhighway* conveys the idea of information traveling at a high rate of speed among homes and businesses. Just as a highway allows physical travel from one place to another, so the information superhighway allows homes and businesses to be connected by the rapid flow of information. Almost 200 million people around the world are able to communicate by Internet, and that number will soon double. "Servers" such as Prodigy, America Online, and Compuserve allow electronic access to libraries of information. Some programs sift, sort, and transmit images, sound, and video. Electronic mail (e-mail) allows people to zap messages without regard to national boundaries. This is the future, a world linked by almost instantaneous communications, with information readily accessible around the globe and few places that can be called "remote."

The implications of the information superhighway for national and global stratification are severe. As discussed in the box on the digital divide on page 271, on the national level, we could end up with information have-nots, primarily inner-city residents, which would perpetuate present inequalities. On the global level, the question is, Who will control the information superhighway? The answer, of course, is obvious, for it is the Most Industrialized Nations that are developing the communications system. This leads to one of the more profound issues of the twenty-first century—will such control destine the Least Industrialized Nations to a perpetual pauper status? Or will their access to this new technology be their passport to affluence?

*T*HE GROWTH MACHINE VERSUS THE EARTH

Of all the changes swirling around us, perhaps those affecting the natural environment hold the most serious implications for human life.

Underlying today's environmental decay is the globalization of capitalism, which I have stressed throughout this text. To maintain their dominance and increase their wealth, the Most Industrialized Nations, spurred by multinational corporations, continue to push for economic growth. At the same time, the Industrializing Nations, playing catch-up, are striving to develop their economies. Meanwhile, the Least Industrialized Nations are anxious to enter the race: Because they start from even farther behind, they have to push for even faster growth.

Many are convinced that the earth cannot withstand such an onslaught. Our global economic production creates extensive pollution, and faster-paced production means faster-paced destruction of our environment. If the goal is a **sustainable environment,** a world system in which we use our physical environment to meet our needs without destroying humanity's future, we cannot continue to trash the earth's natural resources. In short, the ecological message is incompatible with an economic message that it is OK to rape the environment for the sake of profits.

Before looking at the social movement that has grown around this issue, let's examine major environmental problems. We'll begin with pollution in the Most Industrialized Nations.

sustainable environment a world system that takes into account the limits of the environment, produces enough material goods for everyone's needs, and leaves a heritage of a sound environment for the next generation

Boondocks © 2000 by Aaron McGruder. Distributed by Universal Press Syndicate. Reprinted with permission. All rights reserved.

Environmental Problems in the Most Industrialized Nations

Although even tribal groups produced pollution, the frontal assault on the natural environment did not begin in earnest until nations industrialized. The more extensive the industrialization, the better it was considered for a nation's welfare. For the Most Industrialized Nations, the slogan has been "Growth at any cost."

Industrial growth did come, but at a high cost to the natural environment. Today, for example, formerly pristine streams are polluted sewers, and the water supply of many cities is unfit to drink. When Los Angeles announces "smog days" on radio and television, schoolchildren are kept inside during recess, and everyone is warned to stay indoors. The accumulation of hazardous wastes is a special problem. Despite the danger to people and the environment, in many cases the waste has simply been dumped. The Social Map below shows how the worst hazardous waste sites are distributed throughout the United States. The Down-to-Earth Sociology box on page 651 discusses how *corporate welfare* contributes to pollution.

corporate welfare the gifts or financial incentives (tax breaks, subsidies, and even land and stadiums) given to corporations in order to attract them to an area or induce them to remain

Figure 22.2 SOCIAL MAP: WHERE ARE THE WORST HAZARDOUS WASTE SITES?

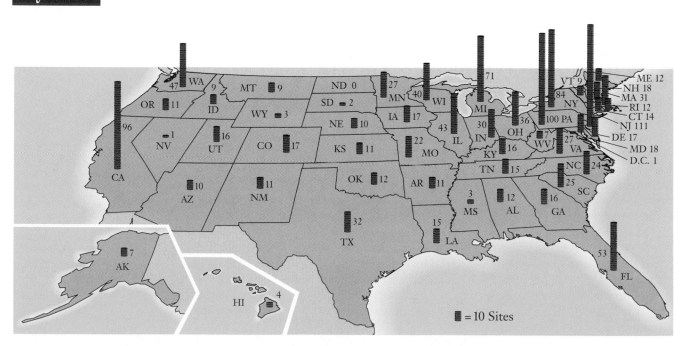

Source: Statistical Abstract 1999:Table 414.

Sociology

Down-to-Earth

CORPORATIONS AND BIG WELFARE BUCKS: HOW TO GET PAID TO POLLUTE

Welfare is one of the most controversial topics in the United States, arousing the ire of many wealthy and middle-class Americans. They view the poor who collect welfare as parasites. But have you heard about corporate welfare?

Corporate welfare refers to handouts given to corporations. A state offers a company tax breaks so it will relocate within the state, or remain in the state if it has threatened to leave. A state may even provide land and factories at bargain prices. The reason: jobs.

Corporate welfare even goes to companies that foul the land, water, and air. Borden Chemicals in Louisiana has released hazardous chemicals so thick that several times the police have had to shut down the highway that runs near the plant. The company has also burned hazardous wastes without a permit. It also contaminated groundwater beneath the plant site, threatening the aquifer that provides drinking water for residents of Louisiana and Texas. Borden's pollution cost the company dearly: $3.6 million in fines, $3 million to clean up the groundwater, and $400,000 for local emergency response units. That's a total of $7 million, quite a fine.

But if we consider corporate welfare, the company didn't make out so badly. Its $15 million in reduced and cancelled property taxes gave it a net gain of $8 million (Bartlett and Steele 1998). And that's not counting the savings the company racked up by not having to properly dispose of its toxic wastes in the first place.

Louisiana has added a novel twist to corporate welfare. It offers an incentive to help start-up companies. This itself isn't novel; the owners of that little "mom and pop" grocery store on your corner may have gotten some benefits when they first opened. Louisiana's twist is whom it counts as start-up operations. You may have heard of some of them. One of these little start-up companies is called Exxon Corp. Although Exxon opened for business about 120 years ago, it had $213 million in property taxes canceled under this program. Another little company that the state figured could use a nudge to get going was Shell Oil Co., which had $140 million slashed from its taxes (Bartlett and Steele 1998). Then there were International Paper, Dow Chemical, Union Carbide, Boise Cascade, Georgia Pacific, and another tiny one called Procter & Gamble.

Of course, you can always improve welfare programs. If the recipients themselves get to design them, you can be certain they'll come up with some good ones. Let's suppose poor people were polluting, and the state issued them credits to reduce their pollution. They could then spend those credits to continue to pollute, or they could sell them to others, giving them the right to pollute.

Naw, too far fetched.

Yet, that is just what U.S. industry has arranged. According to a treaty negotiated in Kyoto, Japan, by the year 2008 the United States must reduce its emissions of greenhouse gases to a specified level. To reap billions of dollars from this treaty, U.S. industries proposed a new corporate welfare law. The government will issue credits to companies that reduce their emissions. They may even count reductions that took place years before the treaty. The companies can use these credits to continue to pollute—or they can sell them for billions of dollars to companies that have not reduced their emissions, giving them the legal right to continue to pollute (Cushman 1999). Now that's a great way to clean up—without cleaning up. ■

Many aspects of pollution in the Most Industrialized Nations are worth discussing. Our follies include harming the ozone layer in order to have the convenience of spray bottles and air conditioners. With limited space, however, I would like to focus on an overarching aspect of our environment, the burning of fossil fuels.

Fossil Fuels and Environmental Degradation The burning of fossil fuels for factories, motorized vehicles, and power plants has been especially harmful. Fish can no longer survive in some lakes in Canada and the northeastern United States because of **acid rain:** The burning of fossil fuels releases sulfur dioxide and nitrogen oxide, which react with moisture in the air to become sulfuric and nitric acids (Luoma 1989).

An invisible but infinitely more serious consequence is the **greenhouse effect.** Like the glass of a greenhouse, the gases emitted from burning fossil fuels allow sunlight to enter the earth's atmosphere freely, but inhibit the release of heat. It is as though the gases have closed

acid rain rain containing sulfuric and nitric acids (produced by the reaction of sulfur dioxide and nitrogen oxide with moisture when released into the air with the burning of fossil fuels)

greenhouse effect the buildup of carbon dioxide in the earth's atmosphere that allows light to enter but inhibits the release of heat; believed to cause global warming

the atmospheric window through which our planet breathes. Most scientists say that we now face **global warming.** The polar ice caps may melt and inundate the world's shorelines, the climate boundaries may move north about four hundred miles, and many animal and plant species will become extinct (Smith and Tirpak 1988; Thomas 1988; Weisskopf 1992; Begley 1997). Alarmed, in 1997, 160 nations approved an environmental treaty to reduce "greenhouse gases." Not all scientists agree that we face a danger, however. Some even doubt that a greenhouse effect exists (Robinson and Robinson 1997).

The Energy Shortage and Multinational Corporations If you ever read about an energy shortage, you can be sure that what you read was false. There is no energy shortage, nor can there ever be. We have the potential to produce unlimited low-cost power, which could help raise the living standards of humans across the globe. The sun, for example, produces more energy than humanity could ever use. Boundless energy is also available from the tides and the winds. In some cases, we need better technology to harness these sources of energy; in others, we need only to apply technology we already have.

We know that burning fossil fuels in internal combustion engines is the main source of pollution in the Most Industrialized Nations. Vast sources of alternative energy are available for us to use. Why, then, don't we develop the technology to use these alternative sources of energy? From a conflict perspective, these abundant sources of energy present a threat to the multinationals' oil monopoly. To maintain their profits, these corporations make certain that internal combustion engines remain dominant. The practical development and widespread use of alternative sources of power will wait until the multinationals have cornered the market on the technology that will harness them—so they can continue to reap huge profits.

The Environment, Race, and Social Class Conflict and unequal power have led to what sociologists call **environmental racism**—minorities being the ones who suffer most from the effects of pollution (Moberg 1999). This is because polluting industries locate where land is cheaper, places where the wealthy do not live. As a result, low-income communities, which are often inhabited by minorities, are exposed to more pollution. Sociologists have studied, formed, and joined environmental justice groups that fight to stop polluting plants and to block construction of polluting industries.

Environmental Problems in the Industrializing and Least Industrialized Nations

Severe consequences of industrialization, such as ozone depletion, the greenhouse effect, and global warming, cannot be laid solely at the feet of the Most Industrialized Nations. With their rush to be contenders in the global competition, along with a lack of funds to pay for pollution controls, and few anti-pollution laws, the Industrializing Nations make their own enormous contributions to this problem. Breathing the air of Mexico City, for example, is the equivalent of smoking two packs of cigarettes a day (Durbin 1995).

The former Soviet Union is a special case. Until this empire broke up, pollution had been treated as a state secret. Scientists and journalists were forbidden to mention pollution in public. Even peaceful demonstrations to call attention to pollution could net participants two years in prison (Feshbach 1992). With protest stifled and no environmental protection laws, environmental pollution was rampant: Almost half of Russia's arable land has been made unsuitable for farming, about a third of Russians live in cities where air pollution is more than ten times greater than permissible levels in the United States, and half of Russia's tap water is unfit to drink. Pollution is so severe that the life expectancy of Russians has dropped, a lesson that should not be lost on the rest of us as we make decisions on how to treat our environment.

With their greater poverty and swelling populations, the Least Industrialized Nations have an even greater incentive to industrialize at any cost. These pressures, combined with almost nonexistent environmental regulations, destine the Least Industrialized Nations to become the earth's major source of pollution.

Their lack of environmental protection laws has not gone unnoticed by opportunists in the Most Industrialized Nations, who use these countries as garbage dumps for hazardous wastes and for producing chemicals that their own people will no longer tolerate

global warming an increase in the earth's temperature due to the greenhouse effect

environmental racism the greater impact of pollution on the poor and racial–ethnic minorities

(LaDou 1991; Smith 1995). Alarmed at the growing environmental destruction, the World Bank, the monetary arm of G7, has placed pressure on the Least Industrialized Nations to reduce pollution and soil erosion (Lachica 1992). Understandably, the basic concern of these nations is to produce food and housing first, and to worry about the environment later.

Although the rain forests cover just 7 percent of the earth's land area, they are home to *one-third to one-half* of all plant and animal species. Despite our knowledge that the rain forests are essential for humanity's welfare, we seem bent on destroying them. For the sake of timber and farms, we clear the rain forests at a rate of 2,500 acres *each hour* (McCuen 1993). In the process, we extinguish thousands of plant and animal species. Some estimate that we destroy 10,000 species each year–about 1 *per hour* (Durning 1990). Others say that this number is conservative, that we extinguish 100 plant and animal species a day, 4 per hour (Wolfensohn and Fuller 1998). Whatever the number, as biologists remind us, a species once lost is gone forever.

As the rain forests are destroyed, so are the Indian tribes who live in them. With their extinction goes their knowledge of the environment, the topic of the Perspectives box below. Like Esau who exchanged his birthright for a bowl of porridge, we exchange our future for some lumber, farms, and pastures.

PERSPECTIVES | Cultural Diversity Around the World

THE RAIN FORESTS: LOST TRIBES, LOST KNOWLEDGE

Since 1900, 90 of Brazil's 270 Indian tribes have disappeared. Other tribes have moved to villages as settlers have taken over their lands. With village life comes a loss of tribal knowledge.

Tribal groups are not just "wild" people who barely survive despite their ignorance. On the contrary, they have intricate forms of social organization and possess knowledge that has accumulated over thousands of years. The 2,500 Kayapo Indians, for example, belong to one of the Amazon's endangered tribes. The Kayapo use 250 types of wild fruit and hundreds of nut and tuber species. They cultivate thirteen types of bananas, eleven kinds of manioc (cassava), sixteen strains of sweet potato, and seventeen kinds of yams. Many of these varieties are unknown to non-Indians. The Kayapo also use thousands of medicinal plants, one of which contains a drug that is effective against intestinal parasites.

Until recently, Western scientists dismissed tribal knowledge as superstitious and worthless. Now, however, the West is coming to realize that to lose tribes is to lose knowledge. In the Central African Republic, a man whose chest was being eaten away by an amoeboid infection lay dying because he did not respond to drugs. Out of desperation, the Catholic nuns who were treating him sought the advice of a native doctor. He applied crushed termites

to the open wounds, and the man made a remarkable recovery.

The disappearance of the rain forests means the destruction of plant and animal species that may hold medicinal or nutritional value for humans (Mendelsohn and Balick 1995). Some of the discoveries from the rain forests have been astounding: A flower from Madagascar is used in the treatment of leukemia; a frog in Peru produces a painkiller more powerful, but less addictive, than morphine (Wolfensohn and Fuller 1998); and the needles from a Himalayan tree in India contain taxol, a drug that is effective against ovarian cancer.

On average, one tribe of Amazonian Indians has been lost each year for the past century—because of violence, greed on the part of non-Indians who want their lands, and exposure to infectious diseases against which they have little resistance. Ethnocentrism underlies much of this assault. Perhaps the extreme is represented by the cattle ranchers in Colombia who killed eighteen Cueva Indians. The cattle ranchers were perplexed when they were put on trial for murder. They asked why they should be charged with a crime since everyone knew that the Cuevas were animals, not people. They pointed out that there was even a verb in Colombian Spanish, *cuevar*, which means "to hunt Cueva Indians." So what was their crime, they

Along Sega is the headman of the Penan tribe of the Sarawak rain forests in Malaysia. With their way of life threatened, the Penan are among the last rain forest nomads in the world.

asked? The jury found them innocent because of "cultural ignorance." ■

Sources: Durning 1990; Gorman 1991; Linden 1991; Stipp 1992; Simons 1995; Nabhan 1998.

The Environmental Movement

Concern about environmental problems has produced a worldwide social movement. In some countries, *green parties*, political parties whose central issue is the environment, are active and successful. Germany's Green party has even won seats in the national legislature (Steinmetz and Rohwedder 1998).

Activists in the environmental movement generally seek solutions in politics, education, and legislation. Despairing that pollution continues, that the rain forests are still being cleared, and that species are becoming extinct, some activists are convinced that the planet is doomed unless immediate steps are taken. Choosing a more radical course, they use extreme tactics to try to arouse indignation among the public and thus force the government to act. Convinced that they stand for true morality, many are willing to break the law and go to jail for their actions. Such activists are featured in the following Thinking Critically section.

Thinking Critically

ECOSABATAGE

Chaining oneself to a giant Douglas fir slated for cutting; pouring sand down the gas tank of a bulldozer; tearing down power lines and ripping up survey stakes; driving spikes into redwood trees and sinking whaling vessels—are these the acts of dangerous punks who are intent on vandalizing and who have little understanding of the needs of modern society? Or are they the acts of brave men and women who are willing to put their freedom and even their lives on the line on behalf of the earth itself?

To get some idea of why **ecosabotage** is taking place, consider the Medicine Tree, a 3,000-year-old redwood in the Sally Bell Grove near the northern California coast. Georgia Pacific, a lumber company, was determined to cut down the Medicine Tree, the oldest and largest of the region's redwoods, which rests on a sacred site of the Sinkyone Indians. Members of Earth First! chained themselves to the tree. After they were arrested, the sawing began. Other protesters jumped over the police-lined barricade and planted themselves in front of the axes and chain saws. A logger swung an axe and missed a demonstrator. At that moment, the sheriff radioed a restraining order, and the cutting stopped.

ecosabotage actions taken to sabotage the efforts of people thought to be legally harming the environment

As concern about the enviroment has grown, a social movement to try to change the course of events has developed. Protest groups have rallied around several issues, including whales and dolphins. Another is the destruction of the redwoods in northern California.

Twenty-four-year-old David Chain's dedication cost him his life. The federal government and the state of California made a deal to purchase 10,000 acres of pristine redwoods for half a billion dollars. As last-minute negotiations continued, loggers from the Pacific Lumber Company kept felling trees, and Earth First! activists kept trying to stop them. One felled tree struck David Chain in the head. He died of a crushed skull.

How many 3,000-year-old trees remain on this planet? Do fences and picnic tables for backyard barbecues justify cutting them down? It is questions like these, as well as the slaughter of seals, the destruction of the rain forests, and the drowning of dolphins in mile-long drift nets that spawned Earth First! and other organizations devoted to preserving the environment, such as Greenpeace, Sea Shepherds, and the Ruckus Society.

"We feel like there are insane people who are consciously destroying our environment, and we are compelled to fight back," explains a member of one of the militant groups. "No compromise in defense of Mother Earth!" says another. "With famine and death approaching, we're in the early stages of World War III," adds another.

Radical environmentalists represent a broad range of activities and purposes. They are united neither on tactics nor goals. Most espouse a simpler lifestyle that will consume less energy and place less pressure on the earth's resources. But some want to stop a specific action, such as the killing of whales, or to destroy all nuclear weapons and dismantle nuclear power plants. Others want everyone to become vegetarians. Still others want the earth's population to be reduced to one billion, roughly what it was in 1800. Some even want humans to return to hunting and gathering societies. These groups are so splintered that the founder of Earth First!, Dave Foreman, quit his own organization when it became too confrontational for his tastes.

Radical groups have had some successes. They have brought a halt to the killing of dolphins off Japan's Iki Island, achieved a ban on whaling, established trash recycling programs in many communities, and saved hundreds of thousands of acres of uncut trees, including, of course, the Medicine Tree. ■

For Your Consideration

Who, then, are these people? Should we applaud ecosaboteurs or jail them? As symbolic interactionists stress, it all depends on how you view their actions. And as conflict theorists emphasize, your view likely depends on your location in the economic structure. That is, if you are the owner of a lumber company you will view ecosaboteurs differently from the way a camping enthusiast would. How does your own view of ecosaboteurs depend on your life situation? What effective alternatives to ecosabotage are there for people who are convinced that we are destroying the very life support system of our planet?

Sources: Carpenter 1990; Eder 1990; Foote 1990; Parfit 1990; Reed and Benet 1990; Courtney 1995; Satchell 1998; Skow 1998; Nieves 1999.

Environmental Sociology

In about 1970, a subdiscipline of sociology emerged called **environmental sociology.** Its focus is the relationship between human societies and the environment (Dunlap and Catton 1979, 1983; Buttel 1987; Freudenburg and Gramling 1989; Laska 1993; Redclift and Woodgate 1997). Its main assumptions are:

1. The physical environment is a significant variable in sociological investigation.
2. Human beings are but one species among many that depend on the natural environment.
3. Because of intricate feedbacks to nature, human actions have many unintended consequences.
4. The world is finite, so there are potential physical limits to economic growth.
5. Economic expansion requires increased extraction of resources from the environment.
6. Increased extraction of resources leads to ecological problems.
7. These ecological problems place restrictions on economic expansion.
8. Governments create environmental problems by trying to create conditions for the accumulation of capital.

environmental sociology a subdiscipline of sociology that examines how human activities affect the physical environment and how the physical environment affects human activities

As you can see, the goal of environmental sociology is not to stop pollution or nuclear power but, rather, to study how humans (their cultures, values, and behavior) affect the physical environment and how the physical environment affects human activities. Environmental sociologists, however, generally are also environmental activists, and the Section on Environment and Technology of the American Sociological Association tries to influence governmental policies (American Sociological Association n.d.).

Technology and the Environment: The Goal of Harmony   It is inevitable that humans will continue to develop new technologies. But the abuse of our environment by those technologies is not inevitable. To understate the matter, the destruction of our planet is an unwise choice.

If we are to live in a world that is worth passing on to coming generations, we must seek harmony between technology and the natural environment. This will not be easy. At one extreme are people who claim that to protect the environment we must eliminate industrialization and go back to some sort of preindustrial way of life. At the other extreme are people who are blind to the harm being done to the natural environment, who want the entire world to continue industrializing at full speed. Somewhere, there must be a middle ground, one that recognizes not only that industrialization is here to stay but also that we *can* control it, for it is our creation. Industrialization, controlled, can enhance our quality of life; uncontrolled, it will destroy us.

As a parallel to the development of technologies, then, we must develop systems to greatly reduce or eliminate their harm to the environment. This includes mechanisms to monitor the production, use, and disposal of technology. The question, of course, is whether we have the resolve to take the steps to preserve the environment for future generations. What's at stake is nothing less than the welfare of the entire planet. Surely that is enough to motivate us to make the wise choices.

SUMMARY AND REVIEW

■ How Social Change Transforms Society

What major trends have transformed the course of human history?

The primary changes in human history are the four social revolutions (domestication, agriculture, industrialization, and information); the change from *Gemeinschaft* to *Gesellschaft* societies; capitalism and industrialization; **modernization;** and global stratification. Social movements indicate cutting edges of social change. Ethnic conflicts threaten the global divisions G7 is working out. Pp. 634–638.

■ Theories and Processes of Social Change

Besides technology, capitalism, modernization, and so on, what other theories of social change are there?

Evolutionary theories presuppose that societies are moving from the same starting point to some similar ending point. *Unilinear* theories, which assume the same path for everyone, have been replaced with *multilinear* theories, which assume that different paths can lead to the same stage of development. In *cyclical* theories, civilizations are viewed as going through a process of birth, youth, maturity, decline, and death. Conflict theorists view social change as inevitable, for each *thesis* (basically an arrangement of power) contains an *antithesis* (contradictions). A new *synthesis* develops to resolve these contradictions, but it, too, contains contradictions that will have to be resolved, and so on. This is called a **dialectical process.** Pp. 638–639.

What is Ogburn's theory of social change?

Ogburn identified technology as the basic cause of social change, which comes through three processes: **invention, discovery,** and **diffusion.** The term **cultural lag** refers to symbolic culture lagging behind changes in technology. Pp. 639–640.

■ How Technology Changes Society

How does new technology affect society?

Because **technology** is an organizing force of social life, changes in technology can have profound effects. The automobile and the computer were used as extended examples. The automobile changed the development of cities, buying patterns, architecture, and even courtship and women's roles. The computer is changing the way we practice medicine, learn, work, and do business. The information superhighway is likely to perpetuate social inequalities both on a national and global level. Pp. 641–649.

■ The Growth Machine Versus the Earth

What are the environmental problems of the Most Industrialized Nations?

The environmental problems of the Most Industrialized Nations are severe, ranging from smog and **acid rain** to the **greenhouse effect.** The greenhouse effect may cause **global warming** that will fundamentally affect our lives. The burning of fossil fuels in internal combustion engines lies at the root of many environmental problems, but alternative sources of energy are unlikely to be developed until the multinational corporations can turn them into a profit. Due to the location of factories and hazardous waste sites, environmental problems have a greater impact on minorities and the poor. Pp. 649–652.

What are the environmental problems of the Industrializing and Least Industrialized Nations?

The worst environmental problems are found in the former Soviet Union, a legacy of the unrestrained exploitation of resources by the Communist party. The rush of the Least Industrialized Nations to industrialize is adding to our environmental decay. The world is facing a basic conflict between the lust for profits through the exploitation of the earth's resources and the need to produce a **sustainable environment.** Pp. 652–653.

What is the environmental movement?

The environmental movement is an attempt to restore a healthy environment for the world's people. This global movement takes many forms, from peaceful attempts to influence the political process to **ecosabotage,** attempts to sabotage the efforts of people thought to be legally harming the environment. Pp. 654–655.

What is environmental sociology?

Environmental sociology is not an attempt to change the environment, but a study of the relationship between humans and the environment. Environmental sociologists are generally also environmental activists. Pp. 655–656.

Where can I read more on this topic?

Suggested Readings for this chapter are at the back of this book.

Sociology & the Internet

All URLs listed are current as of the printing of this book. URLs often change. Please check our Web site, **http://www.abacon.com/ henslin,** for updates.

1. How is our society responding to environmental problems? Go to **http://www.envirolink.org,** a site maintained by Envirolink, the online environmental community. You can find out what is being done to protect our environment by clicking on "Actions to Take." From the list of topics, click on a few that are of interest to you. This will give you information on activities in which you can get involved. When you have finished exploring this site, use your sociological imagination to write a paper on societal responses to environmental threats. What are some of the ways individuals and groups can get involved and make a difference?

2. The diffusion of new technology is uneven. Many factors influence why some social groups have access to a new technology before others do. Let's look at an attempt to address these factors and close the technology gap. Go to **http://arachne.cns.iit.edu/ ~livewire** and click on "General Information." What is this site trying to do? What is the mission and history of the Street-Level Media Project? How has it tried to get new technologies into the hands of inner-city youth? Write a paper about this program. Discuss its purposes, the measures it is taking to accomplish its goals, and the social changes that it hopes will occur as a result.

3. This chapter presents the idea of a sustainable environment, a world system in which the physical environment is used to meet human needs without destroying humanity's future. How can this be achieved? Who is responsible? Who—or what—will have to change in order for us to reach this goal? In this exercise you will take a look at efforts to create sustainable environments. Go to **http://solstice.crest.org.** Read the information on Solstice and browse around the home page. Then click on "Related Net Sites." Click on "Search Database" to see a list of sites dedicated to issues of environmental concern. Browse through several of them in order to gain a better understanding of the issues and strategies involved in creating a sustainable environment.

Write a short paper in which you answer these questions: Is the sustainable environment theme aimed only at the Most Industrialized Nations, or is it global? What are some policies and practices that you think might work with nations at different levels of industrialization? Are there any that would be practical in nearly all countries? How likely is it that any of these policies will be adopted by nations around the globe? What do you think the future holds: the growth machine or a sustainable environment? Is it possible for the two to coexist? If so, how?

4. Not everyone embraces new technologies or is comfortable with the changes that result. Your text discusses how the term *Luddite* developed out of a violent reaction to the textile machines that were replacing skilled craftsmen. Today there is a movement of neo-Luddites. They are concerned that modern technology is threatening our very humanity. You can learn more about the original Luddites and the neo-Luddites at **http://www.cudenver. edu/~mryder/itc_data/luddite.** Check some of the resource sites and read some of the articles. You can even read the Unabomber's manifesto by clicking on "Kaczynski." When you have finished, put together a panel of students who will make a presentation to the class on this issue of resisting new technology. Are the Luddites right? Why or why not?

Glossary

acculturation the transmission of culture from one generation to the next

achieved statuses positions that are earned, accomplished, or involve at least some effort or activity on the individual's part

acid rain rain containing sulfuric and nitric acids (produced by the reaction of sulfur dioxide and nitrogen oxide with moisture when released into the air with the burning of fossil fuels)

acting crowd Herbert Blumer's term for an excited group that collectively moves toward a goal

activity theory the view that satisfaction during old age is related to a person's level and quality of activity

Afrocentrism an emphasis on African-American traditions and concerns

age cohort people born at roughly the same time who pass through the life course together

ageism prejudice, discrimination, and hostility directed against people because of their age; can be directed against any age group, including youth

agent provocateur someone who joins a group in order to spy on it and to sabotage it by *provoking* its members to commit illegal acts

agents of socialization people or groups that affect our self-concept, attitudes, behaviors, or other orientations toward life

aggregate individuals who temporarily share the same physical space but do not see themselves as belonging together

agricultural revolution the second social revolution, based on the invention of the plow, which led to agricultural society

agricultural society a society based on large-scale agriculture, dependent on plows drawn by animals

alienation Karl Marx's term for the experience of being cut off from the product of one's labor that results in a sense of powerlessness and normlessness

alterative social movement a social movement that seeks to alter only particular aspects of people

anarchy a condition of lawlessness or political disorder caused by the absence or collapse of governmental authority

animism the belief that all objects in the world have spirits, some of which are dangerous and must be outwitted

anomie Emile Durkheim's term for a condition of society in which people become detached, cut loose from the norms that usually guide their behavior

anti-Semitism prejudice, discrimination, and persecution directed against Jews

anticipatory socialization because one anticipates a future role, one learns parts of it now

apartheid the separation of races as was practiced in South Africa

appearance how an individual looks when playing a role

applied sociology the use of sociology to solve problems—from the micro level of family relationships to the macro level of crime and pollution

ascribed statuses positions an individual either inherits at birth or receives involuntarily later in life

assimilation the process of being absorbed into the mainstream culture

authoritarian leader a leader who leads by giving orders

authoritarian personality Theodor Adorno's term for people who are prejudiced and rank high on scales of conformity, intolerance, insecurity, respect for authority, and submissiveness to superiors

authority power that people consider legitimate; also called *legitimate power*

back stage where people rest from their performances, discuss their presentations, and plan future performances

background assumptions deeply embedded common understandings, or basic rules, concerning our view of the world and of how people ought to act

barter the direct exchange of one item for another

basic demographic equation growth rate = births − deaths + net migration

bilateral (system of descent): a system of reckoning descent that counts both the mother's and the father's side

blended family a family whose members were once part of other families

born again a term describing Christians who have undergone a life-transforming religious experience so radical that they feel they have become new persons

bourgeoisie Karl Marx's term for capitalists, those who own the means to produce wealth

bureaucracy a formal organization with a hierarchy of authority; a clear division of labor; emphasis on written rules, communications, and records; and impersonality of positions

capital punishment the death penalty

capitalism an economic system characterized by the private ownership of the means of production, the pursuit of profit, and market competition

capitalist class the wealthy who own the means of production and buy the labor of the working class

capitalist world economy the dominance of capitalism in the world along with the international interdependence that capitalism has created

cargo cult a social movement in which South Pacific islanders destroyed their possessions in the anticipation that their ancestors would send items by ship

caste system a form of social stratification in which one's status is determined by birth and is lifelong

category people who have similar characteristics

centrist party a political party that represents the center of political opinion

charisma literally, an extraordinary gift from God; more commonly, an outstanding, "magnetic" personality

charismatic authority authority based on an individual's outstanding traits, which attract followers

charismatic leader literally, someone to whom God has given a gift; more commonly, someone who exerts extraordinary appeal to a group of followers

checks and balances the separation of powers among the three branches of U.S. government—legislative, executive, and judicial—so that each is able to nullify the actions of the other two, thus preventing the domination of any single branch

church according to Durkheim, one of the three essential elements of religion—a moral community of believers; a second definition is the type of religious organization described on page 508, a large, highly organized group with formal, sedate worship services and little emphasis on personal conversion

circular reaction Robert Park's term for a back-and-forth communication between the members of a crowd whereby a "collective impulse" is transmitted

citizenship the concept that birth (and residence) in a country impart basic rights

city a place in which a large number of people are permanently based and do not produce their own food

city-state an independent city whose power radiates outward, bringing the adjacent area under its rule

civil religion Robert Bellah's term for religion that is such an established feature of a country's life that its history and social institutions become sanctified by being associated with God

class conflict Karl Marx's term for the struggle between capitalists and workers

class consciousness Karl Marx's term for awareness of a common identity based on one's position in the means of production

class system a form of social stratification based primarily on the possession of money or material possessions

clique a cluster of people within a larger group who choose to interact with one another; an internal faction

closed-ended questions questions followed by a list of possible answers to be selected by the respondent

coalition the alignment of some members of a group against others

coalition government a government in which a country's largest party aligns itself with one or more smaller parties

coercion power that people do not accept as rightly exercised over them; also called *illegitimate power*

cohabitation unmarried couples living together in a sexual relationship

collective behavior extraordinary activities carried out by groups of people; includes lynchings, rumors, panics, urban legends, and fads and fashions

collective mind Gustave LeBon's term for the tendency of people in a crowd to feel, think, and act in extraordinary ways

colonialism the process by which one nation takes over another nation, usually for the purpose of exploiting its labor and natural resources

common sense those things that "everyone knows" are true

community a place people identify with, where they sense that they belong and that others care what happens to them

compartmentalize to separate acts from feelings or attitudes

conflict theory a theoretical framework in which society is viewed as composed of groups competing for scarce resources

conspicuous consumption Thorstein Veblen's term for a change from the Protestant ethic to an eagerness to show off wealth by the elaborate consumption of goods

contradictory class location Erik Wright's term for a position in the class structure that generates contradictory interests

control group the group of subjects not exposed to the independent variable

control theory the idea that two control systems—inner controls and outer controls—work against our tendencies to deviate

convergence theory the view that as capitalist and socialist economic systems each adopt features of the other, a hybrid (or mixed) economic system will emerge

corporate capitalism the domination of the economic system by giant corporations

corporation the joint ownership of a business enterprise, whose liabilities and obligations are separate from those of its owners

correspondence principle the sociological principle that schools correspond to (or reflect) the social structure of society

cosmology teachings or ideas that provide a unified picture of the world

counterculture a group whose values, beliefs, and related behaviors place its members in opposition to the broader culture

credential society the use of diplomas and degrees to determine who is eligible for jobs, even though the diploma or degree may be irrelevant to the actual work

credit card a device that allows its owner to purchase goods but to be billed later

crime the violation of norms that are written into law

criminal justice system the system of police, courts, and prisons set up to deal with people who are accused of having committed a crime

crude birth rate the annual number of births per 1,000 population

crude death rate the annual number of deaths per 1,000 population

cult a new religion with few followers, whose teachings and practices put it at odds with the dominant culture and religion

cultural diffusion the spread of cultural characteristics from one group to another

cultural goals the legitimate objectives held out to the members of a society

cultural lag William Ogburn's term for human behavior lagging behind technological innovations

cultural leveling the process by which cultures become similar to one another, and especially by which Western industrial culture is imported and diffused into industrializing nations

cultural transmission in reference to education, the ways in which schools transmit a society's culture, especially its core values

cultural universal a value, norm, or other cultural trait that is found in every group

culture the language, beliefs, values, norms, behaviors, and even material objects that are passed from one generation to the next

culture of poverty the assumption that the values and behaviors of the poor make them fundamentally different from other people, that these factors are largely responsible for their poverty, and that parents perpetuate poverty across generations by passing these characteristics to their children

culture shock the disorientation that people experience when they come in contact with a fundamentally different culture and can no longer depend on their taken-for-granted assumptions about life

currency paper money

debit card a device that allows its owner to charge purchases against his or her bank account

defensive medicine medical practices done not for the patient's benefit but in order to protect a physician from malpractice suits

deferred gratification forgoing something in the present in the hope of achieving greater gains in the future

degradation ceremonies rituals designed to strip away an individual's self-identity and stamp a new identity in its place; for example, a court martial or the defrocking of a priest

dehumanization the act or process of reducing people to objects that do not deserve the treatment accorded humans

deinstitutionalization: the release of patients from mental hospitals into the community while receiving treatment within a network of outpatient services

democracy a system of government in which authority derives from the people; the term comes from two Greek words that translate literally as "power to the people"

democratic leader a leader who leads by trying to reach a consensus

democratic socialism a hybrid economic system in which capitalism is mixed with state ownership

demographic transition a three-stage historical process of population growth: first, high birth rates and high death rates; second, high birth rates and low death rates; and, third low birth rates and low death rates; a fourth stage may be appearing, birth rates being lower than death rates

demographic variables the three factors that influence population growth: fertility, mortality, and net migration

demography the study of the size, composition, growth, and distribution of human populations

denomination a "brand name" within a major religion, for example, Methodist or Baptist

dependency ratio the number of workers required to support dependent persons—those 64 and older and those 15 and under

dependency theory the view that the Least Industrialized Nations have been unable to develop their economies because they grew dependent on the Most Industrialized Nations

dependent variable a factor that is changed by an independent variable

depersonalization dealing with people as though they were objects; in the case of medical care, as though patients were merely cases and diseases, not persons

deposit receipts a receipt stating that a certain amount of goods is on deposit in a warehouse or bank; the receipt is used as a form of money

deterrence creating fear so people will refrain from breaking the law

deviance the violation of rules or norms

dialectical process each arrangement, or thesis, contains contradictions, or antitheses, which must be resolved; the new arrangement, or synthesis, contains its own contradictions, and so on

dictatorship a form of government in which power is seized by an individual

diffusion the spread of invention or discovery from one area to another; identified by William Ogburn as the final of three processes of social change

direct democracy a form of democracy in which the eligible voters meet together to discuss issues and make their decisions

disabling environment an environment that is harmful to health

discovery a new way of seeing reality; identified by William Ogburn as the second of three processes of social change

discrimination an *act* of unfair treatment directed against an individual or a group

disengagement theory the view that society prevents disruption by having the elderly vacate (or disengage from) their positions of responsibility so the younger generation can step into their shoes

disinvestment the withdrawal of investments by financial institutions, which seals the fate of an urban area

divest to sell off

divine right of kings the idea that the king's authority comes directly from God

division of labor the splitting of a group's or a society's tasks into specialties

documents in its narrow sense, written sources that provide data; in its extended sense, archival material of any sort, including photographs, movies, and so on

domestication revolution the first social revolution, based on the domestication of plants and animals, which led to pastoral and horticultural societies

dominant group the group with the most power, greatest privileges, and highest social status

downward social mobility movement down the social class ladder

dramaturgy an approach, pioneered by Erving Goffman, analyzing social life in terms of drama or the stage; also called dramaturgical analysis

dumping the practice of sending unprofitable patients to public hospitals

dyad the smallest possible group, consisting of two people

e–cash digital money that is stored on computers

ecosabotage actions taken to sabotage the efforts of people thought to be legally harming the environment

ecclesia a religious group so integrated into the dominant culture that it is difficult to tell where the one begins and the other leaves off; also called a *state religion*

economy a system of distribution of goods and services

edge city a large clustering of service facilities and residential areas near highway intersections that provides a sense of place to people who live, shop, and work there

education a formal system of teaching knowledge, values, and skills

egalitarian authority more or less equally divided between people or groups, in this instance between husband and wife

ego Freud's term for a balancing force between the id and the demands of society

electronic community individuals who more or less regularly interact with one another on the Internet

"electronic primary group" individuals who regularly interact with one another on the Internet, who see themselves as a group, and who develop close ties with one another

emergent norms Ralph Turner's and Lewis Killian's term for the development of new norms to cope with a new situation, especially among crowds

empty nest a married couple's domestic situation after the last child has left home

endogamy the practice of marrying within one's own group

enterprise zone the use of economic incentives in a designated area with the intention of encouraging investment there

environmental racism the greater impact of pollution on the poor and racial ethnic minorities

environmental sociology a subdiscipline of sociology that examines how human activities affect the physical environment and how the physical environment affects human activities

epidemiology the study of disease and disability patterns in a population

estate stratification system the stratification system of medieval Europe, consisting of three groups or estates: the nobility, clergy, and serfs (or peasants)

ethnic (and ethnicity) having distinctive cultural characteristics

ethnic cleansing a policy of population elimination, including forcible expulsion and genocide. The term emerged in 1992 among the Serbians during their planned policy of expelling Croats and Muslims from territories claimed by them during the Yugoslav wars

ethnic work activities designed to discover, enhance, or maintain ethnic and racial identification

ethnocentrism the use of one's own culture as a yardstick for judging the ways of other individuals or societies, generally leading to a negative evaluation of their values, norms, and behaviors

ethnomethodology the study of how people use background assumptions to make sense out of life

euthanasia mercy killing

evangelism an attempt to win converts

exchange mobility about the same numbers of people moving up and down the social class ladder, such that, on balance, the social class system shows little change

exogamy the practice of marrying outside one's group

experiment the use of control groups and experimental groups and dependent and independent variables to test causation

experimental group the group of subjects exposed to the independent variable

exponential growth curve a pattern of growth in which numbers double during approximately equal intervals, thus accelerating in the latter stages

expressive leader an individual who increases harmony and minimizes conflict in a group; also known as a socioemotional leader

extended family a nuclear family plus other relatives, such as grandparents, uncles and aunts, who live together

face-saving behavior techniques used to salvage a performance that is going sour

fad a temporary pattern of behavior that catches people's attention

false consciousness Karl Marx's term to refer to workers identifying with the interests of capitalists

family two or more people who consider themselves related by blood, marriage, or adoption

family of orientation the family in which a person grows up

family of procreation the family formed when a couple's first child is born

fashion a pattern of behavior that catches people's attention, which lasts longer than a fad

fecundity the number of children that women are capable of bearing

fee for service payment to a physician to diagnose and treat a patient's medical problems

feminism the philosophy that men and women should be politically, economically, and socially equal, and organized activity on behalf of this principle

feminization of poverty a trend in U.S. poverty whereby most poor families are headed by women

feral children children assumed to have been raised by animals, in the wilderness isolated from other humans

fertility rate the number of children that the average woman bears

fiat money currency issued by a government that is not backed by stored value

folkways norms that are not strictly enforced

formal organization a secondary group designed to achieve explicit objectives

front stage where performances are given

functional analysis a theoretical framework in which society is viewed as composed of various parts, each with a function that, when fulfilled, contributes to society's equilibrium; also known as functionalism and structural functionalism

functional equivalent in this context, a substitute that serves the same functions (or meets the same needs) as religion, for example, psychotherapy

functional illiterate a high school graduate who has difficulty with basic reading and math

functional requisites the major tasks that a society must fulfill if it is to survive

fundamentalism the belief that true religion is threatened by modernism and that the faith as it was originally practiced should be restored

gatekeeping the process by which education opens and closes doors of opportunity

Gemeinschaft a type of society in which life is intimate; a community in which everyone knows everyone else and people share a sense of togetherness

Gesellschaft a type of society dominated by impersonal relationships, individual accomplishments, and self-interest

gender the social characteristics that a society considers proper for its males and females; masculinity or femininity

gender age the relative values of men's and women's ages in a particular culture

gender role the behaviors and attitudes considered appropriate because one is a female or a male

gender socialization the ways in which society sets children onto different courses in life *because* they are male or female

gender stratification males' and females' unequal access to power, prestige, and property on the basis of their sex

generalizability the extent to which the findings from one group (or sample) can be generalized or applied to other groups (or populations)

generalization a statement that goes beyond the individual case and is applied to a broader group or situation

generalized other the norms, values, attitudes, and expectations of people "in general"; the child's ability to take the role of the generalized other is a significant step in the development of a self

genetic predispositions inborn tendencies, in this context, to commit deviant acts

genocide the systematic annihilation or attempted annihilation of a people based on their presumed race or ethnicity

gentrification the displacement of the poor by the relatively affluent, who renovate the former's homes

gerontocracy a society (or some other group) run by the elderly

gestures the ways in which people use their bodies to communicate with one another

global warming an increase in the earth's temperature due to the greenhouse effect

globalization the extensive movement of capital and ideas among nations due to the expansion of capitalism; also the extensive interconnections among nations due to the expansion of capitalism

globilization of capitalism capitalism (investing to make profits within a rational system) becoming the globe's dominant economic system

goal displacement a goal displaced by another; in this context, the adoption of new goals by an organization; also known as goal replacement

gold standard paper money backed by gold

grade inflation higher grades given for the same work; a general rise in student grades without a corresponding increase in learning or test scores

graying of America a term that refers to the rising proportion of older people as a percentage of the U.S. population

greenhouse effect the buildup of carbon dioxide in the earth's atmosphere that allows light to enter but inhibits the release of heat; believed to cause global warming

gross national product (GNP) the amount of goods and services produced by a nation

group defined differently by various sociologists, but in a general sense, people who have something in common and who believe that what they have in common is significant; also called a social group

group dynamics the ways in which individuals affect groups and the ways in which groups influence individuals

groupthink Irving Janis's term for a narrowing of thought by a group of people, leading to the perception that there is only one correct answer, in which to even suggest alternatives becomes a sign of disloyalty

growth rate the net change in a population after adding births, subtracting deaths, and either adding or subtracting net migration

hate crime crimes to which more severe penalties are attached because they are motivated by hatred (dislike, animosity) of someone's race–ethnicity, religion, sexual orientation, or disability

health a human condition measured by four components: physical, mental, social, and spiritual

health maintenance organization (HMO) a health care organization that provides medical treatment to its members for a fixed annual cost

hidden curriculum the unwritten goals of schools, such as obedience to authority and conformity to cultural norms

homogamy the tendency of people with similar characteristics to marry one another

Horatio Alger myth the belief that due to limitless possibilities for success anyone can get ahead if he or she tries hard enough

horticultural society a society based on cultivating plants by the use of hand tools

hospice a place, or services brought into someone's home, for the purpose of bringing comfort and dignity to a dying person

household people who occupy the same housing unit

human ecology Robert Park's term for the relationship between people and their environment (natural resources such as land)

humanizing a work setting organizing a workplace in such a way that it develops rather than impedes human potential

hunting and gathering society a human group dependent on hunting and gathering for its survival

hypothesis a statement of the expected relationship between variables according to predictions from a theory

id Freud's term for our inborn basic drives

ideal culture the ideal values and norms of a people, the goals held out for them

ideal type a composite of characteristics based on many specific examples ("ideal" in this case means a description of the abstracted characteristics, not what one desires to exist)

ideology beliefs about the way things ought to be that justify social arrangements

illegitimate opportunity structures opportunities for crimes that are woven into the texture of life

impression management the term used by Erving Goffman to describe people's efforts to control the impressions that others receive of them

in-groups groups toward which one feels loyalty

incapacitation to take away someone's capacity to commit crimes, in this instance, by putting the offender in prison

incest sexual relations between specified relatives, such as brothers and sisters or parents and children

indentured service a contractual system in which someone sells his or her body (services) for a specified period of time in an arrangement very close to slavery, except that it is voluntarily entered into

independent variable a factor that causes a change in another variable, called the dependent variable

individual discrimination the negative treatment of one person by another on the basis of that person's perceived characteristics

Industrial Revolution the third social revolution, occurring when machines powered by fuels replaced most animal and human power

industrial society a society based on the harnessing of machines powered by fuels

inflation an increase in prices

institutional discrimination negative treatment of a minority group that is built into a society's institutions; also called *systemic discrimination*

institutionalized means approved ways of reaching cultural goals

instrumental leader an individual who tries to keep the group moving toward its goals; also known as a task-oriented leader

intentional family people who declare themselves a family and treat one another as members of the same family; originated in the late twentieth century in response to the need for intimacy not met due to distance, divorce, and death

intergenerational mobility the change that family members make in social class from one generation to the next

interlocking directorates the same people serving on the board of directors of several companies

internal colonialism the policy of economically exploiting minority groups

interview direct questioning of respondents

interviewer bias effects that interviewers have on respondents that lead to biased answers

invasion–succession cycle the process of one group of people displacing a group whose racial-ethnic or social class characteristics differ from their own

invention the combination of existing elements and materials to form new ones; identified by William Ogburn as the first of three processes of social change

involuntary memberships (or involuntary associations) groups in which people are assigned membership rather than choosing to join

labeling theory the view, developed by symbolic interactionists, that the labels people are given affect their own and others' perceptions of them, thus channeling their behavior either into deviance or into conformity

laissez-faire capitalism unrestrained manufacture and trade (literally, "hands off" capitalism)

laissez-faire leader an individual who leads by being highly permissive

language a system of symbols that can be combined in an infinite number of ways and can represent not only objects but also abstract thought

latent functions the unintended consequences of people's actions that help to keep a social system in equilibrium

leader someone who influences other people

leadership styles ways in which people express their leadership

leisure time not taken up by work or required activities such as eating, sleeping, commuting, child care, and housework

life course the stages of our life as we go from birth to death

life expectancy the number of years that an average newborn can expect to live

life span The maximum length of life of a species

living will a statement people in good health sign that clearly expresses their feelings about being kept alive on artificial life support systems

lobbyists people who influence legislation on behalf of their clients

looking-glass self a term coined by Charles Horton Cooley to refer to the process by which our self develops through internalizing others' reactions to us

machismo an emphasis on male strength and dominance

macro-level analysis an examination of large-scale patterns of society

macropolitics the exercise of large-scale power, the government being the most common example

macrosociology analysis of social life focusing on broad features of social structure, such as social class and the relationships of groups to one another; an approach usually used by functionalist and conflict theorists

mainstreaming helping people to become part of the mainstream of society

Malthus theorem an observation by Thomas Malthus that although the food supply increases only arithmetically (from 1 to 2 to 3 to 4 and so on), population grows geometrically (from 2 to 4 to 8 to 16 and so forth)

mandatory education laws laws that require all children to attend school until a specified age or until they complete a minimum grade in school

manifest functions the intended consequences of people's actions designed to help some part of a social system

manner the attitudes that people show as they play their roles

marginal working class the most desperate members of the working class, who have few skills, little job security, and are often unemployed

market any process of buying and selling; on a more formal level, the mechanism that establishes values for the exchange of goods and services

market competition the exchange of items between willing buyers and sellers

market forces the law of supply and demand

market restraints laws and regulations that limit the capacity to manufacture and sell products

marriage a group's approved mating arrangements, usually marked by a ritual of some sort

marriage squeeze the difficulty a group of men or women have in finding marriage partners, due to an imbalanced sex ratio

mass media forms of communication, such as radio, newspapers, and television, that are directed to mass audiences

mass society industrialized, highly bureaucratized, impersonal society

mass society theory an explanation for participation in social movements based on the assumption that such movements offer a sense of belonging to people who have weak social ties

master status a status that cuts across the other statuses that an individual occupies

material culture the material objects that distinguish a group of people, such as their art, buildings, weapons, utensils, machines, hairstyles, clothing, and jewelry

matriarchy a society in which women dominate men

matrilineal (system of descent) a system of reckoning descent that counts only the mother's side

means of production the tools, factories, land, and investment capital used to produce wealth

mechanical solidarity Durkheim's term for the unity or shared consciousness that comes from being involved in similar occupations or activities

medicalization the transformation of something into a matter to be treated by physicians

medicalization of deviance to make deviance a medical matter, a symptom of some underlying illness that needs to be treated by physicians

medicine: one of the major social institutions that sociologists study; a society's organized ways of dealing with sickness and injury

medium of exchange the means by which people value goods and services in order to make an exchange, for example, currency, gold, and silver

megalopolis an urban area consisting of at least two metropolises and their many suburbs

melting pot the view that Americans of various backgrounds would blend into a sort of ethnic stew

meritocracy a form of social stratification in which all positions are awarded on the basis of merit

metropolis a central city surrounded by smaller cities and their suburbs

metropolitan statistical area (MSA) a central city and the urbanized counties adjacent to it

micro-level analysis an examination of small-scale patterns of society

micropolitics the exercise of power in everyday life, such as deciding who is going to do the housework

microsociology analysis of social life focusing on social interaction; an approach usually used by symbolic interactionists

millenarian movement a social movement based on the prophecy of coming social upheaval

milling a crowd standing or walking around as they talk excitedly about some event

minimax strategy Richard Berk's term for the effort people make to minimize their costs and maximize their rewards

minority group people who are singled out for unequal treatment, and who regard themselves as objects of collective discrimination

modernization the process by which a *Gemeinschaft* society is transformed into a *Gesellschaft* society; the transformation of traditional societies into industrial societies

monarchy a form of government headed by a king or queen

money any item (from seashells to gold) that serves as a medium of exchange; today, currency is the most common form

monopoly the control of an entire industry by a single company

monotheism the belief that there is only one God

moral panic a fear that grips large numbers of people that some evil group or behavior threatens the well-being of society, followed by intense hostility, sometimes violence, toward those thought responsible

mores (MORE-rays) norms that are strictly enforced because they are thought essential to core values

multiculturalism (also called **pluralism**) a philosophy or political policy that permits or encourages ethnic variation

multinational corporations companies that operate across many national boundaries; also called transnational corporations

nationalism a strong identity with a nation, accompanied by the desire for that nation to be dominant

natural sciences the intellectual and academic disciplines designed to comprehend, explain, and predict events in our natural environment

negative sanction an expression of disapproval for breaking a norm, ranging from a mild, informal reaction such as a frown to a formal prison sentence or an execution

neocolonialism the economic and political dominance of the Least Industrialized Nations by the Most Industrialized Nations

net migration rate the difference between the number of immigrants and emigrants per 1,000 population

new social movements social movements with a new emphasis on the world, instead of on a condition in a specific country

new technology the emerging technologies of an era that have a significant impact on social life

noncentrist party a political party that represents marginal ideas

nonmaterial culture a group's ways of thinking (including its beliefs, values, and other assumptions about the world) and doing (its common patterns of behavior, including language and other forms of interaction)

nonverbal interaction communication without words through gestures, space, silence, and so on

norms the expectations, or rules of behavior, that develop out of values

nuclear family a family consisting of a husband, wife, and child(ren)

objectivity total neutrality

official deviance a society's statistics on lawbreaking; its measures of crimes, victims, lawbreakers, and the outcomes of criminal investigations and sentencing

oligarchy a form of government in which power is held by a small group of individuals; the rule of the many by the few

oligopoly the control of an entire industry by several large companies

open-ended questions questions that respondents are able to answer in their own words

operational definitions the way in which a variable in a hypothesis is measured

organic solidarity solidarity based on the interdependence brought about by the division of labor **out-groups** groups toward which one feels antagonisms

panic the condition of being so fearful that one cannot function normally, and may even flee

pan-Indianism a movement that focuses on common elements in Native-American culture in order to develop a mutual self-identity and to work toward the welfare of all Native Americans

participant observation (or **fieldwork**) research in which the researcher participates in a research setting while observing what is happening in that setting

pastoral society a society based on the pasturing of animals

patriarchy a society in which men dominate women

patrilineal (system of descent): a system of reckoning descent that counts only the father's side

patterns recurring characteristics or events

peer group a group of individuals roughly the same age linked by common interests

personal identity kit items people use to decorate their bodies

personality disorders the view that a personality disturbance of some sort causes an individual to violate social norms

Peter principle a bureaucratic "law" according to which the members of an organization are promoted for good work until they reach their level of incompetence, the level at which they can no longer do good work

pluralism the diffusion of power among many interest groups, preventing any single group from gaining control of the government

pluralistic society a society made up of many different groups

pluralistic theory of social control the view that society is made up of many competing groups, whose interests manage to become balanced

police discretion the practice of the police, in the normal course of their duties, to arrest someone for an offense or to overlook the matter

political action committee (PAC) an organization formed by one or more special-interest groups to solicit and spend funds for the purpose of influencing legislation

polyandry a marriage in which a woman has more than one husband

polygyny a marriage in which a man has more than one wife

polytheism the belief that there are many gods

population the target group to be studied

population pyramid a graphic representation of a population, divided into age and sex

population shrinkage the process by which a country's population becomes smaller because its birth rate and immigration are too low to replace those who die and emigrate

population transfer involuntary movement of a minority group

positive sanction a reward or positive reaction for approved behavior, given for following norms, ranging from a smile to a prize

positivism the application of the scientific approach to the social world

postindustrial society a society based on information, services, and high technology, rather than on raw materials and manufacturing

postmodern society another term for postindustrial society; its chief characteristic is the use of tools that extend the human abilities to gather and analyze information, to communicate, and to travel

poverty lacking resources to meet your basic needs

poverty line the official measure of poverty; calculated to include those whose incomes are less than three times a low-cost food budget

power the ability to get your way despite the resistance of others desires

prejudice an *attitude* or prejudging, usually in a negative way

prestige respect or regard

primary deviance Edwin Lemert's term for acts of deviance that have little effect on the self-concept

primary group a group characterized by intimate, long-term, face-to-face association and cooperation

primary sector that part of the economy that extracts raw materials from the environment

private ownership of the means of production the ownership of machines and factories by individuals, who decide what shall be produced

proactive social movement a social movement that promotes some social change

profane Durkheim's term for common elements of everyday life

profession an occupation characterized by rigorous education, a theoretical perspective, self-regulation, authority over clients, and service to society (as opposed to a job)

professionalization of medicine the development of medicine into a field in which education becomes rigorous, and in which physicians claim a theoretical understanding of illness, regulate themselves, claim to be doing a service to society (rather than just following self interest), and take authority over clients

proletariat Karl Marx's term for the exploited class, the people who work for those who own the means of production

propaganda in its broad sense, the presentation of information in the attempt to influence people; in its narrow sense, one-sided information used to try to influence people

proportional representation an electoral system in which seats in a legislature are divided according to the proportion of votes each political party receives

Protestant ethic Weber's term to describe the ideal of a self-denying, highly moral life, accompanied by hard work and frugality

public a dispersed group of people who usually have an interest in the issue on which a social movement focuses; the sympathetic and hostile publics have such an interest, but a third public is either unaware of the issue or indifferent to it

public opinion how people think about some issue

pure or **basic sociology** sociological research whose purpose is to make discoveries about life in human groups, not to make changes in those groups

qualitative research methods research in which the emphasis is placed on observing, describing, and interpreting people's behavior

quantitative research methods research in which the emphasis is placed on precise measurement, the use of statistics and numbers

questionnaires a list of questions to be asked

race inherited physical characteristics that distinguish one group from another

racism prejudice and discrimination on the basis of race

random sample a sample in which everyone in the target population has the same chance of being included in the study

rapport a feeling of trust between researchers and subjects

rationality the acceptance of rules, efficiency, and practical results as the right way to approach human affairs

rationalization of society a widespread acceptance of rationality and a social organization largely built around this idea

rational-legal authority authority based on law or written rules and regulations; also called *bureaucratic authority*

reactive social movement a social movement that resists some social change

real culture the norms and values that people actually follow

recidivism rate the proportion of people who are rearrested

redemptive social movement a social movement that seeks to change people totally

redlining the officers of a financial institution deciding not to make loans in a particular area

reference groups Herbert Hyman's term for the groups we use as standards to evaluate ourselves

reformative social movement a social movement that seeks to change only particular aspects of society

rehabilitation the resocialization of offenders so that they can become conforming citizens

reincarnation in Hinduism and Buddhism, the return of the soul after death in a different form

relative deprivation theory in this context, the belief that people join social movements based on their evaluations of what they think they should have compared with what others have

reliability the extent to which research produces consistent results

religion according to Durkheim, beliefs and practices that separate the profane from the sacred and unite its adherents into a moral community

religious experience a sudden awareness of the supernatural or a feeling of coming in contact with God

replication repeating a study in order to test its findings

representative democracy a form of democracy in which voters elect representatives to govern and make decisions on their behalf

research method (or research design) one of six procedures sociologists use to collect data: surveys, participant observation, secondary analysis, documents, unobtrusive measures, and experiments

reserve labor force the unemployed; unemployed workers are thought of as being "in reserve"—capitalists take them "out of reserve" (put them back to work) during times of high production and then lay them off (put them back in reserve) when they are no longer needed

resocialization the process of learning new norms, values, attitudes, and behaviors

resource mobilization a theory that social movements succeed or fail based on their ability to mobilize resources such as time, money, and people's skills

retribution the punishment of offenders in order to restore the moral balance upset by the offense

revolution armed resistance designed to overthrow a government

riot violent crowd behavior aimed against people and property

rising expectations the sense that better conditions are soon to follow, which, if unfulfilled, creates mounting frustration

rituals ceremonies or repetitive practices; in this context, religious observances or rites, often intended to evoke a sense of awe of the sacred

role conflict conflicts that someone feels *between* roles because the expectations attached to one role are incompatible with the expectations of another role

role the behaviors, obligations, and privileges attached to a status

role extension the incorporation of additional activities into a role

role performance the ways in which someone performs a role within the limits that the role provides; showing a particular "style" or "personality"

role strain conflicts that someone feels *within* a role

romantic love feelings of erotic attraction accompanied by an idealization of the other

routinization of charisma the transfer of authority from a charismatic figure to either a traditional or a rational-legal form of authority

ruling class another term for the power elite

rumor unfounded information spread among people

sacred Emile Durkheim's term for things set apart or forbidden, that inspire fear, awe, reverence, or deep respect

sample the individuals intended to represent the population to be studied

sanctions expressions of approval or disapproval given to people for upholding or violating norms

Sapir-Whorf hypothesis Edward Sapir and Benjamin Whorf's hypothesis that language creates ways of thinking and perceiving

scapegoat an individual or group unfairly blamed for someone else's troubles

school choice parents being able to choose the school their child will attend; often used in the context of expecting for-profit schools to compete for vouchers issued by the state

science the application of systematic methods to obtain knowledge and the knowledge obtained by those methods

secondary analysis the analysis of data already collected by other researchers

secondary deviance Edwin Lemert's term for acts of deviance incorporated into the self-concept, around which an individual orients his or her behavior

secondary group compared with a primary group, a larger, relatively temporary, more anonymous, formal, and impersonal group based on some interest or activity, whose members are likely to interact on the basis of specific roles

secondary sector that part of the economy that turns raw materials into manufactured goods

sect a group larger than a cult that still feels substantial hostility from and toward society

secular belonging to the world and its affairs

secularization the process by which spiritual concerns are replaced by worldly concerns

secularization of culture the process by which a culture becomes less influenced by religion

secularization of religion the replacement of a religion's "otherworldly" concerns with concerns about "this world"

segregation the policy of keeping racial or ethnic groups apart

selective perception seeing certain features of an object or situation, but remaining blind to others

self the unique human capacity of being able to see ourselves "from the outside"; the picture we gain of how others see us

self-administered questionnaires questionnaires filled out by respondents

self-fulfilling prophecy Robert Merton's term for an originally false assertion that becomes true simply because it was predicted

serial fatherhood a pattern of parenting in which a father, after divorce, reduces contact with his own children, serves as a father to the children of the woman he marries or lives with, then ignores them after moving in with or marrying another woman; this pattern repeats

sex biological characteristics that distinguish females and males, consisting of primary and secondary sex characteristics

sex typing the association of behaviors with one sex or the other

sexual harassment the abuse of one's position of authority to force unwanted sexual demands on someone

shaman the healing specialist of a tribal society who attempts to control the spirits thought to cause a disease or injury; commonly called a witch doctor

sick role a social role that excuses people from normal obligations because they are sick or injured, while at the same time expecting them to seek competent help and cooperate in getting well

sign-vehicles the term used by Goffman to refer to how people use social setting, appearance, and manner to communicate information about the self

significant other an individual who significantly influences someone else's life

slavery a form of social stratification in which some people own other people

small group a group small enough for everyone to interact directly with all the other members

social change the alteration of culture and societies over time

social class according to Weber, a large group of people who rank closely to one another in wealth, power, and prestige; according to Marx, one of two groups: capitalists who own the means of production or workers who sell their labor; most commonly, a large number of people with similar amounts of income and education who work at jobs that are roughly comparable in prestige

social cohesion the degree to which members of a group or a society feel united by shared values and other social bonds

social control a group's formal and informal means of enforcing its norms

social environment the entire human environment, including direct contact with others

social facts Durkheim's term for the patterns of behavior that characterize a social group

social inequality a social condition in which privileges and obligations are given to some but denied to others

social institutions the organized, usual, or standard ways by which society meets its basic needs

social integration the degree to which people feel a part of social groups

social interaction what people do when they are in one another's presence

social location the group memberships that people have because of their location in history and society

social mobility movement up or down the social class ladder

social movement a large group of people who are organized to promote or resist social change

social movement organization an organization developed to further the goals of a social movement

social network the social ties radiating outward from the self that link people together

social order a group's usual and customary social arrangements, on which its members depend and on which they base their lives

social placement a function of education that funnels people into a society's various positions

social promotion passing students to the next grade even though they have not mastered basic materials

social sciences the intellectual and academic disciplines designed to understand the social world objectively by means of controlled and repeated observations

social setting the place where the action of everyday life unfolds

social stratification the division of large numbers of people into layers according to their relative power, property, and prestige; applies to both nations and to people within a nation, society, or other group

social structure the framework that surrounds us, consisting of the relationships of people and groups to one another, which give direction to and set limits on behavior

socialism an economic system characterized by the public ownership of the means of production, central planning, and the distribution of goods without a profit motive

socialization the process by which people learn the characteristics of their group—the attitudes, values, and actions thought appropriate for them

society people who share a culture and a territory

sociobiology a framework of thought that views human behavior as the result of natural selection and considers biological characteristics to be the fundamental cause of human behavior

sociological perspective an approach to understanding human behavior by placing it within its broader social context

sociology the scientific study of society and human behavior

special-interest group a group of people who have a particular issue in common who can be mobilized for political action

spirit of capitalism Weber's term for the desire to accumulate capital as a duty—not to spend it, but as an end in itself—and to constantly reinvest it

split-labor market workers split along racial, ethnic, gender, age, or any other lines; this split is exploited by owners to weaken the bargaining power of workers

state a political entity that claims monopoly on the use of violence in some particular territory; commonly known as a country

state religion a government-sponsored religion

status the position that someone occupies in society or a social group; social ranking

status consistency ranking high or low on all three dimensions of social class

status inconsistency (or **status discrepancy**) ranking high on some dimensions of social class and low on others

status set all the statuses or positions that an individual occupies

status symbols items used to identify a status

stereotypes assumptions of what people are like, based on previous associations with them or with people who have similar characteristics, or based on information, whether true or false

stigma "blemishes" that discredit a person's claim to a "normal" identity

stockholders' revolt the refusal of a corporation's stockholders to rubber-stamp decisions made by its managers

stored value the backing of a currency by goods that are stored and held in reserve

strain theory Robert Merton's term for the strain engendered when a society socializes large numbers of people to desire a cultural goal (such as success) but withholds from many the approved means to reach that goal; one adaptation to the strain is crime, the choice of an innovative means (one outside the approved system) to attain the cultural goal

stratified random sample a sample of specific subgroups of the target population in which everyone in the subgroups has an equal chance of being included in the study

street crime crimes such as mugging, rape, and burglary

structural mobility movement up or down the social class ladder that is attributable to changes in the structure of society, not to individual efforts

structured interviews interviews that use closed-ended questions

subculture the values and related behaviors of a group that distinguish its members from the larger culture; a world within a world

subjective meanings the meanings that people give their own behavior

subsistence economy a type of economy in which human groups live off the land with little or no surplus

suburb the communities adjacent to the political boundaries of a city

suburbanization the movement from the city to the suburbs

superego Freud's term for the conscience, the internalized norms and values of our social groups

survey the collection of data by having people answer a series of questions

sustainable environment a world system that takes into account the limits of the environment, produces enough material goods for everyone's needs, and leaves a heritage of a sound environment for the next generation

symbol something to which people attach meanings and then use to communicate with others

symbolic culture another term for nonmaterial culture

symbolic interactionism a theoretical perspective in which society is viewed as composed of symbols that people use to establish meaning, develop their views of the world, and communicate with one another

system of descent how kinship is traced over the generations

taboo a norm so strong that it brings revulsion if violated

taking the role of the other putting oneself in someone else's shoes; understanding how someone else feels and thinks and thus anticipating how that person will act

teamwork the collaboration of two or more people to manage impressions jointly

techniques of neutralization ways of thinking or rationalizing that help people deflect society's norms

technology in its narrow sense, tools; its broader sense includes the skills or procedures necessary to make and use those tools

tertiary deviance "normalizing" behavior considered deviant by mainstream society; relabeling behavior as nondeviant

tertiary sector that part of the economy that consists of service-oriented occupations

the iron law of oligarchy Robert Michels's phrase for the tendency of formal organizations to be dominated by a small, self-perpetuating elite

the quiet revolution the fundamental changes in society that occur as a result of vast numbers of women entering the work force

the scientific method the use of objective, systematic observations to test theories

the social construction of reality the process by which people use their background assumptions and life experiences to define what is real for them

theory a general statement about how some parts of the world fit together and how they work; an explanation of how two or more facts are related to one another

Thomas theorem William I. Thomas' classic formulation of the definition of the situation: "If people define situations as real, they are real in their consequences."

total institution a place in which people are cut off from the rest of society and are almost totally controlled by the officials who run the place

totalitarianism a form of government that exerts almost total control over the people

tracking the sorting of students into different educational programs on the basis of real or perceived abilities

traditional authority authority based on custom

traditional orientation the idea, characteristic of tribal, peasant, and feudal societies, that the past is the best guide for the present

transformative social movement a social movement that seeks to change society totally

triad a group of three people

underclass a group of people for whom poverty persists year after year and across generations

underemployment the condition of having to work at a job beneath one's level of training and abilities, or of being able to find only part-time work

underground economy exchanges of goods and services that are not reported to the government and thereby escape taxation

universal citizenship the idea that everyone has the same basic rights by virtue of being born in a country (or by immigrating and becoming a naturalized citizen)

unobtrusive measures various ways of observing people who do not know they are being studied

unstructured interviews interviews that use open-ended questions

upward social mobility movement up the social class ladder

urbanization the process by which an increasing proportion of a population lives in cities

urban legend a story with an ironic twist that sounds realistic but is false

urban renewal the rehabilitation of a rundown area, which usually results in the displacement of the poor who are living in that area

validity the extent to which an operational definition measures what it was intended to measure

value(s) the standards by which people define what is desirable or undesirable, good or bad, beautiful or ugly

value cluster a series of interrelated values that together form a larger whole

value contradiction values that contradict one another; to follow the one means to come into conflict with the other

value free the view that a sociologist's personal values should not influence social research

variable a factor or concept thought to be significant for human behavior, which varies from one case to another

Verstehen a German word used by Weber that is perhaps best understood as "to have insight into someone's situation"

voluntary association a group made up of volunteers who have organized on the basis of some mutual interest

voluntary memberships (or voluntary associations) groups that people choose to join

voter apathy indifference and inaction on the part of individuals or groups with respect to the political process

war armed conflict between nations or politically distinct groups

WASP a White Anglo-Saxon Protestant; narrowly, an American of English descent; broadly, an American of western European ancestry

wealth property and income

welfare (or **state**) **capitalism** an economic system in which individuals own the means of production, but the state regulates many economic activities for the welfare of the population

white-collar crime Edwin Sutherland's term for crimes committed by people of respectable and high social status in the course of their oc-cupations; for example, bribery of public officials, securities violations, embezzlement, false advertising, and price fixing

white ethnics white immigrants to the United States whose culture differs from that of WASPs

working class those who sell their labor to the capitalist class

world system economic and political connections that tie the world's countries together

zero population growth a demographic condition in which women bear only enough children to reproduce the population

Suggested Readings

CHAPTER 1 The Sociological Perspective

Berger, Peter L. *Invitation to Sociology: A Humanistic Perspective.* New York: Doubleday, 1963. This delightful analysis of how sociology applies to everyday life is highly recommended.

Charon, Joel M. *Symbolic Interactionism: An Introduction, an Interpretation, an Integration,* 6th ed. Englewood Cliffs, N.J.: Prentice Hall, 1998. As it lays out the main points of symbolic interactionism, this book provides an understanding of why symbolic interactionism is important in sociology.

Henslin, James M., ed. *Down to Earth Sociology: Introductory Readings,* 11th ed. New York: Free Press, 2001. This collection of readings about everyday life is designed to broaden the reader's understanding of society, and of the individual's place within it.

Mills, C. Wright. *The Sociological Imagination.* New York: Oxford University Press, 2000. This classic work provides an overview of sociology from the framework of conflict theory.

Willis, Evans. *The Sociological Quest: An Introduction to the Study of Social Life,* 3rd ed. New Brunswick, N.J.: Rutgers University Press, 1997. A user-friendly introduction to sociology.

Journals

Applied Behavioral Science Review, Clinical Sociology, Clinical Sociology Review, International Clinical Sociology, Journal of Applied Sociology, The Practicing Sociologist, and *Sociological Practice Review* report the experiences of sociologists who work in a variety of applied settings, from peer group counseling and suicide prevention to recommending changes to school boards.

Humanity & Society, the official journal of the Association for Humanist Sociology, publishes articles that "serve to advance the quality of life of the world's people."

About a Career in Sociology

The following pamphlets or brochures are available free of charge from the American Sociological Association: 1307 New York Avenue NW, Suite 700, Washington, D.C. 20005-4701, tel: (202) 383-9005, fax: (202) 638-0882

Careers in Sociology. American Sociological Association. What can you do with sociology? You like the subject and would like to major in it, but. . . . This pamphlet provides information about jobs available for sociology majors.

Majoring in Sociology: A Guide for Students. American Sociological Association. This brochure provides an overview of the programs offered in sociology departments, possible areas of specialization, and how to find information on jobs.

Ferris, Abbott L. *How to Join the Federal Workforce and Advance Your Sociological Career.* American Sociological Association. This pamphlet gives tips on how to find employment in the federal government, including information on how to prepare a job application.

Huber, Bettina J. *Embarking Upon a Career in Sociology with an Undergraduate Sociology Major.* American Sociological Association. Designed for undergraduate sociology majors who are seeking employment, this brochure discusses how to identify interests and skills, pinpoint suitable jobs, prepare a résumé, and survive an employment interview.

Miller, Delbert C. *The Sociology Major as Preparation for Careers in Business.* American Sociological Association. What careers can a sociology major pursue in business or industry? This brochure includes sections on job prospects, graduate education, and how to practice sociology in business careers.

These two books are also useful if you are considering a career as a sociologist: the first provides background information; the second is more specific.

Hess, Beth B. *Individual Voices, Collective Visions: Fifty Years of Women in Sociology.* Philadelphia: Temple University Press, 1995. During the past fifty years, women have played an increasingly larger role in sociology, which, like the other sciences, has been dominated by men. The author examines this change.

Stephens, W. Richard. *Careers in Sociology,* 3rd ed. Boston: Allyn and Bacon, 1997. How can you make a living with a major in sociology? The author explores careers in sociology, from business and government to health care and the law.

CHAPTER 2 Culture

Chagnon, Napoleon A. *Yanomamo: The Fierce People,* 4th ed. New York: Harcourt, Brace, Jovanovich, 1992. This fascinating account of a preliterate people whose customs are extraordinarily different from ours will help you to see the arbitrariness of choices that underlie human culture.

Cohen, Mark Nathan. *Culture of Intolerance: Chauvinism, Class, and Racism in the United States.* New Haven: Yale University Press, 2000. The author analyzes how ideas of race, intelligence, and competence permeate U.S. culture.

Fouts, Roger, and Stephen Tukel Mills. *Next of Kin: My Conversations with Chimpanzees.* New York: Daniel M. Barber, 1999. As Fouts recounts his experiences with Washoe, he explains not only the complexities of reasoning by chimpanzees but also why he concludes that it is immoral to lock chimpanzees in cages.

Gitlin, Todd. *The Twilight of Common Dreams: Why America Is Wracked by Culture Wars.* New York: Metropolitan Books, 1997. "Culture wars" refers to fundamental disagreements about the way life should be lived, and to the way certain groups push their own agendas and disparage those of others. The author expresses hope that we can build "cultural bridges" so we once again can dream "common dreams."

Harris, Marvin. *Cannibals and Kings: The Origins of Cultures.* New York: Vintage Books, 1991.

Harris, Marvin. *Cows, Pigs, Wars, and Witches: The Riddles of Culture.* New York: Vintage Books, 1990.

Harris, Marvin. *Good to Eat: Riddles of Food and Culture.* New York: Simon & Schuster, 1986.

To read Harris' books is to read about cultural relativism. Using a functional perspective, this anthropologist analyzes cultural practices that often seem bizarre to outsiders. He interprets those practices within the framework of the culture being examined.

Smith, Shawn Michelle. *American Archives: Gender, Race, and Class in Visual Culture.* Princeton, N.J.: Princeton University Press, 2000. The photos in this book show how gender, race, and class have been conveyed in U.S. history in order to maintain white dominance.

Zellner, William W. *Countercultures: A Sociological Analysis.* New York: St. Martin's, Press, 1995. The author's analysis of skinheads, the Ku Klux Klan, survivalists, satanism, the Church of Scientology, and the Unification Church (Moonies) helps us understand why people join countercultures.

Journals

Qualitative Sociology, Urban Life, and *Visual Sociology Review* focus on qualitative research on social life.

CHAPTER 3 Socialization

Epstein, Jonathon S., ed. *Youth Culture: Identity in a Postmodern World.* Oxford, U.K.: Blackwell, 1998. Analyses of how youth find their identity: in sexuality, music, politics, education, interaction, goals, and frustrations.

Gilmore, David D. *Manhood in the Making: Cultural Concepts of Masculinity.* New Haven, Conn.: Yale University Press, 1991. A survey of societies around the world aimed at determining if masculinity is constant; contains fascinating anthropological data.

Lieberman, Alicia F. *The Emotional Life of the Toddler.* New York: Free Press, 1995. The author analyzes challenges in socializing young children and presents many interesting case materials on problems that toddlers confront.

Lieberman Van Hoorn, Judith, Elzbieta Suchar, Akos Komlosi, and Doreen A. Samuelson, eds. *Adolescent Development and Rapid Social Change: Perspectives from Eastern Europe.* Albany: State University of New York Press, 2000. Based on the premise that when society changes, we change, this book examines the effects of social change on adolescents in eastern Europe.

Mead, George Herbert. *Mind, Self and Society from the Standpoint of a Social Behaviorist.* Charles W. Morris, ed. Chicago: University of Chicago Press, 1974. First published in 1934. Put together from notes taken by Mead's students, this book presents Mead's analysis of how mind and self are products of society.

Mead, George Herbert. (Mary Jo Deegan, ed.) *Play, School, and Society.* New York: Peter Lang Publishing, 2000. The editor reorganizes notes taken by Mead's students, placing the focus on how play is a central component in the formation of the human mind.

Rymer, Russ. *Genie: An Abused Child's Flight from Silence.* New York: HarperCollins, 1993. This moving account of Genie includes the battles among linguists, psychologists, and social workers, who all claimed to have Genie's best interests at heart.

Sociological Studies of Child Development: A Research Annual. Greenwich, Conn.: JAI Press. Along with theoretical articles, this annual publication reports on sociological research on the socialization of children.

CHAPTER 4 Social Structure and Social Interaction

Goffman, Erving. *The Presentation of Self in Everyday Life.* New York: Doubleday, 1990. First published in 1959. This classic statement of dramaturgical analysis provides a different way of looking at everyday life.

Helmreich, William B. *The Things They Say Behind Your Back: Stereotypes and the Myths Behind Them.* New Brunswick, N.J.: Transaction, 1984. Spiced with anecdotes and jokes, yet sensitively written, the book explores the historical roots of stereotypes. The author also illustrates how stereotypes help produce behaviors that reinforce them.

Lennon, Sharron J., and Kim K. Johnson, eds. *Appearance and Power.* Oxford, England: Berg Publishers, Ltd., 2000. Because we know that appearance is important, we try to put our best foot forward. The authors of these articles analyze how significant appearance, especially clothing, is for what happens to us in social life.

Schellenberg, James A. *Exploring Social Behavior: Investigations in Social Psychology.* Boston: Allyn and Bacon, 1993. The author takes the reader on an intellectual journey, exploring such "mysteries" as identity, conscience, intelligence, attraction, and aggression.

Tönnies, Ferdinand. *Community and Society (Gemeinschaft und Gesellschaft).* New Brunswick, N.J.: Transaction, 1988. Originally published in 1887, this classic work, focusing on social change, provides insight into how society influences personality. Rather challenging reading.

Vinitzky-Seroussi, Vered. *After Pomp and Circumstance: High School Reunion as an Autobiographical Occasion.* Chicago: University of Chicago Press, 1998. In this analysis of high school reunions, the author examines the relationship between the self and the past and future.

Walker, Beverly M., ed. *Construction of Group Realities: Culture, Society, and Personal Construction Theory.* New York: Praeger, 1995. Our views of life, what we believe, even what we perceive have a group basis to them.

Whyte, William Foote. *Street Corner Society: The Social Structure of an Italian Slum.* New York: Irvington, 1993. Originally published in 1945. The author's analysis of interaction in a U.S. Italian slum demonstrates how social structure affects personal relationships.

Journals

The following three journals feature articles on symbolic interactionism and analyses of everyday life: *Qualitative Sociology, Symbolic Interaction, Urban Life.*

CHAPTER 5 How Sociologists Do Research

Berg, Bruce Lawrence. *Qualitative Research Methods for the Social Sciences,* 3rd ed. Boston: Allyn and Bacon, 1998. Explains how to collect, organize, and make sense of qualitative data.

Kelley, D. Lynn. *Measurement Made Accessible: A Research Approach Using Qualitative, Quantitative, and Quality Improvement Methods.* Walnut Creek, CA: Altamira Press, 2000. In this analysis of both quantitative and qualitative methods for gathering data, the author explains how to develop questionnaires, improve reliability and validity.

Merton, Robert K., Marjorie Fiske, and Patricia L. Kendall. *The Focused Interview: A Manual of Problems and Procedures,* 2nd ed. New York: Free Press, 1990. Interviewing techniques are outlined; of value primarily to more advanced students.

Neuman, William Lawrence. *Social Research Methods: Qualitative and Quantitative Approaches,* 4th ed. Boston: Allyn and Bacon, 2000. This "how-to" book of sociological research describes the major ways in which sociologists gather data and the logic that underlies each method.

Scully, Diana. *Understanding Sexual Violence: A Study of Convicted Rapists.* New York: Routledge, 1994. The author's examination of the rationalizations of rapists helps us understand why some men rape and what they gain from it.

Spradley, James P. *Participant Observation.* New York: Holt, Rinehart, and Winston, 1998. The book explains the value of participant observation and summarizes interesting studies. From it, you may understand why *you* are uniquely qualified for doing participant observation.

Webb, Eugene J., Donald T. Campbell, Richard D. Schwartz, Lee Sechrest, and Janet Below Grove. *Unobtrusive Measures: Nonreactive Research in the Social Sciences.* Chicago: Houghton Mifflin, 1981. This clear overview of unobtrusive measures also contains concise summaries of a great deal of research.

Whyte, William Foote. *Creative Problem Solving in the Field: Reflections on a Career.* New York: Altamira Press, 1997. Focusing on his extensive field experiences, the author provides insight into the critical involvement of the self in this research method.

Writing Papers for Sociology

The Sociology Writing Group. *A Guide to Writing Sociology Papers,* 4th ed. New York: St. Martin's Press, 1998. The guide walks students through the steps in writing a sociology paper, from choosing the initial assignment to doing the research and turning in a finished paper. Also explains how to manage your time and correctly cite sources.

Cuba, Lee J. *A Short Guide to Writing about Social Science,* 3rd ed. Glenview, Ill.: Scott, Foresman, 1997. The author summarizes the various types of social science literature, presents guidelines on how to organize and write a research paper, and explains how to prepare an oral presentation.

Journal

Visual Sociology Review. A specialized journal in qualitative sociology that focuses on the analysis of social life through visual means such as photos, movies, and videos.

CHAPTER 6 Societies to Social Networks

Forschi, Martha, and Edward J. Lawler, eds. *Group Processes: Sociological Analysis.* New York: Nelson-Hall, 1994. How do your associates, friends, family—and even strangers—influence you? Among other topics, these authors explore such influences.

Fleisher, Mark S. *Beggars and Thieves: Lives of Urban Street Criminals.* Madison: University of Wisconsin Press, 1995. Based on years of participant observation, the author presents an inside view of thieves, gangs, addicts, and lifelong criminals.

Homans, George. *The Human Group.* New York: Harcourt, Brace, 1950. Homans develops the idea that all human groups share common activities, interactions, and sentiments and examines various types of social groups from this point of view.

Janis, Irving L. *Groupthink: Psychological Studies of Policy Decisions and Fiascoes,* 2nd ed. 1982. New York: Houghton Mifflin. Janis analyzes how groups can become cut off from alternatives, interpret evidence in light of their preconceptions, and embark on courses of action that they should have seen as obviously incorrect.

Mills, Theodore M. *The Sociology of Small Groups.* Englewood Cliffs, N.J.: Prentice Hall, 1984. Mills provides an overview of research on small groups, focusing on the interaction that occurs within them (group dynamics).

Zellner, William W., and William M. Kephart. *Extraordinary Groups: An Examination of Unconventional Lifestyles,* 4th ed. New York: St. Martin's Press, 1991. This sketch of the history and characteristics of eight groups—the Old Order Amish; Oneida Community; Gypsies; Church of Christ, Scientist; Hasidim; Father Divine Movement; Mormons; and Jehovah's Witnesses—illustrates the effects of groups on their members.

CHAPTER 7 Bureaucracy and Formal Organizations

Devereaux, James A. *Designing Bureaucracies: Institutional Capacity and Large-Scale Problem Solving.* Stanford, Calif.: Stanford University Press, 1995. Bureaucracies will remain a part of the foreseeable future. The author explains how they can live up to their potential.

Dupuy, Francois. *The Customer's Victory: From Corporation to Co-Operation.* Bloomington: Indiana University Press, 1999. Written to help managers better understand the organizations they manage.

Geneen, Harold. *Synergy and Other Lies: Downsizing, Bureaucracy, and Corporate Culture Debunked.* New York: St. Martin's Press, 1999. A scathing critique of the way U.S. business is done, and a defense of conglomerates, written by an acquisitive CEO.

Herkscher, Charles, and Anne Donnellon, eds. *The Post-Bureaucratic Organization.* Beverly Hills, Calif.: Sage, 1994. By any other name, is a bureaucracy still a bureaucracy? The authors of these articles explain how bureaucracies can be modified to better reach the organization's goals and to better meet human needs.

Hummel, Ralph P. *The Bureaucratic Experiment: A Critique of Life in the Modern Organization,* 4th ed., New York: St. Martin's Press, 1994. The author explores the perils and promises of bureaucracies, with an emphasis on how bureaucracies can become better tools for human needs.

MacDonald, Keith M. *The Sociology of the Professions.* Newbury Park, Calif.: Sage, 1996. Using a symbolic interactionist framework, the author analyzes how jobs are turned into professions.

Parkinson, C. Northcote. *Parkinson's Law.* Boston: Houghton Mifflin, 1997, Bucaneer Books. Although this exposé of the inner workings of bureaucracies is delightfully satirical, if what Parkinson analyzes were generally true, bureaucracies would always fail.

Wilson, Gerald L. *Groups in Context: Leadership and Participation in Small Groups,* 5th ed. New York: McGraw-Hill, 1998. An overview of principles and processes of interaction in small groups, with an emphasis on how to exercise leadership.

CHAPTER 8 Deviance and Social Control

Feld, Barry C. *Bad Kids: Race and the Transformation of the Juvenile Court.* New York: Oxford University Press, 1999. In this overview of the juvenile court system, the author analyzes the trend to remove serious offenders from the juvenile system.

Fleisher, Mark. S. *Dead End Kids: Gang Girls and the Boys They Know.* Madison: University of Wisconsin Press, 1999. This fascinating participant observation study provides an insider's perspective on gang life.

Girshick, Lori B. *No Safe Haven: Stories of Women in Prison.* Boston, Mass: Northeastern University Press, 1999. Do women occupy a special status in the criminal justice system? The author analyzes the life stories of forty imprisoned women to help understand the answer.

Goffman, Erving. *Stigma: Notes on the Management of Spoiled Identity.* New York: Simon & Schuster, 1986. A reprint of a 1968 classic that outlines the social and personal reactions to "spoiled identity," appearances—due to disability, weight, ethnicity, birth marks, and so on—that do not match dominant expectations.

Jankowski, Martín Sánchez. *Islands in the Street: Gangs and American Urban Society.* Berkeley: University of California Press, 1992. The author presents an overview of urban gangs in the United States; findings from this book are featured in the box on page 205.

Messner, Steven F., and Richard Rosenfeld. *Crime and the American Dream,* 2nd ed. Belmont, Calif.: Wadsworth, 1997. Explains how the "American Dream" produces a strong desire to make money but fails to instill adequate desires to play by the rules. Supports Merton's strain theory featured in this chapter.

Rafter, Nicole Hahn. *Creating Born Criminals.* Champagne: University of Illinois Press, 1998. Documents how our thinking about the cause of criminality has changed, with an emphasis on "born" criminals and the eugenics movement.

Reinarman, Craig, and Harry G. Levine, eds. *Crack in America: Demon Drugs and Social Justice.* Berkeley: University of California Press, 1998. Examines the consequences of a repressive drug policy, and explores constructive alternatives.

Scott, Kody. *Monster: The Autobiography of an L.A. Gang Member.* New York: Penguin Books, 1994. This intriguing inside view of gang life provides a rare glimpse of the power of countercultural norms.

Wright, Richard T., and Scott Decker. *Burglars on the Job: Streetlife and Residential Break-ins.* Boston: Northeastern University Press, 1996. For an understanding of how burglars think, as well as how they "work," this book is highly recommended.

CHAPTER 9 Social Stratification in Global Perspective

Carpenter, Ted Galen, ed. *NATO's Empty Victory.* Cato Institute, 2000. The author analyzes why NATO invaded Kosovo, although no NATO country had been invaded and the U.N. Security Council was divided on the issue.

Hajnal, Peter I., and Sian Meikle. *The G7/G8 System: Evolution, Role and Documentation.* Burlington, Ver.: Ashgate Publishing, 1999. An analysis of the development of G7 and its role in world affairs.

Kempadoo, Kamala, ed. *Sun, Sex, and God: Tourism and Sex Work in the Caribbean.* Lanham, Md.: Rowman and Littlefield, 2000. The authors analyze the connections between the global economy and the women, men, and children who sell sex; contains suggestions for changing the situation.

Kibria, Nazli. *Family Tightrope: The Changing Lives of Vietnamese Americans.* Princeton, N.J.: Princeton University Press, 1995. To change one's culture challenges almost all aspects of the self. The author analyzes how Vietnamese families are adjusting to their new lives.

Lane, David, ed. *The Rise and Fall of State Socialism: Industrialist Society and the Socialist State.* New York: Polity Press, 1997. The author analyzes political and economic changes in Russia, the consequences of which are being felt throughout the world.

Miles, Rosalind. *The Woman's History of the World.* New York: HarperCollins, 1990. The author examines the importance of gender in human history.

Thomas, Hugh. *The Slave Trade: The Story of the Atlantic Slave Trade: 1440–1870.* New York: Touchstone Books. An overview of slavery from 1444, when slaves from Africa were first taken to Portugal, until the 1860s, when the last African slave ships arrived in Cuba.

United Nations. *World Economic & Social Survey 1999.* New York: United Nations Publications, 1999. This survey of the economic characteristics of the world's nations provides a detailed contrast between the rich and poor nations.

Wilkins, David E. *American Indian Sovereignty and the U.S. Supreme Court: The Making of Justice.* Austin: University of Texas Press, 1998. The author traces the relationship of Native Americans and the U.S. government by analyzing fifteen decisions made by the U.S. Supreme Court.

Zakaria, Fareed. *From Wealth to Power: The Unusual Origins of America's World.* Princeton, N.J.: Princeton University Press, 2000. The author analyzes how growing wealth and the passing of power from the states to the federal government allowed the United States to become a world power.

CHAPTER 10 Social Class in Contemporary Society

Dent, David J. *In Search of Black America: Discovering the African-American Dream.* New York: Simon and Schuster, 2000. The author, a journalist, examines the life of middle-class African Americans, who live in what is largely a segregated world.

Domhoff, G. William. *State Autonomy or Class Dominance? Case Studies on Policy Making in America.* Hawthorne, New York: Aldine de Gruyter, 1996. The author, a conflict theorist, applies his analysis of social class and power to the development of major U.S. policy decisions.

Duncan, Greg J., and Jeanne Brooks-Gunn, eds. *Consequences of Growing Up Poor.* New York: Russel Sage, 2000. Examines how neighborhoods and families influence children's intellectual development and adolescent behavior.

Gatewood, Willard B. *Aristocrats of Color: The Black Elite, 1880–1920.* Fayetteville: University of Arkansas Press, 2000. Analyzing the rise and decline of the African-American upper class that developed after the Civil War, the author focuses on marriage, occupations, education, religion, clubs, and relationships with whites and with African Americans of lower classes.

Kushnick, Louis, and James Jennings, eds. *A New Introduction to Poverty: The Role of Race, Power, and Politics..* New York: New York University Press, 1999. In this analysis of major causes and characteristics of U.S. poverty, the authors also analyze why poverty persists.

Levine, Rhonda F., ed. *Social Class and Stratification: Classical Statements and Theoretical Debates.* New York: Rowman and Littlefield, 1998. An overview of sociological perspectives on social class and social inequality.

Liebow, Elliot. *Tally's Corner: A Study of Negro Streetcorner Men.* Boston: Little, Brown, 1999. This reprint of a 1968 classic of participant observation research of a group of Washington, D.C., African-American men provides remarkable insight into the dynamics of decision making and relationships.

Newman, Katherine S. *Falling from Grace: Downward Mobility in the Age of Affluence.* Berkeley: University of California Press, 1999. The focus of this analysis of downward social mobility is on what happens to people who lose their jobs and are unable to find decent work.

Oliver, Melvin L., and Thomas M. Shapiro. *Black Wealth/White Wealth: A New Perspective on Racial Inequality.* New York: Routledge, 1997. This book is the first comparison of the wealth (not income) of African Americans and whites. It shows how deep the divide is.

Richardson, Chad. *Batos, Bolillos, Pochos, & Pelados: Class and Culture on the South Texas Border.* Austin: University of Texas Press, 1999. An analysis of class, conflict, cooperation, and identity among Mexican Americans, Anglos, African Americans, and immigrants in the Valley of South Texas.

Wilson, William Julius. *When Work Disappears: The World of the New Urban Poor.* New York: Knopf, 1997. The author analyzes consequences of the disappearance of unskilled jobs near the inner city: the destruction of inner-city businesses, the flight of the middle class, and the stranding of poor people with few alternatives.

Zweigenhaft, Richard L., and G. William Domhoff. *Diversity in the Power Elite: Have Women and Minorities Reached the Top?* New Haven: Yale University Press, 1998. In answering the question asked in the subtitle, the authors explain how the recent arrival of minorities, including women, is affecting corporate culture.

CHAPTER 11 Inequalities of Gender

Amott, Teresa. *Caught in the Crisis: Women and the U.S. Econom,* 2nd ed. New York: Monthly Review Press, 2000. A short, readable overview of women's economic roles from a leftist perspective.

Disher, Sharon Hanley. *First Class: Women Join the Ranks at the Naval Academy.* Annapolis, MD: United States Naval Institute, 1998. This account by the first woman to graduate from the U.S. Naval Academy provides insight into the breaking of a male bastion of power.

Farganis, Sondra. *The Social Reconstruction of the Feminine Character,* 2nd ed. Lanham, Md.: Rowman & Littlefield, 1996. An overview of feminist theory that emphasizes how views of women are shaped by concrete situations.

Ferree, Myra Marx, Judith Lorber, and Beth B. Hess, eds. *Revisioning Gender.* Thousand Oaks: Sage, 1999. An analysis of changes occurring in gender roles, with an emphasis on the potential for changing human relations.

Gilman, Charlotte Perkins. *The Man-Made World or, Our Androcentric Culture.* New York: Charlton, 1911. Reprinted in 1971 by Johnson Reprint. This early book on women's liberation provides an excellent view of female–male relations at the beginning of this century.

Goldberg, Steven. *Why Men Rule: A Theory of Male Dominance.* Chicago: Open Court, 1993. A detailed explanation of the author's theory of male dominance featured in this chapter.

Kimmel, Michael S., and Michael A. Messner, eds. *Men's Lives,* 2nd ed. New York: Macmillan, 1993. These authors examine major issues of sex and gender as they affect men. An excellent companion, and often counterpoint, to the Anderson book.

Lefkowitz, Bernard. *Our Guys: The Glen Ridge Rape and the Secret Life of the Perfect Suburb.* New York: Vintage Books, 1998. This account of a rape that made national news provides insight into how subcultures that center on competitive male athletics can encourage aggression, violence, and rape.

Lorber, Judith. *Paradoxes of Gender.* New Haven, Conn.: Yale University Press, 1994. The author focuses on two vital issues: how gender is constructed and how gender is a primary component of social inequality.

Madriz, Esther. *Nothing Bad Happens to Good Girls: Fear of Crime in Women's Lives.* Berkeley: University of California Press, 1997. The author uses interviews to explain how women's fear of crime contributes to gender inequalities and the social control of women.

Pierce, Jennifer L. *Gender Trials: Emotional Lives in Contemporary Law Firms.* Berkeley: University of California Press, 1995. Using participant observation combined with interviews, the author explains how "doing gender" maintains gender stratification in high-pressure law offices.

Proweller, Amira. *Constructing Female Identities: Meaning Making in an Upper Middle Class Youth Culture.* Albany: State University of New York Press, 1998. The author analyzes what it means to be female in the United States today and how class, race, and education merge in the formation of a female identity.

Tannen, Deborah. *The Argument Culture: Stopping America's War of Words.* New York: Ballantine, 1999. In this argument that Americans argue too much (including too much public debate), the author, a psycholinguist, also reviews basic differences in how boys and girls express agreement and aggression.

Williams, Christine L. *Still a Man's World: Men Who Do Women's Work.* Berkeley: University of California Press, 1995. Based on in-depth interviews with men and women in nursing, elementary school teaching, librarianship, and social work, the author concludes that, due to the high value placed on masculinity, men who work in traditionally women's occupations find a "glass escalator" instead of a "glass ceiling."

Journals

These journals focus on the role of gender in social life: *Feminist Studies; Gender and Society; Gender, Place and Culture: A Journal of Feminist Geography; Journal of Gender, Culture, and Health; Sex Roles;* and *Signs: Journal of Women in Culture and Society.*

CHAPTER 12 Inequalities of Race and Ethnicity

Blea, Irene I. *U.S. Chicanas and Latinas within a Global Context.* New York: Praeger, 1998. By examining the global context, the author explains why Chicanas and Latinas sometimes feel more in common with women of the Least Industrialized Nations than with feminists in their own country.

Chin, Ko-Lin, and Douglas S. Massey. *Smuggled Chinese: Clandestine Immigration to the United States.* Philadelphia: Temple University Press, 2000. Based on interviews with illegal immigrants, the authors analyze the conditions that illegal immigrants from China face on their journey and after their arrival; includes information on safe houses.

De Anda, Roberto M., ed. *Chicanas and Chicanos in Contemporary Society.* Boston: Allyn and Bacon, 1996. An overview of the economy, family, religion, crime, justice, education, and politics of Americans who trace their origins to Mexico.

Du Bois, W.E.B. *Black Reconstruction in America: An Essay Toward a History of the Part Which Black Folk Played in the Attempt to Reconstruct Democracy in America, 1860–1880.* New York: Harcourt, Brace 1935; London: Frank Cass, 1966. This analysis of the role of African Americans in the Civil War and in the years immediately following provides a glimpse into a neglected part of U.S. history.

Klinkner, Philip A., and Roger M. Smith. *The Unsteady March: The Rise and Decline of Racial Equality in America.* Chicago: University of Chicago Press, 2000. Examines the conditions under which racial equality increases and decreases and proposes steps to increase racial equality.

Lytle, Clifford M., and Deloria Vine, Jr. *The Nations Within: The Past and Future of American Indian Sovereignty,* 2nd ed. Austin: University of Texas Press, 1998. Analyzes the relationship between legislation and the self-determination of Native Americans.

Press, Riv-Ellen. *Fighting to Become Americans: Jews, Gender, and the Anxiety of Assimilation.* Boston: Beacon Press, 1999. An analysis of the upward mobility of Jews in the U.S. racial-ethnic structure, and how their stereotypes reflect their aspirations and anxiety.

Reskin, Barbara F. *Realities of Affirmative Action in Employment.* Washington, D.C.: American Sociological Association, 1998. The author analyzes how affirmative action works, including the effects it has on employees and employers.

Rodriguez, Roberto. *Justice: A Question of Race.* Tempe, Ariz.: Bilingual Review Press, 1997. The author was arrested and beaten by the police for taking photos of them beating a mentally confused man. He recounts his own victimization and his subsequent trial against the Los Angeles Police Department.

Smith, Barbara E., ed. *Neither Separate nor Equal: Women, Race, and Class in the South.* Philadelphia: Temple University Press, 1999. A special focus of this anthology is the relationship among racial-ethnic groups and the role of a changing economy in shaping those relationships.

Walker, Samuel, Cassia Spohn, and Miriam Delone. *The Color of Justice: Race, Ethnicity, and Crime in America,* 2nd ed. Belmont, CA: Wadsworth, 2000. The authors analyze racial, ethnic, and gender discrimination in the criminal justice system.

Wilson, William Julius. *The Bridge over the Racial Divide: Rising Inequality and Coalition Politics.* Berkeley: University of California Press, 2000. The author analyzes how monetary, trade, and tax policies increase social inequality; includes recommendations to increase multiracial political cooperation.

CHAPTER 13 Inequalities of Age

Blaikie, Andrew. *Ageing and Popular Culture.* Cambridge, England: Cambridge University Press, 1999. Examines how the extended leisure that has come with the growing numbers of elderly is breaking down the distinction between middle and old age.

Dychtwald, Ken. *Age Power: How the 21st Century Will Be Ruled by the New Old.* Los Angeles: J. P. Tarcher, 2000. Speculates on how the growing numbers of elderly will affect society, and suggests how we should prepare for the coming change.

Furman, Frida Kerner. *Facing the Mirror: Older Women and Beauty Shop Culture.* Boston: Routledge, 1997. This ethnography of Julie's, a beauty parlor, illustrates how women come face to face with and adjust to the realities of aging.

Gubrium, Jaber F. *Living and Dying at Murray Manor.* Charlottesville: University of Virginia Press, 1998. In this ethnography of a nursing home, the author analyzes how staff and patients relate to one another, how patients pass time, and how they react to death.

Quadagno, Jill S. *Aging and the Life Course: An Introduction to Social Gerontology.* New York: McGraw Hill, 1999. This textbook which reviews the major issues in

gerontology, and stresses that the quality of life that people experience in old age is the result of earlier choices, opportunities, and constraints.

Roszak, Theodore. *America the Wise: The Longevity Revolution and the True Wealth of Nations.* New York: Houghton Mifflin, 1999.The author's thesis is that as the numbers of elderly grow, they will have more wealth and political power, leading to a more compassionate and wise society.

Stoller, Eleanor Palo, and Rose Campbell Gibson. *Worlds of Difference: Inequality in the Aging Experience.* 3rd ed. Thousand Oaks, Calif.: Pine Forge Press, 2000. The authors document extensive inequalities borne by the U.S. elderly and explain the social conditions that create those inequalities.

Journals

The Gerontologist, Journal of Aging and Identity, Journal of Aging and Social Policy, Journal of Aging Studies, Journal of Cross-Cultural Gerontology, Journal of Elder Abuse and Neglect, Journal of Gerontology, and *Journal of Women and Aging* focus on issues of aging, while *Youth and Society* examines adolescent culture.

CHAPTER 14 The Economy: Money and Work

Amott, Teresa. *Caught in the Crisis: Women and the U.S. Economy Today.* New York: Monthly Review Press, 2000. An analysis of how the transformation of the economy is affecting women.

Bales, Kevin. *Disposable People: New Slavery in the Global Economy.* Berkeley: University of California Press, 1999. The author documents the relationship between the globalization of capitalism and current slavery in Brazil, India, Mauritania, Pakistan, and Thailand.

Bluestone, Barry, Bennett Harrison, and Richard C. Leone. *Growing Prosperity.* New York: Houghton Mifflin, 1999. An emphasis on how we can continue economic growth: also focuses on the need for a more just distribution of our wealth.

Blumenberg, Werner. *Karl Marx.* New York: VideoBooks, 1999. Written by a member of the underground that fought against Hitler, this classic biography of Marx explores both his personal and public life.

Bonilla, Frank, Edwin Melendez, Maria de Los Angeles Torres, and Rebecca Morales, eds. *Borderless Borders: U.S. Latinos, Latin Americans, and the Paradox of Interdependence.* Philadelphia: Temple University Press, 1998. Analyzes how the globalization of capitalism is affecting U.S. Latinos, their identity, and their relationship to their home country.

Drucker, Peter F. *The Frontiers of Management: Where Tomorrow's Decisions Are Being Shaped Today.* New York: Penguin, 1999. An analysis of global trends and management practices in business, including hostile takeovers and career gridlocks.

Harrison, Bennett. *Lean and Mean: Why Large Corporations Will Continue to Dominate the Global Economy.* New York: Guilford Press, 1998. As the author examines the role of the giant corporations in technological innovations and economic growth, he explains why a permanent workforce is threatened by the rise in part-time and temporary jobs.

Katz, Richard. *Japan, the System that Soured: The Rise and Fall of the Japanese Economic Miracle.* New York: M. E. Sharpe, 1998. The author analyzes Japan's stunning recovery following World War II and the factors that brought it economic depression.

Sennett, Richard, and Bob Sennett. *The Corrosion of Character: The Personal Consequences of Work in the New Capitalism.* New York: W. W. Norton, 2000.An examination of how the "new efficiencies" of the multinational corporations affect workers; contains case studies.

CHAPTER 15 Politics: Power and Authority

Aho, James A. *This Thing of Darkness: A Sociology of the Enemy.* Seattle: University of Washington Press, 1994. This book provides insight into how people develop a collective perception of a broad conspiracy to destroy their way of life, even a shared, impassioned hatred of what they term "the enemy."

Amnesty International. *Amnesty International Report.* London: Amnesty International Publications, published annually. The reports summarize human rights violations around the world, listing specific instances country by country.

Chirot, Daniel. *Modern Tyrants: The Power and Prevalence of Evil in Our Age.* Princeton: Princeton University Press, 1996. From Hitler and Stalin to Trujillo, Mao, and Pol Pot, the author analyzes the political expediency that underlies tyranny.

Domhoff, G. William. *Who Rules America?: Power and Politics in the Year 2000,* 3rd ed. Mountain View, Calif.: Mayfield Publishing Company, 1998. An analysis of how the multinational corporations dominate the U.S. government.

Kerbo, Harold R., and John A. McKinstry. *Who Rules Japan?: The Inner Circles of Economic and Political Power.* Westport, Conn.: Praeger, 1995. An analysis of the "iron triangle" that wields power in Japan—the tightly bound group of corporate, bureaucratic, and political elites.

Mills, C. Wright. *The Power Elite.* New York: Oxford University Press, 1956. This classic analysis elaborates the conflict thesis summarized in this chapter that U.S. society is ruled by the nation's top corporate leaders, together with an elite from the military and political institutions.

Osiel, Mark J. *Obeying Orders: Atrocity, Military Discipline, and the Law of War.* New Brunswick, N.J.: Transaction Publishers, 1999. The author examines the social basis of constraint and freedom in the military and how orders can lead to atrocities.

Simes, Dimitri K. *After the Collapse: Russia Seeks Its Place as a Great Power.* New York: Simon and Schuster, 1999. The author, a Russian expatriate, analyzes the political turmoil in Russia and makes recommendations for U.S. policy toward Russia.

Stiglmayer, Alexandra, ed. *Mass Rape: The War Against Women in Bosnia-Herzegovina,* Marion Faber, trans. Lincoln: University of Nebraska Press, 1994. Giving chilling accounts, the authors explain why mass rape sometimes accompanies war, as it did in Bosnia.

Zweigenhaft, Richard L., and G. William Domhoff. *Diversity in the Power Elite: Have Women and Minorities Reached the Top?* New Haven: Yale University Press, 2000. The authors explore the extent to which Jews, women, blacks, Latinos, Asian Americans, and homosexuals have joined the power elite.

Journals

Most sociology journals publish articles on politics. Three that focus on this area of social life are *American Political Science Review, Journal of Political and Military Sociology,* and *Social Policy.*

Research in Political Sociology: A Research Annual. Greenwich, Conn.: JAI Press. This annual publication is not recommended for beginners, as the findings and theories are often difficult and abstract. It does, however, analyze political topics of vital concern to our well-being.

CHAPTER 16 The Family: Initiation into Society

Bergen, Raquel Kennedy. *Wife Rape: Understanding the Response of Survivors and Service Providers.* Newbury Park, Calif.: Sage, 1996. To understand the experience of women who have been raped, and how agency workers fail to help them, the author interviewed women who had taken refuge in shelters.

Coontz, Stephanie, Maya Parson, and Gabrielle Raley, eds. *American Families: A Multicultural Reader.* Boston: Routledge, 1999. The authors of these articles analyze the diversity of U.S. family life, illustrating the point in the text that there is no such thing as *the* family.

Hackstaff, Karla B. *Marriage in a Culture of Divorce.* Philadelphia: Temple University Press, 2000. Through in-depth interviews with couples married in the 1950s and 1970s, the author looks at how the meaning of marriage and divorce has changed.

Hansen, Karen V., Anita Ilta Garey, and Ronnie J. Steinberg, eds. *Families in the U.S: Kinship and Domestic Politics.* Philadelphia: Temple University Press, 1998. The authors of the 62 articles that make up this anthology cover the definition, structure, and economics of family, community, parenthood, kinship, marriage, divorce, caregiving, violence, and housework.

Hays, Sharon. *The Cultual Contradictions of Motherhood.* New Haven, Conn.: Yale University Press, 1996. The author's premise is that our changed ideology of child rearing ("intensive mothering") forces such great demands on mothers that it drives them to exhaustion.

Hochschild, Arlie Russell. *The Time Bind: When Work Becomes Home and Home Becomes Work.* Owl Books, 1998. Do parents really want to spend more time with

their families and less at work? Or do parents flee families, finding work a respite from family pressures? The author presents some surprising answers.

LaRossa, Ralph. *The Modernization of Fatherhood: A Social and Political History.* Chicago: University of Chicago Press, 1997. The author's exploration of how ideas of fatherhood have changed over time, and how they have varied from one group to another, sheds light on our current ideas of fatherhood.

McAdoo, Harriette Pipes, ed. *Black Families,* 3rd ed. Newbury Park, Calif.: Sage, 1996. An analysis of the experiences of black families and the pressures they experience.

Rubin, Lillian. *Families on the Faultline: America's Working Class Speaks about the Family, the Economy, Race and Ethnicity.* New York: HarperCollins, 1996. Based on interviews, this book maps primary concerns of the working class, allowing us to better understand the tensions they face.

Staples, Robert, ed. *The Black Family: Essays and Studies,* 6th. ed. Belmont, CA: Wadsworth, 1999. As the authors analyze black families–from the time of slavery to postindustrial society–they review gender roles, marriage and divorce, family life, parenthood, adolescence, health, violence, sexual relationships, and public policy.

Strasser, Mark. *The Challenge of Same-Sex Marriages: Federalist Principles and Constitutional Protections.* New York: Praeger, 2000. Based on challenges to state laws that limit marriage to people of the opposite sex, the author analyzes same-sex marriages in light of the U.S. Constitution.

Strasser, Mark. *Legally Wed: Same-Sex Marriage and the Constitution.* Ithaca, N.Y.: Cornell University Press, 1997. Based on the Hawaiian case mentioned in this chapter, the author analyzes same-sex marriages in light of the U.S. Constitution.

Journals

Family Relations, International Journal of Sociology of the Family, Journal of Comparative Family Studies, Journal of Divorce, Journal of Family and Economic Issues, Journal of Family Issues, Journal of Family Violence, Journal of Marriage and the Family, and *Marriage and Family Review* publish articles on almost every aspect of marriage and family life.

CHAPTER 17 Education: Transferring Knowledge and Skills

Anyon, Jean. *Ghetto Schooling: A Political Economy of Urban Educational Reform.* New York: Teachers College Press, 1998. An analysis of how race, class, and politics interweave to create the crisis faced by inner city schools.

Garrod, Andrew, and Colleen Larimore, eds. *First Person, First Peoples: Native American College Graduates Tell Their Life Stories.* Ithaca, N.Y.: Cornell University Press, 1997. Written by graduates of Dartmouth College, these essays recount the anguish minority students feel in a predominantly white college.

Kozol, Jonathan. *Ordinary Resurrections: Children in the Years of Hope.* New York: Crown Publishers, 2000. To listen as these children from a dismal neighborhood in South Bronx talk about life is to become aware of the high potential that schools have to reach children in poverty and to transform their lives.

Matthews, Jay. *Class Struggle: What's Wrong (and Right) with America's Best Public High Schools.* New York: Times Books, 1999. As the author, a reporter, analyzes the experiences of students at Mamaroneck High School in New York, one of the best public schools in the nation, he focuses on how students from privileged and impoverished backgrounds are served by the emphasis on advanced classes.

Miller, L. Scott. *An American Imperative: Accelerating Minority Educational Advancement.* New Haven: Yale University Press, 1998. The author proposes a national policy to reduce the economic, social, cultural, and institutional barriers to the educational advancement of minorities.

Padilla, Felix M. *The Struggle of Latino/Latina University Students: In Search of a Liberating Education.* New York: Routledge, 1997. The author draws on his students' journal entries and on his own educational experiences to analyze how Latino/a students construct their education in a white university.

Powell, Arthur G. *Lessons from Privilege: The American Prep School Tradition.* Cambridge, Mass.: Harvard University Press, 1998. The author explains why private schools work so well and suggests how public schools can apply those principles to improve the education of their students.

Reagin, Joe, Vera Hernan, and Imani Nikitah. *The Agony of Education: Black Students at a White University.* New York: Routledge, 1996. Based on interviews with African-American students and their parents, the authors analyze the dilemmas these students face and the decisions they make.

Schiell, Timothy C. *Campus Hate Speech on Trial.* Lawrence: University of Kansas Press, 2000. An analysis of where free speech, which lies at the center of personal freedom, and its limits on the college campus.

Journals

The following journals contain articles that examine almost every aspect of education: *Education and Urban Society, Harvard Educational Review,* and *Sociology of Education.*

CHAPTER 18 Religion: Establishing Meaning

Berger, Peter L., and Jonathan Sacks, eds. *The Desecularization of the World: Resurgent Religion and World Politics.* New York: William B. Eerdmans, 1999. The authors analyze the continuity or resurgence of religion in world affairs.

Galanter, Marc. *Cults: Faith, Healing, and Coercion.*, 2nd ed. New York: Oxford University Press, 1999. What do Alcoholics Anonymous, the Unification Church, and the mass suicide in Jonestown have in common? This book, rich in ethnographic materials on charismatic cults, provides answers: however, the sociological reader will have to wade through some unacceptable psychiatric interpretations.

Helmreich, William B. *The Enduring Community: The Jews of Newark and Metrowest.* New Brunswick, N.J.: Transaction, 1999. An analysis of the subcultural forces that help Jews maintain their identity in the face of declining religiosity.

Lewis, David C. *After Atheism: Religion and Ethnicity in Russia and Central Asia.* New York: St. Martin's Press, 2000. The author reports on changes in religion since the downfall of communism in Russia.

Mazur, Eric Michael. *The Americanization of Religious Minorities: Confronting the Constitutional Order.* Baltimore: Johns Hopkins University Press, 2000. What happens when religious beliefs conflict with U.S. law? The author analyzes the experiences of Jehovah's Witnesses, Mormons, and Native Americans.

Stark, Rodney, and William Sims Bainbridge. *Religion, Deviance, and Social Control.* New York: Routledge, 1997. Does religion prevent crime, delinquency, suicide, or drug abuse? If so, under what circumstances? The authors answer questions such as these.

Thibodeau, David, and Leon Whiteson. *A Place Called Waco: A Survivor's Story.* New York: PublicAffairs, 2000. A first-person account of life inside the Branch Davidian compound, written by one of only four survivors of the fire who were not sentenced to prison.

Williams, Miriam. *Heaven's Harlots: My Fifteen Years As a Sacred Prostitute in the Children of God Cult.* Deerfield, Mass.: Eagle Brook, 1999. A first person account of membership in the Children of God, a pseudo Christian group with international membership.

Journals

The following three journals publish articles that focus on the sociology of religion: *Journal for the Scientific Study of Religion, Review of Religious Research,* and *Sociological Analysis: A Journal in the Sociology of Religion.*

CHAPTER 19 Medicine: Health and Illness

Cockerham, William C. *Health and Social Change in Russia and Eastern Europe.* New York: Routledge, 1999. The author examines the health crisis in Russia and its former satellites, tracing the social causes that have led to an unprecedented drop in life expectancy.

Fox, Renée C., and Judith P. Swazey. *Spare Parts: Organ Replacement in American Society.* New York: Oxford University Press, 1992. The authors explore moral and ethical aspects of organ replacement, a social issue destined to grow in importance as medical technology continues to advance.

Grob, Gerald N. *The Mad Among Us: A History of the Care of America's Mentally Ill.* New York: Free Press, 1995. From colonial to contemporary times, a detailed history of attitudes and approaches toward the mentally ill, some enlightened, most repressive.

Jones, James H. *Bad Blood.* New York: Free Press, 1993. An account of the syphilis experiments conducted by the U.S. Public Health Service at Tuskegee Institute, which were carried out on unwitting African Americans.

Karp, David A. *Speaking of Sickness: Depression, Disconnection, and the Meaning of Illness.* New York: Oxford University Press, 1997. Written by a sociologist who has suffered from depression for many years, this book provides deep insight into people's experience with this illness.

Kolata, Gina Bari. *Flu: The Story of the Great Influenza Pandemic of 1918 and the Search for the Virus That Caused It.* New York: Farrar, Straus, and Giroux, 2000. The author recounts the worst pandemic of the 20th century, in which perhaps 40 million people died within a year.

Resnik, Susan. *Blood Saga: Hemophilia, Aids, and the Survival of a Community.* Berkeley: University of California Press, 1999. An analysis of how the medical community is implicated in the widespread transmission of AIDS to hemophiliacs.

Smith, Barbara Ellen *Digging Our Own Graves: Coal Miners and the Struggle over Black Lung Disease.* Philadelphia: Temple University Press, 1987. The author relates the coal miners' struggle to get black lung disease recognized by the medical community.

Journals

Health: An Interdisciplinary Journal for the Social Study of Health, Illness and Medicine, Journal of Health and Social Behavior, Research in the Sociology of Health Care, Social Science and Medicine, and *Sociological Practice: Health Sociology* publish research articles and essays in the field of medical sociology.

CHAPTER 20 Population and Urbanization

Anderson, Elijah. *Code of the Street: Decency, Violence, and the Moral Life of the Inner City.* New York: W. W. Norton & Co., 2000. An insider's perspective of how the need and demand for respect dominates social relationships in the inner city, and how this is related to violence, unemployment, and drugs.

Baxandall, Rosalyn Fraad, and Elizabeth Wewn. *Picture Window: How the Suburbs Happened.* New York: Basic Books, 1999. Analyzes how the suburbs were a response to the pivotal issues of U.S. life following World War II.

Benfield, F. Kaid, Donald D. T. Chen, and Matthew D. Raimi. *Once There Were Greenfields: How Urban Sprawl Is Undermining America's Environment, Economy, and Social Fabric.* New York: Natural Resource Defense, 1999. The authors' thesis is that urban sprawl is deteriorating our quality of life; they offer suggestions for what they call "smarter growth."

Brown, Lester R., Gary Gardner, and Brian Halweil. *Beyond Malthus: Nineteen Dimensions of the Population Challenge.* New York: W. W. Norton & Co., 1999. The thesis is that Malthus was right, and unless governments take strong steps the world will be unable to feed its growing population.

Department of Agriculture. *Yearbook of Agriculture.* Washington, D.C.: Department of Agriculture, published annually. The yearbook focuses on specific aspects of U.S. agribusiness, especially international economies and trade.

DeRosier, Linda Scott. *Creeker: A Woman's Journey.* Lexington: University Press of Kentucky, 2000. The author recounts her life growing up in the "hollers" of Appalachia; provides a good understanding of community and a way of rural life that is fast disappearing.

Duany, Andres, Elizabeth Plater-Zyberk, and Jeff Speck. *Suburban Nation: The Rise of Sprawl and the Decline of the American Dream.* San Francisco, CA: North Point Press, 2000. Lays out a vision of how to plan cities and suburbs so they meet human needs and become inviting places to live.

Moe, Richard, and Carter Wilkie. *Changing Places: Rebuilding Community in the Age of Sprawl.* New York: Henry Holt, 1999. Suggests steps we can take to preserve our urban heritage.

Mosher, Steven W. *A Mother's Ordeal: One Woman's Fight Against One-Child China.* New York: HarperCollins, 1994. This book puts a human face on China's coercive family planning policies.

Newman, Katherine S. *No Shame in My Game: The Working Poor in the Inner City.* New York: Knopf, 1999. Another look at the residents of the inner city, this time with a focus on the working poor, those who strive to get ahead but are held back by lack of opportunities and education.

Ross, Andrew. *The Celebration Chronicles: Life, Liberty and the Pursuit of Property Values in Disney's New Town.* New York: Ballantine Books, 2000. An analysis of Disney's planned utopian community in Florida, written by a social scientist who lived in Celebration for a year.

Weeks, John R. *Population: An Introduction to Concepts and Issues,* 7th ed. Belmont, CA: Wadsworth, 1999. Focusing on both the United States and the world, the author analyzes major issues in population.

CHAPTER 21 Collective Behavior and Social Movements

Barkan, Steven E., and Lynne L. Snowden. *Collective Violence.* Boston: Allyn and Bacon, 2000. The authors analyze riots, revolutions, terrorism, cults, militia, and hate groups.

Brunvand, Jan Harold. *Too Good to Be True: The Colossal Book of Urban Legends.* New York: W. W. Norton, 2000. In this collection of over 200 urban legends, you'll probably find some that you heard and thought were true.

Buechler, Steven M. *Social Movements in Advanced Capitalism: The Political Economy and Cultural Construction of Social Activism.* An analysis of why our current state of economic and political development produces social movements.

Gitlin, Todd. *The Sixties: Years of Hope, Days of Rage.* New York: Bantam, Revised edition, 1993. The author, now a sociologist, was a leader in the peace movement that arose during the social unrest of the 1960s. He combines personal experience with a sociological perspective.

Goode, Erich. *Paranormal Beliefs: A Sociological Introduction.* Bellevue, Wash.: Waveland Press, 2000. An examination of how the acceptance or rejection of belief in paranormal events is related to social structure.

Goode, Erich, and Nachman Ben-Yehuda. *Moral Panics: The Social Construction of Deviance.* New York: Blackwell, 1994. An overview of moral panics, one of the forms of collective behavior discussed in this chapter, with an emphasis on the process by which something is determined to be a moral threat.

Hanagan, Michael P., and Leslie T. Moch, eds. *Challenging Authority: The Historical Study of Contentious Politics (Social Movements, Protest, and Contention).* St. Paul: University of Minnesota Press, 1999. The authors analyze how social movements challenge the political order and lead to social change.

Jasper, James M. *The Art of Moral Protest: Culture, Biography, and Creativity in Social Movements.* Chicago: University of Chicago Press, 2000. A primary thrust of this book is how protest movements shape moral thinking.

Lofland, John. *Social Movement Organizations: Guide to Research on Insurgent Realities.* Hawthorne, N.Y.: Aldine de Gruyter, 1996. An advanced analysis of social movement organizations.

Luker, Kristin. *Abortion and the Politics of Motherhood.* Berkeley: University of California Press, 2000. Based on documents and interviews with pro-choice and pro-life advocates, the author demonstrates how people's moral positions on abortion are related to their views on sexual behavior, the care of children, and family life.

CHAPTER 22 Social Change, Technology, and the Environment

Arnold, Ron, and Alan M. Gottlieb. *Trashing the Economy: How Runaway Environmentalism Is Wrecking America.* Bellevue, Wash.: Merrill Press, 1999. Taking the opposite view of the Rensenbrink book, the author advances the thesis that the environmental movement can wreak the natural resource base of the U.S. economy.

Breton, Mary Joy. *Women Pioneers for the Environment.* Boston: Northeastern University Press, 1999. The stories of 40 women who stepped out of their traditional roles to spearhead environmental campaigns.

Brown, Lester R., ed. *State of the World.* New York: Norton, published annually. Experts on environmental issues analyze environmental problems throughout the world; a New Malthusian perspective.

Council on Environmental Quality. *Environmental Quality.* Washington, D.C.: U.S. Government Printing Office, published annually. Each report evaluates the condition of some aspect of the environment.

Cross, Gary, S., and Rick Szostak. *Technology and American Society: A History.* Englewood Cliffs, N.J.: Prentice Hall, 1995. The authors analyze how technology, a driving force in social change, is having fundamental effects on our lives.

Gaard, Greta Claire. *Ecological Politics: Ecofeminists and the Greens.* Philadelphia: Temple University Press, 1998. Examines the ideological connections between feminist theory and social activism in the environmental movement, with a special emphasis on Green politics.

Gates, Bill. *Business @ the Speed of Thought: Using a Digital Nervous System.* New York: Warner Books, 1999. The premise is that the speed of business is increasing and that to keep up businesses must develop a "digital nervous system" to gather, manage, and use information.

Rensenbrink, John. *Against All Odds: The Green Transformation of American Politics.* Gray, Maine: Leopold Press, 1999. The thesis is that to have a "just and self-renewing society" the United States needs a new political system based on "ecological wisdom."

Stead, W. Edward, and Jean Garner Stead. *Management for a Small Planet.,* 2nd ed. Newbury Park, Calif.: Sage, 1996. The authors examine how we can reconcile our need for economic production with our need to protect the earth's ecosystem.

Veltmeyer, Henry, and James F. Petras. *The Dynamics of Social Change in Latin America.* New York: St. Martin's Press, 2000. Analyzes the interrelationship of the globalization of capitalism, ideology, social class, politics, and the economy of Latin America.

Journals

Earth First! Journal and *Sierra,* magazines published by Earth First! and the Sierra Club respectively, are excellent sources for keeping informed of major developments in the environmental movement.

References

Aberle, David. *The Peyote Religion Among the Navaho.* Chicago: Aldine, 1966.

Aberle, David F., A. K. Cohen, A. K. David, M. J. Leng, Jr., and F. N. Sutton. "The Functional Prerequisites of a Society." *Ethics, 60,* January 1950:100–111.

Ackernecht, Erwin H. "The Role of Medical History in Medical Education." *Bulletin of the History of Medicine, 21,* 1947:135–145.

Addams, Jane. *Twenty Years at Hull-House.* New York: Signet, 1981. First published in 1910.

Adler, Patricia A., and Peter Adler. *Peer Power: Preadolescent Culture and Identity.* New Brunswick, N.J.: Rutgers University Press, 1998.

Adler, Patricia A., Steven J. Kless, and Peter Adler. "Socialization to Gender Roles: Popularity Among Elementary School Boys and Girls." *Sociology of Education, 65,* July 1992:169–187.

Adorno, Theodor W., Else Frenkel-Brunswick, D. J. Levinson, and R. N. Sanford. *The Authoritarian Personality.* New York: Harper & Row, 1950.

Aeppel, Timothy. "More Amish Women Are Tending to Business." *Wall Street Journal,* February 8, 1996:B1, B2.

Aguirre, Benigno E., E. L. Quarantelli, and Jorge L. Mendoza. "The Collective Behavior of Fads: The Characteristics, Effects, and Career of Streaking." In *Collective Behavior and Social Movements,* Russell L. Curtis, Jr., and Benigno E. Aguirre, eds. Boston: Allyn and Bacon, 1993:168–182.

Ahlburg, Dennis A., and Carol J. De Vita. "New Realities of the American Family." *Population Bulletin, 47, 2,* August 1992:1–44.

Akol, Jacob. "Slavery in Sudan." *New African,* September 1998.

Albert, Ethel M. "Women of Burundi: A Study of Social Values." In *Women of Tropical Africa,* Denise Paulme, ed. Berkeley: University of California Press, 1963:179–215.

Aldrich, Nelson W., Jr. *Old Money: The Mythology of America's Upper Class.* New York: Vintage Books, 1989.

Allen, Katherine R., and David H. Demo. "The Families of Lesbians and Gay Men: A New Frontier in Family Research." *Journal of Marriage and the Family, 57,* February 1995:111–127.

Allport, Floyd. *Social Psychology.* Boston: Houghton Mifflin, 1954.

Alter, Joel. *Recidivism of Adult Felons.* St. Paul: State of Minnesota, January 1997.

Alter, Jonathan. "From the Prison of the 'Isms.'" *Newsweek,* January 1, 2000:31.

Altman, Lawrence K. "AIDS Virus Transmitted by Deep Kissing." *New York Times,* July 11, 1997.

Altman, Lawrence K. "Researchers Trace the AIDS Virus to a Subspecies of Chimpanzee in Africa." *New York Times,* February 1, 1999.

Amenta, Edwin, Bruce G. Carruthers, and Yvonne Zylan. "A Hero for the Aged? The Townsend Movement, the Political Mediation Model, and U.S. Old-Age Policy, 1934–1950." In *Social Movements: Readings on Their Emergence, Mobilization, and Dynamics,* Doug McAdam and David A. Snow, eds. Los Angeles: Roxbury Publishing, 1997:494–510.

American Federation of Teachers. *Survey and Analysis of Teacher Salary Trends 1998.* Washington, D.C.: American Federation of Teachers, 1998.

American Sociological Association, "Section on Environment and Technology." Pamphlet, no date.

American Sociological Association. "Code of Ethics." Washington, D.C.: American Sociological Association, August 14, 1989; Spring 1997.

Andersen, Margaret L. *Thinking About Women: Sociological Perspectives on Sex and Gender.* New York: Macmillan, 1988.

Anderson, Chris. "NORC Study Describes Homeless." *Chronicle,* 1986:5, 9.

Anderson, Elijah. *A Place on the Corner.* Chicago: University of Chicago Press, 1978.

Anderson, Elijah. *Streetwise.* Chicago: University of Chicago Press, 1990.

Anderson, Elijah. "Streetwise." In *Down to Earth Sociology: Introductory Readings,* 10th ed., James M. Henslin, ed. New York: Free Press, 1999:193–202.

Anderson, Nels. *The Hobo.* Chicago: University of Chicago Press, 1923.

Anderson, Nels. *Desert Saints: The Mormon Frontier in Utah.* Chicago: University of Chicago Press, 1966. First published in 1942.

Anderson, Philip. "God and the Swedish Immigrants." *Sweden and America,* Autumn 1995:17–20.

Anderson, Teresa A. "The Best Years of Their Lives." *Newsweek,* January 7, 1985:6.

Angell, Marcia. "Euthanasia in the Netherlands—Good News or Bad?" *New England Journal of Medicine, 335,* 22, November 28, 1996.

Annez, Patricia. "Livable Cities for the 21st Century." *Society, 35,* 4, May–June 1998:45–50.

Annin, Peter, and Kendall Hamilton. "Marriage or Rape?" *Newsweek,* December 16, 1996:78.

Ansberry, Clare. "Despite Federal Law, Hospitals Still Reject Sick Who Can't Pay." *Wall Street Journal,* November 29, 1988:A1, A4.

Ansberry, Clare. "Nannies and Mothers Struggle over Roles in Raising Children." *Wall Street Journal,* May 21, 1993:A1, A6.

"Anybody's Son Will Do." National Film Board of Canada, KCTS, and Films, Inc. 1983.

Aptheker, Herbert. "W.E.B. Du Bois: Struggle Not Despair." *Clinical Sociology Review, 8,* 1990:58–68.

Arías, Jesús. "La Junta rehabilita en Grenada casas que deberá tirar por ruina." *El Pais,* January 2, 1993:1.

Ariés, Philippe. *Centuries of Childhood.* R. Baldick, trans. New York: Vintage Books, 1965.

Arlacchi, P. *Peasants and Great Estates: Society in Traditional Calabria.* Cambridge, England: Cambridge University Press, 1980.

Armitage, Richard L. "Red Army Retreat Doesn't Signal End of U.S. Obligation." *Wall Street Journal,* February 7, 1989:A20.

Arndt, William F., and F. Wilbur Gingrich. *A Greek-English Lexicon of the New Testament and Other Early Christian Literature.* Chicago: University of Chicago Press, 1957.

Asch, Solomon. "Effects of Group Pressure Upon the Modification and Distortion of Judgments." In *Readings in Social Psychology,* Guy Swanson, Theodore M. Newcomb, and Eugene L. Hartley, eds. New York: Holt, Rinehart and Winston, 1952.

Ashe, Arthur. "A Zero-Sum Game That Hurts Blacks." *Wall Street Journal,* February 27, 1992:A10.

Ashford, Lori S. "New Perspectives on Population: Lessons from Cairo." *Population Bulletin, 50,* 1, March 1995:1–44.

Ashley, Richard. *Cocaine: Its History, Uses, and Effects.* New York: St. Martin's, 1975.

Associated Press. "Clinton Will Announce Welfare Rolls Are at Their Lowest Level in 30 Years." *Wall Street Journal,* January 25, 1999.

Associated Press. "Future Medicine Looks Futuristic." December 2, 1995.

Atchley, Robert C. "Dimensions of Widowhood in Later Life." *Gerontologist, 15,* April 1975:176–178.

Auerbach, Judith D. "Employer-Supported Child Care as a Women-Responsive Policy." *Journal of Family Issues, 11,* 4, December 1990:384–400.

Ayittey, George B. N. "Black Africans Are Enraged at Arabs." *Wall Street Journal,* interactive edition, September 4, 1998.

Baca Zinn, Maxine. "Adaptation and Continuity in Mexican-Origin Families." In *Minority Families in the United States: A Multicultural Perspective,* Ronald L. Taylor, ed. Englewood Cliffs, N.J.: Prentice Hall, 1994:64–81.

Badgett, M. V. Lee, and Heidi Hartmann. "The Effectiveness of Equal Employment Opportunity Policies." In *Economic Perspectives in Affirmative Action,* Margaret C. Simms, ed. Washington, D.C.: Joint Center for Political and Economic Studies 1995:55–83.

Bai, Matt. "Anatomy of a Massacre." *Newsweek,* May 3, 1999:25–31.

Bainbridge, William Sims. "Collective Behavior and Social Movements." In *Sociology,* Rodney Stark. Belmont, Calif.: Wadsworth, 1989:608–640.

Bales, Robert F. *Interaction Process Analysis.* Reading, Mass.: Addison-Wesley, 1950.

Bales, Robert F. "The Equilibrium Problem in Small Groups." In *Working Papers in the Theory of Action,* Talcott Parsons et al., eds. New York: Free Press, 1953:111–115.

Ballantine, Jeanne H. *The Sociology of Education: A Systematic Analysis.* Englewood Cliffs, N.J.: Prentice Hall, 1983.

Baltzell, E. Digby. *Puritan Boston and Quaker Philadelphia.* New York: Free Press, 1979.

Baltzell, E. Digby, and Howard G. Schneiderman. "Social Class in the Oval Office." *Society, 25,* Sept/Oct, 1988:42–49.

Bannon, Lisa. "How a Rumor Spread About Subliminal Sex in Disney's 'Aladdin'." *Wall Street Journal,* October 24, 1995:A1, A6.

Barbeau, Clayton, "The Man–Woman Crisis." In *Marriage and Family in a Changing Society,* 4th ed. James M. Henslin, ed. New York: Free Press, 1992:193–199.

Barberis, Mary. "Egypt." *Population Today, 22,* 6, June 1994:7.

Barkun, Michael. "Reflections After Waco: Millenialists and the State." *Christian Century,* June 2–9, 1993:596–600.

Barnes, Fred. "How to Rig a Poll." *Wall Street Journal,* June 14, 1995:A14.

Barnes, Harry Elmer. *The History of Western Civilization,* Vol. 1. New York: Harcourt, Brace, 1935.

Baron, Robert, and Gerald Greenberg. *Behavior in Organizations.* Boston: Allyn and Bacon, 1990.

Barry, Paul. "Strong Medicine: A Talk with Former Principal Henry Gradillas." *College Board Review,* Fall 1989:2–13.

Bartlett, Donald L., and James B. Steele. "Paying a Price for Polluters." *Time,* November 23, 1998:72–80.

Bazell, Robert. "Medical Errors a Major Killer." NBC Nightly News, November 29, 1999.

Beals, Ralph L., and Harry Hoijer. *An Introduction to Anthropology,* 3rd ed. New York: Macmillan, 1965.

Beck, Allen J., Susan A. Kline, and Lawrence A. Greenfeld. "Survey of Youth in Custody, 1987." Washington, D.C.: U.S. Department of Justice, September 1988.

Beck, Scott H., and Joe W. Page. "Involvement in Activities and the Psychological Well-Being of Retired Men." *Activities, Adaptation, & Aging, 11,* 1, 1988:31–47.

Becker, Howard S. *Outsiders: Studies in the Sociology of Deviance.* New York: Free Press, 1966.

Beckett, Paul. "Even Piñatas Sold in Mexico Seem to Originate in Hollywood Now." *Wall Street Journal,* September 11, 1996:B1.

Beckman, Linda J., and S. Marie Harvey. *The New Civil War: The Psychology, Culture, and Politics of Abortion.* New York: American Psychological Association, 1998.

Beeghley, Leonard. *The Structure of Social Stratification in the United States,* 2nd ed. Boston: Allyn and Bacon, 1996.

Beeghley, Leonard. *The Structure of Social Stratification in the United States,* 3rd ed. Boston: Allyn and Bacon, 2000.

Begley, Sharon. "Twins: Nazi and Jew." *Newsweek, 94,* December 3, 1979:139.

Begley, Sharon. "Odds on the Greenhouse." *Newsweek,* December 1, 1997:72.

Belkin, Lisa. "A Brutal Cure." *New York Times Magazine,* May 30, 1999.

Bell, Daniel. *The Coming of Post-Industrial Society: A Venture in Social Forecasting.* New York: Basic Books, 1973.

Bell, David A. "An American Success Story: The Triumph of Asian-Americans." In *Sociological Footprints: Introductory Readings in Sociology,* 5th ed., Leonard Cargan and Jeanne H. Ballantine, eds. Belmont, Calif.: Wadsworth, 1991:308–316.

Bellah, Robert N. *Beyond Belief.* New York: Harper & Row, 1970.

Benales, Carlos. "70 Days Battling Starvation and Freezing in the Andes: A Chronicle of Man's Unwillingness to Die." *New York Times,* January 1, 1973:3.

Bender, Sue, "Everyday Sacred: A Journey to the Amish." *Utne Reader,* September–October 1990:91–97.

Bender, William, and Margaret Smith. "Population, Food, and Nutrition." *Population Bulletin, 51,* 4, February 1997:1–47.

Benet, Sula. "Why They Live to Be 100, or Even Older, in Abkhasia." *New York Times Magazine, 26,* December 1971.

Bennett, Neil G., Ann Klimas Blanc, and David E. Bloo. "Commitment and the Modern Union: Assessing the Link between Premarital Cohabitation and Subsequent Marital Stability." *American Sociological Review, 53,* 1988:127–138.

Bergen, Raquel Kennedy. *Wife Rape: Understanding the Response of Survivors and Service Providers.* Newbury Park, Calif.: Sage, 1996.

Berger, Peter L. *Invitation to Sociology: A Humanistic Perspective.* New York: Doubleday, 1963.

Berger, Peter L. *The Capitalist Revolution: Fifty Propositions About Prosperity, Equality, and Liberty.* New York: Basic Books, 1991.

Berger, Peter L. "Invitation to Sociology." In *Down to Earth Sociology: Introductory Readings,* 10th ed., James M. Henslin, ed. New York: Free Press, 1999:3–7.

Bergmann, Barbara R. "The Future of Child Care." Paper presented at the 1995 meetings of the American Sociological Association.

Bergström, Hans. "Pressures Behind the Swedish Health Reforms." *Viewpoint Sweden, 12,* July 1992:1–5.

Berk, Laura E. *Child Development,* 3rd ed. Boston: Allyn and Bacon, 1994.

Berk, Richard A. *Collective Behavior.* Dubuque, Iowa: Brown, 1974.

Berle, Adolf, Jr., and Gardiner C. Means. *The Modern Corporation and Private Property.* New York: Harcourt, Brace and World, 1932. As cited in Useem 1980:44.

Bernard, Jessie. *The Future of Marriage.* New York: Bantam, 1972.

Bernard, Jessie. "The Good-Provider Role." In *Marriage and Family in a Changing Society,* 4th ed., James M. Henslin, ed. New York: Free Press, 1992:275–285.

Bernard, Viola W., Perry Ottenberg, and Fritz Redl. "Dehumanization: A Composite Psychological Defense in Relation to Modern War." In *The Triple Revolution Emerging: Social Problems in Depth,* Robert Perucci and Marc Pilisuk, eds. Boston: Little, Brown, 1971:17–34.

Bernstein, Jonas. "How the Russian Mafia Rules." *Wall Street Journal,* October 26, 1994:A20.

Bernstein, Richard. "Play Penn." *New Republic,* August 2, 1993.

Bird, Chloe E. "Gender Differences in the Social and Economic Burdens of Parenting and Psychological Distress." *Journal of Marriage and the Family, 59,* August 1997:1–16.

Bishop, Jerry E. "Study Finds Doctors Tend to Postpone Heart Surgery for Women, Raising Risk." *Wall Street Journal,* April 16, 1990:B4.

Blackwelder, Stephen P. "Duality of Structure in the Reproduction of Race, Class, and Gender Inequality." Paper presented at the 1993 meetings of the American Sociological Association.

Blau, Francine D., and Lawrence M. Kahn. "The Gender Earnings Gap: Some International Evidence." Working Paper No. 4224, National Bureau of Economic Research, December 1992.

Blau, Peter M., and Otis Dudley Duncan. *The American Occupational Structure.* New York: John Wiley, 1967.

Blauner, Robert. "Death and Social Structure." *Psychiatry, 29,* 1966:378–394.

Bloom, Dan, Veronica Fellerath, David Long, and Robert G. Wood. *LEAP: Interim Findings on a Welfare Initiative to Improve School Attendance Among Teenage Parents.* New York: Manpower Demonstration Research Corporation, May 1993.

Blumer, Herbert George. "Collective Behavior." In *Principles of Sociology,* Robert E. Park, ed. New York: Barnes and Noble, 1939:219–288.

Blumer, Herbert. "Sociological Implications of the Thought of George Herbert Mead." *American Journal of Sociology, 71,* 1966:535–544.

Blumer, Herbert. *Industrialization as an Agent of Social Change: A Critical Analysis,* David R. Maines and Thomas J. Morrione, eds. Hawthorne, N.Y.: Aldine de Gruyter, 1990.

Blumstein, Alfred, and Jacqueline Cohen. "Characterizing Criminal Careers." *Science, 237,* August 1987:985–991.

Blumstein, Philip, and Pepper Schwartz. *American Couples: Money, Work, Sex.* New York: Pocket Books, 1985.

Bobo, Lawrence, and James R. Kluegel. "Modern American Prejudice: Stereotypes, Social Distance, and Perceptions of Discrimination Toward Blacks, Hispanics, and Asians." Paper presented at the 1991 annual meetings of the American Sociological Association.

Bogardus, Emory S. *A History of Social Thought,* 2nd ed. Los Angeles: Jesse Ray Miller, 1929.

Bolgar, Robert, Hallie Zweig-Frank, and Joel Paris. "Childhood Antecedents of Interpersonal Problems in Young Adult Children of Divorce." *Journal of the American Academy of Child and Adolescent Psychiatry, 34,* 2, February 1995:143–150.

Booth, Alan, and James M. Dabbs, Jr. "Testosterone and Men's Marriages." *Social Forces, 72,* 2, December 1993:463–477.

Boulding, Elise. *The Underside of History.* Boulder, Colo.: Westview Press, 1976.

Bourgois, Philippe. "Crack in Spanish Harlem." In *Haves and Have-Nots: An International Reader on Social Inequality,* James Curtis and Lorne Tepperman, eds. Englewood Cliffs, N.J.: Prentice Hall, 1994:131–136.

Bowles, Samuel. "Unequal Education and the Reproduction of the Social Division of Labor." In *Power and Ideology in Education,* J. Karabel and A. H. Halsely, eds. New York: Oxford University Press, 1977.

Bowles, Samuel, and Herbert Gintis. *Schooling in Capitalist America.* New York: Basic Books, 1976.

Bradley, Martin B., Norman M. Green, Jr., Dale E. Jones, Mac Lynn, and Lou McNiel. *Churches and Church Membership in the United States 1990.* Atlanta: Glenmary Research Center, 1992.

Brajuha, Mario, and Lyle Hallowell. "Legal Intrusion and the Politics of Fieldwork: The Impact of the Brajuha Case." *Urban Life, 14,* 4, January 1986:454–478.

Brannon, Linda. *Gender: Psychological Perspectives,* 2nd ed. Boston: Allyn and Bacon, 1999.

Brauchli, Marcus W. "China Cranks Up Propaganda Machine and Releases Dissident in Olympics Bid." *Wall Street Journal,* September 15, 1993a:A11.

Brauchli, Marcus W. "A Satellite TV System Is Quickly Moving Asia into the Global Village." *Wall Street Journal,* May 10, 1993b:A1, A8.

Brauchli, Marcus W. "Wary of Education But Needing Brains, China Faces a Dilemma." *Wall Street Journal,* November 15, 1994:A1, A10.

Bray, Rosemary L. "Rosa Parks: A Legendary Moment, a Lifetime of Activism. *Ms., 6,* 3, November–December 1995:45–47.

Breaux, Kia Shante. "Foundation Acknowledges Jefferson Fathered Heming's Child." Associated Press, January 27, 2000.

Brecher, Edward M., and the Editors of Consumer Reports. *Licit and Illicit Drugs.* Boston: Little, Brown, 1972.

Breen, Richard, and Christopher T. Whelan. "Gender and Class Mobility: Evidence from the Republic of Ireland." *Sociology, 29,* 1, February 1995:1–22.

Bretos, Miguel A. "Hispanics Face Institutional Exclusion." *Miami Herald,* May 22, 1994.

Bridgman, Ann. "Report from the Russian Front." *Education Week,* April 6, 1994:22–29.

Bridgwater, William, ed. *The Columbia Viking Desk Encyclopedia.* New York: Viking Press, 1953.

Brilliant, Ashleigh E. *Social Effects of the Automobile in Southern California During the 1920s.* Unpublished doctoral dissertation, University of California at Berkeley, 1964.

Brines, Julie. "Economic Dependency, Gender, and the Division of Labor at Home." *American Journal of Sociology, 100,* 3, November 1994:652–688.

Brink, Susan. "Elderly Empowerment." *U.S. News & World Report,* April 26, 1993:65–70.

Brinton, Crane. *The Anatomy of Revolution.* New York: Vintage Books, 1965.

Broad, William J. "The Shuttle Explodes." *New York Times,* January 29, 1986, A1, A5.

Broad, William J., and Judith Miller. "Rocky Start for U.S. Plan to Stockpile Vaccines to Fight Germ Warfare." *New York Times,* August 7, 1998.

Brockerhoff, Martin. " 'City Summit' to Address Global Urbanization." *Population Today, 24,* March 1996:4–5.

Bromley, David G. "The Satanic Cult Scare." *Culture and Society,* May–June 1991:55–56.

Bronfenbrenner, Urie. "Principles for the Healthy Growth and Development of Children." In *Marriage and Family in a Changing Society,* 4th ed., James M. Henslin, ed. New York: Free Press, 1992:243–249.

Bronner, Ethan. "In Israel, New Grade School Texts for History Replace Myths With Facts." *New York Times,* August 14, 1999.

Brooke, James. "Amid U.S. Islam's Growth in the U.S., Muslims Face a Surge in Attacks." *New York Times,* August 28, 1995:A1, B7.

Brooks, Virginia R. "Sex Differences in Student Dominance Behavior in Female and Male Professors' Classrooms." *Sex Roles, 8,* 7, 1982:683–690.

Brooks-Gunn, Jeanne, Greg J Duncan, and Lawrence Aber, eds. *Neighborhood Poverty, Volume 1: Context and Consequences for Children.* New York: Russell Sage Foundation, 1997.

Browne, Andrew. "Education Seen as the Solution." *Reuters On Line.* September 8, 1995.

Browning, Christopher R. *Ordinary Men: Reserve Police Battalion 101 and the Final Solution in Poland.* New York: HarperPerennial, 1993.

Brownstein, Ronald, and Robert A. Rosenblatt. "Extra Serving of Surplus to Elderly Raises Eyebrows." *Los Angeles Times,* February 2, 1999.

Brunvand, Jan Harold. *The Vanishing Hitchhiker: American Urban Legends and Their Meanings.* New York: Norton, 1981.

Brunvand, Jan Harold. *The Choking Doberman and Other "New" Urban Legends.* New York: Norton, 1984.

Brunvand, Jan Harold. *The Study of American Folklore.* New York: Norton, 1986.

Bryant, Clifton D. "Cockfighting: America's Invisible Sport." In *Down to Earth Sociology: Introductory Readings,* 7th ed., James M. Henslin, ed. New York: Free Press, 1993.

Brzezinksi, Matthew. "Where Cash Isn't King: Barter Lines Pockets in Ex-Soviet States." *Wall Street Journal,* May 1, 1997:A14.

Buechler, Steven M. "Beyond Resource Mobilization: Emerging Trends in Social Movement Theory." *Sociological Quarterly, 34,* 2, 1993:217–235.

Bumiller, Elisabeth. "First Comes Marriage—Then, Maybe, Love." In *Marriage and Family in a Changing Society,* 4th ed , James M. Henslin, ed. New York: Free Press, 1992:120–125.

Bumiller, Elisabeth. "Weekend Excursion: In Amish Land, Witnesses to Old and New." *New York Times,* June 26, 1998.

Bureau of Labor Statistics. "News: U.S. Department of Labor." February 4, 2000.

Bumpass, Larry L., James A. Sweet, and Andrew Cherlin. "The Role of Cohabitation in Declining Rates of Marriage." *Journal of Marriage and the Family, 53,* November 1991:913–927.

Bureau of the Census. "Income, Poverty, and Valuation of Noncash Benefits: 1994." *Current Population Reports* P60–189. Washington, D.C.: GPO, 1996.

Burgess, Ernest W. "The Growth of the City: An Introduction to a Research Project." In *The City*, Robert E. Park, Ernest W. Burgess, and Roderick D. McKenzie, eds. Chicago: University of Chicago Press, 1925:47–62.

Burgess, Ernest W., and Harvey J. Locke. *The Family: From Institution to Companionship.* New York: American Book, 1945.

Burnham, Walter Dean. *Democracy in the Making: American Government and Politics.* Englewood Cliffs, N.J.: Prentice Hall, 1983.

Bush, Diane Mitsch, and Robert G. Simmons. "Socialization Processes Over the Life Course." In *Social Psychology: Sociological Perspectives*, eds. Morris Rosenberger and Ralph H. Turner. New Brunswick, N.J.:Transaction, 1990:133–164.

Butler, Robert N. *Why Survive? Being Old in America.* New York: Harper & Row, 1975.

Butler, Robert N. "Ageism: Another Form of Bigotry." *Gerontologist, 9,* Winter 1980:243–246.

Buttel, Frederick H. "New Directions in Environmental Sociology." *Annual Review of Sociology, 13,* W. Richard Scott and James F. Short, Jr., eds. Palo Alto, Calif.: Annual Reviews, 1987:465–488.

Butterworth, Katharine M. "The Story of a Nursing Home Refugee." In *Social Problems 92/93,* LeRoy W. Barnes, ed. Guilford, Conn.: Dushkin, 1992:90–93.

Callahan, Daniel. *Setting Limits: Medical Goals in an Aging Society.* New York: Simon & Schuster, 1987.

Canavan, Margaret M., Walter J. Meyer, III, and Deborah C. Higgs. "The Female Experience of Sibling Incest." *Journal of Marital and Family Therapy, 18,* 2, 1992:129–142.

Cannon, Lou. *Official Negligence: How Rodney King and the Riots Changed Los Angeles and the LAPD.* New York: Times Books, 1998.

Cantril, Hadley. *The Psychology of Social Movements.* New York: Wiley, 1941.

Caplow, Theodore. "The American Way of Celebrating Christmas." In *Down to Earth Sociology: Introductory Readings,* 6th ed., James M. Henslin, ed. New York: Free Press, 1991:88–97.

Cardoso, Fernando Henrique. "Dependent Capitalist Development in Latin America." *New Left Review, 74,* July–August 1972:83–95.

Carlson, Lewis H., and George A. Colburn. *In Their Place: White America Defines Her Minorities, 1850–1950.* New York: Wiley, 1972.

Carpenter, Betsy. "Redwood Radicals." *U.S. News & World Report, 109,* 11, September 17, 1990:50–51.

Carr, Deborah, Carol D. Ryff, Burton Singer, and William J. Magee. "Bringing the 'Life' Back into Life Course Research: A 'Person-Centered' Approach to Studying the Life Course." Paper presented at the 1995 meetings of the American Sociological Association.

Carrasquillo, Hector. "The Puerto Rican Family." In *Minority Families in the United States: A Multicultural Perspective,* Ronald L. Taylor, ed. Englewood Cliffs, N.J.: Prentice Hall, 1994:82–94.

Carrington, Tim. "Developed Nations Want Poor Countries to Succeed on Trade, But Not Too Much." *Wall Street Journal,* September 20, 1993:A10.

Cartwright, Dorwin, and Alvin Zander, eds. *Group Dynamics,* 3rd ed. Evanston, Ill.: Peterson, 1968.

Casper, Lynne M., and Martin O'Connell, "State Estimates of Organized Child Care Facilities." Annual meetings of the Population Association of America, March 1997, as contained in *Population Today, 25,* 5, May 1997:6.

Cauthen, Nancy K., and James M. Jasper. "Culture, Politics, and Moral Panics." *Sociological Forum, 9,* 3, September 1994:495–503.

Centers for Disease Control. *HIV/AIDS Surveillance Report, 11,* 1, June 1999.

Cerulo, Karen A., and Janet M. Ruane. "Death Comes Alive: Technology and the Re-Conception of Death." In *Science as Culture,* forthcoming 1996.

Cerulo, Karen A., Janet M. Ruane, and Mary Chayko. "Technological Ties That Bind: Media-Generated Primary Groups." *Communication Research, 19,* 1, February 1992:109–129.

Chafetz, Janet Saltzman. *Masculine/Feminine or Human? An Overview of the Sociology of Sex Roles.* Itasca, Ill.: Peacock, 1974.

Chafetz, Janet Saltzman. *Gender Equity: An Integrated Theory of Stability and Change.* Newbury Park, Calif.: Sage, 1990.

Chafetz, Janet Saltzman, and Anthony Gary Dworkin. *Female Revolt: Women's Movements in World and Historical Perspective.* Totowa, N.J.: Rowman & Allanheld, 1986.

Chagnon, Napoleon A. *Yanomamo: The Fierce People,* 2nd ed. New York: Holt, Rinehart and Winston, 1977.

Chalfant, H. Paul. "Stepping to Redemption: Twelve-Step Groups as Implicit Religion." *Free Inquiry in Creative Sociology, 20,* 2, November 1992:115–120.

Chalkley, Kate. "Female Genital Mutilation: New Laws, Programs Try to End Practice." *Population Today, 25,* 10, October 1997:4–5.

Chambliss, William J. "A Sociological Analysis of the Law of Vagrancy." *Social Problems, 12,* Summer 1964:67–77.

Chambliss, William J. "The Saints and the Roughnecks." In *Down to Earth Sociology: Introductory Readings,* 10th ed., James M. Henslin, ed. New York: Free Press, 1999:260–274. First published in *Society, 11,* 1973.

Chandler, Tertius, and Gerald Fox. *3000 Years of Urban Growth.* New York: Academic Press, 1974.

Chandra, Vibha P. "Fragmented Identities: The Social Construction of Ethnicity, 1885–1947." Unpublished paper, 1993a.

Chandra, Vibha P. "The Present Moment of the Past: The Metamorphosis." Unpublished paper, 1993b.

Chapman, Gary. "Are Computers on a Pathway to Replace the Human Species?" *Los Angeles Times,* March 15, 1999.

Charlier, Marj. "Little Bighorn from the Indian Point of View." *Wall Street Journal,* September 15, 1992:A12.

Chavez, Linda. "Rainbow Collision." *New Republic,* November 19, 1990:14–16.

Chen, Edwin. "Twins Reared Apart: A Living Lab." *New York Times Magazine.* December 9, 1979:112.

Chen, Kathy. "China's Women Face Obstacles in Workplace." *Wall Street Journal,* August 28, 1995:B1, B5.

Cherlin, Andrew. "Remarriage as an Incomplete Institution." In *Marriage and Family in a Changing Society,* 3rd ed., James M. Henslin, ed. New York: Free Press, 1989:492–501.

Cherlin, Andrew, and Frank F. Furstenberg, Jr. "The American Family in the Year 2000." In *Down to Earth Sociology,* 5th ed., James M. Henslin, ed. New York: Free Press, 1988:325–331.

Chodorow, Nancy J. "What Is the Relation Between Psychoanalytic Feminism and the Psychoanalytic Psychology of Women?" In *Theoretical Perspectives on Sexual Difference,* Deborah L. Rhode, ed. New Haven, Conn.: Yale University Press, 1990:114–130.

Chu, Henry. "China's Declining Health." *Los Angeles Times,* December 24, 1998.

Chua-Eoan, Howard. "Tripped Up by Lies." *Time,* October 11, 1993:39–40.

Clair, Jeffrey Michael., David A. Karp, and William C. Yoels. *Experiencing the Life Cycle: A Social Psychology of Aging,* 2nd ed. Springfield, Ill.: Thomas, 1993.

Clark, Candace. "Sympathy in Everyday Life." In *Down to Earth Sociology: Introductory Readings,* 6th ed., James M. Henslin, ed. New York: Free Press, 1991:193–203.

Clark, Lindley H., Jr. "How the Biggest Lobby Grew." *Wall Street Journal,* January 27, 1994:A14.

Clay, Jason W. "What's a Nation?" *Mother Jones,* November–December 1990:28, 30.

Clingempeel, W. Glenn, and N. Dickon Repucci. "Joint Custody After Divorce: Major Issues and Goals for Research." *Psychological Bulletin, 9,* 1982:102–127.

Cloward, Richard A., and Lloyd E. Ohlin. *Delinquency and Opportunity: A Theory of Delinquent Gangs.* New York: Free Press, 1960.

Cnaan, Ram A. "Neighborhood-representing Organizations: How Democratic Are They?" *Social Science Review,* December 1991:614–634.

Cockerham, William C. "The Social Determinants of the Decline of Life Expectancy in Russia and Eastern Europe: A Lifestyle Explanation." *Journal of Health and Social Behavior, 38,* June 1997:117–130.

Cohen, Adam. "The Great American Welfare Lab." *Time,* April 21, 1997:74–76, 78.

Cohen, Joel E. "How Many People Can the Earth Support?" *Population Today,* January 1996:4–5.

Cohen, Steven M. "Hey NCR—We're the Shareholders, You Work for Us." *Wall Street Journal,* December 19, 1990:A16.

Cole, Jeff, and Sarah Lubman. "Weapons Merchants Are Going Great Guns in Post-Cold War Era." *Wall Street Journal,* January 28, 1994:A1, A4.

Coleman, James S., and Thomas Hoffer. *Public and Private Schools: The Impact of Communities.* New York: Basic Books, 1987.

Coleman, James William. *The Criminal Elite: The Sociology of White Collar Crime.* New York: St. Martin's Press, 1989.

Coleman, James William. "Politics and the Abuse of Power." In *Down to Earth Sociology: Introductory Readings,* 8th ed., James M. Henslin, ed. New York: Free Press, 1995:442–450.

Collins, Randall. *Conflict Sociology: Toward an Explanatory Science.* New York: Academic Press, 1974.

Collins, Randall. *The Credential Society: An Historical Sociology of Education.* New York: Academic Press, 1979.

Collins, Randall. *Theoretical Sociology.* San Diego, Calif.: Harcourt, Brace Jovanovich, 1988.

Collins, Randall, Janet Saltzman Chafetz, Rae Lesser Blumberg, Scott Coltrane, and Jonathan H. Turner. "Toward an Integrated Theory of Gender Stratification." *Sociological Perspectives, 36,* 3, 1993:185–216.

Conahan, Frank C. "Human Experimentation: An Overview on Cold War Era Programs." Washington, D.C.: U.S. General Accounting Office, September 28, 1994:1–11.

Conrad, Peter. "Public Eyes and Private Genes: Historical Frames, New Constructions, and Social Problems." *Social Problems, 44,* 2, May 1997:139–154.

Cooley, Charles Horton. *Human Nature and the Social Order.* New York: Scribner's, 1902.

Cooley, Charles Horton. *Social Organization.* New York: Schocken, 1962. First published by Scribner's, 1909.

Coolidge, David Orgon. "At Last, Hawaiians Have Their Say on Gay Marriage." *Wall Street Journal,* April 23, 1997:A19.

Cooper, Helene. "Offering Aerobics, Karate, Aquatics, Hospitals Stress Business of 'Wellness.' " *Wall Street Journal,* August 9, 1993:B1, B3.

Cooper, Kenneth J. "New Focus Sought in National High School Exams: NEH Backs Approach Used in Europe and Japan to Assess Knowledge Rather Than Aptitude." *Washington Post,* May 20, 1991:A7.

Corbett, Thomas. "Welfare Reform in the 104th Congress: Goals, Options, and Tradeoffs." *Focus, 17,* 1, Summer 1995:29–31.

Corbett, Thomas. "Poverty: Improving the Measure After Thirty Years, A Conference." *Focus, 20,* 2, Spring 1999:51–55.

Corbin, Robert K. "The President's Column." *American Rifleman,* December 1993:56.

Cose, Ellis. "The Good News About Black America." *Newsweek,* June 7, 1999:29–40.

Coser, Lewis A. *Masters of Sociological Thought: Ideas in Historical and Social Context,* 2nd ed. New York: Harcourt Brace Jovanovich, 1977.

Cottin, Lou. *Elders in Rebellion: A Guide to Senior Activism.* Garden City, N.Y.: Anchor Doubleday, 1979.

Couch, Carl J. *Social Processes and Relationships: A Formal Approach.* Dix Hills, N.Y.: General Hall, 1989.

Coughlin, Ellen K. "Studying Homelessness: The Difficulty of Tracking a Transient Population." *Chronicle of Higher Education,* October 19, 1988:A6–A12.

Courtney, Kelly. "Two Sides of the Environmental Movement: Radical Earth First! and the Sierra Club." Paper presented at the 1995 meetings of the American Sociological Association.

Cousins, Albert, and Hans nagpaul. *Urban Man and Society.* New York: McGraw-Hill, 1970.

Cowen, Emory L., Judah Landes, and Donald E. Schaet. "The Effects of Mild Frustration on the Expression of Prejudiced Attitudes." *Journal of Abnormal and Social Psychology.* January 1959:33–38.

Cowgill, Donald. "The Aging of Populations and Societies." *Annals of the American Academy of Political and Social Science, 415,* 1974:1–18.

Cowley, Geoffrey. "Attention: Aging Men." *Newsweek,* November 16, 1996:66–75.

Cowley, Geoffrey. "Sobering Up About AIDS." *Newsweek,* June 26, 1998.

Cowley, Joyce. *Pioneers of Women's Liberation.* New York: Merit, 1969.

Crary, David. "Internet Gives Elderly Link to Life." Associated Press. November 21, 1999.

Croal, N'Gai, and Jane Hughes. "Lara Croft, the Bit Girl." *Newsweek,* November 10, 1997:82, 86.

Crossen, Cynthia. *Wall Street Journal,* November 14, 1991:A1, A7.

Crossette, Barbara. "U.N. Documents Inequities for Women as World Forum Nears." *New York Times,* August 18, 1995a:A3.

Crossette, Barbara. "Worldwide Study Finds Decline in Election of Women Legislators." *New York Times,* August 27, 1995b.

Crossman, Donna K. "Global Structural Violence Against Women." Paper presented at the 1995 meetings of the American Sociological Association.

Cumming, Elaine. "Further Thoughts on the Theory of Disengagement." In *Aging in America: Readings in Social Gerontology,* Cary S. Kart and Barbara B. Manard, eds. Sherman Oaks, Calif.: Alfred Publishing, 1976:19–41.

Cumming, Elaine, and William E. Henry. *Growing Old: The Process of Disengagement.* New York: Basic Books, 1961.

Curtin, Sharon. "Nobody Ever Died of Old Age: In Praise of Old People." In *Growing Old in America.* Beth Hess, ed. New Brunswick, N.J.: Transaction, 1976:273–284.

Curwin, E. Cecil, and Gudmond Hart. *Plough and Pasture.* New York: Collier Books, 1961.

Cushman, John H., Jr. "Industries Press Plan for Credits in Emissions Control." *New York Times,* January 3, 1999.

Dabbs, James M., Jr., and Robin Morris. "Testosterone, Social Class, and Antisocial Behavior in a Sample of 4,462 Men." *Psychological Science, 1,* 3, May 1990:209–211.

Dabbs, James M., Jr., Timothy S. Carr, Robert L. Frady, and Jasmin K. Riad. "Testosterone, Crime, and Misbehavior Among 692 Male Prison Inmates." *Personality and Individual Differences, 18,* 1995:627–633.

Dabbs, James M., Jr., Marian F. Hargrove, and Colleen Heusel. "Testosterone Differences Among College Fraternities: Well-Behaved vs. Rambunctious." *Personality and Individual Differences, 20,* 1996:157–161.

Dahl, Robert A. *Who Governs?* New Haven, Conn.: Yale University Press, 1961.

Dahl, Robert A. *Dilemmas of Pluralist Democracy: Autonomy vs. Control.* New Haven, Conn.: Yale University Press, 1982.

Dahrendorf, Ralf. *Class and Class Conflict in Industrial Society.* Palo Alto, Calif.: Stanford University Press, 1959.

Daniels, Roger. *The Decision to Relocate the Japanese Americans.* Philadelphia: Lippincott, 1975.

Dannefer, Dale. "Adult Development and Social Theory: A Reappraisal." *American Sociological Review, 49,* 1, February 1984:100–116.

Danzi, Angela D. "Savaria, The Midwife: Childbirth and Change in the Immigrant Community." In *Contemporary Readings in Sociology,* Judith N. DeSena, ed. Dubuque, Iowa: Kendall/Hunt, 1989:47–56.

Darden, Christoper. *Contempt.* New York: HarperCollins, 1997.

Darley, John M., and Bibb Latané. "Bystander Intervention in Emergencies: Diffusion of Responsibility." *Journal of Personality and Social Psychology, 8,* 4, 1968:377–383.

Darnell, Victor. "Qualitative-Quantitative Content Analysis of Graffiti in the Public Restrooms of St. Louis, Missouri, and Edwardsville, Illinois." Master's thesis, Southern Illinois University, Edwardsville, May 1971.

Darwin, Charles. *The Origin of Species.* Chicago: Conley, 1859.

Davis, Ann. "Artificial Reproduction Arrangers Are Ruled Child's Legal Parents." *Wall Street Journal,* March 11, 1998a:B2.

Davis, Ann. "High-Tech Births Spawn Legal Riddles." *Wall Street Journal,* January 26, 1998b:B1.

Davis, Fred. "The Cabdriver and His Fare: Facets of a Fleeting Relationship." *American Journal of Sociology, 65,* September 1959:158–165.

Davis, Kingsley. "Extreme Social Isolation of a Child." *American Journal of Sociology, 45,* 4 Jan. 1940:554–565.

Davis, Kingsley. "Extreme Isolation." In *Down to Earth Sociology: Introductory Readings,* 10th ed., James M. Henslin, ed. New York: Free Press, 1999:133–141.

Davis, Kingsley, and Wilbert E. Moore. "Some Principles of Stratification." *American Sociological Review, 10,* 1945:242–249.

Davis, Kingsley, and Wilbert E. Moore. "Reply to Tumin." *American Sociological Review, 18,* 1953:394–396.

Davis, L. J. "Medscam." In *Deviant Behavior 96/97,* Lawrence M. Salinger, ed. Guilford, Conn.: Dushkin, 1996:93–97.

Davis, Nancy J., and Robert V. Robinson. "Class Identification of Men and Women in the 1970s and 1980s." *American Sociological Review, 53,* February 1988:103–112.

Davis, Nanette J. "Prostitution: Identity, Career, and Legal-Economic Enterprise." In *The Sociology of Sex: An Introductory Reader,* rev. ed., James M. Henslin and Edward Sagarin, eds. New York: Schocken Books, 1978:195–222.

Deck, Leland P. "Buying Brains by the Inch." *Journal of the College and University Personnel Association, 19,* 1968:33–37.

Deegan, Mary Jo. "W. E. B. Du Bois and the Women of Hull-House, 1895–1899." *American Sociologist,* Winter 1988:301–311.

De George, Richard T. *The New Marxism: Society and East European Marxism Since 1956.* New York: Pegasus 1968.

DeMause, Lloyd. "Our Forebears Made Childhood a Nightmare." *Psychology Today 8,* 11, April 1975:85–88.

"Democracy and Technology." *The Economist,* June 17, 1995:21–23.

Denney, Nancy W., and David Quadagno. *Human Sexuality,* 2nd ed. St. Louis: Mosby, 1992.

Denzin, Norman K. "The Suicide Machine." *Society,* July–August, 1992:7–10.

DePalma, Anthony. "Rare in Ivy League: Women Who Work as Full Professors." *New York Times,* January 24, 1993:1, 23.

DeParle, Jason. "Report to Clinton Sees Vast Extent of Homelessness." *New York Times,* February 17, 1994:A1, A10.

DeParle, Jason. "Bold Effort Leaves Much Unchanged for the Poor." *New York Times,* December 30, 1999.

Derber, Charles, and William Schwartz. "Toward a Theory of Worker Participation." In *The Transformation of Industrial Organization: Management, Labor, and Society in the United States,* Frank Hearn, ed. Belmont, Calif.: Wadsworth, 1988:217–229.

Dervarics, Charles. "Is Welfare Reform Reforming Welfare?" *Population Today, 26,* 10, October 1998:1–2.

deYoung, Mary. "The World According to NAMBLA: Accounting for Deviance." *Journal of Sociology and Social Welfare, 16,* 1, March 1989:111–126.

Diamond, Edwin, and Robert A. Silverman. *White House to Your House: Media and Politics in Virtual America.* Cambridge, Mass.: MIT Press, 1995.

Diamond, Milton, and Keith Sigmundson. "Sex Reassignment at Birth: Long-term Review and Clinical Implications." *Archives of Pediatric and Adolescent Medicine, 151,* March 1997:298–304.

Dickey, Christopher. "The Death of Innocents." *Newsweek,* September 2, 1996:51.

Diekmann, Andreas, and Henrietta Engelhardt. "The Social Inheritance of Divorce: Effects of Parent's Family Type in Postwar Germany." *American Sociological Review, 64,* December 1999:783–793.

DiGiulio, Robert C. "Beyond Widowhood." In *Marriage and Family in a Changing Society,* 4th ed., James M. Henslin, ed. New York: Free Press, 1992:457–469.

Dillin, John. "Congress Begins Search for Answers in Waco Tragedy." *Christian Science Monitor,* April 22, 1993:1, 4.

Diver-Stamnes, Ann C., and R. Murray Thomas. *Prevent, Repent, Reform, Revenge: A Study in Adolescent Moral Development.* Westport, CT.: Greenwood Press, 1995.

Dixon, Celvia Stovall, and Kathryn D. Rettig. "An Examination of Income Adequacy for Single Women Two Years After Divorce." *Journal of Divorce and Remarriage, 22,* 1–2, 1994:55–71.

Doane, Ashley W., Jr. "Bringing the Majority Back In: Towards a Sociology of Dominant Group Ethnicity." Paper presented at the annual meetings of the Society for the Study of Social Problems, 1993.

Dobash, Russell P., and R. Emerson Dobash. "Community Response to Violence Against Wives: Charivari, Abstract Justice and Patriarchy." *Social Problems, 28,* June 1981:563–581.

Dobash, Russell P., R. Emerson Dobash, Margo Wilson, and Martin Daly. "The Myth of Sexual Symmetry in Marital Violence." *Social Problems, 39,* 1, February 1992:71–91.

Dobash, Russell P., R. Emerson Dobash, Margo Wilson, and Martin Daly. "Marital Violence Is Not Symmetrical: A Response to Campbell." *SSSP Newsletter, 24,* 3, Fall 1993:26–30.

Dobriner, William M. "The Football Team as Social Structure and Social System." In *Social Structures and Systems: A Sociological Overview.* Pacific Palisades, Calif.: Goodyear, 1969a:116–120.

Dobriner, William M. *Social Structures and Systems.* Pacific Palisades, California: Goodyear, 1969b.

Dobyns, Henry F. *Their Numbers Became Thinned: Native American Population Dynamics in Eastern North America.* Knoxville: University of Tennessee Press, 1983.

Dollard, John, et al. *Frustration and Aggression.* New Haven, Conn.: Yale University Press, 1939.

Domhoff, G. William. *Who Rules America?* Englewood Cliffs, N.J.: Prentice Hall, 1967.

Domhoff, G. William. *The Powers That Be.* New York: Random House, 1979.

Domhoff, G. William. *Who Rules America Now? A View of the '80s.* Englewood Cliffs, N.J.: Prentice Hall, 1983.

Domhoff, G. William. *The Power Elite and the State: How Policy Is Made in America.* Hawthorne, N.Y.: Aldine de Gruyter, 1990.

Domhoff, G. William. "The Bohemian Grove and Other Retreats." In *Down to Earth Sociology: Introductory Readings,* 9th ed., James M. Henslin, ed. New York: Free Press, 1997:340–352.

Domhoff, G. William. *Who Rules America? Power and Politics in the Year 2000,* 3rd ed. Mountain View, Calif: Mayfield Publishing, 1998.

Domhoff, G. William. "The Bohemian Grove and Other Retreats." In *Down to Earth Sociology: Introductory Readings,* 10th ed., James M. Henslin, ed. New York: Free Press, 1999:391–403.

Donelson, Samuel. "World News Tonight." Television broadcast. May 25, 1992.

Dove, Adrian. "Soul Folk 'Chitling' Test or the Dove Counterbalance Intelligence Test." no date. (Mimeo)

Drucker, Peter F. "There's More Than One Kind of Team." *Wall Street Journal,* February 11, 1992:A16.

Du Bois, W.E.B. *The Souls of Black Folk: Essays and Sketches.* Chicago: McClurg, 1903.

Du Bois, W.E.B. *Black Reconstruction in America: An Essay Toward a History of the Part Which Black Folk Played in the Attempt to Reconstruct Democracy in America, 1860–1880.* New York: Frank Cass, 1966. First published 1935.

Du Bois, W.E.B. *The Philadelphia Negro: A Social Study.* New York: Schocken Books, 1967. First pubulished in 1899.

Du Bois, W.E.B. *The Autobiography of W. E. B. Du Bois. A Soliloquy on Viewing My Life from the Last Decade of Its First Century.* New York: International, 1968.

Du Bois, W.E.B. *Black Reconstruction in America, 1860–1889.* New York: Atheneum, 1992. First published in 1935.

Dudenhefer, Paul. "Poverty in the Rural United States." *Focus, 15,* 1, Spring 1993:37–46.

Duffy, Michael. "When Lobbyists Become Insiders." *Time,* November 9, 1992:40.

Dugger, Celia W. "Wedding Vows Bind Old World and New." *New York Times,* July 20, 1998.

Dunlap, Riley E., and William R. Catton, Jr. "Environmental Sociology." *Annual Review of Sociology, 5,* 1979:243–273.

Dunlap, Riley E., and William R. Catton, Jr. "What Environmental Sociologists Have in Common Whether Concerned with 'Built' or 'Natural' Environments." *Sociological Inquiry, 53,* 2/3, 1983:113–135.

Dunleavey, M. P. "Reforming the 3 R's: Blueprints for the Schools of Tomorrow." *Publisher's Weekly,* February 21, 1994:33–35.

Durbin, Stefanie. "Mexico." *Population Today,* July–August, 1995:7.

Durkheim, Emile. *The Division of Labor in Society.* George Simpson, trans. New York: Free Press, 1933. First published in 1893.

Durkheim, Emile. *The Rules of Sociological Method.* Sarah A. Solovay and John H. Mueller, trans. New York: Free Press, 1938, 1958, 1964. First published in 1895.

Durkheim, Emile. *Suicide: A Study in Sociology.* John A. Spaulding and George Simpson, trans. New York: Free Press, 1966. First published in 1897.

Durkheim, Emile. *The Elementary Forms of the Religious Life.* New York: Free Press, 1965. First published in 1912.

Durning, Alan. "Cradles of Life." In *Social Problems 90/91,* LeRoy W. Barnes, ed. Guilford, Conn.: Dushkin, 1990:231–241.

Easterbrook, Gregg. "The Revolution in Modern Medicine." *Newsweek, 109,* Jan. 26, 1987:40–74.

Ebaugh, Helen Rose Fuchs. *Becoming an EX: The Process of Role Exit.* Chicago: The University of Chicago Press, 1988.

Ebomoyi, Ehigie. "The Prevalence of Female Circumcision in Two Nigerian Communities." *Sex Roles, 17,* 3/4, 1987:139–151.

Eder, Donna. *School Talk: Gender and Adolescent Culture.* New Brunswick, N.J.: Rutgers University Press, 1995.

Eder, Klaus. "The Rise of Counter-culture Movements Against Modernity: Nature as a New Field of Class Struggle." *Theory, Culture & Society, 7,* 1990:21–47.

Edgar, Gary. Author's interview with Gary Edgar of the Surveillance Branch of the CDC, March 28, 1994.

Edgerton, Robert B. *Deviance: A Cross-Cultural Perspective.* Menlo Park, Calif.: Benjamin/Cummings, 1976.

Edgerton, Robert B. *Sick Societies: Challenging the Myth of Primitive Harmony.* New York: Free Press, 1992.

Edwards, Richard. *Contested Terrain: The Transformation of the Workplace in the Twentieth Century.* New York: Basic Books, 1979.

Egan, Timothy. "Many Seek Security in Private Communities." *New York Times,* September 3, 1995:1, 22.

"Egipto prohibir la ablacion femenina y adoptar medidas contra infractores." *El Pais,* July 19, 1996:22.

"Egypt." *Population Today,* December 1998:7.

Ehrenreich, Barbara, and Deidre English. *Witches, Midwives, and Nurses: A History of Women Healers.* Old Westbury, N.Y.: Feminist Press, 1973.

Ehrlich, Paul R., and Anne H. Ehrlich. *Population, Resources, and Environment: Issues in Human Ecology,* 2nd ed. San Francisco: Freeman, 1972.

Ehrlich, Paul R., and Anne H. Ehrlich. "Humanity at the Crossroads." *Stanford Magazine,* Spring–Summer 1978:20–23.

Erlich, Paul R., and Anne H. Ehrlich. *Betrayal of Science and Reason: How Anti-Environmental Rhetoric Threatens Our Future.* Washington, D.C.: Island Press, 1997.

Eibl-Eibesfeldt, Irrenäus. *Ethology: The Biology of Behavior.* New York: Holt, Rinehart, and Winston, 1970.

Eichler, Margrit. *Nonsexist Research Methods: A Practical Guide.* Winchester, Mass.: Unwin Hyman, 1988.

Eisenhart, R. Wayne. "You Can't Hack It, Little Girl: A Discussion of the Covert Psychological Agenda of Modern Combat Training." *Journal of Social Issues, 31,* Fall 1975:13–23.

Ekman, Paul. *Faces of Man: Universal Expression in a New Guinea Village.* New York: Garland Press, 1980.

Ekman, Paul, Wallace V. Friesen, and John Bear. "The International Language of Gestures." *Psychology Today,* May 1984:64.

Elder, Glen H., Jr. "Age Differentiation and Life Course." *Annual Review of Sociology, 1,* 1975:165–190.

Elkins, Stanley M. *Slavery: A Problem in American Institutional and Intellectual Life,* 2nd ed. Chicago: University of Chicago Press, 1968.

Ellis, Caroline. "Punish and Be Damned." *New Statesman and Society, 17,* 1991:17.

Ellul, Jacques. *The Technological Society.* New York: Knopf, 1965.

El-Meligi, M. Helmy. "Egypt." In *Handbook of World Education: A Comparative Guide to Higher Education and Educational Systems of the World,* Walter Wickremasinghe, ed. Houston, Texas: American Collegiate Service, 1992:219–228.

Epstein, Cynthia Fuchs. "Inevitabilities of Prejudice." *Society,* September–October 1986:7–15.

Epstein, Cynthia Fuchs. *Deceptive Distinctions: Sex, Gender, and the Social Order.* New Haven, Conn.: Yale University Press, 1988.

Epstein, Cynthia Fuchs. Letter to the author, January 26, 1989.

Erik, John. "China's Policy on Births." *New York Times,* January 3, 1982: IV, 19.

Ernst, Eldon G. "The Baptists." In *Encyclopedia of the American Religious Experience: Studies of Traditions and Movements,* Vol. 1, Charles H. Lippy and Peter W. Williams, eds. New York: Scribners, 1988:555–577.

Escalante, Jaime, and Jack Dirmann. "The Jaime Escalante Math Program." *Journal of Negro Education, 59,* 3, Summer 1990:407–423.

Evans, Peter, and James E. Rauch. "Bureaucracy and Growth: A Cross-National Analysis of the Effects of 'Weberian' State Structures on Economic Growth." *American Sociological Review, 64,* October 1999:748–765.

"Executive Pay." *Wall Street Journal,* April 8, 1999:R1.

Ezekiel, Raphael S. *The Racist Mind: Portraits of American Neo-Nazis and Klansmen.* New York: Viking, 1995.

"Faddish Justice." *Wall Street Journal,* May 2, 1995:A19.

Famighetti, Robert, ed. *The World Almanac and Book of Facts 1995.* Mahwah, New Jersey, 1994.

Famighetti, Robert, ed. *The World Almanac and Book of Facts.* Mahwah, New Jersey, 1999.

Faris, Robert E. L., and Warren Dunham. *Mental Disorders in Urban Areas.* Chicago: University of Chicago Press, 1939.

Farkas, George. *Human Capital or Cultural Capital?: Ethnicity and Poverty Groups in an Urban School District.* New York: Walter DeGruyter, 1996.

Farkas, George, Robert P. Grobe, Daniel Sheehan, and Yuan Shuan. "Cultural Resources and School Success: Gender, Ethnicity, and Poverty Groups Within an Urban School District." *American Sociological Review, 55,* February 1990a:127–142.

Farkas, George, Daniel Sheehan, and Robert P. Grobe. "Coursework Mastery and School Success: Gender, Ethnicity, and Poverty Groups Within an Urban School District." *American Educational Research Journal, 27,* 4, Winter 1990b:807–827.

Farney, Dennis. "They Hold the Cards, But After All, They Do Own the Casino." *Wall Street Journal,* February 5, 1998: A1, A6.

Faunce, William A. *Problems of an Industrial Society,* 2nd ed. New York: McGraw-Hill, 1981.

FBI Uniform Crime Reports. Washington, D.C.: U.S. Government Printing Office, published annually.

Feagin, Joe R. "The Continuing Significance of Race: Antiblack Discrimination in Public Places." In *Majority and Minority: The Dynamics of Race and Ethnicity in American Life,* 6th ed., Norman R. Yetman, ed. Boston: Allyn and Bacon, 1999: 384–399.

Featherman, David L. "Opportunities Are Expanding." *Society, 13,* 1979:4–11.

Featherman, David L., and Robert M. Hauser. *Opportunity and Change.* New York: Academic Press, 1978.

Federal Trade Commission. *Federal Trade Commission Report to Congress for 1994 Pursuant to the Federal Cigarette Labeling and Advertising Act.* Washington, D.C.: U.S. Government Printing Office, October 9, 1996.

Feinglass, Joe. "Next, the McDRG." *The Progressive, 51,* January 1987:28.

Feldman, Saul D. "The Presentation of Shortness in Everyday Life—Height and Heightism in American Society: Toward a Sociology of Stature." Paper presented at the 1972 meetings of the American Sociological Association.

Felsenthal, Edward. "Maine Limits Liability for Doctors Who Meet Treatment Guidelines." *Wall Street Journal,* May 3, 1993:A1, A9.

Felsenthal, Edward. "Justices' Ruling Further Defines Sex Harassment." *Wall Street Journal,* March 5, 1998:B1, B2.

Fendrich, James Max, and Kenneth L. Lovoy. "Back to the Future: Adult Political Behavior of Former Student Activists." In *Collective Behavior and Social Movements,* Russell L. Curtis, Jr., and Benigno E. Aguirre, eds. Boston: Allyn and Bacon, 1993:429–434.

Ferguson, Thomas. *Golden Rule.* Chicago: University of Chicago, 1995.

Ferguson, Trudi, and Joan S. Dunphy. *Answers to the Mommy Track: How Wives and Mothers in Business Reach the Top and Balance Their Lives.* New York: New Horizon Press, 1991.

Feshbach, Murray. "Russia's Farms, Too Poisoned for the Plow." *Wall Street Journal,* May 14, 1992:A14.

Feshbach, Murray, and Alfred Friendly, Jr. *Ecocide in the USSR: Health and Nature Under Siege.* New York: Basic Books, 1992.

Fialka, John J. "Demands on New Orleans's 'Big Charity' Hospital Are Symptomatic of U.S. Health-Care Problem." *Wall Street Journal,* June 22, 1993:A18.

Field, Mark G. "The Health Crisis in the Former Soviet Union: A Report from the 'Post-War' Zone." In *Readings in Medical Sociology,* William C. Cockerham, Michael Glasser, and Linda S. Heuser, eds. Englewood Cliffs, New Jersey: Prentice Hall, 1998:506–519.

Filkins, Dexter. "61 Slain as Violence Rocks the Caste System in India." *Seattle Times,* December 3, 1997, electronic version.

Finckenauer, James O., and Elin J. Waring. *Russian Mafia in America: Immigration, Culture, and Crime.* Boston: Northeastern University Press, 1999.

Fineman, Howard. "Pressing the Flesh Online." *Newsweek,* September 20, 1999:50–53.

Finke, Roger, and Roger Stark. *The Churching of America, 1776–1990: Winners and Losers in Our Religious Economy.* New Brunswick, N.J.: Rutgers University Press, 1992.

Finkelhor, David, and Kersti Yllo. "Marital Rape: The Myth Versus the Reality." In *Marriage and Family in a Changing Society,* 3rd ed., James M. Henslin, ed. New York: Free Press, 1989:382–391.

Finkelhor, David, and Kersti Yllo. *License to Rape: Sexual Abuse of Wives.* New York: Henry Holt, 1985.

Fischer, Claude S. *The Urban Experience.* New York: Harcourt, 1976.

Fish, Jefferson M. "Mixed Blood." *Psychology Today, 28,* 6, November–December 1995:55–58, 60, 61, 76, 80.

Fisher, Julie. "Is the Iron Law of Oligarchy Rusting Away in the Third World?" *World Development, 22,* 2, February 1994:129–143.

Fisher, Sue. *In the Patient's Best Interest: Women and the Politics of Medical Decisions.* New Brunswick, N.J.: Rutgers University Press, 1986.

Flanagan, William G. *Urban Sociology: Images and Structure.* Boston: Allyn and Bacon, 1990.

Flavel, J. H., et al. *The Development of Role-Taking and Communication Skills in Children.* New York: Wiley, 1968.

Fleming, Joyce Dudney. "The State of the Apes." *Psychology Today, 7,* 1974:31–38.

Fletcher, June. "Address Envy: Fudging to Get the Best." *Wall Street Journal,* April 25, 1997:B10.

Flexner, Abraham. *Medical Education in the United States and Canada: A Report to the Carnegie Foundation for the Advancement of Teaching.* Bulletin No. 4. Boston: Merrymount Press, 1910.

Flink, James J. *The Automobile Age.* Cambridge, Mass.: MIT Press, 1990.

Foley, Douglas E. "The Great American Football Ritual." In *Down to Earth Sociology: Introductory Readings,* 10th ed., James M. Henslin, ed. New York: Free Press, 1999:454–467.

Foley, Linda A., Christine Evancic, Karnik Karnik, Janet King, and Angela Parks. "Date Rape: Effects of Race of Assailant and Victim and Gender of Subjects on Perceptions." *Journal of Black Psychology, 21,* 1, February 1995:6–18.

Foote, Donna. "And Baby Makes One." *Newsweek,* February 2, 1998:68–69.

Foote, Jennifer. "Trying to Take Back the Planet." *Newsweek, 115,* 6, February 5, 1990:24–25.

Ford, Constance Mitchell. "South Africa Is Drawing Enthusiasm from Wall Street." *Wall Street Journal,* December 23, 1993:C1, C21.

Form, William. "Comparative Industrial Sociology and the Convergence Hypothesis." In *Annual Review of Sociology, 5,* 1, 1979, Alex Inkeles, James Coleman, and Ralph H. Turner, eds.

Foster, J. Todd. "Russian Mafia Too Savvy for Deed." *The Oregonian,* March 21, 1998.

Fox, Elaine, and George E. Arquitt. "The VFW and the 'Iron Law of Oligarchy.' " In *Down to Earth Sociology,* 4th ed., James M. Henslin, ed. New York: Free Press, 1985:147–155.

Franklin, Clyde W., II. "Sex and Class Differences in the Socialization Experiences of African American Youth." *Western Journal of Black Studies, 18,* 2, 1994:104–111.

Freese, Jeremy, Brian Powell, and Lala Carr Steelman. "Rebel Without a Cause or Effect: Birth Order and Social Attitudes." *American Sociological Review, 64,* April 1999:207–231.

Freudenburg, William R., and Robert Gramling. "The Emergence of Environmental Sociology: Contributions of Riley E. Dunlap and William R. Catton, Jr." *Sociological Inquiry, 59,* 4, November 1989:439–452.

Friedl, Ernestine. "Society and Sex Roles." In *Conformity and Conflict: Readings in Cultural Anthropology.* James P. Spradley and David W. McCurdy, eds. Glenview, Ill.: Scott, Foresman, 1990:229–238.

Frisbie, W. Parker, and Kasarda, John D. "Spatial Processes." In *Handbook of Sociology,* Neil J. Smelser, ed. Newbury Park, CA: Sage, 1988:629–666.

Fritz, Jan M. "The History of Clinical Sociology." *Sociological Practice, 7,* 1989:72–95.

Froman, Ingmarie. "Sweden for Women." *Current Sweden, 407,* November 1994:1–4.

Frumkin, Robert M. "Early English and American Sex Customs." In *Encyclopedia of Sexual Behavior,* Vol. 1. New York: Hawthorne Books, 1967.

Fuchs, Victor R. "A Tale of Two States." In *The Sociology of Health and Illness: Critical Perspectives,* Peter Conrad and Rochelle Kern, eds. New York: St. Martin's Press, 1981:67–70.

Fuller, Rex, and Richard Schoenberger. "The Gender Salary Gap: Do Academic Achievement, Internship Experience, and College Major Make a Difference?" *Social Science Quarterly, 72,* 4, December 1991:715–726.

Furstenberg, Frank F., Jr., and Kathleen Mullan Harris. "The Disappearing American Father? Divorce and the Waning Significance of Biological Fatherhood." In *The Changing American Family: Sociological and Demographic Perspectives,* Scott J. South and Stewart E. Tolnay, eds. Boulder, Colo.: Westview Press, 1992:197–223.

Furtado, Celso. *The Economic Growth of Brazil: A Survey of Colonial to Modern Times.* Westport, Conn.: Greenwood Press, 1984.

Galbraith, John Kenneth. *The Nature of Mass Poverty.* Cambridge Mass.: Harvard University Press, 1979.

Galinsky, Ellen, James T. Bond, and Dana E. Friedman. *The Changing Workforce: Highlights of the National Study.* New York: Families and Work Institute, 1993.

Galinsky, Ellen, and Peter J. Stein. "The Impact of Human Resource Policies on Employees: Balancing Work/Family Life." *Journal of Family Issues, 11,* 4 December 1990:368–383.

Galliher, John F. *Deviant Behavior and Human Rights.* Englewood Cliffs, N.J.: Prentice Hall, 1991.

Gallmeier, Charles P. "Methodological Issues in Qualitative Sport Research: Participant Observation among Hockey Players." *Sociological Spectrum, 8,* 1988:213–235.

Gallup Opinion Index. *Religion in America, 1987.* Report 259, April 1987.

Gallup, George, Jr. *The Gallup Poll: Public Opinion 1989.* Wilmington, Dela.: Scholarly Resources, 1990.

Gans, Herbert J. *The Urban Villagers.* New York: Free Press, 1962.

Gans, Herbert J. *People and Plans: Essays on Urban Problems and Solutions.* New York: Basic Books, 1968.

Gans, Herbert J. "Urbanism and Suburbanism." In *Urban Man and Society: A Reader in Urban Ecology,* Albert N. Cousins and Hans Nagpaul, eds. New York: Knopf, 1970:157–164.

Gans, Herbert J. *People, Plans, and Policies: Essays on Poverty, Racism, and Other National Urban Problems.* New York: Columbia University Press, 1991a.

Gans, Herbert J. "The Way We'll Live Soon." *Washington Post,* September 1, 1991b:BW3.

Garbarino, Merwin S. *American Indian Heritage.* Boston: Little, Brown, 1976.

Gardner, R. Allen, and Beatrice T. Gardner. "Teaching Sign Language to a Chimpanzee." *Science, 165,* 1969:664–672.

Garfinkel, Harold. "Conditions of Successful Degradation Ceremonies." *American Journal of Sociology, 61,* 2, March 1956:420–424.

Garfinkel, Harold. *Studies in Ethnomethodology.* Englewood Cliffs, N.J.: Prentice Hall, 1967.

Garrett, Laurie. "Global Warning." *Los Angeles Times,* March 1, 1999.

Gatewood, Willard B. *Aristocrats of Color: The Black Elite, 1880–1920.* Bloomington, Ind.: Indiana University Press, 1990.

Gay, Jill. "The Patriotic Prostitute." *Progressive,* February 1985:34–36.

Gecas, Viktor. "Context of Soicalization." In *Social Psychology: Sociological Perspectives,* Morris Rosenberg and Ralph H. Turner, eds. New Brunswick, N.J.: Transaction, 1990:165–199.

Geis, Gilbert, Robert F. Meier, and Lawrence M. Salinger. *White-Collar Crime: Classic and Contemporary Views,* 3rd ed. New York: Free Press, 1995.

Gelles, Richard J. "The Myth of Battered Husbands and New Facts about Family Violence." In *Social Problems 80–81,* Robert L. David, ed. Guilford, Conn.: Dushkin, 1980.

Genetski, Robert. "Privatize Social Security." *Wall Street Journal,* May 21, 1993.

Gershenfeld, Neil A. *When Things Start to Think.* New York: Henry Holt, 1999.

Gerson, Kathleen. *Hard Choices: How Women Decide about Work, Career, and Motherhood.* Berkeley: University of California Press, 1985.

Gerth, H. H., and C. Wright Mills. *From Max Weber: Essays in Sociology.* New York: Galaxy, 1958.

Gibbs, Nancy. "The Littleton Massacre." *Time,* May 3, 1999:25–36.

Giddens, Anthony. *Emile Durkheim.* New York: Penguin Books, 1978.

Giele, Janet Zollinger. *Women and the Future: Changing Sex Roles in Modern America.* New York: Free Press, 1978.

Gilbert, Dennis L. *The American Class Structure: In an Age of Growing Inequality.* Belmont, Calif.: Wadsworth Publishing, 1997.

Gilbert, Dennis, and Joseph A. Kahl. *The American Class Structure: A New Synthesis.* Homewood, Ill.: Dorsey Press, 1982.

Gilbert, Dennis, and Joseph A. Kahl. *The American Class Structure: A New Synthesis.* 4th ed. Homewood, Ill.: Dorsey Press, 1993.

Gilham, Steven A. "The Marines Build Men: Resocialization in Recruit Training." In *The Sociological Outlook: A Text with Readings,* 2nd ed., Reid Luhman, ed. San Diego, Calif.: Collegiate Press, 1989:232–244.

Gillborn, David. "Citizenship, 'Race' and the Hidden Curriculum." *International Studies in the Sociology of Education, 2,* 1, 1992:57–73.

Gilligan, Carol. *In a Different Voice: Psychological Theory and Women's Development.* Cambridge, Mass.: Harvard University Press, 1982.

Gilligan, Carol. *Making Connections: The Relational World of Adolescent Girls at Emma Willard School.* Cambridge, Mass.: Harvard University Press, 1990.

Gilman, Charlotte Perkins. *The Man-Made World or, Our Androcentric Culture.* New York: 1971. First published 1911.

Gilmore, David D. *Manhood in the Making: Cultural Concepts of Masculinity.* New Haven, Conn.: Yale University Press, 1990.

Gitlin, Todd. *The Twilight of Common Dreams: Why America Is Wracked by Culture Wars.* New York: Metropolitan Books, 1997.

Glenn, Evelyn Nakano. "Chinese American Families." In *Minority Families in the United States: A Multicultural Perspective,* Ronald L. Taylor, ed. Englewood Cliffs, N.J.: Prentice Hall, 1994:115–145.

Glick, Paul C., and S. Lin. "More Young Adults Are Living with Their Parents: Who Are They?" *Journal of Marriage and Family, 48,* 1986:107–112.

"The Global Giants." *Wall Street Journal,* September 26, 1996: R26–R29.

"The Global Giants: U.S, and Tech Firms Gain Ground in Annual Survey." *Wall Street Journal,* September 27, 1999:R29.

Glueck, Sheldon, and Eleanor Glueck. *Physique and Delinquency.* New York: Harper & Row, 1956.

Goble, Paul. "Russia: Analysis from Washington—Organized Crime's Three Faces." Radio Free Europe, November 5, 1996.

Goffman, Erving. *The Presentation of Self in Everyday Life.* New York: Doubleday, 1959.

Goffman, Erving. *Asylums: Essays on the Social Situation of Mental Patients and Other Inmates.* Chicago: Aldine, 1961.

Goffman, Erving. *Stigma: Notes on the Management of Spoiled Identity.* Englewood Cliffs, N.J.: Prentice Hall, 1963.

Goffman, Erving. "The Presentation of Self in Everyday Life." In *Down to Earth Sociology: Introductory Readings,* 10th ed., James M. Henslin, ed. New York: Free Press, 1999:117–127.

Gold, Ray. "Janitors Versus Tenants: A Status–Income Dilemma." *American Journal of Sociology, 58,* 1952:486–493.

Goldberg, Carey. "Most Get Work After Welfare, Studies Suggest." *New York Times,* April 17, 1999.

Goldberg, Steven. *The Inevitability of Patriarchy,* rev. ed. New York: Morrow, 1974.

Goldberg, Steven. "Reaffirming the Obvious." *Society,* September–October 1986:4–7.

Goldberg, Steven. *Why Men Rule: A Theory of Male Dominance.* Chicago: Open Court, 1993.

Goldberg, Susan, and Michael Lewis. "Play Behavior in the Year-Old Infant: Early Sex Differences." *Child Development, 40,* March 1969:21–31.

Goldman, Kevin. "Seniors Get Little Respect on Madison Avenue." *Wall Street Journal,* September 20, 1993:B6.

Goleman, Daniel. "Spacing of Siblings Strongly Linked to Success in Life." *New York Times,* May 28, 1985:C1, C4.

Goleman, Daniel. "Pollsters Enlist Psychologists in Quest for Unbiased Results." *New York Times,* September 7, 1993:C1, C11.

Gomez, Carlos F. *Regulating Death: Euthanasia and the Case of the Netherlands.* New York: Free Press, 1991.

Goode, Erich. *Drugs in American Society,* 3rd ed. New York: Knopf, 1989.

Goode, Erich. "The Ethics of Deception in Social Research: A Case Study." *Qualitative Sociology, 19,* 1, 1996:11–33.

Goode, William J. "Encroachment, Charlatanism, and the Emerging Profession: Psychology, Sociology, and Medicine." *American Sociological Review, 25,* 6, December 1960:902–914.

Goodwin, Glenn A., Irving Louis Horowitz, and Peter M. Nardi. "Laud Humphreys: A Pioneer in the Practice of Social Science" *Sociological Inquiry, 61,* 2, May 1991:139–147.

Gordon, David M. "Class and the Economics of Crime." *The Review of Radical Political Economics, 3,* Summer 1971:51–57.

Gorman, Peter. "A People at Risk: Vanishing Tribes of South America." *The World & I.* December 1991:678–689.

Gotschall, Mary G. "A Marriage Made in Hell." *National Review, 46,* 6, April 4, 1994:57–60.

Gottfredson, Michael R., and Travis Hirschi. *A General Theory of Crime.* Stanford, Calif.: Stanford University Press, 1990.

Gottschalk, Peter, Sara McLanahan, and Gary Sandefur, "The Dynamics and Intergenerational Transmission of Poverty and Welfare Participation." In *Confronting Poverty: Prescriptions for Change,* Sheldon H. Danziger, Gary D. Sandefur, and Daniel H. Weinberg, eds. Cambridge, Mass.: Harvard University Press, 1994.

Gourevitch, Philip. "After the Genocide." *New Yorker,* December 18, 1995:78–94.

Gourevitch, Philip. *We Wish to Inform You That Tomorrow We Will Be Killed with Our Families: Stories from Rwanda.* New York: Farrar, Straus, and Giroux, 1998.

Gracey, Harry L. "Learning the Student Role: Kindergarten as Academic Boot Camp." In *Down to Earth Sociology: Introductory Readings,* 10th ed., James M. Henslin, ed. New York: Free Press, 1999:418–430.

Graham, Ellen. "Christian Bikers Are Holy Rollers of a Different Kind." *Wall Street Journal,* September 19, 1990:A1, A6.

Grant, Nigel. *Soviet Education.* New York: Pelican Books, 1979.

Greeley, Andrew M. "The Protestant Ethic: Time for a Moratorium." *Sociological Analysis, 25,* Spring 1964:20–33.

Greeley, Andrew. "A Religious Revival in Russia." *Journal for the Scientific Study of Religion, 33,* 3, September 1994:253–272.

Greeley, Andrew M., and Michael Hout. "Americans' Increasing Belief in Life After Death: Religious Competition and Acculturation." *American Sociological Review, 64,* December 1999:813–835.

Greenberg, Brigitte. "One Drink Reduces Stroke Risk." CBS News, November 23, 1999.

Greenberg, Larry M. "Take Two Tablespoons of Mustard and Call If You Don't Feel Better." *Wall Street Journal,* February 22, 1994:B1.

Greenhalgh, Susan, and Jiali Li. "Engendering Reproductive Policy and Practice in Peasant China: For a Feminist Demography of Reproduction." *Signs, 20,* 3, Spring 1995:601–640.

Gross, Jane. "In the Quest for the Perfect Look, More Girls Choose the Scalpel." *New York Times,* November 29, 1998.

Grossman, Lawrence K. *The Electronic Republic: Reshaping Democracy in the Information Age.* New York: Viking, 1995.

Guice, Jon. "Sociologists Go to Work in High Technology." *Footnotes,* November 1999:8.

Guidubaldi, John, Joseph D. Perry, and Bonnie K. Nastasi. "Growing Up in a Divorced Family: Initial and Long-Term Perspectives on Children's Adjustment." *Applied Social Psychology Annual, 7,* 1987:202–237.

Gupta, Giri Raj. "Love, Arranged Marriage, and the Indian Social Structure." In *Cross-Cultural Perspectives of Mate Selection and Marriage,* George Kurian, ed. Westport, Conn.: Greenwood Press, 1979.

Haas, Jack. "Binging: Educational Control Among High-Steel Iron Workers." *American Behavioral Scientist, 16,* 1972:27–34.

Haas, Jack and William Shaffir. "The Cloak of Competence." In *Down to Earth Sociology: Introductory Readings,* 7th ed. New York: Free Press, 1993:432–441. (orig. pub. 1978).

Hacker, Helen Mayer. "Women as a Minority Group." *Social Forces, 30,* October 1951:60–69.

Haddad, Angela, and Robert Newby. "Members Comment on ASA's Publication on Affirmative Action." *Footnotes,* May–June 1999:9.

Hakansson, Stefan. "New Ways of Financing and Organizing Health Care in Sweden." *International Journal of Health Planning and Management, 9,* 1, January 1994:103–124.

Hall, Edward T. *The Silent Language.* New York: Doubleday, 1959.

Hall, Edward T. *The Hidden Dimension.* Garden City, N.Y.: Anchor Books, 1969.

Hall, Edward T., and Mildred R. Hall. "The Sounds of Silence." In *Down to Earth Sociology: Introductory Readings,* 10th ed., James M. Henslin, ed. New York: Free Press, 1999:95–103.

Hall, G. Stanley. *Adolescence: Its Psychology and Its Relations to Physiology, Anthropology, Sociology, Sex, Crime, Religion, and Education.* New York: Appleton, 1904.

Hall, J. A. *Nonverbal Sex Differences: Communication Accuracy and Expressive Style.* Baltimore: Johns Hopkins University Press, 1984.

Hall, Richard H. "The Concept of Bureaucracy: An Empirical Assessment." *American Journal of Sociology, 69,* July 1963:32–40.

Hambler, Brandon, and Sharon Lewis. "An Overview of the Consequences of Violence and Trauma in South Africa." Witt University: Centre for the Study of Violence and Reconciliation, 1998.

Hamermesh, Daniel S., and Jeff E. Biddle. "Beauty and the Labor Market." *American Economic Review, 84,* 5, December 1994:1174–1195.

Hamilton, Kendall, and Susan Miller. "Internet U—No Ivy, No Walls, No Keg Parties." *Newsweek,* March 10, 1997:12.

Hamilton, Richard F. *The Social Construction of Reality.* New Haven, Conn.: Yale University Press, 1996.

Hardy, Dorcas. *Social Insecurity: The Crisis in America's Social Security and How to Plan Now for Your Own Financial Survival.* New York: Villard Books, 1991.

Hardy, Quentin. "Death at the Club Is Par for the Course in Golf-Crazed Japan." *Wall Street Journal,* June 16, 1993a:A1, A8.

Harlow, Harry F., and Margaret K. Harlow. "Social Deprivation in Monkeys." *Scientific American, 207,* 1962:137–147.

Harlow, Harry F., and Margaret K. Harlow. "The Affectional Systems." In *Behavior of Nonhuman Primates: Modern Research Trends,* Vol. 2, Allan M. Schrier, Harry F. Harlow, and Fred Stollnitz, eds. New York: Academic Press, 1965:287–334.

Harpaz, Beth J. "Report: Drug-Resistant TB Spreads." Associated Press, October 29, 1999.

Harrington, Michael. *The Other America: Poverty in the United States.* New York: Macmillan, 1962.

Harrington, Michael. *The Vast Majority: A Journey to the World's Poor.* New York: Simon & Schuster, 1977.

Harris, Chauncy D. "The Nature of Cities and Urban Geography in the Last Half Century." *Urban Geography, 18,* 1997.

Harris, Chauncey, and Edward Ullman. "The Nature of Cities." *Annals of the American Academy of Political and Social Science, 242,* 1945:7–17.

Harris, Diana K. *The Sociology of Aging.* New York: Harper, 1990.

Harris, Marvin. "Why Men Dominate Women." *New York Times Magazine,* November 13, 1977:46, 115, 117–123.

Harrison, Paul. *Inside the Third World: The Anatomy of Poverty,* 3rd ed. London: Penguin Books, 1993.

Hart, Charles W. M., and Arnold R. Pilling. *The Tiwi of North Australia.* New York: Holt, Rinehart, and Winston, 1970.

Hart, Hornell. "Acceleration in Social Change." In *Technology and Social Change,* Francis R. Allen, Hornell Hart, Delbert C. Miller, William F. Ogburn, and Meyer F. Nimkoff. New York: Appleton, 1957:27–55.

Hart, Paul. "Groupthink, Risk-Taking and Recklessness: Quality of Process and Outcome in Policy Decision Making." *Politics and the Individual, 1,* 1, 1991:67–90.

Hartley, Eugene. *Problems in Prejudice.* New York: King's Crown Press, 1946.

Harwood, John. "For California Senator, Fund Raising Becomes Overwhelming Burden." *Wall Street Journal,* March 2, 1994:A1, A13.

Harwood, John, and Geraldine Brooks. "Other Nations Elect Women to Lead Them, So Why Doesn't U.S.?" *Wall Street Journal,* December 14, 1993:A1, A9.

Haslick, Leonard. *Gerontologist, 14,* 1974:37–45.

Haub, Carl, and Diana Cornelius. "World Population Data Sheet." Washington, D.C.: Population Reference Bureau, 1999.

Haub, Carl, and Nancy Yinger. "The U.N. Long-Range Population Projections: What They Tell Us." Washington, D.C.: Population Reference Bureau, 1994.

Hauser, Philip, and Leo Schnore, eds. *The Study of Urbanization.* New York: Wiley, 1965.

Hauser, Robert M., Howard F. Taylor, and Troy Duster. "The Bell Curve." *Contemporary Sociology, 24,* March 1995:149–161.

Hawley, Amos H. *Urban Society: An Ecological Approach.* New York: Wiley, 1981.

Hayes, Donald P., and Loreen T. Wolfer. "Have Curriculum Changes Caused SAT Scores to Decline?" Paper presented at the annual meetings of the American Sociological Association, 1993a.

Haynes, Richard M., and Donald M. Chalker. "World Class Schools." *American School Board Journal,* May 1997:20, 22–25.

Haynor, Anthony L., and Joseph A. Varacalli. "Sociology's Fall From Grace: The Six Deadly Sins of a Discipline at the Crossroads." *Quarterly Journal of Ideology: A Critique of Conventional Wisdom, 16,* 1 & 2, June 1993:3–29.

Heckert, D. Alex, Thomas C. Nowak, and Kay A. Snyder. "The Impact of Husbands' and Wives' Relative Earnings on Marital Dissolution." Paper presented at the 1995 meetings of the American Sociological Association.

Heilbrun, Alfred B. "Differentiation of Death-Row Murderers and Life-Sentence Murderers by Antisociality and Intelligence Measures." *Journal of Personality Assessment, 64,* 1990:617–627.

Hellinger, Daniel, and Dennis R. Judd. *The Democratic Facade.* Pacific Grove, Calif.: Brooks/Cole, 1991.

Hendrix, Lewellyn. "What Is Sexual Inequality? On the Definition and Range of Variation." *Gender and Society, 28,* 3, August 1994:287–307.

Henley, Nancy, Mykol Hamilton, and Barrie Thorne. "Womanspeak and Manspeak." In *Beyond Sex Roles.* Alice G. Sargent, ed. St. Paul, Minn.: West, 1985.

Henslin, James M. *The Cab Driver: An Interactional Analysis of an Occupational Culture.* Washington University Ph.D. dissertation, September 1967.

Henslin, James M. *Introducing Sociology: Toward Understanding Life in Society.* New York: Free Press, 1975.

Henslin, James M. "It's Not a Lovely Place to Visit, and I Wouldn't Want to Live There." In *Studies in Qualitative Methodology, A Research Annual: Reflections on Field Experiences,* Robert G. Burgess, ed. Greenwich, Conn: JAI Press, 1990a:51–76.

Henslin, James M. "When Life Seems Hopeless: Suicide in American Society." In *Social Problems Today: Coping with the Challenges of a Changing Society.* Englewood Cliffs, N.J.: Prentice Hall, 1990b:99–107.

Henslin, James M. "Centuries of Childhood." In *Marriage and Family in a Changing Society,* 4th ed., James M. Henslin, ed. New York: Free Press, 1992:214–225.

Henslin, James M. "Trust and Cabbies." In *Down to Earth Sociology: Introductory Readings,* 7th ed., James M. Henslin, ed. New York: Free Press, 1993:183–196.

Henslin, James M. *Social Problems,* 4th ed. Englewood Cliffs, N.J.: Prentice Hall, 1996.

Henslin, James M. "On Becoming Male: Reflections of a Sociologist on Childhood and Early Socialization." In *Down to Earth Sociology,* 10th ed., James M. Henslin, ed. New York: Free Press, 1999:142–153.

Henslin, James M. "Sociology and the Social Sciences." In *Down to Earth Sociology: Introductory Readings,* 10th ed., James M. Henslin, ed. New York: Free Press, 1999:8–18.

Henslin, James M. "The Survivors of the F-227." In *Down to Earth Sociology: Introductory Readings,* 10th ed., James M. Henslin, ed. New York: Free Press, 1999:251–259.

Henslin, James M. "How Sociologists Do Research." In *Down to Earth Sociology: Introductory Readings,* 10th ed., James M. Henslin, ed. New York: Free Press, 1999:33–44.

Henslin, James M. *Social Problems,* 5th ed. Upper Saddle River, N.J.: Prentice Hall, 2000.

Henslin, James M., and Mae A. Biggs. "Behavior in Pubic Places: The Sociology of the Vaginal Examination." In *Down to Earth Sociology: Introductory Readings,* 10th ed., James M. Henslin, ed. New York: Free Press, 1999:226–237. Original version published as "Dramaturgical Desexualization: The Sociology of the Vaginal Examination." In *Studies in the Sociology of Sex,* James M. Henslin ed. New York: Appleton-Century-Crofts, 1971:243–272.

Hentoff, Nat. "Fifth Grade Freedom Fighters." *Washington Post,* August 1, 1998:A15.

Herbert, Bob. "The Real Jobless Rate." *New York Times,* August 4, 1993:A19.

Herring, George C. "Vietnam War." *World Book Encyclopedia, 20.* Chicago: World Book, 1989:389–393.

Hertzler, Joyce O. *A Sociology of Language.* New York: Random House, 1965.

Hewitt Associates. *Summary of Work and Family Benefits Report.* Lincolnshire, IL: Hewitt Associates, 1995.

Hibbert, Christopher. *The Roots of Evil: A Social History of Crime and Punishment.* New York: Minerva, 1963.

Higginbotham, Elizabeth, and Lynn Weber. "Moving with Kin and Community: Upward Social Mobility for Black and White Women." *Gender and Society, 6,* 3, September 1992:416–440.

Higley, John, Ursula Hoffmann-Lange, Charles Kadushin, and Gwen Moore. "Elite Integration in Stable Democracies: A Reconsideration." *European Sociological Review, 7,* 1, May 1991:35–53.

Hilliard, Asa, III. "Do We Have the Will to Educate All Children?" *Educational Leadership, 49,* September 1991:31–36.

Hiltz, Starr Roxanne. "Widowhood." In *Marriage and Family in a Changing Society,* 3rd ed., James M. Henslin, ed. New York: Free Press, 1989:521–531.

Hippler, Fritz. Interview in a television documentary with Bill Moyers in *Propaganda,* in the series "Walk Through the 20th Century," 1987.

Hirschi, Travis. *Causes of Delinquency.* Berkeley: University of California Press, 1969.

Hochschild, Arlie Russell. "The Sociology of Feeling and Emotion: Selected Possibilities." In *Another Voice: Feminist Perspectives on Social Life and Social Science,* Marcia Millman and Rosabeth Moss Kanter, eds. Garden City, N.Y.: Anchor Books, 1975.

Hochschild, Arlie. *The Second Shift: Working Parents and the Revolution at Home.* New York: Viking, 1989.

Hochschild, Arlie. "Note to the Author." 1991.

Holden, Benjamin A., and Frederick Rose. "Two Policemen Get 2 1/2-Year Jail Terms on U.S. Charges in Rodney King Case." *Wall Street Journal,* August 5, 1993:B2.

Holtzman, Abraham. *The Townsend Movement: A Political Study.* New York: Bookman, 1963.

Homblin, Dora Jane. *The First Cities.* Boston: Little, Brown, Time-Life Books, 1973.

Hornblower, Margot. "The Skin Trade." *Time,* June 21, 1993:45–51.

Horowitz, Ruth. *Honor and the American Dream: Culture and Identity in a Chicano Community.* New Brunswick, N.J.: Rutgers University Press, 1983.

Horowitz, Ruth. "Community Tolerance of Gang Violence." *Social Problems, 34,* 5, December 1987:437–450.

Horwitz, Tony. "Dinka Tribes Made Slaves in Sudan's Civil War." *Wall Street Journal,* April 11, 1989:A19.

Hostetler, John A. *Amish Society,* 3rd ed. Baltimore: Johns Hopkins University Press, 1980.

Houtman, Dick. "What Exactly Is a 'Social Class'?: On the Economic Liberalism and Cultural Conservatism of the 'Working Class'." Paper presented at the 1995 meetings of the American Sociological Association.

Howe, Henry, John Lyne, Alan Gross, Harro VanLente, Aire Rip, Richard Lewontin, Daniel McShea, Greg Myers, Ullica Segerstrale, Herbert W. Simons, and V. B. Smocovitis. "Gene Talk in Sociobiology." *Social Epistemology, 6,* 2, April–June 1992:109–163.

Howells, Lloyd T., and Selwyn W. Becker. "Seating Arrangement and Leadership Emergence." *Journal of Abnormal and Social Psychology, 64,* February 1962:148–150.

Hoyt, Homer. *The Structure and Growth of Residential Neighborhoods in American Cities.* Washington, D.C.: Federal Housing Administration, 1939.

Hoyt, Homer. "Recent Distortions of the Classical Models of Urban Structure." In *Internal Structure of the City: Readings on Space and Environment,* Larry S. Bourne, ed. New York: Oxford University Press, 1971:84–96.

Hsu, Francis L. K. *The Challenge of the American Dream: The Chinese in the United States.* Belmont, Calif.: Wadsworth, 1971.

Huber, Joan. "Micro-Macro Links in Gender Stratification." *American Sociological Review, 55,* February 1990:1–10.

Huber, Joan, and William H. Form. *Income and Ideology.* New York: Free Press, 1973.

Huddle, Donald. "The Net National Cost of Immigration." Washington, D.C.: Carrying Capacity Network, 1993.

Hudson, Christopher G. "The Social Class and Mental Illness Correlation: Implications of the Research for Policy and Practice." *Journal of Sociology and Social Welfare, 15,* 1, March 1988:27–54.

Hudson, James R. "Professional Sports Franchise Locations and City, Metropolitan and Regional Identities." Paper presented at the annual meetings of the American Sociological Association, 1991.

Hudson, Robert B. "The 'Graying' of the Federal Budget and Its Consequences for Old-Age Policy." *Gerontologist, 18,* October 1978:428–440.

Huffstutter, P. J. "God Is Everywhere on the Net." *Los Angeles Times,* December 14, 1998.

Huggins, Martha K. "Lost Childhoods: Assassinations of Youth in Democratizing Brazil." Paper presented at the annual meetings of the American Sociological Association, 1993.

Hughes, H. Stuart. *Oswald Spengler: A Critical Estimate,* rev. ed. New York: Scribner's, 1962.

Hughes, Kathleen A. "Even Tiki Torches Don't Guarantee a Perfect Wedding." *Wall Street Journal,* February 20, 1990:A1, A16.

Humphreys, Laud. *Tearoom Trade: Impersonal Sex in Public Places,* enlarged ed. Chicago: Aldine, 1970.

Humphreys, Laud. *Tearoom Trade: Impersonal Sex in Public Places,* enlarged ed. Chicago: Aldine, 1975.

Humphreys, Laud. "Impersonal Sex and Perceived Satisfaction." In *Studies in the Sociology of Sex,* James M. Henslin, ed. New York: Appleton-Century-Crofts, 1971:351–374.

Hurtado, Aída, David E. Hayes-Bautista, R. Burciaga Valdez, and Anthony C. R. Hernández. *Redefining California: Latino Social Engagement in a Multicultural Society.* Los Angeles: UCLA Chicano Studies Research Center, 1992.

Huttenbach, Henry R. "The Roman *Porajmos:* The Nazi Genocide of Europe's Gypsies." *Nationalities Papers, 19,* 3, Winter 1991:373–394.

Hwang, Suein, L. "Letter from a Tobacco Company to an Art Professor, August 1970." *Wall Street Journal,* July 21, 1995:B1.

Ikels, Charlotte. *The Return of the God of Wealth: The Transition to a Market Economy in Urban China.* Stanford, Calif.: Stanford University Press, 1996.

"Immigration's Costs and Benefits Weighted." *Population Today, 25,* 7/8, July/August 1997:3.

Inkeles, Alex. *One World Emerging? Convergence and Divergence in Industrial Societies.* Boulder, Colo.: Westview Press, 1998.

Iori, Ron. "The Good, the Bad and the Useless." *Wall Street Journal,* June 10, 1988:18R.

Isikoff, Michael. "The Waco Flame-Up." *Newsweek,* September 6, 1999:30.

"Italy's Revolving-Door Prime Minister." *The Economist 353:16,* December 25, 1999.

Itard, Jean Marc Gospard. *The Wild Boy of Aveyron.* Translated by George and Muriel Humphrey. New York: Appleton-Century-Crofts, 1962.

Jacobs, Charles. "Money Talks." *The Boston Globe,* February 19, 1999.

Jacobs, Margaret A. "'New Girl' Network Is Boon for Women Lawyers." *Wall Street Journal,* March 4, 1997:B1, B7.

Jaggar, Alison M. "Sexual Difference and Sexual Equality." In *Theoretical Perspectives on Sexual Difference,* Deborah L. Rhode, ed. New Haven, Conn.: Yale University Press, 1990:239–254.

Jekielek, Susan M. "Parental Conflict, Marital Disruption, and Children's Emotional Well-Being." *Social Forces, 76,* 3, March 1998.

James, Daniel. "To Cut Spending, Freeze Immigration." *Wall Street Journal,* June 24, 1993:A13.

Janis, Irving. *Victims of Groupthink.* Boston, Mass.: Houghton Mifflin, 1972.

Jankowiak, William R., and Edward F. Fischer. "A Cross-Cultural Perspective on Romantic Love." *Journal of Ethnology, 31,* 2, April 1992:149–155.

Jankowski, Martín Sánchez. *Islands in the Street: Gangs and American Urban Society.* Berkeley: University of California Press, 1991.

Jasper, James M. "Moral Dimensions of Social Movements." Paper presented at the annual meetings of the American Sociological Association, 1991.

Jasper, James M., and Jane D. Poulsen. "Recruiting Strangers and Friends: Moral Shocks and Social Networks in Animal Rights and Anti-Nuclear Protests." *Social Problems, 42,* 4, November 1995:493–512.

Jáuregui, Gurutz. "El poder y la soberana en la aldea global." *El País.* July 19, 1996:11.

Jerrome, Dorothy. *Good Company: An Anthropological Study of Old People in Groups.* Edinburgh, England: Edinburgh University Press, 1992.

Johnson, Benton. "On Church and Sect." *American Sociological Review, 28,* 1963:539–549.

Johnson, Cathryn. "The Emergence of the Emotional Self: A Developmental Theory." *Symbolic Interaction, 15,* 2, Summer 1992:183–202.

Johnson, Colleen L., and Barbara M. Barer. "Patterns of Engagement and Disengagement Among the Oldest Old." *Journal of Aging Studies, 6,* 4, Winter 1992:351–364.

Johnson, Dirk. "Growth of Gambling on Tribal Land Starts Trek Back Home by Indians." *New York Times,* January 17, 1999.

Johnson, Kenneth M. "The Rural Rebound." *Reports on America, 1,* 3, Population Reference Bureau, September 1999.

Johnson, Norris R. "Panic at 'The Who Concert Stampede': An Empirical Assessment." In *Collective Behavior and Social Movements,* Russell L. Curtis, Jr., and Benigno E. Aguirre, eds. Boston: Allyn and Bacon, 1993:113–122.

Johnson, Paul. *A History of the American People.* New York: HarperCollins, 1998.

Johnston, Drue M., and Norris R. Johnson. "Role Extension in Disaster: Employee Behavior at the Beverly Hills Supper Club Fire." *Sociological Focus, 22,* 1, February 1989:39–51.

Johnston, Lloyd D., Patrick M. O'Malley, and Jerald G. Bachman. *National Survey Results on Drug Use from The Monitoring the Future Study, 1975–1994.* Rockville, Md.: U.S. Department of Health and Human Services, 1995.

Johnston, Lloyd D., Patrick M. O'Malley, and Jerald G. Bachman. *The Monitoring the Future National Results on Adolescent Drug Use .* Bethesda, Md.: U.S. Department of Health and Human Services, 2000.

Jones, James H. *Bad Blood: The Tuskegee Syphilis Experiment,* 2nd ed. New York: Free Press, 1993.

Jordon, Mary. "College Dorms Reflect Trend of Self-Segregation." In *Ourselves and Others,* 2nd ed., The Washington Post Writer's Group, eds. Boston: Allyn and Bacon, 1996:85–87.

Josephson, Matthew. "The Robber Barons." In *John D. Rockefeller: Robber Baron or Industrial Statesman?* Earl Latham, ed. Boston: Heath, 1949:34–48.

Judis, John B. "The Japanese Megaphone." *New Republic, 202,* 4, January 22, 1990:20–25.

Kagan, Jerome. "The Idea of Emotions in Human Development." In *Emotions, Cognition, and Behavior,* Carroll E. Izard, Jerome Kagan, and Robert B. Zajonc, eds. New York: Cambridge University Press, 1984:38–72.

Kahn, Joseph. "P&G Viewed China as a National Market and Is Conquering It." *Wall Street Journal,* September 12, 1995:A1, A6.

Kalb, Claudia. "A Debate on the Origins of a Plague." *Newsweek,* December 13, 1999:77.

Kalb, Claudia. "The War on Disease Goes Miniature." *Newsweek,* January 1, 2000:89.

Kalichman, Seth C. "MMPI Profiles of Women and Men Convicted of Domestic Homicide." *Journal of Clinical Psychology, 44,* 6, November 1988:847–853.

Kalish, Susan. "International Migration: New Findings on Magnitude, Importance." *Population Today, 22,* 3, March 1994:1–2.

Kanabayashi, Masayoshi. "Work Week." *Wall Street Journal,* August 20, 1996:A1.

Kanter, Rosabeth Moss. *Men and Women of the Corporation.* New York: Basic Books, 1977.

Kanter, Rosabeth Moss. *The Change Masters: Innovation and Entrepreneurship in the American Corporation.* New York: Simon & Schuster, 1983.

Kanter, Rosabeth Moss, ed. *Innovation: Breakthrough Thinking at 3M, DuPont, GE, Pfizer, and Rubbermaid.* New York: HarperBusiness, 1997a.

Kanter, Rosabeth Moss. *World Class: Thriving Locally in the Global Economy.* New York: Touchstone Books, 1997b.

Kanter, Rosabeth Moss, Fred Wiersema, and John J. Kao, eds. *Innovation: Breakthrough Thinking at 3M, DuPont, GE, Pfizer, and Rubbermaid.* New York: Harper, 1997.

Karnow, Stanley, and Nancy Yoshihara. *Asian Americans in Transition.* New York: Asia Society, 1992.

Karp, David A., Gregory P. Stone, and William C. Yoels. *Being Urban: A Sociology of City Life,* 2nd ed. New York: Praeger, 1991.

Karp, David A., and William C. Yoels. "Sport and Urban Life." *Journal of Sport and Social Issues, 14,* 2, 1990:77–102.

Kart, Cary S. *The Realities of Aging: An Introduction to Gerontology,* 3rd ed. Boston: Allyn and Bacon, 1990.

Kaufman, Joanne. "Married Maidens and Dilatory Domiciles." *Wall Street Journal,* May 7, 1996:A16.

Kazman, Sam. "Here's to Honesty in Liquor Sales." *Wall Street Journal,* February 18, 1999.

Keith, Jennie. *Old People, New Lives: Community Creation in a Retirement Residence,* 2nd ed. Chicago: University of Chicago Press, 1982.

Kelling, George L., and Catherine M. Coles. *Fixing Broken Windows: Restoring Order and Reducing Crime in Our Communities.* New York: Free Press, 1998.

Kelly, Joan B. "How Adults React to Divorce." In *Marriage and Family in a Changing Society,* 4th ed., James M. Henslin, ed. New York: Free Press, 1992:410–423.

Kemp, Alice Abel. "Estimating Sex Discrimination in Professional Occupations with the *Dictionary of Occupational Titles.*" *Sociological Spectrum, 10,* 3, 1990:387–411.

Kempadoo, Kamala, ed. *Sun, Sex, and Gold: Tourism and Sex Work in the Caribbean.* New York: Rowman and Littlefield, 2000.

Keniston, Kenneth. *Youth and Dissent: The Rise of a New Opposition.* New York: Harcourt, Brace, Jovanovich, 1971.

Kephart, William M., and William W. Zellner. *Extraordinary Groups: An Examination of Unconventional Life-Styles,* 5th ed. New York: St. Martin's Press, 1994.

Kerr, Clark. *The Future of Industrialized Societies.* Cambridge, Mass.: Harvard University Press, 1983.

Kerr, Clark, et al. *Industrialism and Industrial Man: The Problems of Labor and Management in Economic Growth.* Cambridge, Mass.: Harvard University Press, 1960.

Kershaw, Terry. "The Effects of Educational Tracking on the Social Mobility of African Americans." *Journal of Black Studies, 23,* 1, September 1992:152–169.

Kettl, Donald F. "The Savings-and-Loan Bailout: The Mismatch Between the Headlines and the Issues." *PS, 24,* 3, September 1991:441–447.

Kibria, Nazli. *Family Tightrope: The Changing Lives of Vietnamese Americans.* Princeton, N.J.: Princeton University Press, 1993.

Kifner, John. "Building Modernity on Desert Mirages." *New York Times,* February 7, 1999.

Kinsella, Kevin, and Cynthia M. Taeuber. *An Aging World.* Washington, D.C.: U.S. Bureau of the Census, 1993.

Kitsuse, John I. "Coming Out All Over: Deviants and the Politics of Social Problems." *Social Problems, 28,* 1, October 1980:1–13.

Klandermans, Bert. *The Social Psychology of Protest.* Cambridge, Mass.: Blackwell, 1997.

Klee, Ernst, Willi Dressen, and Volker Riess, eds. *"The Good Old Days": The Holocaust as Seen by Its Perpetrators and Bystanders.* New York: Free Press, 1991.

Klonoff, Elizabeth A., and Hope Landrine. "Sex Roles, Occupational Roles, and Symptom-Reporting: A Test of Competing Hypotheses on Sex Differences." *Journal of Behavioral Medicine, 15,* 4, August 1992:355–364.

Kluegel, James R., and Eliot R. Smith. *Beliefs About Inequality: America's Views of What Is and What Ought to Be.* Hawthorne, N.Y.: Aldine de Gruyter, 1986.

Knaus, William A. *Inside Russian Medicine: An American Doctor's First-Hand Report.* New York: Everest House, 1981.

Kohfeld, Carol W., and Leslie A. Leip. "Bans on Concurrent Sale of Beer and Gas: A California Case Study." *Sociological Practice Review, 2,* 2, April 1991:104–115.

Kohlberg, Lawrence. *The Psychology of Moral Development: Moral Stages and the Life Cycle.* San Francisco: Harper and Row, 1984.

Kohlberg, Lawrence. "Moral Education for a Society in Moral Transition." *Educational Leadership, 33,* 1975:46–54.

Kohlberg, Lawrence. "A Current Statement on Some Theoretical Issues." In *Lawrence Kohlberg: Consensus and Controversy,* Sohan Modgil and Celia Modgil, eds. Philadelphia: Falmer Press, 1986:485–546.

Kohlberg, Lawrence, and Carol Gilligan. "The Adolescent as a Philosopher: The Discovery of the Self in a Postconventional World." *Daedalus, 100,* 1971:1051–1086.

Kohn, Alfie. "Make Love, Not War." *Psychology Today,* June 1988:35–38.

Kohn, Melvin L. "Social Class and Parental Values." *American Journal of Sociology, 64,* 1959:337–351.

Kohn, Melvin L. "Social Class and Parent–Child Relationships: An Interpretation." *American Journal of Sociology, 68,* 1963:471–480.

Kohn, Melvin L. "Occupational Structure and Alienation." *American Journal of Sociology, 82,* 1976:111–130.

Kohn, Melvin L. *Class and Conformity: A Study in Values,* 2nd ed. Homewood, Ill.: Dorsey Press, 1977.

Kohn, Melvin L., and Carmi Schooler. "Class, Occupation, and Orientation." *American Sociological Review, 34,* 1969:659–678.

Kohn, Melvin L., and Carmi Schooler. *Work and Personality: An Inquiry into the Impact of Social Stratification.* New York: Ablex Press, 1983.

Kohn, Melvin L., Kazimierz M. Slomczynski, and Carrie Schoenbach. "Social Stratification and the Transmission of Values in the Family: A Cross-National Assessment." *Sociological Forum, 1,* 1, 1986:73–102.

Kolata, Gina. "Pushing the Limits of the Human Life Span." *New York Times,* March 9, 1999.

Komter, Aafke. "Hidden Power in Marriage." *Gender and Society, 3,* 2, June 1989:187–216.

Korbin, Jill E., Georgia Anetzberger, and J. Kevin Eckert. "Elder Abuse and Child Abuse: A Consideration of Similarities and Differences in Intergenerational Family Violence." In *Perspectives in Social Gerontology,* Robert B. Enright, Jr., ed. Boston: Allyn and Bacon, 1994:165–173.

Korda, Michael. *Male Chauvinism: How It Works.* New York: Random House, 1973.

Kornhauser, William. *The Politics of Mass Society.* New York: Free Press, 1959.

Kotlowitz, Alex. "A Businessman Turns His Skills to Aiding Inner-City Schools." *Wall Street Journal,* February 25, 1992:A1, A6.

Kramer, Josea B. "Serving American Indian Elderly in Cities: An Invisible Minority." *Aging Magazine,* Winter–Spring 1992:48–51.

Krause, Neal. "Race Differences in Life Satisfaction Among Aged Men and Women." *Journal of Gerontology, 48,* 5, 1993:235–244.

Krauthammer, Charles. "A Second American Century." *Time,* December 27, 1999:186.

Kraybill, Donald B. *The Riddle of Amish Culture.* Baltimore: Johns Hopkins University Press, 1989.

Krog, Antjie. *Country of My Skull: Guilt, Sorrow, and the Limits of Forgiveness in the New South Africa.* New York: TimesBooks, 1999.

Krysan, Maria, and Reynolds Farley. "Racial Stereotypes: Are They Alive and Well? Do They Continue to Influence Race Relations?" Paper presented at the 1993 meeting of the American Sociological Association.

Kübler-Ross, Elisabeth. *On Death and Dying.* New York: Macmillan, 1969.

Kübler-Ross, Elisabeth. *Living with Death and Dying.* New York: Macmillan, 1981.

Kübler-Ross, Elisabeth. *Death: The Final Stage of Growth.* Englewood Cliffs, N.J.: Prentice Hall, 1989.

Kuhn, Margaret E. "The Gray Panthers." In *Social Problems,* 2nd ed., James M. Henslin, Englewood Cliffs, N.J.: Prentice Hall, 1990:56–57.

Kuntz, Phil. "Reno, FBI Orders New Investigation of Use of Flammable Devises in Waco." *Wall Street Journal,* August 27, 1999.

Kurian, George Thomas. *Encyclopedia of the First World,* Vols. 1, 2. New York: Facts on File, 1990.

Kurian, George Thomas. *Encyclopedia of the Second World,* New York: Facts on File, 1991.

Kurian, George Thomas. *Encyclopedia of the Third World,* Vols. 1, 2, 3. New York: Facts on File, 1992.

Kurzweil, Ray. *The Age of Spiritual Machines: When Computers Exceed Human Intelligence.* New York: Penguin Books, 1999.

La Barre, Weston. *The Human Animal.* Chicago: University of Chicago Press, 1954.

Lacayo, Richard. "The 'Cultural' Defense." *Time,* Fall 1993a:61.

Lacayo, Richard. "In the Grip of a Psychopath." *Time,* May 3, 1993b:34–36, 39–43.

Lachica, Eduardo. "Third World Told to Spend More on Environment." *Wall Street Journal,* May 18, 1992:A2.

LaDou, Joseph. "Deadly Migration: Hazardous Industries' Flight to the Third World." *Technology Review, 94,* 5, July 1991:46–53.

Lagaipa, Susan J. "Suffer the Little Children: The Ancient Practice of Infanticide as a Modern Moral Dilemma." *Issues in Comprehensive Pediatric Nursing, 13,* 1990:241–251.

Lagnado, Lucette. "Another Peril: Smoking Doubles Risk of Old-Age Blindness, Two Studies Say." *Wall Street Journal,* October 9, 1996:B8.

Lamb, Michael E. "The Effect of Divorce on Children's Personality Development." *Journal of Divorce, 1,* Winter 1977:163–174.

Lancaster, Hal. "Managing Your Career." *Wall Street Journal,* November 14, 1995:B1.

Landtman, Gunnar. *The Origin of the Inequality of the Social Classes.* New York: Greenwood Press, 1968. First published in 1938.

Lang, Kurt, and Gladys E. Lang. *Collective Dynamics.* New York: Crowell, 1961.

Langan, Patrick A., and Mark A. Cunniff. "Recidivism of Felons on Probation, 1986–89." Washington, D.C.: U.S. Department of Justice, February 1992.

Lannoy, Richard. *The Speaking Tree: A Study of Indian Culture and Society.* New York: Oxford University Press, 1975.

LaPiere, Richard T. "Attitudes Versus Action." *Social Forces, 13,* December 1934:230–237.

Larson, Jeffry H. "The Marriage Quiz: College Students' Beliefs in Selected Myths About Marriage." *Family Relations,* January 1988:3–11.

Lasch, Christopher. *Haven in a Heartless World: The Family Besieged.* New York: Basic, 1977.

Laska, Shirley Bradway. "Environmental Sociology and the State of the Discipline." *Social Forces, 72,* 1, September 1993:1–17.

Lauer, Jeanette, and Robert Lauer. "Marriages Made to Last." In *Marriage and Family in a Changing Society,* 4th ed., James M. Henslin, ed. New York: Free Press, 1992:481–486.

Lawlor, Julia. "Women Gain Power, Means to Abuse It." *USA Today,* January 12, 1994:1A, 2A.

Lazarsfeld, Paul F., and Jeffrey G. Reitz. "History of Applied Sociology." *Sociological Practice, 7,* 1989:43–52.

LeBon, Gustave. *Psychologie des Foules (The Psychology of the Crowd).* Paris: Alcan, 1895. Various editions in English.

Leacock, Eleanor. *Myths of Male Dominance.* New York: Monthly Review Press, 1981.

Lee, Alfred McClung, and Elizabeth Briant Lee. *The Fine Art of Propaganda: A Study of Father Coughlin's Speeches.* New York: Harcourt Brace, 1939.

Lee, Sharon M. "Asian Americans: Diverse and Growing." *Population Bulletin, 53,* 2, June 1998:1–39.

Lee, Sharon M., and Keiko Yamanaka. "Patterns of Asian American Intermarriage and Marital Assimilation." *Journal of Comparative Family Studies, 21,* 2, Summer 1990:287–305.

Leland, John, and Gregory Beals. "In Living Colors." *Newsweek,* May 5, 1997:58–60.

Lemann, Nicholas. *The Promised Land: The Great Black Migration and How It Changed America.* New York: Random House, 1991.

Lemann, Nicholas, "The Myth of Community Development." *New York Times Magazine,* January 9, 1994, p. 27.

Lemert, Charles. "A Classic from the Other Side of the Veil: Du Bois's *Souls of Black Folk.*" *Sociological Quarterly, 35,* 3, 1994:383–396.

Lemert, Edwin M. *Human Deviance, Social Problems, and Social Control,* 2nd ed., Englewood Cliffs, N.J.: Prentice Hall, 1972.

Lemonick, Michael D. "Doctors' Deadly Mistakes." *Time,* December 13, 1999:74–76.

Lenski, Gerhard. "Status Crystallization: A Nonvertical Dimension of Social Status." *American Sociological Review, 19,* 1954:405–413.

Lenski, Gerhard. *Power and Privilege: A Theory of Social Stratification.* New York: McGraw-Hill, 1966.

Lenski, Gerhard, and Jean Lenski. *Human Societies: An Introduction to Macrosociology,* 5th ed. New York: McGraw-Hill, 1987.

Lerner, Gerda. *Black Women in White America: A Documentary History.* New York: Pantheon Books, 1972.

Lerner, Gerda. *The Creation of Patriarchy.* New York: Oxford, 1986.

Lesser, Alexander. "War and the State." In *War: The Anthropology of Armed Conflict and Aggression,* Morton Fried, Marvin Harris, and Robert Murphy, eds. Garden City, N.Y.: Natural History, 1968:92–96.

Lester, David. *Suicide in American Indians.* New York: Nova Science Publishers, 1997.

Levinson, D. J. *The Seasons of a Man's Life.* New York: Knopf, 1978.

Levitt, Steven D. *The Quarterly Journal of Economics,* May 1996.

Levy, Judith A. "The Hospice in the Context of an Aging Society." In *Perspectives in Social Gerontology,* Robert B. Enright, Jr., ed. Boston: Allyn and Bacon, 1994:274–286.

Levy, Marion J., Jr. "Confucianism and Modernization." *Society, 24,* 4, May–June 1992:15–18.

Lewis, Dorothy Otnow, ed. *Vulnerabilities to Delinquency.* New York: Spectrum Medical and Scientific Books, 1981.

Lewis, Oscar. "The Culture of Poverty." *Scientific American, 115,* October 1966a:19–25.

Lewis, Oscar. *La Vida.* New York: Random House, 1966b.

Lewis, Richard S. *Challenger: The Final Voyage.* New York: Columbia University Press, 1988.

Liben, Paul. "Farrakhan Honors African Slavers." *Wall Street Journal,* October 20, 1995:A14.

Liebow, Elliot. "Tally's Corner." In *Down to Earth Sociology: Introductory Readings,* 9th ed., James M. Henslin, ed. New York: Free Press, 1997:330–339.

Liebow, Elliot. *Tally's Corner: A Study of Negro Streetcorner Men.* Boston: Little, Brown, 1967.

Light, Donald W. "Perestroika for Russian Health Care?" *Footnotes, 20,* 3, March 1992:7, 9.

Lightfoot-Klein, A. "Rites of Purification and Their Effects: Some Psychological Aspects of Female Genital Circumcision and Infibulation (Pharaonic Circumcision) in an Afro-Arab Society (Sudan)." *Journal of Psychological Human Sexuality, 2,* 1989:61–78.

Lind, Michael. *The Next American Nation: The New Nationalism and the Fourth American Revolution.* New York: Free Press, 1995.

Linden, Eugene. "Lost Tribes, Lost Knowledge." *Time,* September 23, 1991:46, 48, 50, 52, 54, 56.

Linton, Ralph. *The Study of Man.* New York: Appleton-Century-Crofts, 1936.

Lippitt, Ronald, and Ralph K. White. "An Experimental Study of Leadership and Group Life." In *Readings in Social Psychology,* 3rd ed., Eleanor E. Maccoby, Theodore M. Newcomb, and Eugene L. Hartley, eds. New York: Holt, Rinehart and Winston, 1958:340–365. (As summarized in Olmsted and Hare 1978:28–31.)

Lipset, Seymour Martin. "Democracy and Working-Class Authoritarianism." *American Sociological Review, 24,* 1959:482–502.

Lipset, Seymour Martin. "The Social Requisites of Democracy Revisited." Presidential address to the American Sociological Association, Boston, Massachusetts, 1993.

Lipton, Michael. *Why Poor People Stay Poor: Urban Bias in World Development.* Cambridge, Mass.: Harvard University Press, 1979.

Lofland, John F. *Protest: Studies of Collective Behavior and Social Movements.* New Brunswick, New Jersey: Transaction Books, 1985.

Lofland, John. "Collective Behavior: The Elementary Forms." In *Collective Behavior and Social Movements,* Russell L. Curtis, Jr., and Benigno E. Aguirre, eds. Boston: Allyn and Bacon, 1993:70–75.

Lombroso, Cesare. *Crime: Its Causes and Remedies,* H. P. Horton, trans. Boston: Little, Brown, 1911.

Loose, Cindy. "Billionaire to Give $100 Million for Free Online University." *Washington Post,* March 16, 2000.

Lopez, Julie Amparano. "Study Says Women Face Glass Walls as Well as Ceilings." *Wall Street Journal,* March 3, 1992:B1, B8.

Lorber, Judith. *Paradoxes of Gender.* New Haven, Conn.: Yale University Press, 1994.

Lublin, Joann S. "Trying to Increase Worker Productivity, More Employers Alter Management Style." *Wall Street Journal,* February 13, 1991:B1, B7.

Lublin, Joann S. "Women at Top Still Are Distant from CEO Jobs." *Wall Street Journal,* February 28, 1996:B1.

Lublin, Joann S. "Living Well." *Wall Street Journal,* April 8, 1999.

Lundberg, Olle. "Causal Explanations for Class Inequality in Health—An Empirical Analysis." *Social Science and Medicine, 32,* 4, 1991:385–393.

Luoma, Jon R. "Acid Murder No Longer a Mystery." In *Taking Sides: Clashing Views on Controversial Environmental Issues,* 3rd ed., Theodore D. Goldfarb, ed. Guilford, Conn.: Dushkin, 1989:186–192.

Lurie, Nicole, Jonathan Slater, Paul McGovern, Jacqueline Ekstrum, Lois Quam, and Karen Margolis. "Preventive Care for Women: Does the Sex of the Physician Matter?" *New England Journal of Medicine, 329,* August 12, 1993:478–482.

Mabry, Marcus. "The Price Tag on Freedom." *Newsweek,* May 3, 1999:50–51.

MacDonald, Heather. "Law School Humbug." *Wall Street Journal,* November 8, 1995:A23.

MacDonald, William L., and Alfred DeMaris. "Remarriage, Stepchildren, and Marital Conflict: Challenges to the Incomplete Institutionalization Hypothesis." *Journal of Marriage and the Family, 57,* May 1995:387–398.

Mack, Raymond W., and Calvin P. Bradford. *Transforming America: Patterns of Social Change,* 2nd ed. New York: Random House, 1979.

Mackay, Charles. *Memories of Extraordinary Popular Delusions and the Madness of Crowds.* London: Office of the National Illustrated Library, 1852.

Mackey, Richard A., and Bernard A. O'Brien. *Lasting Marriages: Men and Women Growing Together.* Westport, Conn.: 1995.

MacKinnon, Catharine A. *Sexual Harassment of Working Women: A Case of Sex Discrimination.* New Haven, Conn.: Yale University Press, 1979.

MacShane, Denis. "Lessons for Bosses and the Bossed." *New York Times,* July 19, 1993:A15.

Magnuson, E. "A Cold Soak, a Plume, a Fireball." *Time,* February 17, 1986:25.

Mahoney, John S., Jr., and Paul G. Kooistra. "Policing the Races: Structural Factors Enforcing Racial Purity in Virginia (1630–1930)." Paper presented at the 1995 meetings of the American Sociological Association.

Mahran, M. *Proceedings of the Third International Congress of Medical Sexology.* Littleton, Mass.: PSG Publishing, 1978.

Mahran, M. "Medical Dangers of Female Circumcision." *International Planned Parenthood Federation Medical Bulletin, 2,* 1981:1–2.

Maier, Mark. "Teaching from Tragedy: An Interdisciplinary Module on the Space Shuttle *Challenger.*" *T.H.E. Journal,* September 1993:91–94.

Main, Jackson Turner. *The Social Structure of Revolutionary America.* Princeton, N.J.: Princeton University Press, 1965.

Malinowski, Bronislaw. *Sex and Repression in Savage Society.* Cleveland, Ohio: World, 1927.

Malinowski, Bronislaw. *The Dynamics of Culture Change.* New Haven, Conn.: Yale University Press, 1945.

Malmberg, Bo, and Gerdt Sundström. "Age Care Crisis in Sweden?" *Current Sweden, 412,* January 1996:1–6.

Malson, Lucien. *Wolf Children and the Problem of Human Nature.* New York: Monthly Review Press, 1972.

Malthus, Thomas Robert. *First Essay on Population 1798.* London: Macmillan, 1926. Originally published in 1798.

Mamdani, Mahmood. "The Myth of Population Control: Family, Caste, and Class in an Urban Village." New York: Monthly Review Press, 1973.

Mander, Jerry. *In the Absence of the Sacred: The Failure of Technology and the Survival of the Indian Nations.* San Francisco, Calif.: Sierra Club Books, 1992.

Manski, Charles F. "Income and Higher Education." *Focus, 14,* 3, Winter 1992–1993:14–19.

Marcus, Amy Dockser. "Mideast Minorities: Kurds Aren't Alone." *Wall Street Journal,* September 5, 1996:A12.

Marger, Martin N. *Elites and Masses: An Introduction to Political Sociology,* 2nd ed. Belmont, Calif.: Wadsworth, 1987.

Markson, Elizabeth W. "Moral Dilemmas." *Society,* July–August, 1992:4–6.

Markusen, Eric. "Genocide in Cambodia." In *Down to Earth Sociology,* 8th ed., James M. Henslin, ed. New York: Free Press, 1995:355–364.

Marolla, Joseph, and Diana Scully. "Attitudes Toward Women, Violence, and Rape: A Comparison of Convicted Rapists and Other Felons." *Deviant Behavior, 7,* 4, 1986:337–355.

Marshall, Gordon. *In Search of the Spirit of Capitalism: An Essay on Max Weber's Protestant Ethic Thesis.* New York: Columbia University Press, 1982.

Marshall, Samantha. "It's So Simple: Just Lather Up, Watch the Fat Go Down the Drain." *Wall Street Journal,* November 2, 1995:B1.

Marshall, Samantha. "Vietnamese Women Are Kidnapped and Later Sold in China as Brides." *Wall Street Journal,* August 3, 1999.

Martin, William G., and Mark Beittel. "Toward a Global Sociology: Evaluating Current Conceptions, Methods, and Practices." *Sociological Quarterly, 39,* 1, 1998:139–161.

Martineau, Harriet. *Society in America.* Garden City, N.Y.: Doubleday 1962. First published in 1837.

Marx, Gary T. "The New Surveillance." *Technology Review,* May–June 1985:43–48.

Marx, Gary T. "Monitoring on the Job: How to Protect Privacy as Well as Property." *Technology Review,* November–December 1986:63–72.

Marx, Gary T. "Thoughts On a Neglected Category of Social Movement Participant: The Agent Provocateur and the Informant." In *Collective Behavior and Social Movements,* Russell L. Curtis, Jr., and Benigno E. Aguirre, eds. Boston: Allyn and Bacon, 1993:242–258.

Marx, Gary T. "The Road to the Future." In *Triumph of Discovery: A Chronicle of Great Adventures in Science.* New York: Holt, 1995:63–65.

Marx, Karl. "Contribution to the Critique of Hegel's Philosophy of Right." In *Karl Marx: Early Writings*, T. B. Bottomore, ed. New York: McGraw-Hill, 1964:45. First published in 1844.

Marx, Karl, and Friedrich Engels. *Communist Manifesto*. New York: Pantheon, 1967. First published in 1848.

Masheter, Carol. "Postdivorce Relationships Between Ex-spouses: The Role of Attachment and Interpersonal Conflict." *Journal of Marriage and the Family, 53*, February 1991:103–110.

Massey, Douglas S., and Nancy A. Denton. *American Apartheid: Segregation and the Making of the Underclass*. Cambridge, Mass.: Harvard University Press, 1993.

Matthews, Marvyn. "Long Term Trends in Soviet Education." In *Soviet Education in the 1980s*, J. J. Tomiak, ed. London: Croom Helm, 1983:1–23.

Maugh, Thomas H., "AIDS Care Costs Overstated, Says Rand Study." *Los Angeles Times*, December 24, 1998.

Mauss, Armand. *Social Problems as Social Movements*. Philadelphia, Penn.: Lippincott, 1975.

Maybury-Lewis, David. "Tribal Wisdom." In *Sociology 95/96*, Kurt Finsterbusch, ed. Sluice Dock, Conn.: Dushkin, 1995:16–21.

Mayo, Elton. *Human Problems of an Industrial Civilization*. New York: Viking, 1966.

McAdam, Doug, John D. McCarthy, and Mayer N. Zald. "Social Movements." In *Handbook of Sociology*, Neil J. Smelser, ed. Newbury Park, Calif.: Sage, 1988:695–737.

McCabe, J. Terrence, and James E. Ellis. "Pastoralism: Beating the Odds in Arid Africa." In *Conformity and Conflict: Readings in Cultural Anthropology*, James P. Spradley and David W. McCurdy, eds. Glenview, Ill.: Scott, Foresman, 1990:150–156.

McCarthy, John D., and Mark Wolfson. "Consensus Movements, Conflict Movements, and the Cooperation of Civic and State Infrastructures." In *Frontiers in Social Movement Theory*, Aldon D. Morris and Carol McClurg Mueller, eds. New Haven, Conn.: Yale University Press, 1992:273–297.

McCarthy, John D., and Mayer N. Zald. "Resource Mobilization and Social Movements: A Partial Theory." *American Journal of Sociology, 82*, 6, 1977:1212–1241.

McCarthy, Michael J. "James Bond Hits the Supermarket: Stores Snoop on Shoppers' Habits to Boost Sales." *Wall Street Journal*, August 25, 1993:B1, B8.

McCartney, Kathleen, et al. "Teacher-Child Interaction and Chid-Care Auspices as Predictors of Social Outcomes in Infants, Toddlers, and Preschoolers." *Merrill-Palmer Quarterly, 41*, 3, July 1997:426–450.

McCartney, Scott. "People Most Needing Transplantable Livers Now Often Miss Out." *Wall Street Journal*, April 1, 1993:A1, A7.

McCormick, John. "Change Has Taken Place." *Newsweek*, June 7, 1999:34.

McCoy, Elin. "Childhood Through the Ages." In *Marriage and Family in a Changing Society*, 2nd ed., James M. Henslin, ed. New York: Free Press, 1985:386–394.

McCuen, Gary E., ed. *Ecocide and Genocide in the Vanishing Forest: The Rainforests and Native People*. Hudson, Wis.: GEM Publications, 1993.

McGowan, Jo. "Little Girls Dying: An Ancient & Thriving Practice." *Commonweal*, August 9, 1991:481–482.

McGregor, James. "China's Aging Leader Seems Set to Carve Reformist Idea in Stone." *Wall Street Journal*, March 20, 1992:A9.

McGregor, James. "Running Bulls." *Wall Street Journal*, September 24, 1993:R16.

McIntyre, Jamie. "Army Rape Case Renews Debate on Coed Training." April 30, 1997: CNN Internet article.

McKenna, George. "On Abortion: A Lincolnian Position." *Atlantic Monthly*, September 1995:51–67.

McKeown, Thomas. *The Modern Rise of Population*. New York: Academic Press, 1977.

McLanahan, Sara, and Gary Sandefur. *Growing Up with a Single Parent: What Hurts, What Helps*. Cambridge, Mass.: Harvard University Press, 1994.

McLemore, S. Dale. *Racial and Ethnic Relations in America*. Boston: Allyn and Bacon, 1994.

McLuhan, Marshall. *Understanding Media: The Extensions of Man*. New York: Mentor, 1964.

McNeil, Donald G., Jr. "In Angola's Capital, Life Does Not Yet Imitate Art." *New York Times*, January 25, 1999.

McPhail, Clark. "Blumer's Theory of Collective Behavior: The Development of a Non-Symbolic Interaction Explanation." *Sociological Quarterly, 30*, 3, 1989:401–423.

McPhail, Clark. *The Myth of the Madding Crowd*. Hawthorne, N.Y.: Aldine de Gruyter, 1991.

Mead, George Herbert. *Mind, Self and Society*. Chicago: University of Chicago Press, 1934.

Mead, Margaret. *Sex and Temperament in Three Primitive Societies*. New York: New American Library, 1950. First published in 1935.

Meek, Anne. "On Creating 'Ganas': A Conversation with Jaime Escalante." *Educational Leadership, 46*, 5, February 1989:46–47.

Meier, Barry. "Health Studies Suggest Asbestos Substitutes Also Pose Cancer Risk." *Wall Street Journal*, May 12, 1987:1, 21.

Melloan, George. "Apartheid Is Dead—Now Comes the Hard Part." *Wall Street Journal*, November 22, 1993a:A15.

Melloan, George. "Italy 'Steps into the Tunnel' Toward Change." *Wall Street Journal*, April 26, 1993b:A15.

Meltzer, Bernard N., John W. Petras, and Larry T. Reynolds. *Symbolic Interactionism: Genesis, Varieties, and Criticism*. London: Routledge & Kegan Paul, 1975.

Melucci, Alberto. *Nomads of the Present: Social Movements and Individual Needs in Contemporary Society*. Philadelphia: Temple University Press, 1989.

Menaghan, Elizabeth G., Lori Kowaleski-Jones, and Frank L. Mott. "The Intergenerational Costs of Parental Social Stressors: Academic and Social Difficulties in Early Adolescence for Children of Young Mothers." *Journal of Health and Social Behavior, 38*, March 1997:72–86.

Mendels, Pamela. "Rights Group Develops 'Hate' Filter." *New York Times*, November 11, 1998.

Mendelsohn, Robert, and Balick, Michael J. "Drugs and Tropical Forests." *Economic Botany*, June 1995.

Menzel, Peter. *Material World: A Global Family Portrait*. San Francisco: Sierra Club, 1994.

Mersereau, Adam G. "The Military Should Fight Wars, Not Sexism." *Wall Street Journal*, March 17, 1998:A18.

Merton, Robert K. *Social Theory and Social Structure*. Glencoe, Ill.: Free Press, 1949, Enlarged ed., 1968.

Merton, Robert K. "The Social-Cultural Environment and *Anomie*." In *New Perspectives for Research on Juvenile Delinquency*, Helen L. Witmer and Ruth Kotinsky, eds. Washington, D.C.: U.S. Department of Health, Education, and Welfare, 1956:24–50.

Merwine, Maynard H. "How Africa Understands Female Circumcision." *New York Times*, November 24, 1993.

Messner, Michael. "Boyhood, Organized Sports, and the Construction of Masculinities." *Journal of Contemporary Ethnography, 18*, 4, January 1990:416–444.

Meyrowitz, Joshua. "Shifting Worlds of Strangers: Medium Theory and Changes in 'Them' vs 'Us.' " Paper presented at the 1995 meetings of the American Sociological Association.

Michael, Robert T. "Measuring Poverty: A New Approach." *Focus, 17*, 1, Summer 1995:2–13.

Michalowski, Raymond J. *Order, Law, and Crime: An Introduction to Criminology*. New York: Random House, 1985.

Michels, Robert. *Political Parties*. Glencoe, Ill.: Free Press, 1949. First published in 1911.

Milbank, Dana. "Working Poor Fear Welfare Cutbacks Aimed at the Idle Will Inevitably Strike Them, Too." *Wall Street Journal*, August 9, 1995b:A10.

Milbank, Dana. "No Fault Divorce Law Is Assailed in Michigan, and Debate Heats Up." *Wall Street Journal*, January 5, 1996:A1, A6.

Milgram, Stanley. "Behavioral Study of Obedience." *Journal of Abnormal and Social Psychology, 67*, 4, 1963:371–378.

Milgram, Stanley. "Some Conditions of Obedience and Disobedience to Authority." *Human Relations, 18,* February 1965:57–76.

Milgram, Stanley. "The Small World Problem." *Psychology Today, 1,* 1967:61–67.

Milkie, Melissa A. "Social World Approach to Cultural Studies." *Journal of Contemporary Ethnography, 23,* 3, October 1994:354–380.

Miller, Dan E. "Milgram Redux: Obedience and Disobedience in Authority Relations." In *Studies in Symbolic Interaction,* Norman K. Denzin, ed. Greenwich, Conn.: JAI Press, 1986:77–106.

Miller, Judith, and William J. Broad. "Clinton Describes Terrorism Threat for 21st Century." *New York Times,* January 22, 1999.

Miller, Laura L. "Women in the Military." In *Down to Earth Sociology: Introductory Readings,* 10th ed., James M. Henslin, ed. New York: Free Press, 1999:516–531.

Miller, Lisa. "Son of Elijah Muhammad Preaches Gentler Islam in Tune With the Times." *Wall Street Journal,* July 9, 1999.

Miller, Michael W. "Dark Days: The Staggering Cost of Depression." *Wall Street Journal,* December 2, 1993:B1, B6.

Miller, Michael W. "Survey Sketches New Portrait of the Mentally Ill." *Wall Street Journal,* January 14, 1994: B1, B10.

Miller, Walter B. "Lower Class Culture as a Generating Milieu of Gang Delinquency." *Journal of Social Issues, 14,* 3, 1958:5–19.

Miller-Loessi, Karen. "Toward Gender Integration in the Workplace: Issues at Multiple Levels." *Sociological Perspectives, 35,* 1, 1992:1–15.

Mills, C. Wright. *The Power Elite.* New York: Oxford University Press, 1956.

Mills, C. Wright. *The Sociological Imagination.* New York: Oxford University Press, 1959.

Mills, Karen M., and Thomas J. Palumbo. *A Statistical Portrait of Women in the United States: 1978.* U.S. Bureau of the Census, *Current Population Reports,* Series P-23, no. 100, 1980.

Miner, Horace. "Body Ritual among the Nacirema." In *Down to Earth Sociology: Introductory Readings,* 10th ed., James M. Henslin, ed. New York: Free Press, 1999:75–79.

Minkler, Meredith, and Ann Robertson. "The Ideology of 'Age/Race Wars': Deconstructing a Social Problem." *Ageing and Society, 11,* 1, March 1991:1–22.

Mintz, Beth A., and Michael Schwartz. *The Power Structure of American Business.* Chicago: University of Chicago Press, 1985.

Mitchell, G., Stephanie Obradovich, Fred Harring, Chris Tromborg, and Alyson L. Burns. "Reproducing Gender in Public Places: Adults' Attention to Toddlers in Three Public Locales." *Sex Roles, 26,* 7/8, 1992:323–330.

Mizruchi, Mark S., and Thomas Koenig. "Size, Concentration, and Corporate Networks: Determinants of Business Collective Action." *Social Science Quarterly, 72,* 2, June 1991:299–313.

Moberg, Mark. "Strategies of a Multiracial Environmental Coalition in Southern Alabama." *Enviro-Tech,* Spring 1999:4–8.

Mohawk, John C. "Indian Economic Development: An Evolving Concept of Sovereignty." *Buffalo Law Review, 39,* 2, Spring 1991:495–503.

Money, John, and Anke A. Ehrhardt. *Man and Woman, Boy and Girl.* Baltimore: Johns Hopkins University Press, 1972.

Montagu, M. F. Ashley. *Introduction to Physical Anthropology,* 3rd ed. Springfield, Ill.: Thomas, 1960.

Montagu, M. F. Ashley. *The Concept of Race.* New York: Free Press, 1964.

Moore, Stephen D., and Ron Winslow. "Health-Care Systems in 12 Countries Near Crisis, Drug Maker Study Says." *Wall Street Journal,* September 15, 1993:B6.

Moravec, Hans P. *Robot: Mere Machine to Transcendent Mind.* New York: Oxford University Press, 1999.

Morgan, Lewis Henry. *Ancient Society.* 1877.

Morris, Aldon. "Black Southern Student Sit-In Movement: An Analysis of Internal Organization." In *Collective Behavior and Social Movements,* Russell L. Curtis, Jr., and Benigno E. Aguirre, eds. Boston: Allyn and Bacon, 1993:361–380.

Morris, J. R. "Racial Attitudes of Undergraduates in Greek Housing." *College Student Journal, 25,* 1, March 1991:501–505.

Morrow, Betty Hearn. "Urban Families as Support after Disaster: The Case of Hurricane Andrew." Paper presented at the 1995 meetings of the American Sociological Association.

Moscos, Charles, C., and Sydney Butler. *All That We Can Be: Black Leadership and Racial Integration the Army Way.* New York: Basic Books, 1997.

Mosca, Gaetano. *The Ruling Class.* New York: McGraw-Hill, 1939. First published in 1896.

Mosher, Steven W. "Why Are Baby Girls Being Killed in China?" *Wall Street Journal,* July 25, 1983:9.

Mosher, Steven W. "Too Many People? Not by a Long Shot." *Wall Street Journal,* February 10, 1997:A18.

Mount, Ferdinand. *The Subversive Family: An Alternative History of Love and Marriage.* New York: Free Press, 1992.

Moyers, Bill. "Propaganda." In the series "A Walk Through the 20th Century." 1989. (video)

Moynihan, Daniel Patrick. "Social Justice in the *Next* Century." *America,* September 14, 1991:132–137.

Muehlenhard, Charlene L., and Melaney A. Linton. "Date Rape and Sexual Aggression in Dating Situations: Incidence and Risk Factors." *Journal of Counseling Psychology, 34,* 2, 1987:186–196.

Muir, Donal E. " 'White' Fraternity and Sorority Attitudes Toward 'Blacks' on a Deep-South Campus." *Sociological Spectrum, 11,* 1, January–March, 1991:93–103.

Murdock, George Peter. "Comparative Data on the Division of Labor by Sex." *Social Forces, 15,* 4, May 1937:551–553.

Murdock, George Peter. "The Common Denominator of Cultures." In *The Science of Man and the World Crisis,* Ralph Linton, ed. New York: Columbia University Press, 1945.

Murdock, George Peter. *Social Structure.* New York: Macmillan, 1949.

Murphy, Kim. "Last Stand of an Aging Aryan." *Los Angeles Times,* January 10, 1999.

Murray, Charles. "The Coming White Underclass." *Wall Street Journal,* October 29, 1993:A16.

Murray, Charles, and R. J. Hernstein. "What's Really Behind the SAT-score Decline?" *Public Interest, 106,* Winter 1992:32–56.

Myers, Henry F. "Look for Jobless Rate to Stay High in '90s." *Wall Street Journal,* March 2, 1992:1.

Myers, Steven Lee. "Airman Discharged for Refusal to Take Anthax Vaccine as Rebellion Grows." *New York Times,* March 11, 1999.

Nabhan, Gary Paul. *Cultures in Habitat: On Nature, Culture, and Story.* New York: Counterpoint, 1998.

Nachman, Sharon. "Elder Abuse and Neglect Substantiations: What They Tell Us About the Problem." *Journal of Elder Abuse and Neglect, 3,* 3, 1991:19–43.

Naj, Amal Kumar. "Some Manufacturers Drop Efforts to Adopt Japanese Techniques." *Wall Street Journal,* May 7, 1993:A1, A12.

Naj, Amal Kumar. "MIT Chemists Achieve Goal of Splitting Nitrogen Molecules in the Atmosphere." *Wall Street Journal,* May 12, 1995:B3.

Nakao, Keiko, and Judith Treas. "Occupational Prestige in the United States Revisited: Twenty-Five Years of Stability and Change." Paper presented at the annual meetings of the American Sociological Association, 1990. (As referenced in Kerbo, Harold R. *Social Stratification and Inequality: Class Conflict in Historical and Comparative Perspective.* 2nd ed. New York: McGraw-Hill, 1991:181.)

Narayan, Shoba. "A First in Child Care." *Boston Globe,* December 5, 1994:19–20.

Nash, Gary B. *Red, White, and Black.* Englewood Cliffs, N.J.: Prentice Hall, 1974.

Nathan, John. *Sony: The Private Life.* New York: Houghton Mifflin, 1999.

National Center for Education Statistics. *Digest of Education Statistics.* Washington, D.C.: U.S. Government Printing Office, 1991.

National Institute of Child Health and Human Development. "Child Care and Mother-Child Interaction in the First 3 Years of Life." *Developmental Psychology, 35,* 6, November 1999:1399–1413.

National School Safety Center. "The School Associated Violent Death Report," 2000.

National Women's Political Caucus. "Factsheet on Women's Political Progress." Washington, D.C., June 1998.

National Women's Political Caucus. "News and Opinions; 1998 Election Results." November 5, 1998.

Naughton, Keith. "Cyberslacking." *Newsweek,* November 29, 1999:62–65.

Nauta, André. "That They All May Be One: Can Denominationalism Die?" Paper presented at the annual meetings of the American Sociological Association, 1993.

Neikirk, William, and Glen Elsasser. "Ruling Weakens Abortion Right." *Chicago Tribune,* June 30, 1992:1, 8.

Neugarten, Bernice L. "Middle Age and Aging." In *Growing Old in America,* Beth B. Hess, ed. New Brunswick, N.J.: Transaction, 1976:180–197.

Neugarten, Bernice L. "Personality and Aging." In *Handbook of the Psychology of Aging,* James E. Birren and K. Warren Schaie, eds. New York: Van Nostrand Reinhold, 1977:626–649.

"The New Alchemy: How Science Is Molding Molecules into Miracle Materials." *Business Weekly,* July 29, 1991:48–55.

Newdorf, David. "Bailout Agencies Like to Do It in Secret." *Washington Journalism Review, 13,* 4, May 1991:15–16.

Niebuhr, H. Richard. *The Social Sources of Denominationalism.* New York: Holt, 1929.

Nieves, Evelyn. "Lumber Company Approves U.S. Deal to Save Redwoods." *New York Times,* March 3, 1999.

Noah, Timothy. "White House Forms Panel to Investigate Cold War Radiation Tests on Humans." *Wall Street Journal,* January 4, 1994:A12.

Nsamenang, A. Bame. *Human Development in Cultural Context: A Third World Perspective.* Newbury Park, Calif.: Sage, 1992.

Nuland, Sherwin B. "Immortality and Its Discontents." *Wall Street Journal,* July 2, 1999.

Oberschall, Anthony. *Social Conflict and Social Movements.* Englewood Cliffs, N.J.: Prentice Hall, 1973.

O'Brien, John E. "Violence in Divorce-Prone Families." In *Violence in the Family,* Suzanne K. Steinmetz and Murray A. Straus, eds. New York: Dodd, Mead, 1975:65–75.

O'Connell, Martin. "Where's Papa? Father's Role in Child Care." Population Trends and Public Policy no. 20. Washington, D.C.: Reference Bureau, September 1993.

Offen, Karen. "Feminism and Sexual Difference in Historical Perspective." In *Theoretical Perspectives on Sexual Difference,* Deborah L. Rhode, ed. New Haven, Conn.: Yale University Press, 1990:13–20.

Ogburn, William F. *Social Change with Respect to Culture and Human Nature.* New York: W. B. Huebsch, 1922. (Other editions by Viking in 1927, 1938, and 1950.)

Ogburn, William F. "The Hypothesis of Cultural Lag." In *Theories of Society: Foundations of Modern Sociological Theory,* Vol. 2, Talcott Parsons, Edward Shils, Kaspar D. Naegele, and Jesse R. Pitts, eds. New York: Free Press, 1961:1270–1273.

Ogburn, William F. *On Culture and Social Change: Selected Papers,* Otis Dudley Duncan, ed. Chicago: University of Chicago Press, 1964.

O'Hare, William P. "A New Look at Poverty in America." *Population Bulletin, 51,* 2, September 1996a:1–47.

O'Hare, William P. "U.S. Poverty Myths Explored: Many Poor Work Year-Round, Few Still Poor After Five Years." *Population Today: News, Numbers, and Analysis, 24,* 10, October 1996b:1–2.

Ohmae, Kenichi. *The End of the Nation State: The Rise of Regional Economies.* New York: Free Press, 1995.

Oliver, Pamela E., and Gerald Marwell. "Mobilizing Technologies for Collective Action." In *Frontiers in Social Movement Theory,* Aldon D. Morris and Carol McClurg Mueller, eds. New Haven, Conn.: Yale University Press, 1992:251–272.

Olmsted, Michael S., and A. Paul Hare. *The Small Group,* 2nd ed. New York: Random House, 1978.

Olneck, Michael R., and David B. Bills. "What Makes Sammy Run? An Empirical Assessment of the Bowles-Gintis Correspondence Theory." *American Journal of Education, 89,* 1980:27–61.

O'Malley, Jeff. "Sex Tourism and Women's Status in Thailand." *Society and Leisure, 11,* 1, Spring 1988:99–114.

O'Neill, Helen. "Strange, Strange Worlds." *Alton Telegraph,* April 6, 1997:A10.

Olshansky, S. Jay, Bruce Carnes, Richard G. Rogers, and Len Smith. "Infectious Diseases—New and Ancient Threats to World Health." *Population Bulletin, 52,* 2, July 1997:1–51.

Ono, Yumiko. "By Dint of Promotion Japanese Entrepreneur Ignites a Soccer Frenzy." *Wall Street Journal,* September 17, 1993:A1, A6.

Ono, Yumiko, and Jacob M. Schlesinger. "With Careful Planning, Japan Sets Out to Be 'Life Style Superpower.' " *Wall Street Journal,* October 10, 1992:A1, A11.

Orlans, Harold. "Members Comment on ASA's Publication on Affirmative Action." *Footnotes,* May–June 1999:8.

Ortega, Bob. "Portland, Ore., Shows Nation's City Planners How to Guide Growth." *Wall Street Journal,* December 26, 1995:A1, A8.

Ortega, Suzanne T., and Jay Corzine. "Socioeconomic Status and Mental Disorders." *Research in Community and Mental Health, 6,* 1990:149–182.

Orwell, George. *1984.* New York: Harcourt Brace, 1949.

Ouchi, William. *Theory Z: How American Business Can Meet the Japanese Challenge.* Reading, Mass.: Addison-Wesley, 1981.

Ouchi, William. "Decision-Making in Japanese Organizations." In *Down to Earth Sociology: Introductory Readings,* 7th ed., James M. Henslin, ed. New York: Free Press, 1993:503–507.

Paddock, Richard C. "Russians Bank on Bartering." *Los Angeles Times,* December 28, 1998.

Paddock, Richard C. "Patient Deaths Point to Depth of Russian Crisis." *Los Angeles Times,* March 13, 1999.

Pagelow, Mildred Daley. "Adult Victims of Domestic Violence: Battered Women." *Journal of Interpersonal Violence, 7,* 1, March 1992:87–120.

Parfit, Michael, "Earth First!ers Wield a Mean Monkey Wrench." *Smithsonian, 21,* 1, April 1990:184–204.

Park, Robert Ezra. "Human Ecology." *American Journal of Sociology, 42,* 1, July 1936:1–15.

Park, Robert Ezra, and Ernest W. Burgess. *Human Ecology.* Chicago: University of Chicago Press, 1921a.

Parker-Pope, Tara. "Making a Stand." *Wall Street Journal,* April 9, 1998.

Parkinson, C. Northcote. *Parkinson's Law and Other Studies in Administration.* New York: Ballantine Books, 1957.

Parsons, Talcott. "An Analytic Approach to the Theory of Social Stratification." *American Journal of Sociology, 45,* 1940:841–862.

Parsons, Talcott. *The Social System.* New York: Free Press, 1951.

Parsons, Talcott. "Illness and the Role of the Physician: A Sociological Perspective." In *Personality in Nature, Society, and Culture,* 2nd ed., Clyde Kluckhohn and Henry A. Murray, eds. New York: Knopf, 1953:609–617.

Parsons, Talcott. "The Sick Role and the Role of the Physician Reconsidered." *Milbank Memorial Fund Quarterly/Health and Society, 53,* 3, Summer 1975:257–278.

Partington, Donald H. "The Incidence of the Death Penalty for Rape in Virginia." *Washington and Lee Law Review, 22,* 1965:43–75.

Passell, Peter. "Race, Mortgages and Statistics." *New York Times,* May 10, 1996:D1, D4.

Pasztor, Andy. "U.S., Grumman Reach Accord in Pentagon Case." *Wall Street Journal,* November 23, 1993:A3.

Paul, Ron. "Congressman Ron Paul." Newsletter issued April 1994.

Pearlin, L. I., and Melvin L. Kohn. "Social Class, Occupation, and Parental Values: A Cross-National Study." *American Sociological Review, 31,* 1966:466–479.

Peart, Karen N. "Converts to the Faith." *Scholastic Update, 126,* 4, October 22, 1993:16–18.

Pennar, Karen, and Christopher Farrell. "Notes from the Underground Economy." *Business Week,* February 15, 1993:98–101.

Perrin, Kathleen. "Rationing Health Care: Should It Be Done?" In *Perspectives in Social Gerontology,* Robert B. Enright, Jr., ed. Boston: Allyn and Bacon, 1994:309–314.

Perrow, Charles. "A Society of Organizations." *Theory and Society, 20,* 6, December 1991:725–762.

Persell, Caroline Hodges, and Peter W. Cookson, Jr. "Where the Power Starts." *Signature,* August 1986:51–57.

Peter, Laurence J., and Raymond Hull. *The Peter Principle: Why Things Always Go Wrong.* New York: Morrow, 1969.

Peterson, James L., and Nicholas Zill. "Marital Disruption, Parent–Child Relationships, and Behavior Problems in Children." *Journal of Marriage and the Family, 48,* 1986:295–307.

Phillips, Barbara D. "TV: America's Forgotten Plague." *Wall Street Journal,* February 9, 1998:A15.

Phillips, John L., Jr. *The Origins of Intellect: Piaget's Theory.* San Francisco: Freeman, 1969.

Piaget, Jean. *The Psychology of Intelligence.* London: Routledge & Kegan Paul, 1950.

Piaget, Jean. *The Construction of Reality in the Child.* New York: Basic Books, 1954.

Pillemer, Karl, and Beth Hudson. "A Model Abuse Prevention Program for Nursing Assistants." *Gerontologist, 33,* 1, 1993:128–131.

Pillemer, Karl, and J. Jill Suitor. "Violence and Violent Feelings: What Causes Them Among Family Caregivers?" *Journal of Gerontology, 47,* 4, 1992:165–172.

Pillemer, Karl, and Rosalie S. Wolf. *Elder Abuse: Conflict in the Family.* Dover, Mass.: Auburn House, 1987.

Pilling, D., and M. Kellmer Pringle. *Controversial Issues in Child Development.* London: Paul Elek, 1978.

Pines, Maya. "The Civilizing of Genie." *Psychology Today, 15,* September 1981:28–34.

Piotrow, Phylis Tilson. *World Population Crisis: The United States' Response.* New York: Praeger, 1973.

Platt, Tony. " 'Street' Crime—A View from the Left." *Crime and Social Justice: Issues in Criminology, 9,* 1978:26–34.

Pollak, Lauren Harte, and Peggy A. Thoits. "Processes in Emotional Socialization." *Social Psychological Quarterly, 52,* 1, 1989:22–34.

Pollard, Kelvin M., and William P. O'Hare. "America's Racial and Ethnic Minorities." *Population Bulletin, 54,* 3, September 1999:3–47.

Polsby, Nelson W. "Three Problems in the Analysis of Community Power." *American Sociological Review, 24,* 6, December 1959:796–803.

Polumbaum, Judy. "China: Confucian Tradition Meets the Market Economy." *Ms.,* September–October 1992:12–13.

Pope, Liston. *Millhands and Preachers: A Study of Gastonia.* New Haven, Conn.: Yale University Press, 1942.

Population Reference Bureau. "World Information Data Sheet." Washington, D.C., May 1995.

Population Today, 26, 9, September 1998.

"Population Update." *Population Today, 25,* 4, April 1997:6.

"Population Update." *Population Today, 28,* 1, January 2000.

Portés, Alejandro, and Ruben G. Rumbaut. *Immigrant America.* Berkeley: University of California Press, 1990.

Postman, Neil. *Technopoly: The Surrender of Culture to Technology.* New York: Knopf, 1992.

Powell, Bill. "Yeltsin's Legacy." *Newsweek,* January 4, 1999:72.

Power, Carla. "The New Islam." *Newsweek,* March 16, 1998:34–37.

Presley, Cheryl A., Philip W. Meilman, and Rob Lyerla. *Alcohol and Drugs on American College Campuses.* Carbondale, Ill.: Southern Illinois University, 1993.

Pressley, Sue Anne. "The Curious Continue Waco Siege." *Washington Post,* August 28, 1993:A1, A12.

Preston, Howard L. *Automobile Age Atlanta: The Making of a Southern Metropolis, 1900–1935.* Athens: University of Georgia Press, 1979.

"Price of Entry into China Rises Sharply." *Wall Street Journal,* December 19, 1995:A12.

Prud'Homme, Alex. "Getting a Grip on Power." *Time,* July 29, 1991:15–16.

Rabinovitz, Jonathan. "Working Parents Use Internet to Check on Children in Day Care." *New York Times,* December 9, 1997.

Raney, Rebecca Fairley. "Study Warns of Risks in Internet Voting." *New York Times,* March 8, 1999.

Rathus, Spencer, and Jeffrey Nevid. *Human Sexuality in a World of Diversity.* Boston: Allyn and Bacon, 1993.

Ray, J. J. "Authoritarianism Is a Dodo: Comment on Scheepers, Felling and Peters." *European Sociological Review, 7,* 1, May 1991:73–75.

Read, Piers Paul. *Alive. The Story of the Andes Survivors.* Philadelphia: Lippincott, 1974.

Reat, Noble Ross. *Buddhism: A History.* Berkeley, Ca: Asian Humanities Press, 1994.

Reckless, Walter C. *The Crime Problem,* 5th ed. New York: Appleton, 1973.

Redclift, Michael, and Graham Woodgate, eds. *The International Handbook of Environmental Sociology.* Cheltenham, England: Edward Elgar, 1997.

Reed, Susan, and Lorenzo Benet. "Ecowarrior Dave Foreman Will Do Whatever It Takes in His Fight to Save Mother Earth." *People Weekly, 33,* 15, April 16, 1990:113–116.

Reibstein, Larry. "Managing Diversity." *Newsweek,* November 25, 1996:50.

Reich, Michael. "The Economics of Racism." In *The Capitalist System,* Richard C. Edwards, Michael Reich, and Thomas E. Weiskopf, eds. Englewood Cliffs, N.J.: Prentice Hall, 1972:313–321.

Reich, Robert B. *Good for Business: Making Full Use of the Nation's Human Capital, The Environmental Scan.* Washington, D.C.: U.S. Department of Labor, March 1995.

Reitman, Valerie. "Japan's New Growth Industry: Schoolgirl Prostitution." *Wall Street Journal,* October 2, 1996:A8.

Reitman, Valerie, and Oscar Suris. "In a Cultural U-Turn, Mazda's Creditors Put Ford Behind the Wheel." *Wall Street Journal,* November 21, 1994:A1, A4.

Renteln, Alison Dundes. "Sex Selection and Reproductive Freedom." *Women's Studies International Forum, 15,* 3, 1992:405–426.

Reskin, Barbara F. *The Realities of Affirmative Action in Employment.* Washington, D.C.: American Sociological Association, 1998.

Rich, Spencer. "Number of Elected Hispanic Officials Doubled in a Decade, Study Shows." *Washington Post,* September 19, 1986:A6.

Richards, Bill. "Doctors Can Diagnose Illnesses Long Distance, to the Dismay of Some." *Wall Street Journal,* January 17, 1996:A1, A8.

Richter, Paul. "CIA Director Warns of Terrorist Threat." *Los Angeles Times,* February 3, 1999.

Ricks, Thomas E. "Pentagon Considers Selling Overseas a Large Part of High-Tech Weaponry." *Wall Street Journal,* February 14, 1994:A16.

Ricks, Thomas E. "'New' Marines Illustrate Growing Gap Between Military and Society." *Wall Street Journal,* July 27, 1995:A1, A4.

Ricks, Thomas E. "Defense Chief Won't Segregate Sexes in Basic Training, Despite Panel's Views." *Wall Street Journal,* March 17, 1998:A20.

Rieker, Patricia P., Chloe E. Bird, Susan Bell, Jenny Ruducha, Rima E. Rudd, and S. M. Miller, "Violence and Women's Health: Toward a Society and Health Perspective." Unpublished paper, 1997.

Riesman, David. *The Lonely Crowd.* New Haven, Conn.: Yale University Press, 1950.

Riessman, Catherine Kohler. "Women and Medicalization: A New Perspective." In *Dominant Issues in Medical Sociology,* 3rd ed., Howard D. Schwartz, ed. New York: McGraw-Hill, 1994:190–211.

Rifkin, Jeremy. *The End of Work: The Decline of the Global Labor Force and the Dawn of the Post-Market Era.* New York: Putnam, 1995.

Rigdon, Joan E., and Alecia Swasy. "Distractions of Modern Life at Key Ages Are Cited for Drop in Student Literacy." *Wall Street Journal,* October 1, 1990:B1, B3.

Riley, Nancy E. "Gender, Power, and Population Change." *Population Bulletin, 52,* 1, May 1997:1–47.

Risman, Barbara H. *Gender Vertigo: American Families in Transition.* New Haven, Conn.: Yale University Press, 1998.

Rist, Ray C. "Student Social Class and Teacher Expectations: The Self-Fulfilling Prophecy in Ghetto Education." *Harvard Educational Review, 40,* 3, August 1970:411–451.

Ritzer, George. *Sociological Theory,* 3rd ed. New York: McGraw-Hill, 1992.

Ritzer, George. *The McDonaldization of Society: An Investigation into the Changing Character of Contemporary Life.* Thousand Oaks, Calif.: Pine Forge Press, 1993.

Robertson, Ian. *Sociology,* 3rd ed. New York: Worth, 1987.

Robinson, Arthur B., and Zachary W. Robinson. "Science Has Spoken: Global Warming is a Myth." *Wall Street Journal,* December 4, 1997:A22.

Rodash, Mary Flannery. "The College of Midwifery: A Sociological Study of the Decline of a Profession." Unpublished doctoral dissertation, Southern Illinois University at Carbondale, 1982.

Rodriguez, Richard. "The Education of Richard Rodriguez." *Saturday Review,* February 8, 1975:147–149.

Rodriguez, Richard. *Hunger of Memory: The Education of Richard Rodriguez.* Boston: Godine, 1982.

Rodriguez, Richard. "The Late Victorians: San Francisco, AIDS, and the Homosexual Stereotype." *Harper's Magazine,* October 1990:57–66.

Rodriguez, Richard. "Mixed Blood." *Harper's Magazine, 283,* November 1991:47–56.

Rodriguez, Richard. "Searching for Roots in a Changing Society." In *Down to Earth Sociology: Introductory Readings,* 8th ed., James M. Henslin, ed. New York: Free Press, 1995:486–491.

Rodriguez, Victor M. "Los Angeles, U.S.A. 1992: 'A House Divided Against Itself . . .'" *SSSP Newsletter,* Spring 1994:5–12.

Rodwin, Marc A. *Medicine, Money, and Morals: Physicians' Conflicts of Interest.* New York: Oxford University Press, 1993.

Roethlisberger, Fritz J., and William J. Dickson. *Management and the Worker.* Cambridge, Mass.: Harvard University Press, 1939.

Rogers, Joseph W. *Why Are You Not a Criminal?* Englewood Cliffs, N.J.: Prentice Hall, 1977.

Rohen, Thomas P. *Japan's High Schools.* Berkeley: University of California Press, 1983.

Rosaldo, Michelle Zimbalist. "Women, Culture and Society: A Theoretical Overview." In *Women, Culture, and Society,* Michelle Zimbalist Rosaldo and Louise Lamphere, eds. Stanford: Stanford University Press, 1974.

Rose, Frederick. "Los Angeles Tallies Losses; Curfew Is Lifted." *Wall Street Journal,* May 5, 1992:A3, A18.

Rose, Steven. "Stalking the Criminal Chromosome." *Nation* 242 (20), 1986:732–736.

Rosenbaum, David E. "U.S. Breaks a Ring That Smuggled in Thousands of Workers." *New York Times,* November 21, 1998.

Rosenberg, Charles E. *The Care of Strangers: The Rise of America's Hospital System.* New York: Basic Books, 1987.

Rosenthal, Elisabeth. "China's Chic Waistline: Convex to Concave." *New York Times,* December 9, 1999.

Rosenthal, Robert, and Lenore Jacobson. *Pygmalion in the Classroom: Teacher Expectation and Pupils' Intellectual Development.* New York: Holt, Rinehart, and Winston, 1968.

Ross, Catherine E., and Marieke van Willigen. "Education and the Subjective Quality of Life." *Journal of Health and Social Behavior, 38,* 3, September 1997:275–297.

Rossi, Alice S. "A Biosocial Perspective on Parenting." *Daedalus, 106,* 1977:1–31.

Rossi, Alice S. "Gender and Parenthood." *American Sociological Review, 49,* 1984:1–18.

Rossi, Peter H. *Down and Out in America: The Origins of Homelessness.* Chicago: University of Chicago Press, 1989.

Rossi, Peter H. "Going Along or Getting It Right?" *Journal of Applied Sociology, 8,* 1991:77–81.

Rossi, Peter H. "Half Truths with Real Consequences: Journalism, Research, and Public Policy." *Contemporary Sociology,* 1999:1–5.

Rossi, Peter H., Gene A. Fisher, and Georgianna Willis. *The Condition of the Homeless of Chicago.* Amherst: University of Massachusetts, September 1986.

Rossi, Peter H., James D. Wright, Gene A. Fisher, and Georgianna Willis. "The Urban Homeless: Estimating Composition and Size." *Science, 235,* March 13, 1987:1136–1140.

Rotello, Gabriel. "The Risk in a 'Cure' for AIDS." *New York Times,* July 14, 1996.

Rothman, Barbara Katz. "Midwives in Transition: The Structure of a Clinical Revolution." In *Dominant Issues in Medical Sociology,* 3rd ed. Howard D. Schwartz, ed. New York: McGraw-Hill, 1994:104–112.

Rothschild, Joyce, and J. Allen Whitt. *The Cooperative Workplace: Potentials and Dilemmas of Organizational Democracy and Participation.* Cambridge, England: Cambridge University Press, 1986.

Rubin, Lillian Breslow. *Worlds of Pain: Life in the Working-Class Family.* New York: Basic Books, 1976.

Rubin, Lillian Breslow. "The Empty Nest." In *Marriage and Family in a Changing Society,* 4th ed., James M. Henslin, ed. New York: Free Press, 1992a:261–270.

Rubin, Lillian Breslow. "Worlds of Pain." In *Marriage and Family in a Changing Society,* 4th ed., James M. Henslin, ed. New York: Free Press, 1992b:44–50.

Rubin, Zick. "The Love Research." In *Marriage and Family in a Changing Society,* 2nd ed., James M. Henslin, ed. New York: Free Press, 1985.

Ruffenbach, Glenn. "Nursing-Home Care as a Work Benefit." *Wall Street Journal,* June 30, 1988:23.

Ruggles, Patricia. "Short and Long Term Poverty in the United States: Measuring the American 'Underclass.' " Washington, D.C.: Urban Institute, June 1989.

Russell, Diana E. H. "Preliminary Report on Some Findings Relating to the Trauma and Long-Term Effects of Intrafamily Childhood Sexual Abuse." Unpublished paper.

Russell, Diana E. H. *Rape in Marriage.* Bloomington: Indiana University Press, 1990.

Ryan, John, and William M. Wentworth. *Media and Soceity: The Production of Culture in the Mass Media.* Boston: Allyn and Bacon, 1999.

Rybczynski, Witold. "The Virtues of Suburban Sprawl." *Wall Street Journal,* May 25, 1999.

Sahlins, Marshall D. *Stone Age Economics.* Chicago: Aldine, 1972.

Sahlins, Marshall D., and Elman R. Service. *Evolution and Culture.* Ann Arbor: University of Michigan Press, 1960.

Salholz, Eloise. "The Push for Power." *Newsweek,* April 9, 1990:19–20.

Sampson, Robert J., Jeffrey D. Morenoff, and Felton Earls. "Beyond Social Capital: Spatial Dynamics of Collective Efficacy for Children." *American Sociological Review, 64,* October 1999:633–660.

Samuelson, Paul A., and William D. Nordhaus. *Economics,* 13th ed. New York: McGraw-Hill, 1989.

Samuelson, Robert J. "The Elderly Aren't Needy." *Newsweek,* March 21, 1988:68.

Sanchez, Laura. "Gender, Labor Allocations, and the Psychology of Entitlement Within the Home." *Social Forces, 13,* 2, December 1994:533–553.

Sandefur, Gary D. "Children in Single-Parent Families: The Roles of Time and Money." *Focus, 17,* 1, Summer 1995:44–45.

Sapir, Edward. *Selected Writings of Edward Sapir in Language, Culture, and Personality.* David G. Mandelbaum, ed. Berkeley, Calif.: University of California Press, 1949.

Satchell, Michael. "A Whale of a Protest." *U.S. News Online,* October 5, 1998.

Savells, Jerry. "Social Change among the Amish." In *Down to Earth Sociology: Introductory Readings,* 10th ed., James M. Henslin, ed. New York: Free Press, 1999:507–515.

Sayres, William. "What Is a Family Anyway?" In *Marriage and Family in a Changing Society,* 4th ed., James M. Henslin, ed. New York: Free Press, 1992:23–30.

Saxe, G. B. "Candy Selling and Math Learning." *Educational Researcher, 17*(6), 1995:14–21.

Scarr, Sandra, and Marlene Eisenberg. "Child Care Research: Issues, Perspectives, and Results." *Annual Review of Psychology, 44,* 1993:613–644.

Schaefer, Naomi. "Slavery in Africa Is Largely Ignored by U.S. Black Leaders and Major Media." *Massachusetts News,* May 12, 1999.

Schaefer, Richard T. *Sociology,* 3rd ed. New York: McGraw-Hill, 1989.

Schaefer, Richard T. *Racial and Ethnic Groups,* 8th ed. Upper Saddle River, N.J.: Prentice Hall, 2000.

Schatz, Thomas A. "Medicare Fraud: Tales from the Gypped." *Wall Street Journal,* August 25, 1995:A8.

Schellenberg, James A. *Conflict Resolution: Theory, Research, and Practice.* Albany: New York University Press, 1996.

Schlesinger, Jacob M. "For What Ails Japan, Some Think the Cure Is a Good Hot Slogan." *Wall Street Journal,* January 31, 1994:A1, A7.

Schlesinger, Jacob M., and Jathon Sapsford. "Japan, Shaken by Plunging Stocks, Mulls Further Economic Measures." *Wall Street Journal,* December 1, 1993:A14.

Schlossberg, Nancy. *Overwhelmed: Coping with Life's Ups and Downs.* Boston: Lexington Books, 1990.

Schmalleger, Frank. *Criminology Today: An Integrative Introduction.* Upper Saddle River, New Jersey: Prentice Hall, 1999.

Schmemann, Serge. "Russia's Precapitalist Economy: How Can You Have a Bust If You Never Had a Boom?" *New York Times,* December 27, 1998.

Schor, Juliet B. "Americans Work Too Hard." *New York Times,* July 25, 1991:A21.

Schottland, Charles I. *The Social Security Plan in the U.S.* New York: Appleton, 1963.

Schrieke, Bertram J. *Alien Americans.* New York: Viking, 1936.

Schur, Edwin M. *Labeling Women Deviant: Gender, Stigma, and Social Control.* New York: Random House, 1984.

Schwartz, Felice N. "Management Women and the New Facts of Life." *Harvard Business Review, 89,* 1, January–February 1989:65–76.

Schwartz, Mildred A. *A Sociological Perspective on Politics.* Englewood Cliffs, N.J.: Prentice Hall, 1990.

Schwendinger, Julia R., and Herman Schwendinger. *Rape and Inequality.* Beverly Hills, Calif.: Sage, 1983.

Scott, Ellen Kaye. "How to Stop the Rapists: A Question of Strategy in Two Rape Crisis Centers." *Social Problems, 40,* 3, August 1993:343–361.

Scully, Diana. *Understanding Sexual Violence: A Study of Convicted Rapists.* Boston: Unwin Hyman, 1990.

Scully, Diana, and Joseph Marolla. "Convicted Rapists' Vocabulary of Motive: Excuses and Justifications." *Social Problems, 31,* 5, June 1984:530–544.

Scully, Diana, and Joseph Marolla. " 'Riding the Bull at Gilley's': Convicted Rapists Describe the Rewards of Rape." *Social Problems, 32,* 3, February 1985:251–263.

Seabrook, Jeremy. *Travels in the Skin Trade: Tourism and the Sex Industry.* New York: Pluto Press, 1997.

Searle, John R. *The Construction of Social Reality.* New York: Free Press, 1995.

Seaver, W. J. "Effects of Naturally Induced Teacher Expectancies." *Journal of Personality and Social Psychology, 28,* 1973:333–342.

Seib, Gerald F. *Wall Street Journal,* "Click Here for Democracy." *Wall Street Journal,* January 1, 2000:R45–R46.

Seltzer, Judith A. "Consequences of Marital Dissolution for Children." *Annual Review of Sociology, 20,* 1994:235–266.

Shanker, Albert. "Education Contract with America." *Wall Street Journal,* September 15, 1995:A10.

Sharma, S. S. "Untouchables and Brahmins in an Indian Village." In *Haves and Have-Nots: An International Reader on Social Inequality,* James Curtis and Lorne Tepperman, eds. Englewood Cliffs, N.J.: Prentice Hall, 1994:299–303.

Sharp, Deborah. "Miami's Language Gap Widens." *USA Today,* April 3, 1992:A1, A3.

Sharp, Lauriston. "Steel Axes for Stone-Age Australians." In *Down to Earth Sociology: Introductory Readings,* 8th ed., James M. Henslin, ed. New York: Free Press, 1995:453–462.

Sheldon, William. *Varieties of Delinquent Youth: An Introduction to Constitutional Psychiatry.* New York: Harper, 1949.

Shellenbarger, Sue. "The Aging of America Is Making 'Elder Care' a Big Workplace Issue." *Wall Street Journal,* February 16, 1994a:A1, A8.

Shellenbarger, Sue. "How Some Companies Help with Elder Care." *Wall Street Journal,* February 16, 1994b:A8.

Shellenbarger, Sue. "Work and Family." *Wall Street Journal,* May 3, 1995b:B1.

Shenon, Philip. "Arguments Conclude in Army Sex Hearing." *New York Times,* August 26, 1997 (electronic version).

Sherif, Muzafer, and Carolyn Sherif. *Groups in Harmony and Tension.* New York: Harper & Row, 1953.

Sherkat, Darren E., and John Wilson. "Status, Denomination, and Socialization: Effects on Religious Switching and Apostasy." Presented at the annual meetings of the American Sociological Association, 1991.

Sherman, Spencer. "The Hmong in America." *National Geographic,* October 1988:586–610.

Shibutani, Tamotsu. *Improvised News: A Sociological Study of Rumor.* Indianapolis, Ind.: Bobbs-Merrill, 1966.

Shibutani, Tamotsu. "On the Personification of Adversaries." In *Human Nature and Collective Behavior,* Tamotsu Shibutani, ed. Englewood Cliffs, N.J.: Prentice Hall, 1970.

Shirouzu, Norihiko, and Michael Williams. "Pummeled by Giants, Japan's Small Firms Struggle with Change." *Wall Street Journal,* July 25, 1995:A1, A5.

Shively, JoEllen. "Cultural Compensation: The Popularity of Westerns Among American Indians," Paper presented at the annual meetings of the American Sociological Association, 1991.

Shively, JoEllen. "Cowboys and Indians: Perceptions of Western Films Among American Indians and Anglos." *American Sociological Review, 57,* December 1992:725–734.

Shreve, Herbie. Personal communication, 1991.

Signorielli, Nancy. "Television and Conceptions About Sex Roles: Maintaining Conventionality and the Status Quo." *Sex Roles, 21,* 5/6, 1989:341–360.

Signorielli, Nancy. "Children, Television, and Gender Roles: Messages and Impact." *Journal of Adolescent Health Care, 11,* 1990:50–58.

Sills, David L. *The Volunteers.* Glencoe, Ill.: Free Press, 1957.

Sills, David L. "Voluntary Associations: Sociological Aspects." In *International Encyclopedia of the Social Sciences, 16,* David L. Sills, ed. New York: Macmillan, 1968:362–379.

Simmel, Georg. *The Sociology of Georg Simmel,* Kurt H. Wolff, ed. and trans. Glencoe, Ill.: Free Press, 1950. First published between 1902 and 1917.

Simmons, Ann M. "Survivors of Rwandan Genocide Fear Guilty Will Get Away With Murder." *Los Angeles Times,* December 26, 1998.

Simon, David R., and D. Stanley Eitzen. *Elite Deviance,* 4th ed. Boston: Allyn and Bacon, 1993.

Simon, Julian L. *The Ultimate Resource.* Princeton, N.J.: Princeton University Press, 1981.

Simon, Julian L. *Theory of Population and Economic Growth.* New York: Blackwell, 1986.

Simons, Marlise. "The Amazon's Savvy Indians." In *Down to Earth Sociology: Introductory Readings,* 8th ed. James M. Henslin, ed. New York: Free Press, 1995:463–470.

Simpson, George Eaton, and J. Milton Yinger. *Racial and Cultural Minorities: An Analysis of Prejudice and Discrimination,* 4th ed. New York: Harper & Row, 1972.

Simpson, Glenn R. "Now Showing on an E-Mail Screen Near You: Your Congressman." *Wall Street Journal,* January 7, 2000.

Skeels, H. M. *Adult Status of Children with Contrasting Early Life Experiences: A Follow-up Study.* Monograph of the Society for Research in Child Development, *31,* 3, 1966.

Skeels, H. M., and H. B. Dye. "A Study of the Effects of Differential Stimulation on Mentally Retarded Children." *Proceedings and Addresses of the American Association on Mental Deficiency, 44,* 1939:114–136.

Skow, John. "The Redwoods Weep." *Time,* September 28, 1998:70–72.

Small, Albion W. *General Sociology.* Chicago: University of Chicago Press, 1905. As cited in Olmsted and Hare 1978:10.

Smart, Barry. "On the Disorder of Things: Sociology, Postmodernity and the 'End of the Social.' " *Sociology, 24,* 3, August 1990:397–416.

Smith, Beverly A. "An Incest Case in an Early 20th-Century Rural Community." *Deviant Behavior, 13,* 1992:127–153.

Smith, Clark. "Oral History as 'Therapy': Combatants' Account of Vietnam War." In *Strangers at Home: Vietnam Veterans Since the War,* Charles R. Figley and Seymore Leventman, eds. New York: Praeger, 1980:9–34.

Smith, Craig S. "China Becomes Industrial Nations' Most Favored Dump." *Wall Street Journal,* October 9, 1995:B1.

Smith, Daniel Scott, and Michael Hindus. "Premarital Pregnancy in America, 1640–1971: An Overview and Interpretation." *Journal of Interdisciplinary History, 4,* Spring 1975:537–570.

Smith, Douglas A., and Robert Brame. "On the Initiation and Continuation of Delinquency." *Criminology, 32,* 4, 1994:607–629.

Smith, Harold. "A Colossal Cover-Up." *Christianity Today,* December 12, 1986:16–17.

Smith, Joel B., and Dennis A. Tirpak. *The Potential Effects of Global Climate Change in the United States.* Washington, D.C.: U.S. Environmental Protection Agency, October 1988.

Smith, Kristen F., and Vern L. Bengston. "Positive Consequences of Institutionalization: Solidarity Between Elderly Parents and Their Middle-Aged Children." *Gerontologist, 19,* October 1979:438–447.

Smith, Lee. "The War Between the Generations." *Fortune,* July 20, 1987:78–82.

Smith, Wesley J. "Dependency or Death? Oregonians Make a Chilling Choice." *Wall Street Journal,* February 25, 1999.

Smith-Lovin, Lynn, and Charles Brody. "Interruptions in Group Discussions: The Effects of Gender and Group Composition." *American Sociological Review, 54,* 1989:424–435.

Smock, Pamela J., Wendy D. Manning, and Sanjiv Gupta. "The Effect of Marriage and Divorce on Women's Economic Well-Being." *American Sociological Review, 64,* December 1999:794–812.

Snow, David A., Louis A. Zurcher, Jr., and Sheldon Ekland-Olson. "Social Networks and Social Movements: A Microstructural Approach to Differential Recruitment." In *Collective Behavior and Social Movements,* Russell L. Curtis, Jr., and Benigno E. Aguirre, eds. Boston: Allyn and Bacon, 1993:323–334.

Snow, David A., Louis A. Zurcher, and Robert Peters. "Victory Celebrations as Theater: A Dramaturgical Approach to Crowd Behavior." In *Collective Behavior and Social Movements,* Russell L. Curtis, Jr., and Benigno E. Aguirre, eds. Boston: Allyn and Bacon, 1993:194–208.

Snow, Margaret E., Carol Nagy Jacklin, and Eleanor E. Maccoby. "Birth-Order Differences in Peer Sociability at Thirty-Three Months." *Child Development, 52,* 1981:589–595.

Snyder, Mark. "Self-Fulfilling Stereotypes." In *Down to Earth Sociology: Introductory Readings,* 7th ed., James M. Henslin, ed. New York: Free Press, 1993:153–160.

Solomon, Jolie. "Companies Try Measuring Cost Savings from New Types of Corporate Benefits." *Wall Street Journal,* December 29, 1988:B1.

Son, Johanna. "Changing Attitudes Key to Ending Child Sex Trade." InterPress Service, January 23, 1995.

Sorokin, Pitirim A. *Social and Cultural Dynamics.* 4 vols. New York: American Book Company, 1937–1941.

Sorokin, Pitirim A. *The Crisis of Our Age.* New York: Dutton, 1941.

Sourcebook of Criminal Justice Statistics. Washington, D.C.: U.S. Government Printing Office, published annually.

South, Scott J. "Sociodemographic Differentials in Mate Selection Preferences." *Journal of Marriage and the Family, 53,* November 1991:928–940.

Sowell, Thomas. "Effrontery and Gall, Inc." *Forbes,* September 27, 1993a:52.

Sowell, Thomas. *Inside American Education: The Decline, the Deception, the Dogmas.* New York: Free Press, 1993b.

Soysa, Indra de, and John R. Oneal. "Boon or Bane? Reassessing the Productivity of Foreign Direct Investment." *American Sociological Review, 64,* October 1999:766–782.

Specter, Michael. "Plunging Life Expectancy Puzzles Russians." *New York Times,* August 1, 1995:A1, A6.

Spector, Malcolm, and John Kitsuse. *Constructing Social Problems.* Menlo Park, Calif.: Cummings, 1977.

Spencer, Herbert. *Principles of Sociology.* 3 vols. New York: Appleton, 1884.

Spengler, Oswald. *The Decline of the West,* 2 vols. Charles F. Atkinson, trans. New York: Knopf, 1926–1928. First published in 1919–1922.

Spitz, Renée. "Hospitalism." *Psychoanalytic Study of the Child, 1,* 1945:53–72.

Spitzer, Steven. "Toward a Marxian Theory of Deviance." *Social Problems, 22,* June 1975:608–619.

Spragins, Ellyn E. "To Sue or Not to Sue?" *Newsweek,* December 9, 1996:50.

Sprecher, Susan, and Rachita Chandak. "Attitudes About Arranged Marriages and Dating Among Men and Women from India." *Free Inquiry in Creative Sociology, 20,* 1, May 1992:59–69.

Srole, Leo, et al. *Mental Health in the Metropolis: The Midtown Manhattan Study.* New York: New York University Press, 1978.

Stack, Carol B. *All Our Kin: Strategies for Survival in a Black Community.* New York: Harper, 1974.

Stampp, Kenneth M. *The Peculiar Institution: Slavery in the Ante-Bellum South.* New York: Vintage Books, 1956.

Stark, Elizabeth. "Friends Through It All." In *Marriage and Family in a Changing Society,* 3rd ed., James M. Henslin, ed. New York: Free Press, 1989:441–449.

Stark, Rodney. *Sociology,* 3rd ed. Belmont, Calif.: Wadsworth, 1989.

Starna, William A., and Ralph Watkins. "Northern Iroquoian Slavery." *Ethnohistory, 38,* 1, Winter 1991:34–57.

Starr, Paul. *The Social Transformation of American Medicine.* New York: Basic Books, 1982.

Starrels, Marjorie. "The Evolution of Workplace Family Policy Research." *Journal of Family Issues, 13,* 3, September 1992:259–278.

State of American Education: A 5-Year Report Card on American Education." U.S. Department of Education, February 22, 2000.

Statham, Anne, Eleanor M. Miller, and Hans O. Mauksch. "The Integration of Work: Second-order Analysis of Qualitative Research." In *The Worth of Women's Work: A Qualitative Synthesis.* Statham, Anne, Eleanor M. Miller, and Hans O. Mauksch, eds. Albany, N.Y.: State University of New York Press, 1988:11–35.

Statistical Abstract of the United States. Washington D.C.: Bureau of the Census, published annually.

Stecklow, Steve. "SAT Scores Rise Strongly after Test Is Overhauled." *Wall Street Journal,* August 24, 1995:B1, B12.

Stein, Leonard I. "The Doctor–Nurse Game." In *Down to Earth Sociology: Introductory Readings,* 5th ed., James M. Henslin, ed. New York: Free Press, 1988:102–109.

Steinberg, Jacques. "Academic Standards Eased as a Fear of Failure Spreads." *New York Times,* December 3, 1999

Steinberg, Laurence, Stanford Dornbusch, and Bradford Brown. *Beyond the Classroom.* New York: Simon & Shuster, 1996.

Steinhauer, Jennifer. "Angry at Managed Care, Doctors Start Fighting Back." *New York Times,* January 10, 1999.

Steinmetz, Greg, and Cacilie Rohwedder. "Green Party Grows Strong on Soil Peculiar to Germany." *Wall Street Journal,* April 20:1998:A15.

Stengel, Richard. "South Africa's Mandela's First Year." America Online, May 4, 1995.

Stevens, Amy, and Sarah Lubman. "Deciding Moment of the Trial May Have Been Five Months Ago." *Wall Street Journal,* May 1, 1992:A6.

Stevenson, David Lee, and David P. Baker. "Shadow Education and Allocation in Formal Schooling in Japan." In *Haves and Have-Nots: An International Reader on Social Inequality,* James Curtis and Lorne Tepperman, eds. Englewood Cliffs, N.J.: Prentice Hall, 1994:352–359.

Stevenson, Richard W. "U.S. Debates Investing in Stock for Social Security." *New York Times,* July 27, 1998.

Stinnett, Nicholas. "Strong Families." In *Marriage and Family in a Changing Society,* 4th ed., James M. Henslin, ed. New York: Free Press, 1992:496–507.

Stipp, David. "Einstein Bird Has Scientists Atwitter over Mental Feats." *Wall Street Journal,* May 9, 1990:A1, A4.

Stipp, David. "Himalayan Tree Could Serve as Source of Anti-cancer Drug Taxol, Team Says." *Wall Street Journal,* April 20, 1992:B4.

Stockard, Jean, and Miriam M. Johnson. *Sex Roles: Sex Inequality and Sex Role Development.* Englewood Cliffs, N.J.: Prentice Hall, 1980.

Stockwell, John. "The Dark Side of U.S. Foreign Policy." *Zeta Magazine,* February 1989:36–48.

Stodgill, Ralph M. *Handbook of Leadership: A Survey of Theory and Research.* New York: Free Press, 1974.

Stone, Gregory P. "City Shoppers and Urban Identification: Observations on the Social Psychology of City Life." *American Journal of Sociology, 60,* November 1954:276–284.

Stone, Michael H. "Murder." *Psychiatric Clinics of North America, 12,* 3, September 1989:643–651.

Stouffer, Samuel A., Arthur A. Lumsdaine, Marion Harper Lumsdaine, Robin M. Williams, Jr., M. Brewster Smith, Irving L. Janis, Shirley A. Star, and Leonard S. Cottrell, Jr. *The American Soldier: Combat and Its Aftermath,* Vol. 2. New York: Wiley, 1949.

Straus, Murray A. "Victims and Aggressors in Marital Violence." *American Behavioral Scientist, 23,* May–June 1980:681–704.

Straus, Murray A. "Explaining Family Violence." In *Marriage and Family in a Changing Society,* 4th ed., James M. Henslin, ed. New York: Free Press, 1992:344–356.

Straus, Murray A., and Richard J. Gelles. "Violence in American Families: How Much Is There and Why Does It Occur?" In *Troubled Relationships,* Elam W. Nunnally, Catherine S. Chilman, and Fred M. Cox, eds. Newbury Park, Calif.: Sage, 1988:141–162.

Straus, Murray A., Richard J. Gelles, and Suzanne K. Steinmetz. *Behind Closed Doors: Violence in the American Family.* New York: Anchor/Doubleday, 1980.

Straus, Roger A. "The Sociologist as a Marketing Research Consultant." *Journal of Applied Sociology, 8,* 1991:65–75.

Strauss, Neil. "Critic's Notebook: A Japanese TV Show That Pairs Beauty and Pain." *New York Times,* July 14, 1998.

Stryker, Sheldon. "Symbolic Interactionism: Themes and Variations." In *Social Psychology: Sociological Perspectives,* Morris Rosenberg and Ralph H. Turner, eds. New Brunswick, N.J.: Transaction, 1990.

Sullivan, Andrew. "What We Look Up to Now." *New York Times,* November 15, 1998.

Sulloway, Frank J. *Born to Rebel: Birth Order, Family Dynamics, and Creative Lives.* New York: Vintage Books, 1997.

Sumner, William Graham. *Folkways: A Study in the Sociological Importance of Usages, Manners, Customs, Mores, and Morals.* New York: Ginn, 1906.

Sun, Lena H. "China Seeks Ways to Protect Elderly." *Washington Post,* October 23, 1990:A1.

Sun, Lena H. "A Great Leap Back: Chinese Women Losing Jobs, Status as Ancient Ways Subvert Socialist Ideal." *Washington Post,* February 16, 1993:A1.

Sutherland, Edwin H. *Criminology.* Philadelphia: Lippincott, 1924.

Sutherland, Edwin H. *Principles of Criminology,* 4th ed. Philadelphia: Lippincott, 1947.

Sutherland, Edwin H. *White Collar Crime.* New York: Dryden Press, 1949.

Sutherland, Edwin H., and Donald Cressey. *Criminology,* 9th ed. Philadelphia: Lippincott, 1974.

Sutherland, Edwin H., Donald R. Cressey, and David F. Luckenbill. *Principles of Criminology,* 11th ed. Dix Hills, N.Y.: General Hall, 1992.

Suzuki, Bob H. "Asian-American Families." In *Marriage and Family in a Changing Society,* 2nd ed., James M. Henslin, ed. New York: Free Press, 1985:104–119.

Swedish Institute, The. "Health and Medical Care in Sweden." July 1990:1–4.

Swedish Institute, The. "Fact Sheets on Sweden." February 1992.

Sweezy, Paul M., and Harry Magdoff. "Globalization—to What End? Part II." *Monthly Review, 43,* 10, March 1992:1–19.

Sykes, Gresham M., and David Matza. "Techniques of Neutralization." In *Down to Earth Sociology: Introductory Readings,* 5th ed., James M. Henslin, ed. New York: Free Press, 1988:225–231. First published in 1957.

Szasz, Thomas S. *The Myth of Mental Illness,* rev. ed. New York: Harper & Row, 1986.

Szasz, Thomas S. "Mental Illness Is Still a Myth." In *Deviant Behavior 96/97,* Lawrence M. Salinger, ed. Guilford, Conn.: Dushkin, 1996:200–205.

Szasz, Thomas S. *Cruel Compassion: Psychiatric Control of Society's Unwanted.* Syracuse: Syracuse University Press, 1998.

Szelenyi, Szonja. "Social Inequality and Party Membership: Patterns of Recruitment in the Hungarian Socialist Workers' Party." *American Sociological Review, 52,* 1987:559–573.

Tannen, Deborah. *You Just Don't Understand: Women and Men in Conversation.* New York: Morrow, 1990.

Tannen, Deborah. "But What Do You Mean? Women and Men in Conversation." In *Down to Earth Sociology: Introductory Readings,* 10th ed., James M. Henslin, ed. New York: Free Press, 1999:165–170.

Tanouye, Elyse. "Researchers Say Chinese Medicine May Aid in Prevention of Liver Cancer." *Wall Street Journal,* September 6, 1995:B1.

Tanouye, Elyse. "SmithKline to Pay $325 Million to Settle Federal Claims of Lab-Billing Fraud." *Wall Street Journal,* February 25, 1997:B8.

Tapia, Andres. "Churches Wary of Inner-City Islamic Inroads." *Christianity Today, 38,* 1, January 10, 1994:36–38.

Taylor, Chris. "The Man Behind Lara Croft." *Time,* December 6, 1999:78.

Taylor, Howard F. "The Structure of a National Black Leadership Network: Preliminary Findings." Unpublished manuscript, 1992. As cited in Margaret L. Andersen and Howard F. Taylor, *Sociology: Understanding a Diverse Society.* Belmont, Calif.: Wadsworth, 2000.

Taylor, Raymond G., and Alexander I. Mechitov. "Russian Schools and the Legacies of the Soviet Era." *Education, 115,* 2, Winter 1994:260–263.

Taylor, Verta. "Social Movement Continuity: The Women's Movement in Abeyance." In *Social Movements: Readings on Their Emergence, Mobilization, and Dynamics,* Doug McAdam and David A. Snow, eds. Los Angeles: Roxbury Publishing, 1997:409–420.

Teacher's College Record. "Brown Plus Forty." New York: Columbia University Teacher's College, *96,* 4, 1995:601–788.

Thayer, Stephen. "Encounters." *Psychology Today,* March 1988:31–36.

Thomas, Paulette. "EPA Predicts Global Impact from Warming." *Wall Street Journal,* October 21, 1988:B5.

Thomas, Paulette. "U.S. Examiners Will Scrutinize Banks with Poor Minority-Lending Histories." *Wall Street Journal,* October 22, 1991:A2.

Thomas, Paulette. "Boston Fed Finds Racial Discrimination in Mortgage Lending Is Still Widespread." *Wall Street Journal,* October 9, 1992:A3.

Thomas, R. Roosevelt, Jr. "From Affirmative Action to Affirming Diversity." *Harvard Business Review, 90,* 2, March–April, 1990:107–117.

Thomas, William I., and Florian Znaniecki. *The Polish Peasant in Europe and America.* Chicago: University of Chicago Press, 1918.

Thompson, William E. "Hanging Tongues: A Sociological Encounter with the Assembly Line." In *Down to Earth Sociology: Introductory Readings,* 9th ed., James M. Henslin, ed. New York: Free Press, 1995:193–202.

Thornburg, David. "Why Wait for Bandwidth? Schools Can Teleconference, Even with Ordinary Phone Lines." *Electronic Learning, 14,* 3, November–December 1994:20.

Thorne, Barrie. "Children and Gender: Constructions of Difference." In *Theoretical Perspectives on Sexual Difference,* Deborah L. Rhode, ed. New Haven, Conn.: Yale University Press, 1990:100–113.

Thorne, Barrie, and Zella Luria. "Sexuality and Gender in Children's Daily Worlds." In *Down to Earth Sociology: Introductory Readings,* 7th ed., James M. Henslin, ed. New York: Free Press, 1993:133–144.

Thornton, Russell. *American Indian Holocaust and Survival: A Population History Since 1492.* Norman: University of Oklahoma Press, 1987.

Thrasher, Frederic M. *The Gang.* Chicago: University of Chicago Press, 1927.

Tilly, Charles. *From Mobilization to Revolution.* Reading, Mass.: Addison-Wesley, 1978.

Timasheff, Nicholas S. *War and Revolution.* Joseph F. Scheuer, ed. New York: Sheed & Ward, 1965.

Timerman, Jacobo. *Prisoner Without a Name, Cell Without a Number.* New York: Knopf, 1981.

Tobias, Andrew. "The 'Don't Be Ridiculous' Law." *Wall Street Journal,* May 31, 1995:A14.

Toby, Jackson. "To Get Rid of Guns in Schools, Get Rid of Some Students." *Wall Street Journal,* March 23, 1992:A12.

Toch, Thomas. "Violence in Schools." *U.S. News & World Report, 115,* 18, November 8, 1993:31–36.

Tocqueville, Alexis de. *The Old Regime and the French Revolution.* Stuart Gilbert, trans. Garden City, N.Y.: Doubleday Anchor, 1955. First published in 1856.

Tocqueville, Alexis de. *Democracy in America,* J. P. Mayer and Max Lerner, eds. New York: Harper & Row, 1966. First published in 1835.

Tolchin, Martin. "Surgeon General Asserts Smoking Is an Addiction." *New York Times,* May 17, 1988:A1, C4.

Tolchin, Martin. "Mildest Possible Penalty Is Imposed on Neil Bush." *New York Times,* April 19, 1991:D2.

Tönnies, Ferdinand. *Community and Society (Gemeinschaft und Gesellschaft),* with a new introduction by John Samples. New Brunswick, N.J.: Transaction, 1988. First published in 1887.

Tordoff, William. "The Impact of Ideology on Development in the Third World." *Journal of International Development, 4,* 1, 1992:41–53.

Toynbee, Arnold. *A Study of History,* D. C. Somervell, abridger and ed. New York: Oxford University Press, 1946.

Treas, Judith. "Older Americans in the 1990s and Beyond." *Population Bulletin, 50,* 2, May 1995:1–46.

Treiman, Donald J. *Occupational Prestige in Comparative Perspective.* New York: Academic Press, 1977.

Trice, Harrison M., and Janice M. Beyer. "Cultural Leadership in Organization." *Organization Science, 2,* 2, May 1991:149–169.

Troeltsch, Ernst. *The Social Teachings of the Christian Churches.* New York: Macmillan, 1931.

Tucker, Belinda M., and Claudia Mitchell-Kernan. "New Trends in Black American Interracial Marriage: The Social Structural Context." *Journal of Marriage and the Family, 52,* 1990:209–218.

Tumin, Melvin M. "Some Principles of Social Stratification: A Critical Analysis." *American Sociological Review 18,* August 1953:394.

Turnbull, Colin M. "The Mountain People." In *Sociology 95/96,* Kurt Finsterbusch, ed. Sluice Dock, Conn.: Dushkin, 1995:6–15. First published in 1972.

Turner, Bryan S. "Outline of a Theory of Citizenship." *Sociology, 24,* 2, May 1990:189–217.

Turner, Jonathan H. *American Society: Problems of Structure.* New York: Harper & Row, 1972.

Turner, Jonathan H. *The Structure of Sociological Theory.* Homewood, Ill.: Dorsey, 1978.

Turner, Ralph H. "Collective Behavior." In *Handbook of Modern Sociology,* Robert E. L. Faris, ed. Chicago: Rand McNally, 1964:382–425.

Turner, Ralph H. "Race Riots Past and Present: A Cultural-Collective Behavior Approach." Paper presented at the annual meetings of the American Sociological Association, 1993.

Turner, Ralph H., and Lewis M. Killian. *Collective Behavior,* 2nd ed. Englewood Cliffs, N.J.: Prentice Hall, 1987.

Tye, Larry. "After Waco, the Focus Shifts to Other Cults." *The Boston Globe,* April 30, 1993:1, 22.

Udy, Stanley H., Jr. "Bureaucracy and Rationality in Weber's Organizational Theory: An Empirical Study." *American Sociological Review, 24,* December 1959:791–795.

Ullman, Edward, and Chauncey Harris. "The Nature of Cities." In *Urban Man and Society: A Reader in Urban Ecology,* Albert N. Cousins and Hans Nagpaul, eds. New York: Knopf, 1970:91–100.

Ullman, Sarah E. "Does Offender Violence Escalate When Rape Victims Fight Back?" *Journal of Interpersonal Violence,* 13, 2, April 1998:179–192.

UNESCO: Institute for Statistics, 2000.

UNICEF. *The State of the World's Children.* New York: Oxford University Press, 1995.

Uniform Crime Reports. Washington D.C.: FBI, published annually. United Nations.

United Nations Statistical Yearbook 1985–1986. New York: The United Nations, 1987.

United Nations Statistical Yearbook 1990–1991. New York: The United Nations, 1992.

United Nations Statistical Yearbook 1995–1996. New York: The United Nations, 1997.

U.S. Bureau of the Census. *Statistical Abstract of the United States: The National Data Book.* Washington, D.C.: U.S. Government Printing Office. Published annually.

U.S. Department of Energy, Advisory Committee on Human Radiation Experiments. Final Report, 1995. Available online at http://tis.eh.doe.gov/ohreroadmap/achre/report.html.

U.S. Department of Health and Human Services, Public Health Service. *Healthy People 2000.* Washington, D.C.: U.S. Government Printing Office, 1990.

Usdansky, Margaret L. "English a Problem for Half of Miami." *USA Today,* April 3, 1992:A1, A3, A30.

Useem, Michael. *The Inner Circle: Large Corporations and the Rise of Business Political Activity in the U.S. and U.K.* New York: Oxford University Press, 1984.

Vande Berg, Leah R., and Diane Streckfuss. "Prime-Time Television's Portrayal of Women and the World of Work: A Demographic Profile." *Journal of Broadcasting and Electronic Media,* Spring 1992:195–208.

Van Lawick-Goodall, Jane. *In the Shadow of Man.* Boston: Houghton Mifflin, 1971.

van den Haag, Ernest. *Punishing Criminals: Concerning a Very Old and Painful Question.* New York: Basic Books, 1975.

van Den Haag, Ernest, and John Conrad, eds. *The Death Penalty: A Debate.* New York: Plenum, 1983.

Vasil, Latika, and Hannelore Wass. "Portrayal of the Elderly in the Media: A Literature Review and Implications for Educational Gerontologists." *Educational Gerontology, 19,* 1, January–February 1993:71–85.

Vaughan, Diane. "Uncoupling: The Social Construction of Divorce." In *Marriage and Family in a Changing Society,* 2nd ed., James M. Henslin, ed. New York: Free Press, 1985:429–439.

Veblen, Thorstein. *The Theory of the Leisure Class.* New York: Macmillan, 1912.

Vega, William A. "Hispanic Families in the 1980s: A Decade of Research." *Journal of Marriage and the Family, 52,* November 1990:1015–1024.

Vernon, JoEtta A., J. Allen Williams, Jr., Terri Phillips, and Janet Wilson. "Media Stereotyping: A Comparison of the Way Elderly Women and Men Are Portrayed on Prime-Time Television." *Journal of Women and Aging, 2,* 4, 1990:55–58.

Violas, P. C. *The Training of the Urban Working Class: A History of Twentieth Century American Education.* Chicago: Rand McNally, 1978.

Volti, Rudi. *Society and Technological Change,* 3rd ed. New York: St. Martin's Press, 1995.

Von Hoffman, Nicholas. "Sociological Snoopers." *Transaction 7,* May 1970:4, 6.

Waddington, Conrad H. *The Man-Made Future.* New York: St. Martin's, 1978.

Wagley, Charles, and Marvin Harris. *Minorities in the New World.* New York: Columbia University Press, 1958.

Waldholz, Michael. "Computer Brain Outperforms Doctors in Diagnosing Heart Attack Patients." *Wall Street Journal,* December 2, 1991:7B.

Waldholz, Michael. "AIDS Spreading to Teenage Girls in Parts of Africa." *Wall Street Journal,* September 15, 1999:B1, B4.

Waldman, Peter. "Riots in Bahrain Arouse Ire of Feared Monarchy as the U.S. Stands By." *Wall Street Journal,* June 12, 1995a:A1, A8.

Walker, Alice, and Pratibha Parmar. *Warrior Marks: Female Genital Mutilation and the Sexual Blinding of Women.* New York: Harcourt Brace, 1993.

Wallace, Anthony F. C. *Religion: An Anthropological View.* New York: Random House, 1966.

Wallerstein, Immanuel. *The Modern World System: Capitalist Agriculture and the Origins of the European World-Economy in the Sixteenth Century.* New York: Academic Press, 1974.

Wallerstein, Immanuel. *The Capitalist World-Economy.* New York: Cambridge University Press, 1979.

Wallerstein, Immanuel. *The Politics of the World-Economy: The States, the Movements, and the Civilizations.* Cambridge, England: Cambridge University Press, 1984.

Wallerstein, Immanuel. "Culture as the Ideological Battleground of the Modern World-system." In *Global Culture: Nationalism, Globalization, and Modernity,* Mike Featherstone, ed. London: Sage, 1990:31–55.

Wallerstein, Judith S., and Joan B. Kelly. "How Children React to Parental Divorce." In *Marriage and Family in a Changing Society,* 4th ed., James M. Henslin, ed. New York: Free Press, 1992:397–409.

Wark, Gillian R., and Dennis L. Krebs. "Gender and Dilemma Differences in Real-Life Moral Judgment." *Developmental Psychology, 32,* 1996:220–230.

Warner, W. Lloyd, and Paul S. Hunt. *The Social Life of a Modern Community.* New Haven, Conn.: Yale University Press, 1941.

Warner, W. Lloyd, Paul S. Hunt, Marchia Meeker, and Kenneth Eels. *Social Class in America.* New York: Harper, 1949.

Warr, Mark. "Age, Peers, and Delinquency." *Criminology, 31,* 1, 1993:17–40.

Watson, J. Mark. "Outlaw Motorcyclists." In *Down to Earth Sociology: Introductory Readings,* 5th ed., James M. Henslin, ed. New York: Free Press, 1988:203–213.

Webb, Eugene J., Donald T. Campbell, Richard D. Schwartz, and Lee Sechrest. *Unobtrusive Measures: Nonreactive Research in the Social Sciences.* Chicago: Rand McNally, 1966.

Weber, Max. *Economy and Society,* G. Roth and C. Wittich, eds. Berkeley: University of California Press, 1978. First published in 1922.

Weber, Max. *From Max Weber: Essays in Sociology.* Hans Gerth and C. Wright Mills, trans. and ed. New York: Oxford University Press, 1946a.

Weber, Max. *The Theory of Social and Economic Organization,* A. M. Henderson and Talcott Parsons, trans., Talcott Parsons, ed. Glencoe, Ill.: Free Press, 1947. First published in 1913.

Weber, Max. *The Protestant Ethic and the Spirit of Capitalism.* New York: Scribner's, 1958. First published in 1904–1905.

Weber, Max. *Economy and Society.* Ephraim Fischoff, trans. New York: Bedminster Press, 1968. First published in 1922.

Webster, Pamela S., and A. Regula Herzog. "Effects of Parental Divorce and Memories of Family Problems on Relationships Between Adult Children and Their Parents." *Journal of Gerontology, 50B,* 1, 1995:S24-S34.

Weeks, John R. *Population: An Introduction to Concepts and Issues,* 5th ed. Belmont, Calif.: Wadsworth, 1994.

Wei, William. *The Asian American Movement.* Philadelphia: Temple University Press, 1993.

Weintraub, Richard M. "A Bride in India." *Washington Post,* February 28, 1988.

Weisburd, David, Stanton Wheeler, and Elin Waring. *Crimes of the Middle Classes: White-Collar Offenders in the Federal Courts.* New Haven, Conn.: Yale University Press, 1991.

Weisskopf, Michael. "Scientist Says Greenhouse Effect Is Setting In." In *Ourselves and Others: The Washington Post Sociology Companion,* Washington Post Writers Group, eds. Boston: Allyn and Bacon, 1992:297–298.

Weitzman, Lenore J. *The Divorce Revolution.* New York: Free Press, 1985.

Wells, Joseph. "Report to the Nation on Occupational Fraud and Abuse." Association of Certified Fraud Examiners.

Welsh, Stephanie. "A Dangerous Rite of Passage." *Nation,* May 7, 1995.

Wenneker, Mark B., and Arnold M. Epstein. "Racial Inequalities in the Use of Procedures for Patients with Ischemic Heart Disease in Massachusetts." *Journal of the American Medical Association, 261,* 2, January 13, 1989:253–257.

Wertz, Richard W., and Dorothy C. Wertz. "Notes on the Decline of Midwives and the Rise of Medical Obstetricians." In *The Sociology of Health and Illness: Critical Perspectives,* Peter Conrad and Rochelle Kern, eds. New York: St. Martin's Press, 1981:165–183.

Wessel, David. "As Populations Age, Fiscal Woes Deepen." *Wall Street Journal,* September 11, 1995:A1.

West, Candace, and Angela Garcia. "Conversational Shift Work: A Study of Topical Transitions Between Women and Men." *Social Problems, 35,* 1988:551–575.

Whetstone, Muriel L. "What Black Men and Women Should Do Now (About Black Men and Women)." *Ebony,* February 1996:135–138, 140.

White, Jack E. "Forgive Us Our Sins." *Time,* July 3, 1995:29.

White, James A. "When Employees Own Big Stake, It's a Buy Signal for Investors." *Wall Street Journal,* February 13, 1991:C1, C19.

Whorf, Benjamin. *Language, Thought, and Reality,* J. B. Carroll, ed. Cambridge, MA: MIT Press, 1956.

Whyte, Martin King. "Choosing Mates—The American Way." *Society,* March–April 1992:71–77.

Whyte, William H. *The City: Rediscovering the Center.* New York: Doubleday, 1989.

Whyte, William H. "Street Corner Society." In *Down to Earth Sociology: Introductory Readings,* 9th ed., James M. Henslin, ed. New York: Free Press, 1997:59–67.

Whyte, William Foote. "Street Corner Society." In *Down to Earth Sociology: Introductory Readings,* 10th ed., James M. Henslin, ed. New York: Free Press, 1999: 61–69.

Will, George F. "AIDS Crushes a Continent." *Newsweek,* January 10, 2000:64.

Willhelm, Sidney M. "Can Marxism Explain America's Racism?" *Social Problems, 28,* December 1980:98–112.

Williams, Christine L. *Still a Man's World: Men Who Do Women's Work.* Berkeley: University of California Press, 1995.

Williams, Robin M., Jr. *American Society: A Sociological Interpretation,* 2nd ed. New York: Knopf, 1965.

Willie, Charles V. "Caste, Class, and Family Life Experiences." *Research in Race and Ethnic Relations, 6,* 1991:65–84.

Wilson, Edward O. *Sociobiology: The New Synthesis.* Cambridge, Mass.: Harvard University Press, 1975.

Wilson, James Q. "Is Incapacitation the Answer to the Crime Problem?" In *Taking Sides: Clashing Views on Controversial Social Issues,* 7th ed., Kurt Finsterbusch and George McKenna, eds. Guilford, Conn.: Dushkin, 1992:318–324.

Wilson, James Q. "Lock 'Em Up and Other Thoughts on Crime." *New York Times Magazine,* March 9, 1975:11, 44–48.

Wilson, James Q., and Richard J. Hernstein. *Crime and Human Nature.* New York: Simon & Schuster, 1985.

Wilson, William Julius. *The Declining Significance of Race: Blacks and Changing American Institutions.* Chicago: University of Chicago Press, 1978.

Wilson, William Julius. *The Truly Disadvantaged: The Inner City, the Underclass, and Public Policy.* Chicago: University of Chicago Press, 1987.

Wilson, William Julius. *When Work Disappears: The World of the New Urban Poor.* Chicago: University of Chicago Press, 1996.

Winslow, Ron. "Study Finds Blacks Get Fewer Bypasses." *Wall Street Journal,* March 18, 1992:B1.

Winslow, Ron. "More Doctors Are Adding On-Line Tools to Their Kits." *Wall Street Journal,* October 7, 1994:B1, B4.

Winslow, Ron. "Smoking Increases Heart-Attack Risk Fivefold for People in Their 30s and 40s." *Wall Street Journal,* August 18, 1995:B5.

Wirth, Louis. "Urbanism as a Way of Life." *American Journal of Sociology, 44,* July 1938:1–24.

Wirth, Louis. "The Problem of Minority Groups." In *The Science of Man in the World Crisis,* Ralph Linton, ed. New York: Columbia University Press, 1945.

Wohl, R. Richard, and Anselm Strauss. "Symbolic Representation and the Urban Milieu." *American Journal of Sociology, 63,* March 1958:523–532.

Wolfensohn, James D., and Kathryn S. Fuller. "Making Common Cause: Seeing the Forest for the Trees." *International Herald Tribune,* May 27, 1998:11.

Wolff, Michael, et al. *Where We Stand: Can America Make It in the Global Race for Wealth and Happiness?* New York: Bantam Books, 1992.

Wolfgang, Marvin E., and Franco Ferracuti. *The Subculture of Violence: Toward an Integrated Theory in Criminology.* London: Tavistock, 1967.

Womack, James P., Daniel T. Jones, and Daniel Roos. *The Machine That Changed the World: The Story of Lean Production.* New York: Harper Perrenial, 1991.

Woodward, Kenneth L. "Heaven." *Newsweek, 113,* 13, March 27, 1989:52–55.

World Health Organization. *Constitution of the World Health Organization.* New York: World Health Organization Interim Commission, 1946.

"The World of the Child 6 Billion." Population Reference Bureau, 2000.

Worsley, Peter. *The Trumpet Shall Sound.* London: MacGibbon and Kee, 1957.

Wouters, Cas. "On Status Competition and Emotion Management: The Study of Emotions as a New Field." *Theory, Culture & Society, 9,* 1992:229–252.

Wray, Linda A. "Public Policy Implications of an Ethnically Diverse Elderly Population." *Journal of Cross-Cultural Gerontology, 6,* 1991:243–257.

Wright, Erik Olin. *Class.* London: Verso, 1985.

Wright, Lawrence. "One Drop of Blood." *New Yorker,* July 25, 1994:46–50, 52–55.

Wright, Lawrence. "Double Mystery." *New Yorker,* August 7, 1995:45–62.

Wrong, Dennis H. "The Over-Socialized Conception of Man in Modern Sociology." *American Sociological Review, 26,* April 1961:185–193.

Yearbook of American and Canadian Churches. Nashville, Tenn.: Abingdon. Various editions.

Yellowbird, Michael, and C. Matthew Snipp. "American Indian Families." In *Minority Families in the United States: A Multicultural Perspective,* Ronald L. Taylor, ed. Englewood Cliffs, N.J.: Prentice Hall, 1994:179–201.

Yinger, J. Milton. *Toward a Field Theory of Behavior: Personality and Social Structure.* New York: McGraw-Hill, 1965.

Yinger, J. Milton. *The Scientific Study of Religion.* New York: Macmillan, 1970.

Young, Laurie E. "The Overlooked Contributions of Women to the Development of American Sociology: An Examination of AJS Articles from 1895–1926." Paper presented at the 1995 meetings of the American Sociological Association.

Zachary, G. Pascal. "Behind Stocks' Surge Is an Economy in Which Big U.S. Firms Thrive." *Wall Street Journal,* November 22, 1995:A1, A5.

Zald, Mayer N. "Looking Backward to Look Forward: Reflections on the Past and the Future of the Resource Mobilization Research Program." In *Frontiers in Social Movement Theory,* Aldon D. Morris and Carol McClurg Mueller, eds. New Haven, Conn.: Yale University Press, 1992:326–348.

Zald, Mayer N., and John D. McCarthy, eds. *Social Movements in an Organizational Society.* New Brunswick, N.J.: Transaction, 1987.

Zampa, Frederick P., and Albert E. McCormick, Jr. " 'Proxy Power' and Corporate Democracy: The Characteristics and Efficacy of Stockholder-Initiated Proxy Issues." *The American Journal of Economics and Sociology, 50,* 1, January 1991:1–16.

Zellner, William W. *Countercultures: A Sociological Analysis.* New York: St. Martin's, 1995.

Zerubavel, Eviatar. *The Fine Line: Making Distinctions in Everyday Life.* New York: Free Press, 1991.

Zey, Mary. *Banking on Fraud: Drexel, Junk Bonds, and Buyouts.* Hawthorne, N.Y.: Aldine de Gruyter, 1993.

Zola, Irving K. *Socio-Medical Inquiries.* Philadelphia: Temple University Press, 1983.

Zorbaugh, Harvey W. *The Gold Coast and the Slum.* Chicago: University of Chicago Press, 1929.

Zou, Heng Fu. " 'The Spirit of Capitalism' and Long-Run Growth." *European Journal of Political Economy, 10,* 2, July 1994:279–293.

Zuboff, Shoshana. "New Worlds of Computer-Mediated Work." In *Down to Earth Sociology: Introductory Readings,* 6th ed., James M. Henslin, ed. New York: Free Press, 1991:476–485.

Zuger, Abigail. "Fever Pitch: Getting Doctors to Prescribe Is Big Business." *New York Times,* January 11, 1999.

Name Index

Abraham (of Old Testament), 516, 518
Addams, Jane, 3, 18, 19
Adhieu, 232
Adler, Patricia, 83
Adler, Peter, 83
Adorno, Theodor, 328
Alex (a parrot), 57
Alger, Horatio, 281
Ali, 517
Allah, 523
Allende, Salvador, 402
Alter, Jonathan, 439
Anderson, Chris, 140–42
Anderson, Elijah, 96
Ansberry, Clare, 267
Appiah, Kwame Anthony, 320
Applewhite, Marshal, 522
Arafat, Yasser, 112
Arc, Joan of, 420–21
Archimedes, 483
Ariés, Philippe, 86, 88
Aristotle, 478
Aron, Arthur, 451
Arquitt, George, 185
Asch, Solomon, 167–69

Baehr, Ninia, 462
Bai, Matt, 477–78
Bainbridge, William, 614
Balch, Emily Greene, 18
Bales, Robert F., 165
Banks, Laurie, 22
Barnes, Fred, 132–33
Baron, Robert, 138
Barry, Paul, 504
Becker, Howard S., 198
Becker, Selwin, 166
Beeghley, Leonard, 257
Beittel, Mark, 33
Bell, Alexander Graham, 431
Bell, Daniel, 390
Bellah, Robert, 510
Berger, Peter, 5, 419, 625
Bernall, Cassie, 478
Bernard, Jessie, 450–51
Bernard, Viola W., 436
Berk, Richard, 610
Biggs, Mae, 120
Bird, Chloe E., 142
Blumer, Herbert, 153, 609–10
Blumstein, Philip, 462
Bobo, Lawrence, 325

Bond, James T., 448
Boulding, Elise, 153
Bowles, Samuel, 492, 493
Brahma, 520
Brajuha, Mario, 143
Brauchi, Marcus W., 483
Bronfenbrenner, Urie, 466–67
Brooks, Garth, 257
Brunvand, Jan, 617
Bumiller, Elisabeth, 452
Burgess, Ernest, 18, 25, 592
Burmeister, Walter, 149, 157
Burns, Lucy, 297
Bush, George, 213, 612
Bush, Neil, 213
Butler, Richard, 329
Buzzanca, Jaycee, 461
Buzzanca, John, 461
Buzzanca, Luanne, 461
Byrnes, David, 642

Callahan, Daniel, 371
Calment, Jeanne Louise, 361, 362
Calvin, John, 176, 515
Cantril, Hadley, 613
Capela, Stanley, 21
Cappell, Ross, 22
Capucci, Monsignor, 112
Carey, Sgt., 87
Cartwright, Dorwin, 165
Case, Stephen, 259
Castillo Balderas, Carmen, 227–28
Castle, John, 260
Castro, Fidel, 48, 396
Cerulo, Karen, 380
Chafetz, Janet, 291, 297, 313
Chagnon, Napoleon, 197–98
Chain, David, 655
Chalkley, Kate, 294
Chambliss, William, 121, 207–8
Chandak, Rachita, 452
Charlemagne, 240
Charles VII, King, 420
Cherlin, Andrew, 469
Chrysler family, 264
Chunlan, Zhao, 365
Clare, Elizabeth, 526
Clarke, Edward, 302
Clay, Jason W., 439
Clinton, Bill, 402–3
Cloward, Richard, 210, 211
Cobb, Jonathan, 273

Coleman, James, 501
Collins, Randall, 239, 484
Columbus, Christopher, 640
Comte, Auguste, 3, 11–12, 17, 27
Confucius, 521
Conrad, Peter, 56
Cooley, Charles Horton, 23, 68–69, 156, 452
Cose, Ellis, 592
Coser, Lewis, 30
Coskun, Nijla, 436
Coughlin, Ellen K., 140–42
Cowen, Emory, 328
Cox, Courteney, 367
Crawford, Cindy, 624
Croft, Lara, 78
Crossen, Cynthia, 131–32
Croteau, David, 274–75
Cumming, Elaine, 368
Curtin, Sharon, 376–77
Custer, George, 351

Dahrendorf, Ralf, 30, 239
Dancel, Genora, 462
Darden, Christoper, 341
Darley, John, 164, 598
Darwin, Charles, 11–12, 54–55
d'Autriche, Elisabeth, 262
Davidson, John, 614
Davis, Kingsley, 63–64, 237–38, 487
Davis, Nanette, 206
Day, Dorothy, 297
Degler, Jeffrey, 113
de Klerk, Fredrik Willem, 422
de Leon, Ponce, 384
De Martin, Joseph R., 21
DeMause, Lloyd, 88
Denny, Reginald, 612
Deparle, Jason, 140–42
Diana, Princess, 104, 616
DiCaprio, Leonardo, 113
Dickson, William J., 138
Dirkson, Everett, 213
Dirmann, Jack, 504
Dobriner, William M., 99
Dodd, Molly, 115
Dole, Bob, 553
Dollard, John, 328
Domhoff, William, 241, 259, 433
Doane, Ashley W., Jr., 323
Dove, Adrian, 489
Du Bois, W. E. B., 3, 18–19, 20, 29, 231, 349

Dugger, Celia, W., 452
Du Pont family, 264
Durkheim, Emile, 3, 13–14, 16, 17, 27, 33, 106, 107, 155, 208–9, 224, 382, 399–400, 508, 587
Dutton, Donald, 451
Dye, H. B., 66–67

Eaton, Isabel, 18
Ebaugh, Helen, 114
Ebomoyi, Ehigie, 294
Eder, Donna, 302
Edgerton, Robert, 40–41, 199
Einstein, Albert, 12, 101
Eisner, Michael, 259
Ekman, Paul, 73–74
Ellul, Jacques, 641
Engels, Friedrich, 510
Engelberg, Stephen, 431
Epstein, Arnold, 327
Epstein, Cynthia Fuchs, 288
Escalante, Jaime, 503–4
Esau (of Old Testament), 653
Eukleides, 483
Evans, Peter, 182
Ezekiel, Raphael, 332–33

Fahd, King, 402
Falcon, Pedro, 48
Farkas, George, 495–96
Farley, Reynolds, 325
Farrakhan, Louis, 519
Faunce, William, 573
Feagin, Joe, 341
Finke, Roger, 533
Finkelhor, David, 471
Fischer, Edward, 451
Fisher, Ann, 307
Fisher, Gene A., 140–41
Fisher, Sue, 550, 551
Flanagan, William, 603
Flexner, Abraham, 544
Flink, James, 645
Foley, Douglas, 302
Ford family, 264
Ford, Henry, 643, 644
Foreman, Dave, 655
Fox, Elaine, 185
Francis of Assissi, Saint, 512
Franklin, Benjamin, 648
Freud, Sigmund, 12, 72–73, 222
Friedman, Dana E., 448
Froman, Ingmarie, 447
Fuller, Rex, 304–5
Futsu, K'ung (Confucius), 521

Gaillot (Bishop), 535
Galbraith, Kenneth, 249–50
Galinsky, Ellen, 448
Gallambos, Louis, 399
Galliher, John, 15
Gans, Herbert, 596–98
Garcia, Aracelia, 456
Gardner, Allen, 57
Gardner, Beatrice, 57
Garfinkel, Harold, 84–87, 118–19, 216–17

Gates, Bill, 193, 258
Gautama, Siddhartha, 520, 521
Gay, Jill, 252
Genie (neglected child), 67, 68, 70
Genovese, Catherine, 596, 598, 599
Gerassimow, Alexander, 395
Germain, Sophie, 18
Gerson, Kathleen, 460
Gibbs, Nancy, 477–78
Giele, Janet, 313
Gilbert, Dennis, 263–65
Gilligan, Carol, 72
Gilman, Charlotte Perkins, 18
Ginsberg, Ruth Bader, 307
Gintis, Herbert, 492
Goering, Hermann, 166
Goffman, Erving, 84–87, 112–13, 115–16, 198
Gold, Ray, 262
Goldberg, Steven, 289
Goldberg, Susan, 76
Golden, Drew, 499
Goleman, Daniel, 132–33
Gonzalez, Elián, 611
Goodall, Jane, 57
Goode, Erich, 561
Gottschalk, Peter, 279
Gourevitch, Philip, 317–18
Gracey, Harry, 490
Graham, Ellen, 532
Gray, William H., III, 326
Gray Squirrel, 540
Greeley, Andrew, 534
Green, Leslie, 21
Greenberg, Gerald, 138
Gupta, Gira Raj, 452
Gutenberg, Johann, 104, 535

Haag, Ernest van den, 219
Haas, Jack, 550
Hacker, Helen, 295
Hagar (of Old Testament), 518
Hall, Edward T., 111–12
Hamilton, Alice, 18
Hare, Paul, 150
Harlow, Harry, 67–68
Harlow, Margaret, 67–68
Harrington, Michael, 250–51, 279
Harris, Chauncey, 594
Harris, Eric, 477–78
Harris, Marvin, 296, 322–23
Hart, Charles, 355–56
Hartley, Eugene, 328
Hawking, Stephen, 101
Hawn, Goldie, 363
Hawthorne, Nathaniel, 100, 216
Hayakawa, S. I., 343
Hayes, Donald, 497
Heckert, Alex, 467–68
Heimbold, Charles, 259
Hellinger, Daniel, 258
Hemmings, Sally, 352
Henry VIII, King, 234
Henry, William, 368
Henslin, James M., 35, 51, 120, 142, 144

Herod (of New Testament), 517
Higgenbotham, Elizabeth, 272
Higgens, Elizabeth, 461
Hill, Zettie Mae, 267
Hilliard, Asa, III, 504
Hippler, Fritz, 330
Hirohito, Emperor 351
Hirschi, Travis, 205
Hitler, Adolf, 65, 119, 121, 166, 320–21, 328, 332, 351, 421, 639
Ho, David, 560
Hoan, Nguyen Thi, 295
Hochschild, Arlie, 448–50
Hoffer, Thomas, 501
Holbein, Hans, the younger, 634
Holyfield, Evander, 131
Hornblower, Margot, 251
Horowitz, Ruth, 204
Hostetler, John, 513
Htoo, Johnny, 438
Htoo, Luther, 438
Howells, Lloyd, 166
Hoyt, Homer, 593
Huddle, Donald, 583–84
Hudo, Buba, 125, 126
Hudo, Cindy, 125, 126
Huggins, Martha, 246
Huizenga, Wayne, 260
Humphreys, Laud, 143–44
Hussein, Saddam, 426, 624
Hyman, Herbert, 158

Isaac (of Old Testament), 516
Isabell (isolated child), 63–64
Ishmael (of Old Testament), 518
Ivester, Douglas, 259

Jackson, Jesse, 339
Jacob (of Old Testament), 516
Jacobson, Lenore, 495
Jaggar, Alison, 313
James, William, 23
Janis, Irving, 169
Jankowiak, William, 451
Jankowski, Martín Sánchez, 212
Jarrell, John, 262
Jarrell, Sandy, 262
Jasper, James, 626
Jáuregui, Gurutz, 439
Jefferson, Thomas, 352, 424, 479
Jekielek, Susan, 466
Jerrome, Dorothy, 369
Jesus, 9, 109, 381, 478, 483, 511–12, 513, 517, 522, 532, 620
Joan of Arc, 420–21
Johns, Charlie, 90
Johns, Eunice, 90
Johnson, Benton, 521–24
Johnson, Jimmy, 450
Johnson, Lyndon Baines, 372–73
Johnson, Miriam, 302
Johnson, Mitch, 199
Johnson, Norris, 614–15
Johnston, Drue, 614–15
Jones, Jim, 522
Jordan, Michael, 503, 616, 624

Joseph (of Old Testament), 516
Joyner-Kersie, Jackie, 503
Judas, 627
Judd, Dennis, 258
Juliet, 331

Kaczynski, Ted, 641
Kagan, Jerome, 71
Kahl, Joseph, 263–65
Kanter, Rosabeth Moss, 186–88
Karp, David, 275, 598, 601
Kelly family, 227–28
Kelley, Florence, 18, 19
Kempadoo, Kamala, 251
Kenistron, Kenneth, 88
Kennedy family, 264
Kennedy, John F., 169, 260, 350, 422
Kennedy, Rose, 260
Kephart, William, 513
Kevorkian, Jack, 552–55
Khomeini, Ayatollah, 422
Killian, Lewis, 611
King, Martin Luther, Jr., 338, 510, 613
King, Rodney, 612–13
Klebold, Dylan, 477–78
Klonoff, Elizabeth, 542
Kluegel, James, 325
Kohlberg, Lawrence, 71–72
Kohn, Melvin, 79–80, 269, 455
Koresh, David, 507, 525–26
Kornhauser, William, 625
Kraybill, Donald, 109
Kroc, Ray, 180
Krysan, Maria, 325
Kübler-Ross, Elisabeth, 381, 382
Kuhn, Margaret, 375

Lamont, Blanche, 480
Landes, Judah, 328
Landrine, Hope, 542
Larson, Gary, 79, 162
Latané, Bibb, 164, 598
Lauer, Jeanette, 472
Lauer, Robert, 472
LeBon, Gustave, 609
Lee, Lois, 23
Lee, Sharon M., 344
Lehrer, Joshua, 326
Lemert, Edwin, 206–7
Lenin, Vladimir Ilyich, 242, 395, 510
Lenski, Gerhard, 239, 262
Leo III, Pope, 240
Lerner, Gerda, 229, 291, 296
Lewis, Dorothy, 201
Lewis, Michael, 76
Lewis, Nancy, 279–80
Lewis, Oscar, 249–50, 279
Lewis, Ted, 279–80
Liebow, Elliot, 96, 281
Light, Paul, 133
Lightfoot-Klein, A., 294
Linton, Ralph, 39
Lippitt, Ronald, 165–66
Lippman, Julia, 550
Locke, Gary, 345
Locke, Harvey, 25

Lofland, John, 616–17
Lorber, Judith, 313
Louis, XIII, King, 88
Ludlum, Ned, 641
Luther, Martin, 517

Mackay, Charles, 608
Mackey, Daniel, 113
Mackey, Jennifer, 113
MacKinnon, Catharine, 307
Mahran, M., 294
Malthus, Thomas, 572–73, 575
Mandela, Nelson, 422
Mann, Horace, 479–80
Manson, Charles, 522
Mantle, Mickey, 557
Marcus, Amy Dockser, 439
Maris, Roger, 74, 598
Mark, Reuben, 259
Marshall, Joe, 351
Martin, Joe, 496
Martin, Sheila, 526
Martin, William, 33
Martineau, Harriet, 3, 17
Mary, Mother of Jesus, 512
Marx, Gary, 191, 627
Marx, Karl, 3, 12–13, 14, 30–31, 175–77,
    181, 235–37, 242, 256, 263, 281, 396,
    513, 514, 534–35, 635, 639, 643
Massey, Douglas, 48
Matza, David, 205–6
Mayo, Elton, 137, 138
McAdam, Doug, 625
McAuliffe, Christa, 633
McCarthy, John, 628
McCartney, Bill, 513
McCaughey, Bobby, 461
McCaughey, Kenny, 461
McCaughey, Mikayla, 461
McCaughey septuplets, 461
McCormick, John, 592
McGwire, Mark, 74, 598
McKinney, Gene, 308
McLanahan, Sara, 279
McPhail, Clark, 610
Mead, George Herbert, 23, 69–70
Meek, Anne, 504
Mellon family, 264
Merton, Robert King, 27, 158, 210, 495
Merwine, Maynard H., 294
Messner, Michael, 85
Michelangelo, 512
Michels, Robert, 185
Milgram, Stanley, 159–60, 167–69
Milkie, Melissa, 77
Mills, C. Wright, 3, 4, 19, 91, 239, 258–59,
    432–33
Minkler, Meredith, 375
Mohammed, W. Dean, 519
Monroe, Marilyn, 412
Montagu, Ashley, 319
Moore, Wilbert, 237–38, 487
Morgan family, 264
Morgan, Lewis Henry, 638
Morris, Eva, 362

Mosca, Gaetano, 238–39
Moses (of Old Testament), 509, 516,
    518
Mosher, Steven, 585
Moseley-Braun, Carol, 312
Moyers, Bill, 330
Moynihan, Daniel, 278
Muhammad, 517–18, 524
Muhammad, Khalid Abdul, 329
Muir, Donald, 325
Mulleta family, 227–28
Murdock, George, 55, 291–92
Murphy, Kim, 329
Murray, Charles, 279
Mussolini, Benito, 328, 639

Nash family, 264
Nation, Carrie, 620
Nelkin, Dorothy, 626
Niebuhr, Richard, 530
Nkongoli, 318
Norris, Chuck, 116
Nowak, Thomas, 467–68

Ocalan, Abdullah, 436
O'Connell, Martin, 454
O'Connor, Sandra Day, 307
O'Malley, Jeff, 251
Ogburn, William, 25, 58, 638–40
Ohlin, Lloyd, 210, 211
Ohmae, Kenichi, 439
Olmsted, Michael, 150
Orwell, George, 417–18, 646
Ottenberg, Perry, 436
Ouchi, William, 191

Paltrow, Gwyneth, 116
Park, Robert E., 592, 609
Parker, Alisha, 213
Parks, Rosa, 338
Parmar, Pratibha, 294
Parsons, Elsie Clews, 18
Parsons, Talcott, 3, 19, 487, 541
Partingon, Donald, 220
Paul, Alice, 18
Pepperberg, Irene, 57
Perdue, Frank, 400
Perot, Ross, 427
Pettie, Sam, 607, 608, 610
Phede (Fred), 335
Piaget, Jean, 71
Pillemer, Karl, 378
Pines, Maya, 67
Plato, 478
Poma de Ayala, Felipe Guaman, 177
Pope, Liston, 521–24
Portés, Alejandro, 350, 429
Postman, Neil, 641
Powell, Colin, 236, 612
Presley, Cheryl A., 562
Presley, Elvis, 616
Prynne, Hester, 216–17
Purcell, Philip, 259

Ram, Arun Bharat, 452
Ram, Manju, 452

Ramsey, Jon Benét, 310
Rauch, James, 182
Reagan, Nancy, 377
Reagan, Ronald, 377, 425
Reckless, Walter, 205
Redl, Fritz, 436
Reeve, Christopher, 100
Reskin, Barbara, 350
Ricks, Thomas E., 87
Rieker, Patricia P., 142
Rifkin, Jeremy, 413
Riis, Jacob, 236
Rimland, Ingrid, 329
Rist, Ray, 494–95
Ritzer, George, 180
Robertson, Ann, 375
Robertson, Ian, 48, 242, 510
Robertson, Pat, 529
Rockefeller, John D., 394
Rockne, Knute, 99
Rockwell, Norman, 150
Rodriguez, Richard, 82, 273, 601
Roethlisberger, Fritz J., 138
Roosevelt, Franklin D., 169, 184, 345–46, 370
Roosevelt, Theodore, 426
Rosenthal, Robert, 495
Rossi, Alice, 289
Rossi, Peter, 140–42
Rothman, Barbara Katz, 545
Rothschild, Joyce, 190
Ruane, Janet, 380
Rubin, Lillian, 453, 455–56
Rumbaut, Ruben, 350, 429
Runge, Ann, 615
Russell, Diana, 471
Russell, Kurt, 363
Ruth, Babe, 503

Salk, Jonas, 183
Samuelson, Paul, 257
Samuelson, Robert, 371
Sandefur, Gary, 279
Sanders, Howard, 592
Sapir, Edward, 45–46
Sarah (of Old Testament), 516, 518
Sayres, William, 444
Schaet, Donald, 328
Schoenberger, Richard, 304–5
Schuler, Robert, 429
Schulz, Charles M., 366, 529
Schwartz, Felice, 306–7
Schwartz, Pepper, 462
Scott, Ellen, 623
Scully, Diana, 142, 145–46, 551
Seabrook, Jeremy, 251
Sega, Along, 653
Seinfeld, Jerry, 360
Selleck, Tom, 367
Sennett, Richard, 273
Shaffir, William, 550
Shakespeare, William, 101
Sharp, Deborah, 48
Sherif, Carolyn, 330, 331
Sherif, Muzafer, 330, 331

Shibutani, Tamotsu, 438
Shiva, 520
Shively, JoEllen, 52
Shreve, Herbie, 532
Sills, David, 184–85
Simmel, Georg, 161–63
Simon, Julian, 583
Simpson, Alan, 371
Simpson, George, 331, 334
Simpson, O. J., 341
Singh, Thaman, 579
Skeels, H. M., 66–67
Small, Albion, 18, 150
Smith, Joseph, 525
Snell, Pamela, 461
Snyder, Kay, 467–68
Snyder, Mark, 108
Son, Johanna, 251
Sosa, Sammy, 74
Sowell, Thomas, 497
Spencer, Diana, 616
Spencer, Herbert, 3, 11–12, 27
Sprecher, Susan, 452
Springer, Jerry, 204
Stalin, Josef, 426
Stallone, Sylvester, 260
Stark, Roger, 533
Starr, Ellen G., 18
Stein, Leonard, 552
Stepick, Alex, 335
Stinnett, Nicholas, 472
Stockard, Jean, 302
Stohr, Oskar, 65, 119, 330
Stone, Gregory, 601
Stouffer, Samuel, 302
Straus, Murray, 470
Straus, Roger, 140
Suitor, Jill, 378
Sultan, Bandar bin, 402
Sumner, William Graham, 39
Sutherland, Edwin, 202, 211–12
Suzuki, Bob, 459
Sykes, Gresham, 205–6
Szasz, Thomas, 222–23

Taft, Howard, 427
Takewell, Terry, 267, 556
Teresa, Mother, 181
Thomas, William Isaac, 23, 119, 321
Timasheff, Nicholas, 434–35
Tocqueville, Alexis de, 183, 626
Tönnies, Ferdinand, 107, 109, 587
Tolchin, Martin, 431
Townsend, Francis, 369–70
Toynbee, Arnold, 639
Treiman, Donald J., 261
Troeltsch, Ernst, 521–24
Trotsky, Leon, 242
Trudeau, Garry, 448
Trump, Donald, 264–65
Tubman, Harriet, 352
Tucker, Karla Faye, 220
Turnbull, Colin, 75
Turner, Ralph, 611
Tyson, Mike, 131

Ullman, Edward, 594
Usdansky, Margaret L., 48
Useem, Michael, 401–2

Vanderbilt, Cornelius, 236
Vanderbilt, Gladys, 236
Veblen, Thorstein, 389–90
Ventura, Jesse, 425
Vishnu, 520

Wagley, Charles, 322–23
Walker, Alice, 294
Wallace, Anthony, 534
Wallerstein, Immanuel, 248–49
Washington, George, 352, 485
Washoe (a chimpanzee), 57
Watson, Mark, 207
Watts, J., 426
Wayne, John, 52
Weber, Lynn, 272
Weber, Max, 3, 14, 16, 17, 18, 33, 175–79, 180, 187, 235–37, 256, 263–65, 281, 390, 418, 419, 423, 514–15, 635–36
Webster, Noah, 479
Weintraub, Richard M., 452
Wells, H. G., 613
Wells, Orson, 613
Welsh, Stephanie, 294
Wenneker, Mark, 327
White, Ralph, 165–66
Whitt, Allen, 190
Whorf, Benjamin, 45–46
Whyte, Martin King, 452, 453
Wilder, L. Douglas, 339
Williams, Christine, 306
Williams, Damian, 612
Williams, Robin, 50–51
Willie, Charles, 340
Willis, Georgianna, 140–41
Wilson, Edward, 56
Wilson, James, 220
Wilson, William Julius, 339–40, 600
Winfrey, Oprah, 257
Winslet, Kate, 113
Wirth, Louis, 321, 596
Wolfer, Loreen, 497
Woods, Tiger, 320
Wright, James D., 140–42
Wurabuti, 357

Xena, 77, 78

Yinger, Milton, 331, 334
Yllo, Kersti, 471
Yoels, William, 598, 601
Young, Laurie E., 18
Yufe, Jack, 65, 119, 330

Zald, Mayer, 619, 628
Zander, Alvin, 165
Zellner, William, 49, 513
Zerubavel, Eviatar, 46
Zeus, 516
Zuboff, Shoshana, 191
Zundel, Ernst, 329

Subject Index

Abkhasians, 356–57
Ablution, 232
Abortion, 29, 621, 629–30
Abuse
  child, 470–71, 615
  elderly, 376–77, 378
  family, 125, 469–71, 622–23
  gender and, 309–10, 469–71, 622–23
  as a research topic, 126–39
  social inequality and, 470–71
  spouse, 125–39, 310, 470, 471, 622–23
Acculturation, 478
Achievement
  as core value, 50
  and violence of husbands, 130
Acid rain, 651
Acting crowds, 609–10
Activity theory, 369
Acupuncture, 565
Adaptation, 509
Adolescence, 88–89
Affirmative action, 350
Africa, 294, 577, 653
African Americans, 337–42
  and civil rights, 338–39
  in Congress, 338
  and deprivation theory, 625–26
  and education, 20, 338–39, 340
  and the family, 456–58
  gains of, 338–39
  and Harlem, 591–92
  and homicide, 339
  and housing, 326–27
  and Islam, 519
  losses of, 339
  lynching of, 18, 607–8, 610
  and Million Man March, 619
  and mortgage discrimination, 326–27
  and networking, 160
  and racial caste system, 233–34
  rising expectations of, 338
  and slavery, 230–31
  and social class, 339–341
  well-being of, 339
Afrocentrism, 342
Age
  at first marriage, 462
  and religious affiliation, 528
  and voting patterns, 428
Age cohort, 367
Ageism, 365–66

Agent provocateur, 626–27
Aggregate, 155
Aggression and testosterone, 290–91
Aging, 355–84. *See also* Elderly
  activity theory of, 369
  changing perceptions of, 364–66
  in China, 365
  conflict perspective on, 369–75
  and disengagement theory, 368–69
  functionalist perspective on, 367–69
  future of, 383–84
  and gender, 363, 367
  global aspects of, 355–62, 363–64
  and industrialization, 357–58, 365
  and labeling, 362–63
  and life expectancy, 358–62
  and mass media, 367
  and new technology, 383–84
  and poverty, 277
  social construction of, 356–57
  and Social Security, 369–73
  symbolic interactionist perspective on,
    362–67
  and timetables, 363
Agricultural revolution, 153
Agricultural societies, 151, 152–53, 389,
    391–92
Agriculture and U.S. economy, 405
Aid to Families with Dependent Children
    (AFDC), 501
AIDS, 335, 542, 557–60, 618
Aladdin, 615–16
Alcohol
  and health, 561–62
  and spouse abuse, 125, 130, 137
Al-Ghazaly Islamic School, 519
Algiers, 37–38
Alienation
  and bureaucrats, 181, 182
  in cities, 596
  defined, 181
  resisting, 181–82
  and technology, 643
Alzheimer disease, 377, 378
Amazon, 151, 653
American Association of Retired Persons
    (AARP), 371, 375, 377
American Dream, 397, 592
American Federation of Teachers, 497
American Journal of Sociology, 18
American Medical Association, 289, 544–46

American Sociological Association, 142, 157
American Sociological Society, 19, 32
Amish, 108, 109, 513, 524–25
Analects, 521
Anarchy, 432
Andaman Islanders, 434
Angioplasty, 647
Angola, 247, 575
Animal rights activism, 623
Animals and language, 56–57
Animism, 516
Anomie, 14, 155, 210–211
Anthropology, 7
Anticipatory socialization, 84
Anti-Malthusians, 574–77
Anti-Semitism, 516
Antithesis, 639
Apartheid, 233
Apathy, 430
Apostles, 517
Appearance, 115, 108, 110, 287
Applied sociology, 19, 21–22, 32–33,
    139–40
Arabs, 232, 351
Architecture, 644
Arkansas, 499, 532
Arunta, 434
Aryan Nations, 329
Aryans, 320–21, 584
Asian Americans
  assimilation of, 344–45
  diversity among, 344
  education of, 340, 344
  and the family, 458
  income of, 344
  location of, 344
  in politics, 345
  well-being of, 339
"Asian tigers," 252
Assimilation, 333, 334–35
Atheism, 513
Australia, 58–59, 355, 357
Authoritarian personality, 328–29
Authority
  charismatic, 420–21
  collapse of, 419
  defined, 30, 418
  egalitarian, 446
  in the family, 446
  as ideal type, 422
  and legitimate violence, 419

Authority, *continued*
  rational-legal, 420
  and social movements, 622–23
  traditional, 419–20
  transfer of, 422–23
Automobile, impact of, 643–45
Average, ways of measuring, 131
Aztecs, 423, 511

Background assumptions, 118
Back stage, 112, 113
Baghdad, 588
Baha'is, 516
Banaro, 444
Band wagon, 624
Bar mitzvah, 512
Barbie doll, 59, 401
Barter, 393, 398
Basic demographic equation, 584
Basic needs, 103, 105
Batapur, Pakistan, 230
Battering, 470
Battle of Little Big Horn, 351
Battle of New Orleans, 5
Beauty, standards of, 287
Beijing, 590
Benares, 520
Benin, 231
Beverly Hills Supper Club, 614–15
Bhagavad-Gita, 519
Bible, 532
"Big Brother," 417–18
Bikers, 207, 222, 532
Bilateral system of descent, 446
Biology
  and culture, 286–91
  and race, 319
Birth order, 455
Births to unmarried women, 28, 463–64
Black Liberation Front, 627
Blended families, 460
Body
  building, 49
  decoration of, 41, 126
  images of, 116–17
  piercing of, 616
  and subcultures, 49
  tattooing of, 126
  uncovering of, 48
Bolivia, 198
Bombay, 590
Boot camp, 87, 490
Born again experience, 512, 517
Bosnia, 438, 638
Boston, 596–98
Bourgeoisie, 30, 235
Boxing, 131
Brahman, 231, 519
Branch Davidians, 507, 525–26
Brazil, 5, 72, 197, 198, 246–47, 320, 439, 653
Bronx, 181
Brown v. the Board of Education of Topeka, 32
Brown University, 326
Buddhism, 516, 520

Budget surplus, myth of, 372–73
Bulgaria, 575
Bull Moose party, 426–27
Bullfighting, 40, 42
Bureau of Alcohol, Tobacco, and Firearms (ATF), 507, 525–26
Bureau of Indian Affairs, 348
Bureaucracy(ies)
  careers in, 186–87
  characteristics of, 177–79
  communication within, 178
  and corporate culture, 186–87
  dysfunctions of, 180–82
  and formal organizations, 177–83
  and goal displacement, 182–83
  "ideal" versus "real," 179
  impersonality of, 179
  incompetence in, 182
  perpetuation of, 182–83
  sociological significance of, 183
  structure of University, 178

Cabbage Patch dolls, 616
Caesarian births, 17
California, 362, 438, 486, 622, 654–55
California Achievement Test, 347
Calvinism, 176, 515
Cambodia, 318, 346
Camel ad, 562
Canada, 637
Capilano River, 451
Capitalism
  and advertising, 397
  and Calvinism, 176, 515
  changes in, 396–97
  and class conflict, 30
  compared to socialism, 393, 395–96
  corporate, 402
  criticism of, 12, 396
  globalization of, 33, 59, 191–94, 387–414, 649
  ideology of, 395–96
  laissez-faire, 393
  and Protestant ethic, 14, 514–15, 635–36
  and rationality, 174–75
  and religion, 514–15
  state, 393
  welfare, 393
  as world economic system, 393–95
Capitalist class, 13, 30, 214, 234, 236, 263–65
Capitalist world economy, 249
Capital punishment, 220
Carcasonne, France, 588
Card stacking, 624
Cardinals, 598
Cargo cult, 620
Carnegie Foundation, 544
Casey v. Planned Parenthood, 629
Caste system, 231–34
Category, 155
Catholic schools, 501
Cause and effect, 137
Centers for Disease Control, 558–60
Centrist parties, 427
CBS Records, 193

Challenger, 633
Charisma, 423, 522
Charismatic leader(s), 420–21, 522
Chechnya, 439
Checks and balances, 432
Cheerleaders, 81
Chicago, 141
Child abuse, 470–71
Child rearing
  and birth order, 455
  and day care, 81, 454–55, 615
  and life cycle, 453–55
  by married couples, 454
  and nannies, 455
  by single mothers, 454
  and social class, 269, 455
Childbirth
  extremes in, 575
  and life cycle, 453
  and marital satisfaction, 453
  and medical profession, 17, 545
  and midwifery, 545
  and race-ethnicity, 460
  and social class, 453
  to unmarried women, 28, 459
Childhood
  historical perspective on, 86–88
  and life course socialization, 86–87
Childless couples, 460, 461
Children
  in Brazil, 72, 246–47
  as economic assets, 571, 577–79
  feral, 64
  institutionalized, 66–67
  and the Internet, 209
  isolated, 64, 66
  as miniature adults, 86–87
  and poverty, 277–78
  slavery of, 230–31, 232
  socialization of, 4–5, 28, 63–68
  in workplace, 390
Chile, 402
China
  aging in, 365
  and arms sales, 435
  Confucianism in, 521
  economy of, 398–99
  female infanticide in, 584–85
  foot binding in, 297
  and global capitalism, 398, 412
  health care in, 566–67
  "one child policy in," 584–85
  repression in, 116–17
  social change in, 635
  and technology, 44
  women in, 295, 297
"Chinatowns," 345
Chinese Americans, 345
Chinese folk religions, 516
Christianity, 511–12, 514, 516, 517, 522–23
Christian Motorcyclists Association (CMA), 532
Christian Solidarity International, 232
Church of England, 524, 531
Church membership, 527

Church(es), 508, 523, 527, 528, 530
Cigarettes, 561–62
Cinco de Mayo festival, 342
Circular reaction, 609
Citizenship, 424
City(ies)
    and automobiles, 644
    communities within, 596–97
    defined, 588
    development of, 588, 592–93
    edge, 591
    fastest growing, 591
    Industrial Revolution and, 588–89
    life in, 594–99
    revitalization of, 602–3
    shrinking, 591
    versus suburbs, 600–1
    world's largest, 590
City-states, 423
Civil religion, 510
Civil rights, 338–39, 619
Civil rights movement, 619
Civil War, 231, 337, 426, 514
Class
    capitalist, 13, 30, 213
    marginal working, 215
    working, 214–15
Class conflict, 12, 214–15, 239
Class consciousness, 235–36
Class system, 235
Classless state, 639
Cliques, 159
Coalition government, 427–28
Coalitions, 163
Coca Cola, 198
Cockfighting, 134
Coercion, 418
Cohabitation
    growth of, 463
    and marital satisfaction, 9, 10
Collective behavior, 608–18
    and circular reaction, 609
    and crowds, 608–12
    and fire, 614–15
    forms of, 612–18
Collective mind, 609
College
    in China, 483
    and drug abuse, 561
    graduates of, 480
    in Japan, 481–82
    in U.S., 480, 483, 493, 494
Colombia, 653
Colonialism, 248
Columbine High School, 478–79, 499
Common sense
    and language, 45–46
    and race, 319
    and research, 126
    and sociology, 8–10
Communication. See also
        Cybercommunication, Internet, New
        Technology
    electronic, 5, 45, 161, 162, 209, 646–49
Communism
    and Marx, 12

and religion, 513–14, 533–34
Communist party, 242–43, 510
Community(ies)
    in cities, 596–97
    defined, 594
    electronic, 161, 162
    gated, 599
    religious, 513
    and social integration, 13–14
Compartmentalize, 334
Competition, and education, 485
Computers. See also Cybercommunication,
        Electronic community, Internet, New
        technology, Technology
Concentric zone model, 592–93
Conflict perspective on
    aging, 369–75
    class conflict, 12, 239
    crime, 214–15
    education, 488–94
    the family, 448–50
    globalization of capitalism, 402–4
    health care, 542–46
    humanizing a work setting, 190–91
    mass media, 104
    population, 575
    power elite, 432–33
    religion, 513–14
    ruling class, 432–33
    social class, 235–36
    social control, 200
    social institutions, 105–6
    social stratification, 238–39
    society, 12, 30–31
    work, 190–91
Confucianism, 516, 521
Congress, U.S., 338, 342, 426, 431, 562
Conspicuous consumption, 389–90
Consumption, 616
Contradictory status locations, 263
Control group, 136–39
Control theory, 205
Convergence theory, 399–400
Cooperatives, 190
Coors Brewery, 188
Core nations, 249
Corporate capitalism, 402
Corporate culture
    hidden, 186–87
    humanizing the, 187–91
Corporate welfare, 651
Corporations, 400–1, 403, 651. See also
        Bureaucracy
Correlation, 137
Correspondence principle, 492–93
Cosmology, 512
Cosmopolites, 597
Counterculture, 49–50
Courtship, 451–52, 645
COYOTE (Call Off Your Old Tired Ethics),
        206
Credential society, 484
Crime
    conflict perspective on, 214–15
    defined, 202
    functionalist view of, 208–14

and gangs, 212
and gender, 213, 214
hate, 220, 221
illegitimate opportunity and, 211–14
strain theory of, 210–211
street, 211
"in the suites," 211–14
symbolic interactionist view of, 202–208
white collar, 211–14
Criminal justice system
    conflict perspective on, 214–15
    and reaction to deviance, 217–22
    sentencing in, 218–19
    and social class, 121–22, 207–8, 215, 270
Crowd(s), 608–12. See also Collective
        behavior
    the acting, 609–10
    and a collective mind, 609
    minimax strategy of, 610
    rationality of, 610–12
    and transformation of the individual,
        608–10
Crude birth rate, 580
Cuba, 169, 343, 458, 611, 628
Cueva Indians, 653
Cult(s), 521–23, 620
Cultural diffusion, 58, 59, 152
Cultural diversity. See Diversity
Cultural goals, 210
Cultural lag, 58, 640
Cultural leveling, 58–59
Cultural relativism, 40–41, 42
Cultural transmission, of values, 484
Cultural universals, 55
Culture
    corporate, 186–87
    defined, 38
    "ideal" versus "real," 55
    internalization of, 39–40
    material, 38–39, 41, 58
    nonmaterial, 38–39, 58
    overview of, 38–41
    peer, 486
    symbolic, 42–50
    and taken-for-granted orientations, 39–40
Culture conflict, 507, 524–26
Culture of poverty, 249–50
Culture shock, 39
Culture wars, 54
Currency, 391–92
Cybercommunication, 5, 45, 161, 162, 191,
        192, 209, 329, 496, 535, 646–49
Cyberslacking, 192
Czech Republic, 575

Day care
    as agent of socialization 80–81
    corporate, 189–90
    and moral panics, 615
    research on, 81, 454–55
Days sick, 548
Death
    and AIDS, 557–60
    causes of, 546
    and dying, 381
    sociology of, 380–83

Death, *continued*
  stages of, 381
Death penalty, 220, 420
Declaration of Independence, 531
Deferred gratification, 281
Degradation ceremonies, 84–86, 216–17
Dehumanization, 436–38
Deindustrialization, 601
Deinstitutionalization, 539, 548
Delinquency
  as crime, 221
  and differential association, 203–204
  among "Saints and Roughnecks," 121–22,
    207–8
Delta Force, 507, 525–26
Democracy
  as core value, 10
  defined, 423
  direct, 424
  and education, 479–80
  as form of government, 423–24
  representational, 424
Democratic party, 157, 426
Democratic systems in Europe, 427–28
Demographic transition, 574
Demographic variables, 580–84
Demography, 572
Denmark, 395, 445
Denominations, 524
Denver, 477–78, 499
Dependency ratio, 372
Dependency theory, 249
Dependent variable, 136–39
Depersonalization, 550
Deposit receipts, 391
Deprivation theory, 625–26
Deprived animals, 67–68
"Desert Storm," 435
Deterrence, 219
Detroit, 232–33
Deviance
  and anomie, 210–211
  control theory of, 205
  and criminal justice system, 217–222
  defining, 198–200
  and differential association, 202–4
  explanations of, 201–2
  and the family, 203–4
  functionalist perspective on, 208–214
  humane approach to, 224
  illegitimate opportunity theory of,
    211–14
  labeling theory of, 205–8
  mainstreaming of, 204
  medicalization of, 222–24
  and mental illness, 222–24
  and norms, 200–201, 208
  official, 200
  primary, 206
  reactions to, 216–224
  relativity of, 198
  secondary, 206
  and social change, 209
  and social control, 197–224
  sociological perspective on, 198–202
  strain theory of, 210–11

and subcultures, 204
symbolic interactionist perspective on,
  202–8
tertiary, 206
in tribal versus industrial societies,
  199–200
Dharma, 519
Dialectical process, 639
Dialysis, 557
Dictatorship, 424–26
Differential association theory, 202–4
Diffusion,
  of culture, 58, 59, 152
  of responsibility, 596, 598–99
Digital divide, 271
Dinkas, 231, 232
Disabilities, 100, 101, 221
Disabling environments, 563
Discovery, 639–40
Discrimination. *See also* Racism, Race-
    ethnicity, Sexism
  defined, 324
  and elderly, 365–66
  and gender, 293, 298, 299, 311–13
  in health care, 298, 299, 327
  in housing, 9, 10, 326–27
  individual, 326–27
  institutional, 326–27
  and Japanese Americans, 345–46
  in mortgages, 326–27
  and prejudice, 9, 10, 324–25
  and stereotypes, 331
  and U.S. racial caste system, 233–34
Disengagement theory, 368–69
Disinvestment, 601
Distance learning, 496
Diversity
  and the Amish, 109
  in the corporation, 188
  and immigrant experience, 82
  inequality and, 160
  and in-groups and out-groups, 158
  and Japanese corporations, 194
  and language, 46, 48
  and marriage and the family, 444–47,
    451–52
  and norms, 199
  and racial-ethnic mix projections, 582
  and rape, 203
  and sexuality, 199
  in social networks, 160
  and suicide, 199
  training, 188
  in U.S. families, 456–62
Divest, 394
Divine right of kings, 240, 241
Division of labor, 106, 151, 152, 153, 177,
  179, 399–400
Divorce
  children of, 466–69
  conflict perspective on, 31
  and ex-spouses, 469
  and fatherhood, 468–69
  functionalist perspective on, 27–29
  in industrialized nations, 466
  measuring of, 465–66

no-fault, 468
numbers of, 26, 465
patterns of, 467–68
rates, 25
and remarriage, 469
and social class, 269
in Sweden, 447
symbolic interactionist perspective on,
  25–26
Documents, 134, 135–36
Domestication, of plants and animals, 151,
  152
Domestication revolution, 151, 152, 153
Dominant group(s)
  defined, 322
  distribution of, 324
Downsizing, 412–14
Downward social mobility, 271
Dramaturgy
  and gynecological examinations, 120–21
  and symbolic interactionism, 112, 113–19
Drugs, 198, 561–62
Dumping, 556
Dupont Circle, 95–96
Dyad, 161–62, 163
Dysfunctions, 510–11

Early older years, 90
Earnings. *See* Income
Earth First!, 654–55
East Los Angeles, 503–4
Ecclesia, 523–24
Economic production, and the family, 27–30
Economic systems of the world, 393–99
Economics
  as a social institution, 103
  as a social science, 6–7
Economy, the, 387–414
  and computers, 648–49
  defined, 389
  of industrialized societies, 389–90
  and information age, 390–91
  and immigration, 583–84
  of postindustrial societies, 390–91
  of preindustrial societies, 389
  subsistence, 389
  underground, 407–9
Ecosabatage, 654–55
Education, 477–504
  of African Americans, 20, 338–39, 340
  of Amish, 109
  in China and U.S., 483
  college, 480–83, 493–94
  and competition, 485
  computers in, 648
  conflict perspective on, 488–94
  as core value, 51
  and correspondence principle, 492–93
  costs of, 491, 492
  defined, 478
  and democracy, 479–80
  development of, 478–80
  discrimination in, 489–92
  in Egypt, 483–84
  employment in, 484–85
  and expenditures for, 491, 492

and family background, 493
and family functions, 488
functionalist perspective on, 484–88
funding of, 491–92
gatekeeping in, 487
in global perspective, 481–84
and individualism, 485
in Industrializing Nations, 479–482
and I.Q. testing, 489–91
in Least Industrialized Nations, 483–84
mediocrity of, 496–98
in Most Industrialized Nations, 481–82
and patriotism, 485
and performance by nation, 492
and personal change, 487
and poverty, 275–77
problems in, 496–99
and racism, 32
restructuring of, 503–4
sexism in, 17, 293, 299–301
site-based management, 502
and social change, 487–88
and social class, 269
as a social institution, 103
and social integration, 485–87
and social placement, 487
solutions for problems in, 500–4
symbolic interactionist perspective on, 494–96
tracking in, 487, 494–95
and transmission of values, 484–85
and unemployment, 411
and voting patterns, 428
Efficiency, as core value, 50
Egalitarian, 446, 447
Ego, 73
Egypt, 483–84, 516, 518
Elections, 425, 426–27
Electronic church, 529, 535
Electronic communication, 5, 45, 161, 162, 209, 646–49
Electronic community, 161–162
"Electronic primary group," 161, 162
Elder abuse, 378
Elder care, and sandwich generation, 464
Elderly, 355–84. See also Aging
abuse of, 378
changing sentiment about, 371
dependency of, 375–79
domiciles of, 375
empowerment of, 375
future of, 383–84
geographical distribution of in U.S., 361
health care costs of, 374
isolation of, 375
longevity of, 356–57
and new technology, 383–84
in nursing homes, 376–78
and payroll taxes, 359
percentage worldwide, 358
and poverty, 374, 378–79
suicide of, 382–83
Embarrassment, 115
Emergent norms, 611–12
Emigrants, 581
Emoticons, 45

Emotions
and gender, 74
universality of, 73–74
Employee stock ownership, 189
Employment, and voting patterns, 428
Empty nest, 455–56
Endogamy, 231, 446
"English only" movement, 343
Enquirer, The, 104
Enterprise zone, 602–3
Environment, 649–56
and ecosabotage, 654–55
as emerging value, 53–54
and Industrializing Nations, 652–53
and Least Industrialized Nations, 652–53
and Most Industrialized Nations, 649–52
sustainable, 649
and technology, 656
Environment versus heredity, 65
Environmental movement, 654–56
Environmental racism, 652
Environmental sociology, 655–56
Epidemiology, 546
Equality, as core value, 51
Eritrea, 480
Eskimos, 199, 364, 434
Estate system, 234, 240
Estonia, 575
Ethics of research, 142–44
Ethiopia, 227–28, 322, 439, 481, 575
Ethnic cleansing, 334
Ethnic villagers, 597
Ethnicity. See also Race-Ethnicity, Discrimination, Racism
and aging, 361–62
defined, 321
in the U.S., 336
and work, 323
Ethnocentrism, 39–40
Ethnomethodology, 118–19
Etruscans, 451
Eureka Springs, 532
Euro, 438
Europe, 637–38
Euthanasia, 553
Evangelism, 523
Everyday life
and eye contact, 9, 10
and touching, 9, 10
Evolution, 638
Exchange mobility, 272
Execution, 419
Executive Order 9066, 346
Exogamy, 446
Experiment(s),
the Asch, 167
Cold War, 564
on conformity, 167
design of, 138
explained, 136–39
on group dynamics, 164–66
the Hawthorne, 138
on leadership, 165–66,
the Milgram, 167–69
misguided, 143, 563–64

model of, 138
on peer pressure, 167
on sexual attraction, 108–9, 110, 451
on teacher expectations, 495
on teen mothers, 500
Tuskegee Syphilis, 563–64
Experimental group, 136–39
Exponential growth curve, 573
Expression(s), online, 45
Ex-spouses, 469
Exxon Corporation, 651

Face-saving behavior, 115–16
Fads, 616–17
False consciousness, 236
Family(ies), the
African-American, 456–58
Asian-American, 458–59
battering in, 471
blended, 460
child abuse in, 471–72
childless, 460
and common cultural themes, 445–46
conflict perspective on, 448–50
dark side of, 469–71
defined, 444–45
and deviance, 203–204
diversity of, 445–45, 456–62
and economic production, 27–30
and education, 488
extended, 445
functionalist perspective on, 24, 27, 446–48
future of, 472–73
gay and lesbian, 460, 462
in global perspective, 444–47
in historical perspective, 27–30
in hunting and gathering societies, 151
in later life, 455–56
Latino, 458
life cycle of, 451–56
in Mexico, 571
Native American, 458–59
and new technology, 461
nuclear, 445
one-parent, 459–60
of orientation, 445
of procreation, 445
rape in, 471
size of, 571, 572, 575, 577–79
and social class, 79–80, 268–69
as social institution, 103
and socialization, 79–80
in Sweden, 447
trends in, 462–64
universality of, 447
Family background, 493
Famines, 578–79
Fashion, 617
Father, absent, 468–69
Fecundity, 580
Federal Bureau of Investigation (FBI), 507, 525–26, 612, 627
Federal Reserve Board, 327
Fee for service, 546
Female circumcision, 294
Female genital mutilation (FGM), 294

Feminism
and nursing, 552
rise of, 297–98
"second wave" of, 297–98
Feminist perspective on
Freud, 73
social institutions, 106
Feminization of poverty, 277, 469
Feral children, 64
Fertility, 580
Fertility rate, 580
Fictive kin, 457
Fieldwork. *See* Participant observation
Filipino Americans, 345
Finance, computers and, 648–49
Fire, and collective behavior, 614–15
First estate, 234, 240
First social revolution, 151, 152–53
Fitness, as emerging value, 53
Flu epidemic of 1918, 560–61
Florida, 335, 361, 362, 379, 384, 599, 633
Food production, 577
Football, as social structure, 99
Footbinding, 297
Ford Motor Company, 412
Foreign aid, 132
Formal organizations, 177–83
Fossil fuels, 651–52
Fourth social revolution, 151, 154–55
France, 369, 420, 423, 435, 588, 626, 637
Freedom, as core value, 50–51
French revolution, 10, 11
Front stage, 112, 113
Functional equivalent, 510
Functional illiterate, 498
Functional requisites, 105
Functionalist perspective on
aging, 367–69
crime, 208–14
deviance, 208–214
divorce, 27–29
education, 484–88
family, 24, 27, 446–48
global capitalism, 399–402
illness and health care, 541–42
mass media, 104
religion, 509–11
social control, 200
social institutions, 105
social stratification, 237–38
Functions
of education, 484–86
of incest taboo, 447
latent, 484
manifest, 484
of religion, 509–11
Fundamentalism, 107–8, 518

G-7, 436, 439, 637–38
Ganges River, 508, 520
Gangs, urban, 203, 212
Gated communities, 599
Gatekeeping, 487
Gay and lesbian families, 460, 462
Gaza, 575

Gemeinschaft, 107–108, 109, 578, 587, 596, 635
Gender
and age at first marriage, 462
and aging, 363, 367
and advertising, 77
and AIDS, 559
and biology, 286–91
and body images, 116–17
and college degrees, 299–301
and crime, 213, 214
and criminal justice system, 310
defined, 286
and differences in morality, 3, 72
and discrimination in medicine, 298, 299
and division of labor, 151, 153
education and, 17, 293, 299–301
and emotions, 74
in estate system, 234
and eye contact, 9, 10
and the family, 76
and global stratification, 235, 291–95
housework and, 448–51, 645
and inequality, 77, 79, 291–97, 297–309, 301–2, 514
and infanticide, 584–85
and isolation, 375
and labor force participation, 303
and literacy rates, 293
in mass media, 76–77, 116–17
and meaning of marriage, 450
and pay gap, 9, 10, 293, 302–5
peer groups and, 83
and politics, 293, 311–13
and poverty, 277, 378–79
and power, 145–46
and rape, 309
and religion, 514
in research, 142, 272
sex and, 286–91
and sick role, 542
and slavery, 229
social institutions and, 106
socialization into, 76–79, 83
and sports, 85, 301
and stereotypes, 78, 85, 108, 110
and stratification, 227–28, 235, 285–313
television portrayls of, 77
and touching, 9, 10, 128
tracking by, 299–301
and video games, 77–79
violence and, 309–11
and voting, 428
and work, 291–93, 302–9
Gender aging, 363, 367
Gender gap
in pay, 9, 10, 293, 302–5
in politics, 430
Gender relations, future of, 313
Gender roles, 76–77, 85. *See also* Gender
Gender stratification, 227–28, 235, 285–313
General Motors, 400
Generalizability , 134–35
Generalized other, 69
Genes, and human behavior, 55–56, 201
Genocide, 149, 317–318, 321, 332–34

Gentrification, 591
Georgia cotton mill, 390
Geography of church membership, 527
Geopolitics, 636–38
Germany, 318, 321, 358, 410, 421, 423, 425–26, 435, 438, 511, 575, 626
Gerontocracy, 364
Gesellschaft, 107, 109, 587, 596, 635
Gestapo, 425
Gestures, 42–43, 113
Glass ceiling, 305–6
Glass escalator, 305–6
Glittering generality, 624
Global aspects of
aging, 355–64
AIDS, 558–60
beauty, 287
births to unmarried mothers, 28, 463–64
capitalism, 33, 59, 191–94, 248–49, 388–415
courtship, 451–52
disease, 558–61
the economy, 388–415
education, 481–84
environment, 649–56
ethnic conflicts, 636–38
gender inequality, 291–97
group dynamics, 169
health care, 542–43
intergroup relations, 332–49
marriage and family, 444–47, 451–52
population growth, 573–75, 577–86
self, reasoning, and morality, 72
social networking, 160
stratification, 227–52, 542–43
technology, 57–58
Global capitalism. *See* Globalization of capitalism
Global stratification
and environment, 649–56,
and four worlds of development, 243–248
and health care, 542–43
history of, 248–50
and income of world's nations, 244
and Industrializing Nations, 246
in Least Industrialized Nations, 247
maintenance of, 250–52
and Most Industrialized nations, 243
and technology, 241, 252
and women, 227–28, 235, 251
Global village, 57–58, 390, 400
Global warming, 652
Globalization. *See also* Global aspects of, Globalization of capitalism
of capitalism, 33, 59, 191–94, 248–49, 388–415
defined, 33
of the economy, 388–415
and stratification, 227–52
Globalization of capitalism
conflict perspective on, 402–4
and cultural diffusion, 592
and the economy, 388–415
and the environment, 649–56
and foreign ownership of U.S. business, 404

functionalist view of, 399–402
future of, 412–14
and Japan, 191–94
and stratification of nations, 248–49
as trend shaping future, 33
and U.S. ownership in other countries, 405
Goal displacement, 182–83
Government, types of, 423–26
Grade inflation, 498
Gray Panthers, 375
Graying of America, 358–62
Great Britain, 153, 241–42, 404, 557, 637, 638
Great Depression, 369–70, 584
Greenhouse effect, 563, 651
Group dynamics, 161–70
Group of seven (G7), 436, 439, 637–38
Group size
  diffusion of responsibility, 164
  effects on attitudes and behaviors, 164–65
  and relationships, 161–4
  and stability and intimacy, 161–64
Groups
  control, 136–39
  defined, 102, 150
  dynamics of, 161–70
  ethnic, 336
  experimental, 136–39
  focus, 140
  involuntary membership in, 102
  primary, 156
  reference, 158–61
  religious, 521–26
  secondary, 156–57
  small, 161–64, 189
  social, 150
  and social institutions, 103
  subcultures, 49–50
  voluntary membership in, 102
Groupthink, 169–70
Growth rate, 584
Gynecological examinations, 120–21

Haiti, 232, 335
Haitians, 335
Hale-Bopp comet, 522
Hara-kiri, 199
Harijans, 231–32
Harlem, 591–92
Harlow experiments, 67–68
Harvard, 320, 493
Hate crimes, 221
Hawaii, 462
Hazardous waste site, 650
Health. See also Health care
  and alcohol, 561–62
  components of, 540–41
  in historical perspective, 546–47
  and social class, 267–68
  symbolic interactionist perspective on, 540–41
  threats to, 557–64
Health care. See also Medicine
  as commodity, 547
  conflict of interest in, 550–51
  conflict perspective on, 542–46

costs of, 374, 547, 555–57
discrimination in, 327
dumping, 556
fraud in, 551
functionalist perspective on, 541–42
in global perspective, 565–67
global stratification of, 542–43
in Industrializing Nations, 566–67
and inequality, 539, 547
and insurance, 555–56
issues in, 547–57
in Least Industrialized Nations, 566–67
and lifestyles, 565
monopoly of in U.S., 543–46
in Most Industrialized Nations, 566–67
and prevention, 565
rationing of, 556–57
right to, 547
symbolic interactionist perspective on, 540–41
Health Maintenance Organizations (HMOs), 555
Heart transplant operation, 542
Heaven's Gate, 522
Helena, Montana, 641
Heredity versus environment, 65
"Hidden" corporate culture, 186–87
Hidden curriculum, 489
High school
  dropouts from, 481, 500
  and drug abuse, 561
  graduates of, 480
Hinduism, 508, 512, 514, 516, 519–20
Historical change, Marx's model of, 639
History, 351
HIV, 557–560
Hmong, the, 203
HMOs, 555
Holland, 445, 460, 554–55
Hollywood, 412
Holocaust, 329, 516
Holy communion, 512
Homeless
  author's experience with, 3–4, 95–96, 134, 142, 255, 539, 586–87
  counting the, 140–42
  in Japan, 193
  and mental illness, 223–24
  micro-level analysis of, 31–32
  shelters, 3–4, 181
  silence of, 4
  urban, 600
Homicide. See Murder
Homogamy, 453
Homosexuals, 221, 318, 444–45, 460, 462
Hook story, 617
Hopi Indians, 45–46
Horatio Alger myth, 281
Hospices, 381–82
House calls, 544
Household
  defined, 445
  heads of, 457
Housing
  and African Americans, 325–37

and Latinos, 327
  segregation of, 325–27
Housework, 448–51
Hula Hoop, 616–17
Huli Tribe, 640
Hull-House, 18
Human ecology, 592
Human nature, 64
Humanitarianism, as core value, 50
Humanizing a work setting, 187–91
Hunting and gathering societies, 150–52, 389
Hutus, 317–18
Hypothesis, 128

Id, 73
Ideal type, 179
Ideological commitment, 626
Ideology, 230, 643
Ifaluk, 74
Ik, 75
Illegitimate opportunity theory, 211–14
Illness
  functionalist perspective on, 541–42
  symbolic interactionist perspective on, 540–41
Immigrants
  entrepreneurial, 429
  place of birth of, 583
  politics of, 429
Immigration
  and cultural diversity, 582
  debate concerning, 349–50
  illegal, 408
  Irish, 337, 429
  and population growth, 581–84
  projections of, 350, 582
Imperialism, 10–11
Impression management, 115
Imprisonment, as reaction to deviance, 217–18
Incapacitation, 220
Incas, 423
Incest, 471
Incest taboo, 447
Inclusion, 486–87
Income
  of CEOs, 259
  defined, 256
  distribution of, 257
  and inflation, 409, 410
  inverted pyramid of, 391
  of men, 305
  and religious affiliation, 527
  and voting patterns, 428
  of women, 305
  of workers in U.S., 409, 410
Indentured service, 230–31
Independent variable, 136–39
India
  and Buddhism, 520
  caste system in, 231–32
  child labor in, 390
  democracy in, 421
  female infanticide in, 585
  marriage in, 452

Individualism
  as core value, 50
  and education, 485
Indonesia, 86, 247, 578
Indus, 588
Industrial Revolution, 9–10, 30, 151, 153–54,
    234, 236, 588–89
Industrialization
  and aging, 357–58, 365
  and development of sociology, 9–15
  and dying, 380
  and the economy, 389–91
  and education, 479–80
Industrialization, *continued*
  effects of, 409–11
  and inequality, 153–54
  and population growth, 585
  and rationality, 174–76
  of society, 153–54
Industrializing Nations
  and distribution of land and population,
    243
  education in, 482
Inequality
  in educational funding, 491–92
  gender, 286–313
  and health care, 539, 547–48
  and industrialization, 153–54
  and social networks, 160
Infant mortality, 543
Inflation, 409, 410
Information
  control of, 240–41
  and postindustrial society, 154–55
  and social stratification, 240–41
Information age, 390–91
Information superhighway, 649
Infrastructure, 589
In-groups, 157–58
Innovators, 210
Institute of Medicine, 549–50
Institutional death, 381–82
Institutional means, 210
Italy, 575, 637
Intelligence, 67
Intergenerational conflict, 370–75
Intergenerational mobility, 271
Intergroup relations, global patterns of,
    332–49
Interlocking directorates, 403–4
Internal colonialism, 333, 334
Internal Revenue Service (IRS), 409
International Olympic Committee, 116–17
International Telephone & Telegraph
    Company (ITT), 402
Internet
  and children, 209
  and cyberslacking, 192
  and digital divide, 271
  and electronic communities, 161–62
  hatred on, 329
  and online expressions, 45
  pornography on, 209
  religion on, 529, 535
  and social change, 646–49
  Viagra on, 553

Internet cafe, 42, 107, 249
Interracial marriage, 325, 453
Interview, 133–134
Interviewer bias, 133, 142
Intrauterine device (IUD), 585
Invention
  defined, 639
  of microchip, 151
  of plow, 151, 152–53
  of steam engine, 153
  of tools, 152–53
I.Q. testing, 489–91
Iran, 422
Iraq, 426, 435, 439
Iron law of oligarchy, the, 185–86
Islam, 516, 517–19
Islamic fundamentalism, 107–8, 518

Jackson, 338
Jains, 516
Jakarta, 590
Japan
  corporations in, 161, 191–94
  cultural diffusion in, 58
  cultural diversity in, 400
  education in, 481–82
  homelessness in, 193
  lobbying efforts of, 431
  as regional power, 637
  religion in, 514
  and suicide, 9, 10,, 199
Japanese Americans, 345–46
Japanese corporate model, 191–94
Jen, 521
Jerry Springer Show, 204
Jersey City, 519
Jerusalem, 517
Jews, 318, 321, 322, 332, 351, 438, 479, 512,
    516–17
Jim Crow laws, 337
Jonesboro, Arkansas, 499
Judaism, 516–17

Kalahari of South Africa, 479
Kamikaze pilots, 199
Kennedy Space Center, 633
Kentucky, 614–15
Kentucky Fried Chicken, 617
Khmer Rouge, 318
Kiev, 397
Kindergarten, 490
Kinship networks, 448
Klahanie, Wahsington, 599
Koran, 422, 517
Koreans, 612
Kosovo, 232, 438, 638
Kotzebue, Alaska, 459
Kshatriya, 231
Ku Klux Klan, 157, 158, 328, 332–33, 618,
    627
Kurds, 439
Kwanzaa, 342, 457

Labeling
  and aging, 362–63
  and perception, 207–8

  and prejudice, 333
Labeling theory, 205–8
  and bikers, 207
  and prostitutes, 206
  and "Saints" and "Roughnecks," 207–8
  and social class, 207–8
Labor force participation, 303, 406–8
Laissez-faire capitalism, 393
Lancaster county, Pennsylvania, 109
Land, and population distribution, 243
Language, 43–47
  defined, 43
  and goal directed behavior, 44
  and human behavior, 56–57
  in Miami, 48
  and perception, 46–47
  and race, 46
  and shared future, 44
  and shared past, 44
  and shared perspectives, 44
  significance of, 43–45
  universality of, 43
Laos, 346
Latent function, 81
Later middle years, 90
Later older years, 90
Latinos
  in Congress, 343
  defined, 342
  diversity among, 343
  and education, 340
  and the family, 458
  heritage of, 342
  and housing, 327
  location of, 342–43
  numbers of, 342–43
  origins of, 342–43
  and Spanish language, 343
  well-being of, 339, 344
Latvia, 575
Law
  conflict view of, 214–14
  and oppression, 215
  as social institution, 103
Leader(s)
  authoritarian, 165
  charismatic, 420–21, 522
  democratic, 165
  expressive, 165
  instrumental, 165
  laissez-faire, 165
  socioemotional, 165
  types of, 165
Leadership, 165–66
Leadership styles, 165–66
Learning, Earning, and Parenting (LEAP), 500
Least Industrialized Nations
  child birth in, 571, 577–79
  child labor in, 390
  and dependency theory, 249
  and distribution of land and population,
    243
  education in, 483–84
  health care in, 542–43
  and global stratification, 245–46, 247,
    542–43

population growth of, 571, 575, 577–80
symbolic interactionist perspective on births in, 571, 577–79
Legitimate violence, and authority, 419
Leisure
 as emerging value, 53
 and hunters and gatherers, 151
 patterns of, 409–10
 trends in, 410
Liason Agency Network, 233
Life course
 defined, 86
 socialization through, 86–91
 sociological significance of, 90–91
Life cycle of family, 451
Life expectancy, 358–62
 by country, 361
 and ethnicity, 361–62
 and health care, 543
 by year of birth, 360
Life span, 360–61, 383–84
The Lion King, 615
Literacy rates, 293
"Little Havana," 379, 611
The Little Mermaid, 615
Littleton, Colorado, 477–78
Living will, 553, 554–55
Lobbyists, 430–31, 432
Looking-glass self, 68–69
Los Angeles, 548, 590, 612–13, 650
Lottery, 262
Love
 and courtship, 451–52
 in global perspective, 451–52
 and marriage, 25–26
 romantic, 51, 451
Lower middle class, 265
Loyalty, 157–58
Luanda, 247
Lynching, 18, 607–8, 610

Macao, 575
Machismo, 458
Macropolitics, 418
Macrosociological perspective on
 culture, 98
 social class, 98–99
 social status, 99
 social structure, 97–102
Macrosociology, 96–102, 121–22
Mafia
 Russian, 243
 trenchcoat, 477–78
Magic Kingdom, 615
Maine, 549
Mainstreaming
 of deviance, 204
 in education, 486–87
Malabar, 445
Malaysia, 653
Mali, 575
Malpractice, 548–50
Malthus theorem, 572
Mandatory education laws, 480
Manifest function, 81
Manner, 115

March of Dimes, 182–83, 184
Marijuana, 560
Marines, 87
Marital history, 469
Market, 389
Market competition, 393
Market forces, 395
Market restraints, 393
Marketing research and applied sociology, 139–40
Marriage. *See also* Family
 age at first, 462
 arranged, 452
 battering in, 470
 changing meanings of, 25
 and children, 453
 conflict perspective on, 448–50
 and cultural themes, 445–46
 defined, 445
 functionalist perspective on, 446–48
 future of, 472–73
 in global perspective, 444–47
 interracial, 453
 intimacy in, 451
 and life cycle, 452–53
 and misuse of statistics, 472
 postponing of, 462–63
 power in, 31
 and rape, 471
 roles in, 25, 27–29
 same sex, 444–45, 460, 462
 satisfaction in, 9, 10
 successful, 472
 symbolic interactionist perspective on, 25–26, 450–51, 472
 two-paycheck, 448–50
Marriage squeeze, 458
Martians, 613
Marx on Marxism, 12
Masada, 516
Mass media, 103, 623–25
 and aging, 366–67
 and body images, 116–17
 changing images of women in, 78
 conflict perspective on, 104
 as emerging social institution, 103, 104
 as gatekeepers of social movements, 623–25
 and gender messages, 76–77, 78
 and Native Americans, 52
 and prejudice, 329–330
 and public opinion, 623–25
 and school shootings, 499
 and violence against women, 311
Mass society, 625
Mass society theory, 625
Massachusetts, 479–80
Mate selection
 norms of, 446
 and social class, 268
Material comfort, as core value, 50
Math, 503–4
Matriarchy, 289, 446, 447
Matrilineal system of descent, 446
Mattell Toys, 59, 401

Mauritania, 231
McDonaldization of society, 180
McDonald's, 180
McGill University, 18
Mdewakanton Dakotas, 349
Mean, 131
Meaning, ultimate, 509
Means of production, 235, 263, 393
Mecca, 519
Mechanical solidarity, 399, 587
Median, 131
Medicaid, 546
Medical care. *See* Health care
Medical incompetence, 549–50
Medical insurance, 555–56
Medical profession. *See also* Health care, Medicine
 and childbirth, 17
 monopoly of, 544–46
Medicalization of deviance, 222–224
Medicalization of society, 552
Medicare, 370, 374, 546, 551, 557
Medicine. *See also* Health care, Medicine
 alternatives to, 564–67
 computers in, 647
 defensive, 548–49
 monopoly of, 543–46
 and new technology, 647
 professionalization of, 544–46
 rationing of, 556–57
 sexism in, 298, 299, 551–52
 as a social institution, 103
 socialized, 566
 sociological perspective on, 540
Medicine Tree, 654–55
Medieval city, 588
Medina, 518
Mediterranean, 420, 588
Mediums of exchange, 391–93
 in agricultural societies, 391–92
 in industrial societies, 392–93
 in postindustrial societies, 393
Megalopolis, 589
Melanesian Islands, 620–21
Melting pot, 323
Men. *See also* Gender
 and eye contact, 9, 10
 and pay gap, 9, 10
 and touching, 9, 10
Menonites, 524
Mental health
 historical perspective on, 547
 and social class, 268, 539, 547–48
Mental illness
 and deviance, 222–24
 and the homeless, 223–24, 539
 and social class, 268, 539, 547–48
 symbolic interactionist perspective on, 450–41
Mental retardation, 66–67
Meritocracy, 238
Mesopotamia, 588
Metropolis, 589
Metropolitan Life Insurance Company, 178
Metropolitan Statistical Area (MSA), 590–91

Mexico
  economy of, 388
  ethnic conflicts in, 637
  the family in, 571
  gestures in, 42, 43
Mexico City, 590, 595
Miami, 48, 379, 517, 611
Michigan, 554–55
Mickey Mouse, 615
Micronesia, 74
Micropolitics, 418
Microsociological perspective on,
  eye contact, 112
Microsociological perspective on, *continued*
  interaction in everyday life, 108, 110–21
  touching, 112
Microsociology, 96–97, 108–21
  and symbolic interaction, 108, 110–12
Middle years, 89–90
Midwifery, 545
Migration, 580–81
Military
  and sexual harassment of women, 308–9
  as a social institution, 103
Millenarian movements, 620
Million-Man March, 619
Milwaukee Open, 320
Minimax strategy, 610
Minnesota, 425, 572
Minority group(s)
  defined, 322
  distribution of, 324
  emergence of, 322
  shared characteristics of, 322–23
  women as, 295–97
Mission Indians, 434
Mississippi, 338
Mobility, social, 235, 270–75
  downward, 271
  exchange, 272
  intergenerational, 271
  structural, 272
  upward, 271, 274–75
  and women, 272
Mode, 131
Model T, 645
Modernization, 514, 635–36
Mommy track, 307
Monarchy, 423
Money, history of, 391–93
Monogamy, 50, 51
Monopolies, 394, 543–46
Monotheism, 516
Monument Valley, Arizona, 292
Moral holidays, 47–48
Moral issues, 626
Moral panics, 615–16
Morality
  development of, 71–72
  gender differences in, 72
Mormons, 50, 513, 525
Morocco, 37–38, 119
Morphing, 642
Morristown, New Jersey, 376
Mortality, 580
Mortgages, 326–27

Moscow, 395, 434
Mosques, 519
Most Industrialized Nations
  and dependency theory, 249
  and distribution of land and population,
    243
  education in, 481–82,
  and environment, 649–52
  and global stratification, 243
Mothers, unmarried, 28, 463–64
Mourners, 580
Movement for the Restoration of the Ten
  Commandments of God, 522
Mozambique, 296
Multiculturalism, 333, 335, 350–52, 412
Multinational corporations, 250–52, 399,
  404, 409, 651–52
Multiple-Nuclei Model, 594
Murder
  of African Americans, 339
  in schools, 499
  of women, 309–10
Muslims, 516, 517–19
Myths
  of a budget surplus, 372–73
  Horatio Alger myth, 281
  about poverty, 277
  of race, 318–21
  of shool shootings increasing, 499
Myanmar, 439

Name calling, 624
Nannies, 455
National Association for the Advancement of
  Colored People (NAACP), 19, 21, 618
National Enquirer, 104
National health insurance, 556
National Islamic Front, 232
National Opinion Research Center (NORC),
  140–42
National Organization for Women (NOW),
  618
National Women's Party, 297
Nationalism, 438, 439
Native Americans
  aging among, 364
  and casinos, 349
  democracy among, 423–24
  diversity among, 347
  and education, 340
  and the family, 459
  genocide of, 332–33, 347–48
  as invisible minority, 348–49
  and marriage, 444–45
  and mass media, 52
  and population transfer, 347–48
  and separatism, 349
  treaties with, 347–48
  well-being of, 339
Natural disasters, 9, 10, 614
Natural sciences, 6
Natural selection, 55–56
Nature versus nurture, 55–56, 201,
  286–291
Navajo, 292
Nayar, 445

Nazis, 158, 166, 167–69, 217, 318, 329, 330,
  425–26, 482, 613, 618
Nebraska, 203, 427
Neelyville, Missouri, 446
Neighborhood, as agent of socialization,
  82
Neocolonialism, 250
Neo-Nazis, 158, 332–33
Net migration rate, 581
Networking. *See also* Social networks
  and African-Americans, 160
  and women, 160
Networks. *See* Social networks, Networking
Neutralization, techniques of, 205–06
Nevada, 564
New England, 616
"New girl" network, 160
New Guinea, 444, 640
New Malthusians, 573–74, 575–76
New Mexico, 540
New Orleans, 255
New Technology
  and aging, 383–84
  and communication, 5, 45, 161, 162
  and cyberslacking, 191, 192
  defined, 57
  and digital divide, 271
  and dying, 380, 553–55, 557
  and electronic communities, 161, 162
  and the family, 461
  and fears of the future, 272–73
  and global capitalism, 412–14
  in the global village, 57–58
  and Internet, 329
  and Internet University, 496
  and mass media, 329
  and medical rationing, 557
  and politics, 425
  and religion, 535
  and replacement of humans, 60
  and reproduction, 461
  and social change, 646–49
  and social class, 270, 271
  and social stratification, 241, 649
  and work, 410–11, 412–14
New World Order, 401–2, 438–40
New York City, 542
Nicotine, 561–62
Niger, 575
Nigeria, 439
Nile, 588
Nirvana, 520
Noncentrist parties, 427
Nonmaterial culture, and technology, 58
Nonverbal interaction, 31
Norm of noninvolvement, 596, 598–99
Norms
  and deviance, 199, 200–1, 208
  emergent, 611–12
  explained, 47–48
  and social institutions, 103
North American Free Trade Association
  (NAFTA), 438
North Vancouver, 451
Norway, 445, 460
Nursing homes, 376–78

Objectivity, 15
Occupations, prestige of, 260–61
Ogburn's theory, 639–40
Oil-rich, nonindustrialized nations, 248
"Old boy network," 160
Older years, and life course socialization, 90
Oligarchy, 424
Oligopoly, 402
Oman, 575
One-parent families, 459–60
Operational definition, 128
Opium of the people, 513–14
Oregon, 554–55, 648
Organic solidarity, 400
Organizations
    social, 642–43
    and social institutions, 103
Orlando, 599
Oromos, 439
Orphans, 56–57
Out-groups, 157–58
Oxygen bar, 563

Pacific Rim nations, 252
Pakistan, 230
Pan-Indianism, 349
Panics, 613–15
Parenthood, changing meanings of, 25
Parris Island, South Carolina, 87, 308
Participant observation, 134–35
Party affiliation in U.S., 426–27
Patriarchy, 289, 295–97, 446
Patrilineal system of descent, 46
Patriotism, 485
Pay gap, 9, 10, 293, 302–5
Pearl Harbor, 169, 345–46
Peer groups
    and educational performance, 498
    and gender, 83
    and socialization, 83
Peking, 588
Penan tribe, 654
Pequots, 349
Perception
    and ideology, 20–28
    and labels, 207–8
    and language, 46, 47
    selective, 331
Peripheral model, 594
Periphery, 249
Persia, 588
Personal change, 487
Personal identity kit, 85
Personal Responsibility and Work
    Opportunity Reconciliation Act, 280
Personal space, 37–38, 110–112
Personality, development of, 72–73
Personality disorders, 202
Peru, 653
Peter principle, 182
Pietá, 512
Pilgrims, 531
Plain folks, 624
Plant cultivation, 151, 152–53

Plessy v. Ferguson, 337
Pluralism. See also Multiculturalism
    functionalist perspective on, 432
    and religious groups, 528
Pluralistic society, 50, 333, 335
Pokemon, 58
Pokot people of Kenya, 199
Poland, 149
Police discretion, 222
Polio, 182–83
Political Action Committees (PACs), 431
Political parties, 426–27
Political science, 6
Political system of U.S., 426–31
Politics, 418–40
    and gender discrimination, 293, 311–13
    and social class, 269–70
    as social institution, 103
Pollution, 650–56
Polyandry, 444
Polygyny, 50, 444, 518, 525
Polytheism, 516, 520
Population, 571–86. See also Population growth
    conflict perspective on, 575
    and distribution of world's land, 243
    in global perspective, 572–80
    growth of, 573, 574, 580–86
    and income distribution in U.S., 391
    projection of U.S., 586
    shrinkage, 575
    as study group, 129–30
    transfer, 333, 334
Population growth
    demographic variables affecting, 580–84
    forecasting, 584–86
    and immigration, 581–84
    and industrialization, 585
    in Least Industrialized Nations, 571, 575, 577–80
    in a single day, 573
    over two thousand years, 574
    world, 579–86
Pornography, on the Internet, 209
Postal Service, U.S., 179
Postmodern society, 641–42
Potato, 572
Poverty, 273–82
    by age, 277
    and aging, 277, 378–79
    author's experience with, 282
    and births to married women, 279
    and births to unmarried women, 279
    and characteristics of the poor, 279
    and children, 277–78
    culture of, 279
    defined, 273
    duration of, 279
    dynamics of, 279
    in early U.S., 29
    and education, 275–77
    feminization of, 277, 469
    and gender, 277, 378–79
    geography of, 274
    myths about, 277

    patterns of, 276
    and race-ethnicity, 275, 277, 379
Poverty line, 273
Power
    defined, 258, 418
    functionalist perspective on, 432
    Mill's model of, 433
    and rape, 145–46
Power elite, 19, 258, 432–33
Precipitating event, 613
Prejudice
    defined, 325
    and discrimination, 324–25
    extent of, 325
    and fraternity membership, 325
    and labels, 331
    and mass media, 329–330
    sociological perspectives on, 329–31
    theories of, 328–32
    on U.S. campuses, 325–26
Prestige
    display of, 261–62
    and occupations, 260–61
Primaries, 426
Primary groups, 156
Princeton, 493
Prisoners
    characteristics of U.S., 218
    growth in number of U.S., 217
Private ownership of means of production, 393
Prochoice movement, 621, 629–30
Production
    in traditional societies, 175–76
    in nontraditional societies, 175–76
Profane, 508
Professionalization of medicine, 544–46
Progress, as core value, 50
Prohibition, 620
Proletariat, 12, 30, 234, 235–36
Prolife movement, 629–30
Promise Keeper's, 513
Propaganda, 623–25
Property, distribution of, 256–57
Proportional representation, 427
Proposition 209, 350
Props, 115
Prostitution, 23, 206, 251, 285
Protestant ethic, 14, 175–76, 390, 514–15, 635–36
Protestant reformation, 634
Protestants, 14, 175–76, 390, 512–13, 514–15
Psychology as a social science, 7
Public opinion, 623–25
Puerto Rico, 458
Purple Berets, 622

Qualitative analysis, 128–29
Qualitative research methods, 139–40
Quality circles, 188–89
Quantitative analysis, 129,
Quantitative research methods, 139–40
Questions, in research, 132–33
Questionnaires, 133
Quiet Revolution, 25–26, 27, 407–8

Race
defined, 318
and myth, 318–21
in sociological perspective, 318–21
Race-ethnicity, 317–52. *See also*
Discrimination, Racism
and African Americans, 337–342
and AIDS, 559, 560
and Asian Americans, 344–47
and capital punishment, 220
and childbirth, 460
and college attendance, 299, 493, 494
and death penalty, 220
and digital divide, 271
and the family, 456–59
and global politics, 636–38
and hate crimes, 221
heightened sense of, 323
and high school completion, 493
and identity construction, 323
and language, 46
and Latinos, 342–44
and multiracial identity, 320
and Native Americans, 347–49
and poverty, 275
and projections for future, 349–50, 582
and religion, 527–28
and suicide, 383
and unemployment, 411
and voting patterns, 428
and white Americans, 337
Racism. *See also* Discrimination, Race-
ethnicity
and capital punishment, 220
as core value, 51
and education, 32
environmental, 652
in everyday life, 341
and lynching, 18, 607–8, 610
in syphilis experiment, 563–64
in U.S. South, 18–19, 20
Racist mind, 332–33
Rain forests, 653
Random sample, 130–31
Rape
and gender, 309
marital, 471
and power, 145–46
research on, 145–46
Rapport, 134
Rationality, 174–75
Rationalization of society, 174–76
Reality, social construction of. *See* Social
construction of reality
Reasoning skills, stages in development
of, 71
Rebellion, 211
Recidivism rate, 219
Red Sea, 480
Red tape, 181
Redlining, 601
Redwoods, 54, 654–55
Reference groups, 158–61
Reform Party, 427
Rehabilitation, 219–20
Reincarnation, 520

Relative deprivation theory, 626
Reliability, 128
Religion, 507–35
as agent of socialization, 80
and capitalism, 14, 175–76, 390, 514–15
conflict perspective on, 513–14
and culture conflict, 507, 524–26
defined, 508
and economic development, 14
functionalist perspective on, 509–11
future of, 533–35
and gender, 514
and guidelines for everyday life, 509
and hate crimes, 221
and inequality, 514
and Internet, 529, 535
and membership, 527–28, 530, 533
and new technology, 535
and persecution, 511
and Protestant ethic, 14, 175–76, 390,
514–15
and race-ethnicity, 527–28
and rationality, 175–76
science and, 534
secularization of, 530–33
and social change, 14
and social class, 269, 527
as social institution, 103
and support for government, 509–10
symbolic interactionist perspective on,
511–13
in the U.S., characteristics of, 526–33
of the world, 515–21
Religiosity, as core value, 51
Religious affiliation, 527–28, 530, 533
Religious experience, 512–13
Religious groups
characteristics of, 528–29
commitment to, 529
and competition, 528–29
diversity of, 528
and electronic church, 529, 535
membership in, 527–28, 530, 533
pluralism, 528
and recruitment, 528–29
toleration of, 529
types of, 521–26
Relocation camps, 346
Remarriage, 469
Replication, 129
Republican Party, 426–27
Research, 126–46
and common sense, 126
ethics in, 142–44
gender in, 142
methods of, 129–42
models of, 126–29
purposes of, 15–21
and theory, 145–46
Research design, 128, 129–42
Research methods, 128, 129–42
improper, 132–33
qualitative, 139
quantitative, 139
selecting, 139, 140–42
Research model, 126–29

and analyzing results, 128–29
and choosing a method, 128
and collecting data, 128
and defining the problem, 127
and formulating a hypothesis, 128
and reviewing the literature, 127
and selecting a topic, 126–27
and sharing results, 129
Reserve labor force, 330, 413
Resocialization, 84–86
Resource mobilization theory, 628
Retreatism, 211
Retribution, 219
Revolution(s)
agricultural, 151, 152–53, 634–35
American, 10
and collapse of authority, 419
domestication, 151, 152, 153
four social, 9–10, 151, 155, 634–35
French, 10, 12
Industrial, 9–10, 151, 634–35
Revolution of 1917, 482
Revolutionaries, 211
Riots, 612–13
Ritual pollution, 231
Ritualism, 210–211
Rituals, 512
Roe v. Wade, 629
Role conflict, 114
Role extension, 615
Role model(s), 78, 85
Role performance, 112, 113–14
Role strain, 114
Role taking, 69–71
Roles
explained, 101–2
significance of, 102
and social institutions, 103
Roman Catholic Church, 234, 240, 345, 421,
479, 511, 513, 524
Romance, 51, 451–52
Romans, 511–12
Rome, 451, 516, 517, 525
Routinization of charisma, 423
Rubik's Cube, 616
Ruling class, 19, 258, 432–33
Rumors, 615–16
Rural rebound, 601–2
Rural-urban makeup of U.S., 590
Russia. *See also* Soviet Union (former)
barter in, 398
births in, 575
capitalism, 242–43, 397
crime in, 243
education in, 482
and geopolitics, 637
health care in, 561, 566–67
religion in, 533–34
and wars, 434, 439
Rwanda, 317–18, 435

Sabbath, 531
Sacred, 508
St. Alban's School, 489
"Saints" and "Roughnecks," 121–22, 207–08
Salem witch hunts, 511

Same sex marriage, 444–45, 460, 462
Sample, 130–31
San Francisco, 586–87
San Marino, California, 575
Sanctions
    explained, 47
    negative, 47, 216
    positive, 47, 216
Sandwich generation, 464
Santa Rosa, California, 622
Sao Paulo, 590
Sapir-Whorf Hypothesis, 45–46
SAT scores, 173, 497–98, 501, 503
Satanists, 615
Saudi Arabia, 203, 249, 402–3
Scapegoats, 328
Scholastic Assessment Test (SAT), 481
School choice, 502
Schools
    as agent of socialization, 81–83
    and hidden curriculum, 82
    shootings at, 477–78, 498–99
Science
    and core values, 50
    defined, 6
    and religion, 534
    as a social institution, 103
Scientific method, 11
Seattle, 612
Second estate, 234, 240
Second shift, 448–50
Second social revolution, 151, 152–53
Secondary Analysis, 134, 135
Secondary Groups, 156–57
Sect, 523
Secularization of culture, 531–33
Secularization of religion, 530–31
Segregation
    in education, 32
    in housing, 9, 10, 326
    patterns of, 333, 334
    self, 326
    in South, 325, 338
Selective perception, 331
Self
    defined, 68
    development of, 68–71
    as object, 70
    as subject, 70
Self-administered questionnaires, 133
Self-fulfilling prophecy, 495
Self-fulfilling stereotypes, 108–110
Self-fulfillment, as emerging value, 53
Self labeling, 206
Semiperiphery, 249
Senate, U.S., 186, 431
Sentencing, 218–19
Serial fatherhood, 468–69
Sex
    defined, 286
    and gender, 286–91
    and voting patterns, 428
Sex change operation, 289–90
Sex education, 488
Sex tourism, 251
Sexism. See also Gender, Women

in education, 17, 293, 299–301
in everyday life, 301–2
in China, 584–85
in criminal justice system, 310
female circumcision, 294
global perspectives on, 291–95
and housework, 448–51
in medicine, 298, 299, 551–52
in politics, 311–13
and sexual harassment, 307–9
and social stratification, 227–28, 235,
    285–313
in the U.S., 297–309
and work, 291–93, 302–9, 408
Sexual harassment, 307–9
Sexual orientation, and hate crimes, 221
Shamans, 150–51, 540
Shanghai, 590
Shell Oil Company, 651
Shintoists, 516
Shrinking paychecks, 409, 410
Shudras, 231–32
Shunning, 513
Sick days, 548
Sick role, 541–42
Sick Societies, 40–41
Sign vehicles, 115
Significant other, 69
Single mothers, 28, 463–64
Sikhs, 516
Silverado, 230–31
Sinai Desert Arabs, 5
Sing Sing Prison, 419
Sinkyone Indians, 654–55
Site-based management, 502
Slavery, 20, 229–31, 232
Slavs, 318
Slovakia, 14
Slovenia, 575
Small work groups, 189
Small world phenomenon, 159–60
Snake handling, 105
Social change, 633–49
    and automobiles, 643–45
    and computers, 646–49
    defined, 634
    and deviance, 209
    and education, 487–88
    natural cycles of, 638–39
    in postmodern society, 641
    processes of, 638–41
    and religion, 14, 510
    and social movements, 636
    and technology, 641–49
    theories of, 638–41
    and value contradictions, 51
Social class, 255–82
    and African Americans, 339–341
    and the automobile industry, 266
    and child birth, 453
    and childrearing, 269, 455
    components of, 236–37
    conflict perspective on, 235–36
    consequences of, 367–70
    and criminal justice system, 121–22,
        207–8, 215, 270

defined, 98, 256
determinants of, 235–37
and divorce, 269
and education, 269, 488–94
and family life, 268
and labeling, 207–8
macrosociological perspective on, 98–99
Marx's view of, 263
and mate selection, 268
and mental health, 268, 539, 547–48
and new technology, 270
and physical health, 267–68
and politics, 269–70
and power, 236–37
and prestige, 236–37
and property, 236–37
and religion, 269, 527
sociological models of, 263–67
and sports, 85
and stratification, 235–37
Social cohesion, 106–8
Social construction of reality
    and aging, 356–57
    and the body, 552
    and childbirth, 545
    and germs, 119–20
    and gynecological examinations, 120–21
    and health, 540
    and women's reproductive organs, 551
Social control
    conflict perspective on, 200
    and deviance, 197–224
    functionalist perspective on, 200
    and norms, 199, 200–1, 208
    pluralistic theory of, 200
    and religion, 509
    and the self, 74–76
Social Darwinism, 11–12
Social inequality. See Gender, Race, Social
    class, Social stratificaion
Social institution(s)
    and basic needs, 103
    defined, 102
    economics as, 103
    education as, 103
    family as, 103
    and groups, 103
    in industrial societies, 103
    law as, 103
    mass media as emerging, 103
    medicine as, 103
    military as, 103
    and organizations, 103
    overview of, 103
    politics as, 103
    in postindustrial societies, 103
    religion as, 103
    and roles, 103
    science as, 103
    and social structure, 102–8
    sociological significance of, 102, 103
    and values, 103
Social integration
    and community, 13
    and education, 485–87
    and suicide, 13

Social interaction
  defined, 31, 96
  and microsociology, 96–97
Social location, 91
Social mirror, 75
Social mobility, 235, 270–76
  pain of, 273
  types of, 270–72
  women and, 272
Social movement(s), 618–30
  and abortion, 621, 629–30
  alterative, 619–21
  and authorities, 622–23
  defined, 618
  and the environment, 654–56
  failure of, 628–30
  membership in, 621–22
  new, 621
Social movement(s), *continued*
  proactive, 618
  publics of, 621–22
  reactive, 618
  reasons for joining, 625–28
  redemptive, 620
  reformative, 620
  and resource mobilization, 628
  and social change, 636
  success of, 628–30
  tactics of, 621–23
  transformative, 620
  types of, 619–21
Social movement organizations, 618–19
Social networks, 159–61, 241
Social order, 201
Social organization, 642–43
Social placement, 487
Social promotion, 498
Social relationships, 643
Social research
  microsociological, 31
  purposes for, 15–21
  values and, 14–15
  women in, 142, 272
Social Research Corporation, 22
Social revolutions, 634–35
Social sciences compared, 6–7
Social Security, 369–73, 431
Social Security Administration, 372–73
Social setting, 115
Social solidarity, 509
Social stratification, 227–52. *See also* Social
    class
  and caste system, 231–34
  and class system, 234–35
  comparative, 241–43
  conflict perspective on, 235–36
  and education, 488–94
  and estate system, 234, 240
  in former Soviet Union, 242–43
  functionalist perspective on, 237–38
  and gender, 227–28, 235, 285–313
  global aspects of, 227–52
  in Great Britain, 241–42
  in India, 231–33
  maintenance of, 240–41
  and slavery, 229–31

  and social class, 235–37
  and social mobility, 235
  in South Africa, 233
  systems of, 229–35
  and technology, 241
  three worlds of global, 243–48
  universality of, 237–39
  and U.S. racial caste system, 233–34
Social structure
  changes in, 106
  cohesion, 106–8
  defined, 97
  and poverty, 30
  sociological significance of,
    97–98
Socialism
  changes in, 397–98
  compared to capitalism, 393,
    395–96
  components of, 395
  criticisms of, 396
  democratic, 395
  ideology of, 395–96
Socialization
  and adolescence, 88–89
  agents of, 79–84
  anticipatory, 84
  of children, 4–5, 28, 63–68, 86–87
  and early older years, 90
  and emotions, 73–76
  into gender, 76–79, 83
  and individuality, 91
  and later middle years, 90
  and later older years, 90
  through life course, 86–91
  and middle years, 89–90
  and neighborhoods, 82
  and older years, 90
  into the self, mind and emotions,
    68–76
  and social control, 74–76
  of twins, 65
  and young adulthood, 89
Society(ies)
  agricultural, 151, 152–53, 389, 391–92
  defined, 150
  horticultural, 151, 152, 153, 389
  hunting and gathering, 150–52
  industrial, 103, 151, 153–54, 389–90,
    392–93, 445, 466
  modern, 636
  pastoral, 151, 152, 153, 389
  pluralistic, 50
  postindustrial, 103, 151, 154–55, 390–91,
    393, 445
  rationalization of, 174
  and social groups, 150
  traditional, 636
  transformation of, 150–55, 634–38,
    642–49
Sociobiology, 55–56
Sociological analysis
  levels of, 96–97
  and macrosociological perspective, 96–102
  and microsociological perspective, 96–97
Sociological perspective, 4–5, 32

Sociological theory. *See also* Conflict
    perspective, Functionalist perspective,
    Symbolic interactionist perspective
  main perspectives, 22–32
  and testability, 9
Sociology
  applied, 19, 21–22, 32–33
  basic, 19, 21–22, 32,
  clinical, 32–33
  and common sense, 9, 10
  defined, 6
  development of, 9–15, 17–22
  environmental, 655–56
  pure, 19, 21–22, 32
  purposes of, 15
  sexism in, 17
  as a social science, 7
  theoretical perspectives in, 22–31
  uses of, 15
Solar Temple, 522
Solidarity
  mechanical, 106
  organic, 106–7
  social, 509
Somalia, 438, 575
Sons of Samoa, 203
Sony, 191
South Africa
  apartheid in, 233
  government of, 422
  Kalahari Desert, 479
  murder rate of, 233
  reserve labor in, 413
  social stratification in, 233
  transfer of power in, 422–23
South Carolina, 325
Soviet Communist party, 482
Soviet Union (former),
  barter in, 398
  economy of, 397–98
  education in, 482
  government of, 426
  social stratification in, 242–43
Spain, 42, 419, 423, 434, 575, 648
Special-interest group, 430–31
Special Olympics, 640
Spirit of capitalism, 14, 175–76, 390, 514–15
Spiritualists, 516
Split-labor market, 330
Sports
  as agent of socialization, 84
  and gender, 85, 301
  and social class, 85
Spouse abuse, and alcohol, 125, 130, 137
Spurious correlation(s), 137
St. Alban's School, 489
St. Louis, Missouri, 144, 598
St. Patrick's Day, 376
Starvation, 576–77
State, 419, 423
State capitalism, 393
State religion, 510–11
Status
  achieved, 99–100
  ascribed, 99–100
  master, 100

Status consistency, 262, 263
Status discrepancy, 100–1, 263
Status inconsistency, 100–1, 262, 263
Status set, 99
Status symbols, 100
Stereotypes
    and discrimination, 331
    in everyday life, 108, 110
    gender, 78, 85, 108, 110
    self-fulfilling, 108, 110
Stigma, 198
Stockholders revolt, 401
Stop-ERA, 618
Stored value, 391–92
Straffordshire, England, 362
Strain theory, 210–211, 212
Stratification. See Social stratification
Stratified random sample, 130–31
Street corner men, 96
Street crime, 201, 211
"Stroller effect," 79
Structural mobility, 272
Structured interview, 133–34
Subculture(s), 49–50
Subsistence economy, 389
Suburbanization, 600–1
Suburbs, 600–1
Sudan, 231, 232
Suicide
    cross-cultural perspective on, 199
    and cults, 522
    and elderly, 382–83
    among Japanese, 9, 10, 199
    medically assisted, 552–56
    methods of committing, 382
    and race-ethnicity, 383
    rates of, 13, 14
    and social integration, 13
"Super bugs," 560–61
Superego, 73
Supreme Court, 337, 629
Surveys, 129–34
Survivalists, 49
Sweden, 377, 395, 445, 447, 566–67,
    614
Symbolic interactionist perspective, overview
    of, 23–27
Symbolic interactionist perspective on
    aging, 362–67
    births in Least Industrialized Nations, 571,
    577–79
    crime, 202–208
    deviance, 202–208
    divorce, 25–26
    divorce, 25–26
    education, 494–96
    health and illness, 540–41
    marriage, 450–51
    religion, 511–13
Symbols. See also Symbolic interactionist
    perspective
    cow as, 512
    and crescent moon and star, 512
    cross as, 512
    defined, 24, 42
    and divorce, 25–26

electronic communication and, 45
    and everyday life, 23–24
    religious, 511–12
    and society, 24
    Star of David as, 512
Synthesis, 639
System of descent, 446

Table, how to read, 130
Taboo, 49
    and global domination, 252
Tact, 115
Tahitians, 288
Taking role of other, 69
Tartars, 637
Tasmanians, 58–59
Tattoing, 126
Taxes, 359
TB, 561, 616
Teacher expectations, 495–96, 503–4
Teamwork, 115
Tearooms, 144
Techniques of neutralization, 205–206
Technological lifespace, 380
Technology. See also New technology
    and alienation, 643
    and college registration, 173–74
    and communication, 5, 45, 161, 162
    and control of workers, 191, 192
    and cultural leveling, 58–59
    and death, 380
    defined, 57
    displacement of existing, 644
    and the environment, 656
    and global domination, 252
    in global village, 57–60
    and nonmaterial culture, 58
    in postmodern society, 641–49
    and replacement of humans, 60
    and social change, 641–49
    and social organization, 642–43
    and social stratification, 241
    and surveillance, 191, 192
    transformation of, 642
    and transformation of society, 642–49
    and work, 191, 192, 410–11, 412–14
Teen pregnancy, 498, 500
Television, 77
Terrorism
    biological, 436, 437
    chemical, 436
    nuclear, 436
Testimonials, 624
Texas, 342, 507, 525–26
Theory
    main perspectives, 22–32
    of prejudice, 328–31
    and research, 145–46
    and testability, 9
Thesis, 639
Third estate, 234, 240
Third parties, 426–27
Third revolution, 151, 153–54
Thomas theorem, 119–20
"Three strikes," 218–19
Tiwi, 355–56, 357, 364

Tobacco industry, 562
Tokyo, 563, 590
Torah, 479, 516
Tornado, 614
Total institution, 84–86
Touching
    and gender, 9, 10, 128
    microsociological perspective on, 112
Townsend Plan, 369–70
Toyota, 132
Tracking, 487, 494–95
Trading blocks, 401–2
Traditional orientation, 10, 174–75
Traditional societies, 13, 445
Trail of Tears, 348
Transfer, 624
Trenchcoat mafia, 477–78, 499
Tretyakov Gallery, 395
Triad, 163
Trobriand Islanders, 445
Tuberculosis (TB), 561, 616
Tunisia, 285
Tutsis, 317–18
Twins, 65, 289–90, 439

Uganda, 75, 575
Ukraine, 397, 398, 637
Underclass, 265–66
Underemployment, 396
Underground economy, 407–9
Undocumented workers, 408
Unemployment, 411
Union Bank of Monterey, California, 189
United Nations, 438, 439, 575, 637
United Negro College Fund, 326
United We Stand Party, 427
Universal citizenship, 424
University of Alabama, 325
University of California, 18
University of Chicago, 17, 18, 23, 48, 138
University of Colorado, 513
University of Kansas, 17
University of Oklahoma, 426
University of Rochester, 564
Unmarried mothers, 28, 463–64
Unobtrusive measures, 136
Unstructured interview, 134
Untouchables, 231–32
Upper middle class, 265
Upward social mobility, 271, 274–75
Urban dwellers, types of, 597–98
Urban flight, 601
Urban growth, 601
Urban legends, 617–18
Urban patterns, 589–91
Urban renewal, 597, 602–3
Urban revitalization, 597, 602–3
Urbanization, 586–603. See also Cities
    defined, 589
    in Least Industrialized Nations, 595
    and models for growth, 592–94
    problems of, 600–3
    and revitalization, 602–3
    and social policy, 600–3
U.S. Census Bureau, 590
U.S. Department of Transportation, 188

U.S. Justice Department, 612

Vaishva, 233
Validity, 128
Value cluster(s), 53–54
    emerging, 53–54
Value contradictions, 51
Values
    as blinders, 54
    core, 50–51
    explained, 47–48
    overview of U.S., 50–55
    and social institutions, 103
    and social research, 14–15
    transformation of, 643
Vanderveer Group, 21
Variable, 128, 136
Venezuela, 5
Verstehen, 16–17
Veterans of Foreign Wars (VFW), 185
Viagra, 553
Vietnam, 169, 291, 438
Vietnam veterans study, 290–91
Vietnamese Americans, 346–47
Violence
    family, 469–71
    and husband's achievement, 130
    and mass media, 311
    school, 498–99
    against women, 293–94, 309–11, 470,
        584–85
Voluntary Associations, 183–86
    functions of, 184–85
    oligarchy of, 185–86
    and shared interests, 186
Voter apathy, 430
Voting patterns, 428–31
    age and, 428
    by characteristics, 428, 430
    in presidential election, 428, 430
    and social integration, 429–30

Waco, 507, 525–26
Walkman, 193
Walt Disney Company, 599
War, 434–38
    and arms sales, 435–36
    costs of, 435
    defined, 434
    and dehumanization, 436–38
    reasons for, 434–35
    universality of, 434
War of 1812, 5
War of the Worlds, 613
Washington, D.C., 95–96, 489
Washington University, 144
Watergate, 169

Wealth
    defined, 256
    distribution of, 257
Web. See Internet
Webster v. Reproductive Health Services, 629
Welfare, 9, 10, 279–80
Welfare capitalism, 393
Welfare reform, 280
Western Electric Company, 138
Western Sahar, 575
White Anglo-Saxon Protestant (WASP), 337
White-Collar crime, 211–14
White ethnics, 337
White Europeans, 337
White House, 402–3, 437
Whites
    and education, 340
    and home mortgages, 327
    well-being of, 339
Widowhood, 420, 456
Witch hunts, 511
Women. See also Gender, Sexism
    and abortion, 621, 629–30
    and biased medical treatment, 298, 299
    in China, 295
    and circumcision, 294
    and college degrees, 299–301
    and crime, 213, 214
    in criminal justice system, 310
    and divorce, 467–68, 469
    domestic role of, 645
    and education, 17, 293, 299–301
    and estate system, 234
    and eye contact, 9, 10
    global stratification of, 235, 291–95
    and gynecology, 121
    and housework, 448–51, 645
    and inequality, 201–2, 297–309
    and labor force participation, 303, 406,
        407, 411
    and literacy rates, 293
    in the military, 308
    and networking, 160
    and pay gap, 9, 10, 293
    in politics, 293, 311–13
    and poverty, 277
    and professional degrees, 299–301
    and sexual harassment, 307–9
    slavery of, 229
    and social mobility, 272
    social movement of, 298, 629–30
    subjugation of, 153, 229
    and touching, 9, 10
    violence against, 293–94, 309–11, 469–71
    and work, 291–93, 405–8,
        411
Women's movement, 298, 629–30

Woolworth's, 338
Work
    as core value, 50
    conflict perspective on, 190–91
    ethnicity and, 323
    gender and, 291–93, 302–9
    humanizing, 187–88
    and leisure, 409–10
    patterns of, 409–11
    and pay gap, 302–5
    prestige of, 292–93
    sexism in, 291–93, 302–9, 408
    and sexual harassment, 307–9
    technology and, 191–192, 410–11,
        412–14
    in U.S. society, 405–12
    and women, 291–93, 302–9, 405–8,
        411
Work force, characteristics of, 405–7
Workers
    exploitation of, 234, 236
    and Industrial Revolution, 9–10, 234,
        236
    and shrinking paychecks, 409
Working class, 265
Working poor, 265
Workplace, the
    as agent of socialization, 84
    and anticipatory socialization, 84
    computers in, 648–9
World Cup, 301
World economic systems, 393–99
World Health Organization, 559
World system theory, 248–49
World Trade Organization, 612
World War I, 625
World War II, 199, 250, 318, 345, 438, 482,
    516
Wounded Knee, 348

"XYY" theory, 201

Yale, 493
Yanomamo Indians, 4–5, 197, 198, 199
Yellow River, 588
Yemen, 575
Young adulthood, 89
Youngness, as emerging value, 53
Yugoslavia, 637
Yuppies, 262

Zaire, 561
Zapotec Indians, 199
Zero population growth, 585–86
Zero tolerance, 501
Zhongshan, China, 399
Zimbabwe, 73

Photo Credits

Chapter Opener Art Credits (*continued*)

Chapter 14: *Making Butter Cookies* by Franklin McMahon, 1970. Pen or ink and acrylic on paper, 30 x 22 in. Franklin McMahon/ Corbis.

Chapter 15: *Visitors Viewing the United States Constitution and Bill of Rights* by Franklin McMahon. Pen or ink and acrylic on paper, 30 x 22 in. Franklin McMahon/Corbis.

Chapter 16: *Family Supper* by Ralph Fasanella, 1972. Oil on canvas, 70" x 50". Ellis Island Immigration Museum. Courtesy of ACA Galleries, New York and Eva Fasanella.

Chapter 17: *Training Ground #2* by Phoebe Beasley, 1989. Collage, 24" x 48". © Phoebe Beasley/Omni-Photo Communications.

Chapter 18: *Creative Mind* by Tsing-Fang Chen, 1988. Acrylic on canvas, 66" x 48". Lucia Gallery, New York City/TF Chen/ SuperStock.

Chapter 19: *Medicine and Technology* by Vicky Rabinowicz, 1997. Gouache on paper. Vicky Rabinowicz/SIS.

Chapter 20: *Bus Stop in Beijing* by Phoebe Beasley, 1983. Collage, 24" x 36". © Phoebe Beasley/Omni-Photo Communications.

Chapter 21: *Follow the Leader* by Diana Ong, 1997. Brush and colored ink. Diana Ong/SuperStock.

Chapter 22: *Globes Interconnected* by Pete Whyte, 1996. Pastel on paper. © Pete Whyte/SIS.

Photo Credits

p. 5 © Herve Collart Odinetz/ Corbis Sygma; **p. 11** Mary Evans Picture Library; **p. 12** (top) The Granger Collection, New York; (bottom) North Wind Picture Archive; **p. 13** Corbis/Bettmann; **p. 14** (left) © Charles Gupton/ The Stock Market: (right) © Eastcott/ Momatiuk/ Woodfin Camp & Associates; (bottom) The Granger Collection, New York; **p. 17** The Granger Collection, New York; **p. 18** (top) North Wind Picture Archive; (bottom) Photographs and Prints Division, Schomburg Center for Research in Black Culture/ The New York Public Library, Astor, Lenox and Tilden Foundations; **p. 23** University of Chicago Library; **p. 24** © Ronnie Kaufman/ The Stock Market; **p. 27** Alinari/Regione Umbria/ Art Resource, NY; **p. 29** Culver Pictures; **p. 41** (top/left to right) © SuperStock, Inc.; © Art Wolfe/All Stock/ PictureQuest; (center/left to right) © Romano Cagnoni/ Still Pictures; © Art Wolfe/All Stock/ PictureQuest; © Ben Mangor/ SuperStock, Inc.; (bottom/left to right) © Gill Moti/ Still Pictures; © Art Wolfe/All Stock/ PictureQuest; © 2000 Stuart McClymont/ Stone; **p. 42** © Charles Kennard/ Stock, Boston; **p. 43** © Michael Newman/ PhotoEdit; **p. 44** © Graham Earnshaw/ Reuters-Archive; **p. 47** © Jim Pickerell/ Stock, Boston; **p. 48** © Mirror Syndication International; **p. 49** © Owen Franken/ Stock, Boston; **p. 51** © Esbin-Anderson/Photo Network/ PictureQuest; **p. 52** Photofest; **p. 53** © Chuck Savage/ The Stock Market; **p. 54** Courtesy Clarke Memorial Museum, Eureka, California; **p. 56** © Ron Kimball Photography; **p. 57** © Moshe shai Photography; **p. 58** © Scott Houston/ Corbis Sygma; **p. 59** © Mattel, Inc. Photo © Reuters-Archive Photos; **p. 65** © Charlyn Zlotnik/ Woodfin Camp & Associates; **p. 66** © Kate Brooks/ SABA; **p. 67** © Harlow Primate Laboratory/ University of Wisconsin; **p. 69** © Marleen Ferguson/ PhotoEdit; **p. 70** © 2000 Charles Thatcher/ Stone; **p. 74** © William Greenblatt/ Gamma-Liaison; **p. 78** (top) © Eidos Interactive Ltd.; (bottom) © INTERFOTO/ Sipa Press; **p. 81** © George Mars Cassidy/ The Picture Cube; **p. 83** © Michael Newman/ PhotoEdit; **p. 86** © David Austen/ Stock, Boston; **p. 87** © Eddie Adams/ Liaison Agency; **p. 89** © Michael MacIntyre/ The Hutchison Library; **p. 90** AP/ Wide World Photos; **p. 97** © John Neubauer/ PhotoEdit; **p. 100** © Brad Markel/ Liaison Agency; **p. 101** © Abe Frajndlich/ Corbis Sygma; **p. 104** © Bill Aron/ PhotoEdit; **p. 105** © Francois Perri/GIMR/ Liaison Agency; **p. 107** (left) © Charles Gupton/ The Stock Market; (right) © I. Uimonen/ Corbis Sygma; **p. 109** © Dennis MacDonald/ PhotoEdit; **p. 110** (left) © 2000 James Darell/ Stone; (right) © Mark C. Burnett/ Stock, Boston/ PictureQuest; **p. 111** (left) © Alain Evrard/ Photo Researchers. Inc.; (right) © Frans Lanting/ Minden Pictures; **p. 112** (top) © J. C. Francolon/ Gamma-Liaison; (bottom) © 2000 Nick Dolding/ Stone; **p. 113** (top) AP/Wide World Photos ; (bottom) Photo © Kelvin Jones/ MPTV; **p. 116** (left) © Andrew Ramey/ Woodfin Camp & Associates; (right) Photo © Richard Corkery/ NY Daily News; **p. 118** © Heidi Levine/ Sipa Press; **p. 126** © Andrew Lichtenstein/ Impact Visuals; **p. 131** © Lash/ Sipa Press; **p. 134** © Stuart Cohen/ Comstock; **p. 135** (top) © Lannis Waters/ The Palm Beach Post; (bottom) © Rhoda Sidney/ PhotoEdit; **p. 141** © Patrick Forstier/ Corbis Sygma; **p. 143** © Robert McElroy/ Woodfin Camp & Associates; **p. 150** © 1945 the Norman Rockwell Family Trust; **p. 151** © Carlos Humberto/ Contact Press Images; **p. 156** (top) © David Young-Wolff/ PhotoEdit; (bottom) © Jean-Claude Coutasse/ Contact Press Images; **p. 157** (top) © The New Yorker Collection 1979 Robert Weber from cartoonbank.com. All Rights Reserved. [for: 1979 10 01 046. RWE.HG Club]; (bottom) © Bob Daemmrich/ The Image Works; **p. 158** (left) © Bill Losh/ FPG International; (right) © Michael Newman/ PhotoEdit; **p. 159** © Ron McKenzie/ Courtesy American Sociological Association; **p. 161** © Fujifotos/ The Image Works; **p. 164** © 2000 Don Smetzer/ Stone; **p. 166** AP/Wide World Photos; **p. 168** © 1965 by Stanley Milgram. From the film Obedience, distributed by Pennsylvania State University, Audio Visual Services; **p. 174** © Faula Lerner/ Woodfin Camp & Associates; **p. 176** © The Bowers Museum of Cultural Arts/ CORBIS; **p. 177** The Granger Collection, New York; **p. 178** Courtesy MetLife Archives; **p.179** © Charlyn Zlotnik/ Woodfin Camp & Associates; **p. 180** AP/Wide World Photos; **p. 181** © Jean Marc Giboux/ Liaison Agency; **p. 183** © March of Dimes; **p. 186** AP/Wide World Photos; **p. 187** Photo © Peter Simon/ Courtesy Rosabeth Moss Kanter; **p. 190** © 2000 Billy Hustace/ Stone; **p. 193** © Michael Wolf/Visum/ SABA; **p. 198** © Jeremy Hormer/ Panos Pictures; **p. 199** © Hulton-Deutsch Collection/ CORBIS; **p. 202** © Jim Henslin; **p. 203** © Andrew